A HISTORY OF THE
TWENTIETH CENTURY

BOOKS BY MARTIN GILBERT

THE CHURCHILL BIOGRAPHY

Volume III: 1914–1916
Document Volume III: (in two parts)
Volume IV: 1917–1922
Document Volume IV: (in two parts)
Volume V: 1922–1939
Document Volume V: 'The Exchequer
Years' 1922–1929
Document Volume V: 'The Wilderness
Years' 1929–1935
Document Volume V: 'The Coming of
War' 1936–1939

Volume VI: 'Finest Hour' 1939–1941
Document Volume VI: 'At the Admiralty'
September 1939–May 1940
Document Volume VI: 'Never Surrender'
May–December 1940
Volume VII: 'Road to Victory' 1941–1945
Volume VIII: 'Never Despair' 1945–1965

Churchill: A Photographic Portrait
Churchill: A Life

OTHER BOOKS

The Appeasers (with Richard Gott)
The European Powers 1900–1945
The Roots of Appeasement
Children's Illustrated Bible Atlas
Atlas of British Charities
Atlas of American History
Atlas of the Arab–Israeli Conflict
Atlas of British History
Atlas of the First World War
Atlas of the Holocaust
The Holocaust: Maps and Photographs
Atlas of Jewish History
Atlas of Recent History (in preparation)
Atlas of Russian History
The Jews of Arab Lands: Their History
in Maps
In Search of Churchill

The Jews of Russia: Their History in Maps
Jerusalem Illustrated History Atlas
Sir Horace Rumbold: Portrait of a Diplomat
Jerusalem: Rebirth of a City
Jerusalem in the Twentieth Century
Exile and Return: The Struggle for Jewish Statehood
Auschwitz and the Allies
The Jews of Hope: The Plight of Soviet Jewry Today
Shcharansky: Hero of Our Time
The Holocaust: The Jewish Tragedy
The Boys, Triumph over Adversity
First World War
Second World War
The Day the War Ended
Empires in Conflict: A History of the
Twentieth Century 1900–1933
Descent into Barbarism: A History
of the Twentieth Century 1934–1951

EDITIONS OF DOCUMENTS

Britain and Germany Between the Wars
Plough My Own Furrow: The Life of Lord Allen of Hurtwood
Servant of India: Diaries of the Viceroy's Private Secretary 1905–1910

A HISTORY OF THE TWENTIETH CENTURY

Volume Three: 1952–1999

MARTIN GILBERT

Perennial

An Imprint of HarperCollins*Publishers*

A hardcover edition of this book was published in Great Britain in 1999 by HarperCollins Publishers.

A revised paperback edition of this book was published in Great Britain in 2000 by HarperCollins Publishers.

The first U.S. edition was printed in hardcover in 1999 by William Morrow and Company.

HarperCollins books may be purchased for educational, business, or sales promotional use. For information please write: Special Markets Department, HarperCollins Publishers Inc., 10 East 53rd Street, New York, NY 10022.

First Perennial edition published 2000.

The Library of Congress has catalogued the hardcover edition as follows:
Gilbert, Martin.
   A history of the twentieth century / Martin Gilbert.
      p. cm.
   Includes bibliographical references and index.
   Contents: v. 3. 1952-1999
   ISBN 0-688-10066-X (v. 3)
    1. History, Modern—20th century.   I. Title.
D421.G55   1999
909.82—dc21   97-13627
CIP

ISBN 0-380-71395-0 (pbk.)

01 02 03 04 RP/RRD 10 9 8 7 6 5 4 3 2

This three-volume history is dedicated to my mother, Miriam Gilbert, who has lived through all but the first decade of this century.

This third volume is dedicated to my wife Susie, who has been my companion and helper for almost thirty years, and has always encouraged me to tell the story of the twentieth century, both in many of its aspects, and in the wider perspective.

CONTENTS

LIST OF ILLUSTRATIONS

LIST OF MAPS

ACKNOWLEDGEMENTS

IT IS TO THE WORK of fellow historians that my first and foremost thanks are due. I am also indebted to those journalists who, with regard to so many of the episodes of the century, reported from the scene, often at considerable risk, and whose accounts constitute a vivid commentary of our times: those on whose articles I have drawn are listed in the Bibliography. My thanks also go to friends, colleagues and strangers who have sent me material, or answered my queries, on specific episodes covered in this book, among them Neal Becton (Foreign Desk, *Washington Post*), Jeremy Carver CBE, Bethine Church, Lyn Cianflocco (National Center for Statistics and Analysis, Washington DC), Barbara Coffin (Eurovision Mission to Europe), Marion Coope, Ruth Davey (Refugee Council), Dr Michael Dingle, Ellis Douek, Hugh Fox, Helen Goldberg, Richard Gott, Eytan Kohlberg, David Littman (Christian Solidarity International), Sean McCoy, Antony Marcil (World Environment Centre), Fay Miller (Information Resource Center, United States Embassy, London), Jonathan Mirsky, William Nagel, Aditya Nehru, His Excellency Vidhya Rayananonda, Ambassador of Thailand, Erik S. Root (Claremont Institute), Erich Segal, Andrzej Sitkowski, Sir Harry Solomon, Barbara E. Spicer, Marina Temkina, Robert Tomlin, Michael Tregenza, Alan Virta (Special Collections, Boise State University), Michael P. Walsh (Maryknoll Mission Archives), Hedy M. Weinberg (Executive Director, American Civil Liberties Union Foundation of Tennessee), and the archives of the *National Geographic*, Washington. For answering queries with regard to the United States, I am grateful to Morris J. Massel. The Librarian and staff of the London Library have, as always, been most supportive. I am also grateful to Erica Huningher for her helpful suggestions. Kay Thomson read the manuscript and helped with many inquiries.

In my search for photographs I was given access to the Hulton Getty Picture Collection (photographs 1–15, 17–23, 25–41, 43 and 51) where

Luigi Di Dio enabled me to roam the stacks, and to the Associated Press photographic archive (photographs 16, 24, 42, 44–8, 50 and 52), where Bettina Elberg helped me to fill several gaps. I am grateful to both these archives for permission to reproduce their photographs. My son Joshua helped me with the picture layout. During the indexing stage, I was helped by my son David.

Special thanks are due to Tim Aspden, who transformed my very rough maps drafts and ideas, both for this volume and its two predecessors, into maps, of the highest quality, enabling the reader to locate all the places and regions mentioned, and the areas of conflict.

Family, friends and publishers have all been supportive at every stage of this enterprise, which has now reached its conclusion. Arabella Pike at HarperCollins and Beccy Goodhart at William Morrow have supported the project at every stage. I also wish to thank Carol O'Brien and Hilary Rubinstein for enabling me to embark upon the enterprise more than a decade ago.

Final thanks go to my wife Susie, who scrutinized the text of this volume, as of its two predecessors, who has supported this project from its inception a decade ago, and to whom this volume is dedicated.

INTRODUCTION

ON 15 JULY 1998 I handed in the typescript of Volume Two (1933–1951) of this book to the publisher. On the following day the newspapers reported the death in the United States, at the age of eighty-two, of General Nguyen Ngoc Loan. His obituaries on television and in the newspapers worldwide were accompanied by a single photograph: the 'moment of horror', as the British *Daily Telegraph* described it, when the general executed a bound Vietcong prisoner in a street in Saigon in 1968 by shooting him at almost point-blank range in the head. The photographer, Eddie Adams of the Associated Press, won a Pulitzer Prize for the picture. A newsreel film taken at the same time by Vo Suu, which also won several prizes, showed the prisoner dropping to the ground with a fountain of blood arcing from his head into the dust.

The impact of the photograph was immediate. Harry McPherson, one of President Johnson's speech writers, recalled how after seeing it 'You got the sense of the awfulness, the endlessness of the war – and though it sounds naive, the unethical quality of a war in which the prisoner is shot at point-blank range.' The United States involvement in the Vietnam War ended seven years after the photograph was taken. General Loan was among tens of thousands of Vietnamese who found refuge in the United States. He was proud of the photograph which had made him famous, and hung it on the wall of the restaurant which he opened in Dale City, Virginia.

In this third volume the war in Vietnam, including General Loan's act of killing, has its place in the confrontation between East and West, and between totalitarian and democratic values, a confrontation which was an integral part of the century's last four decades. Also integral to how events were perceived, and policies often changed, was the part played by press photographs and film, such as that which caught the moment of General Loan's act of summary execution. The Vietnam War was increasingly performed on the public stage, with television film having its repeated impact.

As the century draws to its close, newspaper and television images bring every element of the global struggle to the homes and sitting rooms of hundreds of millions of people. In the week in 1998 in which General Loan's photograph was reprinted, other images in the newspapers brought scenes of fighting: in the Yugoslav province of Kosovo, and reports of forty-four ethnic Albanians – members of the Kosovo Liberation Army – killed in the conflict. There were also reports of political–sectarian violence in the British Isles, in Northern Ireland, in which three young children died; of villagers beaten up by soldiers in the Indonesian village of Cibedug when they tried to reclaim land from the estate of the deposed dictator Suharto, which he had expropriated from them twenty-six years earlier; of a failed suicide bomb in a crowded Jerusalem street; of eleven people killed in a village south of Algiers, part of a pattern of killing in which fifty people had been murdered in the previous five days and several thousands since the beginning of the year; of an undersea volcanic eruption in the Pacific, the resultant seismic wave from which killed more than two thousand people in the coastal towns of Aitape and Wewak in Papua New Guinea; and of famine in Sudan – in which hundreds of thousands of people were at risk of death through starvation.

This list of such turmoil during the course of a single week was typical of almost every week. Equally typical were the efforts being made throughout the globe to secure peace and compromise, such as the plan made known that week in Nigeria for the President, General Abdulsalam Abubakar, to announce a gradual return to civilian rule. Even in the sphere of natural disasters, significant efforts were being made to anticipate dangers and to deal with them speedily: 1998 was the penultimate year of the United Nations Decade for Natural Disaster Reduction.

In 1952, the year this volume opens, the population of the world was approaching 3,000 million (three billion). In the second half of the century it had more than doubled, to six billion, of whom 1,000 million live in China and at least 950 million in India. Merely to maintain life at a minimum level had become a struggle for at least a quarter of the governments of the world. The refugee population had also doubled. At the same time, the destruction of the resources of the planet had increased. From fish in the oceans to trees in the rain forests, the failure of human restraint had begun to lead to irreversible changes in the ability of the planet to sustain the existing level of well-being. In many areas of the globe, that well-being is itself minimal.

Every historian has his own perspective, derived from personal experiences and interest over many years, in my case over a period of thirty-eight years of research and writing. Some events are central to any presentation of a historical period, and it would be a rash writer who omitted them. This is true of many of several hundred of the episodes in this volume, such as the deaths of Stalin or Mao Tse-tung, the assassination of President Kennedy, the Vietnam War, or man's landing on the Moon. Hundreds more episodes are part of this narrative because they illustrate my general themes, or some aspect of the unfolding years. Events that made an impact at any given time may subsequently have faded from the public mind, and I have tried, in view of their importance when they took place, to include them, and also to include the names of those – now largely forgotten – whose names and stories bestrode the pages of the newspapers and whose images filled the television screens for their brief period of achievement or notoriety. Recent anniversaries, such as the eightieth anniversary of the ending of the First World War, the sixtieth anniversary of the Kristallnacht in Germany, or the fiftieth anniversary of the ending of the Second World War, also present the historian with new material uncovered as a result of the upsurge in public interest and the testimony of those who were alive at the time; and provide a bridge between those who witnessed events and subsequent generations whose lives have been unconsciously influenced by them.

General history can be as sharply focused as detailed studies. Over many years I have tried to interweave the wider sweep of events with the stories, and with the names, of those who made their contribution, often in small corners or without fanfare. 'Lest we forget', the cry of pain that lies behind so many memorials and memorial meetings, is a testimony to the desire of the human spirit not to turn away from the individual, not to overlook the stories of individual heroism, suffering, achievement and hope. During my work on these three volumes, it is the part of the individual on which I have tried to focus: not only individual actions, but the struggle for the rights of the individual, for civil rights and human rights, in every land. By the end of the century those rights are better understood, and more widely respected, than in earlier decades, but not universally. Every decade since the century began has seen a diminution of human rights somewhere on the globe, as well as their advancement. Real progress is not a law of nature; setbacks as well as progress can be found in each year covered by these pages. Gradually, however, human beings see their lives and livelihoods enhanced, even in countries such as the Soviet Union – since 1991 a thing of the past – where they had long been at the margin of national policy or ideology; and gradually the achievements of the century, including those in technology and medical science, become more and more widely available; but, despite that, the struggles for a better life with which the century began do not end as the century ends, and, although the nature of those struggles has often changed, the search for a better life – for human fulfilment – will certainly challenge, frustrate and inspire the twenty-first century as well.

MARTIN GILBERT
Merton College
Oxford
21 June 1999

CHAPTER ONE

1952

. . . an absolute refusal to yield . . .

DISTINGUISHED UNIT CITATION

An unexpected prospect of extending life emerged with an operation at the Pennsylvania Hospital in Philadelphia. It took place on 8 March 1952, when an artificial heart kept a patient alive for eighty minutes. There were parts of the globe, however, where daily life was dominated by war, and by the premature and violent abridgement of the human species.

In Vietnam, 1952 began with France still striving to hold on to control of the areas beyond the Red River Delta. But within a month the Vietminh had succeeded in closing the strategically important Black River to French naval traffic, and had closed all French access to the air base at Hoa Binh. In this offensive action the French lost five thousand men, the Vietminh more than five thousand. The French had begun to realize that the Vietminh battle plan, as devised by General Giap, did not pay much heed to the scale of the Vietminh casualties. This boded ill for the future of French military control outside the main cities.

The architect of the French military plan of defence, General de Lattre de Tassigny, died of cancer in Paris on January 11. A few hours before his death he was told that he had been promoted to the highest French military rank of all, that of Marshal of France. His successor, General Raoul Salan, withdrew from Hoa Binh and continued to fortify the De Lattre Line. Behind that line the Vietminh mounted a series of guerrilla attacks, forcing General Salan to institute special mobile units to keep even his internal lines of communication open. But for the modern artillery and other military equipment that De Lattre had succeeded in securing from the United States, it is doubtful whether the French could have held on to the Red River Delta.

In Chinese-controlled prisoner-of-war camps, British officers and men who had been captured in Korea were subjected to political and physical pressures that were strictly forbidden under the Geneva Conventions for prisoners of war. In January, Major E. D. Harding, who had been captured almost a year earlier during the stand of the Glosters on the Imjin River, was accused together with his commanding officer Lieutenant-Colonel J. P. Carne, of 'disrupting the study programme' and of having 'a generally hostile attitude towards the Communists'. For three weeks the two men were kept in small cells with only sorghum to eat twice a day, while their Chinese captors searched for evidence of their 'misdeeds'. Both were sentenced to six months in prison.

Most of the 170,000 Chinese and North Korean prisoners of war held by the United Nations forces were being held in camps on Koje Island. On February 18, some of their guards entered one of the compounds to find out which prisoners of war were Korean civilians who had been forced to join the North Korean army, and did not want to be repatriated. As the guards attempted to begin the screening procedure, there were riots by prisoners armed with iron bars, clubs and barbed wire. The guards opened fire, and seventy-five prisoners were killed. On May 7 the prisoners took hostage the camp commandant, an American, Brigadier-General Dodd, and demanded the right to establish a Communist organization within the camp, complete with telephones and mimeograph machines. Their demands were met and Dodd was released.

The seizure of Dodd coincided with the arrival in Tokyo of a new commander-in-chief of the United Nations forces, General Mark Clark, who took up his command on May 12. He immediately reneged on the agreement with the prisoners, demoted Dodd and replaced him, and ordered the prisoner-of-war camp to be broken up. The Chinese prisoners were taken to Cheju and many of the North Koreans to the nearby island of Pongam. More riots followed, in which thirty-one prisoners and one American were killed. On December 14 there was an attempted break-out by Communist prisoners on Pongam Island, during which eighty-two prisoners were killed.

The screening procedure to which the Communists objected was finally completed, with more than half the prisoners being held by the United Nations refusing to be repatriated to either China or North Korea. This led to a heated exchange at the armistice talks at Panmunjom between the senior Korean delegate, General Nam Il, and his American counterpart, General William K. Harrison, who was a descendant of both the ninth and twenty-third Presidents of the United States. General Nam Il spoke first:

It is solely in the interest of a handful of munitions merchants and war-mongers of your side that the soldiers of seventeen nations have been driven by your side to come far from their native countries and carry out inhuman destruction and murder against the innocent people of Korea at the cost of their own lives, although people throughout the world who uphold peace and justice unanimously condemn your side for launching and carrying on this unjust war . . .

When your outrageous proposition of forceful retention of war prisoners has gone bankrupt and you can no longer use it as a camouflage to play deceit, your side cannot but resort to vituperation and distortion in these conferences.

General Harrison replied that some of General Nam Il's language 'is what we civilized countries associate with common criminals or persons who through ignorance or stupidity are unable to speak logically or convincingly. In their frustration they resort to efforts to insult.'

General Nam Il's insistence that all Chinese and North Korean prisoners of war be repatriated was rejected. Those who had elected not to return to Communist rule were allowed to remain in South Korea, or go to Taiwan.

Following a typhus epidemic in Manchuria and North Korea at the beginning of the previous year, which decimated many Chinese military units, both China and North Korea had begun to accuse the United States of deliberately and systematically deluging the Communist forces with germ-laden insects – flies, fleas, mosquitoes. The Americans were even said to have dropped clams, having bred cholera organisms in them. The Americans were denounced in the North Korean and Chinese newspapers as the 'new Nazis'.

On February 22 a formal charge of carrying out germ warfare was laid against the Americans by the North Korean Foreign Minister, Pak Hen. The charge was repeated at a Communist-organized World Peace Conference in Oslo three days later. The Communist nations took up the charge in various forms. On February 27 the head of the Hungarian Red Cross, Dr Istvann Florian, telegraphed to the International Red Cross headquarters in Geneva: 'American troops have again seized the bacteriological arm! They have hurled from their planes sickened insects at the Korean People's Army, the Chinese Volunteers and the rear territories . . . The International Red Cross must raise its voice against these inhuman atrocities.'

Two more days and the Red Cross of Communist Poland made a similar protest, concluding that 'all inactivity in this matter signifies solidarity with the criminals'. On March 6 the Roumanian Red Cross demanded immediate action 'to stop this bacteriological war of mass extermination'. Basing itself on the charges that American pilots were carrying out germ-warfare attacks on its soldiers, the Chinese government claimed an even wider germ-warfare plot. A 'Hate America' campaign was launched, which an Australian journalist then in China, Denis Warner, described:

> The population was mobilized to take preventive measures to kill flies, mosquitoes, fleas and rats, to clean up garbage, to destroy everything that might be a carrier or a breeding ground for America's filthy pestilences. In the first year of this campaign Peking listed the destruction of 120 million rats, and nearly one and a half million pounds' weight of flies, mosquitoes and fleas.
>
> A hundred and sixty million tons of garbage, including some that had been there since Ming times, were carted away from the streets: 280,000 kilometres of drains and ditches were filled; forty million cubic metres of earth were used to fill up stagnant pools. Big contingents of Chinese scientists went to Korea and came back laden with US-made containers and 'contaminated' insects . . .
>
> It was the greatest propaganda hoax in history; but that it succeeded in its purpose in China there is no doubt.

On March 7 the United States Secretary of State, Dean Acheson, reiterated earlier American denials of the germ-warfare charges, informing the President of the International Committee of the Red Cross, Paul Ruegger: 'The United States has not engaged in any form of bacteriological warfare.' But as if to trump the denials and make a mockery of them, the Chinese published the 'confessions' of American prisoners of war in Chinese hands, stating that they had participated in germ-warfare activities by dropping 'infected insects' on North Korea.

Seventy-eight American airmen had been interrogated. After as long as five months' solitary confinement and torture – both physical and mental – thirty-eight had 'confessed'. It was by describing the duress under which these confessions had been obtained that the United States was eventually able to reveal that no such germ warfare had taken place. The issue came to a head when, after the war, the germ-warfare accusations were raised by the Soviet delegation in the United Nations in New York. In answering the charges Dr Charles Mayo, the United States delegate, explained the technique of brainwashing that had been used to secure the confessions. Dr Mayo's account not only laid the charges themselves to rest, but gave articulate and painful expression to yet another element of the breakdown of civilized behaviour and the erosion of humane values in the twentieth century:

> It is a method obviously calculated by the Communists to bring a man to the point where a dry crust of bread or a few hours' uninterrupted sleep is a great event in his life. All the prisoners victimized were subjected to the same pattern of intimidation, deprivation of basic physical needs, isolation and physical and mental torture . . .
>
> The techniques varied only in detail . . .
>
> The total picture presented is one of human beings reduced to a status lower than that of animals, filthy, full of lice, festering wounds full of maggots, their sickness regulated to a point just short of death, unshaven, without haircuts or baths for as much as a year, men in rags, exposed to the elements, fed with carefully measured minimum quantities and the lowest quality of food and unsanitary water served often in rusty cans, isolated, faced with squads of trained interrogators, bulldozed, deprived of sleep and browbeaten with mental anguish . . .

The United States then proposed that the United Nations set up a commission to investigate both American charges of Communist atrocities and Communist charges of American germ warfare. With that, the Russians on the United Nations General Assembly's Political Committee changed the subject.

On the battlefield in Korea a struggle had begun during the early months of 1952 for possession of a small horseshoe-shaped hill known as the Hook. In scenes reminiscent of the struggle for Hill 60 in the Ypres Salient in the First World War, the Hook was captured, lost and then recaptured by American marines. So heavy were their losses, and so exhausting the struggle, that they were taken out of the line. They were replaced by British soldiers. Commanded by Brigadier Angus Irwin, the British held out against repeated attacks for several days, digging themselves deep trenches of the First World War variety.

Brigadier Irwin had fought in the retreat to the Channel ports in 1940, been captured, and held prisoner by the Germans for five years. More recently he had fought in Kenya in operations against the nationalist Mau Mau fighters there. In this new battle in Korea, when machine-gun and rifle magazines were emptied, and before they could be reloaded, he and his men used their rifle butts and even their steel helmets to hold off the Chinese. Although at one moment the British soldiers on the Hook were completely surrounded and outnumbered by the Chinese, British artillery support enabled them to launch a counter-attack, and the Hook was held.

Far from the Korean battlefield, the British in Egypt were facing a serious political setback. The British military presence in Egypt was intended as part of a defence strategy involving freedom of naval movement through the Suez Canal, and a military presence astride the land bridge from Africa to Asia. In a series of violent disturbances, Egyptian nationalists, encouraged in part by their own government, attacked British property and demanded an end to the British military presence. The first serious violence took place on January 12 at the village of Tel el Kebir. At this very village, seventy years earlier, British troops had defeated the Egyptian army under Arabi Pasha, established the first British military garrison in Egypt, and acquired a much prized battle honour.

To protect the British forces in Egypt, reinforcements were brought from Cyprus, and British artillery deployed against the rioters. On January 25 the fighting spread to Ismailia, where forty-one Egyptians were killed. Indignant at the loss of life, on the following day Egyptians attacked several British institutions in Cairo, and ten British subjects were killed. In an attempt to defuse the crisis King Farouk dismissed his Prime Minister, Nahas Pasha, and replaced him with Aly Maher Pasha, who promised to maintain order and punish those responsible for the riots. The violence subsided. But the underlying Egyptian resentment at Britain's continuing presence remained. So too did Egyptian determination to extend its full sovereignty over the Sudan. Britain was committed to Sudanese self-determination.

Within Britain, the death of King George VI on February 6 created an upsurge of sorrow and emotion. The King, who was only fifty-six years old at the time of his death, had not been a flamboyant or demonstrative personality. He had come to represent the virtues of calm reliability, even of shyness. Few photographs had made such an impact on the British public as that in which, with Queen Elizabeth, he was seen looking at the damage caused to Buckingham Palace after a German wartime air raid. Following his death, ten days of national mourning were declared. At the Lying-in-State of the

King in Westminster Hall, which took place over a period of three days, more than 300,000 people paid their respects, standing for many hours in rain, sleet and snow as the line moved slowly forward across the Thames bridges and along the Embankment.

The new sovereign, Queen Elizabeth II, was also proclaimed 'Head of the Commonwealth', the first time that this term was used. The burdens about to be thrust upon her had been understood by her father, who had apparently spoken of her as a 'poor lonely girl . . . she will be lonely all her life'.

On February 26 Winston Churchill, who had become Prime Minister at the head of a Conservative administration at the end of 1951, announced that Britain possessed its own atom bomb. It had been planned and produced in utmost secrecy by the Labour government of his predecessor, Clement Attlee, and was tested on Monte Bello Island, off the west coast of Australia, that October. What later became known as nuclear proliferation had begun.

In 1952, the possession of the atom bomb was thought to give Britain a greater say in the counsels of the North Atlantic Treaty Organization. But Britain could not compete numerically with either the United States or the Soviet Union. On November 6, thirty-four days after the British atom bomb was tested, the United States exploded the first-ever hydrogen bomb, at Eniwetok island in the Pacific. In order to carry out the test, the H-bomb – as it became known – was suspended from a tower. The explosion blew the tower, and the island on which it was built, out of existence, leaving a 'hole' in the ocean several hundred feet deep. The atom bombs dropped on Hiroshima and Nagasaki had each generated the equivalent explosive power of 120,000 tons – as compared to the largest wartime bombs of 20,000 tons. The new H-bomb had an explosive power greater than five million tons.

On April 28, with the coming into force of the Japanese Peace Treaty, Japan became once more a sovereign and independent State. Hirohito remained Emperor, but with parliament and not the imperial palace as the centre of legislative power. The Japanese Prime Minister, Shigeru Yoshida – a pre-war Japanese ambassador in London – made it clear that same day that Japan would pursue an anti-Communist policy and would align itself with the United States and the 'free nations'. The Soviet Union refused to admit the validity of the peace treaty, and vetoed Japan's request to join the United Nations, but, accepting the reality of the situation, agreed to withdraw the head of the Soviet military mission to Japan, General Kislenko, and substantially to reduce the size of the mission. Also on April 28, the Japanese government, in a further intimation of where its international alignment lay, signed a treaty of friendship with the Nationalist Chinese government on Taiwan.

One of the first measures of the new government was to pass a law that facilitated the release of convicted Japanese war criminals. Nobosuke Kishi, one of the Class A war criminals accused of masterminding Japan's aggression, who had been arrested in September 1945 but never brought to trial, entered national politics and within five years was Prime Minister.

Within a month of Japan returning to independence the West German provinces occupied by the Western Allies since May 1945 also became a separate, unitary State, with its capital in Bonn. One of the first acts of the Bonn government was to sentence the leader of the neo-Nazi Socialist Reich Party, Otto Remer, to three months in prison. The Nazi Socialist Reich Party was then declared 'unconstitutional', and banned.

As a thirty-two-year-old army major in 1944, Remer had played a decisive part in Berlin in maintaining Hitler's power in the immediate aftermath of the bomb plot. He had ended the war a major-general. By 1952 his party consisted of just over 10,000 members. Evading arrest, he fled to Egypt.[1]

The Transition Agreement of May 26, which established West Germany as a separate State, included a clause recognizing its obligation to make amends for the damage done during the Nazi era. On the following day a treaty was signed in Paris establishing the European Defence Community. The Federal German Republic was one of the signatories, as were France, Italy, Belgium, the Netherlands and Luxembourg. It was intended and assumed that the western frontier of Germany, the scene of German aggression in 1870, 1914 and 1940, would never again be crossed by Germany in war. It was also intended to protect the new community from external aggression from the east. Following the signature of the Treaty, the British and American governments, joined by France, issued a tripartite declaration that any action 'from any quarter' that threatened the European Defence Community would be regarded as a threat to their own security. The North Atlantic Treaty Organization immediately offered reciprocal guarantees, thus

[1] In 1994, having returned to Germany, Remer was sentenced to twenty-two months in prison for 'inciting hatred, violence and racism'. He escaped again, this time to Spain, where he died in 1997.

tying the United States and Canada into the Western European security system.

Later that year, as part of the integration of the new Federal German Republic with the rest of Western Europe, Britain and Germany signed the London Debt Agreement, resolving Germany's long-outstanding First World War reparations debts. A much reduced scale of payment of these debts had first been agreed in 1930, on the eve of Hitler's coming to power. In 1935 Hitler had declared a moratorium on these debt payments. In the 1 August 1952 agreement the West German government agreed to make a final set of token repayments, in order to clear the way for future economic loans designed to revive the West German economy.

On September 10, in Luxembourg City Hall, West Germany signed an agreement with the State of Israel. Under this Luxembourg Treaty the West German government agreed to pay $865 million to Israel – which had been in existence for only four years – as reparation for 'material damage' suffered by the Jews at the hands of the Nazis. The sum was a substantial one, and served as the basis for regular cash payments to many thousands of individual survivors in Israel over the next half-century. The signing ceremony lasted thirteen minutes, and was conducted in complete silence. The signatories were the Federal German Chancellor, Konrad Adenauer, and the Israeli Foreign Minister, Moshe Sharett. East Germany declined utterly to take any part in the negotiations or to accept any liability for what had been done in the Nazi years.

In a separate agreement signed that day in New York, Israel agreed that $110 million of the West German payment would go to the relief of Jewish victims outside Israel. Abba Eban, the Israeli diplomat who signed the New York agreement, commented: 'The Germans, who wanted to wipe the Jews off the face of the earth, are now signing a contract of compensation with the Jewish State.' There was much for the reparation money to be used for at the time of the Luxembourg and New York agreements. That summer there were still 1,845 Displaced Persons, among them five hundred children, living in what – seven years earlier – had been Dachau concentration camp. They were among tens of thousands of Jews still in Europe who needed help to move on to other countries and to build new lives.

There was also a new category of refugee recognized that year – people fleeing from Communist rule and persecution. At the end of 1951 President Truman had set up the American President's 'Escapee Programme': 1952 was its first full year. Work was also in full spate that year by the United Nations Works and Relief Agency for Palestine (UNWRA) which was responsible for the feeding and welfare, including education, of 873,000 Arab refugees who had fled from Palestine during the Israeli War of Independence four years earlier. They had come to rest in refugee camps in Lebanon, Syria, Jordan and Gaza. Some of their camps were run by the host government, but 35 percent of the refugees were under direct UNWRA supervision. The United Nations financed this operation with more than $70 million a year, by far the largest single refugee expenditure worldwide.

The workings of Soviet Communism were becoming more and more shrouded in mystery. Between May and July 1952 a series of trials were held in utmost secrecy in Moscow. Those accused were leading Jewish writers, actors, poets, translators and physicians. One Jew who could not be brought into the show trial was the great comic actor, Solomon Mikhoels, who had been murdered on Stalin's orders four years earlier. All those who were put on trial had served, at the request of the Soviet government, on the wartime Jewish Anti-Fascist Committee. As members of the committee they had been sent to Britain and the United States to explain the Soviet war effort and the suffering of the Soviet people. This they had done. One of them, Solomon Abramovitch Lozovsky, was an old Bolshevik from revolutionary days, a former Deputy Foreign Minister, who, as the wartime head of the Soviet Information Bureau, had met many times with Stalin. One of the first of the group to be arrested, he had been held in prison for more than three years before the trial.

Fourteen of the arrested Jews were brought to trial. All but one were sentenced to death and shot. The fortunate one was the only woman among them. The Soviet newspapers trumpeted the success of 'exposing internal enemies'. In Czechoslovakia, the former Secretary of the Czech Communist Party, Rudolf Slansky, who had been arrested the previous year, together with eleven other former senior Communist Party officials – all of them, including Slansky, were Jews – were accused of a range of espionage and treason charges. These charges related to the failures of the government as a whole, such as setting industrial production targets 'too low' and building new plants whose productive capacity was no greater than those which they replaced. The accused were also charged with wanting to separate Czechoslovakia from the Communist bloc and restoring capitalism.

The trial took place in the court room of a prison. All the accused were found guilty, and nine of the twelve, including Slansky, were hanged.

*   *   *

In the United States, a setback to the Korean War came when the country's steel mills, eighty-eight in all – which were producing a record tonnage for the war effort – fell victim to a wage dispute and were in imminent danger of closing down. The management had refused to negotiate with the main union involved, the United Steel Workers, and a full-scale strike, involving 650,000 men, was in prospect. The Secretary of Defense, Robert A. Lovett, warned Truman that the 'entire combat technique' of the army, navy and air force fighting in Korea depended upon the fullest use of the industrial capacity of the continental United States. In Lovett's words, 'we are holding the line with ammunition, and not with the lives of our troops'. Any curtailment of steel production would, Lovett warned, 'endanger the lives of our fighting men'. Truman took swift action. On April 8, the day on which the strike was due to begin, having authorized an increase in wages, he went on national television and radio to explain that, by means of Executive Order, he was taking the steel mills into government ownership.[1]

As a result of the Executive Order, the steel mills continued to work. But within a few days the steel industry went to the courts, and after a prolonged legal wrangle, on April 29, a Federal district judge in Washington, David A. Pine, declared that the seizure of the mills was illegal. In the judge's words: 'I believe that the contemplated strike, if it came, with all its awful results, would be less injurious to the public than the injury which would flow from a timorous judicial recognition that there is some basis for this claim to unlimited and unrestrained executive power.'

The case was taken to the Supreme Court, and there, on June 2, by a majority of six to three, Truman's action was declared unconstitutional. It was only the third time in United States history that the Supreme Court had placed a specific restriction on Presidential authority.[2] The crucial sentences of the judgment, read out by Justice Hugo L. Black, read: 'We cannot with faithfulness to our constitutional system hold that the Commander in Chief of the Armed Forces has the ultimate power as such to take possession of private property in order to keep labor disputes from stopping production. This is a job for the Nation's lawmakers, not for its military authorities.'

[1] In 1917 Churchill, when Minister of Munitions, had taken over a British aircraft factory for the government, to ensure that production would be maintained at a critical time for aircraft on the Western Front – where Truman was an artillery officer.
[2] The two previous occasions were in October 1864 when the Supreme Court overruled the conviction of conspiracy imposed by a military commission (part of the executive branch of government) against L. P. Milligan; and in 1935 when the Supreme Court ruled that Roosevelt had acted unlawfully in removing a member of the Federal Trade Commission (Humphrey).

And not, it would seem, for its President either. The presidential aspect was commented on by Judge Douglas, one of the majority. 'Today a kindly President uses the seizure of power to effect a wage increase and to keep the steel furnaces in production,' he wrote. 'Yet tomorrow another President might use the same power to prevent a wage increase, to curb trade unionists, to regiment labor as oppressively as industry thinks it has been regimented by this seizure.'

As soon as the Supreme Court verdict was made known the wage increase was annulled and the steel strike began. The losses in production were enormous: twenty-one million tons of steel. By the time a settlement could be reached by agreement with the steel bosses which included a rise in wages and a rise in the cost of steel, the military output for the year had been cut by a third.

On June 23 the United Nations forces in Korea, which had watched with alarm the build-up of Chinese forces during the ceasefire negotiations, carried out a bombing attack on power plants in North Korea. One of these plants was near the Yalu River, the border between North Korea and Chinese Manchuria. The Indian Prime Minister, Jawaharlal Nehru, who had for several months been trying behind the scenes to work for a truce in Korea, declared himself 'aghast'. In Britain there was unease that the United States had not consulted its British ally before ordering the air strikes so close to the border. Anthony Eden, the British Foreign Secretary, called the lack of consultation 'regrettable'. The American government apologized.

The fighting in Korea was no longer taking place up and down the peninsula, but in a narrow front across it, about fifty miles north of Seoul. Both sides were agreed that in any truce there should be a Demilitarized Zone (the DMZ) across the peninsula, along the line of the facing armies. But negotiations stuck on the issue of prisoners of war. The North Koreans wanted all 140,000 of their captured soldiers sent back. The United Nations insisted that half of them wanted to stay in the South, and that they should be allowed to do so. The conditions in the prisoner-of-war camps were bad. In one riot on Koje Island – the second – five prisoners and one American soldier were killed. In a further riot on Koje the American commander of the island was held hostage until better conditions were promised. At two other camps, at Cheju and on Pongam Island, riots, in part instigated by Communist prisoners demanding their return to the North, were suppressed by armed troops, and 138 prisoners killed. An attempt by the Soviet Union to condemn the United States for 'brutalities' on Pongam was defeated at the General Assembly by forty-five votes to five, the Soviet bloc countries joining the Soviet Union in the condemnation, but the ten Asian and Arab countries abstaining – much to Soviet chagrin.

On July 23 a coup d'état in Egypt brought to an end the sixteen-year rule of King Farouk – who had come to the throne at the age of sixteen. He was overthrown, without bloodshed, by a group of army officers, led by General Mohammed Neguib, who resented Egypt's lack of assertiveness in the Arab and Muslim world. Farouk went as an exile, first to Italy and then to Monaco. Neguib took dictatorial powers for himself, and within a year proclaimed Egypt a republic. Such influence as Britain had been able to retain through the King was ended.

In Persia, a government headed by Dr Muhammad Musaddiq was also challenging both British and United States interests in his country, and doing so successfully. Supported by popular acclaim in the streets, and bypassing the moderate stance of the Shah, Musaddiq nationalized all foreign oil interests in his country. Since 1914 the British government had been a majority shareholder in the Anglo-Iranian Oil Company. This agreement had been negotiated by Winston Churchill on the eve of the First World War when he was First Lord of the Admiralty. Almost forty years later, as Prime Minister, Churchill had to watch one of his most successful financial arrangements being destroyed.

Britain appealed for judgment to the International Court of Justice at The Hague. The Persians argued that the Court could not intervene in their country's internal affairs as this would be a violation of the United Nations Charter. The British argued that an Anglo-Persian Oil Convention of 1933 constituted an international treaty, and that Persia was therefore under an obligation to accept the verdict of the Court. By nine votes to five the International Court decided, on July 22, that it had no jurisdiction in the case.[1]

The cruellest of the British overseas conflicts was in the Kenya Colony, where the Mau Mau secret society declared that its aim was to drive all Europeans from Kenya – rulers, farmers and tradesmen. One section of the Mau Mau oath read: 'When the reed buck horn is blown, if I leave a European farm before killing the European owner, may this oath kill me.' There was

[1] Sir Arnold Macnair, a British judge on the Court since 1946, and President of the Court at the time of the judgment, concurred in the decision that the Court had no jurisdiction.

indignation in the House of Commons when the Mau Mau oath was read out by the Colonial Secretary, Oliver Lyttelton. In his memoirs, Lyttelton wrote: 'The driving force of the Mau Mau movement was, nakedly, – power, and the expulsion of the white man: its methods of gaining adherents were the methods of African witchcraft,' and he continued:

The Mau Mau oath is the most bestial, filthy and nauseating incantation which perverted minds can ever have brewed. I am not unduly squeamish, but when I first read it I was so revolted that it got between me and my appetite. It shocked even lawyers who had prosecuted or defended in cases of ritual murder in Africa. Its political object was simply to outlaw and ostracize from the tribe and tribal customs anyone who had taken it.

I can recall no instance when I have felt the forces of evil to be so near and so strong. As I wrote memoranda or instructions, I would suddenly see a shadow fall across the page – the horned shadow of the Devil himself.

Those Kikuyu who were Christian rejected the barbarous pagan practices of the Mau Mau, including forceful mutilation. Between June and September more than sixty Kikuyu were murdered by the Mau Mau for refusing to join them. The killing of White Europeans began in the first week of October. Farmers and coffee planters were the principal victims. Thirty European civilians were murdered between October 1952 and the end of 1954, but, as law and order were enforced, only two in the five following years. During that same period more than 1,800 African civilians were murdered. 'The facts are grim,' wrote Lyttelton, 'and they show that the overwhelming weight of the Mau Mau attack fell upon their fellow Africans.'

On October 7 Chief Waruhiu, who had ruled the Kikuyu for thirty years, and who wanted to work with the British, was forced out of his car on the road near Nairobi and killed. A few days earlier he had issued a condemnation of the Mau Mau. At the end of the month Oliver Lyttelton visited Kenya. In his memoirs he described the activities of the Mau Mau from day to day:

Concerted operations were rare, but on one occasion a gang pressed home repeated attacks upon a police post, in spite of heavy losses. This was unlike their usual mode of warfare, but was explained when it was found that their fanaticism had been hopped up by smoking hemp.

The White settlers, living generally in isolated farms, gave an example of steady nerves. They did not know whether to trust their Kikuyu boys or overseers. At night they barricaded their farms and kept loaded rifles at their side. They must have waited tensely for the sound of the door or the windows being tried, or for footfalls in the darkness. In the day-time they went about armed, and could never be certain that a gang would not spring upon them.

Lyttelton was under no illusions as to the reality of eventual political control over the colony. There were more than six million Africans in the country, of whom a million were Kikuyu. Living among them, but mostly in the towns, were 150,000 Asians and 60,000 Whites. It was essential, Lyttelton told the Whites when he met them, that the confidence of the Africans should be gained by giving them, however gradually, a share in government. To a delegation of White settlers Lyttelton stated:

Sixty thousand Europeans cannot expect to hold all the political power and to exclude Africans from the legislature and from the Government. The end of that will be to build up pressures which will burst into rebellion and bloodshed.

You are suspicious and critical of what you term in a pejorative sense 'Colonial Office rule'. When, as the result of over-conservative or traditional policies you provoke an explosion, you are not slow to ask the British Government and the Colonial Office, which at other times you attack, for troops, aeroplanes and money to suppress a rebellion.

I warn you that one day you will be let down, and therefore besides force, which must now be used and which we will furnish, you must turn your minds to political reform, and to measures which will gradually engage the consent and help of the governed.

The security of your homes, the security of the money, hard work and skill which you have lavished upon your farms, and upon the industries which you have begun to build, cannot rest upon battalions of British troops: it can only rest upon the building of a multi-racial society.

On October 20 a State of Emergency was declared in Kenya. Two months later the Mau Mau leader Jomo Kenyatta – who had been educated at a Scottish missionary school, and spent many years in England – was arrested and brought to trial, charged with administering unlawful oaths. He was sentenced to life imprisonment.

As well as in Kenya, British colonial rule was being challenged in Nigeria, the Central African Federation and Uganda. There were also uprisings in the Malayan Federation and British Guiana. For the British national servicemen, confronted at the age of eighteen by the possibility of various foreign postings, each of these countries represented a perilous destination. In Malaya, a British-officered police force of 60,000 men had to maintain order among five million people. Of his own visit to Malaya, five months after the murder of the High Commissioner there, Lyttelton wrote: 'Morale amongst planters, tin miners, and amongst Chinese loyalists and Malays, was at its lowest. The grip of the terrorists was tightening, and the feelings of the loyalists could be summed up in one word, despair.'

Tens of thousands of Malays were in detention. At any given time more than five thousand were being held in prison without trial. Those found guilty of murdering British soldiers were executed. Chinese Communists – who predominated in the Malay insurgency – were deported to China. In the conflict between the police and the insurgents, 2,578 insurgents were killed, of whom more than two thousand were Chinese.

The British government was committed to maintaining the colonial administration until such time as it could win the war against the insurgents. In his paper to the Cabinet on his return to Britain, Lyttelton set out a formidable list of aids to control which were needed, including armoured vehicles, arms and equipment. It was obtained from the United States, as was earth-shifting equipment, and chemical defoliants to clear the jungle on either side of the main roads. Within five years law and order were restored, and power transferred to the Malays.

In the Caribbean, pressure for independence was resisted by Britain. When a former Second World War bomber pilot, Billy Strachan – the first ethnic West Indian to be commissioned as an officer in the Royal Air Force – began a tour of the Caribbean islands to advocate independence and union for all the islands, he was barred by the colonial authorities from proceeding, and deported from Trinidad.

In South Africa, over which Britain had no control, the African National Congress warned the government in January, by letter, that unless the 'unjust laws' of apartheid were repealed by the last day of February, there would be protest meetings held throughout the country. The letter read, in part:

> The Government, through its repressive policy of trusteeship, segregation and apartheid, and through legislation that continues to insult and degrade

the African people by depriving them of fundamental human rights enjoyed in all democratic communities, have categorically rejected our offer of co-operation. The consequence has been the gradual worsening of the social, economic and political position of the African people, and a rising tide of racial bitterness and tension.

It was a source of 'supreme satisfaction', the African National Congress continued, 'to know that we have the full support and sympathy of all enlightened and honest men and women, Black and White, in our country and across the seas, and that the present crisis and tension have been brought about, not by the African leaders, but by the Government'. In reply, the Prime Minister, Dr D. F. Malan, warned that if a campaign of civil disobedience began the government 'will make full use of the machinery at its disposal to quell any disturbances and, thereafter, deal adequately with those responsible for initiating subversive activities of any nature whatever'. Malan added, in justification of the separations imposed by apartheid, that the differences between the Black Africans and the Whites were 'permanent and not man-made'.

On March 20 there was a triumph for the African National Congress when the country's Supreme Court ruled that the apartheid legislation of Malan's government was unconstitutional. A month later, on April 22, Malan introduced legislation to parliament – where he had a clear majority – making parliament itself a High Court, so that the Supreme Court ruling would be of no consequence, and the apartheid legislation would remain on the statute book unchallenged. One piece of legislation that was thereby 'legalized' was an amendment to the Native Laws Amendment Act, whereby no African was allowed to stay in an urban area for more than seventy-two hours unless he or she had lived there for fifteen years or worked for the same employer for ten years. Under another piece of legislation, entitled the Natives (Abolition of Passes and Co-ordination of Documents) Act, all Black male adults had to carry at all times a so-called 'reference book' containing details of birth, taxation, movement and employment. This was the first of the 'pass laws' that were to be at the centre of Black and liberal White protest in South Africa for many years to come.

As apartheid was reaffirmed and intensified, the African National Congress embarked, on June 26, on a campaign of civil disobedience against 'unjust laws'. One form that the defiance took was to enter a railway station through the 'Europeans only' entrance. Those violating the law would be taken to court. Crowds of supporters would gather outside the court. The police would order them to disperse and they would refuse. The police would then use force. Several Europeans joined the protest movement, among them Patrick Duncan, the son of a former Governor-General of South Africa. By the end of the year, more than six thousand Africans were in prison.

There were also deaths. After two Africans had been arrested at a railway station in Port Elizabeth, riots followed and seven Africans and four Europeans were killed. One of the Europeans was a fifteen-year-old schoolboy. During a riot in Kimberley thirteen Africans were shot dead. In East London rioters set fire to an African training college, a Roman Catholic church and a Christian mission hall. A European nun who had spent her life at the mission was burned to death in her car.

In an attempt to deter European supporters of the African National Congress, legislation was promulgated on November 28 whereby 'any person who uses language or behaves in a manner calculated to cause natives to resist or contravene any law shall be guilty of an offence'. At the same time it was forbidden for more than ten Africans to meet without official permission. In justifying the new regulations, the Minister of Justice, C. R. Swart – who in 1960 was to be the last Governor-General and in 1961 the first President of the Republic of South Africa – told his Nationalist Party followers: 'You cannot fight the law of the jungle with the rule of law. We are faced with a situation which we, as bearers of White civilization, can no longer tolerate.'

Swart embodied the new laws in a measure that gave the government sweeping powers of arrest and detention: the Suppression of Communism Act. As a result of the act, Sam Kahn, a South African Jew and one of the three members of Parliament who represented African interests in the Assembly, was removed from Parliament altogether. Another South African Jew who had championed the cause of the African workers, E. S. Sachs – who had been Secretary-General of the Transvaal Garment Workers' Union for twenty-four years – was forbidden to attend any public meetings. During a protest march by his supporters against this ruling, Sachs was arrested. Protests by British and French trade unionists failed to secure his release.

In the United States the activities of Senator Joseph McCarthy in seeking to find and imprison Communists were unceasing. Under the Port Security Programme, which was given a spurious legitimacy by the alleged demands of the Korean War, employment tests were authorized for all maritime and dock workers in American ports. Many dockers lost their jobs, principally union leaders and those who were active in union affairs. Even after a court decision declared the programme unlawful, and ordered the firings to cease, blacklisting continued.

'The real pressure', wrote a British visitor to the United States, Kingsley Martin, on July 5, 'is a continuous day-by-day affair which has the effect of rewarding mediocrity, cowardice and sycophancy, and silencing independent and creative talent.' In August fourteen leaders of the Communist Party in California were each sentenced to five years in prison. In October a Senate Judiciary Sub-Committee examined the records of American employees at the United Nations. Thirteen refused to answer questions on the ground that they might incriminate themselves. This was a basic constitutional right: the Fifth Amendment.

A Grand Jury investigation reported a month later that 'an overwhelmingly large' group of Americans employed at the United Nations were 'disloyal' to their country. A New York State law banning Communists from teaching in the State was upheld by the Supreme Court. But a 'loyalty oath' imposed by the State of Oklahoma on teachers was judged unconstitutional. Within the State Department, diplomats had to appear before a Loyalty Board. It was a witch-hunt of the most virulent sort, nationwide and relentless. One of its victims was the British-born actor and film-maker Charlie Chaplin, who was accused of having connections with 'subversive' causes. When that charge failed, Chaplin's residency was revoked on suspicion that he had encouraged his lover to have an abortion. For Truman's Attorney-General, James McGranery – a devout Roman Catholic – this was as severe a suspicion as the political one, albeit equally tendentious. Leaving the United States, Chaplin vowed never to return. The banishment was a personal tragedy for Chaplin, and a severe loss to the film industry and culture of his adopted country. It was to be twenty-one years before he returned to the United States, at the age of eighty-four, to receive his second Academy Award (he had won his first in 1928).

That year the film *High Noon* was nominated for an Oscar. The screenplay had been written by Carl Foreman, who was among those being investigated by McCarthy. After Foreman refused to testify before McCarthy's committee, the Oscar went elsewhere, and was granted to Foreman only posthumously, thirty-two years later. Foreman, placed on a blacklist that prevented him from working in Hollywood, or in any American film studio, went to live in Britain.[1]

---

[1] It was in Britain that he wrote the screenplay for *The Bridge on the River Kwai* (1957), which won four Oscars.

Despite there being a Democrat majority of ten in the Senate, Truman could do little to staunch the flow of prejudice and alarm. Southern Democrat Senators did not usually follow a liberal line. On June 25 an Immigration Bill was passed, over Truman's veto, that established quotas according to national origin, a system which the President considered restrictive and racist. His attempt to transfer more than 20,000 federal jobs from the realm of patronage to that of regular civil service recruitment was defeated in the Senate. Truman had no problem, however, in winning Congressional support for a measure arising directly from the Korean War, the Veterans' Readjustment Assistance Act – known, as was its Second World War predecessor, as the GI Bill of Rights. Under this legislation service personnel returning from Korea to the United States were eligible for educational grants, housing assistance and loan guarantees.

The United States to which these soldiers returned was one in which, for the first time since 1881, no lynching had been reported.

Throughout the autumn the talks on a Korean ceasefire had continued at Panmunjom. Various attempts were made to break the deadlock, including one by the government of India – which both Russia and China rejected, much to Nehru's annoyance – and one by a United Nations delegation. It too failed, on the North Korean insistence that all prisoners of war should be repatriated, not merely those who wanted to return.

On October 5, while the United Nations proposal was still under consideration, the Chinese forces in North Korea launched their heaviest offensive of the year. Attacking with artillery and tank support along two-thirds of the front line, they engaged the United Nations forces in fierce fighting. Several hill positions held by United Nations forces on the road to Seoul were overrun. But there was no breakthrough and, as on the Western Front in the First World War, the attacking force lost heavily in being halted and eventually repulsed, with as many as 23,000 Chinese troops being killed in two weeks. Among those who halted the Chinese advance were soldiers of the Royal Thai Expeditionary Force. In the two-week struggle for Pork Chop Hill that began on October 31 they were awarded thirty-nine medals by the Americans, including a Legion of Merit, and a Distinguished Unit Citation which read:

Charged with the defense of a vitally contested hill, the battalion girded itself to withstand an attack, and exhibiting an absolute refusal to yield, repulsed repeated charges by large numbers of the enemy.

When the battalion's outpost position was attacked by two enemy companies with supporting fire from heavy weapons, a furious hand to hand struggle took place in the bunkers, trenches, and communications positions. Although enemy Bangalore-torpedoes caused extensive damage, the battalion held and the enemy withdrew but immediately began to regroup for a second attack.

The enemy forces soon launched another, more savage attack using heavy supporting fire. Refusing to be defeated, the battalion fought courageously, and, failing to breach the battalion's position, the attackers were forced to withdraw with heavy losses in dead and wounded, abandoning a large amount of supplies and equipment.

The extraordinary heroism and resolution exhibited by the members of the Royal Thailand Battalion reflect great credit on themselves and the military service of the Kingdom of Thailand.

In all, 252 Thai soldiers were killed in action in Korea fighting with the United Nations forces.

In the United States, the issue of the Korean War held centre stage in the Presidential election campaign throughout the autumn. Truman was not standing: the Democrat candidate was Adlai Stevenson, who gave his full support to Truman's conduct of the war. Under the American system, Truman would remain President for two months after the election, whoever won. The Republican candidate was General Eisenhower, who, calling upon all his authority as a soldier – and until April the Supreme Commander, NATO – made use of the widespread weariness with the war to denounce Truman's handling of it, and to brand it as 'Truman's war'. In a national television broadcast on October 24, Eisenhower described Korea as 'the burial ground for twenty thousand American dead' and promised that if he was elected President he would end the war. 'I shall go to Korea,' he said.

If Eisenhower had a way of ending the war, an angry Truman told an audience in Winona, Minnesota, he should tell him at once, and thus 'save a lot of lives'. What was the point of waiting until after the election. 'If he can do it after he is elected, we can do it now.'

The issue of Korea was brought before the seventh Assembly of the United Nations on October 24, the day of Eisenhower's dramatic pledge to end the conflict. At the opening session Dean Acheson appealed to China and Korea to instruct their negotiators at Panmunjom to reach agreement and avoid further bloodshed. The Soviet Union, Mexico, Chile and India each put forward proposals: India's was the one that most effectively tried to bridge the gap between forcible and voluntary repatriation of North Korean prisoners of war. This involved the creation of an 'umpire' to decide who should and who should not be sent back. After five weeks of debate, the Indian resolution was accepted by fifty-four votes to five. The Soviet Union objected, and the Soviet bloc followed suit.

Then the Chinese Foreign Minister, Chou En-lai, also rejected it, in public, and the proposal failed.

The American presidential election took place on November 4. Eisenhower was elected by an overwhelming majority, winning all but nine of the forty-eight States, including Stevenson's Illinois and Truman's Missouri. He then flew to Korea, as he had promised to do, spent three days touring the front lines, and returned to the United States. The way in which the war was being handled from Washington, he said, was 'intolerable'. When Truman was shown a poll in which forty-three per cent of those questioned thought it had been a mistake for the United States to have gone to war in Korea, he wrote in a private note for himself: 'I wonder how far Moses would have gone if he'd taken a poll in Egypt? What would Jesus Christ have preached if he'd taken a poll in Israel?' It was not polls or public opinion which counted. 'It's right and wrong.'

In the struggle between Communism and the West, the award of a Stalin Peace Prize to Paul Robeson, the Black American singer, actor and political activist, served only – in the words of his *New York Times* obituary twenty-four years later – to 'close many minds to his artistic merits as a singer and actor'. For several years vigilante groups had disrupted Robeson's concerts, and professional concert halls had refused him bookings. His earnings, which in 1947 stood at $100,000, had dropped by 1952 to $6,000.

In Britain, to reduce the housing shortage that had continued since the end of the war seven years earlier, a new pattern of construction, 'the people's house', was introduced. In the first six months of the year more than 100,000 houses were built. The Minister of Housing, Harold Macmillan – who had fought in the trenches in the First World War – remembered the pledge of the post-war government in 1918 to create 'homes fit for heroes'. The new homes had one less problem to contend with than the old: the number of large households prevalent three decades earlier had considerably decreased.

London faced an unexpected enemy that winter: smog, in which the light of day turned dull, and sometimes to deep darkness, as a result of concentrations of sulphur dioxide and other pollutants in the air. During a four-day smog in December, four thousand Londoners died.

In that year of its restored sovereignty, Japan became a pioneer in radio technology which was to affect the lives of hundreds of millions of people, with the marketing by the Sony company of the first pocket-sized transistor radio. Television also saw an innovation that year which was eventually to make its impact in all democratic societies, the one-minute television commercial. It was first used by Eisenhower as part of his successful presidential campaign.

Globally, the constructive advances in commercial flying were in contrast to the destructive effects of aerial warfare in Korea. On May 2 the world's first regular commercial jet airliner service was opened. It was between London and Johannesburg: a once-weekly service that was soon increased to three times weekly. A journey that until then, using propeller planes, had taken twenty-eight hours, was completed in eighteen hours and forty minutes, with stops at Rome, Beirut, Khartoum, Entebbe and Livingstone.[1]

With the help of the International Civil Aviation Organization, almost a million dollars were given to different countries to help them train pilots and flying experts. India, Pakistan and Turkey were among the beneficiaries of this scheme. With the accession of Japan to the organization at the end of the year, its membership reached fifty-eight.

By the end of the year, thirty-seven national airlines were flying on intercontinental routes. These included twelve on the North Atlantic route – the most developed – and four that flew from Europe to Australia, all on a regular and at least weekly basis. The second half of the century, still mired in the ancient curse of war, was becoming a period of mass communication and mass travel.

---

[1] In 1998 the fastest, non-stop commercial flight from London to Johannesburg took ten hours and fifty minutes.

CHAPTER TWO

1953

There will be no sudden miraculous and sensational
victory over the powers of darkness.

HUGH SETON-WATSON

On 6 January 1953 an Asian Socialist Conference convened in Rangoon.
Socialism was the aspiration of all the delegates for their respective countries,
though the only country in Asia in which a Socialist government was then
in power was one of the smallest, Israel, on the western edge of the continent.
The head of the Israeli delegation was the Foreign Minister, Moshe Sharett,
who in the previous year had signed the Luxembourg agreement for reparations from West Germany. As an immediate result of the contacts made
in Rangoon, Burma sent farmers to Israel to be trained in modern agricultural
techniques. In return Israel sent officers and equipment to modernize the
Burmese army. An Israeli goodwill mission was even sent to Communist
China, though it would be four decades before full diplomatic relations were
opened between the two countries.

Within three weeks of the opening of the Asian Socialist Conference in
Rangoon, the United Nations forces in Korea carried out a small experimental
assault, Operation Smack. It was designed as a joint ground–air experiment:
a daylight raid on a North Korean position known as T-Bone Hill by two
infantry platoons supported by tanks and tactical air forces. It was to be
observed by a large number of air and ground generals, and by fifteen
journalists.

The aim of the operation was to capture North Korean and Chinese soldiers
and take them back for interrogation. But no prisoners were taken, although
more than thirty of the defenders of the hill were killed. Three of the
attackers were killed and sixty-one wounded. There was an outcry in the
United States when the journalists who had been invited to witness the

operation wrote it up as if it had been mounted solely for the entertainment of the visiting generals. 'Some newspapers', the American Commander-in-Chief, General Mark Clark, recalled bitterly, 'went so far as to compare the operation with the death orgies held for the pleasure of Roman nobles and ladies in the Coliseum.'

It was left to Forrest Edwards, of the Associated Press, to set the American mind at rest by assuring his readers that despite the failure of the raid it had been preceded by 'weeks of intense, careful planning', and had in no way been a public relations exercise. In fact, for Mark Clark, the failure of Operation Smack was overshadowed by the very real shortage of ammunition supplies in the rear area stockpiles, which had forced him to set strict quotas for artillery attack: similar quotas had been needed for the British artillery on the Western Front during the First World War.

The Korean death toll continued to mount. On May 13 a Canadian soldier, Private Robert Frederick Girard, was killed. He was the third soldier from the small town of London, Ontario, to die in Korea. The town war memorial does not list their names, or mention Korea; but alongside its First and Second World War tributes to 'The Glorious Dead', are incised the years '1950–1953'.

Asia would remain in the spotlight and its struggles continue to dominate the world headlines and concerns that year. Latin America seemed less central to the world outside it. In a broadcast talk towards the end of the year a former British Ambassador to Argentina, Sir David Kelly, stated that the whole Latin American region was so mismanaging its internal affairs that he no longer had faith in its claim to be 'the land of the future'. Yet United States business and banking interests invested $5,700 million in Latin America that year, more than double the figure of a decade earlier, and representing forty per cent of the total United States overseas investment. This made the problem of Communism seem all the more acute from the perspective of the United States.

In October, John Moors Cabot, the United States Assistant Secretary of State for Inter-American Affairs, warned in blunt terms: 'No regime which is openly playing the Communist game can expect from us the positive co-operation we normally seek to extend to all of our sister republics.' This warning was aimed primarily at the activities of the Guatemalan government. But, in a popular campaign against United States owned companies, that government expropriated 234,000 acres of as yet uncultivated land that had been acquired for eventual fruit cultivation by the American-owned and -managed United Fruit Company.

John Cabot qualified his warning remark about Communism with one that caused satisfaction among the more dictatorial of the Latin American countries. 'We cannot take the attitude', he said, 'that we can afford to feud with every Government whose internal politics do not altogether meet our approval.' President Juan Perón of Argentina had recently announced – not long after the death of his wife Evita – that he was trying to create a South American bloc capable of resisting 'dollar imperialism'. The Assistant Secretary's caveat was a welcome respite from the prospect of active and hostile intervention by the United States.

Hoping to benefit Argentina's working class, with whom his wife had a close rapport, Perón signed a pact of economic collaboration with Chile, then persuaded both Paraguay and Ecuador to join it. But it was to the United States that he had to turn – and did turn – before the end of the year to receive the technical and financial help that was essential for him to proceed as he wished with a major plan of industrialization, and the increase in his oil productive capacity. For large-scale economic plans the 'Colossus of the North' was an indispensable partner, no matter what the political implications might be.

In Colombia, the dictatorial regime of President Laureano Gomez was overthrown in the summer, in a bloodless coup organized by the Commander-in-Chief of the army, General Gustavo Rojas Pinilla, who became President. Those guerrillas who had fought against the previous regime were pardoned, and Dr Gomez himself was allowed to go into exile in the United States. In Bolivia, the revolutionaries who had seized power the previous year in a bloody coup in which a thousand people were killed, retained power and strengthened it. The tin mines on which the national economy depended had been nationalized after the coup, and two counter-revolutionary attempts by right-wing groups during 1953 were quickly crushed. Despite the failure of the government to compensate United States stockholders of the nationalized mines, the American government continued to provide Bolivia with financial and technical help, including a $9 million grant that enabled Bolivia to purchase two thousand tons of wheat from the United States.

The Latin American governments, always proudly independent, often torn by internal dissent, were always watched over closely by the United States. Not since the German Nazis had made considerable efforts to establish their influence in the Argentine a decade and a half earlier had any other European or Asian power been able to dislodge the United States predominance.

Tyranny and dictatorship continued to flourish in many different forms and guises. Taking a leaf from Stalin's book, the Czech President, Klement Gottwald, turned against those Czechoslovak farmers who were resisting collectivization, denouncing them as 'kulaks' and 'village rich' who were acting as 'leeches' on the co-operative farming body. A tax based on the expected agricultural income of all farms was imposed on the independent farmers, who were regularly denounced as 'kulaks and speculators'. In a further punitive measure all 'kulaks' were denied food rations and clothing coupons, even if their agricultural delivery quotas had been fulfilled.

In Poland, a Polish government decree on February 9 gave the State the right to make and end all appointments within the Catholic Church, and to obtain an oath of loyalty to the Communist system from individual churchmen. In Egypt, on February 10, General Neguib, who less than a month earlier had dissolved all political Parties, was voted dictatorial powers by an emasculated parliament. Six days later, on February 16, at the other extremity of Africa, the passing by another emasculated parliament of the Public Safety Act gave the Governor-General of South Africa, and in some cases the Minister of Justice, power to declare a state of emergency and issue regulations that would override existing Acts of Parliament.

In South Africa the Acts of Parliament continued to be repressive. That year the Native Labour (Settlement of Disputes) Act made strikes by Africans illegal, and refused recognition to Black trade unions. The Reservations and Separate Amenities Act restricted many urban facilities – including beaches and swimming pools – according to racial considerations. The African National Congress spoke out against these measures, but its members faced the prospect of arrest if they fell foul of the laws designed to inhibit Black political activity. They were unable to preach the weapon of strike without immediate arrest and imprisonment. Some ANC members advocated violence, others called for restraint.

Among those who were caught up in this debate was a thirty-five-year-old lawyer, Nelson Mandela, who in 1952 had given up his law practice in order to travel the country advocating the need for a democratic and multi-racial society. During 1953 he took up the cause of the 60,000 and more Africans who were being forced, under the guise of 'slum clearance', to leave their Johannesburg suburbs – Sophiatown, Martindale and Newclare – and move to a tract of land bought by the government at Meadowlands, thirteen miles away. In his memoirs Mandela recalled a protest meeting that took place a few days after an order banning him from speaking in public had expired:

> The crowd that night was passionate, and their emotion undoubtedly influenced mine. There were a great many young people present, and they were angry and eager for action. As usual, policemen were clustered around the perimeter, armed with both guns and pencils, the latter to take notes of who was speaking and what the speaker was saying. We tried to make this into a virtue by being as open with the police as possible to show them that in fact we had nothing to hide, not even our distaste for them.
>
> I began by speaking about the increasing repressiveness of the government in the wake of the Defiance Campaign. I said the government was now scared of the might of the African people. As I spoke, I grew more and more indignant. In those days, I was something of a rabble-rousing speaker. I liked to incite an audience, and I was doing so that evening.

Mandela recalled how, 'as I condemned the government for its ruthlessness and lawlessness, I overstepped the line: I said that the time for passive resistance had ended, that non-violence was a useless strategy and could never overturn the white minority regime bent on retaining its power at any cost. At the end of the day, I said, violence was the only weapon that would destroy apartheid and we must be prepared, in the near future, to use that weapon.' Tension and anticipation mounted:

> The crowd was excited; the youth in particular were clapping and cheering. They were ready to act on what I said right then and there.
>
> At that point I began to sing a freedom song, the lyrics of which say, 'There are the enemies, let us take our weapons and attack them.' I sang and the crowd joined in, and when it was finished, I pointed to the police and said, 'There, there are our enemies!'
>
> The crowd again started cheering and made aggressive gestures in the direction of the police. The police looked nervous, and a number of them pointed back at me as if to say, 'Mandela, we will get you for this.' I did not mind. In the heat of the moment I did not think of the consequences.

In the conflict between tyranny and liberalism, as between Communism and its enemies, there were many warriors: anti-apartheid warriors who wanted injustice righted by violence, Cold War warriors in the West who wanted to see Stalinism overthrown by force, anti-imperialists and anti-capitalists who wanted to see the whole apparatus of industrial western society crumble. In a reflection on which way the future conflicts should turn, the historian Hugh Seton-Watson wrote at the beginning of 1953:

> There will be no sudden miraculous and sensational victory over the powers of darkness. Even the dollar cannot prefabricate a Complete Utopia to outwit the Kremlin. Even the most high-minded ideologists cannot manufacture 'a new faith' to convert those wooed by communist propaganda. But much less than this can ward off the Stalinist onslaught.
>
> The western nations have sufficient military, diplomatic and economic resources to force Stalinism back and to accelerate its collapse, without war. They will achieve this if they will remember three things: that their own freedom must be defended; that the Russian and other enslaved nations are not their enemies but their friends; and that only they themselves can remedy the evils that infect their own society.
>
> Every blow against injustice in a British or French village or workshop is a blow against Stalinism. But the blow should be struck, not because it will weaken Stalinism but because it will lessen the volume of injustice in the world. Those who see in social and political reforms no more than tricks to defeat communism, will achieve few reforms, will do their countries small good, and will perhaps not even defeat communism.

'Poverty and tyranny, social oppression and race hatred are evil things,' wrote Seton-Watson. 'These every man of good will should fight, in his own country or outside it, as long as mind and limbs have strength.'

On February 23 Josef Stalin was at his holiday dacha at the Black Sea resort of Sochi. During the morning he was shown reports of the interrogation of five Jewish doctors, all of whom had worked at different times as doctors at the Kremlin, looking after sick members of the Politburo. They had been charged with seeking to murder Stalin. That evening the chief of the Soviet Security Service, the MVD, Lavrenti Beria, arrived at the dacha. Three Soviet leaders close to Stalin – Malenkov, Bulganin and Khrushchev – were the other guests. Beria told them that the doctors, working with other 'enemies of the regime', had been 'surreptitiously shortening the lives of the leadership for a long time'. Among their victims, he said, had been Zhdanov, whose electrocardiogram 'was simply falsified'. Beria explained that Zhdanov had

had a heart attack but that the doctors 'let him go on working and going about his business and this soon laid him low'.

Beria went on to stress to Stalin and his other listeners that 'the main point is that the whole thing was the work of the agency for the Jewish bourgeois-nationalist organization, the "Joint". The threads run deep and are linked to party and military officials. Most of the accused have confessed.' Those confessions, though Beria had no need to spell this out to his master, had relied heavily on all the proven techniques of isolation, threats and torture. The 'Joint' to which Beria referred was the American Jewish Joint Distribution Committee, set up in 1914 to help Jewish refugees on the Eastern Front, and active since then in providing shelter, funds and transit for Jewish refugees and displaced persons everywhere. It had no political purpose or agenda.

On the last day of February Stalin discussed the case of the Jewish doctors with his guests. Beria was again a main participant. Bulganin, Malenkov and Khrushchev were also present. Stalin told Beria to arrange for public trials of the accused. Beria promised full confessions to make the trials possible. 'Arrange it,' was Stalin's comment. Those present had no doubt that a trial of the Jewish doctors would be used as a general accusation against all the Jews of the Soviet Union – more than two million – and that mass deportations to Siberia, where new camps were already believed to have been prepared, and even some sort of bloodbath, might well follow.

The discussion went on until four in the morning of March 1. Stalin was criticizing people in the Soviet leadership who thought, as he put it, that they could 'get by' on their past merits. 'They are mistaken,' he said angrily. The listeners could not know if any or all of them were the ones he was talking about. Then, without as much as a 'good night' to his guests, he broke off his remarks in mid-sentence, left the room and went to bed. During the night he had a brain haemorrhage. Throughout March 1 no member of his staff ventured to find out why their master had not emerged. At 6.30 in the evening – it was already dark outside – a light went on and the staff relaxed, waiting for their master to summon them. By nine in the evening, there still being no sound from him, no bell ringing as usual, they became alarmed. At eleven his bodyguard, M. Starostin, went into the room with the day's correspondence, as an excuse. Stalin was lying on the floor. He had clearly been there for several hours. A copy of *Pravda* was near him, and an open bottle of mineral water on the table. When lifted on to a divan, Stalin tried to speak, but could utter only incoherent sounds. Soon he lost consciousness. Four days later, at 9.50 on the morning of March 5, he died. He was seventy-four years old.

The death of Stalin sent a shockwave of distress through the Soviet Union. Parents and children, young and old, war veterans and factory workers, teachers and pupils wept when they heard that the leader of the nation for more than a quarter of a century, the victor over Germany and Japan, the 'all-seeing' father, was dead. The crowds that mourned in Moscow were so thick that several people were crushed to death. Even amid the outpouring of grief there were those who dared to hope that a change would come over their lives, that fear and tyranny would disappear. But in the first days and weeks after Stalin's death such hopes were seldom spoken.

All Russians who were alive that day recall where they were and how they reacted to the death of Stalin, much as all Americans recall the moment when they learned of the assassination of President Kennedy in 1963. On the day of Stalin's death, Alexander Solzhenitsyn had just completed eight years as a denizen of Soviet prison and labour camps. 'On 5 March 1953,' he later wrote, 'I walked the streets of a town, a free but exiled man. An old deaf woman woke me up one morning and forced me to go out and listen to a communiqué broadcast by the local radio station. Stalin's death was announced. It was my first day of freedom.'

Stalin's funeral took place on March 9 in Moscow. A thirty-gun salute was fired: and fired at the same time in the capitals of all the Soviet republics. After the funeral the body was taken away to be embalmed, and eight months later to take its place next to the body of Lenin in the mausoleum in Red Square, below the walls of the Kremlin. Among those at Stalin's funeral was the Czechoslovak President, Klement Gottwald, founder of the Slovak Communist Party in 1924, Chief Secretary of the Czech Communist Party since 1927 and an exile in Moscow from 1939 until the end of the war. Aged fifty-eight at the time of Stalin's death, he caught pneumonia at the funeral and died five days later.

In the immediate aftermath of Stalin's death, senior Soviet political figures were locked in rivalry to be his successor, among them Nikita Khrushchev and Georgi Malenkov. It was Malenkov, one of Stalin's closest and most zealous associates during the forced collectivization of the 1930s, who, for a short time, emerged as the leader. Five months before Stalin's death, Stalin had appointed Malenkov Deputy Prime Minister. He was forty-six years old. His primacy in the hierarchy of power lasted only two weeks, however, when Khrushchev became First Secretary of the Central Committee of the Communist Party of the Soviet Union – Stalin's position for many years – though at first it was a temporary appointment, unconfirmed by the Party at large.

More alarming to Western observers and leaders than the struggle for power in Moscow was the immediate increase in tension between East and West in the days following Stalin's death. On March 4 the Danish authorities had detained a Polish Russian-built jet fighter which had landed on Born-holm Island in the Baltic. Three days later seven Danish fishing vessels were seized by the Poles off the Hel Peninsula: the vessels were in Polish waters, sheltering from a gale while salmon fishing. On March 10 a United States jet fighter on its way to Berlin was attacked and shot down by Czechoslovak jet fighters – also Russian-built – while over Federal German territory near the border with Czechoslovakia, fifteen miles inside the American Zone. The pilot bailed out and was saved. Two days later Soviet jet fighters shot down a British bomber, also flying to Berlin, in the international Hamburg–Berlin air corridor, on the Soviet side of the German zonal border. Of the crew of seven, six were killed. After lengthy negotiations the Soviet Union declined to give an undertaking that Soviet planes would not fire on aircraft that strayed outside one of the designated air corridors between Berlin and the West.

These confrontations subsided; within a few months of Stalin's death the first cracks began to appear in the Soviet Union's control of the satellite countries. In Poland, Jerzy Turowicz, the Editor-in-Chief of the Catholic newspaper *Tygodnik Powszechny* (Universal Weekly) refused to publish a eulogy of Stalin's alleged contributions to the well-being of post-war Poland. He and his staff were sacked, and kept away from the paper for the next three years. Food and housing shortages in Czechoslovakia were widespread, and there were protest demonstrations in many of the cities. In the industrial centres, factory workers went on strike. In Prague and Bratislava there were protest marches, in which many students took part. During rioting at Plzen the Red Flag was torn down and the busts of Lenin and Stalin were thrown into the streets. Portraits of Masaryk and Beneš – who had become 'non-persons' in the Communist pantheon – were hoisted aloft.

The riots and demonstrations were stopped by force. When tanks arrived the rioters in Plzeň dispersed. Many of them were arrested and imprisoned. East Germany saw a similar turmoil, born of hope that with Stalin's death the Communist regime could be challenged with relative impunity. Tens of thousands of East Germans crossed into West Germany and sought refuge there. There was no wall at that time dividing East and West Berlin, and in a single day in March six thousand East Germans crossed the divide between the two sectors and obtained asylum in West Berlin. Within three months the number of asylum seekers had reached 184,793.

On May 1 – the traditional day of celebration for Communists and workers worldwide – the Communist authorities in East Germany and East Berlin withdrew the meat, fat and sugar ration from those who were neither workers nor children under fifteen. This stimulated a further exodus. On May 28, in a further much resented government order, it was announced that workers must significantly increase their productivity but would receive the same wages as before. Resentment grew, and on June 17 the workers in East Berlin went on strike and organized street demonstrations. At first the police made no attempt to disperse the demonstrators, hoping to show that democratic freedoms obtained in the East as much as in the West of the city.

The demonstrations in Berlin were a serious public challenge to Communist rule and Soviet control. Compared to the earlier demonstrations in Czechoslovakia – themselves not minor – they were revolutionary. Members of the People's Police (the much feared Vopos) threw away their weapons and joined the demonstrators. To put down the uprising, Soviet troops and tanks were ordered from their barracks and deployed in the streets. Many East Berliners, not having weapons, beat on the sides of the tanks with their fists, or threw bricks and stones at them. Several Communist Party buildings were set on fire. The Red Flag, flying on the Brandenburg Gate as it had done on the day of the Soviet conquest of Berlin in 1945, was torn down.

On the afternoon of June 17 the Soviet Commandant of Berlin proclaimed a state of emergency. Summary courts were set up where accusation, trial and execution could take place within an hour. Several hundred demonstrators were hanged or shot. Nine days after the crushing of the revolt in East Berlin, Lavrenti Beria, head of the MVD and the most feared figure in the Soviet Union, met his end. Forty years later, the death of Beria was described by an eye-witness, Major Hiznyak Gurevich, who had fought at Stalingrad and the battle for Berlin, and who was a senior Kremlin guard in 1953. Forty-five years after the event, the *Sunday Times* published an account of how, on the evening of June 26, Major Gurevich was handed a list naming fifty trusted men and ordered to arm them heavily:

They were to wait outside the Borovitskie gates of the Kremlin, the entrance now used by Yeltsin's motorcade.

Beria's time had come. Nikita Khrushchev, manoeuvring to assert him-self as supreme leader of the Soviet Union, had established sufficient sup-port to ensure the downfall of his most dangerous rival.

At a meeting inside the Kremlin, Beria was denounced as a traitor and arrested. When he was searched, guards found a crumpled piece of paper on which the word 'alarm' had been written in red. He is thought to have scribbled it in a panic during the session in the hope of alerting his personal guards.

'I was told only at the last minute that Beria was being arrested and that we were to escort the convoy carrying him,' recalled Gurevich.

'I was shocked. This was the most powerful man after Stalin. But I was told that he was an enemy of the people. Orders are orders.'

At midnight a black government car left the Kremlin. Beria was forced to kneel on the floor of the vehicle, surrounded by his captors. Gurevich and his men took Beria to a cellar underneath Osipenko Street in central Moscow:

'He had not slept all night and his arrest had obviously taken him by surprise,' said Gurevich. 'I offered him some soup and put it on his table. He was furious. He grabbed the plate and threw it at me.

'His cell was 20 metres square, had no windows and was completely bare except for a wooden bed, two chairs and a table. The light was kept on at all times.

'That night I was commanded to guard and serve Beria and to make sure nothing happened to him before the trial. In the event of the bunker coming under attack, I was under strict orders to execute him.'

During the next six months Gurevich lived and slept in a cell adjacent to Beria's. The two cells were connected by a bell which Beria rang whenever he needed anything. 'I did everything for him,' Gurevich recalled. 'I shaved him, ran his bath, cut his hair, bought food for him with money given to me from his bank account. I cooked all his meals and tasted all his food first to ensure that nobody had tampered with it.' Every day Gurevich escorted Beria to his trial, which began in strictest secrecy, and under heavy guard, in November 1953. When the death sentence was passed Gurevich brought Beria a black suit which he was made to wear. He then tied Beria's hands to a steel ring and led him to another cell where five officers were waiting:

'He knew he was going to die but he did not panic,' Gurevich said. 'He let me understand that he wanted me to seek out his son to tell him what had happened. He was a clever man. He was not a coward and he knew how to behave with dignity. At one point he went pale and his left cheek began to tremble. That was his last and only sign of emotion.'

Minutes later Major-General Pavel Batitskii, Chief of Staff of the Air Force, shot Beria at close range. Gurevich and his fellow officers were then instructed to follow suit.

'I drew out my pistol and shot once, hitting him from a distance of two yards,' said Gurevich. 'Then everybody else pulled the trigger.'

The death of Beria, following nine months after the death of Stalin, led to an upsurge in hope within the Soviet Union. The Central Committee of the Communist Party received a deluge of letters from those who had been or still were prisoners in the Gulag, and from the relatives of prisoners, expressing their defiant protest at the incarcerations, and their hopes that the nightmare would soon be ended. Much of the burden of this appeal fell on Nikita Khrushchev, who on September 12 was formally and officially confirmed as First Secretary, and he responded in a decisive manner. Those who had fabricated the charges against the Jewish doctors, and against the Leningrad leaders, were arrested and shot. Those who had been shot as a result of false charges were posthumously rehabilitated. Khrushchev ordered a commission of inquiry to examine the whole nature of the camps and punishments, using the records of the NKVD – the Soviet Security Service from 1934 to 1941. Within three years he was ready to make it public.

Revolutions in Latin America were almost invariably greeted with scepticism elsewhere. The image of rotating dictatorships, each one little different to its predecessor, was a strong one. But in the half-century following the final end to Spanish rule, the aspirations of millions of Latin Americans continued to centre around the search for less harsh, less corrupt government. On July 26 an attempt was made in Cuba by a group of revolutionaries to overthrow the newly installed regime of Fulgencio Batista – the former army sergeant who had earlier ruled Cuba from 1935 until the end of the Second World War, and had recently returned to power. The rebels offered to establish a new Cuba, as promised in their 'Hymn':

Cleansing with fire
Which will destroy this infernal plague
Of bad governments
And insatiable tyrants
Who have plunged Cuba into evil.

The rebels began their struggle with an attack on an army barracks in the town of Santiago de Cuba, the capital of Oriente Province, as far away from the capital, Havana, as any town in Cuba. They were outnumbered by ten to one, but hoped to capture the barracks by surprise and superior zeal. They failed to do so, six of the 134 attackers being killed. As the rebellion collapsed many of those who were captured were tortured and killed. The rebel leader, Fidel Castro, was fortunate: he was captured while sleeping by a humane army officer, brought to trial and imprisoned. 'With what joy I would bring revolution to this country from top to bottom,' he wrote from prison; and after reading Victor Hugo's *Les Misérables* he praised the revolutionary speeches in it as 'full of poetic faith in liberty, and holy indignation against outrages'.

Castro had been sentenced to fifteen years in prison, but within two years he was released under amnesty and allowed to go to Mexico. There, he and his followers planned their return. Inside Cuba, Batista imposed harsh prison sentences on political opponents, and dictatorial control over the press, the universities and the national congress. After student riots, many students were arrested and tortured. The Special Police (the SIM) were notorious for their brutality.

On the day after the attempted coup in Cuba, the long-drawn-out negotiations for a truce in the Korean War came to an end. That day, July 27, an armistice agreement was signed at Panmunjom. The American forces newspaper, *Stars and Stripes*, which eight years earlier had announced the end of the wars in Europe and then in Asia, again celebrated the moment when the troops could look forward to going home.

Since the beginning of the year the armistice negotiations at Panmunjom between the North Koreans and Chinese on the one side, and the United Nations on the other, had been drawing to a close. In April the Chinese had agreed to repatriate badly wounded United Nations prisoners of war. On July 28 the prisoners of war in all the camps inside China were paraded by their captors in their respective places of incarceration. A British National

Serviceman, Albert Tyas – a plumber by trade – who had been held prisoner for more than two years, and was, like all the captives, badly scarred by his isolated and often cruel incarceration, later recalled:

> The camp commander said that at 10.30 that morning General Mark Clark (UN Commander) had signed an agreement for the cessation of hostilities and it was a triumph for the peace-loving peoples of the world. Personally we didn't know if such people existed, but if they did we were eternally grateful to them. At last after two years and four months we knew we were going home.
>
> On about 20 August we set off on our homeward trip, travelling in Russian lorries driven by Chinese soldiers. There were twenty men in each truck. We travelled the eighty miles to Manpojin, a city divided by the Yalu River into two halves. It was strange to see a city with one half standing and one half flattened, but this was a strange war. Even though nothing was left standing where we were, the railway lines were intact.
>
> We travelled in Russian-type trucks all the way back to Panmunjom, but never saw a village, town or city with more than one brick on another. The devastation was total; the whole nation had moved underground to survive.
>
> Handing us back was quite an experience. Twenty-five British prisoners a day was the ration. On the Russian wagons we sat down on each side and waited our turn. Three big Yanks approached the tailboard and lowered it gently: 'Okay, you guys, you're free now. There's no rush, when I call your name walk slowly to me.' Two Yanks lifted us down and supported us into Freedom Village – what a feeling!

Within two weeks of the signing of the armistice at Panmunjom the United States had signed a mutual defence treaty with South Korea. As had been the case before the start of the war two years earlier, North and South Korea became a symbol of the East–West divide.

That divide was to remain a factor in international relations for almost four more decades, but was to undergo many changes of nature. Following the death of Stalin a series of episodes indicated that the monolith might change, even if the suppression of the Berlin uprising had been both bloody and decisive. Beria's disappearance in June from the central control of internal repression was seen by the West as a hopeful sign. So also was the resumption, on August 30, of diplomatic relations between Hungary and Yugoslavia:

not every Soviet satellite was willing totally to boycott the errant Tito regime. Khrushchev's appointment as First Secretary raised hopes that he would lead his people towards a less monolithic regime. But reading the omens was always a speculative venture. On September 26, exactly two weeks after Khrushchev's elevation in the Soviet Union, the Primate of Poland, Cardinal Stefan Wyszynski, was arrested in Warsaw. Throughout the year Wyszynski had defended the Roman Catholic Church against a series of attacks, including a death sentence and long prison sentences on priests accused of espionage, and a decree of February 9 under which the State arrogated to itself the right to make or terminate all ecclesiastical appointments.

Cardinal Wyszynski had protested in public sermons, one of which, in Warsaw on June 4 – the feast of Corpus Christi – had been listened to by a great crowd. When the Bishop of Kielce was sent to prison in September, Wyszynski protested to the Polish Communist leader, Boleslaw Bierut. His protest was made public on September 24. Two days later he was arrested.

In March, and again in May, the Polish pilots of Polish air force MiG-15 Soviet fighters, flying across the Baltic Sea, landed on the Danish island of Bornholm, where they sought, and received, asylum. On June 20 the captain of the Polish passenger liner *Batory*, Jan Cwiklinski, and the ship's surgeon, Dr Takaeter, left the ship at Hebburn, on the North Sea coast, where the ship had been refitting for the previous month, and asked for asylum. Dr Takaeter went ashore first, claiming that he was ill and needed medical help. Captain Cwiklinski then followed, saying that he was going to telephone the police to report the doctor as missing. Both men were granted asylum.

The *Batory* was the flagship of Poland's merchant fleet. During the Second World War she had been an Allied troopship. Ironically, four years earlier a German refugee American Communist, Gerhard Eisler, had used the ship to escape from the United States to Europe: he later became the chief of the East German Information Service. Having been refused permission by the United States to make use of American ports, the ship was on the Gdynia–Southampton–Bombay run.

In an attempt to show that unrest would be dealt with severely, the main celebration of Poland's National Day on July 22 took place in Katowice, which had been renamed Stalinogrod in honour of the dead Soviet leader. The centrepiece of the event was a large military march-past at which the salute was taken by Marshal Rokossowski. As part of Poland's commitment to the Communist bloc, a two-year agreement was signed with North Korea at the end of the year for 'Polish aid' in the form of steel, and industrial equipment.

In October an unusual Polish dash for freedom took place in Korea, when the interpreter with the Polish inspection team in the Demilitarized Zone presented himself to the Americans in the Zone and asked for asylum. He too became an exile and an émigré. Nine days after the interpreter turned his back on Communism, a leading Polish delegate to the United Nations in New York, Professor Marek Korowicz, likewise sought asylum. He was followed five days later by the Polish Consul-General in New York, who fled to Latin America.

Professor Korowicz was in a position to give many details about the nature of the Polish regime, and did so at a press conference in New York on November 24. There were at least seventy-three forced-labour camps in Poland, he said, with about 300,000 people confined in them. 'Many a time on my bus trips from Katowice to Cracow,' he said, 'I passed the labour camp at Jaworzno, where there were approximately 20,000 forced labourers.' Thirty per cent of all prisoners were women. The *New York Times* gave an account of his press conference:

> Everyone in Poland knows that these prisoners, labeled 'class enemies' and 'capitalists', are ordinary citizens, artisans, shopkeepers, farmers and others innocent of crime but arrested and imprisoned because of alleged discontent with the 'shameful' conditions of exploitation and poverty which now prevail in Poland.
>
> They also include a percentage of young men who formed the backbone of resistance against the Nazis.
>
> They are condemned by special commissions that do not even pretend to follow court procedure.

Forced labour was also a feature of life in Communist Czechoslovakia. Short-term conscription of labour had been introduced by law on May 28. Twelve days' labour service a year was the required period. People could be taken to their labour tasks at the weekends or while on holiday. In factories, extra 'peace shifts' took place on Sundays. Soldiers and civilians were also employed in work brigades to build houses. Much of this work was voluntary, but when three volunteers absented themselves they were sent to prison: a warning that absenteeism would be punished.

*   *   *

A crisis broke out in the autumn when Italy and Yugoslavia disputed the future of the Free City of Trieste. On August 24 the Italian Prime Minister, Giuseppe Pella, warned that Italy regarded Trieste as 'important' to it. The Yugoslavs were alarmed at this and announced that they might have to re-examine their own policy with respect to the small but emotionally much longed-for territory. It was believed in Italy that this announcement was a prelude to the annexation by Yugoslavia of the southern, largely rural, area of the Free City.

On August 30 the Italian government ordered its troops to move closer to the border in the area of Gorizia. The Yugoslavs then charged that a platoon of Italian soldiers had crossed the border north-east of Gorizia and 'advanced fifty metres'. Italian warships moved into the upper Adriatic, though they kept more than twenty miles from the disputed coastline. Speaking near the border, Tito demanded the internationalization of Trieste city and the incorporation of the hinterland into the Slovene republic of Yugoslavia. The Italian Prime Minister countered by demanding a plebiscite of the whole disputed area. Tito rejected this.

Unwilling to see a crisis develop that might give Tito the port of Trieste, and a dominant influence in the northern Adriatic, the United States and British governments took the initiative on October 8 by announcing that they would bring to an end the Allied Military Government in the fifteen-mile-long coastal strip running north-west from Trieste city, and hand it over to Italy. If this happened, Tito replied, he would send in Yugoslav troops.

On November 4, the day Italy celebrates the end of the First World War, a massive Italian demonstration was held close to the frontier. The Italian Prime Minister was present. Several thousand Italians tried to march through the coastal strip to Trieste city, to join hands with the Triestini. The Allied Military Government turned most of the Italians back, but several hundred managed to get through. When the Allied Military Government forces, mainly British but with an American detachment, refused to let them raise the Italian flag on Trieste town hall there were riots and arrests. The rioting continued for two more days, and on November 5 three people were killed. On November 6 a large group of rioters, shouting 'Get out, Britain!', were chased into the church of Sant' Antonia in the Piazza dell'Unità d'Italia. Six rioters were killed, all Triestini, two of them boys of fifteen. The Italian Prime Minister protested to the British general at the 'profanation' of the church. The general replied that the police had shown 'admirable restraint' in the face of extreme provocation. 'A number of British vehicles have been overturned and set afire,' Vincent MacLennon reported in the *News Chronicle* in London on November 7. 'US troops are popular and are received with cheers and applause. British soldiers get a considerable amount of abuse.'

The crisis ended when Italy and Yugoslavia agreed to withdraw their troops behind the frontiers of Trieste to avoid further confrontation. The Allied Military Government remained in place.

The checking of Communist ambitions in Korea was felt by the West to be a victory, even if North Korea remained under the most rigid type of Communist control. But there was a sense throughout the West of the need for vigilance in face of the apparently continual efforts of Communists worldwide to take advantage of national discontent. When it seemed that Communism might be successful in British Guiana, borne to victory on the votes won by the People's Progressive Party (the PPP), Britain sent troops to take over the colony. The troops landed on October 6. Three days later the British Governor suspended the constitution and ruled under a state of emergency. The leaders of the PPP were arrested.

Not only Communism, but Islam, was offering an alternative political system to parliamentary democracy. On November 2 the Constituent Assembly in Pakistan declared the country a republic and designated it the 'Islamic Republic of Pakistan'. Henceforth laws based upon Muslim religious principles were to have an important place in national legislation. In Iran, Islamic clerics, among them the fifty-year-old Ayatollah Khomeini, were building up opposition to the secular aspects of the rule of the Shah and waiting for the day when they could denounce it publicly. The Shah, although autocratic, was trying to modernize his country and – much as Atatürk had done in Turkey two decades earlier – to set it upon a predominantly secular path, open to Western social and cultural influences. Two years earlier he had offered all his crown land, including eight hundred villages, for sale to the tenant farmers. The Islamic clerics saw no virtue in this: they wanted Iran ruled according to the tenets and ethics of Islam.

In Britain's African colony of Kenya the challenge to British rule that had been mounted by the Mau Mau continued. Entering British farms, groups of Mau Mau, using their traditional double-edged knives, known as pangas, slaughtered all the cattle they found. In an attack near Timau, in the foothills of Mount Kenya, 360 cattle were killed: hamstrung, disembowelled, their flanks slashed and their tails cut off. In a raid on a nearby police station, the Mau Mau killed five African policemen.

One of the leaders of the armed struggle in Kenya was Dedan Kimathi, a brilliant orator, deeply versed in the Bible. 'At times,' wrote a Kenyan-born British Intelligence officer, 'he seemed to believe that the Bible had been specially written for him. He carried an Old Testament written in Kikuyu wherever he went. He spoke in parables, and his harangues were larded with allusions to and quotations from the Bible.' Calling himself 'Prime Minister Sir Dedan Kimathi' – the self-conferred knighthood was that of the 'African Empire' – in September Kimathi sent a list of his aims to the British Colonial Office and also to the United Nations. Six of its seventy-nine articles read:

We want an African government in Kenya now . . .
We reject the foreign laws in Kenya, for they were not made for Kenya and are not righteous.
Our real fight is not against the white colour, but is against the systems carried on by the white rulers.
Fighting for our stolen land and our independence is not a crime but a revolutionary duty.
Nothing is more precious than independence and freedom . . .
We reject to be called Mau Mau. We are the Kenya Land Freedom Army.

Kimathi established a self-proclaimed Kenyan parliament in his forest hideaway. 'I do not lead rebels,' he said, 'but I lead Africans who want self-government. My people want to live in a better world than they met when they were born. I lead them because God never created any nation to be ruled by another for ever.' Against Kimathi and his fighters the British sent Royal Air Force bombers. In response Kimathi wrote to the British Labour Member of Parliament, Fenner Brockway – who had been a pacifist in the First World War: 'We are not fighting for everlasting hatred, but are creating a true and real brotherhood between White and Black so that we may be regarded as people and as human beings.'

On March 26 the Mau Mau, under Kimathi's increasingly autocratic leadership, massacred ninety-seven villagers at Lari, in the Rift Valley. The Lari massacre turned many Kikuyu irrevocably against the Mau Mau methods. Three years later it was Kikuyu police, including many men who had defected from the Mau Mau ranks, who finally managed to capture Kimathi. He was brought to trial and found guilty, his guilt upheld by three African assessors. Four months later he was executed. Ian Henderson, the British officer who had spent two years tracking Kimathi down, later wrote of his adversary:

> He was hardly a political figure, but he was a criminal of the first rank. It was appropriate that he should fall at last to a party of Kikuyu tribal policemen, representatives of that gallant body of tribal loyalists who had stood firm with Government and decency when the star of Mau Mau seemed to be rising.
>
> It was a final illustration of the great part that the Kikuyu people themselves played in the defeat of the Mau Mau. The young Kikuyu children of the future would be able to stand outside their homes and look up at the distant mountain and say: 'That is where the evil past is buried.'

In all, Mau Mau killed 1,800 Africans and sixty-eight Europeans. In the fight between the British army, the Kenyan security forces – who were able to make use of helicopters – and Mau Mau, as many as 11,000 Mau Mau were killed. Their adversaries lost 166 men. Eleven years after Kenyatta's imprisonment, following a general election, he became President of an independent Kenya. The process of decolonization was following a familiar pattern for many of the once hunted leaders of the national struggle: rebellion, imprisonment, amnesty, negotiation, political leadership and rule.

The British port of Southampton was witness to several scenes of the aftermath of the Korean War, as the prisoners of war came home, to be met by a barrage of journalists and photographers, as well as by their families. Not every story was a celebratory one. On October 13 the *News Chronicle* reported that Bessie Newby, having received a telegram from her husband, Lance-Corporal Kenneth Newby, that he was 'fit and well' after more than two years as a prisoner of war, was on her way to Southampton to greet him when she received a second telegram, stating that her husband had 'died in hospital' while homeward bound.

On October 14 the *Empire Orwell* docked, with 150 former prisoners of war on board: 're-united this morning' with their loved ones, as many British newspaper photographs declared in their enthusiastic captions. Among those who arrived that day was Colonel James Carne, commanding officer the 1st Battalion, The Gloucestershire Regiment, and a hero of the Imjin River battle. He docked with seventy-six of his officers and men. Like him, and like Corporal Newby, they had been prisoners of war of the Chinese. Carne had been forced to spend much of his time as a prisoner – seventeen months – in solitary confinement. When the men followed their Colonel ashore,' *The Times* reported, 'there were happy scenes as they ran to meet their families.' One of those who disembarked that day was Rifleman James Hibbert. Eight years earlier he had returned to Britain after three and a half years in a Japanese prisoner-of-war camp.

In a speech at the quayside Colonel Carne praised the fighting qualities of his men:

> I think they were magnificent before they were captured, and from all I have heard the majority kept their heads up amazingly well afterwards. Soon after the Glosters reached the prison camps conditions began to improve slowly, but in the following months many of us showed signs of beri-beri or had other ailments due to vitamin deficiency. Under such conditions, life and health are not wholly dependent on food, shelter and clothing; it is to their own resolution and optimism that some of the credit must be given for the fact that few British soldiers died in captivity.

Colonel Carne added that 'many NCOs and men with strong characters came to the fore, exposing the inaccuracies of the Communist propaganda and presenting their own more rational opinions. Most of them suffered for thus openly expressing their views. The Chinese methods of punishment were often primitive and unpleasant, sometimes terrible, experiences.' As to the effect of that treatment, Carne said, 'I know that some men have been converted to Communism, but there are also some who are far more anti-Communist than they were before.'

One of those who had apparently been 'converted to Communism' during the brainwashing sessions in captivity was the British Vice-Consul in Seoul, George Blake. A civilian and a diplomat he had been captured and interned in June 1950. He was released after three years as a prisoner. Ten years later, after working since his release in the British Foreign Office, he was discovered to be a Soviet agent.

The Korean War was over, but the travails of South-East Asia in the context of the East-West conflict were not yet ended. On April 9 the Communist Vietminh forces commanded by General Giap, which had been badly mauled the previous year in their continuing struggle against the French in northern Vietnam, turned elsewhere for their victories, crossing the border from Vietnam into Laos. The main Laotian towns were defended by French troops as well as the Laotian army. But as Giap's forces swept southward the French were driven back, losing more than two thousand men during their retreat to the Plain of Jars. Only the coming of the monsoon prevented a Vietminh attempt to capture the Laotian royal capital, Louang Prabang, which Giap had surrounded, and in which French and Laotian troops and the Laotian ruler, King Sisavang Vong, were trapped. Giap ordered his troops to withdraw from the siege and to regroup beyond the city, to recruit Laotian guides, and to stockpile rice, in preparation for a future offensive.

At the end of the year the French commander, General Salan, took an initiative that seemed a harbinger of continued success. On November 26 French airborne troops captured the village of Dien Bien Phu, in the north of Vietnam, wresting control of the village and its fortified defences from the Vietminh, and thereby controlling the road from Hanoi to Laos. Amid the turmoil, injury and death of battle, one Frenchman in Vietnam was fortunate: after seven years in captivity, R. F. Boilot, a Christian missionary, was released by the Vietminh. He had been held captive since the end of the Second World War.

Thirteen years had passed since the outbreak of that war, and seven since it had ended. But what one survivor of Auschwitz, Hugo Gryn, later called the 'unfinished business' of the war remained. It existed in many forms, opening old wounds or aggravating those which had never been fully healed. For some, it was a simple bureaucratic act which shocked, such as the extension of the patent, on 5 January 1953, to J. A. Topf and Son, of Wiesbaden, for a crematorium furnace in which to burn corpses. It was this same furnace design by Topf which had burned so many bodies in Auschwitz.

For other survivors of the war there was the shock of a spate of exoneration for war crimes, such as the posthumous pardon granted on February 28 by a German Denazification Court to General Jodl, hanged as a war criminal at Nuremberg scarcely six years earlier. For yet others the unfinished business related to accusations of military incompetence or failure. Admiral Kimmel had long been accused of failing to be ready for the Japanese surprise attack on Pearl Harbor when he was Commander-in-Chief of the Pacific Fleet. On July 20 Admiral Halsey, commander of an aircraft-carrier group in 1941, wrote to Kimmel – who had tried to enlist Halsey's support: 'Certainly we did not discard the possibility of an attack on Pearl, but with the evidence we had, the most logical inference was that the attack would be against the Philippines and to the southward.'

Admiral Halsey continued, in defence of his superior: 'Had we been in possession of the "Magic" messages with clear implication from the Japs, by their anxiety to be constantly informed of ships' berthing, that an attack on Pearl was intended,' he wrote, 'and the further pointed fact that the date was Dec. 7th, the *Enterprise* and *Lexington* would never have gone on their missions to Wake and Midway. And further, the Fleet would not have been in Pearl Harbor on that date.'

Admiral Kimmel continued to feel aggrieved that his case, even as supported by Admiral Halsey, had not been heard, and that he remained the person considered primarily responsible for the disaster, even though he had not been shown the 'Magic' messages. In his memoirs he wrote bitterly: 'I cannot excuse those in authority in Washington for what they did. And I do not believe that thousands of mothers and fathers whose sons perished on that tragic seventh day of December Nineteen Hundred and Forty-one will excuse them. They will be judged at the bar of history. In my book they must answer on the Day of Judgment like any other criminal.'

In Europe, those judged in the post-war trials to have been criminals were returning home. At the beginning of 1954, SS General Kurt Meyer had his life sentence for the murder of Canadian prisoners of war reduced by the Canadian government to fourteen years, with further time off for good behaviour. On September 7 he was back in his home village of Niederkrüchten. A month later, on October 9, Helmut Knochen, of the feared and hated Paris Gestapo, was sentenced to death. Three and a half years later his death sentence was reduced to forced labour for life. A year and a half after that, it was reduced again, to twenty years' penal servitude. In 1963, within nine years of his death sentence, he was released and sent home to Baden Baden.

Exploration could still excite the public mind on a globe where so much had been seen and visited. When the summit of Mount Everest was conquered for the first time on May 29, by Edmund Hillary, a New Zealander, and Sherpa Tenzing Norgay, there was a sense of a far frontier having been reached. The news reached London in the early hours of June 2, the morning of the coronation of Queen Elizabeth II; it was shouted triumphantly by newsboys as they sold their papers to those who had spent the night along the coronation route.

Forty-five years after Sherpa Tenzing's triumph, his son Jamling Norgay was campaigning to clean up the slopes of Everest from the oxygen canisters, tents and sleeping bags discarded by more than seven hundred climbers who had followed in his father's footsteps and conquered the peak. More than 150 had lost their lives in the attempt: many of their bodies remained on the slopes, frozen and abandoned.[1]

As in the previous few years, television continued to make advances during 1953. Here too a new frontier was reached when both the inauguration of Eisenhower as President on January 20 and the coronation of Queen Elizabeth II on June 2 were televised as 'live' events, and transmitted simultaneously into the living rooms of millions of people. In the world of science and medicine, the discovery by Francis Crick and James Watson of the double-helix structure of DNA, the basic material of heredity, opened up areas of understanding of human life hitherto unimagined – they called it the 'code of life'. In due course it was to provide a method of identification which could eliminate uncertainty over a wide range of otherwise unsolvable mysteries, including the identity of murderers, and the victims of murderers. As I write these words in the summer of 1998, it has confirmed the identity of Tsar Nicholas II, shot down by the Bolsheviks at Ekaterinburg in 1918. As with so many discoveries, others had been working in the same field. At King's College, London, Rosalind Franklin and Maurice Wilkins were in the very final stages of their own successful research on DNA, a full account of which appeared in the journal *Nature* only a month after the 'code of life' pronouncement from Cambridge.

Figures made public in 1953 showed that life expectancy in the industrialized Western nations had risen dramatically since the start of the century. In the United States it was 68.4 years, having been 47 years in 1900, an increase of twenty-one years. In Britain there had been an increase of eighteen years. But in the two largest nations, India and China, the growth in population had hardly kept pace with the availability of food and medicine to sustain a life expectancy that never reached fifty years. The population of China had risen in the previous fifteen years from 475 million to 500 million, that of India from 310 million to 357 million. Each was to more than double its population in the half-century ahead. The effect of the Second World War had been devastating with regard to food production. The year 1953 marked the first year that per-capita food production worldwide had reached its 1939 level.

---

[1] Jamling, who made his own successful climb of Everest in 1996, announced in 1998 that he wanted to clean the mountain and bring down the corpses of the dead climbers. 'The most important thing my father ever taught me was to respect the mountain,' he said.

The cure and pattern of diseases were also changing. In the United States a vaccine designed by an American physician Jonas E. Salk, which promised to eliminate infantile paralysis (polio), was being used for the first time, and plans were being made to vaccinate half a million children. It was exactly a hundred years since the first British Act of Parliament making smallpox vaccination compulsory. In Britain, it was announced that deaths from lung cancer had overtaken those from tuberculosis, with 9,000 people having died of tuberculosis in the previous year and 14,000 from lung cancer.

Scientific investigations carried out in Britain and the United States in 1951 and 1952, and fully analysed in 1953, gave details of the relationship between smoking and cancer, and suggested that the risk of cancer was proportionate to the amount of tobacco smoked. Other research, in which a British professor, George Clemo, was prominent, showed another link with cancer, that of atmospheric pollution in large cities. In a research paper that September, Professor Clemo showed how he had isolated from atmospheric soot a dark-orange compound, chemically related to benzopyrene, that had been shown to be carcinogenic as early as 1932.

The two Nobel Prizes for medicine in 1953 went to Professor Hans Krebs of the University of Sheffield, who had done research into the release of energy into the body from carbohydrate foods, and Dr Fritz A. Lipmann of the University of Harvard, who was working on the influence of the thyroid gland on the control of energy in body tissues. Both men were fifty-four years old. Both had been German Jewish refugees from Nazi persecution. Lipmann had received his doctorate from the University of Berlin in 1922; after researching at the University of Heidelberg he went first to Denmark and then, in 1939, to the United States. Krebs had done his research at the University of Freiburg. Like Lipmann, he was one of many thousands of doctors and medical researchers, scientists and men of letters, who had been driven out of Germany by the Nazis after 1933, whose work both benefited the life of the countries which gave them refuge and enriched humanity.

During 1953 another group of refugees met at the Hamburg Conference on Science and Freedom. One of those who inspired them in their task was Michael Polanyi, a Hungarian-born Jew who in 1933 had been forced to give up his work as a professor of chemistry in Germany, and had emigrated to Britain. He and the scientists and philosophers who joined him were determined that science should not serve totalitarianism, as it had done a decade earlier with such disastrous results for humanity. But scientific neutrality, Polanyi was convinced, could lead only to nihilism or servitude. 'The cultivation of detachment in the face of an advancing foe', he warned, 'is a certain way to enslavement.'

Scientific service in totalitarian regimes continued to enhance their powers. In the Soviet Union the resources of science were being used intensively by the defence establishment to seek Cold War advantages. To counter this, the United States continued to test its own atomic bombs. On March 17, at Yucca Flats, Nevada, more than two thousand marines were given the order, seconds after a massive explosion, to charge across the desert to their 'objective' – the destroyed fortifications, trenches and arsenals of an imaginary enemy.

The 'real' enemy was the Soviet Union. At a conference held in Bermuda in December, Churchill pressed Eisenhower and Dulles to begin talks at the 'summit' with Stalin's successors. Eisenhower was not in a receptive mood, focusing at first on Korea, and telling Churchill – in the words of the top-secret minutes of the meeting – that, if there were a 'deliberate breach' by the Communists of the Korean armistice, the United States 'would expect to strike back with atomic weapons at military targets'. Speaking, as he was determined to do, about future relations with the Soviet Union, Churchill told Eisenhower that he would 'not be in too much of a hurry to believe that nothing but evil emanates from this mighty branch of the human family, or that nothing but danger and peril could come out of this vast ocean of land in a single circle so little known and understood'.

Eisenhower was dismissive of Churchill's approach. The new Soviet Union, he said, like the Soviet Union under Stalin, was 'a woman of the streets', and he added: 'Despite bath, perfume or lace, it was still the same old girl.' There had been no change, Eisenhower argued, in the Soviet policy 'of destroying the Capitalist free world by all means, by force, by deceit or by lies'. This, he insisted, 'was their long-term purpose. From their writings it was clear there had been no change since Lenin.'

Churchill continued to press Eisenhower, both at the Bermuda Conference and after it, to contemplate a meeting with Stalin's successors. He failed in his efforts. Nine months later, in a letter to Eisenhower which likewise fell on stony ground, Churchill set out his hopes yet again. 'Now, I believe, is the moment for parley at the summit,' he wrote on 8 August 1954. 'All the world desires it. In two or three years a different mood may rule either with those who have their hands upon the levers, or upon the multitude whose votes they require.'

Churchill had seen how, in the years between 1933 and 1945, whole nations had clamoured for war, conquest and domination. He was amazed that the United States did not grasp the opportunity at least of exploring a summit meeting. 'Fancy that you and Malenkov should never have met,' he told Eisenhower, 'or that he should never have been outside Russia, when all the time, in both countries, appalling preparations are being made for measureless mutual destruction.' Churchill added, in a final argument in favour of East–West discussions at the highest level: 'After all, the interests of both sides is survival and, as an additional attraction, measureless material prosperity of the masses.'

CHAPTER THREE

1954

> . . . it is better to face the fact of our disagreement than
> to raise false hopes and mislead the peoples of the world
> into believing that there is agreement where there is
> none.

UNITED NATIONS STATEMENT

IN HIS STATE OF THE UNION MESSAGE on 7 January 1954 President Eisenhower stated that his aim during his second year of office would be 'to reduce the Communist menace without war'. This would be done, he explained, by greater United States activity in the economic as opposed to the military sphere. He wanted the emphasis to be on foreign trade, increased international co-operation in the peaceful use of atomic energy, defensive preparations based on new scientific discoveries, and 'vigilance' against Communist subversion inside the United States. 'We shall not be the aggressor,' Eisenhower declared, 'but we and our Allies have and will maintain a massive capacity to strike back.' While 'determined to use atomic power to serve the usages of peace, we take into full account our great and growing number of nuclear weapons and the most effective means of using them against an aggressor if they are needed to preserve our freedom.'

Five days after Eisenhower's speech, his Secretary of State, John Foster Dulles, announced what became known as the 'New Look' policy – a reference to the clothing industry's annual 'new look' in women's fashion. The defence capacity of the United States, Dulles explained, would henceforth be based upon 'a great capacity to retaliate, instantly, by means and at places of our own choosing'. The head of the Democratic Party, Adlai Stevenson – Eisenhower's unsuccessful competitor for the presidency in 1952 – challenged the New Look defence policy and asked if it was devised in such a way as to leave the United States, in the event of Communist aggression anywhere on the globe, with 'the choice of inaction or a thermo-nuclear holocaust'.

The immediate testing point was Korea. The truce in Korea signed at the end of 1953 was still holding, although the subsequent negotiations at Panmunjom for a peace treaty had broken down that December. At midnight on 22/23 January 1954, in accordance with the dates and arrangements set down in the truce, Indian guards acting for the Neutral Nations Repatriation Commission released from the Demilitarized Zone 14,000 Chinese and 8,000 North Korean anti-Communist prisoners of war who did not wish to return to Communist rule. The Chinese went to Formosa and the Koreans to South Korea. At the same time 330 South Koreans, twenty-one Americans and one Briton who refused to be repatriated from the North were handed over to Chinese Red Cross officials.

On January 25 the Soviet, American, French and British Foreign Ministers met in Berlin, in an attempt to resolve the issue of the still-divided Germany, and the still-divided Austria. They were in effect seeking to move forward from the decisions made at Potsdam almost nine years earlier, whereby both Germany and Austria had been divided into zones and occupied by the Four Powers.

The Berlin Conference lasted for more than three weeks. On the first day the nature of the division among the former Allies was made clear when the Soviet Foreign Minister, Vyacheslav Molotov, proposed that the Communist Chinese government should be asked to join their deliberations, and extend them to include South East Asia. This was rejected out of hand, the American Secretary of State, John Foster Dulles, pointing out, somewhat acerbically, that the Four Powers were there because they were the four occupying Powers in Germany and Austria, which were the countries under discussion. He added that it was 'useless' to speak of a conference involving Asia while the Chinese government was holding up the political settlement in Korea.

Molotov then asked that representatives of East and West Germany should be admitted to their deliberations. This too was rejected, on the ground that Britain, France and the United States regarded East Germany as a puppet administration controlled by Moscow.

Speaking with the support of the Americans and the French, the British Foreign Secretary Anthony Eden put forward Britain's proposed solution. There should first of all be 'free elections' throughout Germany, with a secret ballot, held under United Nations supervision. On the basis of these elections a national assembly should be convened. The national assembly should then draft a constitution and prepare the bases for treaty negotiations with the former Allies. The constitution should then be adopted, and a German government formed which would conclude the peace treaty. The treaty would then be signed and come into force. A united – and democratic – Germany would then be in existence as a sovereign, independent State.

Molotov expressed his support for a united Germany and a peace treaty. What he rejected was the first of Eden's proposals, on which all else depended: the free elections held under United Nations supervision. How essential such elections were in the Western perspective was underlined by Dulles on February 2 when he described in detail how the East German election results had been falsified. He also noted that since the holding of these elections almost half a million Germans had fled from the Soviet Zone to the West.

As the discussions proceeded it was clear that no agreement would be reached. Molotov went so far as to insist that Russia retain control over East Germany and remain in occupation of Austria 'indefinitely'. In his final speech, Dulles told the conference that the fundamental difference between the Western participants and the Soviet Union 'revolved around the question of whether it was right, or indeed safe, to give men and nations a genuine freedom of choice'.

Eight months later, on October 3, a nine-power conference in London devoted to the theme of European unity agreed that West Germany should become a member of NATO. Within three weeks, on October 23, Britain, France and the Soviet Union agreed to end the occupation of Germany. That same day, the Western European Union was established, and voted to allow both Italy and Germany to accede to the Brussels Treaty of 1948. Three days later, France and Germany signed an economic and cultural agreement. As the post-war structures of occupation and control were dismantled in West Germany, the cause of European union advanced.

On the morning of March 1 a Japanese fishing vessel, the *Fukuryu Maru* (Lucky Dragon), having earlier had a disappointing search for tuna fish off Midway Island, had made its way to the Marshall Islands in the hope of a better catch. That morning her twenty-three-man crew were fishing east of Bikini Atoll, twenty miles outside the area that had been declared a 'danger zone' by the United States. As they were fishing, a vast explosion occurred, and they and their ship were covered with ash. The explosion was an American hydrogen bomb. The ash was radioactive.

The hydrogen bomb tested at Bikini was more than five hundred times more powerful than that dropped on Hiroshima nine years earlier. It was large enough to destroy the centre of any city in the world: there had been total devastation for a radius of four miles, and serious damage for a radius of eight. Seventy-five naval vessels, known as Joint Task Force One, deliberately anchored at different distances from the explosion, had been either totally destroyed or badly damaged, among them three American battleships and two American aircraft carriers with aircraft crowded on their decks.

James Cameron, a British journalist who witnessed the explosion, noticed pigs running around the island. A scientist next to him commented: 'I feel like apologizing to those pigs. They belong to a reasonable and uncomplicated people, not without a certain grace. At least they aren't crazy.'

On their return to their home port – Yaizu – the fishermen of the *Fukuryu Maru* were found to be suffering from the effects of atomic radiation. The United States Ambassador in Tokyo expressed his 'deep regret', but the Japanese did not regard this as an adequate apology. There was added anger in Japan when the United States government refused to suspend its hydrogen-bomb experiments during the period from November to March, the season for tuna fishing. The market for tuna fish slumped.

Pressure grew in Japan for a ban on the testing of atomic weapons in the atmosphere. By the end of the year the National Anti-Bomb Council of Japan presented a petition with fifteen million signatures. What was later to become the worldwide 'ban the bomb' campaign had begun. On September 23 the wireless operator of the *Fukuryu Maru* died of radiation sickness. The United States Ambassador again apologized. His government offered $1 million in compensation. The Japanese government asked for seven times as much. But even as the debate over the American liability gained momentum, a new scourge was revealed. Japanese meteorologists reported that radioactive rain had fallen on Japan. Its source was not the hydrogen bomb exploded by the United States, but a series of hydrogen-bomb tests by the Soviet Union.

The first Soviet hydrogen bomb had been tested on September 14, in the southern Urals, near the town of Totskoe. It was exploded as part of a troop exercise in the area. Forty years later, details of the test were revealed by the Russian Minister of Defence, Pavel Grachev, who told a combined Russian–American military exercise being held at Totskoe: 'Those who today oppose this peacekeeping exercise should remember 1954, when the whole population for eighteen miles around were kicked out of their homes and had to hide in ditches. It was a barbaric event, threatening the destruction even of our own people.'

Anatol Lieven, a correspondent of *The Times*, who was present when Grachev spoke, commented:

Today, the epicentre of the explosion is marked by a treeless bowl, more than half a mile across, in the middle of the quiet forested hills north of Totskoe. The soil was too pulverized to support trees but smaller plants and grass cover the area.

The Soviet high command did not drop its bomb directly on to the 44,000 troops assembled for the Totskoe exercise. They were grouped in attack formation three miles to the south. Film shot at the time showed soldiers ducking into trenches as the shock wave swept over them. Forty minutes after the blast, the order to advance was given and the lead elements reached the epicentre two hours later. No thought was given to the deadly health effects.

The demand for an end to atmospheric tests intensified. But the realization that such tests were part of the global Cold War made a test ban less likely, especially as Japan had committed itself to the Western part of the confrontation. That year, following the signature on March 8 of a mutual defence agreement with Japan, the United States agreed to supply Japan with $150 million of military equipment, and was to help in the training of the Japanese forces to whom this equipment was sent. The United States also agreed to sell Japan $50 million of surplus wheat and barley, and then to use twenty per cent of the money to finance the development of Japan's military industries: armaments and weapons of war needed for the defence of the home islands. The Japanese Empire was no more. Hirohito retained the title of Emperor, but had agreed to Allied demands that he renounce his 'divinity'.

United States forces had begun to move out of the Japanese mainland. In July the defence of Hokkaido Island – with the exception of air and radar units – was handed over to the Japanese forces and a Japanese general. The size of the Japanese land, sea and air forces was raised from its previous limit of 120,000 to 165,000, and a ban on the employment of former senior officers of the Imperial Japanese Army was removed.

Japan was becoming an increasingly equal partner in the Western defence system. On September 12, in a statement from Moscow, Molotov warned a group of Japanese journalists that 'all would be well' between the Soviet Union and Japan if only Japan would cease 'to bow to the dictates from

Washington'. At the same time, a joint Sino-Soviet statement demanded the evacuation of all 'foreign troops' on Japanese soil.

Inside the United States, liberal opinion was attempting to move away from the segregation and isolation of the past, and to do so on a nationwide basis. On May 17 the Supreme Court ruled, in the case of *Brown* v. *Board of Education* (of Topeka, Kansas), that racial segregation in schools was unconstitutional, stating in its judgment: 'Separate educational facilities are inherently unequal.' This case was one of thirty-two that the Black lawyer Thurgood Marshall took to the Supreme Court (on which he himself eventually served). He won twenty-nine of those cases, including those which eliminated all-White primary elections and all-White juries.[1]

The *Brown* v. *Board of Education* judgment was based on the assertion by the Court, overruling current prejudice, that it was their environment, not their genes, that made Black Americans 'inferior', and that no physiological or mental inferiority existed. While the Court was limited by its legal brief to segregation in schools, by natural extension its ruling clearly applied to segregation in all public facilities. It was to take a decade, however, before a President – Lyndon Johnson – felt strong enough and motivated enough to put civil rights at the top of his agenda.

New nationwide links were also seen in communications. On July 12 the Vice-President, Richard M. Nixon, announced the construction of a network of interstate highways. These would enable cars to travel across the United States, and between States, without encountering a single crossroads or traffic light. They were also seen as part of a defensive network, and as providing rapid exits from the major cities in the event of nuclear war.

City centres would be freed from the financial and environmental damage caused by long-haulage trucks. Drivers would have a more rapid inter-city road system. The motor-car industry flourished: by the end of 1954 General Motors announced that it had produced its fifty-millionth car.

The main impact of the inventiveness of the United States was made in the sphere of national defence. On April 7 the United States announced, in conjunction with Canada, that a chain of radar defence stations was being set up to warn of any hostile aircraft approaching from the north: a Soviet

---

[1] Nicole Seligman, one of Thurgood Marshall's clerks when he was a Supreme Court judge, was one of President Clinton's legal team during his impeachment trial in the Senate in 1999.

surprise air attack across the Arctic Circle would thereby be noticed in time for counter-measures to be taken. This was the three-thousand-mile Mid-Canada Line, which followed the 55th parallel, and consisted of almost a hundred radar warning stations. On September 27 a second chain of radar stations, located above the Arctic Circle, and stretching from Alaska to Greenland, was begun. Two-thirds of the cost would be borne by the United States, one-third by Canada. This was the Distant Early Warning Line (DEW Line). Three days after it was announced, the first atomic-powered submarine, the *Nautilus*, was commissioned by the United States Navy. Within two months, on December 11, the world's largest aircraft carrier, the 59,650-ton *Forrestal*, was launched in an American naval yard.

Internally, the spectre of McCarthyism had continued to haunt and to bedevil American politics. After the United States Army discovered that one of its officers, Major Peress, was a Communist, he was given an honourable discharge. McCarthy protested that 'honourable' discharge was a scandal, and sought to examine the man responsible, Major-General Zwicker. The Secretary of the Army, Robert T. Stevens, refused to allow Zwicker to be cross-examined. Stevens was himself then summoned to appear before McCarthy's committee. He refused to do so, but did agree, at an informal meeting with the Republican members of the committee, to let McCarthy have the names of all those involved in the discharge of Major Peress. The Democrats were outraged, as were a growing number of Republicans. On March 9 a Republican Senator, Ralph E. Flanders, made the first Republican attack on McCarthy on the floor of the Senate. McCarthy, he said, 'dons his warpaint. He goes into his war dance. He emits his war-whoops. He goes forth to battle and proudly returns with the scalp of a pink Army dentist. We may assume that this represents the depth and seriousness of Communist penetration in this country at this time.'

Senator Flanders' attack held McCarthy up to ridicule. 'Is he a hidden satellite of the Democratic Party,' Flanders asked, 'to which he is furnishing so much material for quiet mirth?' Even more destructive of McCarthy's hold on the moral indignation of the United States was a television programme produced by Ed Murrow that exposed McCarthy's methods of interrogation, innuendo and guilt by association.

On April 6 Eisenhower himself entered the McCarthy debate, during a radio broadcast to the American people. 'We do not have to be hysterical,' he said, speaking of the strength of the Soviet Union and the other Communist nations. 'We can be vigilant. We can be Americans. We can stand up and hold up our heads and say "America is the greatest force that God has ever allowed to exist on His Footstool."' But as well as the fear of 'Communist penetration' there was another fear about which he wished to speak:

> The fear that we will use intemperate investigative methods, particularly through Congressional committees, to combat such communistic penetrations.
>
> Now, as I pointed out before, it is minute. The great mass of governmental people, governmental workers – civilian and in uniform – of people in our schools and everywhere else that we can think of are just as dedicated as you and I. They are just as loyal.
>
> But the fringe still have to be hunted out. And, as I say, you will get a full report of what the FBI is doing on this.
>
> Now the Congressional committee – one of its functions when it was first set up – the Congressional Investigative Committee – was to be your protection against the unwarranted attacks of an overpowering Executive. It was to look after your civil liberties. To make certain that your liberties were not eroded away.
>
> Now, ladies and gentlemen, I admit that there can be very grave offenses committed against an innocent individual if he's accused falsely by someone having immunity of Congressional membership. He can lose his job. He can have scars that will be lasting. But in the long run, you may be certain of this – America believes in and practices fair play, and decency and justice.
>
> In this country, public opinion is the most powerful of all forces. And it will straighten this matter out wherever and whenever there is real violence done to our free rights.

A series of televised hearings of McCarthy's committee began on April 22 and continued until June 17. There were angry exchanges between McCarthy and those who sought to challenge his right to probe in the way he was doing. McCarthy's frequent interruption of the proceedings with the words 'point of order' became a national and much mocked catchphrase. In the course of an argument over his right to quote a secret Federal Bureau of Investigation memorandum, McCarthy publicly invited all federal employees who had information about corruption or treason to give it to him, whatever directives to the contrary they might have had from their superiors. There was widespread indignation at this incitement to disregard the law, which was specifically repudiated by the Attorney-General. In a further distancing of the administration from McCarthy, and to protect himself, Eisenhower took action to prevent the disclosure of the private conversations of presidential advisers.

It was becoming clear, as the hearings went on, that, while a hard core of McCarthy's followers continued to support him, large sections of the public on whose tacit support he was dependent had started to turn away from him. On July 30 the Senate began a debate on whether McCarthy should be censured for 'conduct unbecoming to a Senator', and a committee of Senators was appointed to examine his conduct. Two months later, on September 27, he was found to have acted 'improperly' in urging federal employees to hand over documents to him. McCarthy did his own cause no good by denouncing the Senate committee as a 'lynch party' and as the 'unwitting handmaidens of the Communist Party'. On December 2 his witch-hunt was finally ended, when a Senate vote of sixty-seven to twenty-two passed censure upon him. The Republican Senators had been evenly divided (twenty-two to twenty-two) for and against him.

While the fall of McCarthy was in progress, one of those against whom he had directed his accusatory shafts was in serious trouble. Robert Oppenheimer was one of the inventors of the atom bomb. Without his contribution, there might have been no Hiroshima or Nagasaki, and no Bikini Atoll. An inquiry into his political sympathies – 'past association with Communists' – had led to him being refused any future security clearance. It emerged that the main charge against Oppenheimer was his unease about the development of the hydrogen bomb. The United States Atomic Energy Commission endorsed his exclusion from future secret work, citing as its reason both his 'indiscreet associations with fellow travellers' and his 'lack of enthusiasm' for the hydrogen bomb. The protest of a distinguished scientist was made to look like lack of patriotism, even treachery.

Inside the Soviet Union, the impact of the death of Stalin was beginning to be felt. In the first decree signed solely by Nikita Khrushchev, local Communist Party organizations were ordered to take a less harsh attitude towards the Russian Orthodox Church, and not to permit 'methods likely to hurt the feelings of believers'. The extent to which such an attitude would prevail, or be allowed to spread to other spheres, was uncertain. The publication of an article in the journal *Novy Mir* (New World) in which the author suggested with considerable deference that writers should 'obey the dictates of their own consciences' led to the dismissal of the journal's editor.

Overseas, the Soviet authorities sought to keep a careful watch on their representatives, but were not always successful, despite the eagle eye of the Security Service personnel (MVD). When a Soviet diplomat in Australia, Vladimir Petrov, left the Soviet Embassy in Canberra and sought political asylum, with his wife, the Soviet Union broke off diplomatic relations with Australia. Other defectors had an almost equal impact. That same year M. N. Khokhlov, himself an MVD official, was sent from Moscow to kill the head of one of the Russian émigré organizations in the West. When he surrendered to the American authorities in Germany and revealed the truth about his mission, the Western perception of Soviet iniquity was considerably heightened. Much knowledge about the iniquities of the Soviet espionage and secret police systems had also been revealed by a Soviet diplomat and defector, Victor Kravchenko, whose book *I Chose Freedom* became a descriptive classic and was a political warning.

The future of Germany remained unresolved, highlighting the confrontations of the Cold War in Europe. On April 16 Eisenhower pledged United States support to the six countries of the European Defence Community – though this whole structure was destroyed four months later when the French parliament voted against ratification. At a meeting of the Foreign Ministers of the fourteen North Atlantic Treaty Organization countries a week later, another potential difficulty was seen in the numerical superiority of the Soviet troops in Eastern Europe over those of the NATO countries. In addition, almost all the Soviet Union's fighter planes stationed in Eastern Europe, and two-thirds of its light bombers, were jet aircraft. Another difficulty pointed out at the NATO meeting was that the Soviet air force had been active in enlarging and improving military airfields throughout the Eastern bloc.

One factor that seemed in NATO's favour was that the Soviet Union had no equivalent to the long-range B-47 bomber. But it was accepted that continual vigilance, and where possible a constant matching and upgrading of forces, was essential. This included the expenditure of more than $100 million to complete a jet-fuel pipeline and storage system.

As part of its contribution to NATO defences, Canada transferred 164 jet fighters to Greece and Turkey. Atomic weapons were also a part of the NATO arsenal, the United States providing pilotless bombers capable of delivering an atom bomb, and atomic cannons and guided missiles. That October, it was agreed that the German Federal Republic should enter NATO.

While the military defence of Western Europe was predominantly the concern of NATO, the economic well-being of the non-Communist countries of the continent was being given a new impetus by the five-year-old Organization for European Economic Co-operation (OEEC). One initiative taken in 1954 was to reduce the indebtedness of the debtor countries by the creation of an instalment system, not unlike that which had been put in place after the First World War. Another initiative was a drive to reduce import restrictions on goods crossing from one member country to another. Britain took a lead in this, reducing the restricted goods by eighty per cent. The French followed swiftly along the same track, removing restrictions on seventy-five per cent of their commercial imports within a period of ten months. In a parallel measure of economic easement, the six members of the European Coal and Steel Community – France, West Germany, Italy, the Netherlands, Belgium and Luxembourg – had established a single market for coal, coke, iron ore, steel and iron.

An important measure of support for the European Coal and Steel Community came on April 23, when the United States made a loan of $100 million towards the modernization of colliery installations and the building of power stations among the Community members. The United States also promised to stimulate American investment in the Community. A smaller but important loan from France enabled miners to be relocated in areas where pits were more productive. The most important development of all that year, an extension of which was to be one of the mainstays of the European Union fifty years later, was the creation of a European Labour Card, holders of which – drawn from all six participating nations – could obtain work anywhere within the Community, free of restrictions based on nationality.

Western Europe was fortunate that its disputes and development centred upon the gradual coming together of nations in search of greater economic harmony. In Eastern Europe and the Balkans it was the stresses and strains of Communism that overshadowed the development of nations that were still struggling to overcome the long-term effects of the Second World War. In January the Yugoslav Communist Party expelled its Chairman, Milovan Djilas, who had argued strenuously in favour of greater freedom of expression. Djilas, who had had several talks with Stalin in Moscow a few years earlier, had a profound contempt for the Communist system as it had developed in the Soviet Union. With his authority as a Vice-President of Yugoslavia – and as a wartime partisan leader in Bosnia and his native Montenegro – Djilas had written a series of articles in the official Communist Party journal *Borba* (Struggle) and in his own magazine *Nova Misao* (New Thought) calling for greater liberalization, and warning that it was in the nature of oligarchies throughout the

Communist world to usurp and preserve the class distinctions they had been expected to abolish.

Still overshadowing the behind-the-scenes discussions about Korea was the question of whether, in the event of a Chinese violation of the tenuous ceasefire, the United States would be prepared to use the atom bomb. In strict secrecy Brigadier General Edwin H. J. Cairns, the Secretary to the Joint Chiefs of Staff, was asked to prepare a memorandum on this subject. His conclusion was emphatic. 'In the light of the enemy capability to launch a massive ground offensive,' he wrote on April 17, 'US air support operations, including use of atomic weapons, will be employed to inflict maximum destruction of enemy forces.' As well as the use of atomic weapons, Cairns proposed a naval blockade of the China coast, seizure of the offshore islands, and the use of Chinese national-ist forces to launch armed raids on the Chinese mainland.[1]

Not war planning, however, but peacemaking, dominated the public efforts of the former belligerents that spring. In the search for a permanent settlement in Korea, all the previously warring powers agreed to meet at Geneva, though not under the auspices of the United Nations. Both Korea and Indochina were on the agenda. The Geneva Conference opened on April 26. For the first time Communist China was present as a Great Power, represented by its Prime Min-ister and Foreign Minister Chou En-lai.

As had happened during the Berlin Conference two months earlier, at Geneva the division between East and West was absolute, making it certain from the outset that a unified independent Korea was no more possible than a unified independent Germany. The basis for unification proposed by the United Nations Powers was the same as for Germany – free elections for an assembly that would represent the whole country. These elections should be supervised by a 'neutral' international body. It was the word neutral that proved the point of irreconcilable difference. The Communist States wanted the word to apply to any country that had not taken part in the fighting. The non-Communist States regarded the participation of countries like Poland and Czechoslovakia in the supervision of free elections – such as did not exist in those countries – as a sham and a danger. North Korea added another dimension of disagreement when its senior delegate said he understood that the 'supervision' of elections would involve no more than 'observation'.

---

[1] This document remained secret for forty years. It was made available at the National Archives in Washington in December 1994.

As the debate continued, the prospect of Korea being united under an independent government dissolved. The breakdown in the talks came when the United Nations Military Armistice Commission, and the Neutral Nations Supervisory Commission, found that they could monitor the movement of United Nations troops without hindrance, but that the Chinese and North Korean authorities impeded every effort to check what troops were leaving and what were entering North Korea. There were five specified ports of entry in the North, but the observers were given details with regard to only two of them, making the process of monitoring impossible. The Swedish and Swiss members of the Neutral Nations Supervisory Commission complained that their Polish and Czech colleagues were impeding the work by means of their veto power, which they used to prevent the essential spot-checks on the movement of men and materials.

The Geneva Conference reached a crisis point, and with it acceptance that the ideal of a unified Korea would not come to pass. Those members of the United Nations at the Geneva Conference who had sought the outcome of a united Korea issued a statement in mid-June which put an end to any hopes the outside world might have had that the conference would reach a solution. The statement explained that the Communist delegations at Geneva had rejected two 'fundamental principles' without which there could be no equitable resolution of the Korean question:

(1) We accept and assert the authority of the United Nations. The Communists repudiate and reject the authority and competence of the United Nations in Korea and have labelled the United Nations itself as the tool of aggression. Were we to accept this position of the Communists it would mean the death of the principle of collective security and of the United Nations itself.

(2) We desire genuinely free elections. The Communists insist upon procedures which would make genuinely free elections impossible. It is clear that the Communists will not accept impartial and effective supervision of free elections. Plainly, they have shown their intention to maintain Communist control over North Korea. They have persisted in the same attitudes which have frustrated United Nations efforts to unify Korea since 1947.

'We believe, therefore,' the United Nations statement concluded, 'that it is better to face the fact of our disagreement than to raise false hopes and mislead the peoples of the world into believing that there is agreement where there is none.'

American, British and Chinese troops were slowly withdrawn from their respective areas of military control north and south of the ceasefire line. There was indignation in the United States and Britain when it was learned that, after the withdrawal of the Chinese troops from North Korea, they were replaced by others, but beyond verbal protest there was no action. Although South Korea was the country to whose aid the United Nations had come, it pursued its own policy of hostility to the United Nations forces and administrators on its territory, and sought the removal of the Neutral Nations Supervisory Commission. At the same time, the South Korean government quickly spent the $98 million contributed by United Nations members to the reconstruction of the South, through the United Nations Korean Reconstruction Agency (UNKRA).

Of the money spent, sixty-five per cent had been provided by the United States and sixteen per cent by Britain. A further $110 million was allocated for the following year. The need was urgent. Among the first projects to benefit from the funds was a training centre for South Korean doctors and nurses, staffed by a Swiss technical assistance team, the rebuilding of the country's three most important cotton mills, and the restoration of rail and port facilities.

Having failed to create a united Korea, the Geneva Conference went on to discuss Vietnam. The position of the Vietminh had been much enhanced during the previous twelve months. They had been provided by China with the latest American military equipment, captured by the Chinese from the Americans in Korea, and in many respects superior to the American equipment being sent direct to the French forces from the United States.

A new French commander-in-chief, General Henri Navarre, recognized the impossibility of maintaining French control in northern Vietnam. Even the 'waist' of the country – Annam – was so dominated by the Vietminh that the French had given up the coastal and inland roads, and went by sea between the three large coastal towns which they did control – Da Nang, Hué and Nha Trang. Navarre, returning to Paris, proposed dividing Indochina into a northern and a southern military area, along the 18th parallel. North of the parallel the French forces would take up defensive positions and avoid a major battle with the more numerous Vietminh. South of the parallel France would launch a substantial 'pacification programme', and also seek to regain control of Annam.

A major achievement by General Navarre was to persuade an American military mission, sent to Vietnam by President Eisenhower, to endorse the French plan of campaign, and to agree to supply a massive amount of military aid – at least $400 million. The head of the American military mission, General John W. O'Daniel, even tried to persuade Navarre to turn his defensive plan for the Red River Delta into an offensive one.

It was General Navarre who decided, in a directive issued at the end of 1953, that the fortress of Dien Bien Phu, a strategic focal point in the north, 'must be held at all costs'. In November 1953 his troops had seized Dien Bien Phu from the Vietminh, in the hope of disrupting the Vietminh supply lines into northern Laos. In Navarre's mind Dien Bien Phu formed an essential barrier to the Vietminh penetration of northern Laos. He also envisaged it being used as a base for attacking the Vietminh in the surrounding region. What Navarre had not anticipated was that the Vietminh would themselves besiege Dien Bien Phu, making it, not a launching pad for future French initiatives, but a trap for all those inside it.

On January 20 Navarre unleashed what he regarded as the key to maintaining French control in Vietnam, the attack on the Vietminh positions in the narrow central area, Annam. But the Vietminh fought back and forced the French to withdraw into the main towns. In February the Vietminh attacked French positions inside the De Lattre Line in the Red River Delta, cutting the Hanoi–Haiphong road for several days at a time. By March 13 the Vietminh had encircled Dien Bien Phu and the French troops there were besieged.

By an intense effort, the Vietminh maintained four separate supply routes from the Chinese border to the Dien Bien Phu front. Their two main methods of supply were the use of eight hundred Soviet and two hundred American trucks – most of the American trucks had been captured by the Chinese in Korea and transferred to the Vietminh – and ten thousand local workers, both men and women, who carried supplies by hand. In a decisive effort to reduce the French capacity to supply Dien Bien Phu by air, General Giap succeeded in infiltrating saboteurs to the two main French air bases in the Delta, which destroyed eighty-seven aircraft on the ground, most of them transport aircraft – half the total French transport force available.

In April the United States Air Force provided transport aircraft to fly a French battalion to northern Vietnam to participate in the defence of Dien Bien Phu. They also provided United States Air Force mechanics to help with the repair of French aircraft. But all these efforts were to no avail.

The 49,000 Vietminh combat soldiers were surrounding 7,000 French and Vietnamese fighting men, and overlooked them from the high ground less than two and a half miles away. The Vietminh could therefore direct their artillery fire on the French positions in Dien Bien Phu by visual observation, aiming 'down the tube'. As the siege intensified, many of the local Vietnamese defenders, particularly those from the T'ai tribe, became 'internal deserters', taking no part in the fighting and living in holes dug near the Nam Yum River. By the end of the battle as many as four thousand men had pulled out of the conflict.

The ability of the Vietminh to maintain their supply lines, despite continuous French aerial attack, was decisive. An original French assessment gave the Vietminh enough artillery ammunition for only five or six days' intensive fire. In the event the Vietminh were able to bombard Dien Bien Phu for the whole fifty-five days of the siege, firing at least 93,000 rounds into the fortress. Colonel de Castries, the besieged French commander, sent a message from his command post on April 3: 'I expect every man to die at the position assigned to him rather than retreat an inch.' He then ordered his staff officers, the headquarters clerks and cooks and the crews of grounded aircraft to man the trenches around the fort.

A meeting was held in the White House in Washington on April 3 at which President Eisenhower, several senior Senators and the President's military advisers considered a plan to send an American bombing force to destroy the Vietminh attackers around Dien Bien Phu. The bombing plan was put forward by the Chairman of the United States Joint Chiefs of Staff, Admiral Arthur Radford. He proposed a raid by seventy-five to a hundred American bombers, based in the Philippines, taking place over three consecutive nights. There was even talk about dropping three atomic bombs on the Vietminh positions.

At the meeting on April 3, Admiral Radford made three points in support of an American bombing raid to help the defenders of Dien Bien Phu:

(1) South-East Asia and Indochina were important to the national security of the United States;

(2) the French were about to collapse in Vietnam and the Communists would take the country;

(3) the United States must take a decisive action *now* if it wished to avoid a much more costly commitment later.

During the questioning of Admiral Radford it became clear that he envisaged a substantial American commitment to the French struggle in Vietnam. Such a commitment was supported by both the Secretary of State, John Foster Dulles, who wanted an international coalition of allies to prevent a Communist takeover in South-East Asia, and by the Vice-President, Richard Nixon, who was willing to see American ground forces sent to Vietnam if the bombing offensive failed.

One of the Senators present at the meeting on April 3, Lyndon Johnson, asked what countries the United States had sounded out as allies. The answer was, none. Then, on April 6, to the surprise of Radford, Dulles and Nixon, the French government informed the United States that French 'public opinion' would no longer support the war in Indochina, and that henceforth a negotiated settlement was the prime French aim. In the French view – as also that of the British Foreign Secretary Anthony Eden – the Indochina talks about to take place in Geneva would be the ideal forum for negotiations.

With Dien Bien Phu still besieged, Admiral Radford did not despair of enlisting British support in a joint Anglo-American military venture. On April 24 he flew to Britain where, at an emergency meeting of the British Cabinet on the following day – a Sunday – Eden recommended that Britain should 'decline' to be associated with what he called 'any immediate declaration of intention to check the expansion of Communism in South-East Asia' or to join in any 'precipitate military intervention' in Indochina.

Admiral Radford went to see Churchill, who told him bluntly: 'The British people would not be easily influenced by what happened in the distant jungles of SE Asia; but they did know that there was a powerful American base in East Anglia and that war with China, who would invoke the Sino-Russian Pact, might mean an assault by hydrogen bombs on these islands.' Churchill tried, as the secret notes of the meeting recorded, 'to impress on Admiral Radford the danger of war on the fringes, where the Russians were strong and could mobilize the enthusiasm of nationalist and oppressed peoples'. His policy, Churchill explained, 'was quite different; it was conversations at the centre'. Such conversations 'should not lead either to appeasement or, he hoped, to an ultimatum; but they would be calculated to bring home to the Russians the full implications of Western strength and to impress on them the folly of war'.

The British and United States governments had reached a parting of the ways with regard to Vietnam. The American policymakers felt strongly that neither Churchill's belief in conversations with the Russians nor Eden's belief in negotiations at Geneva could help the French defenders in Dien Bien

Phu. At Geneva, on May 2, Eden made Britain's disagreement with United States and French policy clear when he insisted that Britain 'must decline to be drawn into the war in Indochina or even into promising moral support for measures of intervention of which the full scope was not yet known'.

On May 7 the French garrison at Dien Bien Phu was overrun. The French will to try to hold on to northern Vietnam was broken. The talks that took place in Geneva on May 8 centred on an attempt to provide a unified government for the country. As with Germany and Korea, however, the issue of free elections proved the insuperable obstacle. While it was agreed that the elections would be held under joint French and Vietminh auspices, the structure of the international control commission that would supervise them was in dispute.

Once more the Soviet Union, supported by China, wanted Poland and Czechoslovakia to be among the 'neutral States'. The French, and the Vietnamese supporters of the Emperor Bao Dai, replied that this was 'totally unacceptable'. When the seven neutral members of the Commission were proposed by neighbouring Cambodia – India, Pakistan, Burma, Japan, the Philippines, Italy and Canada – Molotov reiterated that Poland and Czechoslovakia must be included. Speaking for China, Chou En-lai said that not only must the Communist States not be 'arbitrarily' excluded from the international commission, but they must have the right of veto on anything that was being decided. At the United Nations Security Council, Thailand complained on May 29 that the activities of the Communists in Indochina threatened Thailand's security.

As a gesture of conciliation in its negotiations with France, on May 29 the Vietminh released from captivity Geneviève de Galard-Terraube, known to the French soldiers as 'the Angel of Dien Bien Phu'. The only woman nurse in the besieged fortress, she had insisted on remaining behind with the wounded. The casualties of war have always included those who reported it to the wider public, both journalists and photographers. Four days before the release of the Angel of Dien Bien Phu, the photographer Robert Capa was killed when he stepped on an anti-personnel mine at Thai Binh. He was forty years old. In the course of two decades he had covered the Reichstag fire, the Spanish Civil War (where he photographed a soldier at the moment when he was killed in action), the Sino-Japanese War and the Second World War. 'It is bad luck for everyone', his friend Ernest Hemingway wrote in an epitaph, 'that the percentages caught up with him.'

* * *

Partition of Vietnam was inevitable, as it had been in Germany and Korea. On July 2, as an indication of the imminence of partition, the French evacuated the southern part of the Red River Delta. Under the agreement reached at Geneva on July 20 a dividing line was drawn between Vietnam and the area under the control of the Vietminh – the People's Republic of Vietnam – at approximately the 17th parallel. The People's Republic, to the north of the divide, had a population of 12,750,000. Vietnam, to the south of the divide, had 9,300,000 people.

The French government agreed to withdraw its troops from North Vietnam. The Vietnamese Communists agreed to evacuate South Vietnam and to take their troops out of neighbouring Laos and Cambodia. Ho Chi Minh would form an interim government in North Vietnam. Elections would be held throughout the country in two years' time. On October 8, Ho Chi Minh's forces entered Hanoi, which was proclaimed the Vietminh capital. Six months later, when the last French troops left the port of Haiphong, their commander General Cogny went as a final gesture to the Haiphong Military Cemetery, to salute the soldiers buried there. They represented eighty years of French colonial endeavour.

The United States felt strongly that the cause of a unified Vietnam should not be abandoned. 'In the case of nations now divided against their will,' the State Department announced, 'we shall continue to seek to achieve unity through free elections, supervised by the United Nations to ensure that they are conducted fairly.'

The division of both Korea and Vietnam into Communist North and non-Communist South seemed to give urgency in Washington, Canberra, London, Paris and other non-Communist capitals to the creation of an anti-Communist defensive alliance spanning the Pacific. Negotiations were swift and a pact was signed on September 8 in the Philippines capital, Manila. The signatories were the United States, Australia, New Zealand, Pakistan, Thailand, the Philippines, Britain and France. Known as the South-East Asian Defence Treaty, it established as its operative arm the South-East Asia Defence Treaty Organization (SEATO), with its headquarters in Bangkok.

Within China, events of momentous significance were taking place in the lives of hundreds of millions of people. Famine and flood were age-old curses in China, and they recurred cruelly that year. During floods in September a tenth of the country's cultivated farmland was under water: an area of more than twenty-six million acres, or twice the total land area under cultivation in Britain. In a draconian – and unsuccessful – attempt to redress the balance of rural poverty, the Soviet system of forced collectivization was introduced. Mao Tse-tung in 1954, like Stalin fifteen years earlier, tackled the scale of the problem with drastic and severe measures. Chou En-lai explained: 'The people have to bear some hardships for the time being . . . in order that in the long run we shall live in prosperity and happiness.'

During the first eight months of the year 100,000 collective farms had been established. At Mao Tse-tung's insistence, and amid great hardship, during the following six months the number rose to more than half a million. In the province of Heilungkiang a State grain farm was established in which the agricultural machinery was provided by the Soviet Union. In the new Chinese constitution introduced that year, friendship with the Soviet Union was part of the preamble.

The Soviet Union also withdrew its troops from Port Arthur – which Japan had seized from Russia in 1905 – and returned the port to China. Russia gave up its 1945 agreement with China whereby there was to be a joint Russo-Chinese administration in the port for thirty years, and handed over the Soviet installations there without seeking compensation. The territorial integrity of Communist China, with the exception of Taiwan, was complete. Tibet also lay within the Communist Chinese sphere, its leaders in exile, and its Buddhist creed and national aspirations under the repressive rule of Peking.

For the first half of the century, much of Chinese life had been dominated by the warlords who controlled their respective areas, and gave their allegiance for a price to those whom they considered were in the ascendant, or withheld their allegiance to gain greater concessions in their region. The Communist government sought to eliminate hitherto integral parts of Chinese traditions and culture by making the Communist Party the sole and strong repository of all power, responsible to, and responsive to, the rulers in Peking. To this end Liu Shao-chi, who had been the principal theoretician of the Chinese Communist Party for almost a decade, insisted that the Party itself must 'heighten' its discipline, and that even high-ranking Party cadres were guilty of 'a lack of understanding . . . of the importance of unity and of collective leadership'. There were even those, he warned, at the highest level of provincial rule who 'regard the region or department under their leadership as their individual inheritance or independent kingdom'.

As a step towards central control, the government abolished the Administrative Committees which had been set up by the Communist Party to govern the six regions into which China had earlier been divided, and made the provincial administrators directly responsible to the central government. These changes were studied by China-watchers outside China with intense concentration. What was becoming known as the Bamboo Curtain denied experts, critics and well-wishers alike any clear scrutiny of events inside China. The American historian Kenneth Scott Latourette, Professor Emeritus of Missions and Oriental History at Yale University, after praising the reconstruction, railway rebuilding, land reclamation, irrigation and flood-prevention projects being undertaken by the Communist regime, as well as the improvement of urban utilities, the control of 'gangsterism' and the elimination of prostitution, commented:

Yet this record had been made possible at a terrific cost in lives, liberty, moral integrity, and China's inherited traditions. At a conservative estimate from 3,000,000 to 5,000,000 had been executed in the first two years of Communist mastery.

Most of this was by shootings in large groups which the public were encouraged or required to attend. In despair untold thousands had committed suicide. Many suffered from mental breakdowns. Class consciousness was created and nurtured and with it class hatred. Mass hysteria was fomented. A strict censorship of the printed page and the radio was enforced.

Scott Latourette added, almost despairingly, that in the new China 'telling the truth was subordinated to the cause of the revolution. Lies were used boldly whenever they were deemed to serve the people's cause.'

In South Africa, where apartheid was the fixed policy of the State, the path of the Nationalists in parliament was not always smooth, despite their ninety-four seats and absolute majority. The opposition United Party, with fifty-one seats, continued to seek to assert greater measures of fairness and of 'integration' for the Black and Coloured population, and challenged all Nationalist legislation, leading to acrimonious debates. The leader of the United Party, J. G. N. Strauss, proposed a relaxation of some of the main discriminatory legislation, as well as a substantial house-building programme for non-Whites, and a revival of the Native Representational Council which the Nationalist government had suspended.

Strauss and his opposition Party were confronted by an opponent of particular zeal – Hendrik Frensch Verwoerd. During the Second World War, Verwoerd had opposed both South Africa's participation in the war on the side of the Allies and the admission to South Africa of Jewish refugees from Nazism. In 1950 he had become Minister of Native Affairs, and in 1954 he began to introduce legislation that went beyond the previous legislation in its immediate and visible effectiveness. His most controversial measure, the Natives Resettlement Act, gave the government powers to remove Black settlements that were considered too close to or too intertwined with White areas. The first to be removed was the Black township of Sophiatown, in the centre of Johannesburg. Its inhabitants were told to leave, and it was bulldozed to the ground, to make way for White development. A Bill was also introduced into parliament which brought to an end the 'mixed' trade unions, in which European and non-European workers fought in one organization for their collective rights. Henceforth, all existing trade unions would have to have separate European and non-European branches, and new trade unions would have to be either White or non-European. The integration thus drastically curtailed had been enshrined in the Industrial Conciliation Act thirty years earlier.

Another piece of legislation introduced by Dr Verwoerd was the Bantu Education Act, which gave the government control of the education of Africans, in many cases taking it out of the hands of essentially liberal-minded Church missionaries. The Anglican Church was particularly affected, and outraged, so much so that a special service for South Africa was held in St Paul's Cathedral, London. In a letter announcing the service, which was to be one of 'prayer and intercession', George Bell, Bishop of Chichester – ten years earlier an outspoken opponent of the bombing of German cities – and Canon John Collins, Chairman of Christian Action, wrote to *The Times*:

> It is in no spirit of self-righteousness that this day is to be observed. The communities are conscious of how often Christians in this country fail in their attitude and conduct towards people of other colours and races resident here. Nor do they question the sincerity of many in South Africa who believe conscientiously in *apartheid*. But they are distressed by the intolerant and increasing restrictions imposed upon thousands of fellow-human beings in South Africa, simply on account of their race or colour

– a refusal to them of elementary human rights and a denial of the sacredness of persons for whom Christ died.

*

Nine years after the ending of the war in Europe, the repatriation of prisoners of war was still not completed. A United Nations High Commissioner who had been appointed in 1950 to resolve this issue reported in November that in the previous year 27,899 Japanese soldiers and more than nine thousand German soldiers had been repatriated: only 13,646 German prisoners of war were still held in Eastern Europe, and a thousand Japanese soldiers and civilians in the Soviet Union and China. The United Nations appealed for these too to be allowed to go home.

In the case of the Germans still held as prisoners of war in the Soviet Union, many of their home towns had been incorporated into Poland. Their final destination was, in the main, West Germany, where several million refugees from the former eastern provinces of Germany asserted their claims to financial help and resettlement through a specially created Ministry of Refugees and Expellees. For many years the maps issued by the ministry refused to recognize that the eastern provinces had been annexed, but showed them as temporarily occupied.

The office of the United Nations High Commissioner for Refugees had become a permanent feature of the post-war world. Its successes were many, but the tasks confronting it were enormous and increasing. During the year it had provided help for 14,000 destitute refugees of European origin in China, and resettled a further 3,000 of them in Europe. Over a two-and-a-half-year period it had assisted 250,000 refugees in Europe to emigrate, mostly to the United States, Canada, Australia and Latin America. Those who found refuge outside Europe, as well as in Britain, included among their numbers both the victims of wartime persecution and some of the perpetrators of that persecution. Argentina proved a popular haven: Adolf Eichmann, one of those who had organized the mass murder of millions of Jews, was one of many former Nazis who had made their home there, living incognito.

Other perpetrators of crimes against the Jews, many of them Ukrainian, Latvian and Lithuanian SS auxiliaries and policemen, gained entry into the United States and Canada by making false declarations on their immigrant visas, denying any wartime wrongdoing. It was these false declarations that led, thirty and forty years later, to their being deported. Fifty-three years after the end of the war the Latvian government was being asked to extradite from Melbourne, Australia, two former Latvian officers, Karlis Ozols and

Konrad Kalejs, who were alleged to have been involved in the murder of tens of thousands of Jews in 1941 in Latvia and Byelorussia. Melbourne, in which they had chosen to settle, was one of the cities in which many Jewish survivors had also made their new homes.

As 1954 came to an end there were still 88,000 refugees living in camps in Europe, nine years after the end of the Second World War. The United Nations was also giving substantial help to the 887,000 Arab refugees from Israel, half of whom were under the age of fifteen. The mandate of the United Nations Relief and Works Agency for Palestine was due to expire in 1955; but it was clear that the problem would not be solved by then, and the mandate was extended for a second five years: it was still in operation half a century after the Arabs left their homes and became refugees. Negotiations to allow at least some of them to return were an integral part of the Oslo peace process which began in 1994.

A disaster at sea in 1954 was among the worst peacetime maritime disasters of the century. During a fierce typhoon a Japanese ferry steamer, the *Toya Maru*, was driven from her anchorage and capsized. More than a thousand passengers and crew were drowned, including fifty Americans, mostly servicemen.

Exploration, after the conquest of Everest, still had its dramatic moments of achievement. During 1954 there were more than twelve climbing expeditions in the Himalayas, including teams – almost emulating the national competitiveness of the Olympic Games – from Britain, the United States, New Zealand, Argentina, Austria and the three wartime belligerents, transformed after less than a decade into friendly competitors: Germany, Italy and Japan. It was an Italian expedition that conquered K2 – Mount Godwin Austen – at 28,252 feet the second highest mountain peak on the globe. The summit, only 700 feet lower than Everest, was scaled, unlike Everest, without the use of oxygen.

In the Antarctic, the United States set up a series of temporary scientific bases, including one at the South Pole, to study the movement of the polar ice, magnetic storms, weather patterns and cosmic rays. In the Arctic the Soviet Union, using motor vehicles, tanks and helicopters, established two survey stations on drifting ice floes in the Arctic Ocean. One of the stations was drifting at the rate of six miles a day. The object of the stations was both to collect scientific data relating to the weather and ocean currents and to find a sea route along the northern coast of Russia, to eastern Siberia.

Pollution had become a serious health hazard in all industrial nations. Raw sewage was a pollutant that affected poor nations. At sea, the effects of oil spillage from tankers knew no national or class boundaries. Marine life suffered, and with it the food chain. In response to the growing and often visible danger, an international convention for the prevention of the pollution of the sea by oil was signed in 1954: but oil spills were to remain a problem. Twenty countries subscribed to the new convention. The first to take legislative action was Britain, whose parliament passed an Oil in Navigable Waters Act, which made it an offence for British ships – other than Royal Navy vessels – to discharge oil within a designated area of the North Sea.

An advance in medicine that year was the confirmation of the link that had recently been established between lung cancer and smoking. At the sixth international congress on cancer, held that year at São Paulo, Brazil, attended by more than a thousand experts from fifty countries, statistics were presented, gathered by the American Cancer Society, which it had not been thought would be ready to be presented for at least another three years. They related to a statistical study of 187,000 men, all smokers, between the ages of fifty and seventy. After the death from cancer of five thousand of the men in two years, a rate that was far in excess of any other cause of death among non-smokers, it was decided to announce that the link was definitely established.

In answer to the smog that had killed four thousand Londoners in four days in 1952, a Clean Air Act was introduced in Britain, making it a punishable offence to emit smoke from any city chimney. The emission of grit and dust from factory chimneys was curtailed, and 'smokeless zones' created. This was an example of what could be done by legislation to improve the environment, though it had required a catastrophe to bring it into being.

The year 1954 saw another example of ecological progress, the development by the Bell Telephone Company in the United States of a solar battery capable of converting the sun's rays into electricity. Half a century later, many homes all over the world were being heated by solar power, and even street lamps, though still on a minuscule scale globally. At the first demonstration of solar power for electricity, sufficient electricity was generated to supply the power needed for a telephone conversation. The first regular colour television broadcasts were transmitted in 1954, in the United States. They began on the first day of the year. One of their highlights later in the year was the televising throughout the United States of the 'Miss

America' beauty competition held in Atlantic City, New Jersey, and seen by television viewers in their living rooms from coast to coast.

Commercial flight continued to gain in its scope, despite several crashes, including two British Comet jet airliners, one of which crashed near Elba on January 10, killing thirty-five passengers, and the other north of Messina on April 9, killing twenty-one passengers. On July 15, in the United States, another four-engined jet passenger aircraft, the Boeing 707, made its maiden flight, a harbinger of things to come.

It was not only in Vietnam that a new conflict had emerged, during the process of France's withdrawal. In Algeria, it was the refusal of France to give up its sovereignty that was leading to armed and violent conflict. During October 30 and November 1 there were more than sixty attacks on French soldiers and police throughout Algeria by Algerian Muslim nationalists. This co-ordinated assault marked the beginning of a sustained attempt by the Front pour la Libération Nationale (FLN) to establish an independent Algeria entirely free from French control. The struggle was momentarily set aside in September, when more than a thousand Algerians were killed during an earthquake at Orléansville. But that was a pause of only a few days. During December, the French reinforced their garrisons in Algeria with 20,000 men. The new arrivals were plunged at once into the daily fears, hatreds, injuries and death of another colonial war.

CHAPTER FOUR

1955

We are always being told that we live in a hard age.
Certainly it offers no pity to the laggard. But was there
ever a time of absolute ease and serenity?

PIERRE MENDÈS-FRANCE

For several years the United States had regarded the future of the
defeated Chinese Nationalists – living in virtual exile on Taiwan, still led
by Chiang Kai-shek – as a crucial element in establishing Western barriers
against European and Asian Communism. On 17 January 1955 the Chinese
Communists began a heavy aerial bombardment of Chinese Nationalist positions on the Tachen Islands (also known as the Pescadores), just west of
Taiwan. On the next day an amphibious force of Communist Chinese landed
on the small island of Yikiang, which the Nationalists did not have sufficient
manpower or arms to defend.

Eisenhower and his advisers were divided on how to respond. Going before
Congress on January 24, Eisenhower asked for the authority of Congress to
employ American forces 'for the purpose of securing and protecting Taiwan
and the Pescadores'. The House of Representatives endorsed this by 409
votes to 3. In four days the President received the powers he sought. Henceforth, the security and survival of the Chiang Kai-shek regime on Taiwan
became the declared and active policy of the United States. There were those
who feared that the United States was about to embark on an all-out war
against Communist China. In left-wing circles in Britain there were protests
that the United States was about to plunge the whole world into war. There
was, however, a limit to what the United States administration was prepared
to risk. Eisenhower quickly put pressure on Chiang Kai-shek not to use the
Nationalist setback in the Pescadores to draw in the United States as a
belligerent.

On February 7 the United States Seventh Fleet began the evacuation of 14,000 Chinese Nationalist troops and 18,000 Chinese civilian refugees from the islands. Six days later, when the evacuation was completed, the Chinese Communist forces took over the islands. The crisis was not yet over. The issue moved elsewhere in the region, and began to turn, as such issues often do, on a tiny point of the globe, in this case the two small islands of Quemoy and Matsu, north of Taiwan, which lay close to the Chinese mainland, and which were under Nationalist control. Suddenly every schoolboy and every conscripted soldier in a dozen nations was watching these islands on the maps presented daily in the newspapers, and wondering if the United States would go to war to keep them within Nationalist Chinese rule. In an attempt to dissuade the Americans from taking such a course, Anthony Eden, who was then in Bangkok, urged John Foster Dulles not to go to war for these two islands, so far distant from Taiwan, to whose defence both the United States and Britain were committed. Eden went so far as to urge the Nationalists to evacuate the islands.

Opinion was moving against the United States. On March 19, the Canadian Foreign Minister, Lester Pearson, announced publicly that Canada would not fight to 'save' Quemoy and Matsu. A week later there was a moment of alarm in Washington when it was rumoured that Eisenhower's advisers wanted him to respond to an attack on Quemoy and Matsu – which was believed to be imminent – by an all-out atom-bomb attack on cities on the Chinese mainland. The rumour had come from Admiral Charney, the Chief of Naval Operations. Eisenhower at once denied the rumour. In a gesture of conciliation towards China, the State Department allowed seventy-six Chinese Communist students, who had been detained in the United States, to return home. Among those allowed to leave was the rocketry expert, H. S. Tsien, who had been held in the United States for five years. On his return to China he began work on creating China's own rocket and ballistic-missile programme.

The talk of war receded. On May 29 the Chairman of the Joint Chiefs of Staff, Admiral Radford, was sent from Washington to Taiwan to impress on Chiang Kai-shek that the United States, while willing to defend the Nationalists on Taiwan, would not go to war with China for the two small offshore islands. Unexpectedly, the Chinese Prime Minister, Chou En-lai, expressed his willingness to negotiate. As Congress, fearing a hard-line response from Eisenhower, pressed the administration to respond favourably, it was announced, first by Dulles and then by Eisenhower himself, that the

United States was prepared to negotiate a ceasefire with regard to the islands without even involving the Nationalists – with whom Chou En-lai had refused to enter negotiations. The war crisis ended, and Quemoy and Matsu, remaining in Nationalist hands, receded into the obscurity from which they had sprung.

During the crisis between Communist and Nationalist China, Winston Churchill was coming to the end of his political career, about to stand down as Prime Minister in favour of Anthony Eden. Six weeks before his resignation, in a speech in the House of Commons on March 1, he introduced a defence budget that included considerable expenditure on the hydrogen bomb. 'We live in a period, happily unique in human history,' he said, 'when the whole world is divided intellectually and to a large extent geographically between the creeds of Communist discipline and individual freedom, and when, at the same time, this mental and psychological division is accompanied by the possession by both sides of the obliterating weapons of the nuclear age.'

Churchill warned that the antagonisms of the 1950s were as deep as those of the sixteenth-century Reformation and the reactions to it that led to the devastation of the Thirty Years War: 'But now they are spread over the whole world instead of only over a small part of Europe.' Casting his mind back even further in history, he reflected: 'We have, to some extent, the geographical divisions of the Mongol invasion in the thirteenth century, only more ruthless and more thorough. We have force and science, hitherto the servants of man, now threatening to become his masters.'

Clement Attlee, Churchill's predecessor, had authorized the building of the British atom bombs. The 'grave decision' to build British hydrogen bombs was one that Churchill had taken. Many people believed, he said, that but for American superiority in nuclear weapons 'Europe would already have been reduced to satellite status and the Iron Curtain would have reached the Atlantic and the Channel.' To protect mankind from nuclear destruction it had become essential, Churchill said, to seek disarmament, but this had to be based on 'an effective system of inspection'. This was the 'only sane policy' for the world for the next few years.

Churchill believed that, while nuclear weapons maintained the freedom of the Western World, their deterrent power had a much greater implication. 'These deterrents may at any time become the parents of disarmament, provided that they deter,' he said. To this end he still considered, as he had done for the past five years, that a summit meeting of the American, Soviet and British leaders was essential. 'It may well be', he said, 'that we shall, by a process of sublime irony, have reached a stage where safety will be the sturdy shield of terror, and survival the twin brother of annihilation.'

There was a distinction that Churchill wished to make, and with which he ended his presentation of the possible path from deterrence to disarmament. 'I have a strong admiration', he said, 'for the Russian people – for their bravery, for their many gifts, and their kindly nature. It is the Communist dictatorship and the declared ambition of the Communist Party and their proselytizing activities that we are bound to resist, and that is what makes this great world cleavage . . .'

Soviet policy continued to lurch from one view of the outside world to another. On February 8 the Soviet Prime Minister, Georgi Malenkov, resigned. He had been proposing a serious programme of arms reduction, in the hope of being able to divert resources to domestic industrial production and the improvement of agriculture. His proposals having been rejected, he was succeeded as Prime Minister by Nikolai Bulganin – who as a young soldier forty years earlier had fought in the Tsarist army. The high point of Bulganin's military achievement had come in the Second World War, in 1941, when, as a lieutenant-general, he helped organize the defence of Moscow. As Prime Minister, despite a high profile at home and abroad, he took second place to Khrushchev, who continued to lead and control the Communist Party machinery, as he had done virtually since Stalin's death.

In the East-West alignment, a further shoring up of the Western defences came on February 24 – while Churchill was still Prime Minister in Britain – when Turkey and Iraq signed a treaty of alliance, the Baghdad Pact. The basis of the new agreement was mutual support against Communist activity within their respective borders, and any Communist threat from beyond them. Within six weeks the British parliament voted to adhere to the Pact. By the end of the year Iran had joined it.

Whether any nation could eventually avoid being caught up in the Cold War was much debated. There was indignation among many of the countries set up only after the Second World War that they should have to take a stance in a quarrel that they did not see as their own. One response was to form their own organization, and this was done, starting on April 18, at Bandung, Indonesia, the opening day of the first Afro-Asian Conference.

The heads of twenty-nine 'non-aligned' nations, among which Communist China was included, gathered at Bandung. They came at the invitation of the Indonesian President, Achmed Sukarno, a Muslim who had collaborated with the Japanese occupation forces during the war in the hope of gaining independence after the defeat of the Dutch. Sukarno had then fought the Dutch (who before the war had imprisoned him for eleven years). His anti-imperial credentials were an important asset in his leadership of the 'non-aligned bloc' established at Bandung. Among those who were invited to Bandung was Archbishop Makarios, who made a strong plea to the assembled delegates to support the Cypriot islanders' struggle against Britain and in favour of union with Greece. Also present was Haj Amin al-Husseini, the Grand Mufti of Jerusalem, exiled by the British from Palestine seven years earlier, and no less an exile from the Jordanian-ruled East Jerusalem since 1948. 'Some of those present', Paul Johnson has written, 'were subsequently to plot to murder each other; others to end their lives in gaol, disgrace or exile. But at the time the Third World had not yet publicly besmirched itself by invasions, annexations, massacres and dictatorial cruelty. It was still in the age of innocence when it was confidently believed that the abstract power of numbers, and still more of words, could transform the world.'

When the Bandung Conference ended on April 24 a new global alignment was in place. Its members were exclusively from Asia and Africa. A leading influence on the deliberations was that of the Indian Prime Minister, Jawaharlal Nehru, who challenged the concept of Communist 'imperialism', and looked to India's 'five principles of coexistence' with China as proof that there was no imperialistic intent on behalf of the Chinese government. When the Prime Ministers of Ceylon and Pakistan expressed their worries about Chinese Communist intentions, Nehru warned that for the conference to endorse those worries would 'thwart' its purpose, which was to avoid taking sides in the wider global confrontation.

The main thrust of the Bandung Conference was hostility to the United States. Considerable excitement was caused when Chou En-lai told the other delegates that 'the population of Asia will never forget that the first atom bomb exploded on Asian soil'. Resolutions were passed in favour of global arms reduction and the abolition of nuclear weapons. Among the leaders who were prominent at Bandung was the new Egyptian President, Colonel Gamal Abdul Nasser. He presented himself both as a leader of the non-aligned nations and as a would-be leader of the Muslim Arab world.

The United States did not intend to leave the non-aligned States unwooed. On April 20, two days after the opening of the Bandung Conference, Eisenhower asked Congress for $3,530 million in foreign aid appropriations. The

Soviet Union also offered aid, and, as the United States had done, arms. On May 14, three weeks after the Bandung Conference ended, eight Communist countries, meeting in Warsaw at the initiative of the Soviet Union, signed a Treaty of Friendship, Co-operation and Mutual Assistance. At the centre of this 'Warsaw Pact', as it was known, was a unified military command for all its members – the Soviet Union, Albania, Bulgaria, Czechoslovakia, East Germany, Hungary, Poland and Roumania. The command was put under one of the most senior Soviet officers, Marshal I. S. Koniev.

Two Central European countries were able to maintain their neutrality amid the contending blocs. One was Finland, which was allowed to remain neutral under the Soviet umbrella: 'Finlandization' became a slogan later on among those Soviet satellites seeking a measure of greater freedom. The other country allowed to be neutral, even more effectively than Finland, was Austria. On April 15, in a bilateral agreement with the Soviet Union, Austria had promised to remain 'permanently neutral' on what was called the 'Swiss model', in return for which Soviet troops would withdraw before the end of the year. A month later, on May 15 – the day after the creation of the Warsaw Pact – the Soviet Union, Britain, France and the United States signed a treaty in Vienna restoring Austrian independence. The conditions for independence included one that in 1919 had been an integral part of the Versailles Treaty, that Austria should not join Germany. The other main condition was that Austria should join neither of the Cold War alignments. The Allied zones of occupation disappeared, and the occupation forces withdrew.

Most appreciated by Austrian opinion during the negotiations was the elimination in the preamble to the treaty of any reference to the responsibility of Austria with regard to the Second World War. Within Austria those individuals who had taken part in the Nazi mass murder and persecution policies breathed a sigh of relief. Five months after the treaty was signed, the death was announced of Cardinal Innitzer, who, seventeen years earlier, had welcomed Hitler to Vienna.

On June 30, as Austria began its first steps as a neutral country, the West German government signed a military aid agreement with the United States. Those who were in exile from countries under Communist rule tried to organize their own circle of self-help, and hope. On July 4 – American Independence Day – an Assembly of the Captive European Nations, after a four-day meeting in Strasbourg, passed a resolution on the importance of keeping the plight of the peoples of Eastern and Central Europe before the international community and the United Nations. The 1948 Universal Declaration on Human Rights gave every person in the world the rights that are associated with free speech and freedom of movement; but, unless the widespread violation of these rights was constantly publicized, the Assembly knew that there was no chance of any change. Even with publicity, and perhaps further declarations and internationally negotiated commitments, no one could guarantee that – or forecast when – the tyrannies which affected so many hundreds of millions of people would come to an end.

Numerous schemes were mooted to help those held captive. One of them, which originated in Britain, involved British university students, often immediately after graduation, travelling to Communist countries, entering into a 'marriage of convenience' with someone who was desperate to leave, and returning with them to Britain – where an amicable divorce would be effected and the short-term partner would remain in freedom.

In Cyprus, the movement for union – *enosis* – with Greece, on behalf of which Archbishop Makarios had spoken at Bandung, gained a new impetus that year. In April it was able to launch a military campaign against British rule, through the National Organization of Cypriot Fighters (EOKA), a guerrilla organization which targeted British military personnel, and also their families. Led by George Grivas, the guerrillas resorted to a series of terrorist actions. Here was yet another destination, and more danger, for British national servicemen.

Powerful support for the demand for union with Greece was provided by Makarios as the head of the self-governing Orthodox Church in Cyprus. As well as his appeal at Bandung, Makarios took the cause of Cypriot separation from Britain to London, Athens and New York. The British hoped that he would use his influence to appeal for an end to the violence, but he declined to do so. At the beginning of September he called on the Greek Cypriots to embark on 'a new stage of passive resistance'. What began as passive soon became active. There were attacks on British soldiers – mostly national servicemen conscripted for a two-year period – and on September 17 the British Institute in Nicosia was burned down. British reinforcements were sent to the island and on November 26 the new Governor, Field Marshal Sir John Harding – the former Chief of the Imperial General Staff – declared a State of Emergency. All the apparatus of British colonial resistance to challenge was asserted with vigour. Severe penalties were enacted for terrorist activity, and public meetings other than church services were banned.

In Malaysia, both Malaya and Singapore were given new constitutions, with elected assemblies and a ministerial system of government. In Singapore there were strikes and riots by the predominantly Chinese People's Action Party, which regarded self-government as inadequate and demanded complete independence. During a riot on May 12 four people were killed. There was anger in Britain when it was learned that an active part was taken in the riots by organized groups of schoolboys from the Chinese middle schools. There had been similar anger when Greek Cypriot schoolboys had participated in the civil disturbances on the island.

As often happened in the final phases of the anti-colonial struggle, the authorities eventually opened negotiations with those whom – like Makarios in Cyprus – they had earlier sworn to crush. Sometimes negotiations would start as a result of the armed struggle being uncrushable, sometimes because of the exhaustion of the colonial power and a failure of national will. In the case of Malaysia, the authorities had won the upper hand. The result was that the Chief Ministers of the two self-governing administrations met the Chinese leader, Chin Peng, in a special area that had been declared a neutral zone and was guarded by British soldiers. After the two Chief Ministers made it clear that they would never recognize the Communist Party in their respective territories, or agree to any terms for a settlement that did not start with a military surrender, Chin Peng withdrew from the talks and into the jungle, declaring that he and his followers would fight on 'to the last man'. Among the troops that entered the jungle to seek him out was a contingent from Australia.

It was the French government which, in its efforts to bring self-government to the French colonies, especially in North Africa, faced the harshest manifestations both of anti-colonialism and of the determination of the local French settlers to retain as much as possible of their positions of authority. The French government, led since June 1954 by Pierre Mendès-France, hoped to find a compromise for Algeria acceptable to the Muslims who made up the majority of the country's inhabitants. Known as a policy of 'integration', this included the teaching of Arabic in schools, the admission of more Muslims to government employment, local self-governing Muslim institutions, and an end to French control over the Muslim religion. A few years earlier, such a plan might have been an acceptable way forward. It was rejected, however, by the Muslims, as not offering enough – and was denounced by the French settlers as offering far too much.

The failure of the efforts by Mendès-France to reach a compromise in

Algeria was to be his downfall. In February the left-wing Parties in his coalition condemned his failure to offer more, and he was forced out of office after only 230 days as Prime Minister. Later that year, in a book recalling his wartime capture, trial by the Vichy authorities, imprisonment and escape, he appealed to his fellow Frenchmen not to lose sight of their wider goal. Recalling the victory ten years earlier, he wrote:

> The error so many people were tempted to make was to believe that the eternal values which were in danger of extinction and for which so much blood was spilt and so much suffering endured, could be rescued and preserved once and for all. They are and always will be threatened, if not from outside, then by our own weaknesses and failures.
>
> We are always being told that we live in a hard age. Certainly it offers no pity to the laggard. But was there ever a time of absolute ease and serenity?

Mendès-France then looked back a decade earlier, to 1945, and to the events since then. 'Victory and liberation did not provide our country with the opportunity to relax its efforts, but with the opportunity of forging its own destiny,' he said. 'It is perhaps more difficult to keep the flame alight when minor temptations and diversions offer themselves on all sides. But the stakes are always the same – freedom and self-respect. And they must be fought for daily at the cost of unrelenting struggle.'

In Morocco, nationalists led by the Front de la Libération Nationale (the FLN) fomented anti-French riots on August 20. That same day Algerian nationalists again attacked French soldiers and police throughout Algeria. At North Constantine, near Philippeville, seventy-one Europeans and fifty-two Muslims were massacred. In an army reprisal, 1,273 'rebels' were killed. In Morocco, on the day of the North Constantine massacres, fifty of the eight hundred Europeans in the town of Oued-Zem were massacred, including many women and children. John Wallis, the *Daily Telegraph* special correspondent in Morocco, called it 'one of the largest and most horrible massacres of Europeans, even in the savage history of Morocco'.

Moroccans who refused to join in the killing were themselves killed by the mob. Jews 'were also victims of the tribesmen's savagery'. When the French Foreign Legion entered the European Quarter five and a half hours after the attack began it found the quarter in ruins and 'littered with mutilated victims'. Looking at the scene, a French lieutenant told his men: 'Take no prisoners.' John Wallis himself, entering Oued-Zem on the following morning, wrote of a 'smoking, ruined town, over which hung the stench of death. I saw a burnt-out lorry with the burnt body of the driver lying in the road. Wherever I looked I saw corpses.'

The new French Prime Minister, Edgar Faure, spoke out on the radio: 'All of France's honour and its humane mission obliges us absolutely, unequivocally, and outspokenly to keep Algeria for France, and in France.' He was answered by Albert Camus, Algeria's most famous French writer – who was later to be awarded the Nobel Prize for Literature: 'Algeria is not France, it isn't even Algeria, it is that unknown land which a cloud of blood hides from its incomprehensible natives, bothersome soldiers and exotic Frenchmen. Algeria is the absent one, whose memory and abandonment pains the heart of a few people.' Camus' proposal: 'That the present two parties simultaneously promise in public not to touch the civilian population in any circumstances.'

The violence spread. As it did so, the French government was obliged to withdraw military units from the NATO command in Europe in order to reinforce its garrisons. When the year began there were 76,000 French troops in Algeria. When it ended the number had reached 170,000, and was still rising. On September 30, at the United Nations General Assembly, where it was expected that French rule in Algeria would be under criticism, France withdrew from the Assembly until the critical item was deleted from the agenda, which it was two months later.

In Tunisia the process of the transfer from French rule to independence involved compromises that emerged only after long and complex negotiations. This was especially true with regard to the transfer of police control to the Tunisians, the continued use of the French language in schools and official documents, and the rights of French residents to representation on the Tunisian town councils. The Tunisian national leader, Habib ibn Ali Bourguiba – who had spent two years in prison for his uncompromising call for full independence – and who had hitherto been hostile to the compromises being worked out, agreed to participate in the final talks in Paris. On June 3 agreement was reached. Tunisia would obtain full internal self-government, to be followed a year later by full independence. Bourguiba returned to Tunis a hero, and as Prime Minister – and President – in waiting.

A resolution also emerged by the end of the year to the conflict in Morocco. Internal dynastic rivalries were resolved when the Pasha of Marrakech, El Glaoui, agreed to recognize the claim of the Sultan, Ben Arafa, to the throne.

Throughout the autumn there were negotiations in France, as a result of which a Treaty of Independence was crafted. Morocco would achieve self-government, followed by complete independence. The first entirely Moroccan government was formed on December 7.

In divided Vietnam, both North and South struggled to develop their economies and to build their nations with half the national resources. A majority of the voters in a referendum in South Vietnam on October 23 voted to depose the Emperor Bao Dai. Three days later South Vietnam was declared a republic, under Ngo Dinh Diem. A Roman Catholic, he had served in the French colonial administration before the war. In 1945 he had been imprisoned briefly by the Communists.

The French had wanted to continue to support Bao Dai. The United States put their trust in Diem, and the republic. For a while there was friction between Washington and Paris. The Americans persisted, and emerged as the main supporters of the Diem regime, sending him a steady stream of military aid.

On February 9 the final phase began of the expulsion of Black Africans from their homes in Johannesburg. Father Trevor Huddleston, an English priest of the Anglican Community of the Resurrection, who had served as the friend of the Africans for the previous twelve years, held mass especially early that morning – at 5 a.m. – in order to be present during the operation. As he left his church he saw the arrival of 'a detachment of African police under European command' and army lorries being driven to the scene. He walked into Sophiatown, the principal area that was to be cleared. 'Lining the street were thousands of police, both white and black: the former armed with rifles and revolvers, the latter with the usual assegai. A few Sten guns were in position at various points.'

There was no violent resistance. 'Most of our local leaders had been banned or arrested,' Nelson Mandela recalled, 'and, in the end, Sophiatown died not to the sound of gunfire but to the sound of rumbling trucks and sledgehammers.' In all, 60,000 Africans were being moved out, to the Meadowlands development which the South African government had purchased for them. It lay thirteen miles away from the city in which those being expelled had lived for generations, and in which most of them worked. 'The lesson I took away from the campaign was that, in the end, we had no alternative to armed and violent resistance,' Nelson Mandela later wrote.

Over and over again, we had used all the non-violent weapons in our arsenal – speeches, deputations, threats, marches, strikes, stay-aways, voluntary imprisonment – all to no avail, for whatever we did was met by an iron hand.

A freedom fighter learns the hard way that it is the oppressor who defines the nature of the struggle, and the oppressed is often left no recourse but to use methods that mirror those of the oppressor. At a certain point, one can only fight fire with fire.

A year after the explusion, in his book *Naught for your Comfort*, which made the story of Sophiatown universally known, Trevor Huddleston wrote bitterly: 'White Johannesburg had encroached on Black Johannesburg.' He added:

The overwhelming majority of South Africans of the 'white' group have no conception whatever of human relationships except that based on racial domination.

The greatest tragedy, in one sense of the present situation, is the total ignorance of those in responsible positions of government of the way in which young Africa thinks, talks and lives.

'It is not white preservation that is considered a sufficient motive force today,' Huddleston commented, 'it is white *supremacy*, that and nothing less.'

Inside the United States, all manifestations of White supremacy in the South were being challenged by law. In the late autumn the Interstate Commerce Commission, a federal body, ordered an end to segregation in public transport. On November 25 a Black woman, Rosa Parks, was arrested in Montgomery, Alabama, for sitting in the front of a bus, in the section reserved for Whites. Following her arrest Dr Martin Luther King, who had just arrived in Montgomery as Baptist pastor, led 50,000 Black protesters in a boycott of local buses and a demand for an end to segregation. The bus boycott lasted thirteen months.

Following the Senate vote against Senator McCarthy in 1954, the tide of anti-Communist witch-hunts was turning. It had been a period of near hysteria, the search for 'Reds under the bed', and the driving away from the United States of some of its most creative citizens. During 1955 several ongoing accusations against individual Americans were withdrawn. In

January a Federal Judge, Justice Youngdahl, rejected a long-standing indictment against Professor Owen Lattimore, a scholar of China who had been
accused by McCarthy of following 'the Communist line'. In June the Supreme
Court ordered the reinstatement of Dr Peters, Professor of Medicine at Yale
University, who had been removed from government employment on the
ground that there was 'reasonable doubt' as to his loyalty.

The Federal Court of Appeals also overturned one of the most vexatious
aspects of the McCarthyite period, the withdrawal of the right to travel
abroad to those accused of Communist sympathies. Travel to other countries
was a 'natural right', the Court ruled. In another landmark judgment reversing the developments of the previous years, on July 21 the New York Court
of Appeals declared that loyalty oaths – such as the one required by the
New York Housing Association for all its tenants – must no longer be
imposed.

The testing of nuclear weapons in the atmosphere continued, with the Soviet
Union and the United States each seeking the most effective weapon. The
ability to destroy a city, or five hundred cities, became a focal point of
scientific experimentation. It also became a focal point of scientific unease.
In March the Federation of American Scientists appealed directly to the
United Nations 'with some sense of desperation' to collect the evidence of
the effect of these explosions and to take action accordingly. Anxiety was also
expressed in the British House of Commons. But there were countervailing
arguments. A British pioneer in the construction of the bomb, Sir John
Cockcroft, insisted that the world level of radioactive contamination produced
by all the atomic bombs was 'too low to cause anxiety'. He believed that
the existing radioactive level would have to increase 'a thousand-fold' before
it would have any harmful effect.

Another British nuclear scientist, Sir James Chadwick, who had also been
involved in the development of the original atom bomb, took a very different
view to that of Cockcroft, stressing not so much the levels of radiation as
the moral aspect of the new weaponry. 'The original atom bomb is a weapon
not very different from other bombs – of the same kind but more powerful,'
he confided in a private note. 'The H-bomb can hardly be classified as a
weapon at all. Its effect in causing suffering is out of all proportion to its
military effect. The H-bomb does not offer any improvement in the waging
of war, and it brings with it a risk of making the world uninhabitable.'
Chadwick added: 'Most people would agree that it would be morally wrong

to use the H-bomb – the only possible exception could be to use it in retaliation, even though only to the extent necessary to make the enemy stop its use.'

Serious scientific warnings began to proliferate. In April, Albert Einstein was one of seven Nobel Prize winners who signed a statement that 'a war with H-bombs might quite possibly put an end to the human race'. The problem created by the existence of the atom and hydrogen bombs was 'the most serious that has ever confronted the human race'. The statement continued:

In view of the fact that in any future war nuclear weapons will certainly be employed and that such weapons threaten the continued existence of mankind, we urge the governments of the world to realize and to acknowledge publicly that their purposes cannot be furthered by a world war.

We urge them, consequently, to find peaceful means for the settlement of all matters of dispute between them.

Einstein's signature on this statement was received by the organizers on the day of his death. A month later, on May 15, the fourteenth and last United States nuclear explosion of the 1955 atomic test series took place in Nevada, at Yucca Flats. Among the explosions that had been carried out during this test series was the detonation of an atomic air missile at a height of six miles, an underground explosion and an above-ground test against a variety of military equipment. In all there had been twenty-five atomic explosions in the course of the tests.

In June Dr Willard Libby, a member of the United States Atomic Energy Commission, made an official statement with the authority of his fellow commissioners that the explosions then taking place in the testing grounds would produce genetic mutations in humans – though not enough, he insisted, to be noticed among the mutations that took place naturally. A few days later a leading German nuclear scientist, Professor Otto Hahn, issued a much stronger warning. He saw 'a danger to humanity', he said, in the genetic effects of radioactivity, against which there was 'no permanent protection'. Hahn had carried out nuclear research inside Germany during the war. Only after the war did he learn that he had been awarded the Nobel Prize (in 1944) for his pre-war pioneering work in the discovery of nuclear fission.

On July 18, after meeting at Lake Constance – a lake bounded by

Switzerland, Germany and Austria – a group of Nobel Prize winners issued a stark warning. They 'saw with horror', they wrote, 'that science was giving mankind the means with which to destroy itself'. They went on to state, with all the authority of their scientific expertise, that modern weapons of war 'may contaminate the world with radio-activity to such an extent that entire nations may be wiped out'.

Nuclear weapons and nuclear power were very different sides of the same scientific coin. The first atomically generated power station began operation in the United States on the evening of July 17 – the day before the Nobel Prize winners' warning about nuclear weapons. It took place in the small town of Arco, Idaho, where nuclear power was used that night to light some 550 buildings for about a thousand residents of the town. For two hours, between eight and ten o'clock that evening, Arco was taken off the national electricity grid and plugged into the new source of electric power.

The experiment at Arco was judged a success. Henceforth, the development of nuclear power was rapid, first in the United States and then in both Britain and Canada. Before the end of the year the United States produced a catalogue of atomic materials for the production of domestic-use and industrial energy, together with a price list. Nuclear power for domestic use was to become a central feature of modern industrialized life.

On August 8 an International Conference on the Peaceful Uses of Atomic Energy was opened in Geneva. Delegates came from seventy-three countries. As well as the 1,428 delegates there were 1,350 academic and commercial observers. Meanwhile the testing of nuclear weapons in the atmosphere continued. On November 27 the Soviet government announced that it had successfully carried out a series of atom and hydrogen bomb tests. This was indeed known outside the Russian land mass, as radioactive dust from the explosions had been detected by scientists in Japan and in Western Europe, with Siberia as the place of origin. Britain also announced plans to carry out more nuclear tests in the atmosphere in the following year at Monte Bello Island, off the west coast of Australia, and thereafter at Maralinga, in the desert in central Australia.

In the United States, twenty-five young Japanese women, who had left Japan by air on May 5, were being treated for the terrible burns and injuries they had received a decade earlier in Hiroshima. On reaching San Francisco one of the girls commented: 'No bombs in the city! It looked as if nothing happened! In Japan, everything destroyed. In America, no! You couldn't see any sign of war. It was a very big surprise.' Another girl remarked: 'All the

Americans ate so much, no wonder they were so big and energetic. And the country was so big too. No wonder Japan lost. I thought how stupid it had been to go to war with America.'

Even as the nuclear tests were continuing in the atmosphere, the 'Hiroshima Maidens', as they were known, were going through a series of long, difficult and often painful operations in the Mount Sinai Hospital, New York. Three plastic surgeons – Arthur Barsky, Sidney Kahn and Bernard E. Simon – performed 127 operation in all on the twenty-five women. A headline in the New York *World Telegram* proclaimed: 'Surgeon's knife battling A-Bomb'.

In China, the Bamboo Curtain, as impenetrable as the Iron Curtain, cut off the country from outside curiosity and inquiry. Mao Tse-tung's imposition of Chinese Communist rule took place amid secrecy and severity. The elimination of 'warlordism' continued, marked in the early months of the year by the suicide of Kao Kang, the senior Communist Party official in Manchuria, and a Deputy Prime Minister of China, who had been accused of trying to detach Manchuria from China and make himself dictator. Special committees were formed throughout the organizational structure of the Communist Party with the authority to enforce Party discipline and publicly to denounce anyone suspected of seeking 'personal dictatorship'.

Intellectual control was imposed with the same severity as political control. On July 17 it was announced that the author and writer Hu Feng had been arrested. He had earlier made a public criticism of Communism as exerting a 'blighting influence' on literature. The control which the Party exercised over culture, he wrote – he was himself a Party member – 'exhausted' people so that they could no longer think straight. The use of Marxism to judge works of art was 'not based on reality'. The 'weapon' of Marxism, he warned, 'is frightening, because it can stifle the real feelings of creativity and art'.

Accused of being an 'agent' of the Chinese Nationalists, Hu Feng was ordered to make a public apology and an abasement. He did so, but his three lengthy self-criticisms were judged inadequate, and he was sent to prison. With one brief respite, he remained in prison for twenty-four years. Throughout China, meetings were held attacking 'Hu Feng-ism', and asserting the Party's correctness in accelerating the pace of land reform as opposed to private initiative. Other dissidents, accused of counter-revolutionary activity, were executed or sentenced to long periods in prison.

Inside the Soviet Union, widespread public discontent – expressed far more openly than was possible in Stalin's time – at the shortages of foodstuffs, forced the government to make intensive efforts to improve the food situation. Under the leadership of Khrushchev, whose colourful, at times almost eccentric personality was beginning to impress itself on his own people and abroad, a 'Virgin Lands' scheme was devised whereby volunteers would go to the empty, barren wastes of Kazakhstan and begin to cultivate the wilderness. In all, more than seventy million acres of virgin and barren soil were ploughed, and fifty million acres were then planted. This involved the establishment within a few months of more than four hundred collective farms, and the despatch to the region of half a million 'volunteers'.

The scheme did not go well. By the time the planting ought to have been begun, only ten per cent of the planned accommodation had been erected, and only five per cent of the granaries needed to store the grain had been built. In addition, severe drought – endemic to the region – meant that much of the area that was planted produced a poor crop, or no crop at all.

Among Khrushchev's other schemes that year was one to plant maize on all uncultivated meadow and pasture land. The order went out from Moscow for an eight-fold increase in the cultivated area of maize. Khrushchev himself, a visible enthusiast for his plan, travelled the country extolling the virtues of the maize crop to agriculturists. The cob would provide flour, and the stalks would provide silage for feeding cattle. To encourage the planting of maize among cattle farmers, Khrushchev announced that it would be a punishable offence for farmers to buy their fodder instead of producing it themselves. As a result of these threats, and also of an offer to the peasants that they could retain and sell fifteen per cent of the maize they grew, the area under maize cultivation increased from ten million to fifty million acres. But the harvest was a poor one, undermining some of the earlier enthusiasm. At the same time, the heavy hand of Moscow was seen when 30,000 men, most of them without any agricultural experience, were sent out to the collective farms to serve as chairmen, in charge of quotas and organization.

Another of Khrushchev's schemes that year, in an attempt to get round the chronic shortage of metal building materials, was to encourage the use of pre-fabricated concrete building blocks in housing construction. He also encouraged builders to use whatever local building materials were to hand, including straw, rushes and sawdust. As an incentive to builders, ten per cent of all newly built houses were to be reserved for those who built them.

The Soviet Union was struggling to modernize, but its focus on defence spending made it difficult to satisfy the domestic consumer market. Officials who favoured extravagant, ornate or luxury dwellings were dismissed, as were architects who put forward over-elaborate designs. A special decree of November 10 poured obloquy on architects who favoured 'extravagant' building styles. The call was for cheap, standardized dwellings, which might have little or no architectural merit or visual attraction, but which would house the population on whose productivity – and to a lesser extent well-being – the State was dependent.

In Latin America, the widespread poverty was in stark contrast to the evolving prosperity and consumer society further north, in the United States and Canada. Dictatorship, often brought to power by promises of social reform, invariably turned to tyranny and corruption, leaving most dissatisfied those for whom it had seemed to offer the most. In Argentina the initially populist regime of President Perón was under sharp attack by those whom he had alienated by his dictatorial rule.

Perón's refusal, in the name of economic independence, to employ foreign capital and technicians in Argentina's southern oilfields had created considerable economic hardship. He therefore reversed his policy, giving exploration and exploitation rights to the Standard Oil Company of California, and enabling it to establish airfields in the region of its concession. This provoked the opposition both of the army, which claimed that the area would become a United States air base, and of his own Peronista Party, which saw the arrangement – essential for Argentina's economic well-being – as a sellout to the 'Colossus of the North'.

Perón also alienated the Roman Catholic Church, accusing it of subversion and introducing a Bill to curb Church powers. His efforts to legalize prostitution and divorce had created an unbridgeable rift. There were street demonstrations in Buenos Aires by Catholic groups which refused to accept any further diminution of their authority. In retaliation, Perón deported two leading priests, Monsignor Manuel Tato, the Auxiliary Bishop of Buenos Aires, and his assistant, Monsignor Ramon Novoa. The deportations took place on June 15. Ten coaches of police with machine guns escorted the two clergymen to the airport where they were put on board an aeroplane bound for Rome. That day the Vatican announced that everyone who had taken part in the persecution of Catholics in Argentina had been excommunicated. On June 16 a group of naval officers launched a military attack on Perón's headquarters in Government House, while naval aircraft dropped bombs, killing several bystanders. The *Daily Telegraph* reported:

Just when the Perón forces appeared to be dominating the fighting in the city's centre waves of bombers swooped down in a second air raid. A pall of black smoke hung over the centre of the capital around the pink-washed Government House.

At least twelve bombs burst among the big offices of the central area. Heavy casualties were reported among the masses of the Peronista workers who had massed there.

Two warships were reported to be anchored in the river and to be shelling the Government House area. The guns could be heard through the city.

Fighter planes machine-gunned Government House . . .

Civilians and troops loyal to General Perón manned anti-aircraft guns.

During June 16 a rebel broadcast claimed that all three armed services were taking over power. But the army, remaining loyal to Perón, crushed what was essentially a naval revolt. 'I congratulate the army,' Perón declared. 'Not one corporal or soldier failed to fulfil his duty.' That night Peronist gangs attacked the Cathedral and many other churches and set them on fire. At least twenty civilians were killed. Perón sought to draw back from further violent confrontation, however, and released his Catholic prisoners. The Radical Party, many of whose members had also been released from prison in an attempt to win the Party over, demanded more concessions. Its leader, Dr Frondizi, whom Perón allowed to broadcast to the nation on July 27, insisted on the complete restoration of individual freedom.

Perón was unwilling to satisfy the mounting demands. His own supporters would not allow him to do so. They were the beneficiaries of the dictatorship, and did not wish to relinquish the privileges and favouritism which their support brought them. At the beginning of August, Catholic demonstrations were renewed. On August 31 Perón declared: 'The order of the day for every Peronista, whether individually or as a member of an organization, is to answer violent action with another action still more violent. And when one of our people falls, five of them will fall.'

Perón's supporters were issued with arms. On September 1 a state of siege was declared in Buenos Aires. On September 16 the garrison of the city of Córdoba – a Catholic stronghold – rose in revolt, its anti-government forces led by General Eduardo Lonardi, a devout Catholic who declared that his insurrection was 'in defence of Catholic Christianity'. Other garrison towns joined in, demanding Perón's resignation. A senior naval officer, Admiral

Isaac Rojas, threatened a naval bombardment of Buenos Aires unless Perón resigned. In face of such a challenge, the dictator had no forces on which he could fall back.

On September 19 Perón resigned. Four days later, General Lonardi entered the capital and was proclaimed President. His first promise was to restore good relations with the Vatican. Admiral Rojas became Vice-President. The Peronistas were removed from their positions of authority in government, the universities, the law courts and Argentine embassies abroad. The agreement with the Standard Oil Company was cancelled. Perón fled to Spain, where Franco granted him asylum.

General Lonardi's presidency did not last long. Accused of behaving too leniently to the Peronistas, and in particular to the trade unions on which Perón had based so much of his support – their headquarters had been among the buildings bombed on June 16 – he was overthrown in a coup d'état on November 13. The new President was the Chief of the General Staff, General Pedro Aramburu. Admiral Rojas remained as Vice-President. The purge of Peronistas intensified. When the trade unions reacted by calling a general strike, Aramburu sent troops against them, and the defiance was violently crushed. Hardly had the anti-Peronists been released from prison than the prisons filled up again with the supporters of the former dictator, and with soldiers and Catholic leaders, former opponents of Perón, who were nevertheless accused of 'plotting revolution'. Some were sent as exiles to the southernmost part of the Argentine, to live in a harsh, inhospitable terrain.

The realities of tyranny, revolution, imprisonment, exile and revenge were in contrast to the pleasurable enjoyments of life that so many people craved. On July 18, there was a landmark in such pursuits of harmless fantasy when the 'Disneyland' theme park opened at Anaheim, in California. 'For some brief periods,' commented the *New York Times*, 'the ceremonies took on the aspect of the dedication of a national shrine.' Disneyland offered a world of light-hearted entertainment to children and adults alike, and a magical environment that was both clean and without violence – an environment at variance with many of the urban centres in the United States, including some within only a few minutes' drive of Disneyland itself.

In Britain, where some scenes of distant wars and poverty were beginning to appear on television, there was widespread moral indignation among parents at the violence of 'horror comics', and their importation was banned by the government. But real violence, and the arbitrariness of death, were often thrust into the news. In June, during the annual twenty-four-hour motorcar race at Le Mans in France, eighty-three spectators and one driver were killed when a car spun out of control. It was the highest death toll in the history of motor racing. The *Daily Telegraph* Motoring Correspondent, W. A. McKenzie, reported: 'For sixty or seventy yards the sandy ground was drenched with blood. Bodies lay everywhere. A few had been covered by advertisement banners, torn off the palisade that had failed to protect them.'

To the outrage of many of the spectators, the organizers ordered the race to go on, until its end twenty-two hours later. One British driver, Mike Hawthorn, who immediately after the accident said he would not drive again in the race, decided to do so and went on to win.

Aspects of the aftermath of the Second World war continued to be in evidence a decade after it had ended. On September 9, four months after the Federal German Republic became a sovereign State, the Federal German Chancellor, Dr Adenauer, went to Moscow as the guest of the Soviet government. During a gala dinner three days later he and Marshal Bulganin came to an agreement that all German prisoners of war still being held in the Soviet Union would be allowed to return home. Most of them had spent more than ten years in captivity.

The first group to be released was brought to the Soviet-Polish border near Bialystok on October 6, and taken on by train and truck to West Germany. In all, more than nine thousand German wartime soldiers were repatriated by the end of the year. Among those repatriated was General Friedrich Gollwitzer, the officer who had led the nineteen captive German generals through the streets of Moscow in July 1944.

The trials of war criminals from the Nazi era had not ceased. On November 22, alerted by the Central Council of Jews in Germany – mostly survivors of the Holocaust – the police in Kiel arrested Dr Karl Clauberg, who, as a doctor at Auschwitz, had carried out sterilization experiments on Jews and Gypsies. He was accused of 'repeatedly inflicting grave bodily injury'. Seven years earlier he had been tried by the Russians and sentenced to twenty-five years in prison for participating in the 'mass extermination of Soviet citizens'. After less than five years as a prisoner in Russia – half the time spent in captivity by German prisoners of war – he had been amnestied and sent back to West Germany, where he boasted to friends and acquaintances of his wartime 'scientific achievements'. Two years after his arrest in West Germany, on the eve of his trial, he died in a hospital at Kiel.

The refugee problem created by the Second World War was being resolved. In gratitude for the international help that Holland had received during severe flooding two years earlier, the Dutch government announced in March 1955 that it would take in 250 refugee families from Displaced Persons camps still in existence in Austria, Trieste, Greece and Italy. There were also refugees as a result of more recent conflicts: both the 850,000 Palestinian Arab refugees still languishing in refugee camps in the neighbouring Arab countries and 670,000 Chinese refugees who had fled from mainland China to Hong Kong.

At the end of the year the Nobel Peace Prize was awarded to the Office of the United Nations High Commissioner for Refugees. It was decided to use the prize money – £13,000 – to disperse a small camp on the Greek island of Tinos, where 125 refugees from the Balkans had been living in squalor and hunger for a decade, since the end of the Second World War.

A major success story in the sphere of international co-operation and assistance was the announcement in March that the United Nations International Children's Emergency Fund (UNICEF) was allocating more than $4 million for work in thirty-four countries to improve maternal and child health. This included special emergency aid for war-torn Korea, and for India, where hunger and poverty were extreme. By the end of the year it was estimated that thirty-two million children, as well as many pregnant and nursing mothers, had been helped by UNICEF, which among other achievements had provided the equipment and medical supplies for 7,500 clinics worldwide.

A special United Nations scheme was the distribution of powdered milk for children in need. International aid, a gift of the world's few wealthiest countries – predominantly the United States – even when distributed honestly to those for whom it was intended, could not obviate the need for the growth of local prosperity, modern agriculture and efficient industry. But as the poorer nations of the world grew poorer, or struggled to maintain their existing paltry standards of living, outside aid took on a crucial and permanent dimension which it was to retain until the end of the century, and no doubt far beyond.

CHAPTER FIVE
1956

... the dictates of conscience and common humanity.

PETER FRYER

In ALGERIA, martial law and censorship were the principal answers known to the French authorities as they confronted the escalating violence between the French settlers and the Arab nationalists. On 10 January 1956, in the columns of *L'Express*, Albert Camus proposed a civilian truce. Travelling to Algiers he spoke at a series of meetings, appealing to both sides for moderation. On January 22 he told a mixed French and Muslim audience: 'We are in a duel with knives, and the world is moving ahead at the speed of a supersonic jet. The same day that newspapers print the horrible story of our provincial quarrels, they announce European atomic stockpiles. If only Europe could come to terms with itself, waves of richness would cover the continent and overflow as far as our house, making our problems and hatreds obsolete.'[1]

A new French government, under Guy Mollet, announced 'free elections' in Algeria to determine its future. But Camus warned that the Muslim Arabs, encouraged to do so by their militant terrorist arm, the Front pour la Libération Nationale (the FLN), 'are making insane demands for an independent Algerian government, where the French will be considered as foreigners unless they want to convert, and war is inevitable'. Conversion to Islam was indeed a demand being made by extremist Muslims. France would never abandon the French in Algeria, Camus believed, telling a friend: 'She cannot, because she would never agree to throw 1,200,000 Frenchmen into the sea.'

Camus was also emphatic that, as he wrote to a friend, 'the current

[1] Four months later Britain carried out its third nuclear test, on Monte Bello Island.

situation of ignoble massacres of civilians and children by terrorists gives valid arguments to the most hard-headed faction of Frenchmen in Algeria'. As a result of Muslim extremism, 'Bit by bit French public opinion accepts the idea of war, a development that I have tried to make clear to Arabs of goodwill, or at least of less bad will. But the only result, I suppose, is that I have won their mistrust.'

Within Algeria, martial law and censorship remained in place, as the violent clash between extremists on both sides – French European Christians and North African Muslim Arabs – continued. On February 8, Camus resigned from *L'Express* in despair at the paper's support for the Arab nationalists, whose acts of terror were also being applauded by Moscow.

In Moscow itself, on February 25, the Twentieth Congress of the Communist Party of the Soviet Union was reaching the end of its week-long deliberations. It had been an unspectacular set of meetings, open to reporters, in which a succession of worthy speakers set out the achievements of Soviet Communism during the previous year, and indicated future lines of continuing progress. Dmitri Volkogonov, Stalin's biographer, writes of how the Congress had been 'moving uneventfully towards its predictable close' when the Soviet Prime Minister, Nikolai Bulganin, who was presiding, announced that the next session would be a closed one. No reporting of it would be allowed. All foreign Communist observers had to leave the hall; they included the exiled Spanish Communist leader Dolores Ibarruri – La Pasionaria.

The outsiders and the journalists having left, Bulganin called on Nikita Khrushchev, the First Secretary of the Communist Party of the Soviet Union, to speak. 'In a state of shock,' writes Volkogonov,

the nearly 1,500 delegates sat transfixed in total silence, interrupting only occasionally with cries of outraged indignation. They seemed to see a ghost standing at the shoulder of the speaker. The more Khrushchev revealed, the clearer the image of the ghost. It was a moment of rare historic significance. Only hours before the speech, no one could have predicted that the stagnant and deformed party would be capable of performing this genuinely civic feat.

Since Stalin's death almost three years earlier Khrushchev had been confronted by mounting, detailed evidence of Stalin's tyranny, had been shown innumerable letters of protest from ordinary Soviet citizens convinced that they had been falsely imprisoned, and had read appeal after appeal that the injustices of the Stalin era should be rectified, that the camps should be emptied and the development of the Soviet Union put in sane and safe hands.

Khrushchev entitled his speech 'On the Personality Cult and its Consequences'. Much of the evidence of Stalin's tyranny was taken from the 1930s. There was even the implication that Lenin, as well as Stalin, had used terror against his enemies. Speaking for more than three hours, Khrushchev gave details of how innocent people had been accused, how confessions had been extracted, how cases had been fabricated against 'enemies of the people' who had done no wrong. The mass deportation of nationalities from the Caucasus had been carried out with 'no military justification'. Stalin had caused the victory in 1945 to be attributed to himself instead of to the Party and people.

During the course of his speech Khrushchev gave short character sketches of Stalin's actions that amazed the delegates, brought up as they all were on the sure knowledge of Stalin's qualities of genius and vision in peace and war. According to Khrushchev, Stalin 'knew the country and agriculture only from the movies'. During the Second World War he had 'worked out military operations on a globe'.

The delegates were shocked. But they were warned that not a word of this must reach the Soviet people. Thus one of the central elements of Stalinism, rigid censorship of ideas and opinions, was to be maintained. The official published version, issued four months later, contained none of the denunciations, the mockery and the invective. It was limited to an admission that 'serious mistakes' had been committed only 'during the later period of Stalin's life', and stated specifically that it would be wrong to seek the source of the Cult of Personality in the 'nature of the Soviet order'. Communism was not to be challenged. The Cult of Personality had to be abandoned, and Stalin gently relegated to obscurity – it was to take another five years, however, before his mummified body was removed from its place of honour inside Lenin's mausoleum and buried by the Kremlin wall, with no further means of preservation.

Khrushchev's speech was intended as a secret guide to the delegates, not as a discussion paper for the Soviet people. It was not in fact to be published inside the Soviet Union until 1989 – thirty-three years after it was made, and two years before the disintegration of the Soviet Union itself. There were, however, a number of foreign Communist Party delegates among his audience. They had not been asked to leave the hall when he began to speak.

Within a few weeks, details of what he had said began to appear in the Western press. The State Department in Washington published an extremely full version.

There were some who said that the speech could not have been made, that the leaked version must be an anti-Soviet provocation, a crude anti-Communist attempt to discredit Stalin and his works. But the speech was a real one: astounding for those who heard it, and a turning point in the nature of Soviet Communism. One man's tyranny had ended. The tyranny of the system remained, more capable of adapting to criticism, but equally able to shore up any gaps in the loyalty or steadfastness of the Party faithful. The instruments of repression remained, the labour camps for political prisoners continued to serve as a warning to dissenters and a destination for those who took their criticisms beyond what the Party would permit.

Even during his speech, Khrushchev made it clear that the new 'collective leadership' had reintroduced the 'proper' Leninist principles of government. Nor was any error of post-war policy laid at Stalin's feet, other than the breach with Yugoslavia, which was in the process of being healed. Nor did Khrushchev have a hundred per cent support for his criticism of the Cult of Personality. In Stalin's birthplace, Georgia, when accounts of the secret speech circulated there were riots by students loyal to Stalin, and more than a hundred rioters were injured. *Pravda* itself, the Party newspaper, referred to Stalin after the speech as 'one of the greatest Marxists' and went on to criticize those 'rotten elements' who dared to question the wisdom of the Party's policies.

Thousands of Stalin's political prisoners were released from prison and labour camp. But this could not be interpreted as a fully reformist decision, as many of those released were made to remain in the region of their labour camps as 'semi-free labourers'. The 'crimes' of many of those who were released had been trivial in the extreme by any but Stalinist standards. One of those amnestied was the woman who had been arrested in 1949 after telling the people in a queue for milk in Moscow that she understood from her son in the Red Army in Vienna that people were no longer queuing for milk in the West. By the time of Khrushchev's speech she had served seven years of her ten-year labour-camp sentence.

After Khrushchev's speech the Soviet forced-labour system remained in operation. By keeping released prisoners at work in the neighbourhood of the camps, the system was even made more efficient as far as the Soviet economy was concerned. This emphasis on a more efficient economy was behind many of the reforms instituted that year. A minimum wage was established, the standard working week reduced from forty-eight hours to forty-six hours, a maximum of six hours a day placed on work by youngsters aged sixteen to eighteen, maternity leave increased (from 77 days to 112 days), and efforts instituted to reduce accidents at work.

During the course of his speech Khrushchev told the delegates that 7,679 of Stalin's victims had been 'rehabilitated', and he added starkly: 'Many of them posthumously.' The concept of rehabilitation, albeit without compensation for the living or redress for the dead, was a giant step forward in Soviet thinking. Members of the old regime, including Molotov, the Foreign Minister and co-architect of the Nazi-Soviet Pact, were removed from high office, Molotov being made Minister of State Control for a year, before being sent as ambassador to Mongolia. As evidence that Khrushchev was determined to strengthen 'Socialist legality' by deed as well as by word, the Communist Party chief in Azerbaijan in the Stalin era, M. M. D. Bagirov, and three police officials accused of complicity in Beria's crimes were tried and executed.

Before Khrushchev had begun his speech denouncing Stalin, there had been a preliminary revisionist speech at the Congress which served, in retrospect, as something of a trial run. It was by the writer Mikhail Sholokhov, author of the bestselling patriotic novel *Quiet Flows the Don*, who used his appearance on the podium to condemn the head of the Soviet Writers' Union, Alexander Fadeyev, one of Stalin's most conspicuous and prolific supporters.

Following the Congress hundreds of writers returned from the labour camps, rehabilitated and cleared of any wrongdoing. One of those who returned was Ivan Makaryev, a literary critic and, since the revolution, a keen Communist. He had worked closely with Fadeyev for a decade before his arrest in 1937. The historians of the Soviet Writers' Union, John and Carol Garrard, have written:

When Makaryev was arrested and sent to the Gulag, he wrote to Fadeyev appealing for his help, then simply asking for some pencils and paper; he received no reply.

On his return to Moscow after nineteen years in the camps, Makaryev discovered that Fadeyev had co-signed the warrant for his arrest. Confronted with this evidence of treachery, Fadeyev admitted that he had received Makaryev's letters and tried to explain his betrayal: 'Forgive me, I got scared . . . Ivan, spit in my face.'

Makaryev seems to have been crushed by this confession of betrayal; like Fadeyev, he committed suicide . . .

Fadeyev killed himself at the writers' colony of Peredelkino, outside Moscow, a place of privileged retreat for him and his fellow Writers' Union members throughout the harsh Stalin years.

The pattern of national independence was beginning to accelerate throughout the areas ruled by the remaining European empires and colonial governments. This marked out 1956 as the first of several consecutive years in which colonial administrations were replaced by national regimes. The leaders of the new governments – the Heads of State and Prime Ministers – had in the main been the leaders of the national struggle, often the advocates of violent murder, who had hitherto been imprisoned, denounced and vilified. On February 8 a three-week conference in London which had been discussing the future of the Malayan Federation ended with a recommendation that Britain should grant independence within two years. On February 29 the Pakistani parliament passed legislation establishing Pakistan – independent since 1947 but still a British Dominion, like Canada – as an Islamic Republic, remaining in the Commonwealth but having as its Head of State a Pakistani Muslim, Iskander Mirza.

On March 2 France recognized the independence of Morocco. That same day, in Jordan, King Hussein asserted his rights as an independent ruler by dismissing the commander of the Arab Legion, General John Glubb – Glubb Pasha – who had been seen by many Jordanians as the representative of the British government, whose military commission he also held. On March 20 France recognized the independence of Tunisia. Two months later, France ceded its small sovereign enclaves on the Indian coast to the Republic of India. These enclaves were Mahé, on the Arabian Sea, and Pondicherry, Karikal and Yanam on the Bay of Bengal.

In one area of the British colonial empire – Cyprus – there was continuing strife. The British Governor and Commander-in-Chief, Field Marshal Harding, tried to open negotiations with Archbishop Makarios with a view to getting him to use his influence to stop the violent attacks on British troops, and on the families of British troops when they were shopping in the market places. Makarios refused to consider any talks not based upon British recognition of the Cypriot right to self-determination. This raised the problem of who would protect the Turkish minority on the island if British control were removed.

On March 9 Makarios was arrested, together with the Bishop of Kyrenia and two other priests, and deported to the Indian Ocean islands of the Seychelles, then under British rule. Two weeks later a time-bomb was found in Field Marshal Harding's bed, almost ready to go off. Within four months, the British authorities executed eight Greek Cypriots accused of terrorist activity.

After a few months in his Indian Ocean exile, Makarios was allowed to live in Athens, but he was refused permission to return to Cyprus. Just as the imprisoned Kenyatta later became the first President of Kenya, so the exiled Makarios was to become the first President of Cyprus. Those who opposed British rule and were its prisoners did not always have to live very long to become its successors. But, while the struggle continued, there were killings on both the British and Greek Cypriot side, as well as conflict between Greek and Turkish Cypriots on the island. A British suggestion that one solution might be the partition of the island between its Greek and Turkish inhabitants was met with some support in Turkey, where marchers had been demonstrating in the main streets of Istanbul and other cities under the banner and cry of 'Cyprus is Turkish'.

Another country in which British soldiers found themselves fighting, and dying, was the Aden Protectorate, where local insurgents were receiving arms from Saudi Arabia. Strikes in the Protectorate virtually paralysed the docks, the power station, the airport and the oil refinery. The rulers of neighbouring Yemen pressed their claim for control of the Protectorate. They were supported in their determination by Egypt, which agreed to Yemen's association with the military pact signed by Egypt and Saudi Arabia on April 21.

During Khrushchev's anti-Stalin speech he had remarked that he wanted to pursue a policy of 'peaceful coexistence' with the Western world. Seven weeks later he and Bulganin embarked on a Soviet cruiser to visit one of the bastions of the democratic and capitalist world. They reached London on April 18, an onlooker of their first drive through the capital recording in the *Spectator* that 'about 60 per cent of the crowd remained silent, about 20 per cent cheered, about 15 per cent booed (I have never heard booing from an English crowd on these occasions before) and the remaining 5 per cent were either policemen or plain clothes men.'

On April 23 the two Soviet leaders were given a dinner in the House of Commons by the National Executive Committee of the British Labour Party, and the Shadow Cabinet. During a question-and-answer session one of the Labour men present asked Khrushchev about the fate of Social Democrats in the Soviet Union. Khrushchev was so angered by this question that he launched into a vicious attack on the British Labour movement and its leaders. In the *Daily Herald*, the Labour Party newspaper, the journalist Deryk Winterton wrote:

> Mr Gaitskell said that the imprisoned Social Democrats were comrades of the British Labour Party with the same beliefs and he hoped that the amnesty just announced in Poland would be extended to them both in Russia and the satellite countries.
>
> He also put in a plea for the Jewish minority in the Soviet Union and added that Morgan Phillips, Party secretary, would give the Russians a list of about two hundred Social Democrat prisoners in Czechoslovakia, Hungary, Bulgaria, Latvia, Lithuania and Estonia.
>
> Mr Khrushchev, it is understood, refused completely to do anything, declaring that there are no Social Democrats in jail in Russia and that what happened in the satellite countries was no concern of his.
>
> Mr Sam Watson, leader of the Durham miners, and Mr Aneurin Bevan repeated the plea, but Mr Khrushchev answered them with the same 'No' and became very heated.

The Soviet satellites were again in turmoil. In April the Writers' Congress in Prague was outspoken in its criticism of the Czech Communist Party and government. A month later there were student protests in Prague and Bratislava demanding a free Press and parliament, freedom to travel abroad, an end to the jamming of foreign radio broadcasts and a reduction in Marxist–Leninist teaching. On June 28, in the Polish city of Poznan, workers' strikes and riots broke out, starting with a strike at the Stalin Locomotive Works. Demonstrators who filled the centre of the town called out to many of the foreign visitors who were in the town for the annual international industrial fair, the largest of its kind in Eastern Europe after Leipzig: 'This is our revolution. Tell the world what we are doing. We want the Russians to get out and we want better conditions after eleven years. We want bread.'

The demonstrators seized the secret police headquarters and the Poznan Town Hall. They also burned a prison in which opponents of the regime had been held. To suppress the uprising Polish tanks and troops were sent into the centre of the city and opened fire. Dr Heinz Brestel, a German journalist who was covering the fair for the *Frankfurter Allgemeine Zeitung*, sent an eye-witness report of the ensuing scene:

> The first victim lay dead on the cobblestones. The angry mob tore branches from the trees and rushed again against the military, shouting their demand for freedom.
>
> A flag was put over the dead man. Others lifted him and carried the body before them as they surged forward. The second victim was a Polish soldier. He refused to fire his gun. An officer killed him with a pistol.
>
> The soldiers then tried to warn the crowd by firing into the air, but time and again they were attacked by the workers.

Thirty-eight people were killed during the unequal struggle, most of them protesters, but also some Communist officials whom the demonstrators had caught. One of the demonstrators told Dr Brestel: 'Tell the people of West Germany that Poland wants to be free. The dead of June 28 will one day rest in a marble temple and millions will remove their hats.' Marshal Bulganin, visiting Poland a month later, called the riots an 'imperialist provocation'.

In Hungary a similar ferment had arisen following Khrushchev's denunciation of Stalin. The government hastened to emulate the Soviet Union by granting pardons to many of those who had been imprisoned for political reasons. As in the Soviet Union, several of these pardons had, perforce, to be posthumous. In June a group of Hungarian writers and intellectuals, members of a two-year-old secret 'Petöfi Circle' – named after the nineteenth-century Hungarian poet and humanist who had abhorred a servile acceptance of the rules – held its first public meetings and demanded an end to Communist repression. The significance of the use of Petöfi's name was at once apparent to the Communist authorities: he had been to the Hungarian revolution of 1848 what Byron was to Greece. Although his father was a Serb and his mother a Slovak, his intense pride in the Hungarian language shone in his poetry. He had been killed in the Hungarian revolution that he had galvanized.

The last British troops left Egypt on June 13, in accordance with the Anglo–Egyptian Treaty of October 1954. Eleven days later Colonel Nasser was elected unopposed as President of Egypt. One of his first appeals for support was to Britain and the United States for financial help with an ambitious project to build a High Dam at Aswan, on the River Nile. On July 19 both countries declined to help. The United States was especially concerned not to appear to be competing with the Soviet Union – with whom Nasser was even then negotiating – on the matter of foreign aid.

On July 20 Nasser was President Tito's guest in Yugoslavia, on Brioni Island. Nehru was also present. Four days later, on his return to Egypt, Nasser made a strident attack on the United States, during the course of which he declared: 'I look at you Americans and say: "May you choke to death on your fury!"' Two days later he announced that he was nationalizing the Suez Canal. He intended that Egypt alone would be the financial beneficiary of the fees and dues of ships in transit.

The Suez Canal Company was owned partly by Britain and partly by France. On July 30 both countries retaliated by imposing foreign exchange controls to the disadvantage of Egypt. During a debate in the House of Commons on August 2 the leader of the British Labour Party, Hugh Gaitskell, condemned the nationalization of the Canal with the words: 'It is all very familiar. It is exactly the same that we encountered from Mussolini and Hitler in those years before the war.' Herbert Morrison, a former Labour Foreign Secretary, urged Ministers 'not to be too nervous' in their reaction because, he explained, 'if they are too nervous we shall begin to evolve a situation in which countries can set themselves up against international practice, international morals and international interests, and, in that case, we are not helping the peace of the world; we are helping anarchy, conflict and bad conduct among nations'.

On August 16, two weeks after these parliamentary denunciations of Nasser's conduct and assertions of the need for an active response, a conference opened in London chaired jointly by Britain and France. It was attended by twenty-two countries that used the Suez Canal, but boycotted by Egypt. When the conference ended on August 23 eighteen of the nations present supported a plan put forward by the American Secretary of State, John Foster Dulles, for an international Suez Canal Board, associated with the United Nations, that would manage the Canal and ensure that it was kept open to ships of all nations – the Egyptians had refused to allow Israeli ships, or ships bound for Israeli ports, including the port of Eilat on the Red Sea – to use it.

The Dulles Plan was taken to Cairo by a mission headed by the Australian Prime Minister, Robert Menzies. The other members of the mission were the Foreign Ministers of Sweden, Iran – deliberately chosen because Iran

was an Asian nation – and Ethiopia, an African nation, together with the
United States Deputy Under Secretary of State, Loy Henderson. In two talks
with Nasser on the following day, the mission stressed the importance of
the Canal to the maritime nations. But Nasser told the mission that any
form of international administration of the Canal would be 'a new form of
imperialism'. On September 6 there was an acerbic clash between Menzies
and Nasser when Menzies remarked: 'Mr President, your refusal of an international administration will be the beginning of trouble.' As soon as he
heard this Nasser closed the file of papers on his desk and told Menzies:
'You are threatening me. Very well, I am finished. There will be no more
discussions. It is all over.'

Sustained attempts by the Ethiopian and Swedish Foreign Ministers, and
by Loy Henderson, to persuade Nasser that there had been no threat were
in vain. On September 9, Nasser publicly rejected the Dulles Plan. A second
conference, made up of the eighteen countries supporting the Dulles Plan,
was convened in London to discuss the next stage. It met on September 19,
and after three days of deliberation agreed to establish a Canal Users' Association. Two days later, on September 23, Britain and France took the question
of the nationalization of the Canal to the United Nations Security Council
in New York.

On September 30 secret diplomacy replaced the much publicized London
and New York meetings. The participants were France and Israel, and they
met at Montparnasse, in Paris. The Israeli delegation was led by the Foreign
Minister, Golda Meir – a future Prime Minister – and contained another
future Prime Minister, Shimon Peres. The French delegation was headed by
their Foreign and Defence Ministers. The French made it clear to the Israelis
from the outset that they were worried that the United States would devise
a solution that would leave Nasser in control of the Canal. The French and
Israelis then agreed to work out a plan whereby they could co-ordinate
military action against Egypt.

The United Nations Security Council began its discussions about the
future of the Suez Canal on October 5. Seven Foreign Ministers were present,
the largest number that had attended a Council meeting. The British and
French governments argued that under the Suez Canal Convention of 1888
the operation of the Canal had to be international. On October 13, after a
week of discussions, in which Egypt, though not a member of the Council,
was allowed to participate, the Security Council adopted the first part of an
Anglo-French resolution on the Suez Canal, stressing its importance as an

international waterway. The Soviet Union exercised its veto, however, to reject the second part of the resolution, which would have obliged Egypt to comply with a set of principles with regard to the operation of the Canal. These principles, connected with unimpeded passage, would have given outside Powers the right to ensure that no political restraints were imposed on ships using the Canal. Egypt had already made it clear by deed as well as word that it would not allow ships bound for Israeli ports to make the voyage.

Three days after the Security Council failed to support the Anglo-French search for international action, Anthony Eden – who had succeeded Churchill as Prime Minister the previous year – and the British Foreign Secretary, Selwyn Lloyd, travelled to Paris to discuss possible military action against Egypt. Such action was favoured by the French Prime Minister, Guy Mollet, and by his Foreign Minister, Christian Pineau.

The focus of international attention on the events following Nasser's nationalization – called by Nasser 'de-internationalization' – of the Suez Canal was repeatedly and increasingly countered by events in Eastern Europe. As the Suez Crisis grew the Soviet Union was confronted by unrest in both Poland and Hungary. Khrushchev's speech denouncing Stalin had stirred up many embers. The crushing of the Poznan riots at the beginning of the year had failed to curb the anger, frustration and resentment felt by many Poles at the totalitarian nature of Polish Communism, and the government's sub-servience to Russia, Poland's traditional enemy.

Hungary was also in turmoil. In the second week of September the Hungarian Trades Union Congress, meeting in Budapest, had demanded genuine participation of the workers in the conduct of industry. Even more revolutionary, there was a call for Workers' Councils to be established which could represent the needs of the workers in disputes with the Communist Party itself, and with the Party leadership. In the third week of September, as protests spread and courage was gained for public action, the Hungarian Writers' Congress elected critics of the Communist regime to be its officers, in place of the existing Party nominees. On October 6 a State Funeral was held for some of the rehabilitated former Communist Party leaders. A vast crowd participated. Nine days later there was a mass student demonstration in Budapest.

The demands of the students went far beyond anything a Communist government – let alone Moscow – would ever accept: a new parliament and government based on free elections, Hungary's withdrawal from the Warsaw Pact, freedom of the Press and of educational instruction, independent courts of justice, free religious instruction if wanted, the end of forced collectivization and forced delivery of agricultural produce, the right to strike for workers, free communication with the West, the removal of Soviet emblems, an end to uranium deliveries to the Soviet Union and support for the Polish national movement.

In Poland there were renewed riots and unrest, and persistent newspaper criticism of the harshness of the Communist regime. This led to an unprecedented Soviet move, when, on October 19, four Soviet leaders, headed by Khrushchev, flew from Moscow to Warsaw and warned that such criticism must stop. To back up these strong words, Soviet warships were ordered to the Polish coast, and Soviet troops based in Poland moved to the outskirts of Warsaw. An article in *Pravda* complained of Polish 'anti-Socialist insinuations'. But then Khrushchev decided not to force the issue to an open clash of arms. Wladyslaw Gomulka – who had been imprisoned by his fellow Polish Communist leaders less than two years earlier for his 'nationalistic' views – was made First Secretary of the Party. On October 21 it was announced in Warsaw that Poland would go its 'own way' to Socialism.

As Gomulka acted to halt all collectivization, and to allow a small measure of freedom of speech, the 'Polish October' was judged in the West to be a setback for the Soviet Union and a victory for dissent. But Gomulka was careful to stress the binding defence links between Poland and the Soviet Union, insisting that his act of defiance was a variety of Communism, not a breach with it. In an editorial reflecting at least the temporary acquiescence of the Soviet leadership, *Pravda* gave cautious approval to the 'Gomulka variant'.

Five days after the Anglo-French meeting in Paris at which it had been agreed to take military action against Egypt, the Israelis returned to the French capital, once more in strictest secrecy. Nasser had ordered military reinforcements into the Gaza Strip, posing a direct threat to the Israeli heartland. For two days, October 21 and 22, the Israelis and French met in a villa at Sèvres, just outside Paris. The senior Israeli present was the Prime Minister, David Ben-Gurion. His most senior colleague was Moshe Dayan, the Israeli Minister of Defence. They were joined by the French Prime Minister, Guy Mollet, and by the British Foreign Secretary, Selwyn Lloyd, who had travelled secretly from Britain. The discussion focused on how the three countries could co-ordinate their planned action in such a way that it would not seem to be collusion. The Israelis would cross into the Egyptian Sinai and advance towards the Suez Canal. This would give Britain and France the opportunity to intervene militarily, in order to 'protect' the Canal.

For many years, the participants at the Sèvres meeting were to deny that it had taken place, and strenuously to rebut the charge of collusion. Later a British participant, Donald Logan, revealed the central issue of the meeting when he recalled: 'We pressed Dayan for assurance that the Israelis understood that unless their military action posed a threat to the canal, British forces would not act. It did not come easily.' Britain would only move against Egypt – in the role of the protector of the Canal – if the Israeli forces could be seen to threaten it. Dayan gave the assurance that Israel did indeed understand the British method.

As Ben-Gurion returned to Israel and Selwyn Lloyd to Britain, events in Eastern Europe threatened to cause havoc with the ability of Britain and France to concentrate all their efforts on the Suez Canal. Since Gomulka's speech in Poland on October 21 stressing Poland's 'way to Socialism' there had been three days of ferment in Hungary, especially among students in Budapest, Pécs and Szeged. At Györ, the writer Gyula Hay had addressed a mass open-air meeting at which speaker after speaker demanded the withdrawal of Soviet troops from Hungary. On October 22 a deputation of students went to see the Prime Minister, Andreas Hegedus, to demand free elections and the departure of the Russians.

During demonstrations in Budapest on October 23 a giant statue of Stalin was pulled down. It was so sturdily built that blow-lamps had to be used to melt it at the knees. All over the city demonstrators reiterated their support for the Poles, and their demands for an end to Communist rule in Hungary and the establishment of a democratic regime. Their demands were comprehensive. They included the withdrawal of all Soviet troops from Hungary – where they had been stationed for more than a decade – and the release of Cardinal Mindszenty, who had been imprisoned in 1949 and held under house arrest since July 1955. They also demanded the return to power of a former Prime Minister, Imre Nagy, who, having pursued a liberal Communist policy after coming to power in July 1953, had been forced by Soviet pressure to resign in February 1955 and had then been expelled from the Communist Party.

The reaction of the Hungarian government to the demands of the students and the growing demonstrations in the streets was swift and predictable. The First Secretary of the Hungarian Communist Party, Ernö Gerö – who had fought in the International Brigade in the Spanish Civil War – issued an appeal for Soviet troops to enter the capital. Thousands of demonstrators hurried to the main broadcasting studio to have their demands broadcast. The green-uniformed State Security (AVH) guards at the studios used tear gas to try to disperse the crowd. A delegation from the crowd forced its way into the building. An AVH officer then shot and killed one of these delegates. Soldiers and armed workers who were sent to help disperse the crowd joined in with them, distributing their firearms.

On the following morning, October 24, before the Soviet troops summoned by Gerö could arrive, Imre Nagy was appointed Prime Minister and promised immediate reforms, the 'democratization' of Hungary and the withdrawal of Soviet troops from the capital. These withdrawals actually began, and were completed within a week, but at the same time troop reinforcements from inside the Soviet Union were brought up to the Soviet–Hungarian border and ordered to take up positions around the capital. Meanwhile Istvan Bata, the Hungarian Minister of Defence, loyal to the old regime and to the Russians, was issuing orders to the Hungarian armed forces that the anti-Soviet insurgents be crushed. One of those to whom his instructions were sent on October 24 was Colonel Pal Maleter, who recalled a week later how he was ordered, by Bata, 'to lead a formation of five tanks against the insurgents in the Eighth and Ninth districts. Once I arrived there, it quickly became clear to me that those who were fighting for their freedom were not bandits, but loyal sons of Hungary. As a result I informed the Minister of Defence that I was going over to the insurgents.'

Maleter did so, and on October 24 took charge of the Kilian barracks in the centre of the city. But the uniformed officers and soldiers of the security forces opened fire that day to defend the radio station which was under attack by the insurgents, thirty of whom were killed. 'Travellers from Budapest today', the *Manchester Guardian* reported from Vienna, 'told of Russian tanks at every main street intersection in and around the city, with heavy fighting in the streets.' The Russians had 'thrown a cordon round the city, and machine-gun and rifle fire could be heard in many districts. Communist party and other official buildings have been set on fire, and numbers of Russian troops have been killed.' The Hungarian government had announced martial law at dawn throughout the country. In successive broadcasts 'it became clear that civil war, if only on a limited scale was raging'.

From Moscow, the official Soviet news agency Tass reported the 'failure of the anti-people's adventure' and went on to explain:

It is clear that this adventure had been prepared over a considerable period of time, and that foreign reactionary forces have been systematically inciting anti-people's elements to come out against the lawful authorities. The Hungarian Government asked the Soviet Government for help. In accordance with this appeal Soviet Army units – stationed in Hungary in conformity with the Warsaw Pact – assisted in re-establishing order.

That day Soviet tanks formed a ring around Budapest along a twenty-five-mile perimeter.

It was not only in Hungary that the spirit of anti-Soviet defiance was leading to violence on the streets. On the night of October 24 Polish demonstrators in the Silesian industrial town of Legnica – formerly Leignitz – tried to attack the headquarters of the Soviet military command in charge of all satellite troops. For several hours they converged on the building, until dispersed by Polish militia using tear gas. There were also anti-Soviet demonstrations that day in the Polish port of Gdansk, on the Baltic, and in the eastern Polish city of Bialystok, only a few miles west of the Soviet–Polish border.

Gomulka was summoned to Moscow but postponed his visit. In the words of the *Daily Mail* Warsaw correspondent Philip Ben, the 'Polish man-in-the-street' did not like the idea of his leader going to Moscow, 'fearing that the Russians want to lure Gomulka, and that something may happen to him'. Determined that Poland should avoid the fate of Hungary, Gomulka appealed to the Polish people not to call for the withdrawal of Soviet troops. A statement from the Central Committee of the Polish United Workers Party effectively removed Poland from the conflict, and marked a retreat from the confrontation and agitation of the previous weeks. Viewing the 'perilous situation' in Hungary, the Central Committee declared:

At such a moment it is particularly important to keep a complete calm, and to strengthen the unity of the Party and of the Polish people.

In a situation when reactionary elements are trying to raise their voice, proclaiming provocative slogans directed against the Polish-Soviet alliance, and when here and there irresponsible and unreasonable utterances are being made, the working class and all citizens should give them a resolute rebuff – in the name of the independence of the country and of the conquests of Socialism.

Today, there is no time for demonstrations and public meetings.

Calm, discipline, sense of responsibility, rallying around the Party and the people's authority for the realization of our just policy in this difficult and critical time – these are the most important requirements of the moment.

Poland had become a spectator of the drama being enacted to the south: at their closest point, the frontiers of Poland and Hungary are less than sixty miles apart.

On October 25 there was a mass demonstration in front of the parliament building in Budapest. The Hungarian security forces again opened fire, and as many as six hundred demonstrators were killed. Two Soviet leaders, Anastas Mikoyan and Mikhail Suslov, had reached Budapest by air. They ordered the resignation of Gerö as Party Secretary and his replacement by Kádár, hoping thereby to restore order.

All over Hungary towns rallied to the revolution. In Miskolc the local radio announced: 'Stop the slaughter of Hungarians in Budapest. Let the Soviet troops leave Hungary. Make a truce!' But the security forces were still fighting to put down the demonstrators. At Dunapentele six unarmed demonstrators were killed when the security forces opened fire. In Budapest, a mass of demonstrators moved during October 25 to the British and American legations, where they presented a petition urging that the Hungarian demand for free elections and the removal of Soviet forces be put to the United Nations. To the surprise and delight of the revolutionaries, a broadcast by Eisenhower was beamed to them by Western radio stations, in which the President declared: 'The heart of America goes out to the people of Hungary.'

Far from crushing the revolt, the massacre outside the parliament building intensified it. Security force men were hunted down and murdered, their bodies sometimes left hanging on trees. During October 26, groups of 'freedom fighters' attacked individual Soviet tanks, or the last tank in a column of tanks moving along a street, with Molotov cocktails. Some brave individuals climbed on tanks to drop a grenade through the hatch. That day, as fighting continued throughout the city, Mikoyan and Suslov were driven under armed guard to the airport and returned to Moscow. As foreign journalists hurried to Hungary, the border with Austria was no longer controlled by Communist guards. Among those who reached Budapest was Noel Barber, the correspondent of the London *Daily Mail*, who reported that day:

As I moved deeper into the city, every street was smashed. Hardly a stretch of tramcar rails was left intact. The jungle of hanging electric cables was denser even than in Buda. Hundreds of yards of paving stones had been torn up, the streets were littered with burnt-out cars. Even before I reached the Duna Hotel, I counted the carcasses of at least forty Soviet tanks. On the way to Rakoczi Square, where the fighting had been particularly bitter, one street was barred by enormous tree-trunks, not chopped down, but uprooted . . .

At the corner of Stalin Avenue, where you branch right for the British Legation and then the Duna, two monster Russian T-54 tanks lumbered past, dragging bodies behind them, a warning to all Hungarians of what happened to the fighters. In another street, three bodies were strung up on a tree, the necks at ungainly angles but still not looking like bodies, more like effigies. A few corpses dotted the streets, though not so many as I expected.

Among those who crossed the border from Austria was Peter Fryer, a member of the staff of the British Communist newspaper the *Daily Worker*. He reached the town of Magyarovar shortly after the security forces had opened fire on a crowd of demonstrators, killing eighty-seven people. One of the first victims was a small girl who had been standing in the front of the crowd. The security police were then besieged in their headquarters. Fryer, his Communist convictions deeply shaken, wrote:

The townspeople took us in slow, silent procession along an avenue of plane trees to the little chapel and mortuary in the town cemetery. Hundreds went with us; we passed many more coming away, having identified kinsfolk or sweethearts or friends or having stood in homage to dead workmates or fellow-students. Some faces were red and stern, others were contorted with weeping, and I wept myself when we reached the chapel and the mortuary.

The mourners made way for us and gently pushed us to the front, so that we should see and know and tell what we had seen. The bodies lay in rows; the dried blood was still on the clothing. Some had little bunches of flowers on their breasts. There were boys who could not have been more than sixteen. There was a boy of six or so. Already in a coffin, lightly shrouded, lay the corpse of an eighteen-month-old baby.

After eleven years of 'people's democracy' it had come to this: that the security police was so remote from the people, so alien to them, so vicious and so brutal that it turned its weapons on a defenceless crowd and murdered the people who were supposed to be the masters of their own country.

Throughout Hungary the ferment of anti-Soviet resistance was high. In the southern province of Baranja a 'revolutionary council' was established, and ordered Hungarian soldiers loyal to the authorities to hand over their arms. In the eastern city of Miskolc the local radio called for the withdrawal of Soviet troops, the establishment of a new government, and the right to strike.

On October 27 Imre Nagy formed a government. Several non-Communists were made members of his Cabinet, including Béla Kovacs, former secretary of the Smallholders Party, who had spent eight years as a prisoner of the Russians. Five thousand political prisoners were released; their cells were unlocked and they were free to leave. Gerö and Hegedus fled to the Soviet Union – which had a common border with Hungary at the eastern extremity of the country.

On October 28, Imre Nagy ordered the army and security forces to cease firing. On the following day Soviet tanks and troops left Budapest. 'A Hungarian peasant spat at one tank as it passed him an arm's length away,' reported a United Press correspondent on his way into Budapest. 'The Russian crew did not notice. Hatred literally oozed from the Hungarians who silently lined the roadsides watching the Soviets evacuate Budapest.'

The success of the anti-Communist revolution in Hungary was as total as it had been unexpected. A window of liberalism had been opened in the heart of Soviet-dominated Central Europe. Even as the West tried to come to terms with the meaning of this dramatic development, unprecedented since 1945, the focus of attention was shifted away from Europe to the Suez Canal. On October 29 Israeli forces invaded the Sinai peninsula. This was part of the plan that had been devised at the villa near Paris. Israel would advance westward across Sinai and, as it drew near to the Suez Canal, Britain and France would call for it to halt and pull back from the Canal, call on the Egyptians likewise to pull back from the Canal Zone, and then land troops along the Canal in order to protect it from attack and ensure the free passage of ships.

On October 30 Britain and France issued their ultimatum. It was addressed both to Israel – which was expecting it and had agreed in advance to comply with it – and to Egypt, which was required under the ultimatum to remove its troops from areas that were sovereign Egyptian territory. Both sides were told that their troops must be pulled back ten miles from the banks of the Canal. Israel accepted. Egypt refused. Egypt was also required under the terms of the Anglo-French ultimatum to accept the temporary occupation of Port Said, Ismailia and Suez City at the southern end of the Canal, by Anglo-French forces. This too was rejected by Nasser.

In the House of Commons the leader of the Labour Opposition, Hugh Gaitskell, asked Eden for an undertaking that there would be no 'further physical action' against Egypt until the Security Council had taken a decision, or until the House of Commons had had a chance to debate the matter. Eden replied that he could give no undertaking that no action would follow after the twelve-hour ultimatum had expired. Gaitskell then condemned the government's action as 'an attempt to impose a solution by force'. Even if what was proposed was, as Eden was insisting, a 'police action' and not a war, it was wrong, Gaitskell argued, 'to decide on our own that we should take independent action'.

The Security Council met that day, when the United States put forward a resolution calling on Israel to halt its advance through Sinai and withdraw behind its frontiers. This resolution was vetoed by France and Britain. It was the first time Britain had used its veto.

During October 30, Anastas Mikoyan and Mikhail Suslov returned by air from Moscow to Budapest. There were reports that large numbers of Soviet troops had entered north-eastern Hungary and were spreading throughout the country. As many thousands of these troops made their way to Budapest, Cardinal Mindszenty – after six years in prison and under strict house arrest, cut off from the outside world – was released and brought back to Budapest. Dozens of members of the security forces who were caught were beaten to death, or hanged upside down from lamp posts and then killed. Nagy's government announced that free elections would be held. Colonel Maleter, driven from the Kilian barracks to the parliament building, met Imre Nagy for the first time, and placed his troops at the government's disposal.

Two struggles were being fought simultaneously. The Hungarian revolution and the Soviet attempt to crush it; and the Suez War, the crowded, controversial events of which were distracting Britain, France and the United States – indeed the whole United Nations – from events in Hungary. On October 31, British and French warplanes bombed the Egyptian airfields. 'We're going in', declared the British *Daily Sketch* that morning. 'British

Moving on Suez', announced the *Daily Mail*. 'Our troops in Suez today?' was the headline in the *Daily Mirror*. The Labour Party newspaper, the *Daily Herald*, under the headline 'Our troops invade', added ominously: 'Dulles is furious'.

Inside Britain there was also anger on the Left that Egypt had been attacked. In parliament, Eden's repeated description – and defence – of the attack on Egypt as a 'police action' rather than a war was mocked by the Labour Opposition. The *Manchester Guardian* reported on November 1:

A passionate debate in the House of Commons yesterday was to have been foreseen, but it released more violent anger on the part of the Opposition than anyone could have expected; more, indeed, than has been experienced for years. Yet this emotional aspect of the debate was not the most significant. It was the gravest in its content that the House of Commons has heard for a long time.

As one illustration. When before has the Leader of the Opposition (or anyone else) been able to report of an act of Government policy that it does not command the support of the Commonwealth countries – that India condemns it; that the Canadian Government regrets it and its Foreign Secretary says it was not consulted in advance about it; that Australia has been unable to support the British Government in the Security Council; that the Prime Minister of New Zealand also regrets what has been done?

It was a grievous recital. It was the darkest cloud that passed over this stormy debate.

During the debate, Gaitskell denounced what he called 'this reckless war'. Eden refused repeated requests to say what was actually happening in the Canal Zone. He would reveal nothing, he said, of any military action that might be pending. But he did speak of his motives. 'I have been accused of living in the past and being obsessed with the events of the 1930s,' he said. 'However that may be, is there not a lesson to be learned from that period which cannot be ignored – that you best avoid great wars by taking even physical action to stop small ones?' Amid Conservative cheers Eden continued: 'Everybody knows that the United Nations is not yet in a position to do that. We and the French had forces available. This is essentially a police operation. We do not want to stay. We do not intend to stay one moment longer than is necessary, but effective action to re-establish peace will make easier the international solution of the many problems which exist in that area.'

The parliamentary debate continued on the following day. The Conservative-Labour divide was deep and bitter. As disorder grew on the floor of the House, the Speaker suspended the sitting for half an hour: such a suspension had taken place only twice in the previous forty years. There were those in Britain who urged soldiers who felt that it was an unjust war not to take part in it. Demonstrators who marched on parliament shouting, 'We want peace' and 'Eden must go', were dispersed by the police. The demonstrators insisted that they had been manhandled.

Leading the non-aligned nations in protest, Nehru denounced the Anglo-French action as 'clear and naked aggression'. But when Marshal Bulganin suggested to Nehru that India should participate in some as yet undefined joint military action against Britain and France, the Indian leader replied that any step that might lead to a world war would be a 'crime against humanity'. The non-aligned nations would remain non-aligned, and neutral.

In a gesture of disapproval of the attack on Egypt, on October 31 the United States suspended all military and financial aid to Israel. On the following day the Kingdom of Jordan, which was allied to Britain, refused the use of British air bases in Jordan as staging posts for attacks on Egypt. An emergency session of the United Nations General Assembly began two days of deliberations on the Suez War on November 1. John Foster Dulles led the attack on the Anglo-French-Israeli action. At the end of its second day of discussions the assembly passed a resolution demanding an immediate ceasefire, an end to the Anglo-French aerial bombardment of the Egyptian airfields, and the withdrawal of the attacking Israeli forces from Sinai.

On October 31 the atmosphere in Budapest was exhilarating for the Hungarian revolutionaries, and those from Western Europe – journalists and well-wishers who had hastened to Budapest – who were witness to their triumph. A British journalist, Boris Kidel, reported to the *News Chronicle*:

Hungary today breathed its first day of freedom. From the underground, emerged the banned non-Communist parties to re-open their headquarters and district offices.

For the first time since the Communists seized power, 'free' newspapers appeared on the streets. And the revered Cardinal Mindszenty, who had come to symbolize Hungary's struggle against Communism, returned a free man to Budapest.

At the Socialist headquarters I witnessed moving scenes between officials returned from forced labour in coal and uranium mines – reunited for the first time since 1948.

Their veteran leader, 67-year-old Anna Kethly, jailed for four years by the Communists, was re-elected head of the party and tonight was on her way to Vienna to meet representatives of their Socialist International.

They will decide if the party should take part in the Government. Most of the Hungarian Socialist leaders are against joining a government as long as Soviet troops are still in the country.

In the ruined streets, silent Hungarians watched long convoys of Soviet tanks and lorries crammed with tommy-gunners leaving the city.

The most amazing sight was the lorry-loads of junk that the Russians were taking from their barracks.

Broken furniture, prams, mattresses and even bird cages and canaries had all been heaped together. It had the ignominious look of a defeated army in retreat.

The Soviet army was neither defeated nor in retreat. By the morning of November 1 more than 75,000 Soviet troops and 2,500 tanks had crossed the Hungarian–Soviet frontier and were moving rapidly towards Budapest. That morning Imre Nagy summoned the Soviet Ambassador, Yuri Andropov – later to be head of the KGB and later still ruler of Russia – and warned him that if the Soviet troops still in the city, who during the night had begun to mass in the streets, did not return to their barracks, his government would pull Hungary out of the Warsaw Pact and declare neutrality.

During the day the Soviet tanks which had entered Hungary from the east continued to drive towards the city. At two in the afternoon Nagy telephoned Andropov to tell him that Hungary was withdrawing from the Warsaw Pact and renouncing the Warsaw Treaty – which bound all the Communist States of Eastern and Central Europe in a solemn engagement with the Soviet Union. At 6.15 that evening Nagy broadcast over Hungarian radio: 'The Hungarian people desire the consolidation and further development of the achievements of its national revolution without joining any power blocs. The century-old dream of the Hungarian people is being fulfilled.' That evening János Kádár, who earlier in the day had expressed his guarded support for the revolution, left by car for Uzhgorod, a former Czechoslovak town that had been part of the Soviet Union since 1945, just across the Hungarian-Soviet border.

During November 1 the guards in the prison hospital in Budapest heard a persistent banging on one of the locked doors. It was Dr Edith Bone, one of the British subjects who had been falsely imprisoned for espionage in 1949. She had spent seven years in solitary confinement. 'Of course you must be released on the spot,' one of the revolutionaries told her. 'Have you got any things? Go back to your cell and collect them.' Edith Bone returned to Britain. 'Having lived like a hedgehog, bristling in every direction,' she wrote, 'it was indescribably sweet to look on all and everything around me with a friendly eye, and to receive similar glances in return.'

On November 2, Imre Nagy appealed both to the United Nations and to the Western Powers for assistance to repel the Soviet invasion. The Hungarian request, he explained, was that the General Assembly put on its agenda 'the question of Hungarian neutrality and its guarantee by the four Great Powers'. That day the United Nations General Assembly was debating Suez. It was several hours before Hungary was mentioned at all, when the Indian delegate referred to 'some difficulties' that had arisen there. The debate centred around a United States resolution condemning Britain, France and Israel for the attack on Egypt. It was passed by sixty-four votes to five.

On November 3 Nagy formed a new government. Among its members was Anna Kethly, the Social Democrat leader who had been imprisoned in 1948, and who was then in Vienna attending a Socialist conference. Unable to reach Budapest because of a Soviet road block, she returned to Vienna. Colonel Maleter, promoted to general, was appointed Minister of Defence.

Throughout the day news was reaching the United Nations in New York of continuing Soviet military advances towards Budapest, and of the transit of additional Soviet troops into Hungary.

That evening Cardinal Mindszenty broadcast from Budapest. 'Our entire situation', he said, 'depends on what the Soviet empire, the vast empire of 200 million inhabitants, will do with its troops within our borders. The radio has announced that the number of Soviet troops in Hungary has increased. We are neutral. We give the Russian empire no cause for bloodshed. Do not the leaders of the Russian empire realize that we will respect the Russian people even more if they do not oppress us?'

Mindszenty went on to call for free elections: 'We want to live in a constitutional state and in a classless society and to increase democratic progress. We are in favour of private property within just and equitable limits of our society's best interests.'

At eight o'clock in the evening of November 3 General Maleter drove to Soviet army headquarters at Tokol to negotiate a halt to the Soviet military advance and the withdrawal of Soviet troops within a fixed period. The Russians had intimated that they would be willing to withdraw early in the new year. The talks began at ten o'clock. A member of Maleter's bodyguard, Sandor Horvath, later wrote:

Everything appeared to go off perfectly in the office where the talks were taking place. At least that was our impression in the ante-chamber, from the noise of conversation we could hear . . .

Towards midnight, about twenty military policemen in green caps burst into the room. They shouted a password and covered our delegation with their sten-guns . . .

Through the broken door I was watching our boss – the others were pale, only his face didn't change.

'So that was it, was it?' he said to the Russians, standing up calmly.

I seized my own sten-gun, thinking that before dying I would still shoot a few rounds at the men in green caps, but it was too late. Two military policemen were already holding me. I tried to get free of them. There was a struggle; I was the stronger. I had again seized the barrel of my sten-gun when the boss called out: 'Stop it! It's useless to resist.' What could I do? What could I do? His words were my orders and I let my sten-gun be taken away.

It was midnight. The open telephone line between Tokol and the parliament building in Budapest was closed down. According to a subsequent United Nations report the discussions between the Soviet military delegation and the Hungarian military delegation at Tokol were interrupted by the entry of a personage 'who bore no insignia of rank'. It was General I. A. Serov, the Chief of the Soviet Security Police. Accompanied by Soviet officers, Serov announced that he was arresting the Hungarian delegation. 'The head of the Soviet delegation, General Malinin, astonished by the interruption, made a gesture of indignation. General Serov thereupon whispered to him; as a result General Malinin shrugged his shoulders and ordered the Soviet delegation to leave the room. The Hungarian delegation was then arrested.'

By midnight almost all Hungarian industrial centres and military bases were surrounded by Soviet tanks. Budapest airport was also surrounded. After a second appeal from Nagy reached New York, a special session of the Security Council was convened. It deliberated through the night. Just before dawn on the morning of November 4 the United States – on the eve of a presidential election – brought forward a resolution calling on the Soviet Union 'to cease the introduction of additional armed forces into Hungary and to withdraw all its forces without delay from Hungarian territory'. The delegate of the Soviet Union, having denied that any Soviet troops had crossed into Hungary, vetoed the resolution. It was the seventy-ninth time that the Soviet Union had cast its veto in ten years.

At four o'clock on the morning of November 4 the Soviet army entered Budapest. Eleven years earlier it had done so as a liberator, driving out the German army. This time it came to crush the new government and to restore Communist rule. At 5.56 that morning Imre Nagy broadcast over Free Radio Kossuth. His words were urgent and full of foreboding. 'Today at daybreak Soviet forces started an attack on our capital,' he said, 'obviously with the intention of overthrowing the legal Hungarian democratic government. Our troops are fighting. The government is in its place. I notify the people of our country and the entire world of this fact.' An hour later a telephone call from the offices of the Budapest newspaper *Szabad Nep* to the Associated Press office in Vienna reported that 'since the early morning' Soviet troops had been attacking Budapest. 'Please tell the world of this treacherous attack against our struggle for liberty.'

It was a Hungarian reporter on *Szabad Nep* who had made contact through the newspaper's teleprinter with the Associated Press in Vienna. He maintained that link throughout the day.

The disappearance of János Kádár three days earlier and his retreat to Uzhgorod in the Soviet Ukraine was about to be explained. That morning he made a broadcast from Uzhgorod announcing that a Hungarian Revolutionary Workers and Peasants Government, with himself at its head, had 'requested the Soviet Army Command to help our nation in smashing the dark reactionary forces and restoring order and calm in the country'.

The independent radio stations still broadcasting from Hungary continued their appeals to allow Hungary to become a neutral power. That a Communist country was demanding to be neutral was unacceptable to Moscow, and a source of inspiration to democrats everywhere. But it was Britain and France that were in the dock at the United Nations, not the Soviet Union. On

November 4 the General Assembly adopted a Canadian resolution that an international force should be sent to the Middle East. Britain and France both abstained from voting. They did agree, however, that if the United Nations would agree to keep the peace in the Middle East, they would be willing to accept a ceasefire.

There was no military force inside Hungary that could challenge the Soviet tanks, though there were hundreds, even thousands of acts of personal defiance and heroism. Many insurgents acquired arms, and took up positions on barricades. More than a thousand Soviet troops were killed in the fighting. Some deserted to the Hungarian patriots. Others proved so unreliable that they were withdrawn.

By eight o'clock on the morning of November 4, Soviet tanks had reached the parliament building on the bank of the Danube. The Hungarian government was in session inside the building. To avoid capture, Imre Nagy took refuge in the Yugoslav Embassy. Cardinal Mindszenty found sanctuary in the United States Legation, where, protected, housed and fed by American diplomatic goodwill, he remained for fifteen years. As the national heroes took refuge, János Kádár agreed to a Soviet 'request' to form a Communist government consisting of 'revolutionary peasant-workers'.

The Hungarian reporter on *Szabad Nep* who had made contact with the Associated Press in Vienna was transmitting by teleprinter a report of what he could see from the windows of the newspaper building. His account was circulated worldwide by the Associated Press:

8.30. At the moment there is silence. It may be the silence before the storm.

We have almost no weapons. Only light machine-guns. Russian-made rifles and some carbines.

People are jumping up at the tanks, throwing hand-grenades inside and then slamming the drivers' windows. The Hungarian people are not afraid of death. It is only a pity that we can't stand for long.

The tanks are getting nearer and there is heavy artillery.

What is the United Nations doing? Give us a little encouragement.

There were about 250 people – including fifty women – in the newspaper building. The Hungarian reporter's messages became more and more desperate:

9.00. Both radio stations in Budapest are in rebel hands.

We will hold out to our last drop of blood. Downstairs there are men who have only one hand grenade.

9.15. The first Russian bombers – about fifteen of them – were reported over Budapest.

I am running over to the window in the next room to shoot, but I will be back if there is anything new or you ring me.

Don't be mad at the way I am writing. I am excited. I want to know how this is going to end.

The building of barricades is going on. The Parliament and its vicinity is crowded with tanks. The tanks are coming in big lines.

They just brought us a rumour that the American troops will be here within one or two hours.

10.00. A shell just exploded nearby. Now there is heavy firing in the direction of the National Theatre, near us in the centre of the city.

We are strong, even if we are only a small nation. When the fighting is over we will rebuild our unhappy, much-oppressed country.

10.50. Just now, the heaviest fighting is going on in the Maria Terezia barracks. There is heavy artillery fire.

Five minutes after this last message, the teleprinter fell silent.

Soviet tanks and troops battled throughout that afternoon and evening for control of the centre of Budapest, overrunning barricade after barricade, and bombing freedom-fighter strongholds from the air. The United Nations General Assembly meeting in New York that evening – after midnight Hungarian time – called on the Soviet Union to withdraw all its forces from Hungary 'immediately'. The voting was fifty to eight in favour of the resolution, with fifteen abstentions. The Soviet Union took no notice. From Budapest came a spate of despairing, staccato calls from Freedom Radio:

Help Hungary.
Help.
Help.
Help
Hear this tortured appeal.
The shadows are deepening over Hungary.
Extend your brotherly hand.
Save us.

On November 4, as the tragedy in Hungary reached a grim climax, ten thousand British demonstrators in London gathered in Trafalgar Square to protest against the British action against Egypt. At least one of their placards read: 'Save Hungary'. As a small group of marchers proceeded down White-hall, mounted police barred their way to Downing Street, and there were what the newspapers called 'near riot scenes'. Several policemen were injured, and thirty-two of the demonstrators were arrested.

In the early hours of Monday November 5, British paratroops landed at Port Said, at the northern entrance to the Suez Canal. At the same time, French troops landed at Port Fuad, on the opposite side of the Canal, facing Port Said. On the following day, in the United States, Eisenhower – who had suffered a heart attack a year earlier – was re-elected President. He was determined to halt what he saw as the Anglo-French aggression against Egypt, and threatened immediate financial retaliation if the fighting did not stop.

Eisenhower feared that as a result of the turmoil created by the Anglo-French and Israeli military actions the Soviet Union would take advantage, and offer itself as Egypt's protector, bringing Soviet influence to the shores of the Red Sea. His aim, he noted in his diary two days later, was to 'exclude the area from Soviet influence'. He added: 'We can provide Egypt with an agreed-upon amount of arms – sufficient to maintain internal order and a reasonable defence of its borders, in return for an agreement that it will never accept any Soviet offer.'

On November 6, at the General Assembly of the United Nations, the Canadians brought forward a resolution for an Emergency International United Nations Force. The aim of the force would be 'to secure and supervise the cessation of hostilities'. The Canadian resolution was supported by fifty-seven countries and opposed by none. Britain, France, Israel and Egypt abstained, as did the Communist bloc, whose leader, the Soviet Union, had no wish to see United Nations forces being sent that week to areas of violent conflict.

Britain and France agreed a ceasefire, to come into effect that midnight. Israel, which had lost 172 soldiers in the fighting, also agreed. Two newspaper correspondents were also killed during the Suez fighting: Jean Roy of *Paris Match* and David Seymour of the Magnum photographic agency (two years earlier another Magnum photographer, Robert Capa, had been killed in Indochina). The bodies of the two men, the intrepid reporters of a quarrel that was not their own, were later handed over to the United Nations by the Egyptian authorities.

*   *   *

By mid-morning on Monday November 5, Soviet troops were in control of most of Budapest. Forty surviving soldiers in the Kilian barracks agreed to surrender under amnesty, and left the building. They were shot down. The Communist journalist Peter Fryer recalled:

> On the Sunday and the Monday while the din of the artillery bombardment and the ceaseless tank-fire mingled with the groans of the wounded, the battle spared neither civilians nor those bringing aid to the wounded.
>
> Bread queues were fired on by Soviet tanks and as late as Thursday I myself saw a man of about seventy lying dead outside a bread shop, the loaf of bread he had just bought still in his hand. Someone had half-covered the body with the red, white, and green flag.
>
> Soviet troops looted the Astoria Hotel as far as the first storey, even taking the clothes from the porters' rest room . . .

'Some of the rank-and-file Soviet troops', Fryer added, 'have been telling people in the last two days that they had no idea they had come to Hungary. They thought at first they were in Berlin fighting German fascists.' There were even some Soviet troops in Budapest – troops who had been conscripted in the Soviet Far East and Mongolia – who thought that they were in Egypt, defending the Egyptians against British and French attack.

Throughout Western Europe there were spontaneous and angry protests about the Soviet action in Hungary. In Luxembourg, protesters broke into the Soviet Embassy during a reception and hurled furniture out of the window. They then set the furniture on fire. West Germany observed three minutes' silence starting at noon in sympathy with the victims of Russian attacks in Hungary. In Paris laughter and shouts from Communist benches interrupted a 'silent minute' for Hungarians held in the French parliament. In Copenhagen more than thirty of Denmark's most prominent Communist intellectuals published an angry protest against Soviet action in Hungary.

In Bonn 30,000 people marched in memory of the dead in Hungary and Egypt. In Lisbon 5,000 students gathered in the biggest city square and then marched in silence to the National Assembly to protest against the Russian massacres in Hungary. Only in Poland was the message of Budapest taken as a warning, even by anti-Communist Poles. The President of the Polish Republic in exile in London, August Zaleski, appealed to Poland to be 'warned by Hungary' and not attempt a rising:

I address to all citizens of Poland a fervent request that in these tragic days they should remain calm and avoid provocations whose consequences might be incalculable. You are surrounded on all sides by Soviet troops. You are dealing with an enemy of whose perfidy I need not persuade you.

Let the fate of Hungary, with whom we deeply commiserate, serve as an example of what can be expected from the East as well as from the West. With all seriousness I warn you that you cannot count upon any help from the West at the present time.

I pray to God that he may inspire you with prudence and patience.

On November 7 János Kádár returned to Budapest, to take up the position of Prime Minister under the protection of the Soviet guns. On the following day the United Nations General Assembly passed a resolution calling for the immediate withdrawal of Soviet troops from Hungary. The Soviet bloc voted against the resolution, supported in its rejection by the Indian government. The General Assembly also authorized United Nations observers to enter Hungary, but Kádár refused to let them in. He did, however, accept United Nations humanitarian relief.

Some idea of the scale of the conflict in Hungary was revealed by the Indian Prime Minister, Jawaharlal Nehru, who informed the United Nations that according to inquiries made by Indian diplomats in Budapest 25,000 Hungarians and 7,000 Russians had been killed. Most of the Hungarians were civilians, and most of the Russians were soldiers. Having been the least willing to condemn the Soviet Union when the fighting was at its height, Nehru admitted – at the end of the year – that the uprising was a 'national one' in which workers and students had taken part.

One result of the Soviet victory was an exodus of Hungarians desperate to escape while the borders, in particular the border with Austria, was not yet sealed. As many as 200,000 Hungarians fled their country, almost two per cent of the total population. Twenty-nine governments made offers of asylum. Four countries agreed to take in unlimited numbers of Hungarian refugees: Britain, France, Norway and Canada. West Germany took in more than 10,000, and the United States 28,000. Each country that opened its doors was to find many facets of its national life greatly enriched by the newcomers. The British historian David Pryce-Jones has written: 'Many of these refugees were talented and ambitious and Hungary could ill afford to lose them. Perhaps the government thought that if such people were discontented, it would be safer to let them go and not risk another internal explosion.'

The careers of three of the thousands of refugees give a flavour of their quality and contribution. Laszlo Heltay, a pupil of Zoltán Kodaly, established the Kodaly Choir in Britain, was for ten years Director of Music at the Royal Choral Society, and conducted orchestras in New Zealand, Dresden, Dallas – and, after several decades, in Budapest. George Radda, who arrived in Britain as a twenty-year-old student, became Professor of Molecular Cardiology at Oxford in 1984 and Chief Executive of the Medical Research Council in 1996. Miklos Radnai, who was head of the Gallery of Hungarian Art in Budapest when the revolution broke out, became an authority on the Norwich school of British painters.[1]

Inside Hungary, the security police were back in their green uniforms, and back in action. The bodies of security policemen who had been killed by the insurgents were dug up and reburied with military honours. Thousands of Hungarians were arrested and deported to camps in the Soviet Union. Detention without trial was introduced. Arrests were widespread. As many as two thousand of those arrested were executed. More than 20,000 were imprisoned. The border with Austria was sealed and mined.

The Hungarian revolution had been thoroughly crushed, and the Anglo-French attack on Egypt brought to a halt. On November 15, as instructed by the Security Council, the United Nations Emergency Force (UNEF) arrived in Egypt. Within a month there were to be five thousand troops in place, sent from eight countries.[2]

On November 21, six days after the first United Nations troops reached Egypt, the General Assembly passed its first censure on the Soviet Union for its invasion of Hungary. On November 22 a bus arrived at the Yugoslav Embassy in Budapest. The Soviet authorities had offered Imre Nagy a safe conduct out of Hungary. He accepted, and was deported to Roumania, where he was held in a prison at Sinaia.

There was a feeling in the West that, had it not been for the distraction

[1] On the day that I wrote these words (26 March 1998), Miklos Radnai's obituary was published in *The Times*. He was seventy-two. At the time of his death he was working on a catalogue of the seventeenth-century Hungarian still-life and bird painter Jacob Bogdani, and had just returned from a visit to Hungary. On the following day, 27 March 1998, the *Independent* published an obituary of another Hungarian refugee who had settled in Britain, Dr Zoltán Frankl, a leading oral surgeon. A survivor of Mauthausen concentration camp, he was ninety years old at the time of his death.

[2] The eight countries sending troops to the Suez Canal were Canada, Colombia, Denmark, Finland, India, Norway, Sweden and Yugoslavia. In the following year two more countries sent troops, Brazil and Indonesia, bringing the size of the force to six thousand.

and upheaval caused by the Suez War, the West might have been able to take more effective action to help Hungary. What that action might have been it is hard to say. But the spectacle of the United States at loggerheads with Britain and France can only have served as an encouragement to the Soviet Union to press its advantage home. It knew that there could be no Western unanimity, and that the NATO powers, so confident and even formidable on paper, were for the time being in disarray.

One courageous Communist voice that spoke out against the suppression of the Hungarian revolution, and the pusillanimity of his own country, Yugoslavia, in the face of that suppression, was that of Milovan Djilas, former partisan and Vice-President. Accused of 'slandering Yugoslavia' by his criticisms, he was imprisoned for nine months, then rearrested, retried and imprisoned again. While a prisoner he wrote a book, *The New Class*, in which he described the Communist leaders in both the Soviet Union and Yugoslavia as a 'new class' of bureaucrats or oligarchs who used power solely for their own ends.

Peter Fryer, the British Communist who had seen so many of the events in Hungary at first hand, wrote in his account of the uprising, *Hungarian Tragedy*: 'The *Daily Worker* sent me to Hungary, then suppressed what I wrote. Much of what I wrote was concealed even from my colleagues.' For Fryer, as for many Western Communists, the Hungarian bid for freedom, and its destruction, prompted a harsh reassessment. 'Stalinism is Marxism with the heart cut out, de-humanized, dried, frozen, petrified, rigid, barren,' he wrote. 'It is concerned with "the line", not with the tears of Hungarian children. It is preoccupied with abstract power, with strategy and tactics, not with the dictates of conscience and common humanity.'

At the very moment when the Soviet army was battling in the streets of Budapest, the British authorities in Singapore confronted a series of demonstrations by Chinese Communist students. For two weeks the students, angry that their union had been declared a subversive organization and closed down, occupied their schools and refused to leave, despite a government order to do so. When they were forcibly dispersed, they rampaged through the city streets, stoning cars, erecting barricades, looting European-owned shops and setting fire to police posts.

On October 26 Royal Air Force helicopters dropped tear-gas canisters on demonstrators in the city streets as the local police proved unable to disperse them. British and Gurkha troops were sent in to drive the rioters from the city centre. During the fighting that followed, eleven Chinese were killed.

Awareness of the evils of apartheid inside South Africa was enhanced when Trevor Huddleston, who had been active in opposing apartheid since his arrival in the country in 1943, described his experiences in his book, *Naught for your Comfort*. The book, which could not be published in South Africa, was smuggled out and became a world bestseller. As soon as it was published in Britain, Huddleston's Superior in the Community of the Resurrection withdrew him from the country, fearing that he would be arrested. From outside he became an articulate and persistent campaigner for civil and human rights in South Africa – to which, thirty-five years later, he was invited back to be the first speaker at the first conference in freedom of the African National Congress. One of those who had been active in the struggle in Huddleston's days, Nelson Mandela, had not forgotten the Englishman's commitment.

There was a particularly harsh setback for human rights in South Africa that year, when after a year of debate and legal turmoil the Appellate Division of the South African Supreme Court ruled, on November 9, by ten votes to one, that the government of South Africa had been right to establish a separate voting register for Cape Coloured voters – primarily Indians, and people of mixed Black-White parentage. This separate register effectively destroyed any influence the Coloured voters might have in the main parliament. After the earlier parliamentary vote in favour of the change, the Prime Minister, J. G. Strijdom, had received a standing ovation from the Nationalist Party, after which members filed past his desk to shake his hand.

The policy of apartheid continued and was continuously reinforced. During 1956 the authorities began the removal of Indian traders who had stands in the centre of towns which were designated White. They were ordered to move their stands to 'locations' on the outskirts. Despite the hardship involved to the individual traders, the zoning plans on racial grounds proceeded, starting with Cape Town and Johannesburg.

On December 5 the South African police, in a nationwide swoop, arrested 156 members of the African National Congress, the Indian Congress and the Congress of Democrats, three groups implacably opposed to apartheid. Among those arrested were three leaders of the Black South African struggle for equality, Chief Lutuli, Professor Z. K. Matthews and Oliver Tambo, as well as one of the leading Black lawyers, Nelson Mandela. They were accused of treason. 'It is not pleasant to be arrested in front of one's children,' Mandela later wrote, 'even though one knows that what one is doing is right. But children do not comprehend the complexity of the situation; they simply see their father being taken away by the white authorities without an explanation.'

On the following day, in Durban, there was a protest meeting of people of all races at which the writer Alan Paton appealed for funds. He was arrested, charged with addressing an illegal gathering and fined. Those charged with treason faced four years of legal proceedings.

In the United States, the struggle for civil rights reached a very different landmark on November 13 – four days after the South African setback – when the Supreme Court in Washington ruled that the segregation of bus passengers was unconstitutional. This enabled the boycott, begun the previous year in Montgomery, Alabama, to be called off, and pointed the way forward to further challenges to existing inequalities. When the Southern Senators drafted what they hoped would be a unanimous 'Southern Manifesto' against the Supreme Court ruling, three of their number refused to sign it: Albert Gore – the father of a future Vice-President – Estes Kefauver and Lyndon Johnson.

On November 30 the General Council of the Socialist International met in Copenhagen. In March the Council had rejected Khrushchev's appeal for co-operation between Communist and Social Democratic Parties worldwide on the ground that, despite the anti-Stalin denunciations in the speech, the nature of Communism had not changed. At the November meeting the Council called for Soviet troops to withdraw from Hungary, and also for an end to the Arab economic boycott against Israel, which was forcing even non-Arab companies to cease trading with Israel if they wished to continue trading with the Arab world.

When the Council called for the withdrawal of all remaining French troops from Egypt, the French delegates walked out. Political affinities were not enough to overcome national moods. Also rejecting the call for withdrawal were Spain, Israel and the International Jewish Labour Bund – which fifty years earlier had been at the forefront of Russian revolutionary socialism.

Another attempt at revolution was under way in the Caribbean. On the night of November 24/25 the ship *Granma* – a fifty-eight-foot yacht – left Mexico and sailed to Cuba. On board were Fidel Castro, who took the rank of major, and eighty-one followers, including an Argentinian revolutionary,

Ernesto (Che) Guevara. They landed secretly in eastern Cuba. It was the start of a sustained guerrilla war against the dictatorial regime of Fulgencio Batista.

The first attack by the insurgents took place on November 30. Reports of the fighting told of ten dead, most of them soldiers and policemen. Three rebels – a student leader, a telephone worker and an office worker – were also among the dead. A news agency report from Havana described how, at Santiago de Cuba, the capital of the Oriente Province, 'organized bands of uniformed insurgents stormed the headquarters of the police, the harbour police and the Customs House, seizing arms and ammunition and setting fire to a building'.

A second landing of men and arms from the *Granma* took place on December 2. Three days later the main group of rebels was ambushed and twenty-four of them killed. The rest were the object of repeated military searches, even of the use of napalm from the air. The historian Hugh Thomas has written of how, in the Sierra Maestra, the surviving fugitives 'sought something edible among the trees, but found nothing except an occasional parasite plant, in which there was a residue of water. They ate herbs, occasional raw corn, or crabs. Guevara attempted to draw water from a rock with his asthma apparatus, and he and his group narrowly avoided asking for succour at a house where the health of Batista's army was being drunk.' One of the group drank his own urine.

On Christmas Eve the insurgents exploded a number of bombs in several towns in the Oriente Province, causing a blackout at the moment of festivities. Batista ordered immediate reprisals, and twenty-two men, members of different opposition groups, were tracked down and killed. Two were hanged, and their bodies left dangling from trees, as a warning. After further bombs on New Year's Eve, in which two people were badly injured, five more members of the opposition were killed.

In the Sierra Maestra, Castro led a much reduced group of twenty men, with scarcely more than twenty weapons. But they acquired arms and had small but morale-boosting military successes. Steadily Castro augmented his numbers and became more daring in his exploits. With growing peasant support he prepared the path to power.

On December 5 the British and French forces on the Suez Canal began their withdrawal. It was completed by December 22. Not only had the military prowess of two Western nations been found wanting, but their United States ally – and partner in the Cold War confrontations – had been willing to take decisive action against them. The Soviet Union suffered from no military weakness or external restraints as it strengthened its hold upon Hungary. When, on December 8, Hungarian workers called for a general strike in protest at the Soviet intervention, the Communist government of János Kádár declared martial law and arrested all those who dared to take to the streets.

The Soviet Union had exerted its authority over Hungary, and set back the cause of Soviet acceptance by the West for many years. Thousands of Western Communists resigned from the Party as a result of 'Hungary'. Those who did not do so had to answer continuous criticism of their pusillanimity. The Soviet Union had also to tread more warily elsewhere. Following the Poznan riots at the beginning of the year, it had tried to impose some form of control over the Polish Communist Party, but by the end of the year it realized that this was not possible, unless a second bloodbath was to be ordered.

Throughout the first two weeks of December there were intense negotiations in Warsaw. On December 17 agreement was reached. The Poles did not allow the Soviet intimidation of mid-October to weaken the move towards some form of independence within the Soviet sphere. As a result of the arguments put forward by the Polish Communist leader, Wladislaw Gomulka – who had been imprisoned from 1951 to 1956 for his criticism of the Soviet Union – the Soviet troops who had taken up positions around Warsaw were ordered back to their bases. *Pravda* published a Polish answer to its charges of anti-Socialist behaviour, and Marshal Rokossowski, the symbol since 1949 of Soviet authority in Poland, resigned as Polish Minister of Defence, and returned to Moscow.

On the other side of the Communist-dominated world the North Vietnamese government of Ho Chi Minh had embarked on a Land Reform Programme. Its aim was both to give land to the peasants and to establish full Communist control over the countryside. The mastermind of the programme was one of the pre-war founders of the Vietnamese Communist movement, Truong Chinh, who was then Party Secretary. Those who opposed the programme were ruthlessly treated. Wealthier peasants and small landowners were, as in the Soviet Union twenty-five years earlier, arrested and executed. Accusations of antipathy to the programme could lead to execution with the merest semblance of a trial. In all, 100,000 peasants were executed. Agricultural output fell precipitately. Within six months Truong Chinh had been made the scapegoat and was dismissed.

*　　*　　*

A revolution of another, non-political and non-violent sort was about to take place – in the transport of goods from one country to another. A standard container had been devised, capable of being stacked on board ship in considerable quantities. The first container port was opened in the United States, at Elizabeth, New Jersey. Slowly the use of containers, and eventually of container ships, came to dominate the transport of goods from continent to continent. International agreements about the containers' dimensions made it possible for them to be transported by road, rail and sea almost anywhere in the world.

On September 25 the first regular transatlantic telephone service was inaugurated. Within a month, on October 17, the world's first large-scale nuclear power station was opened, at Calder Hall in Britain, at a ceremony presided over by Queen Elizabeth II. One of those who spoke at the ceremony was Academician Tupchiev, the leader of a four-man Soviet scientific delegation. He struck a note of warning as to the future of the new power source, telling the assembled guests: 'The limitless reserves of intra-nuclear energy that have been discovered by man's great genius are a powerful weapon which may contribute to the happiness and welfare of the people or may lead to the extermination of millions of lives and the destruction of material culture.'

Tupchiev then put forward a proposal for the internationalization of nuclear energy. Again, he gave his remarks a warning aspect. 'Soviet people', he said, 'believe that measures should be taken to ensure that all fissionable material – to the last gram – be used in the purpose of peace and progress. This material should be placed in the service of mankind and not for the extermination of human beings.'

That year's Olympic Games, which were held in Melbourne, Australia, were affected by two of the political disputes of the year. In protest against the participation of Taiwan – the last bastion of Nationalist China – Communist China withdrew from the Games. And in protest against the Anglo-French-Israeli action against Egypt, five countries withdrew: Egypt, Lebanon, the Netherlands, Spain and Switzerland.

The main focus of the 1956 Olympics was the Soviet-American rivalry, which was a feature of almost every event. By the end the Soviet Union had won thirty-seven gold medals. The United States won thirty-two, reversing the order of the gold medals at the previous Games, which had been held in Helsinki in 1952. This was the first time that the Soviet Union came top of the gold-medal list. It had done so by a process of rigorous selection and training, using the full resources of the State, and equating successful competitiveness with national patriotism. The Soviet athletes were more or less professionals, taking part in a competition for amateurs. The country closest to the two leaders was Australia, the host country, with thirteen gold medals. Hungary, with Communism only just restored as the Games opened (on November 22), won the next largest number, nine.

That October and November also saw the triumphal appearance of the Bolshoi Ballet in London. It was the first visit of any Soviet ballet company to the West, and the first visit abroad of the Bolshoi in its two centuries of existence. People waited all night in the street at Covent Garden for the chance of a seat to see Galina Ulanova dance. So rigid had the Soviet system remained despite the death of Stalin three years earlier that when the three planes with the dancers were diverted because of fog from Heathrow to a United States air base at Manston, in Kent, Ulanova and her colleagues refused to leave the plane until official permission had been received from Moscow.

The Bolshoi Ballet proceeded with its programme. The opening night, October 3, was before the worsening of the international crises. 'I have never heard such cheering,' one of those in the gods, Alan Palmer, recalled forty years later. 'You have given a most beautiful performance I shall always remember,' the Queen told Ulanova after watching her in *Giselle* on October 12. But as a result of the crushing of the Hungarian revolution the return visit of the Sadler's Wells Ballet to Moscow was cancelled. Alan Palmer was among those who had bought the brochure printed in Russian for the Sadler's Wells company's return visit. On November 6 the General Administrator of Covent Garden, David Webster, telegraphed to the director of the Bolshoi Ballet:

> In view of public opinion in this country, which strongly condemns the renewed suppression by Soviet forces of Hungarian liberty and independence, the Royal Opera House Covent Garden has consulted Her Majesty's Government and the Soviet Relations Committee of the British Council.
> It has been unanimously agreed that in the present circumstances the projected visit of the Sadler's Wells Ballet to Moscow cannot take place.

Also cancelled as a result of the crushing of the Hungarian uprising was a visit of a delegation of Russian lawyers who had been invited to Britain by the Bar Council. The Council made it clear to them that they would not be welcome. Nor did any official British representative go to the reception at the Soviet Embassy to celebrate the thirty-ninth anniversary of the Bolshevik revolution. In Moscow, during the celebration of that anniversary, Moscow Radio declared: 'The Soviet people rejoice from the bottom of their hearts at the victory scored by the Hungarian workers over the forces of reaction. We are firmly convinced that Hungary was, is and will remain a Socialist country.'

Only two Western nations sent representatives to the annual celebratory parade in Red Square: Iceland and Denmark. There was another element in the intensification of the Cold War that year: the passing by the United States Congress of the Federal Aid Highway Act. Senator Albert Gore, who had seen and studied the German autobahn system during his war service in Germany in the Second World War, introduced the legislation. It established a continental road network, known as the National System of Interstate and Defence Highways, which was to lead to the building of 41,000 miles of motorways – fast, limited-access roads. The defence aspect was explained by Eisenhower without prevarication. 'Our roads ought to be avenues of escape for persons living in big cities threatened by aerial attack or natural disaster,' he explained. 'If such a crisis ever occurred, our obsolescent highways would turn into traps of death and destruction.' For more than a decade, this escape route aspect was clearly indicated on the highways themselves.

While Ulanova danced in London to admiring audiences, the refugees from Soviet military repression in Hungary, many of whom had started their life in exile in refugee camps in Austria, were beginning to reach Britain. Others, waiting in Austria to go elsewhere, received food, clothing and medicine from many countries, including the United States, and also a distinguished American visitor, Vice-President Nixon, who was photographed on December 22 surrounded by the eager faces of Hungarian refugees looking forward to a new life – for many of them it would be in the United States.

Also embarking on new lives as refugees were 25,000 Egyptian Jews, who, after many generations contributing to the life, prosperity and culture of Egypt, were forced to leave, following the Suez War and Israel's attack in Sinai. More than half of them went to Israel, where, under a Law of Return passed six years earlier, any Jew arriving in Israel could become a citizen. Most of those who went elsewhere did so as 'stateless refugees', among them Gisele Orebi (later Gisèle Littman), who was to become the acknowledged expert on the plight of Jews and Christians in Muslim lands, and their vigorous champion: her book *The Dhimmi, Jews and Christians under Islam*, written under the pen name Bat Ye'or, brought the issue of continuing discrimination to a wide public. Among those Egyptian Jews who were to make their lives and careers in Britain was the laryngologist and hearing specialist Ellis Douek – who had been educated at the English School, Cairo – and his sister Claudia Roden, the cookery historian and writer. One country's loss was, as so often in the twentieth century, another country's gain.

In China, there seemed to be hope of change, despite the execution of dissidents in the previous year, when Mao Tse-tung announced the start of the Hundred Flowers Campaign. The theme of the campaign was:

> Let a hundred flowers blossom,
> let a hundred schools of thought contend.

In Moscow, the Soviet Communist Party leadership feared that the Hundred Flowers Campaign was the Chinese reaction to the suppression of the Hungarian revolt, and that it would serve to encourage not only Hungary, but also Poland and Czechoslovakia, to seek their own way forward. Within China, Mao Tse-tung himself urged the intellectuals to use the campaign to question the methods of the bureaucratic elite within the Party. They did so, denouncing the Party's aloofness as an expression of the ideology of the old exploiting classes. As the debate grew in intensity, Mao Tse-tung realized that it was going too far, and brought it swiftly to a halt.

At the height of the Suez and Hungary crises there had been a small glimpse of a different future. On November 2 it was announced in both London and Moscow that a British and a Soviet citizen had shared a Nobel Prize. It was the first time the Russians had won a Nobel Prize in science. Their recipient was Professor A. V. Seminov. His fellow prizewinner was Sir Cyril Hinshelwood, Professor of Chemistry at Oxford University and President of the Royal Society. Both prizewinners had worked for the previous twenty-five years in the same field – the mechanisms by which chemical reactions proceed in gases – and had been in close personal touch with each other. 'These contacts', wrote the Scientific Correspondent of the *Manchester Guardian*, 'have persisted in spite of all the Iron Curtain trouble.'

It had been a bad year for such a good omen.

CHAPTER SIX

1957

... a catastrophe for the human race, a catastrophe that must be prevented at all costs.

ALBERT SCHWEITZER

THE CONFRONTATION between the Soviet Union and the United States, with its ominous nuclear overtones, reached a watershed on 5 January 1957, the day on which President Eisenhower set out to Congress what quickly became known as the Eisenhower Doctrine. It was intended to make clear to the Soviet Union that, although the United States had acted in the Suez crisis to bring an end to the hostilities, it was not adopting a pacifist or neutralist stance. In his speech, Eisenhower asked Congress, with specific reference to the Middle East – but clearly with wider implications – to authorize him to 'employ the armed forces of the United States . . . to secure and protect the territorial integrity and political independence of any nation or group of nations requesting such aid against overt armed aggression from any nation controlled by international Communism'. He also asked to be allowed to use 'for the purposes of this resolution, without regard to the provisions of any other law or regulation', a sum not exceeding $200 million. This would provide both military and economic assistance to countries which might otherwise be tempted or cajoled into committing themselves to the Soviet sphere of influence.

The phrase to 'employ the armed forces of the United States' went far beyond the use of American forces within a United Nations authorized conflict, as in Korea seven years earlier. The Democratic National Advisory Committee immediately criticized the new doctrine on the ground that it provided no solution to the actual problems besetting the Middle East – the Arab-Israeli conflict, the future of the Suez Canal and, most ominous for the peace of the region, the shipment of arms from the Communist bloc to the Arab States.

John Foster Dulles, whose belief that the United States had to take an active part against Communist encroachments was a principal stimulus to the doctrine, told the House Foreign Affairs Committee on the day of Eisenhower's statement that the doctrine would 'stop World War III before it starts'. When he was asked what the United States would do if Communists took over a Middle East country by subversion, he replied that the United States would not 'invade any country to overthrow its government however it gets there'. This underlined what many Democrats saw as the chief weakness of the doctrine: if the Soviet Union and its satellites were unlikely to embark on actual physical aggression in the Middle East, but were more likely to penetrate the area by means of internal subversion, then the Eisenhower Doctrine would have been established to deal with a contingency which was the least likely to arise.

Questioned about this by the committee, Dulles admitted that this was perhaps a 'weakness'. He added that it was, however, 'necessary in the world we live in', and went on to stress that the economic element of the doctrine would head off Communist subversion through helping countries in the area to stand more firmly on their own feet. Dulles was certain that the combined assurance of American military and economic backing 'gives as adequate protection against internal subversion as you can have unless you intend to go around the world throwing out governments you don't like'.

In his presentation of the dangers confronting the Middle East, Dulles painted a grave picture of the threat of Soviet Communism, telling the committee:

It would be a disaster for the peoples of the Middle East because they are deeply religious peoples and their spiritual suffering would be grievous if they were subjected to the fate of other religious peoples who have fallen under the rule of atheistic, materialistic Communism.

The disaster would spread far beyond the confines of the Middle East itself. The economies of many free world countries depend directly upon natural products of the Middle East and on transportation through the Middle East. And, indirectly, the entire free world economy is concerned.

Western Europe is particularly dependent upon the Middle East. The vast sacrifices the United States has made for the economic recovery of Europe and military defense of Europe would be virtually nullified if the Middle East fell under the control of international Communism.

Finally a Communist breakthrough in the Middle East would encourage the Soviet rulers to resort everywhere to more aggressive policies. It would severely weaken the pressures within the Soviet world for more liberal policies. It would be a severe blow to the struggling peoples of Hungary and Poland who are so valiantly striving for more independence.

In secret testimony to the committee, Dulles said that if any Communist 'volunteers' were sent to fight in the Middle East, the United States would regard it as 'overt aggression'. Stressing that the Communist encroachments could be imminent, he urged rapid action on the economic as well as the military portion of the doctrine. 'Unless we move quickly into the area the situation will be lost,' he said. It would be 'regrettable' if both the House and the Senate did not approve the doctrine by the end of that month.

Dulles's sense of urgency made its impact: by the end of the month both the House Foreign Affairs Committee – on January 24 – and six days later the whole House gave their approval. Senate approval, where the balance of power was forty-nine Democrats and forty-six Republicans – with one vacancy – took two months longer, but it came.

In the Middle East, Lebanon was enthusiastic. Syria, which was already drawing closer to Moscow, was hostile. To effect a joint Arab response Nasser called a meeting in Cairo attended by the leaders of Egypt, Syria, Saudi Arabia and Jordan. Any vacuum in the Middle East, they said, would be filled 'by a united Arab policy of nationalism'. That the United States could help the cause of Arab nationalism as an honest broker was also evident in the aftermath of the Eisenhower Doctrine, when Dulles persuaded Israel, which was still in occupation of both the Gaza Strip and the entrance to the Gulf of Akaba, to withdraw its troops.

In return, Israel wanted the United States to issue a declaration of support for free navigation through the Straits of Tiran and the Gulf of Akaba to the Israeli port of Eilat, Israel's only direct link to the Red Sea and the Indian Ocean. But Eisenhower would not agree to do this until Israeli troops had withdrawn from the Egyptian territory still under occupation. If the assurances demanded by Israel were given before Israel's withdrawal, Eisenhower said, 'we will, in effect, have countenanced the use of force as a means of settling international differences and through this gaining national advantage'.

Israel agreed to withdraw without conditions. The United States had shown the Arab world that it could be firm against the Jewish State. At the end of the month an attempt to win Arab support nearly backfired, when King Saud of Saudi Arabia arrived on a State visit in the United States, but was met in New York by the refusal of the city – under Mayor Wagner – to give him an official welcome on the grounds that his regime supported both slavery and anti-Semitism, and forbade Roman Catholic priests to say Mass. Eisenhower was able to restore the King's goodwill when he arrived in Washington, by going to the airport in person to greet him, and by explaining that the Eisenhower Doctrine was one which could help preserve the independence of the Arab States. One outcome of the King's visit was that the United States was given permission to continue to use Dhahran air base, initially for another five years, in exchange for further military and economic aid.[1]

On January 10 the United Nations General Assembly established a special committee to inquire into what had occurred during the crushing of the Hungarian revolution. The committee, having been denied entry into Hungary by the re-established Communist government, took its evidence from among the tens of thousands of Hungarian refugees in the West. Its conclusion, made public six months later, was that the Hungarian revolt had been 'spontaneous', arising from grievances against the Soviet Union and conditions inside Hungary. The report added that the Kádár government, which had succeeded that of Imre Nagy at the height of the struggle, had been 'imposed' on Hungary by the Soviet Union. That autumn a special session of the General Assembly passed a resolution condemning the Soviet Union for depriving the Hungarian people of their liberty.

Another initiative by the General Assembly, on January 30, was an appeal to the South African government to reconsider the apartheid policy. The appeal was ignored, and legislation continued to strengthen the racial divide. Separate university education was introduced, and also, under the Medical, Dentistry and Pharmacy Act, racial segregation in the nursing profession.

Elsewhere in Africa great changes were taking place in the relationship between the rulers and the ruled. The colonial structure of the previous half-century and more was beginning to wither away. On March 6 the Gold Coast, renamed Ghana, became the first of Britain's Black African dominions, to become as independent as Canada or Australia. For eleven years the

---

[1] Forty-four years later the United States used Dhahran air base as one of the staging points for the bombing of Iraq during the Gulf War.

Africans had been a majority in the colony's legislative assembly. An eight-year struggle for complete independence had been led, successfully, by Kwame Nkrumah, who had used strikes and intensive propaganda as his first main weapons – and been briefly imprisoned – and then the ballot box.

East and West Germany were drawing further and further apart. On January 7 a Soviet–German agreement was signed, one outcome of which was to give the Soviet Union the right to intervene militarily in East Germany 'in the interests of security'. When, in the context of possible German reunification, the question of free elections in East Germany was brought up in the People's Chamber in East Berlin, in the presence of Khrushchev, the Soviet leader denounced the proposal as 'rank hypocrisy'. The West German politicians, he said, wanted nothing less than to turn East Germany 'into a fief of Junkers and Rhine and Ruhr magnates'.

The economy of East Germany was far less buoyant than that of West Germany. Rationing in East Germany remained in place. Industrial reconstruction was slow. Raw materials continued to be sent to the Soviet Union under post-war agreements that were little less than theft, and in respect of which the Soviet Union was complaining that East Germany was in arrears. In the sphere of human rights, the Professor of Social Sciences at East Berlin University was sentenced in March to ten years in prison for trying to start a movement for liberal political reform. Since 1953 more than 20,000 East Germans had fled to West Germany. During 1957 the westward flow reached five thousand a week. There was still no wall in Berlin to stop the East Berliners leaving, and any East German who came to East Berlin could likewise make the westward journey.

West Germany had moved forward with American loans and a free enterprise economy. It also embarked within NATO on a self-defence policy that was denounced by East Germany as militarist, but served to offer a means of defending what had been secured economically and politically in the previous twelve years. During January registration for military service began in West Germany. Of 100,000 men who were called up, only a hundred registered as conscientious objectors. On January 24 a West German officer was appointed Commander-in-Chief of the central sector of NATO in Europe. He was General Hans Speidel, who had been Chief of Staff to Rommel at the time of the Normandy landings. In July 1944 he had been arrested by the Gestapo after the attempt on Hitler's life, and held in prison until liberated by the Allies.

Aged fifty-nine, Speidel represented a German generation that had seen Nazism and served under it, and wanted to avoid any return to it. He had also seen the eastern third of his country fall under Communist rule, and wanted to ensure that there was no further westward move of the Communist colossus. To this end, West Germany was active in furthering the cause of European economic integration, giving its full support on February 5 when the European Economic Community put forward the idea of a wider European Free Trade Area (EFTA) that would include Britain, the Scandinavian countries, Switzerland and Austria. This would extend the existing economic integration that encompassed 164 million people by a further 78 million. The British government felt unable to move forward on these lines, however, citing Britain's special economic interests with regard to the Commonwealth, imports from which were already receiving preferential treatment.

It was not economic pacts, however, but defence pacts that dominated the concerns of the non-Communist world. On March 9 John Foster Dulles flew nine thousand miles from Washington to Canberra to appeal for a common defence policy throughout South-East Asia against Communist encroachment and subversion. Two days later he spoke at the opening session of the third annual meeting of the Council of Ministers of the South-East Asia Treaty Organization (SEATO). Drawing the delegates' attention to Communist China, he commented critically, with regard to North Korea and North Vietnam, on 'the open support given by Communist China to Soviet colonialism and imperialism'. This had 'ominous implications for all free Asian nations', he said. Communist tyranny, he added, 'went about disguised in the pilfered clothes of liberty'. The United States had no intention of recognizing Communist China.[1]

A remark by Dulles during his speech caused a tremor of unease among the non-aligned nations, and among the public of many of America's staunch allies, when he said, almost as an aside, that the forces of the United States 'almost everywhere are equipped with atomic weapons . . . It is almost a normal part of their equipment.'

In China, the Communist Party had struggled to improve rural productivity, and to create among the peasants of China – who made up seventy per cent of the Party membership – a sense of national effort. The figures for grain

---

[1] Dulles was not to know that a pioneering leap forward in the relations between China and the United States was to be made by the then Vice-President Nixon when, as President, he visited China in 1972.

production revealed, however, that the system was not working. During 1957 grain production rose by one per cent, but the population rose by two per cent. Shortages of cotton cloth led to a cut in the ration. Chou En-lai wanted to offer the peasants greater incentives, including a chance to buy more consumer goods. Mao Tse-tung also wanted to stimulate local Communist Party leadership. When he spoke on February 27 at a secret session of the Supreme State Conference – three months later a version of what he had said was published in Warsaw – his theme was the 'contradictions' among the people of China, and how to rectify them.

According to Mao Tse-tung the principal contradictions that had to be rectified were the 'evils' of bureaucracy, sectarianism and subjectivism. Non-Communists were invited to join a nationwide movement for the denunciation of arrogance, formalism and 'an unduly theoretical attitude' among Communist Party officials. This nationwide criticism was a refinement of the previous year's Hundred Flowers Campaign theme – 'let a hundred schools of thought contend'. In Mao's new presentation there were two types of criticism. One type was 'obnoxious' and should be suppressed. The other type was legitimate. The definition of legitimate criticism was that it benefited the 'Socialist transformation' of the country, consolidated the People's dictatorship, strengthened the leadership of the Communist Party, and was beneficial to international Socialist solidarity.

How deep the dissent had penetrated was intimated on June 8, when the Peking *People's Daily* attacked 'rightist' elements who were calling for an end to Communist Party control. Within three weeks Chou En-lai was attacking the 'rightist' elements. Mao Tse-tung also condemned 'rightist opportunism' as constituting a 'bourgeois trend of thought even more dangerous than doctrinairism'. As the attack gained in verbal violence, three Cabinet Ministers – the Ministers of Communications, the Timber Industry, and Food – were accused of plotting to overthrow the Communist Party leadership. They had been inspired in their opposition to the Party by the Hungarian uprising, having argued – as did so many Western Communists – that, after the Soviet suppression of the Hungarian uprising, Communist Parties worldwide had lost their right to rule.

The three Ministers claimed that while they had hoped to see some form of upper chamber, in which there would be a majority of non-Communists, they had not wanted actively to overthrow the regime. Condemned for their opinions, and thus apparently adequately chastised, they were allowed to remain in their ministerial positions. The leaders of the students who rioted in

June in Hanyang and attacked Communist Party officials were less leniently treated: three of them were executed for their part in the riots.

Mao Tse-tung was indefatigable in his criticisms. Addressing a peasant audience of Communist Party cadres he told them that the peasants, and the cadres themselves, had fallen into a pattern of 'individualism, departmentalism, absolute egalitarianism or liberalism' – an array of sins that must be rectified. Rectification was not to be carried out by gentle means. Towards the end of the year the Communist Party leadership began an experiment – soon to be known as the Great Leap (also known as the Great Leap Forward) – whereby the peasants were to be conscripted and mobilized for massive irrigation and water-control projects. However great the natural obstacles or technical challenges, they must be overcome. Within three months more than 100 million peasants had been set to these harsh tasks. Their wives, left at home, had to take on the agricultural work of their absent husbands, mostly as agricultural labourers. Centralized schemes were devised for child care, and for feeding the wives whose work would make it impossible for them any longer to cook at home. To increase industrial production, some industries were moved from the cities to the countryside.

Members of the Politburo of the Communist Party were made to go into the rural areas to see for themselves the transformation of the Great Leap Forward. The slogan on everyone's lips was: 'More, faster, better, cheaper'.

In an effort to bridge the gap opened in the Anglo-American relationship by the Suez War, in the fourth week of March, in Bermuda, President Eisenhower met Harold Macmillan – who had succeeded a sick Anthony Eden as Prime Minister in January – and agreed to make certain American guided missiles available for the defence of Britain, and to allow them to be stationed on British soil. The only caveat was that the warheads would remain under American control.

While Britain and the United States again drew closer together, the cause of European unity advanced without British participation. On March 25 – the day after the ending of the Bermuda Conference – six European nations signed the Treaty of Rome. 'The Six', as they became known, were Belgium, France, West Germany, Italy, Luxembourg and the Netherlands, the nations which since the end of the Second World War twelve years earlier had been at the forefront of the push for a united Europe.

The Treaty of Rome established a European Economic Community (EEC), also known as the 'Common Market'. It was followed by a further agreement by The Six, also signed in Rome, under which a European Atomic Energy Authority (Euratom) was set up to enable the signatories to share the development of atomic energy for fuel. In a third development towards greater unity of action among the Six, the court that had been set up five years earlier by the European Steel and Coal Community was transformed into the European Court of Justice. These were remarkable strides forward from the divisions and bitterness of the immediate post-war period.

In Britain's African possessions the last phase of the anti-colonial struggle was coming to a less noble end. The previous October, Dedan Kimathi, who for three years had led the armed struggle against British rule in Kenya, had been hunted down by police of his own tribe, the Kikuyu. Wounded and captured, he was manacled to a stretcher and taken to hospital. A White judge and three Black African 'assessors' found him guilty of rebellion. He was hanged in Nairobi prison in April. At the time of his execution he was thirty-six years old.

On April 19 the United States rejected a Soviet proposal made two months earlier for the co-ordination of 'Big Four' policies in the Middle East – the Soviet Union being, with the United States, Britain and France, one of the Big Four. Six days later the Eisenhower Doctrine was put to its first test, when on April 25 King Hussein of Jordan declared martial law to protect his regime against a serious challenge by left-wing and republican elements. Eisenhower at once announced that the integrity and independence of Jordan were a 'vital' interest of the United States and of the Middle East as a whole.

The basis of the Eisenhower Doctrine was unilateral American action, and this the President ordered at once, with units of the American Sixth Fleet sailing from the southern coast of France, where they were then berthed, to the eastern Mediterranean. On April 29 it was announced from Washington that American troops would be ready, if needed, to parachute into Jordan 'in a matter of days'. A second announcement that day concerned the first payment to be made under the Eisenhower Doctrine: $1 million in economic aid to Jordan.

The Jordanian Foreign Minister, Samir Rifai, tried to distance his country from the American initiative, declining the parachute troops and then going so far as to refuse to receive a special envoy from the President. But an American shipment of arms to Jordan that autumn was accepted with alacrity.

*   *   *

In India, the second election since independence led to a new government being formed on May 13. It had been brought to power by the largest electorate in the world, more than 193 million voters. Nehru and the Congress Party retained their predominance nationwide, but in the southern State of Kerala a Communist administration was elected. The decision of the Kerala legislature to nationalize the schools, of which almost a third were run by the local Roman Catholic community, was upheld by the government of India as being constitutionally valid. Less easy to defend was the withdrawal of police protection from the owners of tea plantations in Kerala, and a spate of physical attacks on the planters and their non-Communist workers.

Throughout the year, Nehru and his government pressed ahead with efforts at modernization and standardization. A unified national calendar had been introduced on March 22. Nine days later a national decimal coinage system was proclaimed. As a gesture of independence on the tenth anniversary of the end of British rule, Nehru announced on May 13 that the many fine statues – of emperors, viceroys, generals and governors – erected during the century of the British Raj would be removed, but, in order not to cause ill-feeling with Britain, this was to be done gradually. Sometimes the statues found welcome homes: the equestrian statue of the King-Emperor Edward VII, that had been one of the landmarks of Calcutta, ending up in Canada, as one of Toronto's municipal ornaments.

It was from Britain that India was acquiring its navy. In March, Nehru's sister, Vijaya Lakshmi Pandit, the Indian High Commissioner in London, was present at the launching of the naval frigate *Brahmaputra* at Clydebank. In August a former British cruiser, HMS *Nigeria*, was handed over to the Indian government at Birkenhead, modernized and renamed *Mysore*. In November, in Delhi, British and Indian dignitaries joined together at the dedication of a memorial gateway commemorating 25,000 men – Britons and Indians alike – of the Indian Army and Royal Indian Air Force, who had been killed in action during the Second World War.

The regional and communal conflicts of India were seldom absent from the daily news headlines. In September, near Madras, there were communal riots arising out of caste feuding in which forty people were killed, and almost three thousand dwellings burned down. In the Naga Hills, the rebel leader Zapu Phizo refused to accept an offer from Nehru for a general amnesty, and continued to lead his followers in the remote hills, demanding autonomy for his people.

In Kashmir there was a series of bomb explosions, which the Indian government blamed on Pakistani infiltrators, in which six people were killed. There were more deaths, forty in all, when flooding submerged part of the Kashmir Valley. Nature's depredations also struck Ceylon, when floods and landslides killed more than 280 people in December, and destroyed 300,000 homes. Among the countries that responded to Ceylon's appeal for financial aid were Britain, the United States, India and Australia.

In the United States the legal reversal of many of the McCarthyite judgments was under way when, on May 2, McCarthy died. He was only forty-seven years old. By his denunciations of Communist conspiracies he had caused hysteria and deep divisions in American society. A month after his death the Supreme Court ruled that Federal Bureau of Investigation reports used in criminal files – many of which had helped to secure convictions in the McCarthy era – had henceforth to be made available to the defendant. In a further ruling two weeks later, on June 17 the Supreme Court laid down that membership of the Communist Party was not a sufficient ground for conviction. The Supreme Court stressed that there was a legal distinction, which had not been pointed out by the judge when he addressed the jury before the convictions, between 'advocacy of forcible overthrow' of the United States government, 'as an abstract doctrine' and advocacy 'of action to that end'.

The decisions of the Supreme Court were moderating and liberalizing the American way of life. The Supreme Court was looked to by all defenders of human rights in the United States as the upholder of fair and humane values. But age-old prejudice could not be overcome overnight by legal judgments, however binding those judgments might be constitutionally. A decision by the Supreme Court the previous year declaring racial segregation in buses to be unconstitutional, and supporting racial integration in schools, was followed by a series of ugly incidents, in which the racially motivated Ku Klux Klan was active.

On January 10, in Montgomery, Alabama, four Black churches were blown up by dynamite, and the homes of two Black ministers of religion destroyed. But the progress towards equitable civil rights was being asserted and upheld at the highest level. On August 30 the Senate debated the Civil Rights Bill. Despite an attempt by Senator Thurmond of South Carolina to talk it out – he spoke for a record twenty-four hours and eighteen minutes – the Bill was passed into law by sixty votes to fifteen. The new Act, the first civil rights legislation in the United States of the twentieth century, made the right to vote absolute, irrespective of colour, and gave power to federal prosecutors to obtain court injunctions against any actual or threatened interference with the right to vote. Anyone refusing to obey such an injunction could be imprisoned by a judge, sitting without a jury.

The Supreme Court ruling of 1956 had called for integration in schools with 'all deliberate speed'. This meant that during 1957 Black American children were to be admitted to senior high schools without discrimination based on colour. This was resisted by Southern politicians who drew their support from those Whites who opposed the Supreme Court ruling. A crisis came on September 4, when the Governor of Arkansas, Orval Faubus – himself a Democrat of liberal inclinations – fearing mob violence, tried to prevent the admission of Black children to a school in Little Rock, and used the local National Guard to turn the children away.

The case was examined by a federal judge, who came to the conclusion, on September 20, that the integration of the schoolchildren, as required by law, had been 'thwarted by the Governor of Arkansas and by the use of the National Guard'. The judge then ordered Governor Faubus to remove the National Guard from the school. He did so at once, and on September 23 nine Black schoolchildren entered the school. A crowd of Whites had gathered, and attacked four other Blacks outside the school, thinking, wrongly, that they were also schoolchildren – they were in fact journalists. To avoid further possible violence, the nine children who had entered the school were sent home.

Eisenhower took immediate action. On September 24 he ordered a thousand federal troops – paratroopers from the 101st Airborne Division – into Little Rock, to escort the nine children to school. They obeyed the order, and the children took their place in the classroom.

The opposite trend persisted in South Africa. There, the State-Aided Institutions Act allowed the government to enforce racial segregation in all places that were under local and public authority control. This included libraries, concert halls and sports fields. Another piece of legislation – and the South African parliament was scrupulous in placing racial prejudice on the statute book – was the revised Native Laws Amendment Bill, which began its passage through the Nationalist Party-dominated parliament in March. It was bitterly criticized by the opposition, but, like all such legislation it could not be stopped, given the Nationalist Party majority. The new Bill gave the Minister of Native Affairs the power to evict Africans from towns, to ban their entry into schools, hospitals, clubs and even churches, in the areas designated for Whites only.

The church provision was angrily denounced by Church leaders from the Anglican, Nonconformist and Roman Catholic Churches. The Anglican Archbishop of Cape Town, Geoffrey Hare Clayton, sent a personal letter to the Prime Minister on March 7 warning that the Anglican Church was prepared to disobey the provisions of the proposed law. He died of a heart attack a few hours after signing the letter. The leaders of the Dutch Reformed Church made their opposition known privately, and took no part in the public protests. The Bill was passed on April 4, by seventy-two votes to forty-three.

As it plunged deeper into apartheid, South Africa turned its back on Britain with a series of measures clearly signifying the distancing of the two countries. The measures came in swift succession. On March 5 the Union Jack ceased to be one of the two official flags of South Africa, which it had been since 1927. On April 2 the Royal Navy base at Simonstown was handed over to the South African government, ending 143 years of British naval presence there. On May 2 the playing of 'God Save the Queen' on official occasions was abolished.

Since the beginning of the year the trial had been taking place in Johannesburg of the 156 people – men and women, Europeans, Asians, Africans and Coloureds – who had been seized by police the previous December and charged with treason. Some of the interrogations had been carried out with great brutality. When the trial began there was rioting outside the courthouse. Subsequent sessions were guarded by five hundred armed police, who cordoned off the streets around the courthouse. By the end of the year the case was still proceeding. Although they were allowed out on bail, many of the accused lost their jobs as a result of the charges.

Intercommunal violence also broke out that year in South Africa, when, on September 15, there was fighting between Zulus and Basutos in the African townships near Johannesburg. More than forty people, including women and children, were killed, many with axes. Several of the victims were mutilated. When the killing was over the Minister of Justice, C. R. Swart, refused the request by the city councillors of Johannesburg for an inquiry. There was a widespread feeling among liberal-minded Whites that the conditions under which Africans were forced to live in the townships, large areas of which were slums of the most degrading sort, had been a contributing factor to the riots.

One persistent voice of protest was Alan Paton. That year he was asked by the Natal Indian Congress to write a pamphlet which exposed the harshness of the Group Area Act of 1950, which had forced thousands of members of South Africa's Indian community out of their homes and businesses. In the pamphlet, which he entitled *The People Wept*, Paton described the act as 'a callous and cruel piece of legislation'.

Inside the Soviet Union the rule of Khrushchev was a time of conflicting Communist Party attitudes. The crushing of the Hungarian revolt served as a reminder that dissent could be treated with the utmost severity: the implications for internal Soviet politics were clear. At the same time, following Khrushchev's denunciation of Stalin's excesses, rehabilitation did lead to some redress of wrongs: a decree of February 11 rehabilitated the Chechen, Ingush, Balkar, Karachai and Kalmyk peoples, each of whom had been deported by Stalin from their homelands during the Second World War, to avoid the possibility of their being won over by the Germans. They were allowed to return home, but without the right of compensation. A sixth deported people, the Crimean Tatars, were not mentioned in the decree, and remained in exile.

Several Soviet writers were singled out during 1957 for failing to fill their works with an understanding of 'Socialist realism'. Negative features of Soviet life could be criticized, but only from the point of view of *partiynost* – Party-mindedness. This involved making clear that all the defects described by the author were being 'successfully overcome' by the Party. Particular criticism was levelled at V. Dudintsev, whose novel *Not by Bread Alone* gave what the Party managers called the 'false impression' that the individual Soviet citizen was virtually powerless against the obstruction of Soviet bureaucracy. Dudintsev's error was considered especially grave as his novel had been translated into English.

Of great impact that year was the first publication in the West – in Italian translation – of Boris Pasternak's novel *Doctor Zhivago*. Attempts by the authorities in Moscow to persuade Pasternak to produce a 'corrected' text were in vain. The book, with its realistic portrayal of the Bolshevik revolution, and of the revolution betrayed, was banned inside the Soviet Union. Copies that did circulate, in mimeographed versions, passed surreptitiously from hand to hand, and did so at great risk. Some Russians found other ways of learning about the book. A visitor to the Soviet Union recalled how, while wandering through the art galleries of the Hermitage in Leningrad, a young Russian boy of about fourteen came up to him and asked, in a careful whisper when no one was about, if the visitor could give an outline of the novel. When the visitor had finished, the boy patted him on the back with the one word 'molodyets' ('Good lad').

The Soviet authorities feared a lack of dedication to the Communist cause among the youth, and took action accordingly. A Russian Federation decree contained penalties of up to five years' exile with hard labour for those designated 'anti-social parasitic elements'. The boy who asked about *Doctor Zhivago* could well have fallen into that category. When a vast gathering of foreign students, estimated at more than 34,000, assembled in Moscow for the World Festival of Peace and Friendship, their Soviet student hosts were warned not to accept the 'bourgeois values' which many of these visitors would bring with them. The censorship of Soviet writers was not a subject to which the organizers of the festival referred, or wanted discussed.

The East-West divide appeared unbridgeable. But the Pugwash Conference on World Affairs, founded in 1957, served as a small but significant effort to attempt to bridge it. Named after the Canadian village where it was held, the founders of the conference wanted to maintain international contacts within the scientific community 'in times of great sensitivity for those working in nuclear physics and related areas'. The conference marked a watershed in the nature of protest with regard to atomic weapons. The Cold War had cut off scientists and researchers on each side of the Iron Curtain. Uneasy at the use of their talents and discoveries by governments seeking to maintain a high level of confrontation, these scientists felt the need to talk among themselves on the technicalities and ethics of their work.

One of the founders of Pugwash was Joseph Rotblat. Born in Warsaw before the First World War, a Jew, and the Director of the Atomic Physics Institute at the Free University of Poland from 1937 to 1939, he had emigrated to Britain from Poland just before the Second World War. From 1945 to 1949 he was Director of Research in Nuclear Physics at Liverpool University. Like many of his fellow nuclear physicists he had been sent to the United States during the war to work at Los Alamos on the development of the atom bomb. His part in Pugwash was very much in reaction to what he had done and seen in the war years. He was later (in 1995) awarded the Nobel Peace Prize for what the citation called his 'efforts to diminish the part played by nuclear arms in international politics, and in the longer run to eliminate such arms'.[1]

---

[1] Even later (in 1998) he received a British knighthood for his services to international understanding.

The atom and hydrogen bomb tests in the atmosphere, which the United States, the Soviet Union and Britain had all carried out, were causing growing and grave alarm among scientists and philosophers. John Kenneth Galbraith, Professor of Economics at Harvard, working that year on his book *The Affluent Society*, made the stark comment: 'Western man has escaped for the moment the poverty which was for so long his all-embracing fate. The unearthly light of a handful of nuclear explosions would signal his return to utter deprivation if, indeed, he survived at all.'

Unlike the American and British nuclear tests, the Soviet nuclear tests were not made public, but reports from scientists in Japan, Britain and the United States made it certain that seven Soviet nuclear tests had taken place in the atmosphere in January, March and April. On April 23 the philosopher and philanthropist Albert Schweitzer sent a letter to the Swedish Nobel Committee – the awarders of the Nobel Prizes – pressing them to 'mobilize' world opinion against the tests. Schweitzer, whose appeal was broadcast by the Nobel Committee in Norwegian, French, German, English and Russian, warned of the 'great and terrible danger to our descendants from radio-activity'. Schweitzer's words were emphatic and ominous:

> By the laws of genetics, the damaging effects were cumulative, and the full results would appear only one hundred or two hundred years later. Even if it is true that when speaking of the dangers of internal radiation, we can point to no actual case but only express our fear, that fear is so solidly founded on facts that it attains the weight of reality in determining our attitude.
>
> We are forced to regard every increase in the existing danger through the further creation of radio-active elements by atomic bomb explosions as a catastrophe for the human race, a catastrophe that must be prevented at all costs.

Schweitzer went on to point out that Japan was the only country in which public opinion was demanding an end to nuclear tests. Britain, the United States and the Soviet Union 'had said they wanted an agreement to end them, but the real reason no agreement was reached was that, in these countries, there was no public opinion asking for it. It was folly through thoughtlessness. When the necessary public opinion had been created the statesmen might reach agreement.'

The British officer who was asked to command the task force during

Britain's nuclear tests at Christmas Island, in the Pacific, was David Strange-ways, who had been in charge of deception operations in the Western Desert and Northern Europe in the Second World War. He was so opposed to the bomb on moral grounds that he obtained permission to retire from the army and take Holy Orders. On May 10 the Soviet Union appealed to Britain to stop all nuclear tests. Five days later Britain exploded its first hydrogen bomb that was in the megaton range. Two further British H-bomb tests followed in swift succession, on May 31 and June 19. Five days before the second test, the Soviet delegate at the United Nations, V. A. Zorin, suggested a two- or three-year moratorium on all nuclear tests. He proposed that the moratorium should be supervised by an international agency with monitoring posts in Russia, Britain, the United States and the Pacific Ocean. The United States delegate produced a counter-proposal for a shorter moratorium of ten months, and with the Soviet Union agreeing to halt the manufacture of all nuclear weapons one month after the control system had been put into effect.

Two nations were not willing to accept any moratorium at all on nuclear testing. One was Britain, which wanted to go ahead with a series of tests that were even then being prepared, and the other was France, which wished to enter the nuclear arms race, and to manufacture and then test its own nuclear weapons.[1]

The continuing public debate on whether nuclear tests could be free of radioactive fall-out roused considerable public alarm. On June 25 President Eisenhower was given a report, quickly made public, that the American nuclear devices that had been exploded in the Nevada Desert were 'about 95 per cent free' of radioactive fall-out. But within a month the United States Atomic Energy Commission published a handbook in which it stated that a 'clean' bomb was an impossibility. This report also made it clear that a new type of conflict between States, 'radiological warfare', could be carried out using low-altitude nuclear explosions which could contaminate large areas beyond the range of the physical damage.

The focus of science on weapons of mass destruction continued. Both the Soviet Union and the United States were developing an intercontinental ballistic missile (ICBM) that could carry a nuclear warhead, and had a range of up to five thousand miles. Britain, not wanting to fall too far behind in the arms race, was developing an intermediate-range ballistic missile (IRBM) with a range of two thousand miles. The United States and the Soviet

---

[1] As I write these words (in May 1998) both India and Pakistan have tested nuclear devices.

Union were also developing the intermediate missile. The progress of these developments was not always smooth. When the United States tested an 'Atlas' intercontinental ballistic missile in June it failed to perform as intended. The missile had to be destroyed during flight by remote control.

The Soviet competition appeared to have the edge. At the end of August the official Soviet news agency announced that the Soviet Union had succeeded in testing an intercontinental ballistic missile at an 'unprecedented altitude', that the missile had covered 'a vast distance', and that it had landed 'in a target area'. The announcement ended: 'The results obtained showed that it is possible to direct rockets into any part of the world.'

To counter the threat of a Soviet air or missile attack across the polar regions a far northern radar defence line was completed in 1957 after thirty months of exceptionally hard work by American and Canadian construction teams. Known as the Distant Early Warning (DEW) Line, its transmitter and receiver stations stretched from Cape Lisburne on the tip of Alaska to Cape Dyer in eastern Canada. An eastward extension, first to Greenland and then to Iceland, was being planned, and was later to be built. The politico-military structure within which the system worked was the North American Air Defence Command (later known as NORAD), the headquarters of which were built deep inside Cheyenne Mountain in Colorado. American and Canadian interceptor bomber squadrons were in the air at all times in case of a warning of attack.

To obtain adequate warning of ballistic missiles flying at 24,000 miles an hour and descending on their targets at an angle of twenty-three degrees – something the DEW Line could not do – the United States began to develop an even more sophisticated and expensive system, the Ballistic Missile Early Warning System (BMEWS), also based on the radar principle which had served all air defence systems so well for almost twenty years. Contracts for the building of the new system were put out to tender at the end of the year. Three sites were chosen: Clear in Alaska, Thule in Greenland and Fylingdales Moor in Yorkshire, England. The station at Thule, built on the permafrost, had at times to withstand winds of up to 160 nautical miles an hour – an indication of how high a priority the needs of defence had become, and of the cost and challenge of the Cold War.

The Soviet Union was also building a defensive line, known in the West as the Krasnodar Array. It was thought to have been begun three years earlier, with its central point just north of the Caucasus.

*   *   *

In seeking to bolster the armed forces of its allies and associates, the United States was spending vast sums of money in military aid. In less than two decades starting in 1948, France received from the United States more than $4,000 million, Turkey and Italy more than $2,000 million each, and Britain and Greece more than $1,000 million each for the purchase of weaponry. Much of this weaponry was purchased from American manufacturers.

On October 4 the Soviet Union perturbed the Western world and astounded the non-aligned nations by launching the first artificial earth satellite into space. The news was announced from Moscow just before midnight. The satellite was called *Sputnik*, and circled the earth in the astonishingly short time of ninety-five minutes. In the United States there was acute embarrassment that the Soviet Union was so advanced in its scientific inventiveness. An attempt to belittle the significance of the Soviet success by Rear-Admiral Rawson-Bennett, of the Office of Naval Research, who described *Sputnik* as 'a hunk of iron almost anybody could launch', did not lessen the American sense of being upstaged and out-manoeuvred. In a response which many Americans felt was somewhat feeble, President Eisenhower proposed a nationwide testing of United States high school students, with incentives for those who wanted to take up scientific studies.

On October 10, six days after the Soviets' spectacular success with *Sputnik*, the United Nations General Assembly began a discussion of nuclear disarmament. Twenty-four nations asked that disarmament talks should be held 'as soon as feasible'. A central aspect of the proposed talks was to seek agreement, in the words of the twenty-four-Power resolution, on 'an inspection system designed to ensure that the sending of objects through outer space would be exclusively for peaceful and scientific purposes'. Six weeks later – with considerable effort being put into the debate by India, Belgium and Yugoslavia – this resolution was passed. Meanwhile, the United States had continued with its tests to launch an intercontinental ballistic missile, capable of carrying a nuclear warhead. A second effort in September had again been unsuccessful, with the missile having to be destroyed in flight. But on the night of October 16 the United States Air Force launching centre in New Mexico fired a rocket into space that sent pellets flying beyond the earth's atmosphere at a speed of 33,000 miles an hour.

The pellets had no specific direction, and did not constitute a targeted intercontinental ballistic missile, though they could provide experimental data to enable a missile to be developed. An extraordinary feature of this experiment (which was not made public for a month) was that, as the speed of the pellets was greater than the velocity needed for an object to escape from the earth's gravitational pull, the pellets continued to travel through interplanetary space with nothing to stop them.[1]

So bright was the rocket blast that it was seen at Mount Palomar Observatory, six hundred miles away.

Even as the problems of nuclear weapons and outer space were creating tensions between the United States and the Soviet Union, the application of the Eisenhower Doctrine was raised again. The catalyst was a crisis between Turkey and Syria – whose long common border generated a host of disputes – that seemed likely to draw in active military support for Syria from the Soviet Union. Large quantities of Soviet arms were known to have reached Syria during the summer, and also a large number of Soviet military advisers.

The Soviet Union also offered Syria £35 million in the form of technical, and largely military, assistance. When the Soviet Foreign Minister, Andrei Gromyko, spoke to the Turkish Prime Minister Adnan Menderes about Turkish troop concentrations on the Turkish-Syrian border, he also warned Menderes that the Soviet Union would support Syria in the event of an attack. The implication was that the Soviet Union was prepared to embark upon active military intervention. This interpretation was underlined when the Soviet cruiser *Zhdanov* reached the Syrian port of Latakia, only twenty-five miles south of the Turkish border.

The crisis intensified, with Gromyko warning of the 'grave danger' of world war, while Khrushchev appealed to the Socialist parties of Western Europe to help avert war. The United States countered by warning the Soviet Union not to intervene on Syria's behalf. On October 16 – the day of the launching of America's New Mexico 'pellet' rocket – Dulles issued a statement that if the Soviet Union attacked Turkey, with whom it shared a border, the United States would not be able to restrict its reaction to a 'purely defensive operation'. Accusing Dulles and the Americans of 'brinkmanship', the Soviet Union decided not to push the confrontation further. In a typical Khrushchevian gesture, the Soviet leader turned up unexpectedly at a Turkish diplomatic reception in Moscow and announced that his appearance there was a 'a gesture to peace'.

The year had seen several manifestations of potential nuclear confrontation, from China to Turkey. The debate about whether or not the United States

[1] Perhaps they are travelling there still.

would or should use nuclear weapons had become one of polarities. There were those who argued that an all-out nuclear war had to be contemplated, others who insisted that it should be ruled out entirely as an option. A middle way was also postulated, most persuasively by a Harvard professor, Henry Kissinger, who had left Germany for the United States as a teenager in 1938, and whose book *Nuclear Weapons and Foreign Policy* argued the case for a doctrine of limited nuclear war. 'The enormity of modern weapons makes the thought of war repugnant,' Kissinger wrote, 'but the refusal to run any risks would amount to giving the Soviet rulers a blank cheque.' If the United States decided to limit its options either to a conventional war or to a nuclear war, with nothing in between, it could, he feared, 'play into the hands of the Soviet strategy of ambiguity which seeks to upset the strategic balance by small degrees'.

In *Nuclear Weapons and Foreign Policy* Kissinger highlighted the central issue of deterrence, which was to come to dominate Western thinking over the next forty years. 'The greater the horror of our destructive capabilities,' he wrote, 'the less certain has it become that they will in fact be used.' To devise defence policy based upon 'limited nuclear war', he concluded, 'represents our most effective strategy'.

On October 28 a conference opened in Delhi, under the auspices of the International Committee of the Red Cross (ICRC) in which the delegates of eighty-three nations passed a series of resolutions seeking to prohibit atomic experiments which polluted global air and water. But the resolutions had no impact on the race for nuclear mastery which was being enacted: at a conference in London in November a member of the Soviet Embassy, O. K. Sapounov, gave an account of Soviet scientists who were developing a 'photon rocket' which would be driven by elementary particles – photons – travelling at the speed of light. Four decades later no such rocket had come into being.

On November 4, scarcely a month after the first Soviet success with an orbiting satellite, there was a second Soviet achievement, the launching of *Sputnik 2*. This satellite was placed into orbit with a dog – named Laika – on board. The presence of Laika would enable Soviet scientists to study living conditions in space. 'This second achievement', wrote Anthony Smith, Science Correspondent of the *Daily Telegraph*, 'completely eclipses the first, for the new satellite, weighing half a ton, is just over six times heavier than the first, which weighed 184 lbs, and includes an air-conditioned chamber containing a living dog.'

It was the presence of Laika that created an initial upsurge of anger. From

London, the executive committee of the League Against Cruel Sports called upon 'all humane people in every country to express their horror, disgust and contempt' for the Russian scientists' action. The League urged the United Nations to outlaw 'such foul experiments'. Anthony Smith's report ended: 'The National Canine Defence League is asking dog-lovers to observe a silent minute each day, with special thoughts for Laika's early and safe return to earth. Officers of the League will call at the Russian Embassy at 11 a.m. today to lodge a protest.'

There was also a more universal aspect to Laika's flight in space. In the House of Commons the British Prime Minister, Harold Macmillan, declared that if the 'free peoples' were to defend themselves successfully they must develop a dynamism equal to that of the Soviet Union. 'I believe this to be a real turning point in history,' he said.

It was not the Soviet dog in space, but the nuclear testing programmes of the two Super Powers, that most agitated world opinion that winter. On November 28 Nehru appealed to both the United States and the Soviet Union to suspend their atomic testing programmes. Both Bulganin and Eisenhower said they were willing to do so, as part of a comprehensive global agreement. Meanwhile the testing went on. On December 6 there was a widely publicized attempt at the testing site on Cape Canaveral, Florida, to launch a grapefruit-sized American satellite. The rocket which was to have launched it exploded on the ground. On December 17, however, the American attempt to launch an intercontinental ballistic missile was finally successful. Tested over a more limited range than the earlier failed experiments, one such missile found its target.

Britain was also embarking on long-range missile tests capable of carrying nuclear warheads. At the Woomera rocket range in Australia a British missile with a range of two thousand miles was successfully fired, and travelled towards its target at 2,500 miles an hour.

In France, the debate over Algeria remained a violent one. Other than members of the French Communist Party there were at first few French people prepared to envisage full independence for Algeria. More than any other nation, the French believed in their 'civilizing mission'. Algiers had been annexed to France more than a century earlier. Since 1882 the departments of Algiers, Oran and Constantine had been an 'integral part' of metropolitan France. The will to remain in Algiers was strong. Yet the means of remaining alienated more and more people, especially in academic and intellectual circles. Increasingly well-authenticated stories of the torture of Algerians by the French forces in Algeria caused growing distress. The government of Maurice Bourgès-Manoury, who had succeeded Guy Mollet as Prime Minister in June, countered the atrocity charges by issuing a report showing that the rebel atrocities were 'far worse' than anything of which the French forces were guilty.

Acts of terror, already frequent inside Algeria, spread to France. By July it was estimated that two of the 300,000 Algerians resident in France were being killed every day, many by fellow Muslims who were demanding a stronger commitment to independence. On July 19, five days after the French national day, the government in Paris promulgated special powers of arrest and detention with regard to 'all persons born in Algeria, whatever their place of residence'. Many delegates in the Assembly – not only the Communists – protested that discrimination against French citizens by reason of race, colour, creed or origin was contrary to the Declaration of the Rights of Man, on which French liberties were based.

Inside Algeria, General Massu led a sustained campaign, including the use of parachute troops, against the nationalists. An electrified barrier was built along the border with Tunisia, to prevent arms being smuggled into Algeria. The nationalists were not deterred. After local council elections, a hundred Muslims who took office were murdered by their compatriots. Martial law and censorship remained the only answers used by the French authorities.

Ideological differences were not allowed to interfere with the steady progress of international travel. On December 19 the first regular London-Moscow air service was opened. Nor did ideological differences inhibit the United Nations International Children's Emergency Fund (UNICEF) from carrying on its humanitarian work. Despite the Hungarian government's refusal to allow a United Nations inquiry commission on to Hungarian soil, a feeding programme was set up for ten thousand children in Hungary. By the end of the year, UNICEF estimated that it had extended help worldwide to forty-five million mothers and children in more than a hundred countries. An estimated six million mothers and children, in sixty-nine countries, were in receipt of free milk. The system was not a one-way flow of financial assistance. In most cases the recipient countries had contributed two and a half times as much to the aid programme as the United Nations in what were known as 'matching funds'.

The World Health Organization was also continually extending its areas of operations and effectiveness. During 1957 forty-two million people were tested for malaria and sixteen million vaccinated, bringing the number of those vaccinated in the previous decade to 211 million. In ten countries malaria had been wiped out, and partially eradicated in another sixteen. There were plans to extend the anti-malaria campaign to another thirty-eight countries. Other campaigns were being pressed forward against yaws, trachoma and leprosy. Help was also sent behind the Iron Curtain, with Poland being assisted in its fight against measles and infectious hepatitis, and an anti-tuberculosis vaccination campaign was being devised for five million babies and young people in Yugoslavia. When there was an outbreak of polio in Hungary in August, the United States agreed to a World Health Organization request to send the Salk vaccine there to fight the epidemic.

The efforts of the experts and fieldworkers on these United Nations campaigns received relatively little publicity. The main focus of attention was almost always on the United Nations' political sessions, especially in 1957 on the attempts to regulate the testing of nuclear weapons. But the specialized agencies worked at the grass-roots level where poverty and disease were widespread, but where the means, and the will, to tackle them existed.

More than a decade had passed since the end of the Second World War. Memories were merged into and overtaken by the claims of a new age. On July 1 a hundred-mile section of the once notorious Burma railway, built at such high cost in the lives of Allied prisoners of war and Burmese slave labourers, was reopened to civilian traffic. It was used as an ordinary railway, appearing in timetables, for which tickets could be purchased and journeys made without hazard or fear. The railway, which at one point crossed the bridge over the River Kwai that had been built by Allied prisoners of war in conditions worse than slavery, also became a regular route of pilgrimage for the widows and children of prisoners of war. The Allied cemetery at Kanchanaburi was a focal point of their journey of remembrance. By 1987, thirty years after the railway was opened, a special tourist train of the State Railway of Thailand left Bangkok every morning to make the hundred-mile journey. The rest of the railway, over the mountains into Burma, had long since been swallowed up by the jungle.

Films also recalled the torments of war. David Lean's *The Bridge on the River Kwai*, based on a novel by Pierre Boulle, and starring Alec Guinness, portrayed the cruel plight of the prisoners of war forced to build the bridge.

It was seen by 235 million film-goers within its first two years. Neither of its screenwriters, Carl Foreman and Michael Wilson, were able to receive the Academy Award given for their work, as both were under the frown of the McCarthyite accusations. In the film, to make a dramatic ending, the bridge was destroyed; in reality, it had survived the war. It had taken the slave labourers two months to build; for the film-makers, using professional engineers, it took eight months, on location in Ceylon.

In 1957 an Asian influenza pandemic, known as 'Asian 'flu', constituted the worst global epidemic since the end of the First World War, when a different strain of influenza killed an estimated twenty million people – far more than the war itself. In the 1957 epidemic 7,000 people died in Japan and 16,000 in Britain. In the United States the number of deaths reached 70,000, mostly the very young, the elderly and the infirm. The virus arrived in the United States from Asia in the summer. It was first reported on June 2 in Newport, Rhode Island, where naval exercises were being held offshore. Nine days later it appeared at several army bases in California. By September it was rampant in New York City. By mid-October, when seven million people had been vaccinated in the United States, and another twenty million vaccines were ready for use, the worst was over.

Worldwide, the Asian 'flu killed more than a million people in two years. In Ethiopia, in the following years, a malaria epidemic in the central and northern highlands killed 175,000 people between June and December. By October there were not enough healthy people to care for the sick, and a vast acreage of unattended crops was eaten by wildlife. Hundreds of thousands of infected children who survived were damaged by malaria parasites remaining in their blood, making them susceptible to other infections. In Africa the curse of disease was endemic. In the fight against it, the victories, like those in war, were not always decisive.

CHAPTER SEVEN

1958

I still believe that kinder times will come . . .

BORIS PASTERNAK

On 1 January 1958 the European Economic Community came into being. It consisted of six countries, Belgium, France, West Germany, the Netherlands, Italy and Luxembourg. They constituted a 'common market' which they hoped would eventually embrace the whole of Western Europe, and Eastern Europe as well. This could happen only if the countries under Soviet rule and control – the 'satellites' of current terminology – were to break free. This appeared unlikely in the foreseeable future, given the ill-omen of Hungary two years earlier and the more recent repression in Poland and East Germany. January 1 also saw elements of the West German armed forces – including two armoured divisions – placed under NATO command.

In the Cold War confrontation, NATO was a shield not only for West Germany. In his State of the Union message to both Houses of Congress on January 9, Eisenhower tried to put the minds of the American people at rest, and to give them confidence that there would be no American weakness with regard to the Soviet Union. 'We have now a broadly based and efficient defensive strength,' he said, 'including a great deterrent power, which is, for the present, our best guarantee against war.' Four days later Eisenhower sent Congress a $73 billion expenditure budget of which sixty-four per cent was for defence spending and foreign aid. Eisenhower was confronted by a Democrat-controlled Congress, but as a result of the support which he received from the Senate majority leader, Lyndon Johnson, and the House Speaker, Sam Rayburn, the budget was passed, as was an 'emergency' appropriation of $1.3 billion to accelerate missile and space development.

The Soviet Union realized that NATO was able to gain the support of all nations on the periphery of the Soviet bloc, except those like Austria and

Switzerland that were specifically neutral. In an attempt to dissuade Greece from making a commitment to the Western alliance, on January 20 the Russians threatened to impose economic sanctions if it allowed NATO missiles to be based on Greek soil.

Western European unity continued to be an ideal expressed through small economic groupings. On February 3 the Prime Ministers of three nations, Belgium, the Netherlands and Luxembourg, signed a treaty in The Hague establishing the 'Benelux' Economic Union. The treaty provided for the free flow of capital, services and traffic of persons between the three countries. Also signing the treaty was the Dutch Foreign Minister, Dr Joseph Luns, who was subsequently Secretary-General of NATO and a strong advocate of a common European defence as well as economic policy.

The United States had no intention of allowing the Soviet Union to be the only Power in space. On the morning of January 31 the first United States satellite, *Explorer 1*, was sent into orbit. An army-launched satellite, it weighed far less than either of the Soviet *Sputniks*, but it penetrated deeper into space than either of them. The director of the United States satellite programme of which it marked the first triumph was Dr Werner von Braun, one of the German rocket experts who had worked during the Second World War on the V2 rocket, Hitler's last secret weapon.

The task of *Explorer 1* was to study cosmic rays. Its launch marked a psychological turning point of the Cold War. In the words of the *New York Herald Tribune*: 'At precisely 10.55 p.m. (EST) on January 31, 1958, the United States of America regained its national pride.' Despite the failure of *Explorer 2* to get into orbit six weeks later, four more United States satellites were to be launched in the next six months. *Vanguard 1* was launched on March 17 to test solar cells; *Explorer 3* on March 26 (to study cosmic rays and meteors); another satellite on April 23 (to study radiation above six hundred miles, with a mouse on board); and *Explorer 4* on July 26.

The satellite with the mouse was the one that caused the most public interest. Instead of appearing as was planned at a 'victory press conference' with Eisenhower, as John Thompson reported from New York for the *Daily Express*, 'the mouse met its death in the nose cone of an Air Force rocket that came down several thousand miles short of its target'. Ships had been waiting in the drop zone to rescue the mouse and bring it triumphantly ashore. It was not only, or even primarily, to provide information about animal reactions to conditions encountered in space that the Thor rocket had been launched. Writing in the *New York Times*, Richard Witkin explained:

In the nose cone research, the Air Force is trying out an advanced technique for protecting the nuclear warhead from re-entry heat. This heat is generated by air friction when the missile re-enters the atmosphere from the almost airless upper regions.

Nose cones developed for the Atlas and Thor, first generation intercontinental and intermediate range ballistic missiles, are made of copper and are blunt shaped. They cope with heat by absorption in the thick metal shield, and by creation of shock waves that rapidly slow the descent.

The advanced approach tried last week uses the technique of 'ablation', a term meaning removal, as in surgery. An ablative nose cone is made of light materials, such as Fiberglas, which burn and fall away as the missile re-enters the atmosphere.

The Army uses an advanced ablative nose cone on its Jupiter IRBM. A scale model, fired on the nose of a three-stage Jupiter-C test vehicle, was recovered and displayed on television by President Eisenhower last year. But a number of technical difficulties remain to be ironed out.

And ablative nose cone has several advantages.

It makes its final penetration more sharply and swiftly. This increases the difficulty of anti missile defense. It also makes for greater accuracy by minimizing the time the nose cone will be subjected to atmospheric winds.

Nuclear testing in the atmosphere having roused the concern of scientists worldwide, there was a strong public demand for a halt to what was becoming seen as a long-term life-endangering activity. On February 17 the British Campaign for Nuclear Disarmament (CND) held its first public meeting, in Trafalgar Square. Among the speakers was the philosopher and First World War pacifist Bertrand Russell, who said that the issue of nuclear disarmament was the most important that had ever arisen in the history of man. 'I think it is of the utmost importance to get the world to understand it,' he said. 'I believe if they understood it, everyone would agree with us.' Hydrogen bomb tests were doing damage to mankind which was greater than most people realized, 'and a great deal greater than governments are willing to admit'. Russell went on to warn:

If you give one man cancer deliberately, or cause one child to be born mentally defective, you are thought to be a monster. But if you cause 50,000 cancers you are a great patriot.

It seems odd that the same Governments which spend a great deal of money in expensive research on how to prevent cancer spend a great deal of money on still more expensive research on how to cause cancer.

Russell was pro-Russian as well as anti-nuclear. This made his advocacy of the anti-nuclear cause suspect for those who feared a Soviet threat. Of relations between the Soviet Union and the West, Russell said that 'when Russia made any proposals of any sort we were always told they were insincere'.

The chairman of the meeting, Canon Collins, had another point of criticism, castigating 'the timid Church leaders who fear to give offence to the established set-up'. He had accepted the chair of the meeting, he said, because he believed that 'the question of whether we arm ourselves with nuclear weapons is the supreme moral issue of the day'. Collins added: 'That a so-called Christian nation could even contemplate using hydrogen bombs in defence of even the highest values, seems to me a cause of shame. How can a Christian or a liberal man or woman countenance such a denial of the principle that love alone can cast out fear? The Archbishop of Canterbury, and others in the Church who think or speak like him, appears to think that it is fear that makes the world go round.'

On February 28, eleven days after this first anti-nuclear weapons demonstration, NATO officers in Italy watched an 'Honest John' missile being test fired – without its nuclear warhead.

On March 31 the Soviet Union announced that it was suspending the testing of nuclear weapons for six months. On April 7, a week after the Soviet announcement, CND held a march from the British nuclear research centre at Aldermaston to London. While the marchers were still on their way towards the capital, Eisenhower proposed, on April 8, the establishment of mutually agreed testing as a means of enforcing a total test ban. Eisenhower also continued to try to reverse, at least in the long term, the humiliation suffered by the United States by the launching of the two successful Soviet space satellites. To this end he introduced the National Defense Education Act, which authorized $4 billion of federal assistance over four years for higher education, including student loans, and the teaching of science, mathematics and modern languages.

That summer, on July 29, Eisenhower also created a new federal body, the National Aeronautics and Space Administration (NASA). Its first aim was not to administer space, but to enter it.

*   *   *

On April 16 South Africa went to the polls. The result was another clear victory for the Nationalist Party. In the previous parliament it held ninety-six seats. These were increased to 103. The United Party added only one seat to its previous fifty-two. The Coloureds' representatives and the Africans' representatives received their fixed four and three seats respectively. The only time that a political Party had won more than 103 seats was when the United Party won 111 seats in 1938. In the twenty years since then the White supremacist, apartheid-supporting vote had come to dominate the legislative process.

There was, however, a distorting element in the result, even with the White electorate: most United Party voters were concentrated in a few urban areas, while the voting system gave greater value in electoral terms to rural voters, where the Nationalists predominated. The United Party had actually polled the largest number of votes, 700,000, while the Nationalist Party obtained 650,000. Not only was the central democratic concept of 'one man one vote' completely negated with regard to Coloureds and Africans, but even in the White context it was used in such a way as to negate a demographically fair outcome.

Four months after the election the Prime Minister, J. G. Strijdom, died. He was succeeded by Dr Verwoerd, the Minister of Native Affairs, who had long shown himself an implacable supporter of every element of apartheid. Added to that, his wartime pro-Nazi leanings had long alienated him from the members of the parliamentary opposition, and from liberal-minded South Africans everywhere. The African National Congress was especially dismayed. 'Dr Verwoerd, as Minister of Native Affairs, pursued apartheid in all its naked ruthlessness and callousness,' it declared. 'His appointment is yet another demonstration of the extent to which the Nationalist Party is committed to a policy of reaction and extremism.'

As in previous years, the United Nations General Assembly expressed its 'regret and concern' – during a session on October 21 – at the failure of the South African government to respond to its previous appeals for an end to apartheid. The United Nations also asked South Africa to enter into negotiations with the governments of India and Pakistan with a view to improving the position of South Africans of Indian origin. Both sets of requests fell on deaf ears. Dr Verwoerd was not going to defer to outside pressure any more than J. D. Strijdom had done. Apartheid would continue, and its rules would be meticulously enforced.

*   *   *

Troubled elements of the British imperial past continued to distract the present, with its emphasis on the peaceful transfer of power from rulers to ruled. In the Aden Protectorate a thousand Adeni rebels, encouraged to do so by the ruler of neighbouring Yemen, attacked a platoon of Protectorate government guards in an isolated fort, trapping them and the British resident political adviser inside. For four days the siege continued, until British troops arrived and drove the rebels away.

There were six Protectorate States in Aden. The ruler of one of them, Sultan Sir Ali bin Abdul al Karim, was banned from his territory for failing to co-operate with the British, and allowing the defection to Yemen of two brothers sought by the Governor of Aden for 'attempting to subvert' the loyalty of the Adeni troops serving under the British. The Sultan found refuge in Cairo. The five other rulers travelled to London and agreed to set up a federation, within the British colonial administration, and with British military and financial assistance. At the same time, in Aden itself, the Aden Colony (Amendment) Order reconstituted the Legislative Council, to allow more local elected representation on it. It was to be almost a decade before Britain transferred power to a National Liberation Front, bringing 129 years of British rule to an end, and leading to the formation of a People's Republic of South Yemen.

Cyprus was in even greater turmoil than the Aden Protectorate. After British negotiations for a partnership between the Greek and Turkish governments in any future settlement on the island, Archbishop Makarios announced that after a fixed period of self-government Cyprus should become an independent State linked neither to Turkey nor Greece. Most Greek Cypriots applauded this, as did EOKA, the guerrilla movement under Colonel Grivas.

The period of discussions was paralleled by several different forms of violence. The year began with attacks by Turkish Cypriots on British troops, when five Turkish Cypriots were killed. This was followed by fighting between Turkish Cypriots and Greek Cypriots. Then there were killings by EOKA against Greek Cypriots suspected of not supporting Cypriot independence. A fourth type of killing was that by EOKA against British soldiers and their families. After the wife of a British soldier was shot in the back while shopping in Famagusta on October 3, British troops rounded up 650 Greek Cypriots and beat up 250 of them. As tensions rose, British civilians were armed and a renewed search for EOKA members was carried out, culminating in the killing of a leading EOKA fighter, Kyriachos Matsis.

The colonial struggles that continued to tie down more than a million British National Servicemen, conscripts for a two-year period, included the Malay States, whose Federation, created in 1948, had become independent in 1957. At one moment, to protect the elected government, 40,000 British troops were in action against 3,250 Communist guerrillas. During 1958, after a decade of fighting, the British forces finally drove the remaining four hundred Chinese Communist guerrillas, led throughout this period by Chin Peng, into the wilds of the Malay–Thailand border, after which they continued to operate, but only spasmodically, from the Thai side of the border. The United States as well as Britain encouraged the government of Thailand to take action of its own against these guerrillas.

Among the Great Powers and those associated with them the calls for nuclear disarmament and the strengthening of the opposing power blocs continued in tandem. On May 8 John Foster Dulles, speaking in Berlin, stated that the United States would regard an attack on Berlin as an attack on the Western Allies. The very talk of 'Allies' conjured up the language of the Second World War, though with the Soviet Union clearly on the opposite side, and West Germany within the Western camp.

Soviet scientific prowess was again demonstrated on May 15, when *Sputnik 3* was placed into orbit. Its purpose was to carry out aerodynamic studies. But its launch was accompanied by many Soviet newspaper discussions, all of them officially inspired, on the ability of the Soviet Union to deliver 'annihilating blows', understood to be of a nuclear type, on any enemy that embarked on a nuclear war against it.

Soviet nuclear tests in the atmosphere had continued. Only when a considerable series of such tests was completed did the Soviet government announce that it intended to end nuclear testing 'unilaterally'. There was considerable derision in the West that this announcement came so soon after such a significant bout of testing. But it was also clear that this was an area of considerable public concern worldwide, and one where agreement might be possible. The offer to stop testing unilaterally was made by the Supreme Soviet on March 31. Little over a month later, on May 9, the Soviet Union accepted the Western proposal, that had been put forward a year earlier, for technical talks to be held by the three nuclear powers – the Soviet Union, the United States and Britain – to see if a system was possible to control and monitor the suspension of nuclear testing.

Talks to this end opened at Geneva on July 1. They made some progress, but were impeded psychologically when the Soviet Union announced on September 18 that it was about to resume tests, in order to catch up with the West, which had continued its own test programmes during the summer. Although the talks continued at Geneva, the element of trust needed if a verification system was to emerge had all but disappeared.

On July 3, two days after the first conference of experts had opened in Geneva to discuss the detection of nuclear explosions, the United States and Britain signed their own bilateral agreement for co-operation in the development of nuclear weapons. Twenty days later a nuclear-powered United States submarine, the USS *Nautilus*, left Pearl Harbor. Its engines were powered by uranium. Passing through the Bering Straits – which separate the United States from the Soviet Union between Alaska and Siberia – it made its way under the pack ice on August 1, sailed underneath the North Pole three days later, and emerged from the pack ice east of Greenland on August 5. In its ninety-six-hour journey under the ice it had covered 1,830 miles. Eight days later it docked at Portland, on the south coast of Britain.

More than nine-tenths of the journey of the *Nautilus* had been under water. In a report published in the *Daily Telegraph* on August 9, Hanson Baldwin noted the defence aspects of the submarine's triumph with regard to the confrontation of the Super Powers:

> Three military capabilities for Arctic submarine operations are immediately foreseeable. Potentially the most important in a strategic sense is the use of the Arctic for the launching of guided missiles from submarines.
>
> The fleet ballistic missile *Polaris*, a two-stage solid fuel rocket with a range of 1,000 to 1,500 miles and a powerful thermo-nuclear warhead, is now under development.
>
> It has been designed for launching from a submerged submarine at considerable depths. Nine nuclear powered submarines each capable of launching sixteen of the Polaris type missiles have been appropriated for by Congress.
>
> Each is much larger than the *Nautilus*. The first, complete with missiles, is expected to be ready in late 1960 or early 1961.

Hanson Baldwin noted the comments of Commander Robert McWerthy, a United States Navy specialist on missile technology, who observed that even in the Arctic pack ice there were areas of open water and thin ice through which a submarine could take tactical advantage. Baldwin added:

> Using these open or thin spots in the ice pack to put up a periscope occasionally, a missile firing submarine could range pretty much at will – and secure from detection of any sort – across the Arctic.
>
> She could fire her missiles at points of her own choosing and, as Cdr. McWerthy pointed out, from 'the ice pack east of Spitzbergen' the distance to Murmansk is about 400 miles and it is 1,180 miles to Leningrad and 1,420 miles to Moscow, all well within the range of the ultimate *Polaris*.
>
> The missile firing submarine manoeuvring in the Arctic opens a new strategic frontier. The whole vast Arctic coastline of Russia is potentially open to assault.

The triumph of science, and its indication of America's clear military advantage in the nuclear age, could not mask economic and social problems even in the world's most industrialized and productive nation. In the spring, unemployment had reached above five million. The percentage of the unemployed among the Black population was proportionately higher. Eisenhower announced in March a $3 billion budget for housing and highway construction, and for land reclamation.

The sight of a Republican administration acting along Democrat, interventionist lines puzzled and even angered the Party purists. But on March 10, two days after Eisenhower had announced his public works programme, the Vice-President, Richard Nixon, said that the time had passed in the nation's history when the Federal Government 'can stand by and allow a recession to be prolonged or deepen into a depression without decisive government action'. That action had its effect. By the end of the year more than a million of the unemployed were back at work.

In Algeria, the French air force struck at what it believed were concentrations of Algerian rebels – members of the Front de la Libération Nationale (the FLN) – and their military supplies, on the Algeria–Tunisia border. The raid was intended as a reprisal against the repeated attacks by the FLN on French installations and personnel. The French bombs fell on the village of Sakiet Sidi Youssef, a Tunisian border village half a mile inside Tunisia. Seventy-nine people were killed. Tunisia appealed to the Security Council to censure this 'deliberate act of aggression'. The French replied that Tunisia had become the main staging post for supplies being sent to the FLN.

During the spring the French settlers in Algeria became alarmed at the realization that the French government was willing to negotiate with the Algerian nationalists. On May 15, as the protests deepened, with a massive demonstration by 'National Frenchmen' at the Unknown Soldier's monument in Algiers, General de Gaulle, who had been in effective retirement for more than a decade, expressed his willingness 'to assume the powers of the Republic'. On the following day, as the French settlers continued to demand that no concessions be made to the Muslim Arab demands of the National Liberation Front, a new French government – formed two days earlier by Pierre Pflimlin – obtained parliamentary approval for emergency powers, to last for three months.

Pflimlin promised that he would intensify the military measures against the National Liberation Front. But he also intimated that he was willing to enter negotiations with the FLN for a ceasefire, and to enlist the good offices of both Morocco and Tunisia to this end. Neither the European population in Algeria nor the right wing in France were willing to contemplate such negotiations – except with revulsion. There had already, on May 13, been demonstrations in both Algiers and Paris against any such negotiations. The '13th of May Movement' gathered momentum with every day that passed.

Inside Algeria the settlers demanded stronger French action against the FLN. Inside France opinion was sharply divided between those who wanted the Europeans to be supported and those who wanted negotiations with the nationalists. In Algiers, and the other main towns in Algeria, Committees of Public Safety were set up by the Europeans, who called on de Gaulle to return to power, to form a Government of Public Safety, and to help them maintain the authority of France in Algeria.

In a gesture of defiance, on May 24, despatched by the Algerian settlers' leaders, French parachute units based in Algeria landed in Corsica. There they set up Committees of Public Safety, and called for de Gaulle to come to power and to maintain French rule in Algeria. Senior French army officers stationed in Algeria pledged their support for this call. They were encouraged to do so when de Gaulle, at a press conference on May 19, paid tribute to the 'achievements' of the army in Algeria.

Fearing that those who had carried out the parachute action in Algeria might try to do the same in France, a Committee of National Action for Republican Defence was formed. On May 28 Pflimlin resigned, but agreed to remain in office until a successor could be found. As soon as the news of his resignation became known 200,000 Parisians marched through the capital, fearful of a coup d'état by supporters of the French Algerian army and its leaders. On May 29 de Gaulle was asked by the President, Pierre Coty, to form a government. He accepted, and won a parliamentary majority on June 1, obtaining 329 votes against 224.

On June 2 de Gaulle was granted emergency powers for three months. He at once curbed the powers of the Committees of Public Safety in Algeria, which had been among the strongest supporters of his coming to power. Their call was for 'integration' with France. De Gaulle studiously avoided using the word. Instead, crossing to Algeria, he set out a ten-year programme whereby France would extend education and modernize Algerian industry and agriculture, and he offered all Algerians, including the Muslim majority, the status of 'Frenchmen with full citizenship'. The people of Algeria would not only have the vote, but their vote would 'carry exactly the same weight as those of all other Frenchmen'.

To the distress of those who wanted the FLN crushed, de Gaulle also made several pointed references in his public speeches to the courage of the nationalist rebels, and on June 4 went so far as to offer to 'open the door to reconciliation'. Algeria's political future, he pledged on June 27, would be settled by its elected representatives, Europeans and Muslims alike.

On becoming Prime Minister, de Gaulle had been granted the power to draw up a new constitution for France. The new constitution, establishing a Fifth Republic, was approved on September 23. It included the recognition by France of the right of its overseas territories to independence. A month later de Gaulle announced that he was willing to discuss a ceasefire with the FLN. They rejected his offer of talks, however, and continued with their armed struggle.

In French West Africa and French Equatorial Africa, de Gaulle also tried to meet the growing nationalist aspirations. An important step came when, on July 24, he agreed that the Vice-Presidents of the Government Councils – all of whom were Africans – should have the status and authority of Prime Minister when dealing with matters that came within the sphere of African autonomy.

While France struggled to work out what its future would be in predominantly Muslim Algeria, another Islamic county, Iraq, moved to the centre of world attention – and Western concern – when, on July 14, the royal regime was overthrown and a republic proclaimed. The coup d'état which effected this change was a bloody one. Among those assassinated in Baghdad that day were King Feisal and at least ten members of the royal family. The Prime Minister, Nuri es-Said, escaped in disguise, but was caught on the following day and killed. Nuri had been the pre-eminent Iraqi politician and national leader since after the First World War, when he had been Chief of Staff to the Arab Revolt. He had been Prime Minister at different times for a span of twenty-eight years. Although he had supported Colonel Nasser at the time of Suez, he was not regarded by those Iraqis who shot him down as a sufficiently staunch supporter of Arab nationalism. Egypt and Syria had come together in a loose but much vaunted union, the United Arab Republic (UAR), and made much of their independent, anti-Western and pan-Arab stance.

In turning against the Hashemites who had ruled Iraq since the First World War – they had come from Arabia at the head of the largely Bedouin armies of the Arab Revolt – the new ruler, Brigadier Abdul Karim Kassem, denounced them as 'a corrupt gang imposed on the country by imperialism'. The victory of Brigadier Kassem was hailed by President Nasser as an 'outstanding victory' over imperialism. But the British military garrison at Habbaniya – which had been besieged by Iraqi nationalists in 1941 – was left alone, and Iraq remained a member of the Western-oriented Baghdad Pact, but only until the following year.

Fearing that the Iraqi revolution would spread to, and destabilize, the fragile balance between Christians and Muslims in the Lebanon, on the day of the coup in Baghdad the Lebanese government appealed to the United States for help. That day American troops from the United States Sixth Fleet landed in Beirut. Egypt, China and the Soviet Union protested, but the troops remained. Lebanese government efforts to disarm the local militia met with violent resistance. Lebanese Christian and Lebanese Muslim extremists clashed in the streets, and there was a spate of kidnappings. In an effort to calm the situation, with the active help of American diplomats the new Prime Minister, Rashid Karami, a Muslim, agreed to take Christians into his government. The disarmament of civilians was undertaken with some success, and the American troops withdrew.

The Iraqi revolution also had its impact on Jordan, whose King, Hussein – the grandson of the murdered Abdullah – was a cousin of the murdered Iraqi monarch, and, like him, a Hashemite. To maintain the Jordanian kingdom and monarchy, two thousand British troops were flown into Jordan on July 17 and 18, landing at Mafrak, fifty miles north of the Jordanian capital. Further British troops later arrived by ship at Akaba, on the Red Sea. The Soviet Union, China and Egypt protested. King Hussein appealed for 'mutual forbearance' from his Arab neighbours, and appeased their anger by removing the British troops. But he remained vigilant against a possible Syrian attack, and when his plane was ordered to land at Damascus and then attacked by Syrian MiG fighters as he was flying over Syria on his way to a holiday in Europe, the King ignored the order and returned to Amman. Ill-feeling between the two countries was heightened.

In China, the Great Leap Forward was entering its second year. Mao Tse-tung, having made his second visit to Moscow at the end of 1957, was searching for a different form of Communist activism from that which he had seen in the Soviet Union, which to his mind was more like stagnation than revolution. Thirty years earlier the Soviet Communists had rejected the idea of permanent revolution as a Trotskyist heresy. But, as a historian of modern China, Jonathan D. Spence, has written, 'Mao boldly seized on a similar concept with a different label in an attempt to give "continuing revolution" new respectability as a Chinese contribution to revolutionary theory and practice.' Spence quotes from an internal document that Mao circulated to senior Chinese Communists in February 1958. It was headed 'Continuing revolution':

> Our revolutions come one after another. Starting from the seizure of power in the whole country in 1949, there followed in quick succession the anti-feudal land reform, the agricultural co-operativization, and the socialist reconstruction of private industries, commerce, and handicrafts . . .
>
> Now we must start a technological revolution so that we may overtake Britain in fifteen or more years . . .
>
> After fifteen years, when our foodstuffs and iron and steel become plentiful, we shall take a much greater initiative. Our revolutions are like battles. After a victory, we must at once put forward a new task. In this way, cadres and the masses will forever be filled with revolutionary fervour, instead of conceit. Indeed, they will have no time for conceit, even if they like to feel conceited. With new tasks on their shoulders, they are totally preoccupied with the problems for their fulfillment.

One aspect of the Great Leap Forward was the abolition of private plots of land and the amalgamation of existing co-operative farms into much vaster communes. In April twenty-seven co-operative farms in the Province of Honan were turned into a single commune of almost ten thousand households – in all, 43,000 people. The Communist Party Central Committee called these communes the 'logical result of the march of events', a natural stage in the 'all-round, continuous leap forward in China's agricultural production and the ever-rising political consciousness of the 500 million peasants'.

By the end of the year 740,000 co-operative farms had been merged into 26,000 communes. These encompassed 120 million rural households, virtually the whole Chinese peasantry – the official Chinese figure was 90.4 percent. Hardship, starvation, economic disruption, had no part in the way in which the Great Leap Forward was presented, although they were often its realities. Labour battalions received less than six hours' rest in every twenty-four hours. After working with almost no breaks from 5 a.m. to 6 p.m. the Commune workers had then to do compulsory small-arms drill.

When the Central Committee published the version of the experiment by which it wished it to be judged, there were no such things as failure or setbacks, chaos or confusion, an actual shortfall in grain production, or a drop in steel production as more than a million steel furnaces were dispersed throughout China, literally to become part of a million backyards. The Central Committee promoted the vision:

Community dining rooms, kindergartens, nurseries, sewing groups, barber shops, public baths, happy homes for the aged, agricultural middle schools, 'red and expert' schools, are leading the peasants toward a happier collective life and further fostering ideas of collectivism among the peasant masses . . .

In the present circumstances, the establishment of people's communes with all-round management of agriculture, forestry, animal husbandry, side occupations, and fishery, where industry (the worker), agriculture (the peasant), exchange (the trader), culture and education (the student), and military affairs (the militiaman) merge into one, is the fundamental policy to guide the peasants to accelerate socialist construction, complete the building of socialism ahead of time, and carry out the gradual transition to Communism.

Jung Chang, who was six years old in the autumn of 1958, recalled the reality of the Great Leap Forward, and the steel campaign, as experienced by a child:

Every day on my way to and from school, I screwed up my eyes to search every inch of ground for broken nails, rusty cogs, and any other metal objects that had been trodden into the mud between the cobbles. These were for feeding into furnaces to produce steel, which was my major occupation.

Yes, at the age of six, I was involved in steel production, and had to compete with my schoolmates at handing in the most scrap iron. All around me uplifting music blared from loud-speakers, and there were banners, posters, and huge slogans painted on the walls proclaiming 'Long Live the Great Leap Forward!' and 'Everybody, Make Steel!'

Although I did not fully understand why, I knew that Chairman Mao had ordered the nation to make a lot of steel. In my school, crucible-like vats had replaced some of our cooking woks and were sitting on the giant stoves in the kitchen. All our scrap iron was fed into them, including the old woks, which had now been broken to bits. The stoves were kept permanently lit – until they melted down. Our teachers took turns feeding firewood into them around-the-clock, and stirring the scraps in the vats with a huge spoon.

We did not have many lessons, as the teachers were too preoccupied with the vats. So were the older, teenage children. The rest of us were organized to clean the teachers' apartments and babysit for them.

I remember visiting a hospital once with some other children to see one of our teachers who had been seriously burned when molten iron had splashed onto her arms. Doctors and nurses in white coats were rushing around frantically. There was a furnace on the hospital grounds, and they had to feed logs into it all the time, even when they were performing operations and right through the night.

The reality of the Great Leap Forward in China included not only the failure of the steel campaign, but the arrest of tens of thousands of 'rightists' and 'counter-revolutionaries'. This included three thousand members of the Communist Youth League. There were also charges that 'dangerous separatist activities' had emerged among the Mongol, Turkic and Korean minorities, and that 'rectification' campaigns would be carried out to ensure loyalty and unanimity. So severe was the Tibetan resistance – described officially in the summer as 'subversive plots and splitting activities' – that in October all commercial traffic on the Lhasa–India highway was suspended.

There was no unanimity among the Western Powers as to how to confront the Communist Powers. This was seen publicly on August 14, when Britain and France, both anxious to widen their trading patterns, announced a relaxation on the existing prohibitions on trade with the Communist bloc and Communist China. The United States was unwilling to follow its NATO allies all the way, insisting on maintaining the embargo on trade with China, North Korea and North Vietnam. Within two weeks of the Anglo-French decision to widen trade with the Soviet Union, Soviet scientific ingenuity was again demonstrated when a rocket was fired into space, reaching a height of 279 miles, with two dogs on board. It also brought the dogs safely back to earth.

On August 23 the Chinese Communist government began to bombard the island of Quemoy, off the China coast, which was being ruled and garrisoned by the Nationalist Chinese government on Taiwan. This local event soon had international repercussions. On September 7 Khrushchev issued a declaration that any United States attack on China – presumably in support of Taiwan – would be regarded as an attack on the Soviet Union.

Communist China – officially the People's Republic of China – was not yet a member of the United Nations. A proposal by the Indian government that it should be admitted was rejected by the United Nations on September 19. The world's most populous nation was to have no voice in the council of nations. The fate of its people was harsh, and well hidden from the view of outside eyes. In the wake of the Great Leap Forward came famine. The priority given to the nationwide steel campaign was massively detrimental to agricultural production. Jung Chang has written:

Many of the peasants were exhausted from having to spend long hours finding fuel, scrap iron, and iron ore and keeping the furnaces going. The fields were often left to the women and children, who had to do everything by hand, as the animals were busy making their contribution to steel production. When harvest time came in autumn 1958, few people were in the fields.

The failure to get in the harvest in 1958 flashed a warning that a food shortage was on its way, even though official statistics showed a double-digit increase in agricultural output. It was officially announced that in 1958 China's wheat output had overtaken that of the United States. The Party newspaper, the *People's Daily*, started a discussion on the topic 'How do we cope with the problem of producing too much food?'

My father's department was in charge of the press in Szechwan, which printed outlandish claims, as did every publication in China. The press was the voice of the Party, and when it came to Party policies, neither my father nor anyone else in the media had any say. They were part of a huge conveyor belt. My father watched the turn of events with alarm. His only option was to appeal to the top leaders.

At the end of 1958 Jung Chang's father wrote a letter to the Central Committee in Peking, stating that 'producing steel like this was pointless and a waste of resources; the peasants were exhausted, their labour was being squandered, and there was a food shortage'. In his letter he appealed for urgent action. 'He gave the letter to the governor to pass on,' Jung Chang recalled. The governor was a friend. 'He told my father he was not going to forward the letter. Nothing in it was new, he said. "The Party knows everything. Have faith in it." Mao had said that under no circumstances must the people's morale be dampened.'

In Chengdu, in Szechwan Province, where Jung Chang lived, the monthly food ration for each adult was soon reduced to nineteen pounds of rice, three and a half ounces of cooking oil and three and a half ounces of meat 'when there was any'. Many people, she writes, 'were afflicted by edema, a condition in which fluid accumulates under the skin because of malnutrition. The patient turns yellow and swells up. The most popular remedy was eating chlorella, which was supposed to be rich in protein. Chlorella fed on human urine, so people stopped going to the toilet and peed into spittoons instead, then dropped the chlorella seeds in; they grew into something looking like green fish roe in a couple of days, and were scooped out of the urine, washed, and cooked with rice. They were truly disgusting to eat, but did reduce the swelling.' Jung Chang's recollections continued:

I had little idea that famine was raging all around me. One day on my way to school, as I was eating a small steamed roll, someone rushed up and snatched it from my hands. As I was recovering from the shock, I caught a glimpse of a very thin, dark back in shorts and bare feet running down the mud alley with his hand in his mouth, devouring the roll. When I told my parents what had happened, my father's eyes were terribly sad. He stroked my head and said, 'You are lucky. Other children like you are starving.'

I often had to visit the hospital for my teeth at that time. Whenever I went there I had an attack of nausea at the horrible sight of dozens of people with shiny, almost transparent swollen limbs, as big as barrels. The patients were carried to the hospital on flat carts, there were so many of them. When I asked my dentist what was wrong with them she said with a sigh, 'Edema.' I asked her what that meant, and she mumbled something which I vaguely linked with food.

These people with edema were mostly peasants. Starvation was much worse in the countryside because there were no guaranteed rations. Government policy was to provide food for the cities first, and commune officials were having to seize grain from the peasants by force. In many areas, peasants who tried to hide food were arrested, or beaten and tortured. Commune officials who were reluctant to take food from the hungry peasants were themselves dismissed, and some were physically maltreated. As a result, the peasants who had actually grown the food died in their millions all over China.

Jung Chang was later told by a Communist Party official who had worked in famine relief that in Szechwan Province alone seven million people had died. The total death toll for the whole of China between 1958 and 1961 has been estimated as thirty million.

In Vietnam, the division between North and South was heightened in April when the South rejected an appeal from the North for normal economic relations, the mutual reduction of armed forces and eventual elections. In August the northern President, Ho Chi Minh, indicated that his government was turning from Russia to China for its inspiration. 'We must learn from the Soviet Union,' he said, 'but, our country being nearer to China and having similar conditions, we must learn from China and then advance further to learn from the Soviet Union.'

Inside the Soviet Union, Khrushchev combined, from March 27, the post of Prime Minister and Party Secretary, the positions that Stalin had combined in his latter years. Marshal Bulganin, Khrushchev's former partner in power, was relegated to the position of Chairman of the Stavropol Economic Council in the remote North Caucasus. This was at least an improvement on the Stalinist despatch of rivals to the firing squad or Siberian labour camp. Bulganin lived another seventeen years and died in his bed. The Soviet Union was slowly changing. One sign was the fate of the Machine and Tractor Stations (MTS). It was through these that the State controlled the operations of the collective farms, through their provision of machinery for the farms. Khrushchev abolished the MTS and replaced them with Repair and Servicing Stations which had considerably less power of interference in the running of the farms.

The compulsory delivery of farm produce to the State, which hitherto had gone through the MTS, remained, but it was made more flexible, and more dependent on local farm conditions. Greater emphasis was also put on farms growing the crops most suitable for local conditions, rather than those which the Moscow-based planners and controllers felt were most needed for the centrally managed economy.

Khrushchev took pride, and exuded pride, in Soviet achievements, not merely in space. On August 10 he opened the largest hydro-electric project in the world. It had been built near Kuibyshev, on the Volga. The vast lakes created by the project's dams changed the map of the Soviet Union. Ecologically the dams proved a disaster, leading to the steady shrinking of the Caspian Sea.

The limited nature of the political changes in the Soviet Union was clearly shown by the Soviet government's reaction to the award of the Nobel Prize for Literature to Boris Pasternak, whose novel *Doctor Zhivago* was still not allowed to be published inside the Soviet Union. The award was made on October 23 for 'outstanding achievements in contemporary lyric poetry and in the traditional field of great, Russian prose.' No mention was made of the banned novel. Pasternak, who was living in Moscow, accepted the prize. Soviet newspapers called him 'an enemy of socialism' and denounced the award of the prize as a 'cold war manoeuvre'. These denunciations were intensified when John Foster Dulles said that the award had been made for *Doctor Zhivago* and that the novel had been 'condemned, not printed' in the Soviet Union.

Khrushchev was furious when Dulles' remark was reported to him. In the Stalinist era, which had ended only five years earlier, Pasternak's fate could hardly have been less than arrest and trial, followed by imprisonment and even execution, or – if he were fortunate – expulsion from the Soviet Union. In the Khrushchev era things were different, though far from benign. Four days after Pasternak accepted the award he was expelled from the Soviet Writers' Union. At the same time the State Publishing House was forbidden to reissue any of his earlier books or to sign any contracts with him for new books. There were public calls, carefully orchestrated by the authorities, for his expulsion from the Soviet Union and deprivation of citizenship. In the face of this torrent of abuse, Pasternak withdrew his acceptance of the award.

He then wrote, on October 31, to Khrushchev asking to be allowed to stay in his homeland. His request was granted. He remained alive, unarrested, and in Moscow. In a poem that he wrote entitled 'Nobel Prize' he expressed his isolation:

> Which way? I'm like an animal trapped.
> Somewhere: people, freedom, light.
> Behind me, the howls of the hunt,
> but the exit eludes me.
>
> What am I supposed to have done?
> Am I a murderer? A criminal?
> The whole world wept
> over my beautiful world.
>
> Even so close to death,
> I still believe that kinder times
> will come and overcome
> the angry power of spite.

Doctor Zhivago remained on the banned list. When Pasternak's poem 'Nobel Prize' was published in London a year later he was summoned to the Prosecutor-General and charged with 'treason to the fatherland'. If he were to meet with foreigners, he was warned, he would be immediately arrested. The British Prime Minister, Harold Macmillan, was about to visit Moscow. Pasternak had to give an assurance that he would be absent during Macmillan's visit.

Pasternak died in his bed in 1960, at a writers' colony near Moscow. He was seventy years old, and much respected as the translator into Russian of eight Shakespeare plays, including *Hamlet* and *King Lear*. It was to take another five years before his poetry, though still not *Doctor Zhivago*, was published in the Soviet Union.

In June there was a tragic epilogue to the crushing of the Hungarian revolution almost two years earlier. Imre Nagy, who had been imprisoned in Roumania, was brought back in secret to Hungary and put on trial. The trial was held in secret. On June 17 it was announced from Budapest and Moscow that Nagy had been sentenced to death and shot. General Pal Maleter was also shot, together with two close associates of Nagy, Miklos Gimes and Jozsef Szilagy. 'The death sentences have been put into effect' was the form of words in the official statement.

Another of the revolutionary leaders who had sought refuge in the Yugoslav Embassy in Budapest, and then been deported to Roumania, was Geza Losonczy. He had died in prison before he could be executed. A former Communist Deputy Minister for Cultural Affairs, he had come under the frown of Moscow in 1950 and been imprisoned with several other Party leaders, serving four and a half years in solitary confinement. In 1956 he had been one of the first to call for democratic Socialism. Imre Nagy had given him a post in the revolutionary government. Like Nagy, he had been branded a 'counter-revolutionary' and imprisoned again. 'The dead Losonczy', wrote Vincent Savarius in the *Manchester Guardian*, 'remains victorious over his former fellow prisoners and now Ministers, János Kádár and Gyula Kallai, who, though they are physically alive, are considered in Hungary to be morally dead.'

Imre Nagy's own story encapsulated the bewilderment and anger among those who had spent their lives working for the Communist Party and its cause in many lands, on both sides of the Iron Curtain. Since the age of twenty-one, when he had been taken prisoner by the Russians in the First World War while serving in the Austro-Hungarian army, and had then fought in the Bolshevik ranks in defence of Lenin's revolution, Nagy had spent his life in pursuit of the Communist ideal. As an active member of the Hungarian Communist Party he had been forced to flee from Hungary in 1929, and had lived as an exile in the Soviet Union until 1944. He had served in every post-war Communist government in Hungary, first in 1945 as Minister of Agriculture, and from 1953 to 1955 as Prime Minister, when his opposition to all-out collectivization had led to his resignation.

Imre Nagy's re-emergence as leader during the 1956 uprising had proved unforgivable to the Soviet Union, of which for so many years he had been a loyal disciple. His execution caused widespread anger among those who, until Soviet tanks entered Budapest, had been among the Party faithful. It also marked a further blow to Western perceptions of the essentially reformist nature of the men who had succeeded Stalin. And it led to renewed hesitation in accepting Soviet and Communist-bloc assurances of moderation and change.

In the United States, after the initial success of Eisenhower's public works policy, an economic recession brought the number of unemployed above five million again. At the same time, in Little Rock, Arkansas, which had been the focus of so much attention the previous year, the crisis over racial integration continued. On June 21 a United States District Court judge allowed a two-and-a-half-year suspension in the integration of schools. On September 12 the Supreme Court unanimously overruled this, and ordered the school to admit the nine pupils who had been excluded the previous year. To make integration impossible in practice, three days later Governor Faubus of Arkansas ordered the high schools in Arkansas to close. He then held a referendum in Little Rock, when his decision was upheld by 19,470 votes to 7,565. A Private Schools Corporation was set up, so that White pupils could be taught in spite of the closure of the schools. In Virginia, Governor J. Lindsay Almond followed Faubus's lead and closed the schools rather than accept integration. Of the eleven Southern States, only four had allowed even token integration by the year's end.

Racial tension was also evident in Britain; it had been on the increase since the first shiploads of immigrants had arrived from Jamaica three years earlier. In August, riots broke out in Notting Hill, London, and in Nottingham. It took two days before the police were able to bring the riots in Notting Hill under control. No one was killed, but the outburst was a shock to British liberal opinion. An account in the *News Chronicle* described the scene:

London's Notting Hill area flared last night into new violence against coloured people. Gangs of white people roamed the streets. 'We are out to get those niggers,' boasted a Teddy boy. Not until 1 a.m. did they disperse.

The whites surged around the area – at one time their total was 3,000 – looking for trouble. They gathered outside the homes of coloured people. Windows of homes and shops were smashed. Scuffles were going on in any one of a dozen streets.

They were watched by big forces of police waiting for the signal to rush to the house of any trouble spot.

By the end of the night several of the police were casualties – one was seriously hurt.

Most of the coloured people stayed hiding in their homes – police had warned them to do so.

Ten men – one coloured – were injured. By midnight thirteen arrests had been made – four of those held were coloured men.

At Notting Hill police station, four ambulances arrived and a Black Maria full of women.

Twenty police cars which went to the area were jeered at by both black and white youths and bottles were flung at them.

A fight broke out between a group of ten coloured men and seven whites. One white man was stabbed in the shoulder.

With surrounding streets in uproar white people yelled: 'Look the blackie chivved (knifed) him,' and then joined the mêlée.

When a fifteen-year-old boy was arrested, iron bars, bricks and lumps of concrete were flung at a police car. Truncheons were drawn and the mob dispersed. But not before police were forced back against shop windows which were smashed by flying bottles.

White and Black American servicemen in London were warned by their officers to stay away from Notting Hill. Three years later, in an attempt to avert further violent manifestations of anti-immigrant feeling, legislation was introduced to reduce the flow of 'coloured' immigrants to Britain from colonial and former colonial territories. Four decades later, the annual West Indian carnival at Notting Hill, while always heavily policed, had become a scene of uninhibited merriment and unalloyed festivity.

Space exploration, with its defence implications, continued throughout 1958 to be the most publicized area of East–West rivalry. On October 11 the United States launched its first Moon rocket, *Pioneer*. The launch was a success, and the rocket headed for space. Although it failed to hit the Moon, to orbit around it or to escape the Earth's gravitational pull, it did reach a distance of 79,212 miles from Earth – thirty times further than any man had ever reached – before being drawn back to Earth and falling into the South Pacific.

On November 10 a Ten-Power Conference opened in Geneva to discuss measures that might be taken to prevent surprise attack. Both the Soviet bloc and the Western Powers were represented. But when the conference ended on December 18 no agreement had been reached. Also on December 18 the United States launched its fifth satellite into space – *Atlas* – an experimental radio relay station, which successfully recorded and then rebroadcast back to earth a Christmas message from President Eisenhower.

On December 21 de Gaulle was elected President of France. In by far the largest margin of victory since the beginning of the century, he received

78.5 per cent of the vote. The Communist candidate received 13.1 per cent. A third candidate obtained 8.4 per cent. Under the new constitution of the Fifth Republic, which de Gaulle had promoted while he was Prime Minister, the powers of the President were enhanced.

The crisis in Algeria was momentarily eclipsed for the French government when, on December 30, all six countries of French West Africa – Chad, Congo, Gabon, Mali, Mauritania and Senegal – agreed to form a federation that would remain within the French Community. Elsewhere in Africa the demands of national movements were more vociferous, with 'self-determination' being the call that went out from the All African Peoples' Conference which met in December in Accra, Ghana. Among the resolutions passed by the Conference were the call for an end to 'racialism and discriminatory laws', and condemnation of 'frontiers, boundaries and federations'. Following the Conference a permanent secretariat of independent African countries was set up in Accra, which was also the capital of the first African member State of the Commonwealth to become independent.

By the late 1950s the mixed blessings of the motor car were becoming apparent, as the rate of accidents created a serious depletion of human life and individual productivity. It is impossible to calculate how much the industrialized nations lost in terms of the value of the manpower and productive lives, and future productive enterprise, wiped out in car deaths. In the United States 35,331 citizens were killed on the roads in 1958. In Britain there were 5,970 road deaths. Efforts to reduce road deaths were continuous. In Britain, radar was first used on January 20 to check car drivers for speeding.

Motor vehicles had also begun to crowd the streets of cities. The first parking meters were introduced in London on July 10. As general prosperity increased, and the austerity of the war years receded, air travel, like road travel, was becoming available to more and more people in the Western nations. The cause of faster air travel was advanced by the introduction of the first scheduled transatlantic jet services. On October 4 a British Overseas Airways Corporation (BOAC) Comet jet made a non-stop crossing of the Atlantic from London to New York. Twenty-two days later a Pan American (Pan Am) Airways Boeing 707 jet flew non-stop from Paris to New York.

Commerce also took a forward leap when the Bank of America in California launched the first multi-purpose credit card, and the first American Express credit card was also launched.

* * *

The largest single group of beneficiaries of the concern and wealth of the wider world were children. In 1958 more than fifty million children benefited from United Nations activities on their behalf. The sum of $23 million was allocated to child health and welfare in forty-three countries, a third of it to anti-malaria campaigns. The largest single United Nations donation that year was $2.2 million for the expansion of welfare services in India. The main contributor to this financial and social help was the United States, which provided more than half the total budget for children's welfare.

Refugees continued to be sustained by the United Nations. In his report to the General Assembly the Acting Director of the United Nations Relief and Works Agency for Palestine and the Near East, Leslie Carver – who in the Second World War had been a member of the British War Cabinet secretariat – noted that the number of Palestinian Arab refugees in camps under United Nations supervision had reached 963,958. Of those, 842,493 were in receipt of food rations from the United Nations. More than 25,000 were pregnant or nursing mothers. Schools and vocational training centres had been set up. The annual expenditure was running at more than $36 million. The need for financial support was 'as urgent as ever'. Once again, the United States provided more than half of the annual amount. The oil-rich Arab states made almost no contribution.[1]

In Europe, thirteen years after the end of the war, there were still 30,000 refugees in camps. A quarter of these were children. The hardest to resettle were the 9,600 handicapped refugees, whom few if any countries wanted to take in. The United Nations High Commissioner for Refugees, Dr Auguste Lindt, noted that more than $7 million would be needed if the remaining refugees were to be resettled by 1960, as he hoped. There were also ten thousand European refugees in China who wished to leave, but had no money to do so. Most of them had reached China in their flight from Nazi Germany in 1939, but had no place there any more.

One success story that Dr Lindt was able to report was that of the 20,000 Hungarian refugees who had fled to Yugoslavia across the common Hungarian–Yugoslav border two years earlier. As refugees from Communism they had no wish to live in a Communist country. Their resettlement was completed during 1958. More than 16,000 were found countries willing to

[1] Between 1950 and 1974 the principal contributors to Palestinian Arab Refugee relief were the United States ($577 million), Britain ($133 million), Canada ($32 million), West Germany ($27 million) and Sweden ($26 million). During this same period Saudi Arabia, the most generous of the Arab States, contributed just over $5 million.

take them in – and use their talent. Almost three thousand chose to return to Hungary. Some six hundred wished to stay in Yugoslavia. Of the 180,000 Hungarian refugees to whom the Austrian government had given asylum, eight thousand moved elsewhere, helped by the United Nations.

In order to raise public awareness of the refugee problem, the British government proposed, and the General Assembly accepted, that the period from July 1959 to June 1960 would be declared World Refugee Year. All governments were asked to think of ways to make this known, and a postage stamp was designed that all countries were asked to use.

The most immediate refugee problem came from the East–West divide, as young people, many of them under twenty-five, and many of them professionals, fled from East Germany to West Germany. As many as four thousand were leaving each week, availing themselves of the opportunity offered to go across the open border that divided East and West Berlin. In March the Communist Party leaders in East Germany decided that a far greater stress on the teaching of Marxism had to be placed in the school and university curricula. This stimulated the exodus. The authorities responded by placing much stricter controls on the movement of East Germans to East Berlin. But the lack of any effective border barriers inside Berlin itself, and the ability to take the S-Bahn overground suburban railway from east to west unimpeded, made the sealing of the Iron Curtain impossible in the one city where it was under greatest strain.

The refugees from East Germany were absorbed in West Germany, bringing their energy and talents to their fellow Germans, and further accentuating the political, economic and cultural divide between East and West.

In Poland, with all its borders touching other Communist States, the way out through emigration was effectively closed, and there was no 'West Poland' to which would-be emigrants could go. Internally, a close watch was kept on all dissent – and incipient hostility to the Soviet Union – in the inner corridors of power, and those dubbed 'revisionists' were expelled from the Party. One of those removed from public office was the Minister of Culture, Karol Kurlyuk, who was accused of 'undue leniency' towards a Polish writer, Marek Hlasko, who had announced while on tour in Western Europe that he would not return to Poland. Another person denounced by the authorities was the writer Antoni Slonimski, who, at a meeting of the Polish Writers' Union, had called for a minute's silence in memory of the murdered Hungarian leader, Imre Nagy.

The same strictness prevailed in Czechoslovakia, where the border with neutral Austria was strictly fortified and patrolled. In February a 'former industrialist' was charged with illegally manufacturing sweets, and with writing to his daughter abroad 'slandering' the Czech regime. In March several Czechs were sentenced to hard labour for 'listening to hostile radio stations and passing on the news to their friends in cafés'. In June, a man was sent to prison for four months for 'anti-Communist chatter' in a tram.

It was thirteen years since the start of Communist rule in Eastern and Central Europe. It was more than forty years since the Bolshevik revolution. As the seventh decade of the twentieth century drew near, the prospect loomed of a permanent ideological divide along the Iron Curtain – with a single Communist maverick, Yugoslavia – and of a never-ending conflict between the forces of the rule of law and democratic values on the one hand, and on the other of one-Party rule in which obedience and conformity were imposed at whatever the cost in human rights and dignity.

The 'kinder times' of which Pasternak had written were to elude much of mankind in the ensuing forty years. But the instinct for improvement was strong, seen forcefully in the United States in the work of a nationwide charity, the March of Dimes. Set up by President Franklin Roosevelt in 1933 to combat polio, in 1955 the March of Dimes saw its anti-polio work effectively concluded with the declaration that the Salk vaccine was 'safe, effective and potent'; in the United States alone, an estimated 135 million babies were saved by the vaccine in the ensuing four decades. The success of the polio vaccine led the March of Dimes to turn to a new challenge, saving babies from birth defects and related infant health problems, including mental retardation. By the end of the century the number of infant deaths from respiratory distress syndrome had been halved. Anna Eleanor Roosevelt, a granddaughter of the President, and a national trustee of the March of Dimes, commented forty years after the new orientation: 'Today, we are making a difference. Today, we are saving babies.'

The work of charitable organizations devoted to health and welfare is usually unsung. Yet it constituted a significant feature of national and international efforts for human well-being during the second half of the twentieth century.

CHAPTER EIGHT

1959

All history teaches us that like a turbulent ocean beating
great cliffs into fragments of rock, the determined movement of people incessantly demanding their rights always
disintegrates the old order.

MARTIN LUTHER KING

On 1 JANUARY 1959, as the East–West divide seemed fixated on space
exploration and weapons of mass destruction, there were six satellites in
orbit around the Earth. These included the *Atlas* satellite which had broadcast
President Eisenhower's Christmas message a week earlier, and the Soviet
Union's *Sputnik 3*. But the year began with a sharp focus on a terrestrial
reality, the flight of President Batista of Cuba. As he and those most closely
associated with the repression of his regime flew on January 1 from Havana
airport into exile, to seek sanctuary in Dominica, the Cuban revolutionary
movement led by Fidel Castro saw its goal in sight.

From their small beginnings in the Sierra Maestra, Castro's insurgents
had moved towards Havana, taken their first small town – of a thousand
people – the previous November, and were poised to strike at the dictator
himself. In six years of struggle, as many as two thousand people had died,
many of them peasants killed by Batista's army in its punitive sweeps. In
the immediate aftermath of the dictator's flight a military junta tried to
retain control of the capital, declaring martial law and appointing a provisional President. The new regime was ignored by the revolutionaries, who
proclaimed their own provisional President on the following day.

On January 8 the rebel leader arrived in Havana. 'As I watched Castro I
realized the magic of his personality,' wrote Ruby Hart Phillips of the *New
York Times*, who had lived in Cuba for a quarter of a century. 'He seemed
to weave a hypnotic net over his listeners, making them believe in his own

concept of the functions of Government and the destiny of Cuba.' On February 3 Castro was proclaimed Prime Minister. His regime took swift action against the perpetrators of excess during the latter years of Batista's rule. More than two thousand people were arrested, convicted of crimes against the Cuban people and shot.

From the earliest days of the Castro government, social reform was rapidly implemented, with land being transferred from large-scale landowners to those who would till the soil. Some of this land was provided for the 700,000 unemployed, who were urged to grow their own food. A thousand acres was the maximum area allowed under a single person's ownership. For sugar plantations, rice fields and cattle farms the maximum was three thousand acres. Hitherto one per cent of Cuba's six million inhabitants had owned more than one-third of the total land area. All that came to an end. Within five months, all American-owned sugar mills and sugar plantations were confiscated.

As to the politics of the rebels, five years after they had come to power Che Guevara told Lisa Howard of the American news network ABC, in answer to her question about Castro: 'I knew he was not a Communist but I believe I knew also that he would become a Communist, just as I also knew then that I was not a Communist, but I knew that I would become one within a short time and that the development of the revolution would lead us all to Marxism–Leninism.'

When Castro visited Harvard that spring he was received with great enthusiasm by the students there. Arthur Schlesinger Jr has commented: 'They saw in him, I think, the hipster who, in the era of the Organization Man, had joyfully defied the system, summoned a dozen friends, and overturned a government of wicked old men.' But the American government feared the imposition of Communism, not only in Cuba but by example and subversion elsewhere in Latin America, and in March President Eisenhower ordered the Central Intelligence Agency to train Cuban exiles for the military overthrow of the Castro regime.

From the moment that Castro marched into Havana 'at the head of a ragged, bearded band of amateur soldiers', the historian Richard Gott has written, 'it seemed to many sympathizers throughout Latin America that the Latin American Revolution had begun'. This sense of expectation was expressed a year later by Salvador Allende, the presidential candidate of the Socialist–Communist alliance in Chile. 'The Cuban revolution is a national revolution,' he wrote, 'but it is also a revolution of the whole of Latin

America. It has shown the way for the liberation of all our peoples.' On January 27 the Argentinian-born commander of La Cabaña fortress in Havana, Che Guevara, expressed in a newspaper interview his aspirations for the spread of Cuba's revolutionary success:

> The example of our revolution for Latin America and the lessons it implies have destroyed all the café theories: we have shown that a small group of resolute men supported by the people and not afraid to die if necessary can take on a disciplined regular army and completely defeat it.
>
> That is the basic lesson. There is another, which our brothers in Latin America in economically the same position agriculturally as ourselves should take up, and that is there must be agrarian revolution, and fighting in the countryside and the mountains. The revolution must be taken from there to the cities, and not started in the cities without overall social content.

Fidel Castro visited Washington in April, at the invitation of the American Society of Newspaper Editors. Eisenhower refused to see him, but the Vice-President, Richard Nixon, did so, on April 19. The two men talked for three hours. Nixon then dictated an account of the conversation for Eisenhower, which concluded:

> Whatever we may think of him, he is going to be a great factor in the development of Cuba and very possibly in Latin American affairs generally. He seems to be sincere. He is either incredibly naïve about Communism or under Communist discipline — my guess is the former, and as I have already implied his ideas as to how to run a government or an economy are less developed than those of almost any world figure I have met in fifty countries. But because he has the power to lead to which I have referred, we have no choice but at least to try to orient him in the right direction.

The immediate repercussions of Castro's victory in Cuba were dispiriting for the revolutionaries elsewhere. On May 1 a group of a hundred Panamanians landed on the Caribbean shore of Panama, at Nombre de Dios. They were immediately trapped by the authorities. 'It is true that they left from a Cuban port,' Che Guevara later told the United Nations, 'but they were no more than a group of adventurers'. A month later, on June 1, two planes with rebels on board flew into Nicaragua from Costa Rica. They were quickly overcome. Later that month another rebel attack was launched on the Trujillo regime in the Dominican Republic. The rebels had been trained in guerrilla tactics in Cuba. They too were quickly defeated. Three further revolutionary efforts were launched that year. On August 13 there was an 'invasion' of Haiti by thirty Cubans, led by an Algerian. Three months later a group of eighty guerrillas crossed from Brazil into northern Paraguay: most of them were caught within a week. On November 13 there was a revolt in Guatemala against the presence of an American training base for anti-Castro Cubans. That revolt was also suppressed, and the training went on.

Despite the challenge which a Socialist and revolutionary regime in Cuba presented to Washington, the global power and policing of the United States were continually expanding. On February 9 it began to supply arms to Indonesia, to use against revolutionary insurgents. Two days later it was designated by Laos as the sole arbiter of border and territorial disputes, to the anger of North Vietnam. There were those in the United States who queried the enormously high financial cost that these commitments represented. Eisenhower defended these costs with alacrity. 'Any cut-back of present budgetary levels for our Mutual Security programme', he explained on January 30, 'would require additional outlays for our own security forces, far greater than any amount that could be saved.'

On March 13, in a special message to Congress, Eisenhower again stressed the military aspects, asserting that the foreign aid programme had enabled the allies of the United States to maintain 250 strategically located bases across the globe, to have more than five million men under arms, and to provide pilots and air crews for 30,000 aircraft, of which more than half were jets. Eisenhower also noted that, over the same period during which the United States had contributed $22 billion in military assistance, the countries to which that assistance had gone had themselves spent six times as much.

Critics of high military expenditure could not but be amazed and shocked that so much of the wealth of nations was being spent on arms and armaments, even though this massive outpouring of money was going towards defensive preparations, not offensive action. But more of such expenditure was to come. Having heard Eisenhower's argument, Congress approved a further payment of more than $3 billion to America's allies. This brought the total sum spent on war machinery in the post-Second World War era to $166 billion.

The scientific achievements of the United States in 1959, which also called for a large budget, were in the main related to defence. But they spanned every aspect of the new technologies. Eleven artificial satellites were launched that year. The first and second, *Vanguard 2* and *Vanguard 3*, both launched on February 17, weighed twenty-one and fifty pounds respectively, and were expected to be in orbit – between 301 and 1,790 miles above the Earth's surface – for an estimated fifty years. The aim of *Vanguard 3*, which was to send back photographs of the Earth's surface, failed as a result of the satellite's irregular motions. But every setback served only to stimulate still further the pace and scale of the penetration of space. On March 3 a Moon probe, *Pioneer 4*, was launched, and passed within 37,000 miles of the Moon. Scientific curiosity, competition with the Soviet Union and the Intelligence-gathering aspects of defence policy were all in harmony.

Since the Allied breaking of the Berlin blockade eleven years earlier, the Soviet Union continued to regard Berlin as a test point of its own status as a victorious power; a power that was determined never to allow a militarized united Germany to threaten the Soviet Union, or to have the capability to advance eastward, as it had done to such devastating effect in 1917 and again in 1941. When, on March 2, Khrushchev called for a Soviet–American summit 'to deal with the problem of Germany in all its aspects', the United States took alarm at the thought that this might be a prelude to the permanent division of Germany along the existing East–West line, with Berlin forever vulnerable to a Soviet stranglehold. On March 16 Eisenhower broadcast to the American people his reply to the Soviet request. Although the United States was prepared to enter negotiations with the Soviet Union, he said, 'we shall not retreat one inch from our duty. We shall continue to exercise our right of peaceful passage to and from West Berlin.' The United States would not 'try to purchase peace by forsaking two million free people of Berlin'.

The toughness of Eisenhower's speech, and the firmness of his commitment, left the Soviet Union in no doubt that it could not secure a Soviet- or Communist-dominated Berlin. At one point in his broadcast Eisenhower said – with a reference to the British alliance with Belgium in 1914 which the German Kaiser had mocked as a meaningless 'scrap of paper' – 'We have no intention of forgetting our rights or of deserting a free people. Soviet rulers should remember that men have, before this, died for so-called "scraps of paper" which represented duty, honour, freedom.'

The United States administration, and millions of its citizens, had confidence in the deterrent power of military strength and an unequivocal policy. But a related area of American confidence received a jolt a week later, on March 23. On that day the administration published the figures for United States foreign aid over the previous five years, together with the figures for Soviet foreign aid. It emerged that eighteen non-Communist countries that were in receipt of American military aid were also receiving military aid from the Soviet Union, sometimes more than the American contribution. Thus while the United States provided Egypt with $123 million, the Soviet contributed $626 million.

Afghanistan, to which the United States had given $101 million, had received $159 million from the Soviet Union. India, to which the United States had contributed $1,312 million, had secured a further $394 million from the Soviet Union. The concept of aid had become so closely linked with political influence that from the perspective of Washington the Soviet contributions seemed almost an unfriendly act, especially when the total amount that the Soviet Union had transferred to non-Communist countries amounted in 1958 alone to $1 billion, a fifth of the total aid that the United States was giving to many more countries, including its military allies.

The American public wondered if the foreign aid programme was as effective as it was claimed to be by the administration. At $5 billion a year the total cost of the programme was also regarded as too high. The State Department, called in to explain the wider issues, pointed out that much of this aid had enabled the countries receiving it to buy American goods, thus generating business and employment. From a purely capitalist point of view, this argument was valid. Two-thirds of all United States exports since 1947 had been made as a result of the foreign aid programme. The total sum represented ten per cent more than American imports.

The Soviet Union was not far behind the United States in scientific developments, and in some respects was ahead. On January 4 – the day on which the Soviet Deputy Premier, Anastas Mikoyan, arrived in the United States on a goodwill visit – a Russian attempt to send a rocket to the surface of the Moon missed doing so by only five thousand miles. On May 28 the United States launched two monkeys into space. The rocket in which they were travelling reached a height of three hundred miles, and then returned to Earth, with the monkeys alive. There was a sudden realization around the globe that it might be possible to put a man on the Moon.

Whether the United States or the Soviet Union had the edge on the Moon race was eagerly debated. The overtaking point for the Soviet Union came on September 12, when a Soviet satellite, *Lunik* 2, hit the surface of the Moon. Within a month another Soviet satellite, *Lunik* 3, had passed behind the Moon, taken photographs of its hidden side, and also of its visible side, and then gone into orbit around the Earth.

The Western defence system was strengthened when, on May 7, the United States signed an agreement with Britain which gave Britain the right to buy components of atomic weapons, other than warheads, from the growing United States arsenal. Two weeks later, on May 22, Canada and the United States signed an agreement whereby the two countries would work together to develop the use of atomic energy for 'mutual defence'. The United States also agreed to sell Canada the nuclear warheads it needed for its intercontinental ballistic missile programme. On June 14 the United States agreed to give Greece information about nuclear weapons, and to provide it with ballistic rockets. Eleven days later the Soviet Union proposed a nuclear-free zone in the Balkans and the Adriatic. This was rejected by the United States and Britain.

Atomic power was also being used more and more for non-military purposes. On July 21 the United States launched the first atomic-powered passenger cargo ship, the *Savannah*. All these developments sprang from the intensity of the Soviet–American rivalry. Whether there could be a reconciliation, or at least a meaningful easement – a concept Churchill had favoured a decade earlier – seemed to depend more and more on whether a summit, of the sort Churchill had urged on Eisenhower in vain four years earlier, could be arranged.

On July 22 the American Vice-President, Richard Nixon, reached Moscow, reciprocating Mikoyan's goodwill visit of January. On the following day, in the Kremlin, Khrushchev protested to Nixon about the annual Captive Nations resolution, which had just been passed through Congress, as it had done each year since 1950. The resolution urged Americans to 'study the plight of the Soviet-dominated nations and to recommit themselves to the support of the just aspirations of those captive nations'. Khrushchev told Nixon: 'Hitherto, the Soviet Government thought Congress could never adopt a decision to start a war. But now it appears that, although Senator McCarthy is dead, his spirit still lives. For this reason the Soviet Union has kept its powder dry.'

While he was in Moscow, Nixon went with Khrushchev to the American Exhibition – the first of its kind in the Soviet Union – which was to be opened officially that evening. Their altercation was recorded on a newly devised colour television taping system. In his memoirs Nixon described what happened when the American engineers asked if he and Khrushchev would record greetings that could then be played back during the exhibition:

Khrushchev seemed suspicious, but when he saw a group of Soviet work-men near the display the actor in him took over. Before I knew what he was doing he had scrambled onto the platform and was talking for the cameras and playing the gallery.

'How long has America existed?' he asked me. 'Three hundred years?'

'One hundred and eighty years,' I replied.

Khrushchev was unfazed. 'Well, then, we will say America has been in existence for one hundred and eighty years, and this is the level she has reached,' he said, taking in the whole Exhibition hall with a broad wave of his arm. 'We have existed not quite forty-two years, and in another seven years we will be on the same level as America.' The audience was obviously enjoying his boasting, and he continued. 'When we catch up with you, in passing you by, we will wave to you,' he said, looking over his shoulder and waving good-bye to an imaginary America.

Pointing to a burly Russian worker standing in front of the crowd, he asked, 'Does this man look like a slave labourer? With men of such spirit, how can we lose?'

A second confrontation with Khrushchev took place when they went into a model American kitchen at the exhibition. Nixon later recalled its course:

He was defensive, declaring that Russian houses, too, would have the modern equipment displayed in the American exhibit; and he was aggress-ive, arguing that it was better to have just one model of washing machine than many.

When I asked if it wasn't better to be arguing about the relative merits of washing machines than about the relative strengths of rockets, he shouted, 'Your generals say we must compete in rockets. Your generals say they are so powerful they can destroy us. We can also show you something so that you will know the Russian spirit. We are strong, we can beat you.'

I replied, 'No one should ever use his strength to put another in the position where he in effect has an ultimatum. For us to argue who is the stronger misses the point. If war comes we both lose.'

Khrushchev tried to turn the tables, accusing me of issuing an ultimatum. 'We, too, are giants,' he declared. 'You want to threaten – we will answer threats with threats.'

I told him we would never engage in threats. 'You wanted indirectly to threaten me,' he shouted. 'But we have the means to threaten too.'

Finally he was ready to move to less belligerent ground. He said, 'We want peace and friendship with all nations, especially with America.' I responded, 'We want peace, too.'

Standing next to Khrushchev during this exchange was a member of the Central Committee of the Communist Party of the Soviet Union, Leonid Brezhnev; five years later he was to succeed Khrushchev as First Secretary.

On August 2, while still in Moscow, Nixon gave a press conference, at which he expressed his support for inviting Khrushchev to the United States. This prospective invitation was a small beacon of hope to those who felt that international tensions, and the massive arms bill, could be reduced if the leaders of the two Super Powers were to get together. Nixon told his Soviet audience that in his view the Soviet leader 'still has some very real misconceptions with regard both to our policies and the attitudes of our people. And I think that by going to the United States and seeing at first hand, that this would serve to reduce and remove those misconceptions.'

On the day after Nixon's remarks, Eisenhower announced that Khrushchev would be arriving in the United States that autumn.

Inside the United States the issue of segregation continued to focus on Little Rock, Arkansas. The determination of the Governor of Arkansas, Orval Faubus, not to allow integration, despite the rulings of federal courts, was finally frustrated at the beginning of 1959 when, on January 10, a United States district judge ordered the School Board of Little Rock to carry out a plan of racial integration for the town's schools. Despite the Governor's support for the racial separationists on the school board, they were voted off. Forty-four teachers who had been dismissed from the schools because they were suspected of supporting integration were reinstated.

On August 12 the high schools that the Governor had closed the previous year to prevent integration were opened again, and at two of them five Black students were admitted. It was a small step, but a traumatic one for those who had resisted integration with all the force and conviction of racist zeal. Where Arkansas reluctantly led, other Southern States followed, pushed into integration by their respective State Supreme Courts. The first was Virginia, where on February 2 twenty-one Black schoolchildren were admitted, as a result of the court ruling, to a previously all-White school in Alexandria, Virginia.

Georgia was the next Southern State to accept the mandate of the courts, issuing an order on June 5 forbidding racial segregation in the schools in Atlanta. But that October, in an article in *Liberation* which reflected his almost daily public utterances, Martin Luther King warned against the limitations of the current Supreme Court judgments:

Full integration can easily become a distant or mythical goal – major integration may be long postponed, and in the quest for social calm a compromise firmly implanted in which the real goals are merely token integration for a long period to come.

The Negro was the tragic victim of another compromise in 1877, when his full equality was bargained away by the Federal Government and a condition somewhat above slave status but short of genuine citizenship became his social and political existence for nearly a century.

There is reason to believe that the Negro of 1959 will not accept supinely any such compromises in the contemporary struggle for integration. His struggle will continue, but the obstacles will determine its specific nature. It is axiomatic in social life that the imposition of frustration leads to two kinds of reactions. One is the development of a wholesome social organization to resist with effective, firm measures any efforts to impede progress. The other is a confused, anger-motivated drive to strike back violently, to inflict damage.

King rejected the calls to violence. His answer lay, he explained, in 'the mass boycott, sitdown protests and strikes, sit-ins – refusal to pay fines and bail for unjust arrest – mass meetings – prayer pilgrimages etc'. This, he wrote, was the method used in India against the British. To succeed, such mass action had to be 'persistent and unyielding'. King then set out the Indian example and urged his supporters to follow it:

Gandhi said the Indian people must 'never let them rest', referring to the British. He urged them to keep protesting daily and weekly, in a variety

of ways. This method inspired and organized the Indian masses and dis-
organized and demobilized the British. It educates its myriad participants,
socially and morally.

All history teaches us that like a turbulent ocean beating great cliffs
into fragments of rock, the determined movement of people incessantly
demanding their rights always disintegrates the old order.

It is this form of struggle – non-cooperation with evil through mass
actions – 'never letting them rest' – which offers the more effective road
for those who have been tempted and goaded to violence. It needs the
bold and the brave because it is not free of danger. It faces the vicious
and evil enemies squarely. It requires dedicated people, because it is a
backbreaking task to arouse, to organize, and to educate tens of thousands
for disciplined, sustained action. From this form of struggle more emerges
that is permanent and damaging to the enemy than from a few acts of
organized violence.

King urged all Blacks to use 'every form of mass action yet known –
create new forms – and resolve never to let them rest. This is the social
lever which will force open the door to freedom.' In a clarion call for action,
he declared: 'Our powerful weapons are the voices, the feet, and the bodies
of dedicated, united people, moving without rest toward a just goal. Greater
tyrants than Southern segregationists have been subdued and defeated by
this form of struggle. We have not yet used it, and it would be tragic if we
spurn it because we have failed to perceive its strength and power.'

The ending of empire, colonialism, racial discrimination and foreign control
was everywhere accelerating, but not everywhere uniformly resolved. On
January 4 there were violent disturbances at Léopoldville, in the Belgian
Congo, and five Belgian policemen were injured. The Belgian government
responded by sending in parachute troops. On the following day those troops
clashed with Africans in the city. Fifteen Africans were killed. A report in
the *Daily Telegraph* gave further details:

> At least three African rioters were killed when African troops fired rifle
> volleys on a mob in the main market square. There were renewed clashes
> in other markets.
>
> Sporadic looting continued after last night's shop-wrecking and pillage.

The trouble began with a cancelled political meeting but is attributed basically to discontent among the unemployed.

M. Arthur Pinzi, the African Burgomaster of Kalamu, an African suburb, blamed the spread of the disorders on 'over-hasty' police action.

Fighting continued throughout January 6, when twenty more Africans were killed. The Belgian government announced four days later that it would grant substantial and meaningful reforms to the Congolese.

In London, on February 19, agreement was reached by the Prime Ministers of Britain, Turkey and Greece for the independence of Cyprus. It would not be given to Greece or divided between Greece and Turkey, or between Greek Cypriots and Turkish Cypriots. Instead, it would remain a single entity, with full independence, a republic, with a President, and with the Greek and Turkish Cypriot communities each obtaining a wide measure of autonomy. Britain would retain two sovereign military bases. The desire of EOKA for union with Greece, a desire that had been backed up by force and terrorism, would have to be abandoned.

On February 22, as part of the London Agreement, the British Governor released all Cypriot prisoners held in detention. Five days later an amnesty for EOKA terrorists was declared and Colonel Grivas given a safe conduct to Greece, where he was welcomed as a hero and promoted to general. On March 1 Archbishop Makarios returned to Cyprus from exile. At the end of the year he became the independent Republic's first President. EOKA was disbanded and President Makarios – who had once been the outspoken advocate of union with Greece – worked to reconcile the Greek and Turkish communities. One result of his ameliorating efforts was that former EOKA activists launched several assassination attempts against him. None succeeded.

In Nyasaland, however, the British colonial authorities, unwilling to bow to the threat of force, sought to control the nationalist movement and to curb its activities. Their determination was strengthened after the return to Nyasaland of the African National Congress leader, Dr Hastings Banda, from a prolonged exile. On January 25, meeting at Limbe, two hundred Congress officials, inspired by Banda's leadership, discussed the possibility of sabotage and defiance, and resistance to unpopular laws, even by the use of violence.

Riots broke out within a month, on February 19, in three towns in the north of the country. Airstrip buildings and installations were attacked by stone-throwing crowds. During a mass protest meeting at Karonga, speaker after speaker demanded 'immediate control' of Nyasaland for its African inhabitants. The British District Commissioner, having declared the meeting illegal, arrested the leaders, but the crowd forced him to release them. On the following day there were demonstrations and riots in two other towns, and in Lilongwe an African was killed by police. Ten days later a state of emergency was declared, the African National Congress was declared an illegal organization, and 166 of its members in Nyasaland were arrested, including Dr Banda.

The grounds given for the arrests were that 'a massacre was being planned' by the African leaders in the colony. There was incredulity among those who knew Dr Banda that he was capable of such a course of action, and an official British inquiry confirmed that there had been no such intention. The inquiry went so far as to describe the nature of the British administration in Nyasaland after the state of emergency had been proclaimed as 'no doubt temporarily − a police State', in which the security forces had used 'illegal force in making a number of unnecessary arrests'.

A conference on the future of Nyasaland was planned for the following year. Meanwhile, it was announced that because of the state of emergency the existing constitution would be extended for a year, with minor changes. The African representation on the Legislative Council was increased from five members to seven. The number of British-appointed official members rose from twelve to fourteen. The unofficial local White representation remained at six. As one African member of the Council was in detention and another in self-imposed exile in London − to avoid arrest − four new African members were to be appointed. One of them resigned after his house had been burned down, in an African protest against participation in a governing instrument so tilted against fair representation.

Throughout Nyasaland there were continuing clashes between African demonstrators and the British-controlled police force − itself largely African. When a large number of African protesters tried to release a group of prisoners who were being held on board ship at Nkata Bay, and managed to force their way on to the jetty in the port, troops opened fire and twenty of the protesters were killed. This brought the number of African dead in the disturbances to fifty-two. No European or African members of the security forces were killed.

A further British government inquiry, the Devlin Commission, concluded later in the year that the national aspirations of the Africans in Nyasaland were not limited to a small minority of political activists, but were shared by the 'great majority' of the people.

In Southern Rhodesia the Prime Minister, Sir Edgar Whitehead, seeking to avoid an African national challenge to White authority in his country, declared a state of emergency and banned all four African National Congress Parties. He also introduced legislation which made it much easier for the police to arrest and imprison demonstrators and opponents of the regime with the minimum of judicial process. In neighbouring Northern Rhodesia, the Zambia African National Congress was banned by the British authorities on March 12 for 'intimidation' of Africans who were due to vote in the election eight days later. The Congress had called for an African boycott of the elections. Many Africans did vote, but the system of representation was such, and the mix of official and elected members so contrived, that of the ten members of the Executive Council only two were Africans.

In Kenya, eleven Mau Mau prisoners who were being held by the British at Hola Camp were severely beaten on March 3, and died. The beatings were part of a policy of severe repression which the camp administration had devised to break the morale of the captives. Four days later the news of the deaths was made public. At first the prison authorities announced that the men 'might have died from drinking water from a water-cart serving a working party in intense heat'. Then it was admitted that they had died of injuries. According to the official inquest:

> . . . on March 3 a party of eighty-five unco-operative Mau Mau detainees were taken from Hola, in Coast Province, to dig an irrigation trench. The riot squad was called in and blows exchanged after a group of men started giving a Mau Mau howl.
>
> The howl has an infectious effect and it has been known to demoralize a whole camp. The warders were told to restore order and blows were delivered.
>
> When one of the groups began to wail again, the riot squad went in . . .

There were vigorous protests in both Kenya and Britain against the killing of the eleven prisoners. The killings, far from forcing the other detainees into submission, as had been hoped by the camp authorities, served only to accelerate the pressure for Kenyan independence in the colony, and in Britain. In the words of Iain Macleod, who was shortly to become Colonial Secretary, 'Hola helped to convince me that swift change was needed in Kenya.'

Despite the Hola Camp killings, reconciliation was a central part of the evolution of the British–African connection. On a visit to Britain, Kwame

Nkrumah, Prime Minister of independent Ghana – which Britain had ruled since 1874 – was made a Privy Councillor by Queen Elizabeth II while on a visit to Balmoral. In December the British government agreed that in Tanganyika the elected African members would be able to form a majority in the legislative council – the process that had led to Ghanaian independence.

Singapore, founded by the British in 1819 – and the capture of which by the Japanese in 1942 had been a moment of deep humiliation for Britain – became self-governing on June 3, committed to forestall any attempt at the ascendancy of Communist Chinese, as well as to clamp down on 'sex-obsessed' publications and 'rock 'n' roll' music. A month later, on July 4, Jamaica was granted internal self-government within the West Indies Federation, which had been established two years earlier.

United Nations Trustee territories were also on the verge of independence. On December 6 the General Assembly voted to give the three million people of France's Togoland Trusteeship independence in four months' time. The future of French rule in Algeria awaited the decision of de Gaulle, as to whether or not to challenge the demands of the French settlers there to remain an integral part of France. The slogan chosen by the settlers, *Algérie Française*, had first been heard on the streets of Paris a year earlier, during the events that had brought de Gaulle to power. On September 16 de Gaulle made his decision. It caused disappointment to the settlers and frustration to the Algerian nationalists. De Gaulle offered all the inhabitants of Algeria, Frenchmen and Muslims, a referendum, in which they could choose either continued association with France or independence. The referendum would be held, he said, within four years of an 'effective' end to the Algerian national rebellion.

On December 13 the United Nations voted not to intervene in the political future of Algeria.

In South Africa, the imposition of apartheid was taking harsher and more draconian forms with every piece of legislation. The Promotion of Bantu Self-Government Bill provided for the establishment of eight 'homelands' – which became known as Bantustans – for Africans, in which they would become citizens of their Bantustan, but would lose their already circumscribed right of representation in the Pretoria parliament.

Supporters of apartheid hailed the creation of the Bantustans as showing the 'positive' side of segregation. The government encouraged this interpretation. Explaining what the Bantustans would give the Africans of South

Africa, the government declared: 'For the first time in their history they realize that the European is prepared to grant them full freedom of progress within their own sphere of life; that it is not the European's intention to retard the assignment of powers to them on the ground that the time is not ripe, but that it is the firm intention to give them all the training required for this purpose.'

No timetable was provided in the Bill for the coming into being of self-government. For the Africans whose relegation into homelands was being arranged without their participation in the debate, or even in any discussion of the geographic areas involved, this was a policy of separation and exclusion. Despite the Bantustans, six million Africans would still be living in the White-designated areas, and subjected there to all the rigours of apartheid. When the Bill was about to be put through its very first parliamentary stage, the leader of the opposition, Sir de Villiers Graaff, took the almost unprecedented step of opposing even the introduction of the Bill to parliament. In the end the government used special parliamentary 'guillotine' procedures for cutting short debates in order to push the Bill through with the minimum of critical discussion.

Another piece of legislation passed in Pretoria, the disingenuously named Extension of University Education Act, brought to an end the existing racially integrated education at both Cape Town and Witwatersrand Universities, and set up separate institutions of higher learning for the three officially designated non-White categories, Coloureds, Indians and Africans. This Bill had been introduced to the parliament the previous year, but had been postponed as a result of protests at South African universities and at many universities in Britain and the Commonwealth. Once more the parliamentary opposition was prepared to fight the Bill clause by clause, and once more the government introduced a guillotine motion to halt the discussion.

An earlier piece of apartheid legislation, the Immorality Act, which had come into effect in 1950, was being rigorously enforced. This legislation not only forbade sexual intercourse between Whites and non-Whites, but made even an 'invitation' to commit such an act illegal. Between the introduction of the Act and 1957 there had been almost 2,500 convictions. In 1958 and 1959, as police vigilance intensified, the number of convictions increased considerably.

As a protest against 'ten years of restraints on non-Whites' in South Africa, a member of the Liberal Party, Senator Rubin, published a pamphlet in Britain giving specific examples of how some of the apartheid laws worked in practice. 'If an African, born in a town, has lived there continuously for fifty years,' one of his examples read, 'no friend of his who is an African is entitled as of right to visit and remain with him for more than seventy-two hours.' A second example:

> If there is only one waiting-room on a railway station, it is lawful for the station master to reserve that waiting-room for the exclusive use of White persons, and any non-White person wilfully entering it commits a criminal offence and is liable to a fine not exceeding fifty pounds or to imprisonment for a period not exceeding three months or to both such fine and such imprisonment.

Another of Senator Rubin's examples was no less humiliating: 'No African, lawfully residing in a town by virtue of a permit issued to him, is entitled, as of right, to have his wife and children residing with him.'

The United Nations General Assembly, in what was becoming an annual condemnation of apartheid in South Africa, extended its condemnation to include racial discrimination 'in any part of the world'. Beyond condemnation, however, there was no action, leading to a growing cynicism in liberal circles worldwide about the value of the United Nations as a force for the upholding of democracy and humanitarianism. The work of its specialized agencies gave hope, however, that good could be done in the world by an international body, even if by far the largest single financial contribution to these good deeds came, as hitherto, from the United States. It was, in the last resort, the American taxpayer who was most significantly assisting the well-being of mankind.

China, behind its Bamboo Curtain of secrecy, continued to assert its authority on the periphery of the country, among the non-Chinese groups. Any sign of national identity was treated with harshness. In February there was a national uprising in Tibet. The Chinese took immediate military action. On March 17 Tibetans in Lhasa, the capital, attacked the Chinese garrison there. It was a bold but futile gesture of defiance. To escape capture by the Chinese, the Tibetan spiritual and temporal leader, the Dalai Lama, was smuggled out of Tibet.

With a retinue of ninety people, including his family, the Dalai Lama made his way three hundred miles on horseback to the Indian border, where he was given asylum. His arrival in India was witnessed by a correspondent of *The Times*:

The Dalai Lama was bareheaded: he wore spectacles, robes, and ordinary shoes. With him were his fifty-seven-year-old mother (looking far younger than her years), his sister, and his young brother Nagri Rimpoche, a felt-hatted and alert fourteen-year-old: his senior and junior tutors, three Cabinet Ministers, the Lord Chamberlain, the Master of Ceremonies, the Master of the Robes, and the Master of the Tea; representatives of the Great Sera and Drebung monasteries, an oracle, and various other officials and servants.

At the foothills camp, against the back-drop of high mist-shrouded mountains, the swagger and the good looks of those attendants briefly recreated the atmosphere of imagined Tibet. Turquoise pendant earrings hung agitated from beneath felt hats, brooches glowed beneath woollen robes, and silver sword-scabbards protruded jauntily from voluminous folds of blue and grey.

Anxious not to compromise his position as a leader of the non-aligned nations, or to offend China, Nehru granted the Dalai Lama asylum but made it clear that he would not allow political activities to be carried on 'from one country against another'. When the Dalai Lama gave a press conference in the Indian hill town of Mussoorie, on June 20, he not only stated that the Chinese, in their efforts to eradicate Buddhism in Tibet, had destroyed a thousand monasteries, but declared repeatedly, 'I am my government.' This led to an immediate protest from the Indian External Affairs Ministry. 'So far as the Dalai Lama is concerned,' the protest read, 'the Prime Minister has made it clear on more than one occasion that, while the Government of India are glad to give asylum to the Dalai Lama, and show him the respect due to his high position, they have no reason to believe that he will do anything which is contrary to international usage and embarrassing to the host country.' The Dalai Lama could gain no comfort from this, or from the sentence that followed, which stated bluntly: 'The Government of India want to make it clear that they do not recognize any separate Government of Tibet and there is, therefore, no question of a Tibetan Government under the Dalai Lama functioning in India.'

The Chinese decided to present their own spiritual ruler to the Tibetans: the Panchen Lama. On April 10 he was proclaimed Lama at a short ceremony in Lhasa, in front of the palace of the man he was usurping. Three months later the Chinese began to expropriate monastic land in Tibet and to redistribute it. The power of the Tibetan leadership, and such wealth as it possessed, was systematically destroyed. The 13,000 Tibetan refugees who had crossed into India brought with them tales of Chinese behaviour of the harshest kind. The Panchen Lama was proving a figurehead of the most subservient type.

Nehru's hopes of not offending the Chinese were dashed by the Chinese government itself, which accused India of 'hostile acts' in welcoming the Dalai Lama to India. Nehru rebutted this charge with alacrity, stating that it was 'unbecoming and entirely devoid of substance'. As news of the imposition of Chinese rule on Tibet reached the subcontinent, and as it became evident that the oppression of Buddhism was part of the Chinese intention, there was anger in India, not only among Buddhists. Anti-Chinese demonstrations took place in many cities. In Bombay a portrait of Mao Tse-tung was disfigured. But still Nehru hesitated to have too open a breach with China, and when the Dalai Lama, at a second press conference at Mussoorie, described Chinese rule in Tibet as a 'flagrant act of aggression' and a 'reign of terror', the government of India announced again that there was no question of a Tibetan government in exile functioning in India under the Dalai Lama. Nehru also refused a request from the Tibetan exiles to sponsor Tibet's case at the United Nations. Some accused Nehru of hypocrisy, but he saw as his prime duty maintaining the national interest of India, and judged that to be the avoidance of a conflict with China.

Whether conflict with China could be avoided was a question much debated in India after August 7 – a week before India's twelfth anniversary of independence – when Chinese troops gathered on the Indian–Chinese border along the Indian administered and sovereign North-East Frontier Agency, an area of high, almost inaccessible mountain valleys which China claimed for itself. The dispute over this border centred on two maps, one dating from 1847 and the other from 1914. There had been no more recent survey. The Chinese not only claimed rectification of the border in the North East Frontier Agency, and also in the Ladakh Salient – which bordered on Tibet – but also announced that they intended the 'liberation' of two countries lying between India and China, the small and ancient countries of Bhutan and Sikkim, which even the British, in the heyday of their empire, had not sought to annex.[1]

According to a spate of Chinese propaganda, the Indians had replaced the

---

[1] The British had, however, purchased Darjeeling from Sikkim in 1835 (it is today part of India).

British as the 'imperialists' in these two countries. From 1910 until Indian independence in 1947, British India, which had been the predominant power in Bhutan since 1865, had a treaty with Bhutan guaranteeing its independence from China. Nehru, who regarded the Republic of India as Britain's successor in this regard, had signed a Treaty of Friendship with Bhutan in 1949. A similar treaty arrangement had existed between Britain and Sikkim before 1947, and between India and Sikkim from that year. As the new crisis intensified, India made it clear that both countries would be defended by Indian troops if any Chinese troops crossed into them.

The existing frontier with China, Nehru told the Indian parliament on August 13 amid loud cheers, was 'firm by treaty, firm by usage and right, and firm by geography'. It could not be altered under the threat of force. Eleven days later Nehru informed the Indian parliament that Chinese troops had crossed into Indian territory, captured an Indian patrol and surrounded an Indian military outpost at Longju, several miles inside the Indian border. He then read out the protest he had addressed to Peking. Another charge against China that Nehru revealed that day was that Chinese engineers had earlier built a road through Indian territory – the Ladakh Salient – giving them better access to Tibet. It appeared from the secret correspondence that Nehru then read out, dating back to 1954, that China claimed 32,000 square miles of Indian territory of the North-East Frontier Agency, and fifty square miles in Ladakh.

China countered Nehru's protest with the spurious charge that the incident had arisen from the 'trespassing and provocations of Indian troops'. In a letter to Chou En-lai, Nehru wrote angrily, as he had done a decade earlier, that Chinese maps given wide circulation showed large parts of Indian territory in the North-East Frontier Agency as being Chinese. The government of India 'cannot but express their regret once more', he wrote, 'that large areas of Indian territory continue to be shown in official Chinese maps as part of China. It is most extraordinary that the Government of China could not have found time during the last ten years to withdraw these faulty maps. The continued circulation of these maps is a standing threat to India's integrity and evidence of unfriendliness towards India. Obviously no discussion of the India–China border in any sector can proceed on the basis of maps which have no relation to reality.'

The Soviet Union sought to intervene, appealing to both India and China to settle their border dispute. The Indian public was also uneasy at the thought of war, so much so that Nehru hastened to assure his parliament on September 9 that it would be 'extreme folly' for India to go to war 'for a few mountains'. But he went on to criticize China's 'pride and arrogance of might', and to reject any border rectification under the threat of force.

It was while he was adopting a firm stance towards China that Nehru welcomed President Eisenhower to India with particular warmth, and amid unexpected demonstrations of Indian goodwill. But Nehru's determination not to lose his leadership of the non-aligned nations made him unwilling to take up a stronger anti-Chinese stance on issues other than the border. He would abide by existing treaties, not seek confrontation. For this reason he remained unwilling to be the sponsor of the Dalai Lama in his appeal to the United Nations against the Chinese occupation of Tibet.

The Dalai Lama went ahead alone, appealing on September 9 to the United Nations for international intervention to restore Tibetan independence. The General Assembly responded to the Tibetan appeal a month later with a resolution calling for the restoration of civil and religious liberties in Tibet. The Chinese government poured scorn on the resolution, and refused to implement it. Forty years later the Chinese were still the military and political masters of Tibet.

Inside China, the persecution of Christians, of whom there were more than twenty million, intensified. On October 18, sixty-eight-year-old Bishop James E. Walsh, the superior of the Maryknoll Mission in China, was arrested. He had been in China since 1918, and had been appointed bishop by Pope Pius XI in 1925. Longevity of service to Roman Catholicism in China was his sole crime: he was to spend twelve years in prison. Throughout that time he was allowed no news reports, and only one visitor, his brother – a former Maryland State Attorney – for a single visit in 1960.

On October 20 an Indian police patrol was ambushed by Chinese troops forty miles inside the mountainous Ladakh border, and nine Indians were killed. There was outrage, and war fever grew inside India. China blamed the Indian patrol for the incident. Nehru declared that the Chinese version was 'a travesty of the truth'. On November 6, the defence of Ladakh was transferred from the Indian police to the Indian army. On the following day China offered negotiations, which Nehru accepted, and the dispute was transferred to the realm of diplomacy, with a focus on the possible establishment of demilitarized zones and a mutual withdrawal of troops from both alleged frontier lines.

An unexpected war crisis came to an end. But, in an effort not to be outmanoeuvred by China, Nehru added Nepal to the Bhutan–Sikkim declaration, stating publicly that a Chinese attack on Nepal would likewise be considered an attack on India.

From his exile in India, the Dalai Lama began a long process of seeking redress for his occupied country. On November 14 – the day on which India was celebrating Nehru's seventieth birthday – the International Commission of Jurists went to see the Dalai Lama at Mussoorie. The charge that he set out for the Commission was that the Chinese government was guilty of genocide in Tibet. The United Nations had specifically outlawed genocide, but whatever sympathy the Dalai Lama was able to elicit, the United Nations took no steps to remove China from Tibet: none was proposed and none was in prospect.

India's border crisis with China, and the prospect of war with China, had created fears inside India of a violent conflict. War was averted, however, and with it the danger of large military casualties. But India was not spared a heavy death toll that year. It came, as so often in Indian history, from the elements, when flooding caused several thousand deaths in Kashmir in August, and in Bombay State in September – even while the Indian–Chinese dispute was at its most tense – and thousands more were killed in October when East Bengal and Bihar were struck by a cyclone.

Inside China, Mao Tse-tung pursued with tenacity, and where he felt it was needed with ruthlessness, the previous year's Great Leap Forward. Among the Chinese Christians arrested that year was Allen Yuan, a forty-four-year-old evangelical pastor. Charged with propagating falsehood, he was sentenced to the first of a series of incarcerations in labour camps that were to add up to a total of twenty-two years. Forty years later, and a free man, he was still preaching.

A national mobilization of labour was under way in China, unprecedented in history, even in the Soviet Union under Stalin. The historian Jonathan Spence has noted how, in a speech which Mao Tse-tung made to Party activists in Lushan, he took a 'bellicose and self-justificatory' position on the Great Leap Forward, and on the establishment of the vast communes which were at its centre. Confucius, Lenin and Marx had all made mistakes, Mao Tse-tung said, 'so why be surprised that he had too?' If everyone 'insisted on emphasizing nothing but the negative side' then he himself would 'go to the countryside to lead the peasants to overthrow the government'.

Mao Tse-tung added: 'If those of you in the Liberation Army won't follow me, then I will go and find a Red Army, and organize another Liberation Army.' As for the communes, 'up to now not one has collapsed. We were prepared for the collapse of half of them and if seventy percent collapsed there would still be thirty percent left. If they must collapse let them.' Mao Tse-tung ended his speech 'caustically' – Spence writes – 'addressing those at the conference with language drawn from the rural people, as if to emphasize that he came from the masses whereas so many of the other leaders present did not: "The chaos caused was on a grand scale and I take responsibility. Comrades, you must all analyze your own responsibility. If you have to shit, shit! If you have to fart, fart! You will feel much better for it."'

While Mao Tse-tung was imposing unity on the disparate elements of China, he also maintained the strictest possible control over the national minorities on the periphery, and also in Tibet. At the same time the Soviet colossus, its greatest power and control having been established under the impetus of military victory in 1945, was showing signs of hitherto unacceptable diversity. This was primarily in Poland, where the return to power of Wladislaw Gomulka brought with it an emphasis on the specifically Polish 'road to Socialism'. Gomulka also improved Poland's links with Tito's Yugoslavia, which had broken away a decade earlier from Soviet dominance.

At the Party Congress in Warsaw in March, the conditions for future Party membership were laid down: the previous insistence on 'ideological conformity' was abandoned. Party members were told that a special 'revising' commission had decided that neither a competence in Marxism–Leninism nor a public repudiation of religious belief should any longer be among the qualifications for Party membership. Nor was the Party committed any more to its previous, Soviet-inspired 'struggle against the kulak'.[1]

During a visit to Warsaw in July, Khrushchev himself gave specific support to a pledge by Gomulka that the Polish peasant farmers need have 'no fear' of collectivization.

The situation in Czechoslovakia was more openly Stalinist in outlook and behaviour than that in Poland. Agricultural co-operatives were being extended, with 156,000 private farms being absorbed into them in the previous year. The President, Antonin Novotny, commented ominously that

[1] The Polish Communist Party went under the name of the Polish United Workers' Party (the PZPR).

summer: 'Land is being wasted in the form of gardens attached to private houses.' To combat a growing absenteeism at work, a Communist Party exhortation contained the sentence: 'We shall have to return to a system of visits by comrades.' In a courageous letter published in *Rudé Právo*, a steel-worker wrote of how 'in some sections we slave away as in a treadmill . . . We know neither Sunday nor holiday.'

The need to ensure that literature served the regime was stressed by the Czechoslovak Communist Party. A cultural conference at the beginning of the year stated, as its main resolution, that the work of writers and artists should have 'as its main concept the struggle against bourgeois survivals and ideas hostile to our system'. A novel by J. Skvorecky, *The Cowards*, which disparaged Soviet troops was quickly banned. After a number of literary magazines had been closed down, writers, artists and musicians were warned by the Party leadership: 'Pay heed that your art fully assists the Communist moral and aesthetic education of the working people.'

Trials were also a feature of the continued Czech Communist Party emphasis on the correct path. At the beginning of the year, three theological students were imprisoned for stating publicly that 'there is no religious freedom in Czechoslovakia'. Other people were imprisoned for having hidden such property as they could – including coins, works of art and fine cloth – from post-1948 expropriation. An actor was sent to prison for three years for 'making rude remarks' about the Czech Communist leaders, and for 'admiring everything Western'. Following the abolition of private medical practice, several doctors were sent to prison – one of them for eighteen years – for helping what were described in court as the 'remnants of the bourgeoisie' to obtain private medical attention.

In Hungary, Communist rule was also harsh, with thousands of schoolteachers being 're-educated' in the virtues of Communism. In Roumania, collectivization was being extended by decrees which made it illegal to hire agricultural labour or to rent land. There was also an increase in the State expropriation of such agricultural surpluses as the Roumanian peasant farmers were allowed to keep.

In one country Communism suffered a setback that year. Two years earlier the Communist Party of India – which had previously been banned by Nehru for calling for an armed uprising against the post-independence government – came to power in the southern State of Kerala, a State with a large Christian population. The government was a coalition one, but its Chief Minister,

E. M. S. Namboodiripad, had been a member of the Central Committee of the Communist Party of India for sixteen years. His land reforms and attempts to democratize education met with hostility from the Church, and disturbances which the government put down with force. This led Nehru to dismiss the Communist government, a move that was widely regarded in India as unconstitutional. Nehru's daughter Indira was one of those most emphatic that her father should act as he did. Wryly, Namboodiripad would later remark that it was a 'double irony' that the world's 'first democratically elected Communist government' – his own – should have been removed from power by 'undemocratic means'.

In the daily life of more and more people, the call for cheap cars accessible to all was never ending. In Britain the Mini Minor was launched that year – cheap, small and reliable. Within six years, a million had been manufactured. The British and Americans had begun to construct limited-access highways – motorways – to carry traffic from city to city with even greater speed, and with fewer obstacles such as crossroads and traffic lights. The first section of the first British motorway, the M1, intended to link London and Leeds was opened on November 1. That year, 6,520 people were killed on Britain's roads and 36,223 in the United States.

The often stark contrast between the pleasures of ordinary life and leisure and the pressures of politics and international conflict was seen twice in one month that September: on the 7th, at Farnborough, in Britain, where a festive atmosphere pervaded a display by manufacturers of space rockets and guided missiles, including the Thunderbird guided missile capable of carrying a nuclear warhead; and again on the 20th, when Khrushchev, on a visit to Disneyland in California, was refused entry for security reasons. During a televised lunch at a Hollywood film studio he suddenly waved his arms in the air and then banged the table, the gestures being accompanied by a torrent of complaint, during the course of which he told his somewhat bewildered hosts:

Just imagine. I, a Soviet Prime Minister, a Soviet representative, I was given a programme of what I was to be shown and whom I was to meet. Why cannot I go to Disneyland? Do you have rocket-launching pads there? I don't know. Just listen to the reason I was given: 'We cannot guarantee your security if you go there'.

Is there an epidemic of cholera there or something, or have gangsters taken over the place, who might destroy me? Your policemen are tough enough to lift a bull by its horns. Surely they can restore order if gangsters start something.

Come to our country. I will personally accompany anyone to any place, and no foreign guest will see anything but respect. I thought I had come here not to sit in sweltering heat in a closed car. I thought I had come as a free man as a guest of a free people. The facts can evoke nothing but profound disappointment on my part.

Despite the fracas over Disneyland, Khrushchev's visit marked a turning point in the Cold War. No previous Soviet ruler had visited the United States – not even Lenin in his days as an exile. Khrushchev's arrival began with a reminder of Soviet prowess, when, at the airport, he presented Eisenhower with a model of a small sphere which the Soviet rocket *Lunik 2* had landed on the surface of the Moon two days earlier.

On September 27, from the presidential retreat at Camp David, Eisenhower and Khrushchev issued a joint declaration. The two men agreed that international disputes, including that over Berlin, should be settled 'not by the application of force but by peaceful means through negotiation'. This would be carried out first with regard to Berlin, where 'an understanding was reached' – according to the joint communiqué – that negotiations would be reopened 'with a view to achieving a solution that would be in accordance with the interests of all concerned'.

The Eisenhower–Khrushchev meeting was a breakthrough in Cold War diplomacy. On his return to Moscow, Khrushchev literally changed planes and flew on to Peking, telling Mao Tse-tung: 'We on our part must do all that we can to exclude war as a means of settling disputes.' The Chinese were not responsive to the new mood. It was wrong, declaimed the Communist Party journal *Red Flag*, to believe that the Americans would 'lay down their butcher knife and become Buddhas'. Khrushchev responded to such attacks by comparing Mao Tse-tung's hostility to that of Trotsky in 1918.

'Butcher knife', 'Trotsky' – words of denunciation did not bode well for international harmony. But new international efforts in the spheres of medicine and ecology offered hope to millions of people. That year the Vienna Cancer Institute started the first ever bone-marrow bank; and the International Council for the Conservation of Nature planned a register of all national parks and nature reserves in the world, and launched new efforts to preserve animal species that were in danger.

Films continued to make their impact on millions of viewers. Lewis Milestone's *Pork Chop Hill*, set in the Korean War – written by James R. Webb and starring Gregory Peck – stressed the futility of war, much as, thirty years earlier, Milestone's film of Erich Maria Remarque's *All Quiet on the Western Front* had done. It was only six years since the Korean War had ended. The first film about it to make a wide impact had been released in 1956: *The Rack* told the story of an American soldier who, under torture, had helped the enemy. Starring Paul Newman, it gave a powerful portrayal of the torment of an American soldier in captivity. Attempts to glamorize the cruel nature of war, which had characterized many films about the Second World War, seemed to be at an end.

CHAPTER NINE

1960

> ... we stand today on the edge of a New Frontier – the frontier of the 1960s – a frontier of unknown opportunities and perils – a frontier of unfulfilled hopes and threats.
>
> SENATOR JOHN F. KENNEDY

IN AFRICA, 1960 was the year of the greatest change yet. Many forces had conspired to deprive the European powers of what, at the start of the century, had seemed their permanent – and perpetually well-meaning – place there. During the Second World War many African soldiers had served with the Allied armies and seen something of other methods of government and behaviour. Other Africans had become disillusioned by the poor quality of European administrators who – as war took the better-qualified men away for responsible work elsewhere – came in their place and lacked sympathy. Individual Africans of charismatic appeal emerged.

Prominent among the new African leaders was Dr Nnamdi Azikwe (known as 'Zik'), a founder of the National Council for Nigeria and the Cameroons, who had been advocating self-government for Nigeria since 1937. Azikwe had lived in the United States and had absorbed much of American democratic ideals and methods. His assertion that all Africans had the right to independence and self-determination spread throughout equatorial Africa, 'a sweet sound', the historian M.N. Hennessy, has written, 'even to the illiterate masses so assiduously insulated against outside influence by the Belgians'.

On January 6 the British Prime Minister, Harold Macmillan, set off from London on a month-long visit to Ghana, Nigeria, Northern and Southern Rhodesia and South Africa. On January 18, while he was still on his journey, a Kenya constitutional conference opened in London, at Lancaster House. It was boycotted at first by the African elected members, but on January 25

224 · A HISTORY OF THE TWENTIETH CENTURY

they took their place at the negotiating table. For almost a month they worked on the details of a new constitution.

On February 3, two days before the end of his African journey, Macmillan spoke in Cape Town to the South African parliament. 'The wind of change is blowing through this continent,' he said, 'and our national policies must take account of it.' Those members of the South African parliament who were confident of the superiority and staying power of apartheid were not impressed or influenced by these words, or by the spirit behind them. But British policy elsewhere in Africa, where Britain had the power to influence, was greatly affected by them.

On February 21, within three weeks of Macmillan's 'wind of change' speech, the Kenya constitutional conference in London reached agreement. An end to British rule was in sight. The British government agreed to accept majority rule in Kenya based on universal suffrage, where the White and Black vote would be of identical value, thus ensuring the emergence of Black majority rule. The British government also offered to buy a million acres of the fertile White Highlands of Kenya for redistribution as smallholdings to Black African farmers.

Ghana decided that year to become a republic, but it remained in the Commonwealth. The future of the Central African Federation (in which Rhodesia and Nyasaland had been joined since 1953) was also much debated during the year of change when, on April 1, the Nyasaland nationalist leader Dr Hastings Banda was released from prison after being incarcerated for twelve months as a 'dangerous agitator' and invited to London to discuss the constitutional evolution of the Federation. Two and a half months after Banda's release the state of emergency was ended. A British government report published on October 11 recommended greater participation of Africans in the Federation's Assembly, and an end to racially discriminatory legislation.

A constitutional conference on the future of Sierra Leone – where the first British settlement dated back to 1790 – was opened in London on April 27. Within a week it had proposed full independence for the colony inside the year, and this was obtained without setback. Two months later, on June 26, British Somaliland became independent, and on the following day joined Somalia – one of the former Italian colonies which had been handed to Britain to administer in 1950 as a United Nations Trusteeship. Five days after the independence of British Somaliland the final terms of the independence of Cyprus were agreed between Britain and Cyprus, with the long-awaited transfer of power taking place on August 16. On October 1 the Nigerian Federation became independent, with Dr Azikwe as Governor-General; three years later he was to become the Federal President.

Among those who had been instrumental in ensuring that, with independence, the Nigerian administrative structure would work smoothly was a British civil servant, Foley Newns, who had served in Nigeria for the previous twenty-seven years, and who, in the words of his obituary in *The Times* (in 1998), 'loved the Nigerians, and African people in general'. Following his work for the new Nigeria, he did the same for Sierra Leone, where he remained a government adviser after independence.

The 'wind of change' was not making its impact felt everywhere in the British Empire. In Southern Rhodesia, a Law and Order Maintenance Act, passed on November 25, gave the police extra powers against Black nationalist agitation. The Churches, the legal profession and the White newspapers protested at the severity of the measures, but they were passed into law by the predominantly White parliament. The White settlers were convinced that they could retain power. Their aspirations were to survive, and cause Britain deep anguish, for almost twenty more years.

As well as the British Empire, other empires were also resigned to the reality of national self-determination. On January 20 a month-long conference began in Brussels to move the Congo towards independence. The senior Congolese negotiator was Patrice Lumumba, one of the most active members of the Congolese National Movement (the MNC), who had been released from prison to attend – he was serving a six-month sentence for inciting riots the previous October. The forty-four Congolese African leaders who were present were unanimous in demanding independence at the end of the following six months. When the negotiations ended in the third week of February the details of the passage to full independence had been worked out. What had not been decided – and this was primarily a matter for the African delegates – was whether the independent Congo would be a unitary State, as Lumumba wished, or a federal one, as was especially the demand of the Congolese from the mineral-rich Katanga province in the south-east.

In accordance with the timetable established during the Brussels negotiations, elections were held in the Congo on May 11 and lasted for eleven days. Polling was accompanied by fighting between various tribes and quickly spread to the capital, Léopoldville. After several Africans had been killed in the capital, the Belgians declared martial law. Lumumba ignored the restrictions to continue campaigning. Although his Party did not achieve anything like an overall majority – it won 41 of the 137 seats – his was the largest single-Party bloc.

The Belgian Resident Minister in the Congo asked Lumumba to form a government. He received parliamentary support to do so, by a narrow margin – seventy-four to sixty-three votes in the National Assembly – and became Prime Minister. The transfer of power was accompanied by violent attacks by units of the Congolese army on Europeans, including rape, and looting. Lumumba managed to restore order by dismissing all remaining Belgian officers, and declaring that every soldier in the army would be promoted one rank, with the attendant increase in pay. Outside Léopoldville the attacks on Europeans continued. Most Belgians were forced to flee. They were the local administrators, teachers, technicians and above all doctors whose skills were badly needed in the newly independent State, and who had been willing to commit themselves to the successful evolution of an independent Congo.

With much of the Congolese army in revolt, the situation in the Congo deteriorated rapidly. On July 12 Lumumba appealed to the United Nations for the 'urgent despatch' of military assistance. That same day Belgium ordered its troops who were still in the Congo to maintain law and order. At Léopoldville airport, through which many Belgian refugees were trying to leave the country, six Congolese soldiers were killed in clashes with the Belgian troops trying to maintain order. Two days later a secessionist movement in Katanga province declared independence. Its leader, Moise Tshombe, declared himself Prime Minister. The Belgians, with whom Tshombe had maintained good relations, supported him in his endeavour. Sixty per cent of the Congo's income derived from the resources of Katanga.

Another breakaway region, the Kasai province, under the leadership of Albert Kalonji, declared itself an 'Independent Mining State'. Lumumba sent troops by air – to the provincial capital, Luluabourg – to try to restore the rule of the centre, but Kalonji appealed to Tshombe, who sent troops from Katanga to sustain his neighbour's independent stance. As the Kasai State defended its secession, hundreds of Congolese troops were killed.

Lumumba was desperate to maintain the territorial unity of the Congo. He had already appealed for help to the United Nations, and on July 15 the first United Nations troops – Ghanaian and Tunisian soldiers – arrived in Léopoldville, and took control of the radio station in the capital, and, within a week, of airports throughout the country. Even as they asserted the

1. Yucca Flat, Nevada: on 17 March 1953 more than two thousand United States Marines took part in an atomic test. Having emerged from their foxholes immediately after the explosion, they are seen watching the mushroom cloud.

2. A Soviet tank in East Berlin, following the outbreak of strikes on 17 June 1953.

3. French parachutists dropped over Dien Bien Phu, being watched by parachutists who had landed earlier. This photograph was taken on 26 November 1953.

4. Soviet tanks in the streets of Budapest, 26 October 1956.

5. The head of Stalin, decorated with a traffic sign, is set up in a Budapest street after the statue had been toppled and dragged for two miles through the streets, 31 October 1956.

6. Budapest citizens pass the graves of those who were buried in the street where they fell. A photograph transmitted to the West on 1 November 1956.

7. (*Left*) Port Said: a young Egyptian boy surveys the ruins. Behind him is a British tank. This photograph was taken on 13 November 1956. Two days later the United Nations Emergency Force (UNEF) began to take over from the British.

8. (*Left, below*) Fort Worth, Texas: a new highway intersection, built as a result of the Federal Aid Highways Act of 1956. The press agency caption to this photograph described its four levels as part of 'one of the most ambitious highway schemes ever attempted'.

9. (*Below*) Mao Tse-tung and Nikita Khrushchev in Moscow, 1957.

10. Chinese army trucks crossing one of the high mountain passes on their way to Tibet, to supply their troops after the Tibetan uprising of 17 March 1959.

11. Lhasa, Tibet, 10 April 1959: a Chinese Communist official reads a proclamation from Peking calling on the Tibetans to give their allegiance to the Chinese-supported Panchen Lama, following the flight of the Dalai Lama to India.

12. South Africa: the Sharpeville massacre, 21 March 1960.

13. Senator John F. Kennedy, seeking the Democratic nomination for the Presidential elections, and his wife Jacqueline. On accepting the nomination on 15 July 1960, he spoke of the need for a 'new frontier' and called for a 'peaceful revolution for human rights – demanding an end to racial discrimination in all parts of our community life'.

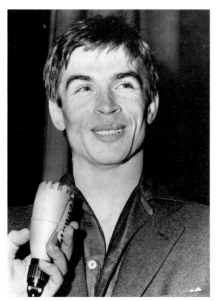

14. The Russian dancer, Rudolf Nureyev, announces that he is seeking asylum in the West: Paris, 22 June 1961.

15. Hendrik Verwoerd, upholder of apartheid, 8 March 1961.

16. Conrad Schumann, the first East German border guard to escape to the West, jumps across barbed wire on what was to be the site of the Berlin Wall, 15 August 1961.

17. 'White Persons Only': a sign at a seaside resort near Cape Town, South Africa.

18. Martin Luther King addressing marchers in Selma, Alabama, 9 March 1965.

authority of the United Nations there were mutinies in the Congolese army. On August 8 the United Nations called for Belgian troops to leave. Within a month they had gone.

On August 12 United Nations troops entered the breakaway Katanga province, together with the United Nations Secretary-General, Dag Hammarskjöld. Among the troops was a detachment from Canada. On September 2 the first Soviet aircraft were sent to the Congo as support for Lumumba's government in Léopoldville. Lumumba used the forces at his disposal to try to unify the country under his control, but he was deposed on September 14 after only eleven weeks as Prime Minister. The troops who seized power in Léopoldville were led by Colonel Joseph Mobutu. A former Congolese sergeant in the Belgian colonial regiment, Mobutu had risen rapidly to prominence since independence four months earlier as he had suppressed the mutinies with harsh measures and summary justice.

In an attempt to heal the secessionist rifts, Mobutu flew on October 16 to Elisabethville, where he and Tshombe agreed that Katanga would remain within the Congo, which would be a State based upon 'unity in diversity'. Soviet, Czechoslovak and other Communist-bloc diplomats and technicians were asked to leave. The Egyptian President, Gamal Abdul Nasser, was accused of 'sustaining rebel elements and hatching plots'. On November 7 the Congo pledged its allegiance to the United Nations Charter. On the following day, as fighting continued in Katanga in the Baluba tribal area, ten Irish soldiers of the United Nations contingent were killed.

Lumumba had been imprisoned by Mobutu but managed to escape. He at once called on the United Nations troops in Léopoldville both to protect him and to help him regain power. They declined to do so, and on November 28 he fled to Kasai province. There he was captured three days later by forces loyal to Mobutu. After being tortured by his captors he was executed on 17 January 1961. When the United Nations demanded an 'impartial' inquiry into the circumstances of his death, Mobutu refused, just as he had earlier refused to allow Red Cross representatives to visit Lumumba in prison. In the Soviet Union, where Lumumba was made a symbol of the anti-colonial struggle, a university in Moscow for foreign students was established and named after him, and honoured him as a 'hero victim of the struggle against colonialism and the rule of mercenaries'.

The struggles for power in the Congo, and the disruption caused by civil war, led to famine on a scale that horrified the United Nations observers sent in to advise. Two hundred Congolese a day were dying of hunger. By the end of the year almost ten million pounds of food, milk and medical supplies had been sent in by the United Nations. Seed corn was being supplied by air, and President Eisenhower set aside $5 million from United States funds as emergency aid.

Elsewhere in Africa, the moves to full independence had proceeded with rapidity. On June 26, Madagascar was proclaimed independent. It had been declared a French protectorate in 1885, after which, during a ten-year struggle, the native Hova dynasty had been suppressed and the Queen, Ranavalona, exiled to Algeria. The Hova people had again rebelled in 1946. Following independence, Madagascar remained within the French Community, and was admitted to the United Nations. Its two official languages were (and are) Malagasy and French.

On July 11 the French government agreed to grant immediate independence to seven of its dependencies, the Republics of Dahomey, Niger, Upper Volta, Ivory Coast, Chad, Central Africa and Congo Brazzaville.[1]

On November 28 Mauritania declared its independence from France, and became an Islamic Republic. Only in Algeria had the Muslim national movement been frustrated. The offer made by de Gaulle of self-determination for Algeria led to riots by the French settlers which broke out on January 24 and continued for a week – 'Barricades Week' in the history of modern France. Settlers, led by a café owner in Algiers – Joseph Ortiz – used paving stones to build their barricades. When police loyal to de Gaulle advanced towards the barricades they were shot down. As wounded policemen tried to crawl away from the barricades to safety, they were shot again. In all, fourteen policemen were killed. De Gaulle appealed on television to the rioters to lay down their arms. They refused to do so, chanting their nationalist slogan *Algérie Française*.

Fearing that the rebels would win control over the French army in Algeria, several of whose leaders had begun to express open sympathy with Ortiz and his fighters, de Gaulle prepared to make a second television broadcast on January 29. France was bitterly divided over the way forward in Algeria. De Gaulle's British biographer, Charles Williams – himself of French Huguenot origin – writes of how the General 'seemed to realize that the Fifth Republic, his own creation, was on the brink of disintegration, and that the

---

[1] After independence the Republic of Dahomey became Benin; Upper Volta became Burkina Faso; Central Africa became the Central African Republic.

speech that he had to make was to be one of the most important of his whole long life'. It was not a successful speech. 'He did not look well: he seemed tired, as though he had not been sleeping. But he had deliberately put on his uniform of brigadier-general, and when he spoke his voice was determined, each point being emphasized by a raised finger in what was otherwise a clenched fist. It was not simply the Head of State who was speaking; it was General de Gaulle.'

In his television broadcast de Gaulle reiterated what he had laid down the previous September as the basis of French policy: 'The Algerians shall have free choice of their destiny.' He then ordered the army not to associate itself with the rebels in any way whatsoever. Its sole duty was to re-establish law and order. No concessions could be made to those 'who dream of being usurpers'. If this were to happen, France would become a 'poor broken plaything adrift on a sea of chance'.

De Gaulle's appeal succeeded. Army unit after army unit in Algeria declared its loyalty, the centre of Algiers was cordoned off and surrounded by troops loyal to the government in Paris. Water and electricity were cut off on orders of the Area Commander, General Crépin. The rebels were on their own. On February 1 Ortiz fled from the city. The men he had led surrendered. They were allowed to leave the city still carrying their arms. Their departure, headed by Ortiz's colleague Pierre Lagaillarde, a member of the Chamber of Deputies, was witnessed by John Wallis, the *Daily Telegraph* correspondent:

At 11.50 Lagaillarde appeared from behind the barricade. He bade farewell to his father, a lawyer who fought in the 8th Army during the war and has been with his son behind the barricade throughout. Then, head high and a tommy-gun slung across his chest, Lagaillarde marched out.

A small crowd of civilians who had been standing in front of the barricade cheered and clapped, shouting 'Algérie française, Algérie française'. Soon six hundred men followed Lagaillarde out singing the 'Marseillaise'.

They formed up between two lines of Foreign Legionaries, and were put in lorries and taken to the Foreign Legion camp at Zeralda, just west of here.

Lagaillarde was driven away in a jeep, sitting beside the driver. Meanwhile a crowd which had gathered on the sea front at the foot of the Post Office Gardens tried to break through the Foreign Legion cordon, to get nearer Lagaillarde and his men.

The Legionaries stopped them and there were some scuffles. The Legion also prevented anyone taking photographs.

Lagaillarde's famous white Bell helicopter was seen to take off from the University Gardens. Immediately two Army Sikorskys gave chase, and forced the helicopter to land back in the gardens.

In it were the pilot and Mme. Lagaillarde, the young Deputy's wife.

In a gesture of reconciliation, Colonel Dufour, the commander of the 1st Parachute Regiment of the Foreign Legion, to whom Lagaillarde and his men surrendered, told them: 'You are surrendering, but you do so as soldiers of France. You need have no anxiety.'

The Algerian Muslim nationalists remained under continual French military pressure. After a terrorist attack on a beach at Chenoua, west of Algiers, on August 1, when twelve people killed included some driving by in their cars and several holidaymakers on the beach, the French army took swift action, and more than thirty Algerians were killed. De Gaulle, meanwhile, continued to seek a means to break the deadlock and move forward the process to Algerian self-government. On June 14 he had appealed to the Algerian provisional government to negotiate a ceasefire. When the response was favourable he invited one of the Front de la Libération Nationale (the FLN) military leaders, Si Salah, to talks in France. Si Salah agreed to participate, and the talks were held at Melun in the summer. But the French conditions, which made the start of negotiations dependent on the FLN laying down its weapons, were rejected, a new Chief of Staff of the FLN, Houari Boumedienne – who had earlier commanded the Algerian nationalist forces in the Oran area – led an intensified military struggle against the French troops.

That September in Paris a manifesto was issued against the continuing war in Algeria. It was signed by 121 intellectuals, among them Jean-Paul Sartre and his wife Simone de Beauvoir. There followed demonstrations in the streets calling for an end to the attempted French military destruction of the Algerian nationalists. De Gaulle was of a like mind. On November 4 he announced that the way forward for France was not *Algérie Française* but *Algérie Algérienne*. There had to be self-government. The settlers were furious. When de Gaulle visited Algeria on December 9 there were four attempts to assassinate him. During his visit, French settlers on the streets indicated their hostility to him at every turn. It was the Algerians who, beneath a flurry of green and white FLN flags, chanted with approval 'Vive de Gaulle!' On December 11, while de Gaulle was still in Algiers, European and Muslim demonstrators clashed in the streets. The police opened fire, and at least 123 people were killed, most of them Muslims.

Returning to France two days after the killings, de Gaulle announced less than a week later, on December 19, that there would be a national referendum on the future of Algeria. The people of France would have to say whether they wanted Algeria to be granted full independence once peace was restored there. The vote, held within three weeks, on 8 January 1961, was in favour of independence. Talks were opened with the Algerian provisional government, and independence followed.

On March 21 there was a demonstration in the South African township of Sharpeville against the pass laws which forced all non-Whites to carry identity cards, and which made it virtually impossible for them to spend the night in a White area, even if it was their place of work. Africans who did not want to join the march were pressed into doing so. Telephone kiosks were wrecked and telephone lines cut. At the height of the protest a crowd of several thousand surrounded the local police station. The crowd was unarmed, the seventy-five policemen inside the station were armed. The police ordered the crowd to disperse, but they would not do so. The police then opened fire.

Fifty-six Africans were killed. Most of them were shot in the back as they tried to flee from the shooting. The scene, a policeman told reporters, resembled 'a world war battlefield, with bodies sprawled all round'.

There was worldwide indignation at the Sharpeville shootings. There had also been deaths at Langa, near Cape Town, during a similar protest demonstration. As police moved in to disperse it there had been cries of 'Kill the white men.' Seven Africans were shot dead. After the shooting at Langa the Africans, angered beyond endurance, set fire to schools, shops and the local administrative centre.

In an unprecedented criticism of the situation inside South Africa, the United States commented through a State Department spokesman:

The United States deplores violence in all its forms and hopes that the African people of South Africa will be able to obtain redress for legitimate grievances by peaceful means. While the United States as a matter of practice does not ordinarily comment on the internal affairs of governments with which it enjoys normal relations, it cannot help but regret the tragic loss of life resulting from the measures taken against demonstrators in South Africa.

On April 1 the United States followed up the State Department criticism by voting at the United Nations Security Council in favour of a resolution which called on the South African government to abandon racial segregation. Henry Cabot Lodge, the American representative on the Security Council – and grandson of the leading isolationist Senator of the same name – urged the South African government to 'reconsider' its racial policies in the interests of peace as well as justice, telling the Council: 'It is not too late to reverse the tide in South Africa.'

The South African government ignored all such pleas and censures. After eleven days of strikes and further protest demonstrations by Africans throughout South Africa, it passed the Unlawful Organizations Act, making demonstrations such as that at Sharpeville illegal and subject to immediate dissolution. It also issued a banning order on both the African National Congress and the Pan-African Congress. The leaders of the banned groups went into hiding. They also formed a guerrilla wing, the Umkonto we Sizwe – the Spear of the Nation. Among those who took a lead in this was Nelson Mandela, one of those who had been arrested for treason four years earlier, and then released while the trial was being prepared. He later recalled:

At 1.30 on the morning of March 30 I was awakened by sharp unfriendly knocks at my door, the unmistakable signature of the police. 'The time has come,' I said to myself as I opened the door to find half-a-dozen armed security policemen.

They turned the house upside down, taking virtually every piece of paper they could find, including the transcripts I had recently been making of my mother's recollections of family history and tribal fables. I was never to see them again.

I was then arrested without a warrant, and given no opportunity to call my lawyer. They refused to inform my wife as to where I was to be taken. I simply nodded at Winnie; it was no time for words of comfort.

As the treason trials began again, a protest against the Sharpeville killings by Bishop Ambrose Reeves of Johannesburg led to his being expelled from South Africa. His 'crime' was to have pointed out that during the killings several of the unarmed Africans had been shot in the back. A further focus on the restrictions and restraints imposed by apartheid came when the Nobel Peace Prize was awarded to one of the African National Congress leaders, Chief Albert Lutuli. For the past eight years Lutuli had been confined under house arrest to a remote farm. Yet from his place of exile he called for racial moderation and urged that resistance to apartheid should not be violent.

South Africa was on the verge of abandoning its last links with Britain, but when the issue of declaring a republic was put to the vote, in a referendum on October 6, the result was close. Only Whites were allowed to vote. In favour of a republic were 52.14 per cent and against 47.42 per cent. The republic came into being the following May. Steadily every facet of moderation was being eroded or bypassed. At the end of the year one of the outspoken critics of apartheid, Alan Paton – who had just returned to South Africa from a World Council of Churches meeting in Geneva – was deprived of the right to travel abroad for a whole decade.

In the United States the government was under public pressure to respond to several recent Soviet appeals for negotiations on disarmament, or to explain whether the Soviet Union's policies constituted a threat to the United States itself. In his State of the Union message on January 7, which was broadcast live on television, Eisenhower told Congress that 'recent Soviet deportment and pronouncements suggest the possible opening of a somewhat less strained period in the relationship between the Soviet Union and the Free World', but he went on to issue a note of caution. 'Neither we nor any other Free World nation', he said, 'can permit ourselves to be misled by pleasant promises until they are tested by performance.'

Within two weeks of Eisenhower's warning, the United States strengthened its defence position in the Pacific when, on January 19, it signed a Treaty of Mutual Co-operation and Security with Japan. This Treaty, which was signed in Washington, also confirmed Japan's position as an integral part of the anti-Communist structure. That such a structure was needed, and even urgently so, seemed suddenly evident when on January 28 one of those charged with national defence, General Thomas S. Power, the head of Strategic Air Command, admitted publicly that within two years the Soviet Union would have sufficient long-range missiles to be able to launch a 'massive' attack on the United States. Four days later the Secretary of Defense, Thomas S. Gates, made a public admission that for the coming three years the Soviet Union was likely to have 'a moderate numerical superiority' in missiles.

General Power sought to calm public anxiety by proposing that there should be a special force of United States bombers 'on alert' in the air at all times. Without such a 'continuous airborne alert', he warned, the Soviet

Union, by launching three hundred missiles simultaneously, could knock out America's bomber striking force at its bases on the ground in thirty minutes. President Eisenhower himself tried to counter the alarm created by General Power's remarks. Enough heavy bombers would always be left after a first strike by any aggressor, he said, to enable the United States to retaliate 'very effectively'.

Eisenhower spoke these reassuring words on February 3. Even as he did so, defence analysts were studying the results of an experiment – held on January 29 – when an Honest John artillery rocket, on its way to a target and capable of carrying a nuclear warhead, was blown up by a Hawk anti-aircraft missile. The rocket warhead never reached its target. Experiments were immediately begun to increase the range of the anti-aircraft missile so that it could intercept and destroy any incoming intercontinental ballistic missile. The new defensive missile was given the name Nike-Zeus. Starting in February, a United States nuclear-powered submarine, *Triton*, sought to circumnavigate the globe without once rising to the surface of the water. It was successful, completing its 41,519-mile circumnavigation in eighty-four days.

The defence preparations of the United States were at the forefront of known experimentation and design. As part of its attempt to counter any possible Soviet submarine offensive, on April 27 the nuclear-powered submarine *Tullibee* was launched in the United States with more tracking devices on board than on any previous submarine. It became known as the 'big ears' of the United States Navy. Within a month, on May 24, the United States space satellite programme launched *Midas 2*. It was instantly known as the 'Spy in the Sky' satellite. Weighing two and a half tons, *Midas 2* carried with it 3,600 pounds' weight of instruments. Its aim was to test the feasibility of setting up a network of orbiting satellites able to send back to Earth almost instantaneous warning of the launching of a ballistic missile attack.

On July 20 the first nuclear-powered submarine, *George Washington*, which had not yet gone out on patrol beyond United States territorial waters, fired a Polaris missile from under water. The missile covered a distance of 1,100 miles. Its essential capacity was that it could be armed with a nuclear warhead. Soviet defence experts noted with alarm that the distance from the Baltic Sea to Moscow was less than five hundred miles, as was the distance from the Aegean Sea to the Soviet naval bases of Odessa and Sevastopol.

Efforts to negotiate a disarmament agreement between East and West took on a new lease of life on March 15, when a ten-Power disarmament committee met at Geneva under the auspices of the United Nations. Talking continued for more than three months. Meanwhile, those who hoped that a way forward could be found to reconcile Soviet-American differences were astonished and dismayed when Khrushchev announced on May 5 to the Supreme Soviet that the Soviet Union had shot down an American high-altitude spy aircraft – the U-2 – above the Ural Mountains, and that the pilot had been captured. He had been on a flight path that began at an air base near Peshawar, in Pakistan, and was taking him over the Urals to Greenland.

The U-2 had been shot down on May 1. Its pilot, Captain Gary Powers, was sentenced by a Soviet military court to ten years' imprisonment for espionage. The United States conceded that while 'extensive aerial surveillance' was 'normally of a peripheral character', it was, as in the case of Captain Powers' flight, 'occasionally by penetration'. The Secretary of State, Christian Herter, who issued this statement on May 9, also insisted that the United States government 'would be derelict in its responsibility' if it did not 'take such measures as are possible unilaterally to lessen and overcome the danger of surprise attack'.

The pressure for nuclear disarmament was growing. At a mass meeting in Manchester, England, on May 13 a message was read out from the German pastor Martin Niemöller. 'We are all in the same boat,' he declared. 'Nuclear disarmament is more than a problem of politics; we must achieve it for mankind's sake and fight for it in the name of right, of humanity, of God himself.'

Two weeks after the U-2 had been shot down, a summit meeting, planned some time before, began in Paris. The Soviet Union was represented by Khrushchev, the United States by Eisenhower, Britain by Macmillan, and France by de Gaulle. The summit began on May 16. It was a stormy encounter of the leaders of the Great Powers. At a private meeting before the formal opening, Khrushchev said that he would only take part in the summit meeting if the United States 'were to declare that in future the United States will not violate the State borders of the USSR with its aircraft, that it deplores the provocative actions taken in the past, and will punish those directly responsible for such actions'. Confronted by these three demands, the most that Eisenhower was prepared to do was to say that all such overflights had in fact been suspended 'since the recent incident'. There would be no apology, and no punishment. Khrushchev then walked out and the formal summit never took place.

The deliberations of the ten-Power disarmament committee which had been meeting at Geneva fared no better. On June 27 the Soviet and East European delegates walked out and the conference came to a premature end.

The international problems of Communism were nowhere great enough to threaten the fabric of its control either inside the Soviet Union or over the nation States of Eastern Europe. The control of the Communist Party inside the Soviet Union was as complete as it had been under Stalin: when a former Red Army journalist Vasily Grossman completed his novel *Life and Fate*, with its description of those who had 'wasted away' in the Gulag, he knew that it could not be published in the Soviet Union, but that the manuscript would have to be smuggled to the West if it were ever to appear in print.

On April 14 the East German government announced that its collectivization of agriculture was 'completed'. In Poland there were riots at the industrial town of Nowa Huta, just outside Cracow, when a plot of land that had been set aside for a church was confiscated by the authorities. In both Hungary and Czechoslovakia there was an intensified effort to extend rural collectivization. In Czechoslovakia, in opposing any reduction of the working week for factory workers, a member of the secretariat of the Central Committee of the Communist Party warned that any free time that resulted from a reduction in hours would encourage 'various petty-bourgeois tendencies, such as shirking participation in public and political events, pottering in the garden, or tinkering with the car'.

In Czechoslovakia a parish priest was sentenced to five years in prison for having 'expressed his opposition to the present social order'. A local Communist Party newspaper attacked what it called a 'considerable part' of the Czech university student body for being 'still under religious influence'. Another newspaper was critical of school teachers, telling its readers on March 22: 'Some teachers may keep to the principles of scientific materialism laid down in the syllabus, but when school is over we find them in church.' The paper went on to warn: 'The atheist education of children and parents will be a long and uphill task.'

To try to keep knowledge and recollections of the inter-war democracy at as great a distance as possible, postal clerks throughout Czechoslovakia were ordered to remove from all letters coming from the United States a stamp, issued to celebrate World Refugee Year, that honoured Thomas Masaryk, the founder of independent Czechoslovakia.

*   *   *

The relationship between the Soviet Union and China was in disarray. There had been anger among the Chinese leadership when the previous year the Soviet Union refused to support China's border dispute with India, to the extent that Khrushchev extended large Soviet monetary credits to the Indian government, and belittled the Chinese territorial claims as 'sad' and 'stupid'. For its part, China repeatedly denounced the Soviet call for 'peaceful coexistence' between East and West, and rejected with contempt the Soviet emphasis on the need to avert war between the contending blocs.

On August 25 the Soviet Communist Party condemned the 'dogmatism' of Mao Tse-tung. The Chinese responded by declaring that all negotiations with the 'imperialist' enemy, and all help given — as the Soviet Union was doing on a growing scale — to non-aligned, non-Communist governments, such as India, weakened the will of the 'revolutionary masses'. The Chinese went so far as to say, contrary to the current Soviet viewpoint, that war itself, even if it delayed the ultimate victory of Communism, could not prevent it.

There were 1,390 Soviet experts working in China, helping on various industrial projects. In September they were summoned back to the Soviet Union. Two of those who returned were nuclear-weapons experts. The Chinese complained that, although they had been sent to China to share their knowledge, they had refused to do so, proving themselves to be 'mute monks who could read but not speak'. On leaving China, the two Russians tore up any documents they could not take with them.

Inside China there was no mitigation of the severity of the Communist regime or of its determination to impose strict ideological conformity. In addition to the famine, which was in its third year, droughts and floods which had created massive hardship in 1959 continued throughout 1960. Tibet, under Chinese rule, was likewise affected by grave natural disasters, as well as by the famine. In Chengdu, Jung Chang was a witness to the continuing famine. One day a three-year-old girl, the daughter of a neighbour, went missing:

> A few weeks later the neighbour saw a young girl playing in the street wearing a dress that looked like her daughter's. She went up and examined it: it had a mark which identified it as her daughter's. She reported this to the police.
>
> It turned out that the parents of the young girl were selling wind-dried meat. They had abducted and murdered a number of babies and sold them

as rabbit meat at exorbitant prices. The couple were executed and the case was hushed up, but it was widely known that baby killing did go on at the time.

Years later I met an old colleague of my father's, a very kind and capable man, not given to exaggeration. He told me with great emotion what he had seen during the famine in one particular commune. Thirty-five percent of the peasants had died, in an area where the harvest had been good — although little was collected, since the men had been pulled out to produce steel, and the commune canteen had wasted a large proportion of what there was.

One day a peasant burst into his room and threw himself on the floor, screaming that he had committed a terrible crime and begging to be punished. Eventually it came out that he had killed his own baby and eaten it. Hunger had been like an uncontrollable force driving him to take up the knife. With tears rolling down his cheeks, the official ordered the peasant to be arrested. Later he was shot as a warning to baby killers.

Despite the ravages of the famine, which killed as many as one in thirty Chinese, the population of China reached 700 million, making it by far the world's most populous nation. The authorities tried to counter the effects of the pressure of population in the cities by enforced internal migration. Hundreds of thousands of Chinese were moved from crowded to empty areas. When life in the remote regions proved even more difficult than it had been in the cities, many of the emigrants returned to their original homes. There, as in the countryside, the use of local people to operate steel furnaces continued to be official policy, and dogma. Again and again the authorities trumpeted, at the insistence of Chairman Mao Tse-tung, that China would soon overtake Britain in its industrial production. Given the fact that China was so much larger than Britain, a fact not mentioned by Mao, this ought not to have been so difficult.

The head of Peking University, Professor Ma Yin-chu, suggested publicly that it was wrong of the authorities to believe that vast numbers of unskilled labourers could equal the scientific and labour-saving devices of the more advanced industrial countries. He was ordered to recant, refused to do so, and was dismissed from his post.

There was also a sustained onslaught inside China on Christian religious worship — many millions of Chinese were Christian. On March 17 it was announced from Peking that the Roman Catholic Bishop of Shanghai,

Monsignor Ignatius Kung Ping-mei, who had been held in prison for the previous five years, had been given a life sentence. Twelve other Chinese Catholics were sentenced to between five and twenty years in prison. Bishop James E. Walsh, the American citizen who had been the head of a Christian mission in Shanghai for many years, was sentenced to twenty years in prison.

The nature of the Chinese catastrophe was understood in the West. On February 12 *The Times* published a remarkable leading article entitled 'The Ravages of Catastrophe', in which it reflected on the historical antecedents of famine and civil war in China. The article was prompted by the publication in Canada of a book by Dr Ho Ping-ti of the University of British Columbia. Dr Ho calculated the Chinese deaths from civil war alone in Szechwan Province from 1932 and 1934 at one million; in the Sino-Japanese war at between fifteen and twenty million; and in the Nationalist-Communist civil war from 1946 to 1949 at between two and three million. *The Times* commented:

> It is a terrible century to look back over. How much is China today affected by memories passed on or by living memory of this frightfulness? When we read of peasant discontent over the communes, over food rationing, over the loss of liberty and the other pressures which they suffer from a Government intent on speedy revolution there is no cause to doubt such complaining. But its significance will be mistaken if the welter of blood and suffering from which China has emerged is not also comprehended.

'The very men who have imposed peace and discipline in the past decade', *The Times* explained, 'are those who saw the catastrophe of the countryside, were incensed by injustice and suffering, and now drive on feverishly towards an unattainable millennium.'

Fifteen years after the ending of the Second World War, the economic reconstruction of the non-Communist economies was manifesting itself in a growing number of regional groupings. Hardly a month passed without some new development in this sphere. On February 18 seven countries in Latin America set up the Latin American Free Trade Association. On May 3 the European Free Trade Association (EFTA) came into force; as a first step, it announced a twenty per cent tariff cut between its members to be effective after two months. On June 21 the United States, Britain, France and the Netherlands signed an agreement to establish an organization in the Caribbean to promote economic and social co-operation throughout the region.

In Turkey, the democratic forces secured a bloodless victory on May 31, when the army, acting as the protector of the rule of law, overthrew the petty-tyrannical regime of Adnan Menderes. The new ruler, General Geman Gursel, promised elections and carried out his promise. The Western Powers, for whom Turkey was an integral part of the anti-Communist parameter, were relieved that there had been no lurch either to Communist or to Islamic control. Menderes was tried for 'plotting against the State' and executed. Ismet Inönü, the former President and Prime Minister, who had been held under house arrest, was allowed his freedom, and his Democrat Party, which Menderes had banned, was restored to vigorous political activity, with Ismet Inönü emerging again as electoral winner and Prime Minister.

On December 14 a further drawing together of West European economic interests and organizations was achieved in Paris. That day a convention was signed to set up the Organization for Economic Co-operation and Development (OECD). The signatories were the eighteen members of the Organization for European Economic Co-operation (OEEC) together with the United States and Canada. This linking of transatlantic interests with those of Western Europe effectively established an Atlantic economic community. Its success was markedly better than that of the Eastern bloc organization, COMECON, dedicated to the same goal of economic partnership.

In the effort to help poorer nations, the World Bank, which had been set up in 1946 under United Nations auspices to make loans for post-war reconstruction, set up an International Development Association with the power to lend money at low interest rates and with long-term repayment commitments. The United Nations Food and Agricultural Organization also tried to focus attention on the problem of global hunger, launching on July 1 a Freedom from Hunger campaign.

The economic power of those countries that produced most of the world's supply of oil also gathered momentum. Meeting in Baghdad, four Arab countries, Iraq, Iran, Kuwait and Saudi Arabia, together with Venezuela, gave notice that they were the ones who would decide the price and rate of flow of the oil – especially the Middle Eastern oil – that was essential for so many world economies. The result of their deliberations was the establishment, within a year, of the Organization of Petroleum-Exporting Countries (OPEC).

Although not every political disagreement between States could be resolved by mutual economic interests, there were many areas of the globe where the need for economic co-operation led to political reconciliation. This was seen most strikingly on September 19, when India and Pakistan – still at loggerheads over Kashmir – signed a treaty on the joint development of the waters of the River Indus, vital to agricultural progress on both sides of the divide.

In the United States, the struggle for racial equality continued with pain and slowness. On February 2 the first of a growing number of sit-ins took place, in Greensboro, North Carolina, to protest against the segregation being enforced there at a luncheon counter in the local F. W. Woolworth's store. Two days later, at Sumter, South Carolina, twenty-six Black American students were sent to prison after they took their seats – carrying their Bibles – at three Whites-only luncheon counters in the town. In Georgia, Martin Luther King was arrested for organizing sit-ins at Whites-only restaurants. He had also organized 'freedom rides' in those towns and rural districts where segregation on buses was maintained. After his release he continued with both these forms of civil rights protest.

On February 6 a bomb blew a hole in the house of Carlotta Watts, one of five Black schoolchildren who had been admitted to the Little Rock High School five months earlier. In New Orleans, four Black schoolgirls had the hitherto Whites-only school to themselves when no White children at all, of the usual 467, arrived for the would-be 'mixed' classes. Elsewhere in the South, as in West Virginia – the most northerly of the Southern States – there were no such demonstrations, and school integration became a fact of Southern life.

The civil rights campaign in the South received unexpectedly strong support from Northern students, White and Black. A special conference of the National Students Association pledged the support of its branches nationwide for the sit-in movement, and for similar direct action. Direct action had become the main weapon of the civil rights campaigners. To protest against the continued segregation inside churches in the South, kneel-in campaigns were organized in Whites-only churches by White and Black Americans who insisted on praying together. The American newspapers reported daily incidents of protest and counter-protest. A news item in the *New York Times* on March 6, headlined 'NEGROES BATTER CARS AT DRIVE-IN', was typical. It began:

Fifty club-wielding Negroes terrorized a white drive-in at Columbia, SC, yesterday in the most recent outbreak of violence accompanying demonstrations against segregated lunch counters.

An already tense situation in Montgomery, Ala., worsened last night with an announcement that the police would break up any attempt by Negroes to hold a mass protest meeting on the State Capitol grounds today, according to The Associated Press.

Peaceful demonstrations were staged in Florida, Texas and Kentucky. But in Houston a Negro suffered a stab wound at the scene of a sit-down protest.

Among the other items in this article was an account of an attempted sit-down at a variety store in Lexington, Kentucky. The store owner put a sign on the counter saying that his store was closed because of a breakdown. When journalists asked him what had broken down, he replied: 'Relations.'

In Washington – itself a town with a Black majority – Eisenhower's government continued to pass legislation to activate its civil rights policies. In the ten Southern States, while sixty-two per cent of all Whites were registered to vote, only twenty-five per cent of Blacks were registered. On February 29 the Supreme Court upheld, in a unanimous decision, the constitutional validity of those sections of the 1957 Civil Rights Act which made it illegal to interfere with Black voting rights. A new Civil Rights Bill was then introduced, intended to end all obstacles being placed in the way of Black voter registration. Opposition to the Bill by Southern Senators opposed to integration led to a 125-hour filibuster in the Senate. It was the longest filibuster on record.

The Civil Rights Bill found a skilful and determined supporter in the Senate, Senator Lyndon Johnson of Texas, who used his own Southern credentials and deep knowledge of the political system to out-manoeuvre the manoeuvrers. The filibustering Senators were forced to accept the political implications of their numerical weakness, and on April 10 the Bill was given Senate approval by 71 votes to 18. Eleven days later the House of Representatives passed it by 288 votes to 99.

As passed into law, the Civil Rights Act gave authority to the courts to appoint federal 'referees' to safeguard what were then called 'Negro voting rights'. Any attempt to obstruct the exercise of those rights by force or threats of violence was made a Federal offence.

*　　*　　*

Following the return to office for the fourth time of President Syngman Rhee in South Korea on March 15, there were widespread student protests against ballot-rigging. Rhee, who was eighty-five, proclaimed martial law. At Masan, fourteen people were killed on election day when the police fired into a university demonstration against the 'tyranny and corruption' of the Rhee government. The demonstrations spread throughout South Korea. On April 19 there was widespread rioting in the capital, Seoul. The police again used live ammunition, and more than a hundred demonstrators were killed. The American government told Rhee that his 'repressive measures' were 'unsuited to free democracy' and withdrew its support for his administration.

Rhee summoned into Seoul a senior army officer, General Song Yo Chan, with an army division, to maintain order. Hardly had the General arrived than he made it clear that he sympathized with the students and wanted to see an end to the Rhee regime. Rhee resigned on April 27. A month later he was allowed to escape to Hawaii. With the rescinding of most of Rhee's restrictions on freedom of assembly, speech and the press, democracy was restored to South Korea. A Supreme Court was established, and the police – on whose repressive measures Rhee had relied – were put under the control of a committee made up of representatives of all political Parties. During a visit to South Korea in June, Eisenhower indicated his support for the constitutional changes.

On September 23, at the United Nations General Assembly in New York, Khrushchev made a strong attack on the Western world. There was a moment of humour, caught by the television cameras, when Khrushchev took off one of his shoes and began banging it on the desk in front of him. Macmillan intervened to ask the President of the Assembly: 'Mr President, perhaps we could have a translation, I could not quite follow.'

The confrontation was more than that of two men, or of public posturing. Five days later NATO announced a unified system of air defence command. Pressure against the implied use of nuclear weapons which such a unified system implied led, on October 5, at the British Labour Party Conference, meeting at Scarborough, to an overwhelming vote in favour of unilateral nuclear disarmament. The card-vote of delegates representing trade union bloc votes was 407,000 in favour of unilateral disarmament and 43,000 against. This vote went against the wishes of the Party's leader, Hugh Gaitskell, who said after the result was announced: 'I stand by the policy of collective security and the membership of NATO.' He added, 'I cannot possibly support a policy of unilateral disarmament or neutralism for Britain which I believe would be profoundly dangerous for the peace of the world and the safety of our country. The parliamentary Party will have to decide its attitude in the light of the various decisions of the conference.'

The Labour Party vote in favour of unilateral nuclear disarmament, a binding vote on Labour policymakers, was to weaken the Party's negotiating position with the Soviet bloc for more than two decades, including fifteen years in government. It was followed less than a month later, on November 1, by an announcement from Harold Macmillan that Britain had agreed to provide the United States with a base and facilities for American submarines armed with Polaris nuclear missiles. The location for the base was Holy Loch, on the western coast of Scotland. It soon became a focal point of protest by the Campaign for Nuclear Disarmament.

The United States continued to press ahead with its defensive preparations at a hitherto unprecedented peacetime pace. On September 24 an atomic-powered aircraft carrier, USS *Enterprise*, was launched at Newport News, Virginia. She had the capacity to sail for several years without refuelling. The focus of interest in the United States had turned, however, to a more personal and directly visible contest, the forthcoming presidential election. The Republican candidate was the forty-seven-year-old Vice-President, Richard Nixon, who had high hopes of stepping into the place vacated by the ailing President Eisenhower. Nixon was challenged by a contender even younger than himself, forty-three-year-old John F. Kennedy, a Democratic Senator. During his six years as a Congressmen – he was first elected in 1946 after naval service in the Pacific war – and his subsequent eight years as a Senator, Kennedy had been an outspoken and eloquent advocate for labour law reform, civil rights legislation and increased United States financial aid for underdeveloped countries.

Criticism of Kennedy's youth had surfaced at the Democrat National Convention in July during his fight for nomination. Former President Truman had urged Kennedy to be 'patient' for another four years. To these criticisms Kennedy answered that if all those under the age of forty-four were to be excluded 'from positions of trust and command', such a rule 'would have kept Jefferson from writing the Declaration of Independence, Washington from commanding the Continental Army, Madison from fathering the Constitution, and Christopher Columbus from even discovering America'.

Kennedy made a particularly strong impact on the American public during his speech at the Memorial Coliseum in Los Angeles on July 15, when he accepted the Democratic Party nomination for the presidency, and called for a 'peaceful revolution for human rights – demanding an end to racial discrimination in all parts of our community life'. Criticizing what he characterized as the outdated conservatism of the Republicans, Kennedy said:

Today there can be no status quo. For I stand tonight facing west on what was once the last frontier. From the lands that stretch three thousand miles behind me, the pioneers of old gave up their safety, their comfort and sometimes their lives to build a new world here in the West . . . Today some would say that those struggles are all over – that all the horizons have been explored – that all the battles have been won – that there is no longer an American frontier. But I trust that no one in this vast assemblage will agree with those sentiments. For the problems are not all solved and the battles are not all won – and we stand today on the edge of a New Frontier – the frontier of the 1960s – a frontier of unknown opportunities and perils – a frontier of unfulfilled hopes and threats.

Kennedy continued:

. . . I tell you that the New Frontier is here, whether we seek it or not. Beyond that frontier are the uncharted areas of science and space, unsolved problems of peace and war, unconquered pockets of ignorance and prejudice, unanswered questions of poverty and surplus.

It would be easier to shrink back from that frontier, to look to the safe mediocrity of the past, to be lulled by good intentions and high rhetoric – and those who prefer that course should not cast their votes for me, regardless of Party. But I believe the times demand new invention, innovation, imagination, decision. I am asking each of you to be pioneers on that New Frontier. My call is to the young in heart, regardless of age – to all who respond to the Scriptural call: 'Be strong and of good courage; be not afraid; neither be thou dismayed.'

On September 26, six weeks before the presidential election was to be held, the two candidates appeared together for a television debate, held in Chicago. It was the first time such a debate had taken place. It was watched by an estimated seventy million Americans. Opinion polls afterwards judged the two candidates to have performed equally well, although Nixon looked older than he was, and gaunt.

In the course of his opening remarks, Kennedy took a strong stance on foreign and defence policy. The question confronting the United States and the world, he said, was whether freedom could be maintained under the 'fiercest attack' it had ever known. He then referred to a historic speech a century earlier:

In the election of 1860 Abraham Lincoln said the question was whether this nation could exist half-slave or half-free.

In the election of 1960, and with the world around us, the question is whether the world will exist half-slave or half-free, whether it will move in the direction of freedom, in the direction of the road that we are taking, or whether it will move in the direction of slavery.

I think it will depend in great measure upon what we do here in the United States, on the kind of society that we build, on the kind of strength that we maintain.

We discuss tonight domestic issues, but I would not want any implication to be given that this does not involve directly our struggle with Mr Khruschchev for survival.

Nixon was not to be upstaged in patriotic zeal. 'This nation cannot stand still,' he said, 'because we are in a deadly competition, a competition not only with the men in the Kremlin but the men in Peking.'

During a second television debate on October 7 Kennedy raised the question of the islands of Quemoy and Matsu, which Communist China continued to claim from Taiwan. It would be unwise, he said, for the United States to be dragged into a war over two islands 'which we have never said flatly we would defend'. Nixon replied that 'we should not force our Nationalist allies to get off them and give them to the Communists. If we do that we start a chain reaction. It isn't two pieces of real estate, or the few people on them that are important, but the principles involved.'

During this second debate, Kennedy spoke forcefully about civil rights. 'The right to vote is basic,' he said. 'I do not believe that the administration has implemented those Bills which represent the will of the majority of Congress on two occasions with vigour.' Kennedy then set out the agenda that he intended to follow were he to be elected President:

There is a very strong moral basis for this concept of equality before the law; not only equality before the law, but also equality of opportunity. We are in a very difficult time. We need all the talent we can get. We sit on a conspicuous stage. We are a gold-fish bowl before the world. We have to practice what we preach.

We set a very high standard for ourselves. The Communists do not. They set a low standard of materialism. We preach in the Declaration of Independence and in the Constitution, in the statement of our greatest leaders, we preach very high standards, and if we're not going to be charged before the world with hypocrisy we have to meet those standards.

I believe the President of the United States should indicate this.

The inequalities which tormented American society were constantly apparent. On October 19, on the same day and almost at the same hour that Kennedy and Nixon were in Miami, Florida, addressing the American Legion on national defence, the Black activist leader Martin Luther King was arrested in a department store in Atlanta, Georgia, for refusing to leave a Whites-only table in the store's restaurant. He was imprisoned, tried and sentenced to four months' hard labour. His wife was then six months pregnant.

Senator Kennedy had already expressed his deep distaste of Southern segregationist policies. Following King's arrest, three Southern State governors warned Kennedy not to intervene on his behalf. On October 25, while he was at the O'Hare Inn, at Chicago airport, preparing to fly to Michigan as part of his punishing electoral campaign schedule, he placed a long-distance call from the inn to King's wife. When they spoke, Kennedy assured her of his concern, and offered to intervene. On the following day Kennedy's brother Robert telephoned the Georgia judge who had imposed the sentence and made a plea for King's release. King was released on October 27.

King's father, a Baptist minister like his son, who a few weeks earlier had endorsed Nixon's candidature on religious grounds, made it known that he had changed his mind. 'Because this man was willing to wipe the tears from my daughter's eyes,' he said, 'I've got a suitcase of votes and I'm going to take them to Mr Kennedy and dump them in his lap.' For Kennedy, who aspired to be the first Roman Catholic President, the endorsement of a prominent Baptist was a turning point. To maximize the effect both of Kennedy's intervention and King's reaction, the Kennedy campaign managers printed one million pamphlets describing what had happened. The pamphlets were then transported by Greyhound bus and distributed to Black churches throughout the country. Following a remark by Nixon's official Press Secretary that the Vice-President had 'no comment' to make on the episode, pamphlets were also distributed in Black churches urging preachers to exhort the faithful to switch their votes from 'No Comment Nixon' to 'The Candidate with a Heart – Senator Kennedy'.

'One cannot identify in the narrowness of American voting of 1960 any one particular episode or decision as being more important than any other in the final tallies,' Theodore White, who chronicled this episode, wrote, 'yet when one reflects that Illinois was carried by only 9,000 votes and that 250,000 Negroes are estimated to have voted for Kennedy; that Michigan was carried by 67,000 votes and that an estimated 250,000 Negroes voted for Kennedy; that South Carolina was carried by 10,000 votes and that an estimated 40,000 Negroes there voted for Kennedy, the candidate's instinctive decision must be ranked among the most crucial of the last few weeks.'

The presidential election was held on November 8. In Harry's Bar in Paris a straw vote was taken of Americans who entered the bar on election day. At the previous presidential election the straw vote at Harry's bar had accurately given Eisenhower and Nixon the victory over Stevenson and Kefauver; under the banner 'Harry's bar is never wrong', newspaper photographers reported the new straw poll result: a Kennedy victory over Nixon by 112 to 108.

In terms of the numbers of votes cast, the real result was incredibly close, with 34,221,531 votes being cast for Kennedy and 34,108,474 for Nixon. Only 113,057 votes separated them. Several minor candidates secured just over half a million votes. It was the closest election result in sixty-six years. It was also, in the words of Theodore White, 'the greatest free vote in the history of this or any other country' – 68,832,818 votes in all, eleven per cent more than in the previous presidential election four years earlier.

Under the established system of State electoral college votes, Kennedy received 303 votes and Nixon 219. Kennedy was massively victorious. He was the youngest President to take office, and also the first Roman Catholic to do so.

In his acceptance speech for the Democratic nomination Kennedy had promised Americans 'a New Frontier', a set of challenges that held out 'the promise of more sacrifice instead of more security'. The choice, he explained, lay 'not merely between two men and two parties, but between public interest and private comfort, between national greatness and national decline, between the fresh air of progress and the stale, dank atmosphere of "normalcy", between dedication and mediocrity'.

Behind these fine oratorical phrases lay several active and inventive policies which had been set out, without equivocation, in the Democratic Party Platform. On civil rights there was a pledge 'to assure equal access for all Americans to all areas of community life, including voting booths, schoolrooms, jobs, housing, and public facilities'. There was a call for greater expansion of federal services: more veterans' benefits, expanded 'programmes to aid urban communities', aid for depressed areas, federal help for schools, a youth conservation corps for the underdeveloped countries, federal 'incentives' for artists, a federal programme of medical care for the aged, and an expansion of federally funded housing. The Party Platform document was given the name 'The Rights of Man'. The rights which it set out were to be paid for, not by increased taxation, but by achieving five per cent economic growth each year.

Following his election, Kennedy waited, as must all victorious American presidential candidates, for the formal handover early the next year. As he waited, the formation was announced in North Vietnam of a National Front for the Liberation of South Vietnam. As well as the political front there would be a military arm, the National Liberation Army, which was known as the Vietcong ('Vietnamese Communists'). The aim of the new front and the new army was to oust the South Vietnamese government and to establish a united – and Communist – Vietnam. Ho Chi Minh had made the deliberate decision to move from the previous, post-Dien Bien Phu phase of 'peaceful, political action' to 'armed revolution'. Military training was to take precedence over political training. Attacks by the Vietcong on villages in the South, and the assassination of village elders, intensified.

On October 21 a North Vietnamese force, travelling through Laos along a trail that was to become its main route southward, mounted an attack on South Vietnamese government frontier posts in Kontum province, but was beaten back. The infiltration of northern forces into the south continued, however, and by the end of the year the Vietcong were in control of large areas of the Mekong Delta and the coastal plains.

The South Vietnamese government was itself in turmoil, with President Diem suppressing civil rights and allowing his family and close associates to benefit from corruption. Non-Communist opposition to his rule culminated on November 11 when a group of South Vietnamese army officers tried to remove him from power. While Diem was besieged in his palace, however, army units loyal to him prevented the rebels from gaining control of the radio station, from which Diem was then able to transmit appeals to army units outside Saigon who were prepared to come to his defence, and rescue. Forty-eight hours after the revolt began, it was over. Its leaders fled to Cambodia.

On the last day of the year, with Kennedy still waiting for the handover from Eisenhower, the Cuban government appealed to the United Nations against United States 'aggression'. In mid-October, before the American presidential election, the Eisenhower government had imposed an embargo on trade with Cuba, after publicly accusing the Soviet Union of secretly sending at least 28,000 tons of arms to Cuba, as well as Soviet technicians to teach the Cubans how to use them.

With the fighting in the former Belgian Congo, a new dimension was added to the world refugee problem. At least 300,000 Congolese were fleeing their homes and seeking refuge in neighbouring countries. Hardly any of them had the means to support themselves, even to purchase the basic essentials of food and shelter. The United Nations High Commissioner for Refugees (UNHCR) had yet another task. The sight of myriad refugees fleeing across African borders, huddled in refugee camps, starving, fearful and without hope was a shock to those who witnessed it, and to those who read about it.

In its survey of refugees still needing help worldwide at the end of 1960, the UNHCR noted that the total number was just over two and a half million. With somewhat clinical yet commendable precision it put the number at 2,558,889. This included 83,000 European refugees, among them 23,000 East Germans who had not yet been found homes in West Germany, and a further 5,000 East Germans who fled through the Soviet Zone of Berlin that Easter. Most of them were farmers whose land had recently been collectivized and shopkeepers whose small businesses had been nationalized. Crossing the zonal border into West Berlin, they were taken to an emergency refugee camp in a West Berlin suburb.

In Asia, there were an estimated one million refugees from Chinese Communism, most of them in Hong Kong, and 40,000 in Portuguese Macao, also without means of support beyond what the UNHCR and the host government could provide. There was also a small but desperately needy group of 6,500 White Russian refugees in Hong Kong, the remnant of the refugees from the 1917 Bolshevik revolution, who after 1949 had been forced to leave their post-revolutionary exile in Manchuria.

More than 1,120,000 Arab refugees from pre-1948 Palestine were receiving help in refugee camps in the Arab lands bordering on Israel, their numbers growing each year as a result of natural increase. Their host countries – including Egypt, Jordan and Lebanon – were unwilling to see them integrate in the local Arab society. Another group of Muslim refugees were the 275,000 Algerians, displaced during the fighting for independence, of whom half were in camps in Tunisia and half in Morocco.

The World Council of Churches was also active helping refugees, and in providing food and shelter for people who were otherwise in desperate straits. That year tens of thousands of earthquake and flood victims in Morocco and Pakistan were being helped under the auspices of the Council, and in South Korea 100,000 people were receiving hot meals every day.

World Refugee Year, which ended in June 1960, had been intended by the United Nations to raise substantial funds for refugees, as well as awareness of their plight. The results disappointed the organizers. Although ninety-seven countries participated in the programme, they raised between them little more than £8 million. National appeals and charities raised a further £20 million, of which the largest single national amount, almost £7 million, was raised in Britain, where fourteen major refugee organizations had participated, with the support of the Churches, all political Parties and the trade unions. The largest single sum allocated to the refugee groups from the sums raised worldwide was £2.8 million for the Palestinian refugees.[1]

One group of refugees for whom the UNHCR did not take responsibility were those who had made their way to Israel. Under the Israeli Law of Return, passed in 1950, any Jew who wished to live in Israel and could make his or her way there became a citizen automatically, and the responsibility, where necessary, of the social resources and services of the State. The numbers of Jews who availed themselves of this law were formidable. Some were idealists who wanted to live in the biblical or political Zion. Others were Diaspora Jews who wished to try their professional and personal luck in a Jewish State. But many were refugees from persecution and expulsion. Among them were many Jews from Arab and Muslim lands, including more than a quarter of a million from Morocco and 129,000 from Iraq. Among the Jewish survivors of the Holocaust who settled in Israel as citizens were more than 150,000 from Poland and 24,000 from Hungary. A further 20,000 Jews had also managed to leave the Soviet Union for Israel in the decade since statehood, despite increasingly severe emigration restrictions imposed

[1] In the money values of 1998, £2.8 million was the equivalent of just over £30 million.

by the Soviet authorities, which eventually reduced the exodus to almost nil. For Israel, a country whose total population at the beginning of the post-war influx was just over 700,000, the vast numbers of new immigrants – more than a million – created tremendous strains, both budgetary and social.

The natural disasters of 1960 were dominated by an earthquake at Agadir, in Morocco, which killed 12,000 people. It was the worst ever recorded earthquake in Africa, and the worst in the western hemisphere since the Lisbon earthquake of 1755, when 40,000 people had been killed. In Agadir, three thousand foreigners – a thousand of them from France – and several hundred tourists, were among the dead. American servicemen stationed in Morocco were among those who rushed to participate in rescue activities. James Dowd, a journalist who flew into the city twenty-four hours after the earthquake, reported in the *Daily Telegraph*:

> Clambering over heaps of rubble I heard many calls from people entombed beneath tons of rubble and rock. Several times I was asked by frantic survivors to help them dig into the remains of their homes.
>
> Many people were still alive beneath tons of masonry who had little prospect of rescue. The damage I saw during my brief visit I can only liken to the very worst wartime bomb devastation I saw in Hamburg, Berlin and Warsaw.
>
> Scrambling over the remains of a café, I heard a faint cry which seemed very near. I then saw the head and one arm of a boy aged about fifteen trapped in the wreckage. He had been there thirty-one hours.
>
> A group of French soldiers looking for survivors came immediately to his aid. They found he was pinned by the legs. They removed huge concrete slabs to release him.

Another earthquake was much less widely reported in Europe, but created equal devastation to that of Agadir. In took place in Chile, in May, where the tremors set off a tidal wave, three southern cities were destroyed, many coastal villages obliterated, and ten thousand people killed. In some areas the sea never fully receded, creating marshlands where partially submerged fences can still be seen. At Puerto Saavedra, on the coast, a few palm trees still sprout from the salty water – 'part of the old town that is no more', in the words of an airline travel magazine feature thirty-eight years later.

The motor car remained one of the century's most persistent killers. In the United States, 36,399 citizens were killed in motor-car accidents in 1960, bringing the total number of motor-car deaths spanning the presidencies of Roosevelt, Truman and Eisenhower to 923,432. This was a terrifyingly high death toll in a country that had avoided war on its soil, and had made continual progress against death from disease. The British road deaths in that same twenty-seven-year period totalled 171,533.

Medical progress in 1960 was remarkable. It included the introduction in the United States of an oral contraceptive tablet for women, 'The Pill'. In Birmingham, England, surgeons developed a mechanical pacemaker for the heart. In the realm of science, space exploration had begun to go beyond the needs of national defence policy. On March 11 the American space probe *Pioneer 5* was launched towards an orbit that took it around the Sun. At a distance of twenty million miles it was still able to send radio signals back to Earth. On April 1 *Tiros 1* was launched, to photograph the world's weather conditions from space.[1]

More down-to-earth plans, relating to below the Earth's surface, were put forward by those who wanted to link Britain and France by means of a Channel tunnel. One problem with the tunnel was that it could not be designed for steam trains, only for electric trains. An alternative suggestion was for a Channel bridge, carrying twin railway tracks and a five-lane road. Plans for the tunnel reached the stage of core samples being taken from below the sea bed, and the charting of the sea bed in detail using a newly developed system of echo sounding. Once these tests were done, however, and the project was found to be feasible, it was allowed to lapse.

Beginning in 1960, West Germany, having signed what were called Global Accords on reparation payments with eleven European countries, began to pay money to those countries which had suffered from German occupation during the Second World War. On March 18, Greece was paid 115 million German marks under one such accord, and France four hundred million that same July. Payments were also made to Poland, which received one hundred million, and, on a much smaller scale, seven and a half million to Russia and eight million to Yugoslavia.

Germany still had its own refugee problem of substantial proportions: Germans from the areas that had been annexed by the Soviet Union and

[1] The name *Tiros* stood for Television and Infra-Red Observation Satellite.

Poland, as well as those driven out of the Sudetenland. These refugees had been held together since 1945 by common bonds of lost homes, lost liveli-hoods, the memories of the ugly scenes of their expulsion, and the continuing hope that they might one day return. A Ministry of Expellees, Refugees and War Victims had been established in Bonn by the Federal Government of West Germany. The very existence of this Ministry kept the refugees' hopes alive, as did the publication of more than thirty volumes of documents describing the expulsions in the most vivid terms.

In 1960, however, in the introduction to the thirty-first volume of docu-ments, the editor, Theodor Schieder, a professor at the University of Cologne, himself a former expellee, wrote of a new path and a new vision which he and his editorial committee wished to stress. The aim of their publications, he wrote, was to 'contribute to encouraging moral forces which may prove capable of overcoming the tensions between the peoples of Eastern Europe and of Europe as a whole. Only if placed in this perspective can the sufferings of our generation bear fruit for posterity.'

For the politicians of West Germany, the existence of a divided Europe, with all its fears and uncertainties, provided an opportunity to enter a new world of defence systems. On September 11 the officers, men and tanks of a West German panzer battalion began a three-week training programme in Britain, at Castlemartin in South Wales. Nine days later journalists were invited to watch the German tanks in action, as they fired their shells into the battered hulks of five British wartime 'Churchill' tanks.

German behaviour during the Second World War had not been a feature of the textbooks being studied in German schools in the 1950s. When a West German student, Gerhard Schoenberner, visited Poland in 1957, he had been shaken by the sites of mass murder of Jews in the Second World War. Returning from Poland he decided to mount an exhibition entitled 'The Past Is Warning'. He also embarked on writing a book to tell the story of the mass murder of the Jews. The book was published in Germany in 1960 – entitled *Der Gelbe Stern* (The Yellow Star). Copiously and starkly illustrated, it had a message for Schoenberner's fellow Germans that he spelled out clearly:

'Bury the past,' demand those who have something to hide. 'Do not sully Germany's name,' cry those who besmirched it with their bloody hands. 'Let bygones be bygones,' the murderers advise us. And there are many people who thoughtlessly repeat their words. They forget that outside

Germany there is a much sharper memory of those years and that the facts which here often still meet with stubborn silence or with incredulous surprise are common knowledge.

Those who kept silent when it was time to speak out talk loudly of forgiving and forgetting. Even well-meaning people speak at the most of shame. But there remains a shared guilt which one cannot easily buy oneself out of, and which cannot be 'made good'. No one can bring the dead back to life. What is done cannot be undone.

Belated moral condemnation and humane regret are not enough. The historical facts must be made known, the social causes that made them possible must be understood, and we must become aware of our own responsibility for what goes on around us.

'We do not escape the past by thrusting it to the back of our minds,' Schoenberner concluded. 'Only if we come to terms with it and understand the lessons of those years, can we free ourselves of the legacy of Hitlerite barbarism. Policies are not preordained by fate. They are made by people and people can change them.'

The war that had been, and the war that might yet be: these were two sides of contemporary concern. The form that a new war might take was a cause for continual public agitation by anti-war and anti-nuclear groups. When, on November 15, the United States sent out the nuclear-powered submarine *George Washington* on its first patrol into the Atlantic, armed with Polaris nuclear weapons, there was fear among those who saw the Cold War leading to nuclear war, but a sense of confidence among those in the Western alliance systems who regarded nuclear weapons, and the ability to deliver them, as the main method of preserving peace.

More than three thousand million human beings were alive in 1960, many of them living in poverty but most of them in peace, however frail or anxious. The bloodletting of two world wars, and of several violent regional and civil conflicts, was behind them. That 'common man' whose century it was, had indeed, in Churchill's words, 'suffered most': he and she had also been the beneficiaries of steady advances in medicine and science whereby life expectancies were being prolonged and the pattern of daily life made easier over large regions of the globe. How far the remaining four decades of the century would prove a continuous progression was unknown, and, as in 1918 and 1945, much hoped for.

CHAPTER TEN

1961

> ... others in earlier times have made the same dangerous
> mistake that the West was too selfish and too soft and
> too divided to resist invasions of freedom in other lands.

PRESIDENT JOHN F. KENNEDY

ON 20 JANUARY 1961 John F. Kennedy was inaugurated President of the United States. At the age of forty-three he was the youngest President in American history. Eisenhower, whom he followed at the White House, was the oldest – at seventy – to leave office. It was on the prospect and note of youth that Kennedy raised so many hopes, and he understood this, telling the American people and the world in his State of the Union message: 'Let the word go forth from this time and place, to friend and foe alike, that the torch has been passed to a new generation of Americans – born in this century, tempered by war, disciplined by a hard and bitter peace, proud of our ancient heritage – and unwilling to witness or permit the slow undoing of those human rights to which this nation has always been committed, and to which we are committed today at home and around the world.' Kennedy added, in words which were spoken with great emphasis, even passion: 'Let every nation know, whether it wishes us well or ill, that we shall pay any price, bear any burden, meet any hardship, support any friend, oppose any foe, to ensure the survival and the success of liberty.'

The rhetoric was genuine; in foreign affairs Kennedy's America stood out as America had done in the days of the Truman Doctrine and the Marshall Plan a decade earlier, as a standard-bearer for democratic values and economic sharing. The magnanimity was based on calculations of stability and a firm front against Communism. But the benefits were real, and the fabric of Western defence, without which there were many dangers of Communist encroachment not only by military means, was enhanced. That the need for public and decisive action was urgent seemed borne out particularly in South-East Asia, where Communist activity by the Pathet Lao forces in Laos had intensified. On March 23 Kennedy announced that the United States 'would not tolerate' the loss of Laos to the Communists. He also ordered an immediate increase in American military aid for the government of Laos, and the movement of American naval and military units already in the country to areas closer to the fighting.

There were miscalculations, however, in the American attempts to confront Communism, which enabled American isolationists and liberals alike to pour scorn on Kennedy's efforts. On April 17 a group of 1,400 Cuban exiles, who had been living in the United States, invaded Cuba. They had been armed, trained and largely controlled by agencies of the United States government. Their point of disembarkation was the Bay of Pigs. After three days on the beachhead, almost the entire invading force had been either killed or taken prisoner. After initial American denials that there was any official involvement, Kennedy announced that he accepted full responsibility for the American government's part in the attack. It was clear that he and his administration had committed themselves to the overthrow of the Cuban Communist regime, hoping – on the basis of poor Intelligence and wishful thinking – that the landings would be followed by a popular uprising against Fidel Castro. Kennedy himself had approved the plans, which the Central Intelligence Agency had devised, and the Chiefs of Staff and the Departments of State and Defense had examined. Kennedy had, however, ruled out direct American military participation, as urged by the CIA. This at least lessened the dangers of international repercussions and United Nations condemnation. Kennedy was rebuked by one leading American commentator, Walter Lippman, for an action 'fundamentally alien to the American character'. Had it succeeded, Lippman wrote, it would only have replaced one Cuban problem by another. But Communist rule – particularly in the western hemisphere – was anathema to the new President, and he sought other means of at least containing it, not by military action or threats but by setting up an 'Alliance for Progress' scheme for social and economic reforms throughout Latin America.

Many people in the United States saw a Soviet nuclear attack as a definite possibility. How far the threat of such an attack could be met was something to which Kennedy felt he must address himself. In July he stated publicly that civil defence preparation was an integral part of insuring against any Soviet 'miscalculation'. There was an immediate increase in the manufacture of fall-out shelters for individual homes. One manufacturer offered one that could be used as an underground garage, another a swimming pool. By the end of the summer, however, only one per cent of the population had acquired a shelter. That still meant more than one million individual shelters had been built. Government money was made available for institutional shelters, especially in hospitals and schools. Many of the school shelters were designed so that they could also be used as gymnasiums and classrooms.

Congress supported the domestic defence measures; but, with regard to social reform, Kennedy, like Roosevelt at the time of the New Deal, found a Congress that did not want to move as fast as he did, although there were sixty-five Democratic Senators as against thirty-five Republicans, and 262 Democratic members of the House of Representatives as against 174 Republicans. To Kennedy's chagrin, of the first 335 measures which he proposed to Congress, only 172 were approved. One of those which was approved was a $435 million job-retraining scheme for the unemployed. But among the proposals against which Kennedy faced fierce opposition was medical care for the aged. One of his most persistent supporters was Senator Frank Church of Idaho, who had been an active member of the Senate Committee on Ageing since he had entered the Senate five years earlier. In a speech supporting Kennedy's measure, Church pointed out: 'Even those with ample incomes have found it necessary to protect themselves against these spiralling costs by taking out insurance policies for medical care and hospitalization. So that the risk of serious illness, and the costs which now attend it, can be spread out over the whole group who are insured.'

Three-quarters of all American families were covered by these private medical insurance policies, which, Church pointed out, 'should be proof enough that insurance represents the most workable answer to the problem of meeting the rising costs of modern hospital care. Unfortunately, private health insurance has not proved a workable answer for the elderly.' Sixty per cent of those aged over sixty-five had incomes of less than $1,000 a year. For them, the problem of finding adequate insurance cover had become 'increasingly acute'.

Senator Church's arguments were forceful, but the provision of medical care for the aged as part of the responsibility, and an urgent part, of government was challenged by those who saw it as unwarranted use of federal funds, and particularly by the American Medical Association, which launched a campaign as strong as Kennedy's own efforts, which were substantial. When the Bill came before Congress, Senator Church was among forty-three

Democrats who voted for it. But twenty-one Democratic Senators joined with thirty-one Republicans to create an unbreachable wall of opposition. Five Republican Senators joined those Democrats who voted in favour of the Bill, but that could not save it, and it was defeated by fifty-two votes to forty-eight. Kennedy was furious.

The scourge of the United States remained civil rights. Blacks were disappointed that Kennedy would not sign an order prohibiting racial discrimination in Federally assisted housing projects. He did, however, press for equality in education, employment and travel. Black activists, helped by a growing number of White civil rights supporters, were determined to introduce measures of integration in the South. On May 4, members of the Campaign of Racial Equality (CORE) left Washington to test the facilities for integration on the route to New Orleans. On reaching Anniston, Alabama, on May 14 these 'Freedom Riders' were attacked by a group of Whites who had been waiting for their arrival. There were more attacks, and even greater violence, when the marchers reached Montgomery, Alabama, on May 20. When some of the Freedom Riders were brought to trial in Albany, Georgia, on charges of disturbing the peace, there was a mass demonstration in their support, and 737 of the demonstrators were arrested, among them Martin Luther King. The protests continued until the arrested men and women were released and the Albany authorities agreed to negotiate the removal of racial barriers.

Inside the Soviet Union, the issue of civil rights had never been on the public agenda. With repeated agricultural failures mocking the collective farm system, Khrushchev instituted a Virgin Lands policy to bring vast regions of fallow land under the plough, especially in Soviet Central Asia. Economic incentives to farmers to produce more grain were combined with harsh political penalties if they failed to do so. The extent of internal problems was highlighted by a decree of May 5, whereby the death penalty was introduced for those convicted of 'large-scale embezzlement of State property', as well as for prisoners in labour camps who used violence against warders or fellow prisoners. A decree of July 1 brought in the death penalty for 'professional speculators'. Many of those who were executed were Jewish: they were identified in the Soviet newspapers by their Jewish-sounding names, leading to an outcry in the West that an anti-Semitic campaign was in progress. The Soviet response was to close down all but one of the synagogues in Moscow.

To ensure general compliance with the dictates of Communist morality, volunteer 'law enforcement squads' and 'comradely courts' were set up, with powers to expose and bring to trial citizens who were regarded as not being zealous in the performance of their Communist duties. Particular crimes that were targeted were obtaining an 'illegal' income by leasing flats or cars, or trading in agricultural or garden produce. A further decree in December made manifestations of 'bourgeois psychology and private-property tendencies' a crime.

The struggle for power in the Congo intensified following the murder of Patrice Lumumba. In Katanga, forces loyal to Lumumba took control of Bakuvu and most of the northern province. In Stanleyville, the capital of the Oriental province, Antoine Gizenga, who had been trained in Prague, proclaimed the province a separate regime, and prepared to defend it with some seven thousand armed men. In one of his first foreign policy initiatives since becoming President, Kennedy issued a warning to the Soviet Union that the United States would defend the Charter of the United Nations 'by opposing any attempt by any government to intervene unilaterally in the Congo'. His warning was heeded.

A resolution adopted by the Security Council on February 21 put in train a concerted effort by the United Nations to avert civil war and to restore parliamentary institutions to the Congo. The Soviet Union refrained from casting its veto, but abstained from voting. Following the resolution, the Congolese Head of State, President Kasavubu, agreed that the Congolese National Army should be reorganized with the help of the United Nations. For its part, the United Nations agreed to supervise the withdrawal of all Belgian military personnel, and all foreign mercenaries serving with the army of the breakaway Katanga province.

As the Security Council had envisaged, the Congolese parliament was reconvened – at Lovanium, near Léopoldville – and a Government of National Unity established. It was opposed by Moshe Tshombe's forces in Katanga. After a mob loyal to Tshombe moved against United Nations personnel at Elisabethville airport, United Nations troops attacked positions held by the foreign mercenaries who made up a significant part of the effective forces of the Katanga army. But the separatist determination of Katanga was strong, and the evacuation of mercenaries, agreed upon by Katanga during negotiations with the United Nations, was halted. At the same time, the United Nations took under its protection 35,000 Baluba refugees fleeing Katanga to avoid being massacred.

During fighting that began on September 13 the United Nations forces were attacked by jet aircraft flown by mercenaries. On the ground, an Irish company of the United Nations force was captured. The United States, under Kennedy's initiative, announced its strong support for continued and forceful United Nations military action. Many Republicans criticized this foreign involvement, but Kennedy had no doubts that the United States had to show that it was behind effective action, if that action was to continue, particularly as both Britain and France were expressing doubts about the United Nations becoming involved in actual ground fighting.

In an attempt to avert greater bloodshed, the Secretary-General of the United Nations, Dag Hammarskjöld, flew from Léopoldville to the Northern Rhodesian town of Ndola, for talks with the Katanganese. His plane disappeared. The next day its wreckage was found, eight miles from its destination. Hammarskjöld was dead. He was posthumously awarded the Nobel Peace Prize.

Although a ceasefire was agreed to by Katanga within a few days, it was soon broken. Violence spread throughout the Congo. On November 11, troops of the regular Congolese army, nominally under United Nations supervision, looted a United Nations base at Kindu and murdered thirteen Italian aircrew members. Another Security Council resolution authorized the new Secretary-General, U Thant, a Burmese, to take 'vigorous action, including the use of the requisite measure of force', to restore the rule of law and the non-violent ascendancy of the Congolese authorities. Tshombe agreed to begin talks with the central government on December 20, and to accept Katanga's subordinate status within the Congo. This agreement, like several before it, was not adhered to, keeping the Congolese situation at the centre of United Nations concerns for another year.

It was not only in the sphere of military activity that the United Nations was active in the Congo. Civilian operations were begun which were based upon training the Congolese in those branches of civic affairs that had hitherto been the province and prerogative of the Belgians and other Europeans. By the end of the year more than a thousand Congolese were being trained under United Nations supervision in the spheres of public health and medicine. Sixty-one 'medical assistants' were sent to France to complete their studies. Twenty-five more were given medical scholarships and intensive training at Lovanium, from which the first Congolese doctors graduated in July. Under the United Nations Educational, Scientific and Cultural Organization (UNESCO) schools were reopened, teaching materials brought in and teachers trained. Public works programmes were set up, with United Nations guidance, to relieve unemployment. Financial experts were sent in to ensure that government expenditure was more stringently controlled. There was also the problem of severe hunger to be tackled in areas where the fighting had been fiercest. At the beginning of the year, in South Kasai, almost two hundred people were dying each day of starvation. Within three months, United Nations relief efforts reduced this to fewer than twenty a week.

In neighbouring Angola, the United Nations was rigidly excluded from any influence, as the Portuguese colonial authorities, faced by a nationalist revolt, took drastic military action against the insurgents. It was action that, as in all such anti-colonial struggles, served only to intensify the determination of those who wished to drive out their European masters. Britain was among the States that publicly criticized the Portuguese for the severity of their reprisals, which were examined by a specially appointed subcommittee of the Security Council. Portugal alleged that the disturbances were caused by foreign intervention. The subcommittee ascribed them, accurately, to the 'genuine grievances of the indigenous population' against the Portuguese administration. A Security Council resolution called upon Portugal 'to desist forthwith from repressive measures'. The call was ignored.

Across the Indian Ocean, the Portuguese were confronted by the determination of the government of India to rid itself for all time of even the tiniest remnant of imperial rule. Nehru declared that, after more than four-and-a-half centuries under the Portuguese flag – and sixty years under the Spanish – foreign enclaves were no longer acceptable. On August 11 the two smallest, Dadra and Nagar-Aveli, were integrated into the Indian Republic without conflict. Neither town had the ability to resist. But the larger enclaves of Goa, Damao (Daman) and Diu refused to give in, and on December 18 were invaded by Indian troops, while Indian aircraft attacked military targets. Both enclaves surrendered the next day. Annexation swiftly followed. At a meeting of the United Nations Security Council, called at the request of Portugal to censure the Indian use of force, the Soviet Union used its veto to prevent the resolution being adopted.

The British Commonwealth was following the logic of Macmillan's 'wind of change' speech. At a three-day conference in Dar-es-Salaam which ended on March 29, the British Colonial Secretary, Iain Macleod, announced that internal self-government for Tanganyika would come into force on May 1, and independence on December 28. The independence date was later moved forward to December 9, so that the many British and foreign dignitaries who were expected to attend the ceremonies would not have to interrupt their Christmas holidays.

One British dependency, the South Atlantic island of Tristan da Cunha, was completely evacuated that year, when the volcano which made up the island, and which had long been believed to be extinct, erupted. All 262 of the island's inhabitants were flown to Britain. There many of them suffered considerably from the British varieties of the common cold, which were unknown in their remote ocean solitude. The island had originally been occupied by Britain to prevent it being used as a base by American warships in the war of 1812.

On May 9 a plebiscite was held in the New Zealand island of Western Samoa in which seventy-nine per cent of the local population voted for independence. The New Zealand authorities accepted this verdict, which had been monitored by the United Nations. Samoa would remain a member of the Commonwealth, but would be given sovereign independence. Inside New Zealand itself, efforts were being made to end the inequalities of the Maori people. With the establishment of a Maori Education Foundation, scholarships and vocational training were to be provided that would match those available to the European population, and enable Maori culture to have an equal place in local educational programmes. A Maori Council was also set up, to deal directly with the central government, and to make it possible for the Maori people to be better represented at national level in discussions with the government: hitherto district and tribal committees had been the main, fragmented means of contact with the central power.

The Cold War exacerbated the relationship even of Allies. On March 13 there was a top-level discussion in British defence circles about what Britain ought to do in the event of a devastating Soviet nuclear attack on the United States, with regard to American atomic weapons at American air bases in Britain. The hope of the British planners was that there should be 'some arrangements' with the United States to release these weapons to Britain, 'but it is doubtful whether this is a subject to raise with the Americans'. In 'any case', suggested the Deputy Permanent Secretary of State at the Ministry of Defence, Frank Mottershead, 'we should get hold of the bombs even if it meant shooting the American officers concerned'.

Such extraordinary deliberations were secret (and not in fact to be made public until the end of the century). The public face of East-West rivalry between the two blocs was more directly confrontational. The West received a considerable shock on April 12, when a Soviet air force pilot, Major Yuri Gagarin, made an orbit of the earth in an artificial satellite. It was not only a triumph for Soviet rocketry – helped by German scientists who had been taken to Russia after the Second World War – but a blow to the morale of the United States, which saw in it a sign of Soviet superiority. Thirty-seven years later, *The Times* could comment: 'It was a demonstration of the capacities of a totalitarian socialist system which was gall to the American belief in the innate superiority of a free-enterprise democracy.'

Frantic efforts were under way in the United States to emulate Gagarin's exploit. This came three weeks later when, on May 5, a United States Navy pilot, Commander Alan B. Shepard, was catapulted to space in a Mercury space capsule on top of a rocket. Unlike Gagarin's flight, Shepard's was sub-orbital and short: fifteen minutes in time and 115 miles in distance. By contrast, Gagarin had orbited the earth. But Shepard's achievement, which on Kennedy's instructions had been broadcast live on radio and television, was greater than that of time or distance. On 23 July 1998, in his obituary in *The Times*, the obituary writer reflected that 'in accomplishing what he did that day, Shepard earned the gratitude of an American space industry and people which had suffered grievous humiliation at the hands of Soviet technology over the previous four years' – from the moment on 4 October 1957 when the first Soviet satellite, *Sputnik 1*, had orbited the earth.

Shepard's success in 1961 marked the start of a 'space race' that was to absorb massive monetary and research efforts, and patriotic zeal, over the coming two decades. Kennedy set the tone when he came before Congress on May 25 to deliver what he called a second State of the Union message. The United States must take, he said, 'a clearly leading role in space achievements, which in many ways may hold the key to our future on earth', so much so that it would become 'a major national commitment' to put a man on the Moon, and to bring him safely back to Earth – and to do so before the end of the decade. A vast sum of money was called for, $1,800 million. Russia and America were in direct confrontation, not on the battlefield or among their respective allies and supporters, but in space. At first the Russians seemed to hold the advantage, seen most dramatically in August when a Soviet pilot, Major G. S. Titov, completed seventeen orbits around the Earth – and did so in just over twenty-five hours. The Americans wanted desperately to send a man around the Earth at least once before the end of the year, but were able to send only a chimpanzee, which in November made two complete orbits. It was not a race, however, that the United States intended to abandon, or to lose.

It was not only in space, but also in the terrestrial sphere, that the rivalries and contrasts between the two systems of government and ideology were marked. On June 16, Rudolf Nureyev, a twenty-three-year-old Soviet ballet dancer touring with the Leningrad-based Kirov Ballet in Paris, was about to fly with his troupe from Paris to London when he was forbidden at the last moment by his Soviet minders from taking the plane, and told – on the tarmac at Le Bourget airport – that he must return to Moscow. He refused, and ran across the tarmac to a French police inspector, crying 'Protect me!' He was given asylum in France. As a student he had refused to join the Communist Youth Organization. On June 23, in his first performance since his defection nine days earlier, he danced in *Sleeping Beauty*. In London, the Kirov Ballet was performing at Covent Garden without him.

There had been an unexpected reminder of the Second World War a year earlier, on May 23, when the government of Israel announced that it had found Adolf Eichmann, one of the senior wartime German organizers of the mass deportation and murder of the Jews of Europe. He had been located in Argentina, captured and abducted to Israel. In preparation for his trial, a mass of documentary evidence and personal testimony was assembled. He did not deny who he was, but argued that he was only a small cog in the machine, acting under the orders of far more powerful superiors. While it was true that his highest rank was that of SS lieutenant-colonel, and that higher-ranking men of extreme evil such as Himmler, Heydrich and Kaltenbrunner had been his bosses, he was clearly shown to have been a bureaucrat of considerable efficiency and persistence, organizing the deportation of Jews from a dozen countries to the death camps that had been set up by the Nazi regime on Polish soil expressly for the purpose of mass murder.

In his inaugural address in Washington on January 20, President Kennedy had set out his approach to the Cold War and East-West relations. 'Let us never negotiate out of fear,' he said, 'but let us never fear to negotiate.' Five months later he flew to Vienna to meet Nikita Khrushchev. It was their first encounter. On the issue that most concerned the world beyond the conference table – the discontinuance of nuclear testing – no progress was made, the Soviet position being that the inspections teams which were central to the American and British test-ban scheme should not be put in place until four years after any test-ban treaty was signed.

On June 5, immediately following the end of the Kennedy-Khrushchev talks, the United States Deputy Secretary of Defense, Rosswell Gilpatric, stated, with the President's authority, that 'if NATO forces are about to be overwhelmed by non-nuclear attack from Communist bloc countries, NATO would respond with nuclear weapons'. American military and air force strength in Europe was increased. So too were the number of West German forces under NATO command: eleven divisions in all, puny compared with the hundreds of divisions that had been deployed during the Second World War, but an earnest of West Germany's determination to be an active partner in the defence of the West, and of the Western values which its constitution, its parliament and its people were espousing. In recognition of the emergence of West Germany as an integral part of the Western defence system, the United States agreed to supply the West German army with both the short-range Sergeant missiles – the nuclear warhead of which could hit a target seventy miles away – and the far more effective 400-mile Pershing missiles and the 700-mile Mace missiles. The nuclear warheads of all these missiles would remain, however, under American control. When, in November, a German admiral was given command of all NATO forces in the Baltic, Moscow sent messages to Norway and Denmark warning them of 'revived German aggressive intentions'. There were, however, no such intentions, nor did NATO make any changes in the naval command. Within NATO there was some satisfaction that the open expression of Soviet fears betokened a genuine weakness that could only help maintain the balance of deterrent power between East and West.

On his return to the United States, Kennedy spoke on television of 'a very sober two days' of talks, during which, he said, 'no major decision was either planned or taken, no spectacular progress was either achieved or pretended'. One element of the idealism with which Kennedy sought to suffuse the American people, and especially the youth, was the establishment of the Peace Corps, which Congress approved on March 1. Its mission, according to the legislation that gave it birth, was to help poorer countries meet their need for trained personnel, to encourage non-Americans to understand Americans better, and to foster greater American understanding of foreign countries. Volunteers worked as teachers, health assistants, small-business advisers and agricultural specialists. Kennedy appointed his brother-in-law, Sargent Shriver, as director. Within three months there had been more than ten thousand applications to join. The first group left the United States that September: a group of twenty-eight surveyors, geologists and civil engineers, who went to Tanganyika. By the end of the year more than five hundred volunteers were at work, in Tanganyika, Ghana, Nigeria, India, Pakistan, the Philippines, St Lucia, Chile and Colombia. No part of the world was excluded. Only the Communist countries, who a decade and a half earlier had rejected the Marshall Plan with all its economic benefits and opportunities, had no interest in seeking to participate. This was at a time when many of them were suffering continued economic hardship, and the Soviet Union imposed upon them unequal economic treaties which drained them of much-needed raw materials and consumer goods.

In the age-old spirit of political partisanship, former President Eisenhower called the Peace Corps a 'juvenile experiment'. But it was much more than that, and at its height, five years after its establishment, it had 15,560 volunteers working outside the United States, in conditions that were far from luxurious, and with a mandate to help and to train and to advance local economic potential. When, in the post-Kennedy era, President Nixon sought to bring the programme to an end, one of his aides, Patrick J. Buchanan, advised against doing so, telling him, in the cynical, dismissive tone of behind-the-scenes bureaucracy: 'Such drastic action would put us crosswise with a number of our friends who have swallowed the propaganda that this is the greatest thing since sliced bread.'

Cynicism of the sort manifested by Eisenhower and Buchanan was not a feature of Kennedy's foreign policy, or of his confrontations with the Soviet Union. On June 4, during his meeting with Kennedy in Vienna, Khrushchev produced a memorandum insisting that the German question must be 'settled' that year and a peace treaty signed. If this were not done, all Western rights in West Berlin would automatically end, and control of access to West Berlin would be handed over by the Soviets to the East German authorities. The East German leader, Walther Ulbricht, added a few days later that, after any German peace treaty, all air and military traffic to West Berlin would also come under East German control. A further East German initiative, on July 6, was the publication of a 'Peace Plan' whereby Germany would be reunited in an All-German Federation, in which equal representation would be given to the seventeen million East Germans and the fifty million West Germans.

On July 25 Kennedy spoke on American television about the Berlin crisis. 'We cannot and will not permit the Communists to drive us out of Berlin, either gradually or by force,' he said. 'We do not want to fight, but we have fought before. And others in earlier times have made the same dangerous mistake that the West was too selfish and too soft and too divided to resist invasions of freedom in other lands.'

Within East Germany, the hardships and tyranny of Communist rule were taking their toll of morale, and the hitherto modest influx of East Germans through Berlin to the West was accelerating. By the end of July it had reached four thousand a week. Many of those who were fleeing were skilled workers, and most of them were young. On August 12 more than 2,400 crossed into West Berlin, the largest number so far. It was clear that, with the Berlin zonal borders having no effective physical barriers – only checkpoints – that the number of those leaving was likely to continue to grow. On August 13 East German troops and police took up positions along the whole length of the Soviet Zone border inside the city. That same night the East German authorities began to build a high brick and concrete wall between East and West Berlin.

As this Berlin Wall was being put in place along the whole length of the border, barbed wire was laid at all the official crossing points. Two days later, a photographer who was standing with onlookers on the West Berlin side of the growing barrier saw an East German soldier running towards it. The photographer took a photograph that was still being reproduced in the newspapers thirty-eight years later. It showed an East German border guard, Conrad Schumann, leaping over the wire and entering West Berlin. 'Many people were standing round,' Schumann later recalled, 'and that was good, because they distracted my colleagues. I was able to swap my loaded sub-machine gun for an empty one before I jumped. The jump was not so difficult then. After that the gun fell noisily on the ground; with a full magazine it probably would have gone off.'

In reaction to the building of the Berlin Wall, the Western governments responsible for the British, French and American sectors of the city protested to Moscow in a joint note four days later, on August 17. The Russian government rejected the protest within twenty-four hours. On August 18 the American Vice-President, Lyndon B. Johnson, flew to Berlin to deliver a defiant message from Kennedy that the United States 'guaranteed' the continued freedom of the people of West Berlin. In order to test Communist intentions, Kennedy ordered a convoy of armed troops to be sent from Western Germany along one of the access roads to West Berlin that traversed East Germany. It was not molested.

The American firmness was decisive. Later, after Kennedy and Adenauer had conferred in Washington, it was announced that the two men had agreed on specific military measures to resist Soviet pressure in Germany. The West European Union had already agreed in May that Germany would be allowed to build destroyers that could be equipped to fire nuclear weapons. That there would not be a serious East-West confrontation over the Berlin Wall became clear – in a somewhat unusual fashion – when, as the Western newspapers were predicting an acceleration of tension, the British Prime Minister, Harold Macmillan, continued his golfing holiday in Scotland. On August 26 Macmillan was asked by journalists if he was not frightened by the crisis. He replied: 'I think it is all got up by the Press. Nobody is going to fight about it.'

In the immediate aftermath of the building of the Berlin Wall, the Soviet Union made a more drastic and potentially decisive challenge to its Cold War adversaries. On September 1, five days after what the London *Spectator* called Macmillan's 'collector's piece of unflappability', the Soviet Union exploded a hydrogen bomb. A truce that had been in place for more than a year was unilaterally broken. On the following day, September 2, at a meeting of the non-aligned nations in Belgrade, Jawaharlal Nehru warned of 'a danger of war coming nearer by the Soviet government's decision to resume nuclear tests'. President Tito, the host of the Belgrade meeting, was particularly aggrieved that the Soviet decision had been announced 'on the day of the opening of this conference of peace'.

The testing of several more Soviet hydrogen bombs followed, in two separate regions: Soviet Central Asia and the Soviet Arctic. The United States responded by announcing on September 5 that it would also resume testing its H-bombs, though it would do so, it said, underground, where the bombs and their aftermath would be rendered 'innocuous'. It was to take almost forty years before the harmful radiation impact of underground testing became public knowledge.

On September 6, in London, members of the ban-the-bomb protest movement, the 'Committee of One Hundred', tried to march to the American Embassy in London to protest against the American resumption of nuclear testing. They then announced that they would organize a public protest in a week's time – a sit-in in Parliament Square of ten thousand people in order to express their criticism of both the United States and the Soviet Union for the resumption of tests. Bertrand Russell, the eighty-nine-year-old mathematician and philosopher, and the senior figure in the appeal for the Parliament Square demonstration, was charged with 'inciting members of the public to commit a breach of the peace', found guilty and sentenced to seven days in prison: in the First World War he had been imprisoned as a conscientious objector.

On September 17 a gathering of 12,000 anti-nuclear protesters took place in Trafalgar Square. They were led by Canon L. J. Collins, the Chairman of the Campaign for Nuclear Disarmament, who had walked to the square from his pulpit at St Paul's Cathedral. In the confrontation with the police, more than a thousand of the protesters were arrested. Eight days later, at the General Assembly of the United Nations, Kennedy made a powerful plea for the abolition of nuclear weapons 'before they abolish us'. Disarmament was no longer a dream, but 'a practical matter of life and death'. He wished to issue a challenge to the Soviet Union, 'not to an arms race but to a peace race', and not only in the sphere of nuclear weapons, but 'step by step, stage by stage, until general and complete disarmament has actually been achieved'. The United States was willing, as a first step in the process, to agree to accept 'effective international control'. The first step should be to end all nuclear tests. In this, the United States already had Britain's agreement.

The Soviet Union baulked at the idea of international control. Verification was not yet an acceptable word in the international diplomatic lexicon. On October 1 the Soviet Union began a series of tests in the Arctic, off Novaya Zemlya. The hydrogen bomb which was exploded in the atmosphere on October 9 as part of this series was estimated to be almost as powerful as the most powerful United States bomb of 1 March 1954: fifteen megatons. On October 23 there was a further explosion. Such was its power that ground and air shockwaves were felt in Sweden, Denmark, Norway, France and Germany. The British atomic research establishment at Aldermaston described it as 'significantly larger than any previously recorded'. It was a fifty-megaton bomb. 'The device today', wrote *The Times*, 'generated the greatest explosive force ever produced by man.'

On October 24, in Britain, a delegation from the Committee of One Hundred, headed by Bertrand Russell, took a letter to the Soviet Embassy in London denouncing the renewal of Soviet tests. When the Soviet Chargé d'Affaires, Vadim Loginov, said that it was all the fault of the 'wicked Americans' and that the Soviet Union 'must take defensive measures in the face of possible attack', Russell replied that he could not 'swallow' such comments about the 'innocence of Russia'. On October 27 Radio Peking broadcast a fall-out warning to all major cities in China.

The dangers to health of nuclear testing had been of intense concern to the international community for more than half a decade, and on October 27 the United Nations General Assembly appealed to the Soviet Union to refrain from carrying out its publicized intention to explode a hydrogen bomb in the atmosphere before the end of the month. Three days later the bomb was exploded.

There was a degree of desperation in the United Nations deliberations that followed. On November 24 the General Assembly called on all member States 'to consider and respect the continent of Africa as a denuclearized zone', and not to use any African territory for testing, storing or transporting nuclear weapons. That same day another resolution declared that the use of thermonuclear weapons was 'contrary to the spirit, letter, and aims of the United Nations, and as such, a direct violation of the Charter'. Fears of nuclear proliferation led, on December 4, to a resolution, sponsored by Ireland, for an international agreement whereby the nuclear powers would refrain from giving nuclear weapons, or the information necessary for their manufacture, to non-nuclear countries. The dangers of such proliferation were powerfully parodied by the American lyricist Tom Lehrer, whose song became a vocal banner for those who feared an imminent nuclear war, the bounds of which would be global and irreversible:

> First we got the bomb and that was good
> 'cause we love peace and motherhood.
> Then Russia got the bomb, but that's okay,
> 'cause the balance of power's maintained that way.
> Who's next?
>
> Then France got the bomb but don't you grieve,
> 'cause they're on our side (I believe).
> China got the bomb but have no fears,
> 'cause they can't wipe us out for at least five years.
> Who's next?
>
> Japan will have its own device,
> Transistorized at half the price.
> South Africa wants two, that's right:

One for the black and one for the white.
Who's next?

Egypt's gonna get one too,
Just to use on you know who.
So Israel's getting tense, wants one in self-defence.
'The Lord's our shepherd,' says the Psalm,
But just in case, we better get a bomb.
Who's next?

Luxembourg is next to go,
And (who knows?) Monaco.
We'll try to stay serene and calm
When Alabama gets the bomb.
Who's next?
Who's next?
Who's next?

As the European empires dissolved, and as new nations emerged, the United Nations was becoming increasingly a global forum. On September 27 it admitted a former British colony, Sierra Leone, which became its hundredth member.[1] The Mongolian People's Republic – a Communist ally and former virtual protectorate of the Soviet Union – and the Islamic Republic of Mauritania – until a year earlier a part of the French overseas empire – swiftly followed. The next member, still before the end of the year, was Tanganyika, once part of the German Empire, and since 1919 under British control. One missing nation in the forum of nations was Communist China. The original Chinese representation had remained since 1945 with the delegates of Taiwan. On December 15 a Soviet proposal to have Communist China admitted was pressed by the Soviet delegate with such frenzied language, especially against Taiwan, that it was rejected by the General Assembly. Among the minority that voted in favour of the Soviet proposal to replace Taiwan by Peking was the Conservative government in Britain.

Even as the horrendous death tolls of war and civil war had scarred previous decades, the new decade saw a push for the saving of life. The achievements

---

[1] As I write these words (in October 1998), there are 185 members of the United Nations.

were not new, but cumulative. On December 15 it was announced that in the fifteen years since its foundation the United Nations International Children's Emergency Fund (UNICEF) had vaccinated more than 134 million people – the majority of them children under the age of sixteen – against tuberculosis, and had treated a further thirty-one million people for yaws, eleven million for trachoma and a million for leprosy.

The work of UNICEF was not only preventative and curative, but concerned with creating conditions in which health could be maintained through hygiene and improvement. The statistics were impressive: 6,500 health centres and 12,300 village centres had been established, mostly in Africa and the Indian subcontinent. More than a thousand medical training institutions (the precise figure given was 1,011) had been set up for child-health, nutrition and welfare workers, and almost two hundred milk-processing plants constructed. A war was being waged against intense poverty, nowhere more urgent than in sub-Saharan and equatorial Africa, and on the Indian subcontinent. The number of individuals in direct receipt of these benefits was calculated at fifty-seven million. An estimated sixty-six million people were protected against the debilitating and often fatal scourge of malaria with insecticides provided by UNICEF. The full extent of the anti-malaria campaign was stressed during a United Nations World Health Assembly in New Delhi in March when it was established that of the 1,336 million people who, two decades earlier, had been at risk from malaria, 298 million were 'free from the scourge' and a further 612 million were protected by the eradication programmes then in operation. As for plague, which at the start of the century had killed millions of people, particularly in India, the recorded death toll worldwide was a mere 360, at most. Smallpox too was on the wane, with the 498,000 cases recorded a decade earlier having fallen to 60,000 in 1961.

In its work in providing technical support for poor countries, the United Nations had set up an Expanded Programme of Technical Assistance. This provided help for every one of the 103 member States that were in need, some in desperate need. Experts were sent to the countries requiring help, and training was given for those in the countries themselves that would eventually operate the facilities and machinery being put in place, much of it connected with irrigation and nutrition. The concept of beneficent imperialism, exercised mostly from European capital cities and by Europeans many of whom spent their lives abroad in the service of their country, was being replaced by a system of international help and increased self-help.

During 1961 almost a third of the technical support budget of the United Nations went to Africa, mostly to former French and British colonies.

An aspect of the East-West divide that was to remain a feature for three more decades was espionage. Twice in 1961 spy trials were held in Britain. In March a ring of five people, led by Gordon Lonsdale, were sentenced for passing on to the Soviet Union information about the underwater warfare establishment at Portland. In May a former British diplomat, George Blake, was sentenced to forty-two years in prison for spying for the Soviet Union.

The world's largest computer was installed that year, at the British atomic energy research station at Harwell. As well as helping atomic research, it was able to make significant advances in weather forecasting. Of equal long-term significance was the work of two chemists, the Englishman Francis Crick and the South African Sydney Brenner, in being able to determine the structure of deoxyribonucleic acid (DNA), offering the prospect of finding and exploring the human genetic code.

Two musical beginnings took place that year that were major events in popular music: the debut of the Beatles at the Cavern Club in Liverpool, and the debut of Bob Dylan at the Gaslight Café in Greenwich Village, New York. Two other eras came to an end, with the last broadcast, in April, of the British radio programme *Children's Hour*, which had been a regular and gentle daily pleasure since 1922, and the last journey, on May 28, of the Orient Express, the train that, in peacetime, each day and night for the previous seventy-eight years had linked Paris to Bucharest.

CHAPTER ELEVEN

1962

> . . . I truly believe that we in this generation must come
> to terms with nature and I think we're challenged, as
> mankind has never been challenged before, to prove our
> maturity and mastery not of nature but of ourselves.
>
> RACHEL CARSON

THE EAST-WEST DIVIDE dominated the new year as it had dominated the old, the spectre of nuclear war adding a dimension that had first emerged with stark clarity during the Korean War a decade earlier, and had become omnipresent. How the conflicting American and Soviet attitudes would affect the balance of power was unclear. At the start of the year the Soviet leaders were able to mock the United States for its failures, and feel a sense of general superiority, which influenced their confidence with regard to any future confrontation.

The collapse of the American stock market on 28 May 1962, when it fell more sharply in one day than at any time since the great Wall Street Crash of 1929, certainly gave the Russians cause for satisfaction – although it was later described by experts as 'a spectacular false alarm' – not only because it seemed general proof of the fallibility of capitalism, but because it encouraged thoughts of a financially weakened, unsound America. Internal divisions in the American South were also much publicized in the Soviet Union, as a sign of America's inner turmoil and weakness. They were certainly real divisions. George Wallace, the newly elected Governor of Alabama, declared in his inaugural address, to the applause of so many of his White constituents: 'Segregation now, segregation tomorrow, segregation for ever.' Defying the United States government, the State of Mississippi refused to allow desegregation in Mississippi University. A Black student, Richard Meredith, had been enrolled. The Federal courts ordered the university to register him.

The university refused to do so. On September 30 Meredith was taken to the university campus under the guard of three hundred United States marshals. Ten times that number of White students began hurling rocks and bottles at the guards. As the confrontation intensified, Kennedy appealed on television for the students and citizens of Mississippi to accept the Federal law on desegregation. His words were a powerful plea for peace and compliance: 'Our nation is founded on the principle that observance of the law is the eternal safeguard of liberty, and defiance of the law is the surest road to tyranny.' Americans were free to disagree with the law, 'but not to disobey it'.

The confrontation on the campus, and in the nearby town of Oxford, Mississippi, continued throughout that night and into the morning. Three thousand Federal troops were sent in to relieve the marshals. In Oxford, White opponents of segregation attacked soldiers, newspaper reporters – who had converged on the town – and Blacks. In the resultant clash with the troops, two anti-segregation demonstrators were killed and seventy injured. Meredith was allowed to enter the classroom. His fellow students, all White, gave him a frosty reception.

Voter registration was another area where segregation had led to democratic rights being withheld. In Macon County, Alabama, with a population of 4,405 Whites and 22,287 Blacks, the White minority had successfully prevented a single Black person from being put on the electoral roll. A Federal court declared this improper. The decision was upheld by the Supreme Court, and on October 22 the voting registrars at Macon were ordered to end their discrimination and to handle all Black voting applications 'expeditiously'. It was a victory through the Supreme Court for the cause of civil rights throughout the American South.

The Soviet Union saw considerable weakness in the civil rights turmoil in the United States, and did not appreciate, when it came, the importance of the Supreme Court verdict, whereby the rule of law, and democratic values, were upheld – as indeed they had been in the Richard Meredith case, albeit at the price of human lives and scenes of appalling prejudice and civil confrontation.

Steadily, the United States was improving its military power and asserting it. In February, Robert McNamara, the Secretary of Defense, told a news conference in Washington that the United States had a 'second strike' nuclear retaliatory capacity greater than the 'first strike' of any other country. This meant that however severe the first nuclear attack might be the United States would be the victor in the second stage. In the defence budget $15,000 million was to be spent on the nuclear deterrent: this sum was the equivalent of all the money being spent by all its European allies for all their military, naval and air preparations. New budget appropriations approved by Congress included the money for two hundred Minutemen intercontinental ballistic missiles and twelve Polaris submarines.

With regard to conventional weapons and armed forces, military assistance was sent to the government of Thailand when it was thought that an attack by Laotian Communist forces might be imminent. The American economic and military presence in South Vietnam was also growing. On February 8 a new American Military Assistance Command for Vietnam was established: four thousand Americans were employed by it, mostly training South Vietnamese soldiers. By the end of the year there were as many as ten thousand United States servicemen training local troops in their struggle against the Vietminh, and providing essential logistic support for military action against the Vietminh. On April 13 the South Vietnamese government announced that during the previous six weeks 2,030 Communist 'rebels' had been killed, for the loss of 540 government troops. The question of whether the Communists represented a force not only of arms but of minds was not addressed. American soldiers were also in combat. In October it was announced by the State Department in Washington that forty-six Americans had been killed in the previous nine months while serving in South Vietnam.

When Chinese Communist forces appeared to be about to enter northern India, Kennedy sent a letter to Nehru promising that the United States would consider 'with sympathy' any Indian request for long-term American help. The United States was also showing its nuclear capacity. After the Soviet Union had exploded more than fifty nuclear devices in the atmosphere during a period of nine months – an average of one every five days – Kennedy authorized the resumption of American tests. The first took place on April 25, in the Pacific Ocean, near two American possessions, Johnston Island and Christmas Island. On July 9 an H-bomb was detonated two hundred miles above Johnston Island. It was the equivalent of two million tons of TNT. The flash of the explosion was so intense that it was seen in New Zealand, four thousand miles away.

The United States was clearly, in terms of military might, the leading nation in the Western world. It was also in many ways the sole arbiter of that world's future. But Kennedy recognized that the United States could not act alone, and that the East-West divide encompassed more than a dozen nations on each side. All these had a part to play in any confrontation, and

– from the Western perspective – in persuading the Communist bloc not to embark on military adventures of political subversion. On June 27 it was in a warning to Communist China that Kennedy revealed, through the toughness of his language, the tone of his thinking. There had been many, growing denunciations by China of the continuing Nationalist presence on the offshore islands of Quemoy and Matsu. These denunciations were exacerbated by the clear indication – confirmed within American diplomatic circles – that Chiang Kai-shek, from his island fastness on Taiwan, wanted to use the islands as launching pads for an invasion of the Chinese mainland, with a view to setting off a popular anti-Communist uprising. The Americans warned him against any such course, and stressed the folly of believing that an uprising was imminent or even in the realm of possibility. But they would defend Chinese Nationalist sovereignty over the two islands, and on June 27 Kennedy warned China that if Quemoy and Matsu were attacked, and if that attack were seen as a prelude to an invasion of Taiwan, the United States would help defend them.

The Chinese government took heed. Even after it shot down a U-2 reconnaissance aircraft over the Chinese mainland, claiming angrily and rightly that this was a 'spy mission', it made no effort to challenge the United States over the islands.

Kennedy's own time spent in London on the eve of the Second World War and while writing his book *While England Slept*, published in 1940, made him advocate a closer and more active association between the nations of Western Europe. Following his description in January of European unity as 'the greatest challenge of all', he obtained the support of Congress for a Trade Expansion Bill, whereby there would be a gradual elimination of tariffs in the United States and the European Economic Community (EEC) on all goods with which, together, the United States and the Community supplied 80 per cent of the world's trade. Other duties would be reduced by up to 50 per cent. In explaining that such a partnership between the United States and the EEC went far beyond the economic and commercial aspects, Kennedy told an audience in Philadelphia – characteristically choosing July 4, the anniversary of the Declaration of Independence, to make his pronouncement – that what was required was 'a declaration of interdependence'. The United States would be 'prepared to discuss with a united Europe the ways and means of forming a concrete Atlantic partnership'. The aims of such a partnership were wide-ranging, and a direct challenge to Communist aspirations from the River Elbe to the Sea of Japan:

We believe that a United Europe will be capable of playing a greater role in the common defence, of responding more generously to the needs of poorer nations, of joining with the United States and others in lowering trade barriers, resolving problems of currency and commodities, and developing co-ordinated policies in all other economic, diplomatic, and political areas. We see in such a Europe a partner with whom we could deal on a basis of full equality in all the great and burdensome tasks of building and defending a community of free nations . . .

Acting on our own we cannot establish justice throughout the world, we cannot ensure its domestic tranquillity or provide for its common defence, or promote its general welfare, or secure the blessings of liberty to ourselves and our posterity. But joined with other free nations, we can do all this and more.

On July 23 the Geneva Conference on Laos concluded its work. The United States, which had been an active participant, agreed to accept its conclusion. American troops would withdraw by October 7, as would the forces of North Vietnam. The neutrality of Laos would be secured, and an International Control Commission would monitor any threat to it. The Commission was made up of members from Canada, India and Poland. All the contending groups within Laos, including the Communist – or far-left – Pathet Lao, under Prince Souphannouvong, would have a place in the new Government of National Unity.

The United States was relieved to be clear of its Laotian commitment. There were heavy pressures elsewhere, not least in Berlin, where the Soviet Union was demanding an end to the Western Zone of Occupation – established in 1945 – and its replacement by the government of East Germany. This was unacceptable to the Western Allies, and on September 7 – with the dispute over Berlin foremost in his mind – Kennedy obtained the authority of Congress to call up 150,000 reservists a year for active service should the foreign situation seem to warrant it.

The geographic range of the United States-Soviet confrontation was wide: Berlin, Laos, Vietnam, even India. Nuclear testing was imposing itself on the vast pristine beauty of the Pacific. But it was close to the continental United States, off the southern tip of Florida, that the most urgent confrontation was emerging. It is only ninety-three miles from Key West in Florida to the Cuban capital, Havana. In January, Communist Cuba had been thrown out of the Washington-based Organization of American States, during the organization's conference at Punta del Este in Uruguay. Shipping and trade with Cuba were to be banned, though Kennedy found it harder to persuade America's allies across the Atlantic to adopt such a stringent course. He persevered, however, being intent on isolating Cuba economically from the capitalist world.

On October 10 an American reconnaissance aircraft brought back photographs showing new building activity in a remote part of Cuba. These photographs, kept strictly secret, were examined by American Intelligence. More detailed scrutiny by reconnaissance aircraft was ordered at once, but had to be postponed for four days because a hurricane made flying impossible. On October 14 both high- and low-level flights took place. They showed that at some of the sites located on October 10 medium-range missiles were already in position. These had a capacity to carry nuclear warheads, and a range of more than a thousand miles. This would put Texas, Oklahoma and Arkansas within range. Washington itself – Kennedy's White House – was only 1,100 miles from the Cuban capital.

As the Intelligence photographs were examined, an alarming picture emerged. At several Cuban airfields, Soviet bombers were identified, of a type that was capable of carrying nuclear bombs. In the photographs these bombers could be seen being uncrated. They had arrived by sea. Other photographs showed sites being prepared to receive even longer-range missiles. On October 16 the photographs were shown to Kennedy. For the next six days a remarkable exercise in secret diplomacy took place. The Soviet motive was understood. Confronted by the sudden announcement that nuclear missiles were already in place that could knock out most, if not all, of America's nuclear capability, Khrushchev could order his troops to occupy West Berlin, and the United States would be too vulnerable at home to retaliate in Europe. Among other distractions in the United States, the mid-term elections were imminent, during which Kennedy would be on the campaign trail, helping Democrat Senators and Congressmen whose seats might be in jeopardy.

Kennedy was not to be distracted. To prevent anything approaching Soviet missile readiness, he came to the decision that he must order the total elimination of the Cuban missile sites before they could be made operational. His military advisers – trained in the art of possible scenarios – warned him that to attack the sites could precipitate a nuclear war. This could develop, they said, if either of the effective methods of attacking the sites were carried out: an American invasion of Cuba, or the bombing of the missile sites. In both cases, it was felt by those who had the task of making accurate assessments of Soviet reactions, that the Soviet Union would respond by embarking upon nuclear war, for which they possessed all the necessary weaponry and means of delivery against, say, the American forces in Europe.

Kennedy did not intend to risk a direct confrontation with the Soviet Union by such drastic measures. Instead he chose a third course, a naval blockade of Cuba. If this blockade did not force the Soviets to remove the missiles, then he was prepared to contemplate direct military action. The blockade made sense in an immediate way. American Intelligence showed that more than twenty-five Soviet or Soviet-chartered ships were on their way to Cuba, many of them inevitably bringing the equipment needed to make the missile bases operational. On October 18 the blockade was put in force. That day Kennedy left Washington for the mid-term election campaigning. Two days later – on the excuse of a cold – he returned to the capital. Then, on October 22, he personally briefed Congressional leaders, and instructed the State Department to brief all American Embassies. That evening, at 7 p.m., Kennedy spoke on television to the American people, reporting for the first time on the presence of the missile sites and the imposition of the blockade – the word 'quarantine' was used instead of blockade, to avoid repercussions in international law, where the legality of blockading a sovereign State could be challenged. The American aim, Kennedy said in his broadcast, was 'to prevent the use of these missiles against this or any other country, and to secure their withdrawal or elimination from the Western hemisphere'.

All ships on their way to Cuba would be stopped and searched. Only those not carrying offensive weaponry would be allowed to proceed. This policy was approved on October 23 by all twenty members of the Organization of American States, with a recommendation that each member State take action – 'including the use of armed force' – to stop the movement of missiles to Cuba. From Moscow came a warning that 'no State which values its independence' could accept the blockade. In secret, Kennedy gave orders that any Russian ship seeking to break the blockade should be sunk.

On October 24 the United States blockade went into effect. That day several Soviet ships known to be carrying jet warplanes and other weapons altered course to avoid the American naval patrols, and abandoned their Cuban destinations. On October 25 the first Soviet ship to reach the American patrols was stopped. It was an oil tanker, and, as it was carrying only oil, was allowed to continue on its course. When, later that day, the Secretary-

General of the United Nations, U Thant, appealed to Kennedy to end the blockade and to Khrushchev to stop the arms build-up in Cuba, Kennedy declined to do so, making it clear that unless the missiles were withdrawn there could be no resolution to the crisis.

On October 26 Kennedy was shown further American air-reconnaissance photographs which indicated that work on the missile sites was continuing. Talks in Washington that day focused on the possibility of direct attacks on the missile sites. As the tension rose, an American reconnaissance plane was shot down over Cuba and its pilot killed. How far the Soviet Union was prepared to risk a direct American attack on the missile sites without retaliation was not known. But on October 27, in what appeared to be a face-saving suggestion, Khrushchev proposed that in exchange for the withdrawal of Soviet air bases in Cuba, the United States would remove its air bases in Turkey. Kennedy rejected this, but wrote a moderately worded letter to Khrushchev, in which he described as 'generally acceptable' the Cuban side of the Soviet proposal: that the United States would end its quarantine and guarantee the 'territorial integrity' of Communist Cuba, in return for the removal of the Soviet bases in Cuba. These would have to be removed, Kennedy wrote, under United Nations supervision, and work on the missile sites would have to stop 'immediately'. If Khrushchev were to give instructions along these lines 'there is no reason why we should not be able to complete these arrangements and announce them to the world within a couple of days'. Were the crisis not to be resolved on these lines, however, it 'would surely lead', Kennedy warned, 'to an intensification of the Cuban crisis and a grave risk to the peace of the world'.

On October 28 Khrushchev backed down. He would, he said, remove all Russian missiles, bombers and troops from Cuba. The American 'quarantine' was at once suspended, while U Thant began negotiations with Fidel Castro for United Nations inspection of the missile sites. On November 1 the negotiations broke down and the quarantine was reimposed. On the following day, Castro agreed to inspection of the sites. At the same time, under United Nations auspices, the Soviet Union agreed that the United States could inspect all departing Soviet ships to ensure that the missiles were being removed.

On November 8 the first Soviet ship with missiles on board, leaving Cuba, was inspected and allowed to pass. The missiles were on their way back to the Soviet Union. Within a few days, forty-two missiles passed through the quarantine and back to Russia. On November 21 the Soviet Union agreed to remove from Cuba all its bombers capable of carrying nuclear warheads. On the following day Kennedy announced the end of the naval blockade.

Castro still refused to allow inspection of the missile sites on the ground, insisting that this would be a violation of Cuban sovereignty. The United States was content to leave this aspect of its concerns to continued aerial reconnaissance, the method which had enabled it to detect the missile sites in the first place.

The missiles were gone. But as many as 15,000 Russian troops and technicians remained in Cuba. When Castro refused to send these away, the United States announced that, while it was willing to give up negotiations on this, it withdrew what was to have been a formal guarantee not to invade Cuba, and pledged to maintain a close aerial scrutiny of all military movements on the island.

The Cuban missile crisis was over. Kennedy had confronted the Soviet Union, and forced it to back down. Inside the Soviet Union, the economic and political problems generated by Communism were proving yet again to be a greater weakness than the economic and racial problems inside the United States. Squandering of government funds was widespread. The Virgin Lands scheme launched the previous year to increase agricultural output had run into formidable difficulties. The 'simple fact' was, Khrushchev told the Central Committee on March 5, 'that we are not producing enough'. Economists, he said, would have to be 'retrained'. In place of the greater individual initiative that the scheme had offered farmers, 'inspector–organizers' were to be set up with wide-ranging powers, able to examine the efforts of farmers over large areas. These inspectors would be 'mobile'; they could turn up in a location at any time, unannounced. Farm chairmen who failed to reach their targets would be 'disciplined'. Many senior local officials were dismissed for their 'failures'. But the underlying problem – how to fertilize the extensive areas that had suddenly been brought under cultivation – could not be resolved. The quantities of fertilizer needed for the Virgin Lands were not available.

Persisting with the themes and denunciations of his anti-Stalin speech of six years earlier, Khrushchev continued to attack the 'Stalin cult'. There were efforts to introduce the Soviet public, through literature, to the failings of the recent Communist past. In his memoirs, Ilya Ehrenburg, who for a while had been one of Stalin's favourite writers, wrote openly of the hardships and tyranny of Soviet life in the 1930s. A novel serialized in the literary magazine *Novy Mir*, Yuri Bondarev's *Silence*, gave an honest appraisal of the hardships suffered by Soviet soldiers after the war. The editor of *Novy Mir*, Alexander Tvardovsky, also persuaded Khrushchev to allow him to publish Alexander Solzhenitsyn's novel *One Day in the Life of Ivan Denisovich*, with its account of conditions in a labour camp in the Stalin era, not in the pre-war but in the post-war years. One scene was set in 1951. The novel was praised by L. F. Ilichev, Secretary of the Central Committee of the Communist Party, in a speech to the Ideological Commission of the Central Committee, attended by many artists, composers, actors and film-makers. 'As you know,' Ilichev told them, 'it deals with a bitter subject, but it is not written from a decadent viewpoint. Works like this inspire respect for the labouring man, and the Party supports them.'

The changes had their limits. After visiting a Russian art exhibition in Moscow on December 1, Khrushchev condemned the paintings as 'miserable imitations of decadent Western formalism' that had been painted by artists using 'a donkey's tail'. Following this criticism, the President of the Academy of Arts resigned. Religious observance was also under attack, the Russian Orthodox Church being accused of 'Stalinist' errors. A number of Atheist Conferences were held, at which those present were told that they must work directly with individual Christian believers to convince them of the error of their beliefs. Churches and monasteries were closed down. National and local newspapers carried a whole spate of articles and news items pointing the finger at worshippers as 'speculators', 'parasites' and 'anti-social elements'.

The decline of European imperialism – already modified and transformed from its turn-of-the-century rigidity to various forms of colonial, commonwealth and autonomous administrations – was accelerating. For almost a decade the Republic of Indonesia had wanted to take control of Dutch New Guinea. On August 15 the Netherlands and Indonesia signed an agreement in New York, whereby the territory would be handed over to the United Nations for six months, and then transferred to Indonesia.

In Algeria, the three-way struggle between France, the European Algerians (mostly French and Christian), and the native Algerians (almost entirely Muslim), was nearing its end, after so many years of strife. Negotiations between France and Algeria had opened at Evian on March 7, between Mohammed Ahmed Ben Bella, the founder of the Front de la Libération National (FLN) and de Gaulle's confidant, Georges Pompidou – who would soon become French Prime Minister. Agreement was reached eleven days later. A ceasefire would come into effect the following day at midday. French troops would withdraw, and there would be a referendum on self-determination. The European Algerians would be able to 'keep their French nationality and return to France whenever they liked'. If they decided to stay in Algeria they would have to choose 'at the end of three years, either to remain French, in which case their linguistic, cultural and religious rights as a foreign minority in Algeria would be respected, or else to become Algerian citizens, in which case they would have minority representation at both local and national levels, in proportion to their numbers'.

The Evian Agreement came into being, and held. As part of the referendum, Algeria would have the right to choose independence. Opposition to this from the Organization de l'Armée Secrète (the OAS) was immediate and violent. There were terrorist bomb attacks not only in Algeria, but in metropolitan France. Ammunition was stolen from army depots. A car bomb in Paris killed two policemen. But the French public turned against the men of violence, their former compatriots, and there were several large anti-OAS demonstrations, in which university teachers and students took a main part. As many as 1,200 OAS members were arrested and held in prison, as were the two leaders of the movement, General Jouhaud and General Salan, both of whom were brought to trial and sentenced to life imprisonment (Jouhaud had been sentenced to death but his sentence was commuted). Two attempts to murder President de Gaulle were foiled. During one of them, on a road three miles outside Paris, shots were fired.

The Algerian referendum was held on July 1. The result was decisive: 5,993,754 voters opting for independence and only 16,478 opposing it. Hardly any Europeans opposed to independence cast their vote. But at first the omens were not bad: in Oran, several hundred Europeans joined a march by Muslim Algerians to celebrate the result. The new government entered Algiers on July 3. But the resentment by extremist Europeans, and the excess of zeal of extremist Muslims, led two days later in Oran to a day of violence in which more than a hundred Europeans were killed. In the immediate aftermath of these killings, thousands of Europeans fled. This was followed by the kidnapping of more than five hundred Europeans suspected of sympathy with the OAS. Some were tortured and then released; others were never seen again. European homes were looted and cars destroyed. By the end of the year 800,000 Europeans – eighty per cent of the total – had left. The hope that they might have made their contribution to the new country was dashed. These were the administrators, teachers, business managers and technicians on whom much depended, particularly in the short term. Within a year of independence, all French-owned estates in Algeria were nationalized.

Internally, the rivals for power struggled to avoid bloodshed. On September 3, troops loyal to Ben Bella marched on Algiers. Two days later agreement was reached among the contenders for the new national leadership that elections would be held as soon as possible. On September 25, before they could be held, Ben Bella was appointed interim Prime Minister at the head of the 'Democratic and Popular Government' of the Algerian Republic. Travelling to New York he was present at the United Nations when Algeria was admitted as the 109th member. In Washington, Kennedy offered him the 'hand of friendship' of the United States. Three days later, in Havana, Fidel Castro offered him Cuba's friendship. Ben Bella reciprocated Castro's gesture by announcing his support for the reversion to Cuban sovereignty of the United States sovereign base of Guantánamo, which the United States had acquired after the defeat of Spain in 1898.

In South Africa, the simmering inequalities of apartheid led on November 21, at Paarl, near Cape Town, to an attack by a hundred Africans armed with knives and axes on a number of White homes. The Africans had earlier failed to secure the release of some fellow protesters who were being held in the local prison. Two Whites were beaten to death and seven Africans shot dead by the police.

Since withdrawing from the Commonwealth and establishing South Africa as an independent republic a year earlier (on 31 May 1961), Hendrick Verwoerd's government was promulgating a series of draconian laws against critics of the regime. On May 12 the innocuously named General Law Amendment Bill imposed the death penalty for all acts of sabotage. Under the Sabotage Act a few months later it became a criminal offence to publish anything said or written by White or Black journalists whose works had been banned. Regulations were put in force at the end of October under which those banned from speaking or writing could be held under house arrest for five years, could not use the telephone, could not receive visitors, and could not communicate with any other banned person. By the end of the year, eighteen such orders had been issued.

Among the leaders of the Black South Africans who were arrested was Nelson Mandela. He was sentenced to five years in prison on conviction for having incited workers to strike, and leaving the country 'without valid documents'.

*   *   *

In China, throughout the early months of the year, the failure of the spring wheat crop as a result of drought brought tens of millions of people to the verge of starvation. Mao Tse-tung's government acted in its usual dramatic and all-encompassing way: town dwellers were ordered out of the urban areas and on to the land. Some of them were peasants who had migrated to the towns in the hope of more food and a better livelihood. They were forced out, as were many people whose life and livelihood had always been as town dwellers. In July it was reported that a third of the population of Canton – one of China's most populous cities – had been forced to migrate to the countryside. Many were students with no experience whatsoever of agricultural work.

From the Kwangtung Province, tens of thousands of dispossessed Chinese fled across the border into Hong Kong, seeking safety under the British flag. The Hong Kong authorities, arguing that the colony was already 'hopelessly overcrowded', sent them back. One country that came to China's rescue was Canada, which sold China, on favourable terms, large quantities of wheat and barley. Smaller quantities of wheat were sold by Australia, the Rhodesian Federation and South Africa.

One effect inside China of sending so many townspeople to the fields was that many industries were denuded of their essential workforce. A further complication came as the Soviet Union and China entered into an ideological dispute – both claiming that the mantle of Marx-Engels-Lenin had fallen on them – with the result that many Soviet technicians in China were recalled. Only the signature in Peking on April 20 of a Sino-Soviet trade agreement brought vehicles and machinery to China in return for tin, mercury and wool. But the loss of the Soviet technicians was not remedied.

On the Chinese border, the attempt by the Chinese to secure a swathe of territory from India – two high mountain passes, one in Ladakh and the other in Assam – led to a protest by India at 'systematic and continuous aggression into Indian territory'. The Chinese persisted. India retaliated by cancelling the 1954 Sino-Indian Trade Agreement, under which China had obtained favourable trading terms for its enterprises in Tibet. As the Chinese would still not withdraw, India closed down all Chinese trade agencies in India and withdrew its own traders from China. On September 8 Chinese troops crossed the 14,000-foot Tangla Ridge, the Chinese-Indian border along the North-East Frontier Agency (NEFA). Fighting began in one of the most inhospitable regions of the world. The Chinese also began to advance in Ladakh. The Indians, who had not expected to be attacked in force at such high altitudes, and so far from any Chinese bases, were driven back. On October 22 Nehru appealed to the Indian people to resist the greatest threat to India since independence.

Indian troops continued to be driven back. In a further appeal, Nehru spoke of Churchill's fortitude in 1940 and of how Britain had stood up to surprise attack and heavy odds. On October 26 India was put on a war footing, and appeals made to the public to donate cash and jewellery for the war effort. Even the Communist Party of India abandoned its ideological stance and denounced Peking's 'treacherous aggression'. This did not stop Nehru from ordering the arrest of many Communist leaders, including the former Chief Minister of Kerala, E.M.S. Namboodiripad, as a precaution.

On November 15 the Chinese began a swift advance through the North-East Frontier Agency, seizing the town of Bomdila, on the border with Bhutan. Walong, on the Burmese border, was also overrun. In India there was widespread panic. Towns were evacuated as the prospect loomed of Chinese troops descending from the hills and penetrating the plains.

While several non-aligned nations, including Egypt, called for Sino-Indian talks, Canada offered India military help. This gave the Commonwealth a sudden revived status in Indian eyes. The United States and Britain both sent weapons to India, and two generals to advise on strategy. This, Peking declared, was 'American imperialism'. But on November 21 China suddenly and unexpectedly announced that its troops would observe a unilateral cease-fire, followed ten days later by a withdrawal to the border. As the withdrawal was completed, the Chinese Foreign Minister, Chou En-lai, insisted that the areas that had been evacuated remained Chinese territory which India was occupying illegally, but against which no further action was planned. China had made its claim, occupied the region it claimed, and then returned it to Indian control. It was a bizarre episode, but a costly one for India, three thousand of whose soldiers were killed. One factor in the Chinese withdrawal was the strong opposition to the Chinese attack on India which had been conveyed by Khrushchev to Mao Tse-tung: the Soviet leader had gone so far as to intimate that all Soviet oil exports to China would cease if the invasion or the occupation of Indian territory continued.

The two Super Powers, with their hydrogen bombs and areas of global confrontation, were not without the means of finding areas of agreement where they could reconcile their defence and scientific interests. On December 5 the Soviet Union and the United States came to an agreement on mutual co-operation for the peaceful use of outer space. Nuclear power for civil use – to provide heat and light for industries and private homes – continued to develop, with two hundred atomic reactors in the United States, and thirty-nine each in the Soviet Union and Britain. But the espionage which had become an integral part of the East-West divide continued without respite, and those who were caught faced severe sentences: on October 22 John Vassall, a British Admiralty clerk who had earlier been stationed in the British Embassy in Moscow, was sentenced to eighteen years in prison for spying for the Soviet Union.

The aftermath of the Second World War, which saw the execution that year of Eichmann in Israel, also saw works of reconstruction, highlighted in Britain on May 25 by the consecration of a new Coventry Cathedral alongside the shell of the old one, burned out in 1940. Among the artists who contributed to the magnificence of the new Cathedral was Graham Sutherland, through tapestry, and Jacob Epstein, through sculpture. Five days later Benjamin Britten's *War Requiem* was given its first performance in Coventry. Its settings of poems by Wilfrid Owen – with lines like 'no mockeries for them from prayers' – and the music to which they were set, brought a note of deep and disturbing realism to the proceedings. Owen himself had been killed in the First World War, in its final weeks. The hope of the organizers that a Soviet soprano, Galina Vishnevskaya, would sing in the requiem was dashed when the Soviet authorities refused her permission to take part.

In the sphere of travel, two new developments were taking place, one of which was to change the nature and the other the speed of commercial travel. The first was the hovercraft, capable of crossing water on an air cushion that lifted it above the water. The Soviet Union was developing these for use on the Don and the Volga rivers; Britain for cross-Channel travel. In the realm of speed, on November 29 Britain and France signed an agreement for the development of a supersonic civil airliner that could fly the Atlantic in less than four hours, at twice the speed of sound: it was given the name 'Concorde', and described as the travel of the future, though in the event it failed to fulfil its promoters' global expectations. But aviation retained its defence aspect, with work on a new concept, the vertical take-off jet aircraft, being sponsored by the NATO powers. Within NATO there was tension, as the European members of the alliance were seeking from the United States the right to an independent nuclear weapons system that could be operated in Europe according to European needs. Britain and France were both emphatic about keeping their own nuclear forces under their own strategic control. The American Secretary of Defense, Robert McNamara, went so far, in a public speech at Ann Arbor, Michigan, on June 16, to call independent nuclear forces 'dangerous, prone to obsolescence, and lacking in credibility as a deterrent'. In a gesture of conciliation, the United States agreed to put five of its Polaris nuclear submarines under NATO command, and to provide all NATO governments with information about the location, capabilities and targets of its nuclear weapons based in Europe. At the end of the year, following the Cuban missile crisis, Kennedy and Macmillan met in the Bahamas. As a result of that meeting, the United States agreed – in return for Britain's pledge to work towards the creation of 'a genuinely multilateral NATO strategic nuclear force' – to provide Polaris missiles to be fired from British submarines. That year NATO also agreed to give economic aid to both Greece and Turkey. The gulf between East and West was as wide as it had ever been, and the contending forces on each side of the Iron Curtain as determined as ever to maintain their military and nuclear strength. But the Cuban missile crisis had shown that, when it came to confrontation, the United States had the greater skills – or the greater nerve.

NATO's opposite number, the Warsaw Treaty Organization, held its spring manoeuvres in Hungary in April. Soviet, Roumanian and Hungarian forces – under the watchful eye of the Soviet Defence Minister, Marshal Malinovsky, participated in 'a simulated attack with tactical atomic weapons'. At the organization's annual meeting in Moscow on June 7, the Chinese, who had hitherto attended as an 'associate' member, were not invited. Albania, which had quarrelled ideologically with the Soviet Union, was also not invited, and protested at its exclusion. Autumn manoeuvres were held in East Germany in September, with Soviet, East German and Czechoslovak forces taking part. In October there were yet more manoeuvres along the border between Poland and East Germany, in which East German, Polish and again Soviet forces participated. During these manoeuvres it was made clear to the West that the armed forces of East Germany were as much an integral part of the Warsaw Pact's military preparations as West Germany's forces were within NATO. The military forces of each multi-power grouping were commanded by a Soviet and an American general respectively, and had been since their formation more than a decade earlier.

The worst natural disaster of 1962 was in Iran, when an earthquake hit the Kazvin-Saveh-Hamadan triangle, and more than 12,000 people were killed.

But it was the determination not to allow the environment to be damaged by man that marked the outstanding event of 1962, the publication by an American writer, Rachel Carson, of *Silent Spring*. In its first 'People of the Century' profile, on 1 January 1999, *The Times* wrote:

> Marshalling empirical evidence of environmental damage done by chemical pesticides, she had exposed with steely authority the arrogance and folly of those who sought to conquer nature, disregarding the integrity of the natural world and the interdependence of all living things. The response of the Establishment was vicious. Carson's scientific credentials were impugned and her status as a childless, unmarried woman belittled. But as evidence of graver ecological damage kept coming in, public opinion remained stalwart. *Silent Spring* planted the seeds of an environmental movement which in the 1970s was to germinate and sprout into a mainstream political issue.

In her first nationwide public interview, on *CBS Reports*, Rachel Carson said: 'We still talk in terms of conquest. We still haven't become mature enough to think of ourselves as only a very tiny part of a vast and incredible universe. Now I truly believe that we in this generation must come to terms with nature and I think we're challenged, as mankind has never been challenged before, to prove our maturity and mastery not of nature but of ourselves.'

Ten years after the publication of *Silent Spring*, the first 'Green Party' was founded, the Values Party, in New Zealand; also that year, in Stockholm, the United Nations held its first environmental conference.

CHAPTER TWELVE

1963

I have a dream that one day this nation will rise up and live out the true meaning of its creed: 'We hold these truths to be self-evident, that all men are created equal.'

MARTIN LUTHER KING

As the rift between the Soviet Union and China intensified, leading to military preparations being increased on both sides of the long border, Khrushchev sought means of strengthening the power of the Communist Party and its centralizing authority. In Moscow, the fusion of the Party and State administrative apparatuses that had been announced the previous year was accelerated. In Soviet Central Asia, the most westerly area of Sino-Soviet contact, power was being transferred from the regional national groups to Russian officials appointed by Moscow, under the auspices of the Communist Party's newly created Central Asian Bureau.

At various points on the Soviet-Chinese border there were clashes. The Soviet Union complained to China of five thousand border violations during the previous year. Chinese troops occupied a number of small, disputed islands – scarcely more than sandbanks – in the Ussuri River. At the frontier station of Naushki, seventy-three Chinese students were detained by the Soviet border authorities for three days after they had resisted Soviet attempts to confiscate the 'anti-Soviet' literature they were attempting to bring into Russia. The slanging match of words intensified. The main Chinese charges were that the Soviet Union, as a result of 'national egoism', was not giving China the economic help it ought to give; and that the Soviet Union was appeasing, and even allying with, the 'imperialist' powers. This latter was most obvious, and most dangerous, the Chinese alleged, in the negotiations that the Soviet Union had begun, principally with the United States, for general disarmament. When these negotiations came to a successful conclusion, a formal treaty was signed banning certain types of nuclear tests. The Chinese were vitriolic in their denunciation of Moscow. But the Cuban missile crisis had curbed Khrushchev's zeal for confrontation: with regard to Berlin, while praising the Wall for strengthening the East German regime – by keeping people in – he moderated Soviet calls for East German control of the city. In May the Soviet Union gave an assurance, to Kennedy's special emissary to Moscow, Averell Harriman, that there would be no attempt by the Soviet Union to breach the neutrality agreement on Laos.

With regard to the most direct area of Soviet-American confrontation, nuclear testing, two developments marked a turning away from the dangers of an escalation of conflict. The first was the announcement on April 5 that the Soviet Union favoured an American proposal for the setting up of a telephonic 'hot line' between Kennedy and Khrushchev whereby the two men could talk directly to each other in the event of a renewed crisis. This would mean that the strident public posturing at the time of the Cuban missile crisis might be avoided. The second development related to the search for an agreement to ban nuclear testing. Hitherto agreement had been impossible to reach because of the Soviet refusal to allow on-site inspection. This refusal was circumvented by excluding underground tests from the ban. All tests above ground, which experts on both sides of the divide recognized as extremely contaminating, were to be banned: they could be monitored from afar. The agreement was signed on June 20. It constituted a break-through which created a sense of relief among those millions who feared both the possibility of a nuclear war and the poisoning of the atmosphere through nuclear testing. With it went an agreement that more than any other pulled the divided world back from the brink: to prevent a surprise attack from space, both sides agreed not to fire nuclear weapons into orbit around the Earth.

Inside the Soviet Union, Khrushchev continued to assert the primacy of the Communist Party and its methods. On March 8 he told a conference of Party officials that the era of the purges had been 'creative', and urged writers to treat controversial areas of Soviet history 'with restraint'. The poet Yevgeni Yevtushenko was made to apologize for his 'immodesty' in writing about the suffering exacted by the Bolshevik revolution in 1917: his account had been published in the French weekly newspaper L'Express. The death penalty for 'economic crimes' which Khrushchev had instituted a year earlier con-tinued to be imposed, amid considerable internal publicity intended to act as a deterrent, and strong external protest. Most of the hundred people executed were not Russians, but officials and 'speculators' from the non-Russian republics, and Russian Jews.

Anti-Jewish measures continued, with more alleged 'speculators' being shot, but the Soviet newspapers made it clear, with official encouragement, that for the identical 'crime' non-Jews did not receive the death penalty. Only when Bertrand Russell protested directly to Khrushchev were the death penalties abandoned. But there was no let-up in anti-religious pressures. The previous year the 30,000 Jews of Lvov had been denied access to a single synagogue; the last synagogue in Minsk was demolished in July. Yevtushenko was criticized for writing a poem, *Babi Yar*, recalling the Nazi massacre of the Jews of Kiev in 1941.

The Christian Churches were also under continual pressure; the release of the Archbishop of Lvov after eighteen years in prison, while welcome in itself, was a stark reminder of the penalties and punishments that the Soviet Union could impose on religious leaders.

Economically, the vast Soviet Union was finding it hard to compete in both the armaments and space races. To the surprise of Western observers, on October 26 Khrushchev announced that Soviet scientists would 'utilize the experience' of their American colleagues in their efforts to land a man on the Moon. The message was a clear one: the Soviet Union expected to take second place in the much publicized 'Moon race'. Defence spending was also cut down to below the previous year's level, though it still stood at 14.6 per cent of the total national expenditure. The Virgin Lands scheme on which Khrushchev had lavished such energy and praise was in considerable difficulty. Nature, in the form of a severe winter followed by a spring drought, combined with the over-ambitiousness of the programme – and the shortage of fertilizers – to reduce the grain harvest that autumn from the maximum of fourteen million tons to only five million. A severe shortage of fodder led to the slaughter of large numbers of cattle.

The isolation of the Soviet Union from world markets could not be maintained in face of the severe grain shortages. After agreeing to pay for all grain purchases in gold, Khrushchev secured the largest ever importation of foreign grain: six and a half million tons from Canada, three million from the United States and almost two million from Australia. One Soviet-bloc country, Roumania, was also encouraged to help out, but was able to provide less than half a million tons.

Economic hardships served to tighten Communist internal controls, not weaken them. This was equally true in Poland, where large numbers of students in religious academies were called up for military service – from which they had hitherto been exempted – and where many convent schools were closed down altogether. For three days there were riots in the south-eastern town of Przemysl when the authorities took over a convent school that was being used to train church organists. But the anti-clerical measures continued, as the Party sought to assert its ascendancy. Nuns were removed from kindergartens where they taught, rival 'peace priests' were appointed to clerical positions, and bishops wishing to attend the Ecumenical Council in Rome were refused permission to leave Poland. Courageously, Cardinal Wyszynski protested against the anti-clerical measures, and spoke of the need for all governments to uphold the 'inalienable human rights' of the individual, including the right to a decent wage.

The Polish government acted to shut down the vehicles of dissent, replacing two liberal weekly newspapers by a Communist Party one. But it also adopted practical measures which were at variance with rigid Communist ideology, one of these being a three-year trade agreement with West Germany, another the acceptance of a permanent West German trade mission in Warsaw. No other satellite country had such a mission. At the same time, a successful effort was made to sign a trade agreement with France, and to continue what was becoming a regular source of grain from the United States and Canada.

There were demonstrations in Warsaw in April, by nurses and doctors, demanding higher wages. In Czechoslovakia the street demonstrations had a more openly political content. On May Day in Prague a group of youngsters were arrested for chanting anti-government slogans. Condemned by the authorities as 'hooligans', the demonstrators were sentenced to up to three years in prison. Two young Czechs were given even longer sentences for trying to cross the frontier into Austria. In December a Czech youth was shot dead by frontier guards when he tried to drive a lorry through the border.

In Czechoslovakia, as in the Soviet Union, modern art was also under attack, the Party newspaper *Rudé Právo* leading an attack on art that was 'detrimental to the interests of socialist society'. There were also official calls for radio and television to give 'unconditional service to socialism and Communism in the spirit of the Party line'.

Czechoslovakia, which between the wars had been a bastion of rugged individual self-expression, was being forced into the mould imposed by Moscow. A teenage girl who was refused the right to study textile designing was told that it was because her parents had escaped abroad when she was three months old, leaving her with her grandparents. University graduates were informed that they had to spend a minimum of three years after graduation at a 'basic place of work' – a factory or building site, collective farm or agricultural co-operative. Archbishop Beran, and four other Catholic bishops, released from prison after twelve years' incarceration, were forbidden to resume their ecclesiastical or pastoral work.

On June 4 the Ayatollah ('sign of God') Khomeini was arrested for preaching in the Iranian holy city of Qom against the rule of the Shah. Part of the Ayatollah's anger was directed against plans proposed by the Shah for the gradual social and political emancipation of women. The Ayatollah's arrest led to protest demonstrations in the capital, Teheran, and other Iranian cities. The Shah sent the Ayatollah into exile: he went first to Turkey, then to Iraq, and finally to Paris, where he formed a focal point for Iranian religious conservatism.

For the rulers and military commanders of South Vietnam, United States support was proving crucial for the maintenance of the national struggle against the North and the Vietcong. American financial aid and military advisers played an essential part in enabling the confrontation between North and South to continue without the North winning repeated advantage. But on January 25 *Life* magazine carried its first major Vietnam War coverage, a fourteen-page spread critical of American involvement. Written by Milton Orshefsky, with photographs by Larry Burrows, the article was headed: 'We Wade Deeper into Jungle War'. The photographs made no attempt to glamorize the war: they showed dirt and grime, suffering and pain.

As well as his confrontation with the Communists, the autocratic President Ngo Dinh Diem, a devout Roman Catholic, had alienated the Buddhist majority. The pressures against the Buddhists intensified throughout the year. On May 8 the government tried to stop Buddhist celebrations in the city of Hué. When the Buddhists tried to continue, peacefully, with their religious rituals, police and soldiers attacked them. In deference to worldwide condemnation of the violence, the authorities began talks with the Buddhists, but the talks were unsuccessful, and on August 21 special forces under the control of Ngo Dinh Nhu – Diem's brother, whom he had made chief of police – attacked pagodas in several towns. Many monks and religious students were arrested, and held without charge or trial. In protest, seven Buddhist monks burned themselves to death.

On September 2, during a television broadcast, President Kennedy made a strong attack on the Saigon government's repressive anti-Buddhist measures. Only 'with changes in policy and perhaps of personnel' could confidence in South Vietnam be restored, he said.

There was further unease throughout South Vietnam when it emerged that Ngo Dinh Nhu had asked the French government to help him seek some sort of accommodation with the Communists in North Vietnam. At the beginning of October, as if to give credence to these rumours, the United States halted all economic aid to South Vietnam, and on October 22 suspended all financial support for the special forces under Ngo Dinh Nhu. When General de Gaulle announced that France might take the initiative in trying to transform Vietnam – one of its former colonies – into a 'unified, neutral State', the United States was horrified. Kennedy himself replied that he would not support any call for the withdrawal of American troops from Vietnam until the Communist guerrilla movement of the Vietcong had been 'crushed'.

On November 1 several senior South Vietnamese officers, led by General Duong Van Minh, took control of Saigon and announced an end to Diem's 'rotten and nepotistic' government. Diem and his brother escaped from the presidential palace just as it was being attacked, but were captured in the suburbs on the following day. Both men were killed. The assassination of Diem was laid by many onlookers at the feet of the United States Central Intelligence Agency. In government circles in the United States there was hope that the military campaign against the Communists would be intensified, and American financial aid was immediately restored. But North Vietnam continued to train and infiltrate guerrilla forces to harass the South Vietnamese forces and their American advisers. That year, more than eighty American soldiers were killed, mostly in helping to drive the Vietcong out of what were designated 'strategic hamlets' which the Vietcong had overrun.

Previously, the United States had set the end of 1965 as the date by which all American forces would be withdrawn from South Vietnam. Kennedy had accepted that. Following the increase in Vietcong activity as 1963 came to an end, however, that date was abandoned.

In the shadow cast by the Second World War, continuing war crimes trials brought forward further details of wartime atrocities. The West German authorities had abolished the death penalty in 1949. Since then more than five thousand Germans had been convicted of Nazi crimes. None had been executed, and less than a hundred had been given life imprisonment. The German public found no fault with this; indeed, the government was being criticized for having allowed the trials to continue for 'so long'. A deadline was set beyond which no trials were to be started: December 1964. This made the trial that began on 20 December 1963 all the more important. It opened in the West German city of Frankfurt and was to become the longest legal case in German history. The twenty-two accused had all worked at Auschwitz as members of the SS. Eight of them had been university graduates before the war. Each of them insisted on his innocence, in the main as having 'followed orders'. One defendant, Wilhelm Boger, told the court: 'I knew only one mode of conduct; to carry out the orders of superiors without reservations.' Another, Hans Stark, told the court: 'I believed in the Führer. I wanted to serve my people.'

For those who had studied the earlier trials, or followed the growing literature about Auschwitz, the details that emerged in the trial were not new. But the fact that they were emerging in a German court of law, under cross-examination and with the highest regard for judicial procedure, gave them an impact as great as that of the Eichmann Trial three years earlier. All but three of the defendants were found guilty. Boger was found guilty of 114 murders and 'complicity in the deaths of 1,000 persons'. He was sentenced to life imprisonment, including five years' hard labour. Stark was found guilty of committing murder, with others, on forty-four separate occasions, one involving two hundred people and another involving at least a hundred. He was sentenced to ten years. For complicity in the murder of at least a thousand people on three separate occasions, another defendant was sentenced to seven years' hard labour.

The independence of Western Germany, and of West Berlin, had become an integral part of United States policy. The line of the Iron Curtain as it ran through Germany constituted the most westerly advance of Soviet power. The United States, as a former occupying power, embraced Western Germany as an essential ally, and a frontline ally, in the confrontation with Communism. On June 23 Kennedy began a five-day journey through Western Germany which included a visit to Berlin. Everywhere he went he repeated the assurance: 'We shall risk our cities to defend yours.' American troops would remain in Europe for 'as long' as they were needed for its defence. In

West Berlin, Kennedy visited the Wall, and then told 150,000 ecstatic onlookers: 'All free men . . . are citizens of Berlin. And therefore, as a free man, I take pride in the words, "Ich bin ein Berliner".' The Germans were nevertheless uneasy at several aspects of America's policy towards the Soviet Union. In one of his last speeches as Chancellor, Adenauer spoke strongly against the American decision to sell wheat to the Soviet Union without attaching any political conditions to the sale.

German unease that the Americans, despite Kennedy's pledge, were contemplating a military withdrawal from Europe, was heightened by 'Operation Big Lift', the movement of an entire armoured division by air from the United States to Western Germany. It was felt that this might be a practice for, or a prelude to, a similarly rapid and substantial movement in the other direction. German fears, which Kennedy had failed to assuage, were more effectively put to rest when Dean Rusk, conscious of the recurrent suspicions, told an audience in Frankfurt on October 27 – during the unveiling of a memorial to General Marshall, the originator of Marshall Aid – that six American divisions would be kept in Western Germany for as long as they were needed there.

South Africa was again the focus of civil rights abuses as the General Law Amendment Bill led to the arrest of several hundred opponents of apartheid. Some of those arrested managed to escape, and from outside South Africa called world attention to the severity of the measures against all dissent, and the strict imposition of apartheid. There were instances of sabotage, and also, as in the previous year, of an African attack on Whites, in which a father, a mother and their two children were hacked to death. Twenty-two Blacks were later sentenced to death for these murders.

A climax to the government's measures to curb protest and dissent came on July 12, when security police surrounded a house in Rivonia, a Johannesburg suburb. Six Whites and twelve non-Whites were seized, among them Walter Sisulu, the former head of the banned African National Congress. Also brought to trial that year was Nelson Mandela, who had been arrested the previous year and sentenced to five years in prison. At his new trial he was charged under the Suppression of Communism Act, and sentenced to life imprisonment. His place of incarceration was to be Robben Island, a maximum security prison from which there was no escape. Three decades later, Mandela recalled the conditions on Robben Island, where he was to remain a prisoner for the next twenty-six years, until 1990:

The cells had been constructed hurriedly, and the walls were perpetually damp. When I mentioned this to the commanding officer, he told me our bodies would absorb the moisture. We were each issued with three blankets so flimsy and worn they were practically transparent. Our bedding consisted of a single sisal or straw mat, and one placed the felt mat on top of the sisal one to provide some softness. At that time of the year, the cells were so cold and the blankets provided so little warmth that we always slept fully dressed.

I was assigned a cell at the head of the corridor. It overlooked the courtyard and had a small eye-level window. I could walk the length of my cell in three paces. When I lay down, I could feel the wall with my feet and my head grazed the concrete at the other side.

Mandela was the 466th prisoner to be admitted to Robben Island in a single year. He was forty-six years old.

Within the United States, the pace of civil rights activities accelerated, as Blacks found a powerful voice in Martin Luther King, and a receptive ear in President Kennedy. The year 1963 marked the hundredth anniversary of Lincoln's Emancipation Proclamation, offering an end to slavery. On February 28, Kennedy asked Congress to grant him wide-ranging powers to introduce civil rights legislation in voting, education and employment. Kennedy pointed out to Congress that a Black person in the United States had about half as much chance as a White person to become a professional; that he had the prospect of earning only half as much as his White counterpart; and that his life expectancy was seven years less. Racial bias, Kennedy warned Congress, marred 'the atmosphere of a united and classless society in which this nation rose to greatness'. Training programmes were set up, and employers and schools were urged to accept the new equality. But there was much resistance, even in the west and north, where half the Black population lived. In cities outside the South which had large Black populations, among them New York, Chicago and Los Angeles, the demand for school integration and equality of employment was as strong as in the South. In the summer, several hundred Blacks were arrested in New York when they tried to prevent people entering or leaving a medical centre building site, hoping to call attention to the need for more Black workers in the construction industry.

In the South, Martin Luther King led a campaign against segregation, choosing Birmingham, Alabama, for the focus of his protest. It was, he said, the 'most thoroughly segregated big city in the United States'. Until the situation was remedied there, he would lead a series of unbroken demonstrations. Starting in April there were daily protest marches through the cities. Each day the city authorities arrested some of the marchers. On May 7 a march of more than two thousand Blacks broke through the police lines and continued to the centre of town. When stones were thrown at the police, the Public Safety Commissioner, Eugene Connor, ordered police dogs and fire hoses to be brought into action. More than three thousand Blacks were put in prison.

There were angry demonstrations elsewhere. When a truce was called in Birmingham, negotiated between the Black leaders and the local Chamber of Commerce, Connor appealed to the Whites not to honour it. 'That's the best way I know', he said, 'to beat down integration in Birmingham.' Bombs were exploded at the home of Martin Luther King's brother, and at a motel that was serving as the headquarters of the demonstrators. During the night of rioting that followed fifty people were injured. On May 12, Kennedy decided to intervene, and ordered Federal troops to Birmingham. He also took steps to bring the local National Guard under Federal auspices. The Governor of Alabama, George Wallace, protested, but Kennedy was determined to put his support behind the forces of integration.

When two Black students tried to enrol at the University of Alabama at Tuscaloosa, Wallace himself barred their way at the entrance. But on June 11, as Kennedy insisted that Federal laws be obeyed, and when the commander of the federalized National Guard ordered Wallace to stand aside he did so, and the two Black students were enrolled. That day Kennedy made another television broadcast – the method that was evolving as by far the most effective means of presidential communication. The troops of the National Guard had been used, he explained, and had had to be used, to enforce a federal court order to ensure the admission to university of 'two clearly qualified young Alabama residents who happened to be born Negro'. Every American should 'stop and examine his conscience about this and other related incidents'.

Hardly had Kennedy finished his television appeal than the Secretary of the National Association for the Advancement of Coloured People (the NAACP) in Mississippi, Medgar Evers, a Black, was shot in the back outside his house in Jackson, Mississippi.

Kennedy pursued his course with vigour and determination, presenting a Civil Rights Bill to Congress of June 19, and urging that policies based on race and on racial discrimination had no place in American life. The Bill had six clauses. The first was to provide the Attorney-General 'with the right, in the last resort, to initiate suits on behalf of individuals who claimed to have been discriminated against by hotels, restaurants, places of amusement or retail establishments'. Any business catering to people travelling between States, or selling goods in inter-State commerce, would be covered by this law.

The second clause was to provide the Attorney-General with the same power 'to act on behalf of persons who complained of school segregation'. The third was to provide federal assistance to schools which were voluntarily desegregating. The fourth was that tax, area redevelopment, public works and education proposals be enacted 'to cope with Negro employment, that other remedial programmes in this area be strengthened, and that measures be taken to eliminate discrimination in employment'.

The fifth clause was aimed at establishing a Community Relations Service 'to identify areas of racial tension, improve communications between the races, and advise local officials about how to proceed'. Until this body could be created by law, Kennedy said that he intended to create it by executive order. The sixth and final clause was that a law be written 'to make clear that the Federal Government was not required to furnish funds to a programme in which racial discrimination occurred'.

Kennedy adopted two parallel tactics to try to ensure that his Civil Rights Bill was passed by Congress. The first – to protect the Bill against fili-bustering tactics on the floor of the House and Senate – was to insist that Congress remain in session for however long it took for the proposed legisla-tion to be passed. At the same time, seeking to prevent a backlash of public resentment, he asked the Black leaders, who had said they would mount massive demonstrations in support of the Bill, to let Congress do its work 'without harassment'. His appeal to the Black leaders was accepted; on August 28 they organized a single but massive march on Washington in which more than 200,000 people took part. After that they pulled back on the number of militant demonstrations.

The Washington march was peaceful. Addressing the vast crowd from the steps of the Lincoln Memorial, Martin Luther King spoke of his dream that the inequalities would pass away: 'I have a dream that one day this nation will rise up and live out the true meaning of its creed: "We hold these truths to be self-evident, that all men are created equal."' The confron-tations that had taken place in the South were, King said, a 'marvellous new militancy', and he declared: 'Go back to Mississippi, go back to Alabama, go back to South Carolina, go back to Georgia, go back to Louisiana, go back to the slums and ghettos of our Northern cities, and know that somehow this situation can and will be changed.'

To Kennedy's disappointment, although he produced a compromise Bill that seemed likely to win the bipartisan support of both Democrats and Republicans, the Republican-dominated House of Representatives Rules Committee prevented any action on the floor of the House for the rest of that year. Across the wider spectrum of social legislation, Congress also impeded Kennedy's plans. He did succeed in pushing through measures designed to help college building, medical schools and vocational training. But two other Bills on which he had set his sights since becoming President, the reduction of taxation and the provision of medical care for the elderly, continued to be blocked by the Republicans. Even the Foreign Aid Bill, for which Kennedy had asked $4,500 million, was passed only after he agreed to a substantial $1,500 million cut. One of Kennedy's problems with regard to foreign aid was that a 'Citizen's Committee' on Foreign Aid which he had appointed, headed by General Lucius D. Clay – the 'hero' of the Berlin blockade – came to the conclusion, which it published, that while foreign aid was 'essential' to the security of the United States, the country was nevertheless 'attempting too much for too many'. Even the provision of wheat to the Communist countries so desperate for food was put in jeopardy.

With elections less than a year ahead, on November 17 Kennedy went to Florida, where he was much encouraged by the enthusiastic crowds that greeted him wherever he went. From Florida he flew to Texas, a State which he had won in 1960 by only a small margin of votes, and where his presence would clearly help the next year's Democratic campaigners. With him was his wife Jacqueline: it was her first public appearance since the death of their prematurely born son Patrick three months earlier. On November 21 they were in San Antonio, Texas, and in Houston, where once again large and enthusiastic crowds cheered their motorcade. That evening they flew to Fort Worth, where they spent the night. So large was the crowd outside their hotel the next morning – an estimated ten thousand people – that before breakfast Kennedy wandered through it, and then made an impromptu speech from an improvised platform. Pondering the East-West divide and the problems of seeking détente with deterrence, he told the large crowd:

No one expects our life to be easy, in this very dangerous and uncertain world . . .

I don't think we are fatigued or tired. The balance of power is still on the side of the free.

From Fort Worth, the Kennedys flew to Dallas, where they had originally intended to drive quickly and directly from the airport to the Trade Mart, where Kennedy was to make a speech to a luncheon meeting. But because of the gathering, as in Fort Worth, of large and enthusiastic crowds throughout the morning, he agreed to a change of plan, and to drive through the centre of the city. During the drive, at 12.30 local time, the President was shot. He died in hospital half an hour later. The announcement of his death shocked the United States and the free world. For liberals everywhere, it seemed as if their sun had set: had plunged precipitately below the horizon. For bigots and reactionaries, his death was less mourned; in some Southern universities, students cheered when the news of his death was reported to them in the classroom.

Kennedy's body was flown back to Washington. With it, on the plane, was his wife Jacqueline, and the Vice-President, Lyndon Johnson. On board the aircraft Johnson was sworn in as thirty-sixth President of the United States, the oath of office being administered by a Federal judge, Sarah Hughes, who was in tears throughout the brief ceremony. Reaching Washington, Johnson told the crowd that had gathered at the airport: 'We have suffered a loss that cannot be weighed. I will do my best. That is all I can do. I ask your help, and God's.'

Kennedy's body was placed in the East Room of the White House, and later moved to the rotunda of the Capitol, where more than 250,000 people filed past it. On November 25, after a requiem mass in St Matthew's Cathedral, he was buried at Arlington Cemetery. Among the mourners was President de Gaulle. The Soviet Union sent Anastas Mikoyan, its First Deputy Prime Minister. That day, in Dallas, Kennedy's assassin was being taken under police custody from the city jail to the county prison, the transfer being televised, when millions of television viewers saw someone walk up to him and shoot him dead.

Even as the shockwaves of Kennedy's assassination continued to distress those for whom he had been a young, vibrant symbol of energy for change, the business of government continued. Johnson had to grapple with many unfinished items of Congressional and national business. In pushing ahead with Kennedy's Civil Rights Bill, Johnson told the Senate – in which the

Republicans were maintaining a stiff opposition: 'No memorial or eulogy could more eloquently honour President Kennedy's memory' than the swift passage of the Bill.

The future of the United States in Vietnam was also a leading item on Johnson's agenda. Kennedy, in face of the most recent Vietcong initiatives, had given up the plan whereby all American troops could be withdrawn by the end of 1965. Yet Johnson had set his heart on social reform. On his first night as President, unable to sleep, he had outlined to his assistants how he would 'revolutionize' America, with federal aid to education. It would be on an even greater scale than that which Kennedy had secured. He would bring in tax cuts to help business, cuts of the sort Kennedy had failed to secure. He would push the Civil Rights Bill into law, and secure important conservation programmes. Jack Valenti, one of those present while Johnson expounded on his plans, later commented, when asked if Vietnam had been discussed: 'Vietnam at the time was a cloud no bigger than a man's fist on the horizon. We hardly discussed it because it wasn't worth discussing.'

Yet Vietnam could not be put aside. On November 24, the day before Kennedy's funeral, Johnson called a group of advisers together to talk to Henry Cabot Lodge, the American Ambassador in Vietnam who had just returned from Saigon to report on the aftermath of the assassination of President Diem. Johnson told them that he was determined not to 'lose Vietnam'. Earlier, when as Vice-President he had been involved in the discussions about whether or not to try to remove Diem, he had been emphatic: 'We should stop playing cops and robbers and get back . . . to winning the war.' At the meeting on November 24 he instructed Cabot Lodge to tell the South Vietnamese generals 'that Lyndon Johnson intends to stand by our word'. In a memorandum for the National Security Council, Johnson stated that the aim of the United States was, as under Kennedy, to help the South Vietnamese to 'win their contest against externally directed and supported Communist conspiracy'.

Johnson sent Robert McNamara to Vietnam to report back to him directly on the prospects for a South Vietnamese victory over the Vietcong. McNamara was pessimistic, telling Johnson that unless the current military trends – with Vietcong control over the villages growing, and the South Vietnamese leaders as incompetent and corrupt as before – were 'reversed in the next two or three months' it would lead to a 'neutralization at best, or more likely to a Communist-controlled State'. The South Vietnamese government's control over the villages in the south, about which McNamara himself had been optimistic in July in a report to Kennedy, had, he told Johnson, 'in fact been deteriorating', and to 'a far greater extent than we realized'. The Vietcong were not being beaten back, nor could they be eliminated. Instead, McNamara reported, they controlled 'larger percentages of the population, greater amounts of territory, and have destroyed or occupied more strategic hamlets, than expected'. President Diem had set up more than two hundred of these 'strategic hamlets' guarding the villages in them with troops and stockades. More than half of them had been abandoned in the previous year.

There were 'more reasons to doubt the future of the effort', McNamara warned Johnson, 'than there are reasons to be optimistic about the future of our cause'. But when Johnson discussed the future of American involvement in Vietnam with the Joint Chiefs of Staff, they were emphatic that they could restore the South Vietnamese victories by 'more forceful moves'. The air force commander, General Curtis LeMay, went so far as to argue in favour of American bombing of North Vietnam. As Le May expressed it: 'We are swatting flies when we should be going after the manure pile.'

Johnson had to stand for election at the end of 1964. This gave him time to delay the decision on Vietnam. At a reception in the White House on Christmas Eve, 1963, he told the Joint Chiefs of Staff: 'Just you get me elected, and then you can have your war.' Johnson later told one of his biographers, Doris Kearns:

I knew from the start that I was bound to be crucified either way I moved. If I left the woman I really loved – the Great Society – in order to get involved with that bitch of a war on the other side of the world, then I would lose everything at home. All my programmes. All my hopes to feed the hungry and shelter the homeless. All my dreams to provide education and medical care to the browns and the blacks and the lame and the poor.

But if I left that war and let the Communists take over South Vietnam, then I would be seen as a coward and my nation would be seen as an appeaser, and we would both find it impossible to accomplish anything for anybody anywhere on the entire globe.

One Far Eastern country kept aloof from the conflicts on the mainland and, having committed itself by treaty not to create armed forces, concentrated on economic recovery. This was Japan, which in February reached agreement with the Soviet Union for Japanese exports of ships and industrial equipment.

Japan would receive timber, oil and coal. In March the Japanese parliament approved an Anglo-Japanese Treaty of Commerce that offered a considerable increase in Japanese exports to Britain. A similar treaty was signed with France in May, and with Australia and New Zealand in August. Japan was steadily reaching out to the markets of the world. As in Germany, the wartime devastation by heavy bombers had meant that in reviving industry, new plants had to be built, and that these could therefore incorporate the latest technology. The Soviet industries in the Urals and Siberia, and many British – and even American – industries, had to work with pre-war and increasingly outdated equipment.

The pattern of Japanese prosperity was becoming clear. In mid-1963 the figures for 1962 were issued: Japan's exports had increased by sixteen per cent and its imports had declined by three per cent compared with the previous year. At the same time, the main vehicle of exports, shipping, was becoming a Japanese economic advantage: Japan's mercantile marine was already the fifth largest in the world, despite having been virtually obliterated at the end of the Second World War.

Illegal drugs that were to become the curse of the final decades of the century were beginning to be used, and to be advocated by some publicly. In the United States, Timothy Leary was dismissed from his lectureship at Harvard University after he supervised a popular series of experiments into the effect of psychedelic drugs. The 'drug culture', not confined to affluent societies, was about to disturb and poison the minds of millions of people. In due course it was to have a marked effect on crime. The need to supply and finance the drug habit, if necessary by theft and violence, undermined the moral outlook of many individuals.

CHAPTER THIRTEEN

1964

Our national honour is at stake. We cannot and will not
shrink from defending it.

SENATOR RICHARD RUSSELL

THE BERLIN WALL, which had been under construction for more than
a year, was finally completed, and East Berlin sealed off from the West, on
5 January 1964. Until that date, an astounding 1,283,918 East Berliners
and East Germans had crossed to the West. With the wall in place, the
East German police showed no compunction in shooting dead anyone who
attempted to scale the wall.

The confrontation between East and West which the Berlin Wall represented did not prevent President Johnson – in election year, and with a
vision of what he called the 'Great Society' uppermost in his mind – from
proposing a decrease in defence spending. His aim, he explained in his State
of the Union message on January 8, was to 'liberate the energies of the
nation' for domestic reforms, of which civil rights was central, and the
elimination of poverty the most urgent. There must, he said, be an 'unconditional war on poverty', and to launch it he called for a budget of little
under $1,000 million. Congress cut off $200 million, but the Bill passed
into law, and the 'war' was begun. To head it, Johnson appointed Kennedy's
brother-in-law, Sargent Shriver, the former head of the Peace Corps. As the
war on poverty received Congressional endorsement, it was revealed that
three days before he was assassinated, Kennedy had asked his advisers to
draft for him a programme against poverty.

Most memorable of the Bills enacted by Congress in the year following
Kennedy's assassination was the Civil Rights Bill, which passed the final
stage on June 19, a year to the day since Kennedy had sent it to Congress,
only to face Republican opposition. Johnson too had been faced by a filibuster

in the Senate which lasted for seventy-five days. The new Bill was only the third Civil Rights Bill to be passed by Congress in almost a hundred years. It was a crucial and indeed revolutionary document, recognizing without prevarication the rights of Black Americans to equality, and to protection of their rights as citizens. Among the places where discrimination or 'refusal of service' was made illegal were all hotels, motels, restaurants, petrol stations, libraries, parks, swimming pools, golf courses and stadiums. Discrimination was also forbidden in any programme that was in receipt of federal assistance, or by any employer or union with a hundred or more employees. It was also made illegal for the illiteracy tests on voters, under which an illiterate person could not vote, to be made more severe for Blacks than for Whites.

Even as the Civil Rights Bill was making its way through Congress, and through the delaying tactics of the filibuster, Black demonstrations had continued. These had led to violent confrontations, and several deaths. In New York, even after the passage of the Bill, racial tension in Harlem led to three days of violence – which also spread to Brooklyn – in which almost a hundred White-owned shops were looted or damaged, and in which one Black rioter was shot dead by the police. There were further acts of violence in Jersey City and in Philadelphia. But what Martin Luther King called the 'marvellous new militancy' – the peaceful marches and pressing of claims through the courts – had been successful. When the Civil Rights Act became law, King himself was awarded the Nobel Peace Prize.

Johnson continued to put forward his vision of the Great Society. In a speech at Ann Arbor in Michigan on May 22, he set out what he felt most needed to be done. 'For half a century,' he said, 'we called upon unbounded invention and untiring industry to create an order of plenty for all. The challenge of the next half-century is whether we have the wisdom to use that wealth to enrich and elevate our national life and to advance the quality of our American civilization.' To this end, he said, work must begin at once, in the cities, the countryside and the classroom. A Food Stamp Act substantially widened the provision of food to the poor and destitute. An Economic Opportunity Act increased educational opportunities for poor children and established a domestic peace corps, Volunteers in Service to America (VISTA).

The real challenge to Johnson's vision did not come from Congress, or from any innate conservatism among the American people – for there was a great will for change. It came instead from one of the most distant regions from the United States, Vietnam. There, the military government which had come to power after the assassination of President Diem was itself overthrown, and a new military government came to power in Saigon, committed to destroy the growing influence and military prowess of the Vietcong. Johnson was at first uncertain how far the United States should support the new regime – headed by a thirty-seven-year-old field commander, General Nguyen Khanh – or whether it should support him at all. But on February 2 he made the pledge that he had given earlier, and Kennedy before him, that the United States would continue to give military aid against the Communist insurgency. He let it be known, in strict secrecy, to General Khanh that if the South Vietnamese were to mount cross-border raids into Laos to try to flush out the Vietcong, the United States would not object. Johnson also gave permission for American air reconnaissance flights over Laos, in the hope of tracking the movement of Vietcong forces.

A new Assistant Secretary for the Far East, William P. Bundy, suggested to Johnson on March 1 that the United States should take more active measures against North Vietnam, blockading Haiphong harbour, bombing North Vietnamese railways and training camps, and informing both the North and South Vietnamese governments that the United States 'will take strong measures to prevent the spread of Communism specifically, and the grab of territory generally, in the area'.

Johnson hesitated to become more deeply involved in Vietnam; indeed, that spring he turned to a Canadian citizen, J. Blair Seaborn, the chief Canadian delegate to the International Control Commission in Vietnam, and through him made an offer to Ho Chi Minh to de-escalate the conflict. If the North Vietnamese agreed to end their support for the Vietnamese Communists in the South, the United States would provide North Vietnam with economic aid, and even with diplomatic recognition. But if such a de-escalation was not acceptable, Johnson warned, the United States would be prepared to contemplate naval and air attacks on North Vietnam. The Prime Minister of North Vietnam, Pham Van Dong, countered Johnson's offer by urging the withdrawal of American troops and advisers from South Vietnam, and Vietcong participation in the South Vietnamese government.

The negotiations collapsed. During the spring, Johnson announced that the number of American advisers there, many of whom were taking a prominent part in the actual combat, would be increased from 15,000 to 20,000. The new men arrived just as the Vietcong were embarking upon their most effective long-term strategy, the creation of a supply line from north to south, the Ho Chi Minh Trail, which would avoid the Demilitarized

Zone (the DMZ) at the border with South Vietnam by running through neighbouring Laos, and cutting back across the Laotian border into South Vietnam at different points between the DMZ and the Mekong Delta.

The trail was to prove effective for the next decade, bringing much-needed supplies, and men, in a continuous stream to the fields and hamlets of the South. It was built by engineers using modern Chinese and Soviet equipment. The roads and bridges constructed along it could carry trucks laden with supplies. Along its five-hundred-mile length, underground barracks, workshops, hospitals, fuel dumps and storage depots were built, essentially safe from aerial bombardment. The first people to use the trail were soldiers of the regular North Vietnamese army, going to the support of largely southern Vietnamese Communist units. By the end of the year as many as ten thousand North Vietnamese troops had used the trail to penetrate the South, and to take up positions around almost all the southern towns.

Senior North Vietnamese officers were sent down the trail to organize the fight against the South Vietnamese army, and did so with conspicuous success. Of the estimated 180,000 Vietcong under arms in the South by the end of the year, 30,000 were in highly trained battalions, with modern weapons many of which had been captured from the Americans, and with an admixture of professional soldiers from the North with experience in fighting against the French.

Johnson was confronted during the summer by a serious challenge from the Republican nominee for President, Barry Goldwater, a Senator from Arizona, who accused Johnson and his administration of being 'soft' on Communism. 'Extremism in the defence of liberty is no vice,' Goldwater told the Republican National Convention during his acceptance speech in San Francisco.

As the Vietcong began to infiltrate more and more effectively into the South, Johnson contemplated the bombing of their supply-lines. This was a relatively easy task on paper. A glance at the map showed where the supply-lines ran. But in many areas they were hidden under a canopy of dense foliage, and constructed with exceptional skill so that the depots, staging posts and even troop concentrations would not be visible from the air, or indeed from a few hundred yards away on the ground. Bombing had been, not only for the Americans, such an established means of making war, both in the Second World War and in Korea, that it seemed inconceivable that the ill-armed, dispersed and struggling Vietcong could be any match for it.

Among Johnson's advisers, Walt Rostow, head of the State Department's policy planning staff, suggested that Johnson could commit the United States to direct military action against North Vietnam without a formal declaration of war, by means of a 'legislative resolution' submitted to Congress. This would avoid the far more difficult course of a full-scale declaration of war, while enabling American forces to go into action, not as advisers, as hitherto, but in their own right. It was by such a legislative resolution that McKinley had committed American troops to China at the beginning of the century: it was a device as old as the Constitution.

Johnson was attracted to the idea of obtaining Congressional approval, in the broadest possible terms, for action. A draft resolution was ready in June, giving him authority to commit United States forces to the defence of any nation in South-East Asia that was threatened by Communist 'aggression or subversion'. An opportunity came within two months. On August 2, after a secret South Vietnamese raid against North Vietnam, in which a United States destroyer, the *Maddox*, took part, three Vietcong torpedo boats attacked the *Maddox* while it was in international waters off the coast of North Vietnam. On the following day two more American destroyers were attacked, and two of the attacking torpedo boats were sunk.

The attack on the *Maddox* provided Johnson with his opportunity. Johnson's resolution – known as the Gulf of Tonkin resolution – was debated by Congress on August 6 and 7. One Democratic Senator, Ernest Gruening of Alaska, warned that 'all Vietnam is not worth the life of a single American boy'. Wayne Morse of Oregon declared that 'the place to settle the controversy is not on the battlefield but around the conference table'. Theirs were very much a minority voice. Richard Russell, the Senator from Georgia who had earlier tried to persuade Johnson not to become more deeply embroiled in Vietnam, caught the prevailing mood – which opinion polls reported as the opinion of 85 per cent of the American public – when he told the Senate: 'Our national honour is at stake. We cannot and will not shrink from defending it.' When the vote was taken, only two Senators, Morse and Gruening, opposed the resolution. In the House of Representatives the vote in favour was unanimous.

Immediately following the passage of the resolution, American bombers attacked five North Vietnamese coastal installations. Four patrol boats and an oil installation were hit. In an address to the American people, Johnson made it clear that the United States, while prepared to limit its retaliatory actions, would not allow itself to be attacked without some form of effective military reaction. At the same time, in secret, he continued his attempt to persuade the North Vietnamese to pull back from war on the basis of the proposals he had already submitted through the Canadian mediator, J. Blair Seaborn. Under these proposals, North Vietnam would receive 'economic and other benefits' in return for giving up its support for the Communist insurgency in the South. But if it continued to support the southern insurgents it would 'suffer the consequences'.

The North Vietnamese rejected what they saw as a solution dominated by a threat. They also felt that victory was within their grasp. The intervention of the United Nations Secretary-General, U Thant, who flew to Washington to see Johnson, was of no avail. Still Johnson acted with caution. The air strikes against North Vietnam, which had taken place after the Gulf of Tonkin resolution, had been limited to one day. Pressure was also put on the South Vietnamese to desist from their covert attacks on the North, which had been a catalyst for the North Vietnamese action on the Gulf of Tonkin.

As election day drew near, Johnson also made a pledge reminiscent of Roosevelt's pledges when war came to Europe in 1939. In Johnson's words: 'We are not about to send American boys nine or ten thousand miles away from home to do what Asian boys ought to be doing for themselves.' But, in the secrecy of the White House discussions, other ideas were being put forward. On September 7 the United States Ambassador in Saigon, General Maxwell Taylor, having flown back from Saigon to give his advice, told Johnson: 'If we leave Vietnam with our tail between our legs, the consequences of this defeat in the rest of Asia, Africa, and Latin America would be disastrous.'

A chance to test the Ambassador's advocacy of 'increased pressure' against the North came on November 1, when Vietcong troops, numbering no more than a hundred, infiltrated an American air base at Bienhoa and, opening fire with mortars, destroyed six B-57 jet bombers on the ground. Five Americans and two South Vietnamese were killed. Ambassador Taylor urged an immediate bombing strike against the North, with a warning that there would be more such strikes if further attacks were mounted against the Americans in the South. When Taylor's advice was studied in Washington, the Joint Chiefs of Staff advocated an even more sustained bombing offensive. American carriers were sent to their aircraft-launching positions off North Vietnam.

It was three days before the American presidential elections. Johnson decided not to strike at all. The attack on the Bienhoa base would be unavenged. On November 3, Johnson was returned in triumph to the White

House which he had entered – unelected – after Kennedy's assassination a year earlier. He had defeated his Republican challenger, Senator Goldwater, by the highest proportion of votes – sixteen million – ever secured by a presidential candidate: far more than Kennedy had achieved. It was the largest popular margin in United States history, sixty-one per cent of the vote, and with an electoral college margin over the Republicans – 486 against 52 – that had previously been exceeded only by Johnson's hero, Franklin Roosevelt, in 1936.

The Democrat majority in both Houses gave Johnson a power for legislative action that was virtually unchallengeable. With regard to Vietnam, however, he hesitated to take the action many of his advisers were advocating – to land American combat troops, as opposed to advisers, in the South, and to send American bombers against the North.

In Britain, a new Labour government, headed by Harold Wilson, came into office on October 16, pledged to move Britain forward into the age of modern science and technology. The government also reflected similar social reform concerns to those of Johnson in the United States. Among Wilson's first measures was the provision of free medical prescriptions.

While the United States found itself more and more deeply drawn into the Vietnamese quagmire, the Soviet Union struggled to balance its enormous spending on defence with the economic needs of its often deprived citizens. Chaos seemed to loom when, with unexpected swiftness, opposition to Khrushchev crystallized at the highest level of the Communist Party hierarchy. Khrushchev's overbearing manner, his crude authoritarianism and above all the failure of the Virgin Lands project, in which he had invested so much energy with so little return, were crucial factors. One catalyst was his indication to his closest and most senior colleagues that he was about to put forward another plan to reorganize agriculture. They did not want more upheaval, or more failure. While he was on holiday at Pitsunde, on the Black Sea coast, the colleagues in whom he had confided about his new agricultural plans met and caballed against him – much as Gorbachev's colleagues were to do in 1991 when Gorbachev too was on holiday not far from Pitsunde, at Foros.

When Khrushchev returned precipitately to Moscow he found that his colleagues – including those who were his nominees – on the Praesidium of the Communist Party had turned against him. Confronting them, he demanded the right to address the full Central Committee. They agreed, but when he spoke on the afternoon of October 14 he was unable to secure a majority. During a marathon session, long even by Soviet standards, one member, Suslov, spoke for five hours against Khrushchev remaining leader. At first Khrushchev's reaction to the onslaught was to lose his temper, and to threaten dire punishment. But in the end he offered his resignation, and it was swiftly accepted.

The announcement that Khrushchev was no longer ruler of the Soviet Union came in a Moscow radio broadcast on the evening of October 15. He was succeeded as First Secretary of the Communist Party by Leonid Brezhnev, one of those most eager to see him ousted. The new Chairman of the Council of Ministers – effectively Prime Minister of the Soviet Union – was Alexei Kosygin. Khrushchev's closest allies, including Vassily Polyakov, who had supported his agricultural initiatives, were removed from office. To show the Communist Party members that the leader's removal was necessary and justified, a few days after his fall a forty-page document was circulated to Communist Party organizations, listing twenty-nine reasons for his downfall. Among the charges were 'nepotism', 'rude personal behaviour', the encouragement of a 'personality cult' – the very charge of which he had earlier accused Stalin – the arbitrary dismissal of officials, 'errors' during the Cuban missile crisis, including the sending of Soviet missiles to Cuba, 'gross errors' in economic planning, and the failure to monitor Chinese scientific progress – a failure, if such it was, that was given striking immediacy on October 16, the day after his public ousting, when the Chinese exploded their first atom bomb.

In space, the Soviet Union was still striving, despite Khrushchev's earlier hesitations, to outdistance and upstage the Americans. On October 12, as the plot against Khrushchev was in its final days, the seventh Soviet-manned spaceship was put into orbit. There were three people on board: the pilot, a doctor and a scientist. The spaceship was brought back safely to earth after twenty-four hours.

In South Africa, the imposition of apartheid was again enshrined in law, with the Bantu Laws Amendment Act of May 6 further limiting the areas around towns in which Blacks could live. In court, the trial of the African nationalists arrested in the Rivonia suburb of Johannesburg had continued for more than a year. Considerable international attention was focused on the trial, during which Nelson Mandela, already a prisoner, but hitherto little known outside South Africa, emerged as a central figure. While admitting that he had been involved in certain acts of sabotage – during which no one had been killed – he claimed that he had been driven to violent action because all forms of non-violent protest had been denied him.

On June 12 eight of the accused men were sentenced to life imprisonment. When the sentence on Mandela was announced there were demonstrations outside South Africa House in London, in which fifty members of parliament took part, and questions were raised at the Security Council of the United Nations. The British government appealed directly to the South African government to reduce the sentences. This so angered the South African authorities that on July 29 Dr Verwoerd announced that his government would not yield to pressure, and the sentences were upheld. He also boasted that he had thrown into the wastepaper basket all the telegrams of protest which he had received from Socialist countries.

Elsewhere in Africa, other forces of disruption were at work. In the Congo, attacks on Congolese Black Christians, and on White and Black missionaries and priests, led to the murder and mutilation of hundreds of people. When an American missionary, Dr Paul Carlson, was among a number of Whites taken hostage, Belgian paratroops were sent in to rescue him. He was shot before he could be saved. One of the hostages who was saved was a Roman Catholic priest, the son of Martin Bormann, the Nazi leader who had disappeared in the ruins of Berlin in the last days of the war.[1]

In Northern Rhodesia, a rebellion led by Alice Mushenga was brutally crushed, and five hundred of her followers killed. They believed, under her guidance, that by calling out the word 'Jericho' they would be immune from bullets.

In the sphere of public health, the United States Surgeon General issued a report that confirmed the link between smoking and lung cancer and disease.

In sport, East-West rivalry reached a climax during the Olympic Games in Tokyo, when the United States won thirty-six gold medals and the Soviet Union thirty. For the first time, television pictures of the Games – indeed the first of any sporting event – were sent by an experimental relay system by satellite, from Tokyo, via space, to the United States, where they could be transmitted locally. From the United States, one set of film was transferred to Europe by jet plane. But the main impact of the Games was on the

[1] Martin Bormann's identifiable remains were found in Berlin during building works in 1998.

re-emergence of Japan, which since its defeat almost two decades earlier had lived with the shame of its wartime record. The Games were opened by the Emperor Hirohito: the man who had agreed to his country's surrender in 1945. Ninety-four nations paraded their athletes before him. This was the first Olympic Games to be held in Asia, fulfilling Japan's desire for Asian paramountcy, not in the political or military, but in the sporting arena. Pride came too as Japan won the third largest number of gold medals – sixteen. In its domestic economy, Japan continued to make impressive strides, with forty per cent of the world's shipping being built in Japanese shipyards.

On Christmas Eve, in Saigon, Vietcong terrorists exploded a bomb in Brinks Hotel, in which American advisers were staying. Two Americans were killed and more than fifty injured. Under the Gulf of Tonkin resolution – and with his massive electoral majority – Johnson could have taken retaliatory action. He refrained from doing so, not wanting to 'jar' the American public during the holiday season. The Vietcong had no such inhibitions. They were already carrying out carefully co-ordinated attacks on villages in the South: one of them, attacked in December, was a Catholic village, Binh Gia, forty miles south-east of Saigon: less than an hour's drive from the capital.

On December 28, as a gesture of defiance and assurance, Binh Gia was occupied by the Vietcong for eight hours. Five days later a South Vietnamese army unit was ambushed near the village and destroyed. As the battle for Binh Gia continued, almost two hundred South Vietnamese troops were killed, as were five American advisers. There was a limit to how long Johnson could resist the mounting clamour from his generals and advisers, and from Ambassador Taylor in Vietnam, for more decisive action. His own mind was not averse to moving the war into a higher gear, though he had repeatedly hesitated, and understood that the American public might not be ready for too dramatic a gesture. When, in the aftermath of the Brinks Hotel bomb and the Binh Gia attacks, Ambassador Taylor advocated air strikes on the North – a solution favoured by many of those in Johnson's advisory circle – it was Johnson who, in his telegram to the Ambassador, put forward what was to create a far greater American entanglement. 'I have never felt that this war will be won from the air,' Johnson wrote, 'and it seems to me that what is much more needed and would be more effective is a larger and stronger use of rangers and special forces and marines, or other appropriate military strength on the ground and on the scene.' He realized, Johnson told General Taylor, that this 'might involve the acceptance of larger American casualties', but, he added: 'I myself am ready to substantially increase the number of Americans in Vietnam if it is necessary to provide this kind of fighting force against the Vietcong.'

The Soviet Union had no such entanglements as were beginning to draw the Americans into a distant land and a military quagmire. Its control over Eastern Europe was complete and mostly unchallenged: it seemed to many seasoned Western observers to be unchallengeable. Considerable progress was also being made to establish Soviet influence outside Europe, and to do so with a potent mixture of anti-Western propaganda and military support. In April, after President Ben Bella of Algeria visited Moscow, a Soviet-Algerian pact for economic and technological co-operation was signed. After President Nasser of Egypt was made a Hero of the Soviet Union, the Soviets, as well as giving a substantial loan to Egypt, of $300 million, offered their support in the Arab-Israel conflict 'in conformity with the legitimate rights of the Arabs'. Soviet arms and military equipment began to flow to Egypt, at first slowly but then with increasing momentum, creating alarm inside Israel that a time would come in the not too distant future when Egypt – which since 1948 had been in occupation of the Gaza Strip – would be tempted to invade its much smaller neighbour.

Indonesia and India both signed agreements that year for arms supplies from the Soviet Union. From Cuba, President Castro – who had secured a trade agreement with Britain, much to the chagrin of the Americans – visited Moscow and signed a new Soviet-Cuban trade agreement.

In Poland, censorship was tightened, and stricter rules applied to the allocation of paper which might be needed by magazines tempted to criticize the Communist regime. Wladyslaw Gomulka, the Polish Communist leader, explained in a speech to the Writers' Union Congress in Lublin in September: 'We assess writing first and foremost from the point of view of the contribution it makes and the part it plays in the ideological struggle between socialism and capitalism.' In Czechoslovakia there were clashes in the streets of Prague between young people and the security forces; arrests and imprisonments followed. There was Communist Party criticism of what was called the 'alarming lack of interest' in Communism among university graduates who were intending to become teachers. In response, the Czechoslovak Communist Party announced that it would be strengthening the university departments of Marxism-Leninism.

Inside the Soviet Union, discrimination against Jews affected school, university and commercial life. At the same time, emigration was virtually impossible. On April 27 a group of Jews in New York founded the Student Struggle for Soviet Jewry. A few weeks later one of the founders, Jacob Birnbaum, called a meeting at Columbia University to call for an improvement of the situation of Christians in the Soviet Union. The international human rights imperative with regard to Soviet violations was small, but vocal, and determined to gain in strength and efficacy. It covered anti-Christian as well as anti-Jewish discrimination. And it was, within a decade, to make its impact on international diplomacy.

The Warsaw Pact countries continued to hold joint manoeuvres throughout the year: in July Soviet forces joined the Czechoslovak manoeuvres, and in September they joined Bulgarian manoeuvres. The North Atlantic Treaty Organization was also active that year, but also divided, and almost in disarray, as a result of an American proposal for the creation of a multinational nuclear force (the MLF), under which twenty-five warships, each armed with eight Polaris nuclear missiles, would be owned, financed and controlled jointly by all members of NATO. An experiment in mixed manning by different national crews and experts was conducted on an American warship, the *Claude Ricketts*.

France, wanting its own nuclear deterrent, remained apart from this project, as did Canada, Norway, Sweden and Denmark. Germany supported it strongly, raising fears among its former adversaries of a 'German finger' on the nuclear button – and leading the American satirist Tom Lehrer to compose the lines:

> Sleep, baby, sleep, in peace may you slumber,
> No danger lurks, your sleep to encumber,
> We've got the missiles, peace to determine,
> And one of the fingers on the button will be German.
>
> Once all the Germans were warlike and mean,
> But that couldn't happen again.
> We taught them a lesson in nineteen eighteen,
> And they've hardly bothered us since then.
>
> So sleep well, my darling, the sandman can linger,
> We know our buddies won't give us the finger,

Heil, hail the Wehrmacht, I mean the Bundeswehr,
Hail to our loyal ally
MLF will scare Brezhnev,
I hope he is half as scared as I.

Partly in response to fears of West Germany's participation in a nuclear-weapons system, Britain's newly elected Labour government under Harold Wilson proposed that Britain's nuclear force should not be merged in the multinational force, but form a 'national contingent'.

One development in the NATO councils in 1964 was a German proposal for a nuclear minefield along the Iron Curtain. This proposal was rejected.

The United States was also active in the Central Treaty Organization (CENTO), established in 1955 with Britain, Iran, Turkey, Pakistan and Iraq, seeking to end the conflict between Greece and Turkey – that had broken out over the future of the Turkish minority in Cyprus. It also hoped to persuade Pakistan to make its dispute with India over Kashmir a part of the defence commitment of the member States. Pakistan was rebuked, however, by the United States, for its closer links with China. The CENTO manoeuvres that year took place in Iran, with 6,800 American troops flown by air from the United States to take part.

In order to bring two members, Turkey and Iran, into closer contact, more than $6 million was paid by the United States for a rail link between the countries: it was built just about in time to be severed by the total collapse of political links between them.

On the morning of October 16 the Chinese government exploded a nuclear device in the atmosphere. Such tests had been banned by the Soviet Union, the United States and Britain under the previous year's Test Ban Treaty. The Chinese test was carried out in the remote Lop Nor desert, but it was monitored closely by the United States, as was the fall-out, which, while considered by American experts to be 'not dangerous to humans', reached western Canada on the morning of October 19 and spread during the following three days to the Great Lakes, the Mississippi valley, Florida and the Atlantic seaboard of the United States and the St Lawrence River.

The United States responded with an underground nuclear test, permitted under the treaty. It was carried out near Baxterville, Mississippi, one of the areas affected by the Chinese fall-out.

*   *   *

Medical science continued to make strides throughout the year, as the ability to save and prolong life offered the prospect of a larger, healthier and longer-living population, not only in the affluent societies, but throughout the globe. The United Nations played its part in trying to ensure that medical advances could make their way to the poorer nations. After five years' intensive research, British scientists announced, prematurely as it emerged, that they had discovered a vaccine for the common cold. But even as advances were being made in tackling illness, it was becoming clearer that the harmful bacteria themselves, against which so much effort was being expended, could not only become resistant to a drug during their lifetime – short though that might be – but could pass on that resistance to their 'offspring'. It even appeared that bacteria could 'catch' resistance from one another, so that a bacterium could become resistant to a drug without having been exposed to it. A battle seemed about to begin, between bacteria and antibiotics, in which scientists would have continually to be searching for new antibiotics that would take the bacteria unawares.

One area of medical science in which marked progress was made was that of organ grafting. Drugs were being developed which could prevent tissue of organ grafts from being attacked, and destroyed, by the body's own immune system.

The development of the computer was also coming to the aid of medical science. That year the Nobel Prize for Chemistry was won by Dorothy Hodgkin of Oxford University, who had been able to determine the structure of biologically important chemicals, including cholesterol, vitamin B12 and a new antibiotic, cephalosporin. Eight years earlier, a typical essential calculation which she needed to make took her three months. By the use of the latest computers, that same calculation – she was working on the complicated structure of the insulin molecule – took her ten minutes: an acceleration factor of 128,000.

Two musicals that were to catch the public imagination and give pleasure for years to come both had their première in New York in 1964: *Hello, Dolly!* on January 16 and *Fiddler on the Roof* on September 22. In the world of popular music, the Beatles achieved the triple success of a single, an album and a film, *A Hard Day's Night*. That year they made their first tour of the United States, as did their British fellow singers the Rolling Stones. For millions of people, popular culture had the power to eclipse the turmoil and strife of a world in conflict.

CHAPTER FOURTEEN

1965

> We often say how impressive power is. But I do not find
> it impressive at all. The guns and bombs, the rockets
> and warships, are all symbols of human failure. They are
> witness to human folly. A dam built across a great river
> is impressive, electrification of the countryside is impress-
> ive, a rich harvest in a hungry land is impressive.
>
> PRESIDENT LYNDON B. JOHNSON

ON 20 JANUARY 1965 Lyndon Johnson began his first term of elected presidential office. In terms of Congressional support he was in a very strong position. Sixty-eight Democratic Senators, three more than in Kennedy's time, and 295 members of the House of Representatives could easily outflank in voting power the 32 Republican Senators and 140 Representatives. Despite the growing Vietnam imbroglio – although as yet no American ground troops had been committed to action – Johnson had an ambitious social reform programme, and was determined to emulate his hero, Franklin Roosevelt, in establishing new parameters of fairness and prosperity.

On January 4, sixteen days before his inauguration, Johnson had delivered a State of the Union address remarkable for the challenges that he set himself: the creation of a Great Society. He promised to provide medical care for the poor (Medicaid) and for the elderly (Medicare) – something that Kennedy had been unable to do. There would also be significant federal financial support for both elementary and secondary education, and supplementary educational, nutritional and health care for disadvantaged children before they enrolled in school (Head Start). Foreign aid would be set at its highest yet. But, as he stressed in his inauguration address on January 20, poverty, hunger, suffering and illiteracy existed in the United States and had to be tackled.

The legislation that followed was wide-ranging. A Higher Education Bill,

for which $2,584 million was voted over a three-year period, included a scheme for national teachers' training, which enabled the federal government to recruit teachers for local communities that could not afford them. Money was also available through this legislation for college classrooms and libraries. Measures were also passed for air and water pollution control, and a special federal commissioner was sent to States with poor records in this regard, to ensure compliance with basic standards. Housing those who were living in deprived areas was also a priority for Johnson, who prevailed upon Congress to vote $7,000 million for the most ambitious federal housing programme yet undertaken in the United States. In all, more than 360 legislative measures were approved before the end of the year.

A centrepiece of Johnson's legislative efforts was civil rights, where the Southern States were putting difficulties in the way of Black voter registration, despite the 1964 Act. In Selma, Alabama, there were demonstrations against the failure of the Alabama legislature to allow Blacks to register, and to ensure that the voting rights secured in 1964 were upheld. Almost three thousand of the demonstrators were arrested. At a specially convened press conference on February 4, Johnson appealed to the whole country to exert 'moral pressure' on behalf of Black would-be voters.

On February 21, while American attention was on Selma, Alabama, the American Black nationalist leader Malcolm X was shot dead while addressing a rally in a ballroom in Manhattan. Born Malcolm Little, he had earlier quarrelled with the leader of the Black Muslims, Elijah Muhammad, under whom he had served for several years, but whom he had recently accused of 'perverting the creed of Islam'. Malcolm X had also been in a dispute with his own splinter group, the Organization of Afro-American Unity, for having addressed a neo-Trotskyite labour rally in New York.

One of Malcolm X's achievements had been to establish small industries for rehabilitating Blacks who had fallen foul of the law. He was also a keen advocate of separate development for American Blacks. His murder led to tension among those extremist Black activists for whom Islam was the creed that seemed to them an essential part of their separate identity. But it was on the continuing struggle for Black voting rights that the mainstream of Black activism was focused. As the Alabama authorities stubbornly ignored the pressure being put upon them to grant Blacks the voting rights accorded to them under the 1964 Act, state highway patrolmen broke up the continuing protest demonstrations with considerable force. During one such confrontation, sixty-seven Black protesters were injured.

On March 9, Martin Luther King went to Selma to protest against the force used by the highway patrolmen against Black voting-rights demonstrators. On the following day five hundred marchers, among them many clergymen, were stopped by troops at the entrance to the town. They knelt, prayed and dispersed. That night, three of the clergymen were attacked by White vigilantes, and one of the clergymen, James Reeb, a Unitarian minister from Boston, was killed.

Johnson himself then took the initiative, summoning Governor Wallace of Alabama to the White House on March 14, announcing that the events seen in Selma would not be repeated, and putting forward to Congress new legislation that would sweep away the voting restrictions that the Southern States had managed to impose despite the 1964 Act. On March 15, in a speech to a joint session of the House of Representatives and the Senate, he insisted that Blacks must be allowed to register as voters without any further hindrance or delay. Using the emotive words of the civil rights movement's protest song 'We Shall Overcome', he told the legislators: 'What happened in Selma is part of a larger movement which reaches into every section and State of America. It is the effort of American Negroes to secure for themselves the full blessings of American life. Their cause must be our cause too. It is not just Negroes, but all of us. And we shall overcome.'

As the new Civil Rights Bill was being debated by Congress, demonstrations in its favour continued. On March 25 a White woman, Viola Liuzzo, who had been taking civil rights workers in her car to one of the demonstrations in Selma, was shot dead. Her killers, who were arrested, were members of the Ku Klux Klan. In a defiant speech, Johnson said he would no more be intimidated by Klan terrorists than by 'terrorists' in North Vietnam.

On August 11 there was rioting in the Black quarter of Los Angeles, after a highway patrolman arrested a Black driver on suspicion that he was drunk. More than 1,500 Blacks turned against the police, burned buildings and looted shops. The National Guard was called out, and a curfew imposed, but the riots continued for four nights, centring on the Black suburb of Watts, and with some seven thousand Blacks rampaging the streets. More than a thousand fires were started. When the riots were finally ended thirty-four rioters were dead and several hundred seriously injured. A commission of inquiry found that resentment at the high Black unemployment was a major cause, as also were the slum conditions in which so many of the Black community lived. On August 15, even as the fires in Watts were still

burning, the new Voting Rights Bill came into law, guaranteeing all American citizens the right to vote, whatever their colour, race or religion.

At the beginning of February two very different emissaries were in Vietnam, but with a not dissimilar agenda. One was the new Soviet Prime Minister, Alexei Kosygin, who urged the North Vietnamese not to do anything that might worsen Soviet-American relations. Kosygin went so far as to suggest that the North Vietnamese use Russia's good offices to try to effect a compromise agreement with the Americans – not unlike that which Johnson had been pushing for earlier. The other emissary was Johnson's National Security Advisor, McGeorge Bundy – whose brother William was Assistant Secretary of State – who on his first visit to Vietnam to report on the situation direct to Johnson was impressed by the strength of the Vietcong in the countryside, and depressed by the weakness and division of the South Vietnamese government.

Whatever advice Kosygin and Bundy might have been about to take back to Moscow and Washington respectively was overtaken by events beyond their respective control. On the night of February 6/7 the Vietcong attacked an American air base near the town of Pleiku, in the central highlands of South Vietnam. It was from Pleiku that South Vietnamese army units had been attacking the Ho Chi Minh Trail as it emerged from the security of Laos and Cambodia. Three miles from the town was Camp Holloway, where American special forces and advisers were stationed. It was heavily guarded, by both American and South Vietnamese troops, as was the airstrip nearby.

In the Vietcong mortar and machine-gun attack on Camp Holloway, eight Americans were killed and ten American warplanes destroyed. That morning, McGeorge Bundy was in Saigon, about to fly back to the United States. He at once telephoned the White House and pressed for immediate American bombing raids against North Vietnam. Although the Vietcong's 'energy and persistence are astonishing', Bundy added in a telegram to Johnson that day (February 7), and although many of the Americans and Vietnamese whom he had consulted during his visit were not sure 'whether a Communist victory can be prevented', it was his view that the 'one great weakness' in the position of the United States in Vietnam was 'a widespread belief that we do not have the will and force and patience and determination to take the necessary action and stay the course'.

Bundy went on to warn Johnson that to negotiate an American withdrawal, along the lines of Johnson's earlier offer to the North Vietnamese, 'would mean surrender on the installment plan'. Only 'continuous' bombing of North Vietnam could have an effect: 'episodic responses' based on specific reprisals for specific incidents – such as the Camp Holloway attack – would 'lack the persuasive force of sustained pressure'. Later that day, to his advisers in the White House, Johnson expressed his own exasperation at doing nothing effective, telling them: 'I've gone far enough. I've had enough of this.'

Johnson retaliated at once, ordering American bombers to strike at strategic targets in North Vietnam. He did so, not by means of a declaration of war, but by virtue of the Gulf of Tonkin resolution which Congress had passed six months earlier. The first target of Operation Flaming Dart was a North Vietnamese army camp at Dong Hoi, sixty miles north of the 17th parallel that divided North and South Vietnam. Ironically, bad weather meant that this first attack was ineffective.

Kosygin returned to Moscow, unable – as the American air strikes intensified – to make a convincing case for the North Vietnamese to sit down with the Americans, or through an intermediary, to discuss a settlement. Ten days after Kosygin's return, the first Soviet surface-to-air missiles reached the North Vietnamese port of Haiphong.

The United States was not technically at war with North Vietnam, nor was it ever to be. In the *New York Times* the columnist James Reston protested. 'The time has come to call a spade a bloody shovel,' he wrote. 'This country is in an undeclared and unexplained war in Vietnam. Our masters have a lot of long and fancy names for it, like escalation and retaliation, but it is a war just the same.' In fact, Operation Flaming Dart had been devised as a one-off retaliatory strike. It was replaced on Johnson's orders by Operation Rolling Thunder, a bombing programme at first envisaged as a continuous eight-week series of unbroken attacks. It was to last for three years. The number of bombs dropped exceeded that of all the bombs dropped in the Second World War in Europe and Asia.

The first bombing attack of Operation Rolling Thunder was carried out on March 2. Six days later the first American combat troops to go ashore in Vietnam did so near the coastal town of Da Nang. Their first assignment was defensive: to protect the existing United States air base there. They were not intended to be a combat force tackling the Vietcong. But they were not to be left unsupported. Johnson told the commander of the American forces in Vietnam, General Westmoreland: 'Assume no limitation on funds, equipment. or personnel.' On April 1 Johnson authorized the despatch to South Vietnam of two additional marine battalions, and at least 18,000 support troops, since, in the words of one of the American historians of the Vietnam War, Stanley Karnow, 'Americans never fight abroad without ample supplies of arms and ammunition, and vast quantities of beer, chocolate bars, shaving cream, and their favourite brand of cigarettes.'

How far the new troops would remain in defensive position was much in doubt. General Westmoreland made it clear that 'a good offence is the best defence' and began to devise his plans accordingly. Ten years later, when he was being made a Doctor of Law at the University of South Carolina – whose students had originally been strong supporters of and volunteers for the war – protesters cried out as the honorary degree cape was being placed around his shoulders: 'Doctor of WAR!'

In his first change of the original plan, Westmoreland persuaded Johnson that his troops could patrol the countryside around the bases they were there to protect. It was a short step from going out on patrol to opening fire on Vietcong, and suspected Vietcong. On April 7, in a speech at Johns Hopkins University in Baltimore, Maryland, Johnson declared that the United States 'will not be defeated', nor would it withdraw from Vietnam either openly 'or under the cloak of a meaningless agreement'. He did, however, put forward proposals to end the conflict: these included a $1,000 million aid programme for the whole of South-East Asia, including North Vietnam, and 'unconditional discussions' on the Vietnamese conflict. The Secretary-General of the United Nations, U Thant, called Johnson's proposals 'positive, forward looking, and generous'. On the following day the North Vietnamese produced proposals of their own: the United States must withdraw all its troops, arms and bases in South Vietnam. The political future of South Vietnam must be settled by the South Vietnamese people themselves, without any foreign interference, 'in accordance' with the programme of the National Front for the Liberation of South Vietnam. Vietnam must then be reunified.

Johnson could not accept what was in effect a complete surrender to North Vietnam. Eight days after the Vietnamese response, he informed the American Ambassador in Saigon, General Taylor, that in addition to the continuing bombing offensive against the North, American troops would be sent out to work, not as advisers, but as an integral part of South Vietnamese army units, entering combat with them. Those, like the Washington lawyer Clark Clifford, a friend who warned Johnson that a substantial United States commitment of troops to Vietnam could be a 'quagmire' without any 'realistic hope of ultimate victory', had their cautions brushed aside by a President who wanted to be told that what he had decided to do was right.

In March, during his speech proposing the Voting Rights Bill, Johnson recalled his time as a schoolteacher thirty-five years earlier, at Cotulla, Texas, where three-quarters of his students were Spanish Americans. 'My students were poor, and they often came to class without breakfast, hungry. They knew even in their youth the pain of injustice. They never seemed to know why people disliked them, but they knew it was so, because I saw it in their eyes. I often walked home late in the afternoon, after the classes were finished, wishing there was more I could do.'

Johnson now had the power to effect a revolution. He had a vision of what could be, if he and those around him were to be able to carry out that revolution successfully. On April 7, while speaking at Johns Hopkins, he said:

> We often say how impressive power is. But I do not find it impressive at all. The guns and bombs, the rockets and warships, are all symbols of human failure. They are witness to human folly. A dam built across a great river is impressive, electrification of the countryside is impressive, a rich harvest in a hungry land is impressive. The sight of healthy children in a classroom is impressive. These – not mighty arms – are the achievements which the American nation believes to be impressive. And if we are steadfast, the time may come when other nations will find it so.

On April 27, three weeks after describing guns and bombs as a 'witness to human folly', Johnson publicly elaborated the American terms for a settlement in Vietnam. The independence of South Vietnam must be preserved. The National Liberation Front must be excluded from any negotiations. The United States would not withdraw until the 'people of South Vietnam can determine their own future free from any external interference'. This was some distance from the 'unconditional discussions' which he had proposed in his offer of April 7.

The American bombing continued. On April 29 the road bridge at My Duc, on the main road linking the region north of the Demilitarized Zone with the rest of North Vietnam, was destroyed: many American newspapers showed photographs of the broken bridge.

On May 11 the Vietcong launched a military offensive on many different points in South Vietnam. Fifty miles from Saigon they occupied the provincial capital of Songbe. American army camps were attacked. As the South Vietnamese army reached near-panic in places, American advisers took command of units that had been left without officers. General Westmoreland called for yet more American troops, telling Johnson bluntly in June, as Vietcong attacks were renewed: 'The South Vietnamese armed forces cannot stand up to this pressure without substantial US combat support on the ground.' Johnson accepted this advice, telling the American public in a television address: 'I have asked the commanding general, General Westmoreland, what more he needs to meet this mounting aggression. He has told me. And we will meet his needs. We cannot be defeated by force of arms. We will stand in Vietnam.'

On July 27 two United States Senators, Richard Russell and Mike Mansfield, urged Johnson to 'concentrate on finding a way out' of Vietnam, a country, they said, 'where we ought not to be' and where the situation was 'rapidly going out of control'. Both men were friends of the President. A decade earlier, Mansfield, a former professor of Asian history, had been a leading advocate of the American involvement in Vietnam. A year earlier he had set out his doubts to Kennedy, but with equal lack of success. A day after the attempt by Russell and Mansfield to persuade him to pull out of Vietnam, Johnson announced that he would be sending forty-four American combat divisions to add to the American troops already in Vietnam, an almost ten-fold increase. Stanley Karnow, a newspaper correspondent in Vietnam at the time, later recalled:

As the war intensified in 1965, the US bombing, shelling, and defoliation of rural areas drove peasants from their hamlets, creating a refugee problem of immense proportions. An estimated four million men, women, and children – roughly a quarter of South Vietnam's population – fled to the fringes of cities and towns in an attempt to survive. They were shunted into makeshift camps of squalid shanties, where primitive sewers bred dysentery, malaria, and other diseases. Thousands, desperate to eke out a living, drifted into Saigon, Danang, Bienhoa, and Vung Tau, cities that now acquired an almost medieval cast as beggars and hawkers roamed the streets, whining and tugging at Americans for money.

For grotesque contrast, no place to my mind matched the *terrasse* of the Continental Palace Hotel, a classic reminder of the French colonial era, where limbless Vietnamese victims of the war would crawl like crabs across the handsome tile floor to accost American soldiers, construction workers, journalists, and visitors as they chatted and sipped their drinks under the ceiling fans.

The refugee influx into the cities was deliberately spurred in many instances by American strategists, who calculated that this 'forced urbaniza-tion', as they termed it, would deny peasant support to the North Viet-namese and Vietcong and thus hamper their ability to subsist in the countryside.

Stanley Karnow added:

Vietnam also served as a laboratory for technology so sophisticated it made James Bond's dazzling gadgets seem obsolete by comparison. American scientists created an array of ultrasensitive devices to detect the enemy through heat, light, and sound refraction, and they even invented an electronic instrument that could smell guerrillas. They produced defoliants and herbicides to destroy jungles and wipe out rice and other crops on which the North Vietnamese and Vietcong relied for food. They perfected rockets like the 'Walley', an air-to-surface missile containing a television camera that enabled a pilot to adjust its course by scanning a screen in his cockpit. And there were bombs of nearly every size, shape, and explosive intensity, from blockbusters to phosphorous and napalm bombs that roasted their victims alive.

Another devastating weapon was cluster bombs, whose hundreds of pellets burst out at high velocity to rip deep into the body of anyone within range. Designed for 'surgical' raids against troop concentrations, the cluster bombs were frequently dropped by American aircraft on populated regions in both North and South Vietnam, killing or maiming thousands of civilians. General Harold K. Johnson, army chief of staff, once attributed the indiscriminate casualties to a lack of precise intelligence about targets. 'We have not enough information,' he said. 'We act with ruthlessness, like a steamroller.'

Along with importing guns and ammunition, oil, spare parts, and other war material, Westmoreland and his logistical experts inundated Vietnam with the luxuries that have become necessities for US forces far from home.

'Not only could American soldiers isolated on remote hilltop fire bases or in jungle camps look forward to receiving cigarettes and beer by helicopter,'

Karnow pointed out, 'but choppers periodically flew in hot meals – and the menu at Thanksgiving and Christmas featured turkey, cranberry sauce and candied yams.'

On the Indian subcontinent, India and Pakistan found themselves in a serious dispute. It began when Pakistan objected at the United Nations General Assembly to India applying provisions of the Indian Constitution to the disputed region of Kashmir. India denounced Pakistan's protest as interference in India's internal affairs, and as part of an ongoing 'hate India' campaign. On March 13 there was fighting between Indian and Pakistani soldiers at many points along their common border in Bengal, Assam and East Pakistan. On March 30 a ceasefire agreement was signed, but within a few weeks fighting broke out in the remote marshland of the Rann of Kutch, an area that was under water for six months of the year. Indian outposts along the disputed border of the Rann of Kutch were shelled by Pakistani artillery, leading India to protest to the United Nations Security Council at Pakistan's 'unprovoked, utterly lawless, and aggressive attacks'.

With British encouragement, a ceasefire was negotiated in the Rann of Kutch. Both sides agreed to withdraw their troops, and to submit the border dispute to an international tribunal. But on June 20, ten days before the final ceasefire terms for the Rann of Kutch were agreed, India complained to the United Nations of forty Pakistani violations of the ceasefire on the Kashmir border – violations, India documented, that had taken place in a six-day period. Other attacks on Indian troops and installations during this period were carried out by Kashmiri Muslims demanding the cession of Kashmir to Pakistan.

On August 5, while India's protest against Pakistani incursions into Kashmir was being studied, more than a thousand Pakistani troops, many of them in civilian clothes, crossed into Indian Kashmir and approached within twenty miles of the capital, Srinagar. In response, India sent troops into the area controlled by Pakistan. A Pakistani tank attack in the last week of August was repulsed. On September 6, after a further Pakistani attack across the border, Indian troops and tanks crossed into Pakistan. Their objective was Lahore, the principal town of the Punjab. Britain – which twenty years earlier had ruled the subcontinent, protested to India at this attack, which was characterized as a full-scale invasion.

War, albeit undeclared, had begun. There were further Indian attacks across the Pakistani border on September 8, one of them against Sialkot in the north, the other towards the town of Hyderabad on the River Indus in the east. As fighting spread, Indian aircraft bombed Pakistani airfields and Pakistani ships shelled Indian shore bases. It was not until September 22 that the United Nations was able to secure a ceasefire. Pakistan was then in possession of a wedge of territory in Kashmir and a considerable amount of land in Rajasthan. India had occupied Pakistani territory near Sialkot, creating a strategic threat to the main agricultural region of the Punjab.

The fighting had lasted for seventeen days. More than three thousand Indian soldiers had been killed, and at least two thousand Pakistani soldiers. Even after the ceasefire, there were accusations by India of continuing Pakistani military incursions across the border. Lal Bahadur Shastri, who had become Prime Minister of India after the death of Nehru a year earlier, was angered by what he regarded as British bias towards Pakistan, and by the greater indignation Britain had expressed against the Indian attack into Pakistan on September 6 than it had expressed against the Pakistani attack into Kashmir a month earlier. India also protested to Washington that United States weapons, sold to Pakistan on the basis that they would be used only for self-defence, had been used against India.

It was the Soviet Union that emerged as the mediator, sponsoring peace talks between India and Pakistan in the Soviet Central Asian city of Tashkent. China took a different stance, giving encouragement to Pakistan by moving troops forward across the Tangla Ridge, the scene of the Sino-Indian conflict three years earlier. India protested, and the Chinese troops withdrew. On the main battlefield, India and Pakistan accepted a United Nations representative, General Tulio Marambio of Chile, who was able to arrange for both sides to withdraw their troops to the pre-war borders.

In other areas that had been under British rule, the post-colonial era was turbulent. On January 29 an attempt in Malaysia by the Pan-Malayan Islamic Party to overthrow the central government in Kuala Lumpur was crushed. The attempted coup had been encouraged by Indonesia, which in the months ahead sent troops across the Malaysian border in Borneo, Sabah and Sarawak. More than ninety Malaysian troops were killed during these incursions. Small groups of Indonesian infiltrators landed on the coast of Johore; other Indonesian saboteurs tried to blow up shipping in Singapore harbour. An attempt by the Japanese government to bring the Malaysian and Indonesian leaders together for talks in Tokyo was rebuffed by Indonesia.

It was internal tensions that destroyed the unity of Malaysia – itself only a recent creation. A climax came when the central government awarded

Singapore an unacceptably small proportion of the textile quotas for the exports of textiles to Britain. There was anger in Singapore when it emerged that some of these textile quotas had been awarded for factories elsewhere that had not yet been built. On August 9 Singapore seceded from Malaysia to become a small, independent and in due course highly prosperous State. It was made a member of the United Nations 'by acclamation' on September 21, and admitted to the Commonwealth a month later.

In the former British African colony of Ghana, where the collapse of world cocoa prices, as a result of global over-production, struck a savage blow at the economy, foreign loans were becoming harder and harder to secure. Government was being conducted by a single political Party, headed by Kwame Nkrumah, with no other parties allowed to stand at election time. In reply to those in the West who disapproved of his regime, Nkrumah published a book entitled *Neo-Colonialism: The Last Stage of Imperialism*, in which he warned of the 'evil forces of international finance', whose headquarters were in New York and Washington, and who controlled and determined the future of all African States. Despite this attack, he did accept the intervention of the World Bank for a restructuring of the Ghanaian economy on the basis of a temporary halt on new projects, a drastic reduction in government spending, and a cut in the price paid to cocoa farmers. One project that did go ahead, being already almost completed, was the electricity-generating plant on the River Volta.

The conflict of previous years between Christian and Muslim Black Africans continued, often in savage form. In the southern region of the Sudan, government troops launched punitive expeditions against Christian communities and several thousand Black Christians were killed: literally hacked to death. Hundreds were murdered inside the Anglican Cathedral at Juba. At Rumbek, the Roman Catholic Vicar-General, Father Archangel Ali, was killed. Similar slaughter took place in the Congo, where many White Christian missionaries and members of their Black congregations were killed, and others tortured.

Independence in Africa continued to be granted to the few countries that were still under colonial rule. On February 18, Gambia, a country with a population of only 320,000, achieved its independence from Britain. But the prospect of independence in Southern Rhodesia, with its White minority determined not to cede power to Black politicians, led on November 11 to a Unilateral Declaration of Independence (UDI) by the White political leaders under the Prime Minister, Ian Smith, to try to ensure continuing White domination. UDI was a blow to Britain's remaining decolonization plans, and a threat to the future of Rhodesia's Black majority. The British government under Harold Wilson struggled to persuade Smith – a Second World War fighter pilot – to withdraw from this provocative stance. In a television broadcast, Wilson declared: 'Mr Smith, think again.' But Smith refused to pull back, and for fifteen years defied all pressures – including a British oil embargo imposed on December 17 with United Nations support – to allow majority rule.

Communist control in the Soviet Union and throughout Eastern Europe seemed unbreakable. A group of Communist Party dissidents in Bulgaria, with some support from the army, tried to overthrow the regime of Todor Zhivkov, but were quickly crushed. Zhivkov, who had set up his first concentration camps for political prisoners six years earlier, boasted that Bulgaria and the Soviet Union 'breathe with the same lungs, and the same blood flows in our veins'.

In the Soviet Union, Alexander Solzhenitsyn was among a number of writers attacked in *Izvestiya* for 'negativism'. The editor of *Pravda*, who came to the defence of the writers, was dismissed from his post. A month later, in September, two Soviet writers, Andrei Sinyavsky and Yuli Daniel, were arrested. They were charged with having smuggled their own writings out of the country, for publication in the West.

While the arts remained under careful scrutiny and restraint, sporting and scientific endeavours were given the strongest support. On March 18 a Soviet astronaut, Lieutenant-Colonel Alexei Leonov, became the first person to 'walk in space', emerging from his capsule for a few minutes while it was in orbit. As the space race, with its strategic as well as scientific implications, continued, an American repeated this feat within three months, Major Edward White leaving his space capsule and drifting alongside it, weightless in space, for twenty minutes. He was attached to the spacecraft by a lifeline, and was able to propel himself about by means of a small hand-held jet.

Determined to put the first men on the Moon, the Americans were accelerating their space launches with growing success. On March 23 a manned spacecraft, *Gemini 3*, was sent into orbit: the first of five to be launched in the United States that year. Its two astronauts, Virgil Grissom and John Young, were the first to manoeuvre a space ship while outside the Earth's gravitational pull. In a plethora of 'firsts', on the following day an unmanned spacecraft sent television pictures back to Earth from a mere 1,300 miles above the surface of the Moon. On April 6 the world's first commercial communication satellite, *Early Bird*, was put into orbit, 22,000 miles above the surface of the Earth. It could transmit both telephone calls – up to 240 simultaneous two-way conversations – and television pictures. These much publicized scientific achievements made all the more galling the dramatic power failure which plunged New York, and a vast number of towns and rural communities – from London, Ontario, to Boston, Massachusetts – into darkness on November 9. The fault was in the massive Canadian–US Eastern Interconnection power grid (Canuse). In New York, 800,000 subway passengers were trapped below ground. It took five hours before the first electricity supplies began to return.

Achievements in space continued, eclipsing terrestrial glitches. On December 4, *Gemini 4* was launched: ten days later it carried out a rendezvous in space with another spacecraft, *Gemini 6*. Both returned safely to Earth.

As the year came to an end, the conflict in South Vietnam continued to draw in fighting men and embroil politicians. On December 17 it was announced from Washington that there were 165,000 American troops in South Vietnam. For the North Vietnamese, this was a presence which their own forces, and the Vietcong in the South, already masters of so much of the countryside, were challenging with every chance of success. The North Vietnamese could also take encouragement from the growth – small at first, but gaining a steady momentum – of the anti-war movement inside the United States, starting with the first 'teach-in' against the war at the University of Michigan at Ann Arbor.

The confidence of the North Vietnamese leaders was seen throughout the year. But when a Commonwealth Peace Mission, established under the initiative of Harold Wilson with a mandate to seek common ground between the adversaries and to initiate negotiations, offered to go to Moscow, Peking and Hanoi, the Soviet, Chinese and North Vietnamese leaders refused even to receive it. Johnson then tried to revive his April offer of 'unconditional discussions', sending emissaries to many Western and non-aligned capitals with the request that his offer be taken up. Johnson did indicate that it might be possible for the National Liberation Front to send representatives to any negotiations – something he had earlier rejected – and he did agree to a pause in American bombing raids to enable the North Vietnamese to formulate their response to his offer, but Ho Chi Minh and the Vietcong were sufficiently confident of success to disdain the American offer and to denounce it as a fraud. When a senior Soviet politician, A. N. Shelepin, visited North Vietnam, hoping to persuade the North Vietnamese to embark on the proffered talks, his efforts were rebuffed. The Chinese government, ever alert to chances to score political points against the Soviet Union, accused the Russians of 'collaborating' with the Americans to defeat the Vietcong in South Vietnam by putting pressure on Hanoi to negotiate. The Chinese added that the arms being supplied by the Soviet Union to the North Vietnamese were obsolete, and imposed a ban on the transfer of Soviet supplies via Chinese air bases. The result was that all such supplies had to go by train, and were subjected to repeated delays in their passage across China. At the same time, Chinese weapons were being sent to North Vietnam, and Chinese military engineers were employed repairing the rail links between southern China and North Vietnam that had been damaged – on the North Vietnamese side of the border – in American bombing raids.

In an interview with the American journalist Edgar Snow, Mao Tse-tung had made it clear in April that China would enter the Vietnamese conflict only if it were attacked by the United States. As a signal to China that such a wider war could not be ruled out, the United States Secretary of State, Dean Rusk, warned that the 'idea of sanctuary is dead': that if China did become involved in the conflict United States retaliation was certain.

China continued to accelerate its nuclear programme. A second Chinese atom bomb was exploded on May 14, more powerful than the first, its strength and nature analysed by Western scientists from the fall-out, which did not respect national borders. Japan and India both protested at the test. Their protests were ignored. The Soviet Union also protested, pointing out that the test was in violation of the 1963 Test Ban Treaty on bombs exploded in the atmosphere. Its protest was likewise ignored.

Inside China, an even more rigorous imposition of Mao Tse-tung's Communist ideas was being imposed. On May 30 the existing system whereby all school and university students spent two months of the year doing physical labour was replaced by a revised scheme, under which the time spent in fields and factories was increased to six months. The idea, the Party explained, was to create a new generation of 'worker–intellectuals'. Art and literature were brought more closely under what was described in the Chinese newspapers as 'the brilliant red banner of Mao Tse-tung's thinking'. Mao had been much angered by the plays of Wu Han, of which *The Dismissal of Han Rui from Office* seemed part of a systematic intellectual attack on Chinese

Communist practice. Commenting on the system of local government, Wu
Han wrote:

> You say the common people are tyrannized,
> but do you know the gentry injures them?
> Much is made at court of the gentry's oppression,
> but do you know of the poverty
> endured by the common people?
> You pay lip service to the principle
> that the people are the roots of the state.
> But officials still oppress the masses
> while pretending to be virtuous men.
> They act wildly as tigers
> and deceive the emperor.
> If your conscience bothers you
> you know no peace by day or night.

Wu Han's call in his play for 'redressing injustices' was officially criticized
on the grounds that 'the peasants of our country have already realized Socialism, possess everything, and have established the great People's Communes'.

Religion in China continued to be repressed. In September all the Buddhist
monks at a monastery in Shansi Province were expelled. In October a British
missionary of Jehovah's Witnesses, Stanley Jones, released after seven years
in prison in Shanghai, spoke of how his treatment had been so much better
than that of the Chinese Christian prisoners incarcerated with him. Not a
single Catholic or Protestant newspaper or magazine was allowed – for an
estimated thirty to forty million Christian Chinese. It was from the new
leader that inspiration had to be sought: one did not need Jesus or Buddha
or even Confucius if Mao Tse-tung was, as the newspapers and wall-slogans
hailed him, 'a beacon light shining over the growing younger generation'.

A statesman whose death recalled the leaders of the Second World War
was Winston Churchill, the last surviving member of the 'Big Three'. Churchill died on January 24 at the age of ninety. His obituaries stressed not
only his wartime leadership, and fortitude in 1940 when Britain was in
danger of invasion, but his long service to social reform. It was Churchill
who, before the First World War, had put forward wide-ranging proposals
for a better life for the working people of Britain, and had placed on the
statute book legislation that enhanced the quality of life for millions of

people. It was not 'fewer hours of work', he said, but 'longer hours of leisure', that were needed by the masses to make life more bearable. As early as his twenty-fifth birthday, in 1899 – when he was in a prisoner-of-war camp in South Africa – he expressed his thoughts on the way the twentieth century would evolve: 'Capitalism in the form of Trusts has reached a pitch of power which the old economists never contemplated and which excites my most lively terror,' he wrote to a friend. 'Merchant-princes are all very well, but if I have anything to say to it, their kingdom shall not be of this world. The new century will witness the great war for the existence of the Individual.'

Always an advocate of negotiations rather than confrontation, or arbitration rather than conflict, Churchill had set out his argument for an East-West summit in 1953: 'I still think that the leading men of the various nations ought to be able to meet together without trying to cut attitudes before excitable publics or using regiments of experts to marshal all the difficulties and objections, and let us try to see whether there is not something better for us all than tearing and blasting each other to pieces, which we can certainly do.' During the final phase of the Korean War, Churchill supported negotiation with the words: 'Communism is a tyrant but meeting jaw to jaw is better than war.'

Throughout the last months of 1965 there was a prolonged debate within the White House as to whether the United States could win the war in Vietnam, and whether the bombing of North Vietnam served any purpose other than destruction without prospect of victory. In November two young American protesters committed suicide by setting themselves on fire: one in front of the Pentagon in Washington, and the other at the United Nations in New York. Opinion polls, which were being used increasingly to monitor shifts and changes in the public mood, and which Johnson studied avidly, showed that more than three-quarters of all Americans favoured a ceasefire initiative. Johnson told his inner circle: 'The weakest link in our armour is American public opinion. Our people won't stand firm in the face of heavy losses, and they can bring down the government.'

On December 17 Johnson assembled his senior advisers at the White House for two days of intensive discussion. Robert McNamara was emphatic that the military solution 'is not certain, one in three or one in two'. He therefore favoured 'a diplomatic solution'. When Johnson questioned him, McNamara replied, 'Our military action approach is an unacceptable way to a successful conclusion.' Johnson, after further questioning, suddenly concurred, with the words 'We'll take a pause.' A bombing halt of thirty-seven days was the result. It did not start until Christmas morning. On Christmas Day, the unilateral American bombing truce came into effect. On the ground, however, the American military commanders sanctioned only a one-day ceasefire, after which they ordered the renewal of American attacks on Vietcong positions and villages believed to be harbouring and helping the Vietcong – there were hundreds of such villages, and the attacks were mounted with considerable force.

CHAPTER FIFTEEN

1966

Each time a man stands up for an ideal, or acts to improve the lot of others, or strikes out against injustice, he sends forth a tiny ripple of hope. And crossing each other from a million different centers of energy and daring, those ripples build a current which can sweep down the mightiest walls of oppression.

ROBERT KENNEDY

IN JANUARY the United States continued with the temporary halt to its bombing operations against North Vietnam, begun at Christmas, in return for an offer to start negotiations. In reply the North Vietnamese government reiterated its earlier insistence that the South Vietnam National Liberation Front – the political arm of the Vietcong – was the only true representative of South Vietnam. This was unacceptable to the Americans, who had invested considerable money and political pressure on the South Vietnamese government to show some respect for the basic concepts of human rights and democratic procedures. In public, Johnson spoke with confidence of the outcome of the war, while not minimizing the severity of the conflict. In his annual State of the Union message, delivered that year on 12 January 1966, he told Congress: 'The days may become months and the months may become years, but we will stay as long as aggression commands us to battle.' In secret, Johnson wrote to Ho Chi Minh three weeks later – the first of five such letters – proposing an end to a war that 'has already taken a heavy toll in lives lost, in wounds inflicted, in property destroyed, and in simple human misery'.

An incident that shocked American liberal opinion was witnessed by the journalist Stanley Karnow. The newly established government of Air Vice

Marshal Nguyen Cao Ky had condemned to death a Chinese merchant, Ta Vinh, on charges of an illegal steel transaction:

> Eager to demonstrate his zeal, Ky had arranged for the supposed culprit's public execution in the square facing Saigon's central market, and I joined the crowd that had assembled to witness the gruesome sight.
>
> A chubby and surprisingly young man, Ta Vinh was dragged to the stake by Vietnamese soldiers as his wife and children, garbed in ritual white mourning dress, let loose bloodcurdling wails of despair. The spectators watched numbly as the firing squad performed its task, and dispersed just as silently when the episode ended.

The public execution of an alleged speculator did not endear the South Vietnamese government to American liberal opinion. There were the beginnings of Senatorial criticism of the American commitment as Senator Fulbright began televised hearings: the war in Vietnam was becoming, in regard both to action and to criticism, the first television war, which millions of Americans could follow from their sitting rooms. But, despite criticism by American liberals – and Democrats – of the American support for the South Vietnamese regime, Johnson, the consummate Democrat politician, was committed to maintain the South Vietnamese government in power. At a meeting with Ky in Honolulu in February, he was flattered when Ky set out a social programme – far from any South Vietnamese reality – which carefully mirrored Johnson's own Great Society. After Ky had described this vision Johnson turned to him approvingly and said: 'Boy, you speak just like an American.'

At the end of the previous year, Johnson had accepted the principle that the National Liberation Front could enter talks. Not only did Ho Chi Minh insist, during the early days of 1966, on the National Liberation Front being the sole representative of South Vietnam at any talks with the Americans, he also insisted, in a speech on January 24, that the supply routes from North Vietnam to the South, against which the Americans had begun to apply heavy bombing tactics, should be restored and developed. Faced by a demand which he regarded as derisory, Johnson ordered the bombing to be resumed. The first new wave of bombers struck at targets along the Ho Chi Minh trail on January 31.

From Paris, President de Gaulle issued a strong condemnation of the United States, demanding the withdrawal of all American troops as a condition of any negotiated peace. De Gaulle favoured a neutralized and unified

Vietnam. His intervention came two weeks before a Buddhist attempt to secure greater powers in the South. Led by Tri Quang, who three years earlier had challenged President Diem, the flag of Buddhist revolt was raised first in Hué and then in Da Nang. In Da Nang the dock workers, whose tasks included unloading American supplies for Ky's regime, went on strike. Violence spread to Saigon. The South Vietnamese officer in charge of central Vietnam, General Nguyen Chan Chi, whom Ky had just dismissed in order to extend his own authority in central Vietnam, joined the Buddhists and took his forces over to the anti-government side. Da Nang and Hué were occupied by General Chi's forces.

The Americans, confronted by the prospect of civil war in South Vietnam between those whom it was supporting, had little option but to throw its authority behind Ky, as Prime Minister, and as the man whom Johnson had so recently met and by whom he had been impressed. In April, Ky moved against General Chi's forces inside Da Nang. The Americans provided transport planes and pilots to bring up four thousand South Vietnamese troops. Ky insisted that the Buddhists, and his South Vietnamese rival, were working for the Communists, an absurd accusation, but one which the Americans did not challenge. It was the American marine commander at the airport who intervened to prevent the two forces coming into conflict, and Ky withdrew. He bided his time; then, on May 14, he sent two thousand Vietnamese troops against Da Nang, without informing the Americans in advance.

The battle inside Da Nang was a fierce one. The destruction of the forces of General Chi and the Buddhists was entrusted by Ky to Colonel Nguyen Ngoc Loan who, using tanks and armoured cars, moved through the city street by street, exacting a fearful revenge. Hundreds of General Chi's South Vietnamese troops, and hundreds of Buddhist civilians, were killed. Most of the civilians who were killed had taken refuge in Buddhist temples.

A week after the capture of Da Nang, Ky ordered the conquest of Hué, the second city held by the Buddhists. In protest against the Saigon government's use of force, at least ten of Tri Quang's followers – monks and nuns – set themselves on fire. Stanley Karnow was again an eye-witness, on the morning of May 29, at a Buddhist temple in Hué:

A Buddhist nun in her mid-fifties, Thanh Quang, had entered the temple compound at dawn, accompanied by a few friends. She assumed the lotus position as one friend doused her with gasoline. Then she lighted a match, immediately exploding into flame as another friend fed peppermint oil to the fire to suppress the stench of scorched flesh. By the time I arrived, her burning body was still erect, the hands clasped in prayer.

The religious rite was fast becoming a political episode. As crowds of spectators knelt before her, appealing to Buddha to ease her suffering, reporters from the local radio station passed among them, recording their cries for later broadcast.

Soon Tri Quang appeared to distribute to the foreign correspondents present copies of a letter that the nun had addressed to President Johnson, condemning America's 'irresponsible' support for the Saigon regime. Tri Quang blamed Johnson for her death, and indicted him for having 'masterminded the repression of the Vietnamese people'.

Johnson clung to other ideals, far removed from repression. On March 22 he had declared: 'I want to leave the footprints of America in Vietnam. I want them to say when the Americans come, this is what they leave – schools, not long cigars. We're going to turn the Mekong into a Tennessee Valley.' This echo of the Roosevelt era, when Johnson had been an eager young Democratic politician, was sincerely meant: the attractive face of post-imperial imperialism. But in a series of lectures at Johns Hopkins University, in Baltimore, Maryland, Senator Fulbright warned that, by its deeper and deeper involvement in Vietnam, the United States was 'in danger of losing its perspective on what exactly is within the realm of its power and what is beyond it'. His conclusion: 'We are not living up to our capacity and promise as a civilized example for the world.'

In June, Ky entered Hué and such opposition as could be mustered was quickly overcome. Once more, Colonel Laon ensured that a rebel city obeyed the conqueror. Hundreds of students and other opponents of Saigon were arrested, given no trial, but sent to prison for many years. Tri Quang, who was arrested while on hunger strike, was detained in a Saigon hospital.

Throughout the internecine South Vietnamese quarrels, and the Buddhist revolt, the American bombing of North Vietnam – Operation Rolling Thunder – had continued. Almost no day passed without a bombing raid. On average, eight hundred tons of bombs were dropped every day. But in August, General Westmoreland admitted, in the secrecy of his official correspondence, that he found 'no indication that the resolve in the leadership in Hanoi has been reduced'. Yet it was to reduce, and to break, that North Vietnamese resolve that the bombing had been launched almost a year and a half earlier.

The advances in social reform in the United States to which Johnson was committed were not eclipsed by the Vietnam War, though the rising cost of the war affected adversely the ability to pay for the measures Johnson would have liked to introduce. When he had spoken during his State of the Union message on January 12 of his confidence that the United States could afford both to fight in Vietnam and to continue the war on poverty, there were many listeners who doubted that this would be possible. Much was done, however. On January 17 Johnson appointed the first ever Black American to a position in the Cabinet: Robert C. Weaver, who became head of the Department of Housing and Urban Development, at the centre of one of the most urgent tasks confronting the administration, the renewal and replacement of millions of substandard dwellings, many of them in the Black ghettos of northern cities, including New York and Chicago. On April 28 Johnson initiated further civil rights legislation to end discrimination in jury service. On October 11 he signed a Bill bringing into law the Child Nutrition Act, whereby impoverished schoolchildren received food funded by the Federal government. A major effort was also made to tackle the problems of the inner cities, many of which looked as if they had been the scene of wartime destruction – they were suffering from virtual disintegration, with terrifyingly high rates of crime and vandalism. On November 3 Johnson signed into law the somewhat clumsily named Demonstration Cities and Metropolitan Redevelopment Act – soon known less clumsily as the Model Cities Act – which provided $1 billion for the rebuilding of more than sixty inner cities across the United States.

The impact of Vietnam on the ability to maintain effective social programmes was not long in being felt. On November 22, Sargent Shriver, the director of the Federal War on Poverty programme, spoke of how there had been a 'retreat on several fronts' because of economic cutbacks. Of the $680 million that had been envisaged that year to help more than nine million Americans, only $200 million was made available, and fewer than three million people were to be its beneficiaries. When Johnson told Congress that $335 million was the 'irreducible minimum' required by the programme, Congress had nevertheless cut $135 million from it. The war, costly and prolonged, was beginning to take its toll on the Great Society.

The needs of the Great Society were many and immediate. When the

Senate rejected a Civil Rights Bill intended to bring to an end discrimination in housing, there was anger in many Black communities, but there were those in Washington who argued convincingly that the public at large was not yet ready to accept integration in residential areas. During a 260-mile protest march in June, the purpose of which was to encourage Blacks to register as voters – something they were entitled to do under earlier legislation – a Black marcher was shot and wounded. On June 7 Martin Luther King joined the march. On June 21, at Philadelphia, Mississippi, gunfire was exchanged between White 'night-riders' and Black 'freedom-marchers'.

The weather that summer was unusually hot. On July 14, after the thermometer had soared to 100 degrees Fahrenheit, there were riots in Chicago and three Blacks were killed. On July 22 there were riots in Brooklyn; an eleven-year-old Black boy was killed by a sniper's bullet. Violence spread to Atlanta, Georgia, to Omaha, Nebraska, and to San Francisco. To the alarm of those in Washington who wished to push ahead with anti-discriminatory legislation, in a Gallup Poll late in the year, fifty-two per cent of those Whites questioned said that they thought the government was moving too fast in the direction of Black civil rights. But the process of change seemed irreversible. The first Black American to sit in the United States Senate was elected on November 8: Edward Brooke, a Republican from – and for – Massachusetts.

The internal racial conflict and the external Vietnamese war came together in a legal judgment on December 5, when the Supreme Court ruled unanimously that a young Black man, Julian Bond, had been wrongly excluded from the Georgia State legislature. Lawfully elected, he had twice been refused the right to take his seat. His 'crime' was not that he was Black, but that he had criticized American policy in Vietnam, and the conscription legislation that had been introduced to maintain, and to increase, the American war effort.

In South Africa, the triumph of the Nationalist Party and of apartheid was complete. On March 18 the government banned as an unlawful organization the autonomous Defence and Aid Fund, under which legal aid was provided for political prisoners, and financial and moral support given to their families. On March 23 a leading barrister, Abram Fischer, was sentenced to life imprisonment for his support of the banned African National Congress and for his membership of the banned Communist Party. During his trial he denounced racial prejudice as a 'wholly irrational phenomenon'. As a Jew, he knew what terrifying results racial prejudice could have.

In the elections held one week after Fischer's sentence, on March 30, the racial policy of apartheid was strengthened yet further when the Nationalists won their highest ever representation in the 170-seat parliament: 126 seats. At the same time, the opposition United Party declined from forty-nine to thirty-nine seats, while the multi-racial Progressive Party obtained only one seat, that of Helen Suzman, an outspoken opponent of apartheid.

The new government, still headed by Dr Verwoerd, was vigilant in banning any public opposition. Six weeks after the election the President of the National Union of Students, Ian Robertson, was banned from attending university or participating in student affairs. A visit by Senator Robert Kennedy, who was as opposed to apartheid in South Africa as to racial discrimination in the United States – against which his assassinated brother had fought – was accompanied by a ban on all non-South African journalists entering the country, so that Kennedy's visit could not be reported impartially. In a speech at the University of Cape Town – from which Ian Robertson had just been banned – Kennedy told a crowd of 15,000 people, many of them students: 'The essential humanity of man can be protected and preserved only where Government must answer not just to those of a particular religion or a particular race, but to all its people.' And in a powerful voice of encouragement for human rights activity everywhere, Kennedy declared: 'Each time a man stands up for an ideal, or acts to improve the lot of others, or strikes out against injustice, he sends forth a tiny ripple of hope. And crossing each other from a million different centers of energy and daring, those ripples build a current which can sweep down the mightiest walls of oppression.'

On September 6 a parliamentary messenger, Demetrio Tsafendas – a mentally unstable Portuguese East African citizen of Greek origin – walked up to Dr Verwoerd as he was sitting in his place, and stabbed him several times. Verwoerd died soon afterwards. Verwoerd's successor, B. J. Vorster, immediately announced that there would be no change in the policies of the government. Apartheid would remain its ideological and administrative base. In reaction to this, on October 27 the United Nations Assembly brought to an end the South African mandate over South-West Africa, the former German colony that in 1920 had been transferred to South Africa as a League of Nations mandate. South Africa rejected the United Nations decision and continued to administer the vast, diamond-rich region, in which, as in South Africa itself, the rules of apartheid were rigidly upheld.

The South African government also remained committed to trading with

Southern Rhodesia, thus effectively neutralizing the blockade imposed by Britain. Portugal, which was seeking to crush the nationalist revolt in the neighbouring colony of Mozambique – where it had 40,000 troops failing to curb the activities of a quarter of that number of guerrillas – also refused to participate in the blockade.

Harold Wilson made strenuous efforts to persuade Ian Smith, the man who had issued the Unilateral Declaration of Independence at the end of 1965, to return to constitutional government, and to help establish an interim administration 'comprising the widest possible spectrum of public opinion of all races in the country'. Talks took place in London, and in the Southern Rhodesian capital, Salisbury. But Wilson's pledge that in any future constitution there would be 'no oppression' of the minority by the majority had no effect.

On August 25, while talks were taking place in Salisbury between several of Harold Wilson's Cabinet Ministers and Smith's Ministers, Smith brought in a Constitution Amendment Bill, which according to the British violated even the minimal human rights provisions of the Unilateral Declaration of Independence constitution. The talks were broken off. In an attempt to persuade Smith to give up the perilous course he had set, against the African majority in Southern Rhodesia, against Britain and against the United Nations, Wilson made a dramatic journey to the western Mediterranean, to meet Smith, for the first time, on board a British warship, HMS *Tiger*. The 'Tiger talks' began on December 2 and continued for three days. Smith finally agreed that he would be willing to embark upon 'talks about talks'. But when he returned to Southern Rhodesia his colleagues rejected even that, and Smith declared: 'The fight goes on.' On the following day Britain asked the United Nations to impose mandatory sanctions on Southern Rhodesia: sanctions that all member States would be obliged to apply, including oil. A British naval patrol at the Mozambique port of Beira prevented oil from being discharged from tankers; but the United Nations had no means of preventing oil from arriving by road from South Africa, and the country's basic needs were supplied.

Within Southern Rhodesia there was an outbreak of African nationalist guerrilla activity. In May a White farmer and his wife were shot dead; in June there were fires and stonings in two African townships; in August seven people were injured when a bomb was thrown into a café in Salisbury. One guerrilla route into the country was across the border from Zambia. These incursions were vigorously combated, the Minister responsible for Law and

Order declaring in a radio broadcast in August: 'We have shot whole gangs of terrorists, not one surviving when they resisted arrest.' White opponents of the breakaway government were also challenged with the full weight of the law. When a number of lecturers and students at the University College of Rhodesia in Salisbury urged the acceptance of Britain's terms, some were first detained and then deported.

Colonial and European rule in Africa was virtually at an end. Other than Southern Rhodesia, the only colonial power with extensive rule remaining in Africa was Portugal: it controlled Portuguese Guinea, the islands of Fernando Po, Principe and São Tomé, the Congolese enclave of Cabinda, and the southern African territories of Angola and Mozambique. Spain still ruled Spanish Sahara and the tiny enclave of Ifni. France had promised an imminent referendum on independence to French Somaliland. Britain had granted both Bechuanaland (Botswana) and Basutoland (Lesotho) independence that year and promised it for Swaziland three years hence. But the troubles in the independent States of sub-Saharan Africa were legion. In Nigeria – which had achieved independence six years earlier – the first of two military rebellions that year took place on January 15, when the Prime Minister and the Finance Minister were among the government leaders killed, as were two of the regional Prime Ministers. A military government was then formed, sustained by troops loyal to the Commander-in-Chief, General Ironsi, who formed a military administration. On May 24, Ironsi issued a decree that abolished the federal regions and replaced them by a unitary State. Five days later, opposition to this led to an outbreak of violence in several regions, and there were attacks by northerners against southerners, and then by northerners against easterners. Several hundred people were killed. These killings led to even more bloody reprisals, and in the ensuing fighting, based on tribal rivalries and bordering on anarchy, General Ironsi was killed.

The new Head of State, General Gowon, a northerner and a Christian, abolished the unification decree. But, stimulated by the fighting and inflamed by the reprisals, the inter-regional divisions were too deep to be assuaged. On September 29, following long negotiations under General Gowon's aegis, an attack by northerners against easterners, starting at Kano, led to slaughter on a hitherto unprecedented scale. At least seven thousand easterners were killed: unofficial estimates put the deaths at closer to 40,000. In addition to the tragedies of killing on such a scale, the east – one of Nigeria's most overpopulated regions – had also to find shelter for more than a million eastern refugees from the northern region. By the end of the year, the country was effectively divided into two States.

In Ghana, the one-Party rule of Kwame Nkrumah was ended by a military coup, carried out while Nkrumah was on an official visit to China. It was Chou En-lai who, in Peking, told Nkrumah that he had been overthrown. He flew first to Moscow, and then to Guinea, from where he conducted a radio propaganda war against the new Ghanaian rulers. They, however, were able to call upon the people to turn their backs on a corrupt and tyrannical regime. Civilian government was restored, Nkrumah's close links to China and the Soviet Union were condemned, the Chinese and Russian advisers whom he had brought in were sent home, and Ghana re-established relations with Britain. The independent judiciary which Nkrumah had undermined was restored. The hut where he had been born fifty-seven years earlier – which he had turned into a place of devoted national pilgrimage – was bulldozed to the ground. For the next six years he lived in exile, dying in a sanatorium in Roumania.

In the former French colonies in Africa, Chad was combating a Muslim rebellion stimulated by neighbouring Sudan. In eight months, 217 of the Muslim rebels were killed. In the Islamic Republic of Mauritania there was distress among the African population when Arabic was made compulsory in all secondary schools. In the ensuing disturbances six people were killed. In the Central African Republic, the Chief of Staff, Colonel Bokassa, seized power, declaring himself to be 'emperor'. Diplomatic relations with China, which the previous government had cultivated, were broken. France, welcomed back, undertook to build the airstrips and roads, and bring in the heavy equipment, needed to develop the country's uranium deposits. In Senegal, there was a breakthrough in the creation of a Black African cultural sensitivity when the first World Festival of Negro Arts was held in Dakar. A total of 2,226 delegates assembled, from thirty-seven countries.

In China, an era of internal destruction had begun. The declared enemy was the 'four olds' – old customs, old habits, old culture and old thinking. Ancient buildings, art objects and temples were destroyed by the Red Guard vigilantes on Mao Tse-tung's directives. Mockingly, Mao declared that the Ministry of Culture in Peking should be renamed the 'Ministry of Mummies'. The reading aloud of Mao Tse-tung's writings, sometimes in vast public gatherings, became a daily feature of Chinese life. The Great Proletarian Cultural Revolution had begun. At the age of seventy-three, Mao Tse-tung was determined to give the Chinese revolution a new impetus, a vigour that he felt it had begun to lose, and a renewed central place for himself.

Violent verbal and physical attacks were made on those who were accused of 'taking the capitalist road' or putting into the Chinese cultural garden 'anti-Socialist poisonous weeds'. Wu Han, whose criticisms of local Party officialdom had so angered Mao Tse-tung, was one of those against whom this latter accusation was raised. He was terribly ill treated for two years, and died in 1969 as a result. Throughout China, encouraged by the authorities, the vilification of those who were accused of deviating from the true path of Communism intensified. Schoolchildren and university students were issued with armbands by the leaders of the Cultural Revolution, who declared the students to be 'Red Guards', through whom the renewed revolutionary path would be secured. In Peking, all the Christian churches were shut down, and red flags flown on the Roman Catholic Cathedral – which in 1900 had been the object of a ferocious attack by the Boxer nationalists.

A swim which Mao Tse-tung took in the Yangtse near Wuhan– where the 1911 Chinese revolution had broken out – was given massive and euphoric coverage in the Chinese newspapers. China's revolutionary achievements, he declared, would exceed even those of the Paris Commune of 1871 – the paradigm revolutionary success – though, having been set up in March that year it had been crushed in May. On August 18, tens of thousands of Red Guards, most of them students, led four days of anti-Western demonstrations in Peking. They were applauded by Mao Tse-tung, who appeared on the Tiananmen Gate as the youngsters paraded in front of him, each one holding up in his hand a copy of the Little Red Book in which Mao Tse-tung's thoughts had been printed. In referring to him, speakers were encouraged to use the words: 'our great teacher, great leader, great supreme commander and great helmsman'.

The demonstrations by the Red Guards soon turned to violence. As well as destroying old buildings, temples and museum pieces that were the pride of ancient Chinese culture, they attacked their schoolteachers, school administrators, local party officials, and even their parents. Many thousands of individuals died under the blows of these attacks. At Mao Tse-tung's insistence, senior Party leaders were dismissed, and they and their families subjected to public criticism and humiliation. Hundreds of leading intellectuals were beaten to death, or committed suicide. Among those who killed themselves was Lao She; his novel Cat Country, published in 1932, had been a powerful criticism of Chinese who turned on each other during the civil war, at a time when danger threatened from Japan. One passage of the novel read: 'The only result of revolution is to increase the number of soldiers in arms and the number of corrupt officials preying on the common people. In this kind of situation the common people will go hungry whether they like it or not.'

Mao Tse-tung was calling on the power and anger of these very 'common people' to turn against Chinese sensitivities and sensibilities that were at the centre both of ancient Chinese culture and of his own earlier revolutionary structures.

In the Soviet Union, there was elation on February 3 when the Soviet spacecraft *Luna 9* made the first soft landing – as opposed to crash landing – on the surface of the Moon. The euphoria took place during the same week that, as a prelude to the trial of the writers Andrei Sinyavsky and Yuli Daniel, set for February 10, there were a series of attacks on the two men in the Soviet newspapers. In the West, forty-nine leading writers signed an appeal in *The Times* for their release. Foreign journalists were refused admission to the court. The writers were accused of smuggling their work to the West and publishing it there: work that was 'being actively used in the ideological struggle against the Soviet Union'. After a four-day trial, during which they pleaded not guilty, Sinyavsky was sentenced to seven years and Daniel to five years in 'strict regime in a corrective labour camp': a sentence normally handed out to hardened and dangerous criminals. Not only Western writers and intellectuals, but almost all the Communist Parties of Western Europe, protested against the sentences. A protest by sixty-two Soviet writers was neither published in the Soviet press nor effective in securing even a reduction of the sentences.

In the most independent of the Soviet literary journals, *Novy Mir*, whose editor, Alexander Tvardovsky, had persuaded Khrushchev to let him publish Solzhenitsyn's *A Day in the Life of Ivan Denisovich* four years earlier, it was announced that a new novel, *Children of the Arbat*, would begin to be serialized. It did not appear. The author, Anatoli Rybakov, had been too outspoken about pre-war Stalinist Russia. Brezhnev was not going to allow the shafts of light of the Khrushchev era to be repeated. It was to take twenty-one years before the novel saw the light of Soviet day.

It was not only intellectual independence of thought that was stimulating the anger of the Soviet authorities. An upsurge in drunkenness and 'hooliganism' was leading to far heavier prison sentences than hitherto. For acts of hooliganism involving the use of an 'offensive weapon', up to seven years' imprisonment could be imposed. Swearing in public was among the minor offences for which a ten- to fifteen-day prison sentence could be imposed: for a second such conviction the penalty was at least six months in prison. In August, a Ministry for the Preservation of Public Order was set up.

In Eastern Europe, aspects of the defiance of the Communist authorities were emerging. In Roumania, the regime of Nicolae Ceauşescu was demanding an end to Soviet troops on Roumanian soil. In East Germany, the Ministry of Culture was criticized by the Party for not keeping a 'tighter rein' on intellectual dissent, and the Minister was dismissed. But this move was not effective with regard to other discontented groups. The Protestant Church in East Berlin, despite warnings from the Communist Party authorities, supported the election as Bishop of Berlin-Brandenburg of a clergyman, Dr Kurt Scharf, who had been expelled from East Berlin after he had protested at the building of the wall five years earlier.

In Poland, amid the celebrations of 1,000 years of Polish statehood, Cardinal Wyszynski was criticized by the Communist regime for having wanted to put the 1,000-year achievements of Poland before the achievements of Communism since 1945. 'This irresponsible shepherd of shepherds puts his illusory claims to the spiritual leadership of the Polish nation above Polish sovereignty,' Gomulka declared. At the millennium celebrations held by the Church at the shrine of the Black Madonna at Czestochowa, the vast gathering of Catholic worshippers – estimated at several hundred thousand – caused the government to fear an upsurge in dissent. Foreign bishops who had been invited to the Church ceremonies were refused permission to enter Poland, and Cardinal Wyszynski was forbidden to go abroad. Four Church seminaries were closed down.

Gomulka meanwhile strengthened Poland's links with the Soviet Union, extending the scope of the previous year's Soviet-Polish Treaty to double the supply of raw materials from the Soviet Union, and agreeing that Polish purchases of wheat – hitherto mainly from Canada – would come henceforth principally from the Soviet Union. Polish writers, in a collective protest, called for clemency on behalf of the imprisoned Soviet writers, Daniel and Sinyavsky, and a young Polish intellectual, Professor Kolakowski – a Marxist philosopher at Warsaw University – declared publicly that without greater intellectual and cultural freedom in Poland there could be no 'genuine democratic freedom'. He was promptly expelled from the Communist Party.

In Czechoslovakia, which unlike Poland had a common border with Western Europe, the main problem confronting the authorities was the number of Czech citizens seeking to cross the border. In July, seventy-eight Czechs were arrested trying to cross into Western Germany. Seven others succeeded in getting across. In the first ten months of the year another phenomenon was revealed: 1,841 'disturbers of the frontier' – as the Czech authorities described them – East German citizens trying to get to West Germany through Czechoslovakia, were caught, and sent back to East Germany. A quarter of a century later, a similar East German exodus, making use of Czechoslovakia, was to be a catalyst in the collapse of the Iron Curtain.

In Prague, student disaffection was manifest in May, when during the annual student festivities placards were waved with the message: 'Long live the Soviet Union – but on its own resources'. In response, Antonin Novotny, who was both President of Czechoslovakia and First Secretary of the Czechoslovak Communist Party, declared that the Party could not accept such a 'destructive' attitude. Journalists, too, were under attack, a Party magazine accusing those who had begun to write about Western art and culture – which between the wars had been an integral part of Czech intellectual life – of 'lacking clear Marxist conceptions of culture, attempting to place art beyond the influence of the Party, and paying too little attention to the socialist culture of the socialist countries'. But the voices of change did not come only from outside Party circles. At the Czechoslovak Party Congress in June, the leader of the Slovak Communist Party, Alexander Dubček, told the delegates: 'The concept that nationalism is the antithesis of internationalism is a persistent relic of the past.' This was not the orthodoxy that Novotny in Prague, or Brezhnev in Moscow, liked to hear. But, as a gesture to the growing criticisms of rigid Party orthodoxy, the anniversary of Czechoslovakia's declaration of independence on 28 October 1918 was restored as National Day. Since the imposition of Communism in 1948, National Day had been condemned as a throwback to bourgeois nationalistic tendencies which the Party deplored.

In Hungary, a decade since the harsh repression of 1956, discontent with the Communist regime was also growing. A number of Roman Catholics who had just been released after a decade in prison were arrested on charges of conspiracy. Priests who had been at liberty since 1956 were accused of 'acting under instructions from their Western contacts'. Tourists from the West were said to have lured churchmen with foreign currency to spy on Hungary. In a gesture of support for the Soviet Union, the Hungarian Prime Minister, János Kádár, made a public speech attacking 'anti-Soviet trends' among the Warsaw Pact powers.

The East-West divide could sometimes be breached in a positive manner. That year the Moscow Radio Orchestra was brought to Britain for four concerts, and the British Royal Ballet toured five Communist capitals: Prague, Sofia, Bucharest, Warsaw and Belgrade. But with the intensification of the war in Vietnam, the sense of East-West conflict was heightened. Fears of an escalation of the war that might draw in the wider alignments of NATO and the Warsaw Pact were prominent in the public mind of many nations.

Johnson had visited Vietnam in October. Speaking to a group of soldiers he told them to 'nail the coonskin to the wall'. On December 13, in a bombing raid in a suburb of Hanoi, more than a hundred North Vietnamese civilians were killed. Eleven days later, on Christmas Eve, Cardinal Spellman, Archbishop of New York, speaking at an American base near Saigon, declared that the war in Vietnam was a war for 'civilization', and that anything less than an American victory was 'inconceivable'. When the British Prime Minister, Harold Wilson, proposed, without success, on December 30, that the United States, South Vietnam and North Vietnam should meet – on British territory – to arrange a ceasefire, his offer reflected the fear of escalation. Its rejection showed how, despite the bombing truce, the struggle had become implacable, and, for the Americans, one from which they could not extricate themselves.

CHAPTER SIXTEEN

1967

> The warriors in the front lines saw with their own eyes
> not only the glory of victory but the price of victory:
> their comrades who fell beside them bleeding, and I
> know that even the terrible price which our enemies paid
> touched the hearts of many of our men.
>
> YITZHAK RABIN

IN CHINA THE CULTURAL REVOLUTION continued on its destructive path throughout 1967. Red Guards, mostly students, and the older 'Red Rebels' who worked alongside them, attacked any individual or institution that was said to have 'taken the Capitalist road'. Almost all their victims were hitherto loyal and hard-working Communist functionaries. Local Party leaders were everywhere denounced for failing to follow Mao Tse-tung's precepts: these, summarized and enshrined in the Little Red Book, were harshly insisted upon and often brutally upheld. Peasants, alarmed at the near-anarchy of the Red Guard actions, began to hoard grain. This in turn reduced the harvest available in the cities, provoking even harsher Red Guard reactions.

Red Guard activity in the factories brought disruption to large areas of industry, including the coalmines of north China, the steelworks in Anhui and the oilfield at Tachung – China's largest. According to Chou En-lai, six months' production was lost by these activities: he himself was criticized, as were his Vice-Premiers. It looked as if China would succumb to total anarchy. Even foreign trade was disrupted by the Red Guards, who often prevented the unloading of foreign goods at Chinese ports.

The Chinese army alone had the power to curb the anarchy. Considerable force was used against those who made use of the Red Guard fervour to establish their own independent centres of power. On February 11 the army placed Peking under military rule and took over the Ministry of Public

Security. In Szechwan, soldiers, attempting to restore some semblance of order, killed thousands of 'radicals'. In Wuhan, in the summer, the army arrested five hundred Red Guard leaders. The response was a massive strike in the factories, and mass protest demonstrations in the streets. The army moved in, and as many as a thousand protesters were killed.

As Chou En-lai appealed, on February 26, for a return to 'order and discipline', Red Guard factions fought each other, using arms and ammunition which they had seized from army depots. There was severe fighting in both Canton and Peking. In August units of the Red Guard occupied the Foreign Ministry in Peking, disrupted all official business, and proceeded to appoint their own 'radical' diplomats as ambassadors worldwide. Insisting that such revolutionary change was essential on 'anti-imperialist' grounds, the Red Guard attacked the British Embassy in Peking and set it on fire.

By September, Mao Tse-tung realized that the Cultural Revolution had gone too far. Far from 'purifying' the revolution, as he had initially declared, it was destroying it. Suddenly 'ultra-left' tendencies were under attack and the army – against which the Red Guard had fulminated for the severity of its actions against them in Wuhan – was praised as a champion of 'proletarian dictatorship'. Student activities which, inspired by Mao Tse-tung, had for nine months been of the most destructive sort, were slowly brought under control. Thousands more Red Guards were killed in fighting with the army. On one occasion five workers, whom Mao Tse-tung himself had sent to the campus of Peking University in order to calm student zeal, were shot dead on the campus by the students themselves.

Workers' organizations were called upon to combat the Red Guards, whose internal divisions were leading to internecine fighting and – fortunately for the authorities who had originally called them into being – weakening their collective strength. A 'Three-Way Alliance' was created of the army, the workers' organizations and the 'revolutionary masses', to combat Red Guard activities in schools, factories and rural communes. First coming into effect in Shanghai, the Three-Way Alliance was able, in large measure because of the army, to restore order, but it was to take a whole year, until the summer of 1968, to do so.

Confronted by the disruption caused by the Cultural Revolution, at the end of 1967 Mao Tse-tung launched yet another nationwide campaign, to bring the violence and anarchy to an end. It was called the Campaign to Purify Class Ranks, and depended heavily upon the army. To ensure that Red Guards who were unrepentant, or who had 'prior connections with the bourgeoisie' – or were formerly connected with the Nationalist Kuomintang, against which the Communists had been victorious in 1949 – did not oppose the new discipline, specially established Workers' Mao-Thought Propaganda teams were set up, drawn from the army and the 'revolutionary masses'. Confessions became the order of the day. For those with no political faults to confess, a 'sincere' confession of some personal failure was better than no confession at all. Silence, or assertions of innocence, could lead to imprisonment or forced labour, not only for the individual, but for his family. 'Disclosure is better than no disclosure,' one Communist Party document explained. 'Early disclosure is better than late disclosure; thorough disclosure is better than reserved disclosure. If one sincerely discloses his whole criminal story and admits his crimes to the people humbly, he will be treated leniently and given a way for safe conduct, and his case will not affect his family.'

On April 21 there was astonishment in the West when Stalin's daughter, Svetlana Alliluyeva, having defected from the Soviet Union, arrived in the United States. She had been on a visit to India when she decided to defect. It seemed incredible that the daughter of the tyrant could be free to travel. Might not this mark a definite stage in the ending of the monolithic Soviet position? Might now the giant be shown to have feet of clay? Five days after reaching New York, Alliluyeva gave a press conference, highly critical of Communism. She had come to the West, she said, 'to seek the self-expression that has been denied me for so long in Russia', and she added: 'I was brought up in a family where there was never any talk about God, but when I became a grown-up person I found it impossible to exist without God in one's heart.'

On April 23, two days after Svetlana Alliluyeva's defection, the Soviet Union launched a manned space ship, the first for more than two years. It was the ninety-seventh anniversary of the birth of Lenin. One of the two astronauts on board, Colonel Vladimir Komarov, was the first Russian cosmonaut to make a second flight in space. The spacecraft, *Union 1*, flew at 18,600 miles an hour, in an orbit between 125 and 139 miles from Earth.

The year 1967 marked the fiftieth anniversary of the triumph of Soviet Communism: as such it was celebrated with considerable fanfare throughout the year, and a six-day public holiday in November. But the Party organs of repression were ever vigilant. A new KGB chief, Yuri Andropov, appointed on May 18, made it clear that there could be no lessening of vigilance. One of his first initiatives was to orchestrate the censure of the United States for 'exploiting' the arrival of 'Soviet citizen Svetlana Alliluyeva' in order to mount 'a broad anti-Soviet campaign'. On the industrial front, a new decree was issued, on November 14 – at the height of the jubilee celebrations – whereby heavier penalties, including prison and labour camp sentences, would be imposed on all factories, trade organizations, planning institutes and railways that fell below the norms that had been set.

Ideological conformity remained a central feature of Soviet art and literature. Efforts to adopt critical or imaginative stances were repeatedly made, but equally repeatedly condemned. The director of the Lenin Komsomol Theatre, Alexander Efros, was sacked for 'systematic refusal to accept Party guidance and criticism'. The annual congress of Soviet writers studiously avoided inviting Alexander Solzhenitsyn. He responded by courageously sending three hundred of the delegates a strong attack on the Soviet censorship of literature. To the anger of the Soviet authorities, this denunciation was then published in full in Paris, in Le Monde, on May 31. Four months later Solzhenitsyn, and Andrei Voznesensky – a fellow writer outspoken in his criticism of the regime – were publicly condemned by the Soviet Writers' Union for providing the West with 'anti-Soviet propaganda'.

It was with regard to Eastern Europe that the Soviet Union faced difficulties that could not be easily resolved or subjected to Communist Party discipline. Roumania, as a gesture which disturbed both the Soviet Union and the other Warsaw Pact powers – most especially Eastern Germany and Poland – established diplomatic relations with Western Germany. In the summer, the Roumanian government further upset the bloc of which it was a part by calling for the disbandment of both NATO and the Warsaw Pact. Neutrality had never been a favoured word in the Communist or Soviet lexicon.

Other Communist Parties sought to maintain the discipline of which Moscow approved. In Poland, a Jewish writer, Nina Karsow, who was writing a book – never published – about secret political trials in Poland, was sentenced to three years in prison for her efforts. A campaign against the Catholic Church was launched, its 'hierarchy' being accused by a Politburo expert on ideology of being 'the bastion of internal forces hostile to Socialism'. Cardinal Wyszynski, always an outspoken defender of the right of worship, was refused a passport to go to the Vatican, and was criticized in the main Communist Party newspaper for his 'unfriendly and disloyal attitude towards the Polish State'.

In Czechoslovakia, Jan Beneš, a short-story and film writer who had organized a public protest against the Soviet trial and imprisonment of

Daniel and Sinyavsky the previous year, was himself arrested, and held in prison for almost two years before being brought to trial. At his trial in Prague, Western journalists were not allowed to be present in the court, nor was a representative of Amnesty International. Beneš was sentenced to five years in prison. The severity of his sentence did not deter other Czechoslovak writers from seeking greater independence. More than a hundred writers signed a manifesto, which was published in the West on September 3, asking for help 'to rescue the spiritual freedom and fundamental rights of every independent artist threatened by the terror of State powers'.

Five days later the Czechoslovak newspapers criticized the manifesto. Several writers believed to have been behind it were expelled from the Communist Party for 'the voicing of thoughts alien to Socialism'. Western observers were impressed by what was clearly the growth of dissent, and the courage of the dissenters in publicizing their views. The Czech authorities reacted with a new press law that further curbed freedom of expression. But student discontent could not be curbed, and student demonstrations at the end of October were broken up by force. Religion was also under constant scrutiny and repression. In August the director of a coalmine was dismissed because his wife had taken the children of a relative to a confirmation ceremony. Repeated government statements that all was well within Czechoslovakia could not hide repeated manifestations of disaffection with the Communist system.

Canada was twice in the international spotlight in 1967. The first time was when, on April 27, as part of its celebrations of a hundred years of existence as a nation, the 1967 World's Fair – Expo – was opened in Montreal. The theme chosen was 'Man and his World', with a stress on ideas and architecture. Expo remained open until October, attracting several million visitors. In July, however, the celebratory euphoria was shaken when General de Gaulle visited Quebec, and gave support to the French-speaking separatists there when, addressing a vast crowd in Montreal on July 24, he called out the separatist slogan: 'Vive le Québec libre.' The Canadian Prime Minister, Lester Pearson, protested that the encouragement of separatism in this way was 'unacceptable' to the Canadian government and to most Canadians, whereupon de Gaulle cancelled his visit to Ottawa – where he was to have addressed the Canadian parliament – and returned to France.

Canada had emerged as a strong supporter of United States action in Vietnam. When, in May, there was parliamentary pressure for Canada to call for a halt in the American bombing of North Vietnam, Lester Pearson insisted that he would not take up a position critical of the United States. But public pressure and public protests grew, so much so that in October the External Affairs Ministry called publicly for a halt to the American bombing, without any prior conditions, as an essential first step towards the start of peace talks. There were even calls for an embargo of all shipments of Canadian war materials to the United States for as long as the war in Vietnam continued, but on this the government in Ottawa refused to act.

Australia had eight thousand troops in Vietnam. The first Australian troops had gone there two years earlier, the year in which the Australian Prime Minister, Robert Menzies, controversially reintroduced National Service, and did so according to a ballot system which meant that some twenty-year-olds would be liable to two years' service anywhere in the world. The ballot was retained until 1972, by which time 47,000 Australians had served in Vietnam, of whom some 15,000 were conscripts. By the end of the fighting, 480 Australian soldiers had been killed in Vietnam. New Zealand also sent regular troops to Vietnam, but never more than five hundred at any one time.

During the summer, the opposition Australian Labour Party made it clear that if it were to come to power it would demand a halt to the American bombing of the North, or else withdraw the Australian troops. Britain refused to make any military commitment. But it was within the United States that opposition to the war was causing Johnson and his policymakers the greatest problems. There were half a million American troops in Vietnam, and conscription notices were going out to hundreds of thousands more. Johnson continued to speak of the war as essential and winnable, but his words were less confident than in the previous year. During his State of the Union message on January 10 he warned that the United States faced 'more cost, more loss, and more agony. For the end is not yet. I cannot promise you that it will come this year – or the next.'

A major military offensive was mounted against the Vietcong at the beginning of the year. Sixteen thousand American troops and 16,000 South Vietnamese troops took part, starting on January 6. The aim was to destroy the 'Iron Triangle', a substantial Communist stronghold in the Mekong Delta north-west of Saigon. In the area of the stronghold were four villages: the Americans evacuated the ten thousand inhabitants before launching the attack. The villages were then totally destroyed: bombed and shelled and burned to the ground. The stronghold itself, which was obliterated in the attack, had been built twenty years earlier, during the Vietnamese struggle against France. On the eve of the American-South Vietnamese assault, the Vietcong defenders fled. Several thousand of them escaped across the border into Cambodia. Seven hundred of those who stayed behind to cover the retreat were killed. The American troops announced a victory, and were elated by it. Within twelve months the Vietcong had returned and the hiding places and fortified points had been rebuilt. Four similar attacks took place against other strongpoints, with similar results: considerable destruction of villages, a sense of victory, and then the quiet, unnoticed return of the Vietcong.

On February 2 Johnson proposed a halt both to the American bombing of North Vietnam and to the 'further augmentation' of United States forces in Vietnam, if Ho Chi Minh would stop the infiltration of troops and supplies from North to South. Ho Chi Minh replied that he had only one condition for entering talks: that the American bombing of North Vietnam should stop. Until that happened, he was not prepared to give any assurance about infiltration from the North. For four days, during the Vietnamese New Year, the American bombing was halted as a gesture of goodwill. The halt was extended for one more day because the Soviet leader, Kosygin, was visiting London, discussing with Harold Wilson the possibility of some international initiative – led by Britain and the Soviet Union – to end the war. As Kosygin had been the intermediary between Johnson and Ho Chi Minh, it was felt in Washington that there would be something particularly provocative if the bombing was resumed while he was himself on a negotiating mission. Harold Wilson tried hard to use the Kosygin visit to move forward the Johnson-Ho Chi Minh dialogue, but failed to do so. The bombing began again on February 13.

Protests against the war grew in number and frequency throughout the United States. It was a war being fought almost ten thousand miles away, for a regime that many regarded as corrupt and oppressive. As American and South Vietnamese troops carried out search-and-destroy missions to find and kill the Vietcong, the civilian death toll mounted. On March 2 an accidental American bombing raid on the South Vietnamese village of Lang Vei killed eighty South Vietnamese civilians. As the bombing of North Vietnam was renewed, a new chant was heard by demonstrators, many of whom called it out with harsh regularity outside the White House while Johnson was inside: 'Hey, hey, LBJ, how many kids did you kill today?' Also in Washington, anti-war demonstrators marched on the Defense Department building and surrounded it. An opinion poll gave the shocking figure – shocking to the President and those who were at his side in the running of the war – of only twenty-three per cent of those polled having confidence in his conduct of the war. Young men who received their draft notices tore them up or burned them in public. Others crossed the border into Canada in order to avoid serving. 'Draft dodger' became for some a term of abuse, for others a term of pride: thirty years later it was to be used, but without success, in the campaign of character-blackening against a presidential candidate, Bill Clinton.

The cost of the war was also impinging on the American public. At the beginning of the year a six per cent war tax surcharge was imposed on all taxpayers: this was increased before the end of the year to ten per cent. In March, Johnson flew to the Pacific island of Guam for three days of talks with the South Vietnamese, and with his own military advisers. During the discussions, Air Vice Marshal Ky, the South Vietnamese Prime Minister, spoke of how the Vietcong were 'on the run' and the North Vietnamese supply-lines to the South 'near paralysis'.

The war continued to intensify. On May 19 the Demilitarized Zone between South and North Vietnam, which both sides had hitherto respected, was occupied by American and South Vietnamese forces. That day, American bombers attacked targets in the centre of Hanoi. In April, American bombers struck at ammunition dumps and power transformers near Hanoi and Hai-phong, but without making any serious impact on North Vietnam's warmak-ing capacity. In June, American bombers struck at oil storage tanks, but much of the oil had already been hidden underground, or in well-camouflaged fuel storage dumps, elsewhere. From his Intelligence analysts, Johnson learned repeatedly that the bombing campaign was not effective in damaging North Vietnam's ability to make war. Destroyed bridges – and hundreds of North Vietnamese road bridges had been destroyed – were quickly repaired. Storage depots were repeatedly dispersed, and the North Vietnamese people made all the more determined to carry on the fight against such a heavy bombardment, not unlike Londoners in 1940.

Only ground forces seemed capable of keeping the Vietcong in check. But, to do that, yet more American troops would be needed in the South. On August 4 Johnson authorized an increase in the number of American troops in Vietnam to over the half-million mark, by an additional 45,000. The arrival of these new troops coincided with the publication of the number of Americans killed in action in Vietnam that year: 9,000, bringing the total over the previous two years to 15,000. That statistic, with all it implied of suffering and waste, and the thousands of bereaved at home, especially widows and orphans, as well as friends, caused many Americans who had hitherto supported the war to think again.

Opposition to the war had begun to emerge at the very centre of political power. That August, Secretary of Defense Robert McNamara, who had been a leading supporter of the bombing offensive launched against North Vietnam in March 1965, told a secret subcommittee of the Senate Armed Services Committee: 'Enemy operations in the south cannot, on the basis of any reports I have seen, be stopped by air bombardment – short, that is, of the virtual annihilation of North Vietnam and its people.' These were not words that Johnson wanted to hear, and in a speech at San Antonio, Texas, on September 29, Johnson said that while he was ready to stop the bombing of the North if this would 'lead promptly to productive discussion' with the North Vietnamese, 'Hanoi has not accepted any of our proposals.' He did not explain that he had always put forward, together with the proposal to halt the bombing and start talks, a condition that Ho Chi Minh had always rejected. That condition was that Ho Chi Minh order an end to the infiltration of North Vietnamese troops and supplies into the South.

At San Antonio, Johnson set out his global perspective on the war. The Communist conquest of South Vietnam could be followed by similar conquests elsewhere in South-East Asia. Communist domination of South-East Asia could bring a Third World War 'closer to reality'. 'But all that we have learnt in this tragic century,' he said, 'strongly suggests that it would be so.' As President of the United States 'I am not prepared to gamble on the chance that it is not so. I am not prepared to risk the security – and indeed the survival – of this nation on mere hope and wishful thinking. I am convinced that by seeing this struggle through now, we are reducing the chance of a larger war, perhaps a nuclear war.'

The American bombing switched in September from North Vietnam to Vietcong strongholds in the South. These were essentially rural and village targets, against which the bombers could send massive destruction but little careful targeting. On one stronghold, Conthien, eight hundred B-52 bombers dropped 22,000 tons of bombs. The jungle around another strongpoint, Dakto, was bombed by three hundred bombers, after which it was hit by American artillery, while chemical warfare units used herbicides to complete the defoliation. A further 40,000 Vietcong soldiers were killed. 'The enemy's hopes are bankrupt,' General Westmoreland declared during a visit to

Washington, but he was wrong. An attempt by the Americans to defend their base at Khesanh from Vietcong attack took five weeks, despite a massive bombing campaign against Vietcong positions during which more than 75,000 tons of bombs and artillery shells descended on them: what Stanley Karnow calls 'the deadliest deluge of firepower ever unloaded on a tactical target in the history of warfare'. After ten thousand of their men had been killed, many by napalm, the Vietcong called off their attack on Khesanh. The Americans lost five hundred marines.

In October there was a mass protest against the Vietnam War in front of the Pentagon, from which the war strategy was being directed. Arthur Miller and Norman Mailer were among those who took part. Johnson, whose portrait was displayed above the words 'WAR CRIMINAL', was both furious and disturbed by the demonstration. The bombing of the North continued. By the end of the year it was estimated that bombing had caused $300 million in damage to North Vietnam. In the raids themselves, confronted by an extraordinarily well-organized and well-directed North Vietnamese anti-aircraft defence, including eight thousand anti-aircraft guns and more than two hundred surface-to-air missile batteries, seven hundred American aircraft had been shot down. Their total value exceeded $900 million. Statistics were easy to use, and to misuse. The American bomber commanders were able to point out, with truth, that in the attacks on power stations and power storage grids, eighty-five per cent of North Vietnam's capacity to generate electricity had been destroyed. But this ignored the equally true fact that – as Robert McNamara had pointed out in his critique of bombing – North Vietnam had been able to meet its war needs with regard to electricity by switching from the destroyed grids to as many as two thousand diesel-driven generators, that could be effectively hidden from aerial bombardment. Food shortages were intense in North Vietnam, but a steady supply of Chinese and Soviet food enabled starvation to be warded off.

Despite the North Vietnamese anti-aircraft defences, and the remarkable system of tunnels and underground shelters which were dug in every town and village, the power of American bombers to kill and maim was almost limitless. In July the village of Vinh Quang was among the targets. Many years later one of the villagers, Ho Thanh Dam, told Stanley Karnow:

The bombing started at about eight o'clock in the morning and lasted for hours. At the very first sound of explosions, we rushed into the tunnels, but not everyone made it. During a pause in the attack, some of us climbed out to see what we could do, and the scene was terrifying. Bodies had been torn to pieces – limbs hanging from trees or scattered around the ground.

Then the bombing began again, this time with napalm, and the village went up in flames. The napalm hit me, and I must have gone crazy. I felt as if I was burning all over, like charcoal, and I lost consciousness. Comrades took me to the hospital, and my wounds didn't begin to heal until six months later. More than two hundred people died in the raid, including my mother, my sister-in-law, and three nephews. They were buried alive when their tunnel collapsed.

A new area of conflict came suddenly to the forefront of world attention when, on May 16, President Nasser of Egypt instructed the United Nations to remove its forces from Sinai. Since 1948 the Sinai Desert, which was Egyptian sovereign territory, and the Gaza Strip (occupied by Egypt since 1948) had been the buffer zone between Israel and Egypt. Both areas were patrolled by a United Nations Emergency Force (UNEF) which had been set up after the Israeli-Egyptian war of 1956, when Israeli troops had occupied Sinai but had then withdrawn, in return for the United Nations presence. When Nasser demanded that the United Nations forces withdraw, they did so without protest, not wishing to find themselves in the firing line. By May 19, almost all 3,400 of them had gone. The United Nations had not even asked Nasser for a week or a month's delay. Israel was suddenly vulnerable to Egyptian attack. At the same time, Syrian forces were on high alert along Israel's north-eastern border.

On May 22, three days after the last United Nations troops had left Sinai, Nasser announced that Egypt refused henceforth to allow Israeli shipping bound for the southern Israeli port of Eilat to proceed through the Straits of Tiran – which were controlled jointly by Egypt and Saudi Arabia, and at which some of the United Nations troops had been stationed. In announcing the blockade, which he did in a speech at an Egyptian air base in Sinai, a hundred miles from Israel's border, Nasser told his pilots: 'We are ready for war.'

Freedom of passage for Israeli ships through the Straits of Tiran had been guaranteed by the United States, Britain and France after the Suez War eleven years earlier. On May 24, having condemned the blockade of Israeli shipping as 'illegal and potentially disastrous to the cause of peace', Johnson

ordered units of the United States Sixth Fleet to take up positions in the
eastern Mediterranean. That day, an armoured brigade from Kuwait reached
Cairo by air, as a gesture of support in what was clearly going to be an
armed conflict. 'Our basic objective', Nasser announced on May 26, 'will be
to destroy Israel. I probably could not have said such things five or even
three years ago. Today I say such things because I am confident.'

Anxious to avoid a drawing in of the nuclear powers into any Middle
Eastern war, Johnson and Kosygin made use, for the first time, of the
Washington-Moscow 'hot line', the recent telephonic link that enabled them
to be in continuous and direct contact. Both men agreed that there would
be no direct military intervention by either the United States or the Soviet
Union. The Israelis were on their own. On May 30 their isolation was
intensified when King Hussein of Jordan flew from Amman to Cairo and
committed himself to join in the attack on Israel. 'We had no right,' the
King later wrote, 'nor could we decently justify a decision, to stand aside
in a cause in which the entire Arab world was determined unanimously to
engage itself.'

A number of States began to work to form an 'international flotilla' of
warships that could sail to the Straits of Tiran and keep them open. The
United States and Britain both supported this. Harold Wilson flew to Canada
to enlist Canadian support. First the Canadian and then the Dutch and
Danish governments agreed to participate. But there were no warships near
enough to reach the Straits for several days. Nasser, hoping to prevent the
arrival of any international naval force, declared on June 2: 'If any Power
dares to make declarations on freedom of navigation in the Straits of Tiran,
we shall deny that Power oil, and free navigation in the Suez Canal.' Dean
Rusk, who had told the Israeli Ambassador in Washington a few days
earlier that the military preparations of the maritime powers had 'reached
an advanced stage', saw the Ambassador again on June 3 to tell him that
'nothing has been firmly decided'.

Israel faced the prospect of having to act alone. It did so, with dramatic
swiftness, in the early hours of June 5, when, in an attempt to pre-empt
Egyptian air strikes on Israeli military and civilian targets, the Israeli air
force struck without warning or declaration of war at more than twenty
Egyptian air bases. As a pre-emptive strike it was wholly effective. One
third of Egypt's warplanes were destroyed on the ground. Israel appealed to
King Hussein not to join in the conflict, but he was persuaded by Nasser
– over the telephone – that Egypt, not Israel, had struck the decisive blow,

and ordered Jordanian troops to attack. At the same time, Syrian, Iraqi and Jordanian aircraft attacked military targets inside Israel.

The Israeli response was immediate and effective. On the ground and in the air the attacking forces were driven off. On June 6, Egypt appealed to the Soviet Union to join the conflict by claiming that the United States and Britain were actively helping Israel, but this was untrue, and the Soviet leaders knew it. They therefore declined to take any active part in the war. The course of the war was as swift as it was decisive. On June 7 Israeli troops occupied the Old City of Jerusalem, which had been under Jordanian rule since 1948. In six days, the Egyptians were driven out of Sinai, the Jordanians were driven off the West Bank, and the Syrians were driven from the Golan Heights. Israel's victory was complete.

On June 9, as the extent of Israel's victory was becoming clear, but was still not certain, Communist Party leaders from every East European country flew to Moscow, where, together with the Communist Party of the Soviet Union, they issued a condemnation of Israeli 'aggression'. On the following day the Soviet Union broke off diplomatic relations with Israel. But it took no steps to commit troops to the Arab side, or to threaten any form of direct military intervention. This led to criticism of Russia in newspapers throughout the Arab world. This criticism was repeated in the most strident form by China, which, as part of the ongoing Sino-Soviet dispute, denounced the Soviet Union for failing to come to the aid of Egypt, Syria or Jordan.

Such verbal abuse could not affect the struggle on the battlefield. By June 10 the war was over. Israel found itself in occupation of territory three times its own size, and of a million Arabs on the West Bank and Gaza Strip, who had begun to call increasingly, not for their return to Egyptian and Jordanian rule, but for autonomy and independence. Israel became an occupying power, to be confronted, and cursed, by the demands and excesses – on both sides of the unequal divide – that all occupation brings in its wake.

During the fighting, 777 Israeli soldiers had been killed. In a speech a few days after the war, the Israeli Chief of Staff, General Yitzhak Rabin, told his listeners, who were basking in the euphoria of such an unexpected and complete victory:

We find more and more a strange phenomenon among our fighters. Their joy is incomplete, and more than a small portion of sorrow and shock prevails in their festivities, and there are those who abstain from cele-bration.

The warriors in the front lines saw with their own eyes not only the glory of victory but the price of victory: their comrades who fell beside them bleeding, and I know that even the terrible price which our enemies paid touched the hearts of many of our men. It may be that the Jewish people has never learned or accustomed itself to feel the triumph of conquest and victory, and therefore we receive it with mixed feelings.

Israel's victory put its troops on the eastern bank of the Suez Canal. Israeli warships patrolled within sight of Port Said. One of them, the *Eilat*, was sunk by Egyptian missiles on October 21 – only four months after Israel's military victory – while outside Egyptian territorial waters. Forty-seven Israeli sailors were killed. In retaliation, Israel began an artillery barrage along the whole length of the Suez Canal. The oil refineries of Suez City were set on fire, and tens of thousands of Egyptian civilians were evacuated from both Suez City and Ismailia.

A year later the artillery duels across the Suez Canal began again. The 'War of Attrition' had begun. There were to be hundreds of casualties on both sides before, following more than twelve months of spasmodic but often intense fire and counter-fire, a ceasefire was achieved under United States and United Nations auspices. The Israeli deaths in the War of Attrition – 593 soldiers and 127 civilians – were almost as high as the deaths in the Six-Day War.

There had also been casualties among those of the United Nations Emergency Force personnel who had not been evacuated by the United Nations on the eve of the Six-Day War. Fifteen had been killed – one Brazilian and fourteen Indians – caught up in a conflict that they had been powerless to prevent.

The East-West confrontation had been avoided in Vietnam, but was acute in the sphere of the development of nuclear weapons' delivery systems and the counter-measures needed to defend against them. The cost of this nuclear arms race was formidable. On September 18 Robert McNamara announced that the United States was spending $5,000 million to create an anti-ballistic missile (ABM) defence system. The Soviet Union was already putting such a system in place. Nor was that the only Soviet move which gave the United States an impetus for further nuclear preparations. On November 3 McNamara gave details both of a new Soviet nuclear bomb, which could be delivered through a low-orbiting space rocket (the Fractional Orbital

Bombardment System – FOBS) and of the American ability to shoot down this bomb at any point during its first orbit. When several members of Congress asked whether the nuclear arms race was not getting out of hand, and expressed their concern that the Soviet Union might be developing weapons, such as the new space bomb, that could prove superior to the American bombs and defence systems, they were assured by the Pentagon, in a statement on November 8, that the United States was still 'in the lead'.

The Pentagon statement sought to give reassurance by means of the statistical balance of nuclear weapons, revealing that the United States possessed at that point in time 1,710 intercontinental ballistic missiles (ICBMs), of which 656 were Polaris missiles in submarines. All these missiles could be fired at targets inside the Soviet Union. The Soviet Union, by contrast, could place no more than five hundred ICBMs above the United States. If the Russians were to carry out a first strike without warning, the Pentagon estimated that nine-tenths of the American missiles that were based on land could survive, and be used against the Soviet Union in a matter of hours.

A further Pentagon announcement on December 14 gave details of a space vehicle which was being developed in the United States, which had the capacity to carry nuclear bombs. Harnessing the knowledge gained during the continuing space research to land a man on the Moon, it could re-enter the Earth's orbit with its bombs and fire them on terrestrial targets anywhere in the Soviet Union, including those few areas that were beyond the range of sea-based Polaris missiles. The new delivery system was known as the Multiple Independent Re-entry Vehicle (MIRV).

ABM, ICBM, FOBS, MIRV: these were the shorthand notations of weapons of mass destruction. How far they could serve as a deterrent to any destruction at all was a matter of theory. Fourteen years earlier, Churchill had expressed his views about the nuclear deterrent. 'These fearful scientific discoveries cast their shadow on every thoughtful mind,' he told the House of Commons,

> but nevertheless I believe that we are justified in feeling that there has been a diminution of tension and that the probabilities of another world war have diminished, or at least have become more remote. I say this in spite of the continual growth of weapons of destruction such as have never fallen before into the hands of human beings. Indeed, I have sometimes the odd thought that the annihilating character of these agencies may bring an utterly unforeseeable security to mankind.

In the field of medicine, the use of laser beams for surgery was entering into common practice. The laser beam had the power to destroy diseased tissue. The first international conference on the application of lasers to medicine was held in Paris in July. Those present learned that, although much of the work was still in the experimental stage, an operating theatre equipped for laser surgery had opened in the United States, at Cincinnati, Ohio. There, the repairing of torn retinas by laser surgery had become a routine operation. A wide range of other uses of laser surgery included the elimination of blockages in blood vessels in the eye, and bone and other surgery where the use of a knife was impossible or dangerous.

Another milestone in medicine was reached on December 3, when a South African surgeon, Dr Christiaan Barnard, carried out the first heart-transplant operation. His patient, Louis Washkansky, survived for eighteen days. In Cleveland, Ohio, an American surgeon, René Favaloro, was developing the coronary bypass operation. That same year, a new technique, mammography – using X-rays – was introduced for the detection of breast cancer. In Britain, in an attempt to reduce the number of road deaths as a result of drinking and driving, the Road Safety Act introduced breath tests; the first ones were conducted on October 10.

In space, the successes of previous years were overshadowed by the first accidental deaths. On January 27 three American astronauts were killed in their Apollo space capsule while it was still on the ground. Within three months, on April 24, a Soviet astronaut, Colonel Vladimir Komarov, who had been successfully launched into space, was killed when the parachute on his spacecraft failed, and he was hurled to Earth. But the imperative of space research, with its military benefits and civilian by-products understood by both contenders, was uninterrupted by these two human disasters. On April 19 an unmanned American lunar probe, *Surveyor 3*, made a soft landing on the Moon, sent back photographs of the Moon's surface, and dug a trench with a mechanical shovel in order to obtain and analyse small rock and dust samples: an essential prerequisite for a manned lunar landing.

The result of the landing of *Surveyor 3* and its experiment was to confirm that the surface of the Moon was safe to land on. The probe had also managed to set down on the Moon's surface with less of a jolt than that felt by a man making a good parachute landing on Earth. The next American experiment – and it was becoming clear that the United States was ahead in the Moon-landing race – was the firing of by far the most powerful rocket ever launched, *Saturn 5*, which at more than three thousand tons weighed as much as a navy destroyer, and on top of which sat the first, unmanned, Apollo space capsule to be sent into orbit. As part of the experiment, the space capsule re-entered the Earth's atmosphere – at 25,000 miles an hour – and then parachuted safely down into the Pacific. Weighing forty-five tons, it was four times heavier than any previous American or Russian space satellite.

As the Americans prepared to carry out a manned Moon landing within the coming two years, they also made available their technology to enable both Australia and Britain to send unmanned satellites into space. Among the instruments on board the British satellite, which was launched from California, was one that could send back information about thunderstorms worldwide. Within the United States, these remarkable space achievements were almost overshadowed at times by news of continuing race riots. In July, rioting and looting broke out in a dozen cities, most ferociously in Detroit, Michigan, and Newark, New Jersey, accelerating the 'flight' of White residents from their homes in the city centres to the suburbs or neighbouring towns. That Black grievances were real was underlined by the report of the Commission on Civil Rights, which Johnson had set up, and which came to the conclusion that racial integration in schools should be speeded up in order to 'reverse' the underachievement of Black children.

In the United States and Europe an era of youthful experimentation and protest was in full swing. In Britain, the first national pop music station was started. As part of the 'Hippie era', the Greyhound Bus company in the United States was offering a 'Hippie Hop' tour of San Francisco. Among the youth, that summer was designated the 'Summer of Love'. With the Vietnam War raging, tens of thousands of young people took to the streets in protest.

In New York, starting on December 5, there were daily marches against the war as part of the 'Stop the Draft Week'. The aim of the marches was to disrupt recruitment at the United States Army recruitment centre in Whitehall Street, at the southern tip of Manhattan. There were also demonstrations outside the United Nations building in New York, where a young man of twenty, Kenneth d'Elia, burned himself to death, 'the sixth self-immolator in the United States during the past two years, and the second to choose his spot outside the United Nations', reported Innis MacBeath to *The Times*.

On December 6, as the New York anti-draft demonstrations continued, they were paralleled in Philadelphia and Buffalo, followed on December 7 by others in Cincinnati and San Francisco. Protesters also marched in Iowa City against the Dow Chemical Company, the manufacturers of napalm. Speaking in the Senate on December 8, Senator Fulbright called the war 'an immoral and unnecessary war' which had 'isolated the United States from its friends abroad, disrupting our domestic affairs and dividing the American people as no other issue of the twentieth century has divided them'. Fulbright added that the United States was 'using its B-52s, its napalm, and all those other ingenious weapons of counter-insurgency to turn a small country into a charnel house'.

As more demonstrations took place each day across the United States, Stop the Draft Week was followed by Peace Week. The child expert and bestselling author Benjamin Spock, who was Chairman of the National Committee Against the War, defended the rowdiness of the demonstrations with the words: 'If we are going to save the world, I don't think we can be particular and have only polite people demonstrating.' As the daily protests continued into their second week, Senator Eugene McCarthy of Minnesota announced that he would stand as an anti-war candidate in the next year's presidential elections. His decision was praised by Robert Kennedy. A mass movement was gaining senior figures in its support. In his second speech in the Senate in one week, Senator Fulbright declared, on December 13, that:

> Industrialists, businessmen, workers and politicians have joined together in a military-industrial complex – a complex which, for all the inadvertency of its creation and the innocent intentions of its participants, has none the less become a powerful new force for the perpetuation of foreign commitments, for the introduction and expansion of expensive weapons systems, and, as a result, for the militarization of large segments of our national life.

Fulbright also spoke that day of America's thirty-two million 'dispossessed children . . . sacrificed to the requirements of the war on Asian Communism'.

CHAPTER SEVENTEEN

1968

... to negotiate, not as victors, but as an honorable
people who lived up to their pledge to defend democracy,
and did the best they could.

WALTER CRONKITE

O<small>N</small> 21 JANUARY 1968 the North Vietnamese made a concerted attack
on the American marine base at Khe Sanh, near the Laotian border, and
against the Demilitarized Zone. General Westmoreland contemplated a
counter-attack against North Vietnam, but had insufficient manpower for
such a major undertaking, about which, in addition, Johnson was uneasy.
Westmoreland reinforced the marines at Khe Sanh, and used powerful B-52
bombers to pulverize the attackers' positions.

Two days after the start of the Khe Sanh attack, the Vietnamese conflict
was briefly eclipsed by an echo of the Korean War. On January 23 North
Korean naval forces captured a United States naval Intelligence ship, *Pueblo*.
The ship had been carrying out its surveillance work outside Korean territorial waters, about fifteen miles offshore in the area of Wonsan. The seizure
of the ship created indignation in Washington. A nuclear-powered aircraft
carrier, *Enterprise*, was ordered to the area, and on Johnson's express orders
14,600 American reservists were called up.

One crew member of the *Pueblo* had been killed in the incident. The North
Koreans announced that they would try the rest of the crew – eighty-two men
in all – as war criminals. In response, the United States warned that any
such action would be considered 'a deliberate aggravation of an already
serious situation'. Despite repeated protests, and prolonged negotiations at
Panmunjom, the North Koreans kept the crew and subjected them to severe
beatings. In order to be released, an officer from the ship had to sign a
document stating – which was false – that the *Pueblo* had been within North

Korean territorial waters. Only when he had signed were the crew released, at the very end of the year.

Even as the diplomatic storm over the *Pueblo* rumbled, a military storm of tremendous intensity was about to break over South Vietnam, where the number of American troops remained above half a million – and the American death toll had reached 16,000. Despite a warning by the Central Intelligence Agency that a North Vietnamese attack was imminent during the Tet (lunar New Year) holiday period that was to begin on January 27, that military storm was not countered. Indeed, with secret negotiations having begun through a Roumanian diplomatic intermediary between the United States and North Vietnam, the Americans gave the South Vietnamese permission for a fifty per cent reduction in their troop strength during Tet – a politically beguiling 'holiday leave'.

Hanoi had proclaimed a truce for the whole seven-day period of Tet. The truce was a skilful act of public deception. Three days into the holiday, on the night of January 30/31, an estimated 70,000 Vietcong troops attacked the American and South Vietnamese forces throughout South Vietnam. The attack gave the Vietcong an initiative which sent the United States reeling. Twenty-four major battles erupted within a few hours. Against Saigon, four thousand Vietcong struck the centre of the city, penetrating the American Embassy. For six-and-a-half hours the battle for the Embassy was seen on television screens throughout the United States. An estimated fifty million Americans watched the chaos and confusion of battle as it took place in the South Vietnamese capital at the very centre of American influence and authority. In the words of Stanley Karnow: 'There, on colour screens, dead bodies lay amid the rubble and rattle of automatic gunfire as dazed American soldiers and civilians ran back and forth trying to flush out the assailants.'

The Vietcong assault on Saigon, during which they also seized the radio station, and attacked both the South Vietnamese General Staff headquarters and General Westmoreland's headquarters at Saigon airport, produced astounding images for the American television viewers. The vulnerability of Saigon was clear, as was the audacity of the Vietcong, and the chaotic nature of the American and South Vietnamese response. Within twenty-four hours, American military authority had been restored in the capital, and almost all the Vietcong attackers killed. But on February 1 an incident took place that was to disturb even more Americans, as they watched it on television or studied it in their newspapers. The man who had harshly crushed the Buddhist insurrection in Hué two years earlier, Nguyen Ngoc Loan, made chief of

the South Vietnam police since then, and promoted general, had lost several
of his men during the Vietcong attack on Saigon, including one who was
shot down in his house together with his wife and children. 'That morning,'
wrote Stanley Karnow, the Associated Press photographer Eddie Adams, and
the Vietnamese cameraman employed by the American National Broadcasting Company who was with him, saw a patrol of South Vietnamese troops
'with a captive in tow'. Karnow's account continued:

> The soldiers marched him up to Loan, who drew his revolver and waved
> the bystanders away. Without hesitation, Loan stretched out his right arm,
> placed the short snout of the weapon against the prisoner's head, and
> squeezed the trigger. The man grimaced – then, almost in slow motion,
> his legs crumpled beneath him as he seemed to sit down backward, blood
> gushing from his head as he hit the pavement.
>
> Not a word was spoken. It all happened instantly, with hardly a sound
> except for the crack of Loan's gun, and the click of Adam's shutter, and
> the whir of Vo Suu's camera.

The next morning every American newspaper reproduced the photograph
of the execution. In the evening the NBC broadcast its 'exclusive' film. It
was edited slightly, Karnow wrote, 'to spare television viewers the spout of
blood bursting from the prisoner's head'. But it made an enormous and
shocking impression, casting a dark shadow on how the South Vietnamese
authorities were regarded by the American public.

In Hué, the Vietcong overran the city and carried out massive reprisals
against those who had supported the South Vietnamese authorities. These
were not recorded by a cameraman or film-maker with instant access to the
television screens of the United States. As many as three thousand people
were murdered. Among those killed was a German physician and his wife,
and two other German doctors. Two French Benedictine missionaries were
also killed: one shot and the other buried alive. In the fighting to recapture
Hué, 150 American marines and 400 South Vietnamese soldiers were killed,
and an estimated five thousand Vietcong. After the Vietcong had been driven
out, South Vietnamese soldiers carried out reprisals of their own. The bodies
of many of those whom they killed were thrown into the same mass graves
as those whom the Vietcong had killed.

Among the American soldiers who witnessed the Tet offensive was Tobias

Wolff, who, on the outskirts of the village of My Tho, which the Vietcong had overrun, saw the American air retaliation:

> For the next couple of days we plastered the town. Their run into My Tho took them right over our compound, sometimes low enough that we could see the rivets on their skin. Such American machines, so boss-looking, so technical, so loud. *Phantoms*. When they slowed overhead to lock into formation the roar of their engines made speech impossible.
>
> Down here I was in a deranged and malignant land, but when I raised my eyes to those planes I could see home. They dove screaming on the town, then pulled out and banked around and did it again. Their bombs sent tremors pulsing up through our legs. When they used up all their bombs they flew off to get more. Flames gleamed on the underside of the pall of smoke that overhung My Tho, and the smell of putrefaction soured the breeze, and still we served the guns, dropping rings of ruination around every frightened man with a radio transmitter.
>
> None of this gave me pause. Only when we finally took the town back, when the last sniper had been blasted off his rooftop, did I see what we had done, we and the VC together. The place was a wreck, still smouldering two weeks later, still reeking sweetly of corpses. The corpses were everywhere, lying in the streets, floating in the reservoir, buried and half buried in collapsed buildings, grinning, blackened, fat with gas, limbs missing or oddly bent, some headless, some burned almost to the bone, the smell so thick and foul we had to wear surgical masks scented with cologne, aftershave, deodorant, whatever we had, simply to move through town. Hundreds of corpses and the count kept rising.
>
> Gangs of diggers sifted through the rubble, looking for survivors. They found some, but mostly they found more corpses. These they rolled up in tatami mats and left by the roadside for pickup. One day I passed a line of them that went on for almost a block, all children, their bare feet protruding from the ends of the mats. My driver told me that we'd bombed a school building where they had been herded together to learn revolutionary history and songs.
>
> I didn't believe it. It sounded like one of those stories that always make the rounds afterward. But it could have been true.

In the Tet offensive and during the month following it, as the last of the Vietcong were rounded up and the captured towns returned to South

Vietnamese rule, two thousand Americans and four thousand South Vietnamese soldiers were killed. As many as 50,000 Vietcong were killed. In March, in the village of My Lai, an American army unit perpetrated a massacre in which a hundred South Vietnamese peasants, women and children among them, were killed. Three Americans in a helicopter chanced upon the scene as the killings were taking place. One of them, Glenn Andreotta, was killed in action three weeks later. The other two were Hugh Thompson and Lawrence Colburn. Twenty-four-year-old Thompson was a helicopter pilot whose mission was to draw enemy fire. Colburn and Andreotta were his crew.

Thirty years later Thompson recalled how, from the helicopter, he and his two companions heard shooting. Flying low, they saw piles of bodies in a ditch. The dead were not soldiers. 'Every time we made a pass there were more bodies. I saw one incident where an American just walked up to a woman and blew her away.' From the helicopter, the three men saw a group of about a dozen Vietnamese – women and children – cowering in a bunker. Thompson put the helicopter down between the Vietnamese and a squad of advancing Americans, drew his gun, and asked one of the Americans, a lieutenant, if the helicopter could evacuate the civilians. 'With a hand grenade,' was the lieutenant's reply.

Thompson then called in another helicopter to help rescue the civilians. While the Vietnamese were hauled on board, Thompson, Colburn and Andreotta drew their weapons in case their fellow Americans started shooting. Those dozen Vietnamese were saved, by the courage of three men. Two men, Lieutenant William Calley and Sergeant David Mitchell, were indicted for the massacre.

American policy in Vietnam was the subject of growing protests – by students, by those who had fought in the war, and by public men. Senator Albert Gore (father of a future Vice-President, Al Gore), who was in his sixteenth year in the Senate, made a number of public appeals during January and February, urging Johnson to get out of 'the morass in Vietnam', and telling a student audience at the University of Idaho, in Moscow, Idaho: 'We are destroying the country we profess to be saving.'

Respected voices had begun to talk of diplomatic negotiations rather than military victory. On February 27 the broadcaster Walter Cronkite, who had just returned to New York from a visit to Vietnam, broadcast over the CBS Television Network. His presentation made a considerable impact on those who had begun to question whether war could in fact go on until the

North Vietnamese and the Vietcong were defeated. 'We have been too often disappointed by the optimism of the American leaders, both in Vietnam and Washington, to have faith any longer in the silver linings they find in the darkest clouds,' Cronkite said.

In Cronkite's view, those American leaders who insisted that Hanoi's 'winter-spring offensive' had been forced on the North Vietnamese 'by their realization that they could not win the longer war of attrition' – and by their hope that any success in the offensive would improve their position for eventual negotiations – might be right. The offensive would indeed improve the North Vietnamese position with regard to negotiations, Cronkite reflected, 'and it would also require our realization, that we should have had all along, that any negotiations must be that – negotiations, not the dictation of peace terms. For it seems now more certain than ever that the bloody experience of Vietnam is to end in a stalemate.'

Fighting would go on. The 'almost certain standoff' in the coming summer would end, Cronkite warned, either 'in real give-and-take negotiations or terrible escalation'. For every means that the United States had to escalate the war 'the enemy can match us, and that applies to invasion of the North, the use of nuclear weapons, or the mere commitment of one hundred, or two hundred, or three hundred thousand more American troops to the battle'. With each escalation, 'the world comes closer to the brink of cosmic disaster'.

These were stern words, but they matched in thoughtful analysis Cronkite's equally thoughtful conclusion – 'realistic, yet unsatisfactory' as he described it – which made a strong impact on his listeners. 'To say that we are closer to victory today', he reflected, 'is to believe, in the face of the evidence, the optimists who have been wrong in the past. To suggest we are on the edge of defeat is to yield to unreasonable pessimism. To say that we are mired in stalemate seems the only realistic, yet unsatisfactory, conclusion.' That conclusion was that – 'on the off chance that military and political analysts are right' – in the next few months the United States 'must test the enemy's intentions, in case this is indeed his last big gasp before negotiations'. But, Cronkite added, 'it is increasingly clear to this reporter that the only rational way out then will be to negotiate, not as victors, but as an honorable people who lived up to their pledge to defend democracy, and did the best they could'.

These words took the edge off any remaining triumphalism about the war: 'to negotiate, not as victors, but as an honorable people who lived up to their pledge to defend democracy, and did the best they could'. It was hardly a war's heroic end as in 1918 or 1945, but it was a way forward, a way out.

The Vietnam War had become the central issue of student protest throughout the United States. There were also student protests in other countries. One such student demonstration was held in London on March 17, outside the American Embassy in Grosvenor Square. German and French student leaders were among those who took part. The police, many of them on horseback, reacted with vigour, and were accused by the students of using excessive force.

Opposition to the war in Vietnam was an important part of the student agenda, but not the only part. In France the demonstrations, culminating in the May Events which brought the centre of Paris to a standstill, were rather more against high French government expenditure on nuclear weapons in contrast to low expenditure on education. One of the leaders of the protest, Daniel Cohn-Bendit – known as Red Danny because of his politics and the colour of his beard – repeatedly denounced the 'fascist repression' of the Sorbonne University authorities, one of whose crimes was to have expelled students who had protested at a lecturer having chosen 'imperialism' as his topic.

Reporting in *The Times* on the pitched battles between police and students on May 6, the second such confrontation in three days, Edward Mortimer wrote: 'Often it came to vicious hand-to-hand fighting, the police charging forward suddenly and laying about them wildly with wooden truncheons.' Eight thousand students took part in the protest, a small number of them wielding iron bars, pick-axe handles and hatchets. More than two hundred students were arrested. No one was killed. The protests were not confined to the streets. At a luncheon in the White House, the Black singer Eartha Kitt told Johnson's wife Lady Bird: 'You send the best of this country off to be shot and maimed. No wonder the kids rebel and take pot.'

American policy in Vietnam was changing. On March 12, five days before the Grosvenor Square demonstration, Senator Eugene McCarthy, challenging President Johnson for the Democratic nomination in the New Hampshire primary, and standing on an anti-Vietnam War ticket, won forty-two per cent of the vote. Though this could not secure him the victory, it was a large enough percentage of the poll to worry Johnson considerably. McCarthy had secured only three hundred fewer votes than the President. The pro-Johnson camp's innuendo against McCarthy in its advertisements – 'The Communists in Vietnam are watching the New Hampshire primary' – had failed to help Johnson win by a decisive margin.

Three days after the New Hampshire result was announced, Senator Robert Kennedy declared his candidature. He too was a critic of Johnson's Vietnam policy: indeed, he had offered not to put his name forward for the presidency if Johnson agreed to 're-evaluate' America's role in Vietnam. Johnson declined to do so, declaring in a public speech on March 17; 'We shall and we are going to win,' and on the following day, 'The time has come when we ought to stand up and be counted, when we ought to support our leaders, our government, our men, and our allies, until aggression is stopped, wherever it has occurred.'

Faced with Johnson's reiterated determination not to 're-evaluate' but to continue the war, Robert Kennedy began his campaign for the Democratic nomination, in opposition to Johnson. Then, on March 31, the Democratic Party was shocked, and the whole nation surprised, when Johnson announced that he would not run for another presidential term. He made his announcement at the end of a television broadcast in which he first announced a partial suspension of the bombing of North Vietnam. Johnson had been much influenced in the decision to curb the bombing by Clark Clifford, his Attorney-General, who had been confirmed in the job on the first day of the Tet offensive. Clifford, who twenty years earlier had helped fashion both the Marshall Plan and the Truman Doctrine, was convinced after the Tet offensive that the United States had to extricate itself from 'an unwinnable war'.

Under the plan announced by Johnson on March 31, American bombing would take place only below the 20th parallel, the area of North Vietnam nearest to the South Vietnam border. Ninety per cent of North Vietnamese territory would be excluded from attack. In secret, Johnson authorized negotiations with the North Vietnamese: the very 're-evaluation' that Robert Kennedy had called for.

Johnson's decision to leave the presidency was not primarily because of Vietnam. He had contemplated announcing his resignation in his State of the Union message at the beginning of the year, before the setbacks of the Tet offensive, and before the McCarthy-Kennedy challenge. His worry, like that of Harold Wilson in Britain six years later, was that ill-health might drive him from office or, in Johnson's case – since he had suffered a severe heart attack in 1955 – kill him in office.

Senators McCarthy and Kennedy battled it out for the Democratic nomination. On May 7, the first time they were both on the ballot paper, Kennedy defeated McCarthy by forty-two per cent to thirty per cent of the votes cast. In Nebraska, Kennedy did even better, polling fifty-two per cent against McCarthy's thirty-one per cent. On May 28 McCarthy won by a five per cent majority over Kennedy. California was the next battle, and a key one. Polling took place on June 4. Kennedy was victorious, by forty-six per cent to forty-two. As he celebrated his California victory he learned that he had won the South Dakota primary by an even larger margin, fifty per cent to thirty per cent. Confident of securing the Democratic nomination, and through it the presidency – which fifty-four months earlier had been held by his assassinated brother, Robert Kennedy told an enthusiastic crowd of his supporters at a celebratory gathering in the Ambassador Hotel, Los Angeles, on June 5, that he was confident that the divisions in the country, whether over race or over Vietnam, could be ended. 'We can start work together. We are a great country. I intend to make that my basis for running.' Then, heading for a room where a press conference was to be held, and taking a short cut through the hotel kitchens to avoid the crowds, he was shot in the head and neck at a range of four feet. On the following day he died. He was forty-two years old, four years younger than his brother had been at the time of the Dallas assassination. Robert Kennedy's assassin, a Palestinian Arab, was arrested, tried and imprisoned for life. Thirty years later he was still in jail.

The first face-to-face talks between the Americans and the North Vietnamese began, in Paris, on May 10. The Tet offensive, dramatic though it had been in confronting the Americans with danger in their midst, had been driven off, leaving the Vietcong seriously mauled. It seemed as if the North Vietnamese might be willing to recognize the independence of South Vietnam. The American negotiators were confident of reaching agreement within a matter of months. But the North Vietnamese had no intention of abandoning their long-term aim of complete control of the whole country. The negotiations dragged on inconclusively. The war, and with it the American bombing of North Vietnam, continued. On June 10 it was announced that the total American combat deaths since the start of the war was more than 25,000.

Inside the United States the scale and intensity of anti-war demonstrations were growing. One of them was held in Chicago at the time of the Democratic

Party's national convention, when Johnson's Vice-President, Hubert Humphrey, was chosen as the Democratic candidate for the presidency. The convention began on August 26. Each night there were protests outside the convention centre. There were many delegates inside the centre who shared the anti-war sentiments of the demonstrators outside. The police and demonstrators clashed, and the television cameramen who had gathered to cover the convention were able to transmit graphic pictures around the world of armed and helmeted American police in action, and of anti-war demonstrators being beaten and chased.

On November 1 the American bombing of North Vietnam was halted. Four days later the voters of the United States elected the Republican challenger, Richard Nixon, as President. In terms of the number of electors on each side the voting was incredibly close: 31,770,237 for Nixon and 31,270,533 for Humphrey. The former Governor of Alabama, George Wallace, who was also standing, secured almost ten million votes. In the electoral college, Nixon emerged the clear victor, receiving 302 votes against Humphrey's 191 and Wallace's 45. It was Nixon on whom the responsibility and burden of Vietnam had devolved. In public he was emphatic: 'I will not be the first President of the United States to lose a war.' But in his National Security Advisor, Henry Kissinger – a pre-war refugee from Nazi Germany – he had a man who was to prove, when called upon, a consummate negotiator, and to whom Johnson had already turned during the short periods when negotiations had earlier been embarked upon.

In Eastern Europe, the Communist world was in varying degrees of turmoil. In Poland an upsurge in anti-Semitism bewildered the 25,000 Polish Jews who were the sole survivors still living in that country of the once substantial Jewish community of three million, the victims of Nazi mass murder a quarter of a century earlier. There was much hidden resentment at the part played by a small number of individual Jews in the imposition of Communism in Poland after the war. There was also State-sponsored anti-Jewish feeling following Israel's victory over Egypt, Syria and Jordan a year earlier: the Polish government had been emphatically on the Arab side. The Jews as a group – some of them having been extremely heartened at Israel's victory – were accused of 'narrow-minded nationalism'. Many thousands were forced to leave their jobs in government, the universities and industry. Many Jewish institutions were closed down. More than 14,000 Jews left the country – allowed to do so by hostile administrators who were glad to see the back of them.

In the Soviet Union there was an upsurge of enthusiasm at Israel's victory among the two to three million Jews. This led to similar antagonism as in Poland, but a refusal to allow more than the tiniest amount of emigration. Hundreds and then thousands of Jews applied to leave and were refused permission to do so. Jews in the West championed the cause of those who wanted to leave. There were protest marches, and appeals to the Soviet authorities to 'let my people go'. A new word was coined, 'refusenik', for any Jew whose request to leave was rejected. Individual Jews were brought to trial and sent to prison and labour camp for publicly demanding the right to leave.

An apparently peaceful revolution was under way in Czechoslovakia. In January the First Secretary of the Czech Communist Party, Antonin Novotny – who had held office for more than fourteen years – was voted out by the Party. His successor was Alexander Dubček. As President, the Party elected General Ludvik Svoboda, a Czech soldier who as a young man had been decorated by the Tsarist army, and who had later led the Czechoslovak Army Corps – a fighting element of the Soviet army – which entered Brno and Prague in 1945: hence his reputation as 'Svoboda the Liberator'.

The censorship of books, magazines and newspapers was all but abolished. Greater freedom of speech was allowed on radio and television than existed anywhere else in the Soviet bloc. What was called by the Czechs a 'Socialist democratic revolution' was under way. Dubček called it 'Socialism with a human face'. The writer Jan Beneš, who the previous year had been sentenced to five years in prison, was pardoned and set free: he emigrated to the United States, where he taught Czech literature at Harvard. The rehabilitation was begun of 50,000 Czech victims of Stalinism, including those who had fought on the republican side in the International Brigade during the Spanish Civil War. It was suggested that the death of Jan Masaryk in 1948 had not been suicide, but political murder.

More than eleven years had passed since the Soviet Union had crushed the Hungarian revolution. Khrushchev was no longer ruler of the Soviet Union or keeper of the Communist conscience. But his successors were no less determined to maintain the uniformity and loyalty of the Communist bloc. On March 23, Dubček was summoned to an emergency meeting of the Warsaw Pact in Dresden, where, after secret talks with the Soviet representatives, he expressed, in the words of several Soviet newspapers, 'certain apprehensions' lest anti-Soviet elements 'take advantage of our process of democratization'. Within a month the Soviet newspapers were attacking those 'elements' – the word Czechoslovakia did not appear – who sought to curb the absolute power of the Communist Party, or to place 'nationalist above internationalist interests'. But during the Dresden meeting, Dubček had been emphatic that 'responsibility for our internal development rests first and foremost with the Czechoslovak Communist Party'.

The ferment inside Czechoslovakia continued. Among the events that angered the Soviet leadership was the formation in Prague of a Club of Committed Non-Party People. On April 5 the Czech Communist Party gave such developments its support by announcing, in its Action Programme, that Socialism could not be built up without 'an open exchange of views and democratization of the entire social and political system'. The Action Programme was wide-ranging and hostile to many basic tenets of Communism: newspaper censorship would be abolished, freedom of assembly would be assured, the right to travel outside Czechoslovakia – to the Communist East or to the capitalist West – would be guaranteed. Public opinion polls must be held, and listened to.

In early May, Dubček was summoned to Moscow. He was followed shortly afterwards by the heads of the Polish, Hungarian, East German and Bulgarian Communist Parties. At the same time 25,000 Soviet troops, ostensibly on Warsaw Pact manoeuvres, took up positions in southern Poland, along the Czech border. On May 17, Kosygin flew to Prague. The pressure on Czechoslovakia mounted. On May 24 it was announced that 'joint command staff exercises', in which Soviet troops were to take part, would be held in June on Czechoslovak and Polish soil.

Starting in mid-June, *Pravda* began attacking individual Czechoslovak Communist Party members by name, denouncing them as 'revisionists'. The Czech government, determined not to give in to pressure, refused a Soviet request to participate in an emergency meeting of Soviet and Eastern European Communist Party leaders in Warsaw. To the anger of the Soviet leadership, both Tito and Ceauşescu flew to Prague to offer the Czech leaders their support. Tito told the Czechs that he could not believe that there existed in the Soviet Union 'people so short-sighted as to resort to a policy of force to resolve Czechoslovakia's internal questions'. Ceauşescu warned that nothing in the Warsaw Pact justified 'interference in the internal affairs of other States'.

In early July the Soviet Union refused to withdraw from Czech soil those Soviet army units that had taken part in the summer joint manoeuvres. An ominous note was struck in *Pravda* on July 11, when it condemned the 'counter-revolutionary forces' in Czechoslovakia and declared that they were more 'treacherous' than those of the Hungarian anti-Communists in 1956. In Prague, the attack in *Pravda* was seen as a warning from the highest level of Soviet power. It was followed three days later by a letter from the Soviet and East European leaders calling on the Czech government to suppress the 'anti-Socialist forces'.

When *Pravda* announced on July 19 that American arms, sent from Western Germany, had been found in Czechoslovakia, exposing 'the perfidious plans of American imperialism and West German revanchism', it seemed a clear attempt to offer a cause for Soviet intervention. That same day the Soviet government informed the Czechs that the western frontier of Czechoslovakia was 'insufficiently protected' against the West, and insisted that Soviet troops should be stationed there.

Dubček and his colleagues were not trying to create a Hungarian-style situation, whereby Hungary turned its back on the Warsaw Pact and effectively pulled itself out of the Soviet system. The Czech aim, from within the Communist Party, was to find a less coercive form of Communism. This was anathema to Moscow. On July 29 the Soviet leaders summoned the whole Czech Praesidium to a meeting at Cierna-nad-Tisou, a Slovak village on Czechoslovakia's eastern frontier with the Soviet Union. In the streets of Prague and other Czech cities, tens of thousands of Czechs signed a petition to their leaders: 'You are writing a fateful page of the history of Czechoslovakia. Write with deliberation, but, above all, with courage. We trust you.' After four days of talks, the Soviets agreed to allow the Czechs their own 'road to Socialism'. For their part the Czechs gave the Soviet Union assurances of 'Socialist solidarity'.

Following the Cierna meeting, on August 3 the Czech leaders met with the Soviet and Eastern European leaders in Bratislava. As a result of the meeting a communiqué was issued in which Czechoslovakia was accorded the right to pursue its 'internal reforms' in return for adhering to its obligations under the Warsaw Pact. On August 5, *Pravda* called the Bratislava Declaration 'a crushing blow to the plans of the imperialists'. But the pressure inside Czechoslovakia to continue the liberalization process was continuous. The Soviet Union was not pleased when first Tito, on August 9, and then Ceauşescu on the following day visited Prague to express, for the second time, their support of the Czech stance. On August 16, as Czech newspapers became more and more outspoken in their demands for a more liberal form of Communism, *Pravda* warned that the Czech leadership still had the obligation to 'introduce elementary order' into the Czech life, and to curb newspaper excesses.

The *Pravda* warning was followed four days later, on the night of August 20/21, by what Dubček and his colleagues had feared most when they sought to put a liberal face on the Communist monolith; and what they hoped they had averted by the agreements reached at Cierna and Bratislava. That night Soviet troops crossed the Soviet-Czech border, and airborne troops were landed at the principal Warsaw Pact air bases inside Czechoslovakia. Also crossing the land border were troops from three of Czechoslovakia's Communist neighbours – Poland, Hungary and Eastern Germany – as well as from distant Bulgaria: in all, half a million men. The Soviet tank commander, General Ivan Yershov, was the Deputy Chief of Staff to the Supreme Commander of the Warsaw Pact.

The principal Czech cities were quickly occupied by predominantly Soviet forces: the tanks that twelve years earlier had filled the streets of Budapest. The Czech government confined its own troops to their barracks, and forbade any armed resistance: just as, in March 1939, there had been no resistance when the German tanks moved in. Czech students no older than the soldiers manning the tanks swarmed into the streets and argued with the soldiers, demanding that they leave. The Soviet leaders gave their own explanation for the occupation: according to a Soviet press statement, 'Party and Government leaders of the Czechoslovak Socialist Republic have asked the Soviet Union and other allied States to render the fraternal Czechoslovak people urgent assistance.'

On August 21, Soviet troops arrested Dubček and most of the Czechoslovak Communist Party leadership. There were clashes in the streets between angry civilian demonstrators and Soviet troops. Many tanks were stoned and some were set on fire. In the confrontations in the streets about eighty Czech civilians were killed. On the following day a Soviet ultimatum demanded the formation of a government from which all Dubček's supporters would be excluded, or military rule would be imposed. In *Pravda* the ultimatum was explained on the grounds that Dubček had sought a 'counter-revolution' aimed at sabotaging the Cierna and Bratislava agreements. On August 23 there was a one-hour general strike in Prague against the occupation and the Soviet demands. That day, the Czechoslovak President, General Svoboda, was flown to Moscow. As he began negotiations in the Kremlin with the Soviet leaders, Dubček and the other Czech Communist leaders arrested with him two days earlier were brought into the meeting.

As the Moscow talks continued, there were half a million foreign troops on Czech soil, and five hundred Soviet tanks patrolled the streets of Prague, which was under curfew. Despite the curfew, however, thousands of young people held a sit-down protest in the main squares. A secret Communist Party congress was held in a Prague factory, and elected a new Central Committee, headed by the absent Dubček. When the Kremlin talks were over Dubček and his colleagues returned to Prague, exhausted and humiliated. His government had given in to all the Soviet demands. On August 28 a mass of young people demonstrated in Wenceslas Square. There was no fighting, and the Soviet conditions were met. In order to ensure this, a Soviet Deputy Foreign Minister, Vasily Kuznetsov, flew to Prague on September 6 and remained there supervising what was called 'normalization'. The Club of Committed Non-Party People was closed down. Anti-Soviet slogans were removed from all buildings. Press and book censorship was reintroduced. 'The sovereignty of each Socialist country', *Pravda* explained on September 26, 'cannot be set up in opposition to the interests of the Socialist world and the interests of the world revolutionary movement.'

On October 16 the Czech government, headed by men loyal to Moscow, or conscious of the power of Moscow to reimpose whatever control it wished, signed a treaty permitting the 'temporary' stationing of Warsaw Pact troops, including Soviet troops, on Czechoslovak soil. They were to remain there, in the words of the treaty, to 'ensure the security of Socialist countries against the increased revanchist strivings of the West German militarists'. In November, at a Polish Communist Party congress, Brezhnev explained the intervention in Czechoslovakia in terms of a doctrinal imperative. 'When internal and external forces that are hostile to Socialism try to turn the development of some Socialist country towards the restoration of a capitalist regime, when Socialism in that country and the Socialist community as a whole are threatened,' he said, 'it becomes not only a problem of the people of the country concerned, but a common problem and concern for all Socialist countries.'

In Moscow, a small demonstration against the Soviet invasion of Czechoslovakia had taken place in Red Square on August 25. The two leaders of the demonstration, Pavel Litvinov – a nephew of Stalin's Foreign Minister, Maxim Litvinov – and Larisa Daniel, both of whom had protested earlier in the year on behalf of several other imprisoned Soviet writers, were brought to trial in October charged with violating public order and slandering the

Soviet State. No Western correspondents were allowed in the courtroom. Litvinov was sentenced to five years' exile and Larisa Daniel to four. A petition for leniency signed by ninety-five intellectuals from around the world, including many Communists, was ignored.

In Czechoslovakia there were anti-Soviet demonstrations in Prague and several other cities at the end of October and in early November. 'Certain quarters of the public', warned *Izvestiya*, one of the voices of the Soviet regime, were still 'under the influence of yesterday'. Dissent inside Czechoslovakia was to be harshly curbed, and clandestine efforts to maintain a liberal outlook stamped on with vigour. But the will to emerge in due course – somehow – from the Soviet orbit was strong, and in many secret circles, some of which maintained a courageous contact with the West, that will was sustained and enhanced.

Western perceptions of the physical threat from the Soviet Union were heightened on September 28, when the British Prime Minister, Harold Wilson, was informed that at least sixty-two of the eighty Soviet diplomats then stationed in London were known to be spies. This fact was set against the knowledge that the Soviet atomic weapons then targeted at Britain had, as Wilson was told by his defence experts, 20,000 times the capacity of the atom bomb dropped on Hiroshima twenty-three years earlier. Targets included the government's Ministry of Defence buildings in London, and the Signals Intelligence centre at Cheltenham, as well as Bomber Command headquarters at High Wycombe, and the headquarters of the 3rd United States Air Force at Ruislip.

In the United States, with Vietnam dominating so much newspaper and television coverage, the racial dissension that Johnson had hoped to curb with his civil rights legislation was rising. On February 8, three Black students were killed in Orangeburg, South Carolina, after they had attempted to play at a bowling alley which had hitherto been segregated – illegally under the existing federal legislation. Many Blacks felt – and Martin Luther King articulated that feeling – that the war in Vietnam was drawing away money and resources that were needed urgently in the South, and in the Black inner-city areas in the North. The legislation was in place, but the means of giving effect to it were being continually curtailed, to meet the needs of the war.

A federal body, the National Advisory Committee on Civil Disorders, reporting on February 29 on the urban riots of the previous year, painted an uncomfortable picture of racism 'pure, simple and ugly' throughout America. Of all the causes of the previous year's disturbances, it concluded, 'the most fundamental is the racial attitude and behaviour of White Americans towards Black Americans. The committee went so far as to warn that the United States was moving towards 'two societies, one Black and one White, separate and unequal'. Martin Luther King was planning a nationwide protest for that summer to draw attention to the continuing inequalities and discrimination. On April 3 he was in Memphis, Tennessee, where he had gone to help organize a strike of Black dustmen. 'I want you to know tonight', he told a large crowd of well-wishers and supporters, 'that we as a people will get to the promised land.'

On the following day, April 4, while standing on the balcony of his hotel, King was shot dead by a White assassin. Four years earlier he had been awarded the Nobel Peace Prize for his efforts to achieve racial harmony and Black equality in the United States. He was thirty-nine years old, a charismatic leader who eschewed violence but believed in the power of public and persistent demonstrations. His assassin, James Earl Ray, was later arrested at London airport, and, taken back to Memphis, sentenced to ninety-nine years in prison.

Following Martin Luther King's assassination, riots, accompanied by looting and arson, broke out throughout the United States. In the words of John A. Garraty and Peter Gay: 'The greatest statesman could not achieve world peace, but a single demented zealot could start a war. Martin Luther King and a host of dedicated followers could not eliminate racial prejudice, but a sordid drifter, shooting King down from ambush, could cause a dozen cities to burn.'

In New York, Black rioters went on the rampage in several smart shopping districts of Manhattan. In all, more than 70,000 soldiers and National Guardsmen were called in, and 24,000 arrests were made. As many as two thousand shops and homes were ransacked, and more than five thousand fires started. Before the riots ended five days later, thirty-six Black rioters had been killed, many of them shot while looting. Four Whites also died. In Washington, despite an evening curfew, Black rioters surged through the streets, setting fire to buildings only a few blocks from the White House. Troops were called in to prevent the rioters reaching the White House itself. The highest number of deaths was in Chicago – with eleven dead – and Washington with ten dead.

It was only after King's funeral on April 9 that calm was restored. On the following day, April 10, Johnson passed into law the Open Housing Bill, prohibiting discrimination in the sale or letting of houses. On May 3, as a testimony to Martin Luther King's influence, the Reverend Ralph Abernathy Jr, one of King's assistants, led a Poor People's March from Memphis, where King had been murdered, to Washington. The march arrived in the capital on June 23, where it established Resurrection City: a hundred huts and temporary buildings within sight of the White House and the Capitol. Within hours, the police ordered the 'city' to be dismantled. When the marchers refused, the police tried to move in. They were confronted by a crowd throwing petrol-filled bottles and flaming sticks at them. The police responded by hurling tear-gas grenades.

On June 24, as the protests continued, the police arrested five hundred of the demonstrators on the steps of the Capitol. They were charged with 'camping without a permit'. Later that day the police moved into Resurrection City, and, behind the shelter of yet more tear-gas grenades, tore down the shanties. A statement from the White House said that Johnson had 'concurred' with the police action. Still the marchers refused to disperse, and on June 25 regular soldiers were brought up, 1,600 in all. *The Times* reported: 'About two thousand Negroes had congregated in the area by early evening, of whom perhaps eight hundred were troublemakers. Shop windows were broken and a jewellery shop looted when hundreds of police intervened. Wearing gas masks, riot helmets and flak jackets, the heavily armed policemen were bombarded with bricks and stones until they smothered the area in tear gas.' The demonstrations were at an end.

Johnson continued his legislative campaign against inequalities. In a move to counter job discrimination he announced a programme of 'affirmative action' whereby all government contractors were obliged to give preference when hiring Blacks and other minority groups. On November 5, Shirley Chisholm became the first Black American woman to be elected to the United States Congress. But success in one area of race equality was not matched by success elsewhere. Hispanics as well as Blacks were expressing their dissatisfaction. Led by César Chávez, head of the United Farm Workers Union, the predominantly Hispanic farm labourers in California boycotted the grape harvest that year in protest against low wages and poor conditions.

In a nation beset with domestic and foreign problems, the successes of the space race came as a tonic, however much some people wondered whether the vast sums of money spent on space exploration might not have been spent elsewhere. On October 11 the *Apollo* 7 spacecraft was launched from

Cape Kennedy (as Cape Canaveral had been renamed) for an eleven-day mission during which it made 164 orbits around the Earth. Live television pictures were transmitted from inside the spacecraft to tens of millions of television viewers, who also saw what the Earth looked like from space. It was a revelation to see the planet as an object not much larger than the Moon as seen from Earth. *Apollo 8* was launched on December 21. Three days later, after a sixty-six-hour flight from Earth orbit to Moon orbit, the three astronauts on board began circling the Moon, each orbit taking two hours. Close-up pictures of the Moon's surface were sent back to Earth, as well as the view of planet Earth as seen from the Moon.

After *Apollo 8* had completed ten orbits of the Moon it returned through space to the Earth's atmosphere, which it re-entered on December 27 at 25,000 miles an hour, before decelerating and splashing down in the Pacific Ocean, a mere six thousand yards from the recovery vessel that was waiting for it. It was clear from this Christmas-time flight that landing a man on the Moon could only be a matter of a year away at the most. On the last day of the year, in a pioneering development within the Earth's atmosphere, the Soviet Union gave a public demonstration of the world's first supersonic aircraft, the Tu-144. Its short but successful flight at speeds above the speed of sound served as a further spur to the Anglo-French supersonic Concorde, which was still being developed.

Also in the terrestrial rather than space realm, sixty-one nations signed a Treaty on the Non-Proliferation of Nuclear Weapons on July 1. The treaty was a landmark in the attempt to prevent the spread of this destructive power to more and more lands, and to more and more areas of conflict. It had taken ten years of negotiation to reach this goal. Three powers that did possess nuclear weapons, the United States, the Soviet Union and Britain, added their signatures. A fourth nuclear power, China, not being a member of the United Nations, was not asked to do so. Four countries rejected the treaty outright: Albania, Cuba, Tanzania and Zambia. Several of the countries who signed it subsequently acquired, or sought to acquire, a nuclear capacity, among them India, Pakistan and Israel.

One aspect of the treaty that offered further hope to those who feared nuclear and military confrontations was that it also called both for continuing measures of general disarmament, with a view to reducing tensions, and for international co-operation and financing in the wider application of atomic power for peaceful purposes.

The world's fifth nuclear power, France, had abstained from voting on the treaty. Eight weeks later, on August 25, it exploded a hydrogen bomb in the South Pacific.

Inventions during 1968 included a whirlpool bath designed by the Jacuzzi brothers of California, makers of farm pumps. A historical injustice was also redressed that year: on December 16, almost three centuries after the expulsion of the Jews from Spain, the Spanish government announced that the 1492 expulsion decree was annulled. Since the expulsion those Jews – known as Sephardi (or Spanish) Jews, many of them still speaking a medieval form of Spanish known as Ladino – had made their homes throughout North Africa, the eastern Mediterranean, the Balkans, and even Holland and the Baltic. Cromwell had admitted them to Britain in the seventeenth century. Hitler had deported them from cities such as Athens and Salonika to the death camps of Central Europe. In Israel they formed half the population, often feeling excluded by the predominant Ashkenazi ('German' or European) Jews, but gradually gaining political influence, and in due course, by the end of the century, considerable political power.

Medical advances continued: the anaesthetic epidural technique to help easier childbirth was announced on September 11. Also in 1968, Dr Christiaan Barnard performed his second heart-transplant operation. The patient lived for a further seventy-four days: fifty-six days longer than the recipient of the first heart transplant the previous year. In Britain, the first heart-transplant patient died forty-six days after receiving his new heart. There was indignation in those medical and public circles which argued that heart transplants were unethical, since life was not really prolonged in any meaningful sense, and that transplant surgeons were 'vultures, waiting for their prey, hovering around the bedsides of potential donors'. But in the case of the British patient who had died it was pointed out that he had been killed by severe complications acquired before his operation. The science and practice of transplant surgery was not, however, to be held back: the transplanting of other organs, including kidneys and the cornea of the eye, were well established. What had been but a few years earlier a theoretical and unknown area of medicine was becoming a standard and life-enhancing procedure, improving in efficacy with every year.

The 1968 Olympic Games were held in Mexico, the first country in the 'developing world' to host them. A few weeks before the Games were to open, student disorders in Mexico City – part of the general student discontent that year, but intensified by the many privations specific to Mexico – were met with severe repression. The Mexican authorities did not want the Games marred by the sights and sounds of anger and protest – as the American Democratic National Convention had been in Chicago the previous month. Police used considerable force, and the Mexican army occupied the university. As in Chicago, the world's newspaper and television correspondents were on hand to transmit the ugly scenes around the world. Several students were killed.

The Games themselves proved once again a competition between the two Super Powers – much as the space race to land a man on the Moon had been. In Mexico, as in space, the United States appeared to have a substantial lead, winning forty-five gold medals to the Soviet Union's twenty-nine. The next closest was Japan. South Africa, which had originally been allowed to participate if its team was racially mixed, travelled together and trained together – conditions which were accepted – was at the last moment asked not to attend. The apartheid regime, even when it made concessions outside South Africa, was still an international pariah.

CHAPTER EIGHTEEN

1969

No progress whatsoever has been made except agreement
on the shape of the bargaining table.

PRESIDENT RICHARD M. NIXON

THE SIGHT OF SOVIET TANKS in the streets of Prague in 1968 had
revived the images of Soviet tanks in Budapest in 1956. Since 1956 the
Hungarian government had pursued a policy in line with that of the Soviet
Union, curbing dissent, and participating – as it had against Czechoslovakia
– in the Soviet agenda. In Czechoslovakia, however, the power of dissent
was harder to curb. On 16 January 1969, in Wenceslas Square in Prague,
a Czech student, Jan Palach, set fire to himself in public, and burned himself
to death, in protest against the continuing presence of Soviet occupation
troops in Czechoslovakia. In his farewell letter, he also demanded an end to
press censorship, and the resignation of those politicians – appointed since
the Soviet occupation – 'who do not enjoy the people's confidence'. In Palach's
honour, more than 200,000 people marched in silence through the streets
of Prague, factories in the capital stopped work for five minutes, and Czech
Radio observed a minute's silence during his funeral, telling its listeners:
'The deepest pain is marked by the deepest silence.' In response to this the
Russian-controlled Radio Vltava was scathing: 'Now we can see the devilish
features of anti-Communism in all its cruelty.'

Following three months of continuing anti-Soviet unease throughout
Czechoslovakia, on March 28 – after the Czechoslovak ice-hockey team had
scored two victories over the Russians in the world championship in Stockholm – there were mass anti-Soviet demonstrations in the streets of Prague
and other Czech cities. In Moscow, *Pravda* launched an attack on the Czech
newspapers and radio for 'stirring up public passions'. Two senior Soviet
officials, the Warsaw Pact army commander Marshal Grechko and a Deputy

Foreign Minister, Vladimir Semyonov, flew to Prague and warned the government that unless anti-Soviet demonstrations ceased, the Soviet Union would intervene militarily without seeking permission first.

The Czech government bowed to the threat of force. Press censorship was tightened and the police force strengthened. The founder of modern Czechoslovakia, Thomas Masaryk, pictures of whom had been defiantly displayed in Wenceslas Square on May Day, was denounced in radio broadcasts relayed from East Berlin. The spirit of defiance was strong among the Czech intelligentsia, however. In June the playwright Václav Havel spoke to trade unionists at the ironworks at Ostrava, although the authorities had declared the meeting illegal. When the authorities closed down the student union at Prague University, there were strikes in the factories in support of the students. The Czech Writers' Union, electing a new committee – of which Havel was a member – called for an investigation into the legality of measures that had been taken against newspapers and magazines. In Slovakia and Moravia, students and workers, distributing leaflets calling for greater liberalism, were arrested and charged with criminal activity. A Soviet delegation visiting a factory in Prague was stoned before it could enter the factory and had to turn away. There were clashes between citizens and Soviet troops in the spa town of Karlový Vary (Karslbad).

On August 21, the first anniversary of the Soviet invasion, the citizens of Prague and all other Czech cities stayed at home: trams, buses, trains, shops, restaurants, cinemas and theatres were empty. During a protest demonstration in Prague against the Soviets four days later, in which 50,000 people took part, two demonstrators were killed by police. There were also deaths during a mass demonstration in Brno.

The Soviet Union acted with decision: in April it had already replaced Alexander Dubček, who had been allowed to remain as Party leader after the previous year's crisis, by Gustáv Husák – 'Iron Gustáv' – who brought in a Praesidium far more amenable to Soviet desires. Flying to the Crimea to meet with the Soviet leaders, Husák agreed to joint Soviet-Czechoslovak manoeuvres to be held on Czech soil within a matter of weeks. On August 27 the Soviet government awarded Husák the Order of Lenin. Two days later he spoke publicly in strong defence of the continuing Soviet occupation. A month later, on a visit to Moscow, he was garlanded with flowers. The public response was hostile: so many Czechs were leaving the country altogether, for the West, that on October 10 severe restrictions were imposed on all emigration, even on tourist travel outside the country. On December

12 Prague radio issued a strong attack on workers who were still 'dissociating' themselves from the Soviet soldiers stationed in their towns. It was also revealed at the end of the year that 'more than a thousand Party workers' had left Czechoslovakia for the West. Thousands more were accused of having gone into 'internal emigration', turning their back on their Communist Party tasks and beliefs. As a sign of how low his star had fallen in Party eyes, Dubček was sent as Ambassador to Turkey. Six months later he was recalled from Turkey, expelled from the Communist Party, and appointed an inspector – one of many – for the forestry administration in Bratislava, where he lived out his days.

The Soviet Union was taking continual, but not always entirely successful, diplomatic steps to shore up its authority in Eastern Europe. Six times in one year Wladislaw Gomulka journeyed to Moscow to consult with Brezhnev. The Warsaw Pact countries were summoned three times in one year, to meetings in Budapest, Prague and Moscow. There were calls for strengthening the armed forces of all Communist States in Eastern Europe. But Gomulka had more success than the Czech leaders in putting forward the case for greater independence within the Communist bloc. At the Moscow World Communist Conference in June – at which delegates from seventy-five countries were present – he set out the 'Gomulka Doctrine', whereby there could be differences, albeit limited ones, in the views of the various Communist Parties, as well as 'great diversity in the worldwide revolutionary process'.

To show that his own Poland did not feel inferior in ideological status to its eastern neighbour, when he raised his glass in a toast to his Soviet hosts Gomulka called them: 'the first among equals'. With regard to the emigration of Jews, Gomulka also distanced himself from the Soviet policy of severely restricted emigration, establishing the 'Gomulka Variant', whereby Polish or Polish-born Jews who wished to leave could do so. This enabled several thousand Jews who were living in the Soviet Union, but who had been born in Poland, to leave Russia for Israel and the West – a Jew born in the Soviet cities of Lvov or Vilna, or in towns such as Brest-Litovsk, Baranovichi, Sarny or Rovno before 1939 would have been a Polish citizen at the time of his birth. The Gomulka Variant enabled these 'Poles' to leave the Soviet Union, in which they had lived for a quarter of a century, following the Soviet annexation of the eastern third of inter-war Poland. These Jews, Gomulka said – his words were reproduced in *Pravda*, causing a ripple of amazement among those normally unexposed to dissenting thought – were not 'tied to Poland by feeling and reason, but to the State of Israel', and he went on to explain: 'They are certainly Jewish nationalists. Can one have a grudge against them for this? Only the same kind of grudge as Communists have against all nationalists, no matter what their nationality is. I suppose that this category of Jews is going to leave our country sooner or later.' To those Jews who considered Israel their 'homeland', Gomulka declared, 'we are ready to give emigration passports'.

Gomulka's independence of thought, and what it implied for Poland's future as a Communist country, was deeply worrying to the Soviet leaders. Not only did Poland take a lead in welcoming a European security conference across the Iron Curtain divide, but it expressed support for the idea of American and Canadian participation in it. On the domestic front, Gomulka encouraged economic changes that would reduce State control, and create incentives for economic expansion and greater productivity. An agreement was signed with France whereby Polish industry could be modernized using French equipment on a long-term credit basis. A Private Traders Association was set up, within which small private enterprises could employ up to a dozen people. Its head was a former Polish aristocrat, Count Ostrowski. But the pattern of dissent which had led to the Soviet invasion of Czechoslovakia in the previous year – in which Polish troops had participated – was carefully and even ruthlessly avoided. During 1968 eighteen university lecturers and students were sent to prison for 'anti-state and anti-Socialist' activities. When a former Minister of Education, Dr Bienkowski, who had been prominent in the 'Polish October' of thirteen years earlier, tried to publish a criticism of the previous year's police attacks on student demonstrations, he was expelled from the Communist Party.

The Party leadership sought to strengthen its control over all Polish universities and magazines: 'Everyone must choose on which side of the barricade to stand' was the Party line. All leading writers – Poland being a lively ferment of writers even at the worst of times – who opposed the Communist Party's cultural ideology were refused admission to the annual Writers' Union Congress. At the same time, following the Chinese model, compulsory manual work was introduced for all Polish students during the university holidays, and a newly established Ideological Commission of the Communist Party was instructed to supervise school and university teaching and textbooks.

In Washington, Richard Nixon was sworn in as President on 20 January 1969. In his inaugural address he set out with stark brevity the dilemma facing the United States. 'We are caught in war, wanting peace,' he said. 'We are torn by division, wanting unity. We see around us empty lives, wanting fulfillment.' The precedent of the Kennedy and Johnson presidencies, of a spate of social reform measures, of a frantic and exuberant first 'hundred days', was not followed. Nor, given the cost of the Vietnam War, could it be. When he finally presented his first domestic programme to Congress on April 14, Nixon told the impatient legislators that peace had been his first priority, and that this was central to many more people than those of the United States alone.

Peace, said Nixon, 'concerns the future of civilization – and even in terms of our domestic needs themselves, what we are able to do will depend in large measure on the prospects for an early end to the war in Vietnam'. Travelling to South-East Asia in July, Nixon stopped in Guam, where he issued the 'Declaration of Guam', stressing that the United States must never again be drawn into a Vietnam-type conflict on the Asian mainland. American troops, he said, would not be used to put down insurrections, even those that were Communist-led.

In an unprecedented move, Nixon also visited Roumania. No American President had been to a Communist country since the start of the Cold War. Roumania's continuing gestures of independence from the Soviet Union, most noticeably in showing sympathy for Dubček's Czechoslovak initiatives the previous year, made it a country that could be wooed by the Americans. But the time for dramatic change had not yet arrived, and President Ceauşescu was careful to stress that from the Roumanian perspective the 'Socialist alliance' remained central.

Throughout the first six months of the Nixon presidency the American Moon-landing preparations gripped the public and held the attention of millions of television viewers. On March 3 the 'lunar module' – the landing vehicle that would in due course have to land on the Moon – was given its first test in space. On May 18 three astronauts were sent into space to test the docking procedures between the service module and the lunar module. On May 22 these three astronauts and their craft approached to within eight miles of the lunar surface in the lunar module before returning to the service craft, and then back to Earth.

Amid unprecedented international interest, on July 16 *Apollo 11* was launched from Cape Kennedy for the actual Moon landing. Three astronauts took part – Neil Armstrong and Edwin 'Buzz' Aldrin, who were to endeavour to land on the Moon, and Michael Collins, who was to remain in the service module just above the Moon's surface. Five days after blast-off, with the spacecraft in orbit around the Moon, the lunar module, codename *Eagle*, was detached from the command module and descended to the surface of the Moon. It was July 20. A ladder was slowly lowered from the lunar module until it touched the surface of the Moon. An estimated 600 million television viewers, as many as eighty million of them in the United States, were watching throughout the world – this viewer in a small hotel in central Portugal – as Armstrong, still on the steps of the lunar module ladder, told mission control in the United States on his radio, 'I am going to step off the LM now,' and, as he stepped on to the lunar surface: 'That's one small step for man, one giant leap for mankind.'

Armstrong was on the surface of the Moon. He was joined by Aldrin. Together, in the less pressing gravity of the Moon, they hopped – seemed almost to bounce – across the Moon's surface, after which they spoke by radio to Nixon, and set up a number of scientific instruments on the Moon's surface. After twenty-one hours and thirty-six minutes on the Moon, the two astronauts lifted off to rendezvous with Collins, and to begin the voyage back to Earth, which they reached on July 24. Their splash-down in the Pacific was witnessed by Nixon himself.

A new era had begun, that was to make space less formidable, and man more adventurous. But the prospect of exploring space could not assuage the widespread sense of 'empty lives, wanting fulfillment' of which Nixon had spoken in his inaugural address. Student unrest, a feature of the previous year in many lands, was accentuated in the United States in 1969 when two weeks of violence at the University of California at Berkeley in February led the Governor of California, Ronald Reagan, to declare 'a state of extreme emergency'. At the University of Wisconsin, at Madison, the refusal of the administration to establish a Black Studies programme led to protest demonstrations by White and Black students marching arm in arm, and to the calling out of the police and National Guard to curb their protest.

Anti-war feeling at Harvard led hundreds of students to protest against the university's Reserve Officers' Training Programme. The militant Black Panthers were also active, marching and clashing with police in a dozen cities across the country. In December, during a police raid on the Black Panther headquarters in Chicago, a former leader, Fred Hampton, was shot dead by police. The Black Panthers charged that there was a government plot to 'wipe out' their leadership. A Federal Government inquiry examined the charge, and dismissed it, though it did say that the movement had been subjected by the police to 'unfair harassment and provocation'.

On October 29, in a major civil rights decision, the United States Supreme Court ordered the immediate integration of thirty schools in Mississippi. The order was obeyed.

The war in Vietnam had become the longest ever fought by the United States: longer than either the First or Second World War. Nixon's imperative was to try to end the war. In January his special negotiator, Henry Cabot Lodge, arrived in Paris to lead the American negotiating team. Various proposals were put forward, including the restoration of the Demilitarized Zone (the DMZ), which the Americans and South Vietnamese had earlier entered and unilaterally brought to an end. When, in February, there was an increase in Vietcong activity against American and South Vietnamese positions, the United States warned that the halt in the American bombing of North Vietnam – which Johnson had instituted the previous November – had 'expired'. When the Vietcong offensive continued, Nixon himself warned the North Vietnamese that the United States 'could not tolerate' such action at a time when it was 'honestly seeking peace' at the conference table.

As an indication that the United States could not isolate and demonize North Vietnam for much longer, on January 10 Sweden became the first Western government to recognize North Vietnam as an independent State. As American casualties grew, Nixon was under pressure, however, especially from fellow Republicans – the voters who had brought him to power – to take some form of retaliatory action against North Vietnam. He declined to do so, and on May 14 announced a series of decisions that were aimed at ending the war within a year. The basis was a mutual withdrawal of American and North Vietnamese troops from South Vietnam, with the last of the American troops that were still in the country being pulled out when the last of the North Vietnamese troops had left. An international supervisory body would verify the troop withdrawals on both sides. Once the non-South Vietnamese troops – American and North Vietnamese among them – had gone, elections would be held.

Under Nixon's scheme, which was not entirely unacceptable to the North Vietnamese, the Communist National Liberation Front would be able to field candidates in the post-withdrawal election, leading up to the formation of a provisional government. This was not acceptable to the South

Vietnamese, and Nixon had an uncomfortable meeting on Midway Island, in the Pacific, with President Thieu of South Vietnam, who had no desire to share power with his Communist adversaries.

Unable to persuade the South Vietnamese to allow the National Liberation Front to share in the electoral contest, Nixon took unilateral action towards reducing America's commitment, announcing on June 8 the imminent withdrawal of 25,000 American combat troops: one in twenty of those fighting in South Vietnam.

The National Liberation Front was in no hurry to conclude a power-sharing deal with the South Vietnamese government. It, and its North Vietnamese allies and sponsors, still looked to the total overthrow of the South Vietnamese regime. At the end of July, Nixon appealed in a secret letter to Ho Chi Minh, to 'move seriously into negotiations which could end the war'. Ho Chi Minh rejected this appeal: his reply reached Nixon three days before the North Vietnamese leader's death on September 3. In despair at the failure of the negotiations, Nixon said that all of them – both the secret and the public – could be summed up in one sentence: 'No progress whatsoever has been made except agreement on the shape of the bargaining table.' He continued, however, to reduce the American military commitment. On August 19 more than a thousand American troops had left their base at Quang Tri with flags flying, but not in triumph. On September 16 Nixon announced that a further 35,000 troops would be withdrawn by mid-December.

Inside the United States, the scale of anti-war protests grew with every month that the war continued. On October 15, in what was called the 'moratorium', several million Americans throughout the country demonstrated against the war. These protests were often silent. There was dismay among the protesters when the Vice-President, Spiro Agnew, belittled their concerns by calling the nationwide demonstrations 'national masochism encouraged by an effete corps of impudent snobs who characterize themselves as intellectuals'. A second mass protest 'moratorium' took place a month later. One cause of continuing concern was the revelation of cruel behaviour by individual American soldiers, in particular the murder of a Vietnamese civilian near Nha Trang in June by a Special Forces colonel and seven of his officers and men. In November, when the full details of the My Lai massacre of the previous year became public, the White House issued a statement, with Nixon's approval, that the incident was in 'direct violation' of American military policy, and 'abhorrent to the conscience of all American people'.

On December 15, Nixon announced a fourth American troop withdrawal: a further 50,000 troops would leave within the next four months. More than a fifth of the American force was on its way home. For the growing number of anti-war Americans, it was not a moment too soon. At the end of the year it was announced that the number of American dead in Vietnam exceeded 40,000.

The Soviet Union had lost the race to put a man on the Moon, but in its own space programme continued to have considerable pioneering success. It was Soviet efforts that year that saw the first joining up of two manned spacecraft in flight, the first transfer of crew from one orbiting spacecraft to another, and the first linking up of two spacecraft to create a temporary orbiting space station. In May, a Soviet satellite landed on the surface of Venus.

Inside the Soviet Union, a new method of dissent had begun to emerge, the clandestine publication and distribution of banned material. Manuscripts that the Communist Party refused to allow to be published were circulated, often in poorly cyclostyled sheets, and eagerly read by those who faced arrest and imprisonment for possession or distribution of these pieces of work, which were known as *samizdat* (privately published). Early in the year a young dissident, Irina Belgorodskaya, was sentenced to one year in a labour camp for having a considerable number of such clandestine publications in her apartment in Moscow. Her trial, on February 19, lasted only a few hours. On the day of the trial the Party newspaper *Izvestiya* made it clear that 'Marxism–Leninism does not recognize classless freedom of speech.'

In May another dissident, Ilya Burmistrovich, was sentenced to three years in prison for giving out copies, produced clandestinely, of works by the imprisoned writers Daniel and Sinyavsky. Other dissidents were not sent to prison, but to mental hospitals, where they were held in secure wards as political prisoners. One such prisoner was a former collective farm chairman, Ivan Yakhimovich. Another was a senior army officer, Major-General P. G. Grigorenko. Both men had spoken out on behalf of dissidents. Yakhimovich was confined in a mental institution in Riga and Grigorenko in one in Moscow.

Trials and sentences did not deter the dissidents; indeed, the threat of punishment stimulated their determination to protest publicly, and to involve the outside world in their struggle. In May a general's son, Pyotr Yakir, joined fifty others in signing an appeal to the United Nations

Commission on Human Rights, calling on the commission to concern itself with violations of human rights inside the Soviet Union. The appeal was wide-ranging, listing for the commission trials and sentences that had been carried out not only against political dissidents but also against 'people seeking national equality and preservation of their national cultures, Jews demanding the right to leave for Israel, and believers seeking religious liberty'.

The signatories of the appeal to the United Nations formed themselves into an Action Group for the Defence of Civil Rights in the Soviet Union. Several of its members were arrested. When the writer Anatoli Marchenko managed to smuggle to the West his account of Soviet prison and labour camp life – *My Testimony* – he was given an additional sentence of hard labour for 'anti-Soviet defamation'.

The extent of the ferment, but also the despair, inside intellectual circles in the Soviet Union was seen in July, when Anatoli Kuznetsov, a writer and journalist who was in favour with the Soviet authorities, defected while on a visit to London, and spoke of how everything that he wrote inside Russia was 'distorted' by the censors, to such an extent that, although his work was regularly published in its censored form, he could 'no longer write, no longer sleep, no longer breathe'. Kutznetsov was denounced in one Communist Party newspaper as 'a Judas who will be hated for ever by his fellow countrymen'.

On November 12, the Soviet Writers' Union expelled Alexander Solzhenitsyn. Although a number of his fellow writers protested at the expulsion, and wanted their protest made public, the Party would not allow their protests to be published. What was published, and given powerful support in all Soviet newspapers and magazines, was a novel by Vsevolod Kochetov, entitled *What Is It You Want?* in which he made a strong plea for the isolation of Soviet youth and culture from the outside world. Ideological conformity required the Iron Curtain to be a barrier of ideas and thought as well as of barbed wire and brick walls.

The Jews of the Soviet Union had been in turmoil since Israel's victory over the Arabs two years earlier. The assertion of Jewishness – so long frowned upon by the Communists – intensified, as did the desire to emigrate to Israel. For the Jews of Kiev, the ravine of Babi Yar on the outskirts of the city became a focal point of Jewish identity. There, more than 33,000 Jews had been massacred by the German occupation forces and SS in September 1941. In memory of that massacre an official Soviet memorial meeting had been held in September 1968. Hundreds of Jews attended. To their intense distress they heard the official speakers denounce, not the wartime mass murder, but the State of Israel. One of the Jews present, Boris Kochubievsky, overheard the following conversation between two Soviet citizens:

Man: 'What's going on here?'
Woman: 'Here the Germans killed a hundred thousand Jews.'
Man: 'That wasn't enough.'

Kochubievsky protested to the authorities. Two months later he was given permission to emigrate to Israel. But after a further nine days he was arrested. His trial began on 13 May 1969. His brother, who wanted to attend, was prevented from entering the court by a 'cordon' of citizens. 'But I am Kochubievsky's brother,' he protested. 'You're not a brother,' one of them replied. 'You're a Yid, a Yid, a Yid.'

On May 16 Kochubievsky was sentenced to three years in a 'severe regime' labour camp. As he left the court he expressed his hope 'that no one else will share my lot because of his desire to go to Israel'. Having served his term he was allowed to emigrate. Many other Jews were later to be forced to share his 'lot' – arrest, trial and imprisonment – as the desire to go to Israel became more widespread.

Many young Soviet Jews had begun secretly to learn Hebrew, and to teach it. The Communist authorities took measures to disrupt and close down all such classes. But the will to assert national consciousness was as strong among the Jews of the Soviet Union as among the many other nationalities whose aspirations were being suppressed. In October, during the Jewish festival of Simchat Torah – the Rejoicing of the Law – thousands of young Jews filled the quarter-mile length of Arkhipov Street, on either side of Moscow's Central Synagogue, singing and dancing, through a cold drizzle, until late in the night. Western observers were surprised by their knowledge of Hebrew and Yiddish songs: songs never taught in Soviet schools, and not openly sung for more than forty years. Some of those present, many of them youngsters, held pieces of paper on which they had written all the Hebrew words they had been able to collect. A movement had been born, with the slogan 'Let my people go!', which was to pit the Soviet Union against Western Jews and, within a few years, against Western governments.

Along its three-thousand-mile border with China, and especially in the Far East, the Soviet Union was confronted with a series of raids and attacks, combined with Chinese calls for a rectification of the border in China's favour. One particular area of conflict was the islands in the Ussuri River which had been acquired by Tsarist Russia in 1860. Peking insisted that the 1860 treaty ceding the area to Russia had been unfairly extracted, and that the islands were rightfully Chinese. On March 2, in a sudden rush, Chinese troops, holding rifles in one hand and waving Mao Tse-tung's Little Red Book in the other, tried to occupy one of these islands, Damiansky Island, but were driven off by the Soviet border guards. In Peking, the Soviet Embassy was besieged by a vast crowd of Chinese protesters demanding the transfer of Damiansky Island to China. The island clash continued. Within a few days thirty Soviet soldiers had been killed. In a further clash twelve more Soviet soldiers were killed. On March 23 the Soviet army newspaper compared Mao Tse-tung to Hitler.

As the dispute with China continued, the Soviet Union put itself forward as the champion of the native peoples of Sinkiang, accusing China of mounting a 'massive colonization' programme in the province in order to turn its Muslim and Mongol inhabitants into a minority. China countered by claiming parts of the Soviet republics of Kirgizia and Kazakhstan, which the Tsars had acquired from China more than a hundred years earlier, including the city of Alma Ata. In June, in an unprecedented attack on a fellow Communist nation, Brezhnev accused China of planning not only a conventional but also a nuclear war on Russia. What was required, Brezhnev told the international Communist Conference in Moscow on June 7, was 'a decisive struggle against Peking's disruptive policy and great power chauvinism'. Western observers could not believe that war was imminent, but the Soviet and Chinese newspapers and radio were each issuing violent verbal assaults. In Moscow, Mao Tse-tung was caricatured as 'an Asian Bonaparte'. Soviet military manoeuvres were held night and day along another of the disputed rivers, the Amur, and the Soviet forces in the region were placed – publicly and ostentatiously – under the command of a military rocket specialist, Colonel-General V. F. Tolubko.

The Soviet Union sought to diffuse the crisis and to persuade the Chinese not to push their border claims. On September 11, on his way back to Moscow from Ho Chi Minh's funeral in Hanoi, Alexsei Kosygin stopped in Peking for talks with Chou En-lai. The two men agreed to begin negotiations, and the Soviet press campaign against China subsided. But for those in Moscow and Peking, as well as for Western observers, the Sino-Soviet physical and verbal violence between April and September had been one of uncertain and dangerous escalation, threatening full-scale war between the world's two largest Communist Powers.

In China, the destruction of the Cultural Revolution was coming to an end. At the Party Conference in April, from which all foreigners and foreign journalists were rigorously excluded, almost no Red Guards were present as a new constitution was presented. The place for the Red Guards, declared the official China News Agency on the anniversary of the first dramatic Red Guard parade in Peking, was 'the countryside, border regions, and stock-breeding areas'.

On July 12 there were riots in Northern Ireland, between Roman Catholics and Protestants in Londonderry. Since 1966 the Catholic minority in this British province had been alarmed by provocative acts by Protestants who were afraid of losing out to the rapidly multiplying Catholic population. In July 1966 a prominent Protestant clergyman, Ian Paisley, had been arrested and imprisoned for unlawful assembly and breach of the peace. In January 1967 the Northern Ireland Civil Rights Association had been set up. The Catholic and Protestant communities were on a collision course. On August 12 there were further severe clashes between Protestants and Catholics in Belfast, when hundreds of houses were destroyed by fire, and several thousand people − four-fifths of them Roman Catholic − were made homeless. Ten people were killed, and more than a thousand injured. Two days later, John Gallagher, a Roman Catholic, was shot through the heart while running for the sanctuary of St Patrick's Cathedral, Armagh. He was the eleventh victim of the renewed violence that was to claim three thousand victims in Northern Ireland and on the British mainland by 1992.

As fighting between Catholic and Protestant extremists spread, Harold Wilson ordered British troops to the province. For a while there was calm, as Catholic women served tea and biscuits to the soldiers, who were protecting the Catholic areas from Protestant attack. The Protestant Loyalists felt that they had been betrayed by Britain, and that keeping the peace was by its very nature a concession to the Irish Republican Army (the IRA). Both sides built up their weaponry, and their grievances. The struggle on which they were embarked was to poison the life of a part of the United Kingdom which most mainland Britons preferred to ignore. But the severity of the struggle was to impinge on mainland politics for the coming three decades.

*   *   *

Pollution was beginning to create concerns in many lands for both the health of the individual and the quality of life of the urban masses. Oil spills were increasingly a cause of coastal pollution: in February 200,000 gallons of crude oil leaked from a mineshaft on to the sea bed off Santa Barbara, California, polluting sixteen miles of beaches. At a conference in Brussels in October, Nixon's adviser on urban affairs, Daniel Moynihan, warned apocalyptically that the world 'may have even less than a 50–50 chance of living until 1980'. Weapons of mass destruction were also having a dangerous impact, even when stored. In Dugway, Utah, in the United States, plague struck sheep near a testing ground for nerve gases.

Throughout the year there had been public pressure – ranging far beyond the continuing student protests in many lands – for an end to those elements of nuclear power that threatened nuclear confrontation, destruction and pollution. On October 7 the United States and the Soviet Union, having worked closely together for many months to work out a way forward, presented at the United Nations in Geneva a joint draft treaty to keep the sea bed free of nuclear weapons. Before the end of October the Soviet Union made public its willingness to proceed with comprehensive Strategic Arms Limitation Talks (SALT). These opened in Helsinki on November 17 and reached a culmination on November 24 when, in ceremonies held simultaneously in Washington and Moscow, a nuclear non-proliferation treaty was ratified. On the following day Nixon renounced, on behalf of the United States, all methods of biological warfare, and ordered the destruction of all biological warfare stocks. In future, he said, biological research would be confined to defensive measures, not attack.

Japan was a beneficiary of the new American policies. On November 21 agreement was reached between Washington and Tokyo that Okinawa would be returned to Japanese sovereignty within three years, and that the United States would remove all nuclear weapons from the island. Japan had other reasons to be confident of its standing in the world: that year, for the first time, its Gross National Product exceeded that of West Germany. Both the defeated nations of 1945 were striding forward to prosperity.

The needs of the environment were gradually being understood, and addressed. In the United States, the National Environmental Policy Act made it mandatory for each government decision to be accompanied by a detailed statement about its environmental impact. A conference on pollution was held in Rome, attended by thirty-nine nations. Chemical weapons dumped in the sea were blamed for the deaths of innumerable sea birds and fish. The destructive effects of the residue of pesticides, in particular DDT, were revealed in both water and soil. The Canadian Prime Minister, Pierre Trudeau, announced a total ban on DDT for more than ninety per cent of the operations using it in Canada.

Minority rights were everywhere being asserted and, in the West, addressed. In Canada, the Official Languages Act made Canada bilingual, thus enabling the French-speaking minority to feel that its needs would be recognized even where there were few French speakers. In the United States, calls were growing by Native Americans – 'Red Indians', the term used hitherto, and even 'Indians', was regarded as belittling – for the return of lands which they claimed had been stolen from them a century and more earlier. President Nixon, in response to these calls, appointed a Mohawk-Sioux, Louis R. Bruce, as Commissioner for Native American Affairs. One of his first achievements was to secure the return of 48,000 acres of tribal land to the Taos Pueblo Native Americans.

In the realm of communications, the first 'jumbo jet' airliner had its maiden flight, on February 9, in the United States. The Anglo-French super-sonic airliner Concorde took successfully to the air in France on March 2. Almost unnoticed at the time but of inestimable importance for the future, the United States Department of Defence established the Arpanet, sub-sequently the Internet – a means of secure and secret communication, which could function even when command centres might be knocked out by nuclear bombs. It could remain fully operational even if telephone landlines, tele-graph poles and radio transmission centres were knocked out. Thirty years later the Internet was becoming the predominant means of communication, and access to information, for hundreds of millions of people worldwide.

CHAPTER NINETEEN

1970

> ... shall we surrender to our surroundings, or shall we
> make our peace with nature and begin to make repar-
> ations for the damage we have done?
>
> PRESIDENT RICHARD M. NIXON

DISSENT IN THE SOVIET UNION marked every month of 1970. On March 19 one of Russia's leading nuclear scientists, Andrei Sakharov, signed a public letter to the Communist Party leadership, in which he protested at the lack of political freedom inside the Soviet Union and called for much wider public discussions of important issues. Sakharov was allowed to remain at liberty – he was far too well known and respected a figure to be incarcerated – but the arrest and imprisonment of those who spoke out against the regime were frequent, and their cases often shrouded in secrecy and anonymity. In April, Amnesty International, a leading Western human rights organization, published a report in which it alleged that there were thousands of Russian 'prisoners of conscience' being held in Soviet prisons, labour camps and psychiatric hospitals specially set up for them. This was not an exaggeration.

The Soviet authorities treated all such criticism with contempt. The business of Communism went on, its public face being one of enthusiasm and inventiveness. April 11, as part of the celebrations for the hundredth anniversary of the birth of Lenin, was declared a 'Day of Voluntary Work'. More than 119 million people were said to have taken part in it. A sustained call by Party officials to follow the 'true path' of Lenin was brought to a climax on November 23 when *Pravda* called on the peoples of the Soviet Union for 'heightened vigilance, decisive struggles against bourgeois ideology and the penetration of views and mores alien to Socialism'.

Those 'alien' views took several forms. One was what Brezhnev himself denounced that summer as 'lawlessness and infringements of labour discipline': the prevalence of drunkenness and absenteeism from work – denounced officially as 'violations of social order' – was affecting national productivity. The existing volunteer citizens law enforcement squads – *druzhinniki* – were expanded and put under police supervision. They could criticize and harass those breaking the laws. Photographs of people picked up drunk were pasted on local bulletin boards.

A setback for the imposition of literary uniformity came on October 8, when the Nobel Prize for Literature was awarded to Alexander Solzhenitsyn. The citation spoke of the 'ethical force' with which he had pursued the traditions of Russian literature. On October 9 the Soviet Writers' Union called the award and the citation 'unseemly'. Solzhenitsyn announced that he would go to Stockholm to receive the award, but later declined to do so, fearing that he might be refused permission to return to the Soviet Union. In support of Solzhenitsyn's award, the cellist Mstislav Rostropovich wrote a letter to *Pravda* and three other Soviet newspapers defending the award. None of the newspapers would publish the letter, but it circulated unofficially, part of the growing dissident literature.

A defection to the West that year intensified the Soviet ire at Western influence and internal dissent. Natalya Makarova, a star of the Kirov Ballet, defected while on tour in London in September. Jewish demands for emigration to Israel were also growing. Among the teachers of Hebrew in Leningrad who sought to revive the Hebrew language, as a base for eventual emigration, was Gilya Butman. In June he was among several hundred Leningrad Jews who protested in public against the Soviet government's refusal to grant them permission to leave. He was also aware of a dangerous enterprise which had its origins among a small group of Jews, most of them from Riga. Their plan was to seize a twelve-seater Soviet civilian aeroplane, fly it across the Soviet border with Finland, land in Sweden, and then, allowing the aeroplane to be returned to the Soviet Union, make their way to Israel.

On June 15, the day the escape was to take place, all those directly involved were seized by the Soviet militia. Six months later the eleven leaders were brought to trial and sentenced to long terms in 'strict regime' labour camps. Two of the would-be hijackers, Mark Dymshits and Edouard Kuznetsov, were sentenced to death.

On December 25, as the sentences were announced in a Leningrad courtroom, cheers of approval broke out from the specially invited citizen-audience. These cheers were drowned out, however, by the shouts of the relatives of the accused. 'Good fellows! Hold on! We are with you! We are waiting for you! We shall be in Israel together!'

Following widespread Western protests, the two death sentences were commuted to fifteen years' imprisonment. The convicted men, nine Jews and two non-Jews, were sent to prison and labour camp. They became known in the West as 'Prisoners of Zion'. Campaigns were launched to release them. It was only after ten years, however, when most of their sentences were due to expire, that all but three of them were released, and allowed to go to Israel. The two non-Jews, Yury Fedorov and Aleksei Murzhenko, remained prisoners, despite the continued efforts of many Jewish and non-Jewish campaigners in the West to have them released. Yosef Mendelevich, the last of the Jews to be held, was released only in February 1981, almost eleven years after being sentenced.

The severity of the Leningrad sentences did not deter those who were now determined to try to emigrate. Two months after the Leningrad sentences, on 26 February 1971, twenty-four Riga Jews marched to the Visa Office to demand the right to leave. Two days later thirty Moscow Jews staged a sit-in at the Supreme Soviet building, in protest against their 'refusal'. But these courageous gestures were overshadowed, within a few weeks, by a second 'show' trial, also held in Leningrad. There were nine defendants, including Gilya Butman, the Hebrew teacher and friend of the first Leningrad prisoners. In a statement to the court Butman declared that the instances of anti-Semitism which he had experienced in the Soviet Union, together with his own studies of Jewish history and the Hebrew language, had brought him 'to the thought of Israel, and the need to struggle to keep Soviet Jews a nation'. It was in that context, he explained, that he had helped the would-be hijackers.

Butman was sentenced to ten years in prison, and, despite many Western protests on his behalf, spent almost a decade in labour camp before being allowed to go to Israel. Henceforth, there were always ten, twenty, even thirty Jews in labour camp for having insisted on the right to leave, or to teach Hebrew. As one was released, another was arrested. But the deterrent effect of such arrests was minimal, and, as the decade proceeded, first hundreds, then thousands and finally tens of thousands of Jews applied to leave. For the next six years the gates were opened and more than 50,000 Jews allowed to leave. Towards the end of the decade, the gates were closed again.

In Vietnam the United States continued to try to disengage as many of its troops as possible, and to negotiate an agreement with the North Vietnamese.

On February 21, in a Parisian suburb, Henry Kissinger, Nixon's National Security Adviser, held his first secret meeting with a North Vietnamese interlocutor, Le Duc Tho, a founder member of the Indochinese Communist Party and the senior Vietminh commissar in South Vietnam during the struggle against French colonial rule. He had spent much of the recent period in the South, in hiding, co-ordinating and enhancing anti-American activity. His negotiating position, which was unacceptable to the Americans, and which Kissinger could not budge, was that after an armistice the South Vietnamese government must be replaced by a coalition in which the Vietcong would be represented. Kissinger hoped to find a formula whereby the North Vietnamese would agree to pull their troops out of South Vietnam without any public announcement, leaving the Vietcong as the sole Communist forces in the South. This was unacceptable to the North Vietnamese, who felt that the Vietcong, left to their own devices, were not strong enough to achieve the Communist objective, the conquest of Saigon and the overthrow of the South Vietnamese government.

On April 20 Nixon announced that another 150,000 American troops would be withdrawn from South Vietnam within a year, leaving fewer than a quarter of a million American troops on South Vietnamese soil. 'We finally have in sight the just peace we are seeking,' Nixon said. Two days later, however, he was discussing with his advisers how to help the Cambodian regime of Lon Nol against North Vietnamese incursions and local Communist insurrection: the Cambodian capital, Phnom Penh, was itself being threatened by Communist attack. The recently deposed Cambodian leader, Prince Sihanouk, had formed a government in exile together with the Communist 'Red Khmers' (the Khmer Rouge) to whom, until then, he had been implacably opposed.

American warplanes had already been involved earlier in April in secret attacks on the Communist insurgents in Laos, the neutrality of which the United States was pledged to uphold. North Vietnamese troops, seeking to extend the Ho Chi Minh trail through Laotian territory, had occupied Saravane and Attopeu, two towns at the northern and eastern edges of the Bolovens Plateau. Newspaper revelations inside the United States of the American air attacks against these positions had angered Nixon intensely. 'We need a bold move in Cambodia to show that we stand with Lon Nol,' he wrote to Kissinger.

Lon Nol's government was the only Cambodian regime in twenty-five years, Nixon told Kissinger – who had just returned from the unsuccessful secret negotiations with the North Vietnamese in Paris – with 'the guts to take a pro-Western and pro-American stand'. From Saigon, General Creighton Abrams – who had succeeded General Westmoreland as commander of the American forces in South Vietnam – argued in favour of the elimination of Communist bases in Cambodia. He warned Nixon that, unless this was done, those bases could serve, at the very moment when so many American troops were being withdrawn from South Vietnam, as staging posts for attacks on the American troops who remained. With his advisers in Washington, Nixon argued, in the secrecy of his long and often rambling discussions, that an attack on Communist bases inside Cambodia would show the North Vietnamese leaders that 'we were still serious about our commitment in Vietnam', and thus encourage them to take the secret Paris negotiations with Kissinger more seriously. Nixon had made up his mind, and, without either consulting or even informing Lon Nol, gave orders for a full-scale American attack into Cambodia: 'the big play', he called it, which would be going 'for all the marbles'.

On April 28, two days before the Americans entered Cambodia, South Vietnamese forces attacked across the border, advancing, as the Americans also planned to do in their wake, towards the two main North Vietnamese and Vietcong bases on Cambodian soil. Nixon announced his decision to move into Cambodia, and the attack itself, in a television broadcast on April 30. As he spoke, 20,000 American troops, supported by American warplanes, were advancing across the border.

Nixon's broadcast was a pugnacious performance. In ordering the attack on Cambodia, he said, he was preferring to follow his conscience. The future of world stability and peace depended on America's success in Cambodia. 'If, when the chips are down, the world's most powerful nation, the United States of America, acts like a pitiful helpless giant, the forces of totalitarianism and anarchy will threaten free nations and free institutions throughout the world.'

American hopes of capturing both the North Vietnamese and Vietcong headquarters in Cambodia were dashed: they overran the locations, but the personnel had gone. Considerable quantities of arms, ammunition and food were captured, but the Soviet Union and China were both willing to replace what had been lost. The United States found itself with a new commitment, the support of Lon Nol and his Cambodian government, itself under continual pressure from local and Vietnamese Communist forces. For the anti-war protesters in the United States, to whom Nixon's withdrawals of American troops from Vietnam had been a positive and encouraging sign, the military entry into Cambodia was a disastrous escalation of the war. Anti-war efforts were renewed and intensified. The Secretary of the Interior, Walter Hickel, opposed the Cambodian venture in public, writing Nixon a letter urging him to listen to the views of young people, and even to the views of his Cabinet. Hickel's letter ended: 'Permit me to suggest that you consider meeting on an individual and conversational basis with members of your Cabinet. Perhaps through such conversations we can gain greater insight into these problems.' Nixon later removed Hickel from his post.

The war intensified. On May 2 the Americans carried out their first bombing raid over North Vietnam since November 1968. In a public petition, more than two hundred State Department officials articulated their opposition. Student demonstrations took place across the country. At Kent State University, in Akron, Ohio, hundreds of students attacked the building used for Reserve Officers training. The Governor of Ohio, James Rhodes, announced – in a reference to the Nazi stormtroops – that the students were 'worse than Brownshirts', and that he would 'eradicate' them. Then, on May 4, Rhodes ordered the National Guard on to the university campus to break up the demonstration. The Guardsmen fired a volley into the crowd. Four students were killed: two boys and two girls.

The Kent State killings – which an FBI report later described as 'not necessary and not in order' – provoked an upsurge of protest. Students and teachers alike went on strike: more than four hundred campuses were closed. Marchers, their numbers estimated at 100,000, marched on Washington and surrounded the White House, demanding an end to the intervention in Cambodia, and an end to the war in Vietnam. All night, night after night, protesters held vigils in the centre of Washington. The largest of these vigils took place on the night of May 9/10, filling the whole area around the Lincoln Memorial and in front of the White House. At five in the morning Nixon himself emerged from the White House, and accompanied only by his valet and a few security men, walked to the Lincoln Memorial, where he talked to the protesters. A few days earlier he had characterized the protesters as 'campus bums'. This hardly endeared him to them. But he sought – belligerent and pathetic in turn – to assure them that what he was doing was right.

The Cambodian incursion backfired, not only on the lawns of Washington. In Congress, by majority vote, American ground troops were barred from entering either Cambodia or Laos. The Ho Chi Minh trail, where it traversed

Laos, would have to be attacked by South Vietnamese troops only, although the United States still bombed the trail.

Nixon was determined to place the anti-war protest movement in a wider context of social disintegration: one which would include two of the established institutions – the courts and the legislature – upon which the checks and balances to presidential power depended. Speaking in Phoenix, Arizona, in November, just before the mid-term elections, he declared: 'For too long the strength of freedom in our society has been eroded by a creeping permissiveness – in our legislatures, in our courts, in our family life, in our universities – and as with all appeasement the result has been more aggression, more violence.'

On May 11, the day after Nixon's walkabout at the Lincoln Memorial amid anti-war protesters, six Blacks were killed in riots in Atlanta, Georgia. They had been protesting against the death of a Black youngster while he was being held in jail in Richmond, Virginia.

In Southern Rhodesia, Britain's four-year struggle to persuade the White separatist regime to return to constitutional rule, and eventual Black majority rule, finally failed. On March 2, Ian Smith's government declared Rhodesia to be an independent republic. On March 3 the British government urged the United Nations Security Council not to recognize the new regime in Rhodesia, and to condemn 'the illegal acts of the racist minority regime' there, including its 'purported assumption of a republican status'. The Security Council responded favourably to Britain's request, calling on all member States of the United Nations not to recognize 'this illegal regime' or to give it any assistance. On May 9 the United States, which Ian Smith had hoped would recognize his republic and thus lead other nations to do likewise, announced that it was closing its Consulate in the Rhodesian capital. Only Portugal and South Africa recognized the pariah republic, and continued to supply it with the fuel oil and basic necessities needed to survive without international support. At the same time, small but determined guerrilla forces entered the country and began to attack government buildings: the guerrillas were mostly members of the Zimbabwe African People's Union (ZAPU), operating from Zambia, and the South African branch of the African National Congress (ANC).

In November, as a gesture of defiance to the international community, and a measure of deliberate separation from the majority Black population,

Ian Smith brought in legislation that would enable the government to declare any residential area to be an 'exclusive area', to be lived in by people of one race only. The title of the legislation – the Property Owners' (Residential Protection) Bill – revealed its purpose.

In South Africa, trials against nineteen Black activists led to the accused being placed under restrictions which prevented them from attending any social, political or educational meeting for five years. In parliament, new legislation tightened still further the noose of apartheid. Under the Bantu Laws Amendment Act, the government could – and did – forbid the employment of Black Africans in a wide range of trades. At the same time, the parliamentary session was the last to be attended by the three White members who had hitherto had the responsibility of representing Coloured voters. That representation was henceforth withdrawn. Figures issued that year showed exactly to what extent demographically, apartheid, and the second-class status of Black and Coloured, was a violation of the Atlantic Charter, which in 1941 had established the principle of one man one vote, and also a breach of the post-colonial concept of majority rule which almost everywhere else in Africa (the Portuguese colonies and Southern Rhodesia being the only other exceptions) had, in the previous decade, come to pass. The figures were: Black population just under fifteen million, White population just under four million, Coloured two million.

Elsewhere in Africa, different violations of human rights were taking place. In Uganda, a policy of a 'Move to the Left' had been put into effect, and in neighbouring Kenya pressure was being imposed on the Indian community to leave. The Kenyan and Ugandan Asians, as they were known, had come from the Indian subcontinent fifty years earlier, many of them brought as workers by the British, or coming as traders. They had become an integral, prosperous and productive element in Ugandan and Kenyan society. But they were not Black Africans, and the tide of prejudice had turned against them. They were prevented from trading and physically harassed. During the year more than five thousand left. Within three years, 20,000 had followed them. Most of them went, as Commonwealth citizens holding British passports, to Britain, where they formed the vanguard of one of the most hardworking, and ultimately most successful immigrant groups – fourteen years after the Communist crushing of the Hungarian revolution had brought in an earlier, dynamic and creative flow of refugees to Britain.

*   *   *

Nigeria was emerging from a civil war in which tens of thousands had been killed, and tens of thousands more had died – and were still dying – of starvation. The province of Biafra having broken away, the central government under General Gowon fought a prolonged war before, on January 15, it secured the breakaway province's surrender. The Biafran leader, General Ojukwu, fled to the neighbouring Ivory Coast. He had hoped to continue the separatist struggle from there, but was only granted asylum on condition that he give it up. Tens of thousands of his former troops remained in Biafra, where they comprised an element of extreme lawlessness, concentrating their efforts on looting and brigandage. The government in Lagos used the deterrent of public executions to try to curb this anarchy, though not to any immediate effect.

Following the Biafran surrender, hunger and starvation still stalked its war-torn regions. Three months after the surrender, as many as three million Biafrans were still being fed by the Nigerian Red Cross. Britain, which had declined to help Biafra when it raised the standard of revolt – only four African States had recognized Biafra as an independent entity – hurried to send food aid and other relief once the authority of the central government had been restored.

Environmental problems were becoming a growing part of the international agenda, and the United States continued to take a lead in placing anti-pollution legislation on the statute book. In introducing legislation on January 1, Nixon warned that pollution had to be checked. 'It is literally now or never,' he said. 'The 1970s absolutely must be the years when America pays its debt to the past by reclaiming the purity of its air, its waters, and our living environment.' He reiterated this theme in his State of the Union message on January 22, telling Congress that the 'great question' of the new decade was 'shall we surrender to our surroundings, or shall we make our peace with nature and begin to make reparations for the damage we have done? Clean air, clean water, open spaces – these should once again be the birthright of every American. If we act now, they can be.'

Nixon asked Congress for a $10,000 million programme to place the most up-to-date waste-treatment plants in all American cities. In a second message to Congress on February 10 he elaborated on his proposals: he wanted the Federal Government to spend $4,000 million over a four-year period to control municipal, industrial and agricultural wastes. The other $6,000 million needed would come from State and local governments. He also proposed the immediate establishment of standards of air cleanliness, with fines of up to $10,000 a day for factories and enterprises which failed to reach the standard.

Across the administrative machine, environmental programmes were being prepared and put into effect. Factories belching smoke and chemicals, hitherto seen as a sign of a healthy economy, were being recognized as a danger to the quality of life of the communities around them, and, indeed, a danger to life itself. The motor car was also being recognized for what it was: a killer not only on the roads — in the single year 1970 a total of 54,633 Americans (of whom almost two thousand were under five) were killed on the roads — but a killer, through pollution, far away from the roadside. Early in the year the Department of Health, Education and Welfare announced new standards for controlling motor-vehicle exhaust. The exhaust gases from cars, explained the department, caused sixty per cent of the air pollution in the United States, more even than that caused by factories. Congress not only placed these standards on the statute book, but insisted on the manufacture of a virtually 'pollution-free' car within six years.

Nixon entered with determination into the anti-pollution arena. New Federal agencies were set up to control pollution. A White House Council on Environmental Quality, working with Nixon's full support, published its first report, warning of the danger of 'ecological disaster' unless considerable changes were made in the' extravagant style' of American life. The report pointed out that the United States, with six per cent of the world's population, used forty per cent of the world's resources. Henceforth, the Council concluded, environmental considerations must be taken into account in all decisions of urban construction. A contemporary British commentator, James Bishop, editor of the *Illustrated London News*, noted: 'In the light of this emphatic official concern it struck many Americans as strange that there were at this time preparations going on in California for the loading of sixty-six tons of nerve gas on board an old Liberty ship which it was planned should then be sailed to the Atlantic and scuttled less than three hundred miles off the coast of Florida.' In spite of widespread protests throughout the United States, the plan for dumping the ship with its lethal cargo on the floor of the Atlantic was carried out on August 18.

Three years after the Israeli defeat of Syria, Jordan and Egypt, the Arab-Israeli conflict continued to flare up. Syria was also reluctant to accept the loss of the Golan Heights, which had fallen to Israel on the final day of the war. On January 30 fighting broke out on the Heights, but Israel retained its positions there. On February 3, Egyptian frogmen sank an Israeli supply ship off the Israeli port of Eilat, in the Gulf of Akaba. In retaliation, Israeli warplanes sank a number of Egyptian minesweepers in the Gulf of Suez. In a further Israeli reprisal attack on February 12 – an air raid on arms and munitions factories near Cairo – seventy Egyptian civilians were killed. On April 8, during another Israeli air raid on Egyptian military targets in the Nile Delta, bombs falling off their target killed thirty children.

As the Egyptian-Israeli War of Attrition continued, the death toll mounted: 593 Israeli soldiers and 127 civilians were killed in the Egyptian artillery bombardments, and almost twice the number of Egyptian soldiers were killed by Israeli artillery and air attacks. The Egyptian civilian deaths were also high. On August 7 both sides, exhausted by the casualties and the need for perpetual vigilance and repeated military action, agreed to a ceasefire. Israel remained in occupation of Sinai, up to the eastern bank of the Suez Canal and the eastern shore of the Gulf of Suez. Egypt remained sovereign along the western bank of the Suez Canal. Egypt agreed not to place any missiles within twenty miles of the Canal. When, after a few months, it began to move missiles up, establishing more than twenty new missile sites, Israel protested, but took no action. Control of the whole of Sinai, an area larger than Israel itself, gave Israelis – population and government alike – a sense of near-invulnerability.

That Israeli invulnerability related to international borders and to the sovereign States that were its neighbours. But a more volatile, less controllable adversary had emerged. The Palestine Liberation Organization (PLO), headed by Yasser Arafat, had become a force whose terror attacks took place far beyond the confines of the Middle East. On February 13, Palestinian terrorists claimed responsibility for the crash of a Swiss airliner near Zurich, with the loss of forty-seven passengers. Seventeen of them were Israelis. That same day, seven elderly Jews were killed in an old people's home in Munich. Again, the PLO claimed responsibility.

In order to have a presence as close to Israel as possible, the PLO had established bases on Jordanian soil; and not only bases, but large areas within which they, and not the Jordanians, exercised effective sovereignty. By the beginning of 1970 there were more than 20,000 PLO activists in Jordan. Their financing and their weapons came from neighbouring Syria, as well as from Iraq and Egypt – and, in the south, from Saudi Arabia, which had sent troops to work inside the PLO-controlled area of Jordan south of the Dead Sea.

Infiltration into Israel from Jordan was the principal source of PLO terror attacks on individual Israelis. On May 22, eight Israeli children between the ages of six and nine were killed when a terrorist shell struck their bus. On November 6, two Israelis were killed when a terrorist bomb went off in the main bus station in Tel Aviv. The pattern of such killings was relentless. Within four years of the end of the 1967 war, 120 Israeli civilians and 183 soldiers had been killed in terrorist attacks. During the same period, Israeli troops killed 1,873 infiltrators, a large number of them before they could carry out their acts of terror. A further three thousand infiltrators were captured and imprisoned.

Inside Jordan, King Hussein governed a population in which Palestinians were almost as numerous as his own Bedouins. He also had more than 100,000 Palestinian refugees, most of them virtually confined to refugee camps throughout his kingdom, a fertile breeding ground of hatred against both Israel and Jordan. The King recognized the threat which the PLO created to his own rule: it was not beyond the bounds of possibility that they might try to seize power in Jordan, and then use Jordan as their power base, both for its own sake, and against Israel.

Every PLO raid that was mounted from Jordanian soil against Israel confronted Hussein with the possibility of Israeli reprisals. On September 6 the King – himself a pilot – was outraged when PLO hijackers seized four international civil aeroplanes, and flew three of them at gunpoint to Dawson's Field, a desert airstrip in northern Jordan – an area that was effectively beyond Jordanian jurisdiction. There, the PLO held many of the passengers hostage until Britain, West Germany and Switzerland agreed to release convicted Palestinian terrorists being held in their respective jails. The PLO then blew the planes up. The King had been made to look, and in this episode was, powerless. At the same time the PLO set its sights on the King's overthrow, and on the creation of a Palestinian government in Jordan.

King Hussein took drastic military action. Starting on September 15, fighting occurred throughout his kingdom. It was particularly savage in the capital, Amman, where, in house-to-house fighting, the Jordanian army drove the PLO militia from their strongpoints and hiding places. Known to the PLO as 'Black September' – the name later given to one of the terrorist groups whose actions were to be among the most bloody – the Jordanian assault was crippling to the PLO. Two thousand PLO fighters, and several thousand more Palestinian civilians, were killed. The PLO withdrew to the northern region of Jordan adjacent to Syria, whose government had cheered them on in the fight with Hussein. Ten months later the PLO were driven out even from this sanctuary. Most of them fled to Syria and Lebanon; Arafat then took up residence in Lebanon, from where he regrouped his forces.

The prospect of agreement between the PLO and Israel was non-existent. The PLO charter called for Israel's elimination. The Israeli Prime Minister, Golda Meir, was adamant that there could not, and would never, be a Palestinian State on the West Bank of the River Jordan – the predominantly Palestinian-inhabited area which Israel had conquered from Jordan three years earlier. Golda Meir was equally adamant, and no less sincerely so, that Israel wished to find a way forward to peace with all its Arab neighbours. Speaking at the end of September in the United States to the bi-annual convention of American trade unionists (the AFL-CIO), she said: 'It will be a great day when Arab farmers will cross the Jordan not with planes or tanks, but with tractors and with their hands outstretched in friendship, as between farmer and farmer, as between human beings. A dream it may be, but I am sure that one day it will come true.'

The State of Israel was only twenty-two years old, but many of its citizens had already fought in three wars. The poet Haim Guri, a veteran of the 1948 War of Independence, wrote, in a passage of anguished prose: 'When, my friends, have we last seen peace? The soil is insatiable. How many more graves, how many more coffins are needed until it will cry out – enough, enough!'

In the West, women's rights were being steadily enhanced. In Britain, the Equal Pay Act made it illegal to discriminate against women – after 1975 – in either wages or conditions of employment. In the United States, the Secretary of Labour, James Hodson, announced that Federal contracts would in future contain a clause making it obligatory for companies with federal contracts to contain a certain quota of women. At the same time, the Attorney-General, John Mitchell, began a series of legal cases under the Civil Rights Act to end discrimination in the employment of Black women. Also in the area of civil rights, on August 31 the first desegregated classes opened in more than two hundred school districts throughout the American South.

In China, a small gesture towards human rights, or at least towards rectifying a human wrong, came on July 10, when Bishop James E. Walsh, who had been imprisoned for the previous twelve years, was taken from

Shanghai prison to the Hong Kong border, and released. On his way back to the United States, and to the Maryknoll Mission of which he was a distinguished son, he was received by Pope Paul VI, who told him: 'You have been a witness, authentic and simple, in joy and in sorrow, then in suffering and humiliation, and finally in separation, from the people you loved so much.'

Natural disasters could drive even the most intense military or political crisis off the front pages of the world's newspapers. On May 31 an earthquake in northern Peru seemed, as the first news of it reached the wire services, to be on a cataclysmic scale. It was: in all, more than 50,000 people were killed, making it one of the worst earthquakes of the century. On November 12, an even higher death toll than in Peru followed a cyclone and tidal wave in East Pakistan (later Bangladesh), when 150,000 people were killed. Nature could be as destructive as any human killing agency.

Man continued to search at the very edge of discovery for healing processes and the means to preserve and prolong life. In West Germany the first successful nerve transplant took place in 1970. Cancer research was continuous: at a cancer conference held in Tokyo towards the end of the year, reports were given by German, Swedish and American scientists on their progress during a year-long worldwide international co-operative programme. Considerable progress was also made in several other areas of medicine, including fertility, artificial hip joints and heart surgery. All heart transplants had been temporarily halted throughout the world in order to overcome the problems of heart rejection. Work was proceeding to good effect, however, on the use of artificial elements – such as plastic pumps, and nuclear-powered heart pacemakers which could last ten years without replacement.

CHAPTER TWENTY

1971

> We have bled too much, committed too many horrors,
> and the time to get out is now. The only way to bring
> our prisoners of war home is to get out now; the only
> way we can renew our commitment to mankind is to
> get out now.
>
> SENATOR VANCE HARTKE

ON 8 FEBRUARY 1971 the South Vietnamese, no longer able to use
American ground troops in support of their activities in Laos, launched an
attack on the Ho Chi Minh trail where it went through Laotian territory.
Whereas the American planners estimated that 60,000 first-class United
States troops would be needed for the task – which they could no longer
undertake as a result of Congressional disapproval – the South Vietnamese
undertook to do it with only 30,000. American bombers were able to devastate the main target, Tchepone. But, even when the South Vietnamese
captured the ruins, the Communist forces managed to surround and bombard
them from all sides.

Among those killed during the incursion into Laos was the American
press photographer Larry Burrows, whose stark photographs of the war eight
years earlier had shocked the readers of *Life* magazine. British-born, Burrows'
first job had been as a tea boy in the London Blitz. He was killed on February
10 when the helicopter he was flying in was shot down. Four other press
photographers were killed with him. The day before his death he had risked
his life to rescue a South Vietnamese soldier from a burning personnel carrier.

After a few weeks, the South Vietnamese withdrew from Laos, leaving the
trail virtually intact. American helicopters evacuated the South Vietnamese
wounded. Many, clinging to the helicopter skids, suffered horrifying injuries

or were killed as the helicopters flew low over the trees to avoid being hit by Communist anti-aircraft fire.

War on one side of the globe did not deter those who were working to eliminate at least one aspect of war – and warlike pollutants – on the other. On February 11, three days after the South Vietnamese had launched their offensive in Laos, supported by American bombers, sixty-three nations, including the United States, signed a treaty banning the use of atomic weapons on the sea bed. In a parallel move, with the emphasis on pollution and the destructive effect of man-made processes in the environment, the Greenpeace international environmental campaign was founded. Giving it impetus were the continuing American nuclear tests.

The origin of Greenpeace came in 1971, after the United States announced plans for a 5.2 megaton underground nuclear test at Amchitka Island, in the Aleutians. Three friends, Jim Bohlen, Paul Cote and Irving Stowe, following the Quaker tradition of 'bearing witness' – protesting injustices by being there to observe them – decided to take a boat to a nuclear test site. On September 15 their ship, the fishing boat *Phyllis Cormack*, set sail for Amchitka. They gave their effort the name 'Greenpeace'. By mid-September ferocious storms forced them to harbour in the Aleutian Islands. The American government had meanwhile announced that, for reasons of the bad weather, the nuclear test would be delayed. The bomb was eventually detonated on November 6.

Although the Greenpeace attempt to stop the atomic test was a failure, it was a catalyst for alerting public opinion and raising awareness. So vociferous were the protests that Nixon cancelled the nuclear-testing programme devised for the following year.

There was a spur to the American anti-war movement on June 13, when the *New York Times* published hitherto secret 'Pentagon Papers', which gave details of American policy planning, and deception, with regard to the prosecution of the war in Vietnam. The government tried to prevent publication of the documents, as such secret material was not usually made public for fifty years or longer, but the Supreme Court upheld the newspaper's right to publish. The United States was fortunate. Amid the conflicts and deceptions which the Vietnam War revealed, and which the Pentagon Papers confirmed, there lay a strong democratic impulse, a scrutiny, a persistent inquiry, a judicial system independent of the executive, a legislature vigilant in its responsibilities.

Within the Soviet Union, no such checks and balances existed. Criticism of institutions, methods, administrative malaise, economic policy, Party lines and the Party leadership carried with it an element of considerable risk. There were outlets for frustration. The humorous weekly magazine *Krokodil* (Crocodile) lampooned in cartoons the failings and foibles of minor bureaucrats, and carried testy readers' letters about faulty chess sets in municipal parks, or trains delayed for hours by defective signals at wayside halts. But there was seldom an attempt to get at the inner problems of the society, and a political movement such as the anti-war campaign in the United States was unthinkable. Yet dissent was never totally silenced inside the Soviet Union. In Moscow a small Human Rights Committee had been formed in 1970 by a group of Soviet writers and intellectuals perturbed by the many violations of human rights in the Soviet Union. One of its founders was Andrei Sakharov, the nuclear scientist, and a senior figure in the Soviet Academy of Sciences. Fifteen years earlier Sakharov had been at the centre of the Soviet development and testing of a hydrogen bomb: his credentials could not have been more patriotic. His first public dissent had been a protest in 1961 against the Soviet atmospheric tests.

At the beginning of 1971 the Chief Prosecutor of the Soviet Union, Roman Rudenko, warned the members of the Human Rights Committee against continuing their activities. The committee members felt confident that the abuses with which they were concerned had to be made public, and that publicity could lead to an end to the abuses. On January 28 the Russian writer and philosopher Vladimir Bukovsky issued a public appeal to Western psychiatrists, urging them to protest as a profession against the Soviet practice of locking up dissidents in psychiatric hospitals. His appeal included two hundred pages of detailed testimony about individuals who were incarcerated. In mid-March, Bukovsky was arrested, and held in a mental hospital. From the West, Amnesty International protested, and was immediately denounced in the Soviet press.

The dissemination of material on human rights abuses, such as that compiled by Bukovsky, was anathema to the Soviet authorities. On March 29 a search was carried out by the KGB at the home of one of the founder members of the Moscow Human Rights Committee, Valery Chalidze. Materials collected by the committee about individual human rights abuse were taken away. In July, in a gesture of defiance, the committee contacted the International League for the Rights of Man in Geneva and obtained affiliation with it. Meanwhile, the KGB resorted to the tactic of listening in to telephone conversations from abroad and cutting them off in mid-flow; and intercepting all letters coming from abroad.

Undeterred by this harassment, in October the Human Rights Committee appealed to the delegates of the forthcoming World Psychiatric Association, that was being held in Mexico, to demand an end to the misuse of psychiatry for political purposes. As a matter of urgency they were asked to demand the release of Bukovsky from his confinement – Bukovsky's mother having been told by the KGB that her son was likely to be declared insane. With regard to Bukovsky, the protest was successful, and he was declared 'normal'.

Trials against Jews continued. Those linked with the Leningrad would-be emigrant hijackers were sentenced to four-, five- and six-year prison terms. Such sentences did not deter the growing pressure for emigration. Small but determined demonstrations took place – one of them in Riga on February 26, in which twenty-four Jews took part – demanding the right to leave the Soviet Union, and to go where they pleased. The demonstrators pointed out that this right was enshrined in the 1948 United Nations Declaration of Human Rights, of which the Soviet Union was a signatory, and for which Sakharov's Committee on Human Rights was campaigning. On May 20 the committee appealed in an open letter to the Supreme Soviet against these sentences, and what it called the 'persecution of Jewish repatriates'. The sole aim of those who were being brought to trial, the committee insisted, was 'to protest against the unlawful refusals to give them visas'.

The trials against Jewish activists continued. In Riga a twenty-three-year-old Jewish nurse, Ruth Alexandrovich, was sentenced to a year in labour camp for distributing six copies of a small privately printed brochure on emigration to Israel and fifteen copies of a brochure about learning modern Hebrew. A Jewish librarian, Raisa Palatnik, was sentenced to two years in labour camp for demanding the right to emigrate. More and more Jews were demanding that right. On applying to leave the Soviet Union, however, many were not only refused permission to emigrate but were thrown out of their professional employment. Once out of work, they were threatened with charges of 'parasitism' – in a society where to be without work was to be in violation of the law. Most were able to get menial jobs, such as working as stokers in boiler houses, road sweepers or lift attendants.

Jewish organizations in the West protested against these pressures and indignities. Taking up the cause of Raisa Palatnik, who was thirty-five years old, a group of British women, calling themselves the '35s', began a tenacious campaign that was to draw public attention to the plight of hundreds of prisoners. In Brussels, the Israeli Prime Minister Golda Meir appealed to the Soviet Union to allow any Jew who wanted to emigrate to Israel to be allowed to do so. On a visit to Canada in October, confronted by Canadian government concern on this issue, Kosygin announced that the number of Jews allowed to leave would be substantially increased: it was – from a mere 1,044 in 1970 to more than 13,000 during the course of 1971.

The repercussions of the war in Vietnam were tormenting the United States. On April 20 the historian Barbara Tuchman noted in her diary the comment by Donald Riegle, a Congressman from Michigan, who had spoken to a couple in his constituency who had lost a son in Vietnam: 'There was no way that I could say that what had happened was in their interest or in the national interest or in anyone's interest.'

On April 24 an estimated 200,000 Americans demonstrated in Washington against the war. Only half that number had been expected. Thousands more, who had come by bus from New York, Philadelphia and Boston, were unable to reach the demonstration as the roads leading to it were blocked by traffic and marchers. Anti-war marches also took place that day in Chicago and San Francisco. Of the Washington marchers, Ian McDonald commented in *The Times*: 'As in previous demonstrations in the nation's capital, the crowds for the most part were made up of the young and the longhaired, mostly college students, dressed in jeans and light shirts. But this time there appeared to be more older people and more Blacks.' There were also Vietnam veterans, many of them in their early twenties, 'wearing camouflage battle dress and floppy field hats and carrying plastic rifles. One older man, dressed in a neat but faded dark suit, walked slowly across the front of the crowd carrying a sign reading: "My son died in Vietnam. What for, America?"'

Addressing the vast crowd, Senator Vance Hartke of Indiana declared: 'We have bled too much, committed too many horrors, and the time to get out is now. The only way to bring our prisoners of war home is to get out now; the only way we can renew our commitment to mankind is to get out now.'

On November 12 Nixon proclaimed an end to America's 'offensive' role in Vietnam, and announced the withdrawal of another 45,000 troops. Only 182,000 remained. American bombers continued to attack Communist supply lines running along the Ho Chi Minh trail, through Laos, but even the American air component, which had wreaked such havoc two and three years earlier, was being reduced. In Paris, American-North Vietnamese negotiations continued.

On the Indian subcontinent, national cohesion was under threat. In two Indian States, Maharashtra and Gujarat, Hindus and Muslims were involved in bloody clashes. In other States, including Bengal, extreme Communists (Naxilites) were seeking to bring organized government to a halt. Several States were quarrelling over borders and water rights. Industrial production was falling. The heavy growth rate in population was eating into, and effectively halving, the five per cent annual growth of the national income. The Congress Party, which had led India to independence in 1947 and ruled it virtually unchallenged since then, had split, and the Prime Minister, Indira Gandhi, unable to draw the factions together, had dissolved parliament.

The general election of March 10 offered the prospect of greater stability, with the re-election of Mrs Gandhi as Prime Minister with a much increased majority. Her section of the Congress Party, known as the Congress (Ruling) Party, won 350 of the 523 seats in the Lower House (Lok Sabha). Her Party also won by far the largest single percentage of the vote, with just over forty per cent of the total electorate of 230 million. Where States were unable to elect stable governments, as in the case of the predominantly Communist West Bengal, Mrs Gandhi imposed her own central rule from Delhi.

The third Indo-Pakistani war since 1947 arose when West and East Pakistan began to break apart. In East Pakistan, a separatist leader, Shaikh Mujib Rahman, leader of the Awami League, won a massive majority in the elections held there, and demanded independence. On February 15 the Pakistani Prime Minister, Zulfikar Ali Bhutto, warned the Awami League to be more flexible, and to work for a federal rather than a separatist solution. His warning was ignored. There were strikes and riots throughout the East Pakistani province of East Bengal, including the capital, Dacca.

Pakistani troops were brought in to maintain order. On March 6 the President of Pakistan, Yahya Khan, broadcast to his nation: 'I will not allow a handful of people to destroy the homeland of millions of Pakistanis.' On March 23 Shaikh Mujib had called again for the transfer of power in East Bengal to the 'elected representatives of the people' – in the elections, 75 per cent of the voters had voted for the Awami League. As a gesture of defiance, the flag of a new nation – Bangladesh – was raised on public buildings in Dacca, while parades of armed 'Bangladeshi' troops marched through the city. On March 25 Shaikh Mujib was arrested by the Pakistani authorities and taken to West Pakistan, where he was held captive. Fighting then broke out between the Pakistani authorities and the East Bengal separatists.

The Indian government stayed aloof, not wanting to become embroiled in the quarrel of its Muslim neighbour at the two extremities of its land mass. In a gesture which did not please West Pakistan, the Indian parliament passed a unanimous resolution of 'sympathy and solidarity' with the people of East Bengal. But words of sympathy were not followed by any practical help, and, much as they would have liked to have done, the East Bengali freedom fighters, the Mukti Bahini, received no weapons from India.

India could not stay aloof for long, however. Hundreds, even thousands of Hindus living in East Bengal were killed by Pakistani troops, and Hindu refugees, numbering hundreds of thousands, began to flee from East Bengal and seek sanctuary across the Indian border. The sight of these refugees in Calcutta was one that shocked even those who could remember the sight of the refugee masses in 1947. On May 31 India appealed to the world for aid to help feed more than a million refugees, and provide them with temporary shelter. By the end of the year the number of refugees had doubled, to two million. Indira Gandhi wrote to Heads of State throughout the world, including Queen Elizabeth II of Britain and President Nixon, for help. It was essential, she said, that with the help of the international community the refugees be allowed to return to their homes, and to do so in safety. India could not shoulder a burden that was essentially Pakistan's creation.

India had another cause for grievance, when it learned that both the United States and China were supplying arms to Pakistan, to help it retain the unity of the two sections of the country. But India (and the imprisoned Shaikh) saw the arms as enabling Pakistan to maintain its dominance over East Bengal.

India began publicly to champion the independence of Bangladesh. In October, having signed a twenty-year treaty with the Soviet Union, Indira Gandhi travelled through Western Europe and the United States, to seek support for an independent Bangladesh. India wanted no Pakistani presence, sovereignty or army to its east, but, instead, a sovereign nation, Bangladesh.

By the end of October, India was training the East Bengali freedom fighters, the Mukti Bahini, on Indian soil, and providing them with arms and ammunition. To relieve pressure on his troops fighting inside East

Bengal, on November 15 General Yahya Khan sent Pakistani troops across the frontier into western India. The Indian forces struck back. On December 3, Pakistani warplanes bombed Indian airfields. There was no declaration of war by either side.

On December 6 India recognized the independence of East Pakistan, under the name of the 'Democratic Republic of Bangladesh'. Within a few days the war had spread to Sind, Punjab and Kashmir in the west, and along the whole East Pakistan border. Within a week Indian troops from West Bengal were advancing towards the East Bengal capital, Dacca, driving the Pakistani forces back to the Brahmaputra River. On December 16 the Pakistani forces in East Bengal surrendered to India. The instrument of surrender was signed in Dacca. That day, India ordered its troops along the border with West Pakistan to cease fighting. They did so, and 90,000 Pakistani troops were taken prisoner of war.

There were territorial gains on both sides, by far the most extensive being by India, which acquired two thousand square miles of Pakistani territory in Sind, including parts of the Rann of Kutch which had been awarded to Pakistan by an international tribunal in 1966, after the previous Indo-Pakistani war. In Punjab, Jammu and Kashmir, India captured and annexed a thousand square miles of disputed territory, as well as thirty-two border posts overlooking the Srinagar-Leh road.

Pakistan gained a few square miles of territory elsewhere, in Jammu and on the Punjab border. More than a thousand soldiers had been killed on both sides. The subcontinent had become three as opposed to two sovereign States: Pakistan, India and Bangladesh (apart from the smaller Himalayan kingdoms of Nepal, Sikkim and Bhutan). President Yahya of Pakistan resigned. Shaikh Mujib was released from prison.

In Africa, in January, there was a military coup in Uganda. Milton Obote, who had been Prime Minister and later President since 1962, was overthrown, and Idi Amin, an army officer and a Muslim, came to power. His was, he said, only a caretaker administration, and his presidency only provisional. He promised an early return to civilian rule after 'free and fair' elections. Two months later, however, he suspended all political activity in Uganda for two years. In May he introduced detention without trial. Unrest at these changes was put down by force. Amin was set not only to remain as President, but to emerge as a dictator.

*   *   *

In Northern Ireland, the violence that had broken out between Catholic and Protestant militants in 1969 neither abated nor seemed capable of a political solution. Roman Catholics generally felt aggrieved at what they called fifty years of British 'misrule', in which their minority rights had been neglected and rebuffed. Protestants felt that the British government – under a Labour Prime Minister, Harold Wilson – was neglecting their majority interests, which had hitherto secured them a clear predominance in the provincial administration.

There was also fighting between two branches of the Irish Republican Army, the 'Provisional' and 'Official' IRA. The main territorial struggle for control was fought in the housing estates of Belfast, where, on January 10, four men were found tarred and feathered. As the British troops in Northern Ireland – whom Harold Wilson had reinforced – tried to interpose themselves between Protestant and Catholic violence, they found themselves abused by both sides. When they tried to tackle the Provisionals, searching for arms in Catholic areas, they were attacked by Catholic girls hurling abuse at them. Shooting between the army and the Provisionals increased. On February 5, Gunner Robert Curtis became the first British soldier to die on active service in Northern Ireland. Television brought in to millions of British homes the sight of British troops being attacked by angry stone-throwing crowds, and having to pull back.

As killings and murder increased, every variety of violence seemed to be perpetrated. On February 9 two BBC engineers and three workmen were killed when a landmine exploded. On February 26 two unarmed policemen were machine-gunned to death. On March 10 three unarmed Scots soldiers, young men in their late teens, who were off duty – two of them were brothers – were lured to a remote country road and murdered in cold blood. The murderers escaped across the border to the Irish Republic.

When IRA gunmen opened fire on a crowd of Protestants returning from a Protestant parade on April 13, there were riots throughout East Belfast. In July there were riots in Londonderry, and two of the Catholic rioters were shot dead by the police. Once again, and not just in Ireland, the human capacity for destruction, for the curtailment of life, for the creation of widows and orphans, was shown to be unlimited. There was talk of civil war, but the mass of the population wanted to pursue their lives without violence. Daily life continued, marred by violent flashpoints – often daily, at other times with gaps of several days, even many days – which became the visual images of a whole society in siege. As so often in the conflicts that tormented divided peoples, the numbers involved were not large. The total population of Northern Ireland was under a million and a half. The non-Catholics constituted, under the most recent census (of 1961), 829,778; the Roman Catholics, 497,547.

Confronted by IRA violence on an increasing scale, on August 9 the British government introduced internment. This effectively deprived those who were held in detention of the basic rights of judicial procedures starting with an arrest warrant and including a trial by jury. With the arrest that day of three hundred IRA men, there were shootings, riots and widespread fires in Belfast, Londonderry and Newry as troops and the IRA fought virtual pitched battles in the streets. When communal violence erupted, and houses were set on fire, 2,000 Protestants and 2,500 Catholics were left homeless. In three days, twenty-two people were killed, among them a Roman Catholic priest.

The detained IRA men were sent mostly to a detention camp at Long Kesh. Under parliamentary pressure, the British government later admitted that the treatment there had been harsh, and that men being interrogated had their heads covered in hoods, were deliberately confused by loud noises, and were made to stand for long periods of time without sufficient rest or nourishment. There was resentment in Britain about another aspect of the conflict: that the two IRA movements both had their headquarters in Dublin, and that the Irish government allowed them to recruit openly and solicit funds. When the British army tried to seal off the roads running from the Republic into Northern Ireland, they came under IRA fire from the Republic side of the border. In one incident a British soldier, two customs officers and a woman were killed by IRA fire. Inside Northern Ireland the second half of the year saw even more IRA killings. On one occasion a Dutch seaman was shot dead in a dentist's surgery. A young Catholic woman in Londonderry who had become engaged to a British soldier was tarred and feathered, and had her hair cut off by a jeering crowd of IRA supporters. In the eight days following December 4 a further twenty-two people were killed. An explosion in a Catholic bar killed fifteen people, including the publican's wife and child. Two days later a factory in Belfast was destroyed by a bomb, and a woman member of the Salvation Army killed.

Protestants and Catholics alike served in the Ulster Defence Regiment. But common service was no protection against those who were becoming known as 'the men of violence'. On December 7 a number of IRA gunmen entered the home of a Protestant member of the Ulster Defence Regiment and shot him dead. On the following day a Roman Catholic UDR man was shot dead in front of his children. Bombs and bullets were dragging an integral part of the United Kingdom into near-anarchy. On December 11 a bomb in a crowded shop in a Catholic district of Belfast killed four people, including a seven-month-old boy.

Amid these storms the life of Queen's University, Belfast, went on, though the faculty were finding it harder and harder to persuade academics from mainland Britain to accept lecture engagements. One faculty member, Dr A. T. Q. Stewart, a lecturer in history, wrote of the escalating violence: 'In Belfast the destruction of property recalled the havoc of the German air raids of 1941, and the city had also to endure a severe water shortage because the autumn was unusually dry. The urban population bore the inconveniences of the troubles with remarkable patience, and courage of a high order was shown by firemen, ambulance drivers, and others whose duties took them into situations of extreme peril.' Stewart also wrote of how, towards the end of the year, 'there were a number of acts of bravery by civilians against the gunmen, the most notable occurring on Christmas Eve, when an unidentified man drove a petrol tanker with a bomb attached away from a street crowded with women and children'.

In one year, 173 people were killed in Northern Ireland. Forty-three of them were British soldiers.

On the night of October 25/26 voting took place at the United Nations in New York for the admission of Communist China. Before the final vote was taken the representative of Taiwan left the chamber, for, as well as voting to admit China, the United Nations voted to expel Taiwan. A fact of international life for more than twenty years had been overthrown. The first of the new Chinese representatives reached New York on November 8. For China this marked an end to isolation and the chance to participate in all the global debates. Speaking at the United Nations General Assembly for the first time, on November 15, the Chinese representatives called for the removal of all American troops from Vietnam. America was already deep in the process of withdrawal.

On November 23 China made its first appearance at the United Nations Security Council. Many unaligned nations had wanted China to be present there as a counterweight to the United States. Once China took its seat, there was no longer a place for Taiwan in any United Nations body or institution. As country after country broke off diplomatic relations with

Taiwan, the Chinese Nationalists on Taiwan, the successors to Chang Kai-shek's Nanking government, had to recognize that their long-cherished hopes of returning to mainland China and supplanting the Communists had been reduced to nil. They could retain their independence, their flag, their currency, an expanding industry, close economic links with the United States; but they could no longer act as 'China' in the councils of the world.

The United States, hitherto Red China's implacable foe, and main adversary at the time of the Korean War two decades earlier, was moving towards the restoration of relations. The idea of so large and powerful a nation as China being kept out of standard international diplomatic and trade relations was fast becoming absurd. On March 15 the United States ended the restrictions on American citizens visiting China. In April, the Chinese invited an American table-tennis team to tour China. These seemingly routine and unexceptional invitations, unique in the annals of Red Chinese-American relations, heralded a turning point in the dialogue between the two Powers. On April 14 Nixon announced that American trade with China would resume, and be put on the same basis as that between the United States and the Soviet Union. The United States also ended the ban on the transfer of dollars to China, so that Chinese-Americans could send financial support to their relatives for the first time since 1949. American-owned ships, if sailing under foreign flags, were allowed to trade in Chinese ports for the first time since the Korean War.

On July 9, Nixon's National Security Adviser, Henry Kissinger – hitherto Nixon's emissary at the secret talks with North Vietnam that were being held in a Paris suburb – was sent, under seal of similar secrecy, to Peking. His visit – sixteen years later the subject of an American opera, *Nixon in China* – lasted for three days. Following the visit the Chinese invited Nixon to China. Despite continuing Sino-American friction over both Vietnam and Taiwan, he accepted.

China had its own hidden agenda with regard to the improving relations with the Americans, and one which Kissinger recognized. The re-emergence of Japan as a Pacific and South-East Asian power was worrying the Chinese government, for whom Japan constituted their largest trading partner. Considerable efforts were made by China to secure better relations with several South-East Asian nations. On August 6 the Burmese President, Ne Win, began a seven-day State visit to Peking. China also established trade relations with Malaysia, widened its relations with Ceylon and – far further afield – developed trading relations with France, Italy and the Scandinavian countries.

In October the State visit to Peking of the Emperor of Ethiopia was a sign that even the most conservative of governments in the Third World was not beyond wooing; and that China's attitude to Africa was not limited to stirring up revolutionary activity. China, despite its totalitarian regime, was seeking – and obtaining – a degree of international respectability that would have been unthinkable a decade earlier. From Britain, China acquired heavy generating equipment and six commercial jet aircraft. Before the end of the year a Chinese trade agreement with Canada secured for China a five-fold increase in the purchase of Canadian grain.

The leaps forward in science that had been so frequent in the previous decade were marked in 1971 by new techniques which were to revolutionize the next three decades. In the United States, Intel introduced the micro-processor, a minute device on a single 'chip' for processing information within a computer. That same year, surgeons developed a fibre-optic endoscope, for looking inside the human body, enabling innumerable probings and diagnoses to be made without the need for incisions. In Britain, in order to co-ordinate the diverse professional skills which the new medical techniques involved, eye surgeons, diamond cutters, titanium technologists and microscope makers joined together in a special Microsurgical Instrumentation Research Association. One of its first developments was the diamond-bladed scalpel, which became the instrument of choice for eye surgeons worldwide. Neurosurgeons and brain surgeons were likewise drawn in to use instruments based on the new technology, including forceps made of titanium alloy: this alloy being lighter than steel and less prone to tarnish. Ironically, the technological advances in this field had come as a result of development with the same alloy for use by the aircraft industry, first in the military and then in the civilian sphere.

The year 1971 also saw advances in the early diagnosis of cancer. But the slow progress of cancer research vexed medical researchers and the general public alike. In May, Nixon called publicly for an 'all-out war' on cancer, putting the full authority of the President of the United States, and his budgetary influence, behind that war. 'There have been some very significant breakthroughs', he said, 'that indicate that we can really look forward to the day that we can find a cure for cancer. It doesn't mean that it's going to come quickly.' The search would not fail, Nixon added, because of shortage of money for research. 'If a hundred million dollars this year is not enough, we will provide more money; to the extent that money is needed, it will be provided.'

One aspect of cancer, and one area of increased medical awareness, was that of the effects of cigarette smoking. In London, in January, the British Royal College of Physicians published a report showing that smoking was a danger to health, and a main cause of lung cancer. In order to spread this information to the public, a pro-active group, Action on Smoking and Health (ASH), was set up, to make information on the dangers of smoking as widely known as possible, and to persuade people to stop smoking. Doctors gave out ashtrays designed in the shape of coffins, and pointed out to the recipients that cigarette smoking was as serious a cause of disease in the 1970s as the 'great epidemic diseases' of typhoid, cholera and tuberculosis had been for earlier generations.

A quarter of a century after this first sustained anti-smoking campaign, great strides had been made in the anti-smoking battle, with non-smoking trains, planes and public places in many countries. But the battle was, even by then, far from won. The failure was seen most clearly in the groups of people smoking outside the front entrances of buildings in which no smoking was allowed.

The United Nations World Health Organization was also active in the anti-smoking campaign. Its method was to encourage tobacco-producing countries to grow other crops. But the main work of the WHO was the campaign to eradicate smallpox worldwide, and to fight the cholera epidemic that reached grave proportions in parts of Africa in March. The WHO also addressed itself to the problem of over-population, financing research into as wide a variety as possible of 'safe, effective and acceptable' methods of birth control.

In the search for a less polluted environment, numerous efforts were being made and developments suggested. In Britain, the Friends of the Earth organization was founded, with an emphasis on the need for reuse and recycling. Its first public action, on May 9, was to dump thousands of Schweppes non-returnable bottles on the doorstep of the firm's headquarters, as part of its call for recyclable bottles. In the United States, one of the most hopeful schemes, from the perspective of 1971, was for a hovertrain to replace the motor-car congestion along the highly urbanized Northeast Corridor between Boston, New York and Washington. The train would run on a slim elevated concrete track, on a thin cushion of air, at 250 miles an hour, and even faster. Experiments were made, with both the track and the air cushion. A special motor was designed. The latest in British technology was enlisted.

French train designs were examined. Enthusiastic newspaper articles were written. But not every human enthusiasm is translated into reality. Twenty-seven years later no such train was in existence: in October 1998 the fastest train then in service on the East Coast line had an average speed of no more than eighty miles an hour.

In Britain, as in the United States, not every beneficent plan reached beyond the drawing board and the prototype. A scheme for an electric car, quiet and pollution-free, but slower than the petrol-driven car, and also for an electric van, had to be abandoned: people were not ready, and were still not ready when the century drew to a close, to give up speed for a more environmentally friendly method of private transport.

The revelation of danger often serves as a catalyst for change. In 1971 it was announced that 250,000 tons of lead were discharged from car exhausts every year in the United States. Doctors and scientists raised the alarm. Lead poisoning, discovered first among the animals in Staten Island zoo, was soon discovered among humans in New York City. Those living closest to busy roads seemed most at risk. Experiments were begun to produce a commercially viable lead-free petrol. Within five years lead-free petrol was to become compulsory in some States of the United States, and in due course in all of them. One health hazard of the modern world had been seriously challenged.

CHAPTER TWENTY-ONE

1972

The real problem is that the enemy is willing to sacrifice
in order to win . . . .

PRESIDENT RICHARD M. NIXON

On Sunday 30 January 1972, in Northern Ireland, there was a Roman
Catholic protest march in Londonderry. The authorities, fearing that the
IRA would use the march to provoke clashes with British troops, had declared
the march illegal, but it had gone ahead nevertheless. The marchers were
protesting against the British government's policy of internment without
trial. As the march was ending, and most of the ten thousand marchers
dispersing, stones were thrown at the troops – members of the Parachute
Regiment – who responded by chasing after the stone throwers. As they did
so, shots were fired, allegedly by IRA snipers. The troops returned fire,
killing thirteen people.

In Dublin the outrage was such that a mob converged on the British
Embassy and burned it down. A British government inquiry, while insisting
that the IRA had opened fire first, admitted that the troops had returned
the fire 'very recklessly'. The tension between the Catholic community and
the British troops mounted. 'Bloody Sunday' became – and remained a
quarter of a century later – a hated symbol of British repression and the
denial of Catholic rights. An IRA bomb on the British mainland, intended
to damage the Parachute Regiment headquarters in Aldershot, killed seven
bystanders. In Northern Ireland itself, there were two IRA bombs, and eight
people were killed. In an attempt to impose some measure of control the
British Prime Minister, Edward Heath, declared direct British rule from
London. But even though one objective of direct rule was to achieve a
measure of conciliation with the Catholics, in the hope of undermining
IRA extremism, on average two British soldiers were killed every week,

intensifying British public hostility. The main streets of many small Northern Irish towns were severely damaged. 'No-go' areas, in which the IRA ruled and British troops did not enter, came into being in Belfast and Londonderry. Heath's order on March 2 that 'intensive' interrogation techniques were no longer to be used on IRA prisoners, while welcomed by human rights groups in Britain, had no impact on the determination of the IRA to make British rule over the province untenable.

On April 15 the leader of the Official IRA, Joseph McCann, was shot dead by British troops in the centre of Belfast. There were widespread riots and considerable destruction of property. A Protestant militia, the Ulster Defence Association (UDA), was formed, to protect Protestant areas from the IRA. Fighting between the two groups regularly took a toll of lives. On the eve of a truce offered by the Provisional IRA on April 26, seven people were killed in the last day's shoot-outs. The truce lasted until July 9, when the Provisional IRA clashed with British troops. In the ensuing gunfight six people were killed, including a Catholic priest. On Friday July 21 the IRA exploded twenty bombs simultaneously in shopping centres and bus stations in Belfast. Eleven people were killed, and 'Bloody Friday' was added to 'Bloody Sunday' in the catalogue of remembrance.

In November, after Edward Heath made his first visit to Northern Ireland since becoming Prime Minister more than two years earlier, the IRA launched a series of rocket attacks on British military bases and strongpoints. Five days before Christmas, five men in a crowded pub in Londonderry were killed by IRA machine-gun fire. The death toll since hostilities broke out in 1969 was 679. Of these 467 had been killed in 1972, including a hundred soldiers. It was to take another quarter of a century, the negotiating skills of several British and Irish governments, and more than three thousand deaths, before the contending parties in Northern Ireland agreed to end their military confrontation, and to embark upon a political compromise.

On February 21 Nixon arrived in China. He was the first American President to set foot on Chinese soil. Seventy-two years earlier American troops had entered Peking as part of a victorious army. Chou En-lai was at Peking airport to greet him, but the streets through which he drove, and Tiananmen Square itself, were deserted. Nixon spent a week in China. During fifteen hours of negotiations with Chou En-lai, he agreed to allow China to purchase considerable quantities of American goods, including locomotives, building equipment, industrial chemicals, trucks and motor-car engines.

The Chinese were anxious to see an end to the conflict in Vietnam that would not throw the North Vietnamese into the arms of the Soviet Union, which was supplying the North with an increasing amount of heavy weaponry. They were relieved when Nixon suggested a reduction of the 8,000-strong American garrison in Taiwan, in return for some form of settlement in Vietnam. The United States would no longer seek to be the policeman or anti-Communist catspaw in South-East Asia.

At the time of Nixon's visit to China he had withdrawn more than 400,000 American troops from Vietnam. In the fighting that was continuing, American combat deaths were fewer than ten a week. Three years earlier they had been three and four times that number. To let the American public know that he was serious in his search for a negotiated settlement, Nixon revealed the existence of the hitherto secret Kissinger talks in Paris.

The North Vietnamese hoped to advance their cause by showing the Americans the extent to which the South Vietnamese were unable to hold the ground unaided. Whether they would be able to do so was already much doubted in Washington. At the end of February the American Secretary of Defence, Melvin Laird, told members of Congress that North Vietnamese and Vietcong attacks on a nationwide scale were 'not a serious possibility'. On March 30, however, these very forces launched a three-front offensive as ferocious as that of the Tet offensive four years earlier. Then it had been the forces already in the South that had attacked the Americans. This time it was divisions based and trained in the North that invaded the South. As many as 120,000 North Vietnamese and Vietcong troops took part. In the first week of the offensive the North Vietnamese troops advanced through the Demilitarized Zone. As a central part of their armoury they had a considerable quantity of first-class Soviet artillery, rockets and tanks. One of the two South Vietnamese divisions facing the attackers who were seeking to surround the provincial capital, Quang Tri – a division many of whose soldiers had never been in combat – panicked and fled. One South Vietnamese divisional commander, General Giai, was tried by court martial for 'desertion in the face of the enemy' and sentenced to five years in prison.

On May 1 the North Vietnamese overran Quang Tri, which they then held for the next three months. Of the tens of thousands of Vietnamese civilians fleeing southward from Quang Tri towards Hué, an estimated 20,000 were killed. Many were killed by North Vietnamese artillery searching for South Vietnamese units, others by American aircraft trying to bomb North Vietnamese troops moving south, still others by American warships in the South China Sea that, with their powerful naval guns, were seeking out North Vietnamese targets up to ten miles inland (the road south, Highway One, ran five to six miles inland).

Of the sixty to seventy thousand American troops still in Vietnam at the time of the North Vietnamese offensive, only six thousand were combat troops. The full weight of the North Vietnamese attack fell on the South Vietnamese who, although numerically far larger – they outnumbered their adversaries by about five to one – were often unable to anticipate where the next attack would come, and were pushed back by the sheer ferocity of it. In the Mekong Delta, from which South Vietnamese troops were withdrawn in order to fight on the other fronts further north, the Vietcong captured more than a hundred abandoned South Vietnamese army posts within two months. The fact that the Mekong Delta was the least important target of the North Vietnamese attack meant that it was less well defended. Monitoring the débâcle from afar, Nixon understood that the policy of Vietnamization – making the South Vietnamese responsible for the main burden of their own defence – was failing. 'The real problem', he wrote privately, 'is that the enemy is willing to sacrifice in order to win, while the South Vietnamese simply aren't willing to pay that much of a price in order to avoid losing.'

Nixon was right: in the battles of 1972 the North Vietnamese and Vietcong lost as many as 50,000 dead. Many of the Communist deaths were a result of the continuing and intensive American air bombing. Against the Communist forces south of the Demilitarized Zone American bombers flew almost five thousand sorties during the March offensive. But while this could lead to massive casualties on the Communist side, it could not prevent the continual erosion of South Vietnamese control. Nixon was aware of this. 'All the air power in the world', he wrote – including the renewed bombing of Hanoi and Haiphong – would not be able to prevent a Communist victory 'if the South Vietnamese aren't able to hold on the ground'.

On April 20 Nixon sent Kissinger on a secret mission to Moscow. In talks with Brezhnev, Kissinger stated that, in order to start negotiations for an end to the war in Vietnam, the North Vietnamese troops who had invaded the South on March 30 should be withdrawn, as a prior condition and first step. Brezhnev passed this on to Hanoi, which could hardly call back the troops that were even then having so much success throughout South Vietnam – albeit at such a heavy loss of life.

Nixon was expected in Moscow for a summit meeting with Brezhnev, who was hoping, despite Vietnam, to make progress on arms control at the meeting. Kissinger had found Brezhnev on April 20 determined on such a summit 'at almost any cost'. On May 5, to accompany new American peace proposals, Nixon ordered the resumption of the bombing of North Vietnam and the mining of Haiphong harbour. The peace proposals that came with the bombing were the most moderate that the United States had yet put forward: the remaining American troops in South Vietnam would leave within four months of a ceasefire and the release of American prisoners of war. The future settlement between the warring factions in Vietnam would be negotiated 'between the Vietnamese themselves'.

The main targets were in and around the capital Hanoi, and Haiphong, the principal northern port. Three days later Nixon ordered American aircraft to lay mines in Haiphong harbour, to prevent the arrival of Chinese and Soviet supply ships. When a Soviet freighter was hit in Haiphong harbour, the Russians protested, but not with particular vigour.

On May 22 Nixon flew to Moscow. As with his visit to China, he was the first American President to make that journey. Both Communist countries had built up a strong propaganda machine against American 'imperialism', portrayed as a diabolical enemy against which the utmost vigilance was needed, and massive arms expenditure. The head of the arch-enemy was within the fortress, as an honoured guest, and with a positive agenda.

Nixon stayed in the Soviet Union, as he had in China, for a week. As Kissinger had anticipated, the Soviet leaders, aware of their country's military weakness with regard to the United States, and of their vulnerability to nuclear attack, were eager to conclude an arms limitation agreement between the two Super Powers. The treaty, signed on May 29, and concluding the first round of Strategic Arms Limitation Talks (SALT 1), marked a turning point in the Cold War. The United States and the Soviet Union agreed to limit the number of defensive nuclear missiles to two hundred each, a hundred to be placed around the capital cities (Moscow and Washington) and a hundred around the sites from which intercontinental ballistic missiles would be launched. The number of offensive nuclear weapons would also be given an upper limit, as would the number of nuclear armed submarines. The actual figures for intercontinental ballistic missiles would be fixed at their existing level, 1,618 Soviet and 1,054 American. As an earnest of his seriousness, Nixon ordered an immediate halt to the work being done at three anti-ballistic missile sites in the United States. Before Nixon left Moscow, he and Brezhnev signed a charter pledging to prevent nuclear war.

Following the Brezhnev-Nixon summit, a substantially expanded trade agreement was negotiated between their two countries, and signed in Washington on October 18. The money owed by the Soviet Union to the United States under the Stalin-Roosevelt Lend-Lease arrangements of the Second World War would be settled and paid, the Americans agreeing to write off much of it. American grain sales to the Soviet Union – then going through a severe grain shortage as a result of a prolonged drought – would be increased to the value of $750 million over three years.

Internally, the Soviet Union was undergoing strains that might have threatened its very fabric, had not the forces of central control and repression been so strong and so experienced. The year marked the fiftieth anniversary of the formation of the Soviet Union, an amalgamation of nationalities, religions and language groups that was essentially a recreation of the Tsarist empire that had preceded it. On February 22 the Central Committee of the Communist Party of the Soviet Union praised the 'great and happy occasion for our multinational people'. But among those people were uneasy partners, on whom the Party authorities in Moscow maintained a vigilant eye. In *Pravda* and *Izvestiya* the Georgians were criticized for falling below the standards expected of Soviet morality. On January 24 *Pravda* had attacked those Young Communists who attended baptisms and church weddings. In the former Baltic States of Lithuania and Latvia – Soviet republics since 1945 – nationalist demonstrations were broken up and their leaders arrested. The Catholic Church in the Baltic was also under continuous pressure. In Lithuania, two priests who had given religious instruction to minors were sent to prison. Two bishops were refused permission to preach and exiled from their bishoprics. The restoration of churches was prohibited, and the teaching of atheism made compulsory in schools. From Moscow, senior Russian Orthodox leaders maintained a discreet acceptance of whatever restrictions were imposed upon them. In March, under the influence of Alexander Solzhenitsyn, and with his participation, an open – and bitter – letter was sent to Patriarch Pimen of Moscow, denouncing the subservience of the Russian Orthodox Church. 'In the olden days they threw martyrs to the lions,' the letter read, 'but today all you have to lose is your affluence.' In April, a senior official of the Swedish Academy who was to have given Solzhenitsyn his Nobel Prize was refused a visa to the Soviet Union.

Religion, too, seemed to be on the increase again, certainly to the extent that the authorities felt they had to issue warnings about it. But the courage of those who wished to practise their religion was evident in March, when 17,000 Lithuanian Roman Catholics sent a petition to the United Nations, and to Brezhnev, demanding the right of open worship. On September 15 there was an article in *Pravda* demanding a more 'militant campaign' to eliminate religion. In particular, *Pravda* rebuked Communist Party and Young Communist (Komsomol) members for participating in church services.

The isolation of the Soviet Union from the West was strictly maintained. Other than Jewish emigration, which reached 30,000 that year, few Soviet citizens could leave the country except on officially sponsored visits from which they had then to return. In February the Soviet troops manning the borderlands were instructed to detain anyone found near the border without permission. There was also an indication of internal unrest in a Supreme Soviet decree in July which created a new type of offence – 'grave crimes' – among which were listed 'banditry', 'disorganizing the functioning of labour camps' and 'mass disorders'.

Freedom of expression inside the Soviet Union continued to draw the sternest of condemnation from the Party and the sternest of surveillance from the KGB. In January, Vladimir Bukovsky was sentenced to seven years' hard labour, to be followed by five years' internal exile in a Soviet city far from Moscow. The charge against him was 'anti-Soviet agitation'. In the months ahead, human rights activists were arrested in Leningrad, Kiev and Vilnius. The main privately printed and clandestinely distributed dissenting magazine, *Chronicle of Current Events*, which scrupulously listed violations of human rights throughout the Soviet Union, was rigorously repressed. Nationalist groups in the Ukraine were harassed. In May, a Roman Catholic worker, Roman Kalantas, burned himself to death in a park in the Lithuanian city of Kaunas in protest against religious repression. As a gesture of solidarity, students demonstrated in the streets of Kaunas and had to be dispersed by the police.

One Soviet response to dissent was expulsion. At the very moment when two dissidents, the astronomer Leonid Lyubarsky and the space scientist Yuri Melnik, were being given five and three years' labour-camp sentences on a charge of 'anti-Soviet agitation', the poet Josef Brodsky was expelled from the Soviet Union. Valery Chalidze, one of the founder members of the Moscow Human Rights Committee, who had earlier been threatened repeatedly with imprisonment, was allowed to leave the Soviet Union for a lecture tour in the United States. Then, while he was out of the country, he had his Soviet citizenship taken away from him.

A similar two-pronged policy affected the Jews of the Soviet Union. While

30,000 were allowed to leave that year, most of them going to Israel – which the Soviet Union was attacking as a 'neo-fascist tool of American imperialism' – other Jews were being arrested and imprisoned for demanding to emigrate, and for encouraging their fellow Jews to leave. When the French Socialist Party leader, François Mitterrand, protested against this discrimination, his Soviet hosts called off his imminent official visit to the Soviet Union.

East of Lake Baikal, in the Buryat Mongol Republic of the Soviet Union, in the heart of Siberia, the Communist authorities had grappled for many years with the Buddhist beliefs of tens of thousands of the region's inhabitants. One of the leading Buddhist scholars of the republic, Bidya Dandaron, had first been imprisoned for his beliefs in 1937, at the height of the Stalinist repression, and had spent eighteen years since then in labour camp. In October, a free man, but unwilling to be silent, he was arrested, with five of his followers, and charged with carrying out 'religious propaganda'. On December 24 – as the Christian world prepared to celebrate Christmas – he was sentenced by a Soviet court to a further five years in labour camp.

Western observers were surprised at how, despite the threat and actual imposition of prison and labour-camp sentences, dissent never faded away. Indeed, in November more than fifty Soviet human rights activists signed a public petition urging an amnesty for all political prisoners. Among the signatories were Andrei Sakharov and Mstislav Rostropovich.

In Czechoslovakia the repression of those who still hankered after a Dubček-style 'Socialism with a human face' continued, as did the Soviet presence inside the country. In September, as many as 100,000 Soviet, Polish, Hungarian and East German troops joined in a widespread series of military manoeuvres throughout Czechoslovakia, an echo of the events of 1968. A renewed collectivization campaign was launched, and the extent of private farming was curtailed. A series of political meetings across the country swore allegiance to the Communist Party and its ideology, while at the same time there was an increase in the trials of dissidents, of whom forty-six, all of them earlier advocates of a more democratic form of socialism, were sent to prison.

As with the Soviet dissidents, their Czech opposite numbers had circulated their ideas in clandestine news sheets, and sought to maintain contact with Western liberals and human rights organizations. All such contact was dangerous. Messages had to be smuggled in and out by means of Western visitors willing to risk arrest and expulsion, and themselves frightened of endangering those for whom they were making the journey across the Iron Curtain. Not only on the map but on the ground the Iron Curtain was a barrier, replete with barbed-wire fences, searchlights and close physical scrutiny of those crossing it. On October 28 a British subject, the Reverend David Hathaway, of the Dewsbury Pentecostal Church, was caught smuggling five thousand Bibles and Christian literature into Czechoslovakia, en route for the Soviet Union. After his arrest he was interrogated and tortured, then sentenced to ten years in prison. Over the previous eight years he had smuggled 150,000 Bibles and New Testaments into Eastern Europe, first into Bulgaria, and later into the Ukraine. He served ten months in prison before British government pressure secured his release.

For the first time since 1968, congresses were held in Czechoslovakia of the principal professional groups among whom dissent had earlier flourished: architects, journalists, dramatic artists, composers and painters. At each congress – they were held almost monthly throughout the year – the call went out for 'Socialist realism'. There was to be no going back to the brief flourishing of cultural diversity of four years earlier. The cinema likewise was purged of the earlier 'new wave' of films that had seemed to mark a way forward for diversity and artistic freedom. In schools, an increase in teachers' pay went hand in hand with a greater vigilance in supervising the political and ideological content of what was being taught, particularly in secondary schools. The Churches, too, were under renewed pressure. Newspapers conducted 'anti-religious' campaigns. The number of theological students was reduced. Priests were 'retired' and were not replaced. When three of the four Roman Catholic bishops died, they too were not replaced. The re-establishment of religious orders and monasteries that had been closed down earlier was refused. Nuns were told that they did not need nunneries and special places of worship, but could undertake 'useful work in hospitals and other social institutions'. The power of Communism to retain its grip on a nation which had prided itself on its independence of thought was demonstrated yet again.

As Israel approached the fifth anniversary of the occupation of the West Bank there were repeated calls from the United Nations, and also from Nixon in Washington, for a complete Israeli withdrawal from the occupied areas. Inside Israel there was a growing realization that some form of compromise was urgent. On May 10 three Japanese gunmen, armed with a machine gun and working for Palestinian terrorists, opened fire in the arrival hall at Lod airport, Israel's main entry point. Twenty-seven passengers were killed, of whom twenty-one were Christian pilgrims from Puerto Rico. Among the other dead was one of Israel's leading scientists, Aharon Katzir, who for six years had been President of the Israel Academy of Arts and Sciences. In September there was yet another act of terror. At the Olympic Games in Munich, eleven Israeli athletes were seized, held hostage, and then killed. German police killed five of the terrorists. Later, following the hijacking of a German Lufthansa airline, the German police released all Arab terrorists who had been imprisoned after the Olympic murders. Inside Israel there was considerable distress that, after the massacre, the Games had continued. The Israeli secret service, the Mossad, undertook to track down and kill the remaining perpetrators of the massacre. They achieved their objective. Once, in Norway, they killed a Palestinian who had nothing to do with the Games.

In London, two weeks after the Munich massacre, Ami Shachori, the Agricultural Attaché at the Israeli Embassy was killed by a letter bomb. These acts of terror inevitably hardened attitudes inside Israel towards peace-making. At the same time, Egypt, under President Sadat, was contemplating a sudden attack across the Suez Canal, with a view to regaining as much as possible of the lost desert. At the same time Syria was making plans to recapture the Golan Heights. Israeli Intelligence followed these various pre-parations, but was confident that, when they neared fruition, they could be negated by a pre-emptive strike, much as in 1967. Many Israelis did not even think a pre-emptive strike was needed. The confidence generated by the victory in 1967 had led to complacency with regard to any possible threat to Israel's extended borders.

On June 28, Nixon announced that no more draftees would be sent to Vietnam. The anti-war movement had obtained one of its main objectives. Vietnam would not become the graveyard of an unending supply of student 'cannon-fodder'. The whole American commitment to sustaining the South Vietnamese government with American troops was being weakened. On October 8, after more than a year and a half of negotiation, Le Duc Tho gave Kissinger the terms of an agreement, the culmination of long and sometimes apparently fruitless negotiations between them, that Kissinger found acceptable. The Americans would agree that the 'mutual' withdrawal of North Vietnamese and American forces would no longer be required as a precondition for a ceasefire. For their part, the North Vietnamese agreed not to insist on the resignation of the South Vietnamese Prime Minister, General Thieu: they felt they had the patience and power on the ground to bide their time.

A ceasefire would be arranged by North Vietnam and the United States without South Vietnamese participation. Once the ceasefire was in place Americans troops would withdraw and all prisoners of war would be exchanged. The future political alignment of South Vietnam would be left – as Nixon had proposed in May – to the Vietnamese themselves. The North Vietnamese had their own ideas as to how this political future was to evolve. Le Duc Tho proposed a Council of National Reconciliation made up of members of the Saigon government, the Communists and 'neutral' representatives – not precisely defined – who would supervise eventual elections. The North Vietnamese proposal assumed that North Vietnamese troops would remain in South Vietnam. Kissinger accepted this, but made it as a condition of their remaining that they would not be resupplied. It was, he later explained, pointless to insist on a North Vietnamese withdrawal. It had been 'unobtainable through ten years of war. We could not make it a condition for a final settlement. We had long passed that threshold.'

On October 21 Kissinger flew to Saigon to obtain General Thieu's acceptance of the agreement. Thieu saw in it nothing but the destruction of South Vietnam and of his government. It was, from his perspective, a victory for North Vietnam – whose troops would remain in the South – and for the Communists, who would be represented, perhaps by a majority representation, on the Council of National Reconciliation. Nixon was so angered by Thieu's reluctance to accept the agreement that he contemplated threatening him that if he did not agree to the terms that had been worked out in Paris the United States would sign a separate treaty with the North Vietnamese. Inside the White House there was even talk of organizing a coup to overthrow Thieu and replace him with someone less hostile to the proposed treaty. Then, on October 24, Thieu publicly denounced the proposed treaty and insisted that the Communist presence in the South 'must be wiped out quickly and mercilessly'. Kissinger sought desperately to revive the treaty and see it brought into effect. In his first White House press conference, on October 26, he said with confidence that all would be well, telling millions of American viewers: 'We believe that peace is at hand. We believe that an agreement is in sight.'

Nixon was on the eve of an election. His challenger was the Democratic Senator George McGovern, on an anti-war ticket. On November 7 Nixon was re-elected President with an increased and substantial majority, obtaining just over sixty per cent of the total vote and winning forty-nine States: he lost only Massachusetts and the District of Columbia. Vietnam remained the dominant focus of his thought and actions. General Thieu was no longer an obstacle to be rebuked or even removed – Nixon had earlier said, 'We are going to have to put him through the wringer' – but an opponent of Communism to be supported.

Thieu had submitted to the United States sixty-nine amendments to the proposed treaty. Nixon instructed Kissinger to take these amendments – which Kissinger regarded as 'preposterous' – to Le Duc Tho. Far from agreement being 'within sight', it had become the subject of interminable differences of opinion. The talks continued, but the agreement drifted apart. On December 13 Le Duc Tho suspended the negotiations and returned to Hanoi for consultations. On the following day, December 14, Nixon warned the North Vietnamese that they had seventy-two hours to begin talking again, and to do so 'seriously' or there would be grave consequences. For four days the North Vietnamese declined to return to the negotiating table. Then, on December 18, the consequences of which Nixon had warned – without spelling them out – were put into operation: a massive American bomber offensive against North Vietnam. For eleven days a total of three thousand sorties were flown, the main targets being within the heavily populated sixty-mile-long corridor between Hanoi and Haiphong. There was only one day on which the bombing was suspended: Christmas Day.

Forty thousand tons of bombs were dropped. The *New York Times* condemned Nixon for having reverted to 'Stone Age barbarism'. The *Washington Post* called the bombing 'savage and senseless'. The death toll was rumoured to be in the thousands. American anti-war activists who visited Hanoi during the bombardment told the city's mayor that he should use the figure of ten thousand. In fact, 1,318 people were killed in Hanoi and 305 in Haiphong. But the impression abroad was of a far larger death toll and utter devastation.

In fact, the American bombers had been able to hit their targets with precision. These targets were all military ones. Civilian houses were hit in error, as was a hospital near Hanoi airport. Of the hundred patients and staff in the hospital at the time of the bombing, eighteen were killed.

The North Vietnamese were not without resources of their own against the Christmas bombing offensive. More than 1,200 surface-to-air missiles were launched against the attackers, of which twenty-six were shot down, and sixty-two American airmen killed. On December 26, following an American request for negotiations to begin again in Paris, the North Vietnamese replied that they would be willing to talk again as soon as the bombing offensive stopped. That offensive was being criticized every day in the American press. On December 27 the columnist Stewart Alsop asked, in the pages of the *Washington Post*: 'What would Nixon do if the North Vietnamese refused to return to the conference table? Nuke Hanoi? Hit the dikes? Or just go on bombing North Vietnam "till hell freezes over"?'

It was not only American critics of the war, but the North Vietnamese themselves, who feared an escalation of the war, either the bombing of the dykes along the Red River or a nuclear strike. Neither was on Nixon's agenda, but there was no way that the North Vietnamese, or American critics of the war, could know this. The very 'madness' with which Nixon's conduct of the war had been portrayed by his critics – the *Washington Post* had doubted his 'very sanity' – made such deadly scenarios seem possible.

The North Vietnamese willingness to talk once the offensive was halted gave Nixon the prospect he sought: on December 30 he ordered a halt. Within a few days, Kissinger and Le Duc Tho arranged to meet again in Paris. They did so on 8 January 1973, and began serious negotiations on the following day – Nixon's sixtieth birthday. Agreement was reached after only five days. The United States could withdraw from its most long-drawn-out, controversial and divisive war.

Concern for the environment had become an annual feature of the international agenda, and one that was gaining in importance and urgency. On June 16 a United Nations conference on the environment, meeting in Stockholm, agreed to a Declaration on the Human Environment which its authors believed could have as great an impact on the quality of life on the planet as the United Nations Declaration on Human Rights was seeking with regard to individual liberty.

The Declaration on the Human Environment recognized the 'sovereign' right of all States to exploit their own natural resources, but added to this right the legal responsibility 'to ensure that activities within their jurisdiction or control did not cause damage to the environment of other States or areas beyond the limits of national jurisdiction'. A quarter of a century later, many aspects of these responsibilities were still being neglected by individual States: but the recognition that the factories and chemical discharges and pollutants of one country could gravely harm life in another had been enshrined in a solemn declaration. By such means alone could there be an international awareness that action was needed, and a monitoring authority with the power, if not to halt pollution, at least to draw attention to it, and call for action.

Five months after the Stockholm declaration, a conference met in London to set rules for the dumping of waste products into the sea. Ninety-one nations attended. It was agreed that certain products could not be dumped at sea at any time or in any quantity, however small. These were radioactive substances, fuel oil, mercury and its compounds, and organo-halogen compounds. For certain waste products special permission was needed if they were to be dumped: these included zinc, chromium and nickel. The enforcement of these rules was to be the responsibility of the signatories. China, a major dumper of pollutants, neither attended the conference nor signed the declaration.

Curbs on the methods of warmaking as well as on industrial pollution were on the United Nations agenda. In April a document with the long but self-explanatory title of the 'Convention on the Prohibition of Development, Production and Stockpiling of Bacteriological (Biological) and Toxic Weapons and their Destruction' was finalized for the signature of all nations. Chemical warfare was not included, but negotiations to include it were continuing. The convention also specifically reiterated the 1925 Geneva Protocol – a high point of the inter-war search for a limitation to the cruelty of war – which had prohibited any combatant from using asphyxiating and poisonous gases as an instrument of war. Going beyond what seemed the current reality of the nuclear deterrent, but certainly an aspiration of the multitude of human beings on the planet, on November 29 the Legal Committee of the United Nations General Assembly adopted a resolution stating that the prohibition of the use of nuclear weapons should be observed by all nuclear powers 'as a law of international life'.

The environment also remained a priority among the Western nations. Once again the United States took the lead, with federal legislation on water-pollution control – the Clean Water Act – the preservation of the Atlantic coastal waterway, and noise control. On July 23 the Americans launched *Landsat 1*, the first satellite that could survey the Earth's resources from space, and monitor their depletion.

CHAPTER TWENTY-TWO

1973

...the ignominious history of those who have strength
but not reason.

SALVADOR ALLENDE

On New Year's Day 1973, Britain formally joined the European Economic Community – the Common Market as it was popularly known. Also joining that day were the Irish Republic and Denmark. The original 'Six' had become the 'Nine'. It was an enlargement that was central to the concept of a United Europe, however defined: economic, monetary or federal. It was twenty years since the British Prime Minister Edward Heath, then a young Member of Parliament, had argued in favour of British entry. He could be proud of his persistence, as well as of his achievement: 'a future of better jobs and a higher standard of living', he called it.

There were early disappointments, which the Labour opposition was quick to exploit. One of the first, on April 6, was the announcement that whereas the British public paid twenty-eight pence per pound for butter, the European Economic Community had sold 200,000 tons of surplus butter to the Soviet Union at eight pence per pound. As a result of the outcry, the British government promised a butter subsidy of two pence in the pound to all purchasers, and a ten pence subsidy (once a month) for five million poor people. On such small but controversial, and much publicized matters, the future of a united Europe was often to seem to turn in future years. But British membership having been accepted, the presence of Britain in Europe became a force for good for Europe as well as a benefit to Britain itself. Almost a quarter of a century was to pass before the 'Euro-sceptics' in the Conservative Party were to contribute, by their divisiveness, to their Party's defeat in a general election.

Before the end of Britain's first year in the Common Market, a project that had been rejected a hundred years earlier because it would constitute too close a link to Europe was taken up again, and agreed upon. This was the Channel Tunnel. A treaty signed by Heath and President Pompidou of France on November 17 constituted a mutual undertaking by both Britain and France to build and operate a Channel Tunnel rail system linking the two countries. A Bill to enable the tunnel to be built was introduced in the House of Commons three days later. Work proceeded, costs mounted, delays proliferated: construction did not begin until 1987.

On January 15 the United States suspended all military action against North Vietnam. Twelve days later, in Paris, the long-awaited ceasefire agreement was signed by all the contending parties: the United States, North Vietnam, South Vietnam and the Provisional Revolutionary Council of South Vietnam (the Communist Vietcong's political arm). The United States had given up any attempt to maintain the independence and territorial integrity of South Vietnam, on behalf of whose government it had fought so long and suffered so much – including disillusionment with the South Vietnamese leaders. The ceasefire agreement reflected this: the 17th parallel – hitherto the border between North and South Vietnam – was described as 'only provisional and not a political or territorial boundary'.

The ceasefire agreement of January 27 enabled the Americans to begin to pull out their remaining forces, and to end their effective state of war – although there had never been a declaration of war – with North Vietnam, against which no further bombing raids were mounted. The United States Defence Department, at the time of the ceasefire agreement, published the statistics of the war, first and foremost the numbers of those killed in Vietnam since the United States became involved in the war on 8 March 1965. In order of magnitude the highest death toll was that of the North Vietnamese civilians and soldiers, and Vietcong, 922,290 in all. The South Vietnamese armed forces lost 181,483 men, in addition to whom 50,000 South Vietnamese civilians were killed. The United States war deaths were 55,337.

More than 150,000 American soldiers had been wounded, some terribly. As the American public turned against the war, it also seemed to turn against the search for adequate provision for the veterans, for adequate recognition of what they had been through. On their return to the United States, many of those who had fought felt spurned and scorned, their suffering of no interest to those among whom they lived and worked. The war had been lost; for millions of Americans it had become a source of shame. Those who had fought it felt that they had been cast as villains and pariahs. It took a decade and more before there was a change. At the turn of the century, at the Vietnam War memorial in Washington, visitors walk in shocked silence along the long list of names. That memorial was not created until 1982.

In the seven years from 1965 to 1973 during which more than 55,000 American servicemen were killed in Vietnam, almost eight times that number of Americans – 414,774 – were killed on the roads in the United States. Indeed, there was not a single year in which fewer people were killed on the roads in the United States than the total seven-year American fatalities in Vietnam.

As the century came to its end, more than three million Americans had been killed on the roads. In 1900 the number killed was thirty-six. In 1972 the total for that one year was 54,589. It was the single worst year in American road history.

Despite the Paris ceasefire agreement, some fighting between the South Vietnamese government forces and the combined North Vietnamese and Vietcong forces then in the South continued. At times it was as fierce as in the past. The North Vietnamese also retained control of those areas of Cambodia which they wanted to use to continue to move troops, weapons and ammunition to the South, where the struggle for control of the Mekong Delta continued. The ceasefire agreement signed in Paris did not include Cambodia. The American air force was therefore still able to bomb the North Vietnamese supply lines running through Cambodia, along the Ho Chi Minh trail, though it could not strike at the trail where it ran through North Vietnam, or where it exited into South Vietnam.

In Laos, as in Cambodia, the North Vietnamese, together with the Laotian Communist Pathet Lao forces, also remained in control of large areas, amounting in all to two-thirds of the country – though only a third of its population. This, too, gave the North Vietnamese a sense that, as regards eventually taking over the whole of South Vietnam, their time would come. One element in their struggle was constant: there was no let-up in the supply of arms and munitions from either the Soviet Union or China. But for the United States the continuing struggle in Indochina was one which it hoped it could henceforth remain clear of. Writing in the *New Republic*, Stanley Karnow noted that the Paris agreement of January 27 'may only be an interlude that precedes the beginning of what could become the third

Indochina war'. The question to be asked was 'whether the struggle that lies ahead can be waged without American involvement'.

On February 12 the first of almost six hundred United States prisoners of war to be set free under the ceasefire agreement were released. The issue of the prisoners of war had been a crucial one in the Kissinger-Le Duc Tho negotiations. One of those released that day was an air force officer, Colonel Robinson Risner, who had been a prisoner of war in Hanoi for seven-and-a-half years. Another of those released, Ronald Bliss, also an air force pilot, shot down over North Vietnam, had been in captivity for seven years. The homecoming of the captives was widely reported on television and in newspapers throughout the United States. More than anything else, these scenes signified that the war was over. There was shock and anger, however, when the former prisoners of war began to talk of their ordeals in captivity. Many had been cruelly tortured, particularly those who refused repeated demands to make public anti-war statements.

Nixon still retained the option that, if the North Vietnamese were to violate the ceasefire terms, the United States might return to an active military role in Vietnam. On March 15, as the last American prisoners of war were released by the North Vietnamese, he indicated that a military response might be called for if the truce was violated. The Secretary of Defence, Elliot Richardson, confirmed that 'we cannot rule out' such an eventuality. These were the last-minute statements of a policy that was about to be rejected altogether. On June 4 the Senate voted to block all United States funding for any further American military activity anywhere in Indochina. Both Nixon and Kissinger made efforts to have this ban delayed until August 15, as American troops were even then bombing North Vietnamese positions in Cambodia, along the Ho Chi Minh trail. Congress rejected even a two-month delay, and the ban came into force. The United States would no longer be able to support the South Vietnamese government militarily, whatever the North Vietnamese might do. With an estimated 150,000 North Vietnamese troops in the South, it was clear that the integrity of the South Vietnamese government – its control over even the main cities – could not long survive a determined North Vietnamese offensive.

The departure of the Americans did not seal the immediate fate of the South Vietnamese government, but it made that fate far more precarious than it had been two years earlier. Inside the United States, any active sympathy that Thieu may have had for his regime and his cause had long ago withered away. When he visited the United States that year – for the first time in his life – there were no lavish banquets and no State ceremonials: the Vice-President entertained him in Washington, and Nixon gave him a small 'family dinner' at his home in San Clemente, California.

Nixon's own presidential authority was under attack. His Special Counsel, John Dean, had accused him publicly of a 'cover-up' with regard to a break-in at the Democratic Party headquarters in the Watergate building in Washington before the 1972 presidential election. It was alleged that Nixon himself had authorized the break-in. Scandal replaced high policy as the area on which the ruler of the world's most powerful nation was having to devote more and more of his time. The attention of the American public became riveted on a sequence of events each of which appeared to show the President in an ever worsening light. A former attorney-general was indicted. Several former White House employees were convicted of criminal charges.

Nixon refused to allow any of his staff to give evidence to a Senate select committee examining the allegations. Then, under growing pressure, he agreed to do so. Each impasse was followed by more pressure and more revelations. Particular zeal in pursuing inquiries, even at a time when there was little general interest in the whole matter, was shown by two reporters on the *Washington Post*, Carl Bernstein and Bob Woodward. As the revelations of cover-up grew, those closer and closer to the President became implicated, and resigned, including two senior presidential assistants, H. R. Haldeman and John Erlichman. Nixon insisted that he wanted justice done, and seen to be done. 'This office is a sacred trust,' he told tens of millions of American television viewers in June, 'and I am determined to be worthy of that trust.'

In the end all trust dissolved, a result of the revelation that tapes had been made in the Oval Office as a matter of course when Nixon was in daily discussion with his closest aides – and the discovery of significant gaps in those tapes at what were clearly key moments. On October 23 Nixon agreed to hand over all nine of the relevant tapes. Seven days later it was announced that two tapes did not exist: a crucial telephone call had been taken by Nixon on an extension that had apparently not been taped, and a meeting between Nixon and John Dean at which, according to Dean, Nixon had spoken about his participation in the cover-up. This was not recorded – according to the White House – because the tape ran out. A third subpoenaed tape was delivered, but had an eighteen-minute inaudible section: this was again a vital meeting between Nixon, Haldeman and Ehrlichman. The President's secretary, Rose Mary Woods, later testified that she had 'pressed the wrong button' on the tape recorder while transcribing the tape and taking a telephone call at the same time.

These details, and the details that were on the tapes, including words used by the President that were referred to repeatedly in the published transcripts as 'expletive deleted' – led to newspaper and Congressional hostility to a President of a sort rarely if ever known before. When the *New York Times* wrote of 'the mania for secrecy, the arrogance towards Congress and the public, the over-centralization of authority, the suppression of internal dissent', it reflected a growing and in due course majority view. The climax of criticism came when the House of Representatives asked its Judiciary Committee to establish whether there was sufficient evidence to impeach the President.

In South America, the left-wing government of Salvador Allende in Chile had caused repeated waves of alarm in right-wing and Republican circles in the United States. Allende, a Marxist, had won the Chilean presidential election in September 1970. For three years he had sought to move Chile along the road to Socialism. His most striking decision was to nationalize Chile's copper mines, previously partly owned by United States companies, including the powerful Anaconda Copper Company. The Chilean Congress supported the nationalization decision across the political divide. Allende also defied the United States by ending Chile's diplomatic and trading boycott of Cuba, a boycott followed at Washington's request by all Latin American countries. In April 1972 he had vetoed a constitutional amendment that would have made the expropriation of private property subject to Congressional approval.

Opposition to Allende's rule culminated in the seizure of power by a military junta, headed by General Augusto Pinochet, on September 11. For two days there was severe fighting in the capital, Santiago. More than 2,500 people were killed. In a defiant message while his presidential palace and suburban home were being bombed, Allende declared: 'I will not resign. I will not do it. I am ready to resist, with whatever means, even at the cost of my life, if this serves as a lesson in the ignominious history of those who have strength but not reason.'

'Either by strength or reason' was the Chilean national motto. Shortly after his message was transmitted, Allende was reported to have committed suicide. Pinochet, the army commander-in-chief who seized power that day, had been encouraged to do so by the Central Intelligence Agency. 'It is the firm and continuing policy that Allende be overthrown by a coup . . .' were the first words of an 'Eyes Only' top-secret message from CIA headquarters at Langley, Virginia, to the CIA Station Chief in Santiago shortly after Allende had come to power. But, from its first days, the nature of the Pinochet regime went against all the tenets of American democracy.

At the very outset of his rule Pinochet ordered more than twenty of Allende's senior advisers to be taken from the presidential palace, where they had been besieged, and confined in an army barracks. There they were tortured and then shot. Among those killed were the co-leaders of both the Communist and Socialist Parties, as well as Allende's chauffeur and doctor. In the months ahead, a total of 2,528 Chileans were arrested and killed. These included parliamentarians, university professors, more than 300 students and 243 trade union leaders.

Among those murdered by the Pinochet regime in its early days was an Anglo-Chilean priest, Michael Woodward. A member of 'Christians for Socialism', he had worked for ten years among the poor of Valparaíso. In an indictment brought against Pinochet twenty-five years later, the charge sheet described how:

> Father Woodward's arms appear to be broken in two by a hammer and his body so scratched it seemed blackened. They gave him no food for days, although sometimes the detainees were fed on beans infested with worms. Father Woodward receives no attention for his broken arms and ribs and, in front of the other prisoners, he and the other priests are accused of sleeping with women. He endures many days with his body broken and eventually he dies.

Also killed in the early days of the Pinochet regime was Carmelo Soria, a Spanish citizen who was working for the United Nations in Chile, and who helped several people escape from Chile. Despite his diplomatic immunity, Soria was dragged from his car, which had United Nations plates, tortured and killed. In close co-operation with the Argentinian, Paraguayan and Uruguayan governments, Pinochet launched Operation Condor, whereby Chileans who fled across the borders for safety were kidnapped and taken back to Chile. When a Lutheran bishop, Helmut Frenz, and his Catholic opposite number Fernando Ariztia, protested to Pinochet, he told them: 'You are priests with the luxury of mercy. I am a soldier and President of the Chilean nation, under attack from the disease of Communism, which must be eradicated. Marxists and Communists must be tortured, otherwise they will not sing.'

For seventeen years Pinochet ruled Chile with an iron hand, with torture as an ever present threat against his political opponents. At the same time he pursued a policy of free-market economics which was to be emulated in Britain by Margaret Thatcher, and widely praised as a means of freeing economic policies from the perceived 'burdens' of State control.

In the Middle East, both Syria and Egypt were looking for an opportunity to win back some, if not all of the territory that Israel had taken from them after the Six-Day War of 1967 – a war they themselves had provoked. Outside Israel, Palestinian Arab terrorism created a focus beyond the potentially endangered borders. Tension was an almost permanent feature of Israel's relations with its Arab neighbours and adversaries. On February 21 more than a hundred passengers, most of them Muslim pilgrims on their way to Mecca, were killed when their airliner, flying eastward from Libya and across the Suez Canal, was mistaken by the Israelis for a hostile aircraft. It had been intercepted by Israeli jets, and crashed in the Sinai Desert. Following several Palestinian Arab threats to 'bomb' Tel Aviv, the Israeli air monitors had feared that this plane was on just such a terrorist sabotage mission. On March 2, Palestinian terrorists in Khartoum murdered the American Ambassador to the Sudan, accusing the United States of 'collusion' with Israel.

Terror was met by reprisal action. On April 9, Palestinian terrorists attacked the home of the Israeli Ambassador to Cyprus: no one was killed. On April 10 there was an Israeli commando raid on Beirut and three Palestinian Arab terrorist leaders were killed. On August 5, four people were killed during a failed terrorist hijacking attempt at Athens airport. On August 10 Israeli planes intercepted another Libyan airliner, en route to Iraq, believing that the Palestinian terrorist leader George Habbash was on board. The plane was forced to land in Israel. When it was clear that Habbash was not a passenger it was allowed to continue on its way.

The war against terror had its own rules and parameters, which Israel felt able to master. The intentions of the Arab sovereign States that were Israel's neighbours were much harder to fathom. Israel was aware of a build-up of Soviet weaponry in both Egypt and Syria. Details of the mass of material which had been sent by sea, and flown in by air, were known to Israeli Intelligence. By the early months of 1973 the amount which Egypt and

Syria had received between them was estimated at $2,000 million. This included 650 Soviet warplanes and 2,500 Soviet tanks reaching Egypt within three years, and 330 planes and 2,000 tanks reaching Syria in that same period. These armaments were of the most modern Soviet types. Some, including hitherto secret anti-tank and anti-aircraft missiles, were of a type that had not yet been sent to Russia's Warsaw Pact partners in Eastern Europe. Were they to be sent into action simultaneously, they would confront Israel with a two-front war which, unless a high state of alert was in place, could be decisive against Israel.

It was one thing to know the odds stacked up on two fronts, another to know if, and how, and when they might be used – if at all. Israelis were used to listening to such threats. As early as 1 May 1972 President Sadat of Egypt had declared, in a public speech in Alexandria: 'In our coming battle, I will not be satisfied with liberating the land. Israel's arrogance and bluster, which has been going on for twenty-three years – all this must be terminated. As I have told them . . . I am ready to pay one million men as the price for this battle. But they too must be ready to pay a million men and more on their side.' Sadat knew, and the Israelis knew that he knew, that while Egypt could, in theory at least, lose a million men in battle and still survive (having a population of fifty million), Israel, with a population of less than four million, could never match man for man such a stupendous toll. But, as nothing untoward followed, Sadat's words were allowed by almost all Israelis to be relegated to the category of bombast. In May 1973 – a year after Sadat's threat – Egypt had conducted massive military manoeuvres on its side of the Suez Canal. The Israeli watchers on the other side were impressed, but not unduly alarmed. On September 13, Syrian and Israeli aircraft clashed on the Golan Heights. The Israelis were surprised by the vigour of the Syrian pilots, but once again they were not unduly alarmed.

On October 4, following a Palestinian Arab terrorist hijacking, the Austrian government agreed to the terrorists' demands to close down a transit camp near Vienna that was housing Jewish immigrants on their way from the Soviet Union to Israel. This incident was headline news in the Israeli papers on the following day, as the Prime Minister, Golda Meir, having made a special journey to Vienna, poured scorn on the Austrians for what she considered their pusillanimity. That same day, and on the following day, Israeli Intelligence circles were studying reports from both Egypt and Syria of increased military activity along the borders. This activity was reported to the Israeli Minister of Defence, Moshe Dayan – a former Chief of Staff –

but he saw no reason to treat it as the sign of an imminent attack. When the commander in the north told him that 1,200 Syrian tanks had taken up positions along a forty-mile front – in June 1941 the German army had deployed 1,400 tanks along a thousand-mile front before invading the Soviet Union – Dayan gave the commander permission to add 110 tanks from the reserve (which was then in the south of the country) to the 57 tanks he had in the north.

October 6 was the Day of Atonement, the holiest day in the Jewish religious calendar. In Israel, as throughout the Jewish world, most Jews fast and spend much of the day in synagogue, in prayer. When the sirens sounded at noon, and the mobilization orders were broadcast over the radio – normally silent on the Day of Atonement – thousands of Israeli soldiers went straight from synagogue to their army camps. It was at two in the afternoon that the co-ordinated offensive began. The plan had been so well guarded that ninety-five per cent of the Egyptian officers taking part in the attack across the Suez Canal had not known until that morning that the manoeuvres on which they had been engaged were in fact a prelude to war.

For twenty-four hours it looked as though Israel might be defeated on both fronts. The Egyptians crossed the Canal and pushed into Sinai, knocking out seventy-seven of the hundred tanks that came up to try to stop them. The Syrians swept forward on the Golan Heights, their first onslaught of 600 tanks faced, as it pushed halfway across the heights, by only 57 Israeli tanks, the whole of Israel's northern tank force. After forty-eight hours, however, by an extraordinary effort of military will and individual courage, Israeli troops and tank reinforcements had halted the armies advancing against them, and were making plans to counter-attack. The fierce battles that followed were longer and far more costly to both sides than the battles of the Six-Day War. None was predictable: but slowly the Israelis pushed back their adversaries, and no single Egyptian or Syrian tank, or soldier, reached the pre-1967 borders of Israel.

From the first day of the war, more than ten thousand Israelis returned from their holidays, work and study abroad in order to serve in their regular or reserve units. On October 10, as the tide of war began to turn, the Soviet Union started an airlift of military supplies to Egypt and Syria. Within ten days almost three hundred planeloads of Soviet arms and military supplies had been flown in. Some were also flown into Iraq, which had a small force fighting on the Golan Heights.

On October 11 the Israelis, having pushed the Syrian troops back to the

1967 ceasefire line on the Golan Heights, advanced into Syria, reaching almost halfway from the border to the Syrian capital, Damascus. On October 16 Israeli troops crossed the Suez Canal and entered Egypt. As both Egypt and Syria felt the weight of fighting behind the 1967 ceasefire lines, they appealed to the Soviet Union for military intervention. There was a momentary belief in the United States that, in the event of direct Soviet participation, America might be drawn in to support Israel. It was suggested that an American threat of nuclear retaliation might have to be made if the Soviet Union did appear about to enter the war. The Soviet Union had no intention, however, of becoming embroiled militarily in the Middle East, or of risking a conflict there – directly or by proxy – with the United States, which, as the war was being fought, had allocated $2,000 million of military aid to Israel.

On October 21 Henry Kissinger – who had become Secretary of State six weeks earlier – was in Moscow for talks with Brezhnev. They agreed that it was the immediate task of the Super Powers to bring the war to an end. Kissinger then flew from Moscow to Tel Aviv, where he obtained Golda Meir's agreement to a ceasefire. Egypt also agreed, but, in an attempt to secure a more impressive foothold on the Egyptian side of the Suez Canal, Israel continued fighting for another day. The ceasefire finally came into effect on October 24. When the fighting ended that day, 2,522 Israeli soldiers had been killed on the two war fronts. The Egyptian and Syrian losses, although kept secret at the time, were even higher: 3,500 Syrian soldiers were killed on the Golan Heights, and even more Egyptians in Sinai.

Unlike 1967, Jordan did not enter the war against Israel, much though it was urged to do by Egypt and Syria. As a result, it neither regained any of the West Bank that it had lost in 1967, nor lost additional territory east of the River Jordan. Throughout the war the bridges between Israel and Jordan remained open for Palestinian civilians, and for Palestinian exports to Jordan. From the third day of the war, Palestinian workers who used daily to cross into Israel for work were allowed to do so.

Following the ceasefire, the Soviet Union lost its enthusiasm for the Egyptian and Syrian cause (at one point in the war Brezhnev had urged the Algerians to 'take all necessary steps' to help Egypt and Syria). On October 26, speaking in Moscow to the Communist-sponsored and -inspired World Peace Conference, Brezhnev avoided any praise for the Egyptian and Syrian armies, which were being much applauded by the fraternal delegates.

The main constructive international involvement in the aftermath of the war came from the United States, and, primarily, from one man, Henry

Kissinger. He made great efforts as a mediator to enable the Egyptian forces trapped on the Sinai side of the Suez Canal to return to Egypt, and to separate the Israeli and Syrian forces on the Golan Heights. On November 5 he made his first journey to several Arab capitals: an early exercise in what was to become known as 'shuttle diplomacy'. On November 11, following an agreement which he reached with Sadat for the 'scrupulous' observance of the ceasefire – an identical agreement was secured that same day with Syria by Kissinger's Assistant Secretary, Joseph Sisco – Egypt and Israel accepted international monitoring of the ceasefire, and a full exchange of prisoners of war. On December 21, after Kissinger had persuaded all but the Syrians to attend, talks began in Geneva to arrange for the disengagement of forces on the Egyptian front.

Kissinger's achievements in the delicate, fraught situation of a war-torn Middle East were remarkable: all the more so because, during the course of the negotiations with regard to the disengagement on the Golan Heights, fifty-four Israeli soldiers and six civilians were killed on the Heights as a result of renewed Syrian shellfire. When signed (on 31 May 1974) the disengagement agreement returned the city of Kuneitra, which Israel had occupied since 1967, to Syria, and established a ten-kilometre zone of limited armaments and forces: within the zone Israel and Syria were each limited to 600 men, seventy-five tanks and thirty-five artillery pieces (in the battle on the Golan Heights, Syria had lost 1,150 tanks).

In the aftermath of the war, there was indignation in Israel when it was learned that forty-two Israeli soldiers had been killed after they had been taken prisoner of war. There was also alarm when it was announced in Washington on November 2 that Egypt had received Soviet 'Scud' surface-to-surface missiles with a range of 160 miles. This would enable them to hit all of Israel from the pre-1967 border. The Scud could be fitted either with high-explosive or nuclear warheads.

The apartheid regime in South Africa could not curb the growing unrest in the Black communities. In the first three months of the year there were 160 strikes by Black workers in the iron, steel, textile and engineering industries. At the height of the strikes the port of Durban, South Africa's third largest city and main seaport, was brought to a standstill. The government made concessions, raising wages and allowing Black workers, for the first time, the right to strike, and a say, albeit small, in the industrial conciliation machinery.

But confrontations between police and Black workers could be violent. On September 11 eleven of two hundred Black miners who were demonstrating in support of their demand for higher pay at the Western Deep Levels goldmine near Carltonville were shot dead by police. It was thirteen years since the massacre at Sharpeville had shocked liberal opinion throughout the world. The Carltonville shootings made a similar impact. 'Today the Black man is everywhere prepared, or is preparing himself to risk the fierce penalties incurred by those who strike or demonstrate, which is deemed illegal and communistic behaviour in South Africa,' wrote *The Times*. 'In mine conditions, of which the world is left as ignorant as possible, this attitude has now provided a shoot out.' In the aftermath of the shootings, John Vorster praised the police for their 'restraint'. This further incensed those who had been horrified by the way in which the police had used, first tear gas, then a baton charge, and finally Sten guns to break up the protest. There was further indignation when it was revealed that, while the mine owners paid out £56 million in wages (in 1992), their profits that year had been £322 million.

The National Union of South African Students was at the forefront of calling for greater liberalization. On February 27 eight of its leaders were banned for five years from holding or participating in any meetings, of however small a group, and denied the right to publish or broadcast their views in any form. On March 8 a similar banning order was placed on eight leaders of the Black South African Student Organization. In all, sixty people were banned that year, the banning being ordered by the government without trial or right of appeal.

The South African Council of Churches, another outspoken body, was also under attack. One of its institutions, the Wildespruit Fellowship Centre, was urging radical social change, and wanted the Churches to take a lead in this. The Prime Minister himself, J. B. Vorster, called on the Council of Churches to clear up what he called 'the den of iniquity'. In November the head of the Centre, Eoin O'Leary, was deported. Throughout the year the South African government passed legislation which strengthened yet further its repressive powers. Among this legislation was an Aliens Control Bill, and a Gatherings and Demonstrations Bill. The concept of law was being used to undermine the rule of law.

Elsewhere in Africa, the horrors of famine had struck most cruelly in Ethiopia, where, following the failure of the rains for three successive years, at least 100,000 Ethiopians died. One of the first Westerners to visit the area was a twenty-nine-year-old British television reporter, Jonathan Dimbleby, who twenty-five years later recalled reaching a former TB hospital on the outskirts of the town of Dessie:

As I walked past the gates the words of my father, Richard Dimbleby, when he went into Belsen concentration camp in 1945 echoed in my mind: 'I entered the world of a nightmare.'

Bodies were scattered on the ground, alive but close to death. The air was filled with the stench of vomit and dysentery. Inside the 'wards' it was worse: women and children lying in their own waste, too weak to take food, moaning, shivering, coughing in their distress.

It was horror beyond belief. Those sounds and images have always haunted me . . .

The camp at Dessie housed 3,000 people but there were no doctors or nurses, only a medical orderly and a monk, who did their best to comfort the sick and dying. The little children were so weak that they could barely stand and so lacking in food and medicine that they were bound to die.

Every morning the orderlies went through the camp in search of those who had died in the cold of the previous night. I shall never forget the first morning when I saw children in rigor mortis. There were three of them, their eyes wide open, their skeletal bodies lying on a pallet made of branches and half-covered with leaves to give them some dignity in death.

We found the same gruesome scenes along the main road north. Altogether there were fourteen camps whose combined death toll was upwards of a thousand a week. Tens of thousands more had perished in the interior, either because they were too weak to leave their homes or because they had succumbed on the long trek in the fruitless search for food.

My calculation that upwards of 100,000 men, women, and children must have died was an under-estimate: the United Nations put the death toll at more than twice that number.

When the scale of the disaster was made known, as a result of the efforts of the United Nations International Children's Emergency Fund (UNICEF), there was an immediate response by many nations able to send medical teams, food and clothing.

Death on a similarly high scale – an estimated 80,000 dead – had come to Uganda, but as a result, not of nature's ravages but of deliberate human cruelty. The new President, Idi Amin, was asserting his power by the most brutal means, in particular against followers of the President, Milton Obote, whom he had deposed the previous year. The civilian and parliamentary government that Amin had promised to bring in was nowhere in prospect, while at the same time the rule of law was being undermined. On February 18 the whole Ugandan judiciary protested to him that members of his security forces were committing 'widespread interference with the course of justice'. Amin ordered the Minister of Justice to take thirty days' leave 'in order to rest'. He was never recalled to his post. Senior army officers who showed unease at the dictatorship were likewise sent on leave, and never called back to office.

Amin – who for many years had been the Ugandan army heavyweight boxing champion – was portrayed in the West as a buffoon, and behaved as if he intended to live up to his reputation. He promoted himself field marshal, and wore flamboyant uniforms which he had designed. On October 28 he turned up uninvited at a meeting of African Heads of State. He expelled almost all the remaining Asians living in Uganda, and proclaimed himself the champion both of Africa and of the Arab cause (he was himself a Muslim). The Soviet Union saw its chance to secure a point of influence. He was fêted by Moscow, and accepted a large quantity of Russian arms.

At a summit meeting in Washington on June 23, Nixon had raised with Brezhnev the need to maintain human rights inside the Soviet Union, but his appeal had been in vain and the pressure on dissidents was maintained. The courage of the dissidents was, however, remarkable. Andrei Sakharov, the nuclear scientist who had once been among the most privileged of Soviet citizens, held a news conference in his Moscow apartment on August 21 in which he told journalists that Western accommodation with the Soviet Union on the terms proposed by the Soviets posed 'a serious threat to the world'. In Sakharov's words, the Russian authorities – whose ways he knew so well – would take technological and economic help from the West, of the sort that had been offered by Nixon during his visit to Moscow, 'while operating domestically behind a wall of secrecy and suppressing of individual rights'.

On September 5, Sakharov was warned by the First Deputy Prosecutor of the Soviet Union, Mikhail Malyorov, that he was 'not immune' from Soviet law. Ignoring this, three days later he called a second news conference at which he accused Soviet psychiatrists of 'complicity' in committing political dissidents to mental institutions. Sakharov's courage in matters of human rights, and his continued opposition to nuclear testing – the French had recently exploded a nuclear device in the atmosphere – led Alexander Solzhenitsyn to issue a statement recommending Sakharov for the Nobel Peace Prize. Solzhenitsyn was himself in trouble, following the publication of his book *Gulag Archipelago* in the West. The book was based on eye-witness accounts which he had assembled of people who had experienced the Soviet labour-camp system from its inauguration in 1918 until 1956. The KGB had searched for the original manuscript of the book for some time. A Leningrad woman, Yelizaveta Voronyanskaya, who knew its whereabouts, had been tortured without a break for five days to reveal them. She did so, and then hanged herself.

The Soviet newspapers denounced Solzhenitsyn for his 'anti-Soviet' work. 'If I am declared killed or suddenly mysteriously dead,' he told an interviewer in August, 'I have been killed with the approval of the KGB.' Solzhenitsyn was to be expelled from the Soviet Union, and Sakharov forced to leave Moscow for internal exile in the city of Gorky, 250 miles east of Moscow, where he was forbidden to talk to foreign journalists. For several dissidents the pressures were too great: in October a Moscow poet, Ilya Gabai, after long questioning by the KGB about his connection with the clandestine *Chronicle of Current Events*, killed himself by jumping from an eleventh-floor apartment.

Amid the horrors of war, amid the persecution of free thought, amid the carnage of road deaths, amid the death toll of natural disasters, the healing processes never abated. With regard to every disease there were those search- ing for a cure. Transplant surgery was making annual and impressive advances: in 1973 there was a breakthrough in the efficacy of kidney trans- plants.

The spur to scientific development could be unexpected. In the aftermath of the Arab-Israel war in October, the Arab oil-producing States had imposed strict oil controls on the Western nations, whom it accused of being biased towards Israel. As a result of the sudden and precipitate rise in the price of oil, there was massive inflation, an economic depression, and, as the cost of fuel oil soared, a drastic reduction in petrol supplies. The high cost of transport had an immediate impact on the cost of the goods being trans- ported, including food.

One effect of the rapid rise in fuel prices was a boost to recycling methods that would enable the use of fuel-based production to be reduced. Among the techniques developed was one for transforming old motor-car tyres into carpet-backing; another was a cheap substitute for asbestos made from a mixture of waste paper and waste plastic. The recycling of paper itself was given a boost. Alternative power sources were also explored with greater zeal, including the harnessing of waves, and even the harnessing of wind, to pumps that could generate electricity. There were experiments in producing gas from sewage and refuse. Research in the use of solar energy was also intensified: with the result that, by means of panels on the roof, private homes could be lit and heated by the harnessing of the sun's energy. Even street lights could be 'lit' by such solar power.

Slowly the awareness of the steady depletion of the planet's resources was penetrating the recesses of government. A turning point in the preservation of wildlife came, in the United States, with the signing by President Nixon on December 28 of the Endangered Species Act. Whether measures for the protection of wildlife, and also of fauna and flora, of the rainforests and coral reefs, of the oceans and the deserts, of the wetlands and the inland seas, would be put in place sufficiently quickly, and sufficiently widely, to prevent an environmental catastrophe in the twenty-first century was not known. But voices were being raised, and American legislation was a pointer to a rescue effort that was at last recognized, and had become urgent.

CHAPTER TWENTY-THREE

1974

Some people talk about bourgeois classical music with
great relish, are mesmerized by it and prostrate themselves before it, showing their slavish mentality for all
things foreign.

PEKING REVIEW

IN THE AFTERMATH of the Arab-Israel War of 1973 and the defeat of
Egypt and Syria, the Arab world established a united front against the
industrialized nations which it blamed for supporting Israel. The Arab oil
embargo remained in place, forcing the price of oil to multiply ten-fold. On
13 February 1974 President Nixon invited the Foreign Ministers of thirteen
industrialized nations – Canada, Japan, Norway and the nine members of
the European Economic Community – to an emergency conference in Washington. At the outset of the discussion, Kissinger warned of an inevitable
'collapse of the world economy' unless urgent and collective measures were
taken. These included conservation of existing fuel, energy-sharing during
the crisis, the development of alternative energy sources, co-operation on
research and development, closer international financial co-operation, and
help from the industrialized nations for the dozens of poor countries for
whom the oil price rise was proving a disaster.

The Washington conference failed to persuade the European nations not
to try to make their own separate arrangements with the Arab oil-producing
States. Britain had jumped the gun before the Washington conference, by
an arrangement announced on January 25 whereby Britain gave industrial
goods worth £110 million to Iran in return for five million extra tons of oil.
On March 4 the European Economic Community announced that it would
make its own approach to the Arabs for a relaxation of the embargo. This
approach was made without consulting the United States, leading Kissinger

to comment acerbically that America's friends posed a bigger problem than its enemies. The United States had no objection to an independent West European policy, he said, 'but it does have an objection when independence takes the form of basic hostility to the United States'. It was essential:

> to bring our friends to a realization that there are greater common interests than simply self-assertiveness and that the seeming victory they are striving for is going to prove hollow in an atmosphere of constant strife and endless competition . . . The question we face is whether the nations of the West and Japan, confronted with an absolutely predictable danger, are able to work cooperatively or whether they are going to act like the Greek city states in the face of Macedonia and Rome and divide among each other and deal competitively with the situation for which there is no competitive solution.

Nixon was equally irate, telling an audience in Chicago that the United States would no longer allow itself to be confronted with 'a situation where the nine countries in Europe gang up against the United States'. Several months of negotiations ensued, during which the Europeans and the Americans agreed that they must consult together in advance of such important initiatives: they also agreed with a plan which Kissinger put forward for a fund of $25,000 million to finance balance-of-payments deficits caused by the high price of oil. It was also agreed, as a result of a further initiative by Kissinger, that the oil-consuming nations would reduce their oil consumption, the United States taking the lead.

Although the Arab-Israel War had ended in an Israeli victory on the battlefield, it did not end the bloodshed in the Middle East. Palestinian Arab terrorists, based in Lebanon, attacked the northern Israeli town of Kiryat Shmona on April 11, killing eighteen men, women and children. The United Nations did not condemn this act, but it did condemn the Israeli air strike that followed it, and, without mentioning the murder of Israeli civilians or Kiryat Shmona, limited its general condemnation to 'acts of violence'. A month later, on May 15, twenty Israeli schoolchildren were killed during a terrorist attack on another border town, Maalot. In further attacks, three Israeli women were killed on Kibbutz Shamir on June 13 and four Israeli civilians in the coastal town of Nahariya eleven days later.

There were further acts of terror in the areas occupied by Israel since 1967. The Palestinian Liberation Organization (the PLO), from its headquarters in

Beirut, announced that all foreign tourists in Israel, including Christian pilgrims, would be considered targets. The PLO also strove for international status and respectability. On October 30 it was recognized by all Arab States as the 'sole representative of the Palestinian people'. Soon afterwards a delegation of PLO officials was received by the United Nations General Assembly. The PLO leader, Yasser Arafat, addressed the Assembly on November 13. On the following day the Assembly voted against allowing Israel to speak in the debate on the Middle East, a signal success for Palestinian Arab pressure. He came, he said, 'bearing an olive branch and a freedom fighter's gun'.

On November 19, four Israeli civilians were killed by PLO terrorists in the town of Beit Shean, in the Jezreel Valley. Three days later, still under the impact of Arafat's presence, the General Assembly voted by eighty-nine votes to eight – with thirty-seven abstentions including Britain and the other Common Market countries – in favour of the right of the Palestinian people to national independence and sovereignty. The United States was one of the eight countries voting against the resolution. A second resolution that day invited the PLO to take part in the Assembly, and other United Nations activities, with the status of 'observer'. That same day, the General Conference of UNESCO voted to exclude Israel from the organization's regional groupings. Israel was isolated and humiliated by this decision.

In an attempt to warn its neighbours not to contemplate another attack, on December 2 Israel announced that it possessed the means to manufacture nuclear weapons. This announcement was taken to mean that such weapons had been produced, or were in the process of manufacture. Within a decade, it was said that Israel had at least two hundred nuclear warheads. Since the nuclear announcement, no Arab State has sent its armies across the Israeli border.

Following the admission of the PLO as a participant in the United Nations debates, pressure on Israel was continuous. On December 13, after 18,000 Jews had reached Israel from the Soviet Union during the course of the year, the Egyptian Foreign Minister, Dr Fahmy, called publicly for an end to all further Jewish immigration to Israel for fifty years. Golda Meir had resigned as Prime Minister for having been taken unawares at the time of the Syrian and Egyptian attack. The new Israeli Prime Minister, Yitzhak Rabin – the first Prime Minister of Israel not to have been born outside the country – pressed for a way forward in the face of apparently implacable Arab hostility. On December 20 Rabin made a public appeal to President Sadat of Egypt to meet him, and to embark on talks for a peace treaty between the two countries, which despite the 1973 ceasefire were still technically at war, and had been since 1948. Sadat made no reply, but Rabin, the Chief of Staff in the 1967 war, was willing to persevere in the pursuit of peace.

The scandal that was evolving around the Watergate break-in and subsequent cover-up led sixty-three per cent of Americans who were questioned to say that they disapproved of the way Nixon was carrying out the office of President. On January 4 he defiantly refused to hand over to the Senate Watergate Committee the tape recordings and memoranda relating to five hundred meetings in the White House. In his State of the Union message on January 30 he said: 'One year of Watergate is enough.' Such a disclaimer was not enough to curb the growing public dissatisfaction with him. He also made a curious slip of the tongue, telling millions of viewers of the need 'to replace the discredited President – er, present – system . . .'.

During March and April several of those connected with various aspects of Watergate were brought to trial, starting with Nixon's former Attorney-General, John Mitchell, and his former White House Chief of Staff, H. R. Haldeman. As the trials were taking place, the Senate continued to demand the tapes that Nixon had refused to hand over. A deadline was set: May 2. Nixon complied, releasing edited transcripts of tapes that amounted to 1,308 pages. They were immediately published in book form, as *The White House Transcripts*, and became a bestseller. Nixon was so confident that the version presented would exonerate him that he arranged for copies to be widely distributed.[1]

On television, Nixon insisted that he had had no prior knowledge of the cover-up until he had been informed of it by John Dean, the White House Counsel, on 21 March 1973. But readers of the transcripts noticed that he was discussing it in detail with Dean on February 28. The same tape showed that Nixon had indeed been aware that the 'dirty tricks' campaign at the time of the election had been under the control of individual members of his White House staff, something he had hitherto strenuously denied. The tapes which he had so eagerly circulated in mid-May were proving his undoing. Equally damaging to him was the fact that eleven tapes were 'missing'. The White House said unconvincingly that nine 'had not been

---

[1] Including to this author, whose copy was sent from the White House in a packet postmarked 13 May 1974.

recorded' and that two 'could not be found'. The published version also had many gaps, marked by 'expletive deleted', 'characterization omitted' and 'inaudible', as well as revealing considerable rambling and disjointed and inconclusive remarks by the man who was supposed to be the leader of the nation. He emerged as more incompetent and incoherent than a President could be imagined to be, or expected to be.

On May 9 the Judiciary Committee of the House of Representatives opened hearings on whether there were grounds to impeach the President. More tapes and transcripts were called for by subpoena. Nixon challenged the subpoena in the court that had issued it. The court asked for a ruling from the Supreme Court. As the arguments were being prepared by both sides for submission to the Supreme Court, further indictments were taking place against those involved in the Watergate break-in. One of those indicted, Dwight Chapin, had been the President's appointments secretary at the time. He was charged with lying to the Watergate Grand Jury, found guilty, and sentenced to a minimum of ten months in prison. Other charges against White House officials were made, and upheld, and sentences passed, throughout the summer. On July 12 the former director of domestic affairs at the White House, John Ehrlichman, was found guilty. Then came the final blow to Nixon: the Judiciary Committee of the House of Representatives issued a fuller version of the tapes than the one presented by Nixon in *The White House Transcripts*. The fuller version filled various gaps in Nixon's edited version. Remarks omitted in the earlier version of one crucial conversation contained the words: 'I don't give a shit what happens. I want you all to stonewall it, let them plead the Fifth Amendment, cover up or anything else if it'll save it – save the plan. That's the whole point. . . . We're going to protect our people if we can.'

'Our people' – those who had carried out the break-in and those in the White House who knew about it – could no longer be protected. On July 24, in a unanimous decision, the Supreme Court ordered the President to hand over the sixty-four tapes he had sought to retain, despite the Congressional subpoenas. Two days later the Judiciary Committee of the House of Representatives voted, by twenty-seven to eleven, to recommend Nixon's impeachment for using the powers of his office 'to delay, impede and obstruct the investigation' of the Watergate break-in 'and to conceal the existence and scope of the unlawful covert activities'. On July 29 the committee added a second article of impeachment, by a vote of twenty-eight to ten: that Nixon had abused his executive power by 'violating the constitutional rights of citizens, impairing the due and proper administration of justice and the conduct of lawful inquiries', and by 'contravening the laws governing agencies of the executive branch and the purposes of these agencies . . .'. A third article of impeachment was added on the following day, that Nixon's refusal to honour the Congressional subpoenas to surrender his tapes was a 'high misdemeanor'. A fourth item of impeachment was rejected by twenty-six votes to twelve, that Nixon had unlawfully concealed from Congress the secret bombing of Cambodia. The Vietnam War was not to be part of the indictment.

On August 1 there were rumours that Nixon was contemplating resignation. Vice-President Gerald Ford, who in such an event would automatically become President, went to see General Alexander Haig, Nixon's White House Chief of Staff. Haig raised with Ford the 'option of a pardon' which a new President could give with regard to his predecessor. Ford heard what Haig had to say, but made no suggestions and no commitment.

On August 5 Nixon handed over yet more tapes, and admitted on television that he had discussed the 'political aspects' of a cover-up of the Watergate burglary within days of the break-in. These further tapes contained one particular disclosure that appeared to substantiate the first two articles of impeachment. The transcripts of Nixon's talks with Haldeman on 23 June 1973 – only six days after the Watergate break-in – showed that Nixon was fully aware of what had taken place at Watergate, and had ordered H. R. Haldeman to call in the Director of the Central Intelligence Agency and tell him to instruct the Federal Bureau of Investigation, whose agents were checking into the burglary, to stop making any further inquiries.

Within twenty-four hours of this new revelation, all ten of the Republican Congressmen who had voted against impeachment in the Judiciary Committee announced publicly that they had reversed their decision. On August 7 a deputation of three senior Republicans, including Senator Barry Goldwater, advised Nixon that he no longer had sufficient support in Congress to escape impeachment. Nixon realized that there was only one way that he could avoid the tensions, exposures and ultimate humiliation of impeachment proceedings, and that was by resigning the presidency, something that had not happened before in American history. On the evening of August 8 he broadcast his intention to resign at noon on the following day, August 9.

Nixon was succeeded as President by Gerald Ford. 'I have not sought this enormous responsibility,' he told the nation in a televised broadcast at his inaugural ceremony that day, 'but I will not shirk it.' Ford added: 'My fellow

Americans, our long national nightmare is over. Our Constitution works, our great Republic is a government of laws and not of men. Here, the people rule. . . . As we bind up the internal wounds of Watergate, more painful and more poisonous than those of foreign wars, let us restore the golden rule to our political process, and let brotherly love purge our hearts of suspicion and hate.'

A month after becoming President, in pursuit of this 'golden rule', Ford granted Nixon a full pardon for all offences against the United States that he might have committed while in office. When a storm erupted over this decision, one result of which was the resignation of Ford's Press Secretary, the new President appeared before a Congressional subcommittee to tell the nation that despite his conversation with General Haig on August 1, 'There was no deal, period.' A final twist to the saga of presidential wrongdoing came on December 19, when Nixon's former Assistant Treasury Secretary, Edward Morgan, was found guilty of assisting Nixon to falsify his tax return four years earlier. More than $500,000 were owed to the Revenue Department. Nixon agreed to pay the money back. Morgan was the twentieth member of Nixon's administration to have been convicted.

One piece of legislation which President Ford opposed, but which Congress passed, over his veto, was the Freedom of Information Act. This became law on November 21. Under it, the United States government was prohibited from denying access to documents 'without good cause' and required federal agencies to supply documents 'without delay' when asked to do so.

President Ford retained the services of Henry Kissinger as Secretary of State. High on the agenda all year had been relations with the Soviet Union, and the process of amelioration known as détente. In July, during a visit by Nixon to Moscow, agreement was reached to ban smaller underground nuclear tests: those hardest to detect. When Ford went to Vladivostok in November, for a summit with Brezhnev, a ten-year pact was outlined for the control and limitation of all offensive strategic nuclear weapons, and nuclear delivery vehicles. Ford and Brezhnev also agreed to set upper limits on strategic nuclear missiles (2,400 each) and heavy bombers (also 2,400). Each country also agreed on a maximum figure of 1,320 each for weapons with multiple nuclear warheads that, although launched by the same vehicle, could hit different targets. The Russians had not yet developed these, but the Americans agreed to include them – and limit their own stockpile of them – according to what was called 'the principle of equality and equal security'.

At Vladivostok, Ford insisted that the Russian search for closer trade relations with the United States would depend on a more liberal Soviet attitude to Jewish emigration, which had fallen from 34,000 to 20,000 in the two previous years. *Pravda* denounced this linkage as having been forced on the President by the 'enemies of détente'. Ford's insistence on this linkage arose as a result of a Congressional vote, the Jackson-Vanik amendment of the previous year. The content and success of this binding legislation was an example of the efforts of an effective American pressure group, the National Conference on Soviet Jewry, which urged that the United States Trade Reform Act of 1972 be amended to include the linkage of emigration with trade. A strong armoury of support had been enlisted. In an open letter to the United States Congress, sent on 14 September 1973, Andrei Sakharov, the Soviet Union's best-known human rights activist – not a Jew, although married to one – had urged support for the amendment on behalf of 'tens of thousands of citizens in the Soviet Union'. These citizens included Jews 'who want to leave the country and who have been working to exercise that right for years and for decades at the cost of endless difficulty and humiliation'.

The Jackson-Vanik amendment had been passed on 11 December 1973. A year later it was an integral part of the Vladivostok negotiations. The Soviet authorities bowed to the pressure, and Jewish emigration grew annually, reaching a peak of 50,000 in 1979.

Within the Soviet Union, the saga of Solzhenitsyn's courageous dissent was reaching a climax. On February 12, after renewed public criticism of his exposure of Soviet labour camp life in *Gulag Archipelago*, he was arrested. On the following day he was deprived of his Soviet citizenship and put on an aeroplane to West Germany. He was not to return to Russia for almost twenty years – when the Soviet Union itself had ceased to exist. A few months after his enforced exile, his researcher, Gabriel Superfin, was sentenced to five years in a labour camp for 'anti-Soviet agitation'. The official message in Superfin's sentence was clear: not every dissident could expect to be sent out of the country. But the pressure of individuals to emigrate was taken up in the West at the highest level. After the British Prime Minister, Harold Wilson, championed the case of the ballet star Valery Panov, he and his wife Galina were allowed to leave. A well-known dissident who was given permission to emigrate after a worldwide campaign on his behalf among human rights groups was Viktor Fainberg, who six years earlier had protested in Red Square against the Soviet-led invasion of Czechoslovakia.

Public protests inside the Soviet Union were rare, and the numbers who had the courage to carry them out were small. After the murder in May of twenty Israeli schoolchildren by terrorist infiltrators from Lebanon, a group of fifty Soviet Jews decided to hold a public protest against the massacre. They gathered outside the Lebanese Embassy in Moscow. One of those who helped organize the demonstration was Anatoli Shcharansky – who had earlier been refused an exit visa. Faced by a line of militiamen, he called out to his fellow protesters: 'Why are you waiting here? We can break the line without any fear.' He then walked forward, and the others followed. It was his first public act of leadership. He and his fellow demonstrators were locked up for twenty-four hours in the cells usually reserved for alcoholics.

Outside the Lebanese Embassy that morning were two leading dissidents, Professor Alexander Lerner, two of whose children had been murdered by the Nazis near Vinnitsa in 1941, and Andrei Sakharov. Their dissident circle was under continual threat. Two weeks after the Lebanese Embassy demonstration, a Jewish doctor, Mikhail Shtern – who had been a Communist Party member for thirty-one years – was arrested in Vinnitsa. The charge against him was of 'bribe-taking and swindling'. His sons knew that his 'crime' was that he had refused a demand by the authorities to renounce their own applications to emigrate.

Soviet repression affected culture as well as human rights. When Alfred Schnittke, the son of a German-Jewish journalist from the town of Engels, in the pre-war Volga German Republic, composed his First Symphony, it was banned by the Moscow authorities for its modernity. Schnittke had been influenced in his composition by the works of Schönberg, Webern and Berg, the scores and tapes of which had been smuggled into the Soviet Union for him. In a courageous act, the conductor Gennadi Rozhdestvensky paid for the entire Moscow orchestra to travel to Gorky, on the Volga, for the first public performance.

Among the official visitors to the Soviet Union was the West German Chancellor, Helmut Schmidt. He offered Russia favourable trade terms for a series of developments, including the provision by German firms of nine thousand 'heavy-duty' trucks, and the construction, by German firms, of a number of chemical plants throughout the Soviet Union. The Russians agreed to increase the existing supply of natural gas. Schmidt also offered the German construction of a nuclear reactor at Kaliningrad (which before 1945, as Königsberg, had been the principal city of East Prussia), from which Russia agreed to supply

Germany with electricity. Schmidt fought hard with Brezhnev, and in the end successfully, to ensure that West Berlin could be supplied with this electricity as it made its way along the power lines to the West.

Yasser Arafat was another visitor to Moscow, when he took the opportunity to thank his Russian hosts for their 'unvarying aid and support'. But Arafat was disappointed when, within a year, the Soviet Union announced that 'all States in the area' had a right to exist. This clearly included Israel. But no mention was made of any prospective or future Palestinian State.

In Vietnam, fighting continued. The initiative lay with North Vietnam, which continued to put its military resources at the disposal of the National Liberation Front, which had set up a Provisional Revolutionary Government in South Vietnam. The ability of the South Vietnamese government to maintain the economic structure of the South was collapsing. But its ability to fight, albeit from a narrower and narrower geographic base, remained formidable. That year 80,000 Vietnamese soldiers and civilians were killed. It was the highest death toll in any one year since the war began.

The military balance in Vietnam had begun to change. The scale of United States supplies to South Vietnam was continually being reduced, at the insistence of Congress. The scale of Soviet and Chinese supplies to North Vietnam was continually growing. When peasants in the area controlled by the Provisional Revolutionary Government tried to flee southward, to South Vietnamese rule, Hanoi banned all movement out of the Communist-controlled zone, and restricted movement within it.

The Cambodian capital, Phnom Penh, was under attack during the winter by the Communist Khmer Rouge forces, but the attack was beaten off. A renewed offensive later in the year was likewise repulsed. But the control of the Phnom Penh government was limited: in addition to the areas controlled by the Khmer Rouge, North Vietnamese Communist forces were in control of the eastern and southern parts of Cambodia, and using them as an integral part of their offensive against South Vietnam. The territorial unity of Laos was also affected by the presence of large numbers of North Vietnamese troops, working alongside the local Pathet Lao Communists. But the agreement reached the previous year for the withdrawal of American and Thai troops was honoured: both met the sixty-day deadline that started on April 5. In place of troops the United States sent economic aid, including support for a substantial hydroelectric project. Thailand also offered to make its contribution to build up the Laotian economy.

In China, the Communist Party was reasserting its power over the army. Leaders who quoted Mao Tse-tung's declamatory phrase 'Political power grows out of the barrel of a gun' were criticized for not completing the phrase, for Mao Tse-tung had gone on to say: 'The Party must control the gun and the gun must never control the Party.' The Party was determined to strengthen its hold over the organizational areas – including agriculture – over which the army, still led by those who had won their spurs in the Long March four decades earlier, exercised considerable control. All that was to end. On July 1, in a leading article to mark the fifty-third anniversary of the founding of the Communist Party of China, both the *People's Daily* and the *Red Flag* announced without ambiguity: 'The Party exercises leadership over everything.' New regional military commanders were appointed, and Party leaders who had been disgraced, humiliated and isolated during the Cultural Revolution were brought back to prominent positions.

The ideological imperatives of the Chinese Communist Party were those of Stalin's Soviet Union of the 1930s. A particularly strong offensive was launched against Western music. Student newspapers stressed that the 'social content' of music by Bach, Mozart, Beethoven, Schubert and Debussy was limited to unacceptable and harmful 'bourgeois' concepts. 'Some people talk about bourgeois classical music with great relish, are mesmerized by it and prostrate themselves before it, showing their slavish mentality for all things foreign,' the *Peking Review* wrote, in explanation of the new campaign. Such people 'are nihilists with regard to national art. Their reverence for foreign things is actually reverence for the bourgeoisie.' If this 'erroneous thinking of extolling foreign things and belittling Chinese things' were not criticized and repudiated, 'then proletarian art and literature will not be able to develop, and Chairman Mao's revolutionary line in art and literature cannot be implemented'.

The target of this campaign was not Western music alone, but also the Prime Minister himself, Chou En-lai, who had been working hard to open up the West to China, and had invited in many Western groups, including musical and operatic ensembles, academics and tourists. In March, Chou En-lai was being attacked by name on wall posters. Mao Tse-tung would brook no rival, nor allow any deviation from the political path he wished to follow. Chou En-lai was in fact gravely ill with cancer and spent long periods of time in hospital. Mao Tse-tung was also ill: the effects of his Parkinson's disease could no longer be controlled, and he appeared in public only with nurses at his side. Even his public speeches contained references to his interest in 'preparing to meet god'. But he retained his iron control over the levers of power. In the battle that he had inaugurated against Western music, new operas and films were produced that extolled 'revolutionary spirit'. They alone – with their 'correct' interpretation of the 'purity of revolutionary activism' – could be performed.

In the sphere of industrial work, the Party stressed the principle that political work must come before the fulfilment of quotas, which had hitherto been the imperative. Production must not be allowed to get in the way of continuing revolution: and revolution involved a constant attack on 'oversized organizational structures'. Mass activism must come from below, with spontaneous zeal, not – as had hitherto been a frequent occurrence – be stimulated by material incentives.

In the struggle against Western influences, Western medicine was among the casualties. There was a call for greater use of – and greater faith in – the 'barefoot doctors' who were itinerant purveyors of ancient Chinese medical remedies, and who numbered more than a million. These doctors were to be preferred to those Chinese surgeons and physicians who used Western techniques, and operated using Western medical equipment.

Local conflicts continued to take their toll. In March, hundreds of Kurdish separatist rebels were killed when Iraqi forces sought to overrun their strongholds on the Iraqi-Turkish border. In February, an IRA bomb on the British mainland killed twelve people – soldiers and their families – who were on a bus. On April 17 the number of those killed in the sectarian fighting in Northern Ireland since 1969 reached a thousand. A month later, on May 17, three car-bomb explosions in Dublin killed thirty-two people. A month later, eleven people were killed by an IRA bomb which was detonated outside Westminster Hall, London. A further five people were killed when the IRA detonated two bombs in public houses in Guildford.

Terrorism had come from Northern Ireland to the mainland, but successive British governments – Labour succeeded the Conservatives as the governing Party five days after the Guildford bombs – were equally determined not to give in to the demands for an end to British rule and the unification of Ireland under the Republic. The violence continued: on November 21, IRA bombs were detonated in two public houses in Birmingham, killing twenty-one people. Harold Wilson's government acted with determination not to allow the IRA to continue to cause death and havoc. On November 28 a Prevention of Terrorism Act was passed through parliament in twenty-four hours –

rather as the 1940 wartime emergency regulations had been. Under the Act, police were given the power to hold terrorist suspects for up to five days without charges being laid against them; and suspects could be banned from the British mainland, or deported from the mainland to Northern Ireland.

In Cyprus, there was turmoil after President Makarios accused the Greek government in Athens of trying to take control of the island. The Greek military junta – which had ruled Greece for the previous seven years – had been pressing its officers in Cyprus to assert the authority of Athens. When Makarios asked the Greek military rulers to give an order to their 650 officers on Cyprus to obey the orders of the Cyprus government, the Greek generals refused to issue any such order. Makarios at once reduced the term of national military service from two years to fourteen months, making four hundred of the Greek officers redundant. He then called on Athens to withdraw all its officers from the island.

The Greek government reacted by sending units of the National Guard, under their Greek officers, into action. On July 15 they attacked the presidential palace with tanks and artillery, and, seizing Cyprus radio, broadcast mendaciously: 'Makarios is dead.' The Greek officers who had carried out the coup were then declared – by the new President, Nicos Sampson – to be 'permanent residents of Cyprus'. A decade and a half earlier, Sampson had fought against the British to secure the union of Cyprus with Greece.

Makarios had in fact escaped from his palace a few minutes before it was overrun. Fleeing to the town of Paphos, on the west coast of the island, he broadcast an appeal to his people to preserve their independence. He was then lifted off by Royal Air Force helicopter to the British sovereign base at Akrotiri, in the south, from where he was flown to Britain.

The Turkish government looked with extreme alarm on the Greek action in overthrowing Makarios and the legitimate and independent government of Cyprus. Under the 1960 Treaty of Guarantee, Turkey, Greece and Britain reserved the right to intervene militarily if no common action could be devised to preserve the Cyprus constitution and the independence of the island. On July 17 the Turkish Prime Minister, Bülent Ecevit, flew to London to propose a joint Anglo-Turkish intervention. The British government declined to act. It also urged Ecevit not to take military action. The United States made a similar plea for moderation. Ecevit returned to Turkey, where on July 19 he and his Cabinet colleagues authorized the invasion of Cyprus.

On July 20, Turkish forces landed in the north – and predominantly Turkish – part of the island. After two days of fierce fighting a ceasefire was called, and the island was effectively partitioned along the ceasefire line. Graeco-Turkish enmity, which had been so fierce fifty-two years earlier during the battle for Western Anatolia, found a new region of confrontation. But, although the island was to remain partitioned, the Greek extremist elements that had pushed the crisis forward were themselves removed: Sampson resigned as President, and, in Athens, the military regime that had sought Greek control of the island was itself overthrown – without violence – on July 23, to be replaced by a democratic administration.

The aftermath of the partition of Cyprus included the need to resettle 200,000 Greek Cypriots who had fled from the Turkish-occupied areas. There were also ten thousand Turkish refugees, who found sanctuary in the British sovereign base. The aftermath also included a breakdown in the ceasefire and a Turkish decision to secure more territory: in three days, between August 14 and 16, Turkish forces secured considerable – and largely Turkish-inhabited – further territory along the northern coast. There was also a terrorist victim of the war: the American Ambassador in Nicosia, Rodger Davies, who was killed by a shot fired through the window of the Embassy by a Cypriot Greek who accused the United States of having supported the Turkish invasion. Ironically, United States hostility to the Turkish action was such that Congress voted to cut off its substantial military aid to Turkey.

A call by the United Nations General Assembly on November 2 for a Turkish withdrawal from the island was rejected by the Turkish government. Instead, a United Nations peacekeeping force took up positions along the ceasefire line, and in the divided capital of Nicosia.

On September 12, in Ethiopia, a military coup deposed the Emperor Haile Selassie. He had been ruler of Ethiopia for forty-four years: six of them in exile after the Italians had conquered his country. A month after having abolished the monarchy, the new military government executed sixty political leaders of the old regime and members of the royal family – they had not been brought to trial. Haile Selassie was held under guard in his palace: he died a year later in unexplained circumstances, at the age of eighty-three.

Man's impact on the global ecological balance was brought to the forefront in 1974, and alarmingly so, when two American scientists, M. Molina and F. S. Rowland, warned that chlorofluorocarbons (CFCs), as used in domestic fridges and as propellants in domestic aerosols – such as hair sprays and deodorants – were likely to be damaging the atmosphere's ozone layer, which filters out ultraviolet radiation from the sun. A quarter of a century later the nations of the world were still struggling to regulate the use of CFCs, and to protect the ozone layer from further damage. But the 'hole' which was identified in the 1970s above Antarctica continued to grow in the following two decades, presenting dangers for the generations yet unborn, unless stronger international – and internationally adhered to – measures could be put in place.

In 1974, as an outcome of the Stockholm conference on the environment, the World Environment Centre was established in New York, founded by an American, Whitman Bassow, as an independent body linking industry, governments and Non-Governmental Organizations (NGOs) in a partnership to minimize waste, reduce industrial pollution at source, prevent industrial accidents, and strengthen environmental laws and institutions. Within two decades, the centre was providing more than a thousand environmental, health and safety experts in voluntary services in thirty-seven countries. A Canadian, Antony Marcil, took over its operations in 1989.

Nature's ravages remained ferocious. A hurricane which struck Honduras in September killed eight thousand people. Famine in India killed several hundred thousand people: Western visitors to Bombay were shocked at the sight of the dead and the dying in the gutters and on the pavements of the main streets of such a modern, bustling metropolis. In Bangladesh the scale of the famine was even greater, with as many as one and a half million people dying of starvation. From this horrific natural disaster came a human act of revitalization: the creation by a young Bangladeshi economist, Muhammad Yunus, from Chittagong, of the Grameen ('village') Bank.

Basing himself on the belief that 'every human being, even one barefoot and begging in the street, is a potential entrepreneur', Yunus established the principle of 'micro-credit'. The Grameen Bank lent tiny sums of money to the poorest of the poor, to people without land, education or even a shelter. More than ninety per cent of the loans went to women, many of whom had never been allowed by their menfolk to handle cash.

Professor Yunus was warned that this was money down the drain, that the poor would never repay. On the contrary, he argued, unlike the rich, the poor could not risk not repaying, for these loans were the only chance they had of escaping from penury. Using meticulous organization and a repayment system adapted to village needs and income levels, Grameen's recovery record was better than ninety-eight per cent – far better than high-street lending to small businesses in Britain. A quarter of a century after it came into being, Grameen was a £1.43 billion business, lending an average of £21 million a month. Micro-credit banks modelled on Grameen have spread to fifty-eight countries, including the United States and Poland.

Twenty-four years after the famine which led to the establishment of the Grameen Bank, the worst floods in Bangladesh's history submerged and destroyed the homes, fields and crops of half of Grameen's two-and-a-half-million clients there, forcing the hard, uncertain task of reconstruction to begin again at the century's end.

In 1974 the population of the world reached, and passed four billion (4,000 million). More than three-quarters of the world's inhabitants were living in poverty, scarcely able to earn enough by their labour, or to produce sufficient food, to feed their families. In March, there were food riots in the Indian State of Bihar. Infant mortality remained high in many nations, particularly in sub-Saharan Africa.

Aware that population and poverty were both on the increase on an unprecedented scale, the United Nations called for a New International Economic Order, in which the development of the Third World would be a priority, towards which the industrialized nations would have to take the main responsibility. To emphasize the urgency, it was announced by the United Nations International Children's Emergency Fund that 500 million children, in seventy poor countries, were facing starvation or severe malnutrition.

CHAPTER TWENTY-FOUR

1975

The division of the planet between north and south, between rich and poor, could become as grim as the darkest period of the Cold War.

HENRY KISSINGER

THE INDUSTRIALIZED WEST had created, and distributed, considerable wealth in the thirty years since the end of the Second World War. But all was not well, and the Arab oil price rises of the previous two years, although stabilized as a result of primarily American and Western European diplomacy, boded ill for the immediate future. In his State of the Union address on 15 January 1975, President Ford told Congress, and the tens of millions of television viewers who watched every such presidential occasion: 'Millions of Americans are out of work. Recession and inflation are eroding the money of millions more. Prices are too high and sales too slow.' The federal deficit and the national debt were both rising. 'Our plant capacity and productivity are not increasing fast enough. We depend on others for essential energy.'

The national need for fuel created conflict with other needs. One of Ford's proposals was to relax the Clean Air Act – an environmentally beneficial measure of the previous year – in order to allow the oilfields of the United States to be more actively exploited. Some measures to conserve fuel were beneficial to the struggle to reduce dependence on high fuel consumption: these included a presidential drive to insulate eighteen million homes across America.

Two assassination attempts were made on Ford within a period of seventeen days, both in California, and both by women. As a result, he was pressed by a concerned American public to reduce the number of his public appearances. He declined to do so, stating, as a matter of public policy in a democracy: 'The American people expect, and I approve of it, a dialogue between them and their President and other public officials. If we cannot have the opportunity of talking with one another, something has gone wrong in our society. Under no circumstances will I, and I hope no others, capitulate to those who want to undercut what's good in America.'

Both would-be assassins, it emerged, were deranged: one was a member of a cult who wanted the imprisoned cult leader released – he was serving a long sentence for murder. The other had earlier asked the police – in vain – to take her into custody, as otherwise, she told them, she might start to 'test the system'.

Another, more traditional test of the system was being made by those who objected to the bussing of schoolchildren from Black areas to White, and White areas to Black, in order to ensure the desegregation of schools. In Louisville, Kentucky, a federal judge, who had ruled that segregation was continuing, ordered the bussing of 11,300 Black pupils from the inner city to the suburbs, and 11,300 White pupils from the suburbs to the inner city. There were riots for four consecutive nights by White protesters incensed by this order. The National Guard were called in to help the police. Protests also took place in Boston a few days later, when similar bussing was ordered.

In a move to enhance and restore democratic procedures in the United States, the House of Representatives abolished its Internal Security Committee, the former all-pervasive House Un-American Activities Committee, which had served to probe the political antecedents of those in public life and the public eye.

From the earliest days of the year, the South Vietnamese government was appealing to the United States for shipments of arms, as the North Vietnamese and Vietcong forces launched a new offensive, overrunning more and more of the Mekong Delta, and pressing closer and closer towards the capital, Saigon. There was no way that Congress – having extracted the United States troops from Vietnam and essentially washed its hands of the struggle there – would agree in time to the commitment involved even in renewed arms shipments. But the United States did call on the eight co-signatories of the Vietnam cease-fire agreement to press North Vietnam to halt its offensive.[1]

As the South Vietnamese appeals – and the Communist attacks – intensified, President Ford did order a strong United States naval task force to

[1] The eight were: Britain, China, France, Hungary, Indonesia, Iran, Poland and the Soviet Union.

coastal waters, but it limited its efforts to reconnaissance flights over Vietnam and Cambodia to observe what was taking place. On February 25, Ford urged Congress to send arms and munitions to the value of $220 million to Cambodia, warning that, unless this was done, Cambodia would be over-run. In a written plea to Congress, Ford asked: 'Are we deliberately to abandon a small country in the midst of its life and death struggle?' Dr Kissinger stressed the extent to which American 'credibility' would be lost if either Cambodia or South Vietnam were to fall to the Communists as a result of the United States disinteresting itself in the struggle.

On March 20 Communist forces overran Da Nang. But still the United States Congress would not contemplate any return of American troops, despite a warning by Kissinger that, if they were to leave the South Vietnam-ese to their own resources, they would be creating a 'massive change in the international environment'. It was, Kissinger said, 'an elementary question of what kind of people we are. For fifteen years we have been involved in encouraging the people of Vietnam to defend themselves. There was never any question that the United States would continue to give economic and military aid to Vietnam, and what we now face is whether the United States will not just stop the loss of American lives, but whether it will deliberately destroy an ally by withholding aid from it in its moment of extremis.'

There were many countries in the world, Kissinger argued, which had no conceivable opportunity to defend themselves without American economic or military assistance: 'And, therefore, if it becomes our national policy that countries must at some point be able to rely entirely on their resources we will have brought about a massive change in the international environment that, in time, will fundamentally threaten the security of the USA as well as the security of our friends.'

There was no time for Congress to take Kissinger's words to heart, even if it had wished to do so. As the Communist forces began their assault on Saigon itself, Ford had no alternative but to authorize the evacuation of the American Embassy there, as well as the Embassy in the Cambodian capital, Phnom Penh. The only task remaining open to the United States was to help evacuate those South Vietnamese who had been its friends and allies, and faced severe reprisals – even execution – if they remained. More than 55,000 were taken out of South Vietnam by the Americans as part of their own evacuation. Thousands more were unable to find a place on the last aircraft – and on the last helicopters – that flew out of Saigon.

On April 13 United States marines helped in America's final evacuation of its remaining diplomatic and military personnel in Cambodia, five years after it had made its first commitment to help sustain the regime against Communist assault. 'It was typical of the American disregard for Cambodians', wrote Henry Kamm, the *New York Times* correspondent most closely associated with Cambodia, 'that the final helicopter evacuation included only 159 Cambodians.' On April 17 the Khmer Rouge captured Phnom Penh. As much of the civilian population fled, thousands were shot down in the streets in cold blood. On April 29 all remaining American personnel were evacuated from Saigon. That same day North Vietnamese troops entered the South Vietnamese capital. On the following day the South Vietnamese government surrendered.

Tension off Indochina remained high. In the second week of May, the Cambodian navy seized an American merchant ship, the *Mayaguez*. The crew of forty was held captive, and their ship guarded by Cambodian troops on the island of Koh Tang. President Ford reacted immediately and forcefully to this challenge to the authority and dignity of the United States, ordering the American aircraft carrier *Coral Sea* – named after the first naval victory over Japan in the Second World War – to the Gulf of Thailand. While American bombers struck at the Cambodian air force, destroying seventeen Cambodian warplanes, American marines landed on Koh Tang and recaptured the *Mayaguez*. During the struggle, fifteen of the landing party were killed. The crew were released, and were recovered at sea in a Thai fishing boat, flying the white flag.

Following the fall of Saigon and the establishment of a unified Communist government based on Hanoi, thousands of South Vietnamese set off by boat, mostly in frail and often hardly seaworthy craft, in search of a place of refuge. Many drowned on the journey. Others were turned away from hostile shores, or, as in the case of Hong Kong, interned in detention camps for years. An Israeli sea captain, who thirty years earlier had himself been a 'boat person' in search of a haven, came across one small ship, adrift on the high seas, took the hungry, frightened refugees on board his freighter, and sailed with them to Israel, where they were given sanctuary.

With the consent of Congress, 132,000 Vietnamese refugees were offered sanctuary in the United States. Some faced cries of 'Go home!' when they reached the town of their destination – especially if it was an area of high unemployment. But many more were met by town bands that marched in parade to welcome them.

On December 3, the government of Laos fell to the Laotian Communists, and the King abdicated. The three nations of Indochina – Laos, Cambodia and Vietnam – the political future of which had drawn in first the French and then the Americans, to bloody wars and bitter defeats, was under the rule of those against whom the outside forces had pitted themselves without respite for thirty years, and at the cost of tens of thousands of lives – the lives of soldiers who had been brought halfway round the world to sustain regimes that had been finally, and amid the harsh violence of civil war, swept away.

In July the United States and the Soviet Union began their first joint venture in space. This was as a consequence of an agreement reached between Nixon and Brezhnev in Moscow the previous year. The aim, as well as an attempt to bring the Super Powers closer together in general détente, was to try to create a workable rescue system in space that both countries could call upon. On July 17 an American Apollo and a Soviet Soyuz spacecraft joined and – 140 miles above the surface of the Earth – two American astronauts made their way from their craft to the Soviet one. From Earth, Ford and Brezhnev sent messages of congratulation.

In the Cold War, new weapons were raising new spectres of danger. The Soviet Union had developed a 'Backfire' bomber that could reach the continental United States and return to the Soviet Union, opening up areas of the United States hitherto beyond Soviet bomber range to nuclear attack. The Soviet Union was also developing – more quickly than the Americans had anticipated – two types of intercontinental missile which had multiple warheads: warheads that, from a single missile, could be sent against different targets many miles apart. The Americans were also developing a new weapon, the 'Cruise' missile, an air vehicle, without a pilot, that could be launched either from an aeroplane or from a submarine: if fired from the White Sea or the Sea of Japan, it could reach many points in the Soviet Union hitherto not within range of nuclear assault.

A proposed arms limitation treaty signing visit by Brezhnev to the United States was postponed, raising fears that the new weaponry might prove incapable of treaty reduction within the Strategic Arms Limitation Talks. One problem was the very definition of 'strategic'. The Soviet Union saw its Backfire bomber as a tactical weapon, but for the United States negotiators any weapon that could bring nuclear attack to the American continent was a strategic one.

One area of Soviet military penetration raised strong American concerns. Angola had become independent from Portugal on November 11. It did so in the midst of a civil war between the factions that had hitherto focused their struggle against the Portuguese. The victorious group, the Marxist–Leninist Popular Movement for the Liberation of Angola (MPLA) was given military help by both the Soviet Union, which sent arms and military advisers, and Cuba, which sent five thousand combat troops. The rival group, the National Union for Total Independence of Angola (UNITA), fought on, but the Soviet weaponry for the MPLA was decisive. On November 24 President Ford warned the Soviet Union that the despatch of weapons, and also of Soviet military advisers, had introduced the rivalry of Great Powers to Africa for the first time since the collapse of European colonial rule fifteen years earlier.

Ford's words were stern ones: 'This Soviet involvement is resented by African nations most of all, but the United States cannot be indifferent while an outside power embarks upon an interventionist policy – so distant from its homeland and so removed from traditional Russian interests.' Were the Soviet Union to continue its interventionist policies, it 'must inevitably threaten other relationships'. On two separate fronts, the nuclear and the diplomatic, the Soviet Union and the United States were on divergent courses.

In Northern Ireland, hopes of peace were raised when an IRA truce that had been called the previous Christmas was allowed to run into January, but on January 16 the IRA resumed its campaign. In all, 245 people died during the year in terrorist attacks by extremist Catholic and Protestant groups. There was also fighting between the extremist groups on either side of the divide: on the one hand between the Protestants groups, the Ulster Defence Association and the Ulster Volunteer Force; and on the other hand between the IRA and the Irish Revolutionary Socialist Party. Children were often the victims of the violence. In June a four-year-old Catholic girl was killed in Belfast by a bomb placed in her father's car. In October a six-year-old Protestant girl was killed by gunmen trying to shoot her father. British businesses began to close down their Northern Ireland offices. Unemployment rose to more than ten per cent, the highest in the United Kingdom. As a gesture of conciliation, on December 5 the British government ended detention without trial. Forty-six IRA prisoners were released. As they left prison they swore to carry on the struggle.

Detention without trial in Northern Ireland had raised protests by human rights groups in Britain. Violations of human rights elsewhere were on a far larger scale. General Pinochet's regime in Chile was condemned by the United Nations in mid-October for the continuing ill-treatment and torture of several thousand political detainees. One detainee, a British subject, Dr Sheila Cassidy, was detained without trial and tortured by electric shock. Only after the firmest British diplomatic protests – and the withdrawal of the British Ambassador – was she released. On December 9 the General Assembly of the United Nations condemned the Chilean government for 'the institutionalized practice of torture'. Its call to Pinochet 'to restore and safeguard essential human rights and fundamental liberties' was ignored.

Many national leaders were approaching the final quarter of the century with a realization that, amid so many advances of science and technology, dangers lurked that could threaten the whole fabric of what had been achieved. One of those was Pierre Trudeau, the Prime Minister of Canada, who, at the Commonwealth Conference, held that year in Jamaica, set out his worries with regard to both the danger of nuclear proliferation and the unequal distribution of wealth in the world. In May the Canadian government announced that it would only provide other countries with nuclear reactors and technology for the peaceful use of nuclear energy if they were signatories of the nuclear non-proliferation treaty. In September, Canada increased its foreign aid allocations to $742 million, or a half a per cent of Canada's Gross National Product. No other country distributed so much in foreign aid. It was sent in the main to the world's poorest nations, for food production, rural development, education, public health and energy.

Canada was also at the forefront of the struggle to protect the environment, and for the better regulation of forests, which were being decimated through-out the world by the demands of the newspaper and packaging industries. Other environmental concerns which had been raised in earlier years received even higher profiles than before. In June, fourteen Federal Agencies in the United States combined forces to call for a ban on fluorocarbon propellants for aerosols within three years, in an attempt to protect the ozone layer, the depletion of which was being spoken of by medical and scientific researchers as a cause of skin cancer, damage to crops and potentially catastrophic effects on the global climate. The phrase 'global warming' was used, indicative of changes that were being caused by man, but which could affect mankind adversely. They were changes which, if action was not taken soon, might prove irreversible.

Many new areas of concern were being opened up by scientific research. These included the danger of cancer among asbestos workers and their families; the effect of excessive intakes of lead on mental retardation; and the increase in mercury poisoning among fishermen in the Mediterranean as levels of mercury, discharged as industrial waste, were continually increasing. Urban pollution was also growing at a rate that caused concern among doctors. So severe was the air pollution in Madrid in January that citizens and visitors were warned only to breathe through their noses, not through their mouths, to take no outdoor physical exercise, and to speak as little as possible except indoors. In Britain, legislation was introduced, as part of the Health and Safety at Work Act, which established the right of any worker, in factory or shop, to be told the details of the work-related pollution that might affect him.

The industrialized nations were faced with the dangers of their own success, and with increasing scientific and medical research that revealed the dangers on their continuing path of industrial development. The Third World countries had no such perspective. For them the raw materials which some – but far from all – of them controlled were a means of survival. Those without raw materials on any significant scale could only turn to the unindustrialized nations as suitors for financial and economic aid. Some could take advantage of the Cold War, playing East and West against each other. Others sought economic security by a definite alignment with one side or the other. But in the main the intense poverty of so much of the Third World was not assuaged. It was augmented in some countries by despotic Presidents stealing the wealth of their own people, sometimes literally sending it out of the country in suitcases to safe havens in Switzerland and elsewhere far away.

Whether the conflict between the wealthy nations and the poor ones could be resolved without some catastrophic collision was not clear. In a speech to the United Nations General Assembly, Henry Kissinger warned of the 'environment of continuing conflicts'. In Paris, at a Conference on International Economic Co-operation, he said that even if the industrial nations and the oil exporters were to work together, they could not supply all the resources needed for Third World development. The developing nations, he stated (in words spoken on his behalf at the United Nations by the American representative, Daniel Moynihan), 'have laid claim for a greater role, for more control over their own destiny, and for a just share in global prosperity'. In contrast, the 'industrially advanced nations have stated their claim for reliable sources of energy, raw materials and other products at a fair price'. He saw no reason to minimize this contradiction, stating without prevarication: 'The division of the planet between north and south, between rich and poor, could become as grim as the darkest period of the Cold War.'

More than a hundred developing countries had no oil to sell. For them the Arab oil-price rises, introduced as a punishment for alleged Western support for Israel two years earlier, but bringing vast profits in their wake for the Arab oil-producing States, crippled any chance of developing their economies. Even industrialized countries like Italy had suffered a drop in industrial productivity of more than seventy per cent as a result of the oil-price rises. Japan's Gross Domestic Product declined for the first time in thirty years. West German industrial output fell seven per cent in six months, as sharp a decline as for the whole of the previous year. Inflation was affecting all countries for whom the massive increase in the price of oil could only be met by depletion of national reserves. In Britain unemployment rose to levels not seen for forty years; but, starting in June, the regular flow of oil from the North Sea offered amelioration for many British economic ills.

Enormous deficits were accumulated by countries whose economies had been struggling for many years to build up some minimal global competitiveness. Non-oil producers accumulated a deficit during 1975 of $35,000 million. One-third of this was owed by four countries: Brazil, Mexico, the Philippines and South Korea. Both Zaire and Zambia lost more than three-quarters of the currency reserves with which they had begun the year. Bangladesh had no reserves at all: it was dependent for its economic survival, and for feeding its population, on Western aid and credit. The oil-producing States were prevailed upon to make a contribution to the global debt, but less than $3,000 million was forthcoming from them. The International Monetary Fund loaned money to countries with the worst deficits, but only by increasing the deficit in the long term. By the end of the year Argentina's national reserves had fallen to $300 million, half of which had been acquired by borrowing. Its foreign indebtedness at the end of the year was $10,000 million.

The world's wealth was represented most clearly by oil; the world's wealthiest nations were almost all of them oil-producing States, including the United States.

In the struggle for survival, the Third World countries had the continuing support of the United Nations agencies set up thirty years earlier. The World

Health Organization was able to report the elimination of viral smallpox in all but three of the thirty countries in which it had been endemic ten years earlier. In the three that remained, it was being rapidly eliminated in two – India and Bangladesh. Ethiopia had yet to tackle that killer.

Another World Health Organization programme, launched in May, was for the elimination of river blindness in the Volta River basin. An international fund was set up, administered by the World Bank, with the United Nations Development Programme covering training and research costs. In the Western world considerable advances were being made in treating infertility. A whole-body X-ray scanner came into use. Skin-grafting techniques were improved. Methods of combating tooth decay were enhanced.

The handicapped were also beginning to receive recognition as a group that should be encouraged to play its fullest possible part in the national life of the Western world. A lead was taken on November 29 in the United States in the Education for All Handicapped Children Act, under which every publicly funded school was required to provide 'appropriate education' for every handicapped school-age child, irrespective of disability. Education also benefited that year, in the widest sense, by the marketing of the first 'personal computer'.

Persistent efforts were being made to help the Third World economically, and to relieve the distress of increasingly widespread poverty. Under the Lomé Convention, fifty-eight Third World countries were given access to Western European markets (in the year that a nationwide referendum in Britain approved British membership of the European Community). In February the United Nations Development Programme agreed that ten 'low-income' countries would be the beneficiaries of technical aid in excess of $80 million. A further $100 million was allocated in June for technical assistance to four developing countries: to Burma for agriculture, forestry and fisheries; to Kenya for rural development; to Kuwait for industry; and to Nigeria for both agricultural development and education. These considerable sums were an injection of cash that could not otherwise have been secured; they were also a temptation to corruption that was not always resisted.

Child poverty was on the increase, and infant mortality affected hundreds of millions of children. Within the United Nations agencies, enormous energies were devoted to the plight of children. In 1974 a World Child Emergency had been proclaimed. In 1975 eight major programmes had been set up under the emergency to bring at least basic food needs and minimum health care to the children most in need. In India more than sixty million people were living on the margin of starvation. India's eastern neighbour, Bangladesh, was the country most at risk. Severe flooding regularly added to the plight of millions of people, whose homes and meagre possessions were washed away. At the same time, political turmoil made any orderly evolution of improvement impossible. In Bangladesh, in January, Shaikh Mujib Rahman declared a one-Party State and established a virtual dictatorship. In August he was murdered by four army majors. His family was murdered with him. There followed a struggle for power within the army. In Africa, those countries which had just acquired independence from Portugal were also in grave economic difficulties, exacerbated in Angola by civil war.

India, which prided itself on being 'the world's largest democracy', was in the process of constitutional turmoil. On January 3, a member of the government, Lalit Narain Mishra, who had been attacked by the opposition for 'corruption in government', was assassinated. The opposition claimed that the government was maintaining power only by devious and corrupt methods, and prepared to put this to the judgment of the courts. On June 12 a judge of the Allahabad High Court held that the election by which the Prime Minister, Indira Gandhi – Jawaharlal Nehru's daughter – had been elected to parliament was void. He then disqualified her from holding public office for six years, on the ground of 'corrupt practices' during the election. But she was allowed to remain Prime Minister pending an appeal to the Supreme Court.

In a swift reaction, Indira Gandhi used her prime-ministerial powers to order the arrest of more than six hundred opposition leaders, including the venerable and much respected Jayprakash Narayan, and one of the best-known Congress Party luminaries, Moraji Desai. On June 26, press censorship was imposed, and a state of emergency declared.

India under Indira Gandhi's emergency parted swiftly from the democratic methods which she insisted were her ultimate objective once the emergency could be set aside. In November, after retrospective changes were made in the election law, the Supreme Court reversed the earlier verdict of 'corrupt practices'. The Press Council of India, set up to protect freedom of the press, was dissolved.

Increased economic well-being gave Indira Gandhi a respite: the grain harvest that year was one of the best on record. The previous year's discovery of oil was proving a substantial one. A viable source of natural gas was also discovered. But the democratic values for which India had fought, and which Indira Gandhi's father had embodied, were suborned.

In Portugal, on the eve of elections in which it was possible that an extreme-left coalition, with full Communist participation, might be established, the army tried to restore the dictatorship. There was fighting in Lisbon on March 11, one man was killed, and General Spinola, the army officer accused of seeking to seize power, fled into exile. On April 25 the Portuguese people went to the polls for the first democratic elections in more than half a century. After negotiations among the political Parties, a government was set up headed by the Socialist leader Mario Suares: although without an overall majority, his Party had won the largest number of votes, 37.9 per cent. The Communists polled 12.5 percent.

Revolutionary Councils were established in Lisbon and elsewhere, and Revolutionary Brigades set up. There were demands, echoing Russia in 1917, for the establishment of a 'dictatorship of the proletariat'. The Cuban model of Fidel Castro was much praised. In a first step to Communist control, a Socialist newspaper was seized by Communist printers. On November 25, soldiers sympathetic to the Communists seized the air force bases around Lisbon, but an anti-Communist force of commandos defeated them. Communists also seized the radio and television stations, from which they broadcast appeals for an uprising. Troops loyal to the government drove them out and halted their inflammatory broadcasts. Street demonstrations in favour of the revolution were dispersed. Democracy was restored.

Portugal's political unrest had repercussions ten thousand miles away. Among the conflicts that broke out in 1975, one was to remain unresolved for the next quarter of a century. Indonesia had been created after the Second World War from the former Dutch East Indies: a vast country of islands and archipelagos, with its capital, Jakarta, on the island of Java. The most easterly island, Timor, had been divided in the seventeenth century between the Dutch and the Portuguese. On Indonesia becoming independent in 1949, West Timor became Indonesian, but East Timor remained Portuguese. In 1975, as Portugal was mired in conflict, the Indonesian army invaded East Timor. A year later the area was annexed. For the following quarter of a century Indonesian security forces fought against the East Timor separatists, and more than 200,000 people were killed.

*   *   *

In Spain, where democracy had disappeared almost forty years earlier, five hundred Spanish civil servants signed a pro-democracy manifesto on February 6. But Franco continued to rule with an iron hand. Basque and Catalan separatists felt the full rigour of police control. After the killing of several policemen, a law was passed whereby a person accused of killing a policeman would be tried by summary court martial, with the death sentence being mandatory on conviction. On September 18 five Basque separatists were convicted of killing policemen, and were sentenced to death. Pope Paul VI made a public plea that their lives should be spared. Fifteen European governments withdrew their ambassadors in protest, including all those of the European Economic Community. At the United Nations, the President of Mexico, Luis Echevarria, called for Spain's expulsion.

Franco ignored the appeals and protests, and the executions were carried out on September 27. There were attacks on Spanish embassies and Spanish government property in Lisbon, Ankara, Rome and Milan. This, Franco said – in a speech from the balcony of the royal palace on October 1, the thirty-ninth anniversary of his becoming Head of State – was proof of 'an international plot of masons, Jews and Communists'.

Two weeks after his speech, the eighty-three-year-old Franco was taken ill with influenza. On November 20 he died. His death was followed two days later by the restoration of the monarchy – under King Juan Carlos – and the promise of the re-establishment of parliamentary government for the first time since the collapse of the republican regime in 1939. Juan Carlos had been 'trained' by Franco from 1960 onwards, and recognized as the heir to the throne by the Franco government in 1969; but as soon as he came to the throne he showed a democratic independence of spirit which Franco's senior advisers hoped they had stamped out. As his first step towards true liberalization, on November 26 the King ordered the release of five hundred of Franco's political prisoners. Six months later the ban on political Parties, which had been in force for more than a quarter of a century, was lifted. Western Europe's longest-lasting dictatorship was at an end.

Throughout the year, Henry Kissinger had conducted persistent shuttle diplomacy to try to bring some resolution to the Middle East conflict. In March he was unable to bring the Israelis and Egyptians to the negotiating table, but in August he succeeded. In Jerusalem he signed with the Israeli Prime Minister, Yitzhak Rabin, and the Foreign Minister, Shimon Peres, a plan for the phased withdrawal of Israel in the Sinai, and the establishment of a United Nations buffer zone between the Suez Canal and the strategic Gidi and Mitla passes. This agreement was then signed between Israel and Egypt in Geneva on September 4. Under it, Egypt undertook not to impede Israeli shipping through the Suez Canal, and to sell Israel oil from the oilfield at Abu Rudeis which Israel was evacuating.

When the United Nations voted on November 10 to condemn Zionism as 'racism', the United States, Britain, France, West Germany and Canada were among thirty-five countries refusing to join in the condemnation. Egypt, however, cast its vote against Israel, as did seventy-four other nations, including all thirteen Communist States. The United States representative at the United Nations, Daniel Moynihan, put the anti-Zionist vote in a wider context, calling it 'a general assault by the majority of nations on the principles of liberal democracy, which are now found only in a dwindling number of nations'.

CHAPTER TWENTY-FIVE

1976

. . . the frantic needs and vulgar tastes of that 'consumer
society' are the complete opposite of a truly happy and
civilized life.

LE DUAN

T HE UNITED NATIONS had more than doubled its size since its establishment thirty years earlier, at the end of the Second World War. At the General
Assembly in 1976, more than 140 nations participated in the debates. As
a sign of the growing recognition of the importance and the problems of
post-colonial Africa, the United Nations Economic and Social Council met
for the first time in Africa, at Abidjan, in the Ivory Coast. A few months
later the fourth session of the United Nations Conference on Trade and
Development met in the Kenyan capital, Nairobi.

In the Security Council, the exercise of veto powers continued: in June
the United States vetoed the admission of Angola for as long as Cuban troops
remained there. Only after the United States agreed, five months later, to
abstain rather than cast its veto, was Angola admitted. The Cuban troops –
20,000 in all by the summer – had by then completed their mission of
helping secure, together with Soviet arms, the victory of the Marxist-led
Popular Movement for the Liberation of Angola. That the civil war would
cease became clear when the United States Senate banned any further American aid to the anti-Marxist groupings.

During a visit to Africa which began on April 23, Henry Kissinger set
out the priorities to which the United States was committed. First and
foremost was an end to the maverick status of Southern Rhodesia, where
the White minority had retained power since its unilateral declaration of
independence eleven years earlier. The British government, headed by James
Callaghan, was insisting that independence must be preceded by majority

rule, and must be achieved in the coming two years: to this the United States gave its full support.

Kissinger offered aid to Mozambique for the loss of trade as a result of the closing of the border with Rhodesia as part of United Nations sanctions; help for refugees who had fled from Rhodesia; and support for an international programme of economic, technical and educational assistance to an independent Rhodesia when the transition came. Kissinger added that Whites as well as Blacks should have 'a secure future and civil rights' in the new republic. On September 19 Ian Smith, the Rhodesian Prime Minister, accepted the principle of majority rule.

In July, Kissinger presided, as Secretary of State, over the final act of United States military involvement in South-East Asia: the evacuation on July 20 of the last American servicemen in Thailand. That presence had begun twelve years earlier. At the height of the war in Vietnam there had been 50,000 Americans in Thailand.

In the new, one-nation, one-Party Vietnam, the Marxist ideology of the North was rapidly becoming all-pervasive. On June 25 the Secretary-General of the Vietnamese Communist Party, Le Duan, announced that those people in the South who 'had attained a living standard much too high for the country's economy and their own working capacity should understand that this prosperity was a sham one. . . . They should know that the frantic needs and vulgar tastes of that "consumer society" are the complete opposite of a truly happy and civilized life.' At the same time, Communist Party officials from the North who went South as part of the reconstruction and re-educational programmes were accused in Party newspapers of having been found susceptible to 'the temptations of southern cities', as well as falling victim to 'the spirit of seeking special privileges and favours'.

A pragmatic element entered into Communist rule, with stress being laid on the need to take advantage of foreign, and even American sources of capital, management and technology, as the 'key to socialism'.

In the Soviet Union, Leonid Brezhnev, having reached the age of seventy, was hailed in the Russian newspapers as a *vozhd* – supreme leader, a term used previously only for Lenin and Stalin. But the apparatus of terror dominated by execution was no more. In its place was a rigid secret police system, prison and labour-camp incarceration for political dissidents; a system that encouraged informers and made criticism dangerous – but no longer fatal. Several dissidents were allowed to emigrate, among them Andrei Amalrik, who had written a book critical of the Soviet Union, and Vladimir Bukovsky, who had published an account of the treatment of dissidents in mental hospitals. Bukovsky was the beneficiary of an exchange: he was permitted to leave for the West when General Pinochet's military regime in Chile released the Chilean Communist leader, Luis Corvalan, from prison, and allowed him to make his home in the Soviet Union.

As had happened in previous Soviet releases, however, the authorities found a way of issuing a warning to those who might be tempted to see the path of dissent as the road to emigration. The Bukovsky-Corvalan exchange took place on December 18. Within three days Bukovsky's associate, Vladimir Borisov, who had helped him collect material on the abuse of mental hospital incarcerations, was himself arrested and confined in a mental institution – on Christmas Day. The new leader of the British Conservative Party, Margaret Thatcher, was outspoken in her condemnation of Soviet tyranny, so much so that the Soviet army newspaper *Red Star* described her as the 'Iron Lady'.

For the first time since the early 1920s, the Soviet Defence Ministry was held by a civilian, the former Leningrad Party Secretary, Dmitri Ustinov; but he was given the rank of general – and later of Marshal of the Soviet Union – to compensate for his lack of a military career.

In June the Soviet Union confronted a serious challenge to its authority in Eastern Europe. This did not take place on the streets or on the barricades, but at a two-day Conference of European Communist Parties, held in East Berlin at the end of June. The Italian Communist Party leader, Enrico Berlinguer, spoke critically of the Soviet Union's invasion of Czechoslovakia almost a decade earlier, and insisted that his Party would continue to criticize policies in the Communist-bloc countries when it felt the need to do so. To the disappointment of the Soviet Union, the final communiqué of the conference made no reference – as all such communiqués had in previous years – to the 'leading role' of the Soviet Union in the Communist movement worldwide.

In the defence sphere, the Soviet Union succeeded in July in introducing a powerful warship, carrying aircraft, into the Mediterranean from the Black Sea. This was the 40,000-ton *Kiev*. Under the Montreux Convention of 1936, to which the Soviet Union was a signatory, no aircraft carriers were allowed to pass through the Straits.[1] The Soviet authorities insisted that although there were aircraft on board, in every respect as an aircraft carrier, the vessel was in fact an anti-submarine cruiser, and thus not covered by the convention. The balance of naval power in the Mediterranean changed overnight: but this was no longer 1938 or 1948, and the likelihood of a conflict with any of the Mediterranean powers was small. Even Egypt, Russia's ally in the eastern Mediterranean, no longer required military support against Israel: its President, Anwar Sadat, was contemplating quite a different, if dramatic movement to break the cycle of hostility and confrontation: a visit to Jerusalem.

Six weeks after the impressive armament and aircraft of the *Kiev* entered the Mediterranean, there was a setback to the Soviet presentation of its military prowess when a Soviet pilot, flying a MiG-25 'Foxbat' fighter and interceptor aircraft, landed in Japan and sought asylum. The Foxbat had been believed by the United States – encouraged in this belief by Soviet secrecy and innuendo – to be the world's 'most advanced' fighter aircraft. Its existence had alarmed the United States defence establishment. When the defector's plane was examined, however, it was found to be less effective as a fighter or as an interceptor – and, critically, far heavier and thus less speedily manoeuvrable – than its American counterparts.

In the United States, 1976 marked the two-hundredth anniversary of independence from Britain. The bicentennial celebration exceeded in zeal the expectation of those who planned them. The British Queen, Elizabeth II, visited Philadelphia, the first British sovereign ever to visit the site of the signing of the Declaration of Independence. The bicentennial year was also election year. The challenger chosen by the Democrats was the Governor of Georgia, Jimmy Carter. Declaring that he was 'twice born' – first at birth and then when he 'committed himself to Jesus' – he promised the American people: 'I'll never knowingly make a misstatement of fact. I'll never betray your trust. If I do any of these things, I don't want you to support me.' In answer to the charge that he was an outsider, a provincial unknown, 'Jimmy who?', not well versed in the ways of Washington, he gained public support by appearing to distance himself from those in Washington who were tarred

[1] The two narrow waterways – the Bosphorus and the Dardanelles, linking the Black Sea with the Aegean Sea (through the Sea of Marmora), each of which was Turkish sovereign territory (Istanbul is on the Bosphorus).

by the stigmas of Vietnam and Watergate. 'I have been accused of being an outsider,' he answered.

I plead guilty. Unfortunately, the vast majority of Americans are outsiders. We are not going to get changes by simply shifting around the same group of insiders, the same tired old rhetoric, the same unkept promises and the same divisive appeals to one Party, one faction, one section of the country, one race or religion or interest group. The insiders have had their chances, and they have not delivered. Their time has run out.

President Ford was facing his first presidential election. Like Truman and Johnson before him he had come to the presidency through the demise of the incumbent. This was his first test as his own man. He lost, and Carter became President. The votes polled were close: 40,249,963 for Carter as against 38,498,496 for Ford. Carter's Congressional support was strong: sixty-one Democrat Senators as against thirty-seven Republicans, and a 290–145 balance in his favour in the House of Representatives. When Carter formed his administration there was criticism that, of the seventeen members of his Cabinet, four were friends of his from Georgia without any particular record of administrative service. But that was the President's prerogative. The merits of the most powerful man in the world – for such the President of the United States had become – would be decided in the years ahead on the basis of his decisions.

In Northern Ireland the sectarian violence continued. On January 6, after fifteen people had been killed in two days, a Special Air Service (SAS) elite unit was sent from the British mainland to try to restore order. On July 21 the British Ambassador to Dublin was murdered. The intensity of sectarian violence reached a pitch of public revulsion on August 10, when three children who were walking with their mother were killed by an IRA car which crashed into them after its driver had been shot dead by soldiers. The death of the Maguire children provoked an instant backlash. Later in the week a group of Catholic women, led by Mairead Corrigan, the children's aunt, and Betty Williams, created a protest movement, the Peace People, which asked women throughout the province to help them bring the killings to an end.

On August 14, after the IRA threatened the leaders of the Peace People with death, ten thousand women, most of them Catholics but including some Protestants, took part in a peace rally in Andersonstown. Two weeks later, on August 28, peace marches were held all over Northern and Southern Ireland: in Belfast, 25,000 people marched, and Protestant and Catholic women marched together, embraced, and wept.

From Germany and Norway came words of admiration for the Peace People, and considerable financial support. The IRA, however, denounced the Peace People and, on October 23, attacked a peace march. Sixteen of the marchers had to be taken to hospital. Five days later a leading republican, Maire Drumm, was shot dead by Protestant gunmen in a Belfast hospital. In November the IRA renewed its attacks against off-duty members of a military arm of the State in Northern Ireland, the Ulster Defence Regiment: fifteen off-duty members were murdered by the end of the year. On December 13 a spate of IRA bombs brought the centre of Belfast to a halt. That year's Christmas truce was restricted to two days, not prolonged into January as in previous years. Indeed, as 1976 came to an end the bombing campaign intensified. The Peace People did not give up their work, but they could not compete with the tyranny of extremism.

As extremists on both sides meted out death in Northern Ireland, in California a law permitted those who were terminally ill to authorize the removal of life-support equipment. In Britain, the Race Relations Act made incitement to race hatred an offence, and established a Commission on Race Equality to monitor discrimination and take steps to reduce it.

In South Africa, student demonstrators in the Soweto Black suburb of Johannesburg began a protest on June 16 against a government proposal for compulsory teaching in Afrikaans. The protest continued for nine days. When police opened fire on the demonstrators, seventy-six students were killed. On July 6 the government dropped its education proposal. But anti-apartheid demonstrations took place throughout the country, and were dispersed by force. By the end of the year, five hundred Blacks had been killed. Many had been shot dead by riot police using automatic rifles.

In the Middle East, civil war had broken out the previous July in Lebanon between the Christian and Muslim communities, with private Christian and Muslim militias in particularly vicious conflict. The PLO under Yasser Arafat was also based in Lebanon, having been expelled by King Hussein from Jordan. It too was divided into warring factions. Iraq and Libya sent troops to support the Muslims. Beirut was divided, with Christian East Beirut and

Muslim West Beirut exchanging frequent shellfire. As street fighting spread in the capital, many non-combatants were killed: massacred by their respective enemies.

In May, six thousand Syrian troops entered Lebanon from the east and advanced on Beirut and Sidon, where pro-Syrian and anti-Syrian Palestinians fought each other for control. On June 16 the American Ambassador, Francis Meloy, accused by the Muslims of favouring the Christians, was kidnapped and murdered. An Arab Peace Force of some ten thousand men was formed by the Arab League, and intervened to try to stop the Palestinian civil war inside Beirut. Like the Syrian troops before it, it failed to do so, and withdrew. On August 12 Tell al-Za'atar – a Muslim enclave in Christian East Beirut – was overrun, and its inhabitants, many of them the families of Palestinian refugees from the 1948 Arab-Israel War, were massacred by the Christian Falangist militia.

On October 17 the warring parties met at Riyadh, under Saudi Arabian auspices, and with Syrian, Egyptian and Kuwaiti participation, to work out conditions for a ceasefire. They were successful: the Arab Peace Force, increased to 30,000 men, was designated a 'deterrent force'. Both sides withdrew from the areas they had overrun. The Lebanese accepted the presence of the PLO in their midst. On November 15 the Arab Peace Force, made up almost entirely of Syrian troops, entered Beirut, establishing its own quasi-military rule. In the course of the fighting, 40,000 people – Lebanese Christians, Lebanese Muslims, and Palestinians – had been killed.

Israel was also caught up in conflict. On June 27 an Air France passenger airliner on its way from Tel Aviv to Paris was hijacked by Arab terrorists shortly after take-off from Athens. The pilot was ordered to fly to Benghazi in Libya, where the hijackers separated out the Israeli and Jewish passengers, and then released the non-Jews. The Jews – ninety-eight in all – were flown on to Entebbe in Uganda, 2,500 miles from Israel, and held hostage at Entebbe airport.

Inside Israel, amid a sense of terrible impotence, the balance of public opinion was that the freedom of the hostages must be secured by complying with the hijackers' demands. These included the release of Fatah terrorists being held in Israeli prisons. Except in the rarest of emergencies, Israeli government ministers do not meet on Saturday – the Sabbath – any more than American, British or French Cabinets meet on Sunday. But on Saturday July 3 the Prime Minister, Yitzhak Rabin, called his Cabinet in order to make a final decision. 'The decision which was taken was in clear opposition to what had recently been the prevailing mood within the Government,' the Minister of Defence, Shimon Peres, later wrote. 'The balance of opinion seemed to be in favour of exchanging the hostages for Fatah terrorists. As Minister of Defence I had worked with my colleagues throughout that week to find another solution – a means of freeing the kidnap victims by an armed intervention of our own.'

Four large carrier aircraft took part in the mission, flying from the southernmost point of the Sinai, Sharm el-Sheikh, directly to Entebbe. Radio silence was imperative; only when the flight was over did a brief radio message come through to the command headquarters in Israel from the commander of the operation, General Dan Shomron: 'We've landed. Don't worry. If anything goes wrong, I'll let you know.'

Almost nothing did go wrong. But one of the hostages, Dora Bloch, an elderly woman who before the rescue raid, when some meat caught in her throat and she began to choke, was taken to the local hospital, was murdered after the raid, while still in the hospital. All the terrorists – Arabs and Germans – were killed during the raid, as were three of the civilian hostages caught in the crossfire. The commander of the rescue mission, Yonatan Netanyahu, was also killed, by a bullet through the heart. Twenty years later his brother Benjamin – who also served as a commando – was to become Prime Minister of Israel.

Reflecting on the Entebbe rescue, Yitzhak Rabin wrote: 'We do not bask in the glory of such victories. We do remember, in sorrow and pride, the men who gave their lives – at Entebbe and elsewhere in the defence of Israel – that this nation should live in peace and dignity in its land.'

On January 8, the Chinese Prime Minister, Chou En-lai, died at the age of seventy-eight. He had been ill with cancer for four years. In the struggle for succession, scorn was poured on the man who hoped to succeed him, Senior Vice Premier, Teng Hsiao-p'ing (known in modern transliteration as Deng Xiaoping) – a prominent 'anti-leftist' – who was denounced as an 'unrepentant capitalist roader'. He had wanted to modernize China's economy along Western lines: his three articles proposing this were condemned as 'three poisonous weeds', and in his funeral oration for Chou En-lai – a funeral Mao Tse-tung did not attend – Teng Hsaio-p'ing spoke of the character of the dead leader in terms that clearly could not apply to Mao Tse-tung, for he called Chou En-lai 'modest and prudent, unassuming and approachable, setting an example by his conduct, and living in a plain and hard-working way'.

Teng Hsaio-p'ing's claims to succeed as Prime Minister were set aside. Hua Kuo-feng, a nominee of Mao Tse-tung, was appointed instead. 'With you in charge, I am at ease,' Mao Tse-tung – who was himself seriously ill – was reported to have said. But the legacy of Chou En-lai appeared to have affected the people directly. On April 4, tens of thousands of Chinese, gathering in Tiananmen Square, in Peking, during the annual memorial ceremonies for deceased ancestors, brought with them wreaths, banners, poems, placards and flowers in homage to Chou En-lai. On the following morning, writes the historian Jonathan D. Spence, 'fresh crowds gathering at the memorial found that all the tributes from the previous day had been removed by the police. Their protests led to scuffles and blows. Police cars were set on fire, and as the crowd swelled to 100,000 or more it forced entry into several of the government buildings that surround the square.' That night several hundred demonstrators were arrested. Many were sent to prison camps to 'reform themselves through hard labour'.

Teng Hsaio-p'ing was discredited: removed from all his official positions 'inside and outside the Party', but permitted to keep his Party membership. In the Chinese newspapers he was compared to Imre Nagy, the black sheep of the Hungarian Communist Party in 1956, said to believe that the class struggle was over, and accused of wanting to restore capitalism.

Mao Tse-tung was by then seriously ill. On May 27 he received the Prime Minister of Pakistan, Zulfikar Ali Bhutto, his last foreign visitor. In June it was announced that he would receive no more foreign visitors. It was rumoured that a neurologist had been flown from Europe to attend to him. In July, Marshal Chu Teh, the commander of the Long March in 1934 and 1935, and victor of the Communist-Kuomintang military struggle from 1946 to 1949, died shortly after his ninetieth birthday. Even he had been singled out for abuse during the Cultural Revolution. While mourning their military hero, the people of China prepared to learn of the demise of their Great Leader. But before they could do so, on July 28, China was hit by an earthquake more severe than any in the history of the world since the sixteenth century.

At least a quarter of a million Chinese were killed, most of them in the city of Tangshan, which was almost completely levelled to the ground. With a stubbornness derived from almost thirty years of rigid Communist rule, all outside help was refused. Even United Nations offers to help were rejected. It was medical teams from all over China that hurried to the succour of the injured: fifty-six medical teams from Shanghai alone. The Chinese army also took a major part in the work of rescue, redeeming itself in the eyes of a people who had been shocked by the army's killing of the mostly student Red Guards during the Cultural Revolution.

On September 9, Mao Tse-tung died in Peking, He was eighty-three years old. Although 300,000 Chinese filed past his body in the Great Hall of the People, the grief was less spontaneous and less widespread than when Chou En-lai had died eight months earlier. The dictator had been a remote and frightening figure, associated increasingly with frenetic and cataclysmic change. Following his death, Hua Kuo-feng became ruler of China. One of his first acts was to order the arrest – and detention in a secret location – of four of those who had been closest to Mao Tse-tung, the four leaders of the Cultural Revolution, including Mao Tse-tung's widow. They were accused of having served as a 'Gang of Four' acting against the orders of the true leader.

In the immediate aftermath of Mao Tse-tung's death there was violence in eleven of China's twenty-nine provinces. Hua Kuo-feng moved quickly to consolidate his power, taking over, in addition to the premiership, the chairmanship of both the Central Committee of the Chinese Communist Party and the Central Committee's Military Commission – the two positions through which Mao Tse-tung had exercised his dictatorial authority.

The power struggle in China was not over. Teng Hsaio-p'ing made his way to Canton, where he was protected by the military governor of the region. In 1976, as in 1926, the power of regional overlords was considerable. That China would change in the aftermath of Mao Tse-tung's death was clear, even in small things: within six months, Beethoven was rehabilitated and the ban on Shakespeare lifted.

While China struggled to adjust to the death of Chou En-lai and Mao Tse-tung, India, the world's second most populous country, entered the second year of Indira Gandhi's emergency. On January 8 the right of an individual to seek the protection of the law courts with regard to freedom of expression, assembly, movement or residence was suspended. Press censorship was maintained, and several newspapers closed down entirely. The independent news agencies were amalgamated into a single government agency, six foreign correspondents were expelled for defying the censorship. Power was being accrued by Indira Gandhi's son Sanjay, who announced a five-point programme for India that was intended to have wide-reaching social effects, and had echoes of Gandhism in it: family planning, tree planting, a ban on dowries, 'each one teach one', and the end to caste discrimination.

As the population of India reached 600 million, Sanjay Gandhi also led a campaign, in conjunction with his family-planning programme, for massive sterilization, of both men and women: this led to an outcry in the West, particularly when in some States the 'reward' offered in return for a vasectomy was a radio. There were many peasants for whom such an inducement was eagerly acceptable.

In international affairs, India under Indira Gandhi's emergency was confronted by the hostility of the United States and Canada. When they refused to contribute heavy water and other crucial materials to India's nuclear-fuel programme, India turned to the Soviet Union. The Soviet Union responded, providing not only the heavy water needed, but also substantial quantities of oil. The American decision to sell light bombers to Pakistan also angered Mrs Gandhi. But, while these arms sales brought her into conflict with the United States, they did not prevent her from seeking to restore relations with Pakistan itself. Diplomatic relations were renewed with Pakistan – with which India had fought three wars within thirty years – and air and rail links between the two countries were restored: the first through train from Delhi to Lahore made its debut on July 22.

With the exception of the Soviet Union, the imperial and colonial era was over. From the Baltic Sea to the Pacific Ocean, and from the Arctic Ocean to the Caspian Sea, the Soviet Union was ruler of many dozens of national groups, each forced to sacrifice its language, flag, national heroes, even religion – for there were several Muslim Republics in Soviet Central Asia – to the greater good, and political will, of Moscow. The United States had relinquished its control over the Philippines. The Netherlands had long seen an end to its possession in the Dutch East Indies. France was almost gone from Africa. Portuguese rule in Africa was ended. Globally, little was left of the British and French Empires. On June 18, Britain conceded independence to the Seychelles, an island group – of 115 islands in all, spread over 400,000 square miles of the Indian Ocean – which had been ceded to it by France in 1810. The Seychelles became the 145th member of the United Nations. Its population, of little more than 50,000, was a mixture of English expatriates, a French upper class, Chinese and Indian traders, and African and Asian workers. It was also becoming a tourist paradise in the era of package-holiday tours.

Within two years of independence, a coup took place and the Seychelles became a one-Party State: a situation that was to last for more than a decade.

* * *

Natural disasters caused far greater loss of life in 1976 than any of the military or civil conflicts that year. In addition to the quarter of a million Chinese killed in the earthquake in central China, 23,000 people were killed in the Central American republic of Guatemala on February 4, when ten towns were completely destroyed, also by an earthquake. Considerable financial help was sent by both the United States and Venezuela; but, just as China had refused all United Nations help, so Guatemala refused any help from Britain, because of a territorial dispute with the self-governing British colony of Belize – which had been known until 1973 as British Honduras.

Whether the needs of the world were exceeded by its resources was much debated. From May 31 to June 11 a special United Nations conference on Human Settlements (Habitat) was held in Vancouver. It proposed a series of definite measures, to be undertaken in the main by the wealthier industrialized nations, whereby basic living needs – shelter, clean water and a decent physical environment – could be made available to every inhabitant of the globe. The seriousness of the resolution was somewhat marred when the Arab States present insisted on adding to it a condemnation of Israel and Zionism. This led to objections from the West, and prevented the resolution from being passed unanimously.

Britain and the United States were also angered during discussions at the United Nations Commission on Human Rights, when the Arab States again put the main focus on a condemnation of Israel for its rule in the occupied West Bank and Gaza Strip. Both the British and American delegates protested at what their governments called a lack of balance. Human rights, warned the American delegate, William Scranton, were being judged, not by independent standards, but by 'vote-gathering' ability.

China having refused any United Nations support for the estimated ten million people who were forced from their homes by the earthquake, there was no shortage elsewhere of recipients for disaster and emergency aid. More than 400,000 Lebanese had been forced from their homes or lost their homes altogether during the Lebanese civil war. There had also been an earthquake in West Irian, floods in Pakistan, and severe drought and crop failure in Cape Verde. Indochina, too, was struggling to recover from the ravages of the Vietnam War: it was the Canadian government that made the first and largest national contribution for humanitarian assistance to Indochina, giving the United Nations a cheque for $250,000. The United States provided $2 million for the last of the campaigns to eliminate smallpox in Ethiopia.

By far the largest national contributions were to the United Nations

Development Programme. In the urgent need to build up agricultural training in the poorest countries, more than $500 million was raised, a fifth of which came from Britain, West Germany and Japan. The irony was not lost on keen-eyed observers that two of the three main donors had been nations which, thirty years earlier, had emerged defeated, devastated and bankrupt from the Second World War.

The Anglo-French Concorde began regular supersonic air passenger services across the Atlantic in 1976, linking London and New York in three hours and twenty minutes – half the time taken by regular jet aircraft. The vexation caused to those on the ground by the loud supersonic bang prevented it, however, from flying above the speed of sound across land. Uninhibited by any such unfortunate defect, that year Apple Computers was founded in the United States, by Steven Jobs and Stephen Wozniak. They were to be part of a worldwide revolution in easier, swifter and more efficient communication, whereby the world of business, the world of administration and the world of leisure were all enhanced.

CHAPTER TWENTY-SIX

1977

> . . . no member of the United Nations can claim that
> violation of internationally protected human rights is
> solely its own affair.
>
> CYRUS VANCE, QUOTING PRESIDENT CARTER

THE SUPER POWERS were edging ever closer to agreement with regard
to their nuclear armaments. In March 1977, the American Secretary of State,
Cyrus Vance, went to Moscow with new proposals for the second Strategic
Arms Limitation Talks (SALT II). These negotiations, although at times
slow and involving disagreement, were already in their sixth year. Talking,
negotiating, defining and redefining positions had become an unthreatening,
if at times frustrating feature of the once bitterly confrontational Cold War.
When the March negotiations broke down, there was no intensification of
the old Cold War rhetoric. Instead, two months later, a 'new framework for
negotiations' was announced, and the talks were taken up again. Ironically,
it was the Western European powers in NATO which took alarm at the
Soviet-American talks on nuclear arms limitation, fearing that any agreement
reached would prevent them, the Europeans, from acquiring long-range
nuclear missiles.

In reality there were no longer flashpoints of potentially violent dispute
between the United States and the Soviet Union. Observers from NATO
were invited to witness Soviet ground/air exercises in Russia in July, and
the details of troop concentrations in Warsaw Pact and Baltic Sea manoeuvres
were reported to NATO as a matter of course under the rules of the multinational Conference on Security and Co-operation in Europe, established in
Helsinki two years earlier by thirty-five States, including the United States
and the Soviet Union. Both East Germany and Poland were in negotiation

with West Germany. The future of Berlin – although the Berlin Wall still divided the city – was no longer an issue threatening blockades.

Vietnam pursued its course as a Communist State, with the reopening of the railway from Hanoi to Saigon (renamed Ho Chi Minh City) as a symbol of the new if politically one-sided unity. No American troops remained in South-East Asia, even on the soil of their ally Thailand. Korea remained divided, but neither the United States nor the Soviet Union was prepared to become embroiled in the continuing disputes between North and South, which, twenty-five years earlier, had brought them both, and China, to the brink of nuclear war. The decision by President Carter to withdraw 33,000 American ground troops from South Korea over the coming four to five years signalled to South Korea just how much it was its own protector, despite assurances by Carter that the United States was 'committed' to the defence of South Korea.

The Chinese Nationalist presence on Taiwan likewise was no longer a source of Great Power confrontation: the United States, after Nixon's visit to China, was as eager as any nation to open up trade links with the Communist government, which, following the death of Mao Tse-tung, was also exploring ways of closer contact, especially at a commercial and industrial level, with the West. The Taiwanese were not pleased when Carter sent his Secretary of State, Cyrus Vance, to Peking, to find new ways of strengthening American-Chinese links. But while Super Power and Great Power rivalries no longer held the element of danger which had earlier been their main focus, global conflicts remained, and continued to lead to heavy loss of life and misery.

In Cambodia, there was a series of border clashes along the border with Thailand. In one incident, the civilian inhabitants of three Thai villages were massacred. They were accused of sheltering Cambodian resistance groups. To help secure his border against infiltration by groups hostile to his dictatorial regime, the Cambodian Prime Minister, Saloth Sar, known as Pol Pot, ordered the depopulation of a strip of territory along its border. This was done with a barbarity seldom seen even in the severity of South-East Asian conflicts. Pol Pot was also perpetrating terrifying crimes inside his country. The total death toll during five years of Khmer Rouge domination was a million and a half, out of a total population of eight million. In the Tuol Sleng prison registry, in Phnom Penh, the notation 'smashed' appears against the names of 107 prisoners during the two days March 17 and 18. Such numbers were an almost daily occurrence. The registry for July 1 records the execution of 114 women: their sole 'crime' was to have been the wives of prisoners who had been executed earlier. On the following day thirty-one sons and forty-three daughters of prisoners were executed. Fifteen of them had been taken from children's detention centres to their execution. Four days after the killing of these children, the prison registry records a further 126 prisoners 'smashed'. By the end of the year, 6,330 prisoners had been 'smashed' in Tuol Sleng. A chilling indication of the scale of the killings is found in the words of the historian Ben Kiernan. 'I first visited Cambodia in early 1975,' he writes. 'None of the Cambodians I knew then survived the next four years.'

In Laos, a full-scale military operation was launched, with the support of Vietnamese troops based in Laos, against the Meo tribesmen who had taken up arms to prevent Communist control of their villages. Dozens of Meo villages were destroyed, and their inhabitants forced out of the hills, to prevent them from supporting the Meo guerrilla groups that fought on.

The main focus of tyranny in Africa was in Uganda. In February there were mass killings of members of the Acholi and Langi tribes. On February 8 the Anglican Archbishop of Uganda, Janani Luwum, met with eighteen Ugandan bishops and drafted a letter to Amin, accusing the security services of torture. 'We have buried many who have died as a result of being shot,' they wrote. There was 'a gun pointed at every Christian in a church'.

The letter of protest was sent to Amin, and a copy smuggled across the border into Kenya, where many Ugandan exiles had gathered. On February 17 Archbishop Luwum, himself a member of the much persecuted Acholi tribe, was found dead. The Ugandan government insisted that he had been killed in a road accident while trying to escape the country. But eye-witnesses had seen bullet holes in the Archbishop's body. Two of Amin's Cabinet Ministers were among those murdered with the Archbishop. On February 24, Amin gave a press conference to 'confirm' that they had been killed in a car crash.

The Ugandan secret police, the innocuously named State Research Bureau, ensured that any opposition to Amin was quickly and ruthlessly suppressed. In June, the European Economic Community, the member States of which accounted for almost half of Uganda's foreign trade, imposed selective economic sanctions: the first of these was to call a halt to all aid payments. Tens of thousands more Ugandans sought asylum outside the country, including Amin's former Ministers of Health, Justice and Information.

In Rhodesia, even as the White government of Ian Smith was being pressed strongly by the United States and Britain to honour its pledge of majority

19. Nelson Mandela shortly before his arrest on 12 June 1964. He was kept in prison for twenty-six years.

20. Jomo Kenyatta, President of the Kenya African Union, shortly after his release in 1961 after nine years in prison. In 1964 he became President of an independent Kenya.

21. Chinese soldiers read from the Little Red Book, which contained what Chinese newspapers called 'the brilliant red banner of Mao Tse-tung's thinking'.

22. A United States warplane casts its shadow over a destroyed North Vietnamese road bridge at My Duc, 29 April 1965.

23. President Lyndon Johnson. His lapel insignia is that of the Silver Star, a military distinction awarded to him during his service as a commander in the Navy in the South Pacific in the Second World War.

24. A street in Hanoi. North Vietnamese prepare to descend into their shelters during an American air raid.

25. South Vietnamese police chief Brigadier-General Nguyen Ngoc Loan executes a Vietcong captive with a single pistol shot to the head, Saigon, 1 February 1968. This photograph was taken by Associated Press photographer Eddie Adams.

26. Prague: Czech demonstrators face a Soviet tank, 26 August 1968.

27. Neil Armstrong (left) and Edwin Aldrin on the surface of the moon, 21 July 1969.

28. United States troops leave their base at Quang Tri, on 19 August 1969, as part of President Nixon's policy of reducing the number of American troops in Vietnam.

29. On 25 August 1969, the first anniversary of the Soviet invasion of Prague, Czech troops keep back Czech pro-democracy demonstrators.

30. A quarter of a million Americans demonstrate against the continuing war in Vietnam, Washington DC on 24 April 1971.

31. Northern Ireland. British troops confront Catholic demonstrators in Londonderry, 30 January 1972. During the ensuing riots, thirteen people were killed.

32. Republic of Ireland. Thirty-two people were killed in Dublin after three car bombs exploded in the Irish capital on 17 May 1974.

33. Super Power summitry: Leonid Brezhnev and Richard Nixon in Washington,
23 June 1973.

34. The Middle East peace process: Henry Kissinger, Yitzhak Rabin and Shimon Peres
sign the Israel/Egypt Interim Agreement in Jerusalem, prior to the signing in Geneva on
4 September 1975. All three were later recipients of the Nobel Peace Prize.

35. Idi Amin in Uganda, at a press conference following the deaths of the Archbishop and two of his Cabinet Ministers, 24 February 1977.

36. President Sadat of Egypt and United States President Jimmy Carter at the White House, Washington, during talks on the Middle East, prior to the Camp David Agreement of 17 September 1978.

rule, a 'war of liberation' was being fought by those who preferred to seize power rather than wait for it to be transferred. It was the thirteenth year of illegal independence, and the two main guerrilla groups, the Zimbabwe African People's Union (ZAPU), under Joshua Nkomo, and the Zimbabwe African National Union (ZANU), under Robert Mugabe, had united to form a single political and fighting force, the Patriotic Front. Rejecting negotiations, it carried out continual attacks on Rhodesian military installations, operating from bases in both Mozambique and Zambia. ZAPU was able to call upon arms and ammunition from the Soviet Union; ZANU from China. In an attempt to achieve a negotiated settlement, the British Foreign Secretary, David Owen, after a visit to eight countries in Africa, including Rhodesia, obtained the support of the United States for a constitutional conference on Rhodesia. The first stage was to be a ceasefire, but this was rejected both by Ian Smith and by the Patriotic Front. A dramatic success for the Front was achieved at the end of the year when more than three hundred young Black Rhodesians from a secondary school at Manama, in the south-west of the country, crossed into neighbouring Botswana and pledged themselves to take up arms against the White regime.

The Smith regime carried out a series of military raids into the countries in which the Rhodesian guerrillas were based. In May, President Kaunda of Zambia declared that his country was 'in a state of war' with Rhodesia. During a Rhodesian army attack into Mozambique in November, 1,200 members of the Patriotic Front were killed. There was widespread international condemnation of this cross-border raid. Inside Rhodesia the killings mounted. In February three Jesuit priests and four Dominican nuns were murdered at the Musami mission station forty-three miles east of the capital, Salisbury, bringing the number of murdered missionaries to thirteen in nine months. The death toll during the year was 1,759 ZANU and ZAPU guerrillas killed, a thousand Black Rhodesians, 244 members of the Rhodesian security forces, and fifty-six White Rhodesians. In measures designed to cut off the guerrillas from local support, the Smith government resettled more than a quarter of a million Africans in 'protected villages'.

In South Africa, defiance was the mood of the Prime Minister, B. J. Vorster, when confronted by continuous pressure from the United States for a modification of the apartheid policy. South Africa would fight 'to the last man' to resist outside interference in the country's internal affairs, he said. But Western scrutiny of the repressive regime was persistent – on average a Black African was dying each month while being held in detention – and there was outrage in the West after the death in police detention of Steve Biko, founder of the moderate 'Black Consciousness' movement. Several South African newspapers expressed their scepticism of the government's claim that Biko had died after going on hunger strike. Donald Woods, the editor of the *East London Daily Express*, said that he would resign his editorship if it could be shown that Biko had in fact died while on hunger strike. Pressure for an inquiry was such that the government gave in: the inquiry revealed that Biko had been kept naked and in shackles while in detention, and had been driven, naked, in the back of a truck all the way from Port Elizabeth to Pretoria while suffering serious brain damage. The cause of death was given as a head injury. The world was shocked at this act of brutality by the White government.

Following Steve Biko's death there was violence in many Black townships in South Africa. In an attempt to bring the full weight of the law against the demonstrators, many of whom were supporters of Biko's Black Consciousness movement, the government banned the organization and detained its leaders. Another civil rights organization, the Christian Institute, which spanned all Christian denominations, was banned at the same time. As if to put the Biko scandal behind it, the government then banned Donald Woods, the editor whose courageous writings had led to the inquiry, and confined him to East London. Also subjected to a banning order, and then detained, was Percy Qoboza, editor of the *World*, which was itself then banned. The *World* had been the mouthpiece of moderate Black South African opinion. But even moderation in support of civil rights was anathema to the custodians of apartheid.

Dyeing his hair and disguising his appearance, Donald Woods defied the order confining him to East London, hitchhiked from there to the border of Lesotho, swam across a flooded river to enter Lesotho, and from there made his way to Britain. A free man once more, he published a book on the Steve Biko affair which he had written in East London in defiance of the terms of his banning order, and which further mobilized Western opinion against the apartheid regime.

Hitherto, the Western nations had hesitated before agreeing to an arms embargo against South Africa. Steve Biko's murder and the subsequent banning orders hardened Western opinion. When the call for a mandatory arms embargo came before the United Nations Security Council, there was no one willing to veto it. Canada, which, as a former Commonwealth partner, had been promoting its trade with South Africa, brought all its promotional activities to a halt. 'By the end of 1977,' wrote Gerald Shaw, Chief Assistant Editor of the *Cape Times*, 'South Africa was standing alone.'

In the Horn of Africa, war had broken out between Ethiopia and Somalia. Somali forces quickly overran much of south-eastern Ethiopia: the Somali-inhabited Ogaden region was almost entirely under Somali control by the end of July. But Soviet military aid to Ethiopia, some of it sent as a matter of urgency by air, enabled Colonel Mengistu's forces to halt the Somali attack before it could overrun the cities of Jigjiga, Harar or Diredawa – the last on the railway line running from Addis Ababa to the coast. The Somali government, hitherto much beholden to the Soviet Union for arms and support, turned against its former patron in anger at the crucial military support given to Ethiopia. Several Russian civilians in Somalia were killed, and on November 13 Somalia expelled several thousand Soviet experts who had been helping create a military and industrial infrastructure for the country. The Soviet-Somali Friendship Treaty was abrogated, and all military facilities that had been accorded to the Soviet Union were withdrawn. Somalia then appealed to the United States, Britain, France and West Germany for arms. They refused to comply until the fighting with Ethiopia ended. Only Saudi Arabia sent arms and munitions. Both West Germany and the United States did agree, at the end of the year, to send agricultural aid and medicines. Somalia was too poor a country to sustain a war and also a reasonably effective subsistence domestic economy. As the fighting continued, the economic plight of most Somalis lapsed from hardship to disaster.

For the Ethiopians, with the Ogaden lost but their main cities secure, internal rivalries led to a struggle even bloodier than that on the battlefield. In Addis Ababa, Ethiopia's Marxist ruler, Colonel Mengistu, murdered his rivals – former colleagues – and instituted a reign of terror in which as many as two thousand opponents of his regime were killed, several hundred during anti-government riots in Addis Ababa on May 4. In coming to power three months earlier he had murdered eight fellow members of the ruling council. By turning for support internationally to the Soviet Union, Mengistu was able to acquire the arms needed to sustain his tyranny. The United States military mission was expelled, and American arms sales were suspended.

In an attack on those suspected of supporting the banned rival Marxist Ethiopian People's Revolutionary Party, a further thousand Ethiopians were killed by government forces. 'It is a historical obligation to clean up vigilantly using the revolutionary sword,' declared Mengistu, in calling for what he described as a 'red terror' against opponents of the regime. At the end of November, Amnesty International put the number of those assassinated by the regime in political killings during the previous eight months at more than ten thousand. Several thousand more were killed in Addis Ababa during December.

The scale of the killings in the Ethiopian countryside was unknown. Mengistu frequently exhorted his troops to root out 'bandits', 'feudalists' and 'anarchists', and they were undoubtedly vigilant, and ruthless, in doing so. The main source of revolt was in Eritrea. There, the insurgent forces, themselves Marxist, which opposed the rule of Addis Ababa, overran all the main Ethiopian strongholds, until Mengistu could only supply the capital, Asmara, by air. The separatists were themselves divided into three warring factions, but two of these managed to come together, increasing the pressure on Ethiopia. They were also able to get military support from Ethiopia's northern neighbour, Sudan, as well as from Kuwait and the United Arab Emirates.

At the edge of the Ethiopian-Somali war and the Ethiopian-Eritrean conflict, France's last African colony, Djibouti (the French Territory of the Affars and Issas), became independent on June 2, after more than a hundred years of French rule. It was both the smallest and the poorest of all the independent African States. To avert civil tension, the new Cabinet was made up of eight Issas, seven Affars and an Arab. To guard against external attack, France agreed to keep 4,500 French troops in the new republic, and to continue sending French economic aid.

In Israel, a new government, headed by Menachem Begin, came to power on June 20. Its philosophy was one that had been excluded from Israeli governing circles since independence almost thirty years earlier: the desire to retain Israeli sovereignty from the Mediterranean Sea to the River Jordan, including the overwhelmingly Palestinian Arab West Bank and Gaza Strip. As a sign of the new attitude, Begin replaced the use of the term 'West Bank' (referring to the formerly Jordanian-ruled western bank of the River Jordan) with the biblical – and British Mandate terms – Judaea and Samaria. When the American Secretary of State, Cyrus Vance, asked Begin, in Washington, if he would accept an Israeli withdrawal to 'mutually agreed and recognized borders on all fronts, phased over years in synchronized steps, and with security arrangements and guarantees', Begin replied tersely: 'In the whole world, there is no guarantee that can guarantee a guarantee.'

When President Carter asked Begin if he would accept a Palestinian State on the West Bank, he replied that such a State would be a 'mortal danger' to Israel: it would become a Soviet base two and a half hours' flying time from Odessa. But he was prepared to offer 'full autonomy' to the Palestinians on the West Bank and in Gaza, and hinted at a possible agreement between Israel and Egypt. To this end his Foreign Minister, the former Labour Party stalwart Moshe Dayan, who had joined Begin's Likud government, made two secret journeys to Morocco, where on September 16 he met the Egyptian Deputy Prime Minister, Hassan Tuhami.

The pace of the secret Israeli-Egyptian negotiations quickened. On November 7, in a speech to the Egyptian parliament in Cairo, Sadat astounded his own parliamentarians, and the Israeli public, by saying that he wanted to address the Israeli parliament (the Knesset) in Jerusalem. 'I am willing to go to the ends of the earth for peace,' he said. Although Jerusalem was only 265 miles from Cairo, in political terms it was indeed the ends of the Earth.

On November 19 Sadat landed, in an Egyptian plane, at Israel's Ben Gurion airport. To Begin, who was waiting on the tarmac with several hundred Israeli dignitaries to greet him, he said: 'No more war. Let us make peace.' Yitzhak Rabin, who had contributed as Chief of Staff to the defeat of the Egyptian armies a decade earlier, was also at the airport. It was the first time the two men had met. 'I was enormously impressed', Rabin later wrote, 'by the poise with which he handled himself in such a unique situation. Here he was meeting all his former arch-enemies, one after another, in the space of seconds, and he nonetheless found the way to start off his visit by saying exactly the right thing to each and every one of them.'

On November 20 Sadat addressed the Israeli parliament, and in front of the incredulous members of the Knesset, and more than a million Israeli television viewers, shook hands with Begin on the podium. It was only four years since their two countries had been locked in fierce war. For its almost thirty years of independence, Israel had been in a state of war with each of its four Arab neighbours – Lebanon, Syria, Jordan and Egypt. Less than two weeks before Sadat's visit it had carried out a full-scale retaliatory raid on southern Lebanon, following a PLO rocket attack on northern Israel which had killed an Israeli woman, a survivor of the Holocaust, who had run outside her house to call her two children into the shelter.

One of the four Arab nations at war with Israel since 1948 was breaking ranks and making peace. The public mood in Israel was full of the expectation of an end to conflict. But it was to take another year before, with the help of the United States, an agreement was reached.

Optimism prevailed at the United Nations about the ability to tackle the challenges of pollution. At a nine-day United Nations Water Conference, held in Argentina in March, the years 1980-90 were designated the decade during which all the peoples of the Earth would have adequate drinking water and sanitation. In the event, no means were found – certainly not in the time set out – of bridging the gap between the developed countries, for whom the main problem was wastage of water, and the developing countries, for whom it was shortage of water, and contamination. At an eleven-day meeting in Nairobi in August, the United Nations Conference on Desertification set out a programme for the gradual reclaiming of desert by the expansion of agriculture and tree-planting. These both depended on water. The schemes were imaginative, but the water resources to make them work were not available, and in many instances political conflicts in the regions most in need – such as the Ogaden Desert in Ethiopia, then occupied by Somalia – made it impossible to establish programmes that would be effective.

Another long-term and hopeful projection was put forward by another United Nations agency, the World Health Organization. It proposed the year 2000 as the time when 'health for all' would have been achieved. To this end, it increased its budget for research into cancer and tropical diseases. Success was reported in the continued elimination of smallpox from India and Bangladesh. But fighting between Ethiopia and Somalia meant that the long-cherished aim of eliminating smallpox in Ethiopia that year could not be fulfilled.

The main work of the United Nations agencies concerning the developing nations, and what had begun to be called the North-South divide, was not projects for improvement but measures to halt poverty and hunger and meet urgent needs. Help for the survivors of earthquakes in Turkey and Roumania – where 1,500 people were killed in March – was one area of urgency. Those affected by drought in Vietnam and Sri Lanka (formerly Ceylon) required massive relief. A tornado in Bangladesh had made hundreds of thousands homeless. On November 19 a tornado, striking southern India, killed more than eight thousand people. Refugees from civil strife in Angola, Rhodesia and the Western Sahara required immediate help: basic shelter and food with which to survive at all.

*   *   *

The advancement of women's rights was a feature of 1977. In November the First National Women's Conference was held in the United States, in Houston, Texas. Also in the United States, the Episcopalian Church decided to ordain women. In Britain, a women's publishing house, Virago, was founded. In India, Indira Gandhi, after a two-year emergency rule, called an election, released the opposition leaders whom she had imprisoned, and, when defeated at the polls by the electorate, laid down the premiership. One by one the measures she had taken to curb freedom of expression were removed.

Human rights remained at the forefront of the international agenda, stimulated by the 1975 Helsinki Agreement. Yet in many regions of the world they were under sustained attack. In Chile, on March 12, all political parties were banned and censorship tightened. But it was in the East-West confrontation that human rights loomed largest as a point of discord. Whereas Soviet military might and defence policy had not led to any increase in East-West tension, the Soviet human rights record did. President Carter was determined to use the Helsinki Final Act – to be debated in Belgrade that October – to spotlight Soviet human rights abuses, in particular the treatment of dissidents. When Brezhnev warned that such matters were of internal Soviet concern only, and if pressed could endanger Soviet-American relations, Carter was not deterred. As Cyrus Vance explained in April: 'It is not our purpose to intervene in the internal affairs of other countries, but, as the President has emphasized, no member of the United Nations can claim that violation of internationally protected human rights is solely its own affair.'

At the Helsinki Final Act conference in Belgrade, the American delegate, Arthur Goldberg, raised many examples of what he called 'violations' of human rights from the Soviet Union. He was answered in more general but scathing terms by the Soviet delegate, Vadim Loginov, who said that the United States 'has no moral right to teach other countries about human rights. Life in the United States is not perfect. It includes the right to go without expensive medical care and the right of minorities to be discriminated against.' Loginov then asked what right a nation which had used napalm and killed 'hundreds of thousands' of people in Vietnam had to speak of human rights.

The Soviet Union was celebrating the sixtieth anniversary of the Bolshevik revolution. Its vast empire was intact. A new constitution – the first since 1936 – stressed the 'leading role' of the Communist Party in the structure and decision making of the State. The right of the citizen to work, housing, health care and education was confirmed, but only in so much as that right did not 'harm the interests of society and the State'. Soviet dissidents pointed out that under the new Constitution the ability of the citizen to defend his civil rights by an appeal to that Constitution was reduced.

Brezhnev was appointed Head of State as well as Party leader. In anticipation of the Helsinki Final Act conference in Belgrade, he authorized strenuous measures against those human rights activists inside the Soviet Union who, under the legal auspices of the Helsinki Agreement, had established Helsinki Monitor groups in several Soviet cities. In February, two members of the twelve-member co-ordinating group of monitors, Dr Yuri Orlov and Alexander Ginzburg, were arrested. Another member, Ludmilla Alekseeva, was 'encouraged' to emigrate. Members of local Helsinki Monitor groups in the Ukraine, Georgia and Lithuania were arrested. Also arrested was one of the spokesmen of the Moscow group, Anatoli Shcharansky, a Jew who had been refused permission three years earlier to emigrate to Israel. He was later sentenced to thirteen years incarceration.

A new feature was evident among the Soviet human rights groups. Hitherto working each for its own agenda – which might be Jewish emigration, or greater freedom for national self-expression in Ukraine or Lithuania – the groups had begun to coalesce and work together. At the same time, a pattern had emerged whereby when one activist who had taken a prominent public position was arrested and sent to labour camp, another came forward in his stead to take the burden of exposure. When, on November 5, the Soviet Union announced a general amnesty for prisoners, the euphoria among human rights activists throughout the world was quickly quashed when it was made clear by the Soviet authorities that the amnesty applied only to criminals, not to political prisoners.

Prison was not the only means of striking at dissent. When a Moscow University philosopher, Alexander Zinoviev, wrote a novel satirizing Soviet society, he could not get it published in Russia. Instead he had it published in Switzerland. As a result, he was dismissed from his job and refused any further academic employment.

In Poland, criticism of the Communist regime was being intensified. When a student at Cracow University was murdered in strange circumstances, his fellow students denounced it as a political murder, and five thousand marched in protest. Following the march a Students Solidarity Committee was set up to replace the official Communist students organization; the committee was warned by the government against 'indulging in sterile arguments about freedom and civil rights'.

In Czechoslovakia, 242 human rights activists signed a petition – Charter 77 – criticizing the violation of human rights by the Czechoslovak government. Following the example of the Helsinki monitors in the Soviet Union, the Charter 77 signatories set up a nationwide movement to monitor violations of human rights. By the end of the year almost a thousand Czechs had signed the Charter. It was a courageous act of defiance. Many intellectuals in the West, including Communist Party members, expressed public support for the Charter's aims. The Czechoslovak government took action to deter scrutiny of its human rights record; many Charter signatories were dismissed from their jobs, some were arrested, brought to trial and imprisoned, among them the playwright Václav Havel – who twenty years later was to be President of Czechoslovakia.

As a gesture of support to Charter 77, the Dutch Foreign Minister, on an official visit to Prague, insisted on seeing one of the three spokesmen of the movement, the seventy-seven-year-old philosopher Professor Jan Patocka. After the Foreign Minister's return to Holland, Professor Patocka – who was already under official displeasure for refusing to apply political criteria for promotions in the Academy of Sciences, whose educational institute he headed – was interrogated at length by the police. Within days of his interrogation he suffered a brain haemorrhage and died.

Human rights violations were not confined to the Communist bloc, and were reported with a regularity that showed how persistent such violations were. On January 17 the European Human Rights Commission found Turkey guilty of torture in Cyprus. On February 7, at the European Court of Human Rights – which had been set up under the auspices of the Council of Europe – the British government admitted 'malpractices' against prisoners in Northern Ireland six years earlier, and promised never again to use the sleep-deprivation techniques which had led to the accusation. On February 21 the Argentine Commission for Human Rights gave a figure of 2,300 as the number of Argentinians killed during the first eleven months of the rule of General Videla. In addition, and deeply disturbing, 20,000 to 30,000 Argentinians had simply disappeared. They were never seen again. It later emerged that the bodies of many of them, after they had been murdered, were flown over the sea and dumped in the Atlantic. On May 18 a report by the International Commission of Jurists estimated that during the first two years of Amin's rule in Uganda between 80,000 and 90,000 people had been killed: and the killings were continuing.

*   *   *

On June 16 Dr Wernher von Braun died in the United States at the age of sixty-five. From 1937 he had directed the German guided-missile establishment at Peenemünde, on the Baltic, where he designed the V1 flying bomb and V2 rocket bomb that brought havoc and death to London, and also to Antwerp, in the closing phases of the Second World War. Working in the United States from 1945, he was director of development operations for the army ballistic missile agency, and later director of the space flight agency, responsible both for America's first intercontinental ballistic missiles (the ICBMs) and for the *Saturn 5* rocket which launched the first man to walk on the surface of the moon.

The past also had an echo in Spain that year, when the Communist Party heroine Dolores Ibarruri – La Pasionara of the Spanish Civil War – who for many years had been an exile in the Soviet Union, was not only allowed back to her native land, but stood successfully for parliament. Her continued defence of Stalin, however, alienated her from the Spanish Communist Party; she became its President, but failed to deflect it from its abandonment of Leninism and support for Eurocommunism, the economic creed of critical but active participation in the capitalist evolution of the European Community.

On August 16 the rock-and-roll singer Elvis Presley died in Memphis, Tennessee. Before being drafted into the army in 1958, he had released fourteen consecutive million-selling records. By the time of his death, at the age of forty-two, he had sold 500 million records. In the five days following his death, eight million were sold. Three years later, another icon of popular culture, Beatles star John Lennon, was murdered by a fanatic outside his New York apartment. He was forty years old.

Václav Havel, the Czech dissident who was then in prison in Ostrava, near the Polish border, wrote to his wife: 'Of all the deaths in the last while, I find myself thinking most about the death of John Lennon. This may be because his death so compellingly reaches beyond itself, as though there were latent in it more tragic connections, problems and aspects pointing to the present world crisis than in any other event. It might even be called "the death of the century" (perhaps even more so than the deaths of Kennedy and King).'

Both the Dakota Building on the steps of which Lennon was gunned down in New York, and Graceland, Presley's house in Memphis, have become destinations of modern pilgrimage.

CHAPTER TWENTY-SEVEN

1978

There will be no check on the demand for human respect;
there will be no quiet acceptance of human starvation.

DAME BARBARA WARD

IN IRAN, OPPOSITION to the rule of the Shah gained in intensity throughout the year. From his home near Paris, the Muslim religious leader, the
Ayatollah Khomeini, who had been in exile for fifteen years, called for
uprisings against the secular authority. In the holy city of Qom, the Ayatollah's spiritual base, rioting took place on 7 January 1978 and again two
days later. Troops loyal to the Shah opened fire and sixty of the demonstrators
were killed. In the course of the forty-day Islamic cycle of mourning the
dead, further riots took place in February in Tabriz, in March in Yazd and
in Tabriz again in April. On May 7 the riots came to the capital, Teheran.

June 17 was declared by the anti-Shah faction to be a nationwide day of
mourning. The Shah relied on his army and security service to staunch the
wave of unrest. On July 23 there were mass demonstrations in the holy city
of Meshed, and several dozen demonstrators were shot down. On August 12
military rule was imposed for the first time in a city where the riots had
begun to get out of hand: Isfahan. Islamic terrorists retaliated by setting a
cinema on fire in Abadan, when 430 people were killed. Political strife was
briefly overshadowed on September 16, when an earthquake killed 21,000
Iranians. World sympathy was roused, and aid flown in from many nations
to help feed the survivors and provide them with shelter.

The impulse of Islamic fervour and its anti-Shah focus grew with every
passing month. In November there were six days of continuous rioting in
Teheran. The Shah, having replaced an unpopular Prime Minister with one
who had reasonable relations with the imams, and having promised to eradicate corruption in the higher echelons of government, was nevertheless unable

to calm the storm demanding an end to the royal regime. On November 6 he appointed a military government, headed by the army Chief of Staff, General Azhari, who proclaimed martial law in the cities. At the same time, Azhari repeated the earlier government's pledge to root out corruption, and promised to pay proper attention to Muslim religious demands. But he could do nothing to stop a strike of oilworkers that paralysed Iran's principal source of foreign exchange. As a result of the strike, which was continued into December, Iran's oil production fell so low that it was no longer adequate even for domestic needs.

The Shah was pressed by the United States to make even more compromises, and to return to civilian rule. On December 10, after the army withdrew from the streets of Teheran, a million people marched against the Shah, called for the Ayatollah Khomeini's return, and the Shah's abdication, threatening to launch a *jihad*, or holy war, against him.

While the Shah battled to prevent the rise of militant Islam, his eastern neighbour, Afghanistan, was succeeding in doing so, and moving to another extreme, Communism. For five years the government of Muhammad Daud had suppressed Islamic groups with severity, moving steadily closer in its international alignments to the United States, and to the Shah's Iran. On April 27, Daud was assassinated, as were many of his closest supporters. The leaders of the predominantly military coup proclaimed a Republican Revolutionary Council, sought immediate support from the Soviet Union – which was forthcoming – and on April 30 proclaimed a Democratic Republic. It was to be run on Marxist lines. The first countries to recognize Afghanistan's new regime were the Soviet Union, India, Cuba and Bulgaria. The United States followed shortly afterwards. On May 7, the new leader, Nur Muhammad Taraki, insisted that he was neither pro- nor anti-Communist, or indeed anti-Muslim, but would decide Afghanistan's alignment according to what financial assistance was available to his country.

China, in the aftermath of Mao Tse-tung and the devastation caused during the Cultural Revolution, was moving towards greater contact with the outside world. In February a massive barter agreement was signed with Japan, under which Chinese oil and coal to the value of $10,000 million was to be exchanged for Japanese steel and advanced-technology industrial plants. Also in February, the European Community and China signed their first agreement. In July, China and Japan signed a peace and friendship treaty. An 'anti-hegemony' clause in the treaty enabled China to break out of what it had seen as a hostile ring of States orchestrated by the Soviet Union. The Soviet leaders had, in fact, warned Japan against making this move towards China, but had warned in vain.

In December the Chinese secured an equally remarkable agreement with the United States. Most decisive for Chinese ambitions was America's agreement to end official diplomatic relations with Taiwan, to withdraw all American troops from the island, and to abrogate the United States-Taiwan treaty of mutual defence. 'The government of the United States of America', the agreement stated, 'acknowledges the Chinese position that there is but one China and Taiwan is part of China.' In return for this commitment, whereby America turned its back on three decades of support for the Chinese Nationalist cause, Communist China agreed, though not in any public statement, that it would not use military means to secure the future joining of Taiwan with China. Even the phrase 'liberation of Taiwan', hitherto an integral part of the Chinese propaganda war against Taiwan, was replaced by the word 'reunification'.

China gained enormously from its agreement with the United States, arguably its most important single agreement since the Communist revolution in 1949. Henceforth, wrote Michael Yahuda, of the London School of Economics, in the immediate aftermath of the agreement, 'China would have access to the world's power-house of advanced technology.'

Domestically, the Chinese government was turning its back on the rigidity of the past. In an appeal to 'intellectuals, former bourgeois groups, the Kuomintang and overseas Chinese', it urged a common front in the development of China. The Chinese People's Political Consultative Conference – which had not met since the Cultural Revolution – spent twelve days in session under the chairmanship of Teng Hsiao-p'ing, whose previous year's exile and denunciation were themselves denounced as having been a serious error.

The principal call of the consultative conference was for people of 'all circles' to work with the Communist Party. Teng Hsiao-p'ing – whose favourite maxim was 'practice is the sole criterion for testing truth' – stressed the harm done to Chinese national unity by the suppression of the conference by the Gang of Four, and the need henceforth for it to be part of the 'democratic consultations on State affairs'. New, more realistic targets were set for economic development by the year 2000. This was one of the first policymaking forums in the world to look as far forward as the millennium in its planning: the World Health Organization had already named 2000 as the year in which disease would be eliminated in the world.

Some of those demoted and most castigated by Mao Tse-tung were brought back into positions of authority, among them Ch'en Yun, who had been removed from the senior echelons of the Party when he criticized the Great Leap Forward in the 1950s: he was brought back as a Vice-Chairman of the Party and given responsibility for ensuring that disciplinary matters were dealt with openly and fairly. Many of the rules laid down by Mao Tse-tung with regard to the outside world were also cast aside. The ban on foreign loans, and the ban on foreign investment in China – bans harmful to China's economic development but on which Mao had insisted – were swept away. Joint Chinese-foreign projects, which he had strongly opposed, were welcomed.

A secret speech which Mao Tse-tung had given to senior Party leaders in January 1962, in which he admitted to 'serious errors', was published officially for the first time on 1 July 1978. Also published by the new regime was a speech by Chou En-lai during the Communist revolution in 1949, in which, 'while praising Mao as a great man, he warned against regarding him as a demigod'. On October 29 Mao Tse-tung's most visible contribution to unity of thought, his Little Red Book, which hundreds of millions of Chinese had read and waved and quoted, was denounced.

The aim of the new leadership in China, which included attaining eighty-five per cent mechanization of work on farms, was to make the country a powerful, modern, Socialist country by the year 2000. The changes needed were to be achieved by scientific, educational and cultural advances towards 'modernity'. One change that caused initial confusion in the West was in the sphere of transliteration: henceforth, under the new official Chinese system of transliteration, Teng Hsiao-p'ing was to be transliterated Deng Xiaoping, Mao Tse-tung as Mao Zedong, and Chou En-lai as Zhou Enlai. Peking became Beijing.

The Soviet Union was also undergoing changes, though strenuous efforts were made to prevent more than rumours of them reaching the West. In April there were riots in the Georgian capital, Tbilisi, when the draft of the new constitution made no reference to Georgian as the official language of the republic. The Party bowed to the public protest. In Estonia, there was growing hostility to the dominance of Moscow.

The determination was still strong of the Russian dissidents who continued to try to monitor the Soviet Union's fulfilment of the human rights clauses of the Helsinki Agreement. But the authorities did not want them to pursue their inquiries, or to publicize them either in Russia or in the West. Active and courageous, the Helsinki monitors who tried to publicize their findings, or to contact Western journalists, were arrested and brought to trial. In every case the sentence was several years in prison, followed by more years of internal exile, barred from returning to their home city. The trials were timed in such a way as to serve as a rolling deterrent. There were six such sentences in rapid succession, each given wide internal newspaper coverage by the Soviet authorities: Yuri Orlov was sentenced on May 18, Vladimir Slepak, who had been refused permission for almost a decade to live in Israel, on June 21, the Lithuanian human rights activist Viktora Petkus on July 12, Alexander Ginzburg on July 14, Anatoli Shcharansky, another of the Jewish 'refuseniks' who had been refused permission to live in Israel, on July 14, and Alexander Podrabinek on August 15.

These were the most highly publicized cases. But for every sentence which the authorities wished to stress, in order to strike fear into the human rights movement, there were several more which created less stir, some of which were kept secret. Among the groups that felt the full weight of official displeasure, and whose leaders were likewise arrested, tried and sentenced, were Crimean Tatars who had been expelled from the Crimea by Stalin in the Second World War and were returning illegally to their homeland, Armenian nationalists and 'unofficial trade unionists' seeking to bring greater accountability to State enterprises.

The Soviet Union under Brezhnev was able to maintain the primacy of the Communist Party and to repress such dissent as arose. The powers of the KGB were not curtailed. No sense of widespread disaffection reached the West. But elsewhere in the Communist bloc there was a more obvious upsurge of unease at the perpetuation of the Communist system. From East Germany a manifesto was smuggled into West Germany, and published in the West German magazine *Der Spiegel*. It had been written by officials of the East German Communist Party who had become disillusioned with Soviet dominance. In it they urged the reunification of Germany, its military neutralization through the withdrawal of both NATO and the Warsaw Pact, and full disarmament, to be followed by elections in which all political Parties would be able to compete for votes, and the emergence of a united Germany. Such a unity, the signatories asserted, would prove both demographically and through free elections to be predominantly Socialist.

One former East German Communist Party official, Rudolf Bahro, who the previous year had published a book critical of the East German regime, was sentenced to eight years in prison, charged with espionage. In a letter smuggled to the West, Bahro said that he still was in favour of East Germany remaining non-capitalist, nor was he hostile to the Soviet Union, but that he wanted a new structure in which there would be a chance of greater freedom for democratic expression.

Poland was in a different sort of turmoil. The disaffection of large numbers of Poles with the Communist authorities found several outlets. Most outspoken was the Students' Solidarity Committee – increasingly known simply as 'Solidarity' – which had active branches in all Poland's university cities. 'Flying academic courses' were organized in private homes, in which lessons were given to challenge the Communist-imposed curricula in the State universities. In January, sixty-five leading Polish intellectuals, scholars and university teachers formed an Educational Courses Society to ensure that the flying courses were as well taught and as effective as possible. The authorities frowned on the venture, but did not suppress it.

A new era had begun in Poland, where more and more groups tested how far the non-Communist and Catholic impetus of the mass of the Poles could be pushed. Free trade unions were being set up, also with the 'Solidarity' label, in most industrial cities. A Peasants' Self-Defence Committee was set up by the quarter of a million Polish farmers who had been allowed, on a small scale, to own and manage their own farms. These farmers refused to pay their State pension contributions, on the ground that they were too high, and demanded the right to be consulted when decisions on farming policy came up. The Party leader, Edward Gierek, bowed to their demands. He had also to take into account a letter signed by several former Party leaders, urging him to institute liberal reforms. Another bastion of Polish life, the Polish Writers' Union, issued a strong criticism of the censorship laws, and elected four well-known critics of the regime to its inner counsel. In response, the Party agreed to set up a system whereby grievances regarding censorship could be heard and remedied.

Throughout this ferment in Poland, the Catholic Church – which also condemned censorship – took the lead in calling for change. The catalyst came on October 16, when Cardinal Wojtyla, of Cracow, was elected Pope, as John Paul II. He was the first non-Italian Pope since 1522, and the first Pole ever to become Pope. For a country with such deep Catholic roots and beliefs, this was an electric moment. The Communist Party, for all its efforts to present itself as a national and economically responsible Party, could not compete with this groundswell of enthusiasm, with its potent combination of widespread religious feeling and strong national identity. A Polish Pope seemed to offer the Poles everything that their powerful Soviet neighbour could not.

Despite the unease of the Communist Party, the Pope's installation Mass in the Vatican was transmitted live on television, and was another example of the power of television to make a political impact. Following the televised ceremony, during which the streets of Poland's cities were virtually deserted, millions of Poles went to churches throughout the country in an unprecedented demonstration, in any Communist country, of religious zeal. During a Mass held in Warsaw a few days later, thousands of worshippers crowded into the church or pressed around the open doors as appeals were made from the pulpit for respect for human rights in Poland, and for an end to the falsification of history: the Party was determined not to allow anti-Soviet facts to be publicized or commemorated. As speaker after speaker called for a new Polish national policy, the worshippers expected the authorities to stop the proceedings. They did not. Power was moving gradually but by perceptible gradations from the Party centres, with all their apparatus of police and undercover control, to the public.

In one other Communist country the flame of dissent burned bright: the members of Charter 77 in Czechoslovakia, their numbers continually increasing, circulated clandestine accounts of violations of human rights. They also held two meetings with dissidents in Poland; a third meeting was prevented by the Czech police. The authorities made persistent efforts to stop the circulation of Charter 77 material, and to arrest those who took part in these activities. So many arrests were made, and so many activists put in prison, that a new opposition group was formed: the Committee for the Defence of Unjustly Persecuted Citizens. One area of dissent, which touched upon worldwide concerns about the environment, was particularly resented by the Czech authorities. This was material circulated by the clandestine opposition drawing attention to the ecological dangers which the Czechoslovak government had created by its attempts to produce nuclear energy.

On March 11 a PLO unit, sailing from the southern Lebanese coast, landed in northern Israel, killed an American-Jewish photographer, Gail Rubin, who happened to be working at the shore where they landed, and hijacked a crowded bus on the main coastal road. When the bus was eventually halted on the highway just north of Tel Aviv, thirty-nine of the passengers were killed. Three days later, in retaliation, Israeli troops crossed into southern Lebanon, occupying a six-mile strip of territory. All PLO installations there were then destroyed. The United Nations called for Israel to withdraw. It did so on June 13, when United Nations troops arrived to take up position between the PLO and the Israeli border, their uniforms and vehicles emblazoned with the initials 'UNIFIL' (United Nations Interim Force In Lebanon). Despite the United Nations military presence in the south – which although 'interim' had lasted twenty-one years by the end of the century – within Lebanon the internal dissension often turned to violence, with Christian Falangists, Lebanese Muslims and the PLO in bitter antagonism. During an upsurge of fighting in Beirut on October 4, five hundred people were killed.

Five days after Israeli troops withdrew from Lebanon, a meeting was held at Leeds Castle, in the south of England, at which the Israeli Foreign Minister, Moshe Dayan, the Egyptian Foreign Minister, Mohammed Ibrahim Kamel, and the American Secretary of State, Cyrus Vance, met to discuss a possible Egyptian-Israeli agreement. President Sadat's surprise visit to Jerusalem almost a year earlier had led to high expectations in Israel that such an agreement could be reached. But Sadat had returned to Cairo with nothing having been even tentatively agreed. Among those in Israel calling for a peace treaty with Egypt after Sadat's visit were a group of army officers, calling themselves 'Peace Now', who wrote to Begin at the start of 1978 urging him to pursue 'the road to peace'. The United States offered its services as an intermediary.

The Egyptian-Israeli negotiations which followed Sadat's visit were a first step. The Leeds Castle meeting had begun a process that made rapid advances. Encouraged by President Carter, and under his auspices, on September 4 Begin and Sadat met at the presidential retreat of Camp David, in Maryland. Carter had invited Jordan, Syria, Saudi Arabia and the Palestinians to participate with Sadat on the Arab side, but they declined to do so. Sadat negotiated tenaciously on his own. Without the other Arab States, however, there could be no peace treaty, as Carter had hoped, to resolve the Middle East conflict. What emerged in its place, after almost two weeks of virtually unbroken talks, was a 'Framework for Peace in the Middle East'. The preamble stated that it would be elaborated into specific peace treaties through future negotiations.

The Camp David Accords were signed on September 17. The first accord

– which was not to take effect even in part for two decades – called for the implementation of an autonomy plan for the Palestinians on the West Bank and in the Gaza Strip, to be followed after five years by a 'permanent settlement'. Under this accord, Israel was committed to recognize, for the first time since its foundation thirty years earlier, 'the legitimate rights of the Palestinian people', and what were called 'their just requirements'.

Whether a peace treaty could be signed between Israel and Egypt remained in doubt. A deadline was set, but it passed with nothing having been concluded. Anxiously, Carter instructed Alfred Atherton, an Assistant Secretary of State, to embark on Kissinger-style shuttle diplomacy in the new year.

In half the nations of Africa there was turmoil. In Zaire, civil unrest, brutal repression and massacres marked the rule of President Mobutu. On Mobutu's return from a visit to the Middle East and Europe in search of aid, he claimed to have forestalled a coup and sentenced nine officers and four civilians to death. International appeals for clemency, including one from the Belgian Foreign Minister, were ignored.

Mobutu had put his military support behind the dissident forces in the Angolan civil war. In retaliation the Angolan government, with Cuban, East German and Soviet support, encouraged anti-Mobutu Zaireans to capture the copper-mining town of Kolweze. Mobutu appealed for help to Belgium, to protect Europeans in the region from massacre by the rebels. The Belgians sent several thousand troops. Four hundred French legionaries were also sent in. But more than a hundred Europeans were massacred before these troops arrived. When, finally, Zairean government troops entered Kolwezi, hundreds of people accused of supporting the rebels were killed.

In Chad, independent from France since 1960, a civil war was being fought, fuelled by Libyan support for the main rebel group. In Equatorial Guinea (formerly Spanish Guinea), ten of the twelve Cabinet Ministers who had been appointed at independence a decade earlier had been murdered, and two-thirds of the members of the Independence Assembly had disappeared. A quarter of the population of 400,000 had fled across the neighbouring borders. Forced labour and cruel tortures were imposed on those who remained. 'The economy is a shambles,' reported the International Commission of Jurists, 'and the infrastructure, both human and physical, is now devastated.'

In Uganda, the tyranny of Idi Amin continued. Amin's security forces dealt ruthlessly with all whom he perceived as his opponents. In March, Raphael Sebugwawo-Amooti, a leading judge and chairman of the Industrial Court, was shot dead. In July the United States Congress voted to suspend almost all trade with Uganda, whose government, the resolution stated, 'engages in the international crime of genocide'. In October, Amnesty International announced that the civilian death toll over the previous eight years was at least 300,000.

The death of Jomo Kenyatta in Kenya pointed up the problems which strong leadership, based on the national struggle for independence, could create. 'He had given political stability to a multiracial, private-enterprise society,' William Tordoff, Professor of Government at the University of Manchester, wrote that year. 'But he also bequeathed glaring social inequality, corruption in high places, mounting pressure on the land from a rapidly increasing population, a serious problem of urban unemployment, and a rising crime rate.' The succession to Kenyatta was fraught with potential inter-tribal rivalry, between leading members of Kenyatta's Kikuyu and the Kalenjin, to which the main contender for the presidency, Daniel arap Moi, belonged. Moi, a former head teacher and Chief Scout of Kenya, won important Kikuyu support, however, and was elected President unopposed. Among his first actions, which were met with widespread approval, was a pledge to root out the smuggling, land-seizures and corruption that had become endemic. As a sign that he intended – in the fifteenth year of Kenya's independence – to follow the path of Western democratic procedures, President Moi released all the political detainees who had been held for opposition activities during the Kenyatta regime. Those released included Professor Ngugi Wa Thiongo, the novelist and playwright who at the time of his imprisonment had been head of the Literature Department at Nairobi University.

In November, President Moi visited France, Belgium and Britain, determined to draw closer to the countries of the European Economic Community. In a move which was applauded by Western environmentalists, he not only upheld Kenyatta's ban, imposed shortly before his death, on the trade in animal skins and other game trophies, but intensified efforts to track down illegal hunters. In December, Moi announced the start of a five-year campaign to combat adult illiteracy.

Kenya was not alone among the States of Africa to move away from autocratic rule. In Burkina Faso – formerly Upper Volta – the military regime voluntarily transferred power to civilian rule, elections were held and an all-civilian government appointed. In Niger, advantage was taken of the four-fold increase in uranium prices since the oil crisis five years earlier, providing much increased revenue; almost half of Niger's uranium exports went to Japan. For Guinea, in the twentieth year of independence, improved relations with France – the former colonial ruler – and an official visit from the French President, Giscard d'Estaing, offered the chance, as for Kenya, of closer ties with the European Economic Community. But, as with so many African States, the shadow of human rights abuse could not be fully removed. In the words of O. E. Wilton-Marshall, a British writer on African affairs: 'As to the large number of political prisoners in Guinea there was no certainty whether they were alive or dead.'

In Rhodesia, the outline of a settlement appeared to be emerging, set out at the end of January at a conference in Malta by David Owen, the British Foreign Minister, and Andrew Young, the United States Permanent Representative at the United Nations, an African-American. At the beginning of April, as an earnest of Ian Smith's desire to accept majority rule, White Cabinet Ministers began sharing their portfolios with Black Ministers. Political detainees were released. The ban on political activity by the Patriotic Front was revoked. But in September forces loyal to the Zimbabwe African People's Union (ZAPU), headed by Joshua Nkomo, using a Soviet heat-seeking missile, shot down an Air Rhodesia passenger aircraft on a domestic flight. Thirty-eight passengers and crew were killed when the plane was hit. Eighteen people survived. Of them, ten were massacred by guerrillas who found the wreckage. In response – having pledged 'more action, less talk', Ian Smith ordered an air attack on a guerrilla camp, and at least three hundred guerrillas were killed. Guerrilla activity intensified. Ian Smith mobilized all White adult males below the age of fifty. But more and more of the country was coming under guerrilla control: in those areas, no taxes were paid to the government in Salisbury, schools and missions were forced to close, and agricultural production was impeded.

On June 23 twelve Britons were brutally murdered at a church mission station. On September 8, guerrilla forces shelled Umtali. In November, when the British Prime Minister, James Callaghan, tried to persuade both sides to begin negotiations, he was rebuffed by both. In December, guerrillas blew up a major fuel-storage depot near Salisbury. The prospect for a settlement looked bleak at the end of a year in which 5,500 Rhodesians – Black and White – had been killed.

In Namibia (formerly South-West Africa), which South Africa had ruled as a mandatory power since the defeat of Germany in 1918, the United Nations was pressing for a full South African withdrawal. But a new South African Prime Minister, P. W. Botha, was as adamant as his predecessor John Vorster that South Africa should continue to administer the diamond-rich region. Guerrillas from the South-West African Peoples' Organization (SWAPO), based in Zambia and Angola, carried out repeated raids across the border, in one of which ten South African soldiers were killed. Against them, South African forces entered Zambia and Angola and sought in vain to destroy the guerrilla bases.

The United Nations Secretary-General, Kurt Waldheim, proposed a cease-fire followed by free elections, under United Nations auspices. Meanwhile, in South Africa itself, there was no let-up in apartheid. At least four thousand Black South Africans, including many of the Soweto schoolchildren who had fled the country earlier, were receiving guerrilla training in Angola, Libya and Tanzania. In March, two bombs were exploded in Port Elizabeth, and two people killed. Banning orders on members of the Black Consciousness movement – of which the murdered Steve Biko had been a leader – continued to be banned from any political activity, or held in detention: seventy-eight of them incommunicado, in solitary confinement.

In Comoro, the Indian Ocean island group which had gained independence from France three years earlier, the autocratic rule of President Ali Soilih came to an end with a coup directed by a French mercenary, Bob Denard. Ali Soilih was killed a few days after being deposed.

With the admission to membership of the Solomon Islands and Dominica, the United Nations counted 151 members: a hundred more than at its foundation thirty-three years earlier. Decolonization was almost complete, and a new community of nations had been created, some of which were far smaller than a small Soviet republic or the average American State. Others were tiny in terms of population. The Solomon Islands – a former British protectorate – although covering an area of almost a quarter of a million square miles, had a population at independence of less than a quarter of a million. Dominica, which had been discovered by Columbus in 1493, and ruled by Britain since 1805, was an island only twenty-nine miles long and sixteen broad. Its population was just above 70,000.

The highlight of the year for the United Nations was the World Conference to Combat Racism and Racial Discrimination. This coincided with another United Nations initiative: Anti-Apartheid Year. But the unity of the anti-racism deliberations was marred by a United Nations resolution passed three years earlier condemning Zionism as racism. This resolution meant that Israel was excluded from all United Nations discussions on racism, with the result that the United States also withdrew from the world conference. The 'Zionism is Racism' resolution had been an initiative of the seventeen Arab States, passed as a result of the built-in majority of the Third World nations, and supported by the Soviet Union and all other twelve Communist States. It had been opposed by all nine members of the European Economic Community including Britain, by the Scandinavian countries, and by Australia, New Zealand, Canada and the United States.

When the deliberations of the World Conference to Combat Racism and Racial Discrimination were over, its resolution echoed the earlier condemnation of Zionism. All the Common Market countries therefore walked out of the conference. Other United Nations initiatives were not affected by the Arab hostility to Israel and its repercussions. But at the third Law of the Sea Conference strong criticism was directed against the United States, Japan, Britain and West Germany for their plans for deep mining of the sea bed in search of oil. Little success was achieved at the United Nations discussions on the control of industrial waste: the industrialized nations did not want to have to curb their industrial production as a result of more stringent waste-disposal controls, and the developing nations did not want any impediment to their industrial expansion.

There was a growing realization in the United Nations that the overriding issue facing more than a quarter of its members was that of poverty: at a meeting of the Economic and Social Council it was revealed that seventeen African nations were suffering from severe drought and increased desertification, as well as from a plague of locusts that was devastating such crops as had managed to survive the drought. Urgent measures had also to be taken, not against drought but against flooding, in both India and Sudan: this was done through the United Nations Disaster Relief Office. Another continuing United Nations battle was being fought by the United Nations High Commissioner for Refugees. Among those to whom his office was giving food and shelter were Black refugees from South Africa and Rhodesia, Zaireans who had fled their country to avoid the civil war, a quarter of a million refugees from Pol Pot's Cambodian regime of terror, who had crossed into Thailand and Vietnam; 200,000 Burmese refugees who had fled to Bangladesh, and tens of thousands of Vietnamese 'boat people'.

The fate of the Vietnamese boat people was shocking. As many as 2,500 of them, on board the freighter *Hai Hong*, were refused sanctuary in Malaysia after a terrifying voyage. The Malaysian government pointed out, in defence of its refusal, that it had already allowed 45,000 boat people ashore: they were being held in camps on the offshore islands. Canada, France and the United States agreed to take in the 2,500 between them. The United Nations High Commissioner for Refugees called a conference in December to try to find countries willing to take in the boat people. Thirty-seven countries agreed to attend. But they would grant only five thousand extra places between them.

Worldwide privation was becoming a concern, not only of the United Nations, but of Christian Churches. Catholic priests had long been active in the desperately poor shanty towns of South America. On July 21 the leaders of the Anglican Church throughout the world met at Canterbury: 440 bishops were present. The economist Dame Barbara Ward spoke to them about the shortage of world resources, and of the growing demand for greater equality that was arising in every land. She told the bishops: 'There will be no check on the demand for human respect; there will be no quiet acceptance of human starvation.'

Among the Anglican bishops present was Desmond Tutu, the first Black to be appointed General Secretary to the South African Council of Churches. He pleaded with his fellow bishops for the identification of the Church with the poor.

The world's worst-ever oil tanker pollution disaster took place on March 16, when the supertanker *Amoco Cadiz* went aground off the coast of Brittany. More than 220,000 tons of oil were spilled into the sea, twice as much as in the previous worst disaster eleven years earlier. A forty-mile stretch of the French coastline was affected. There were to be six more oil spillages in the following nine months, in one of which 50,000 tons of oil polluted the Spanish coast. Following these disasters, stricter rules were brought into force by the Inter-Governmental Maritime Consultative Organization (IMCO).

There was also a victory for the environmentalists that year when the United States banned chlorofluorocarbons (CFCs) as spray propellants, in order to reduce the damage to the ozone layer. Such sophisticated concerns for the future of the planet were in stark contrast to the behaviour of some of the human beings on it. In May, a former Italian Prime Minister, Aldo Moro, was found murdered, after he had been seized for a ransom which the government refused to pay. In June, the President of North Yemen was killed by a South Yemeni parcel bomb. Two days later the President of South Yemen was assassinated by the same group. In September, a Bulgarian dissident author, Georgi Markov, then in exile in London, was murdered on instructions from the Communist secret police in Bulgaria by the injection of a poison pellet through an umbrella. On Christmas Day, Vietnam invaded Cambodia, intent on overthrowing the Khmer Rouge regime and installing a Communist government. Another Indochinese war had begun.

CHAPTER TWENTY-EIGHT

1979

I appeal to you in language of passionate pleading. On
my knees I beg you to turn away from the paths of
violence and return to the paths of peace. Further violence
will only drag down to ruin the land you claim to love
and the values you claim to cherish.

POPE JOHN PAUL II

THE VIETNAMESE INVASION of Cambodia, launched on Christmas Day,
1978, was swift and decisive. By 7 January 1979, a combined force of
Vietnamese troops and Cambodian rebels had captured the capital, Phnom
Penh, and driven out the Khmer Rouge regime over which Pol Pot had
presided with such savagery. An era of tyranny and mass murder was over.
But the Khmer Rouge had been driven out, not defeated, and they were
quickly able to reconstitute themselves as a guerrilla force in both the
north-east and south-west of the country.

The Vietnamese conquerors established a 'People's Republic of Kampuchea' – Kampuchea being the new name for Cambodia – under the rule of
local Communist Party leaders, headed by Heng Samrin. Hundreds of thousands of Kampucheans, facing starvation after the destruction during the
fighting of the previous years of as much as eighty per cent of the country's
arable land, crossed the border into Thailand. There, in the harsh conditions
of refugee camps, they were supplied with food and medical aid sent through
Thailand by the United Nations and the International Red Cross. The Thai
government did not want the refugees on its soil and began to drive them
back into Kampuchea. Harrowing newspaper reports of their plight led to
a direct plea from the Secretary-General of the United Nations, Dr Waldheim, to the Prime Minister of Thailand, not to force any more refugees
back into Kampuchea. The plea was successful. At an emergency conference

of fifty countries, held on November 5, the sum of $210 million was committed to assist the refugees.

In February, Heng Samrin signed a defence treaty with Hanoi. It was under this treaty, the Kampuchean leaders explained in March, that Vietnam had 'agreed that Vietnamese armed forces should assist the Kampuchean people in defending their country'. The fact that the assistance had begun a full month before the treaty was signed was an obvious but unimportant detail. The whole of former French Indochina was under Communist rule.

Not Communism, but Islamic fundamentalism, was struggling to gain power in Iran. On 1 January 1979 the Prime Minister of Iran, General Azhari, who had been appointed to bring an end to the Islamic fervour in the streets, resigned. Despite the use of the army, the police, and the secret police he had been unable to curb the nationwide demand of hundreds of thousands of demonstrators in every city that the Shah be deposed and the exiled Muslim religious leader, Ayatollah Khomeini, be allowed back to Iran.

With Azhari's resignation the Shah offered the premiership to a senior politician, Dr Shahpur Bakhtiar, who agreed to take the job only if the Shah himself left the country while a political settlement was reached with the Islamic movement. Recognizing the ferocity of the Islamic movement's street demonstrations, and realizing that he could not order the army to open fire on such vast masses, the Shah agreed; he left Iran on January 16 for exile, which he hoped would be temporary, first in Switzerland and then in Mexico.

Following the Shah's departure, and despite what this meant with regard to the creation of a power vacuum, Bakhtiar tried to follow General Azhari's policy of not allowing the mob to rule. One of his first acts was to call out the army to restore calm on the streets of Teheran, where the departure of the Shah had been met with jubilation by the fundamentalists. The Ayatollah Khomeini was still in exile in Paris. On February 1, as the street demonstrations for his presence intensified, Bakhtiar invited him to return to Iran. As soon as Khomeini arrived, a number of senior army officers announced their support for him, and for the Islamic revolution which he declared. Briefly, United States marines were called in, by Dr Bakhtiar, to try to restore order in Teheran. After heavy fighting on February 10 and 11, they were forced to withdraw. The accelerating religious fervour swept all before it. The Iranian army – hitherto a bastion of the Shah's authority – declared itself neutral in the conflict in the streets. Within days, Islamic militants had overrun the army barracks in and around the capital. On February 12 Dr Bakhtiar's government resigned and he left for exile.

Ayatollah Khomeini established a government of his supporters. As well as appointing a civilian, secular Cabinet, he also set up a Revolutionary Committee, made up of senior religious leaders, and those secular politicians who had supported his cause while he was in exile. Khomeini, as religious arbiter of the new regime, kept a close watch on government, and made sure that former supporters of the Shah's government who were judged or denounced as enemies of the Islamic revolution were brought to trial and executed. In a referendum at the end of March to decide whether the public wished to set up an Islamic republic, the result, according to the authorities, was a ninety-eight per cent 'yes' vote. The new government, Khomeini announced, would be 'dedicated to Allah'. Political Parties were banned, and all independent and non-Islamic newspapers closed down. Banks and industries were nationalized. People known to be hostile to the new order were attacked in the streets and killed or badly beaten.

Regional opposition, including that of the Islamic religious leader in Iranian Azerbaijan, Shariat Madari, was crushed. Also subjected to military assault were two non-Iranian groups, the Arab minority in the oil-rich province of Khuzestan, and the Kurds in the area around Lake Urmia. Throughout the spring and summer Khomeini had to direct the army against these two centres of revolt, but in neither military campaign was the army fully successful. As Arab guerrilla sabotage of oil installations continued in the south, Khomeini ordered massive repression and executions. His orders were obeyed.

Two potentially hostile groups decided to throw in their lot with Khomeini, and gain influence thereby in the new governing counsels. One was the Tudeh (Iranian Communist) Party, the other the Mujaheddin-i Khalq, a Muslim guerrilla group with Marxist leanings that had been active against the Shah. In Paris, where Khomeini had been an exile until the beginning of the year, Dr Bakhtiar set up an Iranian government in exile.

On October 22, after negotiations in Algiers between Dr Bakhtiar and President Carter's Security Advisor, Zbigniew Brzezinski, the deposed Shah arrived in the United States for medical treatment. On November 4 Iranian students, followers of Khomeini, broke into the American Embassy in Teheran and took sixty-three Americans hostage. The hostages would only be released, said the students, if the Shah was sent back to Iran for trial. Carter refused to do this, and as a reprisal froze all Iranian government financial assets held in the United States – an estimated $8,000 million – and forbade American companies to buy Iranian oil. 'No one', he said, 'should underestimate the resolve of the American government and the American people in this matter.'

The 'hostage crisis' created a sense of powerlessness in the United States. The public awaited a decision. There were demonstrations in several cities against local Iranians (even in Britain a gruesome slogan appeared on the wall of at least one tube station, 'Save fuel, burn Iranians'). On November 19, five days after the freezing of the Iranian assets, thirteen of the hostages were set free. The Iranian government announced that the remaining fifty would be brought to trial as spies. Carter replied that the United States would seek a peaceful resolution to the crisis, but that there were 'other remedies available' to it. He did not say what these were, but it was pointed out by his spokesman that the United Nations Charter included clauses that would justify, in a case such as this, unilateral military action.

Within twenty-four hours of Carter's veiled threat, the American Embassy in Pakistan was attacked by Pakistani sympathizers of the Iranian regime, and two Americans, and two Pakistani employees at the Embassy, were killed. The situation was further inflamed when the Ayatollah Khomeini hinted that the United States was involved in a recent attack by two hundred armed Islamic militants on the mosque in Mecca, Islam's holiest place. The Saudi Arabian government answered that the attack had been the work of Muslim fundamentalists acting alone.

The Shah left the United States on December 15, for Panama. But the hostages were still held, and repeated American appeals for them to be released were rejected by Iran. On her first visit to Washington, the new British Prime Minister, Margaret Thatcher, announced her support for an American request to the United Nations for economic sanctions against Iran. On December 21 Carter ordered a nuclear-powered American aircraft-carrier naval force to the Arabian Sea.

As the Iranian revolution advanced, it eclipsed American concerns elsewhere. But at the beginning of the year the Middle East also had a claim on American attention. Central to the Camp David Accords which had been signed the previous year between Israel and Egypt, with President Carter as a facilitator and co-signatory, was the framework for the conclusion of a peace treaty between Egypt and Israel. After Camp David, efforts to conclude this had failed. In an attempt to move it forward in the new year, Carter had instructed an Assistant Secretary of State, Alfred Atherton, to try to find common ground. As a result of Atherton's shuttle diplomacy in Egypt and Israel, a further meeting was held at Camp David in February between the Israeli and Egyptian Foreign Ministers, Moshe Dayan and Mustafa Khalil. When agreement still seemed elusive, Carter invited Begin to Washington. Carter, aware of the many sensitivities on both sides, then agreed to fly to the Middle East to put the various pieces of the package together. He too embarked on shuttle diplomacy, visiting Sadat in Cairo and Alexandria on March 8 and 9, and then spending four days in Israel, before returning to Cairo.

Carter's efforts were rewarded. Flying to Washington, Sadat and Begin signed a treaty of peace at the White House, in a televised ceremony during which the two former adversaries embraced. In return for an end to the state of war between Israel and Egypt, Begin agreed to give up the whole of the Sinai peninsula. The Labour opposition in Israel – the governing Party from 1948 to 1977 – were surprised about this. Until defeated by Begin in the 1977 election they had stated emphatically that the retention of Sharm el-Sheikh, at the southern extremity of Sinai, and of a strip of territory running down to it, was crucial for Israel, to enable it to keep open the shipping lane to the port of Eilat, on the Gulf of Akaba, and generally defend itself from attack from the south. But Begin had realized that he had to set aside such strategic concepts. He understood that for Sadat only the return of all the lost territory would enable a peace treaty to be signed.

The Israeli withdrawal from Sinai had been made that much more palatable, strategically, when Carter agreed that the United States would build two military airfields for Israel in the Israeli south, in the Negev Desert, in return for the four airfields that Israel evacuated in Sinai. Carter also secured from Congress the largest ever American foreign-aid package for the two signatories: a total of $5,000 million over a three-year period. On May 27 the borders between Egypt and Israel were opened for the first time since 1949, and an air corridor established between the two countries, with regular commercial flights between Cairo and Tel Aviv. Following the signature of the treaty – the first peace treaty between Israel and any of its Arab neighbours, Begin and Sadat were both awarded the Nobel Prize for Peace. On November 19, Sadat took formal repossession of Mount Sinai and of St Catherine's monastery at its base.

The Egyptian-Israeli treaty preserved peace between the two countries for twenty years, and at the end of that period no cause for hostilities was in sight. But the *Washington Post* did draw attention to an aspect of the treaty that held out the prospect of future tension. The treaty, it noted, although it 'holds the marvellous promise of ending the cycle of Mideast wars, simultaneously commits the two countries to negotiate the Palestinian question, truly a rending one'. In the event, after nearly two decades of Palestinian-Israeli confrontation and conflict, the Palestinian question was to be negotiated directly between Israel and the Palestinians themselves.

Following the signature of the Egyptian-Israeli treaty, the United States continued to monitor the situation within Israel with regard to the Palestinians. This too was to be a constant factor in United States-Israeli relations, and disagreements. A first intimation of that was seen in September, when the United States formally condemned Begin's government for allowing Israeli Jews to purchase land in the occupied territories. This, in the words of the State Department protest, was 'contrary to the spirit and intention of the peace process'. But land purchases continued, and within a decade more than a hundred Israeli settlements had been built on the West Bank and in the Gaza Strip, many of them on land bought or expropriated from its Arab owners. An Israeli High Court judgment that the settlement of Eilon Moreh, near the Palestinian Arab city of Nablus, was illegal and should be dismantled led to the settlement being moved to a site only a few miles away. Meanwhile, the eleven Israeli civilian settlements in the northern Sinai, including the small town of Yamit, which all had to be transferred to Egyptian sovereignty under the peace treaty, were deliberately and systematically bulldozed to the ground by the Israeli army to prevent the Egyptians from having use of them.

Even as President Carter was putting the final touches to his Middle Eastern diplomacy, and the triumph of the first treaty of peace between Israel and any of its Arab neighbours, the equally complex and more far-reaching Strategic Arms Limitation Talks with the Soviet Union were proceeding. SALT I had established that agreement could be reached. SALT II had to lay down specific targets. When, on June 18, Carter and Brezhnev met amid the Habsburg splendour of the grand ballroom of the Hofburg Palace in Vienna, the agreement was ready for their signature. This, too, was a moment highlighted on television, which was becoming the main vehicle not only for disseminating news, but bringing it live to hundreds of millions of people: in the United States alone there were 150 million television sets. The agreement set a ceiling of 2,250 strategic missiles or bombers on each side. Of these, no more than 1,320 were to be equipped with multiple warheads or Cruise missiles. In order for the Soviet Union to reach the ceiling, it would have to dismantle 270 strategic missiles, of which it had more than the United States. It was also agreed that no more than ten nuclear warheads would be placed on any new land-based strategic missile, and no more than fourteen on any sea-based missile. The 1972 treaty that had banned anti-ballistic missile systems would remain in force. For its part, the Soviet Union agreed to give up one of its strategic advantages, its ability to bomb United States bases in the Arctic.

With the signing of SALT II on June 18, the Cold War looked as if it was on the wane. But it was not yet dead. Even as the Senate was discussing ratifying SALT II, talks were suspended while the United States protested at the presence of three thousand Soviet combat troops in Cuba. The Russians insisted, truthfully, that the troops were there to train Cuban soldiers: they were not part of any intended offensive force. The United States replied that, whatever its current intentions, the force was a combat one. In defence of the administration's anger, on September 7 Carter told the American people that the United States did have the right 'to insist that the Soviet Union respect our interests and our concerns, if the Soviet Union expects us to respect their sensibilities and concerns'. The word 'respect' was carefully chosen: the time of verbal threats and accelerated military confrontation was over. The Cuban missile crisis, with its truly provocative Soviet action, was long in the past. The United States acted with firmness, but without jeopardizing the SALT II agreement. Intelligence air surveillance of Cuba was increased, and a newly created Rapid Deployment Force was sent to carry out manoeuvres at Guantánamo, the sovereign American naval base on Cuba.

As a measure of caution, Carter announced on December 12 that there would be a small increase in defence spending, of five per cent a year for 1981 and up to four and a half per cent a year for the five following years. Congress, always uneasy at any increase in government spending, was initially critical. But the criticism was swept aside a mere fifteen days after the announcement, when, on December 27, Soviet troops moved into Afghanistan, where there were already at least 1,500 Soviet advisers, most of them military personnel. One result of the Soviet invasion of Afghanistan was that the United States Senate refused to ratify the Strategic Arms Limitation agreement, SALT II, which Carter and Brezhnev had signed in Vienna in June.

* * *

For the twelve months before the Soviet invasion, Afghanistan had been in ferment. A pro-Soviet regime, headed by Nur Muhammad Taraki, which had seized power the previous April, had imprisoned many Islamic religious leaders, who were demanding – as were the Iranian mullahs across Afghanistan's western border – a more religious, Islamic orientation in the government and laws of the State. One source of inspiration for the Islamic fundamentalists was Pakistan, to the east, whose new ruler, Zia al-Haq, insisted that the teaching and tenets of Islam should be a central feature of the national school curriculum. Islamic fervour in the region was deeply disturbing to the Soviet leaders, whose own Central Asian republics, while firmly under the control of secular, atheistic Moscow, were made up almost entirely – other than by a minority of Russian settlers and officials – of Muslims. The cities of Bukhara, Samarkand, Khiva and Ashkhabad, Soviet cities for almost half a century, had all been centres of Islam for many centuries before that.

On February 14 the American Ambassador to Afghanistan, Adolph Dubs, was kidnapped by Afghan Islamic fundamentalists who said they would release him only if the Muslim religious leaders imprisoned by President Taraki were released. The American government began negotiations with the kidnappers, who were holding Dubs captive in a hotel in Kabul. Even while the negotiations were continuing, Taraki, at the suggestion of his senior Soviet advisers, sent Afghan police against the kidnappers. In the resultant gun battle Dubs was killed. The United States protested to the Soviet Union about the role of its advisers in ordering the assault while the Americans were still negotiating with the kidnappers.

The struggle between the pro-Soviet and Islamic movements in Afghanistan was also being fought in the countryside: five thousand Islamic fighters were being held in check in the Konar province, north-east of Kabul, by 12,000 Afghan troops loyal to President Taraki. The government's struggle was intensified in March, when four thousand Iranian fundamentalists entered Afghanistan together with seven thousand Afghan fundamentalists who had earlier sought sanctuary in Iran. Pakistan also gave tacit encouragement to the Islamic movement in Afghanistan.

The Afghan army was riddled with disaffection; desertions to the Islamic guerrilla forces increased during the summer. On August 12 a group of thirty Russians who were visiting a Muslim shrine at Kandahar were murdered by Afghan fundamentalists. There was indignation in the Soviet Union, and fear among the Soviet advisers in Afghanistan that the power of the central government was waning. On September 16 President Taraki was overthrown by Hafizullah Amin. In the gun battle around the presidential palace, Taraki was killed. More Soviet advisers arrived to prop up the Kabul government. But Hafizullah Amin's promise to restore Kabul's authority throughout the country within thirty days was beyond fulfilment – even 300 days would not have sufficed.

The Soviet Union decided to take unilateral action. On Christmas Day – a day recognized as special neither by Soviet Communists nor by Afghan Muslims – Brezhnev ordered a two-day military airlift of Soviet troops into Kabul. It was the largest Soviet troop movement outside Russia's borders since the invasion of Czechoslovakia eleven years earlier. With the arrival of Soviet troops in force, Hafizullah Amin's government was overthrown, and Amin killed. He was replaced by a Soviet nominee, Babrak Karmal. *Pravda* welcomed the new government with enthusiasm, telling its readers: 'True to the treaty of friendship, good-neighbourliness and co-operation with the USSR, which guaranteed lasting peace and security in the region, the Afghan people and State would support and develop their unbreakable fraternal relations with the Soviet Union.'

The word 'unbreakable' echoed the national anthem of the Soviet Union itself – the 'unbreakable union of free republics'. Yet it was by the invasion of Afghanistan that the Soviet leaders lit the slow, and at first unsuspected fuse that was to lead to the break-up of the Soviet Union.

The international repercussions of the Soviet invasion of Afghanistan were immediate. On December 28, as soon as the scale of the invasion was clear, President Carter condemned the Soviet action as a 'blatant violation' of accepted rules of international behaviour, and 'a threat to peace'. He also spoke directly to Brezhnev on the Washington-Moscow hot line. 'He claimed that he had been invited by the Afghan government to come in and protect Afghanistan from some outside third-nation threat,' Carter told the American people in a television broadcast on December 31. This, Carter added, 'was obviously false, because the person that he claimed invited him in, President Amin, was murdered or assassinated after the Soviets pulled their coup'. Carter added that in their telephone conversation Brezhnev 'claimed that they would remove their forces as soon as the situation should be stabilized and the outside threat to Afghanistan eliminated'. These assertions, Carter insisted, were 'completely inadequate and completely misleading'.

What the American response would be, Carter did not elaborate, beyond insisting that his government would make it clear to the Soviet Union that no such action could be carried out without 'severe political consequences'.

In Turkey, religious divisions between Sunni and Shi'ite Muslims led to violent clashes and heavy loss of life. At the beginning of the year martial law was in place in thirteen of Turkey's sixty-seven provinces, set up by Bülent Ecevit, with the support of his Republican People's Party, a left-of-centre alignment with a commitment to secular and democratic procedures. In April there was unrest in the Kurdish regions, and six more provinces were put under martial law. Left- and right-wing political factions were also in violent conflict. Among those murdered was Abdi Ipeçki, the editor of the influential newspaper *Milliyet*, who supported Ecevit's moderate stance.

In dealing with the inter-religious rioting, and even with the Kurdish uprising, Ecevit insisted that the army must, in the final analysis, be account-able to the civil authority. The higher echelons of the army began to associate themselves more actively with the opposition right-wing Justice Party, headed by Süleyman Demirel. On October 15, having failed to restore public order, and after losing his majority in the Senate to the Justice Party in the elections, Ecevit resigned. Demirel, who succeeded him at the head of a right-wing coalition, announced almost immediately that during Ecevit's twenty-two-month premiership, 2,444 people had been killed by terrorists. But killings continued under the new government. Two leading moderates, both professors at Istanbul University, were murdered in November, and four Americans were killed in Istanbul in December. The United States had been hoping to store nuclear warheads at its bases in Turkey. Even Ecevit had refused to allow this, unless the Soviet Union approved, which it did not.

One of Demirel's first actions was to allow the Palestine Liberation Organ-ization to open an office in the capital, Ankara, and to give it the status of a diplomatic mission. This was after Palestinian terrorists had occupied the Egyptian Embassy in Ankara, killing two Turkish policemen and an Egyptian who tried to escape from the building. The PLO was protesting against the Egyptian-Israeli treaty. There was also terrorism inflicted on Turks. This was based on the hatred felt by the Armenians for the massacres carried out by the Turks more than half a century earlier. The son of the Turkish Ambassador at The Hague and the head of the Turkish tourist office in Paris were both among the victims of Armenian terrorist attacks.

*   *   *

Terrorism in Northern Ireland continued throughout the year, but however violent the deaths, and however widespread the destruction of property, neither the Labour government under James Callaghan nor his Conservative successor as Prime Minister, Margaret Thatcher, was prepared to contemplate political change in the province under the threat of violence. Both insisted that direct rule from London would continue until law and order were fully restored. Nor would they agree to give convicted murderers the 'special category' status that they were demanding. Those in prison claimed that they were political prisoners, not criminal murderers.

On the eve of the general election of May 3 that brought Margaret Thatcher and the Conservatives to power, an IRA gunman shot dead the British Ambassador to the Netherlands, Sir Richard Sykes. Eight days later an outspoken opponent of terrorism, the Conservative Member of Parliament Airey Neave, was killed by a bomb in the House of Commons car park. His murder was 'claimed' by the Irish National Liberation Army, a splinter group of the IRA. In April, terrorists in Northern Ireland killed four policemen, a woman prison warder, eight British soldiers and three Ulster Defence Regiment soldiers. Meanwhile, an increasing quantity of money and arms was reaching the IRA from the United States, where pressure from several leading politicians, including Senator Edward Kennedy (the brother of the assassinated President), led to the Carter administration suspending the legal and hitherto unchallenged sale of arms by the United States to the Royal Ulster Constabulary.

IRA violence reached a climax of destructive futility on August 27, when the long-retired Admiral of the Fleet Earl Mountbatten of Burma – who in 1947 had orchestrated the transfer of British power in India – was blown up while on a fishing trip in the Irish Republic. Three people were killed with him, including his grandson. That same day, eighteen British soldiers on patrol in Northern Ireland were killed by landmines detonated from across the border. These deaths brought the total death toll from terrorist violence on both sides of the political divide to two thousand.

After Mountbatten's funeral, Margaret Thatcher met the Irish Prime Minister, Jack Lynch, and prevailed upon him to instruct his army and police forces to co-operate with Britain in cross-border security. This agreement, a courageous one for an Irish Prime Minister to reach, proved his nemesis: it was so widely criticized in the Irish Republic as a craven act of appeasement to Britain that within four months he resigned. His successor, Charles Haughey, had earlier been tried – and acquitted – for smuggling arms to the IRA. His elevation to the premiership enhanced Republican morale on both sides of the border. But the Republican dream, a united Ireland ruled from Dublin – whether achieved by terror or by diplomacy – was not to prove a realistic item in the agenda of what remained of the twentieth century.

On September 29 Pope John Paul II arrived in the Republic of Ireland. He was the first Pope to visit that Catholic country. He knew how much blood had been shed, and was still being shed, in Northern Ireland in the name of religion by both Catholics and Protestants. Speaking to a vast crowd at Drogheda, he said: 'I appeal to you in language of passionate pleading. On my knees I beg you to turn away from the paths of violence and return to the paths of peace. Further violence will only drag down to ruin the land you claim to love and the values you claim to cherish.'

In Africa, starting on April 10, the first multi-racial elections were held in Rhodesia. They lasted for ten days. As a result of the voting the White regime's authority came to an end, and was transferred to a Black majority government under Bishop Abel Muzorewa. Rhodesia was renamed Zimbabwe. On April 11, the day after polling began in Rhodesia, Idi Amin's despotic regime was overthrown in Uganda. Amin fled the country he had ruled with such terror, finding eventual sanctuary, as a Muslim, in Saudi Arabia.

In Equatorial Guinea, Francisco Macias Nguema – the President since independence in 1968 – was charged with 'genocide, treason, embezzlement and systematic violation of human rights'. He had reduced his country to little more than a prison camp, and ordered the deaths of thousands of people. He was found guilty and executed. The firing squad that carried out the execution had been brought specially from Morocco, because local people were afraid that Nguema's spirit was too strong for bullets, and that he would return as a tiger.

In Ghana, after a coup led by a former junior air force officer, Flight-Lieutenant Jerry Rawlings, executions aimed at 'house-cleaning and ridding the country of corruption' were immediate and widespread. General Kutu Acheampong, a former Head of State, and Major-General Emmanuel Utaka, commander of the border guards, having been accused of corruption while in power, were executed on a firing range in front of a large number of onlookers. Six other senior officers were shot ten days later, among them the former commander of the air force and the former commander of the navy. Elections followed, after a ten-year hiatus. They were conducted in an open and democratic fashion, and parliamentary rule was restored. Nigeria also returned to civilian rule. But in Chad, as the government of national unity broke up, and as communal hatreds were intensified, civil war was renewed. In one violent episode in the south as many as five thousand Muslims were massacred. Eleven factions were contending for power, each with an army to back its claims. A truce in August was followed by the establishment of a coalition government three months later, with French troops keeping a watchful but nervous eye over a new government of national unity.

In Eastern Europe, the attempt to assert human rights dominated the agenda. In Czechoslovakia the Communist authorities continued their attempts to destroy the influence of the Charter 77 human rights movement. Václav Havel and five other leaders were convicted of subversion and sentenced to five years in prison. Even the condemnation of the sentences by every Western European Communist Party had no effect. One result, however, was the even more rapid spread of underground pamphlets denouncing human rights abuses, and the proliferation of illegal lectures and theatrical performances. Hundreds of Czechs also found asylum in the West.

In Poland, workers were demanding the right to strike. Catholic, peasant and students groups each called for an end to Communist rigidity. Fifty leading intellectuals, including several Party members, called in a public manifesto for 'a radical change in the politico-social system'. When Pope John Paul paid his first visit to Poland as Pope, crowds estimated at a total of thirteen million turned out to see him. In a speech in Warsaw on June 2, he declared: 'Christ cannot be kept out of the history of man in any part of the globe, certainly not in Poland.' Another blow had been struck against the perpetuation of the system established in Eastern Europe with the arrival of the Soviet army – as liberators – in 1944 and 1945. In September a new opposition group, calling itself the Confederation of Independent Poland, was formed as a political Party, with a secret membership, pledged to secure 'full freedom and independence' for Poland.

The Soviet Union was confronted by an upsurge in individual defections. When the Bolshoi Ballet company toured the United States, three leading members sought, and were granted, asylum. A later tour of the United States by the Soviet State Orchestra was cancelled on orders from Moscow. A Polish joke – always a good indicator of political ferment – ran as follows:

Question: what is the definition of a quartet?
Answer: a Soviet orchestra on the way back from America.

*

Risks to the environment were highlighted in 1979 in the United States. On March 29 there was an accident at the Three Mile Island nuclear power station in Pennsylvania, when radiation from a leak through the ventilation system was detected more than twenty miles away. There were fears of a 'core meltdown' and as many as ten thousand deaths. In the event no such meltdown occurred and there were no deaths. But the measures taken after the leak showed that concern for the harmful effects of radiation was high. Pregnant women and young children were advised to move at least five miles from the power station. Several thousand other people, suspicious of the official denials of danger, left the area altogether. No one was known to have been seriously affected by the leak, but as a precaution twelve other nuclear power stations were closed for checks.

On May 3 a second accident took place at a nuclear power station near Zion, Illinois, when radioactive fumes escaped into the air. In June a leak was found in another Pennsylvania nuclear power station. Henceforth, stringent safety measures were imposed on all nuclear power stations, and Carter insisted that nuclear power was safe, and that it would continue to be used and expanded. One reason was economic, the high price of oil. 'We do not have the luxury of abandoning nuclear power,' Carter explained, 'or imposing a lengthy moratorium on its further use.'

In Britain, there was a leak of radioactive waste at the reprocessing plant at Windscale. Details were also emerging, through a Russian émigré scientist, of a major disaster involving nuclear waste in the Urals two decades earlier. Other environmental concerns were heightened that year by continuing scientific research. The effect of lead in petrol, in damaging the mental development of children, was substantiated. So too was the danger of cancer for those working with asbestos. The impact of pesticides on miscarriages was identified. And a committee of the United States Academy of Sciences announced that as a result of the most recent researches it was certain that the use of halocarbons as the propellants in aerosol cans was depleting the planet's protective ozone layer twice as rapidly as had earlier been calculated. One effect was believed to be a rise in cancer.

Smoking's dangers, likewise mostly with regard to cancer, were emphasized in a 1,200-word report by the office of the United States Surgeon-General which, after examining a mass of recent research, confirmed that smoking causes cancer, and that it was also linked with many other diseases.

*   *   *

The year ended with a noted increase in the number of refugees in the world: five million in all. The majority were fleeing from repressive regimes and from hunger in Africa. The Vietnamese boat people – an estimated 185,000 – were fleeing from Communist rule. More than 30,000 of them were allowed to enter the United States. Tens of thousands of Kampucheans were refugees from a war that had just ended, and from hunger. In Pakistan were tens of thousands of refugees from the civil war in Afghanistan. From the civil unrest in Burma, where several insurgent groups, including the Burmese Communist Party, had taken up arms against the government, tens of thousands had fled to Bangladesh, which had almost no resources to sustain them; during the year, as guerrilla activities in Burma subsided, they were repatriated.

The United Nations High Commissioner for Refugees, enlisting the help of the International Children's Emergency Fund, and the International Red Cross, renewed its efforts to provide the minimal assistance to refugees worldwide, at least to avert deaths by starvation and exposure. Politically, another method was tried that year, and was effective, when the United Nations asked the government of Vietnam 'to stop illegal departures'. The government of Vietnam agreed to do so. Forty years earlier, the British and American governments had done the same to prevent Jewish refugees from leaving Germany: they had asked the German government to 'discourage such travel'. The German government had complied.

For her work in helping the homeless and the dying in Calcutta, many of whom were refugees from the conflict in Bangladesh a decade earlier, the Albanian-born Mother Teresa was awarded the Nobel Peace Prize. She had supervised the setting up of seven hundred shelters and clinics throughout India. The Roman Catholic order of Missionaries of Charity to which she belonged worked throughout the world. Its 158 branches had almost two thousand sisters caring for the poor and the dying.

CHAPTER TWENTY-NINE

1980

It will not be possible for any nation or group of nations to save itself either by dominion over others or by isolation from them. On the contrary, real progress will only be made nationally if it can be assured globally.

BRANDT REPORT

IN HIS STATE OF THE UNION message on 23 January 1980, President Carter announced that he intended to ask Congress to reactivate the selective service system, whereby men of military age would register, and be liable for call-up. The spectre of Vietnam was roused, and although Carter stressed that his plan (which would cost $13 million) was only for registration, not conscription itself, the slogan of those who had not wanted to serve in Vietnam was heard again in the streets in the mouths of a new generation of students: 'Hell, no, we won't go.'

Fears of an accidental nuclear confrontation dogged Carter's desire for a calmer attitude towards international tensions – especially Afghanistan and Iran – when it was revealed that twice in a single week America's nuclear response forces had been alerted and set in motion as a result of a false computer warning. On June 3 the North Atlantic Defence Command computer had reported that a multiple Soviet missile attack had just been launched. One American aircraft with retaliatory nuclear missiles had already taken off from Hawaii, and other bombers armed with nuclear weapons were preparing for take-off, when the false alarm was recognized. Three days later the same NATO computer reported again that a Soviet missile attack had been launched. For three minutes all was readied for a counter-attack, before the mistake was discovered. The computer involved was not used again.

Carter's troubles were domestic as well as international. On the weekend of May 17–19, following the acquittal by an all-White jury of four White policemen charged with beating a Black motorcyclist to death, race riots broke out in Miami, Florida, in which looting, arson and sniping by the rioters was followed by gun battles in which fifteen rioters were killed. This was the highest death toll in racial violence since the immediate aftermath of the assassination of Martin Luther King twelve years earlier. Carter also faced a rise in the murder rate which marked out the United States, among all other Western nations, as crime-ridden to such an extent that on average one American was murdered every half-hour. Among the victims that year was the former Beatle, John Lennon, who was shot dead at the entrance to his apartment block in New York by a former mental patient who had bought his gun legally, in Honolulu.

In the decade that had just begun, more than 275,000 Americans were to be murdered in the United States: five times the number of American servicemen killed in Vietnam. In 1980 alone, a further 51,000 Americans were killed on the roads – almost exactly the five-year Vietnam War death toll. This annual figure scarcely fell. In the decade which started in 1980 almost half a million Americans (the official figure is 460,154) were killed on the roads.

Another statistic, yet to impinge on American consciousness, marked the year 1980: the death of forty people from AIDS (Acquired Immune Deficiency Syndrome). Those affected lost all natural resistance to infection, and there was no known cure. During the previous year, the first in which AIDS deaths were recorded, seven people had died. By 1983 the figure had exceeded two thousand. By 1988 there were 27,909 cases known in the United States alone, and a similar number elsewhere in the world. By 1992, twenty years after the first reported deaths, 170,000 Americans had died of the disease, which could be transmitted by sexual intercourse, or by the inadvertent use of infected needles during blood transfusion or drug use, or by infected blood in blood transfusions. According to the United States Center for Disease Control, an airline steward, who later died, was the individual who had brought the disease to North America, infecting partners in at least ten cities. The origins of the disease were in Africa; and it was in Africa that, within two decades, it was to inflict its greatest toll.

During his State of the Union message, Carter spoke of the fifty-three American citizens who were still being held captive in Iran, 'innocent victims of terrorism and anarchy'. He also spoke of the 'massive Soviet invading forces' that were at that very moment 'attempting to subjugate the fiercely independent and deeply religious people of Afghanistan'. Carter told Congress, and the tens of millions of Americans watching his speech on television:

> In response to the abhorrent act in Iran, our nation has been aroused and unified as never before in peacetime. Our position is clear. We will never yield to blackmail.
>
> We continue to pursue these specific goals to protect the present and future interests of the United States: to preserve the lives of the American hostages and to seek in every possible way their safe release; if possible, to avoid bloodshed which might further endanger the lives of our fellow Americans; to enlist the help of other nations to end this criminal violation of the moral and legal standards of a civilized world; and to persuade Iranian leaders that the real danger to their nation lies to the north from Soviet troops in Afghanistan, and that the unwarranted Iranian quarrel with us hampers their response to this great danger.
>
> If the American hostages are harmed, a severe price will be paid. We will never rest until every one of the victims is released.

How the United States could respond effectively was not clear. On January 1 the Secretary-General of the United Nations, Kurt Waldheim, had flown to Teheran to seek the release of the hostages, but in vain. An American resolution at the United Nations Security Council calling for economic sanctions against Iran was vetoed by the Soviet Union. The United Nations did appoint a special Commission of five members to go to Iran and seek a solution, but their mission was ended when they were refused permission to see the hostages. In March the Iranian students holding the hostages let it be known that they would be willing to hand them over to the ruling Revolutionary Council, a move seen as a way forward to eventual release. But Ayatollah Khomeini intervened, on April 7, to say that the students should continue to hold the hostages at the American Embassy. In response, the United States broke off diplomatic relations with Iran that same day, and banned all trade with Iran except for small quantities of essential foodstuffs and medicine. All Iranian diplomats in the United States were given forty-eight hours to leave.

The United States pressed the nine European Economic Community countries to join the sanctions on Iran. They were reluctant to do so. 'Our restraint is not inexhaustible,' commented Carter's National Security Adviser, Zbigniew Brzezinski, 'and not all the means of redress available to us have been applied.' Carter echoed this sense of frustration, and hint of some possible more dramatic action, when he announced on April 17 that if economic sanctions were not effective in securing the release of the hostages 'the only next step available that I can see would be some sort of military action'. Then, on April 22, the need for such military action seemed to recede, as the EEC Foreign Ministers, meeting in Luxembourg, agreed to introduce sanctions against Iran. They did so in the hope that force could be averted.

Unknown to the European Foreign Ministers when they announced the imposition of sanctions, Carter had already decided to take military action. In strictest secrecy, on April 24, six American transport aircraft, with ninety commandos on board, flew from an air base in Egypt to a remote desert airstrip in Iran. There, they were to rendezvous with eight American helicopters. These were to fly the five hundred miles from their aircraft carrier, *Nimitz* – part of the American naval patrol sent to the Arabian Sea when the hostages were seized. The helicopters were to refuel at the desert airstrip, and then six of them fly on to the outskirts of Teheran, from where the commandos would make their way to the Embassy and, in a rescue reminiscent of the Israeli action at Entebbe fourteen years earlier, bring the hostages out.

At the rendezvous point in the desert, two of the eight helicopters broke down and a third was damaged on landing. As six helicopters were the minimum considered feasible for success, the operation was called off. As the Americans prepared to leave the airstrip, one of the remaining helicopters collided with one of the transport planes: both burst into flames and exploded, and eight Americans were killed. The remaining commandos and planes left Iran. Early on the morning of April 25, Carter went on television to tell the American people: 'I ordered the rescue mission in order to safeguard American lives, to protect America's national interest, and to reduce the tensions in the world that have been caused. It was my decision to attempt the rescue operation. It was my decision to cancel it.'

The Secretary of State, Cyrus Vance, who had opposed the rescue mission, resigned. American sanctions remained in place, but the British government broke ranks with the EEC when it announced in May that it would limit British trade sanctions to new contracts: and that all existing contracts would be fulfilled. In July, one hostage was released because of ill-health. Public American negotiations with Iran, mostly through Algeria, took place throughout the year. Secret American negotiations were also taking place, and secured the release of the hostages at the beginning of 1981 by an unusual – and subsequently controversial – method. Without Congress being informed, arms sales to the Contra rebels in Nicaragua were used, on the President's authority, to pay Iran the money demanded over and above the release of the frozen Iranian assets in the United States.

In Chile, the regime of General Pinochet, which had come to power with strong American support seven years earlier, and had been severely condemned by the United Nations for its use of torture, took a move towards democracy when Pinochet enacted a constitution, approved by national referendum, which restored the rights of the individual which had been so cruelly violated. But there was to be no retrospective justice: as part of the post-dictatorial settlement, Pinochet gave himself an eight-year presidential term, after which he became a senator for life.

The Chilean constitution marked a way forward from dictatorship, but it also enshrined several of the dictator's policies. 'The transition settlement also set in stone the foundations of the economic and social mode,' David Lehman, Director of the Centre of Latin American Studies at the University of Cambridge, later wrote.

> The exceptional majorities required to make certain changes mean that it is in practice impossible to change the semi-privatized education system, the privatized medical and pensions systems, a highly flexible labour market, the constraints on trade unionism, the independent Central Bank, and the consolidation of the military as a financially and professionally self-governing corporation free of any accountability.

*

The Soviet Union had created an international furore by its invasion of Afghanistan, and the installation of a Communist government there. From early in the year there were as many as 80,000 troops in Afghanistan. Although the Soviet troops were in control of the main cities, and the roads between them, the Islamic guerrilla forces had many remote and inaccessible places in which to hide, and from which to attack. Soviet forces were repeatedly ambushed, subjected to hit-and-run attacks in which no quarter was given, and even in the cities liable to be killed if they strayed from their bases or units. By the end of the year, at least a thousand Soviet soldiers had been killed. In retaliation, the Soviet army brought in helicopter gunships and napalm bombs.

In January, all thirty-five nations that were members of the Islamic Conference condemned the Soviet action in Afghanistan. In Teheran, where a year earlier Islamic militants had attacked the Americans, their new target was the Soviet Embassy. On January 4 the United States announced a series of economic measures against the Soviet Union. Sales of high-grade American technology were suspended. Soviet fishing privileges in American waters were curtailed. There was also to be an immediate embargo on the sale of seventeen million tons of grain to the Soviet Union, the next sale that was due. To compensate the American farmers who were selling the grain, the American government bought it up. The other main grain-exporting countries, including all the EEC countries, agreed not to make up the shortfall. Despite American pressure, one of the boycotting States, Argentina, reopened its grain markets to Soviet purchase within a matter of months.

In the United Nations General Assembly there was a substantial majority demanding that Soviet troops leave Afghanistan: 111 votes to 22, with 12 abstentions. But the International Olympic Committee turned down an American appeal either to cancel the Moscow Games or to hold them in another country. Several governments that tried to persuade their national committees to boycott the Games were unsuccessful, with the result that British, Italian and Australian teams did compete. Forty-five governments, however, including the United States, Canada, West Germany and Japan, persuaded their Olympic Committees to boycott the Moscow Olympics, Games that were to have set the seal on Soviet competitive prowess.

Disapproval of the Soviet action did not lead to its total isolation. The French President, Giscard d'Estaing, showed his independence from American and NATO disapproval by flying to see Brezhnev in Warsaw on May 19. On June 30 the West German Chancellor, Helmut Schmidt, flew to Moscow where, in talks with Brezhnev, he reached agreement on a package of Soviet-West German measures for trade and energy co-operation. Philip Hanson, a British expert on the Soviet economy, commented: 'In general Western "retaliation" seemed to disintegrate on contact with Western wallets.' The American attempt to impose a partial embargo on sales of grain to the Soviet Union did not receive total support from the other nations involved. Even control over the movement of grain from the United States producers was incomplete. Existing American controls on the sale of 'military sensitive' machinery and technology to the Soviet Union were tightened, but within six months a Franco-German consortium took over the contract for a large-scale Soviet aluminium project from which an American company had withdrawn because of the embargo. An electric-steel project from which a joint American-Japanese consortium withdrew, in order to conform with the embargo, was taken over by a French group. 'Western wallets' had won the day.

One agreement which the United States itself reached with the Soviet Union was that neither power should become directly involved in the war which broke out, in September, between Iran and Iraq. America's one condition was that the Strait of Hormuz, through which more than forty per cent of the West's oil supplies sailed, should be kept open. The Soviet Union accepted this, and agreed to an American naval task force taking up position in the area.

The Iraqis were determined to gain control of the Shatt al-Arab waterway, which gave Iran control of access to the Tigris and Euphrates rivers, Iraq's waterways. They failed to do so, despite a war that lasted eight years and cost several hundreds of thousands of lives on both sides.

Deeply embroiled militarily in Afghanistan, the Soviet Union watched with grave alarm the political developments inside Poland, its western neighbour and hitherto loyal – or largely loyal – Communist partner. The Catholic Church, buoyed up by the moral and personal support of the 'Polish Pope', criticized in January the divisiveness of Communism in the social structure of Poland, and stated that every society had a right to form independent organizations in search of economic development. There was mockery in the streets when, at the parliamentary elections in March, 99.52 per cent of the votes went to the single Communist-dominated list of candidates. In June, 151 Polish intellectuals – leading writers, scientists and university professors – warned of 'negative changes' that would grow and reach 'avalanche stage, which would threaten open social conflict' unless reforms were instituted. University students, turning their backs on the Party-controlled youth organization, demanded a student association that would not be 'imposing any ideology'.

Strikes began on July 1, with workers demanding free trade unions and better wages. No day passed without a strike in one or other of the shipbuilding yards of the Baltic coast or the mining regions of Silesia. The strikes reached a climax in August, when half a million shipyard workers in Gdansk, Szczecin and other Polish Baltic ports downed tools. They were joined by 200,000 coalminers in Silesia. Catholicism was a strong force in the workers' movement, which had been as affected as any sector of Polish society by the

Pope's visit. In Gdansk, open-air Masses were held under a large portrait of the Pope.

On August 16 a strike committee linking all the striking factories was set up under the leadership of a shipyard worker, Lech Walesa. Quickly the strikers' demands, which at first had been limited to economic conditions, widened to include freedom of speech, an end to censorship, the release of political prisoners and the establishment of·free, independent trade unions. Under the banner of Solidarity, these unions sprang up despite the frown of the authorities. Students and workers found themselves gathering under the same Solidarity banner. Factories declared themselves for Solidarity, and took over the management. In many cases they were helped in organizing their independent activities by Catholic intellectuals, for whom Solidarity demanded the right of access of the Church to the media, and the broadcast of Sunday Mass.

An Eastern European anti-Communist revolution had begun, echoing Hungary in 1956 and Czechoslovakia in 1968. In the last week of August, the Soviet Union sealed the Polish-Soviet border and jammed all Polish radio and television transmissions so that news of the strikes in Poland would not be known to the Russians (for whom Western newspapers were virtually unobtainable). All facilities for dialling abroad from Soviet cities were suspended. After first refusing to do so, the Polish Communist authorities opened negotiations with Walesa in Gdansk. Talks were also opened with the strike committees in Szczecin, Lodz and the Silesian coalfields. The first agreement, with Szczecin and Gdansk, was signed on August 31. It was a triumph for the strikers: Solidarity, which could claim by then to represent eight million workers, was officially recognized as an independent, self-governing trade union. This was the first time that any independent trade union organization had been allowed to function in any Eastern-bloc Communist country. The release of political prisoners, on which Solidarity had insisted, was conceded. Press censorship laws would also be changed. The broadcast of Catholic Mass on radio and television would not only be allowed, but would become a regular Sunday feature of television broadcasting. September 22 was the first strike-free day since July 1.

Poland was desperately short of funds. After an appeal to Moscow, the Polish government secured a loan for $690 million. But Western banks provided far more, $1,300 million in all, and then a further $1,450 million for the purchase of American grain during the coming two years. The Soviet newspapers, reflecting the intense alarm among the Soviet leadership, began to denounce the Polish Communist leaders for their pusillanimity, and to warn of 'anti-Socialist' and 'counter-revolutionary' forces at work inside Poland. The Polish government understood the warning signs, and held back on implementing its agreement with Solidarity. In response, on October 3, several million workers throughout Poland went on a token strike for one hour, an indication of what they could do if the government did not move forward to honour the August 31 agreement in full. Solidarity also added demands: the publication of their own weekly newspaper, and access to the media similar to that which had already been conceded to the Catholic Church.

On October 30, Brezhnev assured the Polish Communist leader Stanislaw Kania that he could have more monetary credits, and that he could rely on Soviet support to curb Solidarity. But the Polish Supreme Court, in a surprise judgment, not only upheld Solidarity's right to organize strikes, but allowed it to delete from its constitution the hitherto compulsory clause acknowledging the 'supremacy' of the Communist Party.

Starting in mid-November East German, Czechoslovak and Soviet newspapers began a sustained attack on Walesa and Solidarity for working 'alongside' anti-Socialist forces in an attempt to overthrow Communism in Poland. Walesa publicly rebutted the charge. Forty Soviet divisions, more than 50,000 men, were then sent to the eastern (Ukrainian) and western (East German) borders of Poland. Poland responded by bringing its own troops in eastern Poland to eighty per cent readiness for combat.

The United States took action to protect Poland from a possible Soviet attack. On December 3, Carter informed the American people that the United States was watching with 'growing concern' what was an 'unprecedented' build-up of Soviet forces along the Polish-Soviet border. The Soviet Ambassador in Washington was called to the State Department and warned that the United States believed that Poland 'should be allowed to solve its domestic problems without outside interference', and that any Soviet intervention would have grave consequences for Soviet-American relations. The United States then announced publicly that it was monitoring all Soviet troop movements. To do this, American radar-warning aircraft with the most sophisticated technology were sent to an American air base in West Germany, from where they could monitor the Soviet-Polish border area from afar.

At an emergency meeting of the seven leading non-Communist industrial powers – the United States, Britain, France, Italy, West Germany, Canada and Japan – which gathered at Venice, Carter declared: 'We are not the

Warsaw Pact, held together by one nation's tanks. We are bound by shared ideals, shared goals, and shared respect for one another.' No Soviet invasion took place. Poland continued on its course of radical reform, moving slowly but steadily away from Communism, and from its Soviet mentor. In Czechoslovakia, by contrast, the dissident movement continued to be harassed and restrained by the Party, police and secret police. It did not give up, however, and was able to announce with pride at the end of the year that as many as two hundred books by banned authors had been published clandestinely.

In Hungary, opposition to the Communist regime took the unusual and – for the authorities – provocative step of the formation of a Foundation to Support the Poor, dedicated to serve the thirty per cent of the population who were believed to be living at or below the socially accepted minimum standard of housing and subsistence. The government warned the Foundation not to 'transgress' the regulations. Opposition activists who spoke out too loudly were dismissed from their jobs, or encouraged to leave the country altogether.

Inside the Soviet Union, dissent was carefully monitored and restrained. Hundreds of known dissidents were forced to leave Moscow during the Olympic Games, to prevent them having any contact with Westerners, several of whom had joined the sporting throng specifically in order to seek out dissidents and offer them moral support. One of the most outspoken dissidents, Andrei Sakharov, was banished from Moscow altogether, and sent to 'internal exile' 250 miles to the east, to the city of Gorky on the River Volga, a city that was out of bounds to foreigners. On the day before leaving, Sakharov signed a statement together with other Russian monitors of the Helsinki Agreement, denouncing the Soviet invasion of Afghanistan.

The number of Jewish exit visas was being continually and systematically cut back, from 51,000 in 1979 to 21,000 in 1980, and just over 2,000 in 1982, at which point it fell to scarcely a thousand, and even lower. Tens of thousands of Jews became 'refuseniks', denied the right (established under the 1948 United Nations Universal Declaration of Human Rights) to emigrate. Several dozen Jews, among them Shcharansky, languished in prison and labour camp for their part in the campaign for emigration, and for their championship of human rights. As well as Jewish activists, Baptists and Russian Orthodox priests who sought greater freedom of worship were arrested, tried and imprisoned. Those who criticized the Soviet abuse of psychiatric detention were likewise sent to prison and labour camp. Three leading activists were expelled from the Soviet Union and forced to go into exile: the satirist Vladimir Voinovich, the historian Lev Kopelev and one of the leaders of the free trade union movement founded two years earlier, Vladimir Borisov. The movement itself was crushed. No Lech Walesa was to be allowed to emerge in the Soviet Union.

In Africa, Rhodesia gained independence, as Zimbabwe, on April 18: in its parliament, eighty seats were allocated to Blacks, and twenty to Whites. In Libya, Colonel Khadaffi, who had been conducting a successful campaign of terror and assassination against Libyan exiles, announced that henceforth only those 'collaborating' with the United States, Israel or Egypt would be hunted down. In South Africa, the Senate, which had been a focus of independent thought, was abolished, and considerable extra powers were given to the President. A sixty-member advisory council set up for the President contained no African members. Bishop Desmond Tutu, a campaigner against apartheid whose voice was becoming increasingly influential abroad, was refused permission to leave South Africa. In June, thirty Africans were killed during clashes with the police in Black townships around Cape Town.

In Turkey, the government of Süleyman Demirel took measures to free the economy from its essentially Socialist orientation: price controls and subsidies were abolished, and with the immediate rise in prices living standards fell. The International Monetary Fund approved, and Turkey obtained substantial new foreign aid. Relations with Greece – strained almost to breaking point after the Turkish occupation of north Cyprus – were improved, and Turkey agreed to the return of Greece to NATO. But terrorism continued, with more than two thousand Turks being killed during Demirel's ten months in office: a higher rate than under his predecessor, Bülent Ecevit. One of those assassinated was a former Prime Minister, Nihat Erim. Another of those killed was the leader of the Turkish metalworkers, Kemal Türkler, a Marxist. In central Anatolia, the Sunni and Shi'ite Muslims (the Sunni were a majority) continued to attack each other.

On September 12 Demirel was overthrown by a military coup. The aim of the army officers involved was to end the terrorism that was disrupting Turkish life, and with which Demirel's minority administration had been unable to cope. Parliament was dissolved and power put into the hands of a National Security Council headed by the Chief of the General Staff, General Kenan Evren, who became Head of State. Martial law was declared, all political activity forbidden, and more than 30,000 people, including the leaders of the political Parties, detained. Demirel, and the former Prime

Minister and opposition leader, Bülent Ecevit, were banned from all political activity.

General Evren appointed a civilian government on September 21. It was headed by a retired admiral. In the month following the military coup, the number of terrorist murders fell to thirty-three, eight being members of the security forces who were attacking the terrorists direct. Armenian terrorists outside Turkey continued their work, however, killing the Turkish Consul-General in Sydney and his bodyguard.

Violence continued to be a scourge in India. On June 22 a thousand people were killed during clashes in Mizoram, Manipur and Tripura by local tribes demanding secession from India. In August, more than a hundred people were killed during Muslim clashes with Hindus in Moradabad, after it was rumoured that Hindus had deliberately placed a pig in a mosque.

Presidential election year in the United States repeats a four-year ritual, one in which the democratic process of choice is surrounded by the pressures and razzmatazz of Party politics, and by unexpected, unplanned and unfortunate episodes that can influence the electorate. Carter, as incumbent, faced as his challenger the former two-term Governor of California, Ronald Reagan – once a Hollywood film star – who at the age of sixty-nine was already beyond the usual retiring age.

Reagan made great play during the campaign on what he described as 'three grave threats to our very existence', blaming these on 'a disintegrating economy, a weakened defence, and an energy policy based on the sharing of scarcity'. For Carter, in electoral terms, the failure of the hostage rescue eclipsed the courage shown in mounting it. His energy proposals had been rejected by Congress, as a result of the opposition of Reagan's own Republican Party. In introducing them, Carter had warned of a 'crisis of our national will'. Reagan was able to take advantage of that crisis by placing it at Carter's door.

Carter's campaign was marred by his personal references to Reagan – references which even his close supporters felt were offensive, and which as the campaign drew to a close Carter promised to halt. In Chicago on October 6, he had caused considerable offence when he said: 'You'll have to determine whether or not America will be unified or, if I lose the election, whether Americans will be separated, Black from White, Jew from Christian, North from South, or rural from urban.' In another speech a few days later he said: 'If you just want to push everyone around, show them a macho United States, that's an excellent way to push us towards war.'

In his 'American Commentary' on October 10, Patrick Brogan wrote in *The Times*: 'It would be altogether in character for Mr Carter to continue hitting Mr Reagan below the belt while protesting that he is motivated solely by Christian charity.' A week later Brogan noted: 'Mr Carter told some old-fashioned, slam-bang, politics, laying into Mr Reagan, calling him "a racialist" and "a danger to the peace of the world".'

Carter was harmed not only by his personal attacks on Reagan, but by the censure passed by his own Justice Department on his brother Billy Carter, for having accepted $220,000 from the Libyan government to act as a lobbyist for it: conduct which the Senate subcommittee that reviewed the case described as 'contrary to the interests of the President and the United States'.

On November 4, the American voters went to the polls. Disappointingly for the democratic process, only 52.9 per cent of those eligible to vote actually did so, the lowest turn-out yet recorded. Reagan was successful, winning all but six States. The defeat of Carter marked the first time since the defeat of Herbert Hoover in 1932 that an elected President had been denied a second term by the electorate. In the senatorial contest, for the first time in almost thirty years the Republicans gained control of the Senate, giving Reagan an unencumbered mandate for whatever legislation he might put forward.

Human rights saw one unexpected area of improvement: China. At the beginning of the year, Christian worship, which had been fiercely repressed during the Cultural Revolution, was again permitted. In June, a Roman Catholic bishop, Deng Yiming, who had been in prison without respite for twenty-two years after refusing publicly to break with the Vatican, was released. The Protestant Churches in China were allowed to reopen their theological seminaries, and to reprint the Bible for the first time in almost a quarter of a century. Buddhist temples, smashed and desecrated during the Cultural Revolution, were repaired at the Communist government's expense, and monks and nuns allowed to worship there. In Chinese-annexed Tibet, Tibetan Buddhists were allowed to visit their holy shrines.

The religious needs of China's Muslims were also given official support, the government making financial contribution to the reopening of more than 150 mosques. The Koran was reprinted, and the Haj, the annual pilgrimage to Mecca, was allowed again. But, for the first year that it was allowed, only sixteen Chinese Muslims made the journey, out of a Muslim population variously estimated at between ten and forty million.

* * *

As two full-scale wars were being fought, in Afghanistan, and between Iran and Iraq, and as tensions mounted, particularly over Poland, between the Soviet Union and the United States, military preparedness was a feature of the global ideological divide. It was calculated by the United Nations that military expenditures worldwide in 1980 were in excess of $500,000 million. The money available for remedial and constructive effort in the regions where it was most needed was less than one per cent of that sum.

On February 13 a commission chaired by the German Social Democrat Willy Brandt published its report on *North-South: a programme for survival*. The report contained a stark statement of the dangers facing the world in the coming decades:

> At the beginning of the 1980s the world community faces much greater dangers than at any time since the Second World War. It is clear that the world economy is now functioning so badly that it damages both the immediate and the longer-run interests of all nations.
>
> The problems of poverty and hunger are becoming more serious; there are already 800 million absolute poor and their numbers are rising; shortages of grain and other foods are increasing the prospect of hunger and starvation; fast-growing populations, with another two billion people in the next two decades, will cause much greater strains on the world's food and resources.

The report went on to stress that 'the industrial capacity of the North is under-used, causing unemployment unprecedented in recent years, while the South is in urgent need of goods that the North could produce'. The current features of global economics – 'rapid inflation, erratic exchange rates, and unpredictable interventions by governments' – were seriously disrupting the trade and investment 'on which an immediate return to world prosperity depends'.

The solutions to this, the report stated, would include 'a large-scale transfer of resources to developing countries'. It would have to include an 'international energy strategy' and a 'global food programme' with increased emergency food aid and 'a system for long-term food security'. These solutions, the report warned,

> will call for readjustment on various planes of the domestic and external life of each nation; there will be some inevitable sacrifices in the short run

and these will doubtless be greater for those with more power and resources to bear them. It will not be possible for any nation or group of nations to save itself either by dominion over others or by isolation from them. On the contrary, real progress will only be made nationally if it can be assured globally. And this global approach cannot be limited to economic problems: it must also take into consideration the great complexity of human society.

That 'human society' was increasingly in dire straits. An earthquake in Algeria in October led to widespread privation and hardship for the survivors, many of whom were destitute: in the earthquake itself more than ten thousand Algerians were killed. Three months later, 400,000 Algerians were still homeless. Fleeing from the war in Afghanistan, 1,200,000 Afghans made their way across the border into Pakistan, and 400,000 to Iran: their lives, in refugee camps where water, food and shelter were the three basic needs, were a misery and a torment.

The more affluent regions of the world continued to find new areas of leisure and improvement. In Japan, the Sony company launched the 'Walkman', a small, portable, personal tape recorder and player. A new American communications satellite, *Intelsat 5*, was launched into orbit around the Earth, able to relay 12,000 telephone calls and two colour television channels at any one time. A new method of sending facsimile letters and documents through the telephone was inaugurated. This was the 'fax' – which was to become ubiquitous within a decade beyond even the Western and industrialized world.

For political reasons, not wanting to expose its citizens to Western ideas, the Soviet authorities tried to exercise stringent control over those who could have access to fax machines. At the end of each Moscow University day, the office fax machines would be dismantled, to prevent students from using them after hours. But control of communications, an essential adjunct to control of thought, was becoming harder and harder to maintain in the face of increasingly rapid and widespread technological developments.

CHAPTER THIRTY

1981

'Anarchy and disarray' . . . 'courage and moderation'

ONE NATION'S PREDICAMENT

THE TRAVAILS OF AFRICA in no way lessened in 1981, or were to lessen in the remaining years of the century. Poverty was too widespread, national indebtedness too high, tribal division too deep, regional rivalries too strong, and the clash of religions and cultures too intense to enable large areas of the continent to find sufficient calm to cultivate the soil, establish a flourishing urban and industrial base, or maintain – let alone raise – standards of living.

Within the sovereign territory of Ethiopia, the Eritrean People's Liberation Front continued to repulse repeated Ethiopian government attacks. In the Tigre province, the Tigre People's Liberation Front succeeded in attacking the provincial capital. Civil war, even when confined to two regions, accentuated the daily burden of subsistence: at almost no time during the year were fewer than four million people in need of emergency relief. Italy, which four decades earlier had been the colonial ruler, became the main national provider of aid.

Somali government troops who had been occupying the Ethiopian province of the Ogaden were almost entirely driven out by the end of the year, when another domestic insurgent group, the Somali Salvation Front, carried out a number of bomb attacks in the capital, Mogadishu. Somalia's problems were compounded as the country suffered a two-year drought. As many as 650,000 refugees from the drought-stricken areas were receiving help from the United Nations High Commissioner for Refugees, in the form of minimal shelter and basic subsistence foodstuffs. Neighbouring Djibouti took in 50,000 refugees from the fighting in the Ogaden.

In Uganda, the removal of President Amin had not ended the scourge of internecine tribal rivalry. Amin's successor, President Milton Obote, lacked the authority, or the necessary troops, to maintain inter-tribal peace. The soldiers – some ten thousand in all – were for the most part northerners. The southerners, and especially the Baganda, were subjected to what amounted at times to a reign of terror by the central government. Torture and murder were a daily occurrence. There were also killings in the north, carried out by Acholi and Langi soldiers. Many thousands of Ugandans fled across the border into Zaire, to join the Ugandan refugees of the 1979 war who had remained in Zaire rather than return and risk more bloodshed. By the end of 1981 there were as many as 200,000 Ugandan refugees in Zaire, and a further 80,000 in Sudan.

Another feature of Ugandan life was the rise in urban crime, amounting at times to near-anarchy. In the capital, Kampala, diplomats and officials involved in international aid joined forces in November to seek assurances from the government of greater personal security. There were also a number of anti-government underground movements, one of which, the Uganda National Rescue Front, was mainly made up of soldiers once loyal to Idi Amin. By the end of the year, seven thousand anti-government activists were in detention, including three thousand of Amin's former army. In one region of Uganda, Karamoja, it was not civil unrest but the curse of famine that was leading to the deaths of hundreds of people. Among those seeking to give succour was Bishop Howell Davies, the only White bishop in Uganda.

In Nigeria, more than four thousand people were killed during Muslim religious riots. In another former British colony, Gambia, the President, Sir Dawda Jawara (the country's first Prime Minister after independence, who had been knighted in 1966), was overthrown while he was in London attending, as Head of State, the wedding of Prince Charles and Lady Diana Spencer. Returning to Dakar he enlisted the help of Senegalese troops to put down the rebellion. As many as a thousand people were killed before his authority was restored. In Ghana, after two spells of power, the first for four months and the second for even less, Flight-Lieutenant Jerry Rawlings was finally ousted. He had first come to power in June 1979, at the head of the Armed Forces Revolutionary Council, pledged to wage a 'holy war against all forms of corruption'. But in September 1981 he admitted failure. 'What I regret most is not having a clearer understanding of the system,' he said.

I thought it was just a question of cleaning it up, getting rid of the rottenness. I did not realize that the return of democracy would permit those same corrupt forces to retain their hold on Ghanaian life. We have not transferred power through the ballot box, we have just transferred administration around members of the same elite. The people know this. They don't even register to vote. They know that democracy is just a veneer to impress the outside. I will admit to naivety when the ARFC was in power. I am less naive now.

*

In January the United Nations, which had overall responsibility for Namibia (until the end of the First World War it had been the German colony of South-West Africa), tried to obtain international agreement for both a cease-fire and elections as a prelude to independence. Negotiations for the timetable for the elections were accepted in principle by the two main contending parties, South Africa – which had administered the territory since the Treaty of Versailles more than sixty years earlier – and the South-West Africa People's Organization (SWAPO). But fighting was renewed that year when South African army units crossed the border to seek out and destroy SWAPO bases inside Angola: 2,500 SWAPO guerrillas were killed during these raids, at a cost of fifty-six South African servicemen. During the raid, quantities of Soviet equipment were seized, and also a Russian non-commissioned officer.

The South African government was also active militarily against the guerrilla forces of the banned African National Congress, who had set up bases in neighbouring Mozambique. On January 29 a South African commando unit, crossing more than twenty miles of Mozambique territory, reached a suburb of the capital, Maputo, and attacked the houses in which ANC members were living. Twelve ANC members were killed. The government of Mozambique, itself largely made up of members of a former guerrilla movement, Frelimo, was also confronted by its own internal guerrilla warfare, conducted by the Mozambique National Resistance Front, which carried out repeated attacks on main roads and strategic villages. Villagers were moved out of these areas and resettled in 'communal villages', where they could be both protected from the guerrillas and educated according to the government's Marxist ideology, characterized by the four-year-old Soviet-Mozambique Treaty of Friendship, and given physical support by the arrival of Soviet warships in the two main ports, Beira and Lourenço Marques.

Efforts at domestic reform were set out by President Machel when he promised, in a series of public speeches, to rid the police and armed forces of those members who carried out 'arbitrary arrests, beatings and torture'.

South Africa faced a rise in sabotage activities. In the centre of Durban, two bombs caused considerable damage. Bombs were also set off in East London and Port Elizabeth. The main targets chosen by the African National Congress were army and police posts, power stations and railway lines. Several daring rocket and grenade attacks were carried out, including one on a building in Cape Town in which pass-law records were kept. The apartheid laws remained in force, and strictly enforced, including residential segregation and the ban on marriage or sexual intercourse across the 'colour line'. Neither Black nor Coloured South Africans were represented in the parliament in Pretoria, where the laws governing their lives were passed. The Black African majority was even to be excluded from citizenship in South Africa: the only way in which it could achieve citizenship was in the quasi-independent 'bantustans', of which Transkei, Ciskei, Venda and Bophuthatswana were the largest. The pernicious nature of this policy was seen when many hundreds of Black squatters, who had come from Transkei and Ciskei in the Cape peninsula, in the hope of work in Cape Town, were declared to be 'aliens' and deported back to their enforced homelands.

In the Soviet Union, new internal laws made it possible to imprison anyone caught 'violating social order' for fifteen days without trial or right of appeal. New rules were also laid down to make it easier to detain or expel foreign citizens. Foreigners were obliged under the new regulations not only to observe Soviet laws but also to 'behave with respect' towards the 'traditions and customs' of the Soviet people. In an attempt to divert attention from the success of the Polish workers in challenging the Communist control of the workplace, 'open letter days' were established at which Party members had to answer criticisms in public. These were not on political questions, or on the question of representation (such questions were part of what the Soviet authorities termed the 'Polish disease') but on local and domestic questions, such as the frequency of bus or train services, the availability of foodstuffs or the state of the public baths.

National agitation was growing. In March there were two protest demonstrations in the Georgian capital, Tbilisi, against the 'russification' of Georgian culture, and demands that more Georgian history should be taught in the republic's schools. In October there was an incident in Estonia when, after a basketball match, several hundred young Estonians vented their anti-Russian feeling. Those dissidents in both Russia and the other republics who had been monitoring Soviet abuses of psychiatry were all but crushed: the last well-known member of the group who was still at liberty, Feliks Serebrov, was sentenced on July 21 to four years' hard labour followed by five years of internal exile. His alleged crime: 'anti-Soviet agitation'.

Towards Poland, the Soviet Union, having failed to prevent the triumph of Solidarity by a show of force on the border, maintained a continual political pressure. In January the Soviet Minister of Defence, Marshal Kulikov, visited Warsaw. The capital, and the country, was in ferment, with as many as 700,000 students and workers striking on January 24 in protest against the privileges granted to Party members, and calling for the removal of 'corrupt and inefficient' Party officials. In reaction to public pressure Stanislaw Kania, while retaining his position as Party Secretary, was replaced as Prime Minister by General Jaruzelski, the Defence Minister. Jaruzelski promised to consult with Solidarity about all new laws, but warned that 'counter-revolution' would be stopped by force. Kania and Jaruzelski were both summoned to Moscow, where they assured Brezhnev that they would act without delay to end 'anarchy and disarray' in Poland. Jaruzelski's call for a three-month moratorium on strikes was agreed to by Solidarity. Lech Walesa, having visited the Pope in Rome, came back with messages counselling 'courage and moderation'.

Despite Moscow's unease, Jaruzelski continued to make concessions to Solidarity. A new labour code was promulgated, granting the right to strike. Following a series of sit-ins by university students, the government agreed to the establishment of an Independent Association of Polish Students. But in March the militia broke into a borough council meeting in Bydgoszcz and beat up Solidarity members who were there. The strike truce was at once broken and half a million Polish workers went on strike in protest. Stanislaw Kania warned that there could be no change of the system in a 'social-democratic direction', but a few days later Jaruzelski bowed to demands that the government recognize the private peasants' trade union, Rural Solidarity.

The first issue of *Solidarity Weekly*, as promised by the August Agreement, was published on April 3. That week the Soviet Communist Party's chief ideologue, Mikhail Suslov, travelled to Warsaw and accused the Poles of 'revisionism'. Forty local Party groups established forums to discuss the future: thirty-nine of them called for internal Party democracy. One, the Katowice Forum, denounced 'creeping counter-revolution'. It was condemned for this by Kania, but applauded in Moscow. In *Pravda*, on June 12, the Polish Communist leadership was accused of making 'endless concessions to anti-Socialist forces'.

Soviet military strength was again demonstrated: first in March and April, during a three-week Warsaw Pact land exercise close to the Polish border, and then in September, with Soviet naval manoeuvres in the Baltic, with the simulated landing of 25,000 troops on the Baltic coast of Lithuania and Latvia, only 150 miles from Poland. It was the largest Soviet amphibious landing exercise since the end of the Second World War.

In September the first Solidarity Congress was held in Gdansk. It called for free parliamentary and local elections. Many members spoke angrily about the continued Soviet pressures. Jaruzelski replied that Polish troops would 'stamp out' what he denounced as growing 'anarchy and anti-Sovietism'. In October Kania resigned, and Jaruzelski became First Secretary as well as Prime Minister. Leading members of Solidarity were harassed. On December 11, Marshal Kulikov made his fifth visit to Warsaw from Moscow. Two members of the Politburo also made the journey: one of them was Yuri Andropov, the head of the KGB. At a meeting of its national commission in Gdansk on December 12, Solidarity again demanded free elections. As its demands were being broadcast, the government cut off all radio and telephone links between the commission and the outside world. At midnight on December 13, Jaruzelski imposed martial law on Poland, and established a Military Council of National Salvation, made up of twenty senior officers, with himself as chairman. Three-quarters of the Solidarity leaders were arrested and interned, as were more than 40,000 democracy activists, workers, academics, journalists, intellectuals and clergy. Strikes throughout the country were broken up by the security forces using armoured vehicles and tear gas. More than two hundred of the demonstrators were killed (the official figure was nine).

Poland, which had begun the year in a euphoric aura of reform, was under military rule. Eighteen years later, in a democratic Poland, students and teachers debated – not entirely as an academic exercise – whether Jaruzelski's action seriously retarded the advent of reform, or whether it prevented a Soviet invasion, with far greater consequences for bloodshed and repression.

More than 100,000 Soviet troops were in Afghanistan. The number of Afghan refugees who had crossed the border into Pakistan was estimated by the United Nations at 2,400,000: the largest number of refugees in any one country. The resources of the United Nations High Commissioner for Refugees could only care – at fullest stretch – for 1,700,000 of them. Within Pakistan there was considerable sympathy for the Afghan Muslims in their struggle against the Soviet Union, and calls for action to support them. But on September 22 the Pakistani President, General Mohammad Zia al-Haq, reported to his people: 'Pakistan cannot wage war against the Soviet Union. But in international forums and through mutual dialogue Pakistan has told the Soviet Union that their action in Afghanistan would never be accepted.' The Soviet Union informed Pakistan that Soviet troops would be withdrawn only after Pakistan recognized the regime of Babrak Karmal. Pakistan rejected this outright. A call on November 18 by the United Nations General Assembly for the withdrawal of foreign troops from Afghanistan was ignored by the Soviet Union. On December 19, Brezhnev celebrated his seventy-fifth birthday. Flying to Moscow from Kabul, the Afghan Prime Minister, Babrak Karmal, presented him with Afghanistan's highest award, the Sun of Freedom.

The United States under a new President, Ronald Reagan, adopted an even sterner stance towards the Soviet Union than it had done under his predecessor. Alexander Haig, the new Secretary of State, warned the Senate Foreign Relations Committee at the beginning of the year – and of Reagan's presidency – of the 'transformation of Soviet military power from a continental and largely land army to a global offensive army, fully capable of supporting an imperial policy'. Reagan himself, at his first press conference, held in the White House on January 29, said that he opposed the ratification of SALT II – which the Senate had refused to pass in the wake of the Soviet invasion of Afghanistan – because it allowed the Soviet Union to continue to build up its nuclear weapons to the accepted level for both countries. He saw no virtue in a treaty that gave the Soviet Union a green light to build more weapons, and in particular its nuclear warheads, rather than to cut back on its existing stocks. He would agree to embark on 'discussions leading to negotiations', he said, but only if the negotiations achieved an actual reduction in the number of nuclear weapons held by both sides. As to the Soviet superiority in strategic, non-nuclear forces, Reagan's Secretary of Defence, Casper Weinberger, announced that he would 'rectify' the imbalance as soon as he could.

This was a strong stance, but not necessarily one that would lead to an impasse, despite the initial Soviet reaction, trumpeted by *Pravda*, that the

Reagan administration intended to embark on an 'orgy' of military spending, and official Soviet government statements that the United States would never be allowed to achieve military superiority. In contrast to the public posturing of the two Super Powers, behind the scenes negotiations continued with a view to agreement. The Soviet leaders recognized that Reagan and his team were not bluffing, and that the United States was pursuing a policy based on military superiority. This gave a new impetus to the agreements that were reached, starting with Reagan's decision, on April 24, to lift the embargo which had been imposed on American exports of grain to the Soviet Union following the invasion of Afghanistan. Negotiations also began, in secret, for a limit to be put by both sides on the number of medium-range nuclear missiles that would be deployed in Europe.

The Reagan administration monitored Soviet military preparations with considerable care. When it became clear that more than $100,000 million a year – at least twelve per cent of the Soviet Gross National Product – was being spent on arms, that 250 intercontinental ballistic missiles had been built in the previous twelve months, and that the number of aircraft and tanks built during that same period was more than four times the previous year, Reagan spoke out publicly and uncompromisingly. It was hypocritical of the Soviet Union to talk about disarmament, he said, when it had decided to embark upon an 'arms race' with such a high level of expenditure and increase in arms production. He added that the Soviet Union could not win the arms race.

Soviet-American arms negotiations did begin, in September, and made progress. Reagan's strong stance was met, as his earlier statements had been, by extremely hostile comments in Soviet newspapers, but that stance reflected a reality that the Soviet leaders could not ignore. They could continue to try to compete in the arms race, but, even by going to the edge of economic risk, they could not win it: the United States was by far the richer country.

Talks on limiting medium- and short-range nuclear weapons opened in Geneva on November 30. The Soviet team was led by the Foreign Minister, Andrei Gromyko, the American team by Alexander Haig. The United States offered to remove all 572 of its intermediate-range nuclear missiles from Europe if the Soviet Union dismantled its medium-range nuclear missiles that were targeting Europe. He also proposed that the Strategic Arms Limitation Talks, which essentially enabled each power to maintain parity with the other even if this meant the weaker power building more, should be started under a new title, the Strategic Arms Reduction Talks (START), and pursue a genuine and substantial reduction of nuclear arms by both sides. As a sign of the seriousness of this proposal, which marked a turning point in the history of Great Power disarmament, the talks, when they began, were held in private. There was to be no public posturing.

A crisis arose, not over the nature of the disarmament plan, but over Poland. With the imposition of martial law in December, Reagan introduced sanctions against the Soviet Union for what he called its 'heavy and direct' responsibility for the crushing of Solidarity. The twice-weekly Aeroflot flights from the Soviet Union to the United States were suspended. The Soviet purchasing commission office in New York was closed. Licences for American firms to export electronic equipment, computers and high-technology materials to the Soviet Union were suspended. Talks on a long-term agreement on American export of grain to the Soviet Union were postponed. Tighter restrictions were imposed on the entry of Soviet merchant ships to United States ports.

Punitive measures were also imposed on Jaruzelski's government. Poland's airline, Lot, was barred from flying to the United States. The Polish fishing fleet was banned from using American territorial waters. In a dramatic personalization of the crisis, the Polish Ambassador in Washington, Romuald Spassowski, was granted political asylum. The 'cruel night of darkness and silence', he said, had descended on his country.

Two assassination attempts failed in 1981, but wounded their victims. One was on President Reagan in Washington on March 30, the other on Pope John Paul II on May 13, in St Peter's Square, Rome. But on October 6, in Cairo, President Sadat was assassinated while on the reviewing stand as units of the Egyptian army passed by in review. An Anglo-Catholic writer, Terence Prittie, a supporter of Israel who had welcomed the Camp David Agreements, wrote after the assassination: 'The vultures of Muslim fundamentalism, once tolerated as safer than Communism, darkened the sky, making Sadat their most illustrious victim and feeding on his failures – neglected infrastructure, imbalance between rich and poor, and suspected corruption.' His greatest crime in the eyes of his assassins was that he had made peace with Israel.

Sadat's successor, the Vice-President, Hosni Mubarak – a Soviet-trained fighter pilot and former air force commander – understood the need to focus more on solving these problems than on Egyptian-Israeli relations, as Sadat had done. Yet during the subsequent two decades Mubarak (still in power in 1999) became closely involved in the emerging Israeli-Palestinian settlement. Nor could the violent clashes between Christian Copts and Muslim fundamentalists, or attacks by Muslim fundamentalists on foreign tourists in Egypt, be eliminated. It was Sadat's efforts, particularly strong in the month before his assassination, to curb the rise of murderous extremism that led to his death. A Coptic bishop was among those killed with him on the saluting stand.

One of Mubarak's first challenges came from across the Libyan border, where Colonel Khadaffi lost no opportunity to make trouble. To meet the danger of a Libyan cross-border attack, Mubarak sent 50,000 troops to the frontier. A joint Egyptian military exercise with the United States, mounted in November not far from the border, served as a further and effective deterrent to Khadaffi. The United States also promised Egypt $3,500 million in aircraft and armoured vehicles over the coming five years.

On June 7, on the orders of the Prime Minister, Menachem Begin, Israel launched an attack on Iraq's nuclear reactor, then under construction near Baghdad. This was the first outside action against Saddam Hussein's military build-up, and came nine months after Iraq had invaded Iran, a war that was to last for eight years. Begin and his expert advisers were convinced that Iraq was about to start manufacturing an atom bomb. The uranium had been supplied, expensively, by France. During the raid the reactor was destroyed. Israel was widely condemned for the action, including by the United Nations Security Council and the British Prime Minister, Margaret Thatcher. Even inside Israel there was criticism, the two most senior Labour opposition figures, Shimon Peres and Yitzhak Rabin – whom Begin was about to challenge in an election – calling it an election ploy. President Reagan was less censorious, intimating that the attack was a legitimate defensive act. Israel's claim that Iraq had frequently expressed the aim of destroying the Jewish state altogether was not fanciful: at the time of Israel's War of Independence in 1948, Iraqi troops had fought in Jerusalem, and in the very centre of the country; in 1973 they had participated in the battles on the Golan Heights.

The raid certainly helped Begin's popularity. In the election, held on June 30, less than four weeks after the raid, his Likud Party won the largest bloc of seats and he remained Prime Minister. On the occupied West Bank, more than eighty Israeli settlements had been built, many of them adjacent to Arab towns and villages, and another forty were planned. With regard to the Camp David Agreements relating to the eventual implementation of Palestinian autonomy – which Begin had signed – a tentative step was taken by Israel when it transferred the administrative authority from military to civilian control, through the formation of sixty village leagues, and plans for a self-governing Palestinian Arab Council. But those Palestinians who rejected the Camp David concept of autonomy, and wanted full independence, murdered a number of leading 'moderates' among their own people who were calling for a working relationship with Israel within the autonomy plan. Other Palestinian Arab protests, both at the continued occupation and at the expropriation of land on which many of the settlements, and the roads leading to them, were built, led to a growing number of commercial strikes, student demonstrations, stone throwing and even fire bombs. In the Gaza Strip, the Israeli Governor of the town of Rafah, Colonel Shahaf, was killed. In retaliation for student participation in the protests, Israel closed down the main West Bank institute of higher education, Bir Zeit University.

It was announced by the United Nations in April that half of the world's ten million refugees were in Africa. Of those, eighty per cent were in the poorest regions. At a United Nations conference attended by ninety-nine States, it was agreed to pledge $560 million – exactly a thousandth of the world's arms bill that year – to help them. The Soviet Union declined to participate in the conference or to contribute to the relief, arguing that it was not responsible for the 'aftermath of colonialism'.

In the Chinese province of Szechwan, severe flooding made one and a half million people homeless. For the first time since the Chinese Communist revolution, the government of China – which was in the process of totally discrediting the excesses of the Cultural Revolution – appealed to the United Nations for help. That help was forthcoming.

The work of the United Nations High Commissioner for Refugees was recognized by the second award of a Nobel Peace Prize. Other United Nations agencies were also battling for the cause of the poor, the dispossessed and those unable to protect themselves from local or international abuses. In a unique request to the Human Rights Commission, three African nations asked for help in restoring human rights in their own countries: Equatorial Guinea, the Central African Republic and Uganda. Ten nations were condemned by the commission for persistent violations of human rights[1].

The World Health Organization faced another burden. As a matter of commercial acumen, several international corporations were promoting both

[1] The ten were South Africa, Namibia, Kampuchea, Afghanistan, Chile, El Salvador, Bolivia, Guatemala, Western Sahara and Israel (the occupied territories).

baby foods and cigarettes in a large number of developing countries. To protect babies, a voluntary code of practice was drawn up, and governments invited to ask their national corporations to subscribe to it. The aim was to ban all advertising of substitutes for breast milk, because of the dangers from the dilution of the substitute milk, or from inadequate sterilization. Only the United States, where the commercial lobby was strongest, opposed the code. The World Health Organization also tried to reduce the massive sums of money spent on advertising cigarettes in the developing world, and the sale there of cigarettes with a higher tar content than was any longer acceptable in the West, where the health dangers from smoking were becoming increasingly evident far beyond the medical profession. The pressure from tobacco manufacturers was, however, hard to counter, even by an international health organization. As the century came to an end, the main source for new and competitive tobacco sales was the mass market of China, which had only recently been exposed to Western imports on a substantial scale. The tobacco manufacturers took full advantage of the novelty of their products in China, the lack of any adequate anti-smoking campaigns, and the social use by the Chinese of cigarettes, as for example before starting a business meeting (much as Westerners might have coffee). By the last year of the century, more than two thousand Chinese were dying every day from lung cancer and other smoking-related diseases: an annual death toll of almost three-quarters of a million.

CHAPTER THIRTY-ONE

1982

The problem is that war belongs to the tragic present
as well as to the tragic past.

ARCHBISHOP ROBERT RUNCIE

FOUR WARS WERE FOUGHT during 1982: but none of them embroiled
the two Super Powers with each other, or threatened the earlier spectre of
nuclear war. In each of the four – the Russian war in Afghanistan, the
Iran-Iraq war, the Israeli invasion of Lebanon and the war between Argentina
and Britain in the Falkland Islands – lives were lost, territory was captured
and recaptured, cities were bombarded and national sentiment was inflamed.
But each of these four wars was limited to the countries by which it was
fought, and drew in no further outside forces. The experience of limited
regional wars was not new, but the survival of such wars – albeit their
vigorous, controversial and bloody survival – into the nuclear age, without
having nuclear repercussions, was a relief to millions of onlookers. Television
made looking on all the more easy and the impact more immediate.

It was more than two hundred years since Britain had acquired the Falkland Islands, and 150 years since the islands had become a British colony.
The Argentine claim to the islands – they were known to the Argentinians
as Las Malvinas – was more than a century old. In 1980 Britain had offered
the Falkland Islanders formal recognition of Argentine sovereignty linked
to a long lease-back agreement which meant that they would remain administered by Britain. The Falkland Islanders rejected any separation from Britain
or loss or diminution of British sovereignty. No serious crisis was anticipated,
and on February 9 Margaret Thatcher defended the British government's
plans to scrap the South Atlantic survey ship HMS *Endurance*, Britain's only
substantial permanent naval presence in the area.

On March 28 five Argentinian warships were sighted near South Georgia, in the South Atlantic. British policymakers took alarm, and on April 1 brought the matter before the United Nations Security Council. The Security Council called for 'restraint and the avoidance of the use of force'. Lord Carrington, the Foreign Secretary, believing that it was South Georgia (which lay 1,500 miles east of the Falklands) that was being threatened, proposed sending a special emissary to Argentina to discuss the South Georgia crisis. The Argentine government rejected his suggestion. For the British newspapers, as for Lord Carrington, the danger was thought to be to South Georgia, not the Falkland Islands, leading to a headline in *The Times*: 'Sabrerattling in the South Atlantic'.

For the public, 'sabre-rattling' was not imminent war. But on April 1 British Intelligence did receive definite information that an Argentine fleet was steaming for the Falkland Islands. On April 2, Argentinian forces landed on the islands and quickly overran them. For three hours, a company of Royal Marines who were stationed there fought to defend the capital, Port Stanley, but were outnumbered, and forced to surrender. That afternoon Margaret Thatcher announced that a British naval task force was being assembled, and that it would 'redress the situation'. At Britain's request an emergency meeting of the Security Council was called in the hope, as Mrs Thatcher expressed it, that 'even at this late hour Argentina would reconsider its rejection of diplomacy'.

The Labour opposition supported the Prime Minister, John Silkin making it clear that 'it is our duty to defend the right of the Falkland islanders to stay British'. When the House of Commons met in emergency session on April 3, the Labour Party leader, Michael Foot, reiterated this position: Britain had a moral duty, and every other kind of duty, to ensure that the right of the Falkland Islanders to keep their association with Britain was maintained. Dr David Owen, the parliamentary leader of the recently formed Social Democratic Party, told the House of Commons of how, five years earlier, when Argentina had made threatening signs, the Labour government of which he was then Foreign Secretary had sent a submarine and other naval vessels to the South Atlantic, and that this deterrent gesture had been effective. Margaret Thatcher replied acerbically that it would have been 'absurd' to send the Royal Navy every time that there was 'bellicose talk' in Buenos Aires.

On April 3 the United Nations Security Council called for the withdrawal of the armed forces of both sides. As Britain's armed forces in the islands were prisoners of war, and the Argentinians the invading and occupying power, this was disingenuous, though it did satisfy Britain's call for an Argentinian withdrawal. When Argentina refused to comply, the Ministerial Council of the European Community agreed to follow Britain's lead and to ban all imports from Argentina, as well as to suspend all financial help. There was pleasure in Britain that France had been particularly supportive of the British stance. The United States, unwilling to jeopardize its influence in South America, took a less censorious position with regard to the Argentinian action, willing at most to try to expedite a diplomatic solution.

The first warships of the British naval task force sailed from Britain on April 4. Two cruise liners were converted into troopships, the *Canberra* and the *Queen Elizabeth II* (popularly known as the *QE2*). That day it was announced that Argentine forces had also landed on South Georgia and raised the Argentine flag.

On April 7 Britain imposed a two-hundred-mile 'exclusion zone' around the Falklands, within which any Argentine naval vessel would be liable to attack. By April 16 the first ships of the task force had reached Ascension Island, just south of the Equator. Meanwhile, with British support, the United States Secretary of State, Alexander Haig, pursued a round of shuttle diplomacy between London, Buenos Aires and Washington in search of a negotiated solution, based on an Argentine withdrawal from the islands.

For more than two weeks Haig found no room for compromise between the positions of the two sides. The Argentinian leader, General Galtieri, insisted that Argentine sovereignty over the islands was not negotiable, and that Argentine troops would remain there 'alive or dead'. Mrs Thatcher insisted that all Argentine forces must withdraw before any negotiations began, and that, when negotiations did begin, the wishes of the people of the islands must be 'paramount'. Haig continued to seek some means of bridging these differences, and at the end of April Mrs Thatcher presented him with a proposal that offered a way forward to negotiations rather than battle. The Argentine forces could remain on the islands in the first instance, but must withdraw at least 150 miles from the capital. The internal administration of the islands would then be put under a commissioner appointed by the United Nations Secretary-General. Negotiations on the future of the islands could then begin 'without prejudice to the rights, claims and positions of the parties and without prejudgment of the outcome'.

The Argentine government's response was not helpful to Haig. Argentinian forces would not withdraw 150 miles but to their 'normal bases and areas of operation'. At the same time, Argentine citizens should be given the same rights as British nationals to enter the islands and to live and work there. Argentina also wanted South Georgia and the Sandwich Islands seven hundred miles east of South Georgia to be included in the negotiations on future sovereignty. These conditions were unacceptable to Mrs Thatcher, whose own compromise proposals greatly strengthened Britain's position internationally. Clearly, in default of negotiations, Britain's naval task force – which was drawing ever closer to the islands – would be in a position to land a substantial force to try to recapture them. On April 24 the European Community agreed to the 'indefinite' continuation of sanctions against Argentina, despite the defection of Italy and the Irish Republic from the unanimity. On April 30 the United States agreed to impose limited military and economic sanctions. Behind the scenes, Reagan and Haig were ensuring that Britain received both military supplies and crucial military and naval Intelligence information.

On April 22 the British naval task force moved into Falkland Islands waters. Three days later a helicopter-borne detachment of Royal Marines landed on South Georgia, where a far larger Argentine force surrendered without fighting. On May 1, British bombers struck for the first time at the Port Stanley airfield. Then, on May 2, came an episode that highlighted the Falklands conflict worldwide: a British submarine, HMS *Conqueror*, torpedoed the Argentine cruiser *General Belgrano*, and 368 Argentine sailors were killed. This ship, then the *Phoenix*, was the last surviving warship of the American fleet attacked by the Japanese at Pearl Harbor in 1941. After the war she had been sold by the United States to Argentina.

There was much international criticism of Britain when it was learned that the *General Belgrano* had been thirty miles outside the naval exclusion zone when she was sunk. The British government defended its action by pointing out that the ship was approaching the British naval task force and was only four or five hours away from it at their combined speeds. Disturbed that the Argentine warship had been sunk outside the exclusion zone, the West German government expressed its 'consternation' at the heavy loss of life and called for a ceasefire.

The Argentinians reacted with martial vigour. On May 4 an Argentine warplane launched an Exocet air-to-sea missile at the British destroyer *Sheffield*. Twenty men on board were killed. Both the warplane and the missile had been sold to Argentine by France, generating a spate of anti-French feeling in Britain. The task force continued on its way, until the moment came when a landing on the Falkland Islands was possible. But on May 9 the leader of the Labour Party, Michael Foot, warned publicly that any frontal assault on the Falklands would be 'a monstrous gamble'.

The assault that did take place was planned to be as tactically effective as possible, making use of the element of surprise and the large number of possible landing places. San Carlos Bay was the area chosen for the initial landings. The first troops ashore were special forces, who made a number of clandestine reconnaissance missions. Then, on May 21, British troops landed at San Carlos Bay. The Argentinian air force struck at the task force ships involved in the landing, sinking three of them – two of them by Exocet missiles. But Argentine losses were heavy: thirty warplanes in the first four days of the landings.

On May 28, British paratroopers captured Darwin and Goose Green. During the attack, seventeen men were killed, including the commanding officer, Colonel H. Jones. More than a hundred Argentine soldiers were killed, and 1,400 taken prisoner. With pride the British Ministry of Defence described the action as 'one of the most brilliant and courageous since World War II'. There was then a ten-day lull in the fighting, as British reinforcements were assembled for the assault on the capital, Port Stanley. During that period, Pope John Paul II visited Britain – a visit planned many months earlier. Although Britain was at war with the largely Roman Catholic Argentina, it was feared that had he postponed his visit it would have been seen as a rebuke for the non-Catholic British, and in some way impugned the loyalty of British Catholics. In his speeches the Pope avoided all reference to the conflict then taking place in the South Atlantic. But speaking in Coventry Cathedral – next to the carefully preserved ruins of the earlier cathedral destroyed in the Blitz in 1940 – he pleaded that war should belong to the 'tragic past', not be part of the present. 'All people must deliberately and resolutely devote themselves to the pursuit of peace,' he said.

On June 2, while British troops in the Falkland Islands were still preparing for their attack on Port Stanley, Mrs Thatcher made a television broadcast in which she stated that she could see no future role for Argentina in the Falkland Islands 'in any thing relating to sovereignty'. She hoped the Argentinian forces on the islands would withdraw without further fighting: many lives would thereby be saved, but she did not 'flinch' from battle. In response, General Galtieri told The Times that Argentina would fight on in the Falklands whatever the outcome of the battle for Port Stanley.

On June 8 a British landing at Bluff Cove in an attempt to shorten the march to Port Stanley was challenged by Argentinian aircraft before the landing force could set up its anti-aircraft defences, and fifty British soldiers were killed. But the attack on Port Stanley continued, and on June 14, after most of the high ground around the capital was in British hands, the Argentine forces surrendered. 'Arrangements are in hand,' the commander of the British land forces, Major-General Jeremy Moore, signalled to London, 'to assemble the men to return to Argentina, to gather in their arms and equipment, and to mark and make safe their munitions. The Falkland Islands are once more under the government desired by their inhabitants. God save the Queen.'

Ten thousand Argentinian soldiers had been taken prisoner of war. They were repatriated as soon as the Argentine government, following the resignation of President Galtieri, whose regime had been autocratic in the extreme, formally acknowledged – as Galtieri had refused to do – that hostilities had ended. It was not until July 11 that this was done; on the following day the British government declared an end to hostilities. Among the weaponry captured by the British were large quantities of French-built Exocet missiles and Soviet-made SAM anti-aircraft missiles, and also early-warning radar systems and night-fighting equipment superior to that in use in the British army. The returning British soldiers were welcomed as heroes. At the service of thanksgiving held in St Paul's Cathedral on July 26, prayers were said both for the 255 British and for the 652 Argentine dead.

The Archbishop of Canterbury, Dr Robert Runcie – who had himself served with the Scots Guards in the Armoured Division in 1944–5, when he had won the Military Cross – spoke in his sermon of how 'people are mourning on both sides of this conflict. In our prayers we shall quite rightly remember those who are bereaved in our own country and the relations of the young Argentinian soldiers who were killed. Common sorrow should do something to reunite those who were engaged in this struggle. A shared anguish can be a bridge of reconciliation. Our neighbours are indeed like us.'

Dr Runcie also spoke of the wider aspects of war. The losses in the Falklands, he said, 'remind us that we possess the terrifying power of destruction', and he continued:

War has always been detestable, but since 1945 we have lived with the capacity to destroy the whole of humankind. It is impossible to be a Christian and not to long for peace. 'Blessed are the peace-makers for they shall be called the Sons of God.' This was one of the themes to which the

Pope repeatedly returned during his visit to this country. His speech in Coventry was particularly memorable when he said 'war should belong to the tragic past, to history. It should find no place on humanity's agenda for the future.'

I do not believe that there would be many people, if any, in this cathedral who would not say amen to that. War is a sign of human failure and everything we say and do in this service must be in that context.

'The problem is', Runcie continued, 'that war belongs to the tragic present as well as to the tragic past,' and he went on to refer to Norman Angell's 'noble book' *The Great Illusion*, first published in 1909, in which 'the irrational character of war in a modern world was precisely described. The thesis is that in a world of economic interdependence you cannot injure another State without damaging your own interests. We flourish and become prosperous, not by raiding and pauperizing our neighbours, but by building them up as ever better markets for our manufactures.' Runcie added:

Yet war, demonstrably irrational and intolerable, has left a terrible mark on this century. It has claimed tens of millions of victims and even now occupies some of the best talents and resources of the nations. The great nations continue to channel their energies into perfecting weapons of destruction and very little is done to halt the international trade in arms, which contributes so much to the insecurity of the world.

In the most heavily armed area, the Middle East, every day seems to bring fresh bad news of man's willingness to resort to the irrational and the intolerable in pursuit of his territorial and ideological ambitions.

Norman Angell was writing 'at the end of a period of relative peace. We cannot be even as sanguine about the human future as he was. . . . This is a dangerous world where evil is at work nourishing the mindless brutality which killed and maimed so many in this city last week. Sometimes with the greatest reluctance force is necessary to hold back the chaos which injustice and the irrational element in man threaten to make of the world. But having said that all is not lost and there is hope.'

Runcie's reference to the killings in London 'last week' was to two simultaneous Irish Republican Army bomb attacks on July 20. One was literally under the horses' feet of a group of ceremonial Horse Guards who were riding from their barracks to Whitehall; the other was under a bandstand where an army band was playing. Eleven soldiers were killed in the two explosions. The public outrage at these killings – which Margaret Thatcher described as 'the product of evil and depraved minds' – did not bring an end to the IRA atrocities. When, in December, a bomb was detonated in a public house at Ballykelly in Northern Ireland, eleven British soldiers and five civilians were killed.

In his sermon at St Paul's, Runcie had referred to the Middle East, where, he said, 'every day seems to bring fresh bad news'. On June 3 the Israeli Ambassador in London, Shlomo Argov, had been gravely injured by a Palestinian gunman – not a PLO member but a member of the smaller, more extreme Iraqi-supported Palestine National Liberation Movement. That same week, PLO units in southern Lebanon, under Yasser Arafat's command, renewed their earlier shelling of towns and villages in northern Israel. No Israelis were killed, but there was considerable public unease inside Israel at the vulnerability of the northern settlements.

On June 6 the Prime Minister, Menachem Begin, ordered Israeli troops to advance into southern Lebanon, and to establish a military buffer zone twenty-five miles deep. His Minister of Defence, Ariel Sharon, had a more ambitious plan, the advance of Israeli forces as far as Beirut, in an attempt to drive the PLO out of Lebanon altogether. It was Sharon's plan that was carried out. By June 9 the Israeli forces were only two miles south of Beirut airport, and had reached the Beirut–Damascus highway, where they were in battle with Syrian army units. There were also violent clashes with the Syrians whose troops were occupying the eastern Beka'a Valley region of Lebanon. On June 9 the Israeli air force destroyed seventeen of the nineteen Soviet-made SAM anti-aircraft missile batteries that Syria had installed in the Beka'a; and in a two-day aerial battle Israeli warplanes, no longer threatened by the SAM missile batteries, shot down more than fifty Syrian MiG fighter planes, also part of the Soviet war supplies sold to Syria.

On June 11 Israel accepted a United Nations call for a ceasefire. But within three days Israeli troops moved forward again, linking up with the Falangist forces in the east of Beirut, and effectively surrounding the PLO controlled areas in the west of the city. On June 15, Peace Now, an Israeli grass-roots movement that had been founded a month earlier by six senior reserve officers protesting against the ill-treatment of Palestinians in the occupied territories, put an advertisement in the Israeli newspapers. It was an outspoken call for peace, and for a move towards recognizing the rights of the Palestinians. The advertisement read:

In this war, the Israeli Army is proving once again that Israel is powerful and self-confident. In this war, we are losing brothers, sons and friends. In this war, thousands are being uprooted from their homes, and towns are being destroyed. Thousands of civilians are getting killed.

What are we getting killed for? What are we killing for? Has there been a national consensus for going into this war? Has there been an immediate threat to Israel's existence? Will it get us out of the cycle of violence, suffering and hatred?

The Peace Now advertisement ended: 'We call upon the Government of Israel: Stop! Now is the time to invite the Palestinian people to join in negotiations for peace. Now is the time for a comprehensive peace based on mutual recognition.'

On June 14, five days after this strong protest against the war in Lebanon, Israel began a sustained air and artillery bombardment of West Beirut. More than four hundred Israeli tanks, firing into the built-up area from positions all around it, and a thousand artillery pieces, many of them firing from the high ground to the east, took part in the bombardment. More than five hundred buildings were reduced to ruins. The bombardment was still being carried out on June 26 when Dr Runcie made his reference to the 'fresh bad news' arriving daily from the Middle East.

On July 3, Peace Now organized a demonstration in Tel Aviv against the war in Lebanon: 100,000 Israelis took part. 'These six weeks', wrote a former Foreign Minister, Abba Eban, in the mass circulation *Ma'ariv* newspaper, 'have been a dark age in the moral history of the Jewish people.' But a counter-demonstration organized by supporters of the war was estimated to have drawn 200,000 people, many of them brought in by bus from distant towns throughout the country.

The Israeli bombardment of PLO positions in West Beirut continued. A hospital was among the buildings hit, the scenes of destruction within its wards being filmed and shown on television screens worldwide. On July 23, after a month of siege, the Israeli army, assisted by Israeli naval units offshore, intensified the bombardment. Hundreds of PLO fighters were killed. On August 1, Sharon ordered fourteen hours of non-stop air, naval and land bombardment. Two days later Israeli troops entered south-east Beirut and sought to engage the PLO forces in direct combat. On August 4 the Burj al-Barajneh Palestinian refugee camp, in which the PLO forces were entrenched, was completely encircled. For twenty hours the Israeli infantrymen fought without respite. But they were able to advance only a quarter of a mile into the camp. That day Israeli troops took control of Beirut airport.

The frustration of the Israeli High Command at being unable to flush out the PLO from Beirut was considerable. On August 11 the Israeli air force began a two-day aerial bombardment. Even while the Israeli bombardment continued, an American envoy, Philip Habib, was trying to effect a ceasefire and settlement. On August 12, following intensive negotiations with Habib, the PLO agreed to leave the city. A multinational force, including 1,800 American marines, was assembled to protect the PLO as it prepared to leave Beirut for Tunis. Its departure was to be by sea. Begin, in an act of chivalry, agreed to let the PLO leave carrying its side arms. On August 30, as Yasser Arafat prepared to leave the city an Israeli sniper had him in his sights. But the Israeli government had specifically ordered that he was not to be killed. That day Arafat left Beirut, and by September 4 the PLO was gone.

On September 1, as the PLO evacuation of Beirut was in progress, Bashir Jemayel, the Christian Maronite President-elect of Lebanon, flew to Nahariya on the Israeli coast, where Begin urged him to sign a peace treaty with Israel. He refused to do so, proposing instead a more limited non-aggression pact. When Sharon, who was also at the meeting, told Jemayel that as Israel had Lebanon in its grasp he would be wise to agree to Begin's request, Jemayal was infuriated, holding out his arms and crying out, 'Put the handcuffs on. I am not your vassal.'

Later that day the 'Reagan Plan' was announced by Washington. It included the principle of 'self-government for the Palestinians of the West Bank and Gaza in association with Jordan'. This new plan was presented by the Americans as the 'next step' in the Camp David peace process. The Begin government was resolved, however, not to relinquish Israeli control of the West Bank (or, in its nomenclature, Judaea and Samaria) and dismissed the American initiative.

Following the departure of the last PLO troops from Beirut, the Syrian troops in the city also left. All was set for Israel's Lebanese ally, the Christian Falange, to take control. But on September 14 Bashir Jemayel was assassinated. His Christian Maronite followers were incensed against the Palestinian Muslims, who claimed responsibility for the assassination, and were determined to take revenge. The Israeli troops were in a situation, far from their own borders, which they could not control. On September 15 they occupied West Beirut 'in order', Begin explained, 'to protect the Muslims from the vengeance of the Falangists'.

The main concentration of Palestinian Muslims was in the Sabra and Chatila refugee camps. Israeli forces sealed off the two camps from the outside world: 'hermetically sealed' was how the Israeli general Rafael Eitan later described it. The Israelis believed that the Falangist soldiers would seek out the Palestinian fighters, not civilians. To help them in this task, Israeli military searchlights illuminated the camps at night. On September 17, Falangist forces entered the two camps and massacred the inhabitants, fighters and civilians alike. When Sabra and Chatila were opened, and newspaper reporters from around the world entered, the bodies (many of them mutilated) of 2,300 Palestinian men, women and children were found. Several hundred PLO fighters had also been killed, as well as twenty-one Iranian Muslims, seven Syrians, three Pakistanis and two Algerians who had thrown in their lot with the PLO: but the military deaths paled in horror beside the civilian ones.

The massacre of Sabra and Chatila shocked the world, and shocked many in Israel, although no Israeli troops were involved in the killings. The Israeli soldiers had expected the Christian Falangists to undertake the mission of clearing out suspected nests of Palestinian fighters. What the Christian soldiers did followed the earlier pattern of the Lebanese civil war, the wreaking of vengeance on the civilian population – vengeance, in this case, in the immediate aftermath of the assassination of Bashir Jemayel.

Those Israelis who had opposed the invasion of Lebanon from its first day, or had been against its extension beyond the first twenty-five miles – the originally declared objective – were distressed that the massacre had not been foreseen and forestalled by the senior Israeli military authorities in the area. On September 25 there was a mass demonstration in Tel Aviv in which 400,000 people – more than ten per cent of the total Israeli population – participated. It was the largest ever demonstration held in Israel. 'No such explosion of public outrage had ever occurred in Israel's history,' wrote the American-Jewish historian Howard M. Sachar fourteen years later.

The cost of the war in Lebanon had been high on all sides, military and civilian alike. The final death toll has been estimated at more than 6,000 PLO troops and Palestinian civilians, 600 Syrian troops, 468 Lebanese civilians and 368 Israeli soldiers. On September 19, Israeli troops began their withdrawal from Beirut. Eventually they fell back to a narrow, three- to four-mile-deep zone of occupation in southern Lebanon, which was still occupied by Israel seventeen years later. In this zone continual battles were fought in the years ahead with some five thousand Iranian-supported Hizbullah – the Party of God – fighters. Hundreds of soldiers were killed on both sides.[1]

The end of the Lebanon war did not end Middle East acts of terror. On November 4 an attack carried out by Shi'ite Muslim suicide bombers on the Israeli military headquarters in the southern Lebanese port city of Sidon killed thirty-six Israelis. On December 6 a bomb exploded in a bus in Jerusalem, killing six Israelis, including two children. The PLO claimed responsibility.

Yasser Arafat made Tunis his headquarters. But an estimated 10,000 PLO supporters were still in southern Lebanon, and more than 40,000 Syrian troops in the Beka'a Valley. Another Middle East battle was over, but the war was not yet ended. Nor was the rest of the region free from conflict. In Syria, Muslim opposition to the secular government of Hafez al-Asad led to rioting and civil war. In February the Islamic Front seized control of the town of Hama. The towns of Homs and Aleppo were likewise seething with Islamic fervour. Asad ordered his troops to attack the Muslim strongholds, using tanks, artillery and the most highly trained of his troops. Against Hama, warplanes were also used, and the centre of the town destroyed, including the historic mosque. At least ten thousand of the insurgents were killed before Asad regained control.

The hopes of greater liberalism in Poland had been set back severely when General Jaruzelski had declared martial law at the end of 1981. The year 1982 saw little reason to revive those hopes. On October 9, Solidarity was banned. Two days later, to show its disapproval, the United States imposed trade sanctions on Poland. Inside Poland, massive demonstrations were held on behalf of Solidarity. Twenty demonstrators were killed in clashes with the security forces. More than ten thousand Solidarity supporters were imprisoned, including the movement's leader, Lech Walesa. Jaruzelski went to Moscow to report to Brezhnev what he had done. A Polish joke had the ailing Brezhnev telling Jaruzelski that Walesa would be released 'over my dead body'. Brezhnev died on November 10. Walesa was released two days later.

Brezhnev had been President of the Soviet Union since 1960, and head

---

[1] Three Israeli soldiers – nineteen-year-olds – were killed in the zone during the week in November 1998 when I was writing this section.

of the Communist Party (for the second time) since 1963; he had been ill for a long time. His successor, Yuri Andropov, had been the head of the KGB for the previous fifteen years. He permitted no relaxation of the Party's control of Soviet life. Sakharov, Russia's best-known dissident, was forced to remain in internal exile far from Moscow. The number of Jews being allowed to emigrate fell to its lowest figure since the death of Stalin thirty years earlier. More Jewish activists were arrested and imprisoned, or threatened with arrest if they did not halt their activities. The Soviet war against the Afghan Muslim guerrillas – the mujaheddin – intensified. When a Soviet military vehicle broke down in the Salang tunnel in November, the Soviet authorities panicked, and, believing (wrongly) that the vehicle had been attacked by guerrillas, sealed the tunnel. As many as a thousand Afghans and Soviet soldiers who were in the tunnel when it was sealed died from the poisonous fumes.

In the war between Iran and Iraq, tens of thousand of soldiers were killed on both sides, but a sustained Iranian attempt to capture the port of Basra, launched on July 14, was unsuccessful. Heavy loss of life seemed no obstacle, however, to a continuation of a struggle that neither side seemed able to win. Ayatollah Khomeini was determined to establish an Islamic republic in all or most of Iraq, and to link it with Iran in a formidable fundamentalist federation. But he also had to deal with agitation inside Iran, at the beginning of the year by the Marxist-oriented Mujaheddin-i Khalq guerrilla group, whose leader was tracked down and killed in February, and throughout the year by the Kurds of western Iran, against whom he launched two military expeditions, but without success. The Kurdish soldiers retreated into the mountains and fought on.

It was not so much the military confrontations of the year, serious though these were, but economic problems, that caused the greatest concern globally. Anxiety among the Western and wealthy nations at Third World indebtedness came to a climax in August, when Mexico defaulted on a loan payment: the interest due on an accumulated short-term foreign debt of $80,000 million. Suddenly the lending nations were confronted by the possibility of widespread defaulting, not only by Mexico, but by four other Latin American countries, Brazil, Argentina, Bolivia and Ecuador, who let it be known that they too would be unable to meet the payments due on their debts – that is to say, the payment of the interest due on what they had borrowed, for the debt itself would remain.

The International Monetary Fund was willing to step in and to reschedule the defaulted debts, but only if the debtor countries involved would agree to strict austerity measures. From the perspective of the poor nations, the wealthy nations were seeking to keep them poor. But the wealthy nations were also suffering from economic recession. In Britain, unemployment had reached the highest figure for more than thirty-five years: three million people were without work. In the United States that figure was twelve million, more than ten per cent of the work force.

The international community had not turned its back on the Third World. The United Nations Educational, Social and Cultural Organization (UNESCO) fixed the year 2000 as the target for the 'eradication' of illiteracy in Africa, and set aside the funds with which it believed this was possible. In the event it proved impossible. In Niger, for example, the illiteracy rate stood at more than eighty-six per cent in 1998, and almost nowhere in Africa had it fallen below fifty per cent. But at the time of the decision hopes were high. What was not understood was the deleterious impact of utter poverty, extreme hunger, crippling civil war and bottomless corruption in many parts of the African continent.

In the West, despite the ebb and flow of economic indicators – dominated by fluctuations in unemployment and inflation – commercialism and the profit motive flourished, as did the expansion of consumerism. Individual enterprise became more highly prized than communal activity. Millionaires gained great esteem, and often political influence as well. In Britain, 'Thatcherism' became synonymous with successful self-advancement, with running ahead of the rat race. With the vaunting of private enterprise came the rapid expansion of trade and profit. On October 7 the New York Stock Exchange announced a record day's trading: more than 147 million shares had changed hands during the day. On November 23, as part of President Reagan's deregulation policy, restrictions on the content and length of television advertisements were removed. That year, as technological advances brought popular culture to a larger segment of the population in the West than ever before, the first Compact Disc (CD) players went on sale.

CHAPTER THIRTY-TWO

1983

> . . . pursue the solution of outstanding problems through
> peaceful means.
>
> MADRID CONCLUDING DOCUMENT

O N 8 MARCH 1983 President Reagan spoke in Orlando, Florida, to the
American Association of Evangelicals. According to *The Times* it was 'one of
the toughest speeches of his presidency'. In it he told the assembled clergymen that 'simple-minded appeasement or wishful thinking about our adversaries is folly'. He went on to warn them to beware 'the temptations of
blithely declaring yourselves above it all and label both sides equally at fault,
to ignore the facts of history and the aggressive impulses of an evil empire'.
The Soviet Union, he added, was 'the focus of evil in the modern world'.

Reagan spoke in this way on the day after he had consulted with Max
Kampelman, the chief United States delegate at the Madrid Conference. On
his return to Madrid, on the day of Reagan's speech, Kampelman added his
own voice of warning – not unlike George Kennan had done in his secret
despatch to Truman from the United States Embassy in Moscow shortly
before Churchill's 'Iron Curtain' speech in 1946. In his remarks, Kampelman
pointed out that those fifty-one Helsinki Monitors who were 'not in Soviet
prisons, labour camps, psychiatric hospitals or in internal exile' had raised
the issue of the 'integrity' of the Helsinki process – the agreed linking of
security and human rights. Kampelman then gave details of what he called
Soviet 'disdain' for the 1975 Helsinki Final Act. 'Only last week,' he said,
'two Soviet human rights activists were given twelve-year sentences for
offences that included seeking to organize a non-official trade union, and
writing poetry which displeased the Soviet authorities.' Since the Madrid
meetings had begun, Kampelman added, five hundred Soviet citizens had
been arrested and convicted for political and religious reasons. 'It is no

wonder', he said, 'that large segments among our people question the wisdom and utility of new promises and new agreements when the old ones continue to be ignored.'

On the day after Reagan's 'evil empire' speech and Kampelman's warning, the British government formally leased to the United States the Indian Ocean island of Diego Garcia, as a nuclear bomber and warship base, through which American bombers could fly on their way to the borders of Soviet Central Asia, and if necessary beyond.[1]

On March 23, fifteen days after his 'evil empire' speech, Reagan spoke on television to the American people. He illustrated his remarks with graphs showing the dimensions of the Soviet build-up, and with aerial photographs which had been classified as secret until a few days earlier. These showed Soviet fighter aircraft and a Soviet Intelligence headquarters in Cuba, Soviet aircraft in Nicaragua, and the building of an airfield with a ten-thousand-foot runway in Grenada.

Reagan then spoke of the future defence of the United States by means of laser weaponry in space. This 'Star Wars address', as it was called, while appearing to be bellicose and war-enhancing, gave the Soviet leaders cause to hesitate. Their expensive, much vaunted nuclear weaponry would, if this space-laser technology could be developed, become obsolete and useless. Yet the Soviet Union did not have the technology or the economic resources to challenge the United States in this innovative and expensive sphere.

More than any single American initiative, 'Star Wars' – although it would clearly take up to a decade to develop – spelt the end of the Soviet-American balance of power, and would tilt it significantly to the American side. As a sign of its seriousness, the American Department of Defense, headed by Caspar Weinberger, announced that prototype laser weapons had already been tested against both incoming missiles and 'attacking' unmanned aircraft. Among those who understood the meaning of Star Wars, and the inevitable Soviet fall from Super Power equality as a result of it, was the recently appointed Communist Party Secretary responsible for Agriculture, Mikhail Gorbachev, a relatively young (fifty-two-year-old) political leader who was being spoken of in Moscow that year as a possible successor to the clearly ailing Andropov. Gorbachev had come to the attention of Western observers

---

[1] Following the independence of Mauritius (of which Diego Garcia had been a part) in 1968, the 1,800 islanders had been sent away to Mauritius, more than a thousand miles to the south-west, and Diego Garcia became a British base.

in March, when he encouraged small groups of peasants to take a more responsible attitude towards agricultural production by increasing their material self-interest through group contracts which gave them a direct stake in the profits of their collective labour. Under the contracts, they would be paid by results. Not pre-selected and rigidly enforced norms, but production targets profitable to the individual – through his group contract – would provide the incentive which collectivization, the Stalinist panacea so long adhered to, had failed to provide.

On September 1 a South Korean civil airliner, a Boeing 747, was shot down by a Soviet military aircraft. It had strayed into Soviet airspace, above the strategically sensitive Sakhalin Island. All 269 people on board were killed, among them an American Congressman, Lawrence McDonald, from Georgia. The plane had been tracked for more than two and a half hours before being shot down by an air-to-air missile. While Andropov remained silent, President Reagan demanded a full explanation for 'this appalling and wanton deed'. Margaret Thatcher denounced the shooting as 'an atrocity against humanity'. Other governments were more hesitant in their condemnation, so much so that Margaret Thatcher said she found it 'inexplicable that we could not get a clearer condemnation by Europe and clearer action in the wider NATO sphere'. Direct commercial flights from Britain to Moscow were suspended, and in a speech in Washington on September 29 she warned that the West was 'confronted by a power of great military strength, which has consistently used force against its neighbours, which wields the threat of force as a weapon of policy, and which is bent on subverting and destroying the confidence and stability of the Western world'.

Despite the shooting down of the airliner, neither President Reagan nor Margaret Thatcher was willing to call a halt to the strategic arms reduction talks that had begun in the spring as a result of an offer by Andropov to find a way to break the deadlock caused by the Soviet invasion of Afghanistan two years earlier. The talks, which were taking place in Geneva, continued, as did the implementation of the most recent Soviet-American grain agreement. Even a suggestion by some Congressmen that the United States reimpose its earlier ban on the sale of pipeline equipment to the Soviet Union was turned down by the administration. The ban had only been lifted in August.

One cause of American hesitation in making too strong a response was the Soviet claim, which the United States soon admitted was true, that an American spy plane, an RC 135, had been in the area earlier. The spy plane had, however, already returned to its base in Alaska when the South Korean airliner was shot down.

Speaking in New York on September 26, at the United Nations General Assembly, Reagan set out in public some of the strategic arms reduction proposals that the United States had made earlier in the year to the Soviet Union, at the talks in Geneva. The principal American proposal was that if the Soviet Union would agree to an equal number of Soviet and American nuclear warheads worldwide, and would reduce the number of its existing land-based medium-range nuclear weapons, then for its part the United States, while retaining the right to deploy its nuclear warheads anywhere in the world, would not in fact redeploy in Europe the nuclear warheads to which, under the equality scheme, it was entitled globally. Reagan also agreed, in his speech of September 26, to an earlier Soviet proposal that the NATO and Warsaw Pact intermediate-range bomber forces should be included in the calculations of the arms reduction talks.

The arms reduction talks continued. The main Soviet counter-proposal was that NATO cancel its plans to deploy the Pershing and Cruise missiles in Europe. Were NATO to do so, Andropov announced, the Soviet Union would reduce its number of SS-20 missiles in Europe by one hundred, to 140. This the United States rejected on the ground that it would leave the Soviet Union with a monopoly of intermediate-range nuclear missiles in Europe. The United States then proposed that both sides should have an equal number of intermediate-range missile warheads in Europe. The Soviet Union rejected this because it would involve the United States introducing Pershing and Cruise missiles to Europe. On November 14, the day of the Soviet rejection, the first American Cruise missiles in Europe arrived at the United States air base at Greenham Common, in southern England. A week later the first Pershing missiles reached American air bases in West Germany. When the Strategic Arms Reduction Talks adjourned in December, the Soviet Union refused to agree to a date when they would be resumed.

The Cold War seemed to have intensified, and yet the imperative for talks remained. Neither side could sustain for much longer the burden of defence spending, or the public unease at the danger of an accidental – or even a deliberate – nuclear confrontation.

In October the focus of international attention turned briefly to the Caribbean island of Grenada, a former British colony which since 1974 had been an independent State within the Commonwealth, a country with a population of little more than 80,000 people. In 1979 the elected government had been overthrown by the New Jewel Movement, and a People's Revolutionary Government set up. Internal disagreements between the members of the government led, on October 16, to the murder of the Prime Minister, Maurice Bishop, and the establishment of a revolutionary Military Council.

Six Caribbean countries, members of the Organization of Eastern Caribbean States (OECS), of which Grenada was also a member, protested at the overthrow of Bishop's government and its replacement by a military council.[1] On October 23, meeting in Trinidad, they agreed to impose sanctions on Grenada. On October 21 the OECS appealed to President Reagan to intervene. Reagan had already ordered a United States naval flotilla which had just set off across the Atlantic on its way to Beirut to be diverted to the Caribbean. There were rumours of an imminent United States invasion of Grenada. But on October 24 the British Foreign Secretary, Geoffrey Howe, assured the House of Commons that there was no reason to believe that such an invasion would take place.

In the early hours of October 25, British Intelligence reported that an American invasion of Grenada was imminent. Margaret Thatcher telephoned Reagan and urged him not to launch an attack. The invasion went ahead nevertheless. Thatcher was unyielding in her opposition to it. 'If you are going to announce a new law,' she said five days later, 'that wherever Communism reigns against the will of the people the United States shall enter, then we are going to have terrible war in the world.'

The six Caribbean countries which had appealed to the United States for action supported the landings, and sent token troop or police forces. Reagan insisted that the lives of as many as a thousand American citizens on the island were at risk, including those of six hundred American medical students. The main landings, of what was codenamed Operation Urgent Fury, were carried out by 1,900 American marines and army rangers. The 636 Cubans who had been building a new airport, under the aegis of a British construction firm, put up no resistance. Forty-three Cuban soldiers who were on the island did put up resistance at the airport, but were quickly overrun. The airport was being designed as a purely tourist one, with a short, nine-thousand-foot, runway.

A further seventy Cuban soldiers fought with the Grenadan soldiers in

---

[1] The six countries – Barbados, Jamaica, Dominica, Antigua, St Lucia and St Vincent – were all members of the Commonwealth.

the hills. When the fighting ended on October 27, eighteen American troops had been killed, forty-five Grenadians and twenty-five Cubans. The United Nations Security Council sought to condemn the invasion, but the United States exercised its veto. The *Washington Post* saw the Communist presence in Nicaragua as a reason for the Grenada action, but was nevertheless sceptical. 'Some Americans will rejoice', it wrote, 'that the United States has finally recaptured a seemingly lost capacity for great-power military response, that it has flashed a warning signal to Nicaragua and other sources of torment, but this is hardly adequate reason to invade a small country.' The *New York Times* was even more critical. Assuming, it wrote, that there were Cuban and even Soviet designs on the small island, Reagan 'will have denied the Russians and Cubans another Caribbean airfield, an auxiliary station for small-arms transfers and a modest source of new recruits for international mischief'. But at what cost, the *New York Times* went on to ask, and then answered its own question with the warning sentence: 'Simply put, the cost is loss of the high moral ground: a reverberating demonstration to the world that the United States has no more respect for laws and borders, for the codes of civilization, than the Soviet Union.'

This severe verdict was later reversed, after a fact-finding Congressional team reported that, as Reagan had claimed, American lives really had been at risk – although no attempt had been made by the military rulers to take the medical students hostage. Congress also supported a series of requests from Reagan to help other Central American governments in their struggle to maintain a semblance of democracy, or at least a robust hostility to Marxist doctrines. Honduras, Costa Rica, Belize and El Salvador each received extra aid for development projects. In addition to this economic aid, El Salvador was given $110 million to help fight left-wing Salvadoran guerrillas. In the three previous years 30,000 Salvadoran soldiers, guerrillas and civilians had been killed. More than five thousand civilians had been murdered in 1982 alone. But Reagan had to assure Congress that he would not send any American soldiers there 'nor', as he promised, 'Americanize the war with a lot of United States combat advisers'. The expanding of the war in Vietnam a decade and a half earlier was still a vivid nightmare in the eyes of many of the American legislators.

United States troops did go, as allies, to Honduras, in a combined naval and army exercise in which 5,600 troops were landed. 'The gringos are here because we called them in,' was the comment of the Honduran Chief of Staff. They were also there because an American-backed Nicaraguan exile army, the Nicaraguan Democratic Force, was using Honduras as the base and safe haven from which to attack into Nicaragua. With regard to Nicaragua, Reagan assured Congress that the United States was not seeking the overthrow of the left-wing Sandinista government there. But, he added, it would not protect that government 'from the anger of its own people'. America's main interest in Nicaragua, he explained, was to make certain that the Sandinista government did not 'infect' its Central American neighbours through the export of subversion and violence. He did not reveal the extent to which the United States was helping the anti-Sandinista guerrilla forces, the Contras.

In a far more distant region, Americans were the victims of anti-American feeling when, on April 18, seventeen American citizens, members of the American peacemaking presence in the war-ravaged city, were killed by a terrorist bomb in Beirut. Six months later, on October 23, a suicide bomber drove a truck filled with explosives into the marine barracks in Beirut. When the truck exploded, 241 American servicemen were killed. Still the American peacemaking efforts continued, culminating in the transfer of all four thousand PLO fighters from Lebanon to Tunisia, where Yasser Arafat had set up his headquarters, and from where he sought to control the Palestinian national movement with a combination of acts of terror and political initiatives worldwide.

Dissent in Eastern Europe was marked in East Germany by the activities of the unofficial 'peace movement', about sixty people in all, known as the 'Jena Group'. Its members, all of them pacifists, were based in Jena but active throughout East Germany. They were welcomed by the authorities when they called for Western disarmament, but when they began to call for Eastern-bloc disarmament as well, and also opposed military training in East German schools and factories, and the sale of war toys and war games, they quickly fell foul of officialdom. That year, twenty of their number were expelled from the country.

In Poland, a second visit by John Paul II since he had become Pope electrified a country whose earlier aspirations had been crushed. Arriving in Poland on June 16, he stayed for eight days. At a meeting with General Jaruzelski early in his visit, he was outspoken in expressing his hopes that the August 1980 agreement with Solidarity – 'the social reforms worked out at the price of such pain' as he called them – would be adhered to. As many as fourteen million Poles in all assembled at the various places where the Pope spoke. It was an incredible demonstration of the strength of Roman Catholicism and the indefatigable spirit of the Polish people. At each meeting, the crowds displayed hundreds of 'V for Victory' signs – the Churchillian symbol of defiance and hope that had been such an inspiration during the Second World War. Everywhere he spoke, the Pope stressed that every society had the right to 'maintain its own identity'. There must be established in every civil society 'social structures which correspond to the nation's requirements'. Only then could one move towards 'the consensus needed by the State'. Whether or not this was traditional Catholic doctrine, it was an inspiration and a challenge for Polish believers. On July 21, a month after the Pope's visit, Jaruzelski ended martial law in Poland.

The political crisis in Poland had taken its toll in the economic sphere. That year industrial production fell by six per cent, national income by eight per cent, and the standard of living by thirty per cent. Inflation was rampant, reaching a hundred per cent. As many as a third of all Poles were living below the poverty line. When the government announced price rises of up to seventy per cent, both the Catholic Church and Solidarity protested. Their power to influence policy may have waned, but their popular influence had not. The award of the Nobel Peace Prize to Lech Walesa boosted his prestige. In a gesture of contempt for the Polish authorities he donated the prize money to the Catholic Church in Poland to be put towards a fund being set up to help private farmers.

In his acceptance speech for the Nobel Prize, Walesa championed the rights of the independent trade unions, and called for the dialogue between government and Solidarity to be renewed. But, harsh though Jaruzelski's rule had become, neither Walesa, nor the Church, nor the vast majority of Poles whom he and the Church between them represented, wanted to do anything against the Jaruzelski regime that might provoke a Soviet intervention.

The Communist authorities in Czechoslovakia ensured that there would be no provoking of the Soviet Union. The dissidents of Charter 77 – after six years of activity calling for the upholding of human rights and greater government accountability – continued to circulate protests and petitions, and to make contact with Western European peace movements, but were under close scrutiny, continually liable to detention and arrest if they ventured too close to public activity. One stimulus to their opposition to government policy came on October 24, with the official announcement that Soviet 'operational-tactical missiles with an enhanced range' would be based in

Czechoslovakia. As in East Germany, so in Czechoslovakia, the dissident movement was trying to press for nuclear disarmament by both sides.

By the end of the year, thirty 'prisoners of conscience' were in prison in Czechoslovakia. In the Soviet Union, twenty-five Russian Jews – 'Prisoners of Zion' – were in prison or labour camp for their part in the continuing pressure for emigration. On October 14 a former prisoner, Josef Begun, was sentenced to twelve years' 'deprivation of liberty': three years in prison, four years in labour camp and five years of internal exile. One of his 'crimes' was that he gave private Hebrew lessons. His wife, Ina Shlemova, desperate for his health – he was fifty-one years old when he began his second sentence – beseeched Western visitors who made contact with her in Moscow to protest on his behalf. It was often the determination of prisoners' wives that alone made it possible for details of their cases to reach the West, and for Jewish organizations throughout the Western world to seek support from sympathetic governments. Each prisoner's wife also had the legal right under Soviet law to be her husband's advocate with the authorities. Ina Shlemova therefore argued that the Hebrew lessons which Begun gave before his arrest were as legitimate as the teaching – permitted under Soviet law – of any 'national' language. Two examples of newly taught national languages that she used, as he used in his trial, were the Avarian language of the Daghestan region of the Caucasus, and the Chukchi language of the Soviet Far East, the revival of which were encouraged by the authorities. Her arguments, like Begun's, were to no avail.

As well as attacks on Jews, the Soviet authorities continued to clamp down on dissent elsewhere. Irina Ratushinskaya was sentenced to seven years for 'anti-Soviet agitation and propaganda' – in her poems.[1]

Peace in Lebanon, and the bustling prosperity for which Beirut was famous throughout the eastern Mediterranean, seemed things of the past. Among the armed groups whose forces could, and did, fight on Lebanese soil were the Maronite Christian militia, the Muslim 'Amal' militia, the Druze (an independent minority then within the Syrian zone of occupation), the Syrian army, Palestinians who had remained in Lebanon after the evacuation from Beirut to Tunis, anti-Syrian fundamentalist Shi'ite Muslims, a quite separate

---

[1] In 1998, Irina Ratushinskaya returned to Russia, with the aim of taking part in Russian politics. In 1999 she published a novel based on her Gulag experiences, entitled *Fictions and Lies*.

Iranian Shi'ite force, and Israeli troops who were gradually withdrawing during the year to a zone in southern Lebanon.

The fighting between Lebanese Christian and Muslim militias, and between Muslim fundamentalist Shi'ite fighters and the Israeli soldiers on Lebanese soil, repeatedly escalated. The American and French peacekeeping forces were under continual attack. Based in the city of Baalbek, Iranian Shi'ite fundamentalists carried out bomb and suicide-bomb attacks, some of which caused heavy loss of life. On April 18 a bomb destroyed the United States Embassy in Beirut, killing eighty-seven people. On October 23 two simultaneous suicide attacks on the peacekeepers' bases led to the deaths of 239 American and 58 French soldiers. On November 4 a suicide bomber who blew up the Israeli military headquarters in the coastal city of Tyre killed twenty-nine Israelis, and thirty-two Lebanese and Palestinian detainees being held in the headquarters.

In reprisals for these attacks, the French bombed the Iranian Shi'ite base in Baalbek, and the Israelis bombed Shi'ite and Palestinian guerrilla concentrations in southern Lebanon. On December 3 the Israelis, having themselves been fired on, bombed Syrian coastal gun emplacements near Beirut. The Syrians, in firing back, hit two American reconnaissance aircraft. American planes then attacked the Syrian bases. During the attack, two of the American planes were shot down by Syrian anti-aircraft fire and two pilots were killed. The Syrians then began to shell American bases. In retaliation, the powerful naval guns of the American warship *New Jersey* pounded the Syrian batteries.

The international community continued to try to keep the peace. Italian and British troops joined the Americans and French. Both American and Saudi Arabian emissaries tried to tackle the root of the problem, to persuade the Maronite Christian minority in Lebanon to redistribute power more evenly to the Muslim majority. But the Maronites, their numerical situation worsening year by year, feared that with Muslim political dominance would come their own political and physical demise.

Amid the destructiveness of war and civil war; amid the fighting that was taking place at any given time on almost every continent; amid the violations of human rights and the struggle of the individual to survive political repression, social inequalities and a shortage of basic needs, every branch of science was contributing to improvements for the lives of hundreds of millions of people.

During 1983 a total of 42,589 Americans were killed on the roads. This figure hid behind its statistical precision enormous human suffering. In Britain the road deaths that year were 5,445. In an attempt to reduce not only the loss of life, but the terrible waste in terms of human resources that such a high death toll represented, the British government introduced the compulsory wearing of seatbelts by drivers and front-seat passengers. The effect was to reduce the number of deaths by a third within a decade.

Environmental concerns were given added impetus that year from two sources. The first was in April, when a Royal Commission in Britain recommended the introduction of unleaded petrol. Within an hour of the publication of the commission's report the government announced that it would act upon it, and that it would introduce unleaded petrol within seven years at the latest. Only a month earlier, a government spokesman had decried such a change on the ground that it would be too difficult to redesign car engines for leadless petrol. The difficulties disappeared when the health hazards were pointed out. Western public opinion was no longer in a mood to dismiss these hazards, or to ignore them.

The second stimulus to environmental change came in June, when the United States government changed its view on 'acid rain'. Hitherto Washington had insisted that sulphur and nitrogen oxide emissions from American power stations were not necessarily the cause of the chemical blight that was affecting millions of trees and polluting thousands of lakes in Canada, as well as in the north-eastern United States. In June, a Federal inquiry described manmade pollutants as 'probably the major contributors' to acid rain. Later that same month the President's science office advised 'meaningful reductions' in sulphur emissions. In Europe the West German government likewise changed its mind, after as much as a quarter of West German forest trees had been damaged by acid rain. Nor did the legislation bring immediate relief: of the 216 coal-fired power stations in West Germany, 205 were exempted from the necessary changes to their operations – which, being costly, would initially reduce their profitability – until some time between 1987 and 1993.

In Eastern Europe the problems of pollution were yet more serious. Factories were older and methods of production even less carefully monitored than in the West. Throughout East Germany and Czechoslovakia the forests which had been an integral part of the landscape, and of the ecological balance of nature, were dying. In the coalmining regions the whole population was at risk; hundreds of thousands of people were suffering from respiratory disorders. The situation in the industrial regions of the Soviet Union, though closed to outside scrutiny, was known to be even worse.

The dangers posed to the environment were highlighted at a conference in Washington at which five hundred scientists, drawn from fifteen countries, discussed what Lloyd Timberlake, the Editorial Director of the environmental magazine *Earthscan*, called 'the ultimate environmental doomsday story'. It concerned how the Earth would be affected by a large-scale nuclear war. First, a cloud would spread over the whole planet, cutting out the Sun's rays and creating a global 'nuclear winter'. The impact of that was set out by Donald Kennedy, the President of Stanford University, California, who told the conference that during the 'nuclear winter' temperatures would be below freezing 'for months' in the north and there would be localized sub-freezing temperatures in the south. Northern crops and southern rainforests would be wiped out. 'When the cloud cleared a damaged ozone layer would let in more than usual ultra-violet rays, with resulting cancers, blindness, lowered disease resistance and genetic mutations. Civilization as humans had built it would be destroyed. Cold, darkness, fire, toxic smog, radiation, violent coastal storms and disease would usher in a new civilization based on misery.'

The 'new civilization based on misery' depended upon a full-scale nuclear war. But other, closer-to-hand miseries were bringing extreme hardship to millions of people without the advent of nuclear war. In the Third World, the desperate search for subsistence had led over the previous decade to over-grazing, over-cultivation and the deforestation of arid and semi-arid lands on a scale hitherto unknown. Each of these dramatically increased the danger of drought, and, when rains came, of flooding. The year 1983 proved to be a crisis year. According to statistics published by the United Nations Food and Agricultural Organization (FAO) in November, 150 million people were at that very moment 'on the brink of starvation'. The most endangered were twenty-two nations in Africa. The FAO added that 'famine has already caused deaths in some countries', among them Ethiopia, from which a stream of starving and destitute refugees was fleeing into the Sudan – where neither food nor shelter awaited them.

It was not Africa alone that was affected by the impoverishment of the land. Bolivia, Peru and Ecuador each suffered severe flooding, accentuated by mudslides that were in many cases created because of the clearing away of trees for development, and which swept away homes and whole villages. The United Nations warned that deforestation, and the 'mismanagement' of watersheds, would make even the advent of typhoons and hurricanes more devastating. When Typhoon 'Georgia' hit Thailand, Kampuchea and Vietnam that October, more than 1,500,000 people were made homeless.

Refugee movements could provoke the most violent of reactions. Among the non-Indian population of India were the Assamese people living in the far north-east of the country whose affinities were far more with Burma and Thailand than with India. The Assamese turned to violence after the arrival in Assam of 300,000 Bengalis, immigrants from Bangladesh, whom the government of India housed in refugee camps.

The Assamese were convinced that the government of India would give the Bengali newcomers – 'true' Indians – preferential treatment. For their part many Bengalis criticized the government for not doing enough to protect them against Assamese hostility. Fighting was widespread. Assamese rebels destroyed more than 1,600 road and rail bridges, in a land of deep river gorges and difficult communications. Reporting in *The Times* on March 24, Trevor Fishlock wrote: 'The very word Assam has become a sort of shorthand for hatred, terror and the collapse of reason and order. Bodies are being found all the time, shot, axed and burnt, even trussed up in sacks in the river. Assam is a madhouse of rage and xenophobia in which the people of varied social groups feel free to fall on their neighbours with knives, spears, staves and guns.'

Fighting between government of India forces and the Assamese led in seven weeks to the death of more than five thousand Assamese.

On September 6 the 'Helsinki process' which had begun eight years earlier came to an end. That day, in Madrid, the long-debated 'Concluding Document' of the European Conference on Security and Co-operation was signed. Thirty-five nations put their signatures to it, most importantly the United States and the Soviet Union. Solemnly secured in the document was an agreement to ensure the freedom of the individual 'to profess and practise religion in line with the dictates of his own conscience'; an agreement to ensure the rights of workers freely to establish and join trade unions, and the right of unions 'to freely carry out their activities in compliance with national laws'; the granting of exit permits for emigration on the basis of family ties, marriage and the reunification of families, the permits normally to be given within six months after application; an agreement to refrain from penalizing would-be emigrants in terms of jobs, housing and social benefit; assured freedom of access for all citizens to foreign embassies, 'with due regard to security requirements'; and an undertaking by all the signatories 'to work for militarily significant, politically binding and verifiable confidence- and security-building measures (CSBMs) to reduce the risk of military confrontation anywhere in Europe'.

Most importantly in the link between human rights and security, the signatories of the Concluding Document were pledged to 'pursue the solution of outstanding problems through peaceful means'. Another stage in the abolition of war between nations had been reached.

CHAPTER THIRTY-THREE

1984

The pace of life cannot, of course, be stopped, but I do think that if man cannot attain spiritual independence from this race for the future, or perhaps from his own self, a catastrophe is imminent.

ANATOLI SHCHARANSKY

IN HIS NOVEL *Nineteen Eighty-Four*, George Orwell, writing just after the Second World War, had envisaged a single, all-embracing totalitarian world order. The signature in 1983 of the Concluding Document of the Helsinki process showed how serious were the efforts of many nations to avert the Orwellian nightmare. But the survival of democratic States had at no point since his forecast been inevitable. Tyrannies had existed then, new tyrannies had established themselves, and the fear of tyranny was ever present in many countries. One optimistic pointer was that the Concluding Document had been signed in Spain, itself a recent returnee to democracy after four decades under Franco's dictatorship. The Soviet Union, however, another of the Madrid signatories, was in no way free from the monolithic rule of the Communist Party. Poland was struggling with a repressive regime.

In Chile, General Pinochet's dictatorship failed to live up to earlier hopes of a gradual relaxation, although press censorship had been relaxed. During 1983 more than a hundred people had been killed in the break-up of street demonstrations against the regime. In the new year those demonstrations grew. On February 6, Socialist and Communist protesters marched together in the streets of Santiago, demanding the legalization of the left-wing political Parties. Pinochet reacted by imprisoning Dr Manuel Almeyda, the leader of the most powerful of those Parties, the Popular Democratic Movement. Members of Pinochet's government held out, nevertheless, the prospect of the legalization of all banned political Parties and the holding of free and fair elections. But after an assassination attempt on General Contreras, the head of the secret police, Pinochet declared a state of emergency, reimposed press censorship, and arrested those who he believed were organizing further demonstrations. He would wage 'a war to the death against Communism', Pinochet promised.

On September 4 a protest demonstration in Santiago was savagely broken up, and one of its leaders, Rodolfo Segual, the head of the metalworkers' union, was beaten on the legs and testicles. In police raids, André Jarlan, a French priest active among the poor, was shot in the head and killed. A former Foreign Minister, Gabriel Valdes, summed up the situation in Chile with the words: 'The government has lost all authority but still has the power.' During a general strike a month later, nine people were killed by the police, and all opposition newspapers were banned.

In the Soviet Union, a change in the leadership always raised hopes of a diminution in the rigidity of the Communist Party system. The death of Yuri Andropov in February was no exception. His successor, Konstantin Chernenko, was very much a member of the old guard, and at the age of seventy-two hardly a man to introduce radical change. But there was some relief in reforming circles that Mikhail Gorbachev, a Party leader twenty years younger than Chernenko, had become Chairman of the Foreign Affairs Commission of the Supreme Soviet, the post which Chernenko had held before his elevation. It was clear that Chernenko was not well – he suffered from emphysema and related heart complaints. From mid-July to early October he was absent from Moscow, on what was said to be a prolonged summer holiday.

The power of the Communist Party, and of the KGB, was undiminished. Pressure for reform was in the economic, not the political sphere, and in economic reform Gorbachev took a lead. Stressing, as he had done the previous year, the need for economic incentives for individual farmers, he also argued the need to bring in to the agricultural sector specialists who would be 'politically mature, literate, and competent organizationally, with a feeling for the new'. That 'new' was still absent in many areas of Soviet behaviour. In May, the Soviet Union withdrew from the Los Angeles Olympic Games in retaliation for the American withdrawal four years earlier from the Moscow Olympics. In place of Los Angeles, the Russians organized the 'Friendship 84' Games in Moscow for all Communist countries.

The Soviet presence in Afghanistan was becoming an increasing burden on the resources of the State. More than 140,000 Soviet soldiers were in the country, unable to prevent repeated guerrilla attacks on their convoys and their bases, and with an ever rising death toll. It was the fifth year of this costly entanglement. In the sphere of human rights, dissidents and Jews active in the emigration movement – despite the clear human rights and emigration provisos of the previous year's Madrid summit – continued to be arrested and sent to labour camps. In September, a Jewish activist, Yuli Edelshtein, was brought to trial on 'drug trafficking' charges. He had been 'caught' reciting the prayer at the end of the Jewish Sabbath in which a spice box is shaken to sweeten the coming week: in Hebrew, the word for 'spices' and 'drugs' is the same. Despite the absurdity of the charge, Edelshtein was sentenced to three years in labour camp.[1] Reflecting on man's destiny, Anatoli Shcharansky wrote from his prison cell in the Gulag to his wife Avital in Jerusalem: 'The pace of life cannot, of course, be stopped, but I do think that if man cannot attain spiritual independence from this race for the future, or perhaps from his own self, a catastrophe is imminent.'

Western campaigns for the release of Soviet political and human rights prisoners were intensified. When Gorbachev visited Margaret Thatcher in Britain in December, she gave him the names of a number of imprisoned Jews and urged their release. He did not make any concessions to her. Among those prisoners was Anatoli Shcharansky, thirty-six years old, and in his seventh year of incarceration, much of it in solitary confinement. Despite mounting Western pressure, Shcharansky remained in prison. Nor, despite similar pressure, was his friend and mentor Andrei Sakharov allowed to return to Moscow from internal exile. On Soviet television a ten-part series sang the praises of an ever alert KGB.

In Poland there was no diminution in the political conflict between General Jaruzelski, desperate not to provoke a Soviet invasion, and the Solidarity movement, eager to return to the reform policies it had so effectively promoted before the imposition of martial law. In emulation of Soviet practice, Jaruzelski made full use of the secret police to curb what he denounced as 'counter-revolutionary forces'. Polish protests were never silenced, however. It is not in the Polish nature to be cowed. When a leading Marxist philosopher and Communist Party member, Professor Schaff, wrote a book critical

---

[1] Following his release in 1987, Edelshtein emigrated to Israel, where he became (in 1996) Minister of Immigrant Absorption. His father, a Russian Orthodox priest, continued to minister to his Christian flock in Moscow. Shcharansky was also to enter the Israeli government in 1996 as Minister of Trade and Industry, and in 1999 to be appointed Minister of the Interior.

of the Party and could not get it published in Poland, he had it published abroad. In it he argued that 'the Party lacked not only credibility but also legitimacy, because socialism had been imported to Poland with Soviet backing'. Schaff was promptly expelled from the Party whose failings he had tried to expose. But his criticism were widely, if clandestinely, circulated inside Poland.

Jaruzelski's government was not without powers of its own, albeit destructive ones. Troops and police were deployed in large numbers to prevent people from laying wreaths at the monuments set up to commemorate those killed in earlier clashes with the authorities. Court procedures were introduced whereby demonstrators could be arrested and imprisoned by the police with the minimum of formality and documentation. Where crucifixes had been put up on schools and other public buildings as a sign of defiance of the authorities, they were torn down by the police. In retaliation, and with the support of the Church authorities, students replaced the crucifixes. The 'war of the crosses' was another indication of the depth of Polish dissent.

Arrests of Solidarity supporters were frequent. House searches became a feature of police activity. At the United Nations, Poland was found to have violated two international conventions, one on freedom of association, and the other on the right of collective bargaining. Expulsion from the International Labour Organization followed. But Solidarity continued to find means of pressing its demands and widening its influence: creating shadow organizations in every large factory. Study circles on the workings of democracy were set up, with the support of Solidarity, in many hundreds of workplaces, and even schools.

On a visit to Moscow, his first since the Brezhnev era, Jaruzelski obtained the support of the new leaders for his repressive measures. He also signed a Soviet-Polish economic co-operation agreement that was to remain in force, according to its preamble, until the year 2000. In July, hoping to diffuse dissent, Jaruzelski granted an amnesty to 652 political prisoners, including the imprisoned Solidarity leaders: 35,000 common criminals were also set free. In welcoming the amnesty, both Lech Walesa and the Church leaders warned that it was not enough: that it was essential to ensure 'implementation of the social accords signed in August 1980'. This Jaruzelski was not prepared to do. The Soviet Union would never have accepted a move to free trade unions.

Towards the end of the year an increasing number of young Roman Catholic priests began to speak in their pulpits in favour of Solidarity, and of Polish national aspirations. The anti-Soviet implications of such patriotism were clear. Among those giving what became known as the 'Masses for the Fatherland' was a Warsaw priest, Father Jerzy Popieluszko, who drew large crowds to his sermons. On October 19 he disappeared. Eleven days later his body was found in the River Vistula. He had been tortured. Popieluszko's murder, Jaruzelski admitted in public, 'has done us a lot of harm'. There was deep unease in Polish government circles that riots would follow the murder. The Pope, having been given an assurance that the government had not been involved in the murder – only 'rogue' secret policemen – was asked to intervene. He did so, appealing for calm.

At Popieluszko's funeral on November 3, a bitterly cold day, 300,000 Poles knelt in the streets around his church, and unfurled banned Solidarity banners that had been brought to Warsaw from all over Poland. During the funeral, Lech Walesa declared: 'Solidarity lives because you, Father Popieluszko, died for it.' A Polish writer and broadcaster living in Britain, Z. J. Blazynski, wrote after the funeral of how, in the wake of Popieluszko's murder, Poland 'became a different, more dangerous but more exalted place, as the cult of a new patriotic saint blossomed around the fresh grave'. One result of the murder was the establishment in Polish intellectual, academic and student circles of a number of human rights groups, charged with monitoring human rights abuses and giving them maximum publicity. At the end of the year four secret policemen were charged with Popieluszko's murder, and imprisoned.[1]

In Czechoslovakia, partly inspired by events in Poland, dissent was growing. There was a mounting demand for religious freedom, with a petition being signed by thousands of people calling on the Pope to visit Czechoslovakia for the 1,100th anniversary of the bringing of Christianity to Czechoslovakia. A Papal visit, however, was something that the Czech Communist authorities refused absolutely to countenance. From their perspective the impact during the previous few years of the Pope's two visits to Poland held grave dangers for Communist control in any country where Christianity had strong roots, not just in Poland, his country of birth. Human rights activists, the Helsinki Final Act circulating among them, called for greater political freedom. Students baulked at the continuing Communist control of literature and the arts.

Charter 77, despite continual harassment, managed to issue more than twenty statements during the year. One of these statements called for the

---

[1] A decade later a secret police captain was sentenced to ten years in prison for Popieluszko's murder. When he appealed against the severity of his sentence, the court of appeal added another three years to it.

support of the human rights monitoring groups that had been set up in Poland in the aftermath of Father Popieluszko's murder. Most embarrassing for the government was the award of the Nobel Prize for literature to the Czech poet Jaroslav Seifert. The 'grand old man' of Czech literature, he had left the Communist Party many years earlier, and was a signatory of Charter 77.

Dissent was also evident in Yugoslavia, where a university lecturer, Dr Yojislav Seselj was sentenced to eight years in prison by a court in Sarajevo for having expressed 'counter-revolutionary views' in an unpublished manuscript. Seven Belgrade students were arrested for having become involved in a 'Free University' where freedom of speech and political assembly were being taught. One of them was found dead in unexplained circumstances shortly after his release from police custody. While the remaining six were being held in custody, Amnesty International adopted them as 'prisoners of conscience'. They were later released and, although denounced officially as 'political terrorists', were not brought to trial.

There was also a revival of national feelings among the Albanian population of the Yugoslav province of Kosovo. The leaders of the movement, some of whom were demanding autonomy within Yugoslavia, others union with Albania, were brought to trial, and imprisoned for terms of up to fourteen years.

Not only tyranny, but civil unrest, marked the internal life of many lands in 'Orwell's year'. In India, intercommunal killings between Hindus and Muslims in the Punjab, and between Sikhs and Hindus – the Sikhs demanding political and religious autonomy – led to more than four hundred deaths. In June, Indira Gandhi ordered the Indian army to remove the Sikh militants who, under their leader, Sant Bhindranwale, had taken over the Sikh holy shrine – the Golden Temple – at Amritsar. Similar military operations were launched simultaneously against thirty-seven other Sikh holy places which had been occupied in protest at the rejection of Sikh demands for autonomy. During the assault on the temple at Amritsar, the soldiers obeyed orders to try to avoid damaging the shrine itself. But when the assault was over, not only had damage been inflicted, but more than seven hundred Sikh militants and ninety Indian soldiers had been killed. The body of Sant Bhindranwale was found in the basement.

On September 25, in response to a pledge by Indira Gandhi, repair work on the Golden Temple was completed. Four days later, Indian troops ended their occupation of the temple. Two days after that, on October 1, three hundred young Sikh militants stormed the building and occupied it, in defiance of the warnings of Sikh officials who, in return for the Indian government's rapid completion of the repairs, had promised that there would be no further occupation. The Indian security forces moved to dislodge the militants, entering the temple and forcing them to leave.

A month later, on October 31, Indira Gandhi was assassinated by two Sikh members of her bodyguard. In an upsurge of anti-Sikh feeling, five hundred Sikhs were killed in Delhi and several hundred more elsewhere. Mrs Gandhi was succeeded as Prime Minister by her son Rajiv Gandhi, who won a substantial victory at the election, gaining more seats for the Congress Party than his grandfather Jawaharlal Nehru had done (400 as opposed to 371). One of his first problems was the impact of the worst industrial accident in modern history, the death of 2,500 people when, in the early hours of December 3 – three weeks before the election – poisonous gas leaked from the American-owned Union Carbide pesticide factory just out-side Bhopal, the State capital of Madhya Pradesh. The placing of a potentially dangerous chemical factory near a population centre and the safety standards being operated by foreign companies based in India were two of the subjects with which Rajiv Gandhi had to grapple, in the wake of popular revulsion at the heavy death toll and indignation at its cruel effects.

In Mexico City, five hundred people had been killed a month earlier, after an explosion at a natural gas processing plant.

A new area of conflict was impinging on world consciousness in 1984: the revolt of Tamil extremists in Sri Lanka (formerly Ceylon). The 'Tamil Tigers', as the insurgents called themselves, were demanding secession from Sri Lanka – they lived mainly in the north of the island, and sought political integration with their fellow Tamils in southern India.

Attacks by Tamil Tigers, and reprisals by Sri Lankan forces, intensified throughout the year. In February, Tamil Tigers blew up an army camp at Jaffna. In March, Sri Lankan air force personnel killed ten civilians in the Tamil town of Chunnakam. In April after Sri Lankan reprisals for further killings grew more frequent, the Catholic Bishop of Jaffna protested against a military attack on a church. After two Sri Lankan sailors were killed onshore, the Sri Lankan navy shelled the fishing village of Valvettiturai. In the last two weeks of November there were more than three hundred violent deaths. A climax to the killings came on December 7, when Sri Lankan soldiers who were travelling in a convoy on a main road were ambushed by Tamil Tigers. A hundred soldiers were killed.

It was the start of conflict and killings that were to continue for the next decade. When, in December, the Sri Lanka government accused the south Indian government of Tamil Nadu of supporting the insurrection, and fired on Indian fishing boats which it accused of running arms to the Tamil Tigers, Rajiv Gandhi, in one of his first actions as Indian Prime Minister, protested.

In Uganda, anti-government forces north of the capital, Kampala, calling themselves the National Resistance Army, were led by a former Minister of Defence, Yoweri Museveni. Over the previous four years, during continuous fighting with government forces loyal to the Ugandan President, Milton Obote, an estimated three-quarters of a million people had been displaced from their homes, and tens of thousands killed. Atrocities were committed by both sides: the massacre of sixteen clergymen in May, including the dean of an Anglican seminary, was believed to have been carried out by a member of the government's own security forces. In August, Elliott Abrams, the United States Under-Secretary of State for Human Rights, criticized the government forces for the 'excesses' they were committing. The situation in Uganda, he said, was 'horrendous'. To try to bring a minimum of food and shelter to the dispossessed, twenty-one refugee camps were operating under the auspices of the international relief agencies.

Elliott Abrams' denunciation of human rights abuses in Uganda included the arrest of newspaper editors who criticized government policy in their editorial columns, and the detention without trial of as many as 1,500 Ugandans for political dissent. A Western human rights organization, the Minority Rights Group, pointed out the inhuman prison conditions in which most of the detainees were being held, and castigated Obote's regime for its 'cynical and flagrant flouting of human rights'. In Guinea, by contrast, following the death – from heart failure, in a heart clinic in Cleveland, Ohio – of Ahmad Sekou Touré, the founding father, dictator for life and brutal murderer of his political opponents, power was seized by a Military Committee of National Redress. One-Party rule was ended, and more than a thousand political prisoners released.

In Northern Ireland the IRA, determined to force a British withdrawal from the province – an integral part of the United Kingdom for three centuries

– continued its policy of bombing and killing. That year, sixty-four people were killed. This figure, commented Brian Walker, Lecturer in Political Science at the Queen's University of Belfast, 'while still very depressing, was the lowest since 1970'. Some had been killed by the IRA, some by Protestant paramilitary organizations, and some by the security forces. There was also an IRA bomb at the Grand Hotel, Brighton, during the Conservative Party conference in October. The target was the Prime Minister, Margaret Thatcher. Five floors of the hotel were badly damaged, including part of the suite in which Mrs Thatcher was staying. Four people were killed in the explosion; a fifth died some weeks later in hospital. Among the dead was a Conservative Member of Parliament, Sir Anthony Berry. Mrs Thatcher, who was in her sitting room working on her conference speech when the bomb went off, was unhurt. 'Life must go on,' was her reaction, to which the IRA retorted: 'Today we were unlucky, but remember we have only to be lucky once.'

In Lebanon, 1,500 American marines formed the main peacekeeping force in and around Beirut. Having failed to stop the warring factions in their seemingly perpetual enmity and bloodletting, with Shi'a Muslim and Druze gunmen having overrun West Beirut, and with Syrian troops still dominating the area to the east of the city, there were calls in the United States for the marines to be withdrawn. On February 7, President Reagan announced that they would all be out of Lebanon within a month. Most of them withdrew from their bases around Beirut to a ship-board watch offshore. After they had left, as a signal to the Lebanese government that it had not lost American support, the United States battleship *New Jersey* opened fire with its powerful sixteen-inch naval guns and bombarded Syrian military positions in the hills above Beirut (in 1915 it was the almost equally powerful fifteen-inch British naval guns that had bombarded the Turkish military defences at the Dardanelles). On September 20, six months after the last of the marines had left, a lorry packed with explosives was driven by a Muslim Shi'ite suicide bomber through the entrance of the American Embassy, where the explosives were detonated. The bomber, and fourteen other people, were killed. It was the third such destructive attack on American property and personnel in Beirut in eighteen months.

Famine increased its devastation in 1984, as Ethiopia suffered another season of drought. Even more than in the previous famine a decade earlier, Western television coverage brought sickening scenes of malnutrition and death from starvation to the homes of tens of millions of well-fed people. A massive international aid effort was mounted, with the United States, Canadian, Western European and Australian governments making the largest contributions. Much of the aid had to go by sea, but emergency air drops, led by a British Royal Air Force team using giant Hercules transport aircraft, were carried out into the heart of the stricken areas.

The aid came too late to save an estimated three-quarters of a million people. But at least ten million more were the beneficiaries of the food that was sent. Not only Ethiopia, but Somalia, Sudan and Chad were affected by the drought. Civil war added to the perils of famine: parts of Ethiopia were under the control of the Tigre People's Liberation Front. Near the coast, the Eritrean People's Liberation Front was fighting: and in a series of battles with the Ethiopian Army, four thousand Ethiopian soldiers were killed.

The insurgents in areas where there was famine also appealed for international aid. A British politics lecturer at the University of Lancaster, Christopher Clapham, noted that 'while all official relief aid was channelled through areas controlled by the central government, and was supervised by the Ethiopian Relief and Rehabilitation Commission, some private relief agencies, especially War on Want, directed their supplies through the Sudan to the insurgent-held areas'. Clapham added that these agencies 'tended to sympathize with the political goals of the insurgents, and publicized charges that aid was being abused for political purposes by the Ethiopian Government. In any event, each side used aid as a means of bringing people in the contested areas under its control.'

In Mozambique – where the Marxist Frelimo regime was beset with guerrilla insurgency from the Mozambique National Resistance Front, supported by South Africa – famine struck as the continuous fighting over large areas made settled agriculture impossible. Within twelve months, as many as 100,000 Mozambicans died of famine. In an attempt to avert further disaster, the President, Samora Machel, met the South African Prime Minister, P. W. Botha, at the border town of Komartipoort, and signed an agreement, known as the Nkomati Accord, whereby, as well as establishing close economic ties, South Africa agreed to end its support for the anti-Machel guerrillas, and Machel agreed to halt his support for the African National Congress.[1]

---

[1] Fourteen years later Nelson Mandela, the hero of the African National Congress – in 1984 a prisoner – married Samora Machel's widow.

Inside South Africa, Black protests at the inequalities of apartheid were renewed. A 'new factor in the unrest', wrote Gerald Shaw, Chief Assistant Editor of the *Cape Times*, 'was the murderous violence directed at local Black leaders who were cooperating with the authorities in the running of local government. Such leaders were castigated as sell-outs or quislings.' In Sharpeville, the scene of a widely condemned massacre eighteen years earlier, fourteen Blacks were killed in intercommunal rioting against alleged quislings. Among the victims was the deputy mayor of the township, who was hacked to death. Others who were accused of 'collaboration' with the authorities were killed by the 'necklace': a car tyre put around their neck and then set alight.

By the end of the year 193 people had died in violence in the Black townships. As police action against the violence in the townships intensified, the South African Catholic Bishops' Conference, known as a cautious and conservative body, astounded and angered the government when it accused the police of 'reckless and wanton violence'. The chairman of the bishops' conference, Durban's archbishop, Denis Hurley, told a press conference that the police action in the townships created 'resentment and antagonism' in the Black community, and was itself contributing to the unrest.

The reaction of Botha's government to all protests was to increase the number of arrests and detentions without trial. Trade union and student leaders were singled out: by the end of the year two hundred were in detention, under a section much condemned by Western human rights organizations, and the United Nations, which allowed for 'indefinite' detention and interrogation. The long-threatened forced removal of Black squatters outside Cape Town, from the camp at Crossroads which they lived in while working in Cape Town or seeking work, was begun. Even the Afrikaner nationalist newspaper editor, Dr Willem De Klerk, protested that there was 'inhumanity' about these forced removals which everyone could see. Botha's government was not deterred. It had already begun to strengthen its various police actions by using the army as an instrument of its apartheid policy. The one chink in the apartheid armour, and it was a small one, was the bringing in to the Cabinet of two political leaders from the Coloured (that is, mixed race and Indian) community, the leader of the (Coloured) Labour Party, the Reverend Allan Hendrickse, and the chairman of the Ministerial Council of the Indian Chamber, Amichand Rajbansi. With this change, wrote Gerald Shaw, 'hope remained that it might yet serve as a catalyst of further change, or at least be a starting-point in that direction. But its central weakness was its denial of political rights for Blacks, and as the year ended, and township unrest appeared to be endemic, Blacks were claiming their rights with increasing impatience.'

As a sign of disapproval of the South African regime, and giving encouragement to anti-apartheid campaigners worldwide, the Nobel Prize for Peace for 1984 was awarded to Desmond Tutu, the Anglican Bishop of Lesotho. In his acceptance speech he said: 'I have just got to believe God is around. If He is not, we in South Africa have had it.'

The award of the Peace Prize to Bishop Tutu – who became Bishop of Johannesburg a few days after receiving the award, and Archbishop two years later – was a political statement by the Nobel Prize Committee of their opposition to apartheid. Tutu was chosen for the award because, as Secretary-General of the South African Council of Churches since 1978, he had championed a non-violent civil disobedience campaign.

The plight of refugees was omnipresent in Africa. Among the most desperate were 45,000 Rwandans who had been expelled from Uganda two years earlier. Rwanda refused to allow them to leave the refugee camps in which they had found some minimum form of shelter. The burden of their survival fell on the international community. In all of Africa, four million people were refugees.

Population growth was increasingly a subject of international concern: at a United Nations Population Conference held in Mexico City from August 6 to 13, delegates learned that during the previous ten years the world population had increased by 770 million – to reach a figure of 4,800 million. In 1974 many developing and poor nations had looked to a rapid increase in their populations as an economic asset: more babies would result in more adults tilling the soil and working in the factories. Western pleas to curb population growth by basic methods of birth control were seen as a means of keeping the poor nations both poor and dependent. By 1984 it had become clear throughout the developing world that the increases in population were creating, not productive hands to generate greater wealth, but more mouths to feed – and in countries many of which had fewer resources than a decade earlier – than the means to feed them.

Disease, the eradication of which had been set a few years earlier at the target year of 2000, proved not to be susceptible to continuous diminution. Malaria-bearing mosquitoes were becoming resistant to the insecticides and anti-malarial drugs being used against them. The World Health

Organization (WHO) caused considerable alarm when it revealed that 150 million cases of malaria had been reported in the previous year, and that this was becoming the average annual figure. One other statistic gave cause for thought, defying imagination then, as it will always do. It came from the United Nations International Children's Fund (UNICEF). While focusing its activities on the child refugees in Africa to whom it could get milk and basic nutrients, and while saving the lives of an estimated half a million children every year – mostly through oral rehydration using a simple solution of water, salt and sugar – UNICEF made it known that throughout the developing world 40,000 children were dying every day.

CHAPTER THIRTY-FOUR

1985

> I cannot claim we had a meeting of minds on such
> fundamentals as ideology and national purpose, but we
> understood each other better.
>
> PRESIDENT RONALD REAGAN

PRESSURE WAS MOUNTING on South Africa to turn away from apartheid.
On 23 July 1985 the British Foreign Secretary, Sir Geoffrey Howe, openly
urged the South African government to release Nelson Mandela and other
African National Congress leaders being held with him. He also urged the
government to begin a 'constructive dialogue' with the Black community,
to end detention without trial, to repeal discriminatory legislation, and to
make 'a commitment to some form of common citizenship'. These demands
were strongly expressed and sincerely meant, but the imperatives of trade
and profit led Britain to oppose the strong economic sanctions on which the
Labour Party opposition and the Commonwealth leaders were insisting. On
July 26, at the United Nations Security Council, Britain joined the United
States in abstaining from the vote on sanctions, and on September 10 cast
its veto against a European Community debate on both economic and cultural
sanctions.

The old imperial adage, 'trade follows the flag', was given an added twist
by Britain's opposition to sanctions. When the Commonwealth heads of
government met in the Bahamas in October, Margaret Thatcher was the
only leader present who refused to contemplate the imposition of increased
trade sanctions on South Africa. She did agree, however, that there should
be a tightening of the existing economic restraints if 'adequate progress' was
not made towards ending apartheid within the following six months, provided the words 'new measures' were used instead of the word 'sanctions'.
The Minister of State at the Foreign Office, Malcolm Rifkind, made it clear,

however, in a debate in the House of Commons on October 23, that the government would not impose sanctions that would do damage to South Africa's economy 'without regard for its people'.

The violence in the South African Black townships, that had been so marked during the previous year, continued without respite. The catalyst was a new constitution which excluded Blacks from parliament. On March 21, the anniversary of the Sharpeville killings of 1966, there was a protest march in the township of Langa, and police in armoured vehicles, using automatic weapons, fired into the marchers, who were unarmed. Twenty-one people were killed. At the same time, within the townships, the assassination of Blacks who were denounced as 'collaborators' continued, and accelerated. By the middle of the year, two or three Blacks were being killed every day, either by police gunfire or by assassination. Destruction of property also intensified: within the townships, as anger spread, schools, churches, shops, buses, cars and homes were destroyed by fire. In August, a peaceful march on Pollsmoor prison, where Nelson Mandela was being held, was broken up by police with whips. Guerrilla activity also increased, with 136 recorded attacks on police posts and other installations that year. Not all the targets were related to the security forces. On December 23, a bomb that was detonated in a shopping centre at Amanzimoti, a seaside resort in Natal, killed five Whites.

In their campaign against the African National Congress, the South African security services crossed the border into Angola in May, and in support of the UNITA rebels there, blew up oil installations in the Cabinda enclave. In June, there was a South African commando raid across the border into Botswana; entering the capital, Gabarone, the attackers killed fifteen suspected African National Congress activists. In a commando raid into Lesotho, nine people were killed.

Economic sanctions were beginning to affect the South African economy. When the United States called in all short-term credits in July, South Africa was forced to announce a moratorium on all repayments. The outflow of foreign capital reached the highest figure ever: in the twelve months ending in September it amounted to 7,700 million Rand. A mere thirty-two million Rand in foreign currency entered the country during that same period. The international community was making it clear that unless there was political change, and a move towards racial equality, there could be no economic amelioration.

*   *   *

At the other end of the political spectrum, the Soviet Union was also in difficulties. In Afghanistan the 140,000 Soviet troops were unable to defeat the Muslim mujaheddin, who continually shelled the main road leading from the Soviet border to Kabul. In an attempt to cut off the mujaheddin from Pakistan, their main source of arms supply, a series of Soviet attacks was launched on the border areas. A sustained Soviet aerial bombing campaign in and around Kandahar not only did serious damage to the city, but destroyed the harvest. The mujaheddin were not deterred. Maintaining their cross-border links with their Muslim allies and emigrés in Pakistan, they also launched repeated attacks on Kabul itself, where the Soviet forces were effectively besieged.

Within the ruling Party in Kabul, which the Soviet Union was determined to maintain in power, division had opened up which threatened the ability of the regime to survive. Two factions had emerged, the Parcham (Flag) and the Khalq (People). In April, at a special assembly of 1,796 tribal leaders from all over the country, President Babrak Karmal secured a unanimous resolution for the Soviet troops to remain. He also took steps to broaden the basis of his regime, with the introduction of eight non-Communists into his twenty-seven-member Cabinet: these included a Hindu and several representatives from the Uzbek and Tajik regions.

Inside the Soviet Union it was not only the rising death toll among Soviet troops in Afghanistan that caused distress; the Soviet public also saw the extent to which Afghan troops loyal to Babrak Karmal were leaving almost all the fighting to Soviet troops. It was not clear to Western observers in Moscow how long the Soviet government could hold back criticism of the Afghan imbroglio. Rajiv Gandhi, the Indian Prime Minister, was among the foreign leaders who, on a visit to Moscow, privately but emphatically expressed their concern at the continued Soviet presence.

There was a sense of some impending and possibly dramatic change of direction in Soviet policy when, on March 10, Konstantin Chernenko died, and was replaced as General Secretary of the Communist Party by Mikhail Gorbachev. As agriculture supremo for the previous seven years, Gorbachev had shown himself keen on a practical, efficient and professional approach to the policies within his sphere. At the time of his emergence as Soviet leader he was fifty-four years old, the youngest member of the Politburo. Within six years he was to transform – and in the end unintentionally to destroy – the Soviet Union.

On April 23, Gorbachev set out his plans to the Central Committee. The inertia which had led to a continual fall in Soviet productivity during the previous decade would be ended. Modern methods would be the order of the day. Corruption, which had become endemic at the highest levels of Party life, would be ended. Industrial productivity, which was only fifty-five per cent of Western standards, would be subjected to 'scientific-technical renovation'. Among Gorbachev's new appointments was a man of his own age, Boris Yeltsin, who was put in charge of construction, and Edouard Shevardnadze, a fifty-seven-year-old Georgian, who was made Foreign Minister. When, towards the end of the year, it became clear to Gorbachev that the Moscow Communist Party apparatus was unhappy with his reforming activities, he appointed Yeltsin to undertake the modernization of the governing of the capital.

In foreign policy, Gorbachev grasped the nettle of disarmament in a way that astounded those analysts, particularly in the United States, who doubted the Soviet commitment to the Strategic Arms Reduction Talks (START). But Gorbachev, having recognized the nuclear superiority of the United States, especially with the imminent advent of a comprehensive, laser-based, American anti-missile system – President Reagan's 'Star Wars' – declared a moratorium on the Soviet deployment of medium-range nuclear missiles in Europe. This opened the way to the renewal of the START talks on the basis put forward a year earlier by the United States. In an echo of Gorbachev's concerns, Edouard Shevardnadze, speaking to the United Nations in New York in September, condemned Star Wars and called instead for a 'Star Peace', with international co-operation in the defence sphere.

Gorbachev saw nuclear disarmament as the key to his determination to modernize the Soviet Union. If he could transfer to the productive world of industry some of the enormous sums of money, and some of the technical and scientific prowess, that were being absorbed by the Soviet defence establishment, and its perceived needs, his internal changes would have a basis in economic reality. In place of the existing slow decline in productivity, Gorbachev set a target of a 3.5 per cent growth. For industries which had declined, this meant an increase well in excess of four per cent. Travelling throughout the Soviet Union in a highly publicized public relations exercise not seen before in a Soviet leader, Gorbachev urged more stringent work discipline and more technical and scientific innovations. In a series of American-style walkabouts, and face-to-face confrontations with the crowds that gathered to see him, Gorbachev took his message of efficiency to the Leningrad region, the Ukraine, Siberia and Kazakhstan.

Reagan and Gorbachev met for the first time at a summit in Geneva in November. In the words of Peter Frank, a British Sovietologist writing early the following year, 'both men had gone to Geneva determined to seek a better understanding of each other as persons and of the other country's point of view. The chemistry worked, not least because of a press blackout during the talks and the lengthy tête-à-tête conversations with only interpreters present.' In the crucial sphere of nuclear disarmament, the outcome of the meeting was positive. Reagan and Gorbachev agreed to instruct their representatives to 'speed up negotiations' when the disarmament talks reconvened. They also agreed to open an American consulate in Kiev and a Soviet consulate in New York, to authorize cultural exchanges, and to pursue joint Soviet-American research on nuclear fusion and air safety.

When the summit ended, and before flying back to Moscow, Gorbachev held an unprecedented ninety-five-minute press conference, telling the assembled journalists: 'The world has become a safer place.' Flying back to the United States, Reagan told Congress: 'I cannot claim we had a meeting of minds on such fundamentals as ideology and national purpose, but we understood each other better.' It was also encouraging, Peter Frank reflected, 'that Gorbachev accepted an invitation to visit the United States in 1986, and invited President Reagan to go to the USSR the year after. Neither side sought to disguise the fact that there were deep differences of opinion left unresolved, or that the dialogue had at times been "sharp" and uncompromising. But at the year's end the "spirit of Geneva" – to which the Soviet media and leadership made frequent reference – seemed still to have real substance. It was a good start.'

A further indication of real change in Soviet policy came when Gorbachev wrote to Reagan – the gist of his letter was made public in December – to say that he would allow American inspectors to visit Soviet underground nuclear testing sites, and offering to negotiate a treaty banning all underground nuclear tests. Reagan responded positively. As a sign of newfound openness, it was agreed that Reagan and Gorbachev would each speak on television to the other's people on New Year's Day.

The Star Wars initiative was not to be America's alone. On December 6 the British government announced that it was joining it. Margaret Thatcher had made a significant commitment to the United States' global security system. By the end of the year it had become clear that the programme, known as the Strategic Defence Initiative (SDI), was no chimera. The United States would spend $33 billion in the coming five years to devise and put in place the technologies that could detect, track and destroy nuclear weapons during their flight. Sensors would both detect the incoming missiles and beam projectiles to destroy them. As its contribution, the British government identified eighteen areas of the programme in which British engineers and scientists could contribute. This included designing software for computers. But the project was highly sensitive, and the specific details remained unknown outside the secret circle.

Within the Soviet Union, the effect of decades of habit and self-satisfaction among Party functionaries was being challenged and swept away. A sustained campaign, led by Gorbachev himself, against corruption, bribery and inefficiency at every level of society resulted in the dismissal of hundreds of officials, and the execution of those judged seriously to have neglected their responsibilities. A campaign against alcoholism led to a considerable increase in the overnight incarceration of drunks in special 'sobering-up' cells in police stations, and the display on public notice boards of the photographs of those who had been taken in, with a warning to all passers-by that these drunken citizens were a disgrace to the nation.

A single theme lay behind all the changes that Gorbachev was aiming for. Its single-word shorthand was 'perestroika' – restructuring. As Gorbachev explained, this was not merely or solely a matter of change in different branches of national life, but a 'restructuring of people's psychology'. Within the parameters of Communist Party rule, and the territorial unity and integrity of the multinational Soviet Union, perestroika offered the prospect of unprecedented change. Speaking to the Writers' Congress on December 18, the outspoken poet Yevgeni Yevtushenko, made a swingeing attack on censorship, on the crimes of the Stalin era and on the contemporary privileges enjoyed by Party officials, and even by State-favoured writers. That Yevtushenko was able to make the speech at all gave courage to those who wanted radical changes in the system; but the omission of the critical sections in the text as published in Literaturnaya Gazeta was a sign that much had yet to be done, even within the framework of a reforming Communism, to bring about real change.

In Poland, the dead hand of repression was still not lifting. Changes to the Penal Code increased the number of political offences that could be punished. Those brought before summary courts were denied the right to legal representation. A Communist Party pronouncement warned the ever-active Polish intelligentsia that they must 'accept the Party's leadership in all aspects of political life, and struggle against any form of opposition'. Book censorship was strengthened. Student autonomy was reduced. Trade union activities were more strictly controlled. In February, in Gdansk, three Solidarity leaders were imprisoned for more than two years for 'participating in activities of an illegal union'. But the instinct of defiance could not be crushed. Several clandestine Solidarity newspapers circulated. More than six hundred book titles, including historical works detailing past Soviet actions against Poland, were published illegally and widely circulated. Each had a print run of about seven thousand copies, was read avidly and was passed from hand to hand, each title reaching tens of thousands of readers. In October, Solidarity demanded the gradual creation of an 'independent society' in Poland, in which the Communist Party and the State would no longer have a monopoly on education, publishing or the media. The government reacted by dismissing more than a hundred 'politically unreliable' senior academic administrators and professors from their posts in fourteen institutions of higher learning throughout Poland.

Gorbachev's spirit of reform alarmed the Communist Party leaders in Czechoslovakia. The Party Secretary, Gustáv Husák, made a special journey to Moscow to seek reassurance that the path of economic reform and efficiency did not have to be followed in Prague. Returning from Moscow, he was able to tell his Party colleagues on the Central Committee that 'we will not take any of the roads based on market-oriented concepts'. The Czechoslovak Communist Party also took the unusual step of issuing a statement doubting that any positive developments would emerge from the Reagan-Gorbachev summit. Particular emphasis was put by the authorities on denouncing the events of 1968 – the 'Prague Spring' of a decade and a half earlier. So angered was Alexander Dubček by these attacks that he emerged from his enforced obscurity as a forestry official to write an open letter to three Czechoslovak newspapers defending what he had done. They refused to publish it.

Muslim fundamentalism was becoming a matter of growing concern to Western Christian countries and to human rights organizations. It was seen most graphically in the punishments imposed in Islamic countries: in the Sudan, cutting off a hand was the punishment for theft. Those convicted of adultery were stoned to death, men being buried up to their waist – if they could struggle free in time they were allowed to live – and women buried up to their armpits. The stones that were thrown had to be not so large as to kill instantly, or so small as to be ineffective. From Colonel Khadaffi's Libya, the government-controlled Radio of Vengeance and Sacred Hate broadcast to other Muslim lands – and in particular to neighbouring Tunisia – criticizing them for not massacring their Jewish populations.

Hijacking also became a focus of international concern, with the predominance of Arab Muslims among the hijackers creating a backlash of public hostility, particularly in the United States. On June 15 two Lebanese Muslim gunmen hijacked a TWA commercial jet airliner with more than a hundred American citizens on board, and forced it to fly to Beirut. It had been en route from Athens to Rome. During its subsequent journeying – from Beirut to Algiers and then back to Beirut – several of the passengers were beaten up and one American was shot dead. The hijackers demanded the release of 766 Shi'ite prisoners held by Israel, most of whom had been captured in the Lebanon. But Reagan announced that the United States would not negotiate conditions with terrorists. Some of the hostages were then taken from the plane and hidden in and around Beirut. Intense behind-the-scenes negotiations began, and after eighteen days, following Israel's release of some of its Shi'ite prisoners, the hostages were also released.

It had been a tense time for the United States. Vice-President George Bush articulated the sense of unease when he said: 'We and our similarly threatened friends must see what actions, militarily and otherwise, can be taken to end this increasingly violent and indiscriminate but purposeful affront to humanity.' Task forces were set up to act as anti-hijack assault teams. Security at airports was strengthened. But, for international terrorists, attacks on innocent civilians, unable to protect themselves and far removed from the cause or even understanding of a quarrel, had long been the instrument of publicizing extremist political demands.

In the Middle East the needs of refugees, including more than a million Palestinian refugees in the Arab States bordering Israel, had always been eclipsed by another need, that of armaments. By far the largest amount of money spent in the region was being spent on arms. In the five-year period from 1984 to 1988 the main suppliers of arms to the Middle East were the Soviet Union and the United States. Of a total worldwide arms trade during the five years that involved the sale of weaponry costing $248,370 million, the Middle East nations received $89,065 million (just over thirty-five per cent of the total). No other region received such a large sum.

Of the sellers of arms – always a source of considerable profit to the seller and the middleman – the Soviet Union was very much at the head of the list, with sales of $33,265 million during the five-year period (37 per cent of the total). The United States came second, with sales of $14,785 million, well under half of the Soviet figure. Britain and France competed closely for the third place in the sale of arms, with Britain's $7,870 million slightly ahead of France's at $7,215 million. Even Communist China managed to sell $900 million worth of arms to the Middle East. Among the recipients of arms, Iran – whose principal supplier, of $2,500 million worth, 83 per cent of its total, was Britain – transferred considerable quantities of weaponry to the Muslim fundamentalist Hizbullah in southern Lebanon, for its fight against Israel. All Israel's arms came from the United States ($6,100 million in the five-year period). Syria's principal supplier was the Soviet Union. Jordan's arms purchases were fairly evenly drawn from East and West.

By contrast to these enormous figures for arms expenditure, the United Nations agencies were able to put together a budget of just under $10,000 million for the coming five-year period, a sum which came from member States, and of which the United States contributed a quarter. The next largest contributions, from the Soviet Union and Japan, were each less than ten per cent of the total. Voluntary fund contributions over the five-year period totalled some $25,000 million. Thus the total spending available to the United Nations agencies, including the High Commissioner for Refugees and the International Children's Emergency Fund, was thirty-nine per cent of the value of Middle East arms sales in that same period, and fourteen per cent of global arms sales.

Natural disasters took their toll without the aid of arms or national rivalries. An earthquake that struck the centre of Mexico City in September killed more than seven thousand people, and made a hundred thousand homeless. Among those who hastened to help with the rescue, and who started a fund for the injured, was the tenor Plácido Domingo. So heavy was the loss of life that the city's baseball stadium had to be used as a morgue. The city's largest maternity ward was among the buildings destroyed by the earthquake, but the fifty-eight new-born babies there at the time were all pulled out alive. A baby's muffled cry had led rescue workers to begin frantically digging, until they came to a cavity in the rubble in which the babies were found.

As in 1984, so in 1985, the worst areas of human suffering were in the famine-cursed regions of Africa. To help the starving millions in Africa, the singer Bob Geldof organized two Live Aid concerts held simultaneously on July 13, one in Wembley Stadium, London, and the other in JFK Stadium, Philadelphia, at which $75 million was raised. The concerts were watched in 160 countries, by more than 1.5 billion people: a quarter of the world's population. The Soviet Union was the only nation that refused to transmit what it denounced as the 'global jukebox'.

More than seven million Ethiopians received international food aid during the year, and it was estimated that as many as six million would need food relief the following year. Civil war continued to impede relief operations: in April, Ethiopian government troops burned down a refugee camp at Ibnat, near Gondar, in which 58,000 people had found shelter. The troops claimed that guerrillas had found shelter in the camp.

An Ethiopian government resettlement drive, moving half a million families from the famine zone to lowland areas in the south and west, was done with utter ruthlessness. Tens of thousands of those intended to be resettled died on the march, lacking the strength to complete the journey, or falling victim to lowland diseases – principally malaria – to which they had not hitherto been exposed. When the French relief agency Médecins sans Frontières, revealed the extent of these deaths, its members were expelled from Ethiopia.

Also leaving Ethiopia, in a clandestine and dramatic military operation, were 25,000 Ethiopian Jews – the Black descendants of Jews who had reached the country from the Arabian peninsula two thousand years earlier. They were airlifted, via the Sudan and Greece, to Israel. Known as Operation Moses, the airlift saved them from the depredations of both famine and civil war.

In Israel itself, a departure from the hitherto inflexible rule that no terrorist threats would be acceded to led in May to the release of 1,150 Palestinian prisoners – 160 of whom were serving life sentences for murder – in return for three Israeli soldiers who had been captured in Lebanon three years earlier. In June, Israeli forces in Lebanon withdrew from all but a three- to four-mile strip of territory along Israel's northern border. After three Israelis had been murdered by Palestinian terrorists in Cyprus in September, the Prime Minister, Shimon Peres, ordered an Israeli air strike against the PLO headquarters near Tunis. In the course of the attack, sixty-five Palestinians and Tunisians were killed. In retaliation, on October 7 the PLO hijacked an Italian cruise liner, the *Achille Lauro*, and shot one of its passengers, Leon Klinghoffer, an elderly, wheelchair-bound American Jew, and threw his body overboard.

The cycle of reprisal and counter-reprisal continued. On November 23 an Egyptian aircraft flying from Athens to Rome was hijacked, and flown to Malta. There, one of the Israeli passengers was killed. On the following day Egyptian commandos, flying to Malta, stormed the plane. Sixty people, including many of the passengers and all but one of the hijackers, were killed in the ensuing shoot-out. Nor was that the final terrorist action of the year. On December 27 fifteen bystanders, Jews and non-Jews, were murdered at Rome airport when Palestinian terrorists opened fire on the El Al Israeli airline ticket counter. Another three people were killed that day at Vienna airport in a similar attack on the El Al check-in counter there.

The Western media tended to focus on the violent incidents in the Middle East to a greater extent than any other region. The Arab-Israeli conflict had become — partly as a result of the PLO's observer status at the United Nations, partly because of the continued and vociferous verbal interventions of the Arab and Muslim States — a conflict covered by newspapers and television to a greater extent than any other thus far. Yet, in terms of loss of life, many other regions were in a far worse situation. For the second year running, Sri Lanka saw the Tamil separatist movement gain in audacity. In January, when Tamil Tigers blew up a troop train, thirty-eight soldiers were killed. In April, soldiers attacked a Tamil village and killed seventy-five villagers. In May, almost a hundred Sinhalese, including many Buddhist monks, were massacred in the holy Buddhist city of Anuradhapura. To escape the fighting, many Tamils fled to southern India, creating a refugee population there of more than 50,000. Within Sri Lanka, a further 40,000 Tamils, fleeing from their homes, were living in refugee camps.

India tried to broker a ceasefire, and Rajiv Gandhi, who took a personal initiative in this, persuaded both the Sri Lankan government and the Tamil leaders to call a halt to the fighting and to begin talks. On June 1 a ceasefire came into effect, and on July 8 talks began in the mountain kingdom of Bhutan, 1,300 miles from the scene of the conflict. The talks reached an impasse when the Sri Lankan government refused to accept even the possibility of Tamil secession. For their part the Tamils rejected any proposal that would involve them giving up their claim to be a 'distinct nation', with the right at least of self-determination. On August 16, while talks dragged on, news reached the negotiators of the murder of two hundred Tamils at Vavuniya. The talks were broken off.

*　　　*　　　*

Scientific research on environmental pollution had begun to alert the international community to the need for serious and immediate collective action. In July the representatives of the thirty-five-nation Convention on Long-Range Transboundary Air Pollution, a convention signed six years earlier, met in Helsinki to establish rules that would be binding on all signatories. It was agreed in a protocol that all the nations present were invited to sign that there should be a thirty per cent reduction in sulphur dioxide emissions that crossed national borders, and that this must be in place within eight years. Not every industrial nation was willing to agree to curbs on its factories, given the expense of anti-pollution measures, and their possible effect on production. Among the countries known as the 'main polluters' who did not sign the protocol were Margaret Thatcher's Britain, Ronald Reagan's United States and General Jaruzelski's Poland.

Environmental concerns, and concerns with regard to public health, increased in July, when the European Commission set out guidelines for farmers within the European Economic Community, regulating the use of pesticides and fertilizers, and creating zones in which they would not be used at all. In September the World Wildlife Fund launched a campaign to conserve the 'wetlands' of the world: the 'swamps, bogs, fens, mires, estuaries, mangrove forests' and other areas that for many years had been regarded as useful wastelands for drainage and development. Their importance to the ecological balance of nature was finally understood, as was the danger to that balance of their disappearance.

France alone of the nuclear powers was insisting on continuing with the atmospheric testing of nuclear weapons. A small but vociferous adversary was the Greenpeace movement, which was prepared to sail a ship, *Rainbow Warrior*, into the test area. To prevent this, French government agents, under orders from Paris, placed a bomb on board the ship, which was then in Auckland harbour. The *Rainbow Warrior* was blown up and sank, and a crewman was killed. The tests went ahead. Later, the French government apologized to Greenpeace for the crewman's death, and to New Zealand for having taken action in an area of New Zealand sovereignty. There was no apology for the nuclear test.

Further research had been done on the effects of a 'nuclear winter' in the event of nuclear war between the Great Powers. It was clear from the final report, made public in September, that the earlier warnings of global disaster were not exaggerated. The research had been sponsored by a highly professional body, the International Council of Scientific Unions. It made clear that the crops grown in the Third World nations north of the equator would be especially at risk. The crops in rice-growing countries, particularly those with large populations – China, Thailand, the Philippines and Bangladesh – would be 'wiped out'. No country would be able to escape a drastic destruction of population and means of subsistence. 'Any disposition to minimize or ignore these effects and the possibility of a tragedy of unprecedented dimensions', the report warned, 'would be a disservice to the human race.'

CHAPTER THIRTY-FIVE

1986

renew . . . reinvigorate . . . restructure.

MIKHAIL GORBACHEV

FROM THE FIRST WEEKS OF 1986, Mikhail Gorbachev made his mark in calling for nuclear disarmament. On January 15, just over a month after Margaret Thatcher had announced her support for President Reagan's Star Wars defence initiative, Gorbachev put forward a comprehensive set of proposals, the declared aim of which was to bring about 'complete, worldwide nuclear disarmament' by the end of the century. During his speech, in an unprecedented comment by a Soviet leader on a Soviet military commitment, Gorbachev described the war in Afghanistan as a 'bleeding wound'. He also promised to deal with 'humanitarian issues' in a new light. To this end the Soviet Jewish activist Anatoli Shcharansky was released in February.

Inside the Soviet Union, Gorbachev continued his efforts to create a modern, technologically efficient, 'restructured' Communist economy and outlook. His promotion of his contemporary, Boris Yeltsin, as Communist Party supremo in Moscow ended the nineteen-year rule of a corrupt and inefficient city administration. At the first Party Congress after he took up his Moscow responsibilities, Yeltsin made a strong attack on privilege, hitherto an accepted and expected aspect of power within the Party at every level.

Gorbachev had set himself a fast and extremely public pace of reform. In his speech at the Party Congress on February 25 he declared that the time had come for the leadership 'to tell the Party and the people honestly and frankly about deficiencies in our political and practical activities, the unfavourable tendencies in the economy and the social and moral sphere, and about the reasons for them'. A 'peculiar psychology', he said, had grown up during the Brezhnev era. It could be summed up as 'how to improve things without changing anything'. It had become necessary to 'renew', 'reinvigorate' and 'restructure' the economy and society. The Soviet Union had to reach the 'highest world levels' of productivity in every sphere, social as well as economic, 'in the shortest possible time'.

In addition to perestroika – restructuring – Gorbachev asked the Communist Party to 'declare a determined and relentless war on bureaucratic practices', and to do so by means of 'glasnost' – openness. The people were henceforth to be informed of what was going on. By this means, there would be a constant check on abuses of authority.

Gorbachev's call for 'openness' was even more electrifying for the Soviet masses than his call for 'restructuring'. Openness was something that the Party and the authorities had never tolerated, much less encouraged. Part of their power lay in secrecy, in the power of the KGB to operate behind the tightest of closed doors, in the restricting of circles of knowledge, in an aura of official self-satisfaction and self-congratulation. To call for openness, as Gorbachev had done, was to put the whole fabric of totalitarian rule on trial.

How far openness was real, and how far it was yet another empty slogan, was put quickly and cruelly to the test. In the very early hours of April 26, two months after Gorbachev's call for openness, the world was confronted – as yet not knowing it – by an event that was initially kept secret by the Soviet authorities, and which, when it became known, was to change many parameters of thought, and help shake to its foundations a system that had been in place for almost sixty years. That morning two explosions destroyed one of four nuclear reactors at Chernobyl, in the Ukraine. The resultant fire was not put out until helicopters, working around the clock, had dropped five thousand tons of lead, limestone, sand and boron.

In the blast of the explosion, and in the radiation poisoning which it generated, 250 people were killed, including two firemen trying to put out the blaze. The figure was withheld from the Soviet people, who were later told that thirty-seven had died. Several hundred thousand people had to be evacuated from the surrounding region. Among the many tons of radioactive material that was shot into the earth's atmosphere by the force of the blast were iodine-131 and caesium-137. The radioactive iodine has a half-life of eight days, the caesium of thirty years. Both are easily absorbed by living tissue.

This was the nuclear accident that scientists and environmentalists had long dreaded: but the Soviet authorities were silent throughout April 26,

27 and 28. The first intimation that something seriously wrong had occurred came when Swedish scientists noted on their instruments high radioactivity in the winds. Even then the Soviet authorities, forgetting the new 'openness', said only that an 'accident' had taken place. As alarm spread on the wings of rumour, Soviet television countered by showing children at play, allegedly in the 'region' where the nuclear reactor was located. When, on May 1, Gorbachev reviewed the May Day parade from the viewing stand in the Kremlin, nothing was said or done to suggest that a momentous, even a catastrophic event had taken place four days earlier.

Not only was the western Soviet Union at risk. A radioactive cloud was also on the move, crossing Poland, Czechoslovakia and Austria, northern Italy and western Switzerland – including Lake Geneva, where the nuclear disarmament talks were taking place. From there it moved over eastern France – on the day that Gorbachev was taking the May Day parade in Moscow – and then on to the English Channel and Britain. Making a swoop off the Atlantic coast of Ireland the cloud then crossed Britain again before traversing the North Sea and, on May 8, reaching the coast of Norway. Winds carried the radioactivity in many other directions, as far south as Greece and Sicily, as far west as Spain and Portugal, as far north as Finland, as far south as Roumania and Turkey. In all, twenty States were affected.

The main effect of the fall-out was an increase in cancer. Calculations of the cancer deaths that would be caused over the following seventy years varied, from a minimum of 5,000 deaths in all to a maximum of 40,000. Some scientists predicted that the number would be much higher, as high as half a million. As to radiation-linked genetic abnormalities, there was no means of predicting what, or on what scale, these would be. It was a cruel case of 'only time will tell'. What did not require time was the sense of outrage, fear and alarm that the Chernobyl nuclear explosion caused; and the anger that the Soviet authorities had kept silent about it for three whole days. Soviet citizens had been taught since the revolution to trust their leaders and their pronouncements. Even when they had been let down in the past, it had not been on a matter touching future life and death so closely.

Governments beyond the Soviet Union were also puzzled as to how to react. The French government denied for several days that the radioactive cloud had passed over France. Food and livestock were affected in all the areas over which the cloud had passed. The West German government was the first to offer monetary compensation to farmers; Sweden did likewise.

For several years British sheep farmers were to have to slaughter contaminated sheep that were judged unsafe for eating. They too were compensated. But monetary compensation could not make up for the fears that the radiation cloud engendered, or for the long-term damage that it might have brought with it. The full effects of this one explosion will not be known until well into the twenty-first century.

The first political casualty was the credibility of the Soviet authorities among their own people. Communist credibility was shaken. In mid-December, after the authorities in Moscow replaced a Kazakh as First Secretary of the Kazakh Republic with a Russian, there were unprecedented riots in the streets of the Kazakh capital, Alma Ata. Cars were set on fire, shops broken into and looted, and a policeman killed. He was the first victim of a process of disintegration that was to end five years later with all fifteen republics of the Soviet Union declaring their independence.

Openness did not die as a result of the initial secrecy that was put up around Chernobyl: indeed, it was accelerated. For the first time, details were broadcast of disasters as they happened: the sinking of a Soviet cruise liner in the Black Sea with the death of four hundred passengers, the attempted hijacking of a Soviet airliner in Siberia, and the sinking, following a fire, of a Soviet nuclear submarine in the Atlantic. Even the clean-up operations at Chernobyl were shown on Soviet television, and the extent of the disaster made clear. In the sphere of human rights, Gorbachev also reversed the policy of his predecessors, from Lenin to Chernenko. After several years in internal exile, Andrei Sakharov was allowed to go abroad for medical treatment, and told that on his return he could resume his scientific work at the Academy of Sciences: he was told of these decisions in a telephone call from Gorbachev himself, an astounding departure from years of cloak-and-dagger relationships between the authorities and the dissidents. One by one, the leading victims of Soviet repression were given their freedom: Yuri Orlov, a founder of the Helsinki human rights monitors in the Soviet Union, was allowed to emigrate, and Irina Ratushinskaya, the poet, was released from prison, and then allowed to emigrate.

In defence of changing what had hitherto seemed the unchangeable, and in answer to the unease of those who were concerned that the changes might go too far from a Communist perspective, Gorbachev asked a gathering of writers in June: 'If not us, who? And if not now, when?'

*   *   *

In Poland, no such liberalization was taking place. When Solidarity groups began to reform, the government warned that such 'destructive actions' could not be tolerated. No action was taken against the new groups, but a plea by Solidarity to be allowed to begin talks with the government was ignored. The Catholic Church continued to warn the government of the dangers of its 'divisive' ideological rigidity, and criticized the newly introduced 'religious knowledge' classes taught by Marxist teachers as 'undermining the value of religion'. A government poll made it clear, however, that in the Church-Party balance, the youth had made up their minds decisively: the opinion poll showed that eighty per cent of young people blamed 'the Party and bribery' for Poland's political and economic crisis, while seventy-five per cent took part in religious activities.

Anti-Soviet feeling, never far from the surface in Poland, was exacerbated after the Chernobyl nuclear accident. After the radioactive cloud had passed over north-eastern Poland, the Polish government announced that it had done so, and that there were dangerous levels of radioactive contamination. In an emergency measure, the sale of milk from grass-fed cows was banned.

In Czechoslovakia, as in Poland, the Communist Party was wary of following Gorbachev's openness. The Party's power depended upon rigid control, and the Czech Party leadership saw, more clearly indeed than Gorbachev, that openness once promoted as a virtue would lead to a questioning, not only of the nature of Party rule, but whether one Party alone was necessarily the way forward. The Czechoslovak government did not reveal the extent to which the Chernobyl fall-out had affected Czechoslovakia, although radiation levels had risen sharply, especially in the eastern, Slovak region, the border of which was only 450 miles from the explosion. In its first reaction, the Czechoslovak government went so far as to attack Western criticisms of the Soviet Union as panic-mongering. It made no public comment when, at the end of the year, Soviet scientists gave the figure of 40,000 as their estimate of the number of additional cancer deaths that would follow in Europe as a result of the explosion.

The dissidents of Charter 77 circulated clandestine criticism of the government for not having told the truth about Chernobyl. They also issued a statement recalling the 'courage' of the Hungarian insurgents of thirty years earlier. When one of the leading Charter 77 members, the playwright Václav Havel, was awarded the much coveted Erasmus Prize, he did not travel to Holland to receive it, lest the Communist authorities refused to let him back into the country. In a speech that was read out on his behalf, however, he stated that the honour was not his alone, but that of the Charter 77 movement. Ironically, as reforms spread in the Soviet Union, more and more Czechs were watching the once derided Soviet television and reading the hitherto conformist Soviet newspapers for signs of how far forward openness could go.

The psychological shockwaves from Chernobyl were also felt in Hungary. In the words of a contemporary British political scientist, George Schöpflin, whose father, when Hungarian Ambassador to Norway, had defected from Hungary in the early 1950s, and whose grandmother had been living in Budapest during the 1956 uprising: 'Unease and ignorance over the impact of Chernobyl, exacerbated by official mendacity, silence and disinformation, only made this worse. The extent of popular ignorance of the real and mythical dangers gave rise to a deep-seated fear, which had no viable outlet but the State.'

In Yugoslavia, the impact of Chernobyl was seen in a series of spontaneous public demonstrations against nuclear power stations. The 'Green' movement, which had begun to take hold in Yugoslavia, was given a strong impetus. When the European Economic Community imposed a ban on imported meat from Yugoslavia, and on certain vegetable products, there was a realization of just how deleterious the explosion had been. In vain did the government try to put the blame for the ban on discriminatory economic policies.

For Yugoslavs, there was a crisis at home that was disturbing the unity of the State: the continuing struggle of the ethnic Albanian majority within Kosovo for greater autonomy. Several Albanian nationalists were brought to trial in both the Kosovo and Macedonian regions, and several Communist Party officials were expelled because of their support for the claims of the Albanians in Kosovo. From the Serbs and Montenegrins living in Kosovo came claims that they were being discriminated against by the Albanian majority. At the Yugoslav Writers' Congress a year earlier it had been alleged that the Serb minority in Kosovo had been the victims of discrimination, persecution, and even 'genocide' at the hands of the Albanians there, and that the authorities in Belgrade were doing nothing effective to protect the Serbs from continuing harassment and violence.

In Asia, the Iran-Iraq War continued, as did the struggle of the Afghan Muslim mujaheddin fighters against the Soviet-supported Marxist regime of Babrak Karmal. In May, Karmal was replaced by the former head of the Afghan secret service, thirty-nine-year-old General Mohammed Najibullah, who travelled the war-torn country calling for 'national reconciliation' and promising that he would respect Islamic traditions. He was not widely believed. The mujaheddin, despite the weight of Soviet weaponry being used against them, were beginning to buy weapons on the international arms market that enabled them to shoot down the Soviet warplanes that had hitherto attacked them with impunity. The new weapons included American-made Stinger anti-aircraft missiles, British-made Blowpipe anti-aircraft missiles and Swiss-made Oerlikon anti-aircraft guns.

Confronted by an end to what had seemed an automatic superiority in the air, the Soviet military authorities in Afghanistan ordered attacks to be made on mujaheddin civilian targets. But they remained reluctant to commit Soviet troops to any direct confrontation with their increasingly active adversary, and, following Gorbachev's description of the Soviet involvement as a 'bleeding wound', the first Soviet troops, eight thousand in all, were withdrawn. Western observers debated the meaning of this withdrawal: some were sceptical that it betokened any real change, especially as more than 100,000 Soviet troops were still in Afghanistan. Other observers recognized that Gorbachev was signalling a change of policy, and that he might soon seek a negotiated political solution in place of the continued and essentially unsuccessful military entanglement.

The war in Afghanistan was entering its eighth year. Among its victims were five million Afghan refugees, a fifth of the country's entire population. Most of them were in vast refugee camps in neighbouring Pakistan and Iran. Those in Pakistan became involved in the communal violence that erupted between the local Pathan tribesmen, and fellow Muslims who were members of a community which had come from India as refugees almost forty years earlier.

In Sri Lanka, where the Tamil separatists were in almost total control of the Jaffna peninsula in the north of the island, only the Sri Lankan army base at Jaffna Fort was under government control. Tamil terrorist attacks took place throughout the island, even in the capital, Colombo. When an Air Lanka passenger plane was blown up at Katunayake airport, most of the thirty-one dead were European and Japanese tourists. In a series of car-bomb and other attacks in the capital, more than thirty Sri Lankan civilians were killed. When the Sri Lankan government contemplated bombing the Tamil strongholds in the north, it was warned against doing this by the Indian government, whose own Tamil region looked with considerable sympathy on their fellow Tamils 'struggling to be free'. Even the government of India took action, however, against violent manifestations of Tamil nationalism on Indian soil: following street fighting in Madras, the Indian army raided a Tamil guerrilla camp in southern India, seizing large quantities of arms and ammunition.

In August, 154 Tamil refugees from Sri Lanka were dumped at sea by the West German cargo ship that had taken them across the Atlantic: they were simply put into lifeboats and set adrift. Rescued by Canadian coast-guards, they were given asylum in Canada.

One environmental hazard that year, although without the element of the unknown generated by Chernobyl, created alarm in Western Europe. In November a fire at a chemical warehouse in Basle, Switzerland, caused tons of pesticides and mercury to be released into the Rhine. It was the start of the hibernation of the eels; almost all of them were killed, as were a great number of other fish. Drinking-water supplies were endangered in West Germany and the Netherlands. It was to take more than three years before the last significant traces of the pollution had gone. Other chemical plants in Switzerland contributed to the environmental disaster. When a herbicidal acid leaked into the river further downstream, in West Germany, the water supplies of dozens of towns had to be shut off while the poison made its way to the sea. Also that year, two clouds of poison gas, one of phenol and the other of phosgene, leaked from chemical factories in Switzerland.

Of greater long-term danger, in many ways on a par with Chernobyl, a 'hole' in the ozone layer above Antarctica – the world's most southerly continent – was found by the British Antarctic Survey. An expedition from the United States which studied the causes of the 'hole' – which was between ten and twenty miles above the earth's surface – ruled out natural causes such as fluxes in solar radiation, or an upswelling of air currents. The expedition confirmed earlier scientific analysis that it was chlorofluorocarbons (CFCs) that were to blame: the use of aerosol propellants in refrigeration units, in the manufacture of foam and as solvents. These innocuous and unspectacular chemical adjuncts to modern life appeared to have a lethal biproduct inconceivable to those who had first developed and used them. Since 1980 the European Economic Union countries had imposed a limit on the production of CFCs, though that limit had come to seem a low one. After the 1986 discoveries, the United States Environment Protection Agency suggested that a higher limit be established worldwide, while warning that if production of the CFC chemicals were to be maintained at the current level, the ozone layer would continue to be depleted, and that, by the year 2025, there would be an extra 142,000 cases of skin cancer every year.

One existing, but still newly discovered, disease was threatening to take a far heavier toll. With no vaccine discovered for AIDS, its prevalence in the United States had reached 25,000 cases, all incurable. In Africa ten times as many people were dying, and the numbers of those infected continued to grow. Rwanda and Zaire were the two African countries worst affected.

In the civil war in Nicaragua, the Sandinista government faced renewed attacks from the Contra rebels. Reagan saw the conflict as a challenge to the ever threatening spread of Communism in Central America. For him, Nicaragua was a 'second Cuba' on America's doorstep. His efforts to secure aid for the Contras were persistent, in the face of considerable opposition. On March 20 the House of Representatives voted by the narrowest of margins, 222 to 210, to deny him a $100 million aid package to the Contras. That vote, he said, was 'a dark day for freedom'. The Senate rallied to Reagan's support, however, reversing the House vote, which then had to be taken again. On June 26 the House passed the aid package by 221 to 209. Two days later the International Court of Justice in The Hague ruled that United States aid to the Contras was in violation of international law, which forbade intervention and the use of force in the internal affairs of a sovereign State. When called upon by the Security Council to comply with the court's judgment, the United States cast its veto.

The $100 million that Congress had voted was not the only money Reagan was able to direct to the Contras. By using the money acquired from America's arms sales to Iran, he was able to send the Contras a substantial amount of arms and ammunition. Such a device, unauthorized by Congress, was illegal, and had to be carried out by the administration in strict secrecy. After a flurry of newspaper revelations, however, details of the transaction were admitted by Reagan in a televised broadcast to the nation on November 13. Twelve days later his National Security Adviser, Admiral Poindexter, resigned, and the man whose brainchild the 'Iran–Contra' link had been, Colonel Oliver North, a much decorated veteran of the war in Vietnam, was sacked from the National Security Council. When asked about the deal by a Congressional inquiry, both pleaded the Fifth Amendment, whereby an American citizen had the constitutional right not to incriminate himself.

The 'Iran-Contra' affair would not go away. As an exercise in clandestine government activity it was not unique, but it had been exposed. The repercussions were to affect many individuals, and inevitably the credibility of Reagan himself. In a politically vigorous democracy, all Republicans were to suffer as a result of it, as the Democrats, who in the mid-term elections had gained control of the Senate, expressed their moral indignation.

The United States was also involved in a violent dispute with Colonel Khadaffi of Libya, whose government was financing terrorist activity in many parts of the world, including Northern Ireland. In March, after a Libyan missile attack on American aircraft exercising in the Gulf of Sirte, American aircraft attacked military targets in Libya. Fifty-six Libyans were killed. In April American bombers, some of them flying from American air bases in Britain, struck at terrorist training camps around the Libyan cities of Tripoli and Benghazi. During the raids, a hundred people were killed. The Libyan support for international terror continued.

In the continuing exploration of space, the American *Challenger* space shuttle was to be yet another small advance in the steady scheme of experiment and familiarity of space exploration. It was launched from Cape Kennedy on January 28. Seventy-four seconds after lift-off, it exploded. The image of its disintegration was seen by hundreds of shocked observers and tourists on the ground at the launch centre, and by millions of shocked television viewers. All seven people on board the shuttle were killed. When, within four months, two unmanned American booster rockets and a European Community rocket had all failed, the space exploration programme was suspended.

One technological development that year was to have extraordinary global repercussions within a decade: the cellular telephone. By the end of the year, there were 115,000 subscribers in Britain, a rate more than a hundred times faster than that of the expansion of the telephone when it first became commercially available.

The anti-democratic forces were active in maintaining their control in many quarters of the globe. In South Africa, as protests against apartheid gathered momentum, President Botha established a state of emergency, and put in place even greater powers of arrest and detention without trial. In August, twenty-one people were killed when police opened fire on demonstrators in the Black township of Soweto. In December, the South African government imposed a stringent ban on newspaper reporting of 'unrest'. In China, in December, police moved on to the streets of Shanghai after three consecutive days of student demonstrations demanding more democracy. The demonstrators were dispersed. When student demonstrations spread to Peking two days later, the police again broke them up, after which the government announced tighter controls on public meetings.

Civil wars also took their annual toll. In August, anti-government forces in Sudan shot down a civilian airliner: all fifty-seven people on board were killed. In South Yemen, in December, during twelve days of fighting between rival factions of the Marxist government, 13,000 Yemenis were killed. During the fighting, boats from the British Royal Yacht *Britannia* took part in the evacuation of foreign nationals. In Angola, the civil war was in its tenth year. Financial aid to the UNITA forces came from the United States: Reagan received UNITA's leader, Jonas Savimbi, in Washington in January. But the European parliament in Strasbourg refused to give Savimbi a hearing: his close links with South Africa put him beyond the pale. South African forces were indeed giving Savimbi help against the Marxist MPLA, mounting a missile attack in August on Namibe harbour, in which two Soviet supply ships were badly damaged.

The civil war in Angola was characterized by an element of warfare that had begun to cause widespread maiming of civilians wherever it was used: the sowing of landmines to prevent the rival faction advancing. Two correspondents of the *Washington Post*, David B. Ottaway and Patrick E. Tyler, wrote on July 27: 'Among the strongest impressions taken away was the extent to which Angola is disintegrating as a functioning State. There are thousands of land mines sown in abandoned cornfields, from which hundreds of thousands of peasants have fled to the cities, making the once self-sufficient country now heavily dependent on food imports.' The human cost of the destruction caused by the landmines, both physically and economically, had been placed in front of the Western conscience.

Terrorism also remained a global phenomenon. In January, in the Christian sector of Beirut, twenty-seven people were killed when Muslim fundamentalists exploded a car bomb. In Spain, nine civil guards were killed in July when their bus was blown up by Basque separatists. In September, when Pakistani commandos stormed a hijacked Pan Am jet airliner at Karachi airport, Palestinian hijackers opened fire on their hostage passengers, and seventeen passengers were killed. On the following day, twenty-one Jews were killed when Arab gunmen opened fire on a synagogue in Istanbul.

Nature's ravages continued to parallel those of man. In Cameroon 1,700 people died in August when toxic gases erupted from the volcanic Lake Nyos. In October nine hundred people were killed when an earthquake struck El Salvador. Each natural disaster, as each war and civil war, created more people in need: the homeless, the dispossessed and the refugees. In an attempt to raise public awareness of the extent of the world refugee problem, the United Nations organized a sponsored 'Race against Time'. The race was inaugurated on May 25, when a Sudanese runner, Omar Khalifa, who had set off from Khartoum, reached the United Nations building in New York. Thirty million runners throughout the world took part in the run, which raised $50 million to help feed the refugees, who, in their crowded camps and tents, had no means of sustaining themselves.

In stressing the principle of 'farming not food', whereby the emphasis for aid would be on enabling famine-stricken regions to be refarmed and revitalized, the United Nations set aside $460 million for the coming three years for the worst affected areas. At the same time, a more ambitious five-year programme, known as the African Priority Programme for Economic Recovery, was launched, with an allocation of $25,000 million a year. Here, too, the intention was to encourage small-scale farming in as wide an area as possible, and to finance similarly small-scale projects to control drought and desertification. Africa, large areas of which were the scene of the world's most concentrated poverty − where civil wars and AIDS were also taking their toll of human life − had become by far the main focus of both humanitarian and agricultural aid.

CHAPTER THIRTY-SIX

1987

> ... to display the principles of democracy and com-
> pliance with the law and with human rights.
>
> THE EUROPEAN SINGLE ACT

THE IRAN-IRAQ WAR was seldom in the headlines of Western newspapers, but it continued to be the most costly war in human terms of any conflict being fought in the world. Starting on 10 January 1987 the Iranians launched an offensive towards the Iraqi city of Basra. Breaking through the Iraqi defences they reached the eastern outskirts of the city. But the Iraqi defences held, and by the end of February the Iranians were driven off: in that one offensive there were 50,000 Iranian dead.

In Lebanon, the struggle for control of Beirut – earlier one between Christian and Muslim militias – reached yet another cruel phase when Muslim was pitted against Muslim. On February 13, Shi'ite Amal militiamen prevented United Nations vehicles with food and medicine from entering the Palestinian refugee camps at Chatila and Bourj-el-Barajneh. As many as 35,000 Palestinians were on the verge of starvation. Amal were also fighting Druze militia in and around the city. On February 22 the Syrian government, whose troops were already in control of the hills to the east of Beirut, and of the Beirut–Damascus highway, took action of its own, sending four thousand Syrian troops into West Beirut. But the Amal siege of the refugee camps continued, and there were many deaths within the camps of those who had suffered so terribly five years earlier, during the fighting for control of Beirut at the time of the Israeli invasion.

It was not until April 7 that Syrian forces reached Chatila, and April 8 before they entered Bourj-el-Barajneh, ending a five-month siege, and making it possible for United Nations food and medical supplies to bring long-awaited relief.

*　　*　　*

The civil war in Sri Lanka, already in its fifth year, escalated. At the end of January a Sri Lankan army operation against the Tamil Tigers in the east coast region of Batticaloa led to two hundred Tamil deaths. At the beginning of April there was fighting among rival Tamil groups. Against Indian advice the previous year, in mid-April the Sri Lankan air force bombed the Tamil-held northern peninsula, damaging the hospital in Jaffna. Retaliation was swift, with 127 people being killed in Tamil attacks on buses near Trincomalee, and eighty in a bomb blast at Colombo bus station. As a reprisal, rebel targets in Jaffna were bombed. When the southern Indian Tamil Nadu provincial assembly voted to send food, medicine and clothing to the Tamils in Jaffna, Sri Lanka accused India 'of helping people to adopt violence against a friendly and democratic neighbour'.

On May 22 the Sri Lankan government launched a full-scale military offensive against the Jaffna peninsula. Six days later Rajiv Gandhi spoke up against what he called the 'cold-blooded slaughter of thousands of Sri Lankan citizens'. On June 3, thirty Buddhist priests were massacred by Tamil gunmen. On the following day, Sri Lankan naval patrol boats turned back an Indian naval flotilla that was trying to bring food and medicine to the Tamils near Jaffna. A day later, the Indian air force dropped humanitarian supplies to Jaffna from the air.

To avoid becoming inexorably drawn in to the civil war in Sri Lanka as the defender of the Tamils, the Indian government offered to open negotiations with Sri Lanka, and if possible to put itself forward as a mediator. Talks followed, and on July 29 the Indian government signed an accord, whereby it agreed to use its good offices to supervise a Tamil Tiger ceasefire.

The Tamil rebels accepted the Indian intervention, and at the beginning of August began to hand over their arms. In return, Sri Lanka released hundreds of Tamils who had been interned. Tamil activists who had been directing the struggle from Madras, and recruiting Tamil supporters there, returned to Sri Lanka. But even as the handing over of arms continued, rival Tamil groups began an internecine struggle, and the handing over of arms, as yet incomplete, came to a virtual halt. As fighting between the Tamil factions intensified, the Indian troops who were meant to be supervising the ceasefire found themselves embroiled in a military confrontation with those whom they were ostensibly helping. On October 11, after breakaway Tamil Tigers attacked Sri Lankan troops, and the death toll began to rise on both sides, the Indian peacekeeping force, some 30,000 men in all, launched an armed attack on Jaffna.

Indian peacekeepers were in battle against the Tamil Tigers. In three days fighting up to October 15, more than two hundred Tamil rebels had been killed. On October 16 Rajiv Gandhi ordered three thousand reinforcements to be flown in. By the end of the month five hundred Indian soldiers had been killed by Tamils. But by the end of the year Jaffna was under Indian army control. It had succeeded where the Sri Lankan army had failed.

From his office in the Kremlin, Gorbachev was casting around for some way of extricating the Soviet Union from Afghanistan. One possibility which he considered was to call back the Afghan king, Zahir Shah, from exile in Italy, in the hope that he might be able to gather both Islamic and Communist support. To make the return of the king all but impossible, Dr Najibullah, the General Secretary of the People's Democratic Party – the country's only legal political Party, hitherto Moscow's nominee – declared himself President.

Annoyed but not deterred, Gorbachev was determined that the days of Soviet intervention in Afghanistan were numbered, and made it known that he would accept a United Nations initiative to reach an internal Afghan settlement. Within the Soviet Union he continued to seek the modernization of the Communist Party, with a view to preserving the Communist ideology and structure of the Soviet Union, and the loyalty to Moscow of all its fifteen republics. At a meeting of the Central Committee on January 27 he called for a 'democratization' of the Party. Despite the 'historic successes' of the past, such as the construction of Socialism and the defeat of Nazi Germany, in the 1970s and early 1980s, he said, 'elements of stagnation and other phenomena alien to Socialism' had begun to make themselves apparent. The Party leadership of the time – he was referring to Brezhnev, although he did not name him – had failed to respond 'appropriately' to the worsening situation. Economic growth rates had fallen, and social problems, including alcoholism and drug abuse, had worsened. Party and State institutions were themselves affected by these tendencies, leading in some cases to 'the abuse of office, intolerance of criticism and even corruption'. In such circumstances, perestroika – restructuring – was not merely an option, it was a necessity.

'We must not retreat and there is no place to retreat to,' Gorbachev declared. Two weeks later he ordered the release of 140 political prisoners from prisons and labour camps throughout the Soviet Union, and promised to review all other cases. Among those released before the end of February was Dr Josef Begun, one of the leading Jewish advocates of emigration to

Israel who, punished for teaching Hebrew, was then in the fourth year of a twelve-year sentence. Within two years all the Jewish 'Prisoners of Zion' had been freed and had left the Soviet Union, most of them for Israel.

The Central Committee then listened to a series of reform proposals the like of which no Soviet leader had put forward before. The main means by which the Communist character of the Soviet Union was to be enhanced, Gorbachev said, lay in 'the extension of Socialist democracy and popular initiative'. The further 'democratization' of Soviet society must be the Party's first priority. To this end, a new law on Socialist enterprise would extend self-management in the workplace. Comparable changes would be made in the organization of collective farms. The role of agricultural co-operatives would be strengthened. Gorbachev went on to say that even the electoral system would be changed, in such a way as to ensure greater 'popular involvement' at all stages of the selection of Communist Party candidates. 'As a rule', voters would be allowed to choose from among several contenders for each vacancy. The Party apparatus itself would be 'democratized'. Party secretaries, from the local to the republic level, would henceforth be elected by secret ballot open to an 'unlimited number' of Party candidates. The same principles might eventually be extended, Gorbachev told the Central Committee, to the Party's own senior enclaves, and to other State organizations. In every case, he said, control 'from above' – to which he insisted that he remained committed – would henceforth be combined with a greater degree of openness and accountability 'from below'.

Within the parameters of central control and the continuing rule of the Communist Party, Gorbachev had opened up a dizzying prospect for change. Within days of his speech, Soviet sources were making it clear to Western diplomats and journalists that there was less than unanimous support for his proposals. But Gorbachev was insistent that they be implemented. From February onwards, the election of local Party Secretaries took place from among at least two candidates, and sometimes more. At the end of March it was announced that 'as an experiment' the local Party elections due to take place in June would allow the nomination of more candidates than there were seats available. Initially this took place in about two per cent of constituencies. It was a small but revolutionary start. The question was, which revolution: the reform of a one-Party system, or the start of a multi-Party one? Gorbachev had taken an enormous risk in introducing the concept of choice, even within the single Party to which he was committed.

Another essentially revolutionary change was the subject of legislation at the June meeting of the Supreme Soviet, when a law was passed which provided for the 'national discussion of important questions of State life'. The new law was intended to provide a legal basis for the existing practice of public discussion of draft items of legislation. But it also provided a procedure for the collection of the results of such discussions, and for their popular dissemination on the basis of 'broad openness'. During the debate in the Supreme Soviet, emphasis was also placed, at Gorbachev's urging, on the promotion of non-Party members to leading positions in all areas of Soviet life.

There was considerable pressure from 'old-guard' Communists to pull back from the brink of rapid change. At a meeting with visiting French politicians in September, Gorbachev spoke in favour of 'Socialist pluralism'. But such pluralism was not at all what the orthodox Communists wanted to encourage. In direct answer to Gorbachev, the head of the KGB, Viktor Chebrikov, publicly accused Western Intelligence agents of trying to 'subvert' Soviet youth and to 'sow the seeds of nationalist discontent', thereby seeking 'to undermine Socialism morally and politically, and to inculcate political and moral pluralism.'

As an indication of their power, at the end of October those senior Party members who were opposed to 'openness' forced Gorbachev to lead an attack on one of his closest allies, Boris Yeltsin, who was forced to resign from his leadership of the Moscow Communist Party apparatus: an apparatus particularly in need of the changes Gorbachev wished to bring about. Yeltsin had demanded an even faster pace of reforms than Gorbachev – who had himself begun to criticize those who wanted to speed up the pace of reform.

On November 2, during a three-hour speech marking the start of the seventieth anniversary celebrations of the Communist revolution, Gorbachev recognized the considerable, and indeed growing, opposition in Communist Party circles to his reform proposals. There was also opposition from those who doubted that the changes would benefit the Soviet people. On a visit to the Soviet space-research city at Baikonur, Gorbachev was asked: 'When is perestroika going to reach us?' One manifestation of reform came on November 14, when the ballet dancer Rudolf Nureyev was allowed to return to the Soviet Union to visit his family, for the first time since his defection twenty-six years earlier.

In foreign affairs Gorbachev pursued a similarly radical and accelerated policy as in domestic Soviet life. When Margaret Thatcher visited him in the spring, four agreements were signed: on Anglo-Soviet co-operation in the peaceful uses of outer space, on the improvement of direct communications between Downing Street and the Kremlin, on greater links in culture, education and information, and on the building of new embassies in London and Moscow. Margaret Thatcher was also allowed to conduct a live television interview with three Soviet journalists.

How far Gorbachev wanted to go, how far he could go, was a subject much debated in the West. Many pressures were put on him, and many suggestions made. Visiting Berlin on June 12, Reagan appealed to him to 'open this gate' and to 'tear down this wall'. Gorbachev made no response. But at his discussions with Margaret Thatcher in Moscow, and eight months later at the Brize Norton air base in Britain on his way to Washington, he first outlined and then described in detail his thinking with regard to a plan he had put forward the previous year, the abolition of an entire category of nuclear weapons: land-based nuclear missiles, of both short and intermediate range. At the Washington summit with Reagan, held between December 7 and 10, this was achieved. The weapons themselves constituted only four per cent of the nuclear weapons of the two Super Powers, but it was the first time since the lapsed Anti-Ballistic Missile (ABM) Treaty fifteen years earlier that such an agreement to disarm had been reached.

Both Reagan and Gorbachev intended the Washington agreement to be only a start. Their stated aim for future talks was to reduce their strategic nuclear arms stocks by fifty per cent, as well as to observe the ABM Treaty, and, most significant of all, with the long-term objective of avoiding a nuclear confrontation, 'to devise measures' which would enable both sides 'to ensure predictability in the development of the US-Soviet strategic relationship under conditions of strategic stability, to reduce the risk of nuclear war'.

Gorbachev took another unprecedented step when, on his return from Washington, he appeared on Soviet television to explain what had been achieved. The treaty, he said, was 'a victory for the new political thinking'. Although only four per cent of all Soviet and American nuclear weapons had been eliminated, 'scientists had calculated that just five per cent was sufficient to destroy the world'. Gorbachev did point out, however – for this was the basis of United States nuclear superiority, and he had been unable to counter it – that the American Strategic Defence Initiative (Star Wars) programme was still in place.

Neither before nor after the Washington summit had there been any pause in the pace or range of openness. Gorbachev was insistent that such hesitation as was being expressed within the Party should not impede his vision. In

November, the Young Communist newspaper *Komsomolskaya Pravda* raised the question, which human rights campaigners in the West had long been disturbed about, of Soviet abuses of psychiatric medicine. The newspaper went so far as to accuse some Soviet psychiatrists of colluding with the police to incarcerate sane and healthy people. Other topics that were aired under the new policy of open and frank debate included the poor treatment of soldiers returning from the Afghan war, drugs, crime, alcoholism and prostitution. Hitherto banned books were published, including Anna Akhmatova's *Requiem* and Boris Pasternak's *Doctor Zhivago*.

In one area of Soviet self-scrutiny, Gorbachev built on what Khrushchev had begun thirty-one years earlier, telling the truth about the Soviet past. In a speech in July to radio, television and newspaper journalists, Gorbachev insisted that the Stalinist purges could 'never be forgotten or justified'. Following his speech, the illustrated magazine *Ogonek* published the first full account of Stalin's purge of the army in 1937–9. The magazine also printed an open letter which had been written to Stalin in 1939 by Fedor Raskolnikov, an 'Old Bolshevik', but never before published in the Soviet Union, in which Raskolnikov accused Stalin of 'wading through the blood of yesterday's friends and comrades'.

Raskolnikov had been a contributor to *Pravda* since 1910. In 1917 he led the Kronstadt sailors in their uprising against the Kerensky government in Petrograd. In 1938, while serving as a Soviet diplomat in Bulgaria, he had been recalled to Moscow, whither many of his fellow diplomats had earlier been recalled, never to be seen again. Fleeing instead to Belgium, he wrote his open letter to Stalin. A few months later he died in unexplained circumstances in the South of France. He was forty-eight years old.

But even for Gorbachev there were limits to what he felt could be revealed. The decision by Stalin to murder tens of thousands of Polish officers in 1940 remained a taboo subject. And in his speech on the seventieth anniversary of the revolution Gorbachev had disappointed many Western observers who imagined that the 'whole truth' was about to be told when he conceded only that 'many thousands' had perished in the purges, rather than the millions who had in fact perished. For Soviet citizens, there was encouraging news when it was announced that a Politburo commission had been set up to investigate the judicial proceedings of the Stalinist period, with a view to rehabilitating parents who had been killed, or husbands who had disappeared without trace.

*   *   *

Nationalism and separatism were potent forces for extremist violence. In June, seventeen Spaniards were killed when Basque separatists carried out a car-bomb attack in Barcelona. In July, forty Hindu bus passengers were killed in India when they were attacked by Sikh extremists demanding Sikh independence. That year the total death toll at the hands of Sikh militants reached more than five hundred. Throughout the year, the Albanian majority in the Kosovo province of Yugoslavia continued to assert its demand for greater autonomy, and clashes between Serbs and Albanians were frequent and at times bloody. In Tibet, in October, three Buddhist monks were among those who were killed when Chinese troops opened fire on unarmed demonstrators protesting against the continuation of Chinese rule.

Islamic fundamentalism took an unexpectedly violent turn in Mecca, the holiest city of Islam. During the annual pilgrimage, Iranian pilgrims, incited by Ayatollah Khomeini, clashed with the Saudi Arabian security forces whose task was to maintain order during the pilgrimage. Four hundred people were killed during the ensuing fighting, including 275 of the Iranians.

One terrorist initiative was forestalled that year, in November, when a Panamanian-registered trawler was boarded by the French authorities in French territorial waters. Its cargo of arms and ammunition was confiscated: it had been loaded in Libya, and was destined for the IRA in Northern Ireland.

As the year came to an end, rebel Black guerrillas in Zimbabwe, which had been ruled for several years by its Black majority, massacred sixteen Whites at a Christian mission near Bulawayo.

Western European unity took a further step towards fulfilment on July 1, when the twelve member States of the European Economic Community signed the Single European Act. The aim of the act, as its preamble stated, was to 'transform relations as a whole among these States into a European Union'. This had first been envisaged, the preamble noted, as early as 1893, in the Solemn Declaration of Stuttgart. High standards were set for the members: 'in particular to display the principles of democracy and compliance with the law and with human rights'. At a practical level, the members of the European Union were committed to abolish trade and employment barriers across their frontiers, to protect the working environment of their citizens, to use their financial resources to 'reduce disparities between the various regions and the backwardness of the least-favoured regions', and co-ordinate scientific research, technological development and public health and safety measures. One aim was the creation of a single currency. Another was the creation of a common foreign policy. A third was the continued extension of the community, of which Spain and Portugal were the most recent members.

When the century began, Europe had been overshadowed by the various empires that were its most powerful entities, and by the British Empire which hovered on its fringe. After the Second World War, Great Power status lay firmly in the hands of the United States and the Soviet Union, the two Super Powers. With the signing of the Single European Act, the European member states – with Britain as an integral if sometimes hesitant part of their collective ideals and institutions – had the capacity to be a 'major player' (in the terminology of the time) in the international economic and political scene.

'Disaster' movies had become an accepted and much enjoyed feature of Western cinema and television screens, and even of what was described as 'in-flight entertainment' for air travellers. But no movie could adequately convey the dangers of real disasters. On September 13, in Goiania, a Brazilian city with more than a million inhabitants, a group of youths broke into a disused private cancer clinic and stole a cylinder from a radiotherapy device. The scrap metal dealer to whom they sold it broke it open, thereby releasing a large quantity of caesium chloride, a highly radioactive, soluble chemical. The chemical, a bright powder, was given to children to play with. It was subsequently blown about in the wind, and carried on a bus. Paper wrapped around the chemical was recycled to make toilet paper. Four people were known to have been killed by the radioactivity thus released. Seventeen more became critically ill. Scientists at the scene estimated that it would be impossible ever to decontaminate the city entirely, and that the radiation would increase the number of cancers in the city for years to come.

At sea, on December 21, more than two thousand people drowned when a ferry capsized in the Philippines. It was the worst peacetime maritime disaster since 1,513 people on the *Titanic* had been drowned in the North Atlantic seventy-five years earlier.

Concern for the environment was reflected in West Germany during the general elections held on January 25, when the Green Party won forty-two seats in the 467-seat parliament. Environmental concerns were further eased in September, when delegates from forty nations, meeting in Montreal, adopted a protocol to the Vienna Convention for the Protection of the Ozone Layer (signed two years earlier) covering all substances known to destroy the ozone layer, including halons – used in many fire extinguishers – which had not hitherto been covered by international agreement. Another step forward in the steady realization of the centrality of environmental concerns, not only for the remaining thirteen years of the twentieth century but for the centuries ahead, was taken in October when the World Commission on Environment and Development, headed by the Norwegian Prime Minister, Mrs Gro Harlem Brundtland, published a report, *Our Common Future*, calling on all governments and international organizations to improve the management of environmental resources, and to do so in such a way that future global economic development could continue in a 'sustainable' manner. While meeting the needs of the current generation, the report stressed, it was important not to 'make it impossible' for future generations to meet their own needs.

Medicine continued to offer new areas of improved health and remedial surgery. That year surgeons at the University of Pennsylvania Hospital in the United States transplanted an entire human knee, while Canadian surgeons used a laser to clear a blocked coronary artery. The first successful five-organ transplant also took place that year, in the United States, when a three-year-old girl received a new liver, pancreas, small intestine and parts of the stomach and colon.

The United Nations relief agencies were again called to act in several emergencies. Parts of Ethiopia, Mozambique and Angola faced famine conditions, compounded by guerrilla warfare that made relief access difficult. In India, a catastrophic failure of the monsoon rains left 250 million people, a third of the country's population, short of water. In Bangladesh, the worst floods for forty years killed more than a thousand people, and left twenty-four million people homeless or facing starvation.

More than eleven million refugees were being helped with basic supplies by the United Nations High Commissioner for Refugees. These included three million Afghans escaping war and civil war by crossing the border into Pakistan. There were also two million Palestinian refugees in Arab lands – the deliberately unresettled refugees and descendants of refugees from the Arab–Israeli wars of 1948 and 1967 – a million Ethiopians who had fled famine and civil war to seek shelter in the Sudan; and half a million Kampucheans (Cambodians) who had fled the continuing civil war to seek sanctuary in Thailand.

Tens of thousands of people were still being killed on the roads each year: 43,390 in the United States and 5,125 in Britain in 1987 alone. In Africa, tens of thousands were dying each year of famine. An ever increasing number were dying of AIDS, including twenty-five per cent of all hospital deaths in Zaire. But the world population continued to rise almost without restraints. On July 11 it was announced that the world population had doubled since 1950, bringing the number of people in the world to 5,000 million. In a public relations effort designed to highlight this moment, the Secretary-General of the United Nations, Pérez de Cuellar, was photographed in a hospital in the Yugoslav city of Zagreb at the birth of 'the world's 5,000 millionth inhabitant'.

This child was one of 220,000 babies born that day. Pérez de Cuellar told the mother that she was lucky, since 'nine out of ten children were born in developing countries'. He refrained from giving her another United Nations statistic, first made public three years earlier, that in those same developing countries 40,000 children were dying each day – still leaving a daily population increase of 180,000 children a day.

CHAPTER THIRTY-SEVEN

1988

How is this bureaucratic monolith to be demolished?

MIKHAIL GORBACHEV

SOVIET COMMUNISM was changing at an accelerating pace that even Gorbachev could not have forecast. In the early months of 1988 a series of events far from Moscow precipitated unpredicted and far-ranging decisions. The scene of the first disturbance was the little known Nagorno-Karabakh Autonomous Region of Azerbaijan, a spot on the map that few Muscovites could have pointed to if asked to locate it.

The population of Nagorno-Karabakh was almost entirely Armenian and Christian. It was surrounded by the Republic of Azerbaijan, the population of which was predominantly Azeri and Muslim. The most authoritative administrative body in Nagorno-Karabakh was the Regional Soviet, a Communist Party bureaucratic institution of the sort that obeyed the orders of Moscow, and had been expected over the decades to show little if any initiative in non-local matters. On February 20, in a vote unprecedented in any Soviet Autonomous Region, the Nagorno-Karabakh Regional Soviet called for the region to be transferred from Azerbaijan – in which it was situated – to Armenia. This was a constitutional and territorial bombshell.

In Yerevan, the capital of the Armenian Soviet Socialist Republic – for each autonomous region and national republic was an integral part of the Soviet Union – an estimated 100,000 Armenians demonstrated on February 22 in front of the city's Opera Square, calling for the transfer and incorporation of Nagorno-Karabakh. The demonstrations were repeated every day until February 26, when Gorbachev himself appealed on television for them to be brought to an end, and promised to examine the situation personally. No Soviet leader had ever made a public appeal for calm before. All might have simmered down, but on February 27 reports reached

Azerbaijan that two Azeris had been killed the previous week by Armenians. When these reports reached the Azerbaijan port city of Sumgait, which had an Armenian minority, there was an anti-Armenian riot. Armenians were attacked in the streets, and Armenian shops were looted and burned. A riot that might have been quickly, and even ruthlessly, put down by Soviet police and army turned into the most traumatic moment of the year for the Soviet system, and for the much lauded 'unbreakable union' of the fifteen Soviet Socialist Republics.

After three days of fighting, thirty-two people had been killed, twenty-six of them Armenians. To the alarm of those for whom Communism was still the only ideology to follow, the Soviet armed forces – invincible hitherto when it came to asserting internal law and order – had been unable to halt the fighting. In Azerbaijan, and in the neighbouring Armenian Soviet Socialist Republic, demands suddenly flared up for secession from the Soviet Union. 'If only Gorbachev had shot the leaders of the Sumgait riots, none of what followed would have taken place,' a Russian historian reflected five years later, as he surveyed the post-Sumgait disintegration of the Soviet Union and the end of Communist Party rule.

On June 15, after Moscow had made it clear that there could be no change in the status of Nagorno-Karabakh, the Armenian Supreme Soviet – another senior Soviet body that had never stepped out of line in its sixty-six years of existence – voted for Nagorno-Karabakh to be transferred to their republic. Two days later the Azerbaijani Supreme Soviet voted this to be a violation of the Soviet constitution. In a counter-move, Azeris inside Nagorno-Karabakh attacked Armenians and demanded greater autonomy within their region. As at Sumgait, Soviet troops tried to stop the disturbances, but failed to do so. Their intervention was simply brushed aside in the intensity of the ethnic conflict. Sixty years of Communist rule, indoctrination, education and all-Union idealism counted for nothing: it was as if it had never been.

As fighting spread, at least thirty Armenians were killed. The Praesidium of the all-Union Supreme Soviet rejected any change in the constitutional status of Nagorno-Karabakh. Realizing that their wish to be a legal part of Armenia would not come to pass, tens of thousands of Armenians fled from Nagorno-Karabakh and sought refuge in Armenia.

Gorbachev was determined to rectify what he saw as past Soviet wrongs with a speed and vision that outflanked his critics by their very audacity. On February 8, in a dramatic initiative, he announced that the Soviet forces in Afghanistan would begin their withdrawal in three months' time. Their painful and humiliating war was about to end, after almost a decade. The Soviet public had been shocked at the scale of the casualties, and humiliated that Afghan rebels, the hostile element of a small neighbour, had been able to defy the northern giant.

In keeping with the openness that was his slogan and inspiration, on March 14 Gorbachev flew to Belgrade for a three-day visit, the first by a Soviet leader since Bulganin and Khrushchev had flown to see Tito in 1955 to try to patch up the Soviet-Yugoslav quarrel. On March 16, while still in Belgrade, Gorbachev expressed his regret at the 'groundless accusations' from Moscow that had led to the breach between the Soviet Union and Yugoslavia in 1948. On the following day, in Geneva, the United States Defence Secretary, Frank Carlucci, announced that the Soviet Union and the United States had created a 'military contact body' the aim of which was to prevent the escalation of military incidents. A substantive improvement in Soviet-American relations had become a priority for Gorbachev, for whom the crippling cost of the arms race was the largest single barrier to his hopes for an economically competitive Soviet Union internationally.

On May 29, President Reagan flew to Moscow. For five days he and Gorbachev held talks on the issues that had long divided the two countries: comprehensive arms control, respect for human rights, disputes over regional conflicts, and joint Soviet-American co-operation. During this summit, on June 1, Reagan and Gorbachev signed the Intermediate-range Nuclear Forces (INF) Treaty which their respective legislative bodies, the Senate and the Supreme Soviet, had ratified a few days earlier. With regard to future nuclear-testing agreements, Gorbachev accepted the American insistence on 'verification'. The open scrutiny implied by this word had been until then an obstacle to agreement. Two months to the day after the signature of the INF Treaty, 'verification' came into being, as the first Soviet intermediate-range nuclear weapons to be dismantled under the treaty were destroyed. This was done in the presence of American observers, at the Sary-Ozek range in Soviet Kazakhstan.

On June 3, Gorbachev allowed – indeed encouraged – Andrei Sakharov to give a news conference at the Soviet Foreign Office, during the course of which Sakharov attacked Soviet human rights policies and called for the release of all dissidents still being held in Soviet labour camps. His call was heeded; during a visit to Moscow four months later the West German Chancellor, Helmut Kohl, was able to announce that the Soviet Union had agreed to release 'all political prisoners'. On June 5, two days after Sakharov's appeal about the prisoners – many of whom had been incarcerated because of their Christian beliefs – a twelve-day celebration began of the millennium of Christianity in Russia. It was celebrated with official approval. Gorbachev gave it his imprimatur by meeting beforehand with the head of the Russian Orthodox Church, Patriarch Pimen. It was the first meeting between a Soviet leader and the Patriarch since 1943, when Stalin had sought Church help in the war against Germany.

The Nineteenth Communist Party Congress opened in Moscow on June 28, and lasted for three days. It was the first Party Congress since 1941, when the Eighteenth Congress had been called as another Second World War emergency means of strengthening Stalin's leadership. Gorbachev, in unravelling Stalin's legacy, was calling into play the same instruments. His speech lasted three-and-a-half hours. It was the most far-reaching, the most daring and the most truly revolutionary that he had made since coming to power. The 'key question', he told the delegates, was how to 'deepen and make irreversible' the process of perestroika which was taking place under the Party's guidance. The three previous years had been 'a turning-point in Soviet life: the whole social atmosphere has changed, and new ideas have begun to make themselves felt throughout the society'. This did not mean, however, that improvements were taking place in all spheres 'or at the necessary speed'.

To be 'realistic', Gorbachev told the Congress, the changes he had outlined had not yet occurred. 'Resistance was still powerful,' many Party organizations were not coping properly with the tasks that lay before them, the 'qualitative changes' that were needed in Soviet society had still to take place. In the view of the Central Committee, the main issue was still the 'radical reform' of the political system.

'Why is such a reform necessary?' Gorbachev asked the delegates, and went on to answer his own question. Partly, he said, it was needed because of the 'deformations' in Soviet political life. These had occurred after the revolution, marked in particular by the 'wave of repressive measures and lawlessness' under Stalin. A 'command system' of political management had grown up which had resisted reform. It had led to the stagnation of the Brezhnev years, when a massive ministerial bureaucracy had developed. There were about one hundred Ministers at the national level, and eight hundred more in the Republics. This bureaucracy had begun to 'dictate its will' in political as well as economic matters. Public life had become far too 'governmentalized', with central direction extending to every sphere of society. A 'wide gap' had opened up between official rhetoric and everyday realities. 'Government by the people' was proclaimed, but what was actually practised was 'centralized authoritarianism'. This had led to widespread public indifference, and to the alienation of working people from public ownership and management. It was this 'ossified system of government, with its command and pressure mechanism', that represented the greatest obstacle to perestroika.

'How is this bureaucratic monolith to be demolished?' Gorbachev asked, and again answered his own question. One way was by an extension of political rights, to ensure that matters of public concern were 'thoroughly debated and evaluated'. What was needed was a Socialism which 'renounced everything that had deformed Socialism in the 1930s, and led to its stagnation in the 1970s'. It was a Socialism which would inherit the 'best elements' of the thinking of its founding fathers, together with the experience of 'other periods and other societies'. A Socialism of this kind would be a system of 'true and tangible humanism in which man is really the measure of all things'. The purpose of all social development, from the economy to 'spiritual life', would be the satisfaction of popular needs. There would be 'a dynamic and advanced economy' based upon a variety of forms of property, and worker participation. A broad measure of central planning would be combined with a 'great degree of autonomy' for individual enterprises. The basic needs of all would be provided for, including health, education and housing, but individual talent would also be rewarded, in both moral and material terms. Such a society would have a high degree of culture and morality. It would be managed by a system of 'profound and consistent democracy'.

The revolutionary nature of this speech shook the Soviet system to its core. Socialism was to be preserved and enhanced – Lenin might not have quarrelled with that – but could the Communist Party and the Soviet system survive such a shake-up? Gorbachev believed that it could. He was mistaken. As a first indication of how radical the changes could be, the leadership agreed to pressure from the mass of the delegates – all of them Communist Party members – for the establishment of a new legislature, the Congress of People's Deputies, in which candidates could come forward for election who were not supporters of the Party line.

On July 4, three days after the Nineteenth Party Congress ended, the use of psychiatric detention for dissidents was abolished. One of the most glaring elements of Soviet human rights abuse was thus swept away. That month Gorbachev promised that a memorial would be built to the victims of Stalin's purges. A competition for the memorial was announced, and entries invited, to be sent for public view to the Donskoy Monastery in Moscow. Writing in the *International Herald Tribune*, Esther B. Fein noted the 'questions that echo' as almost two hundred proposals for a memorial were sent in:

> Would a pyramid of skulls bring to mind the tens of millions of people killed in labour camps and prisons or starved to death in their villages? Would a cube of black granite crushing a sculpted mass of people remind society of the terror felt by millions of Soviet citizens left to the mercy of an oppressive regime? Would a statue of a family entwined in barbed wire keep future generations from letting a despot rule them?

At the end of July, Gorbachev visited Warsaw, where he stated that the 'blank spots' in the history of Russia's relations with Poland should be filled. This opened the way to Soviet admissions of past crimes against hundreds of thousands of Poles, many of whom had been deported by Stalin to Siberia and had perished there. That August, Gorbachev took a dramatic step towards the filling up of another of the controversial blank pages in Soviet history books: the Nazi-Soviet Pact of August 1939. The mantle of fear with regard to knowledge of the past had been such that – twenty-five years earlier – a British historian had been shaken by the intensity of a visiting Soviet teacher from Latvia when she seized him by the arm in his university library and asked – during the few minutes when she was out of sight of the usual Party minder – if she could see the text of the Nazi-Soviet Pact with regard to the Soviet incorporation of the Baltic Republics.

On Gorbachev's instructions, the secret protocol signed in Moscow in August 1939, under which Estonia, Latvia and Lithuania were incorporated into the Soviet Union, without consulting in any way the wishes of their inhabitants, was published. Far from allowing historic wrongs to be set aside, however, publication of the protocol only served to intensify them. Throughout the Baltic Republics there was anger at the continuing heavy hand of Moscow. Couched in a call for Gorbachev's own much vaunted perestroika, restructuring demands emerged in each of the three republics for greater regional autonomy.

A process of questioning and demanding had been set in train in the Baltics, as elsewhere, that was not going to be easy to curb or control.

On November 16 the Estonian parliament, hitherto an essentially docile mouthpiece of Moscow, adopted a constitutional amendment providing it with the right of veto over all legislation emanating from Moscow that concerned Estonia's 'national' interest. One area of grievance over several years had been the location of highly polluting factories in the Baltic without local concerns being taken into account.

On November 26 the Supreme Soviet Praesidium declared the Estonian decision to have been 'unconstitutional'. But it had been made, the grievance had been voiced, and the battle lines drawn for further defiance.

The Eastern European countries were adding their demands on Moscow. At the end of the year, as a result of persistent pressure from the government in Budapest, Gorbachev was forced to withdraw all Soviet nuclear weapons from Hungary. In Poland, Lech Walesa, whose political movement was still banned, appeared on Polish television to demand free trade unions, freedom of the press, a 'final reckoning with the Stalinist past' and the legalization of Solidarity. He then travelled to Paris for the fortieth anniversary celebrations of the United Nations Declaration of Human Rights, and, although holding no public office, was received with full honours by President Mitterrand.

The changes demanded by Gorbachev in the Soviet Union were still being resisted, both by the Polish Communist leadership and by its Czechoslovak counterpart, each fearful of being swept aside completely if any moves were made towards the 'profound and consistent democracy' of which Gorbachev had spoken. In Bratislava, in March, a peaceful religious demonstration was dispersed by force. A gathering in Prague to commemorate the crushing of the Prague Spring twenty years earlier was likewise brought to an abrupt halt, as was a commemorative march on the seventieth anniversary of Czechoslovak independence. In a brief gesture of conciliation, the authorities allowed Alexander Dubček, the architect of the Prague defiance of 1968, to travel to Italy to receive an honorary doctorate at Bologna University, and gave official, though muted, recognition to the founder of Czechoslovakia, Thomas Masaryk. When the year ended the Party made it clear that 'political pluralism', as demanded by Charter 77, was 'out of the question'. A popular joke in Prague likened the Czechoslovak variety of perestroika to the rebuilding of a pig-sty into a modern apartment – with the pig continuing its tenancy.

In Hungary, unlike in Czechoslovakia, several non-Communist groupings emerged, and had been allowed to voice their concerns openly. One of them, the Hungarian Democratic Forum, had a membership of ten thousand by the end of the year. A smaller, equally liberal-minded group, the Alliance of Free Democrats, that also emerged that year, was the successor to the pre-war democratic opposition. Neither had a place in government, but both were outspoken in their suggestions for democratic reforms. The one remaining taboo in public discussions was criticism of Hungary's links with the Soviet Union.

As each Eastern European country tried to come to terms with the changes in the Soviet Union, and its own internal dissenting voices, Roumania embarked, under President Ceauşescu, on a policy of repression that reflected the increasingly bizarre cast of Ceauşescu's thought. In March he put forward a plan to resettle large numbers of farmers and peasants in the towns. His aim was to demolish altogether 8,000 of Roumania's 13,000 villages by the year 2000. As well as destroying the villages, he proposed the pulling down of churches and the demolition of monuments and cemeteries. Roumania, under his vision, was to become a predominantly urban society, with giant 'agro-industrial complexes' to sustain both the food and other consumer needs of the country.

The way in which the cult of personality around Ceauşescu was developing led to protests by the British, Spanish and Swedish governments when, on Ceauşescu's seventieth birthday, messages of greeting from the monarchs of these three countries were read out. The messages had been fabricated by Ceauşescu's supporters – or possibly by Ceauşescu himself. More and more power was also devolving on his wife Elena. On Roumania's National Day, August 23, it was she who delivered the customary presidential speech. Two months later, during a visit to Moscow, Ceauşescu resisted Gorbachev's appeals to allow glasnost and perestroika in Roumania, and, on his return to Bucharest, publicly criticized those Communist Parties that, in line with the Soviet model, were 'withdrawing from the day-to-day administration of government'. In one crucial sense, Ceauşescu was right: once the Communist Parties pulled back from the day-to-day control, supervision and imposition of Party norms and values, the floodgates would be opened for changes far beyond those of internal restructuring or inter-Communist openness. Ceauşescu was determined that Communist rule in Roumania – his rule – would not be weakened or challenged, whatever the Soviet Union might do.

The Bulgarian Communist Party also hesitated to move to Soviet-style changes. Such independent groups as emerged were quickly suppressed. January saw the establishment of the Independent Association for the Defence of Human Rights. By the autumn many of its founder members had been expelled from the country. In March, Bulgarian environmentalists, disturbed by the high level of pollution at Ruse, Bulgaria's fourth largest city, set up a Committee for the Protection of the Environment. The chlorine emissions from a State chemical plant there were polluting both the Bulgarian and Roumanian shores of the Danube. The Party did not like to have this issue brought forward, and the committee was forced to close down. On November 3 a hundred leading Bulgarian intellectuals founded a 'Club for the Support of Perestroika and Glasnost'. It too was forced to close down within a few days. Press censorship was maintained, as it had been since 1945. Two editors who dared to publish articles on historical and cultural topics that did not meet with the Party's approval were dismissed. The 'blank pages' of history which Gorbachev was allowing to be filled in the Soviet Union were to remain blank in Bulgaria.

In Yugoslavia the unity of the republics was under increasing strain. The federal system over which Tito had presided until his death in 1980 was proving inadequate to satisfy the growing and conflicting aspirations – national and religious – of the different regions. Deep ethnic divisions were rising to the surface. In Bosnia-Hercegovina, forty per cent of the population was Muslim. In the Vojvodina there was a large Magyar-speaking minority with historic links to Hungary. The Kosovo province was eighty-five per cent Albanian and Muslim. Croatia was predominantly Roman Catholic, and Serbia Orthodox Christian. Most aggrieved were the Serbs, who saw themselves as the dominant group in both inter-war and post-war Yugoslavia, a country 'created' from the Serb association with the victorious allies in 1918 (the Croats and Slovenes had been part of Austria-Hungary, one of the defeated powers).

During the summer, the head of the Serbian Communist Party, Slobodan Milošević, took steps to bring Kosovo more under the control of the Serb republic. He organized a series of Serb demonstrations at one of which, on September 24, in Niš, 150,000 Serbs participated, demanding an end to the Albanian dominance of Kosovo – from which ten thousand Serbs a year had fled, fearing persecution by the Muslims. The demand of the demonstrators was for greater Serb control over Kosovo. As Milošević's campaign gained momentum, three ethnic Albanians – senior and loyal members of the Yugoslav Communist Party – were forced to resign from their posts for having defended Kosovo's existing provincial autonomy. One of those forced to resign was a member of the central government in Belgrade, Mustafa Pljakić, the Federal Secretary for Transport and Communications.

The Albanians of Kosovo were not without means of protest of their own.

Starting on November 17, there were five days of demonstrations throughout the province, the largest being in the provincial capital, Priština. The Priština demonstration was led by ethnic Albanian miners, demanding continuing autonomy for their province, for their race and for their faith. Islam had begun to re-emerge as a political force in the Balkans, for the first time in three-quarters of a century.

On December 7 the focus on political change was set aside, and Gorbachev, who was then in New York, had to postpone imminent visits to Britain and Cuba, when an earthquake struck Armenia. Several towns were completely destroyed, and 25,000 people were killed. As television showed people throughout the world the extent of the devastation, an upsurge of sympathy led to the collection by many international and national charities of food, blankets and medicine for despatch to Armenia.

Gorbachev flew back from New York to Moscow, and on to the Armenian capital, Yerevan. There, he attacked 'extreme nationalists' in Armenia and Azerbaijan whom he accused of 'using the earthquake disaster for their own political ends'. They were, he said, 'demagogues and adventurists' who, in order to create political instability, inflamed 'nationalist passions' at a time when co-operation was particularly necessary. Armenian demonstrators in Yerevan then used Gorbachev's visit to press their demand for Armenian control of the Nagorno-Karabakh enclave in Azerbaijan. They also protested against the recent arrest of five leaders of the Karabakh Committee campaigning for Armenia to administer Nagorno-Karabakh. When the demonstrators refused to disperse, Soviet troops were called in and opened fire.

Amid this political crisis, rescue efforts continued. But on October 11 a Soviet military transport aircraft flying supplies into Yerevan crashed, killing all sixty-nine servicemen and nine crew on board. International aid and specialists in disaster relief were being rushed to the scene of the earthquake, including five doctors from the French-based Médecins sans Frontières, a World Health Organization 'disaster team' that was based in Copenhagen, and fifteen rescue workers from the British-based International Rescue Corps, which had been active in helping victims of the Mexico and El Salvador earthquakes in 1985 and 1986. The fact that the Armenians were Christian also made its impact. In the words of the Archbishop of Canterbury, Dr Robert Runcie: 'They are a courageous Christian people who have a special claim on the support of all Christian organizations.'

* * *

The war between Iran and Iraq continued into its eighth year. In February the earlier 'war of the cities' was resumed, whereby both Iraq and Iran sent bombers and missiles against Teheran and Baghdad respectively, despite repeated calls from the United Nations that the mutual killing of civilians should be stopped.

In March, Iranian troops captured Halabja, a Kurdish town. Iraq then bombed the town, in which the Kurds were still living, with chemical weapons. Five thousand Kurdish civilians were killed. By using chemical weapons – which were outlawed by international agreement – Iraq earned the condemnation of most members of the United Nations. The Iraqi ruler, Saddam Hussein, had no compunction, however, in using chemical weapons against his Kurdish minority – a minority which, desperate for a less repressive ruler, had supported Iran.

Iran suffered a setback in April when, having mined and damaged an American warship in the Gulf, it faced immediate American retaliation: the destruction of its offshore radar platforms, and the sinking of its few warships. On April 18, two days after the American action, Iraqi forces pushed the Iranian occupation forces out of the Shatt al-Arab, the waterway at the mouth of the Euphrates that Iran had managed to close. Suddenly Iraq was achieving an initiative that had eluded it for eight years. On March 19, Iraqi aircraft seriously damaged Iran's oil-tanker terminal at Kharg, and on May 14 did the same at Larak. Iran's oil exporting facilities and oil revenue were both endangered.

On July 3 the American warship *Vincennes*, on patrol in the Gulf, was involved in a skirmish with Iranian naval vessels near the port of Bandar Abbas. In the course of the skirmish it launched a number of missiles at what it believed to be a hostile Iranian warplane, and shot it down. It was in fact an Iran Air airbus, a civilian airliner, which crashed into the sea. Crew and passengers – 290 people in all – were killed. The Iranians denounced the United States for 'mass murder', but Reagan, while apologizing for the loss of life, stated that it was 'a justified act of self-defence'. The *Vincennes* had believed that it was about to be attacked.

On July 18 Iran accepted the United Nations call for a ceasefire, and a withdrawal to the international boundaries. The ceasefire came into effect in August. The only forces to ignore it were those not under the control of the respective combatants. From Iraq, Iranian anti-Khomeini mujaheddin fighters crossed into Iran and were quickly defeated by Iranian troops.

Inside Iraq, pro-Iranian Kurdish fighters also refused to stop fighting. Iraq again used chemical weapons against them. Tens of thousands of Kurds fled into southern Turkey.

In addition to the ending of the Iran-Iraq War, three other wars ended in 1988. On April 3 Ethiopia and Somalia signed a peace agreement, ending eleven years of conflict, which had also served to displace hundreds of thousands of starving Ethiopians. On May 26 the government of Vietnam announced that it was withdrawing 50,000 of its troops from Kampuchea (formerly Cambodia) and that all those remaining would be placed under Kampuchean control. On August 22 the Angolan and South African governments signed a ceasefire in Angola, and agreed to the withdrawal of South African and Cuban troops; on December 22 Namibia, over which South Africa and Angola had fought, became independent.

Wars ended, but civil wars continued. On August 10 fighting began between the ruling Tutsi and majority Hutu in Burundi. Within a few weeks, thousands had been killed. Terrorism had also become an endemic late-twentieth-century phenomenon. In Northern Ireland, on March 16, three people were killed when a gunman opened fire in a cemetery during the funeral of three IRA men who had been killed by British security forces in Gibraltar. During the funeral of one of those killed at the cemetery, two British soldiers in civilian clothes were seized and brutally murdered. In India, Sikh extremists continued to infiltrate from across the Pakistan border, which Indian troops sealed on April 2. In the three previous months, 645 people had been killed in Sikh-Hindu violence. On May 1, in Sri Lanka, twenty-six bus passengers were killed when Tamil extremists exploded a landmine under their bus. In Greece, on July 11, eleven foreign tourists were killed when Arab terrorists opened fire on a pleasure boat. On December 21 all 258 passengers were killed when a Pan Am passenger airliner was blown up by a terrorist bomb while flying from Britain to the United States. Eleven people on the ground, at the Scottish border town of Lockerbie, were also killed.

As the Soviet Union moved towards greater openness, South Africa maintained the apartheid system with rigidity. On July 18 the imprisoned Nelson Mandela celebrated his seventieth birthday. He had been a prisoner for twenty-four years. Throughout the world there were protest marches demanding his release.

Human rights were everywhere under attack. On October 5, Amnesty

International issued a report in which it gave details of eighty countries, out of 135 countries that it had surveyed, which held political prisoners – 'prisoners of conscience' – and in which torture or ill-treatment had been reported.

The curse of AIDS was highlighted at a three-day conference in London, which opened on January 26, in which Health Ministers and experts from 148 countries pressed governments to take urgent action on what they called 'a serious threat to humanity'. By the end of the previous year, 27,000 Americans had died of the disease.

Toronto, Canada, was the venue for an economic summit of the seven leading industrial nations, who met on June 19 for three days, and agreed by the end of their deliberations that they must reschedule the debts of the world's poorest countries, to enable them to continue to build what they could of infrastructures capable of sustaining growth. But the impact of natural disasters could overwhelm the most tenacious reforming efforts, as when, at the beginning of August more than a million people were made homeless in the Sudan as a result of severe flooding; or at the end of August, when twenty-five million people were left homeless in Bangladesh, and three thousand people killed, when flood waters inundated vast regions, including much of the capital, Dacca. In September, a million people were made homeless when Hurricane Gilbert, the strongest ever recorded in the western hemisphere, hit Mexico in September.

In the steadily increasing awareness of the perils to the environment, two United Nations agencies, the World Health Organization and the Environment Programme, after a fifteen-year monitoring programme carried out in more than sixty countries, announced that most of the 1,800 million people living in towns and cities were breathing air of 'unacceptable' quality. Certain cities, of which Milan, Seoul, Rio de Janeiro and Paris were said to be among the worst, had pollution averages above the World Health Organization limits for safety. Another health hazard that was exposed that year was the incineration of toxic waste at sea. Meeting in Washington in October, the nations that had signed the London Dumping Convention in 1972 agreed to ban the export of toxic waste for incineration. The United States Congress also agreed to ban the ocean dumping of sewage sludge as soon after 1991 as possible. A cruel twist had been given to Tom Lehrer's ironic couplet:

> Fish gotta swim and birds gotta fly
> But they don't last long if they try.

CHAPTER THIRTY-EIGHT

1989

I do not believe that any people can be held in thrall for ever. The machinery of propaganda may pack their minds with falsehoods and deny them truth for many genera-tions of time, but the soul of man thus held entranced or frozen in a long night can be awakened by a spark coming from God knows where, and in a moment the whole structure of lies and oppression is on trial for its life. Peoples in bondage need never despair.
WINSTON S. CHURCHILL, 1949

Let us make sure this revolution keeps on flourishing. . . .
VÁCLAV HAVEL, 1989

THE YEAR 1917 had seen the destruction of the established order in Russia. The year 1933 had seen the destruction of the established order in Germany. From these two traumatic events had come the conflict of Communism and Nazism, the victory of Communism over Nazism, and the imposition of Communist rule throughout Eastern Europe. The year 1989 was to see that tenaciously maintained parameter of world history swept away. No week passed during 1989 without the Soviet Union continuing to astound those in the West who had been convinced that the power and ideological conform-ity of its Communist Party would still be in place, intact, a hundred years after the 1917 revolution.

On 6 January 1989 it was announced from Moscow that all the victims of Stalin's purges during a twenty-year period, from 1930 to 1950, were to be rehabilitated, numbering in their tens of thousands and hundreds of thousands. On February 14 the last Soviet troops left Afghanistan, their departure across the bridge at Termez being witnessed by the world's journalists: a moment of humiliation for the imperial giant, but also a moment of truth. The Soviet Union, like the British Empire whose frontier it had once almost touched in the mountain wilderness of eastern Afghanistan, could no longer impose forms of government beyond its borders.

On March 8, following widespread public demands for greater official 'truthfulness' about the death toll in the immediate aftermath of Chernobyl – as part of the 'openness' which Gorbachev had promised with regard to all the facts of Soviet life – the authorities admitted that the correct death toll had been 250.

On March 26, within three weeks of this admission, the first nationwide elections since 1918 were held in the Soviet Union with candidates from Parties other than the Communist Party. Many Communist Party candidates were defeated, especially in those Republics which had long resented the control of Moscow, but had no means, hitherto, of expressing it. In Moscow, a leading advocate of radical change, Boris Yeltsin, who had earlier been dismissed from the Politburo for wanting to move forward at too swift a pace, won eighty-nine per cent of the vote in his Moscow constituency. Demands for independence had begun to be heard from several Soviet Republics. On April 9, in Tbilisi, demonstrators demanded the right of Georgia to secede from the union. Soviet troops opened fire, and nineteen Georgians were killed. The calls for secession increased.

On July 10 the first of a series of strikes broke out in the Soviet coalfields. Within ten days 300,000 miners were on strike, in seven coalmining regions. Three months later, on October 9, the Supreme Soviet granted the right to strike. This right, a weapon which had helped bring about revolution more than seventy years earlier, had been jealously withheld throughout the Soviet decades. There could have been no greater break with Communist ideology and practice.

The political situation in Eastern Europe was even more fluid, and more rapidly changing, than the situation in the Soviet Union. At the very start of the year, on January 11, the Hungarian parliament passed a law allowing for the formation of political Parties. The forty-year monopoly of the Communist Party was to be broken. But the first by-elections at which non-Communist Parties could put up candidates would not be held until March. Meanwhile, elsewhere in Eastern Europe, it was not at all clear whether such examples of radical change would be repeated. In Czechoslovakia the heavy hand of Communist repression was still in place. On January 16 the police broke up a demonstration in Prague to mark the twentieth anniversary of the suicide of Jan Palach, who had killed himself in protest against the Soviet-led invasion.

East Germany was likewise not ready for drastic change, or so it seemed. On February 5, in East Berlin, border guards shot and killed a man seeking to flee to the West. This had been the deadly response of the East German authorities since the establishment of the Berlin Wall twenty-eight years earlier. In Czechoslovakia, the playwright and leading human rights activist Václav Havel was sentenced on February 21 to nine months in prison for 'inciting public disorder' the previous month.

Much hinged on developments in Hungary. The first blow to Communist and pro-Soviet orthodoxy came in February, when a senior Communist Party member, Imre Pozsgay, publicized the findings of a government commission into the history of Hungary since 1945. The traumatic events of 1956 were no longer described as a 'counter-revolution' – the phrase used hitherto to justify Soviet military intervention – but as a 'popular uprising'. On March 15, in Budapest, two weeks before the first by-elections since 1945 in which all political Parties could be represented, there was a mass demonstration in the streets calling for democracy and national independence. In view of the historical commission's recent findings, this demonstration could no longer be denounced as 'counter-revolutionary'.

The by-elections were held on March 28. For the first time since the Soviet liberation of Hungary forty-five years earlier, candidates representing Parties other than the Communist Party were allowed to stand. Within the hitherto politically monolithic 'Communist bloc' of Eastern Europe, a multi-Party election had taken place. Everywhere the Communist candidates were defeated. Victory went to the candidates of the Hungarian Democratic Forum, whose political platform highlighted 'democracy', integration into Europe, opposition to Communism and the 'preservation of Hungarian values'.

In Poland, as in Hungary, the Communist Party could no longer stand up against the mounting public pressures for change. In Poland, these pressures took the form of an upsurge in strikes, of the sort that had brought Solidarity to power before the imposition of martial law. With new strikes spreading, and street demonstrations growing, on April 5 the Polish government – no longer led by those who had imposed martial law – signed an agreement with Lech Walesa for political and economic reforms. As a first fruit, Solidarity was legalized on April 21.

The power of the individual was being asserted. On April 20 the Czechoslovak government agreed to multi-Party elections, the first in more than forty years. On May 2 the Hungarian government began to dismantle the 218-mile security fence that had long prevented Hungarians from escaping into Austria. In Czechoslovakia, the wind of change continued to be seen when, on May 17, Václav Havel was released from prison, having served less than a third of his nine-month sentence. That day, in Poland, the Roman Catholic Church was given a status hitherto unknown in a Communist country, when the property confiscated from it in the 1950s was restored. It was also given the right to re-establish Catholic schools. On June 4, elections were held in Poland for a new National Assembly. A percentage of seats was reserved for non-Communist political Parties. Solidarity candidates won ninety-nine per cent of these seats. The elections had been free: the figure of ninety-nine per cent, more usually associated with Communist rigged ballots, had been a genuine demonstration of long-suppressed opposition.

As each change took place in Eastern Europe, the spectre of Soviet intervention was raised. But on June 12, in Bonn, the West German Chancellor Helmut Kohl and Mikhail Gorbachev signed a document 'affirming' the right of European States to 'determine their own political systems'. This was a dramatic departure from previous Soviet policy, and practice. In Prague, two months later, there were mass demonstrations on the twenty-first anniversary – August 21 – of the Soviet invasion of Czechoslovakia – an event for which Gorbachev had not apologized. But it was in East Germany that a fuse was lit which was to detonate the powder keg of the Eastern European status quo.

Following the Hungarian government's decision to dismantle its sealed border with Austria and end the stringent border controls that effectively impeded all East-West movement, discontented East Germans, using their Communist documents, made their way through Czechoslovakia to Hungary – travel within the Communist bloc having been a matter of routine for several decades – and then 'escaped' westward into Austria and on to West Germany. The Hungarian government made no attempt to stop them leaving the Communist bloc. The Berlin Wall remained intact, but a way around it had been found. Within three months, 120,000 East Germans had made their way to West Germany by this route.

The Soviet Union itself was not immune from the ferment beyond its western borders. Within the Baltic Republics the Latvian Popular Front was demanding greater autonomy for its republic, as was the Sajudis mass movement in Lithuania, and as were many Estonians. On August 23 more than two million people – Estonians, Latvians and Lithuanians – linked hands to form a 'human chain' of protest on the fiftieth anniversary of the signing of the Nazi-Soviet Pact, as a result of which they had been incorporated into the Soviet Union. Five days later Gorbachev telephoned from his holiday home outside Moscow to the Communist Party leader in Lithuania, Algirdas Brazauskas, to warn him that such demonstrations must be curbed.

The Baltic Republics were not alone in their ferment. During the last week of August there were street rallies in Kishinev, the capital of the Moldavian Soviet Republic, when tens of thousands of demonstrators demanded greater freedom, including official status for the Moldavian language. *Pravda* condemned the demonstrators as 'power-hungry separatists' affected by 'national blindness' and warned that the Moldavian Communist Party leaders had done nothing to halt the protests. Its tone was menacing: 'Those who have led the Moldavian population to ethnic strife, exploiting perestroika slogans as a cover-up, are pursuing their personal aims and seek to take power on the crest of a muddy wave of chauvinism and separatism.'

The denunciation of Moldavian separatism by *Pravda* did not prevent the leading Soviet literary magazine *Novy Mir* from making an astounding break with Communist tradition that month, when it began to serialize Alexander Solzhenitsyn's prison-camp saga, *Gulag Archipelago*. The publication was personally approved by Gorbachev. However much he sought to do so, however, it was impossible to separate the exposure of past errors with the demands for current change beyond what he hoped to achieve, that is, change which would nevertheless preserve the existing structure of the USSR – the Union of Soviet Socialist Republics.

On August 28 Gorbachev travelled to Kiev, where he sought to assert his authority. He did so by removing from office the Ukrainian Party chief, Vladimir Shcherbitsky, who, as a protégé of Brezhnev, had been in power since 1972. Gorbachev had also to try to combat, through a revivified and reformist Communist Party structure, the growing influence of RUKH, a Ukrainian national movement founded a month earlier. RUKH was calling for the preservation and restoration of Ukrainian linguistic and cultural traditions, and for greater autonomy for the Ukraine. Gorbachev was determined not to allow the new movement to usurp the Communist Party as the dominant force in the republic, in the way that similar national movements had done in the Baltic Republics.

In Lvov, on September 17, tens of thousands of Ukrainians marched through the city waving the banned yellow-and-blue flag of the Ukraine, demanding official recognition of the banned Uniate Catholic Church. That evening a Popular Front movement carried out a 'ceremony of mourning' to mark the annexation into the Soviet Union of Lvov and Eastern Galicia, which until 1940 had been part of inter-war independent Poland. Protesters with candles formed a chain of protest in the main streets and squares; others placed candles in their darkened windows.

On September 19 a special plenum of the Central Committee of the Soviet Communist Party met in Moscow to discuss 'ethnic relations' inside the Soviet Union, in the context of the growing national unrest in so many republics. In preparation for the meeting, Soviet newspapers published guidelines laid down the previous week by Gorbachev when he met senior Communist Party leaders from the Baltic Republics. The guidelines conceded 'economic autonomy', but demanded respect for the 'federal character' of the Soviet constitution, and respect for the 'unity' of the Communist Party.

In Warsaw, the newly elected National Assembly began its first session on September 12. It was the first government in Eastern Europe since 1945 that was not under Communist control. Its first public announcement was that forty-five years of Communist rule were at an end. In all future elections, any political group could stand. The apparatus of the Communist regime would be dismantled: was, in fact, disintegrating even without formal acts. The secret police would no longer monitor the opinions of citizens. Censorship would no longer seek to curb expressions of opinion. In a hitherto unprecedented twist in what had been the Eastern European Communist monolith, but was monolith no more, the Polish Communists agreed to join a Solidarity-led coalition government. Five days later the Solidarity candidate, Tadeusz Mazowiecki, was elected Prime Minister of Poland.

In East Germany, the docility imposed by the typical Communist instruments of control and Party vigilance was crumbling. On September 11 a New Forum opposition group came into being, pledged to speak out openly against the continuation of Communist rule. Starting on September 18, large weekly pro-democracy rallies were held in Leipzig.

The unity of Yugoslavia, created after the First World War as a monarchy, and continued after the Second World War under Communism, was also being subjected to fierce internal public debate. On September 27 the Slovenian parliament, one of the member parliaments of the Yugoslav

Federation, approved a number of constitutional amendments which gave it the right to secede from the Federation. The Slovenes wanted to be independent; to be governed from Ljubljana, not Belgrade; to form their own political structure. The fact that they were such a small region, less than eight thousand square miles in extent and less than two million in population, did not deter them: indeed, their desire to be freed from Serb dominance propelled them forward. Two million Slovenes were not going to be deterred from asserting their national rights by any threat of retaliation by ten million Serbs. One particular cause of anti-Serb feeling in Slovenia was the attempt by the Serbs to assert their authority over the ethnic Albanians in Kosovo. During fighting in Kosovo in March, twenty-nine people had been killed, a curfew imposed throughout the region, and the popular Kosovo-Albanian leader, Azem Vlasi, arrested.

On October 7 the East German government embarked on celebrations of the fortieth anniversary of the start of Communist rule. In a gesture of support, Gorbachev flew from Moscow to be present. His presence, and the challenge of the celebrations themselves, provoked massive street demonstrations by East Germans calling for democratic institutions. Riot police were sent in to disperse the protesters.

On October 7, while Gorbachev was in East Berlin, the principal political instrument of Communist rule in Hungary, the Hungarian Socialist Workers' Party, voted, by 1,202 votes to 159, for its own dissolution. It wanted nothing to do, the Party said, with 'the crimes, mistakes and faulty ideas and message' of those who, under its banner, had ruled Hungary for the previous forty years. It also called for guarantees for private property and ownership, and for the privatization or selling-off of State industries. On the following morning the Party newspaper *Nepszabadsag* appeared for the first time without the slogan 'Workers of the world unite!'

Also on October 8 the Latvian Popular Front, holding its first 'annual' conference in Riga, abandoned its call for greater Latvian autonomy and demanded full secession from the Soviet Union. Neither the Lithuanian nor Estonian national movement had gone so far: both limited their calls to political and economic autonomy within the Soviet Union. Another of the demands of the Front was the removal of all non-Latvian Soviet troops from Latvian soil.

On October 11, Poland, whose borders had for so many years represented an 'iron curtain' of controls within the Iron Curtain, opened its western border for refugees from East Germany, and announced that it would accept any refugees who crossed them.

Street demonstrations throughout East Germany continued, undeterred by the repeated efforts of the police to disperse them. In the end, the police gave up: the crowds were too large and the will to disperse them too weak. On October 18, only eleven days after the anniversary celebrations, the East German Party leader and Head of State, Erich Honecker, resigned. His successor, Egon Krenz, went on television to promise 'openness, dialogue and change': a 'turning point' in how East Germany was to be governed. The reaction of the public was that this was 'too little and too late'. The street demonstrations continued.

On October 23, in Hungary, on the anniversary of the 1956 uprising, the Speaker of the parliament, Mátyás Szürös, who had become acting President three days earlier, proclaimed the 'Hungarian Republic' in place of the 'People's Republic' which had been Hungary's designation since 1949.

Everywhere in Eastern Europe the question was being asked: would the Soviet Union take action against what was happening? Would the Gorbachev-Kohl declaration of June 12 be adhered to, as the disintegration of Communist rule in Eastern Europe accelerated? Or would Gorbachev feel forced to renew the iron fist of his predecessors, who had not hesitated in previous decades to crush past manifestations of discontent: in East Berlin, in Hungary and in Czechoslovakia? The last Soviet soldier had left Afghanistan at the beginning of the year. The Soviet army was still a formidable force. But the will to intervene had gone. When it came to the mounting inner turmoil of Eastern Europe, and to Eastern European fears and hatreds of the Soviet Union, the calls for greater openness in Soviet society, even within the parameters of a ruling Communist Party, had undermined the Soviet philosophy of intervention. Nor could the Soviet Union appeal to the fraternal emotions that had helped sustain its rule and control in the immediate aftermath of the defeat of Nazism. The liberator of 1945 had long since become the tyrant. A new generation of Eastern Europeans – millions of students and young workers among them – felt no loyalty to the nation that had made such a major contribution to the destruction of Nazism and the horrors of the German occupation almost half a century earlier.

On October 25 two days after Hungary had dropped its designation of 'People's Republic' – a Soviet spokesman, in a statement made to Western journalists in Moscow, set at rest the minds of those who were apprehensive about a possible hostile Soviet reaction to the events in Eastern Europe. The spokesman was emphatic: the 'Brezhnev Doctrine' of military intervention to 'protect' Communist regimes beyond the Soviet borders was at an end. It had been replaced, he said, by the 'Sinatra Doctrine'. The journalists were momentarily puzzled. Then, with a broad grin, the spokesman said: 'My Way'. Not a weighty statement by Gorbachev, but the catchy title of a Frank Sinatra song ('I did it my way'), gave the green light to the would-be democrats of half a dozen nations. They could make what changes they wished in the way they wished to make them.

In East Germany, as earlier in Poland and Czechoslovakia, the pressure for change continued to be taken to the streets. On October 26 – the day after the Soviet promulgation of the new 'Sinatra Doctrine' – 100,000 pro-democracy demonstrators gathered in the East German city of Dresden. On November 4 there was a huge, peaceful pro-democracy rally in East Berlin, in which half a million people took part. In Bulgaria as many as ten thousand demonstrators marched through the streets of Sofia that day, on the pretext of joining an official ecology protest, and called for democracy and glasnost. There had been no demonstration of this type or size in the forty-five-year rule of the Bulgarian Communist Party.

The pattern and pace of protest continued to grow. On November 6 as many as three-quarters of a million protesters marched through the streets of the six main East German cities. On the following day the East German government resigned, and on November 8 the whole Politburo. The Communist Party leadership had gone. Then, on November 9, the Central Committee of the East German Communist Party took a decision that was to end, and to symbolize the end, of the East-West divide which had been in place since the last days of the Second World War. That night it was announced in East Berlin that the border between East and West Germany was to be opened on the following morning. All East German citizens could leave the country directly and without restriction, through all crossing points through the Berlin Wall and along the 858-mile border with West Germany. The wall itself was to be dismantled.

Starting on the morning of November 10 the physical barrier which had kept the two Berlins and the two Germanys apart was hacked and smashed into hundreds of thousands of pieces, into a million fragments – some of them still on sale a decade later in the souvenir shops of a united Berlin. East Germans poured over the wall, and through the growing number of gaps in the wall, and across the rubble where the wall had stood, linking hands with West Berliners in one of the most powerful symbols of popular will that the twentieth century had witnessed.

Twenty-seven years had passed since the Berlin Wall had been erected. With its fall, a new era dawned for those who had often wondered whether the nightmare of separation, division and control would ever end. The intensified pulse of change was felt throughout Eastern Europe. On November 10, the day on which the Berlin Wall was being pulled down, Bulgaria's Communist leader, Todor Zhivkov, who had been in power for thirty-five years at the head of a rigid Communist dictatorship, resigned. He was the longest-serving leader of any of the Warsaw Pact countries. His successor, Petar Mladenov, the former Foreign Minister, promised to introduce 'pluralist democracy' and a market economy. Within days of his coming into office, the notorious Article 273 of the Penal Code, establishing formidable penalties for 'anti-Socialist agitation', was repealed, and the equally notorious 6th Department of the police – the ideological branch – was dissolved.

On November 20 a new political grouping was established in Czechoslovakia, the Civic Forum. It called on the government to allow free elections and a multiplicity of political Parties. Four days later, on November 24, there were mass resignations of senior Communist Party officials. Called by the people to speak to them, and to link them with the heroic anti-Soviet past, Alexander Dubček addressed a rally of a quarter of a million people. 'The enthusiasm of ordinary people has made the Czechoslovak revolution unstoppable,' wrote a British journalist, Peter Millar, after he had witnessed what he described as 'magical scenes' on Sunday November 26:

> a hands-across-Prague protest designed as a human chain became instead a merry dance, a living tableau from a Brueghel painting, as laughing, skipping people in warm mufflers and long scarves formed an endless twisting snake around the trees, through the snowy park, up to the floodlit spires, the castle itself and the archbishop's palace, then helter-skelter slithered giggling down steep, slippery, narrow cobbled streets and, holding hands with exaggerated formality with a pastiche mazurka, passed across the fifteenth century Charles Bridge, watched by stern statues of all the saints, and on to Wenceslas Square.

Rumours abounded of tanks on the city outskirts. But everyone, including the party, knew the simple truth: without Soviet military and political armour behind it, the threat of armed intervention was hollow.

Also on November 26, in the Bulgarian capital, Sofia, the secret police was dissolved. That same day, a referendum in Hungary voted in favour of dismantling the Communist Party cells in factories. On November 27 a twenty-four-hour general strike throughout Czechoslovakia was seen by all the millions who participated in it as a national referendum calling for an end to Communist rule. Before dawn on December 1, the Czechoslovak Communist Party's Politburo met in emergency session and resolved to admit publicly, and at once, that the 1968 Soviet-led invasion had been 'unjustified and morally wrong'.

Events outside the Soviet Union and Eastern Europe were often eclipsed by the dramas of the collapse of Communism. George Bush, who had succeeded Reagan as President at the beginning of the year, had spoken in his inaugural address on January 20 of how 'the world refreshed by freedom seems reborn', as the 'great nations of the world are moving towards democracy – through the door of freedom'. In domestic policy, he suggested that the United States was 'never wholly herself unless she is engaged in high moral principles'. There was much to be done, he said, pointing among other problems to homelessness and drug addiction.

The Soviet leader was struggling to maintain the unity of the Soviet Empire. On December 1, when he visited the Vatican and met the Pope – the first Soviet leader to do so – Gorbachev took the opportunity to denounce the Lithuanian Communist Party leadership for allowing nationalism and 'social-democratic tendencies' to get out of hand. Amid this domestic consti- tutional turmoil, he tried to maintain the momentum of Soviet-American reconciliation. After a meeting with President Bush on board ship off Malta on December 3, Gorbachev told the first joint presidential press conference ever held that the two Super Powers were entering a 'new epoch'. The Soviet Union would 'never start a war against the United States', he said, and he was 'sure that the President of the United States would never start a war against us'. Gorbachev's spokesman, Gennadi Gerasimov, was even more assertive, telling journalists that the Cold War had 'ended officially' at the close of the last session of the Malta summit that day at 11.45 p.m. Greenwich Mean Time. Asked by a reporter two hours later if the Cold War was really over, Bush gave the thumbs-up sign.

At the Malta summit, neither Gorbachev nor Bush would answer journal- ists' questions about Eastern Europe. Pressed to make a statement, Gorbachev said: 'We should preserve elements of cautiousness – to use the famous phrase of President Bush.' Both world leaders were essentially bystanders in a drama that affected them both, Gorbachev most of all.

Returning to Moscow, Gorbachev spoke on December 6 of the 'advisability of keeping the one-Party system'. On the following day, in an unprecedented act of defiance by a Soviet Republic, the members of the Lithuanian parliament voted by an overwhelming majority to abolish the article in Lithuania's constitution whereby the Communist Party 'directs and leads society' and was 'the hub of its political system'. After thus abolishing the supremacy of the Communist Party, the parliamentarians then voted to add a clause to the constitution whereby 'Parties, social organizations and other legally established movements operate within the framework of the constitution'. This second vote opened the way for non-Communists to stand for election.

On December 6, while Gorbachev was in Moscow stressing the importance of the one-Party system, in Prague the Czechoslovak Communist Party leader, Karel Urbanek, met an opposition delegation headed by several Civic Forum leaders, including Václav Havel. This was the first time that the Party leader had agreed to talk with the opposition. Havel was emphatic that the secret police must be dissolved. Urbanek admitted that it had 'lost its purpose'. That same day, the Czechoslovak Prime Minister, Ladislav Adamec, offered to resign if his government did not meet with public approval.

In East Berlin, a meeting of Communist, opposition and Church groups, holding their first round-table talks, voted to call on the East German government to hold free elections within five months, and to disband the secret police. As in every East European country, it was the secret police that ensured the rule of Communism through an intricate system of informers, the interception of mail, arrests without trial, long periods of incarceration, often incommunicado, and torture. The East German round-table meeting demanded that the secret police Ministry (the Stasi) be replaced by a civilian service under civilian control and accountable to parliament. Stasi offices had already been broken into in several towns and occupied by irate citizens. In Dresden, several members of the Stasi had been injured when the buildings in which they and their families lived had been attacked. In an attempt to calm the situation, the Stasi announced that its members, who were armed, had been given orders 'not to shoot to kill'.

The Soviet Union made no move to counter these measures and decisions of those whom it had once so tightly controlled. The Brezhnev Doctrine was indeed dead. On December 10 a non-Communist coalition government was established in Prague. The President, and Communist Party stalwart, Gustáv Husák, swore in the new Ministers, 'most of whom', commented the British journalist Edward Lucas, 'are committed to undoing his life's work'. Husák then stood down as President, and Václav Havel, whom most people assumed, correctly, would succeed him, announced the news to a vast crowd in Wenceslas Square. They had, he said, achieved a 'peaceful revolution'. He added: 'Let us make sure this revolution keeps on flourishing, but let us not let anyone smear dirt on its peaceful face.'

That day, in Sofia, more than 50,000 Bulgarians gathered in front of the Cathedral to demand the abolition of the clause in the Bulgarian constitution guaranteeing the supremacy of the Communist Party. On the following day, December 11, in Leipzig, 200,000 East Germans were likewise in the streets, demanding the ending of all border restrictions between East and West Germany, and the reunification of Germany as a single geo-political entity. Two days later, on December 13, the first of the 580 watchtowers from which East German guards had controlled the East German border and kept it sealed, were dismantled (at Stapelburg). The East German authorities had abandoned all pretence at retaining the authority of the State. Six days after the dismantling of the watchtowers had begun, all restrictions on travel between East and West Berlin were formally ended.

In Bulgaria, where the first clandestine pro-democracy newspaper had begun to circulate during the summer, all non-Communist political Parties were legalized on December 14, and, for the first time since 1945, demonstrations were permitted without restriction. The Bulgarian Communist Party – long a loyal follower of the dictates of Moscow – had, like its East German counterpart, given up all pretence at maintaining power. From Moscow, there came no lead and no guidance, no protest and no indignation. The Soviet Union, so long used to maintaining a sharp watch on its 'satellites', was struggling with its own internal demons.

Only in Roumania did the Ceauşescu regime, under its authoritarian leader, seek to retain all the elements of centralized and Communist control. Ceauşescu had been in power for twenty-four years, and was determined not to give it up. In January, four journalists, among them Anton Uncu, were imprisoned for publishing an anti-Communist manifesto. Six retired senior Communist Party officials who wrote Ceauşescu a letter of protest for 'violating Roumania's constitution' were put under house arrest. When, in November, Ceauşescu spoke at his Party Congress, he denounced the changes that were taking place elsewhere in Eastern Europe, and, as he spoke, received

125 officially counted and carefully stage-managed standing ovations.

But Ceauşescu could not keep what Churchill had called the 'spark coming from God knows where' from igniting a persistent fire. In the city of Timişoara a Lutheran pastor, László Tökés, an ethnic Hungarian, defiantly ignored all threats that he stop defending ethnic and religious rights. When ordered to move his parish away from Timişoara he refused to do so. On December 16 the Roumanian security forces attempted to remove him by force. His largely Hungarian congregation resisted. On the following day an even larger demonstration took place in his support, a demonstration in which many ethnic Roumanians joined. Security forces and troops opened fire, and a hundred of the demonstrators were killed.

There was indignation throughout Roumania at the killings in Timişoara. But Ceauşescu failed to appreciate the extent of the anger, and left for a three-day official visit to Iran. He returned on December 20. On the following day he decided to hold a mass rally in Bucharest to demonstrate – as at the Party Congress in November – the extent of his popular support. It was a grave miscalculation. The very crowds from whom he had expected unanimous and vociferous adulation turned suddenly against him. Anti-Ceauşescu demonstrations sprang up throughout the capital. As in Timişoara, the security troops opened fire, this time on direct orders from Ceauşcescu. Forty demonstrators were killed. The population of Bucharest, refusing to be cowed, took to the streets in ever-increasing numbers.

Ceauşescu called on the Minister of Defence, General Vasile Milea, to bring the army into Bucharest and restore order. Milea refused to do so. His death shortly after his refusal was widely attributed to Ceauşescu. The army was outraged, and within hours was on the streets joining in with the demonstrators, calling for Ceauşescu's overthrow.

On the morning of December 22, Ceauşescu and his wife sought refuge in the Communist Party Central Committee building. As they did so, a newly formed National Salvation Front, put together by anti-Ceauşescu Communist officials, anti-Communist intellectuals and army officers, announced that it had taken over power. A vast crowd in front of the Central Committee building demanded Ceauşescu's arrest. He and his wife managed to get away by helicopter, but were captured two days later. Then, on December 25, they were subjected to a short and abusive 'judicial' confrontation with their captors, which took place at a secret location, but was later shown on television worldwide. Husband and wife, found guilty of charges that included 'genocide' and corruption, were then shot. The Latin motto *Sic semper tyrannis* (thus always the fate of tyranny) had seldom been given a more graphic representation.[1]

In the final days of the overthrow of Ceauşescu, the secret police, the Securitate, had continued to attack army units and civilians, and several hundred people were killed. It was the only serious bloodletting in Eastern Europe during a year of incredible political turmoil. Elsewhere, the year ended with bloodless triumphs, culminating on December 29 when Václav Havel – writer, dissident, prisoner – became President of Czechoslovakia. He was the first non-Communist President for forty-one years.

When Havel took the oath of office, the 'pledge to Socialism' that had been part of it since 1948 was deleted. In Roumania, as 1989 came to an end, the new government acted quickly to end the village-destruction programme, to bring the secret police under army control, and to end the rigid restrictions on foreign travel.

The events in Eastern Europe had riveted the attention of the world. A revolution was taking place as comprehensive as any seen since the imposition of Communism and the establishment of the Iron Curtain forty-four years earlier. The search for international agreements on a global scale had continued throughout the year. On January 11 a United Nations declaration outlawing the use of poison gas, and toxic and bacteriological weapons, was signed by 149 countries. The imperatives which had caused aerial bombardment to be regulated before the First World War continued to exercise the benign elements of the human psyche, not untinged with the concept of self-preservation.

As the era of Communism evaporated, Islamic fundamentalism was on the rise. On February 14 Ayatollah Khomeini issued a *fatwa* against the British writer, Salman Rushdie, calling for his death for alleged anti-Islamic 'blasphemy' in his book *The Satanic Verses*. Rushdie was forced to go into hiding. In Bradford, British Muslims publicly burned the book. Khomeini died within four months of issuing the *fatwa*, but it remained in force. Rushdie's life became one of unbroken danger. The British government provided him with twenty-four-hour police protection.

Freedom of expression could take many forms; on June 21 the United States Supreme Court ruled that constitutional guarantees of free speech included the act of trampling or burning the national flag. The President,

---

[1] Attributed to Brutus when he stabbed Julius Caesar, *Sic semper tyrannis* was the phrase shouted by John Wilkes Booth when he shot Abraham Lincoln in 1865.

George Bush, and the House of Representatives, expressed their dismay at the ruling. But it was later re-confirmed by the Supreme Court.

In his first nationwide television address, made from the White House Oval Office on September 5, Bush 'declared war' on drugs, launching a $7,800 million campaign to 'mobilize the nation'. Educational institutions that did not implement drugs-education programmes would lose their federal subsidy. Financial help would be given to those in the drug-producing countries of Latin America, principally Colombia, Peru and Bolivia, who were prepared to assist in 'stamping out' the drug trade.

Drug abuse was becoming endemic throughout the world, and the Western world, with its greater affluence enabling individuals to purchase illegal drugs more easily, was no exception. Where money was not available, crime increasingly provided it. In Washington itself, within a mile of the Oval Office, drug trafficking was rampant. The number of drug-related murders in the capital, fifty in the twelve months up to March 1988, had doubled by March 1989. New drugs, including the cocaine derivative 'crack', were continually entering the market, as profits from drug-dealing soared. No sector of society was free from the evil of drug abuse. The Mayor of Washington, Marion Barry, was himself under investigation for drug use. When one of America's leading 'tele-evangelists', Jim Bakker, was defrocked, one of the main charges against him was drug dependency.

The American war on drugs led, in December, to an episode that startled many Americans, and brought down Soviet criticism on the Bush administration. On the night of December 19/20 an American military operation – Operation Just Cause – was launched against Panama, whose military ruler, General Manuel Noriega, was accused by the Americans of drug trafficking on a massive scale. In all, 24,000 American troops took part in the attack, of whom 13,000 were stationed in Panama. Noriega took refuge in the Vatican Embassy in Panama City. The Embassy was then surrounded by American troops, who relayed deafeningly loud pop music through loudspeakers in an effort to disorient him. Noriega gave himself up, and was taken to Miami, where drug charges were laid against him.

As part of his inaugural programme, President Bush had referred to 'welfare dependency' as one of the 'problems' he wished to combat. In Britain, Margaret Thatcher, who by 1989 was the longest-serving British Prime Minister of the century, had taken a lead in trying to create a society in which reliance on State aid and support would be replaced by what had once been considered the essentially Victorian virtue of 'self-help'. In the economic sphere, her policy of privatization relieved the State of the burden, challenge and, as many argued, the duty of running nationwide enterprises and utilities, such as the railways, electricity and waterworks. Putting these utilities into the hands of profit-making entrepreneurs, whose skills at making profits were evident, she considered necessary for the enterprises, many of which had hitherto been an economic burden on the taxpayer, to flourish, and to create wealth for those who managed them. 'Thatcherism' brought Britain great wealth; it also put a stigma on those who failed to master the system.

An echo of the Second World War had a current political dimension. In 1945 the western frontier of Poland had been redrawn to include large areas of what had until then been the eastern regions of Germany: Pomerania, Danzig, the 'Polish corridor', southern East Prussia and Silesia. On November 14, at the end of a six-day visit to Poland, the West German Chancellor, Helmut Kohl, committed Germany to accept the western Polish frontiers, and not to make any claims for any of the land that had been transferred to Poland in 1945. He also put forward a comprehensive plan of 'consultation and co-operation' between Bonn and Warsaw. For its part, Poland promised to ease the life of the small remaining German minority in western Poland.

On December 22 a final act in the drama of the fall of the Berlin Wall was played out at the Brandenburg Gate. That day the gate, a symbol of Prussian nineteenth-century militarism, was opened for the first time to East-West traffic. A British regiment, the Royal Welch Fusiliers, was present, parading with their regimental goat Billy. The British Prime Minister, Margaret Thatcher, had expressed her unease at the prospect of German reunification. At a gathering of historians at her country residence, Chequers, she had listened to and echoed British fears of the power of a single German State. Her fears were answered publicly by a former refugee from Nazism, the publisher George Weidenfeld, who had achieved distinction, and a peerage, in Britain, his home since 1938. In an article in *The Times* he wrote:

A striking feature of West German post-war history has been a conscious, as well as instinctive, aversion to militarism among German youth. Considering that Germany has contracted twice territorially (1918 and 1945) and lost whole provinces, the Federal Republic has fewer elements of right-wing extremism than, say, France or Italy.

The economic and social upsurge of the EC and its member nations should quench fears of a united Germany's disproportionate strength. Any two of the major EC countries combined could rival a united Germany. As the EC expands, Germany's shareholding in the European equity will be diluted.

'As we watch anxiously President Gorbachev's Herculean efforts to keep the Soviet empire from disintegration,' Weidenfeld wrote, 'we should reflect that if there is one country which could focus its inventiveness and skills and, aided by the West and Japan, take the lead in helping to rebuild the infrastructure of Russia, it is Germany.'

Another 'valid reason', in Weidenfeld's view, for the support of German unification 'is the long-term danger in preserving a separate eastern state. The genesis, record, ethos and prospects of the second German State all bode ill: it bears the birthmark of Stalinism.' For two decades it had produced impressive industrial results. The East Germans had taken pride in creating a powerful industrial base in the Soviet sphere. 'Time and again the Ulbrichts and Honeckers proclaimed that the sole *raison d'être* of a second German State was its superior Marxist-Leninist system. Now that that system has gone, why should East Germans not join their kith and kin in the West?'

By the middle of the 1990s, Weidenfeld pointed out, the Federal Republic, 'barring unforeseen events, will have completed half a century of a civil society built by enlightened men. If, then, unity were to crown this achievement, moderation must be seen to triumph.' After the First World War, had Britain and France 'shown a fraction of the compassionate understanding to such moderate men as Rathenau, Stresemann or Brüning which they later lavished on Papen, Ribbentrop and Hitler, we might have been spared a Third Reich and a Second World War'. Weidenfeld added: 'Those who still have a nightmarish vision of a Fourth Reich might banish their fears and put their trust in the enduring continuity of the moral standards set by such humane pragmatists as Adenauer and Heuss, Brandt and Weizsäcker, and in the younger generation of Germans of goodwill.'

These arguments prevailed. Long-ingrained British hostility to Germany was being set aside. The European Union was becoming the forum for collective and moderate decision-making. Economic benefits were overriding historic animosities.

The cause of human rights was unexpectedly advanced in South Africa when, on July 5, Nelson Mandela was allowed out of prison for talks with the South African President, F. W. de Klerk. After a second meeting between the two men on December 12, it was clear that Mandela's release was imminent. Among those present at the December meeting was the Justice Minister, Kobie Coetsee, one of those who had to ensure the operation of apartheid. He announced after the meeting that the discussion with Mandela had covered 'ways and means to address current obstacles in the way of meaningful dialogue'. No such conciliatory words had been heard earlier.

In China, human rights were not asserted successfully. On June 3, in Beijing, protesters in Tiananmen Square demanding greater democratic freedoms for China were fired upon by police and troops. As many as two hundred of the demonstrators were killed. One young man, photographed standing defiantly in front of a line of tanks, caught the imagination of the free world.

Just across the border with China, the British authorities in Hong Kong began the forcible repatriation of Vietnamese boat people to Vietnam on December 11, despite protests by human rights groups. The first fifty-one were seized in the night and deported at dawn. The leader of the Labour Party, Neil Kinnock, asked Margaret Thatcher: 'Don't you realize that you are the only person in this whole shameful episode who cannot make the excuse "I was only obeying orders," for you were the person giving the orders – and those orders are tyrannical?' In reply Margaret Thatcher stressed that 13,000 Vietnamese had been granted refugee status and would not be returned to Vietnam, but that it was 'perfectly in order to return illegal immigrants to their country of origin'. In the debate that followed, the Foreign Secretary, Douglas Hurd, told the House of Commons that the Vietnamese villagers would not abandon their plans to sail for Hong Kong unless it was made clear to them that the colony was not the first stage of 'a voyage to Vancouver or Australia'. Hurd added: 'Unless it is absolutely clear to people in Vietnam that those who do not qualify as refugees will be returned to Vietnam, Hong Kong faces the prospect of tens of thousands more arrivals in 1990. That is simply not an acceptable prospect.'

The Labour foreign affairs spokesman, Gerald Kaufman, accused the government of adopting 'the policy of the three o'clock knock by the police in the morning'. If force had been ruled out for the repatriation, he asked, 'why were 150 riot police equipped with riot helmets, shields and batons needed for the removal of fifty-one people, of whom forty-three were children or women?' David Steel, the Liberal Democrat leader, said that the feelings of the British people at the dawn repatriation of the fifty-one varied from 'unease to repugnance'. The repatriation continued.

* * *

The environment was high on the international agenda, but not all developments were beneficial. Plans for the rapid phasing out of CFCs in order to protect the ozone layer were made, but postponed. On March 24 an Exxon oil tanker struck a reef near Valdez, in Alaska. More than ten million tons of crude oil were spilled. Thousands of birds and hundreds of sea otters were killed. Environmentalists, spurred by the scale of the disaster, established the 'Valdez Principles', urging international agreement to eliminate pollutants that harmed air, water or earth, and called for companies whose products were environmentally damaging to take steps to change them, to restore the environments that they had damaged, and to pay compensation for human injury and ill-health.

The Valdez oil-spill galvanized environmental groups, as no other environmental accident had done before. Opinion polls taken after the spill in the United States showed that, for the first time, a majority considered the environmental issue the 'most important' one facing the nations of the world; seventy-six per cent of those polled said that they considered themselves 'environmentalists'. Many new environmental organizations were set up. In Denmark, where each organization submitted its membership lists, it was found – since many Danes belonged to two or more such organizations – that there were more Danish environmentalists than there were Danes.

Rainforests in South America continued to be burned to make way for agricultural and grazing land. Factories in the industrial nations continued to spew out pollution and create acid rain. East Germany's most recent power station produced more sulphur dioxide, a main component of acid rain, than the whole of Sweden. In the Pacific Ocean, Japan, South Korea and Taiwan resisted attempts to curb deep-ocean drift-net fishing. This method of fishing, covering an area of ocean as large as the continental United States, was such that not only the squid which were its object, but dolphins and other sea mammals, were caught in the nets and killed. In November, New Zealand tried to establish a Pacific maritime convention to have this method of fishing banned, at least in the South Pacific, but its efforts were in vain. In December the United Nations General Assembly imposed a moratorium on the use of these nets after June 1992, but the moratorium was not legally binding on member States.

Environmental issues took up a third of the final communiqué issued by the leaders of the seven major industrial nations at the end of their Paris summit in July. Without agreeing on specific actions, they made it clear that 'decisive action' was needed in order to 'understand and protect the

Earth's ecological balance'. Meanwhile, the immediate demands of famine brought pledges of monetary help from all Western nations for an estimated four million people facing famine as a result of yet another failure of the rains in northern Ethiopia. Civil war meant that the provision of aid could be a hazardous operation. But radio and television appeals in the West had led to an upsurge in the desire to make donations. Following one such public appeal on December 6, £500,000 was raised in Britain alone within three days.

In India, an upsurge of Sikh nationalism led to the murder of nineteen Hindu students in November, shot to death while they were asleep in their hostel in Patiala. The Sikh extremists responsible for the attack were demanding an independent Sikh State, Khalistan. 'Putting out the lives of such bright young people is a despicable act,' said the Prime Minister, Rajiv Gandhi, while commending the Sikhs as a whole for resisting the temptation of extremism. It was five years since his mother had been assassinated by her Sikh bodyguard. The Patiala killings brought to four thousand the number of people killed in the previous two years in similar extremist attacks. More than two hundred policemen had also been killed.

In the United States the slow but steady progress of racial equality, which in earlier years had been worked for by Truman, Kennedy and Johnson, was given a boost that November with the election of Lawrence Douglas Wilder as Governor of Virginia. Not only was Wilder the first elected Black governor of an American State, his victory was all the more remarkable in that more than eighty per cent of the voters were White.

Wilder's story was held up as a model to Black Americans. He had been born in near poverty in Richmond, the former Confederate capital. He had gone to an all-Black school which did not have indoor plumbing. He had fought with distinction in the Korean War. Returning to the United States he had studied law, but been forced to do so outside Virginia, because of its segregationist policies. He had practised law, and become a millionaire. Most remarkable of all, he was the grandson of slaves.

There was one poignant echo of a distant war at the end of 1989 – the arrival in the Philippines in November of thirty Japanese veterans of the Second World War, armed with picks, shovels and maps, with permission to dig up the bones of their dead fellow soldiers and return with them to Japan for burial in the Tomb of the Unknown Soldier.

It was not the past, however, but the future, whose horrors were given the greatest publicity. On December 12 the United Nations International Children's Emergency Fund (UNICEF) announced that more than 100 million children would die from illness and malnutrition in the 1990s. UNICEF pointed out that with $2,500 million a year it could eradicate almost all the causes of these otherwise inevitable deaths. Immunization alone could save the lives of eight thousand children a day. A further seven thousand children died every day from dehydration, and six thousand from pneumonia. Measles, tetanus and whooping cough, which killed three million children a year, were all preventable. The sum involved was the equivalent, UNICEF pointed out, of what Soviet citizens spent annually on vodka, or American cigarette companies on advertising.

CHAPTER THIRTY-NINE

1990

Appeasement does not work. No one should under-
estimate our determination to confront aggression.

PRESIDENT GEORGE BUSH

THE PACE OF CHANGE in Eastern Europe and the Soviet Union, so
unexpected and unprecedented in 1989, hardly slackened during 1990. On
New Year's Day the Roumanian secret police (the Securitate) was abolished.
Four days later the Roumanian government announced an amnesty for every-
one who had been sentenced for political offences since 1947. On 11 January
1990 the focus of anti-Communist activity turned to Albania, the most
Stalinist of all the Eastern European States in its ideological orientation. The
Communist regime there – despite the death five years earlier of the autocratic
Enver Hoxha – did not intend to follow the example of its other Eastern
European counterparts, and on January 11 anti-Communist demonstrations
in the northern city of Shkodër were dispersed by police.

Inside the Soviet Union, more than two hundred Armenians and Azeris
were killed in ethnic clashes in the disputed Nagorno-Karabakh enclave. On
January 18, Azerbaijan declared war on Armenia: this was the first time
since the formation of the Soviet Union that two republics had taken such
a step. On the following day, in the Azerbaijanian city of Baku, sixty
Armenians were murdered in an Azeri pogrom. In Dushanbe, the capital of
the Tajik Soviet Socialist Republic, there were nationalist riots when it was
announced that Armenian refugees from the fighting would be housed in
the city. More than six decades of Communist teaching whereby the Christian
Armenians and the Muslim Azeris and Tajiks would sublimate their religious
traditions to the greater good of the Party, and to the 'unbreakable' union
of republics, were being swept aside.

In Moscow, Gorbachev continued to insist that his call for openness within the Communist Party system offered the only possible path of political change. On February 17 it was announced that Communist Party leaders would no longer be allowed their free country houses (dachas). Changes inconceivable a year earlier were taking place daily. On February 24, in elections in the Soviet Republic of Lithuania, the Communist Party came second to a wide range of nationalist candidates campaigning on platforms opposed to the continuation of Communist and of Soviet rule. Reflecting the ferment inside the Soviet Union, in once-loyal Bulgaria the popular demonstrations against Communism continued. On February 25 an estimated 200,000 people attended an anti-Communist rally in Sofia. On the following day Gorbachev agreed to withdraw all Soviet troops from Czechoslovakia within seventeen months.

A further move away from Communist orthodoxy in the Soviet Union took place on March 5, when the government conceded the right of individuals to run their own small businesses and to employ up to twenty people in them. But, while pressure for economic change fitted Gorbachev's vision of restructuring, it was political change which had become the main public demand, and on March 11, in a move which many forecast would constitute an end to the Soviet Union, as established by Lenin almost seventy-three years earlier, the Communist Party renounced its monopoly on political power. The Party had thus to give up the constitutional guarantee – enshrined in Article Six of the Soviet Constitution – of its 'leading role' in the structure of the State. With Gorbachev's approval, which he had withheld the previous December, the constitution was amended: henceforth the Communist Party would 'share' with other political Parties and social movements the task of forming and administering public policy.

Four days after the Communist Party abandoned its constitutional right to sole political power, like the second tremor that follows an earthquake, Lithuania declared its independence. It was the first of the former Baltic States to break away from the Soviet Union. The Lithuanian move, declared Gorbachev, was 'illegitimate and invalid'. But it had taken place, and the Hammer and Sickle disappeared overnight from the public buildings in a dozen towns and in hundreds of villages, to be replaced by the long-banned Lithuanian flag.

On March 25 Soviet tanks appeared in the streets of the Lithuanian capital, Vilnius. For several hours they passed and repassed the parliament building, inside which the defiant parliamentarians waited. Had the tanks opened fire there could well have been slaughter. Momentarily besieged, the new

Lithuanian government made plans to smuggle out a number of deputies who could establish a government in exile in Sweden. Should the tanks go into action and the country be overrun, the Lithuanian flag would still not be put away or the cause of independence abandoned. After several hours the Soviet tanks withdrew. There was to be no Hungary 1956 or Czechoslovakia 1968 on the territory – or former territory, as it had become – of the Soviet Union.

The successful Lithuanian defiance led Estonia to suspend the Soviet constitution on the territory of the Estonian Soviet Republic, an almost equally brazen act in the eyes of Moscow. But Estonia still hesitated to declare independence. An economic blockade was imposed on Lithuania by the Soviet Union on April 18, and all oil supplies cut off. But the Lithuanians were not to be cowed. Many Western observers, and many Lithuanians, assumed that it was only a matter of time before Soviet troops would re-enter the breakaway republic. But Gorbachev took no further military action: bloodshed would go entirely against the grain of all he had been promising. The example of Lithuania was not, however, immediately followed by any of the other fourteen republics, although, in the immediate aftermath of Lithuania's action, there were growing demands in the Georgian capital, Tbilisi, for independence, and also in both the Estonian capital, Tallinn, and the Latvian capital, Riga.

Gorbachev still believed that he could hold together the unity of the Soviet Union, not by the use of force but by continuing with the policy of openness. On April 22 he authorized the publication of details regarding the full and dangerous impact of the Chernobyl nuclear disaster in the period after the initial deaths, as well as the grant of financial compensation to its victims. But whether such unprecedented telling of the truth could preserve either the Communist system or the unity of the Soviet Union was unclear. On May 1 the traditional Red Square demonstration in Moscow in support of the Party and its leaders was marred, from Gorbachev's perspective, by a counter-demonstration in support of Lithuanian independence. Then, on May 4, Latvia declared itself a sovereign State, the parliament in Riga voting by 138 votes to nil to proclaim Latvia 'an independent democratic republic'. The forty Russian-speaking deputies had refused to take part in the vote. They also rejected the call by the parliament for a return to Latvia of the Abrene region, which the Soviet Union had annexed to the Russian Federal Republic in 1945.

The Estonian parliament voted its declaration of independence on May 8. All three Baltic Republics had detached themselves from the Soviet Union.

*　　*　　*

The impending reunification of West and East Germany led to fears in Poland that a single German State would seek the return of its eastern borderlands, lost in 1945. On March 5, Helmut Kohl renewed his earlier recognition of the post-1945 frontier between Poland and Germany, conceding with all the authority of his Chancellorship that Danzig, Pomerania, Silesia and the southern half of East Prussia would remain a part of Poland. A reunited Germany would, he promised, sign a formal treaty recognizing Poland's sovereignty over that region, once an integral and prosperous part of Germany. The Oder-Neisse Line, established by the victorious Allies, at Stalin's insistence, in 1945, would be the permanent border between Poland and Germany.

The impression of a reformed East Germany was reassuring to the Poles, as well as to the Jews who had never received any form of apology from East Germany during the Communist era for the mass murder of the war years. On April 12 the Speaker of the East German parliament, Sabine Bergmann Pohl, stated publicly: 'East Germany's first freely elected parliament admits joint responsibility on behalf of the people for the humiliation, expulsion and murder of Jewish women, men and children.' The entire parliament then stood in silence in memory of those who had been murdered. Visiting Poland three weeks later, the West German President, Richard von Weizsäcker, who in 1939, as a young soldier, had been among the invading German forces, visited the Nazi death camp at Treblinka, east of Warsaw, and then, on May 3, while still in Poland, pledged that a reunified Germany would never challenge the post-war frontiers.

In search of conciliation in Czechoslovakia, the man who had commanded the Soviet tank forces in Prague in 1968, General Yershov, visited Czechoslovakia and asked Alexander Dubček for 'forgiveness'. Dubček replied: 'You are twenty-two years too late.' To 'forget', he added, 'would be very difficult'. It emerged that Yershov's own career had been harmed when his only daughter married a Ukrainian Jew. The marriage, which he had publicly opposed, ended his hopes of becoming a Marshal of the Soviet Union. Reconciled with his family after six years, the General had spoken, once more in public, of the need for the Soviet Union to apologize to the Czechs.

Czech émigrés began to return, and to play an active part in the restoration of democratic life. Among those who came back was Jan Beneš, whose imprisonment in 1967 had been one of the catalysts for growing dissent.

At the end of the previous year, Czechoslovakia had chosen its leading dissident, Václav Havel, as President. On May 2 Hungary also chose a former dissident, Arpad Goncz, as the country's President. In the aftermath of the 1956 Hungarian uprising, Goncz had been imprisoned for six years. On May 20, Roumania held its first free elections since 1937. Two-thirds of the seats were won by the anti-Communist National Salvation Front, whose leader, Ion Iliescu, was elected President. On May 29, in the largest of the Soviet Republics, the Russian Federation, Boris Yeltsin was elected President, defeating the Communist Party candidate put up by Gorbachev. Within four months, Yeltsin had resigned from the Communist Party, declaring that it was not truly reformist.

Amid the internal political turmoil, Gorbachev recognized that the Soviet Union had to maintain good relations with the United States, particularly if it was not to be isolated further by the Eastern European defections. From May 31 to June 3 he was in Washington, for a summit with President Bush. Both Powers agreed to ban the production of chemical weapons, and to destroy all but five thousand tons of their stockpiles. They also agreed to destroy their stockpiles as soon as a worldwide ban on chemical weapons was agreed. For the first time in fifty years, an agreement was signed 'normalizing' trade relations between the two countries, freeing them from political restraints, and increasing considerably the long-term American grain sales to the Soviet Union.

On June 8, five days after the Washington summit, the new Hungarian President, Arpad Goncz, withdrew Hungary from the Warsaw Pact. Within a month, East Germany ceded sovereignty over economic, monetary and social policy to the West German government.

The force of anti-Communist feeling in Eastern Europe had been most visible in the mass public demonstrations of the previous year. The instrument of the final downfall of Communism was the ballot box. On June 17 there was a constitutional setback for the anti-Communists in Bulgaria when they were able to secure only 144 seats in the election as against 211 seats for the former Communists. But for those who wished to see democracy emerge in Eastern Europe the setbacks were far fewer than the achievements, which continued to astound all those who witnessed them, and to aggravate the Soviet Union, which still tried to prevent such changes within its own borders. The opening of the first stock exchange in Eastern Europe since 1945, in Budapest on June 21, was a particularly strong act of defiance to the whole Communist system.

Within the Soviet Union, similar blows to the established order were taking place. At the Twentieth Congress of the Communist Party, held between July 2 and 13, Gorbachev put forward a wide range of extraordinary changes, each of which was approved: there would be no more economic 'guidelines' for the future Five Year Plan: instead, local needs would be a central part of all projections. Perestroika, explained Gorbachev to the delegates, whose power had already been weakened by the constitutional changes in March, was replacing the 'Stalinist model of Socialism' by a 'civil society of free men and women', the basis of which would be free elections, a multi-Party system, human rights and 'popular self-government'. Gorbachev still hoped that a reformed Communist Party could attract majority support amid the new groups that were bound to take advantage of this new philosophy. In his speech to the Congress, he pleaded with the delegates for a Communist Party that would be 'freed of its ideological blinkers'. It must, he said, be a tolerant Party and a parliamentary Party. It would recognize the independence of its branches in the Republics, albeit within a 'common programme' and common statutes.

Foreign observers had begun to doubt whether such an idealized new Communism could emerge. The forces which had created the original Party structure, ideology, power and privilege were too deeply entrenched and too strongly committed to retain what they already held, or to transform themselves into a part, let alone the leading part, of what Gorbachev told the Congress was his ideal – 'genuine democracy'.

On August 14 Gorbachev issued a series of decrees 'rehabilitating' those who had been murdered by Stalin, or had been imprisoned during the purges. He also restored the citizenship that had been taken away from most exiled dissidents, including Alexander Solzhenitsyn. Six weeks later, on September 26, he presented the Supreme Soviet with a proposed law allowing freedom of religion, halting the active propagation of atheism by the State, and allowing religious activity even in the armed forces. The law was passed by 341 votes to one. Within another three weeks, church services were held in St Basil's Cathedral in the Kremlin, for the first time since 1918.

Islam, which four years earlier Gorbachev had condemned as an 'enemy of progress and Socialism', was given the same freedoms as Christianity. Many new mosques were built throughout the Soviet Central Asian Republics, and donations for Islamic schools and institutions were accepted from Pakistan, Saudi Arabia and Libya.

* * *

Since 1945 the Soviet Union had sought protection against the revival of German power. The division of Germany into two separate States, with Soviet control over East Germany, had made it possible to maintain, for forty-five years, an Iron Curtain less than two hundred miles from the North Sea. A generation of Soviet policymakers had stressed the permanency of the German divide. At midnight on October 2 the German Democratic Republic formally ceased to exist. On the following day the two Germanies announced their unification. The Soviet Union made no protest. It had come to terms with its lost role as the militarily dominant power in Central Europe. That same day, October 3, the Soviet Union reached agreement with the United States to limit the size of their respective conventional forces in Europe. Twelve days later, Gorbachev was awarded the Nobel Peace Prize.

As the year came to an end the spark of anti-Communist revolt was again ignited in Albania, with anti-Communist riots spreading to several cities including the capital, Tirana. Unlike at the beginning of the year the demonstrators were not dispersed. Within three weeks, the Communist government gave permission for the first opposition newspaper to be published and agreed to release two hundred political prisoners.

Within the Soviet Union the policy of openness continued to strike at the very heart of Communist orthodoxy. But Gorbachev's hopes that these changes would help maintain the unity of the vast imperial structure were challenged that autumn when more and more of the republics announced that they would no longer compel their citizens to serve in the Soviet army. On December 1 Gorbachev made it clear that compulsory military service had to be complied with, in every republic. His determination only stimulated further separatist impulses.

In South Africa, the two meetings in 1989 between President de Klerk and Nelson Mandela were the spectacular foretastes of accelerated change. On February 2, within six weeks of his second (December) meeting with Mandela, de Klerk informed the South African parliament – which was quite unprepared for his announcement – that the ban on the African National Congress was over. It, and the two other anti-apartheid movements, the Pan African Congress and the South African Communist Party, could at last take a full part in the political and national debate. Press censorship was relaxed. The execution of convicted prisoners was stopped. All those who had been imprisoned because of their membership of banned organizations were to be released. The government would work for universal franchise and 'respect for human rights'. With firm voice directed towards the White parliamentarians for whom all these changes were anathema, de Klerk announced: 'The season of violence is over. The time for reconciliation and reconstruction has come.'

On February 11, nine days after his revolutionary speech, de Klerk released Nelson Mandela from prison. He had been a prisoner for twenty-seven years, and had become a symbol worldwide of South African repression, and of human rights victims everywhere. Fifty thousand people gathered on the Grand Parade in Cape Town to welcome him. Like Gandhi four decades earlier in the Hindu-Muslim conflict in India, Mandela found himself confronted by intercommunal violence that threatened to destroy his vision of a unified Black-ruled South Africa. Dozens of Blacks were killed in the week after Mandela's release in the internecine fighting between the United Democratic Front, which supported the African National Congress, and the Zulu-based Inkatha movement. On February 25, in an appeal reminiscent of Gandhi's appeal in Noakhali, Mandela urged the fighting factions to stop the killing, and to throw their weapons into the sea. His appeal was not heeded. Nor could he stop the inhabitants of the African homelands – the Bantustans – from attacking their Black rulers, whom they accused of supporting the apartheid regime. In Ciskei, shops were looted, factories burned down, and fifty people killed.

Clashes in the Black townships between the police and the inhabitants also continued. When, at the beginning of April, police broke up a protest march at Sebokeng, near Vereeniging, eighteen protesters were killed and more than two hundred injured. Mandela demanded a judicial inquiry, and de Klerk agreed. When it was published five months later, the police were criticized for having been 'trigger-happy' and for having used force that was 'immoderate and disproportionate to any lawful object'. Of the 281 people killed or injured by police bullets, the report noted, 127 had been shot from behind.

On May 2, Mandela and de Klerk began a three-day meeting at Groote Schuur, near Cape Town. With them were leaders of the White community and of the African National Congress. As a result of the talks, a joint working committee was set up to organize the release of prisoners and the return of the exiles. The African National Congress delegation promised that it would work towards an end of violence and intimidation within the Black community, and between it and the White community. But the White regime could not easily shake off the habits of a generation. In May, eleven Black protesters were shot dead at Thabong, near the gold mining town of Welcom, in the Orange Free State. Following the Thabong killings, Mandela warned de Klerk that there could be no negotiations until the police were brought under control and the 'massacre of Blacks' was ended.

Mandela's authority grew with each day of his freedom. But the forces of reaction challenged de Klerk at every turn. On April 14 right-wing pro-apartheid radicals had raided the Pretoria headquarters of the South African air force and seized small arms, automatic weapons and ammunition. On May 13 more arms were stolen from a South African Defence Force armoury. In the weeks ahead, two offices of de Klerk's National Party were attacked with bombs by pro-apartheid fanatics.

White opposition to de Klerk came to a head on May 26, when Dr Andries Treurnicht, the leader of the Conservative Party, largest of the White opposition parties, addressed a mass meeting of 60,000 ultra-rightists at the Voortrekker Monument, outside Pretoria. Treurnicht declared that Afrikaner conservatives would, if necessary, use armed force to defend their right to a 'white fatherland'. In several parts of the country, including at Welcom, right-wingers were arming and forming vigilante groups under the leadership of the Afrikaner Resistance Movement, and other organizations, allegedly for self-defence. Two White mine employees and fourteen Black miners were killed in mid-May in an outbreak of interracial violence in the Welkom goldmines. On June 9 the Welkom offices of the (Black) National Union of Mineworkers were damaged by a bomb.

Undeterred by this violence, de Klerk instructed his Ministers to resume negotiations with the African National Congress leaders, and these were begun on August 8. The ANC pledged to end the 'armed struggle' against the government, which had been its ideological base for thirty years. Both sides committed themselves to secure change only through negotiation. What neither side could halt was the intercommunal killing. In the Black townships of the Transvaal, five hundred people were killed in the course of a few days. Both the Zulu chief, Mangosuthu Buthelezi, and Mandela appealed for a halt to the killings, but neither man was heeded.

Elsewhere in Africa, the grim cycle of drought and famine was accompanied by civil war. In Somalia, the armed forces under the control of President Mohammed Siyad Barre, himself a general, murdered at least five thousand civilians within two years. The opposition Somali National Movement had also carried out atrocities on a wide scale. In all, according to the human rights group Africa Watch, no fewer than 50,000 civilians, and possibly as many as 60,000, had been killed since the start of the civil war in May 1988. On one occasion, in a stadium in Mogadishu, hecklers had interrupted a speech by President Barre. Troops opened fire on the hecklers, and at least a hundred were killed. In protest against human rights abuses, the United States suspended all financial aid for industrial and commercial development: only humanitarian aid was still sent, as famine intensified. Britain also sent food aid to Somalia.

An echo of the Second World War came when the British government announced that Gruinard Island, off the north-west coast of Scotland, was no longer contaminated with anthrax. The contamination had taken place in 1942 as an experiment in biological warfare. Sheep could once more graze on what had become one of Britain's most isolated, and feared, locations.

In Sri Lanka, the civil war continued, with no diminution in the savagery of the killings. These got so fierce that, on May 30, Amnesty International appealed to the Tamil Tigers to end their 'executions' of political opponents. The appeal was ignored. On June 13 the Tamil Tigers captured ninety Sinhalese policemen in eastern Sri Lanka and executed them. Tamil Tigers also attacked moderate Tamil groups who were calling for restraint and compromise: many of these moderates were forced to seek refuge in Colombo, or fled to India. The Tamil Tigers also turned on the Muslim minority in Sri Lanka. On August 3, 120 Muslims were massacred at a mosque in Kattankudy. Two days later, fifty-eight Muslims were murdered in their villages. When Tamil Tigers captured the fort at Jaffna at the end of August, the Sri Lankan air force bombed the fort with considerable intensity. Among the buildings destroyed in the bombing was the hospital, which had been placed under the control of the International Committee of the Red Cross.

Hundreds of thousands of refugees were on the move. As many as 100,000 managed to cross into India. A further 830,000 were dispersed throughout Sri Lanka. Within the areas controlled by the government, vigilante squads were active, and many people were killed. On October 23 the European Community protested at Sri Lanka's descent into unrestrained killing. Canada did likewise a few weeks later. Indian troops, which had been attempting to keep the peace and to restrain the Tamil Tigers, could do so no longer, and were pulled out. They had lost 1,100 dead during their three-year tour of duty.

The Western world was far removed in its daily concerns from these distant killings. In the United States, the pioneering Americans with Disabilities Act guaranteed to all disabled people the right of access to public facilities, and the right to employment. Computer technology was advancing by leaps and bounds. Substantial progress was made in the mass marketing of CD-Rom compact discs, with almost a million sold before the end of the year (in 1989 the number was 168,000). In Germany and Japan, technologies were being developed to enable road vehicle users to drive to their destination aided by a computer-generated route while sitting at the wheel, a route that took into consideration traffic conditions on the roads they would have to drive as their journey was proceeding. New computer and laser technologies were also providing disabled people with greater mobility and means of communication. Even the ability of a disabled person to make the tiniest movement, such as a slight nod of the head, or indeed a barely detectable blink, was being harnessed to enable meaningful communication.

In a remarkable advance in medical science, surgeons at Guy's Hospital in London performed surgery on a baby in its mother's womb. At the University of Western Ontario, in the Canadian provincial town of London, the first bowel and liver graft transplants were being carried out, enabling the patient to resume a normal diet. In Africa, the World Health Organization was working to eliminate African sleeping-sickness, using an American-developed drug that could restore to perfect health patients whose brains had been invaded by the disease-causing parasite, which had hitherto proved indestructible. The battle against another epidemic African disease, river blindness, was also succeeding, with the decisive breakthrough coming from research done at the Centre for Preventative Ophthalmology at Johns Hopkins University in Baltimore. Of the global killer diseases, only AIDS and cancer still defied the search for successful treatment. And in Africa, in the wake of AIDS, came an upsurge in tuberculosis (TB) among AIDS patients who had contracted TB in their youth. Hitherto their infection had been kept under control, but with the weakening of their immune system by AIDS it returned, killing hundreds of thousands each year.

The Iran-Iraq War was over, but the Persian Gulf was not to be free from further conflict. On July 24 Iraq was reported to have massed 30,000 troops along its border with Kuwait. That number was increased to 100,000 within a week. The reason for such a troop concentration was soon realized. On August 2, Iraq invaded Kuwait.

Saddam Hussein's action was immediately condemned. On the same day, the United Nations Security Council passed a resolution calling for 'immediate and unconditional' Iraqi withdrawal. From Moscow, on August 3, the United States and the Soviet Union issued a joint statement signed by the United States Secretary of State, James Baker, and his Soviet opposite number, Edouard Shevardnadze. Both countries called for an international ban on arms sales to Iraq, much of whose armoury had been provided over the previous decade by the Soviet Union, France and Britain. On August 4 the European Community agreed to impose sanctions on Iraq. Two days later the United Nations made sanctions on Iraq, including oil sanctions, mandatory for all member States. Iraq could neither sell its own oil abroad, nor import oil. Saddam Hussein was internationally isolated.

Kuwait was a country on behalf of whose territorial integrity Britain had landed a military force at the head of the Gulf in 1900, to keep Ottoman Turkish ambitions at bay. The reactions of Queen Elizabeth II's subjects were similar to those of Queen Victoria's subjects, though more vociferous, and more alert to the perils of the region. British public opinion had been outraged earlier in 1990 when an Iranian-born journalist then working for the *Observer*, Farzad Bazoft, had been executed by the Iraqis on a spying charge. There had also been indignation in Britain in April when British customs officials at Teesport had seized a number of large pipes that had been manufactured in Britain for Saddam Hussein as the barrel of a super-gun which he had planned.

On the day of the Iraqi invasion of Kuwait, Margaret Thatcher was in the United States. She not only added her condemnation of the attack without hesitation, but personally pressed President Bush to be as forceful as possible in his response. Bush responded to her arguments, and in a television broadcast on August 8, watched by tens of millions of Americans, he compared Saddam Hussein to Hitler. 'Appeasement does not work,' he said. 'No one should underestimate our determination to confront aggression.' On the following day, Iraq announced the formal annexation of Kuwait. Six days later, on August 13, American and British warships began a naval blockade of Iraq, as an essential part of the United Nations sanctions. Margaret Thatcher had committed two British fighter squadrons and a naval contingent to help enforce the blockade. The Canadian government sent a naval flotilla:

two destroyers and a supply ship. A squadron of Canadian air force jet fighters was sent to provide protection for the three ships, and the 934 sailors and soldiers on board.

On August 19, as the crisis intensified, Saddam Hussein decided to detain foreign nationals caught in Kuwait at the time of the invasion, and to locate them near military installations. This, said President Bush, was against 'all accepted norms of international conduct', and on August 22 ordered the call-up of 40,000 American military reservists. On August 31 Japan offered $1,000 million towards the cost of any multinational force that might be sent to the Gulf. To defend Saudi Arabia against a possible Iraqi attack, twelve Arab League countries agreed to send forces to Saudi Arabia. Saddam Hussein had alienated even his Arab neighbours and potential allies: all but Jordan, which kept open the port of Akaba through which he was able to receive some sanc-tion-breaking supplies. In a gesture of defiance against the Arab coalition building up against him, Saddam Hussein called, on September 5, for the over-throw of King Fahd of Saudi Arabia and President Mubarak of Egypt.

Saddam Hussein had become the object of international condemnation. During a debate in the House of Commons of September 6 and 7, Margaret Thatcher described Iraq's action in invading Kuwait and in taking hostages as a return to the 'law of the jungle'. It was essential, she said, to restore the status quo in Kuwait. For that reason, she explained, she had ordered British ground forces to go to the Gulf. Both she and her Foreign Secretary, Douglas Hurd, made it clear, however, that Britain would not 'use military force without the further authority of the Security Council'. Neil Kinnock, the leader of the opposition, agreed that it was Britain's 'unrelenting purpose' to expel Iraq from Kuwait, to restore the legitimate government there, and to secure the release of all hostages. Nevertheless, while promising the Labour Party's broad support, he cautioned against independent military action without a precise United Nations mandate.

Flying to Helsinki, Bush and Gorbachev held an emergency summit on September 9 to discuss the crisis in the Gulf. In a joint statement the two leaders declared that they were 'united in the belief that Iraq's aggression must not be tolerated', and called upon Iraq 'to withdraw unconditionally from Kuwait, to allow the restoration of Kuwait's legitimate government, and to free all hostages now held in Iraq and Kuwait'. An area of Soviet-American disagreement was made public at the end of the summit, when Gorbachev emphasized the need for a political solution rather than the use of force. The

Americans had made it clear that force was part of their agenda if Iraq did not withdraw from Kuwait.

Speaking to a joint session of Congress on September 11, Bush set out America's objectives: the unconditional withdrawal of Iraqi forces from Kuwait, the restoration of Kuwait's 'legitimate government', the assurance of stability and security within the Gulf, and the protection of United States citizens abroad. He also spoke unequivocally about the economic aspect of the crisis. Stressing the importance of the Kuwaiti oilfields, he said: 'We cannot permit a resource so vital to be dominated by one so ruthless.' Bush ended his statement of September 11 with strong words: 'Iraq will not be permitted to annex Kuwait. That's not a threat, or a boast, that's just the way it's going to be.'

On September 14, Margaret Thatcher ordered an armoured brigade to be sent to Saudi Arabia, which Saddam Hussein had threatened. His troops in Kuwait were at the Saudi Arabian border. The British despatch of an armoured brigade, eight thousand men in all, together with their tanks and armoured vehicles, constituted the largest movement of British troops and armour overseas since the Korean War forty years earlier. If the United Nations' call for Iraq to evacuate Kuwait were not heeded, Tom King, the British Defence Secretary, announced, 'other options' remained available.

Details of Iraqi ill-treatment of Kuwaitis reached the West every day, as did details of Saddam Hussein's efforts to marginalize the Kuwaiti royal family. On September 22 Bush wrote in his diary: 'I've just read a horrible intelligence report on the brutal dismembering and dismantling of Kuwait. Shooting citizens when they are stopped in their cars. Exporting what little food there is. Brutalizing the homes. Dismantling the records. Indeed, making an oasis into a wasteland.' The report that Bush had been shown quoted the Norwegian Ambassador to Kuwait, who, Bush noted, 'attested to the brutality and to the horrible intention' of Saddam Hussein. 'The problem is, unless something happens soon, there may not be a Kuwait – there may be no records – no one will know who Kuwaiti citizens are. There is evidence that he's trying to re-populate Kuwait with Iraqi stooges.' The inference was clear. If 'there ever was a referendum' the vote would go against the Kuwaiti royal family. Saddam Hussein had vowed 'to never withdraw, and he vows that the family should never return'. Bush added: 'This just hardens my resolve. I am wondering if we need to speed up the timetable.'

Bush also pondered a historical precedent. As he later recalled in his memoirs:

In the first weeks of the crisis, I happened to be reading a book on World War II by the British historian Martin Gilbert. I saw a direct analogy between what was occurring in Kuwait and what the Nazis had done, especially in Poland. This in no way diminished the evil crimes the Nazis inflicted upon helpless millions, or the suffering into which they plunged all Europe. The book recounted how the German Army swept through an area, followed closely by special units which would terrorize the population. I saw a chilling parallel with what the Iraqi occupiers were doing in Kuwait. I caught hell on this comparison of Saddam to Hitler, with critics accusing me of personalizing the crisis, but I still feel it was an appropriate one.

I did not have a personal grudge against Saddam Hussein, but I had a deep moral objection to what he had done and was doing. It was unprincipled, and we could not permit it to go on.

On September 25, the Security Council called for air sanctions against Iraq. No Iraqi civilian airlines could fly to any outside airport, and no international carriers fly into Iraq. Slowly, as more and more Western statesmen beat their way to his door, including Edward Heath, the former British Prime Minister, and the former German Chancellor, Willy Brandt, Saddam Hussein released the foreign hostages whom he had taken. But a five-day 'peace mission' to the Gulf and to Iraq, by a Soviet emissary, Yevgeni Primakov, had as its objective to persuade Saddam Hussein to withdraw from Kuwait. Primakov returned to Moscow on October 29, his mission a failure.

The United Nations set 15 January 1991 as the deadline for Iraq to withdraw from Kuwait. Were this not to be done, Bush intimated that military action would follow, with the United States prepared to take the lead in a coalition of naval, air and military forces. There was a growing call inside the United States to avert a military confrontation. On November 20 – the day after Saddam Hussein announced that he was increasing his forces in Kuwait by a quarter of a million men – a group of Congressional Democrats tried to bring an injunction against Bush to prevent him from taking offensive action against Iraq 'without the prior consent of Congress'. One of the most senior Democrats, Senator Edward Kennedy, called for an extension of the January 15 deadline to 2 August 1991.

On November 22 Bush visited the American troops then in the Saudi Arabian desert, and celebrated Thanksgiving with them. That day Britain announced the despatch of a further 14,000 troops to Saudi Arabia, bringing the total number to more than 30,000.

On November 28, following a domestic British political crisis in which Margaret Thatcher was forced from office by those closest to her in government, John Major became Prime Minister. At the age of forty-seven, he was the youngest British Prime Minister for almost a hundred years. He had been both Chancellor of the Exchequer and, more briefly, Foreign Secretary. He took up the power and burden of his new office at the height of the Gulf crisis. On November 29, the day after he became Prime Minister, the Security Council voted to authorize the use of force against Iraq if Kuwait had not been evacuated by 15 January 1991. John Major was as determined as Margaret Thatcher to secure the evacuation of Kuwait. Only two countries, Cuba and Yemen, voted against the acceptance of the use of force. China abstained. No veto was cast.

On the day after the Security Council vote, Bush appeared on television and called for direct negotiations with Iraq. He was prepared, he said, 'to go the extra mile for peace', and suggested that the Iraqi Foreign Minister, Tariq Aziz, should meet him in the White House soon after December 10, and that James Baker should go to Baghdad between December 15 and January 15.

It was up to Iraq to agree to negotiate. The chances that it would were remote, given the way in which the crisis had developed. And yet Saddam Hussein had released many of the hostages. A hallmark of the Iraqi leader's strategy was to cast total uncertainty in the minds of his adversaries as to the way he would move, even though most of his previous movements had been confrontational. Bush expressed his own pessimism when he told the American people during his television broadcast: 'I'm not hopeful we're going to get a lot out of this.'

Bush did try to allay fears of a full-scale war. 'Should military action be required,' he said, 'this will not be another Vietnam. This will not be a protracted drawn-out war.' But any American life lost would be 'paid for in full' by Iraq. On December 6, Saddam Hussein announced the release of all remaining Western hostages in Iraq and Kuwait. On December 24 he stated that Israel would be the 'first target' in the event of war.

The impact of the crisis in the Gulf was widespread. When 100,000 Sri Lanka workers in Kuwait were forced to return home, their regular remittances ceased, with a depressing effect on the Sri Lankan economy. Palestinian workers in Kuwait, who were likewise displaced, could no longer contribute to the welfare of their families in the Palestinian refugee camps in Jordan and Syria.

Dire predictions also came with regard to the environment, should war break out in the Gulf. King Hussein of Jordan warned the World Climate Conference that the environmental impact of such a war would be 'swift, severe and devastating'. The burning of the Kuwait oilfields could, according to several experts, change the climate of the entire region, produce cooler weather and disrupt the monsoon cycle on the Indian subcontinent. Other experts feared the effect of an oil slick that would be slow to clear. One thing was certain, unlike the Korean or Vietnamese Wars, or the war in Afghanistan or the Iran-Iraq War, this war – if it were to take place – would be the first one over which environmental concerns would have been expressed in advance.

The year 1990 certainly saw yet greater awareness of the damage being done to the planet by human intervention and negligence. In the United States the Clean Air Act raised federal standards for toxic emissions by industrial organizations, and ensured that those standards would be enforced. In March, the third International North Sea Conference, held at The Hague, agreed as a matter of urgency to reduce by half, and in some cases by more than half, the levels of pollution from the worst pollutants. In all, thirty-seven pollutants were listed. In the case of lead, mercury, cadmium and dioxin, a minimum cut of seventy per cent by 1995 was deemed essential.

Not only urgent practical measures, but long-term strategies, were on the environmental agenda, and found echoes of support at some of the highest levels of government. In January, at a conference in Moscow of religious leaders and parliamentarians from thirty countries, Gorbachev himself had called, but to no effect, for the creation of an 'International Green Cross' that, acting for the environment as the International Red Cross did for wounded soldiers and prisoners of war, would help nations with ecological problems. Gorbachev also suggested that there should be a United Nations force of 'Green Berets' – again to parallel and contrast with the Red Berets of so many national paratroops – that would intervene whenever there was an ecological disaster. This too did not come to pass, although such disasters were frequent, and the Soviet Union was a major offender.

At the end of April, Soviet rocket fuel, leaked in vast quantities into the White Sea, killing 100,000 seals, and millions of fish and other marine creatures. According to Soviet naval sources, one-third of the sea life of the White Sea had been killed. The Soviet newspaper *Izvestiya* called it 'an ecological tragedy of huge proportions'. The negligence of human beings themselves, within the span of only a century, was putting the very existence of humanity in danger.

CHAPTER FORTY

1991

> ...a helping hand for those who need it; where people
> can get a hand up, not just a hand-out. A country that
> is fair and free from prejudice – a classless society, at
> ease with itself.
>
> JOHN MAJOR

FOR THE FIRST TWO WEEKS OF 1991 the United Nations pressed Saddam
Hussein to withdraw from Kuwait. He adamantly refused to do so. Under
the banner of the United Nations, a coalition was assembled, ready to go
to war to liberate Kuwait. Of crucial importance, on January 12 both Houses
of Congress voted in Washington to authorize American military action in
the Gulf, though Senate support, with fifty-two votes for and forty-seven
against, was a narrow one. This was the first time since the Second World
War that Congress had given its approval for military action.

The United States provided the supreme commander, a Vietnam War veteran, H. Norman Schwarzkopf, and by far the largest contingent, 425,000
military, naval and air personnel, although few of them had experience of battle.
Saudi Arabia provided 45,000 and Egypt 30,000. Britain, which made the next
largest contribution, sent 25,000 troops, some of whom had seen action in the
Falklands War nine years earlier. Syria provided 17,000 soldiers and support
staff, France 15,000, Kuwait 12,000 and the United Arab Emirates 8,000. The
coalition air forces were provided by the United States, Britain, Saudi Arabia,
France and Italy. Not since the Korean War in 1950 had there been such a
universal coalition of active powers: twenty-nine in all.[1] In the words of the
British historian M. R. D. Foot, who had served in the Second World War:

---

[1] In addition to the countries mentioned in this paragraph, troops or logistical support were
provided by Argentina (with which Britain had been at war nine years earlier), Australia,
Bangladesh, Belgium, Canada, Czechoslovakia, Denmark, Germany, Greece, Morocco, the
Netherlands, New Zealand, Niger, Norway, Oman, Pakistan, Poland, Qatar, Senegal and Spain.

They came from every continent and from diverse religious, political and social cultures, including Marxist and Muslim as well as Christian and agnostic, Arab and Slav as well as Latin and Anglo-Saxon. The presence of strangers with entirely foreign customs – such as women wearing visible trousers, or driving motor vehicles – was upsetting to Saudi Arabian society; but the upset was overridden by the urgency of the war's aim, to get the invader out of Kuwait. It had taken prodigious efforts by supply staffs to get the combatants to the theatre of war in time, with adequate supplies of ammunition, fuel and food.

Saddam Hussein commanded the fourth-largest armed forces in the world, as many as a million men, of whom 580,000 were on the Kuwaiti front. Many of them had gained experience of battle in the recent war with Iran. Saddam's arms had come from the world market, where selling arms was one of the most lucrative forms of capitalist enterprise. By far the largest single source of his most modern arsenal, fifty per cent in all, including his Scud missile launchers, came from West Germany. Eight per cent came from Switzerland and five per cent each from Italy and France. The Soviet Union, although making up only two per cent of the total arms sold, had provided more than 800 Scud missiles. One American company provided Iraq with network analysers used to develop missile guidance. A British firm designed and supervised the construction of a missile-testing complex.[1]

United Nations Security Council Resolution 678 of the previous November, authorizing force to be used to end the Iraqi occupation of Kuwait became effective on January 15. An ultimatum was sent to Iraq, and rejected. On January 16 the war began, codenamed Operation Desert Storm. That night air attacks were launched against Iraqi military installations in both Kuwait and Iraq. Baghdad was shaken by the pounding all around it. The American warplanes which made up the main air strike force sought to restrict their bombing to military targets, but there were many civilian casualties. In an astoundingly dangerous effort to ensure that targets were hit with precision, British and American special troops were parachuted deep into Iraq, and, disguised as local Iraqis, placed homing devices at points which were required to be attacked.

Inside Kuwait, the Iraqis found an ally. There were 750,000 Kuwaitis

---

[1] Countries whose arms firms provided less than five per cent of Iraq's arsenal were Brazil (4%), Britain and the United States (3.5% each), Austria (3%), Belgium (2%) and Japan (1.5%).

and 400,000 Palestinians living in Kuwait. 'Many (but not all) of Kuwait's inhabitants of Palestinian origin welcomed and helped the invaders, providing labour and advice about where to loot,' M. R. D. Foot has written. 'The Iraqi army followed sound mediaeval precedent in looting Kuwait city thoroughly. Shops and houses from which the owners had fled, or of which the owners were suspect, were stripped of television sets, washing machines, freezers, fine carpets – anything portable and desirable. This activity went on steadily while battles raged elsewhere.'

In the first twenty-four hours of the war, the highly centralized Iraqi air defence system had its communications network destroyed. The ground control interception stations, from which the anti-aircraft activity was to be directed, were almost all destroyed. By the night of January 17/18 Iraqi anti-aircraft activity was minimal, and the systematic destruction of the road bridges over the River Euphrates proceeded without any serious interdiction. Saddam Hussein was so angered by the failure of his anti-aircraft defences that he ordered the execution of his anti-aircraft commander. In the course of the fighting, the coalition air forces flew 110,000 air sorties. Sixty-seven aircraft were shot down, a tenth of the rate of loss of an equivalent Allied air raid on Germany in the Second World War.

As a substantial part of the anti-Iraq coalition was made up of Arab States, including Saudi Arabia, the American and British governments prevailed upon Israel not to participate. On January 18 the first Iraqi Scud missiles were launched, causing damage to property, but no deaths, in Ramat Gan (just outside Tel Aviv) and Haifa. Despite this act of war, which was repeated on the following day, Israel deferred to renewed pressure from the non-Arab coalition partners, and refrained from retaliation. In an audacious action, authorized by John Major, British special forces were parachuted deep into Iraq, from where they tracked down the mobile Scud launchers – of which there were 108, targeting both Israel and Saudi Arabia – and directed Allied air strikes against them.

On January 20, American planes based at Incirlik, in southern Turkey, attacked Iraqi forces in the north of Iraq. That day Iraq fired Scud missiles at the American air base at Dhahran, in Saudi Arabia, and at the Saudi Arabian capital, Riyadh. American Patriot anti-missile batteries were in action against the Scuds; and on January 21 both the United States and the Netherlands provided Patriots for Israel, which continued to be under Scud attack.

During January 21, Iraq caused considerable indignation among the coalition partners when seven Allied prisoners of war were shown on Iraqi television, and appealed for the war to end. It was announced that they and other prisoners of war would be used as 'human shields' at potential strategic targets. After the war it was learned that they had been tortured before being put in front of the television cameras. That day, British naval units were in action for the first time against Iraqi targets in the Gulf.

Television was showing hundreds of millions of viewers in Allied coalition countries the 'prowess' of their forces. Reporters familiar to American and British audiences were seen in the capital of the enemy, including Peter Arnett of CNN and John Simpson of the BBC. They reported on the attacks, often visible in the sky behind them, of their own national forces. This reportage took place round the clock, and was relayed instantaneously.

Fearful that the Scud missiles that were being fired nightly against Israel would be armed with poison gas, the Israeli government had issued gas masks to all its citizens, and advised all Israelis to create a 'sealed room' inside their homes, to which they could go when an attack was imminent, and, wearing their gas masks, await the worst. The worst never came, but the strain of the nightly retreat to the sealed room was an enormous one, incredibly difficult for a nation that had been born so soon after the destruction of millions of Jews in the gas chambers.

On January 23 Iraq launched its fourth Scud missile attack on Israel. The American Patriot missiles were in place to intercept. To the intense relief of the Americans, that day the Israeli Cabinet, headed by Yitzhak Shamir, agreed to a policy of non-retaliation. During the day the Chairman of the United States Joint Chiefs of Staff, General Colin Powell, announced that the coalition air forces had achieved air superiority over Iraq, and that henceforth their main task would be to concentrate on severing the supply-lines between Iraq and its forces in Kuwait.

The first Kuwaiti territory to be liberated by the coalition was Qaruh Island, in the Gulf, from which the Iraqis were driven on January 24. On the following day, in an act of vandalism, Iraq began to pump crude oil from the Kuwaiti storage tanks into the Gulf. The much feared oil slick quickly formed, thirty miles long and eight miles wide. It was the world's worst crude oil spillage, and it had been done deliberately. It was estimated that more than a million birds would die as a result of it.

On January 28, as the coalition air force bombed Iraqi airfields without respite, 150 Iraqi pilots flew their warplanes – 150 out of a total Iraqi air force of 750 – to Iran, where they sought sanctuary from the bombing. They were to take no further part in the war. The first land battle took place two days later. Iraqi troops, in their first military offensive of the war, crossed the border from Kuwait into Saudi Arabia, and advanced towards the coastal town of Khafji, ten miles south of the border. Khafji was occupied, but within forty-eight hours Saudi and Qatari troops, helped by American marines, drove the Iraqis out: of the 400-strong Iraqi battalion that had occupied the town, sixty-five were killed. The rest surrendered. Twelve marines were also killed.

The bombing of Iraq intensified. On January 31 John Major agreed to an American request to station B-52 bombers in the United Kingdom, from where they could attack targets in Iraq without the need to land again en route.

A new phrase entered the global vocabulary on February 3 – 'friendly fire'. It referred to soldiers killed in error by their own side. On that day it was seven American marines. 'Friendly fire' was to take a heavy toll in the coming days. On February 13 several hundred Iraqi civilians were killed when American planes bombed a bunker in Baghdad. This was not an error in aiming: the bunker was believed to be an Iraqi communications centre, and was the target.

Some of the American planes sent against Iraq were B-52 bombers, the giants of the Cold War, most of which had been decommissioned and mothballed almost two decades earlier. They flew direct from bases in Diego Garcia, Spain and Louisiana, and from Eaker Air Force Base in Arkansas via an American base on British soil, at Fairford in Gloucestershire. One of those who commanded the bomber force, Colonel Tom Sullivan, described the B-52 missions as 'fourteen hours of boredom and ten minutes of terror'.

Iraq began to call for a ceasefire. On February 10 the Soviet emissary Yevgeni Primakov had visited Baghdad, and on February 18 the Iraqi Foreign Minister, Tariq Aziz, flew to Moscow. Talks continued for four days, but the Iraqi 'peace plan' presented by Tariq Aziz was not acceptable to the coalition. Saddam Hussein, in a broadcast on February 21, stated defiantly that Iraq would not surrender, and told the Iraqi people: 'The mother of battles will be our victory.' That day, British troops began their heaviest artillery bombardment in action since the Korean War, on Iraqi targets just north of the Saudi Arabian border. Saddam retaliated by embarking on a scorched-earth policy in Kuwait, setting more than 150 oilwells on fire. The vast plumes of dense black smoke turned day into night over Kuwait City.

The coalition armies had not yet crossed the border into Iraq. But on

February 22 President Bush sent an ultimatum to Iraq, that either Iraqi forces evacuate Kuwait by five o'clock in the evening on the following day, or they would face a 'ground war'. Saddam took no steps to end his occupation. The evening came and night fell. Then, at dawn on February 24, the armies of the coalition launched their ground attack. It involved a thrust through the desert up to two hundred miles west of Kuwait. On the most westerly flank, a French division advanced a hundred miles into Iraq in the first twenty-four hours. Nearer Kuwait, Egyptian, Saudi and American troops were in action, pinning down Iraqi troops that might otherwise have been transferred to the main battlefields deep inside Iraq.

In the first hours of the Allied assault, 5,500 Iraqi troops surrendered. By the end of the first day, 20,000 had surrendered. In Kuwait City, the Iraqi defenders blew up public buildings and hotels, and set a further 150 oilwells on fire, intensifying the pall of black smoke over the city.

Iraq had not lost the ability to retaliate, even against Saudi Arabia. On February 25, twenty-eight American soldiers were killed by a Scud missile attack. In Israel, 1,600 families had their homes destroyed or badly damaged as a result of Scud attacks, and one civilian died of a heart attack when a Scud exploded near him. He was the only Israeli victim of the Scud attacks.

The weight of American bombs on Iraq was formidable. Night after night television had carried pictures to millions of homes around the world of bombs hitting their targets, of the oil slick and the oilwells on fire, and, in one extraordinary image, of an American missile wending its way through Baghdad. On February 26, Saddam Hussein, in a broadcast over Iraqi radio, announced that Iraqi troops were withdrawing from Kuwait. As they withdrew, they took with them as much looted property as they could cram into every car and truck they could commandeer. As the convoy made its way back towards Iraq, along the Mutla Ridge north of Kuwait, it created a four-mile traffic jam, visible from the air and an easy target (it had no anti-aircraft defences). American aircraft attacked, and the convoy was set on fire. A few hours later, Allied troops and war correspondents reached the wreckage. Televised images of the destruction were sent around the world.

American, British, French and Arab forces advanced from Saudi Arabia across the desert deep into Iraq, reaching the River Euphrates at Nasiriyah, and cutting Baghdad off from the port of Basra. In a tank battle that day, as British tanks advanced against Iraqi positions, nine British soldiers were killed when they were accidentally attacked by an American warplane.

On February 27, Allied forces entered Kuwait City. The objective of the United Nations resolution had been secured. Kuwait was declared officially 'liberated'. Almost all its oilwells were on fire, deliberately ignited by the retreating Iraqi forces. In a letter to the United Nations that day, Tariq Aziz agreed to rescind the Iraqi annexation of Kuwait, and to pay reparations for the damage done in the city.

South of Basra, Allied forces surrounded the elite troops of the Iraqi Republican Guard. On the following morning, February 28, while Western television and newspaper readers were still being shocked by scenes of carnage at the Mutla Ridge, President Bush appeared on television to announce the suspension of all hostilities in the Gulf. 'Kuwait is liberated,' he declared. 'Iraq's army is defeated; our military objectives are met.' It was the forty-second day of the war. More than 175,000 Iraqi soldiers were being held prisoner of war by the Allies.

The coalition forces lost fewer than two hundred of their combatants. Of these as many as a quarter had been killed accidentally by their own side, in the ill-named 'friendly fire'. The largest national death toll was the American, 145 killed in action and 121 killed in accidents.[1] The British lost twenty-four men, the Egyptians ten, the United Arab Emirates six and the French two. The Iraqi losses on the battlefield were at least eight thousand. A further five thousand Iraqi civilians were killed during the Allied bombing raids, particularly on Baghdad.

Negotiations to conclude the ceasefire terms were held between the Iraqis and the Allied forces on March 3. Iraq gave the Allies details of the minefields it had sown in Iraq and Kuwait. The Allies promised to return all Iraqi prisoners of war. A prisoner-of-war exchange began on the following day. That day the Emir of Kuwait and his government returned to their capital after seven months in exile. On March 6 John Major flew to Kuwait City. He was the first Allied leader to do so. The city was still reeling from the effects of occupation. Two weeks later the newly installed Kuwaiti government resigned for having failed to restore public services.

United States forces remained in Iraq. In the south, where Saddam Hussein threatened vengeance on the Shi'ite Muslims who had looked forward to his

---

[1] During 1991 more than 40,000 Americans were killed on the roads in the United States. The annual American road death toll remained above 40,000 for each of the remaining years of the century.

overthrow and still sought it, American troops reoccupied positions they had reached during the fighting in order to protect the rebels. On March 1 revolts broke out against Saddam Hussein both among the Shi'ites in the south and among the Kurds in the north. He took immediate and decisive steps to crush both insurrections. In the north, his air force, no longer able to combat Allied air mastery, bombed the Iraqi city of Kirkuk, which was being held by Kurdish rebels.

As American troops withdrew, under the ceasefire terms, from the southern Euphrates valley, Saddam Hussein turned his army and air force against the Shi'ites. Kerbela, the main point of Shi'ite resistance, was bombed. After three weeks of intense fighting the rebellion was at an end. Saddam Hussein, defeated in war, was still master of his country, of his regime and of his powers of repression.

On April 3, Turkey closed its border with Iraq in order to prevent the entry of 200,000 Kurds, who were fleeing from the advance of Iraqi troops. A further 600,000 Kurds had fled their homes during the war. On April 5 the Security Council demanded that Iraq halt the repression of the Kurds. The call was ignored. On the same day, President Bush announced the immediate airlift of humanitarian aid to the Kurds. On April 8, in an attempt to protect the mass of Kurdish refugees on Iraqi soil, an emergency meeting of European heads of government was held in Luxembourg. At the meeting, John Major took a lead in calling for 'safe havens' to be set up in the Kurdish areas of Iraq under Allied protection. His proposal was accepted. That day, in an effort to give air protection to the safe havens, the United States warned Iraq not to send any warplanes north of the 36th parallel. The Iraqis complied.

On April 11 the Gulf War ceasefire came formally into effect. That day, Iraqi ground forces, advancing from the south, attacked the Kurdish safe havens, all of which were on Iraqi territory. Two days later the United States began Operation Provide Comfort, to fly in relief supplies to the Kurds on the Iraq-Turkey border. On April 16 Bush committed American troops to maintain the safe havens, all of which could be supplied across that border. On the following day American, British and French troops based in southern Turkey crossed the border into northern Iraq, to secure the safe havens, to build refugee camps in them, and to distribute food and medicine.

With Allied military help a series of Iraqi attacks on the safe havens were repulsed. After July 15, however, when the Allies withdrew from Iraq, including from the Kurdish region, there was little the Kurds could do but to contemplate negotiations for a settlement on Iraqi terms. For a few months more, as Iraqi troops continued to try to overrun the safe havens, Allied forces operating from bases on Turkish soil drove them off. But an Iraqi blockade of the northern region, despite Allied air drops of supplies, forced the Kurds to come to terms with the enemy they knew, and had negotiated agreements with many times before. In June, British forces began to withdraw from the safe-haven zone: the first town they left was Amadiyah, at the eastern edge of the zone, a town in which Saddam's troops and police – and secret police – had been rounded up five weeks earlier by the British 'humanitarian officer', Lieutenant Rory Copinger-Symes, an anti-tank specialist known locally as the 'the mayor of Amadiyah'. The period of protection had been short.

Inside Iraq, Saddam Hussein had been forced to agree to United Nations inspection teams. In the years ahead he was to court further Allied military intervention by ordering the inspection teams out, or impeding their work. Essentially, they were searching for the weapons of mass destruction, principally nuclear, chemical and biological weapons, which it was believed he possessed, or was developing. When his 'super-gun' was discovered by the United Nations inspectors that autumn, it was destroyed.

It had been the hope of the Allies that the defeat of Iraq would be followed by internal moves to depose Saddam Hussein. This did not happen. The instruments of repression remained in his hands, even as United Nations sanctions bit into his economic solvency. Eight years later he was still ruler of Iraq.

From the first days of 1991 the government of the largest of the Soviet Union's republics, the Russian Federation, led by Boris Yeltsin, challenged the supremacy of Gorbachev's government. As a gesture of defiance, and of contempt for what he considered the far too slow pace of change, Yeltsin had resigned from the Communist Party the previous year. Gorbachev was still unable to contemplate the possibility of the break-up of the Soviet Union. The defection of the Estonian, Latvian and Lithuanian Republics still rankled. On January 13, in a desperate attempt to reverse what many considered to be the inevitable break-up of the Soviet federal structure, Soviet troops still stationed in Lithuania took over the radio and television centres in Vilnius.

In the protests that followed, thirteen Lithuanians were killed. It was a crude and futile assault. On the following day, from Moscow, Yeltsin denounced the violence against the Lithuanians, thereby giving his tacit support to Lithuanian independence. Still Gorbachev refused to face what had surely become the inevitable. On January 20, during a pro-independence rally in the Latvian capital, Riga, he ordered Soviet troops to occupy the Ministry of the Interior building. This was done, and four Latvian demonstrators were killed. This only served as a spur to Latvian national aspirations.

Seeing his economic restructuring measures being ignored in the general chaos, Gorbachev issued a decree giving the Soviet law-inforcement agencies wide new powers to 'compel' economic discipline. But too many changes were taking place in the political and federal structure of the Soviet Union for the necessary calm to prevail through which such essentially long-term reforms could be put steadily in place.

On February 9 the people of Lithuania voted in a national referendum called to confirm the previous year's declaration of independence. The Soviet military action a month earlier had been totally counter-productive. When the votes were counted, ninety per cent of Lithuanians had voted for independence.

In Moscow Boris Yeltsin continued to press for more substantial reforms than those offered by Gorbachev. On February 22 as many as 400,000 demonstrators marched in the centre of the city to support Yeltsin's defiant call. There was a further blow to Gorbachev on March 3 when the Estonian government called for a referendum on independence, in which seventy-seven per cent of Estonians voted in favour of remaining outside the Soviet Union. The proximity of Estonia's eastern border to Leningrad – less than eighty miles – was something that had troubled Soviet leaders since Estonia had secured its independence at the time of the 1917 revolution.

At the time of the collapse of the Tsarist empire at the end of the First World War there had been a brief but unsuccessful attempt by White Russia (Byelorussia) to assert its independence. Since then the region, apart from four years of the most savage German occupation, had been a loyal Soviet Republic, its capital, Minsk, indistinguishable from any other Russian city, its language almost identical to Russian, its nationalism dormant. But from the moment Lithuania, its neighbour to the north-west, had declared independence Byelorussian nationalism had re-emerged, and in April Minsk was brought to a halt by a general strike of Byelorussian nationalists calling for independence. The distance from the eastern border of Byelorussia to Moscow was only 270 miles, little more than the distance from Washington to New York.

On April 9 the Georgian Soviet Socialist Republic declared independence. In Moscow Gorbachev was unable to forestall the demands of the Russian Federation (the Russian Federative Soviet Socialist Republic) for its own elected presidency. Throughout April and May there were demonstrations in favour of this democratic development. Gorbachev was powerless to prevent it and on June 12 Boris Yeltsin was elected to a newly created 'executive' Russian presidency. He was the first Soviet leader in the history of the Soviet Union to be elected by popular vote. Sixty per cent of the citizens of the Federation, which stretched from the Black Sea to the Sea of Japan, and from the Finnish to the Chinese border, voted for Yeltsin.

Not all calls for change were answered. When a congress of Crimean Tatars meeting in Simferopol demanded Tatar sovereignty over the Crimea Soviet troops were sent to the area and no further disturbances took place. Gorbachev's openness was not dead, however: it continued to be carried out in the filling up of the many blank pages in Soviet history books. No aspect of Stalin's crimes was left untouched. On June 17 the KGB announced that 'forty-two million Soviet citizens' had perished in the forced collectivization of the Ukraine between 1928 and 1930 and in the nationwide purges from 1935 to 1952.

Gorbachev, having for almost six years led the forces of change, was himself in perilous retreat and defensive mode. On July 1 he authorized the signature of a protocol dissolving the Warsaw Pact – the military and structural basis of the East-West divide, and of the Soviet Union's defence system with regard to Western Europe, was at an end. That same day Gorbachev ordered the start of the denationalization of all State enterprises. The 'privatization' on whose behalf Margaret Thatcher waged such a successful campaign until her demise the previous year had reached the one country where for more than seventy years it had been ideologically unthinkable.

With Lithuania, Latvia, Estonia and Georgia each having declared independence from the Soviet Union Gorbachev was under pressure by nationalist sentiment in the remaining eleven Soviet republics to accord them 'equal status' with the hitherto dominant Russian Federation, and with each other. In an attempt to preserve the Soviet Union, he put forward an All-Union Treaty in which this equal status was enshrined. The date of August 20 was set for its signature. Within the Russian Federation, changes were taking place far beyond those contemplated by Gorbachev as part of glasnost or perestroika. On July 20 Boris Yeltsin banned the Communist Party from all workplaces and all government establishments throughout the Russian

Federation from Kaliningrad on the Baltic Sea to Vladivostok on the Sea of Japan.

On August 5, in a moment of much needed relaxation, Gorbachev flew to the Crimea (to the very Simferopol in which the Crimean Tatars had demanded sovereignty less than two months earlier) and was driven across the magnificent mountain range to a villa at Foros on the Black Sea. He intended to spend two weeks there before returning to Moscow to sign the All-Union Treaty. But on the last day of his holiday, leading hard-line Communists, under Gennadi Yanaev, who were intent on returning the Soviet Union to Communist rule and restoring the territorial and ideological unity of the Soviet Union, held him incommunicado in his villa and attempted to seize power in Moscow.

The leaders of the anti-Gorbachev coup were emphatic that the All-Union Treaty he had been about to sign constituted a 'threat of disintegration, a break-up of a single economic space and single defence and single foreign policy'. This was true; but there was no longer any popular desire for the unity of the Soviet Union or for the perpetuation of Communist rule. It was almost seventy-four years since Lenin and Trotsky had seized power in Moscow. Against them had been the crumbling will and disintegrating resources of a discredited government and war-weary people. In 1991 the forces of change and reform which Gorbachev himself had unleashed, and by which he had then been left behind, were determined not to lose what had been gained.

From its first hours, the coup was opposed by Boris Yeltsin and those in Moscow who, as a result of their new-found status, wished to retain, even through bloodshed, the enormous degree of territorial and political independence secured during the previous months. Not only did Yeltsin physically impose his authority in Moscow, but he managed, by a series of telephone calls, to secure the support of the Western European leaders. It was John Major, the British Prime Minister, who took the lead that same day in denouncing the coup as hard line and reactionary.

In a desperate measure to reverse the tide of independence the leaders of the coup ordered Soviet naval vessels to blockade the Estonian capital of Tallinn, and Soviet troops to move against the Latvian parliament building in Riga. But Yeltsin and those loyal to him continued to struggle in Moscow against the forces of Communist restoration. A British woman, Kay Thomson, watching these events on television in far away rural England, wrote in her diary at 1.45 p.m. on August 19:

BBC newscaster says that a state of emergency has been declared for a period of six months; people are converging on Red Square despite an order that no protests are allowed.

Scenes are shown of a man trying to haul a soldier out of his tank and of a woman yelling at a soldier from her position on another tank onto which she has climbed.

Gorbachev is reported under house arrest in the 'south of the country'.

Elsewhere in the Soviet Union massive demonstrations took place in denunciation of the coup. On August 20, in Kishinev, the capital of the Soviet Socialist Republic of Moldavia, 400,000 people marched. In Leningrad, part of Yeltsin's Russian Federation, 200,000 took to the streets to denounce the coup. That same day Estonia formally declared its independence: this was specifically recognized by Yeltsin four days later.

For three days those who wanted to see the restoration of Communism and the preservation of the Soviet Union continued to struggle and to fight. On August 21 Soviet 'black beret' police were in action in the Lithuanian capital, Vilnius, and one Lithuanian was killed. That day in Moscow, having for three days defied the attempted coup, several hundred thousand of Yeltsin's supporters established a civilian barricade round the parliament building from which Yeltsin and his government continued to direct their resistance. As tanks failed to break through the barricade in the fighting, three civilians were killed: Dimitri Komar, Ilya Krichevsky and Vladimir Usov.

The attempted coup was defeated. During August 21 Gorbachev returned to Moscow, where, in an address to the Russian Federation parliament, he praised Yeltsin for having done so much to bring the coup to an end. But Gorbachev's authority had gone. He had to watch helplessly as Latvia declared its independence and Lithuania reaffirmed its early separation from the Soviet Union. On the following day, August 22, a triumphant Yeltsin, ruler of a non-Communist Russian Republic, ordered the Hammer and Sickle flag to be replaced with the pre-revolutionary White, Blue and Red.

Following the defeat of the Communist coup the determination of the remaining Soviet Republics to secure their independence could not be restrained. On August 23 Armenia declared its independence and on the following day the Ukraine, the agricultural heartland and industrial power-house of the Soviet Union, also declared its independence. That day, Gorbachev resigned as leader of the Communist Party. He remained President of the Soviet Union. His last official act as Party leader was to disband the Party's Central Committee, through which the Soviet Union had been ruled since 1917. The Soviet Union itself was finally disintegrating. On August 25, Byelorussia declared its independence (taking the name Belarus). That day, in the Ukrainian capital Kiev, the order went out from the new government that all Communist Party property was to be seized, the Party no longer having any rights. Two days later, on August 27, Moldavia declared its independence, taking the name Moldova.

On August 29, five days after Gorbachev's resignation as Party leader, all Communist Party activity was suspended in all the former Soviet Republics. Thus ended the political power, economic privilege and ideological control, hitherto maintained over Soviet society by seventeen million Soviet Communist Party members and their Party bosses at every level in their hierarchy of power, at the top of which was the disbanded Central Committee and its General Secretary.

On August 30 the local Soviet in Baku voted to re-establish the independence of Azerbaijan, which Lenin had destroyed in 1920. On August 31 two of the Central Asian Republics of the Soviet Union, Uzbekistan and Kirgizia, declared their independence. Four days later, on September 4, a newly formed State Council, made up of the most senior figures of the Soviet Republics, met in Moscow and formally recognized the independence of Lithuania, Latvia and Estonia, all three of which were admitted to the United Nations two weeks later.

On September 6 another Central Asian Republic, the Tajik Republic, declared independence. Even the memory of Lenin was to be expunged. On September 6, the day of Tadzhikistan's defiance, the city of Leningrad was renamed St Petersburg, the name it had borne until 1914. The central structures of Communism were also being dismantled. On September 28 the Young Communist League (Komsomol), the basis of Communist indoctrination in schools, was disbanded.

The Soviet Union still existed, though without the Communist Party as its underlying raison d'être, and with its territorial unity in disarray. As a sign that those republics which had declared independence were truly outside the Soviet orbit, on October 3 the State Council in Moscow established diplomatic relations with Lithuania and Estonia. The declarations of independence continued, the Turkmen Soviet Socialist Republic raising its national flag over the parliament building in Ashkhabad on October 27.

Two days later, Gorbachev flew to Madrid, where he held discussions with President Bush about arms control. Then, on the following day, amid all the panoply of the royal palace, together with Bush he opened the first face-to-face talks between Israeli and Palestinian delegates.

On December 1, the people of the Ukraine cast their vote in a referendum for independence: ninety per cent voted in favour of total separation from the Soviet Union. On December 8, the leaders of three Soviet Republics, Russia, Belarus and Ukraine – the heartlands of the Soviet Union – met in Minsk and agreed to establish a Commonwealth of Independent States (CIS) and declared the 'end' of the Union of Soviet Socialist Republics – the USSR, or Soviet Union – which had been a central feature of world power for so many years. They then appealed to the other former Republics to join the CIS.

One Republic, Kazakhstan, had still not broken away from the defunct Soviet Union. On December 16 it declared its independence. Meeting in the Kazakh capital of Alma Ata five days later, on December 21, the leaders of eight more of the former Soviet Republics joined the Commonwealth of Independent States that had been established thirteen days earlier. Only Georgia declined to be a member of the new association. It wanted its independence to be absolute. Four days later, on December 25, Gorbachev formally resigned as President of the dissolved Soviet Union. That day, in Georgia, it was announced that fifty-six people had been killed in Tbilisi in four days, during an opposition attempt to overthrow the post-Communist ruler, President Gamsakhurdia.

On December 26 the Supreme Soviet, which had ruled the Soviet Union since 1917, met in Moscow and dissolved itself. Four days later the leaders of the CIS met in Minsk and affirmed the right of each member State to establish its own armed forces.

In contrast to what became known as 'the former Soviet Union', the People's Republic of China maintained its Communist and totalitarian course. Economic reforms which followed the line of Gorbachev's 'restructuring' were welcomed but political change was not. By the end of the year China was the only world Power subscribing to the political ideologies and structures of Marxism-Leninism. Publicity was given to the punishment and even expulsion of those Communist Party members who 'violated' Party discipline.

In China, natural disasters often overshadowed politics. Floods in 1991 were so severe that in some regions public order broke down, and there were also outbreaks of typhoid, hepatitis, dysentery and malaria.

There was an escape from hunger and civil war in Ethiopia for 14,000 Ethiopian Jews, who were flown to Israel in a thirty-hour airlift starting on May 24. From the disintegrating Soviet Union, which a few years earlier had restricted Jewish emigration almost to nothing, a hundred thousand Jews were allowed to emigrate, and all future emigration was permitted without hindrance.

The civil war in Angola ended formally in 1991. The peace accord, signed in Lisbon on May 31, brought sixteen years of internecine fighting to an end. In Burma, in October, as a signal that democracy even under attack was to be sustained, Daw Aung San Suu Kyi, the Burmese opposition leader who had been under house arrest for the previous three years, was awarded the Nobel Peace Prize.

Yugoslavia was disintegrating as the Soviet Union had done. Tito's stern Communist rule had ended in 1980; his successors had maintained the powers of the central authority with dwindling success for a further decade. Too many ethnic and national aspirations were being roused. On June 25 two of the component parts of the Federal Republic of Yugoslavia, Croatia and Slovenia, declared their independence. Ordered to do so by Slobodan Milošević, Yugoslav troops and tanks – predominantly Serb – advanced towards the respective breakaway capitals, Zagreb and Ljubljana. Several dozen people were killed. After mediation by the European Community, the Serb forces withdrew. The war had lasted ten days.

Slovenia was not attacked again, and settled down to its independent status as one of Europe's smallest nations, with a population of under two million. But, in August, Serb troops re-entered Croatia and fighting between Serbs and Croats intensified. In Osijek, the regional capital of eastern Croatia, a ten-year-old girl was among the three people killed when Serb artillery shelled the town. Three children were among seven civilians killed when Petrinja, a Croat town only thirty miles south of Zagreb, was shelled. On September 4, Serb forces launched a two-pronged attack into Croatia from both Vojvodina and Bosnia. The Croat town of Okučani, on the Zagreb-Belgrade motorway, was captured, and Vukovar besieged. Within a few days, Serb troops reached to within fifty miles of Zagreb, before they were halted.

In October, Serb forces besieged the Croat city of Dubrovnik, on the Adriatic, in which Roman and Byzantine houses had survived for more than 1,500 years. Many were badly damaged by Serbian shellfire.

On October 15, Bosnia-Hercegovina, one of the republics of Yugoslavia, voted to become an independent State. But its multi-racial character – it had a mixed Croat, Serb and Muslim population – made it impossible for any one element within its borders to claim full control, and it was the object of an immediate Croat and Serb military attack. A new war had begun that was to bring death to thousands and destruction to towns and villages that, since the defeat of the Germans in 1945, had struggled to rebuild their shattered lives and poor economies, and had succeeded. As national passions intensified, and ethnic conflict spread, all that had been achieved in almost half a century of endeavour was put in jeopardy.

On November 17 the eastern Croatian town of Vukovar, which had been besieged by Serb forces for eighty-six days, was overrun. A thousand people had been killed during the siege.

Patterns of violence were repeated in Europe, Africa and Asia. In India, in June, Sikh militants attacked two trains in the Punjab, killing more than seventy passengers. In Zaire, more than a hundred protesters were killed when troops opened fire on a demonstration against the autocratic regime of President Mobutu. In South Africa, intercommunal killings continued, despite renewed efforts by Nelson Mandela, in the name of the African National Congress, and Chief Buthelezi of the Zulu Inkatha movement, to calm tensions between their respective followers. On January 12, thirty-five mourners were killed when gunmen attacked an ANC wake in a township near Johannesburg. In the previous four years, five thousand people had been killed in intercommunal violence.

President de Klerk continued on his anti-apartheid course, repealing during the first six months of the year almost all the repressive legislation, including the Land Acts, the Group Areas Act and the Population Registration Acts. After a break of thirty years, on March 27 the International Olympic Committee agreed to readmit South Africa to the Olympic Games.

Among those whom many in Britain called the 'men of violence' – the IRA – efforts continued to try to cause damage on the British mainland. On February 7 a mortar attack was launched on Downing Street from a van parked in nearby Whitehall. Some of the mortar shells exploded outside the Cabinet room while a meeting was in session. John Major instructed his colleagues to carry on with their deliberations, which they did. On February 16 a bomb was exploded at Victoria Station, in London. One person was killed.

Among the projects on which John Major was working was a 'Citizen's Charter' that would give the individual the right to question poor performance in dozens of areas of national life in the public sector. Customs officials would be expected to abide by certain standards, so would the post office and the railways, schools and hospitals – so would each government department. A series of Charters, each designed for a specific area of public contact with officialdom, were intended to ensure that the institutions gave the public good service, and would rectify failings. High standards of service to the public would be set out, and would be enforced. The first version of the Charter made its public appearance on July 22.

Democracy had been strengthened by accountability in the interests of those it was there to serve. But such are the vagaries of politics that there was much newspaper and even public derision, especially from the right wing of his own Conservative Party, directed against the Citizen's Charter. To his critics, Major replied:

> Who are the people who are sneering, saying it's a little idea? They are people who wouldn't recognize a public service if it gripped them by the windpipe – they don't use buses, they never use trains, they don't send their kids to primary school, they don't queue in some grotty surgery, they don't hang around in a hospital waiting for five hours while the surgeon sees forty people ahead of them in the queue. They've got no idea about any of that. They don't understand these frustrations because they don't face them.

Major's defence of the Citizen's Charter betokened a wider agenda, which he set out as he prepared to make his first appeal to the electorate as Prime Minister at a general election, an election in which he and the Conservative Party were successful. 'I want a Britain', he told the electorate, 'where there is a helping hand for those who need it; where people can get a hand up, not just a hand-out. A country that is fair and free from prejudice – a classless society, at ease with itself.'

In the Balkans, the turmoil in 1991 resembled that of the first decade of the century. In the first and second weeks of January, five thousand ethnic Greeks fled from Albania as pro- and anti-Communist factions clashed. As many as 25,000 Albanians also fled, by sea across the Adriatic, seeking sanctuary in Italy, which was reluctant to receive them, and sent as many as it could back to Albania. On February 20 student protesters in the Albanian capital, Tirana, pulled down the statue of the former Communist leader, Enver Hoxha. In Bulgaria, the former Communist ruler, Todor Zhivkov, was put on trial on charges of fraud and embezzlement. In Yugoslavia, twelve Croats were killed in the worst ethnic clashes between Serbs and Croats for forty years.

On November 25 the fourteenth United Nations-brokered ceasefire came into force in Yugoslavia. It was ended twelve days later when Serb forces bombarded the predominantly Croat town of Osijek.

The conflicts of the 1990s included many that had begun in the 1980s. On 18 November 1991 an Englishman, Terry Waite, the envoy of the Archbishop of Canterbury, was freed in Lebanon after having been held hostage since 1987. He was the last of several British hostages to be freed. The remaining American hostages were released by Christmas. The last two German hostages were freed six months later.

In Sri Lanka, fighting between Tamil separatists and Sri Lankan forces continued throughout 1991. On February 18, forty-four Sri Lankan soldiers were killed by an extremist Tamil faction, the Liberation Tigers of Tamil Eelam. On March 2 a car bomb in a Colombo suburb killed sixty Sri Lankans, among them the target of the bomb, the Defence Minister, Ranjan Wijeratne. Another victim of the Sri Lankan violence was the former Indian Prime Minister, Rajiv Gandhi — who had been ousted from the premiership two years earlier, but was on the verge of a return to power. On May 21 he was assassinated while at an election rally in southern India. His assassin was a young woman, an extremist Tamil separatist who had strapped a large explosive charge to her body, and came up to him with a garland to put around his neck. Detonating the explosives, she killed herself and fifteen others at the same time. Inside Sri Lanka, during an army attack on a Tamil village on June 12, more than 150 villagers were killed. A car bomb which was exploded by Tamils in Colombo on June 21, at the Defence Ministry operational headquarters, killed sixty people. In a military operation against Tamil separatists at the end of July, the Sri Lankan army killed two thousand Tamil fighters. Moderate Tamils assisted the Sri Lankan forces in their attempt to eliminate the extremists.

In Chad, three hundred political prisoners were killed by the President, Hissene Habré, before he fled his country. In Algeria, three hundred people were killed in the first five months of the year as the army clashed with Islamic fundamentalists. In Somalia, the civil war, intensifying in October, led to the deaths of 20,000 people by the end of the year. Of Somalia's six million inhabitants, as many as five million were estimated by the United Nations to be 'under-nourished'. The civil war made it almost impossible to get relief supplies to them. In the words of Christopher Clapham, a British expert on the region: 'While in some localities clan elders were able to maintain order, Somalia as a State effectively ceased to exist.'

In all the fighting that year, including the Gulf War, the disintegration of the Soviet Union and Yugoslavia, the continued fighting in Sri Lanka, and the civil war in Somalia, the number of those killed was numbered at most in the tens of thousands. But in the course of a few hours in November, 6,500 people were killed in floods and landslides in the Philippines. And on April 29 between 150,000 and a quarter of a million people had been killed when a cyclone, striking the ever vulnerable Bangladesh, drove the sea ashore, inundated a vast area (the size of south-east England), and made five million people homeless. As winds reached speeds of up to 165 miles an hour, five hundred fishing boats and their crews were swept away, and a million tons of rice were lost to the sea.

On May 13, almost unnoticed in the aftermath of the Gulf War and the disintegration of the Soviet Union, President Bush announced that the United States would no longer contemplate the use of chemical weapons 'for any reason, including retaliation'. It was eighty-four years since the United States had failed to persuade the Great Powers of the day (1907) to give up aerial bombardment as a method of war.

It was yet another small but decisive step forward, amid a world wallowing in violence, towards the sane conduct of international disputes.

CHAPTER FORTY-ONE

1992

I said we should remember this spot because some day
people should know what happened here.

AN EYE-WITNESS

THE CIVIL STRIFE IN YUGOSLAVIA seemed to reach a positive turning
point on 1 January 1992, when Serbia and Croatia agreed to the deployment
of United Nations troops. But violence did not cease. On January 7, five
European Community monitors were killed when their helicopter was shot
down over Croatia. On January 15 the countries of the European Community
formally recognized the independence of Slovenia and Croatia. The Yugoslav
Federation was at an end. A 'unity' of Slav peoples – Serbs, Montenegrins,
Croats, Slovenes; also a unity of religions – Roman Catholics, Orthodox
Christians and Muslims – which had first been put together in 1919, was
over.

On February 21 the United Nations Security Council authorized the
despatch of a peacekeeping force of 14,000 men to Croatia. On March 1
Bosnia-Hercegovina declared its independence. Five weeks later, on April 6,
the United States and the countries of the European Community agreed to
recognize the new State, which was admitted to the United Nations in May.
From the outset of its independence, Bosnia was beset with internal and
external strife. Serbia wished to regain it. Croatia wished to acquire part of
it. Its Muslim population wished to have their rights fully protected. Of the
total Bosnian population of three million, forty-four per cent were Muslims,
thirty-one per cent were Serbs and seventeen per cent were Croats. The
Bosnian Serbs, not wishing to be separated from Serbia, and calling for the
creation of a Greater Serbia of which they would be part, had boycotted the
referendum on independence.

In the fighting which started in March, the Bosnian Serbs were helped by the Serbian troops of what was still called the Federal Yugoslav Army (Slovenia and Croatia, both formerly part of Federal Yugoslavia, had broken away the previous year). Behind the lines, Bosnian Serb soldiers were trying to eliminate the Muslim population by the most terrible of all methods, not with expulsion but by mass murder. Among the Muslims rounded up that April were those in the village of Vlasenica. It was to be four years before their fate became known, when Western journalists entered the area for the first time. One journalist, Stacy Sullivan of *The Times*, spoke to two men who had been in a refugee column that passed through Vlasenica six months later:

The column was led by a 38-year-old metal worker now living in Tuzla. The man, who asked that his name should not be used, said the refugees were hiding in the forest just below the site of the dirt pit on 19 October 1992 – the second day of a three-day journey out of Serb-held territory. 'In the afternoon, a red tractor towing a trailer of corpses drove up to the site and dumped fifteen to twenty bodies along the side of the road. They were men and women of different ages.'

As night fell, the man said the column of refugees ran up the hill and past the bodies. 'Some of them were cut in half, others were partially burnt,' he said. 'I will never forget those three days.' The man said a white summer house stood by the site, and a blue trench-digger was there. It still is – and a small white house, gutted and its roof destroyed, is there too.

The second witness, Maso, is a small dynamic man in his sixties who was in the refugee column. He said: 'I was hiding with thirty-five other refugees by a stream below a dirt pit when I heard what sounded like a truck drive up. It was a tractor with a trailer and it unloaded some cargo. I did not know what the cargo was until that evening when we had to run past a pile of bodies.

'We had to run past a blue forklift and a white summer house. I ran through the bodies up the hill, They were unloaded like logs. I said we should remember this spot because some day people should know what happened here.'

On April 21, in the Bosnian capital, Sarajevo, Serb forces fired on the city centre, which was being held by a combined Muslim and Croat force. Two days later the European Community sent a peace mission, 'monitors' who negotiated a ceasefire. On May 12, however, Serbian shellfire on the centre of Sarajevo was renewed. The monitors left that same day, followed two days later by the United Nations peacekeeping force. On May 18 the United Nations High Commissioner for Refugees announced that a million people had been made homeless as a result of the fighting. Tens of thousands were seeking sanctuary elsewhere in Europe. A new source of refugees, with all their hopelessness and poverty, and potential contribution to the life of the countries that took them in, had been created on the continent of Europe.

On May 26, sixteen people were killed in Sarajevo when Serbian troops carried out a mortar attack on a bread queue. Fighting was endemic throughout Bosnia. To enable humanitarian flights to reach Sarajevo with essential supplies of medical equipment and food for a starving population, the United Nations handed over Sarajevo airport to the Serbs on June 29. In return, the Serbs agreed that the United Nations peacekeeping force could return, and would not be fired on.

To ensure that non-Serb minority groups fled from the areas under Serbian control, thousands of homes were destroyed, thousands of men held in detention camps amid considerable brutality and privation, and thousands more people – men, women and children – were massacred. These killings became known as 'ethnic cleansing', a new phrase in the vocabulary of the century's evil deeds. On July 24, thousands of Bosnian Muslims began fleeing from the northern Bosnian town of Bosanski Novi, to escape 'ethnic cleansing' atrocities. On August 4 the United Nations Security Council condemned the Serbian-controlled detention camps in Bosnia. Ten days later, the Security Council adopted resolutions denouncing 'war crimes' and calling for military action in support of humanitarian relief operations. British troops were among the first to participate in this relief protection.

By the end of August the Federal Serb and Bosnian Serb forces were in control of seventy per cent of Bosnia. They then declared the areas under their rule, which were mainly in the north and east, linked by a narrow corridor, to be the Republika Srpska (Serbian Republic) with its capital at Pale. The remaining thirty per cent of Bosnia declared itself a Muslim-Croat Federation, with its capital at Sarajevo. Serbia and Montenegro, abandoning the Federal designation which no longer held any meaning, proclaimed the foundation of a new Yugoslav State.

As a result of international pressure, the Serbian troops from the new Yugoslavia withdrew from Bosnia. As they did so, they handed over control of the areas they had secured to the local Bosnian Serbs. Bosnia was divided on largely ethnic lines, varying according to military dispositions. But, behind the front lines, mass murder continued. And far from the Balkans, refugees from the conflict were seeking asylum in whatever countries would take them in: that year Sweden received a record number of asylum seekers, 85,000 – 'in spite of signs', Reuters reported, 'that hostility to foreigners is growing'.

The Soviet Union was no more. Its largest geographical component, the Russian Republic, soon to be called the Russian Federation, headed by President Yeltsin, acted as the leader of the Commonwealth of Independent States that was the Soviet Union's successor. On January 8, Yeltsin accepted, on behalf of his Republic, a massive emergency food aid package to the value of $263 million which had been agreed by the European Community, on John Major's initiative, Britain then holding the rotating Community presidency.

It was not Russia alone, however, that had to establish new foreign relations with the rest of the world. Every republic of the former Soviet Union despatched ambassadors abroad and through its foreign ministers began the slow process of establishing a national foreign policy. On January 13 the government of Lithuania signed an agreement with Poland – with which it had a common border – recognizing the border and agreeing to non-interference in each other's internal affairs. Recognition of this border was important, as Poland had strong emotional attachments both historically and in terms of the Polish population to the western region of Lithuania and indeed to the capital Vilnius. On the following day, January 14, Estonia, one of the first breakaway States, established diplomatic relations with the Russian Federation and began negotiations for a similar treaty of non-interference in internal affairs. The next of the new republics to establish relations with a country outside the former Soviet Union was Moldova. On January 16 this small republic of just over four million inhabitants established diplomatic relations with Hungary. The most ambitious of these early treaties was signed by Ukraine on January 29: a barter deal with Iran whereby Iran would provide Ukraine with gas and oil in return for chemicals, concrete and steel piping.

A source of discontent in the three Baltic Republics was the continued presence there of Russian troops, soldiers who had been involved the previous year in several attempts to stifle the independence movement. On February 1 Yeltsin was at Camp David, in Maryland – the scene of the successful Israeli-Egyptian negotiations just over a decade earlier – where he issued a joint declaration with President Bush that Russia and the United States 'no longer regarded themselves as adversaries'. Also on February 1, negotiations were concluded in Moscow between all the members of the Commonwealth of Independent States and the three Baltic Republics for the withdrawal of all troops – the majority of whom were Russian – from Lithuania, Latvia and Estonia. With the implementation of this agreement the people of the Baltic nations could finally feel their independent strength. They also felt more secure.

Lithuania, the largest of the three Baltic States, with a population of 3,700,000, – of whom 8.2 per cent were Russian and 6.9 per cent Polish – contented itself with 4,200 soldiers, 350 sailors and 550 air force personnel. Its air force (as of 1998) consisted of three helicopters but no combat aircraft. Estonia, with a population of 1,400,000 – of whom just over twenty-eight per cent were Russian – had 3,300 soldiers, 150 sailors and no military air force. Latvia with a population of 2,500,000, of whom almost a third were Russian, had a total defence force of three thousand, and an air force of two aircraft and five helicopters. Under an agreement signed in Moscow, Russian forces, stationed at the former Soviet anti-ballistic-missile early-warning station at Skrunda, were to remain until 1999 when the early-warning station would cease to exist.

Flying to Paris on February 7, Presidents Yeltsin and Mitterrand signed the first treaty between Russia and the West; nine months later, during a visit to London, Yeltsin signed an Anglo-Russian treaty of friendship with John Major. Against the background of successful foreign negotiations, Yeltsin was confronted, in Russia itself, by food shortages which led, on February 9, to widespread street demonstrations in Moscow and other cities. On the following day the United States, Canada and the European Community agreed to airlift food to all the former Soviet Republics. Embarking on a military-style operation, given even a military-type codename, Operation Provide Hope, American aircraft flew fifty-four flights from its Rhein-Main air base in Germany, bringing 17,000 tons of food and medical supplies. There was an element of luck in this: the supplies were those that had been accumulated at Rhein-Main for despatch to the American forces in the Gulf, had the Gulf War continued beyond the previous February.

During February an attempt by Yeltsin to persuade the members of the Commonwealth of Independent States to form a unified armed-forces system was rejected, after talks in Minsk, by three former Soviet Republics – Ukraine, Azerbaijan and Moldova. The Moldovan armed forces were to consist of 15,300 military personnel. In the six Muslim republics which had formed part of Soviet Central Asia, the cross-border links were predominantly with Iran. On February 17, after negotiations in Teheran, the six joined the regional Muslim trading group, the Economic Co-operation Organization. Within three weeks one of the six – Turkmenistan – established a joint Chamber of Commerce with Iran.

The new republics were beset with internal and intercommunal disputes. On February 25, in the Armenian enclave of Nagorno-Karabakh, two hundred Muslim Azeris were killed during ethnic clashes with the Christian Armenians. On March 9, after three Russian soldiers had been killed, Russian troops were pulled out of the area. Six days later a truce was signed in Teheran between Armenia and Azerbaijan and the fighting between the two communities came to an end. On March 20, the leaders of the Commonwealth of Independent States, meeting in the Ukrainian capital, Kiev, agreed to send a joint peacekeeping force to Nagorno-Karabakh.

On March 28, a week after the Kiev peacekeeping meeting, there was fighting between Ukrainians and Russians in the predominantly Russian area of Eastern Ukraine, in which eighteen people were killed. Ukrainian hostility towards Russia had led to the establishment of border controls and a considerable amount of mutual recrimination. On April 22, denouncing the 'deception' emanating from Moscow at the time of the Chernobyl disaster, the government of the Ukraine announced that between six thousand and eight thousand people had died in the explosion at the nuclear plant six years earlier. Chernobyl lay just inside the northern border of the Ukraine.

Concerned about the possible disputes between the republics, which might escalate into some form of sustained armed conflict, negotiations were begun for a comprehensive Mutual Security Treaty. These were concluded in the Uzbekistan capital, Tashkent, on May 15. Ukraine declined to participate. Those former Soviet Republics which agreed under the treaty to recognize each other's borders, and which pledged a 'common defence' against aggression were Russia, Armenia and four of the Central Asian Republics, Kazakhstan, Turkmenistan, Uzbekistan and Tajikistan. The longest of all the borders recognized under the treaty was that between Russia and Kazakhstan, which extended for more than two thousand miles, from the Caspian Sea to the Chinese border.

Negotiations between Russia and Ukraine proved much more difficult. At stake was the former Soviet Black Sea fleet, once the pride of the Soviet Union. On August 3 agreement was reached to have three years' joint control of the warships, followed by the division of the fleet equally between Russia and Ukraine.

One area of agreement which was reached during the summer among eleven members of the Commonwealth of Independent States, enabled them to send a 'Unified Team' to the Olympic Games in Barcelona. In previous Olympic Games since the Second World War the Soviet Union had prided itself on its athletic prowess. The Unified Team was able to repeat this, winning the largest number of gold medals (forty-five) as against the United States (thirty-seven). Germany, whose unification had been as dramatic as the disintegration of the Soviet Union, won thirty-three gold medals as a single German team.

In Georgia, independence had been beset from its first days in April 1991 by the secessionist demands of the Abkhazians, 160,000 of whom lived, among 250,000 Georgians, on the Black Sea coast in and around the port of Sukhumi. On August 14 the Abkhazians rose in revolt, demanding their own independent State. In three days of fighting fifty people were killed. Thousands of Georgians living in the region fled as refugees to the Georgian capital, Tbilisi. On August 26 the Georgian government reimposed its authority in Abkhazia.

The year ended with yet more turmoil, with clashes in the Turkmenistan capital, Ashkhabad, between local Turkmen ex-Communists and Turkmens determined to establish an Islamic administration. And in Moscow, on December 14, at the opening of the Congress of People's Deputies of Russia, the deputies rejected President Yeltsin's candidate, Yegor Gaidar, a reformer, and chose instead the more conservative-minded Viktor Chernomyrdin. The revolution for change which Gorbachev had begun, and which Yeltsin had accelerated, was being challenged.

On December 29 the United States and Russia – again taking the lead for all the former Soviet Republics in matters of nuclear defence – agreed on the text of the long-delayed Strategic Arms Reduction Treaty (START II). Under the new treaty, both Russian and American nuclear stockpiles were to be reduced by two-thirds. The United States would help financially in enabling the former Soviet Republics to carry out their side of the agreement. President Bush had already, on October 24, signed a Freedom Support Act, whereby Congress had approved financial and technical assistance 'to support freedom and open markets in the independent States of the former Soviet Union'. One exception was made, to show United States displeasure: no

American assistance to Azerbaijan was allowed under the Act until 'the President determines . . . that the Government of Azerbaijan is taking demonstrable steps to cease all blockades and other offensive uses of force against Armenia and Nagorno-Karabakh'.

For Azerbaijan, this American prohibition was a blow. Armenian forces occupied more than twenty per cent of its territory. More than a million Azerbaijanis were refugees from the occupied region, placing a heavy burden on the Azerbaijani government in Baku. But American support for Armenia was traditional, going back to the early years of the century when the Christian Armenians were persecuted in Muslim Turkey. That the majority of Azerbaijanis were Muslims emphasized the divide and intensified the conflict.

On June 28 the body of Ignace Paderewski, Poland's first President, was taken from Arlington Cemetery, Virginia, and flown to Warsaw. At the time of Paderewski's death in 1941 the American government had pledged that it would be returned to Poland when Poland was free. With Lech Walesa as President, censorship gone, a substantial increase in private ownership in prospect, and a multi-Party government in place in which Solidarity was a part, Poland was as free as it had been since before the Second World War.

On July 17 one more former Communist country began to dissolve. That day the regional parliament of Slovakia issued a 'declaration of sovereignty'. It no longer wished to be part of Czechoslovakia, with which it had first achieved independence in 1918. On December 31, Czechoslovakia ceased to exist. In its place were two separate and independent republics: the Czech Republic, with its capital in Prague, and Slovakia with its capital in Bratislava.

On December 1 a Central European Free Trade Agreement was signed in Cracow between Poland, Hungary, the Czech Republic and Slovakia. Over five years, trade barriers would be reduced, with a view to eventual membership of the European Community. NATO membership also beckoned the new States of Central Europe, thereby giving them a security which they had sought in vain between the two world wars.

The new States were each determined to combat upsurges of extreme nationalism. This was most marked in Poland, where the Polish National Community Party – many of whose members were skinheads, characterized by their closely cropped hair, heavy boots and braces – staged a series of demonstrations against foreigners. On February 15, three hundred members of the Party had carried out an anti-German and anti-Jewish march at the border town of Zgorzelec. Their slogans included: 'Down with Jews and Germans' and 'Poland for the Poles'. The Polish government promised to curb these excesses.

Apologizing for historic wrongs was to become a feature of the 1990s. There was an early example of this on 31 March 1992, when King Juan Carlos – General Franco's successor as ruler of Spain – and the Israeli President, Chaim Herzog, met in a Madrid synagogue to be blessed by a rabbi in what *The Times* described as 'a symbolic gesture' of reconciliation, five hundred years to the day since the Roman Catholic monarchs banished the Jews from Spain. Later that week, in the city of Toledo, a thousand Jews bearing the surname Toledano – whose ancestors had originally come from Toledo – were given the keys to the city. On the following evening Queen Sofia of Spain presided over a concert of reconciliation at which four thousand Jews of Spanish origin listened to a concert played by the Israel Philharmonic Orchestra. The high point of the evening was a composition by an Israeli composer, with the Inquisition as its theme, in which the part of the tormented Jew was sung by Plácido Domingo, himself Spanish-born. Domingo's rendering, in Hebrew, of the prayer 'Hear! Oh Israel!' was a cry of pain across the centuries. An era of apologizing for the past had begun.

On June 1 the government of Taiwan apologized for the deaths, forty-five years earlier, of as many as 28,000 civilians, who had been killed when the army suppressed a series of political protests in 1947. Documentation was called for, so that a list of names of those who had been murdered could be compiled. Reconciliation was also being sought among former wartime combatants. On October 25, German and British military veterans met at El Alamein, in the Egyptian desert, to recall their respective sacrifices in battle fifty years earlier. That same day, the Japanese Emperor Akihito paid the first visit to China by any Japanese monarch: it was half a century since the Japanese atrocities in China, including the 'rape of Nanking', that had marked a low point in the behaviour of human beings towards each other. Japan was unwilling, however, despite mounting pressure that it should do so, to issue a formal or official apology to the tens of thousands of Allied prisoners of war who had suffered in Japanese prison camps and at forced labour during the Second World War.

One conflict that had smouldered, and several times burned, since 1948 found a determined adversary in 1992: the new Prime Minister of Israel,

Yitzhak Rabin. Coming to power after the electoral victory of his Labour-led coalition, on July 13 he set out in his first public speech what he hoped to achieve. His government would embark on the pursuit of peace with a 'fresh momentum'. It was determined to turn 'a new page in the annals of the State of Israel'. Within Israel it would 'strengthen the foundations of democracy and the rule of law, ensure equality for all citizens, and protect human rights'.

Rabin intended that the Palestinians would become partners, not enemies, and that Palestinian rights, perceived in the widest national and personal sense, would be restored. In private conversations he stressed his belief that it would take no more than nine months to reach agreement with the Palestinians. In his first speech he quoted the poet Rachel, who had asked: 'A concerted, stubborn, and eternal effort of a thousand arms, will it succeed in rolling the stone off the mouth of the well?'

In his first speech, as in a presentation later in the year to John Major, Rabin spoke of Israel's place in the world at a time when apartheid was ending in South Africa, when there were hopes of negotiations between the adversaries in Northern Ireland, and when the post-Communist world was coming to terms with a new reality in Eastern Europe. 'It is our duty to ourselves and to our children', he said, 'to see the new world as it is now – to discern its dangers, explore its prospects and do everything possible so that the State of Israel will fit into this world whose face is changing.' Rabin's credo marked a revolution in Israel's thinking:

No longer are we necessarily 'a people that dwells alone', and no longer is it true that 'the whole world is against us'. We must overcome the sense of isolation that has held us in its thrall for almost half a century.

We must join the international movement towards peace, reconciliation and cooperation that is spreading over the entire globe these days – lest we be the last to remain, all alone, at the station.

'The new Government', Rabin told the Israeli parliament, 'has accordingly made it a central goal to promote the making of peace and take vigorous steps that will lead to the end of the Arab-Israeli conflict. We shall do so based on the recognition of the Arab countries, and the Palestinians, that Israel is a sovereign state with the right to exist in peace and security. We believe wholeheartedly that peace is possible, that it is imperative and that it will ensue.'

With the help of his Foreign Minister, Shimon Peres – also a former Prime Minister – Rabin intended to propose to the Arab States and to the Palestinians 'the continuation of the peace talks based upon the framework forged at the Madrid Conference'. But the two men would move swiftly towards a more ambitious outcome. As Rabin explained it:

> As a first step toward a permanent solution we shall discuss the institution of autonomy in Judaea, Samaria, and the Gaza District. We do not intend to lose precious time. The Government's first directive to the negotiating teams will be to set up the talks and hold ongoing discussions between the sides.
>
> Within a short time we shall renew the talks in order to diminish the flame of enmity between the Palestinians and the State of Israel.
>
> As a first step, to illustrate our sincerity and good will, I wish to invite the Jordanian-Palestinian delegation to an informal talk, here in Jerusalem, so that we can hear their views, make ours heard, and create an appropriate atmosphere for neighbourly relations.

Rabin acted with the speed and authority of a man determined to break the earlier mould of stagnation and confrontation. When the army sought permission to enter the Palestinian university campus at Nablus, to search for six armed Palestinians who were believed to be trying to influence student council elections there, Rabin refused. Within a week of his coming to power he ordered a freeze on all new building, including settlers' houses, in the West Bank and Gaza. On August 10 he flew to the United States for a two-day meeting with President Bush at Kennebunkport, the President's summer home in Maine, on the Atlantic Ocean. Two weeks later, on August 24, Israel cancelled deportation orders against eleven Palestinians regarded as a disruptive influence. That same day, talks between Israel and the Palestinians were resumed in Washington. Four days later, Israel released eight hundred of the 7,429 Palestinians whom it was holding in detention. A new, if short-lived, era had begun of Israeli-Palestinian negotiations on the basis of equality.

Racism could flare up almost anywhere on the globe. On April 29, in Los Angeles, after four White police officers, accused of beating up a Black motorist – the beating had been captured on film – were acquitted, race riots broke out, and arson and looting spread. Black attacks were particularly fierce against shops owned by immigrants from South Korea. Six thousand National Guardsmen and four thousand marines and infantrymen were called in, and, during five days of near-anarchy, fifty-eight people were killed. The damage done to property was estimated at $1,000 million. When the riots ended, Bush allocated $19 million for an anti-drug and anti-gang campaign.

In intercommunal violence in the land-locked African State of Burundi, at least a thousand Hutu had been executed without trial after a mutiny was suppressed by the Tutsi-dominated government. News of the executions, which had taken place the previous November, only reached the West five months later. Two thousand Sri Lankans were killed in 1992, as the Tamil revolt continued into its tenth year, with the Jaffna peninsula firmly under the control of the extremist Tamil Liberation Tigers. Muslims and Tamils were also fighting: in one incident, 190 Muslims were massacred, in another, fifty-seven Muslims and fifty-three Tamils were killed. In South Africa, more than seven thousand Africans had been killed in intercommunal violence between African National Congress and Inkatha Freedom Party supporters in the twenty-seven months up to March 1992. In India, on December 6, after Hindu extremists attacked and destroyed a historic mosque in the Hindu holy city of Ayodhya, riots throughout northern India led to four hundred people being killed.

On June 3, delegates from more than a hundred nations, and Non-Governmental Organizations (NGOs) representing two thousand environmental groups – the latter known as the Global Forum – met in Rio de Janeiro for the first Earth Summit. Under the auspices of the United Nations, eleven days of discussion ended with calls for regulations to be set out for an 'environmentally sound' development of the planet. The reality from day to day was dire. In northern Pakistan, two thousand people drowned in severe flooding in September. In Cairo, five hundred people were killed in October in an earthquake. In eastern Indonesia, 1,200 people were killed in an earthquake and resultant tidal wave in December. In its annual slaughter, the motor car – a major and continually growing source of environmental pollution – killed more than 50,000 people that year in India, 40,000 people in the United States, and more than 4,000 in Britain.

In July the United Nations Special Representative in Somalia, Mohammed Sahnoun, a Muslim from Algeria, announced that five thousand people a day were dying of starvation. On President Bush's authority, an American air and sea armada was sent at once: Operation Provide Relief. Under it,

228,000 tons of grain reached Somalia within a month. At least half the grain was then looted by warring factions. With the authority of the United Nations, a Pakistani force of five hundred men was sent to halt the looting, but was unable to do so. The warring factions were well armed and anarchic, and would often shoot to kill without provocation.

By the end of September an estimated 300,000 Somalis had died of famine. Thousands more had been killed in factional rivalry. In October, Amnesty International condemned the Somali warlord, General Mohammed Farah Aydid, for mass executions. For his part, Aydid rejected any further United Nations involvement, claiming that it was an 'affront' to Somalia's sovereignty. The United Nations Special Representative, Mohammed Sahnoun, warned publicly that hundreds of thousands more Somalis would be killed unless the United Nations took immediate and effective action.

On December 3 the United Nations Security Council approved a resolution authorizing direct intervention in Somalia, under the leadership of the United States. On December 4, determined that any more food sent in should go to those who most needed it, President Bush ordered 28,000 American troops to Somalia, to carry out Operation Restore Hope. Before the troops could arrive, food aid which had been unloaded at Mogadishu docks was unable to reach even the north of the city, because rebel forces controlled the suburbs. Western journalists photographed hundreds of bales of aid lying idle at the dockside on December 5. The first marines landed at Mogadishu on December 9, their arrival recorded by the same photographers who had earlier shown the world the food aid that could not be distributed because of civil unrest. Several thousand French troops were also brought by sea to Mogadishu from Djibouti. These forces took over physical control of the famine epicentres in the south of the country, including the inland towns of Baidoa and Baidere, with a mandate to make the food aid available to those who were so desperately in need of it.

On December 8, on the evening before United States troops landed at Mogadishu, the local warlord in Kismayu, Colonel Omer Jess, ordered the murder of more than a hundred of the leading members of a rival clan, among them religious leaders, businessmen and a doctor. The killings went on for three nights. Colonel Jess, a member of the Ogadeni clan, had seized Kismayu seven months earlier, imposing his rule on the local Harti clan, who were now his victims. When President Bush's envoy, Ambassador Robert B. Oakley, reached Kismayu on December 19, Colonel Jess welcomed him warmly, eager to be a recipient of the mass of aid that was already landed at Mogadishu. Questioned by Western journalists about the killings in Kismayu, Oakley said: 'We are not an occupying power, we have no power of arrest. There is nothing in the Security Council resolution about war crimes, as there is with Bosnia.'

On December 28 a joint force of two hundred United States and forty Canadian soldiers arrived by helicopter at the town of Belet Huen, the last of the famine-stricken towns for which humanitarian aid was reaching Somalia. As soon as they secured the airfield, C-130 Hercules cargo planes brought more soldiers. The operation was commanded by a Canadian officer, Lieutenant-Colonel Carol Mathieu. Within seven days, a force of eight hundred Canadians was supervising the distribution of food.

For the United States, which masterminded the landings and the occupation of the towns, the Somalia intervention was a humanitarian commitment on a massive scale, constituting a signal to the world that armed forces could have other uses than combat (in February Operation Provide Hope had seen American aircraft fly fifty-four food missions into the former Soviet Union). On December 31, Bush himself flew to the Somali capital, Mogadishu, and, at the nearby village of La Foule, visited a school and relief centre for mothers and children. Offshore, as a sign of the protective as well as war-making power of the United States, were the aircraft carrier *Ranger*, the amphibious assault ship *Tripoli*, the transport dock *Juneau* and the supply ship *Jack Lummus*.

That year, American non-military economic aid reached its highest-ever level: $6,154 million, voted for by Congress under the Foreign Assistance Act. The two largest beneficiaries were Israel ($1,200 million) and Egypt ($892 million). Following the Camp David Accords five years earlier the United States had been committed to ensuring as best it could the economic stability of these two countries, once bitter adversaries on the field of battle. The next largest amount in foreign aid was $815 million to India. Helping to sustain India's democracy was another American foreign policy goal. The countries of Eastern Europe which had so recently broken free from the Communist system received a total of $431 million between them. Specific sums had also been allocated for refugees from Iraq ($12 million) and for the Palestinian refugees in the refugee camps of the Occupied West Bank and Gaza Strip ($10 million).

Almost every country in Africa was in receipt of American economic aid. The most substantial beneficiaries were Ethiopia, which received $188 million, and Mozambique, which received $117 million. The total United States economic aid to Africa, $1,391 million, was only slightly in excess of the aid to Israel alone. Even when added up, these large sums amounted to only half of one per cent of the total United States national budget outlay for the year. The total sum also constituted slightly less than the amount earned by the United States in that same year from arms sales.

By far the largest purchaser of American arms was Saudi Arabia, which paid $1,111 million for modern weaponry with which to defend itself if attacked by Iraq or Iran. In the seven years following the Gulf War, neither scenario came to pass. Every Western European country except Ireland, Switzerland and Austria, also purchased arms from the United States. The largest purchaser was Spain ($687 million) followed closely by Germany ($572 million).

As well as economic aid, there was yet another source of American money for countries which the United States considered reliable allies: this was military aid. The largest recipient of military aid was Israel ($1,800 million), followed by Egypt ($1,302 million). The three other main recipients were Turkey, Greece and the Philippines. But with the Cold War over and the Soviet Union dissolved, the United States was able, for the first time since before the Second World War, to contemplate a substantial reduction in defence spending. In his State of the Union message on January 28, Bush announced a thirty per cent cut in defence spending: $50,000 million over the coming five years. He added, however, that the United States would continue to 'protect itself', and that it would also continue its world role 'in support of freedom everywhere'.

In September an American citizen, Nathan Cook, died at the age of 106. He was the oldest known United States army veteran, and had fought in China in 1900. His death was a link with America's first military expedition of the twentieth century. On the last day of the year – in the final weeks of George Bush's presidency – the defence aspect of American policy was highlighted when the United States Department of Defence awarded a number of six-year contracts to manufacturers to develop the 'Brilliant Eyes' satellite.

Each 'Brilliant Eyes' satellite was intended to carry sensors that could monitor both space and Earth. These sensors were designed to pinpoint hostile land- or sea-launched missiles shortly after they had been launched, to follow and track them, and to discriminate between multiple warheads and decoys. The sensors would then activate counter-measures against missiles that were within range of ground-based anti-missile defences, or against those that had left the atmosphere. The ones that had left the atmosphere could be shot down by an equally new orbiting firing system, 'Brilliant Pebbles'. Under the Pentagon's User Operational Evaluation System (UOES), in the event of an international crisis, or to provide support in regional conflict, as many as a dozen prototype 'Brilliant Eyes' satellites had been planned to be put into orbit by 1998.

'Brilliant Eyes' and 'Brilliant Pebbles' were to have been America's ultimate defence during the Cold War, and constituted the high point of the Star Wars defence system inaugurated by President Reagan. Under the proposals as contracted for on December 31, between twenty and forty 'Brilliant Eyes' would be in orbit within six years. This whole programme was cancelled by the new President, Bill Clinton, on 13 May 1993, when he announced 'the end of the Star Wars Era'. It was a final affirmation that the Cold War was over.

Another war, which had ended seventeen years earlier, was providing a bonanza for souvenir hunters in 1992. In Ho Chi Minh City – Saigon until it fell to the Vietcong and North Vietnamese in 1975 – tourists, including those from the United States, bought American air force clocks salvaged from planes and ships, and North Vietnamese pith helmets and war medals. Above a bar, a former South Vietnamese photographer for United Press International, Hoang Van Cuong, who had spent six years in prison camps after the war, sold photographs which he had taken in the last weeks of the war. A Western journalist who saw them commented: 'Their theme is despair.'

Another aftermath of war was increasingly impinging on Western consciousness, and consciences. In every armed conflict, whether war or civil war, opposing sides planted anti-personnel mines to keep the other side at bay. These mines, dug into the ground, could kill or maim, not only when the fighting was taking place, but for many years after it, as unsuspecting civilians trod on unsuspected mines. Even those engaged in clearing the vast minefields left by wars were at risk. Among those killed while clearing mines in Afghanistan in 1992 was a twenty-three-year-old English volunteer, Tim Goggs, who was posthumously awarded the George Medal for his bravery in trying to rescue a colleague in the explosion in which he was fatally wounded. He had worked at mine clearance for eighteen months. When he was killed he left a legacy to the charity Christian Aid for a programme to teach people how to recognize mines, and how to mark minefields for later destruction. After his death his parents set up a charity, Tim's Fund, to continue his work.

In the presidential elections in the United States, William Jefferson Clinton – known popularly as Bill – was elected as the first Democratic President since Jimmy Carter. In an editorial on December 29 the *New York Times* saw an opportunity for the new President, once he took up office in the New Year, to give a lead in establishing an international law-enforcement force. There was 'no reason why principles, and UN procedures, need to be ad hoc', the paper wrote. 'Instead of posses the world needs a standby force ready to move quickly under joint command before mass killings start. Like the cop on the beat, the mere existence of such a force could deter genocide, rampages and gross crimes. By moving quickly to articulate new rules and form a permanent peacemaking force, the new Clinton team might finally give real weight to the idea of "the international community".'

In one region where the United States had been used to taking unilateral action, Central America, there was one ray of hope as the year came to an end. In the words of the *Baltimore Sun*: 'El Salvador is celebrating its first peaceful Christmas season in a dozen years thanks to a remarkable exercise in diplomacy by the United Nations. The civil war that claimed 75,000 lives still rages in people's hearts, but national exhaustion and a dramatic change in US policy gave the United Nations the opening it needed for a ceasefire that has held for almost eleven months.'

The rebel armies of the National Liberation Front had been disarmed and demobilized. The Front's leaders had formed an open and freely operating political Party. Land was being distributed among the landless. Peace was bringing economic revival. The United States had written off $500 million in debts. International aid of $800 million was being secured. Whether what the *Baltimore Sun* called 'the appalling gap between a small wealthy upper class and poverty-plagued masses' could be narrowed without renewed conflict, and whether some of the many other global conflicts could be resolved in this way, after so much bloodshed and division, was a question difficult to answer in the affirmative, even in the traditionally optimistic glow of an old year giving way to a new one.

CHAPTER FORTY-TWO

1993

Let us pray that a day will come when we all will say:
Farewell to arms.

YITZHAK RABIN

FOR A DECADE, European leaders had been moving towards greater unity.
The European Community was already debating and acting as a single body
on many issues of foreign policy. The direct involvement in Bosnia was a
European initiative. On 1 January 1993 the European single market came
into being. Economic frontiers between the members of the European Community, and all the European Free Trade Area countries except Switzerland,
were removed. The Maastricht Treaty of the previous year opened up the
prospect, by the year 2000, of a single European currency. Britain had
secured, as a result of John Major's negotiations at Maastricht, an 'opt out'
clause with regard to social legislation: especially the favoured Community-
wide imposition of a national minimum wage to which the Conservative
government was opposed, on the pragmatic ground that it would increase
unemployment, because small businesses would not be able to pay the higher
wages to the full range of their staff.

Essentially, however, the European Community – officially known from
November as the European Union – was a formidable force for collective
cross-border economic action and expansion, with the new States of Eastern
Europe likely to join it, and other States, including Greece and Turkey,
seeking to do so. One of its goals was a single European currency – the Euro
– which eleven member States, but not Britain, Denmark or Sweden, were
to adopt six years later.

For those who shared the aspiration of global harmony, a landmark was
reached on January 15 with the signature in Paris of a convention banning
chemical weapons. It was signed by 120 nations, including the United States

and Russia. For the United States it was the last international act of the Bush presidency. Five days later, on January 20, Bill Clinton was sworn in as President. His success was as a result of a swing towards the Democrats after twelve years of Republican ascendancy.

Recognizing and welcoming America's leading place among the nations of the world, in his inauguration address Clinton called on 'a new generation of Americans to a season of service'. He added: 'Today a new generation raised in the shadow of the Cold War assumes new responsibilities in a world warmed by the sunshine of freedom but threatened still by ancient hatreds and new plagues.' There should be sacrifice 'not for its own sake but for our own sake'. Abroad, the United States should 'not shrink from the challenges'. He would maintain 'American leadership of a world we did much to make'. When 'our vital interests are challenged, or the will and conscience of the international community are defied', America would act 'with peaceful diplomacy when possible, with force when necessary'.

Among Clinton's achievements before the end of the year was to obtain Congressional approval for his signature of a North America Free Trade Agreement (NAFTA), linking the United States, Canada and Mexico in the world's largest free-trade area. Clinton also opened, the day after Congress gave its approval to NAFTA, the first Asia-Pacific Economic Co-operation summit. It took place in Seattle, on the Pacific coast of the United States. Fifteen nations of the 'Pacific rim' took part.

For Western television viewers the year opened with horrific scenes of mass starvation in Somalia, and with the obvious factional lawlessness there which made the distribution of vital food aid so perilous for the United States and French forces that had already landed. Canada and Belgium also sent troops. All were authorized by the United Nations to disarm the warring factions, and ensure that the food being sent in was fairly distributed.

On January 2 a British famine relief worker, twenty-eight-year-old Sean Devereux, was shot and killed by Somali fighters in Kismayu. He was the first Western aid worker to be killed since United States troops had landed. On January 10, a total of fourteen warring factions inside Somalia agreed to a ceasefire so that aid could be distributed. But sniping continued. In Mogadishu, on January 18, the first American marine was killed, Private Domingo Arroyo. Eight days later, also in Mogadishu, a second marine, Corporal Anthony Botello, was killed by a sniper. That day, in Kismayu, in a battle with armed Somali militias, American and Belgian troops killed eight Somali fighters. Four days later, on January 30, seven hundred American troops flown by helicopter to Afgoi failed to find a substantial arms cache believed to be hidden there.

Amid these clashes, food aid continued to be distributed. Among the supplies sent to Somalia were 2,500 tons of biscuits from Britain. These had been baked, packaged and stored during the Second World War, as 'strategic food stocks' in the event of a prolonged war. Declaring that they were 'no longer needed', on March 9 the British Agriculture Minister, John Gummer, authorized their despatch to Somalia, as part of 200,000 tons of British food aid. Although somewhat drier than was acceptable to the British palate, the biscuits remained edible, and with some nutritional value, after half a century. From the needs of a long-ended war had emerged a source of succour for the starving.

At the beginning of June, Somali militiamen tried to seize power in Mogadishu. Twenty-two Pakistani soldiers of the United Nations peace-keeping force were killed. A week later, on June 12, American planes began a series of attacks on the strongpoints of General Aydid. When supporters of Aydid attacked American peacekeeping troops in Mogadishu, the Americans returned fire, and twenty people were killed. On June 16 the United Nations ordered the arrest of General Aydid. In an unsuccessful attempt to seize him, street fighting was renewed. Four United Nations soldiers and a hundred Somalis were killed.

The search for General Aydid led to an American air raid on his command headquarters, in which Aydid escaped injury, but seventy-three Somalis were killed. In revenge, four Western journalists in Mogadishu were set upon by a large crowd and killed. During a sustained mob attack on United Nations peacekeepers in Mogadishu on September 9, American helicopter gunships opened fire in an attempt to disperse the attackers, a hundred of whom were killed. On October 4 twelve American soldiers were killed in a two-day battle against supporters of General Aydid, who continued to evade capture. In response, President Clinton announced two days later that he would double the number of American troops in Somalia.

Unhelped by any outside intervention, the Afar people of Djibouti, who sought independence, were attacked in July by the forces of the ruling Party, the Muslim Popular Rally for Progress. International aid agencies in the area reported that as the government forces overran the area, recapturing the Red Sea coast, they carried out widespread rape, summary executions and the poisoning of wells. Tens of thousands of the Affars fled into Ethiopia, where they joined as many as four million people who were still dependent on international food aid for their survival.

In the Persian Gulf, Saddam Hussein had challenged the United Nations by placing surface-to-air missiles in the 'no-fly zone' that had been declared in southern Iraq. On January 6 the coalition partners issued an ultimatum that he remove the missiles or face renewed attack. For ten days Saddam ignored the ultimatum. Then, on January 16, with the approval of its coalition partners, the United States launched a series of air strikes on strategic sites near Baghdad. Three Iraqi civilians were killed when a hotel in the city was hit in error. There were further attacks on Iraqi missile sites in southern Iraq.

The main American air strikes against Saddam Hussein were carried out by seven B-52 bombers, flying non-stop from Louisiana to Iraq and back. The Pentagon called it 'the longest air combat mission in history'. An air force colonel commented excitedly: 'Any banana republic can have an air force with F-15s, F-16s. But only a Super Power has a long-range bomber.' It was forty-five years since the B-52 had been designed, and the super-bomber put into service.

In June, the United States uncovered an Iraqi plot to assassinate former President Bush. The result was a series of American air attacks on June 26 on targets in Baghdad.

In Bosnia, on January 13, Lance-Corporal Wayne Edwards was the first British soldier of the peacekeeping force to be killed. On the following day the aircraft carrier *Ark Royal* was ordered to sail to the Adriatic, to assist in the protection of aid convoys. On February 22, as further details emerged of atrocities committed during Serb 'ethnic cleansing' operations in northern Bosnia, the United Nations Security Council adopted a resolution (808) on the establishment of an international war crimes tribunal for the former Yugoslavia. This was the first such tribunal to be set up since the International Military Tribunal in Nuremberg and Tokyo after the Second World War. Then, it was the victors in war who had determined that the war crimes of their enemies should be punished. With regard to Yugoslavia, the forum of judgment was truly international, with judges from countries that were not involved in the conflict.

The predominantly Muslim city of Srebrenica had been besieged by Serb forces for three months. The Serbs had refused to allow food into the city, and tens of thousands of people were on the verge of starvation. On March 19 a United Nations humanitarian convoy, led by General Philippe Morillon, managed to reach the city. The 700,000 inhabitants had been saved from a terrible fate. On March 25 the Muslim-led government in Bosnia agreed to a plan put forward by a former American Secretary of State, Cyrus Vance, and a former British Foreign Secretary, David Owen, for the division of Bosnia according to ethnic factors. The Bosnian Serbs rejected the plan.

On March 31 the United Nations Security Council passed a resolution (816) ordering the Yugoslav Serbs not to fly over Bosnia and so intervene in the conflict from the air. The Serbs ignored the resolution. With United Nations approval, NATO agreed to act. On April 12, fifty of its warplanes began to patrol the airspace over Bosnia, to enforce the no-fly zone, and to prevent Serb aircraft attacking Muslim positions. That day, Serb forces on the ground began an intense artillery attack on Srebrenica. Fifty-six Muslims were killed in the city. Six days later the city surrendered to the Bosnian Serbs. On April 26, President Clinton, who was taking an increasingly active part in the Bosnian conflict, ordered the freezing of all pre-1990 Yugoslav assets in the United States, and the implementation of stronger sanctions against Serbia and Montenegro.

The Bosnian Serb leaders were willing to consider the Vance-Owen peace plan, which gave them considerable territory, and on May 2, after talks in Athens, they signed it. But three days later the plan was rejected by the Bosnian parliament. The Serbian government recognized that the Vance-Owen plan gave the Bosnian Serbs as much as they could possibly hope for, even if the fighting were to be prolonged: perhaps even more, for the fighting might go against them. It therefore urged the Bosnian Serbs to accept the plan. When they refused to do so, Serbia imposed an economic blockade on its co-Serbs and erstwhile allies, hoping to convince them to sign. On May 15 the plan was put to a referendum, and was rejected. Four days later the Bosnian Serb leader, Radovan Karadžić, declared: 'The plan is dead.'

The international community intervened. The United States, Britain, Russia, France and Spain announced the establishment of 'safe areas' for the Muslims in Bosnia. Within these, the Muslims would be protected by an international force. Both Serbs and Croats would be allowed to keep the areas of Bosnia which they had occupied. The Bosnian Muslim president, Alija Izetbegović, rejected this.

Bosnian Serb shelling of Sarajevo was renewed. On June 1, a hundred people were injured when shells fell on a football match. Ten days later a

Muslim relief column was attacked, not by Serb but by Croat gunmen. British soldiers escorting the convoy returned fire, and two of the Croats were killed. On June 13, Bosnian Serbs laid down an artillery barrage on the besieged Muslim town of Goražde. Fifty-two people were killed. On the following day Bosnian Muslim troops began a sustained attack on Bosnian Croat villages in the centre of Bosnia, determined to drive the Croats out of the region altogether. Thousands of Croats fled.

A new plan for Bosnia was emerging. After Croat and Serb leaders had met in Geneva they proposed, on June 16, that Bosnia should be divided into three independent 'mini-States': Serb, Croat and Muslim Bosnia. The Council of Europe, meeting in Copenhagen five days later, considered that the result of such a division would be the inevitable destruction of the Muslim area by the Serbs and Croats, who would then partition Bosnia between them. The Bosnian Serbs and Croats each had contiguous external States from which arms and help could come, and by which their part of Bosnia could be annexed. The Muslims had no 'big brother' who could protect or annex them. On June 22 the Copenhagen summit announced that the European Community countries would send troops and money to help protect the Muslim areas in Bosnia. Christian Europe had become the protector of Islam against Christian assault.

The behaviour of the Bosnian Serbs had created widespread revulsion in Western Europe and the United States. This was heightened on July 12 when a Serb mortar shell aimed at the centre of Sarajevo hit a group of people queuing for water. Twelve of those in the queue were killed. Two weeks later, Bosnian Serb troops made a concerted effort to enter Sarajevo. At an emergency meeting of NATO ambassadors in Brussels, it was agreed to make plans for possible air strikes on Serb positions around the city. The Serbs understood the seriousness of the threat, and on July 12 withdrew from their most forward position on Mount Igman. Three days later the Royal Air Force mounted Operation Irma, to bring out by air forty-one of the sick and wounded from Sarajevo for treatment in Britain.

Negotiations for the 'mini-State' solution, whereby Bosnia would be divided on ethnic lines, reopened in Geneva on August 16. The basis of the talks was a detailed United Nations partition plan which David Owen produced with Cyrus Vance's successor, the Norwegian Foreign Minister Thorvald Stoltenberg. Bosnia would be divided into three independent 'mini-States': a Serbian republic, a Croatian republic and a Bosnian Muslim republic. Sarajevo and an area for some ten miles around it would be a republic of its own administered by the United Nations. On September 1 these talks collapsed. But on September 16 the Bosnian Muslim leader, President Izetbegović, and Bosnian Serb representatives, meeting in Geneva, agreed to the establishment of three ethnic States (Muslim, Serb and Croat) under a single sovereign authority, provided that each would have the right to secede after two years. Neither the Serbs nor the Croats were willing, however, to give up land which, under the Owen-Stoltenberg plan, would have been transferred to the Muslim republic.

On November 9, as the internecine fighting continued, one of Bosnia-Hercegovina's – and Europe's – historic monuments, the sixteenth-century bridge in Mostar, was destroyed by Bosnian Serb shellfire. By the end of the year there were 22,000 United Nations troops in the disputed province, the two largest contingents being those of France (3,000) and Britain (2,500). The peacekeepers watched as warmaking went on.

In Russia, President Yeltsin faced increasing opposition from hard-liners, almost all of them former Communists, who were demanding a halt to the reforms. On March 10 there had been a fierce altercation in the Congress of People's Deputies, between Yeltsin and the Speaker of the Congress, Ruslan Khasbulatov. Ten days later, Yeltsin announced the introduction of presidential rule. The Congress immediately began a process which they intended would lead to his impeachment. On March 24 Yeltsin announced that his plans for presidential rule had been dropped.

The hard-liners proceeded with their impeachment plans, but on March 28 failed to get a sufficient majority in the Congress. Six days later, Yeltsin was in Vancouver, where after two days of talks with President Clinton he received a $1,600 million aid package for Russia, and a reduction of American trading restrictions that had remained in force since the Communist era. Yeltsin had to try to deal with a deteriorating situation, however, with regard to the Russian environment. In Siberia, Russia's largest region, leaking oil pipes were damaging hundreds of thousands of square miles; factory emissions were depositing acid rain over vast areas; and on April 7 an explosion at a nuclear reprocessing plant caused radioactive contamination in dozens of towns and villages.

To challenge the hard-liners, Yeltsin called for a referendum on his leadership, and on his economic reforms. He won the referendum, but not by a sufficiently large majority to call early elections, as he had hoped. He remained President, and was determined to continue with the ambitious programme of privatization that he believed would alone enable Russia to survive as a modern State. On July 6 the seven leading industrial nations (the G7) at their summit in Tokyo, agreed to a $3,000 million aid-to-Russia programme to help the privatization programme forward.

Yeltsin's achievement in Tokyo did not lessen the discontent of the hard-liners and former Communists who wanted his overthrow, and whom he further angered when, on August 25, in Warsaw, he laid a wreath at the monument to the Polish officers murdered by Stalin in the Katyn forest in 1940.

On September 21 Yeltsin took drastic action to defend his position by dissolving the Russian parliament. Control of the country, he announced, would be in his hands alone. Elections would be called within three months. Although dissolved, the Russian parliament refused to disband. Its members refused even to leave their building, the White House, overlooking the Moscow River. In an extraordinary session, it voted to strip Yeltsin of all his presidential and constitutional powers, and appointed a leading hard-liner, Alexander Rutskoi, as 'acting President' in Yeltsin's place. On the following day, all telephone links, water and electricity supplies to the building were cut off. Two days later, on September 24, troops loyal to Yeltsin surrounded the building. For thirteen days it was besieged, with many of the parliament-arians and their supporters trapped inside it.

On October 3 pro-Communist demonstrators outside the parliament building tried to break the police and army cordon and release those trapped inside. They were beaten back. Yeltsin declared a State of Emergency, and on the following day, October 4, ordered commando troops, supported by tanks and armoured vehicles, to break into the building. From across the Moscow River, the building was hit again and again by shellfire, as a bloody battle ensued. More than 140 people in the building were killed. When fire broke out as a result of the bombardment, the defiant parliamentarians emerged with their hands up. Yeltsin had asserted his power by the most visible and destructive means.

Destruction was followed by debate, and recourse to the ballot box. On December 12 the elections Yeltsin had promised were held throughout Russia. They were the first democratic elections to be held in Russia since the elections for the Constitutional Assembly in 1918, the results of which Lenin had dismissed with contempt. In the 1993 elections, the largest share of the vote was won by an extremist nationalist, Vladimir Zhirinovsky, who, under the label Liberal Democratic Party, had publicly championed the reconquest of the lost republics. But even Zhirinovsky's share of the vote (23.9 per cent) was less than a quarter of the votes cast. The principal reformist Party, Russia's Choice, led by Yeltsin's ally Yegor Gaidar, came second, with 14.5 per cent of the vote. The Communist Party of the Russian Federation, headed by Gennadi Zyuganov, came third, with 13.6 per cent. In a separate ballot, the electors approved Yeltsin's proposed new constitution. His own presidency had not been on the ballot paper.

Yeltsin did not have to worry about the conflicts elsewhere in the former Soviet Union, which would have been his direct concern had they taken place two years earlier. On September 27 several hundred people were killed when, after an eleven-day siege, Sukhumi, the capital of the Abkhazian region of Georgia, was captured by anti-government forces loyal to the former President of Georgia, Zviad Gamsakhurdia. In central Georgia, Gorbachev's former Foreign Minister, Edouard Shevardnadze, who had been elected President of Georgia, ordered troops loyal to him to crush the remnants of Gamsakhurdia's revolt. Those rebels who survived the military assault fled into Abkhazia, where they helped to sustain the breakaway region.

In Algeria an all-out war was being waged on the Islamic Salvation Front. In January 1992 the government, with army support, had cancelled the country's national elections when it became clear that they were likely to be won by the Front. The Muslim militants, aggrieved at having been cheated of power, took violent action, attacking soldiers and civilians alike. The army responded with ferocity. In the first six months of the year more than four hundred militants were killed. After two French surveyors were kidnapped and killed in September, six thousand foreign residents left the country. By the end of the year twenty-five foreign nationals had been killed, and both France and the United States began taking their own citizens away.

Four years had passed since Ayatollah Khomeini had issued the religious *fatwa* calling for the death of the British author Salman Rushdie, for alleged insults to Islam in his novel *The Satanic Verses*. In February, Khomeini's successor, Ayatollah Khamenei, announced that the *fatwa* was renewed. As a sign of solidarity with Rushdie, John Major received him at Downing Street. Many British Muslims protested at this. In May, when a Turkish newspaper announced that it was going to publish extracts from the novel, the hotel in the city of Sivas where its translator, Aziz Nesin, was staying, was set on fire. Nesin, who had just made a speech attacking Islamic extremism, escaped, but in the ensuing riots thirty-six people were killed, among them several leading Muslim moderates who had defended Rushdie's right to publish the novel, and Nesin's right to translate it. In Oslo, the Norwegian publisher of *The Satanic Verses* was shot in the back and injured.

In Egypt, Islamic fundamentalism took the form of repeated attacks by Muslim militants on Coptic Christians, foreign tourists and the police. During the course of the year, 245 people were killed. The government responded by attacking mosques where militants were hiding. On March 10, twenty-five Muslim extremists were killed in gun battles with police in Cairo and Aswan. Two days later, Islamic extremists in India killed more than two hundred people when they detonated a car bomb in Bombay. Four days later, eighty-six people were killed by car-bomb explosions in Calcutta.

In the Middle East the conflict between Israel and the Palestinians intensified. For five years Palestinian youth in the occupied territories had been carrying on a campaign of harassment and violence against Israeli soldiers and civilians alike: the Intifada. It was the intensity of the Intifada that had convinced Yitzhak Rabin to follow the path of negotiation rather than confrontation. But there was a limit to the provocation that a democratic society could take. Public opinion demanded security. Following the murder of three Israeli soldiers in Gaza at the end of 1992, and the kidnapping of a fourth, Sergeant Nissim Toledano, whose body was found bound and stabbed to death a day later, Rabin ordered the deportation to Lebanon of 1,600 members of the two main Islamic extremist organizations, Hamas and Islamic Jihad.

The killings inside Israel continued. On 15 January 1993 a Palestinian from Gaza stabbed four people to death at the Central Bus Station in Tel Aviv and at a café. One of the dead was a recent Jewish immigrant from Russia. Another was a Lebanese Arab visiting Tel Aviv.

In the midst of these killings, talks had begun, in strictest secrecy, between Israel and the Palestine Liberation Organization, the PLO, with which, until then, successive Israeli governments had refused to negotiate, denouncing it as a 'terrorist organization' and its leader, Yasser Arafat, as a 'man of blood'. The first Israeli-PLO talks took place on January 20, five days after the Tel Aviv killings, at a secluded villa just outside Oslo, and lasted three days. The host was a Norwegian research organization headed by Terje Rod Larsen, who had earlier befriended the Israeli Deputy Foreign Minister, Yossi Beilin. 'The time had come to make good our campaign commitments,' the Israeli Foreign Minister, Shimon Peres, later wrote. 'Rabin had pledged to implement the Palestinian autonomy plan within nine months of our taking office, and that deadline was now approaching. I, too, was impatient to move forward.'

As the secret talks continued in Oslo, the Intifada intensified. On January 27 Israeli troops killed an armed Palestinian in Gaza City. On February 5 they killed a fourteen-year-old boy, Khaled Itawi, in a refugee camp in the Gaza Strip. Three other Palestinian stone-throwers were also shot dead. On February 6, Israeli troops, confronted by a crowd of rock-throwers, killed seventeen-year-old Ashraf Dao'or in Gaza City. Inside Israel there was a fierce debate about these killings. Between August 1992 and January 1993 two-thirds of the Palestinian deaths occurred, according to the Israeli army's own announcements, during incidents where the lives of soldiers were not in danger. Under such circumstances, army regulations forbade any 'lethal' shooting – that is, aiming above the legs when using live ammunition. Most Palestinian deaths therefore occurred as a result of the army's failure to comply with its own regulations. The number of Palestinian children aged sixteen and under who were killed had also risen in the previous six months. When the *Jerusalem Post* wrote of the children sent by their elders to throw rocks and cinder-blocks, 'It is their senders who are guilty of murder, not the soldiers,' Yuval Ginbar, of the Israeli human rights organization Betselem, noted bitterly, 'Our soldiers are never wrong. Who is?'

On February 9 Shimon Peres told Rabin that Israel should 'try to induce' Arafat to leave Tunis and return to the West Bank and Gaza. Rabin agreed. On February 11 the Oslo talks were resumed for another two days, again in strictest secrecy. A draft Declaration of Principles was produced, as well as a paper setting out 'Guidelines for a Regional Marshall Plan'. The Palestinian negotiators were particularly keen on this concept of a Western financial commitment of the sort that the United States had given to Europe after the Second World War. The urgency of finding a new way forward was underlined a month later, when figures were released for the death toll during 1992. Palestinians had killed eleven Israeli soldiers and eleven Israeli civilians during the year. Israeli troops had killed a hundred Palestinians. And Palestinians, mostly members of Hamas and Islamic Jihad, had killed more than two hundred of their fellow Palestinians.

On August 20, Shimon Peres celebrated his seventieth birthday. That night, his were among the initials put on the document at which the negotiators on both sides had worked so long: the Oslo Accords. 'Here', he later wrote, 'was a small group of Israelis, Palestinians and Norwegians – partners to one of the best-guarded secrets ever, a secret whose imminent revelation would mark a watershed in the history of the Middle East.' Peres told his Palestinian opposite number, Abu Ala'a: 'The fate of Gaza can be like that of Singapore. From poverty to prosperity in one sustained leap.'

The PLO, hitherto a pariah for most Israelis, became a partner. The Likud opposition in Israel derided this, condemning Rabin and Peres in the crudest, most threatening language for having shaken the hand of the enemy. But they, in their turn – with the greatest reluctance – were to shake that hand, and to promise publicly to honour the agreements that had been signed by their predecessors. That promise was to be much tested in the years ahead.

On August 30 the Israeli Cabinet approved the grant of self-rule to the Palestinians in the Gaza Strip and Jericho. The PLO put their signature to the plan on September 9. The PLO would administer these areas, fly its flag, tax its people, govern the municipalities and continue negotiations to extend self-rule to all the Palestinian-inhabited areas of the West Bank. Before any public agreement could be reached between them, and before a Declaration of Principles embodying the Oslo Accords could be signed, Israel had been insistent that Yasser Arafat, hitherto the leader of a group that had carried out many spectacular acts of terror, should specifically renounce terror. On September 13, as President Clinton awaited Rabin and Arafat at the White House for the signing, the turning point in the negotiations came at the eleventh hour, for it was only then that Arafat agreed to sign a letter, written to the Norwegian Foreign Minister, which acceded to Israel's demand. In the letter, Arafat agreed that, upon signing the Declaration of Principles, he would include in his public statements the words:

In light of the new era marked by the signing of the Declaration of Principles, the PLO encourages and calls upon the Palestinian people in the West Bank and Gaza Strip to take part in the steps leading to normalization of life, rejecting violence and terrorism, contributing to peace and stability, and participating actively in shaping reconstruction, economic development and co-operation.

The signing of the Declaration of Principles on September 13 took place on the White House lawn, witnessed by President Clinton. The signing ceremony took place at the desk used at Camp David for the signing of the Begin-Sadat agreement in 1978. Immediately after the signing, Rabin's uneasy handshake with Arafat, and his wry smile, were seen by millions of television viewers across the world. As much as any other single act, that handshake symbolized the revolution that had taken place and the new reality that beckoned. Israel had recognized the PLO, was talking to it and was signing agreements with it; the PLO had recognized Israel, and promised to reject violence and terrorism.

Rabin was often asked in the months ahead what had gone through his mind during that handshake. A private, shy man, he did not easily give an answer. But when his 1979 memoirs were reissued three months after Washington, he set down his feelings.

> I knew that the hand outstretched to me from the far side of the podium was the same hand that held the knife, that held the gun, the hand that gave the order to shoot, to kill. Of all the hands in the world, it was not the hand that I wanted or dreamed of touching. But it was not Yitzhak Rabin on that podium, the private citizen who lives on Rav Ashi Street in Tel Aviv, it was not the father of Dalia, and of Yuval, who both completed their army service, or the grandfather of a soldier today, Yonatan – a grandfather who does not sleep too well at nights, and worries like all parents and grandparents in Israel.

Rabin's reflections continued:

> I would have liked to sign a peace agreement with Holland, or Luxembourg, or New Zealand. But there was no need to. That is why, on that podium, on that world stage, I stood as the representative of a nation, as the emissary of a State that wants peace with the most bitter and odious of its foes, a State that is willing to give peace a chance.
>
> As I have said, one does not make peace with one's friends. One makes peace with one's enemy.

During his speech on the White House lawn, Rabin appealed directly to the Palestinians. 'We are destined to live together, on the same soil in the same land,' he told them.

> We the soldiers who have returned from battle stained with blood, we who have seen our relatives and friends killed before our eyes, we who have attended their funerals and cannot look into the eyes of parents and orphans, we who have come from a land where parents bury their children,

we who have fought against you, the Palestinians – We say to you today in a loud and clear voice: Enough of blood and tears. Enough. We harbour no hatred towards you. We have no desire for revenge. We, like you, are people who want to build a home, plant a tree, love, live side by side with you – in dignity, in empathy, as human beings, as free men. We are today giving peace a chance and saying to you: Enough. Let us pray that a day will come when we all will say: Farewell to arms.

On the day after the Washington signing, Rabin flew to Morocco where, in Rabat, he took the first steps towards a peace treaty with Jordan, the outlines of which were initialled that day. King Hassan of Morocco had used his good offices for more than thirty years to try to move the Arab-Israeli conflict towards its resolution.

Racism and ethnic violence continued to scar the final decade of the century. On May 29, five members of a Turkish family were killed in an arson attack on their home in Solingen, in Germany. Neo-Nazis were believed to have been responsible. Anti-Turkish feeling was running high among those – mostly among the unemployed and the unemployable – who resented the large number of foreign workers in Germany. The German government appealed for moderation. In the ethnic struggle between Hutu and Tutsi in Burundi, two thousand people, including the President and six government ministers, were killed in October during a failed military coup.

In Britain, in March, two small boys were killed by an IRA bomb at Warrington in Cheshire. Revulsion at the killings stimulated the peace movements throughout Ireland, North and South. In Dublin, 200,000 Irish men and women marched in protest against the claim of the IRA to represent the people of Ireland. But the killings and counter-killings continued. In October ten people were killed in Northern Ireland in an IRA bomb explosion in a mainly Protestant area of Belfast. A week later seven people died when a revenge shooting was carried out by Ulster Freedom Fighters against a Catholic bar in Londonderry.

Behind the scenes, both John Major and the Irish Prime Minister, Albert Reynolds, were working to find a long-term solution to the Northern Irish imbroglio. On December 15, after the third of three meetings within a few weeks, they issued a Joint Declaration on Northern Ireland (known as the Downing Street Declaration) calling for an end to intercommunal violence, and a lasting political settlement for the province. In the words of the declaration, it was 'for the people of the island of Ireland alone, by agreement between the two parts respectively, to exercise their right of self-determination on the basis of consent, freely and concurrently given, North and South, to bring about a united Ireland' if they so wished. But, the declaration stressed, 'it would be wrong to attempt to impose a united Ireland in the absence of the freely given consent of a majority of the people of Northern Ireland'. In circumlocutory language, it indicated that steps would be taken towards having the contentious claim to jurisdiction over Northern Ireland deleted from the Irish constitution and that, if IRA violence were brought to 'a permanent end' and renounced for the future, Sinn Fein could expect 'to join in dialogue in due course between the governments and the political parties on the way ahead'.

The declaration gained immediate parliamentary, media and popular approval in the Republic of Ireland, where it was judged to have recognized fully all reasonable nationalist and Catholic aspirations; and to have done so without giving cause for the Protestant Unionists to fear that the existing status of Northern Ireland would be altered against their wish. There was a widespread desire in both North and South to call for an immediate end to violence by the paramilitary groups in both communities. Anxiety grew after Christmas, however, when both the IRA and the Loyalist terrorists embarked once more on their murderous courses.

The Downing Street Declaration had been rejected by extremists on both sides. But for a growing majority of the people of Northern Ireland, it represented the only possible way forward: negotiation, compromise and conciliation.

In South Africa, the moves towards the ending of apartheid were also accompanied by ethnic and intercommunal violence. On July 25 a number of Black gunmen burst into a church in a suburb of Cape Town, killing twelve of the mainly White congregation. Could such action be described any longer as a manifestation of frustrated nationalism? Apartheid had been abandoned and discrimination against Blacks was everywhere being dismantled through open debate and through the political process. Nelson Mandela was asserting the rights of Blacks with increasing success and President de Klerk was preparing a legal mechanism whereby apartheid would be dismantled altogether. On the day after the church killings, the draft of South Africa's first post-apartheid constitution was published, inviting a vigorous political debate, far away from the separations and violence of the past. But on July 31 there was another outburst of brutal killing, when a hundred Blacks were killed in intercommunal violence in the townships near Johannesburg. In August an American student, Amy Biehl, who was White, was set upon by a crowd of Blacks in the township of Guguletu, and killed. Four Blacks were later imprisoned for her murder. The Black South African writer, Sindiwe Magona, later wrote:

> All South Africans killed Amy Biehl, for we allowed, even encouraged, the climate that made the attack possible. White hatred of Black people in South Africa resulted in bigotry's becoming law – apartheid. The reverse of this, Blacks' hatred of Whites, may not have achieved such institutionalized status, but that is not to say it does not exist.
>
> To the contrary, it is abundant in Black folklore: it can be found in our jokes, in our stories, in the songs and oral histories of Black townships, villages and squatter camps. And the carelessness with which we talk about White people, in a far from flattering light, in the presence of very young children ensures that these negative sentiments will be ingrained in them, that they will grow up knowing that *abelungu* are horrible people who have no hearts, who have done all manner of evil towards us.
>
> Black South Africans may feel that they have a right to this hatred, that the country's history justifies it. Indeed, ours is a history of White exploitation of Blacks – long before apartheid, as well as during that era and beyond. Yet has the time not come for us to move on? Does harbouring this hate advance the cause of the nation one iota?
>
> The war cry during the days near apartheid's end – 'Boers are dogs!' – was a variation on an old theme, whispered harshly in times of peace, spat out during private outpourings of anger and frustration, spoken far from the White person who provoked it.

Following Amy Biehl's murder, politicians continued to seek a political solution. On September 7 agreement was reached by a Negotiating Council consisting of twenty-three different groups, to establish a Transitional Executive Council, through which apartheid would cease to exist. Forty-five years of inequality, based on racial considerations, would come to an end. It was going to be a process fraught with difficulty, as intercommunal violence proved as ferocious as Black-White violence had ever been. On the day after the Agreement, nineteen Africans were killed when Black gunmen opened fire on a taxi queue in the township of Wadeville near Johannesburg.

As in the Middle East, so in South Africa, the continuation of violence did not deter those who were determined to move forward from confrontation to co-operation. On September 23 the South African parliament passed a Bill setting up the Transitional Executive Council, and instructed the Council to prepare for the country's first multi-racial elections, to be held the following spring. After an appeal by Nelson Mandela at the United Nations on September 24, the United States, the British Commonwealth and the countries of the European Community agreed to lift sanctions on South Africa, the main international weapon against the apartheid regime. On October 15 both Mandela and President de Klerk were awarded the Nobel Peace Prize. De Klerk later recalled the private dinner hosted by the Nobel Committee for himself and Mandela in Oslo, before they went to Stockholm for the main award ceremony. 'It was pleasant and our hosts were courteous and considerate,' he wrote.

But the atmosphere was stiff – particularly from Mandela's side. Before my arrival, he had chosen once again to attack me in interviews. Apparently he was not pleased by the decision to include me in the award. In private conversations, the chairman of the Nobel Committee let me know how controversial their decision to grant the prize to me as well as to Mandela had been. My reception was reserved by comparison with the effusive welcome accorded to Mandela.

De Klerk continued:

The ceremony took place the next afternoon. In my speech I tried to avoid saying anything too contentious. I conveyed my sincere congratulations to Mr Mandela and paid tribute to all those who were working for peace in South Africa. Mandela's response was, for the most part, appropriate and conciliatory.

That evening I accompanied Mandela on to a first-floor balcony at the Grand Hotel to witness what our programme described as a spontaneous torchlight procession. I watched as several hundred people carrying candles filed up the avenue and gathered outside. It was very picturesque and quaint. Then they started shouting ANC slogans. I heard some shouting 'Kill the farmer, kill the Boer!' Others were shouting 'De Klerk, go home!'

Mandela was smiling warmly and waving. It was a very unpleasant situation. However, we stood our ground and faced the crowd, somewhat grimly. But with almost everybody raising their fists in the ANC salute, we slipped back into the hotel.

Next day we flew to Stockholm where I spoke of the constitutional progress we were making in South Africa. Mandela then made a blistering attack on me and the National Party. The Swedes were deeply embarrassed. I was seething. It was only with the greatest self-control that I once again managed to bite my tongue and not shatter the illusion that there was a cordial relationship . . .

Despite the bitter legacy of the past, the process of dismantling apartheid was unstoppable. When the all-race Transitional Executive Council met on December 7, it marked the first time that Blacks had a voice in all executive decisions relating to their, and South Africa's, future. Two weeks later, on December 22, the South African parliament, elected under the apartheid franchise, voted to adopt an interim constitution that would lead to majority rule after an election in four months' time.

In one of the worst maritime peacetime disasters of the century, a thousand people died when a ferry sank off the coast of Haiti on February 18. In July, almost two thousand people died during floods in the Punjab, which made two million Indians homeless. In September, ten thousand Indians were killed when an earthquake struck the Indian State of Maharashtra.

Natural disasters could not be averted, but was there anywhere on the planet that could avoid civil strife or be free of deliberate killing? On August 15, in the remotest Amazon, in Brazil, illegal gold and tin miners were seeking to exploit the region's natural resources. Facing their depredations, and dispossession, were the local Yanomami Indians. In a confrontation between the two cultures, the miners massacred seventy-four of the Indians. It might just as well have been 1493 as 1993. Despicable and barbaric as it was in itself, it also served to point up an extraordinary element of the profit-making imperative in the last decade of the twentieth century – the predominance of greed, and the imbalance of monetary values. The massacre came in the year when five American astronauts, working in space, at the edge of new scientific horizons, repaired the Hubble space telescope at a cost of $360 million; and when, in the course of another pioneering scientific endeavour, $980 million was spent on the American space probe *Mars Observer*, with which, once launched into space, all contact was lost. Space spending in the United States in that one year exceeded $1,340 million. The profit made by the gold and tin miners has been estimated at no less than $1,000 million.

CHAPTER FORTY-THREE

1994

Never, never, and never again shall it be that this beautiful land will again experience the oppression of one by another ... The sun shall never set on so glorious a human achievement.

NELSON MANDELA

IN THE UNITED STATES, President Clinton, like Roosevelt, Kennedy and Johnson before him, had a vision of a fairer society in which those at the lower end of the socio-economic spectrum would be helped by the State – by the taxes of those who were best able to make a contribution to the wider well-being. On 25 January 1994, in his televised State of the Union message, he called for legislation on health insurance, crime prevention and welfare reform, gun control, federal funds for drug treatment, job training for the unemployed, and urban renewal. In a warning to Congress with regard to his health-care proposals – which were strongly endorsed by his wife Hillary – Clinton declared: 'If you send me legislation that does not guarantee every American private health insurance that can never be taken away, you will force me to take this pen, veto the legislation, and we'll come right back here and start all over again.'

Republican hostility to Clinton's social reform measures effectively curtailed or impeded them all. The would-be jewel in the legislative crown, health care, was not to come to pass. Republican hostility was not restricted to policies alone: a sustained public attack on Clinton's alleged financial and personal misconduct was so intense that it threatened to impede the daily business of government. During the mid-term elections on November 8, Clinton's hopes of pursuing his legislative programme were struck a further blow, when Republicans gained control of both the Senate and the House of Representatives. Gaining nine seats in the Senate, the Republicans had

fifty-three Senators to the Democrats' forty-seven. In the House of Representatives the Republicans gained more than fifty seats, securing 230 in all, as
against the Democrats' 204.

With the defence of the West no longer based upon the confrontation with
the East, NATO looked to a pan-European role, as peacekeeper when internal
strife threatened to disintegrate into civil war. On January 11, at the end
of a two-day summit in Brussels, the final communiqué spoke of the establishment of a Partnership for Peace in which the newly democratized States of
Eastern Europe would be invited to join, as well as the neutral States. There
was also an urgent item on the Western agenda: the former Soviet nuclear
arsenal, a proportion of which was under the control of Ukraine.

Yeltsin's Russia, despite its internal turmoil, still had in Yeltsin a strong
leader whose word with regard to the decommissioning of nuclear weapons
could be trusted. Ukraine was a less certain factor. On January 12, Clinton
was in the Ukrainian capital, Kiev, where he urged the dismantling of all
nuclear warheads on Ukrainian soil. On the following day, in Moscow, he
and Yeltsin discussed this with the Ukrainian leaders. After two days of
talks, a tripartite agreement was reached: Ukraine would dismantle the
nuclear weapons which it had inherited from the Soviet Union, and would
sign a Non-Proliferation Treaty (which it did at the end of the year). At
the same time, the last Russian troops prepared to leave Germany. It was
fifty years since they had crossed on to German soil, and fought their way
to Berlin. What many Western observers assumed was a permanent fact of
geo-political life, a Russian military presence on German soil, came to an
end. The last Russian troops left on August 31. A week later the last of the
British, French and American troops who had been stationed in Berlin since
1945 likewise departed.

The disarmament agreed upon in the START strategic arms reduction
treaty signed by Bush and Gorbachev three years earlier was proceeding on
both sides of the former divide. For the United States this included the
physical dismantling – by means of metal guillotines that sheered off tails
and wings – of the B-52 bombers that had once carried out carpet bombing
over North Vietnam, and had twice been used to strike at Saddam Hussein's
warmaking capacity. Of the 744 that had been built, 350 were being
destroyed at the Davis Monthan air force base just outside Tuscon, Arizona.
Giles Whittell, who witnessed this process of disarmament, wrote:

Davis Monthan is an otherworldly place, especially at night. Bigger than the whole of downtown Tucson, it is silent and unlit. The tailplanes of thousands of mothballed fighters, bombers and military transports form long lines of black notches against the moon. B-52s awaiting the guillotine, three miles of them, are drawn up behind a tall barbed-wire fence along the entire east side of the base. These aircraft have been described as looking like pterodactyls. They do have a brooding reptilian quality, but in truth they look more like nuclear bombers. Their nocturnal silhouettes are downright scary.

When the slicing up begins, at 7 a.m. most Tuesdays and Thursdays, it seems somehow excessive. Each aircraft has already been gutted of hundreds of miles of wiring, fuel lines and hydraulics. In most cases the eight oddly puny-looking engines have been unbolted from their paired pods and the dials and gauges have been removed from the cockpits, some to be resold in Beverly Hills at $500 a throw.

A $500,000 crane has been designed and built in Japan to drop the massive hardened steel blade on the back of the fuselage first, chopping off the tail. Then it squeaks on its tracks to each wing in turn. As the second wing is severed the cigar-shaped body rolls on its side with a death rattle of rending metal.

The destruction of the bomber was almost over. In Giles Whittell's words: 'A bulldozer pushes the pieces into a neat heap in which humbled form what was once the pride of the United States' Strategic Air Command will wait ninety days before being sold as scrap at sixteen cents a pound.'

North Korea, under its President Kim Il Sung, had retained the Communist ideology structure. It had also begun to develop a nuclear programme. The main nuclear research facility was the radiochemical laboratory at Yongbyon, a hundred miles north of the capital, Pyongyang. A seven-member United Nations inspection team which visited the site in March was prevented from taking samples. On June 15, after United Nations inspectors were refused permission to return to Yongbyon, President Clinton proposed an arms embargo, and sanctions. A week later, Kim Il Sung agreed to halt his nuclear weapons programme.

On July 8 Kim Il Sung died. He was eighty-two years old, a Communist Party member since 1930, and the leader of the Korean People's Revolutionary Army against the Japanese occupation in the late 1930s and throughout the Second World War. He had ruled North Korea since 1948. 'His rule was personal, dictatorial and absolute,' commented the *Annual Register* in its obituary section. 'To the mass of his people he assumed the likeness of a god. So intense was the cult of personality that 50,000 statues of himself were believed to have been set up for his worship; no dissidence was tolerated, no contact with the outside world permitted for the masses.'

Kim Il Sung was succeeded by his son Kim Jong Il, although, as was natural in such a closed society, no official announcement to that effect was made.

Having returned to the United States from Ukraine, on February 3 Clinton announced that the American economic embargo on Vietnam, which had been in place for nineteen years, was ended. He also authorized the withdrawal of American troops from Somalia, where they had been in violent conflict with the forces loyal to General Aydid. The work of peacekeeping and supervising the distribution of humanitarian aid devolved upon 20,000 United Nations troops from other countries. On March 25, Egyptian troops took over from the Americans at Mogadishu airport, as the last of the Americans returned home.

United Nations troops were also called in that month to Israel, after a Jewish fanatic opened fire on Palestinian Arabs praying in the main mosque in Hebron – in which was located the tomb of Abraham, holy to Jews and Muslims alike – and killed twenty-nine Muslim worshippers. But the killings did not halt the continuing negotiations for Palestinian self-rule, which took place in secret in Bucharest and Cairo, with Shimon Peres, Israel's Foreign Minister, as its chief negotiator. When Rabin and Arafat met in Cairo on May 3, it was to finalize an agreement that built substantially on what had earlier been agreed in Oslo and Washington. Signing was planned for May 4. The world's press gathered to witness the historic occasion. But at the very last minute, well after midnight of May 3, Arafat continued to demand tiny territorial changes to the detailed maps that had been drawn up, and previously agreed upon by his officials after many hours of discussion (there were six detailed maps in all). At one point President Mubarak, who was to preside over the public ceremony, saw Rabin privately to ask him to agree to give Arafat a small area on the Gaza coast that Israel wanted to retain for security reasons, as it was close to some of the Jewish settlements in the Strip. Rabin agreed.

The signing ceremony on May 4 was shown live on television throughout the world. It was Mubarak's sixty-sixth birthday. As the signing ceremony went ahead, millions of television viewers saw Rabin, as he was about to sign the pile of documents that constituted the agreement, stop and go over to the other dignitaries – including Mubarak and the American Secretary of State, Warren Christopher – and point out to them that Arafat had not signed the maps of the Jericho area autonomy. The assembled dignitaries took it in turns to try to persuade Arafat to sign. He would not do so. Rabin remained impassive, his arms crossed, his expression dour. The leaders then left the carefully prepared stage and argued the matter out away from the cameras. Mubarak was said to have used stern language in insisting that Arafat sign. The leaders then returned to the stage, and to the cameras, and Arafat appended his signature to the map.

As finally signed that day, the Cairo Agreement, later known as Oslo I, gave the Palestinian Authority, to be headed by Arafat, 'legislative, executive, and judicial powers and responsibilities', including its own armed police force, and full control over internal security, education, health and welfare. The Palestinian Authority would also be empowered to negotiate agreements with foreign powers on economic matters and regional development, and to sign agreements on cultural, educational and scientific matters. Israel would retain control of foreign affairs and defence. This gave the Palestinian Authority (known to the Palestinians as the Palestinian National Authority) even wider powers than those which the Jewish national institutions had obtained from the British between the two world wars.

By the agreement, Arafat assumed the title of 'Chairman of the Palestinian Authority'. The word used for 'Chairman' in the Arabic text was *rais*, which could equally correctly be translated as 'President', creating for him the aura of Head of State.

The Cairo Agreement was signed on May 4. A few days later, having flown to Johannesburg, Arafat spoke in a mosque of how the Palestinians would 'continue their jihad until they had liberated Jerusalem'. To speak of *jihad* – holy war – so soon after concluding an agreement aimed at peace and coexistence was a shock to the Israeli public, and to Rabin. 'Any continuance of violence and terror', Rabin warned, 'contravened the letter . . . that brought about mutual recognition, and called the entire peace process into question.' Arafat explained that by *jihad* he had meant not 'holy war' but 'sacred campaign'.

To calm the situation in Hebron, where three months earlier the Jewish gunman had massacred twenty-nine Arabs, a United Nations observer force took up position between the Jewish and Arab sections of the city on May 8. The force was known as the Temporary International Presence in Hebron (TIPH). It consisted of 160 unarmed soldiers from Norway, Denmark and Italy. A similar force, the Temporary International Presence (TIP), was despatched to Gaza. It consisted of four hundred unarmed foreign observers. Then, on May 13, only nine days after the signing of the Cairo Agreement, all Israeli troops and administrative personnel were withdrawn from Jericho. Four days later, they were withdrawn from the Gaza Strip. The Palestinian flag, which four years earlier had been hauled down by Israeli troops whenever it flew in national defiance – and those who tried to raise it being often shot, wounded and even killed – was raised over Jericho and over Gaza City. In Gaza, Palestinian self-rule extended to all the 800,000 Arab inhabitants. Excluded from Palestinian control were the sixteen Israeli settlements in Gaza, with a total population of five thousand.

On May 19, two days after the Israeli withdrawal from Gaza, Rabin met secretly in London with King Hussein to draft the outlines of a peace treaty between their two countries. Many of the details were then worked out by Israeli and Jordanian negotiators in the presence of the Jordanian Crown Prince Hassan, in the Royal Palace at Akaba, within sight of the hotels and beaches of Eilat.

On July 1 Yasser Arafat visited Gaza for the first time in twenty-seven years. Eleven days later he returned to the city to take up permanent residence there, and to serve as Chairman of the Palestinian Authority. The housing, education and social welfare of a million Palestinian Arabs, half of them refugees and the descendants of refugees from the war of 1948, had become his responsibility and that of the Authority. Money for his first projects came from the European Union, Japan and the United States. Four years later it was revealed that more than half of the sums received, amounting to hundreds of millions of dollars, never found their way to the projects for which they were designated. In the shadow of some of the worst slums of the Middle East, the Gaza refugee camps, substantial villas were built for the Authority's leaders, using money intended to rehouse the refugees. When Britain and the European Union urged Arafat to audit the sums of money they were sending him, he refused. Five years later the European Union was to stop sending Arafat money until he agreed to a proper accounting and auditing system.

Palestinian Muslim fundamentalists opposed to the autonomy plan, who still spoke of the destruction of Israel and the creation of a Palestinian State from the Mediterranean Sea to the River Jordan, carried out repeated acts of terror, hoping to derail the 'peace process', both between Israel and the Palestinian Authority, and between Israel and Jordan. On July 18 a hundred people, most of them Jews, were killed when Iranian-supported Muslim militants exploded a massive bomb at the Jewish community centre in Buenos Aires. Neither side allowed these acts of terror to derail the peace process. On July 20, Peres flew from Jerusalem to the Dead Sea Spa Hotel, on the Jordanian side of the Dead Sea, where he negotiated with the Jordanians a plan to develop the two countries' water resources, as well as to join their electricity grids. The helicopter flight from Jerusalem to the Jordanian side of the Dead Sea 'took only fifteen minutes', Peres later wrote, 'but it crossed a gulf of forty-six years of hatred and war'. Four days later Rabin and King Hussein flew to Washington, where on the following day, July 25, they signed a declaration ending the state of war between their two countries. One result of that long war had been Jordan's loss of East Jerusalem and the West Bank in 1967.

The imperative of peace appeared to be as powerful as once the imperative of war had been. When, on July 26, fourteen people were injured by a car bomb which caused extensive damage to the Israeli Embassy in London, it was not allowed by either side to affect the momentum of the negotiations. As a gesture of confidence that these negotiations would soon be satisfactorily concluded, on August 3 King Hussein flew at the controls of his royal jet over the city of Jerusalem, circling the golden Dome of the Rock which had recently been gilded as a result of his own munificence. It was the first time that a Jordanian aircraft had flown through Israeli airspace except in war. Jerusalemites looked up in wonderment at the scene, as the King talked over his aircraft radio to Rabin, who was in his office. Five days later, on August 8, the first border crossing was opened between Israel and Jordan, in the Arava valley just north of Eilat and Akaba, for their respective citizens.

The pace of change in the Middle East was rapid; the dangers formidable. On October 14, Rabin, Peres and Arafat were awarded the Nobel Peace Prize as the 'architects' of the Israeli-Palestinian accords. On October 19, twenty-two Israelis were killed when a Muslim suicide bomber blew up a bus near Tel Aviv. Five days later, President Clinton – the ninth American President to involve himself in the Arab-Israel conflict – embarked on what he called 'a mission inspired by a dream of peace'. After a visit to the tomb of President Sadat near Cairo, he held talks in Cairo with Mubarak and Arafat, and then flew to Akaba for the signing of the Israel-Jordan Treaty of Peace.

The Israel-Jordan peace treaty, signed on October 26, ended the nominal state of war along Israel's longest borders. Under the treaty Israel returned to Jordan several strips of land in the Arava valley and just south of the Sea of Galilee. It was a time 'to make the desert bloom', Rabin told the assembled well-wishers headed by President Clinton. King Hussein pledged that the peace between Israel and Jordan would be a 'warm peace' that would enhance the quality of life in both countries. Israelis had long complained that the peace with Egypt was no more than a 'cold peace'.

Three days after the signing of the Israel-Jordan peace treaty, more than two thousand Israeli, Arab, American and European political and business leaders met in Casablanca, at an economic summit hosted by King Hassan of Morocco. It marked a historic widening of the dialogue between Israel and the Arab States, and the start of what was intended to be economic co-operation and joint ventures throughout the Middle East and the Mediterranean. Opening the conference, King Hassan declared: 'We must prove that the Mediterranean can become a region of solidarity and equilibrium, a true Sea of Galilee, around which the three religions and the sons of Abraham, united by historical bonds, will be able to build a magnificent bridge for the century to come.'

The hopes of the Casablanca Conference were real, and were reiterated a year later in Amman. But it could take many years before they are realized. Meanwhile, attempts by Muslim extremists to derail the Israel-Palestinian agreements were continuous. Within Gaza, Islamic fundamentalists battled with the new Palestinian police under Arafat's command. On November 18, fourteen people were killed and two hundred injured in one such clash.

In Bosnia, the Serb struggle for control continued despite the Geneva talks and peace plans. On February 5, sixty-eight people were killed when a mortar bomb exploded in the market place in Sarajevo. Four days later, at their second summit meeting in Brussels in a month, the NATO governments discussed possible military intervention in Bosnia. In combative mood, they issued an ultimatum to the Serbs to withdraw their heavy weapons from around Sarajevo, or to face NATO air strikes on their positions around the city.

In Sarajevo, the British commander of the United Nations forces, General Sir Michael Rose, negotiated a ceasefire on February 9 between the local Muslims and Serbs, in the hope that daily life could continue in the city without the terrible dangers of mortar attack. Two days later the Bosnian Serbs handed over a proportion of their heavy guns. In an attempt to persuade Russia to take an initiative with its fellow Slavs, John Major flew to Moscow to see Yeltsin. Two days later, following Yeltsin's positive response, the Serbs began to withdraw the rest of their heavy artillery.

On February 28, four Serb warplanes penetrated the limits of a NATO no-fly zone established to protect the Bosnian Muslims. All four were intercepted and shot down. It was the first offensive action in the forty-five years of NATO's existence.

In the Muslim enclave of Maglaj, in northern Bosnia, the Bosnian Serbs had imposed a state of siege. On March 13, United Nations observers managed to enter the enclave. They found 20,000 people on the verge of starvation. Considerable efforts were being made by the United Nations to improve the pattern of daily life for those under attack. On March 17 they secured an agreement whereby Bosnian Muslims and Serbs undertook to allow civilians free movement in and out of Sarajevo for the first time in two years. At the same time, Bosnian Muslims and Croats were negotiating in Washington to create a Muslim-Croat federation: this was agreed on March 18, the day on which the British Prime Minister, John Major, visited Sarajevo. The prospect of a return to normal life was emerging. On March 20 more than 20,000 people watched a football match in Sarajevo stadium, one of the buildings which, until the NATO intervention two months earlier, had been subjected to regular Serb mortar fire.

The United Nations had designated the Muslim enclaves in the predominantly Serbian areas of Bosnia as 'safe areas', and had warned the Bosnian Serbs not to attack them. When the safe haven of Goražde was besieged, and no food or medical aid convoys allowed into it, despite renewed United Nations and NATO warnings, NATO planes attacked the Serbian forces surrounding the town. On the following day, as the siege continued, there were further air strikes. NATO was acting as the military arm of the United Nations. But Bosnian Serb nationalism was not easily deterred, and on April 17 neither the United Nations nor NATO were able to prevent Serb tanks from penetrating to the very centre of Goražde.

On April 22, NATO issued an ultimatum to the Bosnian Serbs to withdraw from Goražde. Two days later, as a convoy of United Nations peacekeepers reached the city, the Serbs withdrew. They were not prepared to engage in combat with the United Nations.

An attempt to reach a political solution despite Bosnian Serb attacks reached fruition on June 22, when two parliaments met in Sarajevo and agreed to merge. One was the parliament of the predominantly Muslim Bosnian Republic, and the other was the parliament of the Muslim-Croat Federation, established the previous month. Both this combined Bosnian authority, and the Bosnian Serb legislature in Pale, rejected the Geneva proposals for the partition of Bosnia into three ethnic republics. All communities were determined to secure more territory for themselves than the Geneva plan envisaged, or to take control of the whole of Bosnia.

The Bosnian Serbs felt that they could still overwhelm the Sarajevo administration and those dependent upon it. At the beginning of August they began once more to deploy heavy weapons around Muslim-held enclaves. NATO took immediate action, attacking the heavy-weapon concentrations. The volatility of the situation in Sarajevo remained such, however, that the visit of Pope John Paul II to celebrate Mass there in September had to be cancelled. Two months later, on November 21, NATO carried out its heaviest bombing raid yet, when thirty-nine warplanes attacked a Serb-held airfield in Croatia which was being used by the Serbs to attack the United Nations 'safe area' of Bihać.

Inside Russia, Yeltsin ruled as President with a hostile parliament critical of his every move. The Cabinet announced by the Prime Minister, Viktor Chernomyrdin, on January 20 was made up mainly of conservatives. Several Yeltsin reformers refused to serve in it. A month later, on February 23, the parliament voted overwhelmingly in favour of two amnesties, one for those who were under arrest for their part in the pro-Communist hard-line coup against Gorbachev in August 1991, and the other for those who had taken part in the rebellion against Yeltsin in October 1993. The two leaders of the 1993 rebellion, Ruslan Khasbulatov – an ethnic Chechen – and Alexander Rutskoi, were released from prison three days later.

Dissidents and exiles were also being allowed to return to Russia in freedom. On May 27 Alexander Solzhenitsyn returned after twenty years of enforced exile. He found a country in turmoil, and was distressed that the open, calm pursuit of liberty which he had championed seemed still so far away. Poverty in the streets, long lines of citizens holding up a few apples or packets of cigarettes or a few items of clothing for sale, ostentatious wealth, a new class of super-rich, the often bloody clashes of private Mafia-style gangs – each belied the hopes that had been stirred by the collapse of the Soviet system and Soviet Communism. The Communist Party itself was still active, and gaining adherents. On October 28, Solzhenitsyn addressed the Russian parliament. Russia, he said, was ruled by an oligarchy, concealed by a 'sham democracy'. Privatization, the main economic goal of the Yeltsin administration, was a form of 'privateering' that ought to be punished by the law courts.

Treaty making and economic arrangements between the central government in Moscow and the regions proliferated. In February the Minister for Nationalities in Yeltsin's Cabinet, Sergei Shahkrai, concluded an agreement with the large and oil-rich Muslim autonomous republic of Tatarstan, allowing it to retain its own constitution and sovereignty 'for a long time'. The agreement gave Tatarstan the right to apply Russian federal legislation on its territory only when it chose to do so, although the federal government retained the right to determine the republic's contribution to the federal budget. Another agreement was signed in August with Bashkortostan, also a Muslim autonomous republic, in the southern Urals, which was rich in natural resources. The agreement permitted Bashkortostan to raise its own taxes and to retain its constitution, while confirming the authority of the federal government to set macro-economic policy and to regulate defence and foreign affairs.

Not only the economic but the territorial integrity of the Russian Federation had been challenged by another of the Muslim Autonomous Republics, that of Chechenya. On November 29 Yeltsin ordered all 'illegal military formations' inside Chechenya to lay down their arms. The Chechen 'President', Major-General Dzhokhar Dudayev, refused. On December 11, determined to restore the authority of Moscow over a region that was constitutionally an integral part of the Russian Federation and under Russian sovereignty, Yeltsin ordered Russian forces across the Chechenya border. The Chechens – known through history as doughty fighters – resisted. On December 14 Dudayev announced that his people would 'fight to the death'. Among those who demonstrated in support were the Chechens living in Jordan. They had been sent there, nine hundred miles away, in the days of the Ottoman Empire, two centuries earlier, to serve as a southern border force for the Turks against the Bedouin of the Arabian desert. Demonstrating outside the Russian Embassy in Amman, their placards read: 'Hands off our Chechen brothers'.

On December 19, Russian warplanes bombed the Chechen capital, Grozny. Many civilians were killed. Three days later a Russian ground offensive was launched against Grozny. A new war had begun. A call by Yeltsin that civilian targets should be avoided was ignored by the Russian commanders on the spot. By the end of the year, fifty Russian soldiers had been killed, and eight hundred Chechens. More than 200,000 Chechens fled across the borders of the neighbouring Russian Republics, or struggled through the high mountain passes across the Caucasus mountains into Georgia.

Travelling to Grozny, Sergei Kovalyov, the Human Rights Commissioner of the Russian Federation, a Yeltsin nominee, called for an end to what he described as a 'crazy massacre'. On December 23 the Russian parliament demanded a ceasefire, and the opening of negotiations. Within a few weeks, it was clear that the cost of the war would exceed the ability of the dangerously depleted Russian State budget to finance it. But Yeltsin did not want this exercise in independence within his Russian Federation's borders to succeed. He was supported in the continuation of the war by the Russian Security Council, a group of policymakers who were regarded by some Western experts as almost identical in their attitudes to the Soviet-era Politburo: secretive, hard-line and nationalistic. The leader of the largest political Party in the Russian parliament, Vladimir Zhirinovsky, was emphatic that 'Russian territorial integrity' must be preserved, no matter how high the cost. Within Chechenya, President Dudayev was able to call forth enormous reserves of national, patriotic and Muslim religious fervour. The Chechens were by tradition fighters, and would fight on.

In South Africa, as apartheid was dismantled, intercommunal violence continued. On March 28, sixty people were killed in Johannesburg when Zulu Inkatha demonstrators tried to march to the African National Congress headquarters. White extremists were also active: on April 24 they detonated a car bomb near the ANC headquarters, killing nine people.

Constitutionally, the evolution of a multi-ethnic South Africa could not be halted by violence. On April 25 the White parliament met for the last time and voted itself out of existence. This ended 342 years of White rule – British and Afrikaner – in South Africa. On the following day voting began in the first multi-racial elections ever to be held in South Africa. On April 27, while the votes were still being cast, the new constitution came into effect. Multi-racial government was henceforth a constitutional fact. When the election results were announced on May 6, the largest Party was the African National Congress, with 62.2 per cent of the vote. The National Party (predominantly White) secured 20.4 per cent, and the Zulu Inkatha 10.5 per cent.

On May 10, four days after the election results were announced, Nelson Mandela was sworn in as the first Black President of South Africa. In his speech at his inauguration he said:

Today, all of us do, by our presence here . . . confer glory and hope to newborn liberty. Out of the experience of an extraordinary human disaster that lasted too long, must be born a society of which all humanity will be proud. . . .

We, who were outlaws not so long ago, have today been given the rare privilege to be host to the nations of the world on our own soil. We thank all of our distinguished international guests for having come to take possession with the people of our country of what is, after all, a common victory for justice, for peace, for human dignity.

We have, at last, achieved our political emancipation. We pledge our-selves to liberate all our people from the continuing bondage of poverty, deprivation, suffering, gender and other discrimination.

Never, never, and never again shall it be that this beautiful land will again experience the oppression of one by another. . . .

The sun shall never set on so glorious a human achievement.

Let freedom reign. God bless Africa!

Mandela later recalled how, a few moments after he had spoken:

. . . we all lifted our eyes in awe as a spectacular array of South African jets, helicopters and troop carriers roared in perfect formation over the Union Buildings. It was not only a display of pinpoint precision and military force, but a demonstration of the military's loyalty to democracy, to a new government that had been freely and fairly elected.

Only moments before, the highest generals of the South African Defence Force and police, their chests bedecked with ribbons and medals from days gone by, saluted me and pledged their loyalty. I was not unmindful of the fact that not so many years before they would not have saluted but arrested me. Finally a chevron of Impala jets left a smoke trail of the black, red, green, blue and gold of the new South African flag.

The day was symbolized for me by the playing of our two national anthems, and the vision of whites singing *Nkosi Sikelel' iAfrika* and blacks singing *Die Stem*, the old anthem of the republic. Although that day neither group knew the lyrics of the anthem they once despised, they would soon know the words by heart.

On June 1, after a thirty-three-year absence, South Africa was readmitted to the Commonwealth. President Mandela was not the only former prisoner to become a Commonwealth Head of State: Archbishop Makarios and Jomo Kenyatta preceded him in that, having been prisoners of the British government. But Mandela was the one who had spent the longest in prison, a prisoner of the South African government of which he had become the head.

In July, President Mitterrand of France became the first Western leader to address the South African parliament since Harold Macmillan thirty-four years earlier. In July, a South African cricket team played its first match in England since 1965, at Highclere, watched by the Queen. In July, in London, the same South African cricket team beat England in the Lords Test. In August a South African sports team flew to Canada, where it participated at the Commonwealth Games, in Victoria, British Columbia. South Africa was a pariah nation no more. Visiting Washington in October, Mandela secured $700 million in United States promises of aid.

In Rwanda there were ominous signs of impending violence when, on April 6, the Presidents of both Rwanda and neighbouring Burundi were killed when the plane they were travelling in was shot down by a rocket fired from the ground. The two Presidents were returning from peace talks in Tanzania. It was almost certain that the perpetrators of the double assassination were extremists in the Rwandan Presidential Guard, members of the Hutu majority, who were opposed to peace with the Tutsi-dominated Rwandan Patriotic Front. On the day after the murders, the Rwandan Prime Minister, Agathe Uwilingiyimana, was also killed, in the Rwandan capital, Kigali, together with ten Belgian soldiers who had been detailed by the United Nations to protect her.

These Belgian soldiers were members of a 2,500-strong United Nations force sent to maintain peace in Rwanda, where two groups were in conflict: the majority 6,975,000 Hutu, of Bantu tribal groups common to most of sub-Saharan Africa; and the minority 697,500 Tutsi, the traditional rulers of Rwanda.

Civil war had erupted. On April 12 the Hutu-led government in Kigali fled as rebel Tutsi troops approached the city. As fighting intensified, Hutu attacks on Tutsi reached a fearsome pitch. Hutu human rights activists who protested against the massacres were killed by their fellow Hutu. The United Nations Security Council, fearful for the lives of its own men, voted on April 21 to withdraw all but 270 of the United Nations force from Rwanda. Two days later the International Committee of the Red Cross announced that 100,000 people had been killed in Rwanda in the previous eighteen days. Five days later the toll had doubled to 200,000.

Some of the worst massacres took place inside churches to which the Tutsi had fled for sanctuary. As the genocide continued, a quarter of a million Tutsi refugees fled across the border into Tanzania. On May 17 the Security Council unanimously voted a new resolution (918) agreeing to expand its peacekeeping forces in Rwanda by sending five thousand well-armed soldiers. On the following day the forces of the Tutsi-dominated Rwandan Patriotic Front began a sustained attack on Kigali, which it captured on May 22. Elsewhere the Hutu slaughter of Tutsi civilians continued. Since April 6, half a million Tutsi had been killed.

The international community was horrified, but powerless. At the end of June, another Security Council resolution (929) authorized immediate French 'humanitarian' intervention. The first French troops arrived at Kigali by air on the following day. On July 6 the Rwandan Patriotic Front was in control both of Kigali and of seventy-five per cent of the Rwandan countryside. Declaring itself to be the 'legitimate' government of Rwanda, it gave permission to the French troops to police and protect a refugee zone in the south. It was the turn of the Hutus to flee. By mid-July as many as 1,200,000 Hutus had fled into the French-protected zone, and a further two million into exile in Zaire. It was almost certainly the biggest refugee movement in Africa's tragic history of flight and dispossession.

On August 2, British troops flew to Rwanda to join the French peace-keeping force. At the end of August, however, the French troops withdrew. Thousands of Hutu refugees who tried to cross with them into Zaire were turned back at the border by Zairean troops, and the border closed. On November 8 the Security Council set up an International Criminal Tribunal for Rwanda, charged with prosecuting those responsible for genocide. In Kigali, the Tutsi-dominated government, encouraged to do so by the United

Nations, set about pursuing a policy of reconciliation. Moderate Hutu were given both the presidency and the premiership. One of its most effective measures was to set up military re-education centres where soldiers of the defeated Hutu army could be encouraged by 'harmonization training' to enrol in the new 'patriotic army' in which Tutsi and Hutu served together.

Even without the genocide, the life expectancy in Rwanda was no more than forty-five years for men and forty-seven years for women. A massive task faced any government there that hoped to bring about a subsistence economy and even the smallest measure of normal life, with no violent disruption.

On May 6 Queen Elizabeth II and President Mitterrand opened the Channel Tunnel, linking Britain and France, and making it possible to travel by train from London Waterloo to Paris Gare du Nord in three hours. From the French side of the tunnel, another high-speed link went to Brussels. Using the new link, it was possible to leave London by train in the morning and be in Berlin in time for dinner.

The Downing Street Declaration of the previous year had opened the way for talks between the Catholics and Protestants of Northern Ireland. The declaration had called for an end to violence in the streets. Extremists ignored the call. On June 18, while a group of Catholics were watching a televised World Cup match in a bar, Ulster Volunteer Force gunmen burst in, killing six of the viewers. But John Major persevered in trying to obtain an end to the violence, in which 3,168 people had died during the previous twenty-five years. His efforts were successful: on August 31 the IRA announced that a ceasefire would come into effect that midnight, both in Northern Ireland and on the British mainland.

The ceasefire held, and on September 15, in a dramatic departure from current policy, John Major lifted the ban on broadcasting by Sinn Fein members. Suddenly the voice of Gerry Adams, hitherto transmitted on television and radio through an actor, became a daily feature of the political debate. Major also announced that there would be a referendum on Northern Ireland on the constitutional future of the province. Winston Churchill's advice to Sinn Fein in 1922, 'Quit killing and start talking,' was finally being heeded. On October 13 the three main Protestant paramilitary organizations in Northern Ireland likewise declared a ceasefire.

John Major built rapidly on the new developments. On October 21 he lifted the exclusion orders banning the Sinn Fein leaders from entering mainland Britain. At the same time he announced the reopening of all border crossings between North and South, and offered to start talks between the British government and Sinn Fein by Christmas if they would confirm that the ceasefire was intended to be permanent. The talks began in Belfast on December 7.

In both the Middle East and Northern Ireland there were hopes of ending the spiral of violence. Such hopes seemed more remote in Sri Lanka, where, on October 24, fifty-seven people were killed in a bomb attack. Among the dead was the opposition presidential candidate, Gamini Dissanayake. On November 9 Chandrika Bandaranaike Kumaratunga was elected President, Sri Lanka's first woman Head of State. She set as her goal the restoration of civic calm, and the resolution of the ethnic conflict that had divided the country and taken tens of thousands of lives. She was no stranger to political violence. Her father, a former Prime Minister, Solomon Bandaranaike, had been assassinated in 1959 – by a Buddhist monk – when she was a teenager. Her husband, also a former Prime Minister, had been assassinated in 1988.

From the first days of her presidency, Mrs Kumaratunga opened negotiations with the Tamils, and sent a negotiating team to Jaffna. As in Northern Ireland and the Middle East, the year ended with hopes that the peace process would produce what was spoken of as a 'peace dividend'.

A remarkable achievement in 1994 was that of the United Nations World Food Programme. During the year it helped to feed twenty-five million people, more than half of them women and children. The two main categories of food distribution were to refugees who had fled beyond their national borders, and those who had been displaced – whether by famine or civil war – within their country. Finding countries to allocate the money to pay for this massive amount of aid was becoming increasingly difficult. Only three countries of the sixty wealthiest member States had paid their dues in full: Canada, Australia and Sweden. The United States, which provided a quarter of the United Nations budget, was in arrears by almost $500 million. Russia, whose own budget was in dire peril, and whose contribution was just under seven per cent of the total, had completely defaulted, owing more than $500 million.

Among the United Nations peacekeeping missions active that year were those in Angola, Mozambique, Rwanda, Somalia, South Africa, Western

Sahara, the Aouzou Strip between Chad and Libya, Guatemala, Haiti, Cyprus, the former Yugoslavia, Iraq and Hebron.

On December 15 the United Nations admitted its 185th member. This was the Republic of Palau, the last remaining United Nations Trust Territory in the western Pacific. Also spelled Pelew and Belau, this small island group, consisting of only five small inhabited islands, had been through a chequered history. Becoming part of the Spanish Empire in 1886, they were sold by Spain to Germany in 1899, after the Spanish defeat in the war with the United States. In 1914 the Japanese army conquered the islands from the Germans, and in 1920 the League of Nations gave the islands to Japan as a Japanese Mandate. After fierce fighting in 1944 – the battle for Peleliu and Angaur islands was particularly ferocious – they were captured by the United States. In 1947 the Security Council transferred them to the United States as a United Nations Trust Territory.

The Palau archipelago has an area of little more than 300 square miles and a population of 15,000. A Compact of Free Association, signed on October 1, placed the responsibility for its defence on the United States, for fifty years. It also provided for substantial American financial support. A principal source of independent revenue is the sale of fishing licences to foreign fleets fishing for tuna. Another source of revenue is tourism: more tourists arrive each year than there are citizens.[1]

As in previous years, a maritime disaster had the power to shock even the most cynical. On September 28 more than nine hundred passengers died when the ferry *Estonia* sank in the Baltic Sea. There were only 140 survivors.

On August 26 retrospective compensation was made by the United States to the families of two British officers who were killed in error in northern Iraq that April, when American fighters mistook two United Nations helicopters for Iraqi aircraft, and shot them down. The families of nine British soldiers who had been killed in error during the Gulf War three years earlier were still awaiting compensation.

---

[1] Even a small Pacific island group could create historic waves in the Western world. The year of Palau's independence was also the fiftieth anniversary of the Pacific battles of 1944. The United States Post Office issued a set of commemorative stamps. Other Pacific islands where battles had been fought were commemorated, but not Peleliu or Angaur. Marines who had fought there, where a thousand American soldiers were killed in action (as were more than 10,000 Japanese) protested to President Clinton, but it was too late to alter the stamps.

The value and fragility of human life was nowhere more cruelly exposed than in post-Communist Russia. As a result of an upsurge in crime, a widening gap in incomes between the 'new Russian' rich and the mass of the people, and a substantial increase in the consumption of vodka, life expectancy for men in the former Soviet Union had fallen between 1990 and 1994 by more than eight years. This was the most precipitate recorded fall of the century. Life expectancy for women had fallen by four years. The population itself was falling. Russia's population declined by more than four million in the five years from 1992, to 150 million in 1998, the year in which the population of the United States, with its continuing immigration, exceeded 265 million.

CHAPTER FORTY-FOUR

1995

Another dark day. . . .

MISHA GLENNY

THE EUROPEAN UNION was expanding. On 1 January 1995, Sweden, Finland and Austria were admitted, bringing the total of member States to fifteen. The peace of Western and Central Europe, so violently shattered fifty years earlier, seemed assured. Europe was protecting itself against the national, ethnic and racial conflicts that continued to rage elsewhere. Even in Northern Ireland, efforts were being made by the British and Irish Prime Ministers, John Major and John Bruton, to reach agreement on the voluntary disarming of the IRA and the entry of Sinn Fein into the negotiations on the constitutional future of Northern Ireland. On November 28, on reaching agreement with Bruton on an international body to advise on the decommissioning of arms, John Major said: 'Everyone will need courage to take risks in the search for peace, and I hope they will be prepared to do so.'

Among those who were willing to become involved in the Irish question was President Clinton. Prevented by Republican majorities in both Houses of Congress from pursuing much of his social legislation, he was willing, and constitutionally free, to make considerable efforts as a peacemaker overseas. First Ireland, and then both Bosnia and the Middle East, were to be the beneficiaries of his endeavours. On November 30 he spent the day travelling around Northern Ireland, in support of the Major-Bruton peace initiative. At a metal factory in Belfast he was greeted with a tumultuous ovation by the non-sectarian workforce, and by a Protestant boy and a Catholic girl who held hands to introduce him. Visibly moved, Clinton said that the ceasefire announced fifteen months earlier marked a turning point: 'Now is the time to sustain that momentum and lock in the gains of peace.' The vast majority of Protestants and Catholics wanted, he recognized, to make permanent peace, but there were still a few who would 'never escape the dead-end street of violence'. The people of Northern Ireland 'must not allow the ship of peace to sink on the rocks of old habits and hard grudges'. As long as they pursued peace, 'America will proudly stand with you.'

Beyond Europe, risks for peace were less in evidence than zeal for war. Throughout the first week of January, Russian forces in the Autonomous Republic of Chechenya – an integral part of the Russian Federation – fought to capture Grozny, subjecting the Chechen capital to a harsh daily artillery barrage. In the Chechen town of Chali, thirty people were killed when Russian planes, in bombing the town centre, hit the hospital. At the end of the first week of renewed fighting, President Yeltsin met Sergei Kovalyov, the Human Rights Commissioner of the Russian Federation, who had just returned from Chechenya. When Kovalyov urged Yeltsin to call off the attacks and stop the war, the President, in Kovalyov's words, 'mostly kept quiet, made some isolated remarks, and objected to what I was saying'. Richard Beeston, the Moscow correspondent of *The Times* to whom Kovalyov reported Yeltsin's words, commented: 'It is widely accepted that if the armed forces fail again to take the capital in a ground offensive, as they did a week ago in a bungled assault, the leadership will be under intense pressure at home and abroad to halt the operation and resign in disgrace.'

Russian troops pressed steadily forward through the outskirts of Grozny. On January 7 the general commanding the Russian Ministry of the Interior troops in the assault, Viktor Vorobyov, was killed as he was moving his headquarters closer to the centre of the city. An official spokesman said that at the time of his death he had been 'in charge of liquidating resistance' in Grozny. He was succeeded by another senior official of the Ministry of the Interior, General Anatoli Kulikov.

As the fighting continued, and the Chechens held tenaciously to the centre of Grozny, Russian troops tried to hit Dzhokhar Dudayev's house in the mountains twenty miles south-east of Grozny, where he was known to be staying. The house was hit and destroyed, but Dudayev had left it two hours earlier. The Russian Defence Minister, Pavel Grachev, convinced that Dudayev was in the house when it was hit, announced in Moscow that he had 'information that General Dudayev had been killed or wounded'.

Russian troops were acting with a ferocity that did not always confine itself to the field of battle. In the town of Samashki, as many as 250 Chechen townsfolk were killed in a massacre that led to the dismissal of General Kulikov. On April 15, Kulikov's successor, General Yegorov, launched a ferocious artillery and infantry attack on the town of Bamut, one of the last Chechen strongholds outside the mountains. In Grozny, Yeltsin set up a pro-Russian Government of National Revival.

The Chechens made a dramatic step to advance their cause when, in June, two hundred Chechen fighters mounted a raid on Budenovsk, a Russian city of 100,000 people that lay more than sixty miles from the Chechen border. The raiders captured the town and took two thousand of its inhabitants hostage. As Russian troops counter-attacked, the Chechen raiders retreated with their hostages to the town's hospital. In the fighting, more than a hundred people were killed: Russian soldiers, Chechens, and townsfolk. After receiving authorization from President Yeltsin, who was then in Canada at the G7 economic summit, the Russians mounted two attacks on the hospital. Both attacks were beaten off, with further loss of life on both sides.

Seeking to avert further bloodshed, the Russian Prime Minister, Viktor Chernomyrdin, entered into negotiations over the telephone with the leader of the Chechen raiders, Shamil Basayev. The Russians agreed that in return for the release of the hostages they would allow the Chechens safe passage back to Chechenya. The Chechen terms included six lorries on which they could travel back, and a refrigerated lorry to transport their dead. Chernomyrdin also promised to open peace talks with the Chechen leader General Dudayev.

At the end of July, after five weeks of negotiations, agreement was reached between the Russian government and its Chechen rebel subjects; a ceasefire would come into effect that day, July 30. Russia would release its 1,325 Chechen captives; the Chechens would release the Russians they were holding; all but two brigades of Russian troops would withdraw from Chechenya; the Chechens would disarm; both sides would provide maps of their minefields so that they could be cleared away without further endangering civilians. The constitutional status of Chechenya was left unresolved; this led General Dudayev to denounce the treaty which his negotiators had signed.

Anatoli Kulikov, who since resigning from his Chechen military command had become Russian Minister of the Interior, accepted that the arrangement reached would satisfy neither side. 'This agreement will not be met with delight, either in Grozny, or in the mountains, or in Moscow,' he said. 'There are forces that are interested in the fires of war going on burning, or at least smouldering.' He was right. Two days after the ceasefire was signed, Chechen fighters carried out a series of hit-and-run attacks on Russian forces in Grozny and throughout Chechenya, and six Russian soldiers, as well as several Chechens, were killed. But on December 8 the Russian Prime Minister, Viktor Chernomyrdin, signed an agreement in Moscow with Dudayev's successor as head of the government of the Chechen Autonomous Republic, Doku Zavgayev. Under this agreement Chechenya would receive greater autonomy than that accorded to any other autonomous republic in the Russian Federation. The Chechen government would be able to open consulates and trade missions abroad, and Chechen military conscripts would not have to serve outside the Chechen borders. All separatist fighters who agreed to lay down their arms would be amnestied.

In Latvia, one of the former Soviet Republics that had broken away completely four years earlier, anti-Russian feeling had manifested itself earlier that summer, when on May 4 the Latvian government blew up the Russian radar station at Skrunda, south of Riga. This nineteen-storey early-warning station was meant, under the terms of the Latvian-Russian treaty of 1992, to remain under Russian control for another four years. But Latvia's leader, President Ulmanis, insisted that the radar station had to be destroyed. 'For Latvia,' he said, 'it has always been a symbol of war, occupation and global confrontation.'

In Afghanistan, from which Russia had withdrawn, Islamic fundamentalist Taleban rebels fought to overthrow the government of President Burhanuddin Rabbani. On November 26, three Taleban jets bombed the capital, Kabul, dropping nine bombs and killing thirty-seven people, among them a two-year-old child.

In Bosnia, fighting intensified at the beginning of April. In the Bihać enclave, Bosnian Serbs tried yet again to overrun the Muslims. In the mountains near Tuzla, Bosnian Serbs were trying to hold back an advance by Muslim government forces. The offensive was only held back because of heavy falls of snow. In Sarajevo, Bosnian Serb snipers fired on Croat Catholic church-goers; then, on April 8, they shelled the city centre, killing three civilians. Two days later, the United Nations asked NATO jets to strike at the Bosnian Serb mortar positions, and instructed its peacekeepers on the ground to give the jets details of the targets.

In London, John Major warned the Bosnian Serbs to stop firing and start negotiating. All factions, he said, must respect the ceasefire. 'The parties to the Bosnian conflict should heed this appeal,' he declared. 'They are quite literally playing with fire. If they rekindle all-out war, I do not believe that any of the participants will be able to make lasting gains.' But at the end of April the mainly Muslim Bosnian government rejected United Nations calls to continue the four-month ceasefire when it expired at midday on May 1. It hoped to regain on the battlefield land lost in battle to the Bosnian Serbs, and, at the very moment the ceasefire expired, tried to drive Serb forces back from the Bihać pocket. At the same time, two Croatian jets bombed a Serbian-held bridge in central Croatia, while Bosnian Serbs shelled the Croatian city of Dubrovnik, on the Adriatic Sea. In Sarajevo, a few hours after the ceasefire expired, Bosnian Serb snipers killed two women who were walking from the city centre to the suburbs.

During May 1, Croat forces broke through the United Nations-patrolled ceasefire lines and captured the Serb-held town of Okučani, sixty-five miles east of Zagreb. Thousands of Serbs fled the town by car, tractor and on foot, into the nearest Serb-held area of Bosnia. On May 2, in a reprisal against Zagreb, the Croat capital, Serb missiles, launched from thirty-five miles to the south, killed four people and injured more than a hundred as rockets equipped with shrapnel-spraying cluster bombs landed in the city centre. A second rocket attack on the following day killed one person and injured sixty-four.

In the last week of May, the Bosnian Serbs embarked upon a tactic of seizing United Nations peacekeepers and unarmed military observers, and using them as 'human shields' for their military convoys. More than a hundred had been taken hostage at the Weapons Collection Points (WCPs) set up by the United Nations during the ceasefire. French and Ukrainian troops formed the largest two groups of seized men. Six United Nations observers had been taken to the Bosnian Serb capital of Pale, to locations which the Bosnian Serbs knew might be the targets of NATO jets, among them a strategic bridge and the radio station. Some of these men, including those at the bridge, were chained to the potential NATO targets. After strong United Nations protests, the Bosnian Serb commander agreed that the chaining would stop.

The United Nations announced that it might have to withdraw its whole peacemaking force, 40,000 men in all, from eighteen countries.[1] But the seizures continued. On May 29, at different strategic locations around

---

[1] Principally France (3,835), Britain (3,565), Pakistan (2,978), Malaysia (1,534), Netherlands (1,523), Turkey (1,474), Spain (1,464), Bangladesh (1,239), Sweden (1,015), Canada (631), Norway (712), Ukraine (609) and Russia (507). Smaller contingents had been provided by Belgium, Denmark, Egypt, Jordan and New Zealand.

Sarajevo, Bosnian Serbs seized seventy-six French, forty-five Canadian and twenty-five Russian troops. Thirty-four British soldiers were among those taken captive. In all, 372 United Nations personnel were being held hostage by the end of May. In Britain, John Major responded by sending a further 6,700 British troops to Bosnia, to protect the troops already there. 'I sent out troops to Bosnia,' he said on May 30, 'and I intend to do everything in my power to ensure that our soldiers are released unharmed.' Major was supported in his strong stance by the leader of the opposition, Tony Blair, who stated emphatically that 'there is no question of us putting forward the notion of withdrawal in response to the taking of hostages. If anything, it should lead us to an even tougher enforcement of the United Nations mandate.'

On British and French initiative a Rapid Reaction Force was set up, of troops who could be moved wherever they were needed on the Bosnian battlefield. This strong stance was effective. On June 2 the Bosnian Serbs released 126 United Nations hostages, and promised to release the others within a matter of days. But there was distress among the Allies on the day of the releases, when it was announced that an American jet fighter on a reconnaissance patrol had been shot down in Serb-held north-west Bosnia, near Banja Luka, by a SAM 6 missile. The pilot, Captain Scott O'Grady, was believed to have parachuted out. The American commander of the NATO forces in the area, Admiral Leighton Smith, demanded his immediate return. 'They've got him,' he said. 'I want him back.'

For six days there was no sign of O'Grady, and it was widely assumed that he was dead. Then, on June 8, in a dramatic rescue bid, two American helicopters – supported in the air above the rescue by a multinational NATO fleet of nearly forty aircraft – landed on a pine-covered hilltop where O'Grady, having managed to make radio contact, was hiding. As Bosnian Serb soldiers, alerted by the descent of the helicopters, opened fire, O'Grady was lifted off to safety.

Despite Allied elation at the rescue of O'Grady, a sense of imminent catastrophe affected all the participants in the Bosnian struggle. The Bosnian Serbs had 75,000 soldiers in the field. The Bosnian Muslim and Bosnian Croat soldiers totalled 137,000. The United Nations Protection Force (UNPROFOR) had 24,000 troops. NATO had more than 250 combat air-craft. The 'Battle for Bosnia' appeared to be on the verge of massive intensification. Such fears were not exaggerated. On July 11 Bosnian Serb forces launched an attack on Srebrenica, a town with 40,000 Muslim inhabitants that was one of the United Nations' safe havens. American and Dutch NATO bombers launched two air strikes on the advancing Serbian tanks, knocked out two tanks, but failed to halt the assault. A third air attack was called off at the request of the Dutch Minister of Defence, Joris Voorhoeve, after the four hundred lightly armed Dutch soldiers who constituted the United Nations peacekeeping force in Srebrenica received terrorist threats. As the Serb troops entered the town as many as 30,000 Muslims fled in panic, abandoning their homes. On the following day a Serb mayor was appointed, and the United Nations peacekeepers were told that they were no longer needed.

A second Muslim safe haven, Zepa, was attacked by the Bosnian Serbs on July 14. A hundred Ukrainian soldiers were the United Nations defence for 15,000 people. NATO warplanes flew overhead but took no action. The siege of Zepa continued for eight days. 'We're still holding on,' the mayor, Mehmed Hajrić, broadcast on July 22. 'We can't keep up counting the shells that are landing. Day and night. It doesn't stop at all.' From Zepa, seven thousand Muslims were taken under United Nations guard to Bosnian government-held territory. The Bosnian Serbs encouraged them to leave. But on July 24 the town was overrun, looted and set on fire.

From their earlier conquest, Srebrenica, the Bosnian Serbs had taken away four thousand Muslim men and boys. A further six thousand refugees who had been making their way from Srebrenica to the Bosnian Croat town of Tuzla were unaccounted for, as were three thousand from Zepa. The United Nations Security Council warned that nothing should be done to harm them, and repeated its condemnation of 'ethnic cleansing'. On July 22, John Major called on the international community 'to maximize the political pressure' for the release of those who had been taken away. Dutch United Nations peacekeepers, reaching Zagreb from Srebrenica on July 22, reported having seen Bosnian Serbs shooting Muslims dead in the streets of Srebrenica. One Dutch soldier said he had seen 'a truck full of corpses, apparently dead soldiers', as he was being driven out of the Srebrenica enclave. On the following day, in the town of Ljubovija, two miles from the Serbian border, details were emerging of 'ethnic cleansing' on a vast scale. A British journalist, Louise Branson, reported to the *Sunday Times*:

The stories of mass executions and the burning or burying of bodies are impossible to verify independently, but come from Serbian sources.

The prisoners, estimated to number 4,000, were separated from their families when Srebrenica fell last weekend. They were taken to the nearby town of Bratunac and were placed in three detention centres, including a football field and a school. The Red Cross and other humanitarian groups have been denied access to them.

The town of Ljubovija, two miles from Bratunac on the Serbian side of the Drina river, is awash with tales of horror about what has happened to the Muslim men. The stories are being brought back by Serbs and Bosnian Serb refugees who regularly cross a bridge to visit friends and relatives in Bratunac. They gave their accounts to my Serb translator. They were unaware I was a foreign journalist.

One woman said her husband, who is in the Bosnian Serb army, had told her of mass shootings in the stadium; she believed the number was 3,000. The motive was largely vengeance, she said, for Muslim killings of Serbs both earlier in the war and more recently. Many of the Muslim men were known personally to the Bosnian Serb soldiers, she said. She did not like the 'bad thing' that was happening but accepted it because 'they have done the same to us'.

A man in the Rocket café was equally fatalistic. He said that 'everyone is talking of lots of "Killings"' but shrugged and said: 'You know, that's the way things are around here.'

His cousin from Bratunac, he said, told him that some of the captured Muslims had their throats slit. Most were shot.

One man said he had been told by 'insiders' that the total number of detainees was 4,000. They had been held, he said, in three locations: the Bratunac football field, a school in the nearby village of Hanzari and a camp further afield in Batkovic, near Bijeljina. The sound of constant shooting from the football field, he said, was explained away as celebratory gunfire.

One woman said friends told her they had seen several buses taking bodies to a field to be burned. Others talked of mass burials.

On July 23 the United Nations peacekeepers in Bosnia decided that a priority must be the defence of Sarajevo against a renewed Bosnian Serb assault. From the Rapid Reaction Force, 1,200 British and French soldiers, with artillery and tanks, were sent to Mount Igman, overlooking the city: the same heights from which the Bosnian Serbs had earlier fired down a rain of mortar shells on the city, before being driven off by NATO jets. 'It looks as if we are going to go blow for blow,' a United Nations official commented. 'We are moving to pitched artillery battles between peacekeepers and the Serbs.'

On July 28 the Bosnian conflict took a new and violent twist when Bosnian

Croat forces, together with two heavily armed brigades of the Croatian army – ten thousand men in all – crossed the Croatian border into Bosnia, driving the Bosnian Serbs from several towns inside the Bosnian border, capturing eighty-five square miles of territory, and cutting the Bosnian Serbs off from direct road links with the town of Knin, in Croatia, and from the predominantly Serb-inhabited Krajina region of Croatia, both of which were under Bosnian Serb occupation.

While Croats attacked Serbs, and 13,000 Serbs took to the roads as refugees, the Serbs were massing their forces to try to destroy the Muslim enclave of Bihać, in which 20,000 Muslims were surrounded. Bihać held out. It was the Croat military offensive that succeeded. Despite widespread international condemnation, by August 4, more than 100,000 Croat troops were advancing into the Serb-held areas of Croatia. In Knin, hundreds of Serb civilians were killed during the Croat air and artillery bombardment. According to Mate Granić, the Croatian Foreign Minister, the aim of the offensive was to reintegrate the Krajina into Croatia 'within a week'. After two days of intense fighting, Knin had fallen to the Croats, and 150,000 Serbs were on the road, fleeing across the border into Serb-controlled areas of Bosnia. One of the first Western journalists to enter Knin in the wake of the Croat forces was Misha Glenny, who reported to *The Times*:

A woman with three fingers shot off tells how her family of seven were trundling away from their burning village on a tractor when a Croatian army unit opened fire with automatic weapons, killing three and injuring the rest.

'Now that you've come, they've cleaned up the bodies which were lying in the street until yesterday,' the woman called Dusaska said. 'The civilians were mainly shot as they made their way to the UN compound, but we know of two men at least who had their throats cut.'

Now Croatian army units sweep up and down the roads of Knin with the unmistakable swagger of military conquerors: one hand holding up the V-sign, the other clasping a bottle of beer.

Knin, which has had a majority Serb population for three centuries, will soon have but a handful of Serbs left.

Aside from a few confused old ladies picking their way through the broken glass in front of every shop, there are no civilians visible in Knin.

The head of the United Nations Mission to former Yugoslavia, Yasushi Akashi, appealed to the Serbian population not to leave Knin 'during a temporary passion'. But, as Misha Glenny wrote: 'Unfortunately this is no temporary passion. It stretches back over fifty years to the shattering memory of the Second World War. "All my grandparents and two uncles were killed by Croats," Dusaska explained. "Nobody believes them here, and we are not going to stay."'

The 'symbolic importance' of the fall of Knin could not be overestimated, Glenny wrote. 'It will at last open up Croatia's economy as the town has the key rail junction linking Zagreb with the Dalmatian coast – the goose laying the golden eggs of the tourist industry. But it also signals the end of a centuries-old community.' In acquiring this crucial link to the coast, 'Croatia will have achieved one of its main strategic aims in these dreadful wars. The Serbs of Croatia will be no more. Another dark day for Europe.'

Such sympathy for the Serbs as their fate inside Knin, and their flight from the Krajina, might have evoked was rapidly set aside when details emerged three days later of the mass murder of 2,700 mostly Muslim men and boys from Srebrenica by the Bosnian Serb forces who had driven them out of their homes. On August 10 the United Nations Security Council was shown satellite and U-2 spy plane aerial photographs of four mass graves. The American Ambassador to the United Nations, Madeleine Albright, spoke of the testimony of a sixty-three-year-old Muslim who had survived the massacre by hiding among the dead. 'Those dead were not killed in the heat of battle,' she told the Security Council. 'They were systematically slaughtered on the instructions of the Bosnian Serb leadership.' The Assistant Secretary of State, John Shattuck, who had just returned from Bosnia, reported eye-witness accounts 'of mass executions, beatings, rape and other flagrant violations of human rights'. The Security Council expressed its 'deep concern' about the missing inhabitants of Srebrenica and Zepa, and condemned the refusal of the Bosnian Serbs to allow the Red Cross unrestricted access to the area. It also warned the Croats to stop the war against the Krajina Serbs, and to allow the Serbs to return to their homes. To avoid being captured by the Bosnian Serbs and being used as human shields, the last seventy-seven British, four Norwegian and two Ukrainian soldiers left the Muslim safe area of Goražde a day before they were due to leave.

On August 28, Bosnian Serb mortar-fire on Sarajevo killed thirty-seven people in the market place, and injured a hundred. This episode, not the first or the worst of its kind, proved a catalyst for action. NATO responded both by bombing Bosnian Serb positions around the city, and by issuing an ultimatum that all Bosnian Serb heavy weapons around Sarajevo must be removed. The Bosnian Serbs wanted to defy NATO, but were told by President Milošević of Serbia that they must comply. He recognized clearly that NATO's mood was such that it would take very little more provocation, or collaboration between his Serb forces and the Bosnian Serbs, for Belgrade itself to be at risk from NATO air strikes.

The Bosnian Serbs had little option but to obey Milošević, who was in effect their master's voice. On September 20 they began to remove their heavy weapons. Elsewhere in Bosnia, the Bosnian Serbs were being driven back by Croat and Muslim forces. As the fighting intensified, the American Assistant Secretary of State, Richard Holbrooke, met the Foreign Ministers of Serbia, Croatia and Bosnia in Geneva, to work out a ceasefire, and a territorial settlement. On September 8 they reached agreement 'in principle'. Bosnia would remain a separate sovereign State, divided into two 'democratic, self-governing' entities. Forty-nine per cent of Bosnia would be the predominantly Serb areas and would be known as Republika Srpska (the Serbian Republic). Fifty-one per cent, the predominantly Muslim and Croat areas, would be called the Federation of Bosnia and Hercegovina.

The ambitions of Serbia and Croatia over Bosnia were set aside. Neither Belgrade nor Zagreb would rule the territory their armies had fought over, or had encouraged their ethnic allies to fight over. Bosnian Serbs would not be able to join Greater Serbia. Bosnian Croats would not be able to join Croatia. The sovereign independence of the divided Bosnia would be maintained. There would be a President for all Bosnia, with his capital in Sarajevo, and a Head of State for each of the two regions. The Presidency would rotate, a 'presidential triumvirate' being elected from the Serb, Muslim and Croat communities. The first President was the Muslim leader Alija Izetbegović. There would also be a Council of State for the whole of Bosnia, and two governments – with Prime Ministers, Cabinets and civil servants – one for each region.

The Geneva agreement of September 8 became the basis for negotiations which took place almost immediately, under American auspices, at Dayton, Ohio, at the Wright-Patterson Air Force Base. Talks continued there for twenty-one days, behind the sealed compound of the base. Three Presidents participated, those of Bosnia, Croatia and Serbia. A fourth President, Bill Clinton, kept a close watching brief on the negotiations, acting as a mediator whenever matters came to a serious impasse. Agreement was reached, and initialled, on November 21. In announcing it, Clinton said that it would allow the people in Bosnia to move from 'the horror of war to the promise of peace'. President Izetbegović of Bosnia, one of the signatories, was more restrained. 'To my people I say this,' he commented. 'This may not be a just peace, but it is more than a continuation of war.'

In an extraordinary development, during a NATO meeting in Brussels on November 28 at which the Russian Minister of Defence, General Pavel Grachev, was present, Russia agreed that its forces in Bosnia would henceforth be under American command, as part of a new force that was being devised. Troops from the United States, Russia, Denmark, Norway, Sweden, Estonia, Latvia, Lithuania, Turkey and Poland would all participate. On the day of the Brussels agreement, Clinton spoke on American television, and to members of both Houses of Congress, to persuade them that it was right for American troops, 20,000 in all, to be sent to Bosnia as part of the new force. 'I ask all Americans, and I ask every member of Congress, to make the choice for peace,' he said. 'In the choice between peace and war, America must choose peace.'

The agreement reached at Dayton was taken to Paris and signed there – as the Dayton Peace Treaty – on December 14. Four days later, on December 18, the first American troops reached Bosnia, three days later than scheduled because fog over Bosnia had made it impossible for their planes to land. They were to be part of a NATO-led Peace Implementation Force (IFOR) which on December 20 formally took over from the United Nations Protection Force (UNPROFOR).

The cost of the conflict in Bosnia had been high. At least 200,000 civilians had been killed. Two million people had been made homeless. This was not the region's first torment in modern times. The early years of the twentieth century had seen Bosnia in violent turmoil. The First and Second World Wars had been fought as fiercely on Bosnian soil as anywhere. The last years of the century had seen an upsurge in fighting in the same towns, the same valleys, the same villages.

The decision by President Clinton to meet the Sinn Fein President, Gerry Adams, at a St Patrick's Day reception at the White House had been resented in Britain. In an attempt to help move the Northern Irish peace process forward, and to calm the sudden British hostility, on March 18 Clinton offered to act as an 'honest broker' in trying to persuade the IRA to hand over their weapons. In John Major's plan for peace, this was an essential stage.

*   *   *

In Africa, more than half a million Tutsi had been murdered by Hutus in 1994. Tutsi revenge was not long in coming in 1995. For several months, on Rwandan soil, international aid agencies, a representative of the United Nations High Commissioner for Refugees, and eighty human rights monitors, as well as 5,500 United Nations troops, were trying to protect, feed and provide shelter for more than a quarter of a million Hutu refugees. The area in which their refugee camps were located, in the south of Rwanda, had earlier been under the protection of a French military force. The French had withdrawn, leaving soldiers from Nigeria, Ghana, Malawi, Tunisia and India, commanded by a Canadian general, Guy Tousignant. According to their mandate they had to work 'in co-operation' with the Rwandan government.

The Rwandan government decided to act. On April 18, declaring that the five refugee camps in the south were becoming a 'hotbed' for Hutu guerrillas intent on wreaking vengeance for the Tutsi massacres of Hutus the previous year, it ordered the camps to be closed. The largest was Kibeho camp, with more than 100,000 Hutu refugees. It had a small United Nations military contingent – its role limited to 'peacemaking' – including a Zambian military unit. In the second week of April the Rwandan government ordered the camp to close down, but many of the refugees refused to leave. They were frightened of what might happen to them at the hands of the Tutsi if they returned to their homes.

On the morning of April 22 soldiers of the Rwandan Patriotic Army (RPA) surrounded the camp and opened fire on refugees who were refusing to leave. A United Nations official described the start of the killing: 'Rain started and it looked like people were trying to seek shelter. A couple of shots were fired into the crowd and people started dying. Immediately afterwards there was a mass panic. Everyone ran. The massacre had started.'

Firing continued for up to an hour. Within the army cordon, RPA troops continued to shoot and kill. That afternoon, as thousands of refugees broke through the cordon and tried to flee down the hillside, Rwandan troops opened fire on them. A United Nations soldier who was forced to take refuge in a military post witnessed the scene that followed. 'The soldiers were acting like barbarians, chasing and trapping refugees who had escaped their cordon.' Many of those who were caught were bayoneted to death.

Julian Bedford, a Reuters journalist who reached Kibeho camp while the shooting was still going on, wrote an account of what he saw that was published in newspapers throughout the world. 'At least some of the refugees had their own firearms and used them,' he wrote. 'I saw one armed man shooting with a pistol at the Australian medical staff and then firing in the other direction at the RPA. Makeshift medical centres were overwhelmed by the number of casualties and each seriously wounded Hutu who was selected to be evacuated by helicopter had to be cleared by the RPA.' Bedford added that United Nations helicopters 'were unable to land at the camp until late afternoon because of the anarchy'.

'We're talking of hundreds killed and obviously hundreds wounded,' commented Patrick McCormick, of the United Nations International Children's Emergency Fund. 'Nobody has been able to make an exact count in the confusion.' Twenty-three of the seriously wounded were evacuated to Kigali, but aid officials said they were only 'a small fraction' of those who needed urgent medical attention.

A worker with the charity Médecins sans Frontières, Etienne Quétin, who was in Kibeho at the height of the massacre, told journalists on the following day: 'We saw the army shooting into the backs of people fleeing the camp, old people and women, it was indiscriminate.' A doctor working with Médecins sans Frontières added: 'Yesterday I was walking over bodies. I couldn't even get the car through.' In Paris, the Rwandan Prime Minister, Faustin Twagiramungu, described the army's actions as a 'legitimate response'.

As many as eight thousand Hutu were killed that day. That night two hundred Hutu, some of them armed, made a last stand. Most of them were killed. On the following day, April 23, Sam Kiley, the Africa correspondent of *The Times*, was an eye witness:

Children tugged at their slaughtered parents among the mass of corpses strewn around the ruins of Kibeho refugee camp in Rwanda yesterday, a day after up to 8,000 Hutu refugees were mown down by government soldiers or trampled to death in the panic.

The grim sight of an infant trying to suckle from a murdered mother greeted aid workers who entered the camp. Further torment awaited 80,000 survivors of the Kibeho tragedy as they were force-marched to the town of Butare twelve miles away. Dozens of people dropped from exhaustion on the road, since most had been without shade, food or water for five days.

Sam Kiley added: 'Last night roads around the camp were clogged with dead and dying who lay in thick mud amid the burned remains of their plastic sheeting huts, while babies abandoned or orphaned in the panic crawled helplessly for shelter.'

The ten thousand Hutu survivors of the Kibeho massacre who were marched to the town of Butare were subjected to a horrendous fate. Eve-Ann Prentice, the diplomatic correspondent of *The Times*, wrote on April 25 of how they were 'stoned or hacked with machetes by civilians' as they were being marched to a stadium in Butare where, a year earlier, thousands of Tutsi had been massacred by Hutu.

The Rwandan government insisted that it had to track down the last thousand Hutu still in Kibeho camp. International opinion was divided. While France condemned the camp massacre, the United Nations commander, General Tousignant, spoke of a 'regrettable incident', and the British Minister for Overseas Development, Baroness Chalker, whose Ministry was a leading donor of aid to Rwanda, declared, in line with the Rwandan government's position: 'These camps are full of Hutu extremists with weaponry who were breaking out at night, terrorizing the villages where people have resettled.'

On March 20 a Turkish force of 35,000 men, supported by tanks, artillery and aircraft, advanced across the northern border of Iraq into the area where four years earlier Britain and the United States had established safe havens for the Kurds fleeing from Saddam Hussein's attacks. The objective of the Turkish advance into northern Iraq was to seek out members of the Kurdistan Workers' Party (PKK) who had been carrying out attacks on Turkish army installations inside Turkey, where tens of thousands of Kurds lived, and were seeking greater autonomy.

An attack on Iraq was technically a breach of Iraqi sovereignty; crossing the border in force could be regarded as an act of war. But the Turkish Prime Minister, Tansu Ciller, insisted that the aim of the operation was not to impinge on Iraqi sovereignty in any way, but to 'rip out the roots of the terror operations'. After Mrs Ciller had assured the United States that Turkey had no territorial designs on Iraq, Washington gave its tacit approval for the operation, having long regarded the Marxist-Leninist PKK as a terrorist organization. Russia also raised no objection to the operation, accepting Turkey's assurance that this was a 'one-off action'. On behalf of the European Union the French Foreign Minister, Alain Juppé, reiterated the American view that the PKK was a 'terrorist group' that should not be allowed to have its way, though he did rebuke Turkey for 'violating' Iraqi sovereignty.

After two days of battle, Turkish troops had killed two hundred Kurds. Eight Turkish soldiers were killed. A PKK base at the eastern town of Bote was repeatedly bombed by Turkish fighter bombers, and destroyed. The United Nations High Commissioner for Refugees appealed to the Turks to discriminate between the PKK fighters and the many civilians in the area.

Further east, Islamic militants were seeking to undermine the government of Tajikistan, once a Soviet Central Asian Republic, and for almost four years an independent State associated with the Commonwealth of Independent States. The rebels, having been defeated in their main attempt to seize power shortly after Tajikistan became independent, were based inside neighbouring Afghanistan. From time to time they crossed the border into Tajikistan, and in doing so had killed a number of Russian soldiers stationed there, members of the Russian Federal Border Guard Service.

As rebel cross-border attacks intensified, and thirty-five Russian border guards were killed, the Tajik government appealed to the Russian Federation to help. The commander of the Russian Federal Border Guard Service flew to the Black Sea resort of Sochi, where Yeltsin was on holiday, and gave him the latest details of the rebel attacks. Yeltsin responded at once, ordering Russian jets to fly across the Afghan border and attack the Tajik rebels in their base in the Afghan provincial town of Taloqan. During the attack, which took place on April 13, many houses and shops were destroyed, and a hundred people killed. It was the day of the funeral of eleven of the Russian border guards.

The final phases of nuclear disarmament were under discussion at Geneva. On April 4 Sir Michael Weston, the senior British government representative at the United Nations Conference on Disarmament, announced that Britain would scrap the hundred remaining nuclear bombs carried by the Royal Air Force within three years, nine years earlier than planned. It was already more than four years since Britain's last underground nuclear test in the Nevada Desert. Two days later, on April 6, Weston announced that Britain would give up its right to carry out those underground nuclear explosions that were permitted to check the safety and reliability of weapons systems. The right to carry out these tests 'in exceptional circumstances' had been retained by both Britain and France, which likewise agreed to give up the safety tests. 'We have now formally given up nuclear testing,' a British Foreign Office spokesman commented. 'There'll be no more dimples in the Nevada Desert.' It was almost forty-three years since Britain's first nuclear test, carried out on Monte Bello Island, off Australia, on 3 October 1952.

On August 11, on the fiftieth anniversary of the dropping of the American atom bomb on Nagasaki, Clinton announced that the United States would follow Britain's lead, and no longer carry out nuclear tests, even as provided for, as tests of safety procedures. It was known that the Pentagon had wanted to retain the right to carry out small-scale tests to monitor the 'safety and reliability' of American nuclear weapons stocks. Clinton overruled this. His decision, he said, constituted a 'permanent halt' to such tests, and would enable the world to pull back from the 'nuclear precipice'.

United Nations attempts to extend the Nuclear Non-Proliferation Treaty had run into a difficulty, however. Israel, which had never publicly acknowledged that it possessed nuclear weapons, but which was widely believed to have about two hundred, reiterated on April 6 that it could not renounce them (assuming that it had them) for as long as States such as Iran and Libya openly threatened to destroy the Jewish State. The nature of Israel's concerns was underlined three days later when Islamic extremists in the autonomous Gaza Strip detonated two suicide bombs, killing seven Israelis. One effect of the bombing was to delay yet further the fixing of the date of the withdrawal of Israeli troops from population centres in the West Bank, as agreed in the Oslo and Cairo accords. The first withdrawal had originally been scheduled to take place nine months earlier, but been moved forward to July. With terror bombings continuing, it was likely to be moved forward again.

Arafat responded to the suicide bombs by widespread arrests of members of Islamic Jihad, and by sentencing to fifteen years in prison an Islamic Jihad activist who had been found guilty by a Palestinian Authority court of recruiting child suicide bombers. 'Arafat is implementing Yitzhak Rabin's orders,' was the defiant cry of Islamic militants at the funeral of one of the suicide bombers on April 10. In response to the two bombings, which led to calls inside Israel for the peace process to be halted, Rabin declared that the process must continue. But he warned that the latest attack had 'further eroded the chances of sticking to a peace timetable' and went on to ask: 'If this is what happens when we leave Gaza, what will happen when we leave Jenin, Qalqiliya and Tulkarem?' These were three of the West Bank cities – each only a few miles from Israel's pre-1967 border – from which Israel was due to withdraw as soon as a new timetable could be devised.

On July 25 a suicide bomber, a member of Hamas, the Islamic Resistance Movement, killed himself and five Israelis on a bus in Tel Aviv. It was twenty-four hours before agreement was expected to be reached between Israeli and Palestinian negotiators discussing the timetable of the next phase of the Oslo Agreement, the withdrawal of Israeli troops from seven Palestinian cities on the West Bank. Israel suspended negotiations until after the funerals of the victims, but Rabin, determined not to allow terrorism to deflect the peace process, insisted that it must go on. Any halt in the talks, Rabin told Labour Party activists, would be 'handing victory' to the Islamic extremists. Rabin was helped in his resolve to continue the talks by Arafat, who publicly condemned 'terrorist activities': the first time he had used this phrase when describing attacks on Israelis.

On September 24 agreement was reached between Israel and the Palestine Liberation Organization whereby Palestinian self-rule, already in place in the Gaza Strip and Jericho under Yasser Arafat's leadership, would be extended to most of the West Bank, including all seven Palestinian towns. The agreement included the creation of a 12,000-strong Palestinian police force to supervise the transfer of power. The Israeli troop withdrawal was to be completed within six months, followed twenty-two days later by elections throughout the Palestinian Authority area for a Palestinian Council.

On September 28 Rabin returned to Washington and once again signed an agreement with Arafat. Known as Oslo II, it provided a timetable and a clear pattern for the extension of Palestinian self-rule to the West Bank, going far beyond the Gaza and Jericho transfers of Oslo I. In his speech Rabin referred to the problem of terrorism, urging Arafat to 'prevent terrorism from triumphing over peace'. If that were not done by the Palestinians, Rabin said, 'we will fight it by ourselves'.

Inside Israel, the opposition parties reviled Rabin for Oslo II. Outside his apartment block in Tel Aviv, opponents of the peace process called out, whenever he arrived or left, 'Traitor' and 'Murderer'. Once, when his wife Leah pulled into the driveway underneath her apartment, someone in the crowd shouted out: 'After the next election, you and your husband will hang from your heels in the town square like Mussolini and his mistress. This is what we are going to do to you. Just you wait.'

The Israeli parliament debated Oslo II on October 5 and 6. The leader of the right-wing Moledet Party, Rechavam Ze'evi, told his fellow legislators: 'This is an insane government that has decided to commit national suicide.' Ariel Sharon, the man who had masterminded the invasion of Lebanon in 1982, declared that Rabin and his government had 'collaborated with a terror organization'. When the vote was taken, Oslo II passed with a narrow margin: sixty-one to fifty-nine. After the vote the protests against the extension of Palestinian autonomy continued. The Israeli President, Ezer Weizman, who had emerged as a persistent critic, said that the agreement had been negotiated 'too quickly, and without sleep'. Weizman was critical that so important an agreement had been passed with so small a government majority.

Rabin did not allow such criticism to deter him. At the end of October he flew by helicopter to Jordan for the Amman Economic Conference, the follow-up to the Casablanca Conference of the year before. Amman, like Casablanca, was the forum at which the leaders of Arab States which had hitherto had no contact with Israel, and whose population had been repeatedly inflamed in the past against Israel, were to plan for a common future throughout the region. Several important steps forward were made. Egypt, which had only agreed to come to the conference at the last moment, announced that it was willing to negotiate a comprehensive free-trade agreement with Israel. Qatar agreed to supply Israel with natural gas, to be pumped in Israeli pipelines, within five years. Jordan announced the ending of trade barriers with Israel.

In his speech to the Amman Economic Conference, Rabin noted that, since Casablanca, Israel and its Arab neighbours had begun work on joint projects covering water, transportation, agriculture, environment and energy. Those efforts, inconceivable a few years earlier, were weaving a fabric, he said, of coexistence and co-operation, 'a fabric resistant to the pressures, scepticism and outright sabotage which attempt to disrupt and derail the peace process'.

Those pressures were continuous. At a rally in Jerusalem on October 28, at which the leader of the Likud opposition, Benjamin Netanyahu, was the main speaker, Rabin was denounced by several speakers as a traitor who was abandoning the Land of Israel. During the rally, leaflets were distributed showing Rabin dressed as a Nazi officer. A video film of the meeting was later shown, in which a woman plunged a knife into a photograph of Rabin.

Rabin indeed began to feel that, in terms of public support for the peace process, the government was losing ground. On November 4, a week after the opposition rally in Jerusalem, a mass rally was held in Tel Aviv in support of the government and the peace process. Rabin and Peres were both on the platform. The supporters of Oslo II were determined to show that they were both numerous and vociferous. It was a joyful gathering. Israel – having already left Gaza and Jericho – would be leaving the densely populated areas of the West Bank where so much blood had been shed, and so much hardship endured, in the twenty-eight-year-long occupation of Arab towns, and in violent confrontation with Arab youth.

Rabin spoke from the platform with emotion and understanding about the peace process. 'This is a course which is fraught with difficulties and pain,' he said. 'For Israel there is no path without pain. But the path of peace is preferable to the path of war.' For the sake of the families of soldiers, for their children – 'and in my case for our grandchildren' – 'I want this Government to exhaust every opening, every possibility, to promote and achieve a comprehensive peace. Even with Syria, it will be possible to make peace.'

As the rally came to an end, Rabin, although normally a shy man, joined in the singing of 'The Song of Peace', which had been composed during the Arab-Israel war of 1973:

> Let the sun rise, and give the morning light
> The purest prayer will not bring back
> He whose candle was snuffed out and was buried in the dust
> A bitter cry won't wake him, won't bring him back
> Nobody will return us from the dead dark pit
> Here, neither the victory cheers nor songs of prayer will help
> So sing only a song for peace
> Do not whisper a prayer
> Better sing a song for peace
> With a great shout.

The song over, Rabin left the platform and went to his car. As he did so, an assassin rushed up behind him and shot him in the back.

The man who murdered Rabin was an Israeli and a Jew: a twenty-seven-year-old religious law student who was implacably opposed to Palestinian self-rule. 'I acted alone on God's orders,' he said after his arrest, 'and I have no regrets.' Rabin was seventy-three years old when he was killed. He was succeeded as Prime Minister by the seventy-two-year-old Shimon Peres. The two men, once bitter political rivals, had become partners in the search for a negotiated peace with the former Palestinian, and PLO, enemy. Peres continued the quest, but the shock of Rabin's assassination divided Israeli society. Some argued that to allow the extemists on either side – Jew or Arab – to dictate policy was the road to despair. Others expressed the view that Rabin had been pushing ahead too quickly with the peace process. The Likud opposition, headed by Benjamin Netanyahu, argued that the agreements with the Palestinians gave away too much without adequate guarantees of security for Israel's citizens against future terrorist attacks.

Rabin had been willing to risk the continuation of some terrorist attacks by Muslim extremists in the belief that Arafat and the Palestinian Authority would become responsible partners for Israel, would fight against terror, and embark upon a process of joint economic enterprise, where acts of goodwill could be answered by goodwill. It was something only time could show. Peres was determined to continue on the path of reconciliation, and to honour the agreements Rabin had signed. On November 12, Israeli forces left the West Bank city of Jenin, which came immediately under the rule of the Palestinian Authority. A week later Arafat entered the city – in an Egyptian helicopter – and declared it 'free'. Speaking about the Islamic extremists among the Palestinians who opposed the agreement, and who still pledged themselves to violence in the course of disrupting it, Arafat declared that they had failed. 'My brothers,' he said, 'this is the peace movement in the land of prophecy, and so we should put our hands together in order to build the Palestinian State.'

On December 3 the Israelis began to withdraw their troops from Bethlehem. The seven Palestinian policemen who then entered the town marked the start of the rule of Arafat's Palestinian Authority. Christmas 1995 would be celebrated under the Palestinian flag.

Amid the break-up of nations, and the emergence of others, one country retained its unity despite secessionist pressures. Canada had already faced a referendum in 1980 with regard to the demand of French-speaking Quebec for separation and independence. In November 1995 a second referendum was held. Just as a former Prime Minister, Pierre Trudeau, had fought valiantly and successfully to maintain the unity of Canada, so his successor in 1995, Jean Chrétien, did likewise. The vote was close, but decisive. Writing in the *New Yorker*, Murray Sayle commented (with a reference to the United States as Canada's 'smaller neighbour'):

> Canada and Canada's smaller neighbour to the south are both to be congratulated – with some reservations – on the vote the other day that barely kept the French-speaking province of Quebec from claiming separate

sovereignty and thus breaking up the Canadian federation. True, we have recently seen Chechenya, Rwanda, and Bosnia, among other places ending in 'a', fall into chaos and despair. But Canada?

Warm-hearted, stable, fair to its many minorities, staunch in the cause of justice and democracy, Canada is one of the world's most highly respected countries. As its Prime Minister, Jean Chrétien, told a Montreal rally just before the vote, non-Canadians cannot understand why anyone would want to leave it. Yet a large majority – sixty percent, by some counts – of Mr Chrétien's fellow Quebec-born Francophones voted to do just that. . . .

Murray Sayle commented that, for the 'short term' at least, 'a disaster has been narrowly averted – a switch of a mere thirty-odd thousand votes would have sent the verdict the other way – and we can all be grateful to those who made the vital difference'. And he added:

President Clinton offered the tactful hope that America would remain partners with a stable and strong – that is, a united – Canada. President Jacques Chirac of France said carefully that France would recognize not an independent Quebec but 'the facts' – a pledge that inflamed no one.

And a million or more rest-of-Canadians rallied, sent postcards, made telephone calls, or visited Montreal in person, all delivering the same message: they wanted Quebec to stay in the family. The response from those Quebeckers who voted No was at least unambiguous: they all wanted to remain Canadians.

*

As the century drew to its close, the increase in apologies for the misdeeds of past generations was growing. On April 27, President Herzog of Germany, in a speech at the former Belsen concentration camp, said that Germany was excluding nobody from its memory of Nazi crimes: neither Jews, Gypsies, Russians, Christian activists, trade unionists, Socialists or the handicapped. Germans, he said, were 'responsible not only for what they do, but also for what they allow to happen. Whoever allows others to steal somebody's freedom will ultimately lose his own freedom.'

Two months earlier Herzog had been criticized for a speech in Dresden which made no reference to the sufferings of the Jews and other victims of Nazism during the Second World War. On that occasion, the anniversary of the Anglo-American bombing of Dresden, he had chosen to focus on the German victims of Allied bombing, and on the 'unhappy fate' of millions of Germans forced out of their homes by Soviet forces. His April speech at Belsen redressed that balance. On the day after Herzog's speech, the Polish Foreign Minister, Wladyslaw Bartoszewski, a former inmate of a German concentration camp, told German parliamentarians in Bonn, 'Millions of Jews and Poles were victims of the Hitler dictatorship,' but he went on, to the astonishment – and applause – of his Germans listeners, to apologize for the 'tragedy' of those Germans who had been forcibly expelled from the areas allocated to Poland in 1945. 'We remember that innumerable people from the German population were affected and that Poles were among the perpetrators,' he said. 'I will say this openly: we deplore the individual fates and suffering of individual Germans who were hit by the consequences of the war and who lost their homes.'

On June 1, in Vienna, the Austrian parliament approved the creation of a fund, for the first time since the end of the Second World War, for the victims of Nazism. In 1943, Austria had been declared by the Allies as Hitler's first victims. Successive post-war Austrian governments had therefore been able to ignore the fact that many Austrians were active at every level of Nazi activity, including several death-camp commanders. The vote of June 1 was a recognition that Austrians had participated in Nazi war crimes.

In Switzerland, there was criticism from some Swiss citizens when President Villiger apologized on their behalf, in the Swiss parliament, for the country's wartime treatment of Jews. In 1942 more than ten thousand Jews who had crossed into Switzerland from France, to avoid the German deportation plans, were forced by the Swiss police back into France. Most of those who were sent back had then been deported to their deaths. President Villiger's apology was unprecedented. So also was the posthumous pardon offered in November to Paul Grüninger, the Swiss police chief at St Gallen who was fined, thrown out of the police force and stripped of his pension in 1940 for having allowed three thousand Jews to enter Switzerland illegally. After the Swiss government closed the border to Jews seeking refuge, Grüninger had put a false date-of-entry stamp in their passports. The local Swiss prosecutor who had worked for Grüninger's pardon described it with understandable hyperbole as 'a conquest of history'.

The survivors of Japanese atrocities against Allied prisoners of war between 1941 and 1945 had long felt that they would never be offered a proper apology. To the surprise of the veterans, the mayors of both Hiroshima and Nagasaki made apologetic statements during their respective atom bomb commemorations in August with regard to Japanese wartime behaviour. A written apology from the Japanese Prime Minister, Tomiichi Murayama, reached John Major in advance of the fiftieth anniversary of the defeat of Japan in 1945. It expressed 'profound remorse for Japan's actions in a certain period of the past which caused such unbearable suffering and sorrow for so many people, including prisoners of war'. Such are the vagaries of diplomacy, however, that when Downing Street was asked for the full text of the letter, a spokesman said that it could not be released 'because it was in Japanese and was confidential correspondence to the Prime Minister'.

Many British war veterans continued to press for a public apology. But when John Major's successor, Tony Blair, took up the issue, he too was unable to secure one that satisfied all of the dwindling band of survivors. On August 15, however, on the fiftieth anniversary of the end of the war against Japan, Tomiichi Murayama gave a televised news conference in Tokyo, in which he used the actual Japanese word for 'apology' for the first time, with regard to Japan having pursued a 'mistaken national policy, and through its colonial rule and aggression, caused terrible damage and suffering to the people of many countries'. No such mistake would be made again. 'I regret, in the spirit of humility, these irrefutable facts of history, and express once again my feelings of bitter remorse, and offer my heartfelt apology.' In his remarks, Murayama specifically mentioned the Allied prisoners of war. The only shadow cast on the apology was the unofficial but well-attended ceremony at which nine of Murayama's Cabinet Ministers were present, held later that day at the Yasukuni Shrine in Tokyo, in which were buried, and honoured, many wartime Japanese leaders who had been executed by the Allies for war crimes.

Another apology offered by Murayama was made on July 18, when he described the atrocities committed by Japan against an estimated 200,000 'sex slaves' – known euphemistically as 'comfort women' – who had been seized in Korea and elsewhere during the Second World War for the personal gratification of Japanese soldiers. Such conduct had been 'inexcusable', Murayama said. 'I offer my profound apologies to all those who, as wartime "comfort women", suffered emotional and physical wounds that can never be closed.' The Japanese public would be asked for voluntary contributions to make economic compensation.

In the former Soviet Union, the location known as Perm-36 – one of the evil centres of Stalinist tyranny and of the post-Stalin labour-camp system – whose last political prisoners had been discharged in 1987, was opened in 1995 as the Museum of the History of Political Repression and

Totalitarianism in the USSR. 'The camp has been restored with advice from former inmates, and with the help of volunteer labour by Russian and international student groups,' writes Karen Hewitt of the Institute for Slavonic Studies in Oxford. Much of the funding came from local government and from local businesses. The Governor of Perm Region, Gennadi Igumnov, was on the Board of Directors, as was Alexander Solzhenitsyn, who had recently returned to Russia after a twenty-year exile. Other local town museums, Karen Hewitt adds, 'certainly in Perm Region and, I imagine, elsewhere, have sections devoted to the Gulag, where the camps are presented as a controversial part of the local society and economy'.

Even the much feared Gulag, the region of darkness, the proof for many observers inside and outside Russia of the unchangeable nature of Communist tyranny, had become, before the century reached its end, the subject of exhibitions and inquiry, of discussion and debate.

In China, the human rights activists calling for greater democracy were under continuous pressure. At the beginning of May a group of them petitioned the government to practise political tolerance – 'a spirit with which our country is relatively unfamiliar'. Forty-five intellectuals signed the letter. Two of the signatories were leading Chinese scientists, the seventy-five-year-old Xu Liangying, who in 1957 had been sentenced with his family to twenty years' detention for campaigning for political freedom, and Wang Gangchang, one of the creators of China's nuclear weapons – an echo of the involvement of the Russian nuclear scientist Andrei Sakharov in the Soviet dissident movement. Following the letter, forty-one dissidents were arrested. Most were taken into custody until after the sixth anniversary of the Tiananmen Square uprising. Also arrested before the anniversary was Fang Zheng, who was detained and questioned for five hours. During the uprising, when he was an athletics student at Peking Sports University, he had tried to pull a friend out of the path of an advancing tank, and had lost both his legs. In September 1994 he participated at the Sixth Far Eastern and Pacific Disabled Games as China's discus champion, as well as a medallist in the shot and javelin events. He had been allowed to compete only on condition that he gave no interviews; at the last moment he was flown back to China before he could compete.

Amnesty International, in its 1995 report on China, wrote that six years after the suppression of the 1989 pro-democracy protests 'serious human rights violations continue across the country. The last year was marked by increased political repression and the adoption of new repressive legislation.'

At the end of August, China was host to the United Nations ongoing Fourth World Conference on Women. One of the main associates at the conference, the Non-Governmental Organizations' Forum for Women, headed by a woman activist from Thailand, Supatra Masdit, ended ten days of meetings on September 8 with an official protest at China's 'human rights violations'.

On September 20 the New York Academy of Sciences awarded its Human Rights of Scientists Award to two Chinese dissidents, Professor Xu Liangying and Ding Zilin. In reporting on the award to *The Times*, Jonathan Mirsky noted that Professor Xu, a leading Chinese physicist and member of the Chinese Academy of Sciences, had been detained for twenty years, starting in 1957. He was inspired during those years, he said, by a picture of Albert Einstein with the words: 'Great spirits have always encountered opposition from mediocre minds.'

In 1989 Professor Xu compared Mao Tse-tung to Hitler. He also persuaded forty-two intellectuals to sign a petition calling for democracy, the rule of law, and no further persecution of dissidents. In 1994 he and six other academics wrote to President Jiang Zemin: 'Not everyone in China is dead. There are some people who still petition for human rights.' In May 1995 he organized another letter to President Jiang, urging that China should practise political tolerance.

Professor Xu was being held under virtual house arrest, often not allowed out long enough to buy a newspaper. In a letter to the New York Academy he wrote: 'The dismal human rights record of my country is well known to the world and its improvement will depend on the continual and concerted efforts of all those who are concerned with human rights in and out of China.'

Ding Zilin, a professor at Beijing's People's University, was the mother of a young man shot dead during the Tiananmen killings. For five years she pressed the authorities to provide details of his death. She too was held under house arrest and forbidden to continue her university teaching. Despite reluctance on the part of many of the parents of others killed in 1989, she was able to gather almost a hundred names of victims. In May 1995, shortly before the June 4 anniversary of Tiananmen Square, Professor Ding published a statement signed by twenty-seven women whose children or husbands had been killed on June 4. 'Six years ago,' the statement said, 'the government used its machine to murder and wound people in the streets of Beijing.' The signatories demanded that the National People's Congress investigate the killings and issue an account to the families of the victims.

On the eve of the United Nations Fourth World Conference on Women in Beijing, Professor Ding and her husband were taken from their flat to another part of China, so that she could not make contact with the delegates. In her letter to the New York Academy of Sciences, accepting its award, she wrote that every citizen should 'have the right to choose the kind of society, political system, and individual lifestyle that is compatible with human dignity', and she added: 'These were the dreams of those who gave their lives at Tiananmen.'

Human rights abuses continued on many national landscapes. In Nigeria, the military regime of General Sani Abacha – whose theft of vast sums of money from his own exchequer led to him being dubbed 'lootocrat' – executed nine of its most outspoken public critics, including the writer Ken Saro-Wiwa. On August 11, Kim Sun-Myung, the man whom Amnesty International described as the world's longest-serving 'prisoner of conscience', was released. He was seventy-one years old. Forty-four years earlier, at the age of twenty-seven, he had been imprisoned by the government of South Korea as a North Korean agent. His release came as part of a mass amnesty to mark the fiftieth anniversary of the liberation of South Korea from Japanese rule.

On April 29 a United Nations congress on crime opened in Cairo. Government officials, police and lawyers from 120 countries were present. According to experts at the congress, the 'main fear' for millions of people in the 1990s was no longer war between nations, but 'the safety of their homes and families' from criminal activity. The congress heard that violent crime was increasing worldwide by five per cent every year. Evidence was also presented of international alliances between criminal gangs. Criminals were amassing fortunes more quickly than banks or large corporations, and moving their money from country to country 'at the speed of an electronic signal'.

'The vast amounts of cash generated by money laundering', wrote Stewart Tendler, crime correspondent of *The Times*, who reported on the congress, 'are powerful enough to influence some national economies.' In Russia, where industrial production had fallen twenty-five per cent over the previous five years, total personal income had risen by ten per cent, 'suggesting criminal and shadowy activity'.

The worst natural disaster of 1995 took place in January, when five thousand Japanese were killed after the city of Kobe had been struck by an earthquake.

In May, two thousand Russians were killed when an earthquake struck the northern tip of Sakhalin Island. In the island's main town, Neftegorsk, eighty per cent of the buildings were destroyed. The remoteness of northern Sakhalin inhibited rescue efforts: it was 4,500 miles from Moscow and a thousand miles from the Russian Far Eastern port of Vladivostok, the nearest source of adequate aid supplies.

Such natural disasters made tens of thousands of people temporarily homeless. But a heavy burden of more permanent homelessness was faced by far larger numbers of refugees. On November 16 the United Nations High Commissioner for Refugees, Sadako Ogata, announced that the UNHCR was taking care of twenty-seven million refugees worldwide: nearly three times as many as ten years earlier. Nor did she envisage that number lessening. The 'century of the refugee' that had been spoken of halfway through the century was continuing.

Forty-two years had passed since the end of the Korean War. After the unveiling of the Vietnam War Memorial in Washington by President Reagan in 1984, it was commented on by many of those present that there was no memorial in the capital to those who had fought and died in the Korean War, although more Americans (62,423) had been killed in Korea than in Vietnam (55,437). Efforts were begun to find a suitable form of memorial. It was decided to create a field in which were placed sculptures of life-size soldiers placed to look as though they were advancing. The new memorial was only a few minutes' walk from the Vietnam Memorial.

Ground had been broken on the Korean War Memorial project by President Bush on 14 June 1992. Three years later the memorial was ready. It was opened and dedicated by President Clinton on 27 July 1995. An inscription at the memorial stated: 'Our nation honors her sons and daughters who answered the call to defend a country they never knew and a people they never met.' Another inscription, engraved on a low polished black marble wall, read: 'FREEDOM IS NOT FREE'.

1996

I can still hear their screams.

A SURVIVOR

T HE APOLOGIES FOR PAST WRONGS that had become a feature of the 1990s continued in 1996. In South Africa, the Truth and Reconciliation Commission, set up to hear from all sections of the population about responsibility for the violence of the apartheid years, heard Chief Mangosuthu Buthelezi, head of the Zulu Inkatha Freedom Party – hitherto an opponent of the commission – come before it at the beginning of September and apologize to the African National Congress. As many as 15,000 Africans had been killed in the fighting between the two rival groups during the previous decade. While denying any personal role in the killings, Buthelezi told the commission, headed by Archbishop Desmond Tutu: 'I know that because we are human beings, and therefore sinners, we still hurt each other even tomorrow. I therefore apologize for past hurts.'

Past hurts could be apologized for; present hurts could only exacerbate tensions and lead to greater anguish. In Israel, where Islamic fundamentalists rejected the considerable progress being made towards Palestinian autonomy, suicide bombers killed twenty-five Israelis on February 25 and a further nineteen Israelis on March 3. Pressure on the Prime Minister, Shimon Peres, to call a halt to the peace process was immediate. The President, Ezer Weizman – a former commander of the Israeli air force – called for a halt to the talks that were taking place for the next stage of the Israeli withdrawal from the West Bank. 'We are at war,' he said, as the funerals of the bomb victims were relayed on television to a traumatized Israeli society. 'We cannot go on like this.'

On March 4 a third suicide bomb, in Tel Aviv, killed twelve people. 'The attack came on a day when children in fancy dress were enjoying the festival of Purim . . . a festival that is supposed to celebrate God's protection,' wrote Christopher Walker to *The Times*. The blast of the suicide bomb, he added, 'caused scenes of such appalling human devastation that television companies were forced to issue warnings about the content of their film coverage'. When Shimon Peres visited the scene, an angry crowd, already chanting 'Death to the Arabs,' called out to him: 'Peres, you are next.'

The cumulative effect of the suicide bombs inside Israel affected the relationship between the Israeli government and the newly established Palestinian Authority under its Chairman, Yasser Arafat. Following the suicide bomb of March 4, Peres announced that Israeli troops would act against the Muslim fundamentalist organizations, Hamas and Islamic Jihad, within the areas that had been transferred to Palestinian self-rule.

In an attempt to create an international coalition against terrorism, Peres and the Egyptian President Hosni Mubarak called a summit meeting at Sharm el-Sheikh, the town at the southern tip of Sinai that had been occupied by Israel from 1967 to 1979, and which, having once been a fortified outpost, had become a flourishing Egyptian holiday resort. The one-day meeting took place on March 13. King Hussein came from nearby Jordan. King Hassan, who had helped to broker the early contacts between Israel and the Palestinians, also came. Islamic fundamentalism within their borders was of concern to both kings. John Major represented Britain, Clinton the United States and Yeltsin Russia. Yasser Arafat, Chairman of the Palestinian Authority, also came, and joined all the participants in a condemnation of terror.

No act of Palestinian terror occurred within Israel in the two weeks after the Sharm el-Sheikh summit. But, starting on March 31, Hizbullah fundamentalists in southern Lebanon launched a series of rocket attacks on northern Israel, forcing tens of thousands of Israelis to spend their nights in air-raid shelters on the eve of the Passover holiday, celebrating the exodus from Egypt. In a retaliatory attack within the Israeli security zone in southern Lebanon, Israeli artillerymen accidentally killed two Lebanese installing a water tank and injured a three-year-old child. The government of Israel apologized.

The Hizbullah shelling continued. On April 10, Peres ordered retaliatory air strikes across Israel's northern border, including an attack on Hizbullah positions in the suburbs of Beirut. Twenty-one people were killed. Fearing an Israeli invasion of Lebanon, as in 1982, as many as 400,000 Lebanese left their homes in the south and fled northward. The Israeli attack was given a codename, Operation Grapes of Wrath. An Israeli Cabinet communiqué explained: 'If Israeli civilian facilities are hit, there will be no immunity from strikes on parallel Lebanese facilities. Israel is not limited by time, and has the patience, the fortitude and the ability to continue carrying out the required actions until Hizbullah attacks cease.' The communiqué went on to say that Israel had no intention of returning to Lebanon, as it had done in the 1982 invasion, but warned that 'Hizbullah terrorists and facilities in Lebanon, including those in Beirut, will not enjoy immunity.'

As the Israeli bombardment of Hizbullah positions continued, the building in which several hundred Lebanese civilians were sheltering from the bombardment in the village of Qana was accidentally hit, and ninety-seven Lebanese civilians were killed. Peres issued a full and immediate apology, and offered compensation. President Clinton called for an immediate ceasefire, and sent his Secretary of State, Warren Christopher, to the Middle East, to help secure it. Meanwhile, on April 18, Peres and Arafat agreed to resume talks – broken off after the three suicide bombs – on security co-operation between Israel and the Palestine Authority in tracking down Islamic fundamentalists intent on suicide bombing. On April 25 the Palestine Liberation Organization agreed to strike out of its charter all references to the destruction of Israel – 'the most important ideological change of the century', Peres called it. Elated by this fulfilment of a crucial element of the Oslo Accords, on the following day, April 26, the Israel Labour Party, of which Peres was the leader, withdrew its formal opposition to the eventual creation of an independent Palestinian State.

A ceasefire between Israel and Hizbullah came into effect on April 27 through the good offices of the United States. But, as a result of the continued attacks on its soil, there were calls within Israel for all further Israeli withdrawals on the West Bank to be halted. The Prime Minister, Shimon Peres, was determined that the peace process should continue. But on May 29 the electorate gave a different, if divided verdict. In the parliamentary elections, Peres' Labour Party obtained the largest single block of seats in the parliament. But in that same day's election for Prime Minister – a new constitutional departure – the premiership was won, though by the narrowest of margins, by the leader of the Likud opposition, Benjamin Netanyahu. The votes cast were 1,501,023 for Netanyahu, and 1,471,566 for Peres (50.4 per cent as against 49.5 per cent).

Under the constitutional changes that had been introduced as part of the direct election for Prime Minister, it fell to Netanyahu to try to form a government, even though his Likud bloc was not the parliamentary Party with the largest number of seats. He succeeded in forming a government by piecing together a coalition of right-wing and religious parties, which followed his lead in delaying the further devolution of power on the West Bank to the Palestinian Authority.

By their suicide bomb attacks of February 25 and March 3 and 4, the Islamic fundamentalists had succeeded in setting back a peace process that had begun with high hopes. Whether they could destroy that process altogether was yet to be seen. On September 4, Netanyahu and Arafat held their first ever meeting, at the Erez border crossing between Israel and the Gaza Strip. Netanyahu urged Arafat to curb the Islamic fundamentalists within the areas controlled by the Palestinian Authority. Three weeks later, after Israel had opened the exit to an ancient tunnel running alongside the Temple Mount, the Palestinian Muslim clergy declared this was endangering the foundations of the Al-Aksa mosque – which it was not – and violence flared. Arafat said nothing in public to curb the passions that opening the tunnel – itself a provocative act – had aroused. Within two days, fifty-five Jews and Arabs had been killed on the West Bank and Gaza Strip. It was the highest death toll there in thirty years. One of the dead was an Egyptian officer on the Egyptian-Israeli border, killed by a stray bullet from the Gaza Strip.

On October 1, Arafat and Netanyahu met in Washington, encouraged by President Clinton to try to reach agreement, but they failed to do so. In the event, two years after Netanyahu came to power, he agreed, at the Wye Plantation talks in the United States, under President Clinton's watchful eye and active intervention, to proceed with the territorial withdrawals agreed by his predecessors in the Oslo and Cairo agreements, and to embark within a short time on the 'final status' talks envisaged in the original Rabin-Peres agreements with Arafat. But the promise of progress broke down within a few weeks, and at the beginning of 1999 the withdrawals were suspended by Israel, and Netanyahu called for elections.

In 1996 more than 70,000 people were killed on the roads of India – on average 155 every day. In the United States, which had twenty times more vehicles than India, 43,000 people were killed on the roads that year. Civil violence, while killing far fewer people, was more likely to reach the headlines, and far more likely to pose potential danger to national stability. In Chechenya, continuing strife between the departing Russians and the imminently autonomous Chechens led to a Russian attack on Chechen hostage-takers on January 15 in which sixty people were killed. In the continuing

Sri Lankan conflict, fifty-five people were killed when Tamil extremists exploded a lorry bomb in the capital, Colombo, on January 31.

February saw further acts of civil strife. The IRA decided to end its ceasefire and begin a terrorist bomb campaign on the British mainland. Two people were killed in a bomb explosion in an underground car park in London on February 9. Nine days later an IRA bomb exploded on a bus in London, killing the man who was carrying it to its intended destination. But John Major and John Bruton continued their talks for the revival of the peace process. On May 30, elections were held in Northern Ireland for a 110-member Forum, to provide delegates to all-Party peace talks on the future of the province. At the beginning of June, a four-day official visit to Britain by the Irish President, Mary Robinson, marked a further step forward on the road to reconciliation and agreement. This was followed within a week by the opening, on June 10, at Stormont Castle, Belfast, of the all-Party talks on the future of Northern Ireland, the delegates to which had been elected through the Forum. With the approval and active goodwill of President Clinton, the talks were held under the chairmanship of a former United States Senator, George Mitchell. The IRA were excluded from them because they had refused to restore the ceasefire.

On June 15, as the talks continued, the IRA exploded a bomb in the city centre of Manchester. No one was killed, but 220 people were injured. Two weeks later an IRA mortar rocket was fired against a British army barracks in Germany, but no one was hurt. On July 8 the police fired plastic bullets at Loyalist rioters in Belfast. Two days later John Major ordered a thousand extra British soldiers to the province. Four days later an IRA bomb injured seventeen people in Enniskillen. On October 7 two IRA car bombs were exploded inside a British army barracks, injuring thirty-one soldiers.

The hopes of the Downing Street Declaration seemed dashed. But neither the British nor the Irish government was willing to give up the search for a peaceful solution. The mass of the public in Northern Ireland, and most of their leaders, aspired to nothing less.

In northern Iraq, the Kurdish safe havens which had been set up on the initiative of John Major at the end of the Gulf War had provided sanctuary for tens of thousands of Kurds fearful of the enmity of Saddam Hussein. But for more than a year, starting in the summer of 1995, Kurdish factions had been fighting each other with a ferocity that had led to the loss of three thousand lives by August 1996. The two main political groupings in contention were the Kurdistan Democratic Party (KDP), led by Massoud Barzani, and the Patriotic Union of Kurdistan (PUK), led by Jalal Talabani. 'Outside powers keen to weaken any sign of Kurdish autonomy', wrote one observer, Michael Theodoulou, 'have been quick to exploit the rivalry.' On August 22 the PUK accused the KDP of 'colluding' with the forces of Saddam Hussein. The KDP replied by accusing its rival of using heavy weapons supplied by Iran. Both accusations were immediately denied. Both were true.

A central element in the inter-Kurdish dispute was disagreement over the revenue being obtained – in effect by brigandage – from oil tankers carrying illegal refined petrol from northern Iraq into southern Turkey. The road along which the tankers drove with their illegal cargo passed through territory controlled by Barzani's Kurdistan Democratic Party, which made certain that its rival saw none of the money.

'The KDP's major grievance', wrote Michael Theodoulou, 'is that the PUK has seized control of the city of Arbil, seat of the now defunct Kurdish parliament in which the two factions had evenly shared power after elections in 1992. Since the Gulf War, the area has been protected by Allied air cover, but inter-Kurdish fighting has left a power vacuum and Iranian influence now pervades the region.'

The inter-Kurdish killings continued. The safe havens had turned in upon themselves with a vengeance. On August 31 Saddam Hussein took advantage of these divisions by sending troops and tanks across the hitherto respected border and occupying Arbil. It quickly emerged that the Iraqis had been encouraged to act by Barzani and his Kurdistan Democratic Party, in the hope of seeing its rival, the Patriotic Union of Kurdistan, driven from the city. On President Clinton's orders the United States initiated Operation Desert Strike against Iraq. 'Hussein's objectives may change,' Clinton declared on September 3:

> but his methods are always the same – violence and aggression, against the Kurds, against other ethnic minorities, against Iraq's neighbours. Our answer to that recklessness must be strong and immediate. . . . We must make it clear that reckless acts have consequences, or those acts will increase. We must reduce Iraq's ability to strike out at its neighbours and we must increase America's ability to contain Iraq over the long run.

Operation Desert Strike was carried out by two bombers – which flew from their Pacific island base of Guam – and two guided-missile ships stationed in the Gulf. Twenty-seven Cruise missiles were launched against targets in the south. Several buildings were demolished, and five people were killed. Russia, France, Spain, New Zealand and China condemned the American action. Germany, Japan and Britain supported it, with John Major making it possible for the airborne tankers that refuelled the two bombers in the air to use Diego Garcia atoll in the Indian Ocean.

The struggle between the two Kurdish factions, as a result of which America struck at Iraq, continued. But Iraq gradually extended its territorial control over the Kurdish areas, helped by faction fighting among the Kurds. In the words of John Swain and Marie Colvin, in the *Sunday Times* on September 1: 'The rivalry has saddened ordinary Kurds. At some twenty million, they are the largest group of people in the world without their own country. Yesterday's invasion by Iraq makes their dream of forging their own nation even more remote.'

Inter-Kurdish rivalry intensified: a power struggle that, by the end of 1998, had led to more than 35,000 deaths over a fourteen-year period.

In Algeria, the anger of the Islamic fundamentalists at having been denied the possibility of electoral victory continued to lead to bloodshed. On May 24 the Armed Islamic Front (the GIA) replied: 'We have slit the throats of seven monks.' Seven French Trappist monks, aged between fifty and eighty-two, had been murdered. They had been kidnapped from their monastery, at Medea, two months earlier. Candles had been lit for their release in Notre Dame in Paris by Christians, Muslims and Jews. When news of the killings reached Paris the candles were extinguished by the Archbishop of Paris, Cardinal Jean-Marie Lustiger. 'The candles represented hope for their lives,' he said. 'I wanted them to burn for ever.'

Pope John Paul II condemned the killings as 'barbaric'. In the previous four years 40,000 people had been killed in the violence in Algeria. Most of them were innocent bystanders of the conflict between the government and the fundamentalists. Many of them were children.

In Russia, the economic divisiveness of the break-up of the Soviet Union five years earlier was countered on March 29, when President Yeltsin signed an agreement on 'economic union' with the Presidents of three other former Soviet Republics, Kazakhstan, Belarus and Kirgizstan. He also announced, two days later, the partial withdrawal of Russian troops from Chechenya. This did not prevent him from ordering continual air strikes against rebel

Chechens still holding out in the mountains. On April 21 the leader of the rebels, and former President of the breakaway Chechenya, General Dzhokhar Dudayev, was killed during one of these air strikes south of Grozny.

The first round of presidential elections was held in Russia on June 16. Yeltsin headed the poll with just over a third of the votes. His closest rival, only 3.3 per cent behind him, was the Communist candidate, Gennadi Zyuganov. While the people of Russia awaited the second round of the election, the people of Mongolia, casting their votes on June 30, brought a decisive end to seventy-five unbroken years of Communist rule. The second round of the Russian presidential election, held on July 3, brought outright victory to Yeltsin. The Communists, defeated in this election, but feeling their strength growing, had to bide their time. Within a few days they learned, as did all Russia, that Yeltsin had suffered a mild stroke on the eve of the poll, partially paralysing his left arm.

On August 9 Yeltsin was sworn in as the first democratically-elected President of Russia. He continued to assert Russia's authority in Chechenya as breakaway separatists, led by General Aslan Maskhadov, refused to recognize the earlier Russian-Chechen accord. In the week in which Yeltsin was sworn in as President in Moscow, two hundred Russian soldiers were killed in the fighting in Chechenya. A week later Grozny was under Chechen separatist control. The Russians responded with air strikes which set much of the city centre on fire. Thousands of citizens fled in panic. 'With no electricity, water or food,' *The Times* reported on August 10, 'thousands of residents of Grozny, which used to have a population of 400,000, have been forced to live in makeshift shelters as the street battles raged above them. So far, despite appeals from the International Red Cross, there has been no opportunity to move out the wounded or even to collect the bodies that litter the street.'

Yeltsin sent his security chief, General Alexander Lebed, a former paratrooper, to Chechenya, to warn that the full weight of Russian power would be brought to bear should the rebellion continue. On August 29, Lebed signed a peace agreement with General Maskhadov. The war was over. In all, 90,000 people had been killed. It was agreed to delay the issue of Chechen sovereignty until the year 2001. Believing that Lebed was plotting to overthrow him, Yeltsin dismissed the General on October 17.

In the Republic of Belarus, the revolutionary changes of five years earlier were being reversed. On November 24, as a result of a referendum, President Lukashenko was granted dictatorial powers. The British journalist Richard

Beeston was an eye-witness that day in the capital, Minsk, reporting to *The Times*:

> Thousands of demonstrators, including communists, nationalists and democrats, braved the first snowfall of the winter to protest against the mercurial leader outside the capital's parliament building, until now the centre of opposition to his rule. However, the rally eventually dispersed quietly as it dawned on the opposition that their battle was lost.
>
> 'I am voting against Lukashenko because he is dangerous and power-hungry and will hurt our country,' Sergei Urban, a businessman, said. 'Unfortunately, I know he will win.'

As a result of the referendum, Lukashenko, who was already in control of the army, the security services and the media, obtained the right to appoint half the members of the constitutional court, and many of the deputies in the new parliament. In the Communist era, he had been the director of a collective farm.

In Afghanistan, in which a decade earlier Russian troops had been fighting to preserve a besieged Communist regime, the rebel Taleban Islamic militia tightened their siege of Kabul in June, when in a single day's rocket attack sixty civilians were killed. Keeping up the siege, and the artillery barrages, on September 27 the Taleban overran Kabul and deposed the government of President Rabbani. One of those for whom the Taleban searched on entering Kabul was the former President, Muhammad Najibullah. As chief of police under the Soviet-installed regime of President Karmal, whom he succeeded, Najibullah held, in the words of his obituary in the *Annual Register*, 'a grisly reputation for his cruel and murderous treatment of political prisoners'. On the approach of the Taleban he had sought sanctuary in the United Nations mission in Kabul, but, having left that sanctuary for the airport, he was caught while trying to board a plane, taken away and executed. His bludgeoned body was left hanging from a concrete traffic gantry.

From their first days in power, the Taleban rulers imposed strict Islamic rule. One casualty was the education of women, which was strictly forbidden. Men and women convicted of adultery were stoned to death.

The Dayton Peace Treaty had brought an end to the ethnic fighting in former Yugoslavia, and created a unified yet partitioned Bosnia. Muslims and Bosnian Croats in one geographic area, Bosnian Serbs in another, had to rebuild broken homes and shattered lives, and learn to live in some degree of harmony with the minorities in their midst from each community. There was, however, a great deal of unfinished business with regard to the civil war that had just ended. The United Nations was committed to bringing to trial those Bosnian Serbs who had been identified as war criminals, responsible for the 'ethnic cleansing' of thousands of men, women and children. There were fifty-two names on the initial list submitted to the International War Crimes Tribunal at The Hague. The first to be arrested and indicted was Dušan Tadić, who had been flown from Sarajevo to the Netherlands under NATO guard. On January 30, two more Bosnian Serb officers were arrested, a general and a colonel who had taken a wrong turn and strayed into Bosnian government-controlled territory. They too were flown to The Hague to await trial.

In the many locations where the killings had taken place, United Nations peacekeepers had the task of exhuming the mass graves of the victims. One such place was the site of the Susica camp, near the village of Vlasenica. At the edge of the forest above the town, wrote Stacy Sullivan in a despatch published in *The Times* on January 29,

there is a 40-foot wide dirt pit. Bits of clothing, stray shoes and bullet casings poke out from the flattened earth. A dilapidated blue trench-digger sits perched by its side. Refugees who went through the forest in October 1992 say they saw bodies being dumped. It is impossible to say how many may be buried in the basin because the town has been sealed off to journalists and human rights workers for three and a half years.

Her report continued:

Hundreds, possibly thousands were killed in Vlasenica, site of the Susica detention camp where the United Nations war crimes tribunal estimates 8,000 Muslims were interned. The camp commander has already been indicted for war crimes.

One witness recalled bodies stacked like logs and another a lorry-load of soldiers shouting: 'There you are, dead Muslims. Soon there will be more of you.' Two weeks ago American troops set up a base camp four miles from Susica in the 'ethnically cleansed' village of Gradina, outside Vlasenica, making it possible for journalists to visit the town for the first time since its capture by the Serbs in the summer of 1992. The Americans were horrified as they pitched tents in the gardens of burnt-out houses.

But the horror of the charred village is just the first of the atrocities the Americans face. Besides the forest pit, there are said to be at least two other mass graves in the hills and valleys near by.

The United Nations believed that they had located the site of 187 mass graves. Of these, at least twenty contained more than five hundred bodies each. In March, a United Nations envoy, Elisabeth Rehn, confirmed that at least three thousand Muslims had been murdered by the Bosnian Serb army after the fall of Srebrenica in July 1995. Eight thousand more Muslims were as yet 'unaccounted for'. The United States Ambassador to the United Nations, Madeleine Albright, who was taken in March to see a mass grave near Srebrenica, commented: 'It is the most disgusting and horrifying sight for another human being to see.'

Mass graves were also being found in Cambodia, from Pol Pot's reign of terror twenty years earlier. The search for graves was being undertaken, as in Bosnia, under the aegis of the United Nations. Funding came from the United States, through a Cambodian Genocide Programme. The manager of the programme, Craig Etcheson, gave details of the new discoveries at a press conference in Phnom Penh in February. 'We had anticipated that there could be about one hundred to two hundred of them in the whole country,' he said. 'That is so far off, it is ridiculous. We are finding thousands in individual provinces.'

Whether the war crimes trials would be pursued against the senior per-petrators was much debated. John Major, the first Western leader to visit the Bosnian Serb Republic, stressed, after meeting opposition Bosnian Serb leaders in Banja Luka, that the most senior of all the Bosnian Serb leaders during the conflict, including Radovan Karadžić and General Ratko Mladić, should be indicted for war crimes and handed over to the United Nations tribunal in The Hague. 'I wouldn't be content for them to just fade away,' he said. Major's determination was echoed by his Defence Secretary, Michael Portillo, who said over the BBC: 'The international community will not forget these people. They will never have another quiet day in their lives because one day there will be a knock at the door. There will never be a full peace until people who have committed atrocities are brought to justice.'

On November 29 the United Nations War Crimes Tribunal at The Hague handed down its first sentence. It was on twenty-five-year-old Lance-Corporal

Dražen Erdemović. A Bosnian Serb soldier, he had taken part in the massacres of Muslims at Srebrenica, confessing to the killing of 'at least' seventy people at an execution site where 1,200 unarmed Muslims had been shot dead by Bosnian Serbs. He was sentenced to ten years in prison. The sentence had been made a relatively light one, explained the French judge, Claude Jorda, in view of Erdemović's remorse, and the evidence he had given about other suspected war criminals.

Erdemović was the first person to be sentenced by an international tribunal since the German and Japanese war criminals were hanged at the end of the Second World War. He was, in the words of Ben Macintyre, a journalist who reported on the trial, only 'a small cog in the Bosnian Serb army's genocidal machine'.

In July, seventy Sri Lankans were killed in a bomb explosion in a crowded commuter train in Colombo. In Burundi, three hundred Tutsi were massacred by Hutu rebels on July 20. Five days later, the Tutsi seized power in the capital, Bujumbura.

In neighbouring Rwanda, after an army coup on July 25 in which a Tutsi general, Pierre Buyoya, seized power, more than six thousand Hutu were killed in less than three weeks. Of these, four thousand were unarmed civilians. According to Amnesty International, in a statement issued in London on August 22, 'most of these victims were killed after the army came to their villages, ostensibly to obtain information about movements of rebels. Soldiers then assembled the victims and shot them.'

Inside Zaire, after fierce fighting between the Zairean army and Zairean Tutsi insurgents, the Tutsi captured two provincial capitals at the end of October. They then proceeded to fight and defeat rebel Hutu militiamen who had been terrorizing 700,000 fellow Rwandan Hutu refugees in camps in eastern Zaire. These Hutu militiamen had their own killing squads. Known as the Interahamwe (those who kill together), they had been active inside Zaire for more than a year, terrorizing Tutsis and Zairean civilians alike. On November 8, Sam Kiley reported to *The Times* from Keshero, in Zaire, a mile from 'teeming and disease ridden' Mugungu camp, home to half a million Hutu refugees who were being held captive by their fellow Hutu of the dreaded Interahamwe:

Elizabeth Wimana, 30, said Rwandan Hutus had sneaked out of Mugunga, crept through the rebel front lines, and raided her home on Monday. 'They took all our clothes and food and tried to slice me through the chest. I fell to the ground and they took my son,' she said.

The four-year-old, Philippe, was dragged away screaming while the Interahamwe slaughtered Elizabeth's six neighbours with machetes.

Kiley added:

Kaihura Kanyoni stood stiffly in the throng of people desperate to tell their stories. He had been stabbed three times in the back of the neck and left for dead by the Interahamwe last Saturday. Six members of his family were taken.

Suzannah Ndatukunda, 45, stood next to him. Her eight children were taken on Sunday. Adera, a grandmother, lost her four grandchildren the day before. On the same day the Rwandan Hutus attacked Juma Urimuben-shi, 53 – they took his food, clothes, wife and three children. All he has left of them is snapshots.

More than 700,000 Rwandan Hutus, terrorized for so long by their fellow-Hutu Interahamwe, were liberated in mid-November by the Tutsis. After almost two years of enforced captivity they set off back to their homes in Rwanda: 'a gigantic flood of humanity twenty-five miles long', Sam Kiley reported from the Zairean town of Goma, through which they passed on November 15. The refugee camps, Kiley was told by Ray Wilkinson of the Office of the United Nations High Commissioner for Refugees, 'were now empty of all but the dead'.

One discovery made in the Mugungu refugee camp after the Hutu extrem-ists had been driven out was of a series of documents showing that, despite the United Nations arms embargo imposed on Rwanda on 17 May 1994 – five weeks after the genocide began – a British firm had supplied the Hutu with a considerable quantity of arms. They had avoided the embargo on arms to Rwanda by having them sent to Goma, in Zaire, twenty miles from the Rwandan border, in an area controlled by Hutu. The arms had been shipped over a period of three months. The 'end-user' certificates had given Zaire as their final destination. The first shipment, of almost a million rounds of ammunition, valued at $750,000, had been flown from Israel, as had the second shipment, of more than a million rounds of ammunition and ten thousand grenades. Most of the weapons in the seven shipments had come from former Communist countries in Eastern Europe. The British firm had organized the shipments, and made its customary profit from them, as had the Israeli firms involved. Arms dealing had proved as profitable a business throughout the century as the use of those arms had proved destructive.

The Hutu extremist Interahamwe, fleeing from Mugungu, carried out one further murderous assignment, to kill those in their path as they retreated back into Rwanda. Passing through Kabuti, in eastern Zaire, they hacked to death as many as five hundred civilians. Sam Kiley saw the corpses 'rotting next to burnt-out lorries'. He also spoke to those who had witnessed the atrocities:

Emmanuel Kambali, 23, an artist from Sake, twenty miles east of Kabuti, said the Interahamwe had been slaughtering Zairean villagers on a huge scale, emptying the rich Masisi region of people.

A survivor of the massacre on the road, Jean-Philippe, 42, had been found wandering the lush grasslands by the rebels. His eyes glassy with terror two weeks after the attack, he said his wife and three children were among the bodies next to the five lorries, two of them United Nations water bowsers. 'There were only twenty survivors. We managed to run into the bushes, but the Interahamwe killed everyone else. Many were burnt alive. I can still hear their screams.'

*

On April 6 there was an upsurge in fighting in Liberia, where, for the previous seven years, warlords representing five tribal rivalries had carried out an internecine struggle in which 150,000 people had been killed. The renewed fighting was an attempt by the government in the capital, Monrovia, to drive out the rebel leader, General Roosevelt Johnson. The attempt was unsuccessful, as the general offered to satisfy his enemies through negotiations. In a despatch to *The Times*, published on April 11, Mark Huband commented: 'As hatred, personal enmity, covetousness and deceit are the main elements in the Liberian political debate, it is not surprising that General Johnson decided to plunge the war-racked Monrovia into chaos, seize hostages and barricade himself behind his rocket-propelled grenades as a way of showing his feelings. But just as easily as he exploded, he has now calmed down.'

To save foreign nationals from the inevitable upsurge in fighting, the United States launched a combined naval and military operation, in which, on the first day, 168 foreigners were evacuated, including fifty-four Americans. Even as they were being taken off by helicopter, five hundred Liberians were killed in street fighting. Sixty American troops landed to supervise the continuing evacuation.

Within two days, anarchy had broken out in Monrovia. Helicopter evacuations had to be suspended when the helicopters were fired on. Teenage gunmen attacked the United Nations High Commissioner for Refugees compound in the city. 'There are bodies in the street. This is really wanton carnage,' reported Ruth Marshall of the UNHCR, which was looking after 1,200,000 Liberian refugees who during previous years had fled the fighting elsewhere in the country. A British engineer, John Hare, who worked for the charity Save the Children, decided to remain in the city to help co-ordinate the work of medical aid workers attempting to succour the wounded in the streets.

A series of ameliorations, as welcome as they were unusual, took place as the year came to an end. In Serbia, after five weeks of peaceful but crowded street protests by as many as 200,000 people against repressive legislation, the government agreed in December to set aside corruptly obtained election results, giving more weight to the votes of the democratic candidates. On December 27, the Chinese Prime Minister, Li Peng, on a visit to Moscow, signed a number of agreements, one of which led to the reduction of military forces along the Chinese-Russian border – the longest border between two sovereign States, with direct contact along more than 3,500 miles. On December 29 the last Russian troops left Chechenya. That same day, in a ceremony in Guatemala City, an agreement was reached which ended thirty-six years of civil war in which 150,000 Guatemalans had been killed, 50,000 had 'disappeared' (and were certainly dead) and nearly a million people had been driven from their homes.

In Ukraine, the legacy of Chernobyl was far from ended. The report of an inquiry that had been commissioned by the European Union into the continuing effects of the catastrophe was published in March. It had been carried out by fifty-nine scientists from eight countries. Its conclusion was dire: as many as thirty million Ukrainians, out of a total Ukrainian population of just over fifty million, might be at risk from radioactive contamination. The risk was coming from water being washed by floods from near the crippled reactor into rivers used for drinking, irrigation and fishing. The scientists strongly advised that fishing should be banned at Lake Kozhanov, on the Russian side of the border, 156 miles from Chernobyl. Tests indicated that the fish in the lake were contaminated with radioactivity which exceeded European safety limits by up to sixty times.

On April 10 a four-day conference opened in Vienna, co-sponsored by the United Nations Atomic Energy Agency and the European Commission. It opened with a minute's silence for the 'past, present and future' victims of Chernobyl. Seven hundred delegates heard a Russian radiological expert, Anatoli Tsyb, speak of 'a significant rise' in thyroid cancer in the areas of Belarus, Ukraine and Russia most affected by the radioactive fall-out. Seventy per cent of the fall-out had been deposited on Belarus. The estimated total radioactivity from the Chernobyl accident was two hundred times greater than that from the Hiroshima and Nagasaki atom bombs combined. In the future, as during the previous decade, it was children who would be most at risk.

In the struggle against disease, a further landmark was reached in 1996 when the United Nations World Health Organization announced that all the remaining stocks of the smallpox virus would be destroyed within three years. Only two stocks of the virus remained, at the Centres for Disease Control (CDC) in Atlanta, Georgia, and at the Russian State Research Centre for Virology and Biotechnology in Koltsovo, near Novosibirsk in Siberia. As a result of the worldwide vaccination campaign begun two decades earlier, wrote Nigel Hawkes, the Science Editor of *The Times*, on January 26, 'a scourge of mankind for more than 3,500 years' had been eliminated as a human disease. But, Hawkes explained, destruction of the last remaining laboratory stocks had been opposed both on principle and on scientific grounds:

Some scientists simply oppose destroying any form of life, even a virus estimated to have killed 600,000 people a year in Europe between the sixteenth and eighteenth centuries. 'To wipe out a species is always a concern,' says Dr Brian Mahy of CDC.

Some scientists who work on viruses oppose destruction because there may still be things to learn by studying smallpox. The WHO says scientists have now produced harmless clones of the virus and have its full genetic blueprint, which should provide them with all they need.

The virus will be destroyed by autoclave – an oven that will heat it to fatally high temperatures. The virus will be taken from its locked freezer at a maximum security building by researchers in pressurized space suits and heated to 130 degrees for forty minutes. Then the process will be repeated.

In a communiqué, the World Health Organization said that the eradication of smallpox was 'among the greatest public health achievements of all time'. The last known case of smallpox, which disfigures and causes blindness and even death, was recorded in Somalia in 1977. Destroying the remaining stocks would ensure that there could be no escape of the last preserved amounts of the virus. 'The destruction of smallpox in the wild', Hawkes noted, 'means that mankind is progressively losing any natural resistance to it. In theory at least, that means an escape could set off a major epidemic.'

Another remarkable medical achievement that year was the successful surgery carried out in a Miami hospital on a twenty-nine-year-old Italian who had six transplants: kidney, pancreas, stomach, large intestine, small intestines and liver.

Advances in medical science that were able to prolong life were in shocking contrast both to the wanton killings around the globe and to the failures of many governments to improve the quality of life for their citizens. A World Bank report on global poverty, issued in June, stated that 1,300 million people, a fifth of the world's population, lived on less than $1 a day. A publication that same month, *Caring for the Future*, by the Independent Commission on Population and Quality of Life, an international forum, noted that the world population, which stood at 5,800 million, would continue to grow and would double within the coming hundred years – making the problem of even basic feeding a grave one, and leading to 'rampant poverty' – unless governments were able to stabilize their population growth by 'massive efforts in health, education and the use of development assistance'.

An example of the problems of feeding millions of people was revealed by the United Nations on September 13. Speaking in Beijing, the outgoing director of the United Nations World Food Programme, Robert Hauser, spoke of the problems of North Korea, where, for the second year running, more than ten per cent of all crops had been destroyed in floods. North Korea was 'definitely on a downward spiral', he said. For the previous nine months, twenty-two million North Koreans had been on a daily ration of seven ounces of cereal. 'If you go into the countryside you see only skinny people. Many children have pot-bellies, stick-like arms, visible ribs – symptoms of malnutrition. This year they may just make it, but next year the crisis will be worse.'

'Despite a plea for international help,' *The Times* reported on September 14, 'little more than token aid has arrived. Analysts say Stalinist North

Korea has only itself to blame. No journalists are permitted to view the devastation caused by the floods in the security-sealed State and no pictures appear of hungry children – the kind of photographs that, in Ethiopia for example, evoked worldwide concern.' According to United Nations estimates, North Korea had been able to produce only 3.5 million tonnes of grain annually in recent years, 'well below the 4.8 million tonnes required to meet minimum nutritional needs'.

Inequalities of wealth had been underlined during the negotiations to end the civil war in Guatemala, when it was revealed that ninety-five per cent of the rural population was landless, and that 200,000 people – two per cent of the total population – owned sixty-five per cent of the productive land. In July, a United Nations Human Development Programme Report revealed that half of the world's wealth was owned by just 385 people. Bill Gates, the founder of the American computer software company Microsoft – who, as the world's wealthiest person, was estimated to be worth $39 billion – King Fahd of Saudi Arabia, the Sultan of Brunei and the other 383 members of the so called 'super-rich', possessed more assets than the entire Gross Domestic Product of countries which contained forty-five per cent of the world's population. Per-capita income was also falling in eighty-nine of the world's two hundred countries. Over the previous five years the per capita income in the republics of the former Soviet Union had fallen by an eighth. Nineteen countries, including Liberia, Rwanda, Sudan and Ghana, had lower per-capita incomes than they had had forty years earlier. The Human Development Programme administrator, James Speth, commented: 'If present trends continue, economic disparities between the industrial and developing nations will move from inequitable to inhuman.'

CHAPTER FORTY-SIX

1997

Mine is the first generation able to contemplate the possibility that we may live our entire lives without going to war or sending our children to war. That is a prize beyond value.

TONY BLAIR

In Northern Ireland, terrorist incidents in January included IRA bombings and mortar attacks, together with repeated statements from Sinn Fein that it wished to be part of the political dialogue. The Northern Ireland Secretary, Sir Patrick Mayhew, who was responsible in the British Cabinet for the Province, called this combination of policies 'hard deeds and honeyed words'. Not only the IRA, but Loyalist paramilitaries, were carrying out terrorist activities. The situation seemed to be drifting inexorably to a time before the ceasefires, before the talks, and before the Downing Street Declaration pointed a way forward to constitutional talks with all sides participating in them.

Sinn Fein continued to demand a place in the talks on Northern Ireland's future. On 12 February 1997 the IRA killed a British corporal in Northern Ireland. John Major insisted that there must be a 'credible ceasefire' before Sinn Fein could enter talks. He was strongly supported in this stance by the new American Secretary of State, Madeleine Albright – who had earlier been American Ambassador at the United Nations. She strongly condemned the IRA killings. When invitations went out from the White House for the St Patrick's Day celebration with the President, Sinn Fein was not invited, as it had been the previous year.

Over Easter, the IRA planted a number of bombs on the British mainland. On April 29 they forced the postponement of the Grand National horse race at Aintree, a central fixture of the horse-racing season – before the First

World War a suffragette, Emily Davison, had thrown herself in front of the King's horse at the Epsom Derby as a political protest, and been killed. On May 1, during the British general election, Sinn Fein candidates stood throughout Northern Ireland. Their share of the vote was the highest they had ever received, 16.1 per cent (126,921 votes). The two leading Sinn Feiners, Gerry Adams and Martin McGuinness, were both elected to the House of Commons. Both men refused to swear the oath of loyalty to the Queen, and were disqualified from taking their seats.

In the general election of May 1 the Conservative Party was defeated after eighteen years in power; its 336 seats were reduced to 165. Labour increased its parliamentary representation from 271 to 418. The number of those casting their vote, 73.1 per cent, was the lowest since 1945. The Labour majority, 177, was the largest since 1945. John Major, who had been Prime Minister for almost six years, was succeeded by Tony Blair. Under Blair's leadership, the Labour Party, having made a decisive move away from traditional Labour Socialism before the election, took pride in the name New Labour.

In Northern Ireland, where John Major had worked so hard to secure an agreement, the killings continued on both sides of the sectarian divide. So too did the search for a settlement along the lines that Major had instituted. The Labour government's Secretary of State for Northern Ireland, Mo Mowlam, took swift action, which was followed by a visit to Belfast on May 16 by Tony Blair, who sought to put Loyalist minds at rest when he said that his agenda was 'not a united Ireland'. Support for a ceasefire – previously accepted by the IRA three years earlier – and for renewed negotiations, came from President Clinton, who in a visit to London at the end of May condemned the mentality which said 'we'll talk when we're happy and shoot when we're not'. On July 19 the IRA announced that they would accept a ceasefire from noon on the following day, a Sunday. It came into effect, and on the Monday, Sinn Fein were invited to the all-Party talks at Stormont Castle that had been going on for several months without them.

The talks which Sinn Fein joined had been convened under the chairmanship of the former American Senator, George Mitchell. On September 9, Sinn Fein signed the 'Mitchell Principles'. They were willing to become a political Party committed to debate, compromise, acceptance of the will of the majority, renouncing violence, handing over their arms, and willing to forgo, if that was the wish of the majority, their central aspiration of more than eight decades, a united Ireland. When Blair met Gerry Adams in Belfast on

October 13, it was the British government's first official contact with Sinn Fein since 1921. Within two months, Gerry Adams was invited with a Sinn Fein delegation to Downing Street. The delegation arrived to find rival crowds gathered at the entrance to Downing Street to cheer and jeer them as they walked past the security gates – set up a decade earlier to protect Downing Street against IRA attack – to No. 10. As they passed through the gates there were cries of 'murderers' and 'New Labour, new traitors'.

Rita Restorick, the mother of the last soldier who had been killed in Northern Ireland, thrust a Christmas card containing her son's photograph into Adams' hand and told him that she hoped he was sincere about peace. Adams replied that he hoped the negotiations would make the sufferings of people like her part of 'our painful history'.

During his talk with Adams, which lasted for almost an hour, Blair offered the Sinn Fein leader 'a choice of history' – violence and despair, or peace and progress. 'It is important', Blair said, 'that I look you in the eye and hear you say that you remain committed to peaceful means. If we were to slip back, I believe we would slip back to something worse than what came before.'

Adams stressed his commitment to the principles of democracy and non-violence, but told Blair: 'All the hurt and grief and division which has come from British involvement in Irish affairs has to end.'

The demonstration that had paralysed Belgrade at the end of 1996 continued throughout January 1997. On January 4 the city was brought to a halt when more than 100,000 anti-government protesters took part. Eight days later, 400,000 Serbs packed the streets, demanding reform, in scenes reminiscent of the fall of Communism in Eastern Europe almost a decade earlier. As a result of the demonstrations, opposition majorities were installed in several cities. Later in the year, a considerable measure of press freedom was restored.

For some years, efforts had been made in Belgrade to reach a compromise with the ethnic Albanian majority in Kosovo. In April, talks between Serb officials and representatives of the Kosovo 'government in exile' took place in New York. The Democratic League of Kosovo had committed itself to non-violent advocacy of its constitutional demands. But during the year a change took place, as it became clear that the Serbs were not going to move forward to any meaningful form of self-government. The Kosovo nationalists saw no such Albanian Authority being granted by Belgrade. In Priština, the principal Kosovo town, student demonstrations starting in October and

37. Ayatollah Khomeini at Neauphle-le-Château, near Paris, an exile, awaiting his return to Iran. This photograph was taken on 8 November 1978.

38. Pope John Paul II in Warsaw, 2 June 1979, during his first visit as Pope, with the First Secretary of the Central Committee of the Polish United Worker's Party, Edward Gierek.

39. British soldiers in the Falkland Islands, during the Falklands War, 1982.

40. Argentine soldiers lay down their arms after their surrender in the Falkland Islands, 14 June 1982.

41. *Left* Mikhail
Gorbachev and
Margaret Thatcher,
a photograph taken
at Chequers on
16 December 1984.

42. *Below* Peking,
3 June 1989: tanks and
a lone demonstrator in
Tiananmen Square.

43. Crowds from the British sector in Berlin look over the Berlin Wall, while a child is lowered on to the eastern side of the wall, 10 November 1989.

44. Moscow, 21 August 1991: tanks and demonstrators loyal to Boris Yeltsin defend the Russian parliament building.

45. Mogadishu: Somali dock hands sit on sacks of United States food aid, awaiting the arrival trucks to take the food to north Mogadishu, which was controlled by a rival clan, 5 December 1992.

46. Mogadishu, early morning, 9 December 1992. Press photographers hasten to photograph one of the first United States military special forces to land at Mogadishu. This picture was taken by Robert Borea of Associated Press.

47. The Dayton Peace Accord, signed in Paris, 14 December 1995. Seated: Slobodan Milošević of Serbia, Franjo Tudjman of Croatia, and Alija Izetbegović of Bosnia. Watching them (left to right) are Prime Minister Felipe Gonzales of Spain, President Bill Clinton of the United States, President Jacques Chirac of France, Chancellor Helmut Kohl of Germany, Prime Minister John Major of Britain and Victor Chernomyrdin of Russia.

48. The Sharm el-Sheikh anti-terrorist summit, 13 March 1996. Left to right: King Hussein of Jordan, Shimon Peres, President Clinton, President Mubarak, Boris Yeltsin (waving), King Hassan of Morocco and Jacques Chirac.

49. The Korean War Memorial in Washington: American soldiers advancing.

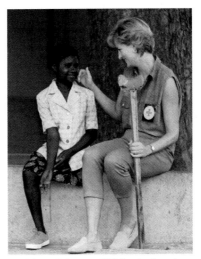

50. Diana, Princess of Wales, in Angola, with thirteen-year-old Sandra Thijica, who lost a leg from an anti-personnel mine while she was working on the land. This photograph was taken by Joao Silva of the Associated Press on 14 January 1997.

51. A Polish sapper, a member of the United Nations Emergency Force (UNEF) clearing mines near the Suez Canal, in the buffer zone between Israel and Egypt. This photograph was taken on 21 March 1974 by a Bulgarian photographer, Encho Mitov.

52. Hutu children wait while food is prepared in a refugee camp near Gisenyi, Rwanda. This photograph was taken by Associated Press photographer Sayyid Azim on 26 June 1997.

continuing until the end of the year demanded full autonomy, even independ-ence. A self-styled Kosovo Liberation Army was formed, and began to attack Serbian security forces. A new violent conflict was in the offing.

In Israel, under the autonomy plan that had been put in place by Rabin and Peres two years earlier, Yasser Arafat exercised political and administrative control in the territory of the Palestinian Authority, including six of the seven Palestinian cities. The peace process took a further step forward on January 15 when Benjamin Netanyahu agreed to transfer eighty per cent of the seventh city, Hebron, to the Palestinian Authority, leaving twenty per cent under Israeli rule. In that twenty per cent area lived almost a thousand Jewish settlers and several thousand Palestinians. Stringent rules were laid down to try to keep the two groups apart. The other six entirely Palestinian towns were already under full Palestinian control. Israeli troops withdrew from Hebron on January 17. Two days later Arafat entered the city to a hero's welcome. It was his first visit there in thirty-two years.

For Israelis, tragedy struck on February 4 when two military helicopters on their way to southern Lebanon crashed in bad weather over Israel. All seventy-three servicemen on board were killed. It was the worst accident in Israeli military history.

On July 30, a suicide bomber killed thirteen Israelis, and injured 170, when he blew himself up in the main market in western (Jewish) Jerusalem. Netanyahu immediately suspended the current peace talks with the Palestin-ians. The perpetrator was a Muslim fundamentalist, a member of Hamas, who opposed any Israeli-Palestinian agreement. In response to the killings, Arafat promised to 'confront this terrorist act' with action. 'We are doing our best,' he said. But Netanyahu's office let it be known that the Israeli Prime Minister had replied: 'You have to do more.'

Arafat was having difficulty controlling Hamas, whose power consisted not only in their weapons but in their activities in providing social services, especi-ally in the refugee camps in Gaza, alongside the slums of which Arafat's friends and political associates were building villas for themselves. In mid-August, Arafat called a two-day forum in Gaza City of his own Palestinian Authority, Hamas and Islamic Jihad. His aim, he said, was 'national unity' talks. He wanted all groups to work together to ensure that Israel continued to observe the Oslo Accords, and pull out of the West Bank. It was noticed by Israelis and Palestinians alike that he did not condemn the Jerusalem suicide bomb.

*   *   *

On January 20, President Clinton was inaugurated for a second term after his victory in the presidential elections at the end of 1996, the first Democrat since Franklin Roosevelt sixty years earlier to be sworn in for a second term. Among his most implacable opponents was Newt Gingrich, who was re-elected Speaker, the first Republican to serve two consecutive terms as Speaker for sixty-eight years. In the political battle of wills between them, Gingrich was not averse to raising matters of personal sexual impropriety with which Clinton was being increasingly linked.

Clinton delivered his fifth State of the Union message on February 4. He asked Congress 'for a bipartisan process to preserve social security and reform Medicare for the long run'. His aim was to 'give more families access to affordable, quality health care'. He wanted measures introduced that would ensure that those temporarily unemployed would not lose their health insurance, that would enhance the existing anti-drug efforts, and that would make two years of college education, supported by tax credits and scholarships, universal in America in the twenty-first century.

Republican hostility to Clinton and his policies ran deep. Every charge of 'sleaze' at the White House was followed up assiduously. A Special Prosecutor, Kenneth Starr, was investigating allegations against Clinton and his wife Hillary with regard to property speculation in his home State, Arkansas, of which Clinton had been Governor before becoming President. Starr caused some consternation among Republicans hostile to Clinton when he announced his intention to resign that August and take up a university post, but he subsequently said his decision had been 'unwise' and that he would see his inquiry through. As the inquiry evolved, Starr began to delve deeply into the sexual-harassment charges being raised against the President, and much discussed in public, with growing media obsession. On May 27 the Supreme Court ruled that the President had no immunity in the courts for private acts.

Clinton persevered with his domestic agenda. On June 14, in San Diego, he launched a year-long 'campaign against racism'. He also prevailed upon the Republicans, despite their initial hostility, to agree to a bipartisan programme designed to balance the Federal budget in the next five years. Although this involved cuts in Medicare and Medicaid, it was compensated for by increased funding for education and health insurance for children, and expanded health care cover for children of parents who could not afford health insurance. The bipartisan legislation to this end was signed by Clinton on August 5. The budget would be balanced by the year 2002. 'We have fulfilled the responsibility of our generation to guarantee opportunity to the next generation,' Clinton told Congress and the American people.

In foreign policy, Clinton persevered with the diplomatic initiatives being evolved following the end of the East-West divide six years earlier. On March 20 he attended a summit in Helsinki with President Yeltsin. One result was the signing two months later of the Russia-NATO Founding Act on Mutual Relations, Co-operation and Security, whereby Russia and its former NATO adversary would become partners, sharing knowledge, weaponry and Intelligence information. The signing took place in Paris. President Yeltsin was so enthusiastic that, without prior discussion or warning, he told the NATO signatories that he would, as a gesture of goodwill, remove the warheads from all Russian nuclear weapons that were pointing at their countries.

All the signatories of the Founding Act were enthusiastic about what they had achieved. 'In the twilight of the twentieth century,' said President Clinton, 'we look forward toward a new century with a new Russia and a new NATO, working together in a new Europe of unlimited possibility.' President Chirac, the Paris summit's host, said that the Act swept away the remnants of the Cold War. 'We will be turning the page on half a century of misunderstanding, of confrontation, of division on our continent,' he said. Tony Blair, attending his first summit, described himself as a child of the Cold War era, 'raised amid the constant fear of a conflict with the potential to destroy humanity. Whatever other dangers may exist, no such fear exists today. Mine is the first generation able to contemplate the possibility that we may live our entire lives without going to war or sending our children to war. That is a prize beyond value.'

Helmut Kohl, the German Chancellor – echoing Churchill's wartime 'blood, toil, tears and sweat' – stressed the far-reaching significance of the Act 'at the end of a century which has seen so much blood, tears and suffering'.

Russia remained uneasy about the enlargement of NATO to include its former Eastern European satellites, but agreed that American-Russian co-operation should include 'consultation, co-ordination and, to the maximum extent possible, joint decision making and action on security issues of common concern'. The concept of joint Russian-American action was new: it had last taken place more than eighty years earlier, when, in 1919, American soldiers had participated in the Allied military intervention to crush Lenin's Bolshevik regime.

One initiative Clinton took was with regard to a scourge from previous wars: the anti-personnel mines sown by the combatants, in both war and civil war, which, for many years after the conflicts had ended, caused death, mutilation and maiming on a massive scale. A lead in the anti-landmine campaign was being taken in Britain by Diana, Princess of Wales, who took her concerns worldwide. On January 14, in the Angolan capital, Luanda, she spoke to a number of landmine victims, among them thirteen-year-old Sandra Thijica, who had lost a leg in eastern Angola three years earlier. On August 9, in the Bosnian town of Zenica, the Princess met a volleyball team, all of whose members had been injured by mines, and who could play only by propelling themselves forward on their hands and haunches.

At the beginning of 1997 President Clinton had issued, with his presidential authority, a unilateral ban on the export from the United States of anti-personnel landmines. But such were the vagaries of national policy that, when an international treaty banning anti-personnel landmines was ready for signature in Ottawa on September 17, the United States declined to sign it. The American government's position was that the Ottawa Treaty failed to exempt South Korea from its provisions. In South Korea, the Pentagon explained, landmines were regarded by both South Korea and the United States as essential to the defence of the country, and of the 37,000 American soldiers stationed there. Justifying this argument, Clinton himself said: 'No one should expect our people to expose our armed forces to unacceptable risks.' Clinton did propose an alternative strategy in the battle against landmines, instructing the Pentagon to develop 'alternative weapons' which would make the landmine obsolete by the year 2006.

The death of Diana, Princess of Wales in a car crash in Paris in August – only three weeks after she had been photographed with the landmine victims in Bosnia – created a worldwide surge of emotion. Many of the film tributes stressed her work on behalf of the charity International Campaign to Ban Landmines. In October the charity was awarded the Nobel Peace Prize. In congratulating Jody Williams, the American co-ordinator of the charity, on the award, President Clinton said that the United States would still not sign the global moratorium which eighty-nine nations had ratified in Ottawa. A few days later it was announced that about three hundred civilians were being killed or maimed each month by landmines in Kampuchea.

Russia had entered a period of erratic personal rule by Yeltsin, and a subculture of violence and Mafia-style business empires. Assassinations of rival gang leaders were frequent: one such shooting took place on the pavement outside the prestigious National Hotel, facing Red Square and the Kremlin. In May, Yeltsin sacked both his Defence Minister and the Chief of the General Staff for failing to 'reform' the army. In response, Lev Rokhlin, the chairman of the defence committee of the parliament (himself a former commanding general in Chechenya) accused Yeltsin of having 'doomed the armed forces to destruction'. In local elections, success went increasingly to candidates of the Popular-Patriotic Union of Russia, an alliance between old-style Communists and new-found nationalists opposed to Yeltsin's economic reforms. The chief of these, privatization, had led to substantial theft of former State property. In November, an international business consultancy published a 'corruption league' table in which Russia was at the top. As the quality of life in Russia declined for the mass of the people, Yeltsin appealed to 'ordinary' Russians to show more compassion for each other in the 'harsh struggle for their daily bread'. There was widespread distress in June when publicity was given to the fact that the life expectancy of the average Russian had been declining in the six years since the fall of Communism. As of 1996, only fifty-four per cent of Russian men over the age of sixteen were likely to reach the age of sixty. The equivalent figure in the United States was closer to seventy.

Yeltsin's personal health and behaviour gave repeated cause for concern. In November 1996 he had undergone a quintuple cardiac bypass operation. In January 1997 he cancelled all his official engagements for a week: the official Kremlin doctors' report of the President's 'mild fever and influenza symptoms' was not widely believed. It soon emerged that he was suffering from pneumonia. His drinking habits had long been notorious, and he spent more and more time out of the public eye. When he did emerge, it could be with bizarre results. On an official visit to Oslo at the end of the year, he appeared to believe that he was in Helsinki – where he had met Clinton nine months earlier.

Humiliation for Russia came after the signature of the Chechen ceasefire, one condition of which was the withdrawal of Russian combat troops from what was still an integral part of the Russian Federation. In January the former commander of the rebel Chechen armed forces, Aslan Maskhadov, was elected President. On May 12, in Moscow, he and Yeltsin signed a formal peace treaty between the two countries, one of which (Chechenya) was constitutionally a part of the other (Russia). Maskhadov made no secret of his desire for ultimate full independence for his autonomous republic. He also introduced Islamic law in place of Russian law, the first autonomous region within the Russian Federation to make such a drastic change. As a first visible example of the effects of new law, convicted murderers were executed in public.

In the north of Afghanistan, a Russian-trained general, Abdul Rashid Dostum, was holding out against the Islamic rule of the Taleban, and had succeeded in asserting his authority in six provinces along the border with the Central Asian States of the former Soviet Union. A former Communist, Dostum (the name means 'everybody's friend') had risen through the ranks of the Soviet-trained Afghan army. By ethnic origin an Uzbek, he controlled a region of Afghanistan that was forty per cent Uzbek. Repeated Taleban attacks failed to dislodge him. In defiant mood, he had even established his own airline, Baulk Air. Elsewhere in Afghanistan, the Taleban were imposing the strictest of Islamic laws, and enforcing them. The place of women in society was to be strictly behind the veil.

Within the Arab and Islamic world, Muslim fundamentalism had become a serious challenge to secular regimes. In Algeria, 50,000 people had been killed in five years of violence, most of the victims of which were civilians, often slaughtered in their beds. In the first week of August, 150 Algerian villagers were killed in an area that had become known as the 'triangle of death' south of Algiers. Those killed included children and a woman in her last month of pregnancy. Most of them had their throats cut. In one attack, four young men playing dominoes outside their house were chained together and then killed. A British journalist, Anthony Loyd, who visited some of the villages where the killings had taken place, spoke to survivors in the village of Bentalha, including a schoolteacher named Ali, and told their stories in *The Times* on October 22:

> The carnage that remained behind them was extreme by any standards. They had set fire to every house they could. Few of the 217 dead had been shot. Most, the majority elderly men, women and children, had had their throats cut. Some had been beheaded. Thirty-four young women were missing, taken away as booty. 'It was the second tragedy I had suffered in a month,' Ali added.
>
> 'Three weeks previously the village of Sidi Rais had been raided in a similar way. I teach at the primary school there. So when I turned up to work one morning I found half my pupils had been killed. Then I lost my neighbours.'

I had already seen Sidi Rais. Its catalogue of survivors' horror stories was almost identical to that of Bentalha: mutilation, beheading, burning, evisceration. One man told of having seen his two-year-old daughter thrown from a rooftop before his wife had her throat cut in front of him.

The terrorists had tried to do the same to him, their knives cleaving through his hand as he put it up to protect his throat, before crawling away to escape.

In Egypt, Muslim fundamentalists continued to attack foreign tourists, and to be hunted down and killed by the security forces. In November fifty-eight European holidaymakers were massacred outside a pharaonic temple in Luxor by members of the Jamaa Islamiyya (the Islamic Group). In Pakistan, in February, thousands of Pakistan's three million Christians were driven from their homes in the Punjab by Muslim extremists. Their homes were then set on fire and thirteen churches destroyed. The Christian village of Shantinagar was one of those that had been looted and set on fire. When police were called in, two rioters were killed before the rest dispersed. But the mandatory death penalty imposed a decade earlier for anyone convicted of blaspheming the name of the Prophet Mohammed remained in force.

From Iran came news in February that any Muslim who killed the British novelist Salman Rushdie, accused of blaspheming the Prophet in his novel *The Satanic Verses*, would be entitled to an even greater monetary reward than hitherto: it had been increased by an Iranian foundation from $2 million to $2,500,000. The British government immediately denounced the move as an 'outrageous infringement' of Rushdie's 'fundamental rights'.

At midnight on June 30, Britain left Hong Kong, which was returned to China after a hundred years as part of the British imperial and colonial domain. The transfer had been agreed upon when Margaret Thatcher was Prime Minister. China promised that the former Crown Colony could develop its democratic system 'in a manner suitable to the Hong Kong reality'. 'At dawn today,' *The Times* reported,

the Chinese army came across the border. More than 5,000 residents of the village of Sheung Shui came out in driving rain to watch troops and armoured vehicles on their main street, where dragon dancers performed and a loudspeaker blasted out patriotic revolutionary songs. Some villagers stopped cars carrying Chinese army officers and presented them with flowers. Four thousand troops and twenty-one armoured personnel carriers moved to positions in six separate districts of Hong Kong.

In Britain, Tony Blair warned the Chinese leaders that Hong Kong would be 'destroyed' if they were to renege on their pledges in the Anglo-Chinese Joint Declaration to allow the existing social system and laws to be 'fundamentally unchanged'.

Apologies for past wrongs continued to be a part of the international agenda, particularly in Europe. On January 21 the German Chancellor, Helmut Kohl – who as a teenager had been a member of the Hitler Youth – and the Prime Minister of the Czech Republic, Václav Klaus, signed an accord expressing mutual regret for the Czech expulsion of Germans from the Sudetenland in 1945. At the same time, the German government made it clear that it would support the Czech Republic's application for membership of the European Union.

In Switzerland, the three largest banks announced on February 6 that they would pay out £55 million for survivors of the Holocaust, in view of the money deposited in Swiss accounts before the war by Jews who had subsequently been murdered, and whose accounts had been frozen. In France, French bishops offered a formal 'repentance' on September 30 for the failure of the Roman Catholic Church to condemn the persecution and deportation of Jews during the Vichy regime in the Second World War. This 'repentance' was all the more impressive because individual bishops had, at the time, spoken out most forcefully against the deportations. The twenty bishops involved in the event explained that they wished to make more widely known to the public, and publicly to condemn, the way in which 'the negative view of Jews which the Church fostered over the centuries helped to create a fertile terrain in which Nazi ideas could be planted without resistance'.

In Britain, 307 soldiers who had been shot for desertion and cowardice in the First World War were given a posthumous apology, but not, as had been hoped by their relatives, a pardon. Medical research in recent years had shown that most of them, far from being 'cowards', had suffered from undiagnosed shell-shock: a condition affecting soldiers that was known in the latter part of the century as 'post-traumatic stress disorder'. The most that the government would offer was 'a deep sense of regret', and a willingness to add the 307 names to books of remembrance and war memorials from which they had been excluded or expunged. The government did agree, however, to introduce legislation that would substitute life imprisonment for all military offences for which execution was still the punishment.

In Burma, nine British and twenty-five Japanese war veterans visited the Allied war cemeteries along the Burma Railway and attended a service of commemoration in February, in a gesture of reconciliation. Those whom they jointly remembered were the 37,000 Commonwealth soldiers who had died in action or as slave labourers, and the 190,000 Japanese soldiers killed in the battles in Burma.

In South Africa, the Truth and Reconciliation Commission continued to hear apologies from both sides of the Black-White divide. Four White policemen who had been involved in the killing of Steve Biko twenty years earlier were among those voluntarily confessing to their crimes and applying for an amnesty. They included Colonel Harold Snyman, who headed the interrogation that led to Biko's death. Donald Woods, the anti-apartheid newspaper editor who had been forced into exile after Biko's murder, said of the amnesty applications: 'It feels good. I've been wondering for years when they would come out of the woodwork. Too much has been hidden for too long.'

The United States continued to apologize for the treatment of Indians – known most recently as Native Americans. In the nineteenth century they had been repeatedly massacred. Treaties had been signed between the 554 Indian tribes in North America – the remnants of a once great nation – and the Federal government, giving them $1,700 million in funds, and exempting them, as 'sovereign governments' according to their individual treaties, from the anti-gambling provisions that applied in most States. This enabled even the smallest of tribes to invest in massive gambling projects. By 1997 there were almost three hundred such gambling sites, run by more than 175 tribes, including Mohicans, Navajos and Sioux. These sites were bringing the tribes $4,000 million a year in revenue. When some Republican Senators threatened to reduce the Federal funds because of the size of the gambling revenue, the only American Indian in the Senate, Ben Nighthorse Campbell, himself a Republican, from Colorado, said that any such legislation would be passed 'over my dead body'.

On January 10 the first trial conducted by the United Nations International Criminal Tribunal for Rwanda took place in a courtroom in Tanzania. The first witness, identified for her own safety only as 'K', spoke of how, on 19 April 1994, she was confronted by the accused, the mayor of the town, Jean-Paul Akayesu, a forty-three-year-old Hutu, and a crowd of men whom he was leading. The 'people' whose fate she witnessed were Tutsis:

'The killers escorted eight people right to the fence of the communal office where they were told to sit down with their arms and legs well out in front of them,' she said. 'At the moment they were going to be killed they raised their arms to beg for mercy but Akayesu said "quickly" giving the order to have them killed.'

Mr Akayesu told the Hutu extremists outside his office to 'go to your own sector and work', meaning to kill, she said.

K said that she was then locked up and from detention watched fellow Tutsis, including teachers, brought outside Mr Akayesu's office and killed.

Some of those murdered, K said, 'were attacked to the point of death and then were put in wheelbarrows and buried alive'. Akayesu was found guilty of the murder of at least two thousand Tutsis.

Even as the war crimes trials were starting, more crimes were being committed. Hutu extremists had continued to harass and persecute the Hutu refugees who had sought sanctuary in Zaire. Some of these refugees had been marched as much as five hundred miles by their fellow-Hutu captors. The British journalist Sam Kiley was again a witness of the plight of these forgotten victims of a distant civil war. Writing from the town of Punia, on the River Congo in central Zaire, he told *The Times*:

Starving Hutu children, their skin hanging from their backsides like baggy pajamas, tottered into a stinking barn for a last bowl of porridge before hitting the road on the orders of extremist leaders prepared to march them literally into the ground. . . .

'We don't know where we are going, nor why any more. Many have died in the forests of disease and hunger,' Jean Kanyamukenke, a former agronomy student from southern Rwanda, said.

The 4,027 tired and hungry refugees in the group moved as if in slow motion as they prepared yesterday to leave Punia, about halfway between Kindu and Kisangani in the north. The Hutu militia leaders had ordered them to march on, as the rebel force approached the town. From the air thousands of others could be seen heading north in a miserable line along a dirt road towards Kisangani.

The Dutch Minister of Development, Jan Pronk, who was in Punia when the marchers were driven through, commented: 'Much more walking and all the refugees will be dead.'

In the jungles of Amazonia, Brazilian searchers after gold continued their penetration of the rainforest reserve inhabited by the Yanomami Indians. The lure of diamonds added to the intensity of the search. Six thousand miners were on the march, more even than in previous years, when their clashes with the Yanomami had led to the deaths of dozens of Indians. On August 28 *The Times* published a report from the region by Gabriella Gamini. 'Health workers said a sharp rise in cases of malaria, tuberculosis and pulmonary infections had been detected among the Yanomami Indians,' she wrote, 'since gold and diamond prospectors, known as "garimpeiros", set up makeshift jungle camps which are polluting and spreading disease along ecologically sensitive rivers.'

Claudio Esteves de Oliveira, one of three doctors working for a pro-Yanomami Indian commission, commented:

When garimpeiros invade the Yanomami lands they plunder their crops, pollute the rivers and shoot any Indian who opposes their presence. The mining pits dug along the rivers are breeding grounds for the mosquitoes which cause malaria epidemics. Drunken garimpeiros regularly raid the villages to rape the Yanomami girls. We have detected an alarming rise in sexually transmitted disease, and dread to think what the outcome would be if we started to test for HIV.

During August, twelve Yanomami Indians were killed in confrontations with armed gold diggers. Three children under three and ten elderly women died from malnutrition before reaching the hospital in Boa Vista, capital of the Brazilian state of Roraima, and the closest city to the two hundred remote Yanomami villages scattered around the reserve.

During a meeting of indigenous leaders with Brazilian authorities in Boa Vista, Davi Kopenawa Yanomami, a chief, told the authorities:

The gold and diamond hunters threaten us with guns and illness. They are killing my people and keep coming into our lands, even though the

Government promised to keep them out. Very soon the Yanomami will be no more and the Earth will be destroyed. My people want to defend the forest from destruction. But the white men have weapons that kill faster than an arrow. The Yanomami cannot fight back against this evil.

In 1991, in response to the threat posed by the miners, the Brazilian government demarcated a third of the State of Roraima as a 'preservation' zone for the Yanomami. Its failure to enforce the zone was criticized by local and international organizations which defend the rights of endangered tribes. According to Non-Governmental Organizations affiliated to the United Nations, which were working in the region, the situation had become 'critical', and if the flow of illegal miners continues the damage could be irreversible.

In the early 1990s the Brazilian police and army had launched Operation Free Jungle to remove 40,000 garimpeiros by force during the gold rush then. But no such operation was planned against the new influx of miners desperate to find gold and diamonds in the protected region. One miner asked Gabriella Gamini when she spoke to him in Boa Vista: 'It's the richest area in the land, full of gold and diamond deposits. Why should the Indians have it all?' Like so many others, she commented, 'he is a migrant from exhausted mines in the poor state of Maranhão. Thousands of others come from backwater towns across the border in Venezuela – such as the Wild West-style Santa Elena de Uieren – which survive on the illegal diamond trade.'

In 1996 the Brazilian government gave $1 million to Brazil's official organization for the protection of indigenous groups. The money, which was meant to be used to renew operations against illegal mining activity, 'has mysteriously vanished', reported Gabriella Gamini. 'Some say it was spent by the cash-strapped organization's headquarters in Brasilia before it ever reached Roraima.'

Missionaries and health workers who live in the Indian villages of Toototobi and Dimini, added Gabriella Gamini, 'have reported seeing huge patches of forest being cut down to build clandestine landing strips for the twin-engined planes which bring miners into the jungle. More than fifty-five *balsas*, or barges, used to drill into riverbeds have also been spotted in the area'. At least 100,000 Yanomami Indians roamed the northern Amazon basin before Spanish colonizers reached the Americas after 1492. An estimated 22,000 members of the tribe survive, 9,400 in Brazil and the rest in

Venezuelan rainforest. Brazilian health workers, who registered a small rise in the Yanomami birth rate in the years 1993–5, when mining activity was almost eradicated, believe that their population is falling again.

While Brazilian forests were being cut down to make way for mining activity, the forests of Indonesia were being burned to create farm land. The result in 1997 was fires which created a cloud of pollution that affected the whole of South-East Asia. According to the World Wide Fund for Nature (WWF) up to 1,700,000 acres of forest were ablaze on September 25. 'Blame for the fires', wrote the British environmentalist Richard Black, 'fell mainly on large landowners, private and corporate, who used fire as a cheap method of felling trees and extending their plots, often illegally. "Slash-and-burn" subsistence farmers were also held responsible.' In Kuala Lumpur, and other parts of Malaysia, people were advised to wear masks if they went outside. Airports had to be closed down. Schools were closed. Hospitals treated hundreds of thousands of people with respiratory ailments.

Among the problems confronting many nations was still that of water shortage. Sometimes pollution was to blame. A government ecology committee in Azerbaijan reported that half the country's factories were polluting lakes and rivers. Other former Soviet Republics had the same dismal story to tell. The Caspian Sea was almost too polluted for the caviar-bearing sturgeon to survive in it. The Aral Sea was drying up. Siberian rivers flowing into the North Polar seas were disgorging high levels of toxic waste and crude oil spillage. In the Russian city of Dzerzhinsk, three hundred miles east of Moscow, the concentration of dioxins in groundwater – a mere eighteen miles from the River Volga – was estimated at fifty times above the acceptable international standard.

On World Water Day, in March, the United Nations warned that eighty countries were short of water. Within a few decades, it forecast, as much as two-thirds of the world's population would be suffering from 'moderate to severe water stress'.

At the beginning of May the focus of world poverty turned to South Asia, when the United Nations Development Programme gave its support to a report, produced by the Human Development Centre in Pakistan, with details of the growing impoverishment of the region. Using every accepted measurement – with regard to per-capita income, education, literacy and diet – the report concluded that South Asia had 'for the first time' fallen behind sub-Saharan Africa, to become 'the poorest, most illiterate and malnourished region on Earth'. South Asia's average per capita annual income was $309. That of sub-Saharan Africa was $555. In South Asia, two-thirds of all children were underweight; in sub-Saharan Africa, one-third. The only statistic that revealed substantial growth in South Asia was that of arms expenditure. India had built up for itself the fourth largest army in the world, Pakistan the eighth largest. Both powers had spent vast sums of money developing nuclear weapons.

India, which ranked 142nd in the world in terms of per capita income, had the world's highest arms import bill. Pakistan, 119th in the income table, had the tenth largest arms bill. The annual expenditure on arms in South Asia – principally India, Pakistan, Myanmar (formerly Burma), Malaya, Singapore and Indonesia – was more than $8,580 million. The region contained twenty per cent of the world's population, but forty per cent of the world's poor. The President of the Human Development Centre, Mahbub ul-Haq, commented: 'The quality of social services, education, transport, drinking water and health is deteriorating. South Asia must reposition itself or it will be marginalized by global forces. If it misses out there will be tremendous dangers of revolution in this society.' Among the exploitations most common was that of child labour. An estimated one million children aged fifteen and under were working in Delhi illegally at the end of the century.

The United Nations World Health Organization had expressed its hope, in the 1980s, that epidemic disease could be eliminated from the planet by the end of the century. But those creatures who were the carriers and causes of epidemics did not go so quietly to their graves. The year 1997 marked the centenary of the discovery, in India, that malaria was spread by mosquitoes. A century later, anti-malarial drugs existed in profusion. But the malaria-bearing mosquito persisted in its dangerous peregrinations, killing three million people every year.

Another disease that was believed to be capable of elimination, tuberculosis (TB), likewise continued to cause death on a wide scale. During 1997 the World Health Organization announced that, despite the existence and availability of effective drug treatments, TB was still 'the world's leading infectious killer' of young people and adults. There was evidence of the emergence of drug-resistant forms of TB; these had led to an increase in the disease on four continents, specifically in Russia, Latvia, Ivory Coast (Côte d'Ivoire), Argentina and India. Although TB was being conquered in most developed countries, the falling rate of TB was offset by the rising rate of asthma.

In the pantheon of death-dealing habits, smoking had emerged as the greatest killer of them all, far exceeding AIDS. The World Health Organization appealed in 1997 to the leaders of all countries to join in the fight against a 'global tobacco epidemic'. In the developed countries, smoking was on the decline, following more than a decade of active anti-smoking governmental campaigns (including graver and graver mandatory health warnings on tobacco advertisements). But in developing countries, and among women generally, lung cancer was massively on the increase. China was the centre of the smoking epidemics. The Chinese were smoking one in every three cigarettes in the world, and two thousand Chinese were dying every day of cancer of the lungs and other diseases directly related to smoking.

Globally, children remained the most vulnerable group in society. In 1997 there were ten million deaths among children under the age of five. Ninety-seven per cent of those deaths were in the developing world. Most of them were due to infectious diseases, pneumonia and diarrhoea, combined with malnutrition.

The computer age came into its own in 1997. That May, the Russian world chess champion, Garry Kasparov, was defeated by Deep Blue, a 'supercomputer' constructed by International Business Machines (IBM) in the United States. A new avenue of global communications had also come into its own, the World Wide Web (www). This had been devised by Tim Berners-Lee at the CERN laboratories in Geneva, as a way of organizing the information on the Internet and making it accessible. Computers linked to the Internet would have an effective – and efficient – browsing system. Computer screens and their operators in any country, at any time of day or night, could be linked with anywhere else in the world, in a matter of seconds, and fragments of seconds. One aspect of this new global system of instantaneous communication was e-mail, a virtually simultaneous global correspondence system, first used by research scientists at American defence establishments in the 1960s, which eliminated the need for pen, ink, stamps, post offices and, most important of all, the passage of time. Instantaneous communication was the final contribution of the twentieth century to the chitter-chatter of mankind, as well as to its serious purposes in the spheres of commerce, government and health.

Meanwhile, ravages of nature, as well as disease, continued to beset the end of the century as they had done its beginning. In May, 2,400 Iranians were killed in an earthquake which made 100,000 people homeless. In November, four thousand Vietnamese, most of them fishermen, were drowned when a typhoon hit the southern coast.

The ability of industrial nations to wreak a different kind of havoc was shown in June, when it was revealed that five of Britain's largest companies were regularly polluting the environment by illegally releasing thousands of tons of toxic gases and dangerous chemicals into the atmosphere. One of the chemical firms involved, Rhône-Poulenc – the world's eighth largest drug and chemical group – was also among the world's leading producers of drugs to help asthma and allergy sufferers, most of whom were the victims of urban and industrial pollution.

CHAPTER FORTY-SEVEN

1998

> By burying the remains of the victims we want to expiate
> the sins of our predecessors. We are all guilty. It is
> impossible to lie to ourselves by justifying the senseless
> cruelty on political grounds. Guilty are those who com-
> mitted this heinous crime, and those who have been
> justifying it for decades – all of us.
>
> BORIS YELTSIN

JUST AS WARS HAD SCARRED the opening years of the twentieth century, well before the outbreak of the First World War, so wars also scarred the century's closing years. In the first weeks of 1998 the focus of world news attention fell on Kosovo, a province of what was left of Yugoslavia. The majority of the population of Kosovo were ethnic Albanians. The province had been an integral part of Albania before the First World War. It was in Kosovo that the Serb prince Lazar fell in battle as the Ottoman invaders swept through the Balkans in 1389.

'Serbs would no more think of yielding Kosovo to Albanians', wrote Brooke Unger in the *Economist* on January 24, 'than would Jews of handing Jerusalem to Palestinians. Serbia's corrupt and brutal rule is supposed to make this clear to Kosovars, but it also feeds an enraged separatism that makes an uprising seem all but inevitable.' Western diplomats, Unger added,

watch this slow dance to disaster with horror. The fear is that domestic violence in Serbia could turn into yet another Balkan war. Macedonia, at least a quarter of whose people are Albanian, might be dragged in, and with it neighbours that have never stopped questioning its newly-won statehood: Bulgarians, Greeks, Yugoslavs and Albanians. If Greece got involved, so might Turkey, its bitter Aegean rival. Their clash would weaken NATO's southern tier. Would Russia, patron to both Serbia and Greece, stand aloof?

On April 27, in an intensification of the Kosovo conflict, Serbian soldiers of the Yugoslav army crossed into the province to confront the national movement. In the first of the renewed skirmishes, twenty Albanians were killed. Fighting resumed in July, when Yugoslav infantry burned down dozens of small villages as they encircled the Kosovo Liberation Army (KLA) in the town of Orahovac and drove them from it. As many as two hundred ethnic Albanians were killed during a four-day battle in the streets of Orahovać, a town of 20,000 people, most of them ethnic Albanians. Some of the dead were killed by Serb tank fire as they tried to flee. Many houses belonging to ethnic Albanians were then destroyed.

President Milošević was summoned to Moscow, where on June 16 he agreed to stop the Serbian attacks inside Kosovo, and to open negotiations with the leader of the Kosovo Albanians, Ibrahim Rugova. When the attacks continued, the United States, Russia and the European Union joined together to renew calls for Milošević to halt the Serbian attacks. They also condemned the financial support being given to the Kosovo Liberation Army by outside forces. On July 8 an American emissary, Robert Gelbard, stated that if the KLA did not agree to a peaceful settlement, 'we will try to interrupt their ability to sustain themselves through the full chain of supply'.

At the end of July, Serb soldiers brought death and destruction to yet more villages. Near the village of Rance, eleven Albanian civilians, mostly women and children, were blown to pieces by a tank shell as they tried to escape on a cart. In an attack on the village of Senik, sixteen civilians were killed. Hundreds of others were forced to flee. Fernando del Mundo, the representative of the United Nations High Commissioner for Refugees in Kosovo, told the British journalist Anthony Loyd that 'the scene I saw there was out of Dante's *Inferno*'. Del Mundo went on to describe how 'a four year old boy had had his head blown off; a child had been killed by shrapnel while in its mother's arms; a dead woman was missing half her face; another casualty was a dead woman whose two-week-old baby, deprived of its mother's milk, died after twenty-four hours'.

For their part, the ethnic Albanians exacted a cruel revenge. Dozens of Serb civilians were taken hostage, then killed. Since the beginning of the year, 173 Serbs had disappeared. It was presumed they had been murdered. A renewed Serb military offensive in the second week of September drove

40,000 ethnic Albanian refugees to try to escape the advancing troops. Fernando del Mundo walked almost two miles along the seven-mile-long refugee column. 'I have just returned from the area,' he told a press conference in Peć on September 9, 'and Serbian troops and tanks are moving towards the refugees from the east. The head of the column is near the village of Krusevać and its tail-end is seven miles to the rear. The dirt road is jammed with tractors, wagons and cars. People are in a panic because they fled villages that were shelled and burnt on Tuesday. They have little water or food and no shelter.'

In all, 400,000 ethnic Albanians – a quarter of Kosovo's population – were on the move, driven from their homes, or fleeing from them to avoid Serb vengeance. In the second week of September, dozens of Albanian villages were burned to the ground. In the rural triangle between the towns of Peć, Dakovica and Klina, Anthony Loyd witnessed the aftermath of the Serb advance:

Though there was little fighting, the zone nevertheless presented a glimpse of the apocalypse. Dense smoke poured into the sky, minarets emerging like rare blooms. Columns of tanks, armoured personnel carriers and vehicle-mounted anti-aircraft guns swept out of the shattered ruins eastwards.

Behind them, scarcely a single Albanian remained. Dead dogs and livestock littered the fields; smashed cars and tractors lay overturned on the verges of empty roads; bandana-clad police looted and burnt whatever the shelling and shooting had left behind.

Throughout the first two weeks of October, as Serb soldiers fanned out through Kosovo, and as more and more reports of rape, looting and murder were verified, the European Union and NATO demanded of the government in Belgrade that it halt the offensive in Kosovo at once. President Milošević at first resisted all demands. But the threat of air strikes by NATO, as in the Bosnian conflict, was effective. A ceasefire was agreed on October 12 between the Kosovo Liberation Army and the Serbs. It was negotiated in Belgrade by President Clinton's special envoy, Richard Holbrooke. The Yugoslav government also agreed that a 2,000-strong 'verification force' could take up positions in Kosovo to monitor the ceasefire. The force, which began to arrive at the end of November, was unarmed. Among its first members to arrive in Kosovo were fifty soldiers from Britain. Two thousand more soldiers were expected within three months, drawn from thirty-five States, members of the Organization on Security and Co-operation in Europe (the OSCE). Its power lay in the threat of NATO airstrikes should the Serbs renew hostilities within their Kosovo region.

In nearby Bosnia the NATO-led Stabilization Force was not only maintaining the peace and patrolling the borders, but was on the lookout for war criminals. On December 2 it captured General Radislav Krstić, who was wanted for trial as a war criminal by The Hague Tribunal. It was Krstić who had overseen the fall of Srebrenica in 1995, after which several thousand Muslims had been massacred. The indictment against him had been kept secret until his arrest, so that he would be caught – as he was – unawares. Three weeks after Krstić's capture, a former Bosnian Croat paramilitary commander, Anto Furundzija, was sentenced to ten years in prison for 'violating the laws or customs of war' after standing by while another paramilitary soldier beat and raped a female detainee near Vitez in 1993. Furundzija was found guilty of torture and of 'outraging personal dignity'.

One aftermath of the Balkan troubles was an influx of refugees to Western Europe. The issue of 'asylum-seekers' entered the British political agenda when the government announced, at the end of November, that social security benefits would be cut by half for those asylum-seekers reaching Britain, in order, in the words of Richard Ford, the Home Correspondent of *The Times*, 'to let the world know that Britain is no longer an attractive destination for economic migrants, rather than genuine refugees'. It was expected by the British immigration authorities that at least 110,000 asylum-seekers then in Britain would have their claims for refugee status rejected, and be forced to leave the country by 2002. In 1997 there had been 32,500 asylum applicants. In 1998 that figure had risen to 38,000. Ten years earlier it had been only four thousand. Britain was far from alone in being confronted by this problem. As the century came to an end the pressure of asylum-seekers from Africa, Asia and the Balkans on every Western European nation was considerable, and growing.

Under the British government's scheme, a new national agency was to be established to provide support for asylum-seekers. Its services would include providing vouchers to be exchanged in shops for food and clothing. The asylum-seekers were to be dispersed around Britain – in bed-and-breakfast accommodation, hostels and disused council housing – to ease the burden on London. The Medical Foundation for the Care of Victims of Torture, which treated more than fifty refugees a day at its centre in North London, criticized the plans. If the asylum-seekers were sent to far-off locations, it said, they would no longer have access to appropriate care or to the community and legal assistance bodies concentrated in the capital. Helen Bamber, the Foundation's Director, denounced the voucher scheme as 'dehumanizing' because it would place refugees in a position of absolute dependency and deny them the opportunity to pay for a bus fare, a public lavatory or a treat for a child.

Meeting in Britain, at Birmingham, in mid-May, the world's seven richest powers – Canada, France, Germany, Italy, Japan, the United Kingdom and the United States – known as the G7, joined with Russia to form the G8, and to discuss the need to reduce, and to collect, the debts owed to them by the world's poorer nations. They also discussed the scale of their foreign-aid commitments. France, which spent the second largest amount on arms of the G8, also gave the largest amount in aid, 0.48 per cent of its Gross National Product (GNP). Canada, with the smallest economy of the G8, and the member spending the smallest amount on arms, gave 0.32 per cent of its GNP in foreign aid. The United States, the richest country in the world as well as the largest spender on arms, gave the lowest level of any industrialized country of its GNP in aid, 0.12 per cent. Of this, one-fifth went to Israel and Egypt, as part of the ongoing peace-negotiation commitments that had begun two decades earlier.

Britain, the least rich of the G8 countries in terms of GNP, and the country which spent the least per capita on health and education, gave 0.27 per cent of its GNP in foreign aid, slightly above the G8 average. Britain also gave the highest proportion (a quarter) of its overseas aid to the least developed countries. 'It is one of the great lessons of the twentieth century', Tony Blair had told a television interviewer on May 17, 'that democracy and prosperity go together.' With regard to foreign aid, Germany was an above-average donor, giving 0.33 per cent of its GNP to that end. As to indebtedness, the two countries that owed Germany the most money for interest-bearing loans were Russia and India. The largest lender of the G8 nations was Japan, which was owed $70 billion in outstanding loans. Japan had the highest per-capita income in the industrialized world.

As the G8 Summit met in Birmingham, a parallel meeting of the People's Summit took place in the city to urge cancellation of the debts of the poor nations of the world. To further this goal, a Jubilee 2000 Coalition was established. Its Director, Ann Pettifor, explained: 'We want to persuade world leaders, on the occasion of the Millennium, to give a billion people a fresh start in life – by writing off the unpayable debts of the poorest countries. . . . Countries whose resources are diverted from health, clean water and sanitation – into unproductive debt service – will be able to concentrate on rebuilding for their own people.'

At the Birmingham summit the situation of Russia was revealed as bizarre. While owing $40 billion, much of it in outstanding loans from the Soviet period, Russia was itself owed $70 billion by the poorer nations on whose behalf the Jubilee 2000 Coalition was campaigning. Russia saw this money as a potential source of foreign exchange, and had joined the Paris Club of creditor–debtor nations as a creditor, in an attempt to collect these debts. The countries that owed Russia money were among the poorest. They included Nicaragua, Vietnam, Yemen, Angola, Ethiopia, Guinea and Mozambique, countries to which the former Soviet Union had lent money as part of its attempt to build up political influence. They were being asked to pay in order to enable the former giant to sustain its own weak economy.

The award of the Nobel Prize for Economics to Amartya Sen stressed the importance of the needs of the developing world. Indian-born, living and teaching in Britain, Sen had stressed the need for equity in the relationship between the industrial and developing world. His book *Poverty and Famines*, published in 1981, had been subtitled 'an essay on entitlement and deprivation'.

The Warsaw Pact nations of Eastern Europe, once a bastion of Soviet power, were being drawn into the NATO orbit. NATO itself had completed a year of military activity in Bosnia, acting as a shield for the Sarajevo government against Bosnian Serb attacks. In seeking to extend the borders of NATO-land as far east as the Russian, Belarus and Ukrainian borders, on May 1 the United States Senate ratified what was known as NATO 'enlargement', to include Poland, Hungary and the Czech Republic in the following year. By this vote, the United States became the fourth NATO country to support enlargement: the others were Germany, Canada, Denmark and Norway. In welcoming this decision, President Clinton said that the expansion of NATO would reduce the prospect of Americans ever being called again 'to fight in the battlefields of Europe'.

The eastward enlargement effectively redrew Europe's former Cold War boundaries, pushing NATO to the borders of Russia, and committing

British, American and other NATO forces to the defence of the three former Warsaw Pact countries. Within the Senate, there had been opposition from ten Democrats and nine Republicans, who claimed that the treaty would reverse the post-Cold War democratic process in Russia, stretch the NATO alliance to breaking point, cost the American taxpayer billions of dollars, and push American soldiers into unwelcome peacekeeping missions. But isolationism, however well argued, was unable to gain anything approaching a majority vote.

Within the United States a grim echo of earlier racism took place at the beginning of June, when three men with suspected links to the Ku Klux Klan chained a disabled Black man, James Byrd, to the back of their pick-up truck and drove him for two miles along an asphalt road in Texas. In the course of the ride his head was torn off. His torso was then dumped in a creek. 'All the evidence shows that the slaying was racially motivated,' said the local sheriff. It was a year since President Clinton's promise in San Diego to develop a plan to heal a nation still divided by attitudes to race.

In Northern Ireland, the persistent efforts of John Major during his premiership, followed by the new initiatives of Tony Blair, the direct intervention of President Clinton and the negotiating skills of George Mitchell, the former United States Senator, served to secure the long-awaited settlement. After talks chaired by Mitchell, agreement was reached on Good Friday, April 10. Cross-border links between Northern Ireland and the Irish Republic were to be strengthened. Catholic participation in Northern Ireland's constitutional, political and economic development would be on a basis of equality. But union between Northern Ireland and the Republic would not come about without the consent of Northern Ireland's Unionist majority.

As an earnest of their desire to draw Sinn Fein into the process as an active negotiating and long-term participating partner, the British and Irish governments allowed several prominent IRA prisoners, men who had been convicted of murders, to leave prison and attend the Sinn Fein conference that was to vote on the Good Friday Accord. The conference had been called for May 11 in Dublin. The prisoners had agreed to express their public support for the abandonment of force.

At its Dublin conference, amid enthusiasm at the presence of the hero–prisoners, Sinn Fein approved the Good Friday Accord – including the pledge that there would be no union with the Republic of Ireland without the agreement of the Ulster Unionists – and voted to pursue its long-term goal and ideological imperative of a united Ireland through politics, not force. The legacy of violence was not denounced, however. Martin Fletcher, the Chief Ireland Correspondent of *The Times*, was present at the Dublin conference. 'The emotional highlight of the day . . .', he wrote, 'was the unexpected entrance of the Balcombe Street gang, which terrorized London in the mid 1970s. Joseph O'Connell, Harry Duggan, Eddie Butler and Hugh Doherty are serving multiple life sentences for their campaign of bombings and shootings, including the murder of Ross McWhirter.'

Ross McWhirter, the editor and compiler of the *Guinness Book of Records*, and a tireless campaigner against terrorism, had been murdered by the IRA in 1975. Martin Fletcher's account continued:

Delegates shouted, whistled and stamped their feet in a deafening ten-minute ovation as they entered the conference hall, punching the air in triumph, and there were even tears as Mr Adams hugged them on stage.

Mr Adams said the intention was not to provoke Unionists, but the men were 'our Nelson Mandelas' enjoying their first day of freedom in twenty-three years and their presence was 'a great delight'. Earlier this year the Home Secretary ruled that they would have to spend the rest of their lives in prison because of the enormity of their crimes. They were transferred from England to Portlaoise jail last week and allowed thirty-six hours' leave to attend the conference yesterday. They will be driven back to prison today.

The convicted murderers were returned to prison. Gerry Adams, who had welcomed them, turned Sinn Fein towards the negotiating tables. 'I recognize how significant this decision is for Republicans,' said Mo Mowlam, the Secretary of State for Northern Ireland in Blair's government, 'and pay tribute to the leadership of Gerry Adams in bringing his party to support the agreement.' Voting was held throughout Northern Ireland on May 23, when seventy-one per cent of the voters endorsed the Good Friday Accord: fifty-five per cent of Protestants and ninety-six per cent of Catholics had cast their votes in favour. In welcoming the result, Blair said: 'Everybody has now said you can make your argument by word, by debate, by argument, by persuasion. But there is no place for the gun and the bomb or violence in the politics of Northern Ireland or any of the island of Ireland. All that is over and gone.'

President Clinton hailed what he called 'a springtime of peace', adding: 'Peace is no longer a dream. It is a reality.'

A massive bomb blast in Omagh on August 15 killed twenty-nine people, most of them women and children. Both Catholics and Protestants were among the dead. The youngest to be killed, Breda Devine, was eighteen months old. Maura Monaghan was twenty months old. The bomb was the work of an IRA splinter group which called itself, provocatively, the 'Real IRA'.

It was the worst single atrocity during almost thirty years of Troubles. But it was not allowed by any of the supporters of the Good Friday agreement to halt the process of talking that had already begun. Outrage at the bomb was expressed by all the political Parties engaged in the talks, including the IRA. Gerry Adams announced: 'I am totally horrified by this action and I condemn it without any equivocation'. Three days after the bomb, the perpetrators announced that 'all military operations have been suspended from midnight'.

The talks continued, unaffected by the Omagh bomb except in the determination of the participants to continue on the path of peaceful and constructive dialogue. In recognition of what had been achieved, the Nobel Peace Prize was awarded that October to the two local politicians, John Hume and David Trimble, who had contributed the most, by their leadership, to Catholic-Protestant reconciliation. 'We hope it is merited,' said Trimble, 'because there is an element of prematurity about this. . . .' Twelve years earlier, the Nobel Peace Prize had gone to Mairead Corrigan and Betty Williams, two Belfast women who had brought thousands of people on to the streets demanding an end to bloodshed.

With 1,200 million inhabitants, China was by far the world's most populous country. On 1 January 1998 a former United States State Department officer, Maxwell Harway, wrote of his most recent visit to China: 'Except for the large picture of Mao in front of his mausoleum, his pictures are rare. We found a few in the art and antique stores, together with pictures of old emperors. In the hotel bookshop, we found *Mao, Man not God*. In other words, he too made mistakes, a thought that a few years ago would have sent the author to the provinces to pick cabbages.'

A month after this observation was published, information reached the West of the less than encouraging Chinese treatment of political dissidents.

On January 24, four Chinese poets in the south-western city of Guiyang were arrested as they planned to publish a new literary review, *China Cultural Renaissance*. In it they had intended to put forward the case for a flourishing of art outside the official ideology. After the poets had been arrested, their homes were ransacked. Other dissident voices were able to make themselves heard. Xu Wenli, who had already spent twelve years in prison for advocating democracy, called publicly for the government in Beijing to open talks with the exiled Dalai Lama. He also called – in an echo of Lech Walesa's call in Poland nearly two decades earlier – for free trade unions to represent the Chinese workers.

One area in which Chinese dissent and democratic yearnings could not easily be cowed was through the Internet. In a despatch from Hong Kong – since the previous year a Chinese city – Michael Sheridan told readers of the *Sunday Times*, after telling them about the arrest of the four poets in Guiyang:

> Although the plight of the poets showed the prevalence of China's state repression, it also highlighted the astonishing persistence of dissent and growing underground network of intellectuals and even party officials who are daring to call for change. They are nourished by the Internet, often communicating by e-mail and in constant contact with an outside world that can no longer be kept behind an electronic great wall.
>
> Between 200,000 and 600,000 people in China are connected to the Internet, and the state council, China's cabinet, has put out regulations banning its use for 'inciting the overthrow of the government or the socialist system'.
>
> According to the United States State Department, Chinese dissidents overseas have already succeeded in sending documents by e-mail to supporters inside the country, even though government technicians block access to some web sites.

Michael Sheridan concluded: 'Power may no longer come out of the barrel of a gun, as Mao said, but from a computer keyboard, and while demonstrators can be shot on the streets, hackers can lurk in any office, creating an authoritarian nightmare.'

On June 25, a few hours before President Clinton landed in China on his first official visit, seventy-nine Chinese dissidents, from nineteen provinces, signed an open letter announcing the creation of the China Democracy Party. Five of those who tried to register the Party officially were arrested. They were detained at an unknown prison, without legal representation or contact with their families: a violation of China's own criminal law. The others continued to insist that they were a legitimate manifestation of political activity. One of the founders of the new Party, Xu Wenli, noted: 'It is not like before, when it was "one soldier swimming alone". Now we go out and do this together.'

Also on the eve of President Clinton's visit to China, a former Secretary-General of the Chinese Communist Party, the seventy-eight-year-old Zhao Ziyang, who had been removed from power for supporting the student demonstrators in Tiananmen Square in 1989, spoke out against the shootings in the square and the subsequent repressions. The massacre in the square, he said, was 'one of the biggest human rights problems this century'. In a public statement, Zhao Ziyang declared: 'In the past, the Communist Party of China has rectified many historical mistakes. Now we are facing the arrival of a new, open, democratic and information-age era. What reason do we have to reject the will of the people, cling to the June 4 problem and block our road to democratic politics?'

Professor Ding Zilin, whose seventeen-year-old son had been killed in Tiananmen Square by an army bullet, and who had long acted as spokesperson for other grieving parents, said that she was pleased to learn of Zhao Ziyang's letter. 'I have been looking forward to such a day for a long time,' she said. 'This makes me confident about the future.'

On June 28, during Clinton's visit, the Chinese people were amazed to see him on their television screens, talking openly with their own President, Jiang Zemin, about human rights, Chinese rule in Tibet, and Tiananmen Square. On the following day, however, the Chinese-language newspapers made no reference to any of the controversial items, nor were Clinton's full remarks replayed on the television evening news. But in a speech on June 29 to students at Beijing University he electrified his young audience with his assertion that no country could prosper or find political stability in the twenty-first century 'without embracing human rights and individual freedom'. Bronwen Maddox, a journalist who was covering Clinton's visit for *The Times*, wrote of how, after the speech, 'now coasting into the easier half of his nine-day visit, Mr Clinton seems exhilarated – and horrified – by the visual evidence of China's transformation: the cybercafés packed with espresso-drinking, Internet-addicted students, just yards away from one-room huts with open fires, all bathed in air so polluted that the other side of the street is hazy'.

In August a book on existing Chinese labour camps published in the United States told of Muslims – mostly Turkic-speaking Uighurs – who had been rounded up in Sinkiang as part of the suppression of separatist sentiment, and put to work in uranium mines where the death rate was between ten and twenty per cent a year. 'Some become ill from black lung disease,' the authors, James Seymour and Richard Anderson, wrote, 'but many do not live long enough to develop that malady, as safety conditions are atrocious.' Also in August, in the town of Shenzhen, across the border from Hong Kong, thirty convicted criminals were executed in a mass firing-squad execution. Their crimes included murder, robbery, theft and dealing in illegal firearms. They had been sentenced in the morning and immediately taken away to be shot. Each was killed by a single bullet to the base of the skull. This was part of Operation Strike Hard, the scale of which had led to criticism from several Western human rights organizations: in 1996 alone, 4,367 criminals had been executed in this way.

In December the United States protested at the arrest of dozens of human rights activists, including Xu Wenli. Another of those arrested, Wang You-cai, had been one of the student leaders during the Tiananmen Square protests in 1989. On December 5, the Associated Press reported from Shanghai that, 'in its crackdown on dissent in cyberspace, China put a computer entrepreneur on trial on charges of giving e-mail addresses to an Internet pro-democracy magazine. Lin Hai, 30, owner of a software company here, went on trial in a closed courtroom on charges of subversion for giving the addresses of 30,000 Chinese computer users to VIP Reference, a journal published by Chinese dissidents in the United States.'

It was on 4 June 1997 that the first issue of an electronic magazine, Tunnel, had appeared in Chinese e-mail boxes. The date had been deliberately chosen: it was the eighth anniversary of the Tiananmen Square massacre. The magazine was almost entirely written by intellectuals inside China, and then distributed to Chinese e-mail boxes from computers in the United States. Tunnel described itself as the first electronic magazine 'dedicated to breaking China's information blockade'. In the words of Greg May, a research associate of Chinese studies at the Nixon Center in Washington: 'The Internet is fundamentally an unruly free-for-all. Just as the United States is able to prosecute only a handful of the child pornographers and con artists on-line, Beijing can hope to catch only a token few of its growing legion of cyber-critics.'

On December 20 the Beijing government allowed Liu Nianchun, a human rights activist for whom President Clinton had intervened, to leave China for the United States, together with his wife and daughter. They flew that day to Detroit. On the following day, December 21, even as news of Liu's release was gaining China goodwill in the West, a court in Beijing sentenced his fellow human rights activist Xu Wenli to thirteen years in prison, and Wang Youcai to eleven years. The next day, after a trial in Wuhan, their colleague Qin Yongmin was sentenced to twelve years in prison.

Human rights abuses in China were much on the Western agenda; inside China it was the ravages of nature that claimed human lives on a vast scale. In July, at least three thousand Chinese were killed in floods in the province of Hupeh, along the Yangtse River.

In Burma, the leader of the opposition, Aung San Suu Kyi, went on hunger strike to protest against her exclusion for the previous decade from political life. Braving official censure, a hundred student members of her National League for Democracy demonstrated and demanded that parliament should be called, and their Party be allowed to participate in free elections. Riot police broke up the demonstration. Suu Kyi ended her strike and was taken home by ambulance. Her long fight to restore democracy in Burma continued, but the military regime made no concessions.

The National League for Democracy continued to draw attention to the Burmese government's exploitation of the country, including the laundering of drug money, and urged the maintenance of the United Nations boycott, imposed because of repeated abuses of human rights. In an interview published in the *Sunday Times* on July 12, Suu Kyi said: 'We have a lot of quiet supporters but any people who come to us today do so with the courage to face whatever it is that the government chooses to do to them. There are those who say that it's all very well for me because I'm exempt from prison, but I'm not. There is no guarantee that I'll not be put into prison. Everybody is vulnerable.'

In Indonesia, on November 14, twelve people were killed in clashes with the police in the capital, Jakarta, after seven hours of fighting. The predominantly student protesters were demanding the introduction of genuine democracy. After more than fifty years of almost continuous dictatorship, and the fall of President Suharto in May, the new regime was struggling to find the way forward to new laws and a new openness. But, in answer to the demonstration, President Habibie ordered a military crackdown against those whom he denounced as 'subversives'. Commented David Watts, correspondent of *The Times* in Jakarta: 'It was hard to see what subversion could achieve in a country that is already on its knees. A hundred million Indonesians live below the poverty line, existing on 2,000 calories a day.' Among those pressing for reforms was Amien Rais, the populist Muslim leader who, like the nineteenth-century reformers in Europe, believed that parliament was the forum through which reforms should come.

In Britain, on November 25, the Law Lords overturned a High Court decision which had spared the former Chilean dictator, General Pinochet, from a Spanish demand for extradition. The Spanish government wanted to bring war crimes charges against him, arising out of his tyrannical rule twenty-five years earlier, and the deaths and disappearance of thousands of people, including many Spanish citizens. The eighty-three-year-old Pinochet, who was in a London hospital receiving medical treatment when the Spaniards made their request, was detained. On 29 March 1999, after prolonged legal arguments, the Law Lords reversed their earlier ruling, thus enabling Spain to seek Pinochet's extradition.

The war crimes tribunals for both Rwanda and Bosnia were continuing their work. In Rwanda, the death sentences passed by the Rwandan courts were to be carried out publicly. Four execution sites were chosen, at each of which those found guilty had perpetrated their crimes. It was the first time since the end of the Second World War fifty-three years earlier that men had been found guilty of genocide. Those to be executed had not been accused of firing shots or wielding machetes, but of giving the orders for mass murder.

One of the execution sites was Kigali. The four who were to be shot there, in public, included Froduald Karamira, who had appealed daily over radio stations controlled by extremist Hutus for the Hutu majority to 'cleanse' their communities of Tutsi 'cockroaches'. Amnesty International had expressed its concern that the defendants had not been provided with sufficient time or opportunity to prepare their defence. Some had been given notice of the date of their trial, and access to their dossiers, only a few days before the trial began. After sentence of death had been passed, Pope John Paul II had appealed for amnesty. But the murder of so many hundreds of thousands of people in the most barbaric circumstances propelled a deep and swift vengeance. The first public executions took place on April 24. A British journalist, David Orr, witnessed the scene in Kigali, and reported it to *The Times*:

Tens of thousands had assembled at the football field by the time the four prisoners appeared. To cheers, three men and a woman were taken from a van and led to four wooden stakes driven into the ground. . . .

The spectators were gathered thirty or forty deep around three sides of the hillside pitch in Nyamirambo, a poor suburb of the capital, Kigali. Armed military patrolled the high ground above the far sideline where the doomed prisoners awaited their fate.

Some young men had climbed into trees to get a better view, others sat, legs dangling, on the crossbars of the goals. A woman held her young daughter aloft so she could see the four.

A well-dressed man said: 'This is justice being done.' A young man in jeans said: 'This will serve as an example to people who might try to organize genocide in future.'

On November 16, in The Hague, three United Nations judges imposed the first international convictions for atrocities committed against Bosnian Serbs. A Bosnian Croat and two Muslims were convicted of murdering, torturing and raping Serb prisoners in 1992. The trial had lasted for twenty months. It was the first in which the tribunal concentrated on atrocities against Serbs – who were blamed for most of the war crimes committed in Bosnia. The prosecutor, Brenda Hollis, had been seconded from the United States Army legal branch.

After listening to the testimony of survivors of Čelebiči camp of how prisoners were murdered, tortured and raped by the camp staff, the Presiding Judge, Adolphus Karibi-Whyte, from Nigeria, sentenced the camp's deputy commander, Hazim Delić, a Muslim, to twenty years in prison. 'You displayed a singular brutality in causing the deaths of two men,' the judge said, 'and a calculating cruelty in the torture and mistreatment of many others.' In their 483-page ruling, the judges said that Delić appeared 'to take a sadistic pleasure in causing the detainees pain.'

The camp warden at Čelebiči was a Bosnian Croat, Zdravko Mučić. He was found guilty of eleven war crimes and grave breaches of the Geneva Conventions for overseeing guards who murdered nine Serbs and tortured six. His conviction was the first by an international court on the basis of 'command responsibility' since the International Military Tribunals at Nuremberg and Tokyo convicted Second World War German and Japanese commanders and superiors for the crimes committed by their subordinates. Mučić was sentenced to seven years' imprisonment. A camp guard, Esad

Landzo, was sent to prison for fifteen years for murdering three inmates and torturing others. He and Hazim Delić were found guilty of having beaten to death one man and nailed a Muslim political Party badge to his head. Landzo also beat a sixty-year-old man to death with a wooden plank.

The Muslim fundamentalist killings in Algeria showed no abatement. A thousand people, almost all of them civilians, were being killed every month. On January 11 the Editor-in-Chief of Algeria's leading independent newspaper, *El Watan*, appealed through the pages of the *Sunday Times* for an international conference to study and condemn the violence in his country:

> Those who kill are well known; they do not try to hide what they have done. Rather, they proudly admit responsibility for it. That was confirmed by the latest bulletin of the Islamic Salvation Front – the main Islamicist political grouping – in which it even revealed details of killers' identities.
>
> The dilemma for all us Algerians, living as we do in anxiety, fear and uncertainty, is how to put an end to their horrible carnage.
>
> Terrorism in Algeria is an extremely powerful force. It has grown out of the Islamist party that succeeded during 1990 and 1991 in winning over thousands of people with its demagogic speeches.
>
> The armed groups consider that they are fighting for their faith. These are young men who are extremely determined and who offer their lives to God. All those who are not with them are denounced as *tawaghit* (ungodly ones) and non-believers. Political Islam in Algeria has produced death and desolation. It is no solution for my country.
>
> However, the current political and military power structure does not give us much hope for the future either. The system functions on the basis of regionalism and nepotism. Corruption is widespread. You cannot expect millions of Algerians to have hope in such a situation.

At least 65,000 Algerians had been killed by Muslim fundamentalists during the previous six years.

In East Africa, car bombs detonated within minutes of each other on August 7 at two American embassies, one in Nairobi and the other in Dar-es-Salaam, killed 184 people, including twelve Americans. Most of the dead were in Nairobi. The perpetrators were Muslim fundamentalists opposed to a diversity of enemies, of whom the United States and Israel headed the list.

President Clinton ordered immediate retaliation, and American warplanes struck at the headquarters of the Saudi Arabian-born prince and multi-millionaire Osama bin Laden in Afghanistan, from which the bombing campaign had been planned, and against a terrorist facility in Sudan. More than fifty Cruise missiles were fired at bin Laden's headquarters near Khost, in southern Afghanistan. In a carefully co-ordinated attack, they were launched from two ships in the Red Sea and four ships and a submarine in the Arabian Sea. Twenty-three people there were killed at the base, including fifteen Western converts to Islam, one Briton among them, who had decided to throw in their lot with the fundamentalists. Bin Laden was not among the dead.

Throughout the area of the American attacks, anti-Western sentiment was inflamed. Most Western aid workers left Afghanistan to avoid being assaulted in the streets; some were evacuated by air. Yeltsin called the American air strikes an 'act of terrorism'. Defending the two attacks on Islamic fundamentalists, Clinton called the perpetrators people 'who wrap murder in the cloak of righteousness and so profane the name of a great religion in whose name they claim to act'. He added: 'Afghanistan and Sudan have been warned for years to stop harbouring these groups.' Tony Blair announced: 'I strongly support this American action.'

Within Afghanistan, the Taleban were strengthening their political control by imposing edicts based on their interpretation of Islamic law. On July 8 it was announced that anyone possessing a television set, satellite dish or video recorder would be punished. After fifteen days, any television set not handed over to the authorities would be smashed. Other laws being strictly enforced forbade women to work, girls from going to school, and men from trimming their beards. Another edict called for painting all downstairs windows black, so that women inside could not be seen from the street. In the fifteen per cent of Afghanistan that was not under Taleban control, Taleban troops were fighting against the forces of General Ahmed Shah Masood, the leader of the country's Tajik minority. On August 10 the northern city of Mazar-i-Sharif fell to the Taleban forces. It had a predominantly Uzbek population, whose lifestyle, in the words of one observer, Christopher Thomas, was 'repugnant to the orthodox Taleban – alchohol is freely on sale, women are mostly unveiled, long hair is popular among men, and girls attend school'. Following the fall of Mazar-i-Sharif, General Masood, a hero of the guerrilla war against Soviet occupation a decade earlier, still controlled a section of the road that led from Kabul to the northern border.

Fleeing from the fighting, one and a half million Afghan refugees were living in camps in north-eastern Iran.

In Iran itself, the relatively more moderate Islamic regime of President Khatami was having to face the threat of Taleban incursions into eastern Iran. It was also confronted by an upsurge of Islamic extremism, by those who saw Khatami as too moderate, and who, as a sign of their determination not to slide back to Western modernity, had begun to execute supporters of free speech. Among those killed were the writer Mohammed Jafar Pouyandeh and the poet Mohammed Mokhtari, both outspoken opponents of censorship.

Apologies for historic wrongs marked the year 1998, as they had done throughout the decade. On a visit to Japan in January, Tony Blair encouraged the Japanese Prime Minister, Ryutaro Hashimoto, to make an apology – not the first from Japan – about Second World War atrocities. The Japanese still declined to pay the £14,000 (just under $20,000) to each surviving prisoner of war that the former prisoners had asked for. They did agree, however, to increase from £600,000 to £800,000 the annual 'reconciliation package' which would involve a joint pilgrimage – funded by the British and Japanese governments – by British and Japanese veterans to the old battlefields and cemeteries in South-East Asia; a programme of one-year scholarships at Japanese schools for the grandchildren of British prisoners of war; and a programme of visits to war graves in Japan, to be doubled to a hundred veterans a year.

For those ten thousand former prisoners of war and several thousand more former civilian internees, most of whom had hoped for individual recompense – of a modest sort – there was, to say the least, deep disappointment. 'The Japanese have refused to offer the compensation we are demanding because they say it will open the floodgates,' commented Arthur Titherington, the chairman of the Japanese Labour Camp Survivors' Association. 'But who made the floods?'

The Japanese refusal to pay compensation was upheld by a Tokyo court on November 26. 'This court rejects the plaintiffs' claims,' said the Japanese judge, Shigeki Inoue, and he added: 'There is no need to examine facts related to maltreatment or to rule on them.' Muriel Parham, on behalf of the Association of British Civilian Internees, said: 'It is disgusting, but I don't see it as a surprise. The Japanese don't see it as a surprise. The Japanese don't want to lose face.' Muriel Parham was five years old when she was captured in Manila with her family. 'We spent three-and-a-half years in utter hell,' she said. 'We were all skeletons when we came out.'

China was also hoping for an apology for the Japanese invasion of 1937 and the destructions and massacres that followed. The visit of the Japanese Prime Minister, Keizo Obuchi, to President Jiang Zemin of China in the last week of November was to have been the occasion for a public apology by Japan for the cruelties inflicted. But, despite intense diplomatic consultations, no formula could be found, and Keizo Obuchi limited himself to a document that contained what many Chinese intellectuals considered the far too ano-dyne phrase 'deep regrets and a heartfelt apology to the Chinese people'. According to a Chinese government spokesman, Tang Guoqiang, however, 'the key is not the signing, it is how to implement the letter and spirit of the document. With regard to Sino-Japanese relations, the most important issues are how to face history, how to have correct perspective with regard to history and how to open up the future for bilateral relations.'

On March 16 the Vatican issued its first apology to the Jews with regard to Roman Catholic passivity during the Holocaust. The statement regretted the 'errors and failures of sons and daughters of the Church' who had failed to save Jews. It also praised those thousands of Catholic priests and laity whose intervention had saved Jewish lives. The statement also looked to the future: 'We wish to turn awareness of past sins into a firm resolve to build a new future in which there will be no more anti-Judaism among Christians or anti-Christian sentiment among Jews, but a shared mutual respect.'

Not all retrospective activity was in search of apology or reconciliation. On the same day that the Vatican apologized for its wartime passivity in the face of the Nazi persecution of the Jews, five hundred veterans of a wartime Latvian Waffen-SS unit, many of them wearing their old SS uniforms, marched in the Latvian capital, Riga, to the National Freedom monument, to lay wreaths in memory of 50,000 of their fallen comrades, killed in action fighting alongside the German army on the Eastern Front, or dying after the war in Soviet prison camps. As the SS veterans made their way to the monument, some of those lining the streets greeted them with applause, while others cried out 'Fascists!' and 'Murderers!'

On the last day of March, in the New Zealand parliament, a Bill was introduced whose aim was to 'close a century of injustices' inflicted on the Maori people of the South Island. The Bill formalized an agreement signed the previous October, under which the Ngai Tahu tribe would receive more than £56 million as compensation for historic wrongs. The new Bill was specifically based on the decision to honour the Treaty of Waitingi, signed between the Maoris and Queen Victoria in 1840. Under the treaty, through which New Zealand became part of the British Empire, the Maoris were promised that they could keep their land, and their 'treasures', which included forests and fisheries. Wars later in the century, fought with great brutality, dispossessed them of these 'treasures' and almost all their land. In introducing the new Bill, and arguing that its passage was a moral as well as a judicial imperative, Doug Graham, the New Zealand Justice Minister, was close to tears.

On the day on which the New Zealand legislation was introduced, Australia handed back to its traditional Aboriginal owners the land at Maralinga used by Britain for atomic testing in the 1950s and 1960s. Almost £40 million had been spent cleaning the desolate and remote area to make it inhabitable again for its indigenous Tjarutja people.

In June the German government apologized to the Hereros of Namibia (the former German colony of South-West Africa) for the massacre of thousands of Herero men, women and children in 1904. Of the 80,000 Herero in South-West Africa at the start of the century, only 15,000 had been alive a decade later.

The German apology was sent in the form of a private diplomatic note, in answer to a petition for compensation sent to Bonn by King Munjuku Nguvana. The note spoke of 'a particularly dark chapter in our bilateral relations' and stated that 'the moral responsibility has to weigh heavily on the consciences of all historically sensitive Germans'. No compensation was offered. But the German Foreign Ministry pointed out that several projects which had received some of the German aid to Namibia did benefit the Herero peoples – themselves a minority in Namibia, partly as a result of Germany's own earlier depredations.

Also in June, five sackfuls of necklaces, rings, bracelets, watches, coins, family silver, cutlery and precious stones stolen by the Germans when they entered Trieste in 1943 were handed back to the survivors of the Jewish community from which they had been taken. Some of those whose belongings were returned had been deported to Auschwitz and killed; others had been murdered in the concentration camp set up by the SS in a flour mill at San Sabba, near the city. The sacks had been found in a vault in Rome. In taking possession of them, the Chief Rabbi of Rome, Elio Toaff, said: 'We are here today to remember those who are no longer with us, those who have left us their evidence shut up inside those sacks.'

On August 2 the Deutsche Bank, Germany's largest commercial bank, issued an apology about the 4,446 kilograms (9,780lb) of Nazi looted gold which it had bought during the Second World War, some of it arriving in sealed sacks from Auschwitz. This included gold smelted from the teeth of victims, wedding rings and jewellery. 'The bank regrets most deeply the injustice that took place,' the bank announced, adding that it 'fully acknowledges its moral and ethical responsibilities for the darkest chapter in history'.

The Deutsche Bank offered no financial recompense, but the Swiss banks, including the government-owned Swiss Central Bank, all of whom had also dealt in Nazi gold and looted Jewish assets, agreed on August 12 to provide $1,250 million for survivor groups, as compensation for unreturned Holocaust-era assets. The offer was announced as twenty States in the United States, and thirty American municipalities, were preparing to impose economic sanctions against the Swiss banks. Six months later, on 16 February 1999, the German government announced that twelve of Germany's largest banks and companies would contribute to a new fund to compensate several hundred thousand surviving slave labourers from the Nazi era. Slave labourers had hitherto been excluded from the German government's post-war payments amounting to $60 billion, paid out to Jewish and other victims of Nazi crimes. The new fund, of $2 billion, would be available for those who had been forced to work, often in horrific conditions, in private companies such as Krupp, Siemens and Volkswagen.

A Russian apology on July 17 was made by President Yeltsin himself when, hand on heart, he offered 'a deep bow of repentance and national atonement' before the remains of the last Tsar of Russia, the Emperor Nicholas II, murdered by the Bolsheviks in 1918. From St Petersburg, where the ceremony took place in the Cathedral of the St Peter and St Paul Fortress, Michael Binyon wrote to *The Times*: 'At the end of a moving ceremony in the Cathedral of the Peter and Paul Fortress Mr Yeltsin, watched by millions of Russians across the country, stood in sombre silence before the vault while his wife, Naina, crossed herself.'

Yeltsin told those gathered in the cathedral: 'The massacre of the Tsar was one of the most shameful pages of our history. By burying the remains of the victims we want to expiate the sins of our predecessors. We are all guilty. It is impossible to lie to ourselves by justifying the senseless cruelty on political grounds. Guilty are those who committed this heinous crime, and those who have been justifying it for decades – all of us.'

On November 10, a memorial to the 'millions' of victims of Stalin's terror was unveiled in Moscow, in a park not far from the Kremlin. It consisted of hundreds of carved stone heads behind a symbolic prison fence of metal bars and barbed wire.

As the century drew towards its close, historical echoes reverberated more and more: anniversaries became the focal point for television and radio programmes and newspaper and magazine articles, even for grand political gatherings. On the fiftieth anniversary of the end of the Second World War, in May 1995, the heads of more than a hundred states had gathered at St Paul's Cathedral in London for a service of reconciliation and remembrance. June 1996 saw the few surviving veterans of the Battle of the Somme – when 20,000 British soldiers were killed in a morning – gather at the site and remember their fallen comrades. In 1998 hardly a day passed without some historical echo being presented to the public. It was not only through anniversaries. On February 11, among forty-eight new Canadians swearing allegiance to their adopted home was Kim Phuc. In 1972 her photograph had appeared in newspapers all over the world – a terrified naked girl running away from her Vietnamese village after an American napalm attack. Her two brothers were killed that day. Fifteen years later, she and her husband had moved from Vietnam to Cuba. In 1992, during an aeroplane stopover in Gander, Newfoundland, they had defected to Canada, where she was granted asylum, and where her two sons were born. As she became a Canadian citizen she was asked what ambitions she had. She replied: 'To take care of my boys. To do my best to help Canada.'

Another Vietnamese story was revived a month later, thirty years after American soldiers had massacred a hundred Vietnamese civilians at the village of My Lai. Three Americans who had tried to halt the massacre were given recognition as heroes in a ceremony in Washington on March 8, when they received the Soldier's Medal, the highest award for bravery not involving contact with the enemy. For one of the three, Glenn Andreotta, it was a posthumous award: he had been killed in action three weeks after the massacre. The other two, Hugh Thompson and Lawrence Colburn, received the award in person. Thompson's medal citation for heroism 'above and beyond the call of duty' was candid. It stated that he had landed his helicopter 'in the line of fire between fleeing Vietnamese civilians and pursuing American troops to prevent their murder'.

Even after thirty years, many Americans were distressed by these revelations. Vietnam remained a scar on the vibrant tissue of American life.

In another echo of the savage past in Indochina, on April 16 news reached the West that Pol Pot, the former Cambodian dictator, was dead. As many as 1,700,000 Cambodians had died during his tyrannical regime. Western journalists who crossed the border that night and saw the body were in no doubt that it was 'Brother Number One', as he had been known by his followers. Whether Pol Pot had died of natural causes, or by his own hand, or violently, was not known. Henry Kissinger thought he might have been killed by the Khmer Rouge whom he had once led, to prevent him being handed over for trial and revealing their connection, and that of their new leader, Ta Mok, with the existing Hun Sen regime in the capital, Phnom Penh.

Almost all of the continent of Africa had been free of colonial rule for the last third of the century. But it had struggled with many demons, from famine and drought to civil war and inter-tribal slaughter. The aspirations of several dozen Black South African leaders, nation builders in their day, had been severely curtailed. One Black African, Nelson Mandela, had emerged – after almost three decades in prison – as the political and moral leader of his nation. Another, the American-educated Kofi Annan, who had been born in Ghana, was the first Black African to lead the United Nations, as its Secretary-General. He had proved a doughty fighter for global reconciliation, and for upholding the rule of law and justice. He was asked by the Security Council, at the suggestion of the United States, to prepare a report on the political and economic future of Africa. Following the bloodletting in Somalia and Rwanda, the United States sought an international consensus on policy towards Africa. Shortly before Annan's report was ready, President Clinton travelled through Africa, urging greater democratization and free-market economies.

One African Head of State, President Museveni of Uganda, had argued that Africa must stop blaming its colonial past for its ills, and 'solve its own problems'. Kofi Annan shared this view. On April 16 he presented his report. 'Today more than ever Africa must look to itself,' he wrote.

The nature of political power in many African States, together with the real and perceived consequences of capturing and maintaining power, is a key source of conflict across the continent.

It is frequently the case that political victory assumes a winner-takes-all form with respect to wealth and resources, patronage, and the prestige and prerogatives of office.

Where there is insufficient accountability of leaders, lack of transparency of regimes, inadequate checks and balances, non-adherence to the rule of law, absence of peaceful means to change or replace leadership, or lack of respect for human rights, political control becomes excessively important, and the stakes become dangerously high.

Annan's report, a blueprint for Africa at the start of the twenty-first century, argued that too many African States were too ready to resort to military force. He proposed that they cap their military spending at 1.5 per cent of their Gross Domestic Product, and make a public commitment to 'zero growth' in their defence budgets for the following ten years. He also called for economic liberalization. State-owned industries should be privatized 'without delay'. Above all, he stressed, what was needed was 'good governance'. Every African State should stamp out corruption, and show respect for human rights, democracy and the rule of law. As for the rest of the world, Annan wrote, it had a part to play as well: by reducing the foreign debts it was owed, and by allowing African goods access to wider markets. All this should be put in train at once: Annan proposed an African Heads-of-State summit in five years' time – in 2003.

The immediate needs of Africa were also much on Kofi Annan's agenda. In the eastern region of the Democratic Republic of Congo (formerly Zaire), ethnic Tutsis, supported by both Uganda and Rwanda, had attacked several towns, including Goma and Bukavu on Lake Kivu, and also Kisangani, the country's third largest city, which controlled shipping on the Congo River. Their aim was the overthrow of President Kabila, who two years earlier had begun his own march to power from this same region. In the words of one Africa watcher, Sam Kiley: 'Dreams of an "African renaissance" led by a new breed of leader have been shattered' by the uprising. In the capital, Kinshasa, Congolese citizens were urged throughout August by Kabila's government to take up 'machetes and hoes' against the Tutsis. On August 12 Sam Kiley reported from Kinshasa that the government had stated on the previous day that it would 'turn the dreams of a Tutsi empire into a nightmare,' as Tutsis living in the capital were rounded up and many of them shot on the spot. 'Rapid Reaction Force police units in Kinshasa hunted down Tutsis yesterday,' Kiley reported. 'Those arrested were considered luckier than Tutsis trapped by civilians or ordinary soldiers. The latter risked a bullet or being stoned to death.'

Despite the intensity of ethnic hatreds, Kofi Annan was able, after a series of tense negotiations, to persuade the two sides to talk. On November 29, after negotiations in Paris, the governments of Uganda and Rwanda, both of which were actively supporting the rebels, and the Congo government, agreed to a ceasefire. The rebels themselves, who still controlled large areas of north-east Congo, swore to continue the fight. But they had lost their two sponsors. Kofi Annan was a realist: commenting on the agreement of Uganda and Rwanda to stop their support for the rebels, he said, 'They committed themselves to accepting an immediate end to hostilities. I hope they do not change their minds at once.' As the year came to an end, President Kabila continued to fight the rebels, enlisting Hutu extremists who had fled into Congo from Rwanda, and sending them into battle against ethnic Tutsis who, together with disaffected Congolese soldiers, constituted the main insurgent forces.

In Nigeria, after the imprisoned Yoruba leader Moshood Abiola died in captivity, ethnic riots led to widespread violence in July, and at least fifteen deaths. In Angola, artillery fire by UNITA rebels, led by Dr Savimbi, killed eight people in Huambo, leading to the evacuation of United Nations staff. In Guinea-Bissau, more than a hundred troops and civilians were killed when mutinous soldiers, followers of a former chief of staff, General Ansumane Mana, challenged government forces in the capital who remained loyal to President Joao Vieira, who, when an army major, had seized power eighteen years earlier. With a population of a million, Guinea-Bissau had one of the world's lowest life-expectancy rates, just under forty-two years for men, and just over forty-five for women. Almost half the population was illiterate.

In the Republic of Congo (formerly the French colony of Congo Brazzaville), a country of fewer than three million people, of whom a quarter were illiterate, more than a thousand people were killed in fighting between the army, loyal to the President, General Sassou-Nguesso, and rebels led by the former Prime Minister, Bernard Kolelas.

In the Sudan, hundreds of thousands of people were dying of hunger, the victims of famine, while civil war made the despatch of aid almost impossible. A temporary agreement to provide aid was reached in July between the Sudanese government, and the rebel forces of the Sudan People's Liberation Army in the famine area, and the United Nations, whose World Food

Programme undertook to co-ordinate relief efforts. Michael Dawes, who had seen the worst of malnutrition and death in the Bahr el Gazal region of the war-torn Sudan the previous year, wrote in the *Independent* on November 21:

> As the famine gripped, aid workers likened their task to bailing out a sinking ship. Their day would start with the count of the dead in the centres. No one was immune from the tangible, panicky desperation. One Belgian nurse on her first assignment cried when she managed to revive a dying old man by forcing the high protein porridge down his rattling throat. She sobbed in relief, but the man died two days later.
>
> After a visit to a feeding centre in Ajiep, I watched as a low-flying Hercules aircraft tipped out its load of food. I started to cry. At that moment it seemed that a beautiful swoop in the sky was bringing inter-national will to a place where there was only despair.
>
> There had been a lot wrong with the aid operation for southern Sudan. This time last year government donors did not want to know, and the United Nations operation was cutting back. The warnings that 1998 was going to see severe food shortages were ignored. But by this summer there was a single overriding tactic. Get the food in. And it came. Eighteen aircraft are now flying regular missions to save lives in southern Sudan. The cost to the United Nations and to other aid groups is put at about £1m a day.
>
> Waiting for his powdered vitamin A at Barrarud, a two-year-old called Adeng Abek clutched at his mother. He had on a necklace which is worn to prevent the spirits of the dead occupying his body. No one can give reliable figures for how many died in this, the latest of Sudan's many tragedies. Perhaps it is time to talk of lives saved.
>
> I left the feeding centre in Bahr el Gazal with the children playing football outside, and stopped off in another province where fields have been flooded since July. The floods have displaced 100,000 people. Even that will not stop the war.

The money for famine relief in Sudan came principally from the United States, which provided almost $200 million of the $284 million for which the United Nations had asked. The European Union and Britain were the next largest donors. The despatch of this aid to the Bahr el Gazal constituted, in the words of Rupert Cornwell, the Senior Foreign Correspondent of the *Independent*, 'the biggest humanitarian airdrop in history'.

It was not famine and food aid alone that made the Sudan part of the international agenda in 1998. The National Islamic Front government in the Sudan, in power since 1989, and driven by Muslim fundamentalist fervour, was carrying out a policy of mass destruction in the predominantly Christian and animist south of the country. An estimated 70,000 villagers were killed in the first six months of 1998. Tens of thousands were taken out of their villages and forcibly resettled in 'peace camps' from which there was no escape. Many were made to do unpaid labour. Boys were abducted and sold into slavery. Others were forcibly converted to Islam. When the United Nations failed to act decisively to challenge these violations of human rights, its Special Rapporteur, Dr Gaspar Biro – a distinguished Hungarian academic – who had urged action, resigned from his post.

Among the Non-Governmental Organizations fighting for human rights in Sudan, Christian Solidarity International, based in Geneva, did what it could to publicize the abuses, pointing out that many Black African Muslims in the Sudan were also being hounded by the Muslim rulers in Khartoum, accused of apostasy. On December 8, a Harvard law scholar, Mary Ann Glendon, wrote in the *New York Times* of how the National Islamic Front government had been 'conducting a genocidal campaign, in the predominantly Christian southern part of the country, that has already claimed more victims than the conflicts in Rwanda, Bosnia and Kosovo combined'. The overwhelming majority of the casualties, she pointed out, 'are not rebels, but civilians who do not share the regime's radical Islamic ideology', and she added:

Tens of thousands of women and children, deemed 'infidels', have been captured as war booty, taken from their families and forced into unpaid labour. Many are routinely beaten and abused. Some have been forced to convert to Islam and given Arabic names.

This year, the Government bombed a Sudanese refugee camp in Uganda and has bombed humanitarian targets – hospitals and feeding centres – at least forty times. Two Roman Catholic priests were tortured while detained on suspicious charges of sabotage. They may face the death penalty, which could mean crucifixion, under the Sudanese penal code.

Elsewhere in Africa, the former famine regions had also seen remarkable amelioration, even transformation. Jonathan Dimbleby, who had seen harrowing sights in Ethiopia twenty-five years earlier, returned to Ethiopia in 1998, and to the town where he had witnessed privation and death, writing in the *Daily Mail* on December 8:

> On this trip, after twenty-five years of unmitigated bad news from Ethiopia, I was looking for good news. But I am now not only older but more sceptical, exceptionally cautious when I hear political leaders, especially in the Third World, bang on about their grand schemes.
>
> It was therefore a relief to discover that Ethiopia's Prime Minister, Meles Zenawi, had no illusions. 'My biggest dream', he told me, 'is for all Ethiopians to have three meals a day, to have some access to education and a minimal level of health care.' A modest enough aspiration, I suggested. 'It's big for Ethiopia,' he replied.
>
> The statistics he had to confront are profoundly depressing. In a hospital in Dessie, I saw children still dying from starvation and related diseases. In Northern Ethiopia, one in five babies still fails to reach its first birthday – much the same death toll as it was when I was first there.
>
> As the population of the country has doubled to sixty million in the same period, it means that more babies die in Ethiopia today than twenty-five years ago. The hospital is the same size as it was when I first came: two hundred beds to serve a catchment area of eight million people. The doctor in charge is a hero. He has less than half his complement of doctors and nurses and lacks basic drugs and medicines. One of his two operating theatres is closed for lack of equipment; there is no laundry – and, in a town where power cuts are a nightly occurrence, no generator.
>
> Although he could earn five times as much in the private sector, he remains. Why? He looks towards a patient and says with gentle sadness: 'These are my people.'
>
> There is hope. The peasants no longer live in fear of officials blathering Marxist slogans. Their rights are respected, their voices are heard and a host of pilot schemes are afoot to lift them from penury.

Dimbleby's account continued:

> At a food 'handout' for the poorest of the poor, I saw men and women who had walked barefoot for over thirty miles to take their elected leaders to task for failing to organize the relief system fairly.
>
> Although the government had to import almost 500,000 tons of relief

grain this year to stave off an emergency (a larger tonnage by far than anywhere else in the world), the regime works.

With a sophisticated 'early warning' system and, crucially, far more trust between the government and the international agencies, distribution of relief is efficient and virtually free of corruption. As a result, the United Nations officials now believe that a repeat of the 1973 or 1984 famines is almost inconceivable.

I asked Meles Zenawi if he looked forward to the day when – in the name of genuine democracy – he might be kicked out of office through the ballot box. He nodded. 'Over time people will become bored with seeing the same faces over and over again . . . . they will choose a different prime minister.

'If we achieve that, we achieve our dreams. If we don't, then we shall have failed.' It is a seductive pitch and it is no surprise that in Western capitals he is regarded as one of the new men of Africa.

Freedom is, however, still a fragile plant in Ethiopia. Human rights are still violated. Yet I am inclined – cautiously – to believe that the nation really is en route from dictatorship to democracy, as the prime minister claims. If he is right, there is hope. If he is wrong, there will be a terrible reckoning.

I use the word 'nation' – and there's the rub. Ethiopia is not one but many nations and they are often in conflict. If these tensions cannot be resolved peacefully, the nascent democracy will collapse.

Even as I write, the future is under renewed threat. Last May, Eritrea (which won independence from Ethiopia in 1992) occupied a triangle of desert inside Ethiopia's border, a piece of real estate that is of precious little use to anyone but which is claimed by both sides.

Today the two armies face one another in a dangerous stand-off. If war erupts again in this corner of Africa, Ethiopia will descend even deeper into penury.

Starvation will stalk the land once again and the fragile dreams of those who love this country will be buried under the rubble.

*

Fears of nuclear proliferation were unexpectedly intensified on May 11, when the Indian government conducted three underground nuclear tests in the desert of Rajasthan. An Indian government spokesman announced with pride that the tests established that India had the capability for a 'weaponized nuclear programme'. In such a poor country, struggling to maintain some basic quality of life for its population of a thousand million, such a pro-gramme seemed to outside observers both an expensive and a dangerous luxury. The danger was that India's neighbour, Pakistan, with which it had fought three wars since partition in 1947, would move ahead with nuclear tests of its own. The Indian tests were also, as the United Nations Secretary-General, Kofi Annan, pointed out 'with deep regret', a breach of the inter-national testing moratorium.

Strong international pressure was put on Pakistan not to test any nuclear devices of its own. But on May 28, at Chagai, near the Afghan border, Pakistan carried out five underground nuclear tests: 'the first Islamic bomb' was how many Western newspapers described them. A sixth test was carried out on May 30. International indignation at both the Pakistani and Indian tests was mirrored in Delhi on August 6, the fifty-third anniversary of the atom bomb dropped on Hiroshima, when five thousand Indians, led by two of India's best-known writers, Arundhati Roy and Khushwant Singh, marched through the streets of Delhi to protest at both the Indian and Pakistani tests. One banner read: 'Bread, not bomb'.

The era of nuclear testing was meant to have ended more than a decade earlier. Like France before them, India and Pakistan had defied the inter-national community, and ignored the risks of radioactive contamination. The spectre of the long-term dangers to world health caused by past tests was revived. Between 1945 and 1975 the United States had tested 1,030 nuclear devices and the former Soviet Union 715. France had tested 210 devices – most recently in 1995 and 1996. Britain's total nuclear tests were only forty-five, the same number as China, which had helped Pakistan develop its nuclear arsenal.

International sanctions were applied against India and Pakistan for their testing. Pakistan was particularly hard hit by this, as it had come to rely heavily on foreign loans and had less foreign currency reserves than India on which to draw for the payment of imports. As Pakistan's economy threat-ened to collapse, President Clinton took a lead in lifting some of the sanctions, while the International Monetary Fund (IMF) agreed, on November 25, to a massive $3,300 million financial aid package. As with all IMF loans, conditions were attached: in the case of Pakistan, these included a provision 'to try to reduce corruption'.

India struggled with considerable communal and regional unrest, and conflict with Pakistan. Along the disputed border of Kashmir, fifty-two people were killed on both sides during rifle and artillery clashes. In western

Assam more than a hundred people were killed when bombs were exploded by the Bodo separatist movement, the Bodo Liberation Tigers. In eastern Assam, another separatist group, the ULFA, damaged oil pipelines and other government installations. More than thirty ULFA members were killed by the security forces. The non-Indian ethnic minorities in these remote regions, adjacent to Burma and China, had long harboured separatist ambitions. The highest death toll came, however, not from man's anger but from the excesses of nature: in June more than a thousand people (Oxfam put the number above ten thousand) were killed when a cyclone hit the district of Kandla, in Gujarat; two hundred died in December when the Brahmaputra River burst its banks, sweeping away crops, houses and villagers.

Epidemic disease continued to mar the final years of the century. On March 19 the World Health Organization warned that three million people were dying every year of tuberculosis (TB), the same number as were dying each year of malaria, and that the TB death rate was rising. In as angry a statement as could be found in the United Nations' annals, it named fifteen countries which, it said, must do more to control the spread of the disease. It also pointed out that eight of those countries had the money needed to take effective remedial action. But they had left it too late to implement the World Health Organization's specially devised emergency programme, the Directly Observed Treatment, Short Course (DOTS), which could have brought the epidemic under control.[1] The other seven countries had also left it too late.[2]

The World Health Organization pointed to another alarming aspect of the TB epidemic. Where people with the disease had failed to finish their six- or eight-month course of treatment – as often happened in 'poor, under-educated and especially nomadic or refugee communities' – the TB bacillus became immune to antibiotics. It was estimated that up to fifty million people were infected with the multi-drug resistant (MDR) form of the disease, 'even if they were not themselves ill'. Even New York 'is still struggling with an outbreak'. In Britain, where TB was relatively under control, there were up to six thousand new cases each year. According to Peter Omerod, of the British Thoracic Society: 'Complacency remains our

---

[1] The eight were: Brazil, Indonesia, Iran, Mexico, the Philippines, the Russian Federation, South Africa and Thailand.

[2] These seven were: Afghanistan, Ethiopia, Myanmar (formerly Burma), Nigeria, Pakistan, Sudan and Uganda.

biggest threat both in the United Kingdom and the rest of the world.'

Disease also struck Irian Jaya, the Indonesian half of New Guinea, where malaria killed at least six thousand people in the first three months of the year. Malnutrition was also taking its toll in Irian Jaya. Dr Ferenc Mayer, an emissary from the International Committee of the Red Cross, who visited the region in March, said that in some villages he went to 'every resident had malaria and up to 95 per cent were suffering malnutrition'.

Not malnutrition, but famine, was stalking North Korea. A report by the international relief agency Médecins sans Frontières said that corpses were lying in the streets in several cities, and that there were authenticated reports of cannibalism. Food aid from the United Nations-sponsored World Food Programme was reaching North Korea, but most of it was immediately diverted to the army for its own consumption, or sold on the black market where only the relatively well-off could afford it. As well as starvation, tuberculosis, typhoid and cholera were spreading.

One battle – an important one – in the environmental war was won in 1998. On April 30, agreement was announced in London and Washington whereby the government of Brazil, the World Wide Fund for Nature and the World Bank would preserve sixty-two million acres of rainforest as an internationally recognized 'protected area'. The World Bank agreed to cover the cost, estimated at no less than $100 million, and almost certainly more. A further 125 million acres were to be added to the protected area by 2005. The urgent need for this agreement was underlined by the fact that, in the three months before it was signed, fires started deliberately – and illegally – to clear the forest for farming and grazing had destroyed an area of forest the size of Belgium. The area to be protected was the size of the United Kingdom.

The worst natural disasters of the year were two earthquakes in Afghanistan. That in February killed four thousand people. That in May killed five thousand. Both earthquakes were in the northern and eastern areas controlled by anti-Taleban warlords. Fighting was suspended as the United Nations co-ordinated a massive airlift of food, medicine and tents. In July, two thousand people were killed when a tidal wave, caused by an underwater volcano, hit coastal towns and villages in Papua New Guinea, washing many villages away and submerging the towns under a wall of mud. In August the Chinese government announced that at least two thousand people had died since June in floods along the Yangtse. That month, several thousand people died, many of them from disease in overcrowded refugee shelters in

Bangladesh, as more than ten million people were driven from their homes by floods. To prevent the death toll rising into the hundreds of thousands, a massive airlift of food and supplies was sent through the United Nations and the International Red Cross.

In November, ten thousand people were killed, many of them buried alive, when a hurricane hit Honduras and Nicaragua (an earthquake in 1972 had killed five thousand people in Nicaragua). The hurricane's devastation was described by a British journalist, David Adams, from the Nicaraguan capital, Managua: 'Television pictures showed dozens of contorted bodies – arms, legs and sometimes only the tops of heads – sticking out of the dark mass of mud, along with tangled driftwood and debris washed down by more than a week of torrential rain. Other bodies lay face down, arms and legs outstretched, where they had been flattened by the mud.'

International aid was swiftly forthcoming. The European Union sent $7.7 million, the United States $3.5 million. A British frigate, HMS *Sheffield*, was helping with rescue work along the coast, together with the United States Coast Guard. The long-term prospects were dire: the storm had wiped out in a few hours seventy per cent of Nicaragua's crops.

There was yet another disease overshadowing both natural disasters and the depredations of malaria and tuberculosis – the two diseases which were killing between them six million people every year. By the summer of 1996, AIDS was approaching a worldwide deadly total of twelve million: more than two million in 1997 alone. According to the World Health Organization's *World Health Report*, published that summer, AIDS would soon be killing as many people as malaria or tuberculosis. While the incidence of AIDS was falling in Europe, in Africa it was rising precipitately. In Botswana and Zimbabwe one in every four adults was HIV-positive. Writing in the *International Herald Tribune*, Michael Specter warned:

Zimbabwe was suddenly turned into the deadly centre of the AIDS epidemic. Recent studies suggest that it may have the highest infection rate on earth.

The optimism of the West is a cruel fantasy in Zimbabwe. There are no treatments, no cure, little hope and in almost every country in Africa – far more pressing problems to face each day.

The savage virus has left few people untouched: it has devastated families, communities and cities. But seen through the weary and often bloodshot eyes of the beleaguered doctors and nurses who must attend to the sick people around them, AIDS is just another word for dying – and it's just another disease.

People here call it *iyoyo* – 'that thing'. In the sparse but spotless clinics of Zimbabwe – where aspirin is available only a third of the time – 'that thing' may not even be the one that matters most. With an average of less than $10 to spend on each person's health every year, most African countries have no money for tests, for fancy drugs or for complicated support networks.

Despite the magnitude of the epidemic, the great majority of people in Africa have no idea if they are infected with HIV, the virus that causes AIDS, and most do not want to know.

Michael Specter noted that Zimbabwe 'once had a health system that was the envy of southern Africa. Yet, fuelled by AIDS and by increasing poverty and instability, illness has begun to overcome the country. Tuberculosis, hepatitis, malaria, measles and cholera – all wholly preventable – have surged mercilessly. So have infant mortality, stillbirths and sexually transmitted diseases.' He was writing from Tsholotsho:

In 1996, during the last heavy rains, this region in the centre of Zimbabwe reported 82,000 cases of malaria – which means that more than half of the local population got sick.

In 1989, one hundred people died of malaria in Zimbabwe. Last year the figure was 2,800. Reported cases of tuberculosis – the sentinel illness of poverty and social decline – have risen to 35,000 last year from 5,000 in 1986. This year it is worse.

'AIDS continued to cut such a grim swath', wrote Helen Rumbelow in *The Times*, 'that it will soon rival the Black Death and Spanish influenza.' The Black Death in the fourteenth century and the Spanish influenza in 1918 and 1919 had each led to the deaths of as many as twenty million people. AIDS was on the way to overtaking them within a decade. After malaria, tuberculosis and AIDS, road deaths were the world's fourth largest killer. In the United States the number of people killed on the roads, averaging more than 45,000 since 1961, reached a total – since 1899 when twenty-six people were killed – of more than three million by 1998. The World Health Organization also looked at 'economically disabling diseases' which prevented people from leading a full and productive life: in this category, 'mental disorders' were on the increase, headed by depression, alcoholism, drug abuse, suicide and violence.

Amid the statistics of death and disability, the United Nations Population Fund announced on July 9 that the population of the world would reach six billion the following summer (the projected date was 16 June 1999). The world population, more than half of whom lived in Asia, had increased by one billion in the previous eleven years. Each year saw a further eighty million people added to the total population.

Notwithstanding statistics, the work of the World Health Organization, enabled people all over the world to be offered the chance of a better life. In November, five months after the publication of the 1996 report, the death was announced of Szeming Sze. He had been born in China, in Tientsin, in 1908, had been educated in England – where he worked as a doctor in a London slum – and had been resident in the United States from 1941. It was he who had helped create and develop the World Health Organization, and served as its Medical Director for twenty years.

Some of the needs of the poor nations for whom the World Health Organization worked had also become the needs of one nation which, a decade earlier, was one of the world's two Super Powers, Russia. For several months towards the end of the year, Russia had been approaching the West for help to feed its population. On October 9, in Moscow, the Russian Prime Minister, Yevgeni Primakov, asked the European Commission President, Jacques Santer, for 'humanitarian aid'. The inhabitants of villages in remote areas of northern Russia were leaving their homes and travelling hundreds of miles in search of food. Hunger was driving Russians in the Murmansk region to cross into Norway to seek asylum. In remote areas the Red Cross had begun to distribute food parcels.

On November 8, Russia signed an agreement with the United States, whereby America would provide Russia with more than three million metric tonnes of food, including $625 million worth of grain, pork and beef. Five days later, on November 13, the Russian government formally applied in Brussels for help from the European Union, submitting a list of urgent needs. The list, which the European Foreign Ministers approved, involved $500 million in aid. It included one million tonnes of wheat, sufficient for 387 million loaves of bread. Also to be sent were half a million tonnes of rye, 150,000 tonnes of beef, 100,000 tonnes of pigmeat and 50,000 tonnes of rice, as well as 50,000 tonnes of milk powder – enough to make 21,000 million glasses of milk, and enough to provide the people of Russia with 140 glasses each.

On November 20, a week after Russia's application for food aid, a Russian rocket was fired from the Baikonur cosmodrome: Baikonur had been rented to Russia from Kazakhstan for twenty-five years under the Caspian Agreement of June. The rocket carried with it the first stage of the International Space Station to be assembled, using more than a hundred components, over the coming five years, by Russia, the United States, the European Union, Canada, Brazil and Japan. The total cost of the project was $20 billion, the bulk of which was to be paid for by the United States. The Russian contribution, cost, almost $5 billion, was ten times the food aid agreed upon by the European Union. Beset by economic hardship, Russia struggled internally against a host of problems. More than 90,000 prisoners, many of them in psychiatric prisons, were suffering from tuberculosis. At the High Security Psychiatric Hospital in Orel, of eight hundred patients, all of them murderers, one-third had the disease. Many had caught it in prison. The medicine, diet and conditions needed to effect a cure were for the most part entirely absent.

Hardly a week passed in Russia without a political, business or 'Mafia' killing. On August 3 the murder was reported of Alexander Shkadov, chief executive of Russia's largest diamond-processing plant, Kristall, in Smolensk. The murder in St Petersburg of a prominent parliamentarian and human rights activist, Galina Starovoitova – shot to death on November 20 as she walked upstairs to her apartment – was likewise ascribed to deliberate contract killing. She had earlier opposed the war in Chechenya, and staunchly defended the rights of Estonians, Latvians and Lithuanians – as well as Poles and Ukrainians – to their independence. She was forty-three years old when she was killed.

In the last two years of the century, Russian neo-fascist youths roamed the streets of many cities, flaunting the swastika banner and calling for death to the Jews. In an attempt to counter this, the Minister of Justice, Pavel Krasheninnikov announced a ban on Nazi symbols and propaganda.

Many of Russia's eighty-nine autonomous republics and regions were in angry mood. In mid-November the thirty-six-year-old President of the Buddhist Autonomous Republic of Kalmykia, Kirsan Ilumzhinov, announced that he would secede from Russia if the subsidies due from Moscow failed to arrive. 'Whereas Chechenya is still receiving certain sums of federal money,' he told Russian television viewers, 'Kalmykia is not getting anything for paying student grants, or for vaccinating children, or for keeping maternity homes, or for implementing a programme for combating plague. So in fact we are not a part of Russia.' In retaliation, President Ilumzhinov was refusing to pay taxes due to Moscow, and was printing his own money.

Violence within the Russian Federation took many forms. In October, three British and one New Zealand engineer, sent to Chechenya by a British telecommunications firm in Weybridge, Surrey, were seized by rebel Muslim fundamentalists, and held for two months in the rebel-dominated town of Ursus-Martan. The rebels demanded a multi-million dollar ransom. On December 7, Chechen commandos loyal to the government in Grozny attacked the rebel hideout. Five gunmen and two commandos were killed. Twelve gunmen escaped with the four hostages. A few hours later the hostages were executed. Their severed heads were found by the roadside at Assinovskaya, on the western border of Chechenya. 'Beheading is not unusual in Chechenya,' wrote Carey Scott and Mark Franchetti in the *Sunday Times*. 'During the war for independence, the severed heads of Russian soldiers would appear in the Grozny market place. These four victims were not soldiers but telecom engineers from Surrey. They were not trying to destroy Chechenya but to rebuild it by helping to re-establish the telephone system wiped out by the war.'

The kidnappers insisted that they were acting in the name of Islam, inspired by both Iran and the Taleban in Afghanistan. A leaflet distributed in Grozny six months earlier, by followers of Arbi Barayev – leader of the fundamentalist Wahabi Muslim sect in Chechenya – declared that the struggle to build an Islamic State justified the kidnapping of Westerners.

The fragility of the secession States of the Soviet Union was highlighted in August, when Ukraine sought help from the International Monetary Fund to prop up its dwindling foreign currency reserves. By comparison with Poland and Hungary, both of which had attracted as much as $20 million in foreign investment since the fall of Communism, Ukraine had attracted only $2 billion. The International Monetary Fund agreed to a loan of $2.2 billion, over a ten-year period.

That December there was news of efforts being made in Russia for reunification with Belarus, one of the former Soviet Republics, and Russia's western neighbour. 'We are now calling for merging our nations in one Union State,'

Yeltsin explained after signing a Christmas Day agreement with the Belarus leader Alexander Lukashenko. Whether these two or any other of the fifteen former Soviet Republics would merge their sovereignties was not, however, either certain or in the realm of probability. Belarus, the closest to Russia linguistically and historically, was the one possible exception: its parliamentarians were pressing for the same national anthem as Russia, and a new name for their relationship, the Union of Sovereign Republics, nostalgically echoing the former Union of Soviet Socialist Republics.

In the third week of October, President Clinton participated in talks at the Wye Plantation near Washington. Also taking part was King Hussein of Jordan, who came to the talks from hospital where he was being treated for cancer. The principal participants were the Israeli Prime Minister, Benjamin Netanyahu, and the Chairman of the Palestinian Authority, Yasser Arafat, who were being urged to come to an agreement to reactivate the suspended Israeli withdrawal from the West Bank.

Arafat already had considerable powers, mainly over the Gaza Strip and six Palestinian cities. In return for his pledge to condemn anti-Israel attacks and root out Palestinian terrorist groups, the agreement held out the prospect of all the remaining Palestinian towns, and five hundred Palestinian villages on the West Bank, also coming under his rule. The negotiations were tense, many disagreements remained, but on October 23 – after a final unbroken twenty-four hours of negotiations in which Clinton took an active part – it was agreed that Israel would continue to transfer land, conquered in 1967, to the Palestinian Authority, and would embark on a move forward to the 'final status' talks, including the future of Jerusalem, as agreed between Arafat and Rabin four years earlier.

As a first fruit of the new agreement, on November 20 the Palestinian Authority took over the West Bank town of Qabatiya, once a centre of the Intifada against the Israeli occupation forces. 'We were the first town to hang a Palestinian for collaborating with Israel during the Intifada,' one resident told Patrick Cockburn, a British journalist who covered the celebrations in Qabatiya that day. 'He was called Mohammed Ayad and he was hanged from an electricity pole.' As part of the Wye Agreement, Israel released 250 Palestinian prisoners that day. One of them was being awaited in Qabatiya. Four days later, on November 24, in the Gaza Strip, Arafat opened the Palestinian airport: Yasser Arafat International Airport. The first plane to touch down on it came from Egypt. A few weeks later Palestine

Airlines inaugurated its first flights, each of its three planes resplendent in their new national livery.

Arafat also gained revenue for his Palestinian Authority from a casino in Jericho, built jointly with Austrian and Palestinian funds. The Islamic Hamas movement denounced the project, but Arafat was not deterred. From the first days of the experiment, hundreds of Israelis drove down to the Jordan Valley to gamble at the tables. It was their money that the Palestine Authority could turn to its own constructive, or private, purposes. Gambling experts from Britain and Denmark were brought in to oversee the tables. From the entrance to the casino could be seen the monastery and cliff edge of the Mount of Temptation.

A change of historic importance, and of future significance, came on November 23, when the office of President Herzog of Germany moved to Berlin. This was the first federal agency of the united Germany to leave Bonn – the West German capital during the five decades of divided Germany, for the designated new capital. In 2000, as in 1900, Berlin was to be the centre of the wealthiest and most powerful nation in Europe. The rebuilding of the post-war wastelands in Berlin – the bombing of which had been a central feature of Allied policy in the Second World War – had been proceeding with incredible energy. The date for the main move of government ministries and offices from Bonn to Berlin was set for September 1999.

The last of the First World War veterans were dying out, their deaths a subject of newspaper comment. In June, Fred Wall, the last-known British survivor of the Ypres Salient battle for Passchendaele died, aged a hundred. He was one of only two hundred soldiers from his battalion who survived 'going over the top' in November 1917. On November 7, under the heading 'Roll Call', *The Times* printed the names of all known British First World War soldiers, sailors and airmen who were still alive: there were 300 names in the list. Three days later, in the former French-ruled port of Dakar, Aboulaye N'Daye, the last Senegalese rifleman known to have fought in the First World War, died at the age of 104.

Modern communications were making the location of details ever easier; on the day of Rifleman N'Daye's death the Commonwealth War Graves Commission announced that whereas it used to receive 50,000 postal inquiries a year from people seeking to locate the graves of relatives killed in war, during the previous forty-eight hours it had received 700,000 – and in the previous week 4,200,000 – inquiries on its website. These 'hits' were an indication of the massive extension of global contact that had been brought about within a decade.

On December 16 the United States, supported militarily only by Britain, launched Operation Desert Fox against military and air targets in Iraq. Saddam Hussein was charged by the United States and Britain with defying the international arms inspectors, who were operating inside Iraq under United Nations auspices. The strikes continued on the three following nights. Twenty-five Iraqis were killed. Having extended the no-fly zone of 1991 northward from the 32nd to the 33rd parallel, the Iraqi missile sites at Hillah and the air bases in the region of Kut were both among the targets. These targets also included several sites not covered by the no-fly zones, including the capital, Baghdad, and the oil refineries of Kirkuk. The cost of Operation Desert Fox was formidable. In three nights of sustained attack, the United States military machine spent as much money as had been set aside by the government during the previous four years on cancer research.

Even as the attack was proceeding against Iraq's military infrastructure, both President Clinton and Tony Blair warned that further attacks would take place if Iraq continued to 'weaponize' its chemical and biological agents. In Britain, Muslim fundamentalists chanted 'Kill Tony Blair', but the Prime Minister insisted that if Saddam Hussein was not prevented from making these weapons 'the consequences to our future peace are real and fundamental'. Russia – on which Clinton had recently imposed sanctions for selling sensitive weapons technology to Iran, Libya and North Korea – led the voices of protest. Marshal Igor Sergeyev, the Defence Minister, stated that the American and British air strikes 'flagrantly violated the norms of international law, and openly ignored the world community's efforts to settle the situation'. In declining to attend a scheduled meeting of the recently created Russia-NATO Council, Sergeyev asked: 'How can we talk about co-operation and partnership with the alliance now, when Russia's opinion is openly ignored?'

In Sierra Leone, a rebel movement dislodged from power early in the year was carrying out a reign of terror. As Barbara Crossette reported in the *International Herald Tribune* on July 30:

> By the hundreds, poor farmers and villagers – men, women and children – have been shot, lacerated, mutilated by having limbs hacked off. Some

have been turned into grisly messengers of death, sent disfigured and bearing letters warning the West African country's president, Ahmad Tejan Kabbah, and the African peacekeeping troops who restored him to office in March that armed resistance will continue and no one is safe.

A refugee, who reached Guinea with only the stumps of his arms, told his story to a representative of Refugees International, a Washington-based advocacy group, which videotaped his testimony along with other accounts. 'You don't want a military government,' the refugee said the rebels told him. 'You say you want a civilian government. Then we will have to cut off your hands. Then go to Tejan Kabbah and he will have to give you new hands.'

Another refugee without hands, shaking with fear, appeared so traumatized on the tape that he repeated again and again his perplexity about how he could not use a toilet without help, when there was so little help to be had.

'What they are doing really is atrocious,' declared Fode Dabor, Sierra Leone's representative at the United Nations. 'I've never seen it before. They've been cutting limbs, gouging the eyes of innocent women and children. This is one of the most vicious rebel organizations in the world.'

In South Africa, the Truth and Reconciliation Commission continued its work. As in Spain after the death of Franco, or Chile after the retirement of Pinochet, there was to be no retributive justice. Among those pardoned in 1998 were the four young Black men who had murdered the White American student Amy Biehl five years earlier. The judges on the Commission explained that the four youths had subscribed to the belief that Whites were their enemies: 'At that moment, to them, Amy Biehl was a representative of the White community.' The Black South African writer, Sindiwe Magona, commented:

In a remarkable show of compassion, Amy's parents have supported the commission's decision. What is more, they have expressed the hope that these young men 'will receive the support necessary to live productive lives in a nonviolent atmosphere'.

If the miracle of 1994 will not be betrayed, the ultimate freedom the people of South Africa must give themselves is freedom from hate.

Past wrongs will not be redressed through mindless violence, blind hate, lawlessness and brutality. Rather, concerted corrective action is called for. And the first step toward that is acknowledging the hate – and then letting go of it. Only then can our energies be truly harnessed and redirected toward healing and the building of a nation.

'If even half of the outrage of August 1993 could be channelled into concrete action,' Sindiwe Magona wrote, 'the country would certainly inch toward the ideal state that Amy Biehl's parents envision. But there can be no cure until there has been a diagnosis. Acknowledging our cancer is the first step, the prerequisite.'

Race hatred, like religious and political extremism, like fanaticism of all forms, has emerged again and again as a theme of twentieth-century life and death. Much unfinished business of past years remained on the international agenda in 1998. On July 31 the first British war crimes procedure began with charges being laid against Anthony Sawoniuk, for the murder of four Jews in his hometown, the White Russian town of Domachevo in 1942. In Germany, President Roman Herzog awarded one of Germany's highest medals to Steven Spielberg, for his film *Schindler's List*, with its graphic portrayal of the Holocaust.

As the righting of historic wrongs also continued, on August 4 the Canadian government signed a treaty with an Indian 'nation', the Nisga'a, whose lands in British Columbia centred on the small town of New Aiyansh, giving its members effective self-government over a 745-square-mile swathe of territory, and unimpeded access to natural resources from which they had been excluded for more than a century. Fifty other Indian groups in British Columbia were pursuing similar claims.

On December 29 the Khmer Rouge made its first public apology for the 'killing fields' reign of terror in the 1970s, during which as many as two million people were murdered. Khieu Samphan, the former Cambodian Head of State, announced that he was 'very sorry'. Two months later, in March 1999, President Clinton apologized to the people of Guatemala, saying that Washington's active support in the 1950s and 1960s for a regime 'which engaged in widespread repression was wrong'.

Ecological dangers were becoming a matter of international alarm. The wild Atlantic salmon was believed to be on the verge of disappearing, defeated by industrial waste, polluted run-off from farms and the construction of dams that prevented its spawning. In July the World Wide Fund for Nature (WWF) announced that some of the most 'exotic' sea creatures to be found around British coasts could be killed off by thousands of metric tonnes of industrial chemicals, heavy metals and oil pollution unless government Ministers meeting at Sintra, in Portugal, took drastic steps to curb marine pollution.

Before the Sintra meeting, a new convention – Ospar – on pollution controls in the north-east Atlantic, was ratified by fifteen countries. Ministers at the Sintra meeting were urged to phase out 'hormone-mimicking' chemicals which change the sex of fish and other sea creatures, making it impossible for them to breed. Many chemicals, as well as heavy metals such as zinc, copper, mercury and arsenic, are so toxic they destroy life in large areas of the sea bed. More than seventy per cent of marine pollution starts on land, entering the sea via rivers, agricultural run-off and the atmosphere. Although deliberate discharge was already banned by international conventions, European seas were being used 'as a rubbish dump', in the words of the World Wide Fund. Considerable pollution came from oil and gas extraction, and from shipping.

The loudest alarm call came with regard to animal life on earth. The World Conservation Union (IUCN), after working closely with more than six hundred scientists worldwide, concluded that twenty-five per cent of all mammal and amphibian species were in danger of extinction, as were thirty-one per cent of all fish species, twenty per cent of all reptile species and eleven per cent of all bird species. Tigers and pandas were among the species that were soon likely to exist only in zoos. The cause of the threat was man's destruction of their habitat, including forests, wetlands, grasslands and chaparral. Of the 233 species of primate in Brazil, seventy per cent faced extinction; in Madagascar and South-East Asia, fifty per cent. Thirty per cent of the world's coral reefs were in critical condition from pollution.

The facts of the decline of species were known. The remedy lay with governments. Natural parks and nature reserves were not enough to curb the downward spiral. A concerted effort of international will was needed to tackle the destructive elements which had been allowed to flourish by international lack of will, and which had created the decline. Another destructive element globally was the aftermath of five decades of war and civil war: the anti-personnel mines which killed and maimed thousands of people every year. In August it was announced from Kuwait that more than 1,700 people had been killed by landmines since the Iraqi forces were driven out eight years earlier. In addition, eighty-four mine-clearing experts had been killed, and two hundred injured, while trying to do their job.

On December 7 a three-day meeting opened in the Bangladesh capital, Dhaka (formerly Dacca), at which it was stated that fifty countries were still manufacturing these mines, among them the United States, France, Spain, Italy and Serbia, but that international agreements were making the manufacture of mines illegal. Under the recently signed Ottawa Treaty, 131 nations had agreed not to assemble the mines, which used the simple technology used for making industrial explosives, and often the same computer chips as used in radios and transistors.

Following the Ottawa Treaty, $500 million had been pledged to mine clearance. The United States agreed to put an extra $200 million to this task for year 1999. Mine Extraction Centres had been established by the United Nations, with the organizational support of the Swiss government, in Cambodia, Bosnia, Mozambique, Angola and Afghanistan, charged with mapping the local minefields, and with training workers to extract the mines. The International Committee of the Red Cross, based in Geneva, had appointed Peter Herby as co-ordinator of a Mines-Arms Unit: he set out his priority at the Dhaka meeting: 'First, we have to ban them, then clear them, and then treat the victims.' Clearing the mines would be a massive task: the State Department in Washington estimated that there were at least sixty million such mines in the ground. Rehabilitation, the human face of the landmine horror, would require enormous financial, medical and psychological resources.

CHAPTER FORTY-EIGHT

1999

> Now, as a thousand years ago, it is the young, old and
> weak who suffer most. In 1999, no less than in 1939,
> the trauma of displacement lingers long after peace and
> shelter have been restored. In that sense, however com-
> plex and politicized refugee crises have become, the
> plight of their victims is timeless.
>
> RICHARD LLOYD PARRY

As the last year of the century began, the veneer of civilization
showed itself in places to be very thin. In Algeria, on 2 January 1999,
Muslim rebels cut the throats of twenty-two people in the village of Oued
al Aatchaane, 240 miles south-west of Algiers, as part of their struggle
against the military regime that had refused to allow elections likely to
lead to an Islamic victory. Fourteen Algerian soldiers were also killed that
week near Gdyel in a rebel ambush. On January 3 the *Sunday Times* estimated
the number of people dying of starvation in North Korea in 1998 at a
minimum of 300,000, stating that the figure could be half a million. As
the famine entered its fourth year, Trevor Rowe of the United Nations
World Food Programme warned: 'Unless we can feed children between the
ages of eight months and seven years, we may be talking about a lost
generation.'

In Sierra Leone, rebels of the Revolutionary United Front, who had sworn
to overthrow the government of Ahmed Kabbah, were joined by three hundred armed mercenaries from Ukraine. Entering the capital, Freetown, they
set fire to the power station, post office, town hall and United Nations
headquarters. A West African peacekeeping force (ECOMOG)[1], sent by

---

[1] ECOMOG is the Nigerian-led peacekeeping force of ECOWAS (Economic Community of
West African States); MOG stands for Monitoring Observer Group.

several other West African nations, challenged the rebels. A thousand people were killed in the fighting. In the part of Freetown held by Nigerian-led peacekeeping forces, French helicopter pilots evacuated citizens to safety. Offshore, a British frigate, HMS *Norfolk*, gave haven to Europeans. Its captain, Commander Bruce Williams, was shocked to see bodies of victims of the fighting floating past. 'There are many cases of mutilations,' he said, 'with arms and hands chopped off those who tried to resist rebel activities. They have not acted with any decorum or principles.'

The United Nations ranked Sierra Leone the poorest country in the world. As a result of the civil war, then in its ninth year, 440,000 citizens – a tenth of the total population – were refugees beyond its borders. Many members of the Sierra Leone government defence force, the Kamajors, men and boys, wore mirrors on their chests, believing this would ward off bullets. Led by Foday Sankoh, the rebels demanded that the country's diamond wealth be taken away from the government. In the areas of Sierra Leone controlled by the rebels, villagers loyal to the government were killed and maimed. At least a thousand civilians were killed during the rebels' six-week occupation of the town of Waterloo.

Massacres were also taking place in Yemen. On January 27 three Roman Catholic nuns who worked for the Missionaries of Charity – of which Mother Teresa had been the guiding light – were killed as they left their clinic in the Red Sea port of Hodeida. Two of them were from India and one from the Philippines.

Starting on January 7, 'death squads' operating in northern Colombia killed more than a hundred villagers. At Playon de Orozco, twenty-seven churchgoers attending a baptismal Mass were brutally murdered. The perpetrators of the killings called themselves the United Self-Defence Forces of Colombia (AUC).

On January 11, American warplanes fired on Iraqi surface-to-air missile batteries. As they did so, Pope John Paul II criticized the previous month's bombing of Iraq: 'International law cannot be the law of the strongest, or of a simple majority of States, or even of an international organization. It must be a law which conforms to the principles of natural and moral law, which are always binding on parties in conflict and the various issues in dispute.'

Within three months, after a hundred air-defence sites in Iraq had been hit by American and British warplanes, the Saudi Arabian government refused to allow American aircraft operating from bases in Saudi Arabia to take part in the raids, despite the personal efforts of the Secretary of Defence, William Cohen, to persuade it to relent.

In the Balkans, on January 9, the British and American monitors in Kosovo, headed by a British officer, General John Drewienkiewicz, prevented Serb soldiers attacking members of the Kosovo Liberation Army in the village of Bajgora. 'We had to persuade them to turn back,' Drewienkiewicz said. 'My people walked the tanks back.' But the intensity of the ethnic conflict defied the most vigilant monitors. On January 16, a week after the averted clash at Bajgora, the bodies of forty-five ethnic Albanians were discovered just outside the village of Racak.

The Racak villagers had been murdered by Serbs. The victims, including three women and a child, had been mutilated. A man, of about sixty-five, had been decapitated. William Walker, the American head of the international monitoring mission, told journalists: 'It is about as horrendous an event as I have seen, and I have been in some nasty situations.' President Clinton commented: 'This was a deliberate and indiscriminate act of murder designed to sow fear among the people of Kosovo.' American and British warplanes were put on a war alert. NATO sent an American general, Wesley Clark, to Belgrade, to urge Milosevic to order a halt to the killings. *The Times* wrote on January 19: 'The countries of Europe must not tolerate massacres in their midst and refugees on their doorstep. At some point it must be conceded that the honourable option of diplomacy has been tried and found wanting. There is nothing to suggest that Mr Milosevic will respond to anything short of the most credible of military threats. The message that General Clark must deliver in Belgrade is unambiguous: air strikes may be a last resort. But Racak has brought that resort very much closer.'

Within two weeks of the Racak killings, twenty-four ethnic Albanians were murdered by Serb soldiers in the village of Rogovo. On January 30 the British Foreign Secretary, Robin Cook, flew to Belgrade to warn Milosevic that unless the killings stopped, NATO would launch air strikes against Serbian positions. Cook then travelled to the Macedonian capital, Skopje, where he warned representatives of the Kosovo Liberation Army that the KLA must also cease fighting and start negotiating. Six nations – the so-called 'Contact Group' of Britain, the United States, Russia, France, Germany and Italy – supported this initiative. In London, one of the founders of the

Kosovo liberation movement, Bardhyl Mahmuti, was urged by the British government to persuade his fellow-fighters to enter negotiations.

In Africa, in the last two weeks of January, at least 178 Hutu civilians were killed in southern Burundi, either by Hutu rebels or in clashes between rebels and government forces. Hutu rebels based in neighbouring Tanzania crossed the border to attack the town of Makamba, killing fifty-nine civilians. In India, in the last week of January, a father and his two sons were burned to death by Hindus because they were Christians, part of a spate of anti-Christian attacks by Hindu fundamentalists.

In the United States, President Clinton was impeached by the Republican-dominated House of Representatives. His trial took place in the Senate, in his absence. The charges related to his private life, to alleged perjury in civil law suits, and to attempts to subvert the course of justice. On January 19, as the Senate trial was in progress, Clinton delivered his State of the Union message, offering American financial help to Russia and other former Soviet republics to enable them to destroy their chemical and biological weapons. Part of the money America would spend on 'threat reduction' would be used to enable 8,000 Russian scientists hitherto employed by the defence industries to work on civilian research, and to dismantle and store nuclear warheads that had been decommissioned.

Clinton – who was acquitted of all impeachment charges by the Senate on February 12 – also sought funding to combat threats to computer networks, setting up a National Defence Preparedness Office to train and equip police, fire and ambulance workers who would be the first on the scene of any biological or chemical weapons attack, within the United States, by those who might try to use computers for terrorism, such as the sabotage of America's electricity grid.

The arms trade continued to flourish. Bulgaria became a transit point for weaponry needed by insurgent groups. Weapons were shipped through the Bulgarian ports of Varna and Burgas to the rebels and warring factions in Angola, Congo, Eritrea, Somalia, the Hutu militia in Rwanda, and Sri Lanka – where Tamil Tigers were the recipients: that October they killed more than a thousand government troops. Bulgaria also produced its own specialist weapon for sale internationally, a version of the Russian Kalashnikov rifle. Raymond Bonner reported in the *International Herald Tribune*: 'Light, durable, easy to maintain, it is ideal for young soldiers slogging through jungles or trekking up mountains.' Two main organizations were involved: Kintex, the Bulgarian State Marketing Agency, and Arsenal, Bulgaria's largest arms manufacturer, which was also State-owned.

Bulgaria faced competition from other countries seeking the large profits available by selling arms to those intent on the violent overthrow of their internal enemies. Two former Soviet Republics, Ukraine and Belarus, as well as Slovakia and Roumania, competed for arms sales to rebel groups, terrorist organizations and religious fanatics, principally Islamic. But it was Bulgaria that secured an order for the shipment of thirty-five tons of weapons to the rebels in Sierra Leone. False certificates indicated that the arms were a legitimate sale to Nigeria.

Israel also entered the world armament trade. Israeli consultants helped the regime in Myanmar to produce small arms and ammunition through a factory in Singapore. But it was the United States which continued to dominate the world arms trade, supplying (in 1997) $15.2 billion worth of arms. Britain, the second largest supplier, provided $5.9 billion, France $4.9 billion and Russia $2.4 billion. The main recipients of United States arms sales were Saudi Arabia, Taiwan, Egypt and South Korea. Russia provided most of the arms bought by India, China and Vietnam.

In defending Britain's arms trading under a Labour government, the Foreign Secretary, Robin Cook, stated: 'The Government is committed to the maintenance of a strong defence industry which is a strategic part of our industrial base.' He was answered by a former Conservative Member of Parliament, Matthew Parris, who wrote: 'Well count me out. We let ship-building die because it wasn't commercial; we stopped the slave trade because it was wrong; the arms trade is commercially doubtful and morally wrong. A world to come will look back on munitions shipments to primitive places as we look back on slave shipments from primitive places, amazed that sane men could justify this.'

While in opposition Cook had singled out Conservative arms sales to Indonesia as 'particularly disturbing'. In the first years of the Labour government, in which Cook was Foreign Secretary, twice as many licenses for the export of small arms and machine guns to Indonesia were granted as in the last year of the Conservative government. The sale of howitzers, mortars and flame-throwers had continued at pre-election levels. This equipment, said Colonel Halim Nawi, Indonesian Defence Attaché in London, in February 1999, had been used to crush dissent in East Timor.

The two main arguments used by the British government departments most involved in the arms trade were that the arms industry employed 410,000 people – a substantial workforce that might otherwise be unemployed – and that foreign companies would 'steal' British contracts if too many restrictions were put on the trade in weapons. The financial stakes were high: on March 1 it was announced in Athens that Greece was planning to spend £10 billion on the 'modernization' of its armed forces. Every international arms-selling nation wanted to be part of this. The United States, which a month earlier had cut off arms sales to Greece on the ground that Greece had supplied top-secret NATO aircraft-jamming codes to Russia, hastened to declare that no such breach of secrecy had taken place.

Non-violent progress also marked the start of the final year of the century. On January 1, eleven member States of the European Union, totalling 290 million people, adopted a single currency, the Euro, thereby abolishing their monetary borders.[1] Three countries decided to remain outside the circle: Britain, Denmark and Sweden. A fourth, Greece, had not met the necessary economic criteria to join. The creation of the Euro made the European Union the most powerful economic bloc after the United States. In the words of Reuters correspondent Nick Antonovics, the eleven 'euro zone' member States 'are taking one of the most extraordinary steps in European history, forging a common future as an integrated economic power when, little over fifty years ago, many were enemies on the battlefield'.

On January 22 agreement was reached between lawyers for Holocaust survivors and a number of Swiss banks, including the Swiss National Bank, ending a dispute that had become an acrimonious part of the unfinished business of the Second World War. The banks agreed to a cash settlement as compensation for assets that had not been returned after the war. Those eligible for a share of the settlement were defined as 'targets and victims of Nazi persecution'.

Those forced into slave labour by the Nazis between 1939 and 1945 were also seeking compensation. Jews and non-Jews alike had been cruelly ill-treated in the factories of the Third Reich. More than 250 German industrial enterprises that had taken advantage of slave labour during the Second World War were still in business fifty-five years later. An American

---

[1] The eleven States were Germany, France, Austria, Belgium, Finland, Ireland, Italy, Luxembourg, the Netherlands, Portugal and Spain.

government negotiator, Stuart Eizenstat, brought together representatives of the industrialists and the former slave labourers in a series of meetings which, by the end of 1999, agreed on a figure that would enable former slave labourers – an estimated three quarters of a million, of whom 135,000 were Jews subjected to the harshest of treatment – to have meaningful monetary support for the rest of their lives.

In Indonesia, President Habibie indicated on January 28 that he might be prepared to grant independence to East Timor. More than 20,000 Indonesian soldiers had been killed since the Indonesian invasion of the former Portuguese colony of East Timor in 1975. The apparent offer of independence did not, however, halt the killings of East Timorese by paramilitary groups trained by the Indonesian army. In the words of Florentino Sarmento, the head of the Indonesian Human Rights Commission in Timor: 'When the East Timorese heard the announcement they initially thought that after two decades of despair the end was in sight. But those hopes quickly faded when it became apparent the army was continuing its terror campaign regardless of what Habibie said.' In mid-April fighting broke out in the East Timor capital, Dili, as pro-Indonesian militias called for a 'cleansing' of those in favour of independence from Indonesia. Within a few months, more than two hundred East Timorese had been killed and thousands of homes burned down by anti-independence militias. Xanana Gusmao, who had led the independence struggle from within Indonesia, sought refuge in the British embassy in Djakarta. Tens of thousands of East Timorese fled into West Timor.

On September 18, warships of the International Peace Force set sail from Australia, commanded by an Australian general, Peter Cosgrove. As a twenty-one-year-old company commander in Korea, Cosgrove had been awarded the Military Cross. Of the nearly eleven thousand troops, more than a third were Australian.[1] Despite continued intimidation, when the referendum was held on August 30, more than eighty per cent of the voters, representing 871,000 people, voted for independence. By the end of the year, a new State, accepted by Indonesia, had joined the international community. The exiled leaders returned: Gusmao in October and José Ramos Horta – who had been in exile for twenty-four years – in December.

[1] The United Nations forces sent to East Timor were from Australia (4,500), Philippines (1,440), Thailand (1,000), New Zealand (800), Canada (600), Italy (600), France (500), South Korea (400), Britain (270 – Gurkhas), Singapore (250), United States (200), Fiji (180), Brazil (50), Argentina (50), Malaysia (30), Sweden (10) and Norway (5).

East Timor was the United Nations' 188th member state. With less than 6,000 square miles of land, it was nevertheless far bigger in both population and land area than the three other newcomers to the United Nations in 1999, each in the Pacific. On July 12 independence came to Kiribati, whose 82,000 people were scattered across 280 square miles and thirty-six islands – formerly the Gilbert, Ocean, Phoenix and Line islands. Tonga, formerly a British-protected island kingdom, with 98,000 people living on islands across 288 square miles of territory, became independent on June 4. But the first of the three to receive independence in 1999, on January 31, was Nauru. Formerly a British Mandate and later an Australian Trusteeship, which had been taken from Germany in 1920, its 11,000 citizens live on an island of only eight square miles.

Human rights abuses saw no abatement in the final year of the century. In China, Lin Hai, the owner of a software company, was found guilty of subversion and sentenced to two years in prison for distributing 30,000 Chinese e-mail addresses to a democracy magazine published in the United States. Lin Hai had been held incommunicado for eight months before charges were laid against him. During that time the number of Chinese Worldwide Web users had more than doubled, from less than a million to more than two million. A further one and a half million accounts were expected to be opened in 1999.

The spread of the Internet in China gave hope to China's first opposition Party for more than half a century, the China Democracy Party. But, on February 26, the Communist authorities arrested the Party's young founder, nineteen-year-old Wang Yingzheng, as he was photocopying an article he had written on corruption within the Communist Party. He was charged with attempting to 'subvert State power'. China was also under the international spotlight for its continuing repression in Tibet. On March 30 a human rights organization charged that one in thirty-three Tibetan male prisoners, and one in twenty female prisoners, of the many thousands held in Tibet's main prison since 1987, had died of maltreatment.

In Iran, as in China, a repressive regime was confronted with the challenge of the Internet, satellite television and the fax machine. Under President Mohammed Khatami, conciliation towards the West had begun. In an interview with John Simpson of the BBC, Esmail Khoi, an Iranian poet living in exile in London, pointed to the fax machine through which he sent his poems to Iran, and commented: 'This is how Iran will eventually change.'

In Indonesia more than 160 people were killed at the beginning of 1999 during inter-religious riots in which churches and mosques were burned. On March 1, a report in the *International Herald Tribune* told of the city of Ambon being turned 'into a battle zone' as Indonesian troops 'fired at Christians and Muslims who were fighting each other with firebombs, machetes and arrows'. By the end of the month two hundred people had been killed in the fighting. Many were hacked to death in disputes over land ownership.

On the Serbian-Albanian border, Serb military engineers were laying tens of thousands of anti-personnel mines during the first two months of 1999. The aim was to prevent arms being smuggled across the Albanian border into Kosovo, for the Kosovo Liberation Army. Although Yugoslavia was a signatory to the 1997 Ottawa Treaty banning the manufacture of mines, its government remained one of the largest manufacturers, among the twenty-five nations still making these outlawed machines. Seven different types of landmine were found at the beginning of 1999 by munitions experts attached to the Kosovo Verification Mission, an international team established by the Organization for Security and Co-operation in Europe (OSCE). A British journalist, James Pettifer, wrote from Kosovo while negotiations between Serbs and Kosovars were taking place in a Paris suburb: 'Whatever the outcome at Rambouillet, the menace of the minefields will remain.'

In March 1999 President Milosevic of Serbia refused to accept the presence of an international force of monitors on Serbian soil, as an assurance that the Kosovar Albanian majority would be granted effective autonomy by Belgrade. The talks between the Serbian and Kosovar leaders at Rambouillet collapsed. In Kosovo, Serb forces continued to destroy ethnic Albanian villages. NATO – which on March 12 had been enlarged to include Poland, the Czech Republic and Hungary – decided to act. On the evening of March 24 the first air strikes were carried out against military targets throughout Serbia. It was the world's largest military campaign since the Gulf War eight years earlier, and the first NATO attack on a sovereign nation since the alliance had been set up fifty years earlier.

The NATO action was given the codename Operation Deliberate Force. It was designed, President Clinton explained, to stop the repression of the Kosovar Albanians by the Serbs: President Milosevic 'must either choose peace, or we will limit his ability to make war'. In the words of the American commander of the NATO forces, General Wesley Clark: 'We're going systematically and progressively to attack, disrupt, degrade, devastate and ultimately – unless President Milosevic complies with the demands of the international community – we're going to destroy his forces.'

The NATO warplanes taking part in the assault on the first day, during which forty Serb targets were hit – and ten Serb civilians were killed – came from fourteen nations.[1] The aircraft in the first assault included eight American B-52 bombers, of Vietnam vintage, which flew from a Royal Air Force base at Fairford, in Britain, and, circling Yugoslavia, launched their missiles from outside Yugoslav airspace. Two of the American warplanes, B-2 stealth bombers, flew non-stop from their base in Missouri to drop satellite-guided bombs. Most of the other aircraft in action flew from air bases in Italy, a NATO member. Missiles were also launched from American warships, and from a British submarine, HMS *Splendid*, in the Adriatic Sea. Among the NATO nations taking part in the action against Serbia was Germany, four of whose jets participated in air strikes near Belgrade on the first night. This was the first German military action beyond its borders since 1945. It came fifty-eight years after the German bombing of Belgrade in the Second World War.

During the first month of the air war, raids were carried out every night against Serbian military targets. Enormous damage was done, with relatively few civilian casualties: less than a hundred in the first thirty days. A further sixty people were killed when NATO aircraft struck in error at a convoy of Kosovar Albanians being driven out of the province. Each day, Serb forces cleared villages, often separating all adult men from women, children and old people. By the third week of April, NATO estimated that 10,000 Kosovars had been murdered in cold blood by Serb troops and paramilitary units. Almost a million Kosovars, many of whom had seen their close relatives murdered, or had passed massacre sites on their way, were forced across the borders with Macedonia, Albania and Montenegro, where international aid agencies – assisted at first by British troops – did their utmost to relieve their physical plight. Their mental anguish could not be assuaged.

Kosovar Albanian refugees were also taken in by Bosnia, Croatia, Bulgaria and Turkey. The first to arrive in Britain, 260 in all, did so at the end of April: 120 of them were women and children whose menfolk were either murdered or missing. The NATO countries, publicly and emphatically committed to the return of the Kosovars to their homes, had perforce to take

---

[1] The United States, Britain, Belgium, Canada, Denmark, France, Germany, Italy, the Netherlands, Norway, Portugal, Spain, Greece and Turkey.

them in as refugees, as the economic and human pressures on Albania and Macedonia, two of the poorest countries in Europe, grew. In the five years before the war, Britain had already taken in 10,000 Kosovars, the same number as that of the German Jewish children brought to Britain in 1939 on the eve of the Second World War. The instinct to help was widespread: Saudi Arabia and Iran sent aid; Israel took in a hundred refugees, all Muslims.

That Milosevic did not break during the first few weeks of the heavy air onslaught was a blow to the hopes of the NATO leaders. But the British and American governments in particular repeatedly voiced their determination that the Kosovars would eventually be able to return to their homes, that their villages – systematically looted and burned by the Serbs – would be restored, and that those Serbs perpetrating ethnic cleansing would be punished as war criminals. 'Our campaign will continue shifting the balance of power against him until we succeed', Clinton wrote in the *Sunday Times* on April 18. Two days later the British Foreign Secretary, Robin Cook, handed Judge Louise Arbour, the Chief Prosecutor of the War Crimes Tribunal at The Hague, a list compiled by British Intelligence, of fifty incidents in which mass murder had been carried out. 'We want to be sure that those brought to justice are not only the thugs who committed the crimes but those who gave the orders,' he said. 'We are determined that those responsible for turning Kosovo into a slaughter house should be brought to justice.' Nineteen days earlier, a British court had convicted seventy-eight-year-old Anthony Sawoniuk to two terms of life imprisonment for the killing, in 1942, of eighteen Jews in the former Polish town of Domachevo, then under German rule. For more than fifty years Sawoniuk had lived in Britain, a post-war refugee. His sentence was the first to be passed by a British court for crimes committed during the Second World War.

In August, a senior Bosnian Serb general, Momir Talic, arrived in Vienna to attend a military seminar. A warrant for his arrest was immediately issued by Judge Arbour. Talic was arrested by the Austrian authorities and flown to The Hague, where he was charged with crimes against both Muslims and Croats in Bosnia in 1992. He was the first war crimes suspect in Bosnia to be arrested outside the territory of former Yugoslavia, and the thirtieth Bosnian Serb to be held in captivity facing trial for crimes against humanity.

Reports of savage crimes committed by Serb forces against the Kosovar Albanians intensified NATO's determination to persevere with the war. On April 21, the British Prime Minister Tony Blair, visited NATO headquarters at Mons, scene of the first German-British clash in the First World War. NATO policy was moving towards the conviction that ground troops would have to be deployed if ethnic Albanians were to be returned to their homes. Blair commented that the Allies were fighting 'a just war in a just cause for the values of civilization itself. We should have no hesitation and every resolve to see the thing through to the end'.

The united Germany took a further step towards integration in July, when the parliament moved from Bonn to Berlin. It was the first time for more than half a century that Berlin was the full and undivided capital. Among the buildings brought into use by the new administration was Hermann Goering's former Aviation Ministry.

Russia continued to fight separatism. In August, more than 400 Muslim separatists were killed in the autonomous region of Dagestan, on the Caspian Sea. Their leader, Shamil Basayev, announced that the fight would go on until Dagestan had been purged of leaders influenced by Boris Yeltsin – 'a faithful servant of Zionist capital'. In neighbouring Chechenya, rebel fighters continued to challenge the authority of Russia and the superior fire power of Russian troops. 'There will be tough measures, and we will restore order in Dagestan and in other regions in the North Caucasus', Boris Yeltsin declared from Moscow on August 16. A month later, the Russian Prime Minister, Vladimir Putin, announced from Moscow that Russia was prepared to resume 'full-scale war' with Chechenya. Daily bombing missions began on September 23, when oil refineries in Grozny were set on fire, and at least fifty Chechen civilians killed. By the end of November the civilian death toll in Grozny had reached more than five hundred. In the fighting on the ground, six hundred Russian soldiers had been killed. In Moscow, at the end of November, the 'Soldiers' Mothers Group' called for an end to the fighting. On December 3, Russian soldiers opened fire on a Chechen refugee column led by a woman carrying a white flag. Forty of the refugees were killed.

By the end of the year Russian troops had crushed the Dagestan revolt. His health failing, Boris Yeltsin resigned. His successor as President, Vladimir Putin, followed in Yeltsin's footsteps by ordering a massive military and air attack on the Chechen rebels still holding out in Grozny and the mountains to the south. Within Russia, as a result of this decisive action, Putin's popularity rose.

* * *

The war between NATO and Serbia ended on June 10, when President Milosevic agreed to withdraw his troops from Kosovo. As a NATO force entered the province, the refugees began returning to their homes, many of which had been deliberately destroyed. At least five thousand Serb soldiers and two thousand Serb civilians had been killed during seventy-eight days and nights of NATO air bombardments.

Within twenty-four hours of entering Kosovo, British and German troops found mass graves of victims of 'ethnic cleansing' at Kacanik, Glogovac, Kusaj, Mali Krusa and Korenica. Shocking scenes of these were shown on television. Within a week a further fifty mass murder sites had been located. Even while the war was being fought the International War Crimes Tribunal at The Hague had indicted Milosevic as a war criminal. When, or whether, he would be brought to justice was an open question.

The twentieth century had begun with collective international military action against China. That year, Germany, Britain and the United States had each taken part in the punitive action. At the end of the twentieth century, each was among the nations participating in the air-strike forces against Serbia. Just as in 1900 China had submitted to the dictates of 'The Powers', with heightened protection of foreign traders and missionaries at Peking and elsewhere, so Serbia in 1999 was in a similar position. She agreed to an international force in Kosovo, the return of the refugees and an autonomous region within which Belgrade could exert no authority. The returning Kosovar Albanian refugees set about rebuilding their homes and livelihoods. As 1999 came to an end the NATO-led peacekeeping force, K-For (Kosovo Force), was headed by a German commander, General Klaus Reinhardt, with British, Russian, Ukrainian, French and Canadian soldiers among the peacekeepers.

It was as 'The Year of Refugees', in the words of Richard Lloyd Parry in the *Independent*, that 1999 became known. Twenty years earlier the United Nations High Commissioner for Refugees had two and a half million refugees under its auspices. That number rose by the end of the century to twenty-two million. 'Now, as a thousand years ago, it is the young, old and weak who suffer most,' wrote Lloyd Parry. 'In 1999, no less than in 1939, the trauma of displacement lingers long after peace and shelter have been restored. In that sense, however complex and politicized refugee crises have become, the plight of their victims is timeless.'

CHAPTER FORTY-NINE

RETROSPECT

. . . patches of brilliance and decline . . .

BARBARA TUCHMAN

THROUGHOUT ITS COURSE the twentieth century has been marked by the most terrible bloodletting of war, civil war and tyrannical dictatorship. It has also generated the most life-enhancing changes in medicine, social welfare, science and technology. Every decade has seen a desire to make improvements for all mankind. In 1977 the United Nations had sufficient confidence – in terms of planning and expectation – to declare as one of its aims the eradication of water shortages by 1990, and of disease by the year 2000. Neither the 1990 nor the 2000 targets have yet been realized.

The weapons with which water shortage and disease, poverty and hunger, were fought and continue to be fought, were not as costly as the weapons used to fight wars and maintain tyranny. But often it was war and tyranny that proved the priority, leaving the social needs of even the poorest countries to be neglected. The cruelties of war and tyranny, on which so much national wealth was spent, affected tens of millions of human beings. Violent, bloody conflicts were perpetuated by the diversion of wealth and human inventiveness from constructive, ameliorative enterprises, and by national and racial extremism.

Human ingenuity, skills, energies and resources made their contribution in equal measure for good and ill. War itself, through which tens of millions of civilians and bystanders perished, had origins not necessarily in conquest and greed. Often it was seen by those who led their nations as the only means available to them to redress grievances, preserve independence or guard the rule of law. The 'just war', wars of self-defence, wars of national liberation, wars to protect the threatened freedom of others, were no less terrible in their effects because they could call upon moral imperatives as justification. Tyrannies that were destroyed, like that of Hitler's Thousand Year Reich, which was laid in ruins after twelve years, were destroyed amid suffering that made little or no distinction between soldier and civilian, military target and hearth and home.

The weapons of war had their own tyranny. Submarines could, in firing a single torpedo, sink a warship on which a thousand or more men drowned. Ever more powerful artillery shells and aerial bombs could destroy not only military fortifications but whole blocks of flats, monasteries, railway stations, even shelters in which people were seeking refuge from the very bombs that killed them. The fifteen-inch naval gun pounding other warships and shore installations, the shelling of Paris by 'Big Bertha' in the First World War, the V2 rocket bombs launched on London in the Second World War, and – in terrible climax – the atom bombs dropped on Hiroshima and Nagasaki; these were all designed, financed and delivered in the twentieth century.

In 1925 Winston Churchill predicted that 'a bomb no larger than an orange' might one day destroy a whole city. Bombs larger than an orange, but capable of destroying far more than a single city, were in existence as the century came to an end, including nuclear warheads capable of hitting any target on the globe, and multiple warheads that, from a single missile, could be aimed to blast a dozen different targets over a wide area. Far less powerful weapons also joined the armoury of defence and attack. The Molotov cocktail – a bottle filled with fuel oil, and with a rag as a wick – was first used by Finnish troops in trying to hold back the Soviet assault in 1939. It later became part of the armoury – often almost the only part – of otherwise unarmed civilians facing tanks in their city streets.

The First World War saw the use of poison gas on the battlefield. The Second World War saw massive aerial bombardment, one result of which, the 'firestorm', killed more than 40,000 citizens of Hamburg in a single night. At least twice as many were killed during a single night air raid on Tokyo. Watching a Royal Air Force film of a British bombing raid on the German town of Wuppertal in 1942, Churchill could almost not believe the new powers for destruction, asking those who had watched the film with him: 'Are we beasts, are we taking this too far?'

The nuclear arms race after 1945 seemed at times to be heading, as during the Korean War, to the brink of what was then called a 'nuclear holocaust'. In the 1950s the United States built highways along which the urban populations of all its great cities could be evacuated in the event of nuclear war. Every citizen, every school, every public institution, was urged to build shelters capable of protection in nuclear attack. In the Soviet Union, whole cities, including the nuclear naval base at Sebastopol, were closed to foreigners in an attempt to keep their military preparations secret. Espionage had a field day. But when the reality of the mutually destructive nature of nuclear war became apparent, and whenever nuclear testing in the atmosphere revealed massive risks to global health, as in an accelerated increase in the incidence of cancer, the Super Powers – the United States and the Soviet Union – drew back from the brink, gradually negotiating an end to nuclear testing. They then began to pursue, with other nuclear powers, a series of treaties seeking to curb nuclear proliferation. As the century came to an end, however, proliferation was not ended. In 1998 the explosion by both India and Pakistan of nuclear devices brought a chilling realization that the danger of nuclear confrontation had re-emerged beyond the control of the principal nuclear powers.

Echoes of the century's wars were a feature of its closing years. On Armistice Day 1998, eighty years after the end of the First World War, surviving veterans gathered in Ypres at the Menin Gate. Inscribed there are the names of the tens of thousands of soldiers whose bodies were never identified, lying in that one sector of the Western Front. Yet as an antidote to war, enormous efforts were made during the century to reduce the range of war, and to abolish war altogether. Two years before the century began, and six years before the Wright Brothers' pioneering flight, aerial warfare was 'abolished', in 1898, with international agreement that no more bombs would be thrown from balloons. In 1907, on the initiative of the President of the United States, Theodore Roosevelt, a conference of the world's then forty-four nations, including all the great empires, met to discuss outlawing aerial bombardment. Twenty-seven of the nations agreed, including the United States and Britain. Germany was one of the seventeen that wanted to retain the right to make war from the air. All forty-four powers did agree, however, to limit aerial bombardment to military targets. These were defined as mostly naval dockyards and military installations. By implication, residential and built-up areas would not be bombed.

Within four years the Italians, signatories to the 1907 convention, used aerial warfare in Libya in their war against Turkey. During the First World War, bombs dropped by German Zeppelins and German bombers destroyed both military installations and homes in London and Paris. After 1918, as a result of the slaughter in the trenches during the First World War, efforts were made to abolish war altogether, much as the slaughter of mid-nineteenth-century wars had led to the creation, if not of a no-war policy, at least of an International Red Cross organization that could mitigate the severity of battlefield wounds and the suffering of prisoners of war.

In 1928, under the auspices of the League of Nations and with the agreement of all the League members, war itself was abolished as a means of resolving disputes among States. This was the achievement of an American, Frank Kellogg, and a Frenchman, Aristide Briand. Both received the Nobel Prize for Peace for breaking the mould of human conflict. Yet the wisdom of 1928 was soon eclipsed. Within a decade wars were again being fought without respite. The Japanese invaded China, the Italians invaded Ethiopia, the Italian army and the German air force intervened in the Spanish Civil War, the Germans invaded Poland, and the Russians attacked Finland – a sombre list, behind which lay great suffering in hundreds of cities and through vast regions of countryside, as well as on the battlefields. In 1932, in a poem in which he spoke of the 'Black Thirties', Siegfried Sassoon, after watching a flight of aeroplanes, warned that the time would come, in the not too distant future, when 'Fear will be synonymous with flight.' Aerial warfare, uninhibited by rules, dominated the Second World War, and preceded it. The Japanese bombing of Chinese cities, the German bombing of the Basque town of Guernica, were preludes to the destruction wreaked by various of the combatants on Warsaw, Helsinki, London, Belgrade, Canton, Nanking and in due course Berlin and Tokyo.

The protections accorded by international convention by no means guaranteed the safety of those on whose behalf the conventions had been signed. Prisoners of war were particularly vulnerable to abuse by their captors. The German treatment of Soviet prisoners of war, and the Japanese treatment of prisoners of war from all the Allied armies, reached extremes of inhumanity. Inhumanity was also the hallmark in the murder of six million Jews, under the cover of war, and of millions of civilians in occupied lands. Treatment of civilians and non-combatants reached an unprecedented level of barbarity, as evidenced by the German reprisals against individuals and whole communities in Poland, Czechoslovakia, Yugoslavia, Greece and France. In the concentration camps, death camps and death marches, soldiers and civilians alike were murdered or died because of deliberate ill-treatment. Five years after the ending of the Second World War, the United Nations soldiers taken prisoner in Korea were held captive in appalling conditions, in which many were tortured and many died. In Vietnam, civilian victims of the war numbered in their hundreds of thousands, many of them killed or maimed by napalm.

The recounting of these wars, seemingly endless in their sequence, is the task of all historians of the twentieth century as they describe its progressions and regressions. My own perspective was influenced by a remark made in 1937 by the Chinese photographer T. C. Lau, a graduate of the University of Pennsylvania who was a practising dentist in Canton. Lau had taken a series of photographs of the Li women of Hainan island, whose heavy five-pound brass earrings distorted their earlobes but were considered, among the Li, a thing of beauty and a mark of status. In 1937 Lau was visited in his home by the Editor of the American *National Geographic* magazine, which published his photographs a year later. By the time the photographs appeared the Japanese army had overrun Canton, and Lau and his family were among tens of thousands of Chinese refugees in Hong Kong. From there he wrote to the Editor: 'Historians may appropriate only a line or two to record this present catastrophe, but it is tremendous to us who are in it.'

I have always tried to devote more than 'a line or two' to such human catastrophes as the Japanese invasion of China, with its terrible cruelties, but there are many catastrophes of the century that do not get the space they might have received, and perhaps ought to have received; and some perforce are absent altogether.

At the beginning of the century the Imperial Powers were in the ascendant throughout the globe. By its close, most were a distant memory. Their colonial rule was over. The British Empire divested itself of India – its 'jewel in the crown' – in 1947. In the decade beginning in 1960 the colonial partitioning of Africa was brought almost to an end. The last surviving empire was that of Russia. The imperial authority of the Russian Tsar, stretching from the Baltic Sea to the Pacific Ocean, survived Japan's Far Eastern victory in 1905. Even when war-weariness and revolution swept away Tsarism in 1917, and the empire was briefly broken up, Lenin successfully regained much of the empire, establishing Communist rule in the Caucasus and Central Asia, and in the Far East, often by brutal force of arms. Lenin's successor, Stalin, recovered, first in 1940 and then in 1944, the Baltic lands which the Tsar had ruled until 1917. Stalin fell, but the territorially vast empire – covering, in the proud Soviet terminology, 'one-third of the earth's surface' – remained, to be characterized by one American President, Ronald Reagan, as the 'evil empire'.

In order to maintain itself, Soviet imperial rule had at its disposal a rigid ideology and a strong secret police system, with labour camps, and labour-camp zones the size of Wales or Massachusetts, to sustain it. No other Imperial Power had such great forces of repression at its disposal. In the three and a half decades following Stalin's death, not one square mile of that empire was given up. In 1988 Gorbachev inherited the borders that Lenin and Stalin had secured. Then, in a few months of turmoil in 1991, the Soviet Union disintegrated. Among the pressures on it had been internal dissent, the growing international focus on human rights, the enormous financial burden of trying to maintain any sort of defence parity with the Western defence systems, and the rapidly widening gap between its own economic performance and that of the capitalist world.

The two nations which the Soviet Union had helped to defeat in the Second World War – Germany and Japan – both represented success in the economic sphere beyond the wildest imaginings of the Communist economic system. The frequently derided and denounced United States, far from collapsing under the 'contradictions' of capitalism, was gaining internal and international strength, as well as respect.

Few revolutions in the twentieth century were so total, so dramatic and so globally significant as the fall and disintegration of the Soviet Union in 1991. Ten years earlier it would have been inconceivable for all but the most visionary to foresee the day, while still in the twentieth century, when a bastion of the Soviet system, the former Ukrainian Soviet Socialist Republic, would replace the Hammer and Sickle with the Ukrainian flag, and discard the ruble; and when the train announcer at Kiev station would announce the departure of the train to St Petersburg, having for seven decades given the train's destination as Leningrad.

Among those set at liberty by the fall of Communism in the Soviet Union, and helping to precipitate that fall, were the nations of Eastern Europe. Their independence between the wars had been eclipsed by German conquest and then Soviet domination. Their struggles for liberation had been in vain: Hungary in 1956, Czechoslovakia in 1968 were high points of national effort, but not until Soviet Communism was on the wane were they able to break free from the Communist mould.

In every decade of the century, nations sought ascendancy, some in their regions, some over whole continents, some even across the world. The British Empire on which 'the sun never set' was by far the most powerful and visible empire when the century began. But even before the outbreak of the First World War another Power, the United States, was emerging with all the characteristics needed to become a dominant world entity. Industrial power marked the first steps to that ascendancy. The power – and will – to intervene overseas was another, not only in the western hemisphere, but in China, where American troops were a leading element in the international expeditionary force of 1900. As an arbiter between other States, America emerged prominently, first as the host to the Treaty of Portsmouth, following the Russo-Japanese War of 1904-5. Twice, the United States emerged as the defender in arms of democracy, first in Europe between 1916 and 1918, and then in Europe and Asia between 1941 and 1945.

After proving itself a decisive element in two world wars, the United States became, after the Second World War, the defender and sustainer of Western values, militarily through the Truman Doctrine and the North Atlantic Treaty Organization, and economically, and thus socially, through the Marshall Plan. The Berlin Airlift depended considerably on the efforts of the United States. The United Nations war in Korea could not have been maintained without the predominant participation of the United States.

Even the United States could abuse its power. Long after it ended, the Vietnam War continued to be a controversial and, for some, a shameful episode in American consciousness. That war served, as had the pre-First World War imperial excesses of Britain, France and Germany, to discredit those for whom the positive aspects of empire – or in the case of the United States the positive aspects of the struggle against global Communism – were central tenets of belief in ultimate good. But just as, after the fall of the British Empire, the Commonwealth emerged as a force for democratic and beneficent action, so after the Vietnam War the United States pursued its own beneficent activity worldwide, predominant in the sphere of global aid, and taking direct action as part of a multinational force, as against Saddam Hussein in Iraq, and in Somalia against famine. Beneficent too was the role taken by the United States as a major paymaster for the United Nations and its agencies. More controversial was the role of the United States, and of those nations in commercial competition with it, in selling arms to threatened States: arms that could also be used, and were often used, as instruments of internal repression and external aggression.

The role of the individual was seen again and again in the twentieth century as decisive. Enormous powers for evil and for good resided in the leaders of the great nations; lesser nations, in the hands of able and ambitious men and women, could change their destiny, and affect the destiny of those around them. The fate of those individuals was often ruled by chance. When the twentieth century began, assassination was regarded as one of the evils of the nineteenth century that would not be perpetuated in 'modern times'. The handiwork of a discredited ideology – anarchism – assassination was thought to have no place in the new century. It did, however, continue, becoming a source of personal, political and international grief. Even a much truncated list reveals the extent and wide-ranging nature of the assassin's work in the past hundred years. Among those assassinated before the First World War were King Umberto of Italy, President McKinley of the United States, several senior Tsarist officials in Russia – Ministers, police chiefs and provincial governors – the whole Serbian royal family, and, in June 1914, the Archduke Franz Ferdinand, whose murder, by a young Serb, precipitated the Austro-Hungarian attack on Serbia, and with it the rapidly evolving road to war of a dozen European nations and global empires, four of which – the Russian, the German, the Austro-Hungarian and the Turkish – were destroyed by the war.

The assassination of Rasputin in Russia was part of the ferment leading to the Bolshevik revolution; the assassination of the Tsar and his family was a culmination of Bolshevik excesses; the assassination of the secret police chief M. S. Uritsky was a reaction to Bolshevik terror. Lenin himself was the victim of a would-be assassin, whose bullet gravely injured him and led to his early death at the age of fifty-four. Trotsky, one of the architects of the Bolshevik revolution, was assassinated while in exile, on orders of Stalin.

The assassination of President Kennedy in 1963 seemed to cut short an era of hope for the United States, and for the world. The assassination of Martin Luther King was a cruel act of racial hatred. President Sadat of Egypt, who made the first peace between Israel and one of its Arab neighbours, was shot down by a flurry of assassins' bullets. The Israeli Prime Minister, Yitzhak Rabin, was assassinated shortly after he had made peace with another of Israel's neighbours, Jordan, and was moving forward in constructive negotiations with the Palestinians.

Tyrants were often the targets of assassins, but not always its victims. Hitler survived several assassination attempts, including one by senior army officers who were prepared to topple the whole Nazi apparatus. He died by his own hand. Stalin and Mao Tse-tung died in their beds. Pol Pot, the man who ordered the murder of a million and a half of his fellow Cambodians, died many years later, old and forgotten, on his sick bed. An African tyrant,

Idi Amin, responsible for the murder of tens of thousands of his fellow Ugandans, lived out his life in quiet exile in Saudi Arabia.

While assassinations have marred the century, the flight and plight of refugees has scarred it irrevocably. What some have called 'the century of the refugee' has included many desperate mass escapes, reminiscent of the biblical Exodus, although for many of the twentieth-century refugees there was no Promised Land at the end of their journey. Most fortunate were those from Belgium in 1914, many of whom found asylum in Britain: they could go back to their country and to their homes when the war ended four years later. Many of the hundreds of thousands of Jews who fled from the German attack that same year, 1914, and found refuge in Russia, had no homes to which to return. This was even more the case in 1945, when the 100,000 survivors of the Holocaust found that, in the main, they were not welcome back in the towns where they and their families had lived for generations. For them, a trek began that often lasted half a decade, before some haven received them – including the newly created State of Israel, whose 1950 Law of Return gave any Jew the right to settle there.

The flight of Serbs from Serbia at the time of the Austrian conquest in the fierce winter of 1915 to 1916 was one which epitomized distress and dispossession. The flight of Armenians from Turkish Anatolia, first in 1915 and again in 1918, was accompanied by ferocious killings. The flight of Turks from Greece and Greeks from Turkey in 1921 and 1922, which was at first vicious in its bloodletting, became the subject of a population-transfer scheme that was held up as a model of peaceful exchange.

The flight from Nazism between 1933 and 1939, of Jews, democrats, Communists, trade unionists, liberals, anti-Nazis and humanitarians affected more than half a million people, depriving them of their homes, livelihoods and family circle. It also highlighted the contribution of the refugees to the world which took them in: far more Nobel Prizes were won by Germans – many of whom were Jews – driven out of Germany than by those who remained in their homeland. As citizens of the countries which took them in, refugees from Nazism made a formidable contribution to scientific and medical research in the post-war world.

After the Second World War, political upheavals and border changes created waves of refugees on a scale never seen before, certainly not in the twentieth century and probably in no previous century of recorded history. In 1945 more than three million Germans fled from Communist rule in

Poland and the Soviet zones of Germany. Another three million German-speaking *Volksdeutsche* (ethnic Germans) fled from Czechoslovakia, from which they were driven by force, and from other Eastern European countries where they and their ancestors had lived for many generations. These 'refugees and expellees', as the West German government called them, and it gave them a Ministry with that name, were for several years a burden on the economy of the regions in which they settled. Millions more Japanese were taken from the Pacific Islands, South-East Asia, China and Manchuria, where hundreds of thousands had been settled by Imperial Japan, and taken back to the Japanese Home Islands, almost all the cities of which had been devastated in the wartime bombing.

In 1947, at the time of the division of India and Pakistan into two independent states, several million Hindu and Muslim refugees fled slaughter and uncertainty. They too became an economic burden on the societies which took them in. More than half a million Palestinian Arabs fled during the Israel War of Independence in 1948 – some were driven out, others fled in the hope of returning in the wake of their fellow Arab conquerors. To this day many are living in camps in neighbouring Arab lands, or, since 1995, in camps within the jurisdiction of the Palestinian Authority. They were not encouraged to merge into the societies which took them in. A special United Nations agency, the Refugee and Works Administration (UNRWA), set up in 1949 to help them, was still supporting almost a million – including the children, grandchildren and great-grandchildren of the original refugees – with health, social and educational facilities, and food, fifty years later. For other refugees, the office of the United Nations High Commissioner for Refugees (UNHCR) undertook the main and formidable responsibility of providing shelter and food. By the end of the century it was helping more than twenty-two million people, in 120 countries: half the countries of the world.

From Communist repression, tens of thousands of Hungarians made their way to the West in 1956. Their contribution, in professional and economic terms, to the countries that made them welcome has been remarkable, as has the contribution of the tens of thousands of Kenyan and Ugandan Asians who were driven out of their homes – and for the most part out of Africa – in 1970–71. Not so fortunate were the two million refugees from the fighting in Bangladesh in 1971. A few were able to make their way to Britain and other Western countries; most remained in India, as refugees, living in conditions of considerable privation.

With Britain having agreed to return Hong Kong to Chinese rule, the late 1980s and early 1990s saw the emigration of tens of thousands of Hong Kong Chinese unwilling to contemplate life under Communism. They too were refugees, though in many cases they were able to take their wealth with them. Large numbers made their way to the Canadian city of Vancouver where, by the end of the century, they had not only prospered but formed the largest single immigrant group, eleven per cent of the city's population. A Hong Kong Chinese, David Lam, even became Lieutenant-Governor – the Queen's representative – of British Columbia. Chinese immigration was also substantial in the United States, making a particular impact on higher education. In Los Angeles, a million Chinese immigrants constituted more than eight per cent of the population in 1991.

It was flight without such final redemption that was the lot of tens of millions of people in the final decade of the century. Most of them were seeking refuge from civil wars – as in the former Yugoslavia – and from tribal killings in Africa, including those in the Sudan and Rwanda. The harrowing scenes on Western television screens of refugee camps and emaciated refugees, especially young children, pointed up the enormous discrepancy between two worlds, both on the same planet.

Economic hardship, and the search for better economic opportunities, also propelled many people to leave their homes and countries in search of new opportunities. In 1991 the number of immigrants to the United States during a twelve-month period was evidence both of the massive migration of peoples that characterized the last decade if the century and of the predominant part which the United States (then with a population of 248,000,000) was taking as a country of asylum, choice and opportunity. Among the largest immigrant groups to America that year were 56,000 from the Soviet Union – most of them Jews – and 55,000 each from the Philippines, Vietnam and Mexico. In all, 704,005 immigrants were admitted to the United States during that one year. They came from almost every country on the globe and from every ethnic group. The scale of immigration to the United States has in no way declined since then.

By the 1990s, immigration was changing the nature of many societies. In Britain, almost two million Muslims were citizens, and there were three-quarters of a million Sikhs and Hindus. In France, Muslim North Africans formed a significant social group. In Germany, anger about the presence of Turkish workers who were needed for the economy (they were known as 'guest workers' in the official parlance) was sometimes expressed in outbreaks of racist violence against them. In 1992 the British government gave asylum to a Sudanese who was living in Germany, on the grounds of 'a well-founded fear of persecution' there. During 1992, Britain, which in the five years ending in 1988 had taken in more than a million immigrants, took in asylum-seekers from twenty countries, including Bosnia (6,000), Sri Lanka (5,000), Iran, Somalia, Ghana, Ethiopia and Uganda.

One particular refugee exodus proved a precursor of political change of the most dramatic sort. The flight from East Germany in 1990 of more than a million people proved the catalyst for the Soviet collapse. Within two years these refugees were able to return to their homes and to a freedom that many of them, even those in their thirties and forties, had never before experienced.

The virtues of patriotism and self-sacrifice have been eclipsed in many lands by self-doubt. Ethnic conflicts and civil wars have largely replaced the power-bloc confrontations of the First and Second World Wars. Yet those two wars have left a permanent reminder, mostly in stone, to the scale of their human destruction. Monuments to the war dead of both those wars, and monuments to the Unknown Soldiers of those wars, exist in many lands. The ultimate tragedy for millions of families was that they never knew where their loved one – son or husband or father – was buried. The First and Second World War battlefields of Europe and Asia are scattered with the remains, or the graves, of those whose bodies were never identified. On the day that I began writing this chapter, a Russian living in the Arctic city of Kandalaksha gave details of some eighty soldiers whose bodies, fifty years after their deaths during the Allied Intervention in 1919, had been found in a building site during the Communist era, and covered in concrete.

The phrase, 'no known grave', first used on the hundreds of monuments set up by the Imperial (later Commonwealth) War Graves Commission, became a feature of many conflicts, and is relevant to millions of civilians as well as soldiers. In the Nazi era, enormous efforts were made by the perpetrators of the killings to burn the corpses of those who had been murdered: and then to grind up the bones and scatter the ashes in rivers, swamps and fields. Those who wish to mourn these victims cannot go to an individual gravestone, only to a desolate site of mass murder. The soil content around the crematoria of the 'death camps' of the Second World War, including Auschwitz-Birkenau, is fifty per cent human ash, more than half a century after the ovens stopped burning.

Mass murder features in another aspect of the twentieth century: the growing imperative in the century's final decade for countries and governments to apologize, officially, for acts carried out many years earlier that were seen as crimes. In the course of the act of apology, facts and details were often released which not only made the apology seem all the more necessary, but added to historical knowledge. Files that had been closed under seal of secrecy were opened, and their contents revealed to the public for the first time in thirty, fifty or even eighty years.

On the Western Front in the First World War, the British military authorities executed more than three hundred men for cowardice. Eighty years later government decisions and television programmes charted a series of apologies, reburials and recognition of the cause of their 'cowardice', often shell-shock, which was not understood medically at the time. The revelation that some of these soldiers had been executed specifically, in the words of the officer deciding the case, to 'make an example' to others, made the apologies all the more poignant.

Apologizing for the past, erecting monuments for past excesses, seeking forgiveness for perceived errors even in previous centuries – these had become regular features of public demand and government response in the 1990s. In 1992 the Spanish government sought reconciliation with the Jewish world for the expulsion of the Jews from Spain five hundred years earlier. The Polish government, once Communism was overthrown, erected a monument in Warsaw for those Poles who had been the victims of Soviet labour camps. A monument in Moscow, unveiled in November 1998, commemorated Stalin's Russian victims of half a century earlier. There was talk in government circles in Britain of apologizing to the people of Northern Ireland for British soldiers having opened fire on civilians on Black Sunday in Londonderry in 1969, less than twenty years earlier.

In the United States there were growing pressures for successive Presidents to apologize for the treatment more than a century ago of the 'Native Americans', more than a million of whom were massacred during the westward expansion of American settlement and civilization. Even their former and familiar name – 'Indians', or 'Red Indians' – had become a term that may not be used because it had become offensive. In Canada, the 'Red Indians' of a generation ago became known as 'First Nations'. They, too, received compensation for ill-treatment of a century and more earlier.

Apologies for mass murder during the Second World War were made by successive German governments over more than a decade. The German government also made financial restitution to the survivors of the 1933-45 anti-Jewish policy. Swiss banks began to come to terms with their 'neutrality'. The Japanese government, pressed to apologize for its wartime treatment of Allied prisoners – both soldiers and civilians – and to make restitution, was less willing to do so in the unequivocal form that the survivors wanted. Japan did, however, apologize to the Korean and other South Asian 'comfort women', as they were called by the Japanese at the time – women forced to serve as prostitutes in Japanese army brothels.

In South Africa, after the fall of apartheid, the Truth Commission laboured to make apology rather than trials and imprisonment the way forward for reconciliation of the races. The American and Canadian governments both apologized to the Japanese-Americans and Japanese-Canadians for having interned them, as a feared potential disloyal fifth column, in the Second World War. The American government was also pressed to apologize to, and to compensate, the many hundreds of American soldiers who, as part of the weaponry of war in Vietnam, used defoliant chemical sprays which affected their health. American and British soldiers whose ill-health started immediately after the Gulf War of 1991, and who claim they were harmed by medicines used to protect them from chemical attack, also seek restitution.

Nuclear power, which was launched with such destructive force in 1945, became within a few decades a source of industrial and domestic energy, of light and heat, for thousands of millions of people. The first town to be lit entirely by nuclear power was in the United States – Arco, Idaho, in 1955. The peaceful uses of nuclear energy in heating and lighting brought global improvements with regard to urban living, not only in the industrialized nations, but increasingly in the developing world. This was despite two much publicized, for the public highly disturbing, accidents at nuclear power stations, the first in 1979 at Three Mile Island in the United States which led to no fatalities, the second in 1986 at Chernobyl, in the Soviet Union, which led to deaths and radiation sickness in parts of the Ukraine, Belarus and Russia, and abnormally high levels of radiation in Sweden, Denmark and Finland.

The twentieth century has seen immense scientific and technological advances. When the century began the motor car was in its infancy and flying machines were part of the world of fiction and fantasy. Yet by the outbreak of the First World War the first regular air service had begun, in the United States, from Tampa to St Petersburg, Florida, a distance over

Tampa Bay of twenty miles, saving twice that distance by land. When the First World War ended, London and Paris were already linked by regular passenger air services. The inter-war years saw the invention of the jet engine. Within three years of the end of the Second World War the sound barrier had been broken by a British test pilot. As I write these words it is being broken several times every day by the civilian supersonic airliner Concorde crossing the Atlantic.

As political barriers fell, commercial aircraft linked cities between which no direct travel was previously possible. In 1995 a commercial airliner made the first direct flight between Israel's Ben-Gurion airport and Amman. Airlines also reflect national identities and new national sovereignties. After the disintegration of the Soviet Union into twelve separate and independent republics, the Soviet airline Aeroflot was fragmented into a dozen national airlines, each proudly displaying its national emblem. Even the poorest nations, such as Bangladesh, can boast a national air carrier. One of the demands of the Palestinian Authority during its negotiations with Israel was for a national airline, and, as agreed to in the Wye Plantation negotiations in 1998, an airport in the Gaza Strip from which to fly it.

Communications spread far beyond travel and flight. By the end of the century the Internet, which had originally been created as a secret American government defence communications system which could not be 'knocked out' by nuclear attack, linked hundreds of millions of people across the globe without any opening or closing hours, weekend respite or waiting time. Like air travel before it, the Internet brings the miracle of rapid communication to vastly larger numbers of people.

Space exploration, which at the start of the century was a whim of the writers of fantasy, became commonplace in the century's final decades. Every new breakthrough brought new excitement. In 1998 the American astronaut John Glenn returned to space at the age of seventy-seven. Although his adventure cost millions of dollars, millions of United States taxpayers were exhilarated by the spectacle. Even on Florida's Space Coast, 300,000 people came out to watch the launch. The flight also caught the imagination of many millions far beyond the United States. It was a triumph, but also a routine, of television reporting and viewing.

Advances in technology, and above all television, brought not only scenes of conflict, but a myriad world of entertainment, into hundreds of millions of homes. The internal combustion engine, a novelty at the beginning of the century, enabled millions of people to travel for work and pleasure, to explore the countryside and to take family holidays. In every land, cars and buses serve as the links between families and communities. Trucks are a vital artery of commerce. Yet the motor car has proved a persistent killer. In the United States more than three million Americans were killed in car accidents between 1918 – the first year in which more than ten thousand people were killed – and 1998. In India, in the last decade of the century, half a million people were killed on the roads. Every four years in Britain, more people are killed on the roads than on the first, horrific day of the Battle of the Somme in 1916. In Israel's first fifty years of its existence more people were killed on the roads than in all its wars.

Yet despite its wars and conflicts, and despite the harsh toll of the motor car, the twentieth century witnessed a greater upsurge of leisure activities for all people than any century before it. Art, literature and music, including jazz, and the pop music that was in its infancy in the 1950s, reached more people than had ever been possible earlier. The games that became popular in Western societies, such as Monopoly, had a flavour of acquisition, wealth and success. Devices for pleasure proliferated, including the consumption of what became known as 'junk food' (because of its essential paucity of nutrition). As early as the Olympic Games of 1904, held that year in St Louis, local German-Americans produced two new food items, the ice-cream cone and the hamburger. Seventy-one years later the first 'drive-in' hamburger restaurant was opened.

Sport likewise found a vastly popular place in the public mind. Football and baseball games were regularly watched by tens of thousands of people, for whom the stadium was a focal point, week after week, of individual and collective enthusiasm. Other sports, including cricket, tennis, basketball, horse racing and ice hockey, could also draw in appreciative spectators. Those who could not attend could listen to commentators on the radio or watch the action itself on television. The Olympic Games became a source of pleasure not only for those who attended but also for those, numbering in their hundreds of millions, who listened on radio, watched on film newsreels or, in the last third of the century, watched on television. As a result of the money generated by advertising, sports sponsorship, bringing with it the commercialization of sport, became a dominant aspect of most competitive games by the end of the century.

Television itself, however, both unites and isolates. In many societies, particularly the more affluent ones, the breakdown of family life, of the family unit itself, has created loneliness and isolation; and in affluent countries a greater dependence on psychiatry, itself a relatively new discipline at the beginning of the twentieth century. The family talk around the dinner table, itself no doubt sometimes idealized in retrospect, has been replaced for many millions of people with living alone, cut off from the outside world, yet linked to it by television, and, increasingly, by the Internet.

The century has been one in which the voice of the individual asserted itself, as did the voice of governments that sought to follow the democratic and liberal mean between the excesses and extremes of totalitarianism. Fascism and Communism, dictatorship and tyranny, religious fundamentalism, have battened on the century like locusts. Tyranny is still a feature of dozens of regimes. But democracy has had the strength to fight its own battle for survival. Votes for women were a feature of that democratic battle before the First World War. Lowering the age of voting, and thus increasing the number of voters, was one of the battles after the Second World War. At the general election of 1955, British National Servicemen under the age of twenty-one had no vote. Soldiers murmured even then how wrong it was that they could be sent to die for their country, at a time when British troops were in conflicts in Kenya, Malaya, Aden and Cyprus, yet could not vote for or against the government whose policy might send them there, possibly to be wounded or killed. The same was true for American servicemen in Vietnam: in the United States votes at eighteen had to wait until 1971. Not only votes, but parliaments, increased and proliferated globally through the century. The spread of genuinely democratic parliaments, whose majorities can be changed by the freely expressed will of the electorate, is one of the most solid achievements – one of the glories – of the twentieth century. The power of money and of the media constantly challenges this. Vigilance, scepticism and continual questioning are no less vital in democracy than under tyranny.

The voice of the individual, as enshrined in 1948 in the United Nations Declaration on Human Rights, became the voice of dissent. The scrutiny carried out by organizations like Amnesty International brought the focus on human rights to a global public. Meeting in Geneva, the United Nations Commission on Human Rights, and the Non-Governmental Organizations which represent specific minority interests at the Commission, cast a strong spotlight on human rights abuse. Two areas in which it was particularly active in the 1970s and 1980s were the inequalities and indignities of apartheid in South Africa, and the struggle of the Jews to emigrate from the Soviet Union without harassment or imprisonment.

The impact of dissent was heightened in the last quarter of the century through the medium of television, which could instantly bring unpopular sights, rousing protest demonstrations, to the homes of hundreds of millions of people. The opposition inside the United States to the Vietnam War was enhanced by television, both by the sights of the horrors and by the scenes of mass protest. The same was true of the women's peace movement in Northern Ireland, a movement which won the Nobel Peace Prize. The pressures for environmental protection were also enhanced by television reports of the destruction of rainforests, wetlands or dwindling species of whales, birds, fish and plants. Ecologically protective movements such as Friends of the Earth, Greenpeace and the 'Green' Parties in politics, one of which entered the governing coalition in Germany in 1998, likewise gained from television exposure of their cause. Damage to the environment, and the rapid consumption – as well as the destruction – of the world's natural resources, adversely affect the affluent, the comfortable, the poor and the destitute alike. Even the wealthiest may not be able to escape the effect of cancer-causing pollutants.

Of the many problems which beset the twentieth century, ill-health and disease were among the most pernicious. Plague in India at the beginning of the century killed more people than Hitler's armies in Russia. The influenza epidemic at the end of the First World War killed at least twice as many people as the war itself. Tuberculosis and poliomyelitis – TB and polio – killed hundreds of thousands of people every year.

Some of the greatest achievements of the twentieth century were in the field of medicine. The humble but efficacious aspirin waited until 1899 before its appearance, thus becoming a twentieth-century life-enhancer, whose beneficial properties continue to be discovered decades later, most recently in the treatment and prevention of heart disease. The steady onward march of medical research and achievement was evident from the early years of the century. In 1903 electro-cardiography was first demonstrated, in Holland. In 1905 the first cornea transplant took place, in Austria. In 1907 the first systematic diagnosis of tuberculosis was made, in France; and in 1910, also in France, the first determination of radiography as a therapeutic agent. In 1922 insulin was first isolated, in London, Ontario; that same year a diabetic patient in Toronto received an insulin injection for the first time.

The greatest of all the medical victories was the victory over bacterial infection. Before the twentieth century doctors could do little about infection.

For 20,000 years those who were regarded as healers practised incantations, or gave potions – many of herbal medicine, including Chinese, Indian and Amazonian medicines – which were valuable in terms of general health, but none of which was very effective against infection. Then, for the first time in recorded history, came the cure. It was a slow, steady, yet dramatic process which began one-third of the way through the century. Bacterial infection, the killer of all preceding centuries and generations, was in the process of being conquered. The start came with Prontosil, a yellow dye which killed germs, and which was discovered by the German industrial giant I. G. Farben in 1932. It is a sad commentary on humanity that ten years later this same I. G. Farben, the healer of 1932, was making use of slave labourers in its wartime industrial plants, where tens of thousands died in the harshest of working conditions, including at a factory within sight of the crematoria at Auschwitz. Compensation for the few slave labourers who survived was resisted for half a century.

During that ten-year period from 1932 to 1942, doctors were searching for even more effective and wider-ranging means of fighting bacterial infection. The crucial breakthrough came with the discovery of antibiotics. The discovery of penicillin on the eve of the Second World War was the achievement of a Scot, Alexander Fleming. Its development during the war as an effective anti-bacterial agent was the work of a German-Jewish refugee, Ernst Chain. The impact of penicillin was immediate. Hundreds of thousands of soldiers who would have died from wound infections, the successors to those soldiers who in previous wars did die, were saved – both to live and, in many cases, to return to the battlefield to fight again, and to be killed.

New antibiotics, discovered after the Second World War, spread their life-preserving powers around the world. The destructive powers of typhoid were defeated by chloromycetin (also known as chloramphenicol). Trachoma, the eye disease which existed in the world on an epidemic and in places endemic scale, was controlled by aureomycin. Cholera and syphilis were likewise combated by antibiotics. Tuberculosis, the greatest killer of them all, had been defeated by streptomycin, but, as the century came to an end, drug-resistant forms of tuberculosis had emerged, raising it once more to epidemic proportions. The same was true of malaria. Having been virtually eliminated by the 1950s, malaria re-emerged in the final decade of the century as a killer of three million people a year.

Other medical achievements followed in the wake of the anti-bacterial victory. Surgery, which by the century's end was taken for granted as a safe

way to fight illness, had in all previous centuries been a gruesome risk, due
to the prevalence of post-operative infections that, irrespective of the surgeon's skill, killed even after successful surgery. Following the ability to
control infection, surgery became a safe way forward. One of the great
advances as a result of the basic safety of surgical techniques was heart-
transplant surgery. By the end of the century there were more than 20,000
successful transplants worldwide: in 1996 alone, four thousand in Britain
and more than two thousand in the United States, with a survival rate for
71.7 percent of all cases for more than four years. The longest surviving
heart-transplant patient in Britain was alive eighteen years after his operation.

The prevention of infection through vaccination was another twentieth-
century victory. Diphtheria was first successfully vaccinated against in 1914.
The polio vaccine, first Salk's in 1955 and then Sabin's in 1957, virtually
eliminated polio within a decade. Until the 1950s polio was a catastrophic
disease, especially, ironically, in 'clean' Western countries, where the need
for cleanliness to fight infections was thought to be understood. Among
those who had been disabled by it was Franklin Roosevelt. Great care was
taken while he was alive not to reveal to the American public the extent of
his disability.

The smallpox vaccine had been known, and used, since the eighteenth
century. But mass vaccination was entirely a twentieth-century phenomenon.
So successful was it that the United Nations World Health Organization
was able to announce, on 26 October 1978, that smallpox had ceased to
exist on Earth. The total elimination of a dreadful disease was one of the
triumphs of twentieth-century medical techniques.

A series of other discoveries have helped to prolong life, and to bring the
miracles of medical research to the benefit, and greater longevity, of millions
of people. The synthesis of hormones (which were themselves discovered in
1902) enabled a hormone needed by the body to be replaced, both to attack
wasting diseases, as in oestrogen to prevent osteoporosis in menopausal
women, and as an anti-inflammatory vehicle for disease, as in cortisone.

One essentially medical advance, accepted as routine at the end of the
century, which was not conceivable when the century began, was genetic
research. On 25 April 1953 Francis Crick and James Watson announced the
discovery of the double helix structure of DNA, the basic material and
vehicle of heredity. The implications of genetic healing are incalculable,
based on the potentiality to correct a genetic defect before a child is born.
Another vital medical advance is X-ray imaging. Few present-day hospital

procedures would be possible without the benefit of X-ray. First discovered in 1895, advances in X-ray technique in the twentieth century included Computerized Axial Tomography (CAT) and Magnetic Resonance Imaging (MRI) scans, with their revolutionary application to diagnosis. Advances in laser and fibre-optic medical techniques enabled diagnosis and surgery to be effectively combined.

Not all medical advances involve operations. Health was also enhanced during the century by the discovery of the properties of vitamins. It was not until 1913 that vitamin A was isolated, and not until the 1930s that the wide range and nature of vitamins were known, and capable of proper dietary use. Pointers to a healthy diet continue to be explored: in a medical lecture in London in the autumn of 1998 the life-enhancing properties of the cocoa bean were extolled, offering to turn chocolate from an indulgence to a cure.

Despite the victories over bacterial infection, disease remains rampant. In the latter part of the century drug abuse became an alarmingly pervasive component in the destruction of the social fabric, leading to an increase in crime, and in the profits made by those who batten on human gullibility, weakness and addiction. Many illnesses, despite continual efforts, still elude cure. As the century comes to an end many forms of cancer, despite massive research initiatives, have yet to be conquered. Deaths from AIDS multiply massively every year, particularly in the poorer countries of Africa, and in India. Many viral infections – and even bacterial ones such as bacterial meningitis – remain killers. The spectre of infant mortality, which was so prevalent over much of the globe when the century began, continued, at the century's end, to cast a shadow in the many countries where poverty and the daily struggle for subsistence still make the worldwide advances in health cruelly remote, and minimally effective.

The contrast between rich and poor nations, as well as between Africa, where the prevalence and spread of AIDS in the late 1990s was most rapid, and other continents, can be seen in the most recent (1997) figures for life expectancy, calculated at birth. In Britain, it was seventy-four for men and seventy-nine for women. In Canada, it was seventy-three for men and almost eighty for women. In the United States, it was seventy-two for men and almost seventy-nine for women. In China, with a population of more than a thousand million, life expectancy was sixty-six for men and seventy for women. In Russia, it was declining for both sexes, from well above sixty in 1991 to well below sixty in 1997. In India, with almost a thousand million people, life expectancy was just above fifty-seven for men and fifty-eight for women. Central and sub-Saharan Africa fared the worst. In Uganda and Malawi the life expectancy for both sexes was forty-one. In Rwanda it was forty-two. In Guinea-Bissau it was under forty-two years for men and just over forty-five for women. In Burundi and Angola it was on average forty-six. In Burkina Faso and neighbouring Benin, it was under forty-six for men and just over forty-nine for women. In Burkina Faso the illiteracy rate was just over eighty per cent.

The twentieth century is characterized by war and the brutal curtailment of human life that war brings; by the enormous energy, inventiveness and willpower that was put behind warmaking; and by the tens of millions who were killed, many of them civilians, and several millions of them children. The century is also characterized by the healing and life-protecting advances which it saw from its first years. More lives were prolonged, and more life-threatening illnesses cured, more starvation averted, more malnutrition warded off, than lives cut short in war. In 1955 there were twenty-one million deaths among children under the age of five. By 1995 that figure had fallen to eleven million.

Yet illness and hunger persist; as the century reached its final year cholera was still endemic in eighty countries. Yellow fever, which killed 30,000 people a year, was showing, in the words of the World Health Organization, 'a dramatic resurgence' in Africa and the Americas. Measles, which the World Health Organization hoped to see eliminated by the year 2000, 'still kills nearly a million a year'. As life expectancy rose, non-communicable diseases gained in their destructive power. Coronary and other heart diseases accounted for more than ten million deaths a year as the twentieth century came to an end, stroke for four-and-a-half million. Cancer killed more than six million a year, pulmonary disease three million. Three communicable diseases, AIDS, tuberculosis and malaria, each killed three million people a year at the approach of the millennium. Of the premature deaths which the World Health Organization stressed were 'preventable', the saddest in many ways were those of the 585,000 women dying every year in pregnancy or childbirth. The risks of such deaths in Europe were one in 1,400; in Asia, one in sixty-five; in Africa, one in sixteen. Infant mortality, like illiteracy, remains the curse of Africa at the century's close.

The instant globalization of communications, the ability to contact individuals and institutions anywhere in the world, at any time of night or day, had yet to play a decisive role in curing global hunger, or in lessening in any significant way the desperate discrepancies between rich and poor. Knowledge of the sufferings and inequalities of the world had yet to encompass the power to help. Realization of the unequal distribution of wealth and resources is only a tiny and first step towards even the minimum amelioration of those inequalities. Wars and conflicts between peoples are a self-inflicted burden, as is destruction of the environment; yet disease, illiteracy and natural disasters are quite sufficient wars to fight.

Historic echoes as the century came to an end included the death in June 1999, in Salisbury, Connecticut, of Anne Sheafe Miller. She was the first person in the United States whose life had been saved by penicillin, in 1942. Her death, aged ninety, was followed a few days later by another echo of the past, the presentation by President Clinton of the Congressional Gold Medal, the highest honour Congress can bestow, to Rosa Parks. Her refusal to give up her seat on an Alabama bus in 1955, and her arrest for this 'crime', had led to the bus boycott that resulted in the Supreme Court's decision that bus segregation was unconstitutional. Admiral Kimmel's long search for vindication, over allegations of negligence in 1941, at Pearl Harbor, was also achieved in 1999, albeit posthumously.

Echoes of past wars abounded. In Britain, the death on June 7 of Air Commodore Donald MacDonell was a reminder of the day when the German air force almost destroyed the ability of Britain to resist the Nazi onslaught: on 15 August 1940, the heaviest German attack of the Battle of Britain, MacDonell shot down two German fighter aircraft of the seventy-five destroyed that day in the air. A year and a half later, he was shot down over France, spending the next three years in German captivity. In the United States, Senator John McCain of Arizona, a former naval aviator who had been shot down over Hanoi in 1967 and been a prisoner of war in North Vietnam for the next five and a half years, was a contender for the Republican nomination for President in the year 2000. As a Senator he took a lead in the campaign to curb the powers of the tobacco industry and its all-pervasive advertising.

The last year of the century, as the first, was marked by war. Even as Serb troops withdrew from Kosovo, fierce fighting was taking place between Ethiopia and Eritrea, with frequent artillery and tank battles along the disputed border. Several thousand soldiers were killed in March in the battle for the border town of Tsorona, where Ethiopian soldiers were forced to advance through a minefield, and hundreds of them blown to pieces. 'I never believed in Hollywood films until I saw this battle,' commented a young Eritrean female fighter, Yordanos Habte.

The connection between poverty and indebtedness was recognized in June 1999 by the leaders of the Group of Seven (G7) industrialized nations, who agreed to write off twenty per cent of the money owed them by the poorest nations. Thirty-six developing countries would be the beneficiaries, including Sudan, Uganda, Bolivia, Mozambique and Guyana. Campaigners of Jubilee 2000 were dismayed that the percentage of debt being written off was not higher.

For the nations bordering on the Indian Ocean there was alarming news that summer which went beyond even the burdens of indebtedness: scientists had discovered an enormous concentration of pollution – covering an area the size of the continental United States – high above the ocean from Somalia to Sumatra. At its densest, along the coastlines of India and Myanmar, it intercepted up to 45 per cent of direct sunlight. Blown by the summer monsoon across the Indian and East-Asia land mass, it combined with the monsoon rains to fall as acid rain. Among those who might suffer the effects of this pollution was the Earth's 6,000 millionth inhabitant, born in the third week of June 1999 – one of more than 25,000 children born on the same day.

Reward and rehabilitation were on many national agendas as the century drew to its close. For his efforts for peace in Northern Ireland, John Major was made a Companion of Honour, the recognition Churchill had received in 1922 for his part in the struggle to reconcile conflicting Irish aspirations. In the continuing Russian efforts at rehabilitation, on June 9 the Prosecutor-General of Russia officially 'cleared' the son of Tsar Alexander II, and three other Romanov princes, of 'wrongdoing'. Each had been executed by the Bolsheviks in 1918. In Moscow the Administration of the Rehabilitation of Victims of Political Repression was reviewing hundreds of cases. In the words of its director, Galina Vesnovskaya, all had been victims of 'political reprisals'. Yet victimization, unfair arrest and human rights abuse continued in many countries, including the world's most populous, China. On June 10 a former civil servant, Fang Jue, who the previous year had distributed a pro-democracy manifesto, was sentenced to four years in prison. His 'crime' included giving Western journalists a paper he had written calling for greater democracy in China.

In London, a human rights group, African Rights, issued a report on the day of Fang Jue's sentence highlighting human rights abuses in Zimbabwe. The report was welcomed by those in Zimbabwe who sought a more democratic society. Trevor Ncube, an independent editor in the Zimbabwe capital, Harare, commented: 'The significance of this report shows that the world is watching us and giving us a thumbs down on human rights. It calls for a new constitution, better land reform and a free Press. The report will fortify and encourage people in our civil society to keep fighting for real change.'

Such 'real change' was also hoped for by many of Israel's electorate when, on May 17, Benjamin Netanyahu's government was defeated at the polls, and replaced by an administration headed by Ehud Barak, a former Commander-in-Chief, who supported the withdrawal of Israeli troops from Lebanon, and a renewal of the Oslo Peace process with the Palestinians.

The natural disasters in the last year of the twentieth century spanned the globe. During earthquakes in August and November as many as 17,000 Turks were killed. In September, in China, torrential rain released massive mudslides: a thousand Chinese were killed and five million − the entire population of Denmark − left homeless. Also in September, 2,000 people were killed when an earthquake struck Taiwan. In October, 8,000 Indians were drowned when a cyclone devastated twelve coastal districts off the Bay of Bengal. In December, 30,000 people lost their lives when floods and landslides devastated the northern coastal region of Venezuela.

At the century's end, for each person living in relative affluence or comfort, adequately fed and at work, four people − often in the same country − are living in penury, unable to earn enough money or grow enough food to maintain a family in minimum security, on the margin of starvation or afflicted by life-shortening diseases. Mustering the will and energy to battle against these global imbalances is among the major challenges that lie ahead. So too is the survival and strengthening of the institutions of democracy, and the prevention of the proliferation of nuclear arms and chemical weapons. In 1984, looking back over the whole span of recorded history, the historian Barbara Tuchman wrote: 'We can only muddle on as we have done in those same three or four thousand years, through patches of brilliance and decline, great endeavour and shadow.' The twentieth century encompassed both extremes.

MAPS

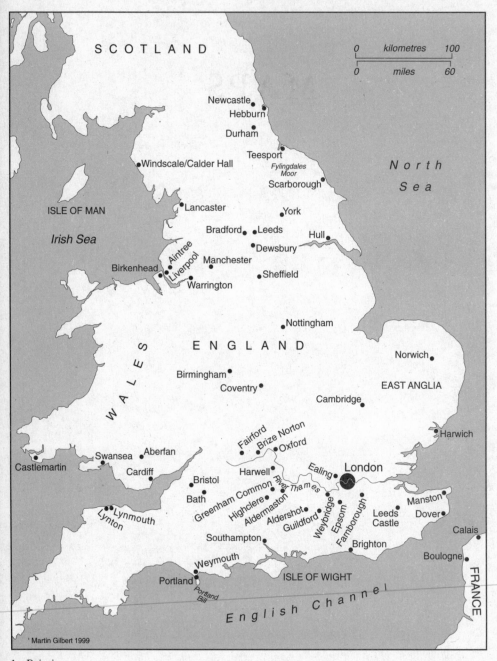

1. Britain

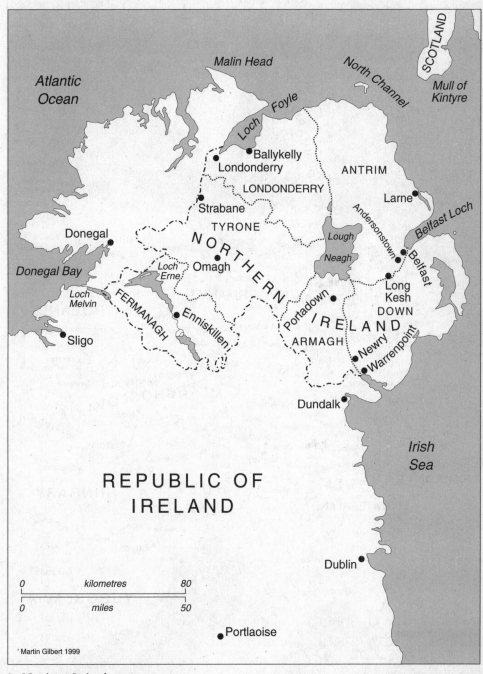

Atlantic
Ocean

Malin Head

SCOTLAND

North Channel

Mull of
Kintyre

Loch *Foyle*

●Ballykelly
●Londonderry

ANTRIM

LONDONDERRY

●Larne

●Strabane

Andersonstown

Belfast Loch

TYRONE

N O R T H E R N

Lough

Neagh

●Belfast

●Donegal

Loch
Erne

●Omagh

Long
Kesh

Donegal Bay

I R E L A N D

DOWN

Loch
Melvin

FERMANAGH

Portadown
●

●Newry

Warrenpoint

●Sligo

●Enniskillen

ARMAGH

●Warrenpoint

●Dundalk

*Irish
Sea*

REPUBLIC OF
IRELAND

| 0 | kilometres | 80 |
| 0 | miles | 50 |

●Dublin

' Martin Gilbert 1999

●Portlaoise

2. Northern Ireland

3. Western and Central Europe

4. Eastern Europe

The borders of the Soviet
Republics, 1945 - 1991

| 0 | kilometres | 500 |

| 0 | miles | 300 |

SWEDEN

FINLAND

Murmansk

Kandalaksha

*White
Sea*

Archangel

*Lake
Onega*

Helsinki

*Lake
Ladoga*

Leningrad
(St. Petersburg)

Tallinn

ESTONIA

Baltic Sea

LATVIA

Skrunda

Riga

LITHUANIA

Kaunas

Vilnius

Kaliningrad

POLAND

Minsk

BYELORUSSIA

Baranovichi

Brest-Litovsk
Domachevo

Kozhanov

Sarny

Chernobyl

Rovno

Kiev

Lvov

UKRAINE

Vinnitsa

Kharkov

MOLDAVIA

Kishinev

ROUMANIA

BULGARIA

CRIMEA

Sevastopol

Simferopol

Foros Yalta
Pitsunde

Black Sea

Krasnodar

Caucasus Mountains

Batum

GEORGIA

ARMENIA

AZERBAIJAN

Baku

Caspian Sea

*Aegean
Sea*

Mediterranean Sea

TURKEY

SYRIA

IRAQ

IRAN

Dzerzhinsk

Gorky
(Nizhni Novgorod)

Moscow

SOVIET UNION

Orel

River Volga

Engels

Perm

Sverdlovsk
(Ekaterinburg)

Ural Mountains

BASHKORTOSTAN
AUTONOMOUS
REPUBLIC

TARTARSAN
AUTONOMOUS
REPUBLIC

Kuibyshev

Totskoe

KAZAKHSTAN

Astrakhan

'Martin Gilbert 1999

5. The Soviet Union

6. Central Asia

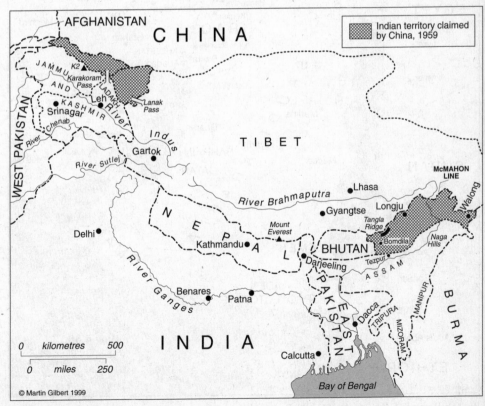

7. The Chinese-Indian conflict

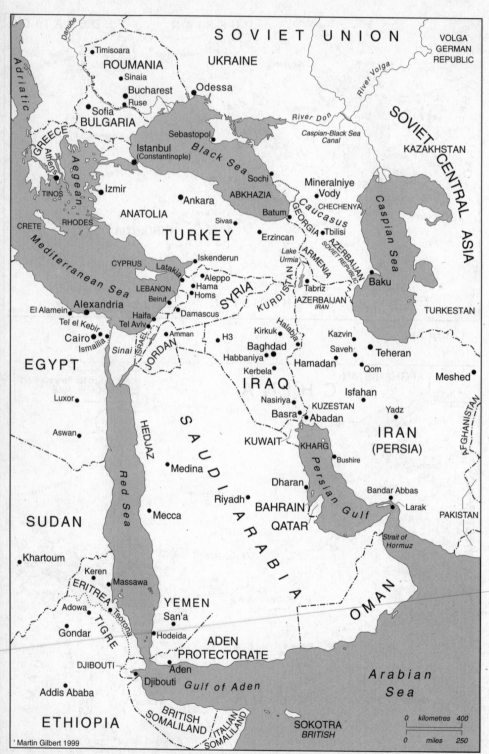

8. The Black Sea region, the Middle East and Arabia

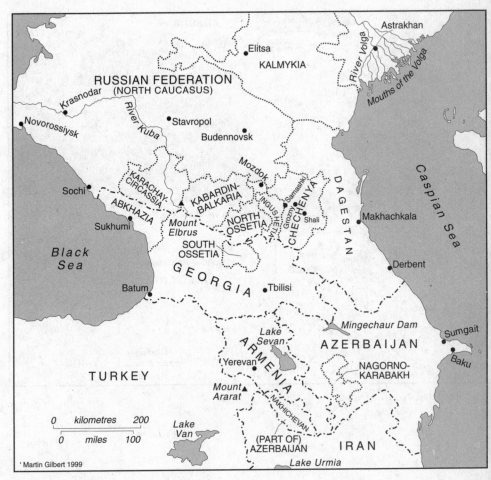

Astrakhan

Elitsa

KALMYKIA

RUSSIAN FEDERATION
(NORTH CAUCASUS)

River Volga

Mouths of the Volga

Krasnodar

River Kuba

Stavropol

Budennovsk

Novorossiysk

Mozdok

KARACHAY-
CIRCASSIA

Sochi

ABKHAZIA

KABARDIN-
BALKARIA

INGUSHETIA

Samashki

Grozny

CHECHENYA

Shali

DAGESTAN

Makhachkala

Caspian Sea

Sukhumi

Mount
Elbrus

NORTH
OSSETIA

SOUTH
OSSETIA

Derbent

Black
Sea

G E O R G I A

Tbilisi

Batum

Mingechaur Dam

Sumgait

Lake
Sevan

AZERBAIJAN

TURKEY

Yerevan

ARMENIA

NAGORNO-
KARABAKH

Baku

Mount
Ararat

NAKHICHEVAN

0   kilometres   200

0   miles   100

Lake
Van

(PART OF)
AZERBAIJAN

I R A N

' Martin Gilbert 1999

Lake Urmia

9. The Caucasus

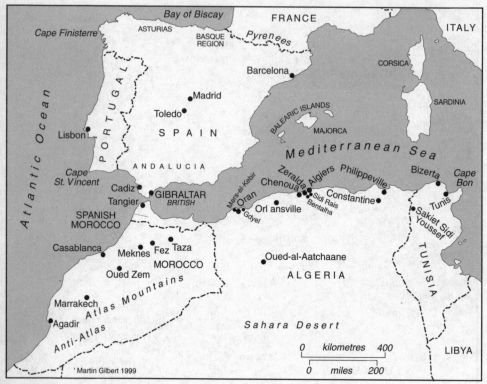

10. Spain and North Africa

Beirut

Beka'a Valley
Baalbek
Litani River
Sidon

Damascus

SYRIA

Mediterranean
Sea

Tyre
Qana

Mount Hermon

Nahariya
Acre
Maalot
Kiryat Shmona
Shamir
Kuneitra
Golan
Heights

Haifa

Sheikh Miskin

Sea
of
Galilee

Jebel
Druze

Caesarea

Beit
Shean
Irbid

Netanya

Jenin
Qabatiya
Tulkarem
Nablus
Qalqiliya
WEST
BANK
Mafrak

River Jordan

Tel Aviv

Lod
Bir Zeit
Ashdod
Jericho
Amman
Jerusalem

Ashkelon
Madaba
Gaza
Erez

Dead Sea

Hebron

JORDAN

SAUDI
ARABIA

Yamit
El Arish
Beersheba
Kerak

ISRAEL

Negev

Sinai
occupied by
Israel,
1967-1980

International borders, 1967-73

West Bank, Gaza Strip and Golan
Heights, occupied by Israel, 1967

▲▲▲▲ Furthest northern advance of Israeli
forces, 1982-83

Israel security zone, under Israeli
military control, since 1983

Petra
Ma'an

EGYPT

0   miles   50

0   kilometres   70

Eilat

SAUDI ARABIA

Gulf of
Akaba
Akaba

Martin Gilbert 1999

11. Israel, Lebanon, Jordan

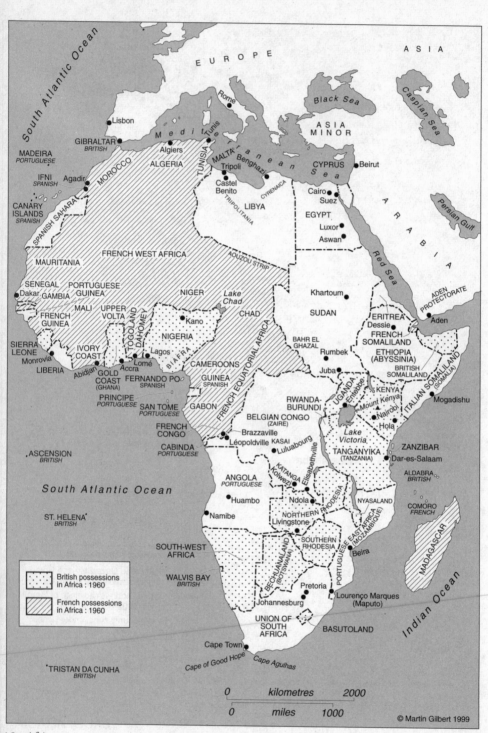

South Atlantic Ocean

EUROPE

ASIA

Rome

Black Sea

ASIA
MINOR

Caspian Sea

Mediterranean Sea

Lisbon

GIBRALTAR
BRITISH

Algiers

Tunis

MALTA

Benghazi

CYPRUS

Beirut

MADEIRA
PORTUGUESE

Tripoli

IFNI
SPANISH

Agadir

MOROCCO

ALGERIA

TUNISIA

Castel
Benito

CYRENAICA

Cairo

Suez

ARABIA

Persian Gulf

CANARY
ISLANDS
SPANISH

SPANISH SAHARA

LIBYA

TRIPOLITANIA

EGYPT

Luxor

Aswan

MAURITANIA

FRENCH WEST AFRICA

AOUZOU STRIP

Khartoum

Red Sea

ADEN
PROTECTORATE

SENEGAL
Dakar

PORTUGUESE
GUINEA

GAMBIA

NIGER

Lake
Chad

SUDAN

ERITREA

Aden

FRENCH
GUINEA

MALI

UPPER
VOLTA

Kano

CHAD

Dessie

FRENCH
SOMALILAND

SIERRA
LEONE
Monrovia

IVORY
COAST

TOGOLAND
DAHOMEY

NIGERIA

Lagos

BIAFRA

CAMEROONS

BAHR EL
GHAZAL

Rumbek

ETHIOPIA
(ABYSSINIA)

BRITISH
SOMALILAND

ITALIAN SOMALILAND
(SOMALIA)

LIBERIA

Abidjan

Lomé
Accra

GUINEA
SPANISH

Juba

Mogadishu

GOLD
COAST
(GHANA)

FERNANDO PO
SPANISH

FRENCH EQUATORIAL AFRICA

UGANDA
Entebbe

KENYA

Mount Kenya
Nairobi

PRINCIPE
PORTUGUESE

SAN TOME
PORTUGUESE

GABON

RWANDA-
BURUNDI

Hola

ASCENSION
BRITISH

FRENCH
CONGO

CABINDA
PORTUGUESE

BELGIAN CONGO
(ZAIRE)

Brazzaville
Léopoldville

KASAI

Luluabourg

Lake
Victoria

TANGANYIKA
(TANZANIA)

ZANZIBAR

Dar-es-Salaam

ALDABRA
BRITISH

South Atlantic Ocean

ANGOLA
PORTUGUESE

KATANGA
Kolwezi

Elisabethville

COMORO
FRENCH

ST. HELENA
BRITISH

Huambo

Namibe

Ndola

NORTHERN RHODESIA
Livingstone

NYASALAND

NORTHERN RHODESIA

PORTUGUESE EAST AFRICA
(MOZAMBIQUE)

MADAGASCAR

Indian Ocean

SOUTH-WEST
AFRICA

BECHUANALAND
(BOTSWANA)

SOUTHERN
RHODESIA

Beira

WALVIS BAY
BRITISH

British possessions
in Africa : 1960

French possessions
in Africa : 1960

Pretoria

Johannesburg

Lourenço Marques
(Maputo)

UNION OF
SOUTH
AFRICA

BASUTOLAND

Cape Town

TRISTAN DA CUNHA
BRITISH

Cape of Good Hope

Cape Agulhas

0   kilometres   2000

0   miles   1000

© Martin Gilbert 1999

12. Africa

13. Central Africa

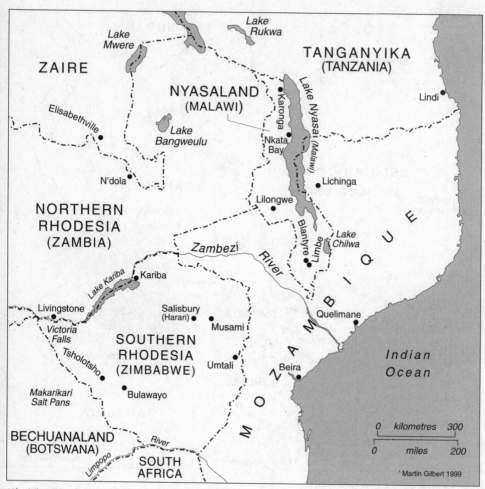

14. The Rhodesias, Nyasaland, Mozambique

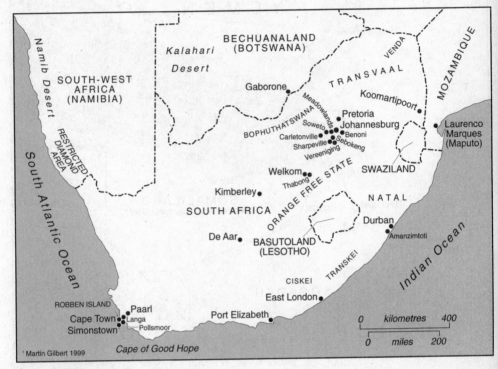

15. South Africa

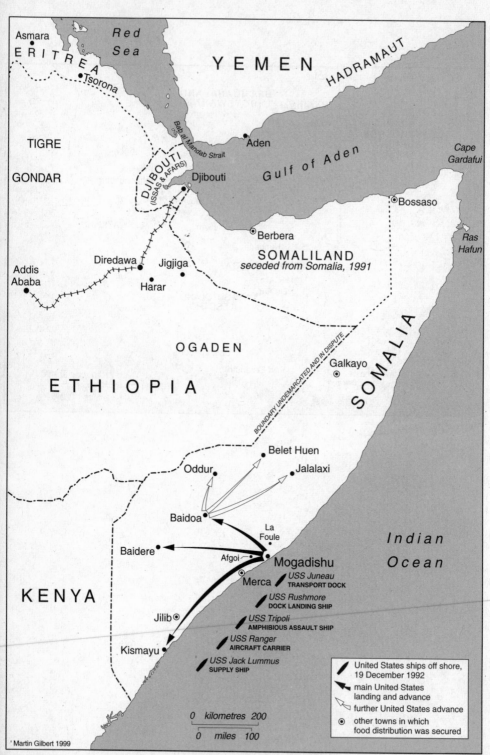

Asmara
ERITREA
Tsorona
Red Sea
YEMEN
HADRAMAUT
TIGRE
Bab al Mandab Strait
Aden
Gulf of Aden
Cape Gardafui
GONDAR
DJIBOUTI (ISSAS & AFARS)
Djibouti
Bossaso
Berbera
SOMALILAND
seceded from Somalia, 1991
Ras Hafun
Addis Ababa
Diredawa
Jigjiga
Harar
OGADEN
ETHIOPIA
SOMALIA
BOUNDARY UNDEMARCATED AND IN DISPUTE
Galkayo
Belet Huen
Oddur
Jalalaxi
Baidoa
La Foule
Indian Ocean
Baidere
Afgoi
Mogadishu
KENYA
Merca
USS Juneau
TRANSPORT DOCK
USS Rushmore
DOCK LANDING SHIP
Jilib
USS Tripoli
AMPHIBIOUS ASSAULT SHIP
USS Ranger
AIRCRAFT CARRIER
Kismayu
USS Jack Lummus
SUPPLY SHIP

United States ships off shore, 19 December 1992
main United States landing and advance
further United States advance
⊙ other towns in which food distribution was secured

0   kilometres   200
0   miles   100

' Martin Gilbert 1999

16. Somalia

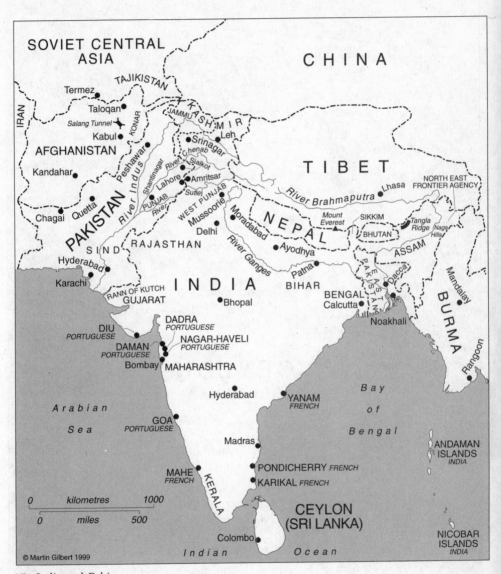

17. India and Pakistan

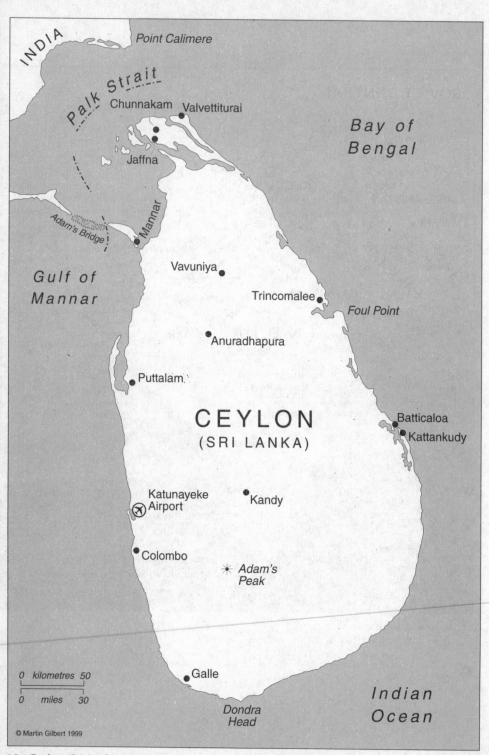

INDIA

Point Calimere

Palk Strait

Chunnakam   Valvettiturai

Bay of
Bengal

Jaffna

Adam's Bridge

Mannar

Gulf of
Mannar

Vavuniya

Trincomalee

Foul Point

Anuradhapura

Puttalam

CEYLON
(SRI LANKA)

Batticaloa

Kattankudy

Katunayeke
Airport

Kandy

Colombo

Adam's
Peak

0   kilometres 50

0   miles   30

Galle

Dondra
Head

Indian

Ocean

© Martin Gilbert 1999

18. Ceylon (Sri Lanka)

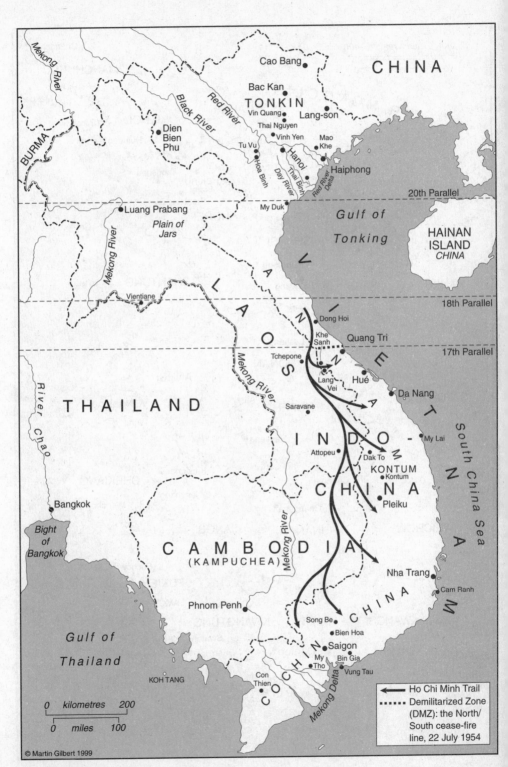

CHINA

Cao Bang

Bac Kan

TONKIN

Vin Quang · Lang-son

Thai Nguyen

Vinh Yen

Mao Khe

Dien Bien Phu

Tu Vu

Hoa Binh

Hanoi

Haiphong

Red River Delta

Mekong River

Black River

Red River

Day River

Thai Binh

BURMA

20th Parallel

My Duk

Gulf of Tonking

HAINAN ISLAND
CHINA

Luang Prabang

Plain of Jars

Mekong River

Vientiane

18th Parallel

Dong Hoi

Khe Sanh · Quang Tri

17th Parallel

Tchepone

Lang Vei · Hué

LAOS

Saravane

Da Nang

THAILAND

River Chao

Mekong River

INDO-

My Lai

Attopeu · Dak To

KONTUM
Kontum

South China Sea

CHINA

Pleiku

Bangkok

Bight of Bangkok

CAMBODIA
(KAMPUCHEA)

Mekong River

Nha Trang

Cam Ranh

Gulf of Thailand

Phnom Penh

Song Be · **CHINA**

Bien Hoa

Saigon

My Tho · Bin Gia

Vung Tau

KOH TANG

Con Thien

COCHIN

Mekong Delta

	Ho Chi Minh Trail
	Demilitarized Zone (DMZ): the North/South cease-fire line, 22 July 1954

0 kilometres 200

0 miles 100

© Martin Gilbert 1999

19. Indochina

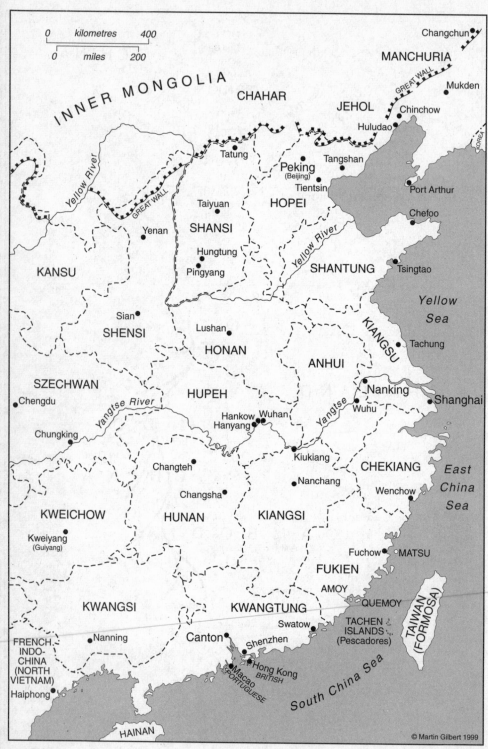

20. China

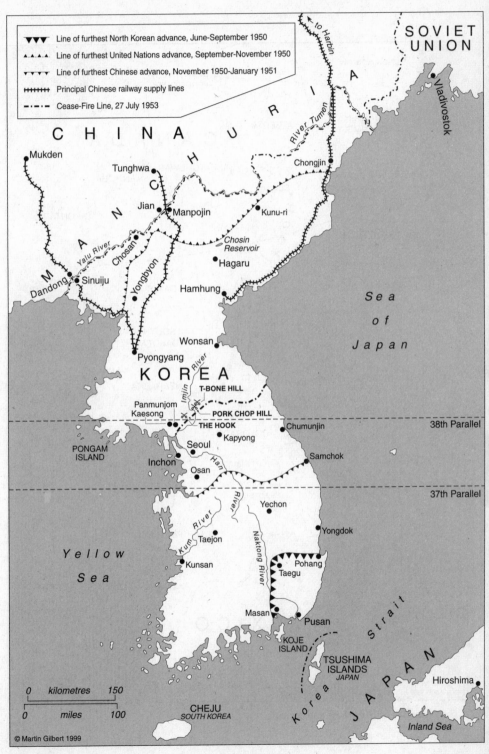

Line of furthest North Korean advance, June-September 1950

Line of furthest United Nations advance, September-November 1950

Line of furthest Chinese advance, November 1950-January 1951

Principal Chinese railway supply lines

Cease-Fire Line, 27 July 1953

SOVIET UNION

Vladivostok

to Harbin

MANCHURIA

CHINA

River Tumen

Mukden

Tunghwa

Chongjin

Jian

Manpojin

Kunu-ri

Yalu River

Chosan

Chosin Reservoir

Dandong

Sinuiju

Yongbyon

Hagaru

Hamhung

Sea of Japan

Wonsan

Pyongyang

KOREA

Imjin River

T-BONE HILL

Panmunjom

PORK CHOP HILL

Kaesong

THE HOOK

Chumunjin

38th Parallel

Seoul

Kapyong

PONGAM ISLAND

Han River

Inchon

Samchok

Osan

37th Parallel

Yechon

Yongdok

Kum River

Taejon

Naktong River

Yellow Sea

Kunsan

Pohang

Taegu

Masan

Pusan

KOJE ISLAND

Korea Strait

TSUSHIMA ISLANDS
JAPAN

Hiroshima

JAPAN

0   kilometres   150

0   miles   100

CHEJU
SOUTH KOREA

Inland Sea

© Martin Gilbert 1999

21. Korea

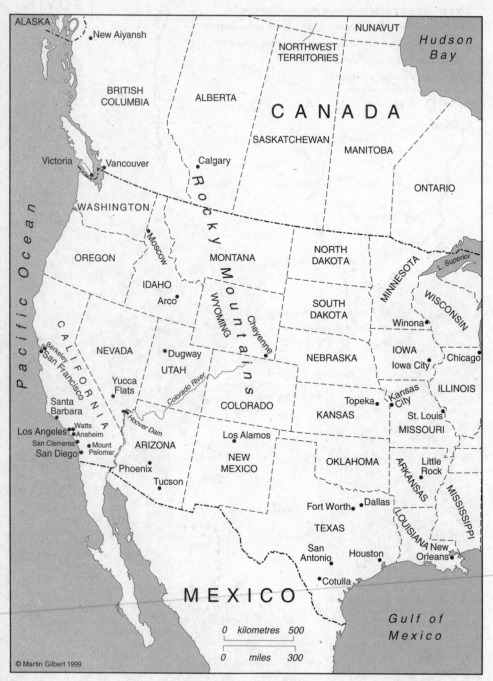

22. The western United States and Canada

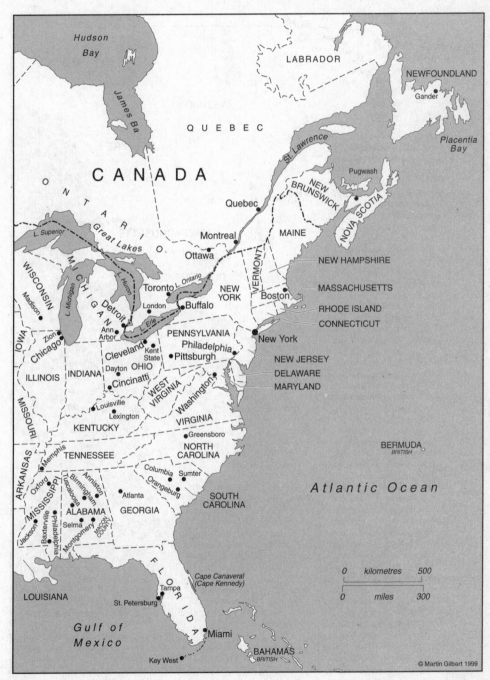

23. The eastern United States and Canada

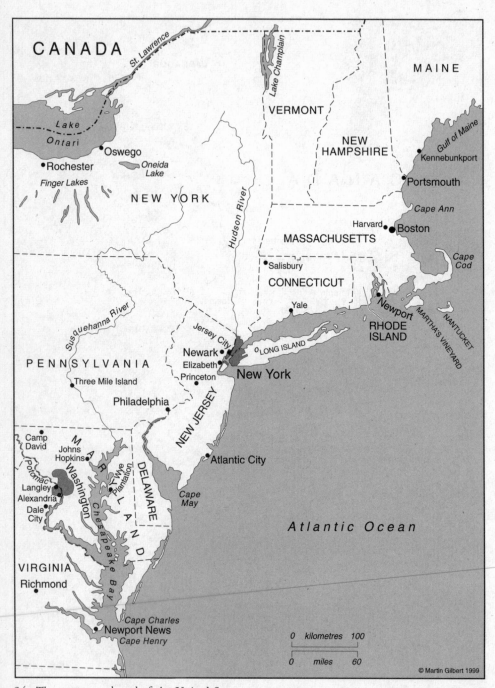

24. The eastern seaboard of the United States

© Martin Gilbert 1999

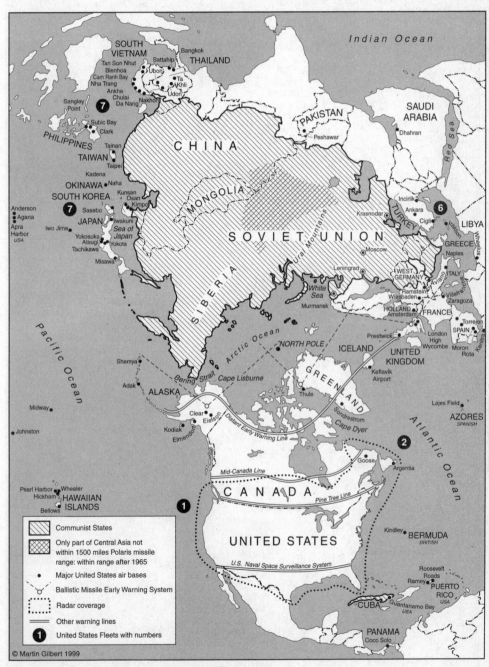

Indian Ocean

SOUTH VIETNAM
Tan Son Nhut
Bienhoa
Cam Ranh Bay
Nha Trang
Ankhe
Chulai
Sangley Point
Da Nang
Bangkok
Sattahip
THAILAND
Ubon
Ta Khli
Udon
Nakhon

PAKISTAN
Peshawar

SAUDI ARABIA
Dhahran

Subic Bay
Clark
PHILIPPINES
Tainan
TAIWAN
Taipei
Kadena
OKINAWA Naha
SOUTH KOREA
Anderson
Agana
Apra Harbor
USA
Sasebo
Kunsan
Osan
Kimpo
Iwo Jima
Yokosuka
Atsugi
Tachikawa
Iwakuni
Yokota
JAPAN
Sea of Japan
Misawa

CHINA

MONGOLIA

SOVIET UNION

Ural Mountains

Moscow

Krasnodar

Incirlik
Ankara
Cigli
TURKEY

LIBYA
Wheelus

GREECE
Naples
ITALY

Iraklion

SIBERIA

Leningrad
White Sea
Murmansk

WEST GERMANY
Ramstein
Wiesbaden
HOLLAND
Amsterdam
Aviano
Villefranche
Zaragoza
FRANCE
Torrejon
SPAIN
Moron
Rota
Kenitra

Pacific Ocean

Shemya
Adak
ALASKA
Bering Strait
Cape Lisburne
Arctic Ocean
NORTH POLE

GREENLAND

Prestwick
ICELAND
Keflavik Airport
UNITED KINGDOM
London
High Wycombe

Midway
Johnston

Clear
Eielson
Kodiak
Elmendorf
Distant Early Warning Line
Thule
Sondrestrom
Cape Dyer

Lajes Field
AZORES
SPANISH

Goose
Argentia

Atlantic Ocean

Mid-Canada Line
CANADA
Pine Tree Line

Pearl Harbor Wheeler
Hickham
Bellows
HAWAIIAN ISLANDS

UNITED STATES

Kindley
BERMUDA
BRITISH

U.S. Naval Space Surveillance System

Roosevelt Roads
Ramey
PUERTO RICO
USA

CUBA
Guantanamo Bay
USA

PANAMA
Coco Solo

Communist States

Only part of Central Asia not within 1500 miles Polaris missile range: within range after 1965

• Major United States air bases

Ballistic Missile Early Warning System

Radar coverage

Other warning lines

① United States Fleets with numbers

© Martin Gilbert 1999

25. United States global preparedness, 1960

Caribbean Sea

WEST INDIES

CURACAO
DUTCH

BARBADOS *BRITISH*

Atlantic Ocean

PANAMA

Caracas

VENEZUELA

TRINIDAD *BRITISH*

BRITISH GUIANA

Panama
Canal

Bogota

Mount
Roraima

Santa Elena

DUTCH GUIANA

FRENCH GUIANA

COLOMBIA

Boa
Vista

Equator

EQUADOR

Quito

River Amazon

MARANHAO

A M A Z O N I A

P
E
R
U

Pernambuco
(Recife)

Lima

B R A Z I L

Bahia

BOLIVIA

Brasilia

La Paz

Goiania

C
H
I
L
E

GRAN
CHACO

PARAGUAY

Rio de Janeiro

Sao Paulo

South
Pacific
Ocean

Cordoba

JUAN
FERNANDEZ
CHILE

Valparaiso

Santiago

URUGUAY

Buenos Aires

Punta del Este

Montevideo

ARGENTINA

Puerto Saavedra

P
A
T
A
G
O
N
I
A

South Atlantic Ocean

FALKLAND ISLANDS
BRITISH

0   kilometres   1000

0   miles   500

TIERRA DEL
FUEGO

SOUTH GEORGIA
BRITISH

© Martin Gilbert 1999

Cape Horn

SOUTH SANDWICH ISLANDS
BRITISH

26. South America

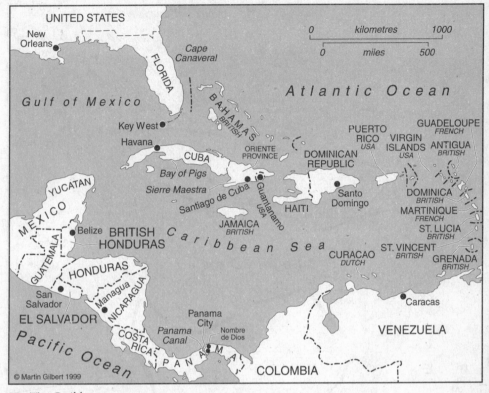

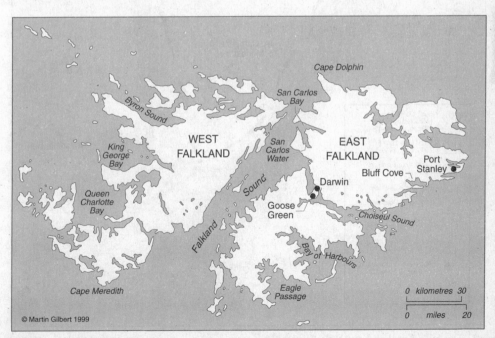

27. The Caribbean

28. The Falkland Islands

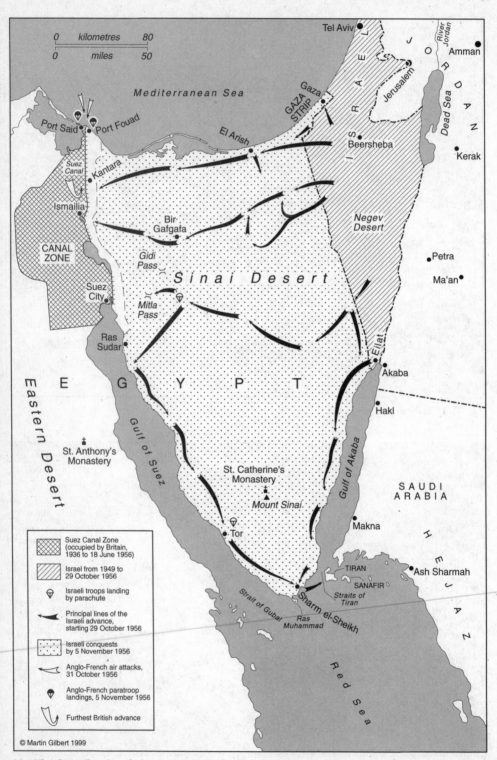

29. The Suez Canal and the Sinai Peninsula

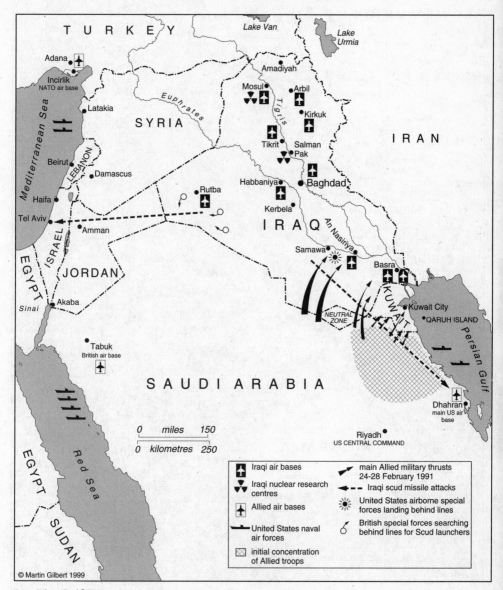

30. The Gulf War

Legend:

- **Iraqi air bases** (air base symbol)
- **Iraqi nuclear research centres** (symbol)
- **Allied air bases** (symbol)
- **United States naval air forces** (symbol)
- **initial concentration of Allied troops** (symbol)
- **main Allied military thrusts 24-28 February 1991** (arrow)
- **Iraqi scud missile attacks** (dashed arrow)
- **United States airborne special forces landing behind lines** (symbol)
- **British special forces searching behind lines for Scud launchers** (symbol)

Map labels:

TURKEY · Lake Van · Lake Urmia · Adana · Incirlik NATO air base · Latakia · Amadiyah · Mosul · Arbil · Kirkuk · SYRIA · Euphrates · Tigris · Tikrit · Salman Pak · IRAN · Mediterranean Sea · Beirut · Damascus · LEBANON · Habbaniya · Baghdad · Haifa · Kerbela · Tel Aviv · Amman · IRAQ · An Nasiriya · Samawa · Basra · ISRAEL · JORDAN · Rutba · KUWAIT · Kuwait City · QARUH ISLAND · EGYPT · Akaba · Sinai · NEUTRAL ZONE · Persian Gulf · Tabuk British air base · SAUDI ARABIA · Dhahran main US air base · Red Sea · Riyadh US CENTRAL COMMAND · EGYPT · SUDAN

Scale: 0 miles 150 · 0 kilometres 250

© Martin Gilbert 1999

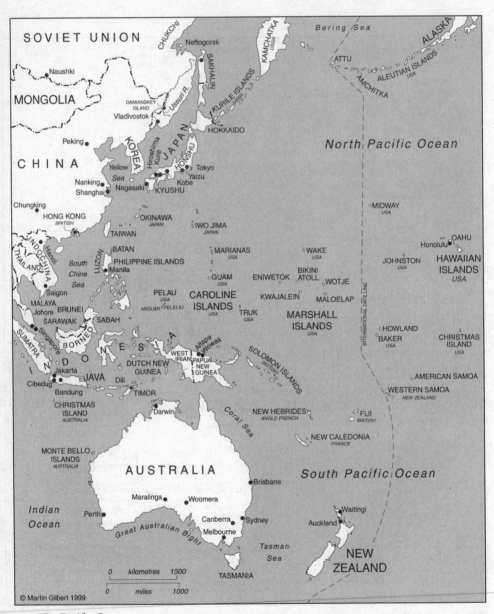

SOVIET UNION

CHUKCHI

Neftogorsk

KAMCHATKA
USSR

Bering Sea

ALASKA

ATTU

ALEUTIAN ISLANDS
USA

AMCHITKA

Naushki

MONGOLIA

SAKHALIN

DAMIANSKEY
ISLAND
Vladivostok

Ussuri R.

KURILE ISLANDS
USSR

HOKKAIDO

North Pacific Ocean

Peking

CHINA

KOREA

JAPAN

HONSHU

*Yellow
Sea*

Hiroshima
Kure

Tokyo
Yaizu

Chungking

Nanking
Shanghai

Nagasaki

KYUSHU

Kobe

MIDWAY
USA

HONG KONG
BRITISH

OKINAWA
JAPAN

IWO JIMA
JAPAN

Honolulu

OAHU

HAWAIIAN
ISLANDS
USA

INDOCHINA

Hanoi

THAILAND

TAIWAN

BATAN

*South
China
Sea*

LUZON

PHILIPPINE ISLANDS

Manila

MARIANAS
USA

WAKE
USA

JOHNSTON
USA

Saigon

GUAM
USA

ENIWETOK

BIKINI
ATOLL

WOTJE

MALAYA
Johore

BRUNEI

PELAU
USA

CAROLINE
ISLANDS
USA

KWAJALEIN

MALOELAP

SARAWAK

SABAH

ANGUAR PELELIU

TRUK
USA

MARSHALL
ISLANDS
USA

HOWLAND

CHRISTMAS
ISLAND
USA

Singapore

SUMATRA

BORNEO

I   N   D   O   N   E   S   I   A

Jakarta

JAVA

Altape
Aitape Wewak

WEST
IRIAN

PAPUA

BAKER
USA

Cibedug

Bandung

Dili

DUTCH NEW
GUINEA

NEW
GUINEA

SOLOMON ISLANDS
BRITISH

AMERICAN SAMOA

WESTERN SAMOA
NEW ZEALAND

TIMOR

CHRISTMAS
ISLAND
AUSTRALIA

Darwin

Coral Sea

NEW HEBRIDES
ANGLO FRENCH

FIJI
BRITISH

MONTE BELLO
ISLANDS
AUSTRALIA

NEW CALEDONIA
FRANCE

AUSTRALIA

Brisbane

South Pacific Ocean

*Indian
Ocean*

Perth

Maralinga

Woomera

Canberra

Sydney

Waitingi

Auckland

Melbourne

Great Australian Bight

*Tasman
Sea*

NEW
ZEALAND

| 0 | kilometres | 1500 |

| 0 | miles | 1000 |

TASMANIA

INTERNATIONAL DATE LINE

© Martin Gilbert 1999

31. The Pacific Ocean

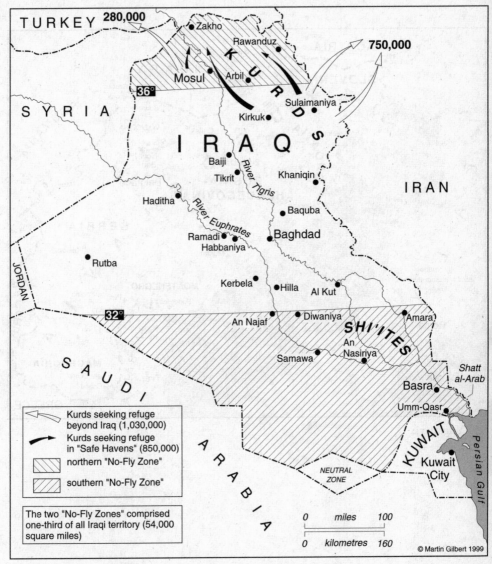

TURKEY **280,000**

• Zakho

Rawanduz

K U R D S

Mosul Arbil

36°

SYRIA

750,000

Sulaimaniya

Kirkuk •

I R A Q

IRAN

Baiji •

Tikrit •

River Tigris

Khaniqin •

Haditha •

Baquba •

River Euphrates

Ramadi •
Habbaniya

Baghdad

JORDAN

• Rutba

Kerbela •

Hilla • Al Kut •

32°

An Najaf •

Diwaniya •

SHI'ITES

Amara •

Samawa •

An
Nasiriya

SAUDI

Basra

Shatt
al-Arab

Umm-Qasr •

ARABIA

KUWAIT

Kuwait
City

Persian Gulf

NEUTRAL
ZONE

⇨ Kurds seeking refuge
beyond Iraq (1,030,000)

➡ Kurds seeking refuge
in "Safe Havens" (850,000)

▨ northern "No-Fly Zone"

▨ southern "No-Fly Zone"

The two "No-Fly Zones" comprised
one-third of all Iraqi territory (54,000
square miles)

0   miles   100

0   kilometres   160

© Martin Gilbert 1999

32. Iraq after the Gulf War

33. Yugoslavia

The Dayton Agreement for Bosnia-Herzegovina

- Area of the Serb Republic (Republika Srpska)
- Area of the Muslim/Croat Federation

AUSTRIA

SLOVENIA

Ljubljana

HUNGARY

River Danube

Zagreb

Okucani

CROATIA

Petrinja

Osijek

EASTERN
SLAVONIA

Rijeka

Vukovar

Novi
Sad

River Danube

POSAVINA
CORRIDOR

KRAJINA

Bosanski
Nova

Banja Luka

Brcko

S
E
R
B
I
A

Bihac

B

Bijelina

Batkovic

CROATIA (DALMATIA)

O

Maglaj

Drvar

Tuzla

S

Vlasenica

Bratunac

Zadar

N

Susica

Ljubovija

Knin

Gornji
Vakuf

Sarajevo

Zepa

Srebrenica

Split

Prozor

Pale

A

Celebici

HERZEGOVINA

Adriatic
Sea

Mostar

Gorazde

River Drina

MONTENEGRO

Dubrovnik

Pec

KOSOVO

Lake
Skadar

Under the Dayton Agreement, the whole of Bosnia-
Herzegovina would have a central government at
Sarajevo, headed by a President. The Serb Republic and
the Muslim/Croat Federation (known as the Federation of
Bosnia and Herzegovina) would each have its own
Prime Minister and government.

ITALY

ALBANIA

Eastern Slavonia, which had been occupied by the Serbs
in 1991 would return to Croatia. Gorazde would remain
a part of the Muslim/Croat Federation with a secure link
to Sarajevo. The status of Brcko, dominating the
Posavina Corridor linking the two Serb areas, would be
decided by international arbitration.

© Martin Gilbert 1999

34. Bosnia-Herzegovina: the Dayton Agreement

35. The NATO air war against Yugoslavia

36. Kosovo

© Martin Gilbert 1999

BIBLIOGRAPHY OF WORKS CONSULTED

Reference books and documents

Amnesty International Report, 1998, Amnesty International Publications, London, 1998.

Herbert Aptheker (ed.), *A Documentary History of The Negro People in the United States*, volumes five (1945–1951) and six (1951–1959), Citadel Press, New York, 1993.

Alan Bullock and Oliver Stallybrass (eds), *The Fontana Dictionary of Modern Thought*, Fontana Collins, London, 1977.

Henry Steele Commager (ed.), *Documents of American History since 1898*, Appelton-Century-Crofts, 7th edition, New York, 1963.

R. E. G. Davies, *A History of the World's Airlines*, Oxford University Press, London, 1964.

James Eayrs (ed.), *The Commonwealth and Suez, A Documentary Survey*, Oxford University Press, London, 1964.

M. Epstein, and others (eds), *The Annual Register, A Review of Public Events at Home and Abroad*, Longmans, Green, London, 1934–66.

John A. Garraty and Peter Gay (eds), *The Columbia History of the World*, Harper and Row, New York, 1972.

George C. Kohn (ed.), *Encyclopedia of Plague and Pestilence*, Facts on File, New York, 1995.

Paul Johnson, *A History of the Modern World: From 1917 to the 1980s*, Weidenfeld and Nicolson, London, 1983.

Harold Josephson (ed.-in-chief), *Biographical Dictionary of Modern Peace Leaders*, Greenwood Press, Westport, Connecticut, 1985.

Surjit Mansingh, *Historical Dictionary of India*, Vision Books, New Delhi, 1998.

Geoffrey Nowell-Smith (ed.), *The Oxford History of World Cinema*, Oxford University Press, Oxford, 1996.

William Outhwaite and Tom Bottomore, *The Blackwell Dictionary of Twentieth Century Social Thought*, Blackwell, Oxford, 1993.

Alan Palmer, *Dictionary of the British Empire and Commonwealth*, John Murray, London, 1996.

Alan Palmer, *Who's Who in World Politics from 1860 to the Present Day*, Routledge, London, 1996.

Philip Rees, *Biographical Dictionary of the Extreme Right since 1890*, Simon and Schuster, New York, 1990.

J. M. Roberts, *The Hutchinson History of the World*, Hutchinson, London, 1976.

Philip Waller (ed.), *Chronology of the 20th Century*, Helicon, Oxford, 1995.

Contemporary works (in chronological order of publication)

Kingsley Martin, 'The American Witch-Hunt', *New Statesman and Nation*, 5 July 1952.

Henry Steele Commager, *Freedom, Loyalty, Dissent*, Oxford University Press, London, 1954.

William H. Whyte Jr, *The Organization Man*, Simon and Schuster, New York, 1956.

Trevor Huddleston, *Nought for your Comfort*, Collins, London, 1956.

Peter Fryer, *Hungarian Tragedy*, Dennis Dobson, London, 1956.

Milovan Djilas, *The New Class, An Analysis of the Communist System*, Frederick A. Praeger, New York, 1957.

Max Lerner, *America as a Civilization, Life and Thought in the United States Today*, Simon and Schuster, New York, 1957.

Henry Kissinger, *Nuclear Weapons and Foreign Policy*, Harper and Brothers, New York, 1957.

John Kenneth Galbraith, *The Affluent Society*, Hamish Hamilton, London, 1958.

Dr Ho Ping-ti, *Studies on the Population of China, 1368–1953*, University of British Columbia, Vancouver, Canada, 1959.

Alan Paton, *The People Wept*, Kloof, Natal, 1959.

Senator Rubin, *This Is Apartheid*, Gollancz, London, 1959.

Martin Luther King, 'The Social Organization of Non-Violence', *Liberation*, New York, 1959.

Thomas Schieder (ed.), *The Expulsion of the German Population from Czechoslovakia*, Federal Ministry for Expellees, Refugees and War Victims, Bonn, 1960.

Rachel Carson, *Silent Spring*, Houghton Mifflin, Boston, 1962.

Guy Wint and Peter Calvocoressi, *Middle East Crisis*, Penguin Books (A Penguin Special), London, 1967.

Walter Cronkite, 'Who, What, When, Where, Why: Report from Vietnam', *CBS Television Network*, 27 February 1968.

Amartya Sen, *Poverty and Famines, an essay on entitlement and deprivation*, Clarendon Press, Oxford, 1981.

Barbara W. Tuchman, *The March of Folly: From Troy to Vietnam*, Michael Joseph, London, 1984.

Martin Gilbert, *The Jews of Hope: The Plight of Soviet Jewry Today*, Macmillan, London, 1984.

David B. Ottaway and Patrick E. Tyler, 'Angola: Two Faces of War', *Washington Post*, 27 July 1986.

Lord Weidenfeld, 'All roads lead to German unity', *The Times*, 19 January 1990.

Letters, diaries, speeches and dispatches

Robert H. Ferrell, *The Eisenhower Diaries*, W. W. Norton, New York, 1981.

Václav Havel, *Letters to Olga, June 1979–September 1982*, Faber and Faber, London, 1988.

John F. Kennedy, 'Accepting the Nomination for the Presidency of the United States', speech, Los Angeles, 15 July 1960: http://www.cs.umb.edu/jfklibrary/speeches.htm

Tom Lehrer, *Too Many Songs by Tom Lehrer*, Methuen, London, 1981.

Ernest R. May and Philip D. Zelikow (eds), *The Kennedy Tapes: Inside the White House during the Cuban Missile Crisis*, The Belknap Press of Harvard University Press, Cambridge, Massachusetts, 1997.

James Seymour and Richard Anderson, *New Ghosts, Old Ghosts: Prisons and Labor Reform Camps in China*, M. E. Sharpe, New York, 1998.

Memoirs

A. Anatoli (Kuznetsov), *Babi Yar*, Jonathan Cape, London, 1970.

Edith Bone, *Seven Years Solitary*, Hamish Hamilton, London, 1959.

George Bush and Brent Scowcroft, *A World Transformed*, Alfred Knopf, New York, 1998.

Jung Chang, *Wild Swans, Three Daughters of China*, HarperCollins, London, 1991.

General Mark W. Clark, *From the Danube to the Yalu*, Harper and Row, New York, 1954.

F. W. de Klerk, *The Autobiography: The Last Trek, A New Beginning*, Macmillan, London, 1999.

Milovan Djilas, *Land without Justice, An Autobiography of his Youth*, Methuen, London, 1958.

Anthony Farrar-Hockley, *The Edge of the Sword*, Frederick Muller, London, 1954.

Mikhail Gorbachev, *Memoirs*, Doubleday, London, 1996.

Nikita Khrushchev, *Khrushchev Remembers: The Last Testament*, André Deutsch, London, 1974.

Oliver Lyttelton, Viscount Chandos, *The Memoirs of Lord Chandos*, Bodley Head, London, 1962.

Nelson Mandela, *Long Walk to Freedom*, Little Brown, London, 1994.

Pierre Mendès-France, *The Pursuit of Freedom*, Longmans, Green, London, 1956.

Arthur Miller, *Timebends, A Life*, Methuen, London, 1987.

Lieutenant-Colonel Colin Mitchell, *Having Been a Soldier*, Hamish Hamilton, London, 1969.

Richard M. Nixon, *The Memoirs of Richard Nixon*, Sidgwick and Jackson, London, 1978.

Irina Ratushinskaya, *Fictions and Lies* (a novel), John Murray, London, 1999.

Matthew B. Ridgway, *The War in Korea*, Barrie and Rockliff, London, 1968.

Arthur Schlesinger Jr, *A Thousand Days*, André Deutsch, London, 1965.

Margaret Thatcher, *The Downing Street Years*, HarperCollins, London, 1993.

Tobias Wolff, *In Pharaoh's Army, memories of a lost war* (Vietnam), Bloomsbury, London, 1994.

Boris Yeltsin, *The View from the Kremlin*, HarperCollins, London, 1994.

Larry Zellers, *In Enemy Hands, A Prisoner in North Korea*, University Press of Kentucky, Lexington, Kentucky, 1991.

Biographies

Jonathan Aitken, *Nixon, A Life*, Weidenfeld and Nicolson, London, 1993.

Peter F. Alexander, *Alan Paton, A Biography*, Oxford University Press, Oxford, 1994.

Nicholas Bethell, *Gomulka, His Poland, his Communism*, Longmans, London, 1969.

Andrew Brown, *The Neutron and the Bomb, A Biography of Sir James Chadwick*, Oxford University Press, Oxford, 1997.

Robert Conquest, *Stalin, Breaker of Nations*, Weidenfeld and Nicolson, London, 1991.

Edward Crankshaw, *Khrushchev: A Biography*, Collins, London, 1966.

Cameron Hazlehurst, *Menzies Observed*, George Allen and Unwin, Sydney, 1979.

Walter Isaacson, *Kissinger, A Biography*, Faber and Faber, London, 1992.

Doris Kearns, *Lyndon Johnson and the American Dream*, Harper and Row, New York, 1976.

Linda Lear, *Rachel Carson: Witness for Nature*, Henry Holt, New York, 1997.

Robert Low, *La Pasionaria: The Spanish Firebrand*, Hutchinson, London, 1992.

David McCullough, *Truman*, Simon and Schuster, New York, 1992.

H. Montgomery Hyde, *Stalin: The History of a Dictator*, Rupert Hart-Davis, London, 1971.

Evgeny Pasternak, *Boris Pasternak, The Tragic Years, 1930–60*, Collins Harvill, London, 1991.

Paul Preston, *Franco, A Biography*, HarperCollins, London, 1993.

Theodore C. Sorenson, *Kennedy*, Harper and Row, New York, 1965.

Dmitri Volkogonov, *Stalin, Triumph and Tragedy*, Grove Weidenfeld, New York, 1988.

Juan Williams, *Thurgood Marshall: American Revolutionary*, Times Books, New York, 1998.

General books

Hilary Beckles, *A History of Barbados: from Amerindian settlement to nation-state*, Cambridge University Press, Cambridge, 1990.

Leslie Bethell (ed.), *The Cambridge History of Latin America*, volume six, Cambridge University Press, Cambridge, 1994.

Olaf Caroe, *Soviet Empire, The Turks of Central Asia and Stalinism*, Macmillan, London, 1953.

Raymond Carr, *Spain 1808–1975*, Clarendon Press, Oxford, 1966.

Christopher Coker, *War and the 20th Century: A Study of War and Modern Consciousness*, Brassey's, London, 1994.

Phillip B. Davidson, *Vietnam at War, The History: 1946–1975*, Sidgwick and Jackson, London, 1988.

Horst Faas and Tim Page, *Requiem: By the Photographers Who Died in Vietnam and Indochina*, Random House, New York, 1997.

Ronnie E. Ford, *Tet: Understanding the Surprise*, Frank Cass, London, 1995.

Robert Frank Futrell, *The United States Air Force in Korea, 1950–1953*, revised edition, Office of Air Force History, United States Air Force, Washington DC, 1983.

John and Carol Garrard, *Inside the Soviet Writers' Union*, The Free Press, New York, 1990.

Patricia Giesler, *Valour Remembered: Canadians in Korea*, Directorate of Public Affairs, Veterans Affairs, Ottawa, Canada, 1982.

Martin Gilbert, *Winston S. Churchill*, volume eight, William Heinemann, London, 1988.

Martin Gilbert, *Israel: A History*, Doubleday, London, 1998.

John Gittings, *The Role of the Chinese Army*, Oxford University Press, London, 1967.

Richard Gott, *Guerrilla Movements in Latin America*, Thomas Nelson, London, 1970.

Philip Hanson, *From Stagnation to Catastroika: Commentaries on the Soviet Economy, 1983–1991*, Praeger, Westport, Connecticut, 1992.

Max Hastings, *The Korean War*, Michael Joseph, London, 1987.

Ian Henderson with Philip Goodhart, *The Hunt for Kimathi*, Hamish Hamilton, London, 1958.

M. N. Hennessy, *Congo, A Brief History and Appraisal*, Pall Mall Press, London, 1961.

R. E. M. Irving, *The First Indochina War, French and American Policy, 1945–54*, Croom Helm, London, 1975.

Kenneth N. Jordan, Sr, *Forgotten Heroes, 131 Men of the Korean War Awarded the Medal of Honor, 1950–1953*, Schiffer Military/Aviation History, Atglen, Pennsylvania, 1995.

Henry Kamm, *Cambodia: Report from a Stricken Land*, Arcade, New York, 1998.

Ben Kiernan, *The Pol Pot Regime: Race, Power, and Genocide in Cambodia under the Khmer Rouge, 1975–79*, Yale University Press, New Haven, 1996.

Leopold Labedz (ed.), *Solzhenitsyn: A Documentary Record*, Allen Lane/The Penguin Press, London, 1970.

Kenneth Scott Latourette, *A History of Modern China*, Penguin, London, 1954.

Robert Leckie, *Conflict: The History of the Korean War, 1950–53*, Putnam, New York, 1962.

Hugh Lunghi, *The Common Cause Story: Freedom, the Common Cause of Mankind*, Common Cause, Fleet, Hampshire, 1995.

Noel Malcolm, *Kosovo: A Short History*, Macmillan, London, 1998.

Arthur Marwick, *The Explosion of British Society, 1914–62*, Pan, London, 1963.

Philip Mason, *Common Sense about Race*, Victor Gollancz, London, 1961.

David Pryce-Jones, *The Hungarian Revolution*, Ernest Benn, London, 1969.

David Rees, *Korea: The Limited War*, St Martin's Press, New York, 1964.

Robert Service, *A History of Twentieth-Century Russia*, Allen Lane/The Penguin Press, London, 1998.

John Darrell Sherwood, *Officers in Flight Suits: The Story of American Air Force Fighter Pilots in the Korean War*, New York University Press, New York, 1996.

Tommie Sjöberg, *The Powers and the Persecuted: The Refugee Problem and the Intergovernmental Committee on Refugees*, Lund University Press, Lund, Sweden, 1991.

Jonathan D. Spence, *The Search for Modern China*, W. W. Norton, New York, 1990.

Gerald Emanuel Stern, *Broken Image, Foreign Critiques of America*, Random House, New York, 1972.

Gustav Stolper, Karl Häuser and Knut Borchardt, *The German Economy, 1870 to the Present*, Weidenfeld and Nicolson, London, 1967.

Hugh Thomas, *Cuba, or The Pursuit of Freedom*, Eyre and Spottiswoode, London, 1971.

Adrian Walker, *A Barren Place: National Servicemen in Korea, 1950–1954*, Leo Cooper, London, 1994.

Theodore H. White, *The Making of the President, 1960*, Athenaeum House, New York, 1961.

Newspaper articles

In addition to unsigned reports by Agence France-Presse, Associated Press, Bloomberg, Reuters and United Press International, I have drawn on the following signed newspaper articles:

John Aglionby, 'Poor invade Suharto ranch in battle against starvation', *Guardian*, 20 July 1998.

John Aglionby, 'Timorese are slaughtered as Indonesia talks peace', *Observer*, 31 January 1999.

R. W. Apple Jr, 'Allies Threaten to "Devastate" Serbian Forces,' *International Herald Tribune*, 26 March 1999.

Randhir Singh Bains, 'Christians in India', *The Times*, 29 January 1999.

Elena Becatoros, 'Discovery of sub wreck confirms survivor's tale', *Sunday Times*, 18 February 1998.

Ernest Beck, 'Hungarian reformers opt for social democracy', *The Times*, 9 October 1989.

Julian Bedford, 'Hundreds die in camp slaughter' (Rwanda), *Sunday Times*, 23 April 1995.

Richard Beeston, 'Yeltsin orders renewed attack on Chechenia', *The Times*, 7 January 1995.

Richard Beeston and Thomas de Waal, 'Grozny burns as rebels encircle 7,000 troops', *The Times*, 10 August 1996.

D'vora Ben Shaul, 'The threat of mass extinction', *Jerusalem Post*, 2 August 1998.

Michael Binyon, 'Russian jets kill 100 in Afghan border raid', *The Times*, 14 April 1995.

Michael Binyon, 'Drink lures Russians to early grave', *The Times*, 3 August 1998.

Anna Blundy, 'Primakov asks for food aid from Europe', *The Times*, 10 October 1998.

Anna Blundy, 'Cash-hit republic seeks break from Russian rule' (Kalmykia), *The Times*, 19 November 1998.

Anna Blundy, 'Russian psychiatrist dreams of Broadmoor', *The Times*, 20 November 1998.

James Bone, 'Investigators obstructed at North Korea nuclear site', *The Times*, 17 March 1994.

James Bone, 'Bosnian Serbs are accused of massacre', *The Times*, 11 August 1995.

Raymond Bonner, 'Bulgaria: Arms Source for World Belligerents', *International Herald Tribune*, 4 August 1998.

Roger Boyes, 'Guarantee by Kohl on 1945 frontiers', *The Times*, 15 November 1989.

Roger Boyes, 'Germany pledges to keep memory of Holocaust alive', *The Times*, 28 April 1995.

Roger Boyes, 'Postwar expulsions regretted by Poles', *The Times*, 29 April 1995.

Roger Boyes, 'Nazi to be tried for killing 500 in death camp', *The Times*, 5 March 1998.

Joel Brand, 'UN withdrawal looms as ceasefire ends in Bosnia', *The Times*, 1 May 1995.

Louise Branson, 'Serbs confirm mass killings', *Sunday Times*, 23 July 1995.

Joan Breckenridge, 'Remembering the heroes of yesterday, A couple lobby for a memorial in Normandy to Canadians who helped liberate Europe', *Globe and Mail*, Toronto, 20 May 1998.

Ian Brodie, 'Pride of Pacific battle found', *The Times*, 21 May 1998.

Ian Brodie, 'Clinton agenda targets terrorist hackers', *The Times*, 20 January 1999.

Ian Brodie, 'US "sorry for death squads": President apologises to Guatemala . . .', *The Times*, 12 March 1999.

Patrick Brogan, 'American Commentary', *The Times*, 10 and 17 October 1980.

Jay Bushinsky, 'Latvian president asked to apologize for murder of Jews', *Jerusalem Post*, Jerusalem, 23 February 1998.

John Carlin, 'Mandela and De Klerk hold first talks', *Independent*, 13 December 1989.

David Childs, 'Otto Ernst Remer', *Independent*, 9 October 1997.

Patricia Clough, 'East Germans demand early free elections', *Independent*, 8 December 1989.

Tim Cooper, 'Mountain of rubbish: His father was the first man to scale Everest, now Tenzing's son wants to clean it up', *Evening Standard*, 24 February 1998.

Rupert Cornwell, 'Lithuania challenges the Party's supremacy', *Independent*, 8 December 1989.

Rupert Cornwell, 'Clark Clifford' (obituary), *Independent*, 14 October 1998.

Peter Crookston, 'Where only Capa dared', *Sunday Telegraph*, 24 May 1998.

Barbara Crossette, 'A Ghastly Campaign of Terror in Sierra Leone', *International Herald Tribune*, 30 July 1998.

Francis Curta, 'Kremlin leaders in meeting to stem nationalist turmoil', *The Times*, 18 September 1989.

Mary Dejevsky, '78 killed as quake rescue plane crashes' (Armenia), *The Times*, 12 December 1988.

Mary Dejevsky, 'Bulgaria leader Zhivkov resigns', *The Times*, 11 November 1989.

Anthony DePalma, 'Canada Signs Historic Treaty with Indian Group', *International Herald Tribune*, 6 August 1998.

Caroline Drees, 'Chernobyl tornado "spread thyroid cancer"', *The Times*, 10 April 1996.

William Drozdiak, 'New Pledge for a Nazi Fund: 12 German Firms to Compensate Wartime Slave Workers', *International Herald Tribune*, 17 February 1999.

Cameron Duodu, 'How the grand lootocracy beggared Nigeria's people', *Observer*, 22 November 1998.

Ross Dunn, 'Peres' Party votes to accept creation of Palestinian State', *The Times*, 26 April 1996.

Valerie Elliott, 'British cities faced 20,000 Hiroshimas', *The Times*, 1 January 1999.

Michael Evans, 'Britain ends 40 years of nuclear test explosions', *The Times*, 7 April 1995.

Esther B. Fein, 'Sculpting Terror: The Stalin Memorial', *International Herald Tribune*, 20 September 1989.

Susan Fishkoff, 'Witness who won't stay silent' (Johnnie Stevens), *Jerusalem Post*, Jerusalem, 5 January 1998.

Trevor Fishlock, 'Assam slaughter goes on with 5,000 dead after seven weeks of slaughter', *The Times*, 24 March 1983.

Martin Fletcher, 'Virginia falls to slave's grandson', *The Times*, 9 November 1989.

Martin Fletcher, 'Clinton abandons nuclear testing', *The Times*, 12 August 1995.

Martin Fletcher and Peter Capella, 'US force sails for Liberia as anarchy imperils rescue', *The Times*, 13 April 1996.

Mark Franchetti, 'Kremlin guard reveals how he shot hated Beria', *Sunday Times*, 4 January 1998.

Martin Gilbert, 'Placido Domingo's cry straddles the centuries in Toledo', *Jewish Chronicle*, 10 May 1992.

Kerry Gill, 'All-clear for anthrax isle after 48 years', *The Times*, 19 April 1990.

John Gittings, 'Internet use lands Chinese man in jail', *Guardian*, 21 January 1999.

Mary Ann Glendon, 'Sudan's Unpunished Atrocities', *New York Times*, 8 December 1998.

Misha Glenny, '150,000 Serbs flee Croat conquerors', *The Times*, 8 August 1995.

John Gregory, 'Galina Ulanova', *Independent*, 23 March 1998.

Ruth E. Gruber, 'Ex-Nazi sentenced to life for Italy's worst massacre' (Erich Priebke), *Jewish Chronicle*, 13 March 1998.

Hugo Gurdon, 'Death catches up with a general who showed no mercy', *Daily Telegraph*, 16 July 1998.

Alan Hamilton, 'Veterans honour the Slapton victims', *The Times*, 28 April 1994.

Alan Hamilton and John Young, 'Japan makes apology for war atrocities', *The Times*, 12 August 1995.

Douglas Hamilton, 'Army pitched into Kosovo battle', *Guardian*, 20 July 1998.

Nigel Hawkes, 'Destruction date is set for the final stocks of smallpox', *The Times*, 26 January 1996.

Simon Hayden, '"Neutral" Sweden's role in war, Reuters, *Hong Kong Standard*, 8 January 1998.

Peter Herby, in conversation with V. K. Dethe, 'The Buried Inferno' (anti-personnel mines), *Times of India*, 2 January 1999.

Louis Heren, 'Washington confrontation prevents spread of rioting', *The Times*, 26 June 1968.

Mark Husband, 'Political struggle gives way to evil war of greed' (Liberia), *The Times*, 11 April 1996.

Hyun-Sung Khang, 'North Koreans flee cannibals', *Sunday Times*, 3 January 1999.

Tina Jackson, 'Where Tourists Fear to Tread' (Yemen), *Big Issue*, 11–17 January 1999.

Douglas Jehl, 'Who Armed Iraq? Answers the West Didn't Want to Hear', *New York Times*, 18 July 1993.

Douglas Jehl, 'Raids Against the Iraqis Begin to Annoy Saudis', *International Herald Tribune*, 23 March 1999.

Tim Jones, 'One more victim in war with no winners', *The Times*, 28 August 1992.

Tim Jones, 'In the event of war, shoot your allies and steal their bombs', *The Times*, 13 October 1998.

Imre Karacs, 'When Conrad Schumann jumped over the Berlin Wall . . .', *Independent*, 24 June 1998.

Bill Keller, 'Solzhenitsyn's "Gulag" comes in from the cold', *New York Times*, 29 August 1989.

Adam Kelliher, 'Troop pullout ends Kurds' bliss', *The Times*, 13 June 1991.

Jane Kelly, 'The shy genius who changed all our lives' (Tom Kilburn), *Daily Mail*, 18 June 1998.

Sam Kiley, '8,000 Rwanda refugees die in Army massacre', *The Times*, 24 April 1995.

Sam Kiley, 'Congo uprising shatters dream of renaissance', *The Times*, 5 August 1998.

Sam Kiley, 'Embattled Congo plans "nightmare" for Tutsi rebels', *The Times*, 12 August 1998.

Sam Kiley, 'Freetown burns as rebels slaughter hundreds', *The Times*, 13 January 1999.

Michael Knipe, 'Mr Vorster praises restraint of riot police', *The Times*, 13 September 1973.

Michael Laris, 'Chinese Dissidents Launch Campaign to Back New Party', *International Herald Tribune*, 17 July 1998.

Wim van Leer, 'After the deluge' (Berlin, August 1945), *Jerusalem Post*, 17 January 1986.

David Lehman, 'Order punctuated by explosions: Chile's legacy of distrust and the problem of Pinochet's return', *Times Literary Supplement*, 18 December 1998.

Anatol Lieven, 'Russia remembers deadly experiment', *The Times*, 10 September 1994.

Anatol Lieven, 'Chechenia signs autonomy deal', *The Times*, 9 December 1995.

Robin Lodge, 'Cold and hunger drive Russians from villages', *The Times*, 11 November 1998.

Anthony Loyd, 'Fever of killing in Kosovo', *The Times*, 31 August 1998.

Anthony Loyd, 'Serbs force Albanian refugees back to a shattered land', *The Times*, 14 September 1998.

Edward Lucas, 'Czech PM offers to quit if new Cabinet fails to please', *Independent*, 7 December 1989.

Edward Lucas, 'Communist rule ended in Czechoslovakia', *Independent*, 11 December 1989.

Innis MacBeath, 'Barriers attacked in New York', *The Times*, 7 December 1967.

Ian McDonald, '200,000 Washington marchers prove that the anti-war movement has not lost its drive', *The Times*, 26 April 1971.

Anne McElvoy, 'Giant gap in the Iron Curtain', *The Times*, 10 November 1989.

Ben Macintyre, 'Americans track down Hirohito treasure sub', *The Times*, 19 July 1995.

Ben Macintyre, 'Bosnia massacre confirmed', *The Times*, 23 March 1996.

Ben Macintyre, 'Annan brokers Congo ceasefire at Paris summit', *The Times*, 30 November 1998.

Sindiwe Magona, 'South Africa's Other Racism: Blacks' Hatred of Whites', *International Herald Tribune*, 5 August 1998.

Greg May, 'Here Comes E-mail, and Beijing Can't Police It', *International Herald Tribune*, 1 March 1999.

Stanley Meisler, 'Remember the Peace Corps?', *Los Angeles Times*, 13 January 1998.

Peter Millar, 'Democracy dances in the Czech boulevards', *Sunday Times*, 3 December 1989.

Jonathan Mirsky, 'More Arrests Despite the "Dialogue" on Human Rights', *International Herald Tribune*, 27 July 1998.

Jonathan Mirsky and James Pringle, 'Crippled victim of Tiananmen protest held by Chinese', *The Times*, 30 May 1995.

Edward Mortimer, 'Hundreds in Paris riots are hurt', *The Times*, 7 May 1968.

Christopher Munnion, 'S. Africa searches for lost war hero honoured by navy', *Daily Telegraph*, 25 April 1998.

Norimitsu Onishi, 'Fear in Sierra Leone as Rivals "Do Their Own" and Nigerians Want Out', *International Herald Tribune*, 1 February 1999.

Matthew Parris, 'Arms and immorality', *The Times*, 16 January 1999.

Grant Peck, 'Saigon thrives on war souvenirs', *Jerusalem Post* (Associated Press), 29 December 1992.

Jane Perlez, 'Somali Killed 100 as US Troops Landed', *International Herald Tribune*, 29 December 1992.

James Pettifer, 'Landmine ban is defied on border', *The Times*, 10 February 1999.

Eve-Ann Prentice, 'Tutsis stone survivors', *The Times*, 25 April 1995.

Michael Prescott and Zoe Brennan, 'Cook sells twice as many guns to Indonesia as Tories', *Sunday Times*, 14 March 1999.

James Pringle, 'Women's forum condemns China for harassment', *The Times*, 9 September 1995.

James Pringle, 'Christians keep faith in China's "secret houses"', *The Times*, 1 June 1998.

James Pringle, 'Smoking leaders' legacy catches up with Chinese', *The Times*, 20 November 1998.

Peter Pringle and Rupert Cornwell, 'Cold War is over, Bush and Gorbachev declare', *Independent*, 4 December 1989.

Tim Radford, 'Undersea jolts create waves of awesome power', *Guardian*, 20 July 1998.

Byron Rogers, 'When the Hood blew up without trace', *Sunday Telegraph*, 24 May 1998.

James Rupert, 'Riots in Nigeria Threaten Wide Ethnic Conflict', *International Herald Tribune*, 9 July 1998.

Murray Sayle, 'The Vote in Quebec', *New Yorker*, 13 November 1995.

Carey Scott, 'Mortar kills Russian general in battle for Chechen capital', *Sunday Times*, 8 January 1995.

Carey Scott and Mark Franchetti, 'Horror in Chechnya', *Sunday Times*, 13 December 1998.

John Simpson, '20 years on, Iran is torn between following the Koran or the Internet', *Sunday Telegraph*, 31 January 1999.

Alex Duval Smith, 'Abubakar prepares to unveil gradual return to civilian rule' (Nigeria), *Guardian*, 20 July 1998.

Dinitia Smith, 'The Sultry Eartha Kitt: Mellower, but Still Proud', *International Herald Tribune*, 5 March 1999.

Geraint Smith, 'Half the world's wealth is owned by just 385 people', *Evening Standard*, 16 July 1996.

R. Jeffrey Smith, 'Battle Devastates a City in Kosovo', *International Herald Tribune*, 24 July 1998.

David Spanier, 'Poor People refuse to quit camp' (Washington DC), *The Times*, 24 June 1968.

David Spanier, 'Mass arrest of Poor People', *The Times*, 25 June 1968.

Michael Specter, '"So Many Sick People" in Zimbabwe, Now the Deadly Center of AIDS', *International Herald Tribune*, 7 August 1998.

Cheryl Stanton, 'On location' (the Chilean earthquake of 1960), *Hemisphere*, United Airlines, May 1998.

Denis Staunton, 'Countess Maria von Maltzan, In defiance of fascism', *Guardian*, 18 November 1997.

Julian Strauss, 'Massacre evidence mounts against Milosevic', *Sunday Telegraph*, 31 January 1999.

Stacy Sullivan, 'Mass graves scar hillsides round former Serb camp', *The Times*, 29 January 1996.

Marcus Tanner, 'Attacks on Croatian towns shatter cease-fire', *Independent*, 4 September 1991.

Marcus Tanner, 'Belgrade's forces slice into Croatia', *Independent*, 5 September 1991.

Stewart Tendler, 'UN tackles rise in world crime', *The Times*, 29 April 1995.

Juliet Terzieff, 'Kosovo Serbs massacre 45 villagers', *Sunday Times*, 17 January 1999.

Michael Theodoulou, 'Fifth Iran dissident is found murdered', *The Times*, 14 December 1998.

Christopher Thomas, 'Taleban poised to take last city', *The Times*, 4 August 1998.

Brooke Unger, 'The Balkans, Europe's roughest neighbourhood', *Economist*, 24 January 1998.

Christopher Walker, 'Suicide bomb kills seven Israelis', *The Times*, 10 April 1995.

Christopher Walker, 'Arafat asks UN to intervene as civil war fears grow', *The Times*, 11 April 1995.

Christopher Walker, 'Terrorists to be attacked in Palestinian areas after suicide bomber kills 12', *The Times*, 5 March 1996.

Christopher Walker, 'Rockets fired into Galilee', *The Times*, 1 April 1996.

David Watts, 'Tiananmen's legacy hangs over Jakarta', *The Times*, 16 November 1998.

Tim Weiner, 'In World's Arms Bazaar, US Keeps the Top Spot', *International Herald Tribune*, 5 August 1998.

Craig R. Whitney, 'Major Nations Urge Halt to Aid for Kosovo Rebels', *International Herald Tribune*, 9 July 1998.

Giles Whittell, 'Bombers Away' (the B-52), *The Times Magazine*, 17 September 1994.

Richard Wigg, 'Super powers clash on human rights', *The Times*, 9 March 1983.

Leslie Yarranton, 'Daughter brings a Red Army commander in from the cold' (General Yershov), *European*, 18 May 1990.

Guy Yeoman, 'Sinking of "Khedive"', *The Times*, 24 February 1994.

Michel Zlotowski, 'Silence is broken over round-up of children', *Jewish Chronicle*, 29 August 1997.

INDEX

compiled by the author

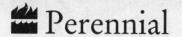
Perennial

Books by Martin Gilbert:

A HISTORY OF THE TWENTIETH CENTURY

"This is history stripped to its essentials, shorn of fads and celebrities
and hoopla, and devoted instead to what was of consequence."

—*The New York Times*

A HISTORY OF THE TWENTIETH CENTURY
VOLUME ONE: 1900-1933
ISBN 0-380-71393-4 (paperback)

This first volume covers the critical thirty-three years that began this remarkable
span of time. From the dawn of aviation through a great war that left six million
soldiers dead and four vast empires destroyed, to the inauguration of Roosevelt as
U.S. President and Hitler as Chancellor of Germany, and the beginning of Stalin's
show trials in the Soviet Union.

A HISTORY OF THE TWENTIETH CENTURY
VOLUME TWO: 1933-1951
ISBN 0-380-71394-2 (paperback)

This second volume documents the attempts to preserve human values, to
maintain the rule of law, and to uphold the rights and dignity of the individual.
It begins as Roosevelt embarks on the New Deal and ends as Kennedy is elected to
the presidency. In this span Gilbert covers the Depression, the Spanish Civil War,
the Japanese aggression in China, the relentless spread of Nazi power, World War II,
the imposition of the Iron Curtain and the growth of the Cold War, the Berlin
Blockade, and the nuclear confrontation.

A HISTORY OF THE TWENTIETH CENTURY
VOLUME THREE: 1952-1999
ISBN 0-380-71395-0 (paperback)

This final volume has been updated from the hardcover publication to include all
of 1999. Careful accounts are made of the wars in Korea, Vietnam, and Bosnia, the
postwar resurrection of Europe, famine in Africa, apartheid, the arms race, the
dawn of the computer age, Neil Armstrong's landing on the moon, the extraordinary advances in medical science, Martin Luther King, Jr. and John F. Kennedy's
assassinations, and when Beijing's Tiananmen Square shocked the world.

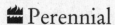
Perennial
An Imprint of HarperCollins*Publishers*

Available wherever books are sold, or call 1-800-331-3761 to order.